Enthofer/Haas

●

Treasurer's Handbook
Handbuch Treasury

Treasurer's Handbook

Financial Markets:
A Practitioner's Guide

edited by

Hannes Enthofer
Patrick Haas

2nd Edition

Handbuch Treasury

Praxiswissen für
den Geld- und Kapitalmarkt

herausgegeben von

Hannes Enthofer
Patrick Haas

2. Auflage

Bibliografische Information der Deutschen Nationalbibliothek

Die Deutsche Nationalbibliothek verzeichnet diese Publikation in der Deutschen Nationalbibliografie; detaillierte bibliografische Daten sind im Internet über http://dnb.d-nb.de abrufbar.

ISBN 978-3-7143-0238-7

© LINDE VERLAG WIEN Ges.m.b.H., Wien 2012
1210 Wien, Scheydgasse 24, Tel.: 01/24 630
www.lindeverlag.at

Druck: Hans Jentzsch u Co. Ges.m.b.H.
1210 Wien, Scheydgasse 31

Dear treasury professionals,
dear treasury professionals to be,
dear ACI community,

We are happy to be able to say that many aspects of the first edition of the Treasurer's Handbook received praise:

- Comprehensive description of the current treasury know-how (approx. 1,300 pages)
- Bilingual: English and German on facing pages in one book
- Up-to-date, including Code of Conduct (governance rules for traders)
- Practical, tried and tested knowledge through long-standing co-operation with traders and ACI – The Financial Markets Association – our thanks go to the many helpful people there
- Lasting knowledge to successfully pass ACI certification exams
- ... not strictly in this vein but important nonetheless: sold out already after a little more than one year.

The second edition offers three major additions:

- Update of the Code of Conduct
- Replacement risk of derivatives
- Integrating commodities into the treasury knowledge

The Treasurer's Handbook was written in special times – during the recovery from the financial crisis. This brought and still brings about a re-focussing of treasury tasks away from increasing the return on risk towards a hedging- and customer-oriented treasury. What remains unchanged is the fundamental treasury knowledge that is necessary to hedge and manage market risks.

To this end the Treasurer's Handbook wishes to make a contribution towards professional work in the money and capital markets. We wish you success in looking up things, reading and studying this book.

Patrick Haas

Hannes Enthofer

Liebe Treasury-Professionals,
liebe Treasury-Professionals in spe,
liebe ACI-Community,

wir konnten feststellen, dass an der ersten Auflage unseres Handbuches Treasury Folgendes geschätzt wurde:

- Umfassende Darstellung des aktuellen Treasury-Wissens (ca. 1.300 Seiten)
- Zweisprachig: Englisch und Deutsch auf gegenüberliegenden Seiten in einem Buch
- Zeitgemäß, inklusive Code of Conduct (Governance Regeln für Händler)
- Praxisnahes Wissen durch jahrelange Zusammenarbeit mit Händlern und dem ACI – The Financial Markets Association, bei deren „Motoren" wir uns herzlich bedanken
- Bleibende Wissensgrundlage zum Erwerb der ACI-Zertifizierungen
- ... und nicht ganz in der Systematik, aber wichtig: nach wenig mehr als einem Jahr bereits ausverkauft.

Die zweite Auflage bietet vor allem drei Erweiterungen an:

- Weiterentwicklung des Code of Conduct
- Wiederbeschaffungsrisiko bei Derivaten
- Integration des Themas Rohstoffe in das Treasury-Wissen

Das Handbuch Treasury ist in einer speziellen Zeit entstanden – während der Aufarbeitung der Finanzmarktkrise. Das brachte und bringt Verlagerungen in der Treasury-Arbeit weg von der Steigerung des Return on Risk hin zu einem hedging- und kundenorientierten Treasury. Was unabhängig von der Fokussierung der Treasury-Arbeit bleibt, ist das Treasury-Wissen, das notwendig ist, um Marktrisiken abzusichern und zu steuern.

In diesem Sinne will das Handbuch Treasury einen Beitrag zur professionellen Arbeit im Geld- und Kapitalmarkt leisten. Wir wünschen Ihnen viel Erfolg beim Nachschlagen, Lesen und Studieren.

Patrick Haas

Hannes Enthofer

25 Years of Finance Trainer

In the beginning was the ACI: In 1986 the Financial Markets Association approached us with the request for a Forex handbook for their members. The result was the ACI-authorised Forex Handbook which was distributed to 1200 traders and ACI members in Germany, Luxembourg, Austria and Switzerland.

In the meantime, a lot has happened:

- Forex was joined by the money market, both fields were enriched by derivatives, the fixed income market gained entry via collateral.
- Finance Trainer has developed the so-called Cyber*School, a trainer-supported online learning programme with integrated benchmarking features. With this highly efficient learning method Finance Trainer was able to prepare ever-growing numbers of ACI certification programme participants and thus make a major contribution to the field of money and capital market training.

On the occasion of the 25th anniversary of Finance Trainer we wished for a more substantial manifestation of our treasury know-how, namely a jubilee edition. This book has not been created overnight. "Whole generations" of trainers and Cyber*Trainers have written, edited, updated and augmented the original text, for which thanks are due. Special thanks go to Jürgen Pfeifer who did the final editing and added introductions, test questions and solutions.

We would also like to thank the many ACI officials who have been supporting us over the years. An extra warm thank you to the drivers of the German-language ACI training efforts Manfred Kunert, Hildegard Pfitzenreuter, Klaus Sturm, Christof Niggli (current Chair ACI International Board of Education) and Manfred Wiebogen (current President ACI worldwide). The international ACI careers of Christof Niggli and Manfred Wiebogen are the direct result of the excellent work of the German-language training initiative that started in the mid-90s.

To do justice to the international nature of the money and foreign exchange markets the book is written in both German and English. This way, it serves not only as a reference book but also as a glossary of commonly used treasury products, techniques and regulations.

We wish you success in your referencing, reading and studying with this handbook.

Patrick Haas   Hannes Enthofer

25 Jahre Finance Trainer

Am Anfang war das ACI: Die Händlervereinigung wollte ein Forex-Handbuch für seine Mitglieder. 1996 haben wir deshalb ein von den ACI-Vereinigungen in Deutschland, Luxemburg, Österreich und der Schweiz autorisiertes Forex Handbuch (wie es damals hieß) herausgegeben und an 1200 Händler und Mitglieder versendet.

In der Zwischenzeit ist viel passiert:

*   Zum Forex kam der Geldmarkt hinzu, dann in beiden Märkten Derivate, über das Collateral der Fixed Income Markt.
*   Finance Trainer entwickelte die Cyber*School, ein Trainer-unterstütztes Online-Lernprogramm mit laufendem Benchmarking. Mit dieser effizienten Lernmethode konnte Finance Trainer die verbreiterten und immer wichtigeren Zertifizierungen des ACI wirkungsvoll vorbereiten und einen wesentlichen Anteil auf dem Gebiet der Geld- und Kapitalmarktausbildung erringen.

Nach 25 Jahren Finance Trainer haben wir uns eine Zusammenschau des Treasury Knowhows, das wir vermitteln, gewünscht. Quasi eine Jubiläumsausgabe.

Dieses Buch entstand nicht von heute auf morgen. „Ganze Generationen" von Trainern und Cyber*Trainern bei Finance Trainer haben geschrieben, redigiert, upgedated und erweitert. Bei ihnen allen bedanken wir uns herzlich. Ein besonderer Dank gilt Jürgen Pfeifer, der sozusagen die „Schlussredaktion" übernommen und das Handbuch mit Übersichten, Kontrollfragen und Lösungen veredelt hat.

Bedanken wollen wir uns auch bei den Verantwortlichen des ACI, die seit Jahren unsere Arbeit nützen und uns unterstützen. Besonders erwähnen möchten wir „die Motoren" der (deutschsprachigen) ACI Ausbildung, Manfred Kunert, Hildegard Pfitzenreuter, Klaus Sturm, Christof Niggli (heutiger Chair ACI International Board of Education) und Manfred Wiebogen (derzeitiger Präsident der weltweiten ACI Organisation). Der Aufstieg von Christof Niggli und Manfred Wiebogen im internationalen ACI zeigt, welch hervorragende Arbeit diese deutschsprachige Ausbildungsinitiative, die Mitte der 90er-Jahre startete, geleistet hat.

Damit das Handbuch dem internationalen Gedanken der Geld- und Devisenmärkte entspricht, haben wir es in zwei Sprachen herausgegeben. Somit kann es nicht nur als Nachschlagewerk, sondern auch als Glossar von gebräuchlichen Produkten, Techniken und Regelungen des Treasury verwendet werden.

Wir wünschen Ihnen viel Erfolg beim Nachschlagen, Lesen und Studieren mit dem Handbuch.

Patrick Haas   Hannes Enthofer

Information:

In conjunction with this book, you may wish to use our online learning programmes – the Finance Trainer Cyber*Schools:

- ACI Diploma Cyber*School (ACI Dipl.)
- Dealing Certificate Cyber*School (ACI DC)
- Operations Certificate Cyber*School (ACI OC)

Details and registration at: www.financetrainer.com

Information:

Zum vorliegenden Buch gibt es auch Online-Lernprogramme – Die FINANCE TRAINER CYBER*SCHOOLS:

- ACI Diploma Cyber *School (ACI Dipl.)
- Dealing Certificate Cyber*School (ACI DC)
- Operations Certificate Cyber*School (ACI OC)

Details und Anmeldung unter: www.financetrainer.com

Contents

Inhaltsverzeichnis

Part II: The Capital Market

Teil II: Der Kapitalmarkt

Teil VI: Risikomanagement

Part VII: Central Banks, Fundamental Analysis
and Technical Analysis

Teil VII: Notenbanken, fundamentale Analyse
und technische Analyse

Part VIII: Annex

P.I

1.1

Teil VIII: Anhang

Part I: The Money Market

Teil I: Der Geldmarkt

The money market is the part of financial markets involving assets with original maturities of one year or shorter. Money market rates are determined by the liquidity situation of the market participants, on the central banks' market policy and the individual maturity. The market is made up of central banks and credit institutions and to a smaller degree of institutional investors such as life insurers and public bodies. The money market provides liquidity funding for the global financial system. It allows acquiring necessary liquid funds as well as investing excess liquidity. In the international markets the market participants are funds, insurance companies, industrial and trading companies, which make extensive of the liquidity transformation function of the markets.

Money market instruments being traded on the international money markets are interbank deposits, certificates of deposit, eligible bills, commercial papers und treasury bills.

The different money market instruments will be described in detail in chapter 2; chapter 1 introduces the basics of quotation and calculation of interest rates for money market instruments. Topics covered range from the typical types of yield curves and the corresponding theories through to methods for calculating interest rates, payment dates and conventions that are used for quoting interest rates.

Chapter 2 gives the reader an overview of the different money market instruments and then provides a precise description for each of these instruments including quotation and conventions of these money market instruments as well as comparisons between different instruments.

The third chapter deals with money market derivatives such as forward rate agreements and money market futures providing further information on conventions and terminology, the margin system and the application of money market futures. Furthermore, a comparison between those two derivatives is made.

Chapter 4 explains repurchase agreements (repos). You will get further information on quotation, terminology and the legal basics as well as the different types of repos and their application and risks.

The final chapter 5 explains a special interest rate swap, namely the overnight index swap and its functionality, conventions, terminology and application. The "normal" interest rate swaps and cross currency swaps are described in chapter 2 of part II.

Included in the following exams:
- **ACI Dealing Certificate**
- **ACI Diploma**
- **ACI Operations Certificate**

Der Geldmarkt ist jener Teil des Finanzmarktes, auf dem kurzfristige Kredite, z.B. Tages- und Monatsgeld, insbesondere zwischen Banken gehandelt werden und Geldmarktpapiere (kurzfristige Schuldtitel) von der Bundesbank zu festgesetzten Geldmarktsätzen an- und verkauft werden. Die Geldmarktsätze richten sich in erster Linie nach der Liquiditätssituation der Marktteilnehmer in Abhängigkeit zur Offenmarktpolitik der Notenbank sowie nach der Fristigkeit. Die Marktteilnehmer sind Notenbanken und Kreditinstitute und in begrenztem Maße Kapitalsammelstellen (z.B. Lebensversicherer) sowie die öffentliche Verwaltung. Der Geldmarkt erfüllt in erster Linie eine Liquiditätsausgleichsfunktion zwischen den Banken. Damit wird zugleich ermöglicht, fristgerecht notwendige liquide Mittel zinsgünstig zu beschaffen oder überschüssige Liquidität anzulegen. An den internationalen Märkten kommen als Marktteilnehmer Fonds, Versicherungen, Industrie- und Handelsunternehmen hinzu, die die Liquiditätsausgleichsfunktion des Marktes im verstärkten Maße für ihre Belange nutzen.

Zu den Geldmarktinstrumenten, die an internationalen Geldmärkten gehandelt werden, zählen Interbank-Depotgeschäfte, Certificates of Deposit, Wechselgeschäfte, Commercial Papers und Treasury Bills. Bevor in Kapitel 2 näher auf die einzelnen Geldmarktprodukte eingegangen wird, vermittelt Kapitel 1 die Grundlagen für die Quotierung und Berechnung der Zinsen von Geldmarktprodukten. Das Themenspektrum reicht von den typischen Formen von Zinskurven und den dahinterstehenden Theorien zur Begründung der verschiedenen Verläufe von Zinskurven bis hin zu Methoden der Berechnung, Zahlungszeitpunkten und Konventionen, die bei der Quotierung von Zinssätzen verwendet werden.

Das Kapitel 2 gibt dem Leser zu Beginn einen Überblick über die einzelnen Geldmarktinstrumente und geht anschließend näher auf die einzelnen Instrumente ein. Dabei werden die Quotierung sowie die Usancen der Geldmarktinstrumente sowie Vergleiche zwischen den Instrumenten näher erläutert.

Das 3. Kapitel beschäftigt sich dann mit den Geldmarktderivaten, also Forward Rate Agreements und Geldmarktfutures. Hier wird näher auf die Terminologien und Usancen, auf das Margin-System und auf die Anwendung der Geldmarktderivate eingegangen. Außerdem wird ein Vergleich zwischen diesen beiden Geldmarktderivaten angestellt.

Das Kapitel 4 setzt sich mit dem Thema Repurchase Agreements (Repos) auseinander. Dabei wird intensiv auf die Quotierung, Terminologien und rechtlichen Grundlagen sowie die verschiedenen Arten von Repos sowie deren Anwendung und Risiken eingegangen.

Abschließend wird in Kapitel 5 auf einen speziellen Zinsswap, nämlich den Overnight Index Swap sowie dessen Funktionsweise, Usancen bzw. Terminologien und Anwendung, eingegangen. Die „normalen" Zinsswapgeschäfte und die Cross Currency Swaps sowie deren Funktionsweise, Usancen bzw. Terminologien und Anwendung werden in Kapitel 2 von Teil II behandelt.

Prüfungsrelevant für:
- **ACI Dealing Certificate**
- **ACI Diploma**
- **ACI Operations Certificate**

1. Methods of Interest Calculation, Yield Curve and Quotation

In this chapter you learn ...

- which methods are used to determine the number of days for interest calculations.
- which methods are used to determine the day basis for interest calculations.
- which conventions are used in the money and capital markets.
- what a yield curve is.
- which three types of yield curves are distinguished.
- which theories there are on the shape of a yield curve.
- how to calculate interest rates for unusual terms using straight-line interpolation.
- how interest rates are quoted.
- what a basis point is.
- when interest is paid for money market transactions with terms of up to one year or more, respectively.

1.1. Methods of Interest Calculation

While calculating interests, the general question is how the interest for one period is determined. The interest calculation methods employed can vary, depending on national and product markets. As a rule, interest can be calculated in the following manner:

$$I = C \times r \times \frac{D}{B}$$

I = amount of interest
C = capital amount
r   = interest rate in decimals (i.e. 5 % = 0.05; 10.3 % = 0.103; etc.)
D = number of days of the term of interest
B = day basis for calculation (fixed number of days per year) (= day base)

There are three methods to determine the **number of days (D)**.

a) **ACT-method (Actual-method): Counting the actual numbers of days that elapse.**
   Term of interest: 1 March – 31 March → 30 days
   Term of interest: 1 March – 1 April   → 31 days

b) **30-method: Each month counts as 30 days (remaining days in a month are subtracted).**
   Term of interest: 1 March – 31 March → 30 days
   Term of interest: 1 March – 30 March → 29 days
   Term of interest: 1 March – 1 April   → 30 days

1. Zinsberechnung, Zinskurve und Quotierungen

In diesem Kapitel lernen Sie ...

- welche Methoden es zur Berechnung der Tage für die Zinsberechnung gibt.
- welche Methoden es zur Berechnung der Basis für die Zinsberechnung gibt.
- welche Konventionen im Geld- und Kapitalmarkt verwendet werden.
- was man unter einer Zinskurve versteht.
- welche drei typischen Formen von Zinskurven unterschieden werden.
- welche Theorien es zur Begründung der verschiedenen Verläufe von Zinskurven gibt.
- wie Zinssätze für unübliche Laufzeiten mithilfe der linearen Interpolation berechnet werden.
- wie Zinssätze quotiert werden.
- was man unter einem Basispunkt versteht.
- wann die Zinsen bei Geldmarktgeschäften mit Laufzeiten bis zu einem Jahr bzw. über einem Jahr gezahlt werden.

1.1. Methoden der Zinsberechnung

Für Zinsberechnungen stellt sich allgemein die Frage, wie die Zinsen für eine Periode zu errechnen sind. Die Art dieser Ermittlung ist in den einzelnen nationalen Märkten unterschiedlich und variiert von Markt zu Markt. Grundsätzlich kann von der folgenden Formel ausgegangen werden:

$$Z = K \times r \times \frac{T}{B}$$

Z = Zinsbetrag
K = Nominalbetrag (Kapital)
r = Zinssatz (5% = 0,05; 10,3% = 0,103 etc.)
T = Anzahl der Tage für die Zinsberechnung (Laufzeit)
B = Berechnungsbasis (festgesetzte Anzahl der Tage pro Jahr)

Für die **Berechnung der Tage** (T) gibt es drei Methoden:

a) **ACT-Methode (Actual-Methode):** Die tatsächlich verstrichenen Tage werden gezählt.

   Zinsperiode: 1. März – 31. März → 30 Tage als Berechnungsgrundlage
   Zinsperiode: 1. März – 1. April → 31 Tage als Berechnungsgrundlage

b) **30-Methode:** Jeder Monat wird mit 30 Tagen gerechnet. Die Resttage innerhalb eines Monats werden subtrahiert.

   Zinsperiode: 1. März – 31. März → 30 Tage als Berechnungsgrundlage
   Zinsperiode: 1. März – 30. März → 29 Tage als Berechnungsgrundlage
   Zinsperiode: 1. März – 1. April → 30 Tage als Berechnungsgrundlage

c) 30E-method: Each month counts as 30 days (the 31st is treated as if it was the 30th; remaining days are subtracted).

Term of interest: 1 March – 31 March   → 29 days
Term of interest: 1 March – 30 March   → 29 days
Term of interest: 1 March – 1 April   → 30 days

This method is used in the Euromarket as well as in some continental European markets.

The correct number of days can be determined by using the ISDA formula for the 30-method and 30E-method:

$$D = (y_2 - y_1) \times 360 + (m_2 - m_1) \times 30 + (d_2 - d_1)$$

D = number of days
y_1 = year in which the period starts
y_2 = year in which the period ends
m_1 = start month
m_2 = maturity month
d_1 = start day
d_2 = maturity day

where for d_1 and d_2:

	30-method	30E-method
d_1	$d_1 = 31 \rightarrow 30$	$d_1 = 31 \rightarrow 30$
d_2	$d_2 = 31 \rightarrow 30$, if d_1 is 30 or 31	$d_2 = 31 \rightarrow 30$

Example
Interest period 1st – 31st March 2004
30-method: $D = (2004 - 2004) \times 360 + (3 - 3) \times 30 + (31 - 1) = 30$
30E-method: $D = (2004 - 2004) \times 360 + (3 - 3) \times 30 + (30 - 1) = 29$

There are three ways to **determine the day basis (B).**

a) 360-method: Assuming that each year has 360 days.

Annual term: 1 March XY – 1 March XZ are 365 days   → day base is 360 days
Annual term: 1 March XY – 3 March XZ*) are 367 days → day base is 360 days
*) e.g. with a weekend

b) 365-method: Assumption that each year has 365 days.

Just as with 360, but generally → day base is 365 days

c) **30E-Methode:** Jeder Monat wird mit 30 Tagen gerechnet. Der 31. eines Monats wird mit dem 30. gleichgesetzt. Resttage werden subtrahiert.

Zinsperiode: 1. März – 31. März $\quad\rightarrow\quad$ 29 Tage als Berechnungsgrundlage

Zinsperiode: 1. März – 30. März $\quad\rightarrow\quad$ 29 Tage als Berechnungsgrundlage

Zinsperiode: 1. März – 1. April $\quad\rightarrow\quad$ 30 Tage als Berechnungsgrundlage

Diese Methode ist im Euromarkt und in einigen kontinentaleuropäischen Märkten üblich.

Um die korrekte Anzahl von Tagen zu ermitteln, kann man auch auf die sogenannte „ISDN-Formel" zurückgreifen. Sie lautet für die 30-Methode und 30E-Methode:

$$D = (y_2 - y_1) \times 360 + (m_2 - m_1) \times 30 + (d_2 - d_1)$$

D	= Anzahl Tage
y_1	= Startjahr der Zinsperiode
y_2	= Endjahr der Zinsperiode
m_1	= Startmonat der Zinsperiode
m_2	= Endmonat der Zinsperiode
d_1	= Starttag der Zinsperiode
d_2	= Endtag der Zinsperiode

Dabei ist für d_1 und d_2 zu beachten:

	30-Methode	**30E-Methode**
d_1	$d_1 = 31 \rightarrow 30$	$d_1 = 31 \rightarrow 30$
d_2	$d_2 = 31 \rightarrow 30$, wenn $d_1 = 30$ oder 31	$d_2 = 31 \rightarrow 30$

Beispiel
Zinsperiode 1. – 31. März 2001   **30-Methode:** $D = (2001 - 2001) \times 360 + (3 - 3) \times 30\,(31 - 1)$ $D = 30$ **30E-Methode:** $D = (2001 - 2001) \times 360 + (3 - 3) \times 30 + (30 - 1)$ $D = 29$

Für die **Berechnung der Basis (B)** gibt es drei Methoden:

a) **360-Methode:** Das Jahr wird mit 360 Tagen gerechnet.

Jahreslaufzeit: 1. März XY – 1. März XZ sind 365 Tage $\quad\rightarrow\quad$ Basis 360 Tage

Jahreslaufzeit: 1. März XY – 3. März*) XZ sind 367 Tage $\quad\rightarrow\quad$ Basis 360 Tage

*) z.B. bei einem Wochenende

b) **365-Methode:** Das Jahr wird mit 365 Tagen gerechnet.

Wie bei der 360-Methode, nur allgemein $\rightarrow$ Basis 365 Tage

c) ACT-method:

In the money market (ISDA-method):

The actual days per year are counted (leap year 366 days, "normal" year 365 days). If a deal runs over two years (one of them being a leap year), the interest calculation is divided into two parts.

Example

2 January 2003 – 2 January 2004 interest calculation Actual/Actual

$$x \cdot \frac{364}{365} + x \cdot \frac{1}{366}$$

In the capital market (ISMA-method):

A year is counted with actual days of the term of interest (multiplied by the number of terms of interest).

Example

Bond with semi-annual interest payments:
1 March XY – 1 September XY are 184 days → day basis is 368 days (184 x 2)

$$x \cdot \frac{184}{368}$$

Generally different ACT-methods are used in the market. The most usual are the ISDA- and the ISMA-Methode, which are called **"Actual/Actual historical" (ISDA)** or **"Actual/Actual Bond" (ISMA)** in the market.

Therefore, theoretically nine combinations of days (D) and basis (B) are possible but **only five of them are practically used: ACT/365, ACT/360, 30/360, 30E/360 and ACT/ACT.**

Daily conventions vary from market to market. In the table below the **conventions for money markets and capital markets** are listed. In the capital markets, however, these conventions may differ in their specifications regarding the international and domestic market and regarding different financial instruments. Therefore, please clarify these conditions before you trade!

c) **ACT-Methode:**

Im Geldmarkt (ISDA-Methode):

Gerechnet wird mit der Anzahl der tatsächlichen Jahrestage (Schaltjahr 366, normales Jahr 365). Fällt ein Geschäft in zwei Jahre, von denen ein Jahr ein Schaltjahr ist, wird die Zinsberechnung in zwei Teile geteilt.

Beispiel
2. Januar 2003 – 2. Januar 2004 Zinsberechnung ACT/ACT $$x \cdot \frac{364}{365} + x \cdot \frac{1}{366}$$

Im Anleihemarkt (ISMA-Methode):

Das Jahr wird mit den echten Tagen der Zinsperiode (mal die Anzahl der Zinsperioden) gerechnet.

Beispiel
Anleihe mit halbjährlicher Zinszahlung: 1. März XY – 1. Sept. XY sind 184 Tage Basis: 368 (184 x 2) $$x \cdot \frac{184}{368}$$

Generell finden im Markt verschiedene ACT-Methoden Anwendung. Die üblichsten sind die ISDA- und die ISMA-Methode, die im Markt auch als **„Actual/Actual historical"** **(ISDA)** oder **„Actual/Actual Bond" (ISMA)** bezeichnet werden.

Von den neun theoretisch möglichen Kombinationen von T und B sind allerdings **nur fünf in Verwendung: ACT/365, ACT/360, 30/360, 30E/360 und ACT/ACT**.

Die Tageskonventionen sind von Markt zu Markt unterschiedlich. In der folgenden Tabelle sind die **Konventionen im Geld- und Kapitalmarkt** aufgelistet. Beim Kapitalmarkt sei jedoch darauf hingewiesen, dass diese Konventionen zwischen dem internationalen bzw. dem Heimmarkt und den unterschiedlichen Instrumenten in der Spezifikation differieren können. Vor dem Handel daher bitte unbedingt die Konditionen nochmals klären!

	Money market		Money market		Capital Market
Australia	ACT/360	Norway	ACT/360	Euro	ACT/ACT
Euro	ACT/360	Poland	ACT/365	Great-Britain	Gilts: s.a.*) ACT/ACT
New Zealand	ACT/360	Sweden	ACT/360	Japan	30/360 or ACT/ACT
Great Britain	**ACT/365**	Switzer-land	ACT/360	Sweden	30/360 or 30E/360
Hong Kong/ Singapore	**ACT/365**	Czech Republic	ACT/360	Switzer-land	30/360 or 30E/360
Japan	ACT/360	USA	ACT/360	USA	30/360 or ACT/ACT

*) semi-annual

Example		
Semi-annual bond, principal 10,000 at an interest rate of 7,5% p.a., last coupon on 1st May, next coupon on 1 November (number of days: 184). On 31st May, the following interest is due:		
Calculation method	**Days of term/Days per year**	**Calculation of interest**
ACT/365	30/365	$10,000 \cdot 0.075 \cdot \dfrac{30}{365} = 61.64$
ACT/360	30/360	$10,000 \cdot 0.075 \cdot \dfrac{30}{360} = 62.50$
30/360	30/360	$10,000 \cdot 0.075 \cdot \dfrac{30}{360} = 62.50$
30E/360	29/360	$10,000 \cdot 0.075 \cdot \dfrac{29}{360} = 60.42$
ACT/ACT	30/368	$10,000 \cdot 0.075 \cdot \dfrac{30}{368} = 61.14$

	Geld-markt		Geld-markt		Kapital-markt
Australien	ACT/360	Norwegen	ACT/360	Euro	ACT/ACT
Euro	ACT/360	Polen	**ACT/365**	UK	Gilts: s.a. ACT/ACT*)
Neuseeland	ACT/360	Schweden	ACT/360	Japan	30/360 oder ACT/ACT
UK	**ACT/365**	Schweiz	ACT/360	Schweden	30/360 oder 30E/360
Hongkong/ Singapur	**ACT/365**	Tschechien	CT/360	Schweiz	30/360 oder 30E/360
Japan	ACT/360	USA	ACT/360	USA	30/360 oder ACT/ACT

*) semi-annual

Beispiel		
Halbjährliche Anleihe, Nominale 10.000 mit 7,5% Zinsen p.a., letzter Kupon am 1. Mai, nächster Kupon am 1. November (Anzahl der Tage: 184). Am 31. Mai sind damit folgende Zinsen angefallen:		
Berechnungsmethode	**Verrechnungstage/ Tage pro Jahr**	**Zinsberechnung**
ACT/365	30/365	$10.000 \times 0,075 \times \dfrac{30}{365} = 61,64$
ACT/360	30/360	$10.000 \times 0,075 \times \dfrac{30}{360} = 62,50$
30/360	30/360	$10.000 \times 0,075 \times \dfrac{30}{360} = 62,50$
30E/360	29/360	$10.000 \times 0,075 \times \dfrac{29}{360} = 60,42$
ACT/ACT	30/368	$10.000 \times 0,075 \times \dfrac{30}{368} = 61,14$

1.2. The Yield Curve

The yield curve (also known as interest rate structure) displays **interest rates of a specific financial instrument for different terms to maturity**. For example the T-bond curve shows the yields of US Treasury bonds ("T-bond") with various terms to maturity. Due to the number of different instruments there are a lot different yield curves such as interest rate swap (IRS) curve, LIBOR-curve, Bund-curve, mortgage bond-curve etc.

There are **three different types of yield curves**:

- **steep yield curve**
  (normal or positive) short-term interest rates are lower than long-term interest rates.
- **flat yield curve**
  interest rates for different terms are the same.
- **inverse yield curve**
  short-term interest rates are higher than long-term interest rates.

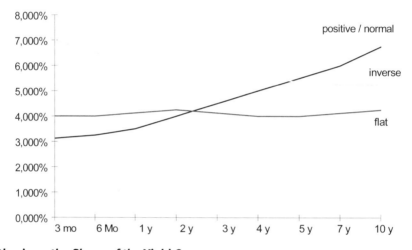

Hypothesis on the Shape of the Yield Curve

There are three theories on the shape of a yield curve:

One of them is the so-called **Interest Expectation Theory**. Therefore, the yield curve represents the expectations of market participants regarding future yields. If the market expects rising interest rates, the yield curve will slope upwards, because market participants will anticipate higher future rates for long-term investments.

According the **Liquidity Preference Theory** the market participants demand a premium for long-term investments compared to short term deals. Therefore, even in a situation where no interest rate change is expected, the curve will slightly slope upwards. This constellation is called "normal interest curve".

The **Market Segmentation Theory** says that different groups of market participants are active in market segments with different duration. This supply and demand mismatch in the various segments leads to different yields for different terms.

Certainly, there are several other factors that have an influence on the yield curve, e.g. interventions of the central bank, preferences of liquidity among market participants, etc.

1.2. Die Zinskurve

Die Zinskurve (bzw. Renditekurve) stellt die **Zinssätze für verschiedene Laufzeiten** eines Finanzinstrumentes dar. So zeigt beispielsweise die „Bundkurve" die Renditen von Deutschen Bundesanleihen (kurz Bund) mit unterschiedlichen Laufzeiten. Aufgrund der Vielzahl von unterschiedlichen Instrumenten gibt es auch eine Vielzahl unterschiedlicher Zinskurven wie z.B. Interest Rate Swap (IRS)-Kurve, Pfandbriefkurve, T-Bond-Kurve, EURIBOR-Kurve etc.

Drei typische Formen von Zinskurven werden unterschieden:

- **ansteigende Zinskurve**
  (normale, steile, positive Zinskurve): Die Zinsen für kurze Laufzeiten sind niedriger als für lange Laufzeiten.
- **flache Zinskurve**
  Die Zinssätze für unterschiedliche Laufzeiten sind gleich hoch.
- **inverse Zinskurve**
  Die Zinssätze für kurze Laufzeiten sind höher als die Zinsen für lange Laufzeiten.

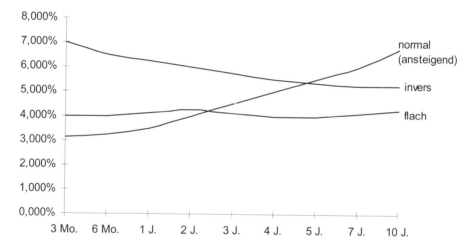

Zinskurventheorien

Zur Begründung der verschiedenen Verläufe von Zinskurven gibt es drei Theorien:

Die **Erwartungstheorie** geht davon aus, dass Erwartungen über zukünftige Zinsänderungen das Angebot und die Nachfrage nach Titeln mit verschiedenen Laufzeiten unterschiedlich beeinflussen. Dadurch ergeben sich unterschiedliche Zinssätze für die unterschiedlichen Laufzeiten.

Gemäß der **Liquiditätspräferenztheorie** wird für eine längere Veranlagung eine Prämie verlangt. Demnach weist die Zinsstruktur auch bei neutralen Erwartungen bezüglich zukünftiger Zinsänderungen eine positive Steigung auf.

Die **Marktsegmentierungstheorie** geht davon aus, dass in den verschiedenen Laufzeitsegmenten unterschiedliche Gruppen von Marktteilnehmern agieren, wodurch sich unterschiedliche Zinssätze in den einzelnen Segmenten ergeben.

1.3. Interpolation

Since there is not always a benchmark at hand, interest rates must sometimes be estimated. In the following, we want to show the most simple method to calculate interest rates for unusual terms: **straight-line interpolation**.

$$r=r_s+\left[\frac{r_l-r_s}{D_l-D_s}\right]\times\left(D-D_s\right)$$

r   = interest rate in decimals
D = number of days of the term of interest
r_s = interest rate in decimals, short-term
D_s = number of days, short-term
r_l = interest rate in decimals, long-term
D_l = number of days, long-term

Example

We calculate the interest rate for a deposit for 1½ months (46 days) on the basis of the following interest rates:
1 month   3½%   (31 days)
3 months 3¾%   (92 days)

$$r=0.035 +\left[\frac{0.0375-0.035}{92-31}\right]\times(46-31)=3.56148\%$$

The method of straight-line interpolation has the advantage that it is **very easy to apply**.

To give a complete overview, we would like to point out, that there exist also methods which take the non-linearity of interest rates into account. These are:

- logarithmic interpolation
- cubic splines

1.4. Quotation

Interest rates are often quoted in **basis points** that lie either below or above a certain benchmark rate. A bank could lend money at LIBOR -3 basis points; or a Dollar bond is issued at T +50: this would mean 50 basis points above the yield of a comparable US Treasury bill. One basis point is equal to **1/100 of 1%, i.e. 0.01%**.

The quotation of interest rates in the money market is done on a p.a. basis, where the **interest is paid at the end of the term**. The interest that is thereby paid is called **simple interest** (e.g. CHF $2^1/_4 - 2^3/_8$% for 6 months).

1.3. Interpolation

Da nicht für jede beliebige Laufzeit eine entsprechende Benchmark zur Verfügung steht, müssen Zinssätze mitunter angenähert werden. In der Folge wird die einfachste Methode der Berechnung von Zinssätzen für unübliche Laufzeiten mit der **linearen Interpolation** vorgestellt.

$$r = r_k + \left[\frac{r_l - r_k}{T_l - T_k}\right] \cdot (T - T_k)$$

r   = Zinssatz in Dezimalen
T   = Laufzeit in Tagen für die zu berechnende Periode
r_k = Zinssatz in Dezimalen, kurze Periode
T_k = Laufzeit in Tagen für die kürzere Periode
r_l = Zinssatz in Dezimalen, lange Periode
T_l = Laufzeit in Tagen für die längere Periode

Beispiel

Wir ermitteln einen Zinssatz für ein Depot von 1½ Monaten (46 Tage) aus folgenden Zinssätzen:

1 Monat   3½%   (31 Tage)
3 Monate   3¾%   (92 Tage)

$$r = 0{,}035 + \left[\frac{0{,}0375 - 0{,}035}{92 - 31}\right] \times (46 - 31) = 3{,}56148\%$$

Der Vorteil der dargestellten Methode der linearen Interpolation liegt in ihrer **Einfachheit**.

Allerdings wollen wir auch auf Methoden hinweisen, die die Nichtlinearität der Zinskurve berücksichtigen:

- Logarithmische Interpolation
- Cubic Spline

1.4. Quotierungen

Zinssätze werden oft in **Basispunkten** quotiert, die über oder unter einer bestimmten Benchmark liegen können. Beispielsweise könnte eine Bank zu LIBOR -3 Punkte Geld leihen oder eine Dollaranleihe könnte zur Quotierung T +50 emittiert werden, das bedeutet 50 Basispunkte über der Rendite einer vergleichbaren US-Treasury-Bill. Ein Basispunkt ist **1/100 von 1%, also 0,01%**.

Die Angabe des Zinssatzes für Geldmarktgeschäfte erfolgt auf einer **p.a.-Basis**, wobei die **Zinsen im Nachhinein am Ende der jeweiligen Laufzeit** auf das Kapital gezahlt werden. Die dabei entrichteten Zinsen nennt man auch **einfache Zinsen** (z.B. CHF $2^1/_4 - 2^3/_8\%$ für 6 Monate).

In the money market, most transactions have terms of not more than one year. Where the **term exceeds twelve months, interest is paid first after one year and then at maturity**. For example, interest payments on an 18-month deposit are due after twelve months for the first time, and finally after 18 months, i.e. at the end of the 6-month period of the second year. Simple interest for a definite period is calculated on the basis of the principal.

There are different methods to calculate interest for individual instruments.

Example

What is the value of a basis point of one year deposit USD 1,000,000?
Since USD is calculated on ACT/360 basis, the value of one Basis point is 1,000,000 x 0.0001 x 365/360 = 101.39 EUR.

Summary

There are three methods to determine the number of days (D): ACT-method (Actual-method), 30-method and 30E-method. There are also three ways to determine the day basis (B): 360-method, 365-method and ACT-method. Theoretically, nine combinations of days (D) and basis (B) are possible but only five of them are commonly used: ACT/365, ACT/360, 30/360, 30E/360 and ACT/ACT.

The yield curve (also known as interest rate structure) shows the interest rates of a specific financial instrument for different terms to maturity. There are three different types of yield curves: steep yield curve, flat yield curve and inverse yield curve. There are three theories on the shape of a yield curve: Interest Expectation Theory, Liquidity Preference Theory and Market Segmentation Theory.

Since there is not always a suitable benchmark available, interest rates must sometimes be estimated. The most simple method to calculate interest rates for unusual terms is the straight-line interpolation.

Interest rates are often quoted in basis points either below or above a certain benchmark rate. One basis point is equal to 1/100 of 1%, i.e. 0.01%. The quotation of interest rates in the money market is done on an annual basis with interest payable at the end of the term. When the term exceeds 12 months interest is paid after one year and then at maturity.

Geldmarktgeschäfte werden üblicherweise bis zu einer Laufzeit von einem Jahr abgeschlossen. In jenen Fällen, in denen die **Laufzeit** von Krediten oder Einlagen im Geldmarktbereich **zwölf Monate übersteigt**, werden die **Zinsen zunächst jährlich und dann bei Fälligkeit** bezahlt. Beispielsweise werden die Zinsen für ein genommenes 18-Monats-Depot erstmals nach zwölf Monaten und zum zweiten Mal nach 18 Monaten bezahlt, also nach dem Ende der 6-Monats-Frist im zweiten Jahr. Einfache Zinsen für eine bestimmte Periode werden auf das gegebene Kapital bzw. auf einen gegebenen Nominalbetrag gerechnet.

Unterschiedliche Zinsberechnungsmethoden für einzelne Instrumente sind jederzeit möglich und beeinflussen den absoluten Wert eines Basispunktes.

Beispiel

Was ist der Wert eines Basispunktes bei einem EUR 1.000.000 Jahresdepot?
Da EUR am Geldmarkt mit ACT/360 gerechnet wird, muss der Wert eines Basispunktes 1.000.000 x 0,0001 x 365/360 = 101,39 EUR sein.

Zusammenfassung

Bei der Zinsberechnung gibt es für die Berechnung der Tage drei Methoden: ACT-Methode (Actual-Methode), 30-Methode und 30E-Methode. Für die Berechnung der Basis gibt es ebenfalls drei Methoden: 360-Methode, 365-Methode und ACT-Methode. Von den neun theoretisch möglichen Kombinationen von T und B sind allerdings nur fünf in Verwendung: ACT/365, ACT/360, 30/360, 30E/360 und ACT/ACT.

Die Zinskurve (bzw. Renditekurve) stellt die Zinssätze für verschiedene Laufzeiten eines Finanzinstrumentes dar. Es werden drei typische Formen von Zinskurven unterschieden: ansteigende Zinskurve (normale, steile, positive Zinskurve), flache Zinskurve und inverse Zinskurve. Zur Begründung der verschiedenen Verläufe von Zinskurven gibt es drei Theorien: Erwartungstheorie, Liquiditätspräferenztheorie und Marktsegmentierungstheorie.

Da nicht für jede beliebige Laufzeit eine entsprechende Benchmark zur Verfügung steht, müssen Zinssätze mitunter angenähert werden. Die einfachste Methode zur Berechnung von Zinssätzen für unübliche Laufzeiten ist die lineare Interpolation.

Zinssätze werden oft in Basispunkten quotiert, die über oder unter einer bestimmten Benchmark liegen können. Ein Basispunkt ist 1/100 von 1%, also 0,01%. Die Angabe des Zinssatzes für Geldmarktgeschäfte erfolgt auf einer p.a.-Basis, wobei die Zinsen im Nachhinein am Ende der jeweiligen Laufzeit auf das Kapital gezahlt werden. In jenen Fällen, in denen die Laufzeit von Krediten oder Einlagen im Geldmarktbereich zwölf Monate übersteigt, werden die Zinsen zunächst jährlich und dann bei Fälligkeit bezahlt.

1.5. Practice Questions

1. Name and describe the three methods to determine the number of days for interest calculation!

2. Name and describe the three ways to determine the day basis for interest calculation!

3. Which of the following currencies in the money market is quoted on an ACT/365 basis for the calculation of interest on interbank deposits?
   a) CAD
   b) CHF
   c) EUR
   d) All answers are false.

4. For which of the following currencies is the interest rate calculated on an ACT/365 day basis in the money market?
   a) GBP
   b) EUR
   c) JPY
   d) USD

5. Which of the following currencies is NOT calculated on a 360 day basis in the euro market?
   a) SEK
   b) CHF
   c) GBP
   d) HKD
   e) EUR

6. What is a yield curve?
   a) It shows historical returns on given products over time.
   b) It is an estimate of market expecations with regard to future interest rates.
   c) It shows market makers what interest rates to ask when lending funds.
   d) It shows the relationship between yields and maturities for a set of similar or identical products.

7. Name and describe the three different types of yield curves!

8. Which of the following situations is reflected by a positive yield curve?
   a) Swap points are at a premium.
   b) Swap points are at a discount.
   c) Long-term interest rates are higher than short-term interest rates.
   d) Short-term interest rates are higher than long-term interest rates.

9. Which yield curve should prevail in a neutral market situation according to the Liquidity Preference Theory?
   a) flat
   b) normal
   c) inverse

1.5. Wiederholungsfragen

1. Nennen und beschreiben Sie die drei Methoden zur Berechnung der Tage bei der Zinsberechnung!

2. Nennen und beschreiben Sie die drei Methoden zur Berechnung der Basis bei der Zinsberechnung!

3. Welche der folgenden Währungen wird am Geldmarkt mit ACT/365 kalkuliert, wenn die Zinsen für Euro-Anlagen errechnet werden?
   a) CAD
   b) CHF
   c) EUR
   d) Alle Antworten sind falsch.

4. Der Zinssatz welcher Währung wird am Geldmarkt auf der Basis ACT/365 berechnet?
   a) GBP
   b) EUR
   c) JPY
   d) USD

5. Welche der folgenden Währungen werden im Euromarkt NICHT mit Basis 360 Tage gerechnet?
   a) SEK
   b) CHF
   c) GBP
   d) HKD
   e) EUR

6. Was ist eine Zinskurve?
   a) Sie zeigt historische Renditen gegebener Produkte im Zeitablauf.
   b) Sie schätzt die Markterwartungen bezüglich des zukünftigen Zinsniveaus.
   c) Sie zeigt Market Makern, welche Zinssätze für Kredite zu verlangen sind.
   d) Sie zeigt den Zusammenhang zwischen Renditen und Restlaufzeiten für eine Anzahl von ähnlichen oder identischen Produkten.

7. Nennen und beschreiben Sie die drei typischen Formen von Zinskurven!

8. Welche Situation spiegelt eine positive Zinskurve wider?
   a) Swappunkte befinden sich im Aufschlag.
   b) Swappunkte befinden sich im Abschlag.
   c) Langfristige Zinssätze sind höher als kurzfristige Zinsen.
   d) Kurzfristige Zinssätze sind höher als langfristige Zinsen.

9. Welche Form sollte eine Zinskurve bei einer neutralen Erwartungshaltung des Marktes gemäß der Liquiditätspräferenztheorie haben?
   a) flach
   b) normal
   c) invers

10. What is the characteristic of the Market Segmentation Theory?
    a) Market participants demand a premium for long-term investments.
    b) The yield curve represents the expectations of market participants regarding future yields.
    c) A supply and demand mismatch leads to different yields for different terms.
    d) All answers are false.

11. According to the Expectation Theory, what is the main influence factor on the shape of the yield curve?
    a) segmentation of market participants
    b) compound interest
    c) preference of market participants for short-term investments
    d) expectations of market participants regarding the future interest rates

12. The 90-day interest rate is 3.1% and the 180-day interest rate is 3.5%. What is the 120-day interest rate?

13. What is a basis point?

14. When is interest paid for money market transactions with a term of up to one year?

15. When is interest paid for money market transactions with a term of more than one year?

10. Was ist das Merkmal der Marktsegmentierungstheorie?
    a) Marktteilnehmer verlangen für längere Laufzeiten einen Aufschlag.
    b) Die Zinskurve wird von der Erwartung über die zukünftige Zinsentwicklung beeinflusst.
    c) Es ergeben sich unterschiedliche Zinssätze aufgrund von Angebots- und Nachfrageungleichgewichten.
    d) Alle Antworten sind falsch.

11. Wovon hängt nach der Erwartungstheorie die Form der Zinskurve ab?
    a) Segmentierung der Marktteilnehmer
    b) Zinseszinsen
    c) Präferenz der Marktteilnehmer für liquide Mittel
    d) Meinung der Marktteilnehmer bezüglich der zukünftigen Zinsentwicklung

12. Der 90-Tage-Zinssatz ist 3,1% und der 180-Tage-Zinssatz ist 3,5%. Was ist der 120-Tage-Zinssatz?

13. Was versteht man unter einem Basispunkt?

14. Wann werden die Zinsen bei Geldmarktgeschäften mit einer Laufzeit von bis zu einem Jahr gezahlt?

15. Wann werden die Zinsen bei Geldmarktgeschäften mit einer Laufzeit von über einem Jahr gezahlt?

2. Money Market Cash Instruments

In this chapter you learn ...

- about the most important money market cash instruments.
- about the differentiate between coupon and discount instruments.
- about the differences in calculating interests using a yield and discount rate.
- about the features of the reference rates LIBOR, LIBID and EURIBOR.
- about the main features of interbank deposits.
- about the main features of certificates of deposit (CDs).
- about the main features of eligible bills.
- about the main features of commercial papers (CPs).
- about treasury bills.

The money market is the interbank market for trading short-term financial instruments. Most of the transactions in the money market have terms up to three months, some up to one year or more.

The most important money market products are:

- interbank loans/deposits
- certificates of deposit (CDs)
- bills of exchange   } tradeable instruments
- commercial papers (CPs)
- repurchase-agreements (Repos)

In contrast to interbank deposits, certificates of deposits, federal savings bonds (T-bills), and commercial papers are negotiable instruments. A negotiable instrument can be sold in the secondary market before maturity (end of the term).

The main goal of banks and other money market participants is to maintain their liquidity. They must, at all times, be able to pay off borrowed money at once, if the need may arise. The existence of a money market for cash products enables banks and other competitors who have a surplus of short-term deposits to earn interest by investing this surplus. On the other hand, those market competitors who demand short-term money can borrow them from a liquid market.

If the money market is very liquid, banks assume that their demand of money can be satisfied easily and immediately. This means that they can work with a smaller amount of capital in order to increase their aggregate earnings.

Banks need liquidity to **satisfy statutory regulations as well as to meet the requirement of fully covering their obligations at any time.**

2. Cash-Instrumente im Geldmarkt

In diesem Kapitel lernen Sie ...

- die wichtigsten Geldmarktinstrumente kennen.
- den Unterschied zwischen Kupon- und Diskontinstrumenten kennen.
- den Unterschied in der Berechnung der Zinsen zwischen der Angabe eines Zinssatzes und eines Diskontsatzes kennen.
- die Referenzzinssätze LIBOR, LIBID und EURIBOR und deren Eigenschaften kennen.
- die wesentlichen Merkmale von Interbank-Depotgeschäften kennen.
- die wesentlichen Merkmale von Certificates of Deposit (CDs) kennen.
- die wesentlichen Merkmale von Wechselgeschäften kennen.
- den Ablauf eines Wechselgeschäfts kennen.
- was man unter Schuldscheinen (promissory notes) versteht.
- die wesentlichen Merkmale von Commercial Papers (CPs) kennen.
- was man unter Treasury Bills versteht.

Der Geldmarkt (Money Market) ist der Interbankenmarkt für den Handel von kurzfristigen Finanzinstrumenten. Die meisten Geldmarkttransaktionen werden mit einer Laufzeit von bis zu drei Monaten, manche auch bis zu einem Jahr oder sogar länger getätigt.

Die wichtigsten Geldmarktinstrumente sind:

- Interbankenkredite/-Depots
- Certificates of Deposit (CDs)
- Wechsel   } handelbare Instrumente
- Commercial Papers (CPs)
- Repurchase Agreements (Repos)

Certificates of Deposit, Wechsel und Commercial Papers sind im Gegensatz zu den Interbankdepots handelbare Instrumente. Man spricht von einem handelbaren Instrument, wenn dieses im Sekundärmarkt vor der Fälligkeit (Laufzeitende) wieder verkauft werden kann.

Banken und andere Geldmarktteilnehmer haben die primäre Aufgabe, ihre Liquidität zu erhalten. Sie müssen jederzeit in der Lage sein, gegebene Einlagen sofort zurückzuzahlen. Die Existenz eines Geldmarkts für Cash-Produkte ermöglicht Banken und anderen Marktteilnehmern mit einem Überhang an kurzfristigen Anlagen, diese gegen Zinsertrag zu investieren. Andererseits können Marktteilnehmer, die Bedarf an kurzfristigen Geldern haben, diese in einem liquiden Markt aufnehmen.

Ist der Geldmarkt sehr liquide, schließen die Banken daraus, dass sie ihren Geldmittelbedürfnissen prompt und sehr einfach nachkommen können. Das bedeutet, dass sie mit geringerem Kapitaleinsatz arbeiten können, um ihren Gesamtertrag zu steigern.

Banken benötigen Liquidität zur **Einhaltung gesetzlicher Bestimmungen bzw. zur Aufrechterhaltung der Bedingung, Verpflichtungen jederzeit erfüllen zu können.**

Also the **national banks**, need the money market to fulfill a number of tasks:

- controlling inflation through active policies in the money market
- managing the exchange rate
- controlling the lending operations of the state

Through these actions by the national banks in the money market they can send **signals about the future development of interest rates in the money market.**

Coupon Instruments vs. Discount Instruments

Most of the instruments are **coupon instruments** i.e. they are **issued at an interest rate (coupon) and face value. Notional amount and interests are paid back** at maturity. Coupon instruments are **Interbank Deposits, CDs and Repos.**

Discount instruments are issued with a **discount from their notional value**; at maturity the **holder receives the notional amount**. The difference between the issuing price and repayment is the buyer's interest result.

Discount instruments are e.g.: **Commercial Papers, T-Bills and Eligible Bills.**

True Yield vs. Discount Rate

A **yield** (interest rate p.a., effective rate) is quoted on the basis of the **invested capital** (= present value) a **discount rate** is calculated on the basis of the **future value.**

Example
You sell 100 EUR at 5% interest rate for 360 days. What are the Cash-Flows?
T0:   100
T1g: 105 $[100 + (100 \times (0{,}05 \times 360/360))]$

Auch die **Nationalbanken der einzelnen Länder** brauchen den Geldmarkt, um einer Reihe von Verpflichtungen nachkommen zu können:

● Kontrolle der Inflation durch aktive Geldmarktpolitik
● Management des Wechselkurses der eigenen Währung
● Kontrolle der Kreditgeschäfte des Staates

Durch die Aktionen der Nationalbanken im Geldmarkt können **Signale für die Zinsentwicklung im Geldmarkt** gesetzt werden.

Kuponinstrumente vs. Abzinsungsinstrumente

Die meisten Instrumente sind sogenannte **Kuponinstrumente**, d.h., sie werden zum **Nennwert und mit einem Zinssatz (Kupon) emittiert.** Am Ende der Laufzeit wird dann der **Nennwert plus Zinsen zurückgezahlt.** Zu den Kuponinstrumenten zählen **Interbank Depots, CDs und Repos.**

Die Cashflows eines Kuponinstruments stellen sich wie folgt dar:

Im Gegensatz dazu werden **Abzinsungsinstrumente (Diskontinstrumente)** mit einem **Abschlag vom Nennwert emittiert** und zum vollen **Nennwert zurückgezahlt.** Aus der Differenz der beiden Beträge ergibt sich der Ertrag für den Käufer.

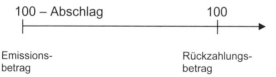

Diskontinstrumente sind beispielsweise **Commercial Papers, T-Bills und Wechsel.**

Zinssatz vs. Diskontsatz

Wird ein **Zinssatz (Rendite)** angegeben, so wird der **Zinsbetrag auf der Basis des Anfangsbetrages** berechnet. In der Folge werden auch die Begriffe per anno Zinssatz (p.a. Zinssatz), Rendite oder effektiver Zinssatz verwendet.

Beispiel

Sie legen 100 EUR zu einem Zinssatz von 5% für 360 Tage an. Welche Cashflows ergeben sich daraus?

Anfangsbetrag: 100
Rückzahlung: 105 $[100 + (100 \times (0{,}05 \times 360/360))]$

If a **discount rate** is quoted, the **discount** is calculated on the **basis of the future value** and not on the basis of the investigated capital.

Example
You buy a bill of exchange 100 EUR at 5% interest rate for 360 days. What are the Cash-Flows? T0:   95 $[100 - (100 \times (0,05 \times 360/360))]$ T1:   100

For both examples the interest amount is 5 EUR. Please note that in the first case the invested capital is 100 EUR and in the second case it is only 95 EUR. Therefore the **yield is in the second case higher than in the first case.**

PLEASE NOTE:

It is essential to differentiate between: **coupon instrument ≠ discount instrument** and **yield ≠ discount rate.** Sometimes discount instruments are quoted on a yield basis. That means the price of the instrument can be calculated by computing the present value of the notional amount. In this case the quoted yield is comparable to the quotation of other interest instruments (e.g. Interbank deposit) – but still the Cash-Flows inherent are different due to the effect that the instrument is still a discount instrument.

Example
You buy a EUR-CP, 100 EUR at 5% interest rate for 360 days. What are the Cash-Flows? T0:   95,238 $[100 / (1 + 0,05 \times 360/360)]$ T1:   100

Wird ein **Diskontsatz** angegeben, so ist gemeint, dass der **Abschlag (Zinsbetrag) auf Basis des Rückzahlungsbetrages** berechnet wird und nicht auf Basis des Anfangsbetrages.

Beispiel

Sie kaufen einen Wechsel über 100 EUR zu einem Diskontsatz von 5% für 360 Tage. Welche Cashflows ergeben sich daraus?

Anfangsbetrag: 95 $[100 - (100 \times (0,05 \times 360/360))]$

Rückzahlung: 100

Bei beiden Beispielen ist der Zinsbetrag 5 EUR. Allerdings ist zu beachten, dass im ersten Fall (Zinssatz-Quotierung) das eingesetzte Kapital 100 EUR ist, bei der Diskontsatz-Quotierung jedoch nur 95 EUR. Somit ist die **Rendite, d.h. das Ergebnis der Veranlagung bezogen auf das Anfangskapital, im zweiten Fall höher als im ersten**.

BEACHTEN SIE:

Die beiden Dimensionen Kuponinstrument bzw. Diskontinstrument und Zinssatz bzw. Diskontsatz sind unbedingt auseinanderzuhalten. So kann es manchmal auch vorkommen, dass Diskontinstrumente auf Renditebasis quotiert werden. Das bedeutet, dass das Instrument zwar mit einem Abschlag zum Nennwert gehandelt wird, der Abschlag jedoch auf Basis des Anfangsbetrages und nicht auf Basis des Rückzahlungsbetrages berechnet wird.

Beispiel

Sie kaufen ein Euro-CP über 100 EUR zu einem Zinssatz von 5% für 360 Tage. Welche Cashflows ergeben sich daraus?

Anfangsbetrag: 95,238 $[100 / (1 + 0,05 \times 360/360)]$

Rückzahlung: 100

2.1. Overview

	Interbank loans/ deposits	CDs	Eligible bills	CPs	T-Bill	Repo
(Main)-issuer	banks	credit institutions (for ex. commercial banks)	corporates	corporates, banks	government	–
Liability	issuer	issuer	beside the obligation of the issuer: credit risk mitigation through goods and an accepting bank	issuer	issuer	a repo agreement is backed by securities
Interest	coupon-instrument	coupon-instrument	discount-instrument	discount-instrument	discount-instrument	coupon-instrument
Quotation	yield basis	yield basis	discount rate	ECP yield basis Domestic CP discount rate	USD, GBP discount rate all others yield basis	yield basis
Secondary market	no	yes	yes	yes	yes	no

2.2. Interbank-Depotgeschäfte

Most banks make deposit deals with each other. The interest rates in the domestic or the euromoney market that are the basis for these operations, depend on the current conditions in the markets and on the volumes that are traded.

Quotation

The interest rate for all standard terms (from overnight to twelve months) is quoted. The highest volume is achieved in the markets of up-to-3-months.

Banks in the market quote **different interest rates**, that **depend on their current liquidity and their current open positions**. Banks with a surplus of liquidity will quote lower in order to receive fewer deposits and will also be willing to accept a lower lending rate. Moreover, banks with high ratings are able to borrow money from the market on better conditions than banks with lower ratings.

The **margin between bid and offer** is **usually 1/8%** (12.5 basis points). For the most liquid currencies the margin is often smaller.

2.1. Übersicht

	Depot	CD	Wechsel	CP	T-Bill	Repo
(Haupt)- Emittent	Banken	Kreditins- titute (z.B. Geschäfts- banken)	Industrie	Banken, Industrie	Staat	–
Haftung	Emittent	Emittent	Emittent, Besi- cherung durch Waren und ak- zeptierende Bank	Emittent	Emittent	Besiche- rung durch Wertpapiere
Zins	Zinssatz nach Verein- barung	Kuponins- trument	Diskont- instrument	Diskont- instrument	Diskont- instrument	Zinssatz nach Verein- barung
Zinsbasis	Rendite	Rendite	Diskont	Rendite oder Diskont (Inlands USD CP, sogenann- te USCPs)	Rendite oder Diskont (USD und GBP T-Bills)	Rendite
Sekundär- markt	Nein	Ja	Ja	Ja	Ja	Nein

2.2. Interbank-Depotgeschäfte

Die meisten Banken tätigen untereinander Depotgeschäfte. Die Zinssätze, zu denen diese Geschäfte (Depots) im Heimwährungsmarkt oder im Eurogeldmarkt gehandelt werden, hängen von den aktuellen Marktkonditionen und von den Volumina ab, die untereinander gehandelt werden.

Quotierung

Die Zinssätze werden für alle Standardlaufzeiten von overnight bis zu zwölf Monaten quotiert. Das größte Volumen entfällt auf Perioden bis zu drei Monaten.

Selbstverständlich **quotieren unterschiedliche Banken unterschiedliche Zinssät- ze**, je nach ihrer **momentanen Liquidität** oder ihren **momentanen offenen Positionen**. Banken mit einem Überhang an Liquidität quotieren niedriger, um keine Einlagen mehr nehmen zu müssen. Sie akzeptieren aber auch Zinssätze zu einem niedrigeren Niveau, wenn sie veranlagen wollen. Darüber hinaus sind Banken mit besserer Bonität in der La- ge, ihre Mittel am Geldmarkt zu niedrigeren Sätzen aufzunehmen als Banken mit schlechterem Rating.

Die **Marge zwischen Geld und Brief** („bid and offer") beträgt **üblicherweise 1/8%** (12,5 Basispunkte). Für sehr liquide Währungen ist sie oft kleiner.

For the euromoney market in London, there exists a so-called reference or **bench-mark rate**: the **London Interbank Offered Rate** (LIBOR). The LIBOR is an internationally accepted reference rate, that has reached its position due to the importance of the City of London as banking center and its importance in the money market (eurodollar market).

LIBOR is the most important reference rate, usually used in fixing of certain maturities (FRAs, interest rate swaps, loans, etc.). It embodies the **average interest rate of certain reference banks** that are chosen for the daily fixing. LIBOR is called the interest rate at which top banks are willing to lend money to one another.

Presently, currencies like USD, GBP, EUR, CHF, JPY, AUD, and CAD are being officially published as LIBOR fixing by the BBA. These rates represent the euromoney market and may differ from the so-called domestic fixing.

LIBOR rates are published daily at **11 o'clock GMT** by the **British Bankers' Association** and exist for terms between 1 and 12 months.

LIBID (London Interbank Bid Rate): In contrast to LIBOR, the LIBID represents the so-called **deposit rate**. **LIBOR minus the usual spread** yields the LIBID (e.g. LIBOR USD 3-month = 3.50%, minus spread of 1/8% equals to LIBID of 3.375%). LIBID is the rate banks are willing to borrow money.

Interbank rates are also quoted in all major financial centers of the world. Furthermore, there is a TIBOR (Tokyo Interbank Offered Rate), PRIBOR (Prague Interbank Offered Rate) and **EURIBOR** (Euro Interbank Offered Rate) that replaced the interbank rates of the 15 Euro-in countries. EURIBOR is derived from the offered rate quotes of **43 panel banks** (as of August 2012). The highest and lowest 15% of all quotes are eliminated and the **average over the remaining quotes calculated**. EURIBOR is published by THOMSON Reuters and is quoted with 3 decimals.

EURIBOR established a dominant position as reference rate for Euro money market transactions. Euro-LIBOR plays a rather negligible role.

Conventions

Start date

Usually, the term of a deposit starts **two working days after the deal has been concluded**.

This does not apply for the following transactions:

Overnight (O/N) – the loan/deposit starts on the **same working day** on which the deal has been agreed on.

Tom/Next (T/N) – the loan/deposit starts **one day after the deal was agreed** on.

Für den Euro-Geldmarkt in London wurde ein sogenannter Referenzsatz bzw. **Benchmark Rate** eingeführt. Das ist der **London Interbank Offered Rate (LIBOR)**. Der LIBOR ist ein international anerkannter Referenzsatz, der sich aus der Stellung des Londoner Bankenplatzes und seiner Wichtigkeit im Geldmarkt (Euro-Dollar-Markt) entwickelt hat.

LIBOR-Sätze werden für Perioden zwischen overnight und zwölf Monaten täglich um **11.00 Uhr London-Zeit** von der **British Bankers' Association** (BBA) **veröffentlicht** und haben sich zum Referenzsatz für viele Arten von Geschäften entwickelt (wie z.B. zum Fixing von FRAs, Interest Rate Swaps oder Krediten etc.). Mit der offiziellen Einführung des Euro gibt es seitens der Euro-Währungen das Bestreben, das Londoner Fixing als Benchmark für den Euro abzulösen.

Mit dem **EURIBOR** wurde das entsprechende Fixing am **01.01.1999** eingeführt.

Interbanksätze werden aber auch in allen größeren Finanzzentren der Welt „gefixt". Mit der Einführung des Euro wurden viele Sätze obsolet (z.B. FIBOR, BIBOR, VIBOR). Der **EURIBOR (Euro Interbank Offered Rate)** ersetzt diese nationalen Interbanksätze. Er ist ein um Extremwerte (obere und untere 15% der Quotierungen werden eliminiert) **bereinigter Durchschnitt von Briefsätzen**, die von derzeit **43 Banken**, genannt werden (Stand: August 2012). Der EURIBOR wird von THOMSON Reuters veröffentlicht und auf drei Kommastellen quotiert.

Der **LIBOR (London Interbank Offered Rate)** war vor Einführung des Euro der wichtigste Referenzzinssatz, der üblicherweise zum Fixieren bestimmter Fälligkeiten (FRAs, Interest-Rate Swaps, Kredite etc.) herangezogen wird. Er bildet den **durchschnittlichen Zinssatz bestimmter Referenzbanken**, die für das tägliche Fixing ausgewählt wurden. Der LIBOR wird auch häufig als jener Satz bezeichnet, zu dem erstklassige Banken bereit sind, untereinander Geld zu leihen.

Derzeit werden die Währungen USD, GBP, EUR, CHF, JPY, CAD und AUD offiziell von der BBA als LIBOR-Fixing veröffentlicht. Diese Sätze repräsentieren den Euro-Geldmarkt und können vom sogenannten Domestic Fixing abweichen.

LIBID (London Interbank Bid Rate) stellt im Gegensatz zum LIBOR den sogenannten **Einlagensatz** dar. Der **LIBOR abzüglich des üblichen Spreads** ergibt somit den LIBID (z.B. 3-Monats-LIBOR EUR = 3,5% abzüglich Spread 1/8% ergibt LIBID von 3,375%). Er wird auch als jener Satz bezeichnet, zu dem Banken bereit sind, Einlagen zu nehmen (werden Funds benötigt bzw. ist das Rating schlecht, wird auch mehr als LIBID geboten).

Usancen

Laufzeitbeginn

Die Laufzeit eines Depotgeschäftes beginnt üblicherweise **zwei Bankarbeitstage nach Abschluss** des Geschäftes.

Ausnahmen:

Overnight (O/N): Das Depot startet **an dem Werktag, an dem der Abschluss des Geschäftes erfolgt.**

Tom/Next (T/N): Das Depot startet **einen Werktag nach Abschluss** des Geschäftes.

End date (maturity)

Usually, the term of a loan/deposit of x months ends x calendar months after the start date. The term of a 3-month loan/deposit with start date on January 3 ends on April 3.

If the end date falls on a **weekend or a bank holiday**, the end date is the **following working day**. If the start date is the **last working day of the month**, the end date will also be the **last working day** of the respective month.

Interest period

The **time between start date and end date** is called interest period.

Interest payments

A **per annum, "p.a.", quote** has become the standard for calculating the interest on deposits. For loans/deposits with **terms shorter than one year**, the interest is paid at the **end of the term**. Therefore, the repayment includes both principal and accrued interest.

For loans/deposits with **terms of more than 12 months**, interest is usually paid **every 12 months** and then at the **end date** of the deal.

For example, if a bank lends money for 18 months, the first interest payment occurs after 12 months and the second one at the end date.

To compare non-annual interest rates with p.a. interest rates, the different dates for interest payments must be considered. To compare a 3-month interest rate with a 12-month interest rate, one usually employs the concept of effective (real) interest. Thereby, **compounding effects** are taken into account.

Example
A 1-month deposit at 6% p.a. (= 0.5% per month) earns more interest than a 12-month deposit at 6% p.a.
1-month deposit at 6% p.a. (0.5% per month) comparable annual yield $$= (1,005)^{12} - 1$$ $$= 0.0616778 \text{ or } 6.16778\%$$
12-month deposit at 6% p.a. comparable annual yield = 6%
The effective interest rate of the comparable 3-month deposit at 5% (= 1.25% quarterly) is: $$(1.0125)^4 - 1 = 0.0509453 = 5.09453\%$$
The effective interest rate is the same as that in the table above.

Note: The formula to calculate the compound interest assumes a steady rate of interest for the respective term. Since most commercial banks pay their interest on a quarterly basis, the fixed interest rate of 5% for a 3-month deposit equals an effective compound interest rate of approx. 5.09% p.a. In practice, it is not certain whether one can re-invest at a rate of 5% for the whole term of the deposit. Therefore, the gains realised from interest payments can eventually be higher or lower.

Laufzeitende

Die Laufzeit eines Depots von x Monaten endet üblicherweise genau x Kalendermonate nach Laufzeitbeginn. Für ein 3-Monats-Depot mit Laufzeitbeginn am 3. Januar endet die Laufzeit am 3. April.

Sollte das Laufzeitende auf einen **Wochenendtag** oder einen **Bankfeiertag** fallen, so ist das Ende der Laufzeit der **nächste Banktag**. Ist der **Laufzeitbeginn** der **letzte Arbeitstag im Monat**, dann ist das **Laufzeitende** auch der **letzte Banktag im Monat** (Ultimo).

Zinsperiode

Als Zinsperiode wird der **Zeitraum zwischen Laufzeitbeginn und Laufzeitende** bezeichnet.

Zinszahlung

Als Standardkonvention für die Zinsberechnung bei Depotgeschäften hat sich eine **p.a.-Quotierung** institutionalisiert. Bei Depotgeschäften mit **Laufzeiten unter einem Jahr** werden die **Zinsen im Nachhinein** für die Dauer der Zinsperiode gezahlt. Bei Rückzahlung erfolgt also die **Zahlung von Kapital und angefallenen Zinsen.**

Für Depotgeschäfte mit einer **Laufzeit von über zwölf Monaten** werden die Zinsen üblicherweise jährlich zum jeweiligen **Jahrestag des Geschäftbeginns** und zu **Laufzeitende** gezahlt.

Veranlagt eine Bank beispielsweise ein Depot für die Laufzeit von 18 Monaten, so werden Zinsen erstmals nach zwölf Monaten und zum Laufzeitende gezahlt.

Um Zinssätze für unterjährige Perioden mit einem Jahressatz zu vergleichen, ist zu berücksichtigen, dass bei einer kurzfristigeren Veranlagung (oder Refinanzierung), die Zinszahlung schon am Laufzeitende fällig wird. Um einen 3-Monats-Satz mit einem 12-Monats-Satz zu vergleichen, wird daher üblicherweise auf das Konzept der Effektivzinsen zurückgegriffen. Die **Berechnung von Effektivzinsen** berücksichtigt etwaige **Zinseszinseffekte.**

Beispiel

Was ist der vergleichbare Effektivzinssatz eines 3-Monats-Depots zu 5%?

$$EZ = \left(1 + \frac{NZ}{ZP}\right)^{ZP} - 1$$

EZ = Effektivzins p.a. in Dezimalen
NZ = Nominalzins p.a. in Dezimalen
ZP = Zinsperioden p.a. (z.B. 2 für halbjährlich, 4 für quartalsweise etc.)

$$EZ = \left(1 + \frac{0{,}05}{4}\right)^{4} - 1 = 5{,}09453\%$$

Anmerkung: Bei dieser Berechnung wird unterstellt, dass die Wiederveranlagung zum gleichen Zinssatz (hier 5%) stattfindet, was in der Praxis nicht gewährleistet ist. Das tatsächlich realisierte Ergebnis kann daher höher oder niedriger ausfallen.

To compare the quoted p.a. interest rates with the respective compound interest rates, consider the following rates for different terms:

Interest period	Interest rate, p.a.	Effective interest rate in %
1 month	5%	5,12%
2 months	5%	5,11%
3 months	5%	5,09%
6 months	5%	5,06%
1 year	5%	5,00%

The Eurocurrency Market

Apart from the interbank market for loans/deposits in the domestic currency, there exists also the eurocurrency market. A eurocurrency is a **foreign currency that is traded outside the borders of the country** where the foreign currency serves as domestic currency. On the eurocurrency market, eurocurrencies are lent and borrowed.

The major foreign currency is the US Dollar. Apart from the Dollar, there are also liquid markets for other euro-currencies, e.g. Euro-EUR, Euroyen, Euroswiss, and Eurosterling. Main centers of eurocurrency trade are in London, New York, Luxembourg, Singapore, and Hong Kong.

Previously, the spread between bid and offer rates in the eurocurrency market was narrower than in the domestic market. Today, this is no longer true, because the differences between domestic currency market and eurocurrency market have grown smaller.

Transactions in the eurocurrency market include foreign currencies, and therefore the supply of those loans is a little delayed. In the eurocurrency market, loans are paid to the borrower usually **two days after the deal has been agreed** on.

2.3. Certificates of Deposit (CDs)

A certificate of deposit is a **bearer instrument** documenting the placing of a deposit for an agreed term at a given interest rate. Therefore, it serves as an **obligation** of the borrower to **pay an agreed amount of capital -including interest- to the owner at the maturity date**.

Certificates of deposit **originally come from the domestic US-Dollar market**. In the euromarket, CDs are very closely related to common interbank loans/deposits. Certificates of Deposit (CDs) are normally issued by credit institutions (for ex. commercial banks). Investment banks and discount houses do not belong to the credit institutions.

Originally, CD issues were on paper. Nowadays, there are data processing systems (e.g. Euroclear) in the market that guarantee the clearing of CDs as well as electronic bookings with the borrowers and creditors.

In London, this has led to the founding of the **Central Money Markets Office (CMO)**, an institution of the Bank of England that serves as an **international clearing unit for CDs**. This in turn, has lead to the almost complete elimination of CDs on paper.

Die Tabelle zeigt die effektiven Zinssätze einer Anlage zu 5% für unterschiedliche Zinsperioden:

Zinsperiode	Zinssatz p.a.	Effektivzinssatz in %
1 Monat	5%	5,12%
2 Monate	5%	5,11%
3 Monate	5%	5,09%
6 Monate	5%	5,06%
1 Jahr	5%	5,00%

Der Euro-Geldmarkt

Neben dem Interbankenmarkt für Depots in der Heimwährung gibt es auch noch den sogenannten Euro-Geldmarkt. Er dient der **Ausleihung und Veranlagung von Geldern in Fremdwährungen**, die außerhalb der Landesgrenzen in jenen Ländern gehandelt werden, in denen diese Fremdwährung Heimwährung ist.

Einige Zeit war der Spread zwischen Geld- und Briefsätzen im Euro-Markt enger gestellt als im Heimwährungsmarkt. Da sich die Unterschiede zwischen Heimwährungsmarkt und Euro-Geldmarkt reduziert haben, ist dies nicht mehr der Fall.

Transaktionen im Euro-Geldmarkt beinhalten Fremdwährungen. Daher ist die Lieferung dieser Depots in Fremdwährung mit Verzögerung verbunden. Bei einem Euro-Geldmarkt-Depotgeschäft werden die Geldmittel dem Ausleiher in der Regel **zwei Werktage nach Abschluss des Geschäftes geliefert.**

2.3. Certificates of Deposit (CDs)

Ein Certificate of Deposit (CD) ist ein **Inhaberpapier,** das die Veranlagung eines Depots für eine vorher bestimmte Periode zu einem gegebenen Zinssatz dokumentiert. Es stellt daher die **Verpflichtung** für den Schuldner dar, **einen bestimmten Kapitalbetrag inklusive Zinsen an den Inhaber am Laufzeitende zu zahlen.**

Certificates of Deposit haben sich **ursprünglich im US-Heimwährungsmarkt entwickelt.** Im Euro-Markt sind CDs sehr eng verwandt mit gewöhnlichen Interbankdepots. Certificates of Deposit werden normalerweise von Kreditinstituten (z.B. Geschäftsbanken) emittiert. Investmentbanken und Diskonthäuser zählen nicht zu den Kreditinstituten.

Ursprünglich sind CDs auf Papier dokumentiert worden. Heute gibt es elektronische Datenverarbeitungssysteme (Euroclear), die sowohl das Clearing der CDs als auch die elektronische Verbuchung bei Schuldnern und Gläubigern sicherstellen.

In London entstand beispielsweise das **Central Money Markets Office (CMO),** eine Einrichtung der Bank of England, die als **internationale Clearingstelle für CDs** fungiert. Dies führte zum Entfall von CDs auf Papierform.

Comparison of Certificate of Deposit vs. Deposits

With a clean deposit, the depositor places an agreed amount of capital at a bank for an agreed period. At the end of the term (maturity date), the depositor gets back both the initial amount and the interest payment.

A CD is a **certificate that entitles the holder to enter a deposit deal**: It is a bearer security (this includes electronic data carriers, too). The underlying amount of capital may be traded by the bearer before maturity.

The main advantage of CDs compared to clean deposits is that the bearer of a CD possesses a **negotiable liquid instrument in the secondary market**. Therefore, the bearer of a CD has the possibility to invest a deposit if there is sufficient demand. At the same time he remains a **flexible liquidity position** during the whole term of the CD.

For this flexibility, the borrower usually has to accept **lower interest rates than the market interest rates**. Usually, the difference between these rates is 1/16% (6.25 basis points) or 1/8% (12.5 basis points).

The nominal amount of capital can vary between a minimum of USD 25,000 and several millions of USD.

Markets and Conventions

CDs are issued and **traded in all major financial centers of the world**. The **main center** is **London**. The Bank of England authorises top banks in London to issue CDs in a number of currencies: GBP, USD, JPY, AUD, CAD, and EUR. Provided that the domestic national bank raises no objections, it is also possible to issue CDs in other currencies.

Terms of CDs

While most CDs are issued with **terms of 1, 3, or 6 months**, "broken-dates" are also possible. Often, CDs are **part of an issuing program** of a bank-consortium, where **terms of 1 year or between 3 and 5 years** are also possible.

CDs are quoted on an interest rate basis upon their issue. Usually, interest payments are due at the end of the term. CDs, running longer than 1 year, have the interest paid annually.

Primary Issue

CDs are issued as **interest instruments**. For example, bank A demands refinancing of 20 m EUR for a period of 6 months. Through a broker, they find a lender at 6%.

Vergleich Anlagezertifikat/Depot

Bei einem normalen Depotgeschäft veranlagt der Einleger eine bestimmte Geldsumme bei einer Bank für einen vorher bestimmten Zeitraum. Am Laufzeitende erhält der Einleger die Geldsumme (Kapital inklusive Zinsen) zurück.

Ein CD ist ein **Berechtigungsschein für ein Depotgeschäft.** Es handelt sich um ein Inhaberwertpapier (auch auf elektronischen Datenträgern); der Inhaber kann den im Zertifikat definierten Betrag vor Laufzeitende an einen Zweiten übertragen.

Der große Vorteil eines CDs gegenüber einem Depotgeschäft besteht darin, dass der Inhaber des CDs über ein **handelbares, liquides Instrument** verfügt, das er **im Sekundärmarkt auch vor Fälligkeit bei Bedarf wieder verkaufen** kann. Somit kann Cash kurzfristig mit einem für die Laufzeit des CDs fixierten Zinssatz angelegt und durch die jederzeitige Handelbarkeit die **Flexibilität in der Liquiditätsposition** trotzdem beibehalten werden.

Als Preis für diese Flexibilität muss der Inhaber des CDs **üblicherweise einen niedrigeren Satz als die im Geldmarkt quotierten Depotsätze** akzeptieren. Dieser liegt normalerweise 1/16% (6,25 Basispunkte) oder 1/8% (12,5 Basispunkte) unter dem jeweiligen Referenzsatz im Depotmarkt.

Das Nominale eines CDs kann zwischen einem Minimalbetrag von etwa USD 25.000 und mehreren Mio. USD liegen.

Märkte – Usancen – Konventionen

CDs werden **in allen wichtigen Finanzzentren der Welt sowohl emittiert als auch gehandelt.** Das **Hauptzentrum** ist **London.** Die englische Nationalbank autorisiert erstklassige Banken in London zur Emission von CDs in einer Reihe von Fremdwährungen: GBP, USD, JPY, AUD, CAD und EUR. Vorausgesetzt die örtliche Notenbank hat keine Einwendungen, können CDs auch in anderen Fremdwährungen emittiert werden.

Laufzeit von CDs

Während die meisten CD-Emissionen über **Perioden von 1, 3 oder 6 Monaten** laufen, gibt es auch gebrochene Laufzeiten (Broken Dates). Oft sind CDs auch **Teil eines Emissionsprogramms einer Bankengruppe,** wodurch es auch zu **Laufzeiten von über einem Jahr bzw. zwischen drei und fünf Jahren** kommen kann.

CDs werden bei ihrer Emission auf **Zinssatzbasis** quotiert. Normalerweise erfolgt die Zinszahlung am Ende der Laufzeit. Bei CDs mit einer Laufzeit von über einem Jahr werden die Zinsen jährlich gezahlt.

Erstemission

CDs werden als **Zinsinstrument** emittiert. D.h., es wird zum Nennwert emittiert und am Laufzeitende werden Nennwert plus Zinsen zurückgezahlt.

Example

Bank A agrees to issue a CD and the deal is agreed for EUR 20 m (4 x EUR 5 m). In other words, four CDs are issued, each for an underlying amount of EUR 5 m. The investor pays the bank EUR 20 m (EUR 5 m per CD).

We assume that the interest period is 183 days. Each CD guarantees the bearer the original amount of capital of EUR 5 m plus interest of EUR 152,500.

The calculation of the repayable amount is made with the simple interest formula:

$$\text{repayable amount} = 5{,}000{,}000 + (5{,}000{,}000 \times 0.06 \times \frac{183}{360}) = 5{,}152{,}500$$

5.000.000   5.152.500

Emissions-   Rückzahlungs-
betrag   betrag in 183 Tagen

Secondary Market

Example

Assume, that the buyer of the CDs (bank B) is willing to sell two of the CDs 3 months after the purchase. Bank B finds a buyer who is willing to buy the CDs at a yield of 5% for the rest of the term (91 days).

Each CD has a value of EUR 5,152,500 at maturity. There are several ways to calculate prices in the secondary market for these instruments.

$$PV = \frac{FV}{1 + \left(r \times \dfrac{D}{B}\right)}$$

PV = present value (capital)
FV = future value
r = interest rate, in decimals
D = number of days
B = day basis for calculation

The buyer of the certificate of deposit (CD) demands a yield of 5%. Each CD is therefore sold for a price of

$$\frac{5{,}152{,}500}{1 + \left(0.05 \times \dfrac{91}{360}\right)} = 5{,}088{,}191$$

Abzinsung 91 Tage mit 5%

5.000.000   5.088.190,92   5.152.500

Emissions-   Sekundärmarktpreis   Rückzahlungs-
betrag   nach 92 Tagen   betrag in 183 Tagen

Beispiel

Bank A hat einen Refinanzierungsbedarf von 20 Mio. EUR für eine Laufzeit von sechs Monaten. Über einen Broker wird ein Kreditgeber (Investor) zu 6% gefunden. Bank A ist einverstanden, ein Einlagenzertifikat zu emittieren. Um die Handelbarkeit zu erhöhen, werden vier CDs á EUR 5 Mio. emittiert. Der Investor zahlt EUR 20 Mio. an Bank A (EUR 5 Mio. für jedes CD).

Angenommen die Zinsperiode dauert 183 Tage, so garantiert jedes einzelne CD dem Inhaber bei Vorlage am Laufzeitende eine Rückzahlung von EUR 5.152.000 (Kapital + 152.500 Zinsen).

Die Berechnung des Rückzahlungsbetrages erfolgt mit der einfachen Zinsformel.

$$\text{Rückzahlungsbetrag} = 5.000.000 + \left(5.000.000 \times 0,06 \times \frac{183}{360}\right) = 5.152.500$$

Emissions-betrag   Rückzahlungs-betrag in 183 Tagen

Sekundärmarkt

Beispiel

Fortsetzung: Nach 92 Tagen entschließt sich der Investor, das CD wieder zu verkaufen. Er findet im Markt einen Käufer, der bereit ist, zu 5% für die Restlaufzeit (91 Tage) zu kaufen. Wie viel erhält er für ein CD?

Um den Sekundärmarktpreis zu ermitteln, wird der Rückzahlungsbetrag (EUR 5.152.500) mit der aktuellen Rendite (5%) abgezinst.

$$BW = \frac{EW}{1 + \left(r \times \frac{T}{B}\right)} \qquad BW = \frac{5.152.500}{1 + \left(0,05 \times \frac{91}{360}\right)} = 5.088.190,92$$

BW = Barwert (d.h. hier Sekundärmarktpreis)
EW = Endwert
r   = Zinssatz in Dezimalen
T   = Anzahl der Tage
B   = Tagesbasis

Somit erhält der Investor im Sekundärmarkt bei einer Rendite von 5% für die Restlaufzeit von 91 Tage EUR 5.088.190,92 pro CD.

Abzinsung 91 Tage mit 5%

5.000.000   5.088.190,92   5.152.500

Emissions-betrag   Sekundärmarktpreis nach 92 Tagen   Rückzahlungs-betrag in 183 Tagen

The **CD's selling price** in the secondary market may be higher or lower than the original buying price, **depending on the current yield curve**.

As a rule, the **re-selling price of a CD** should be **higher than the original purchase price**. With a stable yield curve, the price of a CD should rise steadily. Though, if the rates of interest rise, the value of the CD will fall.

2.4. Eligible bills

An eligible bill is a certificate (several formal regulations have to be adhered to) by which the issuer obliges himself to pay a specific amount of money at a given place and time to the bearer. He has to fulfill this obligation either himself or through someone else.

Conventions

Originally, eligible bills were **specified by the underlying deal**. This means, that an exporter drew a bill on the importer to finance a specific shipment, and then presented it to his bank for acceptance. As soon as the bank signed and therefore accepted the bill, **the bill carried both the risk and the quality of the accepting bank**. The accepting bank obliged itself to pay at maturity. Therefore an eligible bill is sometimes called **"two-name paper"** or **"double-name paper"**, if it holds two signatures (of issuer and endorser).

Now, the accepting bank was able to give the bill for acceptance to another bank, that – provided this bank had better ratings than the original bank – could accept the bill and thereby raise the certificate's value.

The quality of the accepting bank is the main determinant for the interest rate at which the bill is signed. The higher the quality of the bank, the lower would be the interest rate.

Eligible bills are **discount instruments** that are traded on the same basis as T-bills and commercial papers. The main difference risk concerns credit risk. With a commercial paper, only the issuer is liable, but in the case of an eligible bill, the bank assumes responsibility, too.

Der **Verkaufspreis** eines CDs im Sekundärmarkt kann, **abhängig von der aktuellen Zinskurve,** höher oder niedriger als der ursprüngliche Kaufpreis sein.

Als **allgemeine Regel** gilt, dass der **Wiederverkaufspreis eines CDs höher** sein müsste **als der ursprüngliche Kaufpreis.** Bei einer stabilen Zinskurve mit Normalverlauf müsste der Wert eines CDs bis zum Ende der Laufzeit stetig anwachsen. Steigen jedoch die Zinssätze, kann der Wert eines CDs auch fallen.

2.4. Wechselgeschäfte

Ein gezogener Wechsel ist eine vom Aussteller unter Beachtung bestimmter Formvorschriften ausgestellte Urkunde, in der sich der Bezogene durch Akzept verpflichtet, eine bestimmte Geldsumme zu einem festgesetzten Zeitpunkt an einen bestimmten Ort an den als berechtigt Ausgewiesenen zu zahlen.

Usancen

Ursprünglich waren Wechseldokumente **auf das jeweilige Grundgeschäft spezifiziert.** Das bedeutet, ein Exporteur (Aussteller, Gläubiger) hat den Wechsel auf einen Importeur (Bezogener, Schuldner) gezogen, um eine bestimmte Lieferung zu finanzieren, und hat diesen Wechsel in weiterer Folge bei seiner Bank (Indossatar) zum Akzept vorgelegt. Ab dem Zeitpunkt, zu dem diese Bank den Wechsel durch Stampiglie und Unterschrift autorisiert hatte, bekam das Wechseldokument das Risiko und die Qualität des Ausstellers und des Bezogenen (zuvor nur des Bezogenen). Der letzte Wechselnehmer (Gläubiger, Indossatar) in der Kette kann also **Rückgriff (= Regress)** nehmen **auf jeden Indossanten** (ehemalige Gläubiger). Da alle ehemaligen Wechselnehmer als **Gesamtschuldner** haften, **verringert sich das Ausfallsrisiko mit jeder Weitergabe (Indossament).** Der Wechsel wird daher manchmal auch als „**two-name paper**" oder „**double-name paper**" bezeichnet, wenn er zwei Unterschriften (neben jener des Ausstellers auch jene des Indossanten) aufweist.

Wird ein Wechsel zur Diskontierung an eine Bank weitergegeben, erhält der Indossant (Verkäufer) von der Bank (Indossatar) den **Geldbetrag abzüglich eines Zinsabschlags (Diskont).** Bei Fälligkeit legt die Bank den Wechsel dem Bezogenen vor, der dann seine im Wechsel dokumentierte Schuld begleicht.

Wechsel sind **Diskontinstrumente,** die auf der gleichen Basis wie T-Bills und US-Commercial Papers gehandelt werden, d.h. mit einem Diskontsatz. Der wesentliche Unterschied besteht im Bonitätsrisiko. Während bei einem Commercial Paper nur der Emittent haftet, garantiert bei einem Wechsel zusätzlich die akzeptierende Bank. Wechsel werden in den USA auch **Bankers Acceptance (BA)** genannt. Wechsel, die bei der **Bank of England** eingelöst werden können, nennt man „**Eligible Bills**".

Quotation

Eligible bills are quoted at the **discount rate**, i.e. the interest amount is calculated on the basis of the final value.

Example

An eligible bill was drawn for CHF 1 m maturity date is the 1st of October.
On the 1st of August (time to maturity: 61 days) the bill is presented to a bank that re-discounts it at 3½%.

The bank pays on the 1st of August

$$1{,}000{,}000 - \left(1{,}000{,}000 \times 0.035 \times \frac{61}{360}\right) = 994{,}059.44$$

With those two payments (1,000,000 = end value; 994,069.44 = cash value) we can use the following formula to calculate the interest rate:

$$r = \frac{(FV-PV)}{PV} \times \frac{B}{D}$$

$$= \frac{(1{,}000{,}000-994{,}069.44)}{994{,}069.44} \times \frac{360}{61} = 3.520088\%$$

Alternatively, one can also calculate the yield on the basis of the discount rate of 3½%:

$$r = \frac{r_d}{1 - \left(r_d \times \dfrac{D}{B}\right)}$$

$$= \frac{0.035}{1 - \left(0.035 \times \dfrac{61}{360}\right)} = 3.52088\%$$

2.5. Commercial Papers (CPs)

Commercial papers are **short-term bonds** that are negotiable as **bearer certificates**. At maturity, the issuer of a commercial paper pays the capital plus interest to the bearer. For companies, commercial papers are an example of "securitisation", i.e. they can borrow money without drawing on their bank deposits. When issuing, the **banks act as a broker** by passing on CPs to potential investors without investing on their own. In this way, funds go directly from investor to debtor/creditor without placing a deposit in the bank.

Quotierung

Wechsel werden mit einem **Diskontsatz** quotiert. D.h., der Zinsbetrag wird auf Basis des Endwertes (Rückzahlungsbetrages) berechnet.

Beispiel

Es wurde ein Wechsel über USD 1 Mio. gezogen, Fälligkeit: 1. Oktober. Am 1. August (Restlaufzeit 61 Tage) wird dieser Wechsel einer Bank präsentiert, die ihn zu 3½% diskontiert. Wie viel bezahlt die Bank am 1. August?

$$BW = EW - \left(EW \times rd \times \frac{T}{B} \right)$$

BW = Barwert (d.h. hier Kaufpreis Wechsel)
EW = Endwert (d.h. hier Nennwert Wechsel)
rd = Diskontsatz in Dezimalen
T = Anzahl der Tage
B = Tagesbasis

$$BW = 1.000.000 - \left(1.000.000 \times 0,035 \times \frac{61}{360} \right) = 994.069,44$$

Die Bank kauft den Wechsel um USD 994.069,44 an.

Um das Ergebnis mit einem auf Renditebasis quotierten Instrument vergleichen zu können, ermitteln wir aus den beiden Zahlungen einen Zinssatz (Rendite).

$$Rendite = \frac{(EW-BW)}{BW} \times \frac{B}{T}$$

$$Rendite = \frac{(1.000.000-994.069,44)}{994.069,44} \times \frac{360}{61} = 3,52088\%$$

Die Rendite kann auch direkt aus dem Diskontsatz berechnet werden:

$$Rendite = \frac{Diskont}{1 - \left(Diskont \times \frac{T}{B} \right)} \qquad Rendite = \frac{0,035}{1 - \left(0,035 \times \frac{61}{360} \right)} = 3,52088\%$$

2.5. Commercial Papers (CPs)

Commercial Papers sind **kurzfristige, unbesicherte Schuldverschreibungen**, die **als Inhaberpapiere handelbar** sind. Sie werden **typischerweise von erstklassigen Industrie- und Handelsunternehmen begeben** (mittlerweile aber auch von Finanzgesellschaften). CPs sind für Industrieunternehmen ein Beispiel der „Securitization". Das bedeutet, dass Kreditmittel aufgenommen werden können, ohne Bankdepots in Anspruch nehmen zu müssen. **Banken fungieren** bei der Emission von Commercial Papers **als Vermittler**, indem sie die Commercial Papers an potenzielle Investoren weiterleiten, aber keine eigenen Mittel investieren. Auf diese Weise fließen die Mittel direkt vom Investor zum Einlagennehmer bzw. Kreditnehmer, ohne dass ein Depotgeschäft mit der Bank abgeschlossen wurde.

Conventions

Commercial papers are issued as a series of notes, where each note guarantees the bearer a fixed amount of capital at maturity. Each note possesses the following specifications:

- the name of the issuer
- the note's underlying nominal amount of capital
- the issue date
- the maturity date
- the proof of authenticity (evidence of origin by the arranging bank)

Apart from this, each note carries the clause that it is negotiable and that the bearer is entitled by the issuing company to pay or receive payment through the arranging bank.

The issue of commercial papers is made by **investment banks**; CPs are made negotiable for customers (mostly large companies) and are offered to a great number of potential customers. The **margin of a bank's CP dealer is calculated on the basis of the turnover volume**. This margin usually is not more than 2 basis points. For EUR 1 mil., issued for 90 days, the margin would be EUR 50.

The buyer of a commercial paper buys an unsecured debt of a corporate. Since he buys the CP through a bank dealer, he can be sure that if he wants to materialise the CP, the bank accepts the commercial paper at the current market rate. But this obligation is not legally binding.

Origin of the Commercial Paper Market

Like certificates of deposits, commercial papers were **developed in the US capital markets**. Due to the situation in the US banking market ten to fifteen years ago, companies usually had better ratings than domestic banks. Among these companies, a market for the supply and demand of money developed which was run by the banks. The role of banks as simple agents had some advantages for investors as well as for creditors:

- Creditors were able to re-finance cheaper in this way than directly from the bank
- Investors received better yields than the potential yields from a bank deposit operation

US-CPs/Euro-CPs

US-CPs are commercial papers in the national money market of USA. Euro-CPs are in the international money markt (the Euro market) traded CPs.

Konventionen

Commercial Papers werden üblicherweise im Rahmen eines CP-Programms begeben. Darunter versteht man eine **Rahmenvereinbarung zwischen dem Emittenten und den platzierenden Banken.** Der Emittent hat dabei das Recht, aber nicht die Verpflichtung, jederzeit CPs zu begeben. Ein derartiges CP-Programm hat daher den **Charakter einer Daueremission,** da CPs in mehreren Tranchen und über einen längeren Zeitraum hinweg emittiert werden können. Dabei garantiert jeder einzelne Schuldschein dem Inhaber einen **fixen Geldbetrag am Laufzeitende.**

Jeder Schuldschein enthält folgende Daten:

- Name des Emittenten
- Nominalbetrag des Schuldscheins
- Emissionsdatum
- Laufzeitende
- Authentizitätsnachweis (Ursprungszeugnis der Vermittlerbank)

Darüber hinaus enthält jeder Schuldschein noch den Vermerk, dass er handelbar ist und der Inhaber zur Zahlung bzw. zum Empfang der Zahlung durch die Vermittlerbank im Auftrag der emittierenden Gesellschaft berechtigt ist.

Die **Emission** von Commercial Papers wird **von Investmentbanken vorbereitet** und für ihre Kunden – meist größere Industrieunternehmen – **handelbar gemacht** und einer großen Anzahl von Investoren angeboten. Der **Händler von Commercial Papers** bei einer Bank erhält eine **Marge auf das Volumen des Umsatzes.** Diese Marge beträgt üblicherweise nicht mehr als zwei Basispunkte, was bei EUR 1 Mio., emittiert für 90 Tage, einen Betrag von EUR 50 ergibt.

Der Käufer eines Commercial Papers kauft eine ungesicherte Verbindlichkeit eines Industrieunternehmens, aber durch den Kauf bei einer Bank hat er auch die Garantie, dass die Bank das Commercial Paper, sollte er es realisieren wollen, zum dann gültigen Marktpreis zurücknimmt. Diese Verpflichtung ist aber nicht rechtswirksam.

Ursprünge des Commercial-Papers-Marktes

Wie bei den Certificates of Deposit haben sich Commercial Papers auch **ursprünglich im US-Kapitalmarkt** entwickelt und spielen auf dem nationalen Geldmarkt der USA eine große Rolle. Im US-Bankenmarkt Anfang der 80er-Jahre verfügten Industrieunternehmen meist über bessere Bonitäten als örtliche Banken. Unter diesen Industrieunternehmen entstand ein Markt des Geldangebotes und der Geldnachfrage, der über die Banken abgewickelt wurde. Durch die reine Vermittlungstätigkeit ergaben sich folgende Vorteile für die Banken:

- Der Kreditnehmer erhielt eine billigere Refinanzierung als direkt über die Bank.
- Der Investor erzielte eine höhere Rendite als über ein Bankdepotgeschäft.

US-CPs/Euro-CPs

US-CPs sind Commercial Papers im nationalen Geldmarkt der USA. Euro-CPs sind im internationalen Geldmarkt (dem Euro-Markt) gehandelte CPs.

Terms of Commercial Papers

Usually, commercial papers have **terms between seven days and one year (US commercial papers between one and 270 days)**. The average term in the market is around 60 days.

In the **US market**, a **CP issue is only possible in USD**; the benchmark rate is the "Federal Reserve Composite Rate".

In the **euromarket**, issues are done in different currencies: **USD, GBP, EUR, JPY, CHF**; approx. 80% of all issues are, however, done in USD.

Settlement of CPs is on the same day. All issuers must have a credit rating.

Yields of Commercial Papers

Interest rates for US commercial papers are quoted on a **discount basis**, just as for T-bills and eligible bills. In most domestic commercial paper markets, rates are quoted as **discounts from the end value of the amount of capital**. In the **euromarket** (ECP), commercial papers are often quoted on a **yield basis** (just like Interbank deposits and CDs) but still remain a discount instrument (meaning that the final Cash-Flow is 100% and not 100% + interest).

Example

The following **US-CP** is issued:
face value: USD 1.000.000
discount: 5%
term: 30 days
How much is the underwriting revenue?

$$\text{present value} = \text{future value} - \left(\text{future value} \times \text{discount} \times \frac{\text{days}}{\text{basis}} \right)$$

$$\text{present value} = 1{,}000{,}000 - \left(1{,}000{,}000 \times 0.05 \times \frac{30}{360} \right) = 995{,}833.33$$

Example

The following **Euro-CP** is issued:
face value: EUR 1.000.000
yield: 5%
term: 30 days
How much is the underwriting revenue?

$$\text{present value} = \frac{\text{future value}}{1 + \text{interest rate} \times \dfrac{\text{days}}{\text{basis}}} \qquad \text{present value} = \frac{1{,}000{,}000}{1 + 0.05 \times \dfrac{30}{360}} = 995{,}850.62$$

Laufzeiten von Commercial Papers

Für gewöhnlich haben CPs eine **Laufzeit zwischen sieben Tagen und einem Jahr.** Die durchschnittliche Laufzeit im Markt beträgt etwa 60 Tage. Bei **US-CPs** liegt die Laufzeit **üblicherweise nicht über 270 Tagen,** weil darüber ein SEC-Verfahren (Security and Exchange Commission) erforderlich wäre.

Im **US-Markt** sind **Emissionen nur in USD möglich,** wobei die Benchmark die „Federal Reserve Composite Rate" darstellt.

Im **Euro-Markt** werden Emissionen in folgenden Währungen getätigt: **USD, GBP, EUR, JPY, CHF** (wobei etwa 80% aller Emissionen in USD getätigt werden).

Verzinsung von CPs

CPs sind **Diskontinstrumente**, d.h., sie werden mit einem Abschlag zum Nennwert emittiert. Die Verzinsung ergibt sich aus dem **Unterschied zwischen Emissions- (bzw. Kauf-)Betrag und Rückzahlungsbetrag.**

US-CPs werden wie die meisten inländischen („domestic") Commercial Papers auf **Diskontbasis** quotiert (so wie T-Bills und Wechsel).

Euro-CPs hingegen werden auf **Renditebasis** quotiert. Sie können daher rechnerisch wie ein Certificate of Deposit behandelt werden. Es handelt sich dabei jedoch weiter um Diskontpapiere in dem Sinne, dass der Rückzahlungswert 100% des Nominales entspricht.

Beispiel

Folgendes **US-CP** wird emittiert:
Nennwert: USD 1.000.000
Diskont: 5%
Laufzeit: 30 Tage
Wie hoch ist der Emissionserlös?

$$\text{Barwert} = \text{Endwert} - \left(\text{Endwert} \times \text{Diskont} \times \frac{\text{Tage}}{\text{Basis}} \right)$$

$$\text{Barwert} = 1.000.000 - \left(1.000.000 \times 0,05 \times \frac{30}{360} \right) = 995.833,33$$

Beispiel

Folgendes **Euro-CP** wird emittiert:
Nennwert: EUR 1.000.000
Zinssatz: 5%
Laufzeit: 30 Tage
Wie hoch ist der Emissionserlös?

$$\text{Barwert} = \frac{\text{Endwert}}{1 + \text{Zinssatz} \times \dfrac{\text{Tage}}{\text{Basis}}} \qquad \text{Barwert} = \frac{1.000.000}{1 + 0,05 \times \dfrac{30}{360}} = 995.850,62$$

Ratings for Commercial Papers

Investors have neither the possibility nor the time to collect all information concerning the risks of their investments. Therefore, they must rely on the ratings of international agencies that determine the rating of the issuing corporations. A properly working market for CPs can only exist if there are **standard ratings of all issuing corporations**. Those ratings are mostly made by the two leading agencies **Standard and Poor's** and **Moody's**. To make a commercial paper attractive to investors, it needs a rating of at least A1/P1.

2.6. Treasury bills

Treasury bills (T-bills) are **short-term debts (terms up to 1 year)** that are issued within the framework of an auction. Due to their **high liquidity**, T-bills are the most important money market instruments in the US. T-bills are **discount instruments**; i.e. they do not have a fixed interest rate. The yield is computed by using the length of the term and the difference between buying price and nominal value.

Quotation in the Primary Market

T-bills are issued by **price tenders**. Since they are discount instruments, the prices that are quoted during the auction, are the prices at which banks are willing to accept the T-bills.

Example

At a tender for a 1 m, 90 days, US T-bill, a price of 985,350 is quoted. Therefore, the discount is 14,650. With this data, one can easily calculate the discount rate:

$$\frac{14{,}650}{1{,}000{,}000} \times \frac{360}{90} = 5.86000\%$$

To compare the yield to a normal interest rate, one has to convert the 5.86%.

$$r = \frac{r_d}{1 - \left(r_d \times \frac{D}{B}\right)} = \frac{0.0586}{1 - \left(0.0586 \times \frac{90}{360}\right)} = 5.94713\%$$

Bonitätserfordernis für Commercial Papers

Marktteilnehmer (Investoren) haben weder die Möglichkeiten noch die Zeit, über die Kreditrisiken ihrer Veranlagungen Informationen einzuholen. Daher müssen sie sich auf das Rating von internationalen Ratingagenturen, die die Bonität von emittierenden Unternehmen bewerten, verlassen. Ein funktionierender CP-Markt kann daher nur existieren, wenn es **standardisierte Ratings aller emittierenden Unternehmen** gibt. Die Ratings werden vorwiegend von den beiden führenden Agenturen **Standard and Poor's** und **Moody's** vorgenommen. Ein Rating von A1/P1 ist erforderlich, um ein CP für Investoren attraktiv zu machen.

2.6. Treasury Bills

Treasury Bills (T-Bills) sind **kurzfristige Schuldscheine (Laufzeiten bis ein Jahr)**, die im Rahmen einer **Auktion** begeben werden. T-Bills sind in Amerika durch die **hohe Liquidität** das wichtigste Geldmarktinstrument. T-Bills sind **Diskontinstrumente**, d.h., sie sind nicht mit einem fixen Zinssatz ausgestattet. Die Rendite errechnet sich somit aus der Haltedauer und der Differenz von Kaufpreis und Nominalwert.

Quotierung Primärmarkt

T-Bills werden im Rahmen eines **Kurs-Tenders** begeben. Da es sich um Diskontinstrumente handelt, wird bei der Auktion der Preis, zu dem die Bank bereit ist, das T-Bill zu übernehmen, geboten.

Beispiel

Bei einem Tender für 1 Mio., 90 Tage, US-T-Bill, wird ein Preis von 985.350 geboten. Der Diskont beträgt also 14.650. Aus diesem Diskont kann der Diskontierungssatz ausgerechnet werden.

$$\frac{14.650}{1.000.000} \times \frac{360}{90} = 5,86000\,\%$$

Um den Diskontierungssatz mit einem normalen Zinssatz zu vergleichen, müssen die 5,86% umgerechnet werden.

$$r = \frac{r_d}{1 - \left(r_d \times \dfrac{T}{B}\right)} = \frac{0,0586}{1 - \left(0,0586 \times \dfrac{90}{360}\right)} = 5,94713\%$$

Quotation in the Secondary Market

In the secondary market, T-bills are quoted in terms of **discount rates**. In this case, one has to convert the discount rates into yield rates in order to compare T-bills with interest rates of time deposits.

Example

Assume that the discount rate of a US T-bill, with 61 days to maturity, is 6%, the yield can be calculated in the following way:

$$r = \frac{r_d}{1 - \left(r_d \times \dfrac{D}{B}\right)} = \frac{0.06}{1 - \left(0.06 \times \dfrac{61}{360}\right)} = 6.06163\%$$

Excursus: UK Treasury Bills' Conventions

UK Treasury bills are zero-coupon eligible debt securities denominated in GBP and issued by the UK Debt Management Office (DMO). UK Treasury Bills can be held in the depository systems of the CMO and Euroclear.

Tender

Treasury bills are issued at weekly tenders on the last business day (Friday). The quotation is on a money market yield basis (ACT/365) up to three decimal places. The DMO announces the size and the maturity of bills on offer at the preceding week's tender. All participants at Treasury bill tenders must be registered financial institutions, which are regulated by the FSA and are subject to its rules and guidance in their activities.

Nominal

The minimum nominal of the bids at tenders is GBP 500,000. Bids above this minimum must be made in multiples of GBP 50,000. Bids must be submitted by 11.00 (London time) one day after the tender. All payments to holders of UK Treasury bills are made without tax deductions.

Maturity

The minimum maturity is 1 day and the maximum maturity is 364 days. However, weekly tenders are typically for maturities of 1 month (approx. 28 days), 3 months (approx. 91 days) and 6 months (approx. 182 days).
Bills issued at tenders currently mature on the first business day of the week and will be adjusted for weeks including bank holidays.

Summary

The money market is the interbank market for trading short-term financial instruments. Most of the transactions in the money market have terms up to three months, some up to one year or more.
The most important money market products are interbank loans/deposits, certificates of deposit (CDs), bills of exchange, commercial papers (CPs) and repurchase agreements (repos).

Quotierung im Sekundärmarkt

Im Sekundärmarkt werden T-Bills mit **Diskontierungssätzen** quotiert, sodass in diesem Fall nur die Umrechnung von Diskontierungssatz zu Rendite stattfinden muss, um T-Bills z.B. mit Depotzinsen vergleichen zu können.

Beispiel

Wird der Diskontierungssatz für einen US-T-Bill von 61 Tagen Restlaufzeit mit 6% quotiert, so berechnet sich die Rendite wie folgt:

$$r = \frac{r_d}{1 - \left(r_d \times \dfrac{T}{B}\right)} = \frac{0{,}06}{1 - \left(0{,}06 \times \dfrac{61}{360}\right)} = 6{,}06163\%$$

Exkurs: Konventionen bei UK Treasury Bills

UK Treasury Bills sind zentralbankfähige Null-Kupon-Anleihen, lautend in GBP und vom Britischen Debt Management Office (DMO) emittiert werden. UK Treasury Bills können in den Depot-Systemen der CMO und Euroclear gehalten werden.

Tenderverfahren

UK T-Bills werden in wöchentlichen Tendern am letzten Werktag (Freitag) ausgegeben. Die Quotierung erfolgt auf Geldmarkt-Basis (ACT/365) mit drei Nachkommastellen. Das Volumen und die Laufzeit der angebotenen Bills werden vom DMO bei der Ausschreibung der Vorwoche angekündigt. Alle Teilnehmer müssen regulierte Finanzinstitute sein, die den Regeln und Richtlinien der FSA unterliegen.

Nominale

Die Mindestnominale eines Tenders beträgt GBP 500.000. Kaufgebote über diesem Minimum müssen in Größenordnungen von GBP 50.000 erfolgen. Die Gebote müssen einen Tag nach der Ausschreibung bis spätestens 11:00 Uhr (Londoner Zeit) übermittelt werden. Alle Zahlungen an die Inhaber von UK T-Bills erfolgen ohne Steuerabzug.

Laufzeit

Die minimale Laufzeit beträgt einen Tag und die maximale Laufzeit 364 Tage. Allerdings sind wöchentliche Tender in der Regel für Laufzeiten von einem Monat (ca. 28 Tage), drei Monaten (ca. 91 Tage) und sechs Monaten (ca. 182 Tage).
Die Laufzeit von UK T-Bills, die bei einem Tenderverfahren ausgegeben wurden, endet am ersten Werktag der Woche (angepasst um Bankfeiertage).

Zusammenfassung

Der Geldmarkt (Money Market) ist der Interbankenmarkt für den Handel von kurzfristigen Finanzinstrumenten. Die meisten Geldmarkttransaktionen werden mit einer Laufzeit bis zu drei Monaten, manche auch bis zu einem Jahr oder sogar länger, getätigt.
Die wichtigsten Geldmarktinstrumente sind Interbankenkredite/-Depots, Certificates of Deposit (CDs), Wechsel, Commercial Papers (CPs) und Repurchase Agreements (Repos).

Banks need liquidity to satisfy statutory regulations as well as to be able to fully cover their obligations at any time. National banks need the money market too in order to master a number of tasks. Via national banks' actions in the money market signals are sent about the future development of interest rates.

Most instruments are coupon instruments, i.e. they are issued at an interest rate (coupon) and face value. Notional amount and interests are paid back at maturity. Coupon instruments include interbank deposits, CDs and repos. Discount instruments are e.g. commercial papers, T-bills and eligible bills. The difference between the issuing price and repayment is the buyer's interest result. Discount instruments are issued with a discount from their notional value; at maturity the holder receives the notional amount. Discount instruments are e.g.: commercial papers, T-bills and eligible bills.

The yield (interest rate p.a., effective rate) is quoted on the basis of the invested capital (= present value), a discount rate is calculated on the basis of the future value.

Most banks make deposit deals with each other. Interest rates in the domestic or the euromoney market depend on current market conditions and on traded volumes. The interest rate for all standard terms (from overnight to twelve months) is quoted. For the euromoney market in London there exists a so-called reference or benchmark rate: the London Interbank Offered Rate (LIBOR). The LIBOR is an important, internationally accepted reference rate due to the importance of the City of London as a banking center and major money marketplace (eurodollar market). Interbank rates are also quoted in all major financial centers of the world. Furthermore, there is a TIBOR (Tokyo Interbank Offered Rate), PRIBOR (Prague Interbank Offered Rate) and EURIBOR (Euro Interbank Offered Rate) that replaced the interbank rates of the 15 Euro-in countries. LIBID (London Interbank Bid Rate), on the other hand, represents the so-called deposit rate. LIBOR minus the usual spread yields the LIBID. Usually, the term of a loan/deposit starts two working days after the deal has been concluded. Usually, the term of a loan/deposit of x months ends x calendar months after the start date. The term of a 3-month loan/deposit with start date on January 3 ends on April 3.

For deposits with terms shorter than one year the interest is paid at the end of the term. Therefore, the repayment includes both principal and accrued interest. For loans/deposits with terms of more than twelve months interest is usually paid every twelve months and then at maturity.

A certificate of deposit is a bearer instrument documenting the placing of a deposit for an agreed term at a given interest rate. Therefore, it serves as an obligation of the borrower to pay an agreed amount of capital -including interest- to the owner at the maturity date.

The main advantage of CDs compared to clean deposits is that the bearer of a CD possesses a negotiable liquid instrument in the secondary market. Therefore, the bearer of a CD has the chance to invest a deposit if there is sufficient demand. CDs are issued and traded in all major financial centers of the world. The main center is London. CDs are issued as interest instruments. While most CDs are issued with terms of 1, 3, or 6 months, "broken-dates" are also possible. Often, CDs are part of an issuing program of a bank consortium, where terms of 1 year or between 3 and 5 years are also possible.

Banken und andere Geldmarktteilnehmer haben die primäre Aufgabe, ihre Liquidität zu erhalten. Banken benötigen Liquidität zur Einhaltung gesetzlicher Bestimmungen bzw. zur Aufrechterhaltung der Bedingung, Verpflichtungen jederzeit erfüllen zu können. Auch die Nationalbanken der einzelnen Länder brauchen den Geldmarkt, um einer Reihe von Verpflichtungen nachkommen zu können. Durch die Aktionen der Nationalbanken im Geldmarkt können Signale für die Zinsentwicklung im Geldmarkt gesetzt werden.

Die meisten Instrumente sind sogenannte Kuponinstrumente, d.h., sie werden zum Nennwert und mit einem Zinssatz (Kupon) emittiert. Am Ende der Laufzeit wird dann der Nennwert plus Zinsen zurückgezahlt. Zu den Kuponinstrumenten zählen Interbank Depots, CDs und Repos.

Im Gegensatz dazu werden Abzinsungsinstrumente (Diskontinstrumente) mit einem Abschlag vom Nennwert emittiert und zum vollen Nennwert zurückgezahlt. Diskontinstrumente sind beispielsweise Commercial Papers, T-Bills und Wechsel.

Wird ein Zinssatz (Rendite) angegeben, so wird der Zinsbetrag auf der Basis des Anfangsbetrages berechnet. Wird ein Diskontsatz angegeben, so ist gemeint, dass der Abschlag (Zinsbetrag) auf Basis des Rückzahlungsbetrages berechnet wird.

Die meisten Banken tätigen untereinander Depotgeschäfte. Die Zinssätze werden für alle Standardlaufzeiten von overnight bis zu zwölf Monaten quotiert. Für den Euro-Geldmarkt in London wurde ein sogenannter Referenzsatz bzw. Benchmark Rate eingeführt. Das ist der London Interbank Offered Rate (LIBOR). Der LIBOR ist ein international anerkannter Referenzsatz, der sich aus der Stellung des Londoner Bankplatzes und seiner Wichtigkeit im Geldmarkt (Euro-Dollar-Markt) entwickelt hat. Interbanksätze werden aber auch in allen größeren Finanzzentren der Welt „gefixt". Mit der Einführung des Euro wurden viele Sätze obsolet (z.B. FIBOR, BIBOR, VIBOR). Der EURIBOR (Euro Interbank Offered Rate) ersetzt diese nationalen Interbanksätze. LIBID (London Interbank Bid Rate) stellt im Gegensatz zum LIBOR den sogenannten Einlagensatz dar. Der LIBOR abzüglich des üblichen Spreads ergibt somit den LIBID. Der Beginn der Laufzeit eines Depotgeschäftes ist üblicherweise zwei Bankarbeitstage nach Abschluss des Geschäftes. Das Laufzeitende eines Depots von x Monaten ist üblicherweise genau x Kalendermonate nach Laufzeitbeginn. Als Standardkonvention für die Zinsberechnung bei Depotgeschäften hat sich eine p.a.-Quotierung institutionalisiert. Bei Depotgeschäften mit Laufzeiten unter einem Jahr werden die Zinsen im Nachhinein für die Dauer der Zinsperiode gezahlt. Bei Rückzahlung erfolgt also die Zahlung von Kapital und angefallenen Zinsen. Für Depotgeschäfte mit einer Laufzeit von über zwölf Monaten werden die Zinsen üblicherweise jährlich zum jeweiligen Jahrestag des Geschäftbeginns und zu Laufzeitende gezahlt.

Ein Certificate of Deposit (CD) ist ein Inhaberpapier, das die Veranlagung eines Depots für eine vorher bestimmte Periode zu einem gegebenen Zinssatz dokumentiert. Es stellt daher die Verpflichtung für den Schuldner dar, einen bestimmten Kapitalbetrag inklusive Zinsen an den Inhaber am Laufzeitende zu zahlen. Der große Vorteil eines CDs gegenüber einem Depotgeschäft besteht darin, dass der Inhaber des CDs über ein handelbares, liquides Instrument verfügt, das er im Sekundärmarkt auch vor Fälligkeit bei Bedarf wieder verkaufen kann. Somit kann Cash kurzfristig mit einem für die Laufzeit des CDs fixierten Zinssatz angelegt werden und durch die jederzeitige Handelbarkeit die Flexibilität in der Liquiditätsposition trotzdem beibehalten werden.

An eligible bill is a certificate (several formal regulations have to be adhered to) which obliges the issuer to pay a specific amount of money to the bearer at a given place and time. He has to fulfill this obligation either himself or through someone else. The accepting bank may give the bill for acceptance to another bank, that – provided this bank had better ratings than the original bank – could accept the bill and thereby raise the certificate's value. Eligible bills are discount instruments that are traded on the same basis as T-bills and commercial papers. The main difference concerns credit risk. With a commercial paper, only the issuer is liable, but in case of an eligible bill, the bank assumes responsibility, too.

Commercial papers are short-term bonds that are negotiable as bearer certificates. At maturity, the issuer of a commercial paper pays the capital plus interest to the bearer. For companies, commercial papers are an example of "securitisation", i.e. they can borrow money without drawing on their bank deposits. When issuing, the banks act as a broker by passing on CPs to potential investors without investing on their own. Usually, commercial papers have terms between seven days and one year (US commercial papers between one and 270 days). The average term in the market is around 60 days. In the US market, a CP issue is only possible in USD. In the euromarket, issues are done in different currencies: USD, GBP, EUR, JPY, CHF; approx. 80% of all issues are, however, done in USD. Interest rates for US commercial papers are quoted on a discount basis, just as for T-bills and eligible bills. In the euromarket (ECP), commercial papers are often quoted on a yield basis (just like interbank deposits and CDs) but still remain a discount instrument (meaning that the final cash-flow is 100% and not 100% + interest).

Treasury bills (T-bills) are short-term debts (terms of up to 1 year) that are issued within the framework of an auction. Due to their high liquidity, T-bills are the most important money market instruments in the US. T-bills are discount instruments; i.e. they do not have a fixed interest rate. The yield is computed by using the length of the term and the difference between buying price and nominal value.

CDs werden in allen wichtigen Finanzzentren der Welt sowohl emittiert als auch gehandelt. Das Hauptzentrum ist London. Während die meisten CD-Emissionen über Perioden von 1, 3 oder 6 Monaten laufen, gibt es auch gebrochene Laufzeiten (Broken Dates). Oft sind CDs auch Teil eines Emissionsprogramms einer Bankengruppe, wodurch es auch zu Laufzeiten von über einem Jahr bzw. zwischen drei und fünf Jahren kommen kann. CDs werden bei ihrer Emission auf Zinssatzbasis quotiert.

Ein gezogener Wechsel ist eine vom Aussteller unter Beachtung bestimmter Formvorschriften ausgestellte Urkunde, in der sich der Bezogene durch Akzept verpflichtet, eine bestimmte Geldsumme zu einer festgesetzten Zeit an einen bestimmten Ort an den als berechtigt Ausgewiesenen zu zahlen. Wird ein Wechsel zur Diskontierung an eine Bank weitergegeben, erhält der Indossant (Verkäufer) von der Bank (Indossatar) den Geldbetrag abzüglich eines Zinsabschlags (Diskont). Bei Fälligkeit legt die Bank den Wechsel dem Bezogenen vor, der dann seine im Wechsel dokumentierte Schuld begleicht. Wechsel sind Diskontinstrumente, die auf der gleichen Basis wie T-Bills und US-Commercial Papers gehandelt werden, d.h. mit einem Diskontsatz. Der wesentliche Unterschied besteht im Bonitätsrisiko. Während bei einem Commercial Paper nur der Emittent haftet, garantiert bei einem Wechsel zusätzlich die akzeptierende Bank. Wechsel werden in den USA auch Bankers Acceptance (BA) genannt. Wechsel, die bei der Bank of England eingelöst werden können, nennt man „Eligible Bills".

Ein Schuldschein (promissory note) ist eine Urkunde, die die Verpflichtung des Schuldners (Ausstellers) beinhaltet, eine bestimmte Summe entweder zu einem festgesetzten oder noch festzusetzenden Zeitpunkt oder auf Verlangen des Gläubigers zu bezahlen.

Commercial Papers sind kurzfristige, unbesicherte Schuldverschreibungen, die als Inhaberpapiere handelbar sind. Sie werden typischerweise von erstklassigen Industrie- und Handelsunternehmen begeben (mittlerweile aber auch von Finanzgesellschaften). Dabei können Kreditmittel aufgenommen werden, ohne Bankdepots in Anspruch nehmen zu müssen. Banken fungieren bei der Emission von Commercial Papers als Vermittler, indem sie die Commercial Papers an potenzielle Investoren weiterleiten, aber keine eigenen Mittel investieren. Für gewöhnlich haben CPs eine Laufzeit zwischen sieben Tagen und einem Jahr. Die durchschnittliche Laufzeit im Markt beträgt etwa 60 Tage. Im US-Markt sind Emissionen nur in USD möglich. Im Euro-Markt werden Emissionen in folgenden Währungen getätigt: USD, GBP, EUR, JPY, CHF (wobei etwa 80% aller Emissionen in USD getätigt werden). CPs sind Diskontinstrumente, d.h., sie werden mit einem Abschlag zum Nennwert emittiert. Während US-CPs wie die meisten inländischen („domestic") Commercial Papers auf Diskontbasis quotiert werden, werden Euro-CPs auf Renditebasis quotiert.

Treasury Bills (T-Bills) sind kurzfristige Schuldscheine (Laufzeiten bis ein Jahr), die im Rahmen einer Auktion begeben werden. T-Bills sind in Amerika durch die hohe Liquidität das wichtigste Geldmarktinstrument. T-Bills sind Diskontinstrumente, d.h., sie sind nicht mit einem fixen Zinssatz ausgestattet. Die Rendite errechnet sich somit aus der Haltedauer und der Differenz von Kaufpreis und Nominalwert.

2.7. Practice Questions

1. Which of the following statements is true for the EURIBOR?
   a) It is calculated and published by the BBA.
   b) The EURIBOR is calculated from the quotes of presently 57 international banks.
   c) The panel of reference banks consists only of banks from member countries of the Eurozone.
   d) The panel of reference banks consists only of banks from EU member states.

2. Which benchmark replaced the FIBOR on 1.1.1999?

3. If a Eurodollar-CD is issued in London for 12 months, how is the interest usually paid?
   a) semi-annually
   b) at maturity
   c) quarterly
   d) at the start date

4. How is the repayment of an issued CD effected at maturity?
   a) interest only to the original purchaser
   b) principal only to the original purchaser
   c) principal plus interest to the original purchaser
   d) principal plus interest to the bearer of the CD

5. What is the basis of most USD money market transactions in London?

6. Explain the difference between coupon instruments and discount instruments!

7. Name two examples for coupon instruments and discount instruments!

8. Explain the difference between the interest calculation with true yield and with discount rate!

9. What is meant by "LIBOR" and "LIBID"?

10. What is the advantage and the disadvantage of a CD compared to clean deposits?

11. Who is normally the issuer of a Certificate of Deposit (CD)?
    a) industry
    b) government
    c) discount house
    d) investment banks
    e) credit institutions
    f) central bank

12. The maximum term of certificates of deposit (CDs) is …
    a) 3 years
    b) 6 months
    c) 12 months
    d) 5 years

2.7. Wiederholungsfragen

1. Welche Aussage trifft auf den EURIBOR zu?
   a) Der EURIBOR wird von der BBA errechnet und veröffentlicht.
   b) Der EURIBOR wird aus Quotierungen von derzeit 57 internationalen Banken errechnet.
   c) Der EURIBOR wird nur aus Quotierungen von Banken aus Mitgliedstaaten des Euro errechnet.
   d) Der EURIBOR wird nur aus Quotierungen von Banken aus Mitgliedstaaten der EU errechnet.

2. Durch welche Benchmark wurde per 1.1.1999 der FIBOR ersetzt?

3. Wie werden die Zinsen üblicherweise bei der Emission eines 12-Monats-Eurodollar-CDs in London bezahlt?
   a) halbjährlich
   b) bei Fälligkeit
   c) vierteljährlich
   d) am Emissionstag

4. Wie findet die Rückzahlung eines von Ihnen emittierten CDs bei Fälligkeit statt?
   a) Zinsen an den ursprünglichen Käufer
   b) Nominale an den ursprünglichen Käufer
   c) Nominale plus Zinsen an den ursprünglichen Käufer
   d) Nominale und Zinsen an den Inhaber des CDs

5. Auf welcher Basis werden die meisten USD-Geldmarktgeschäfte in London fixiert?

6. Erklären Sie den Unterschied zwischen Kupon- und Abzinsungsinstrumenten!

7. Nennen Sie jeweils zwei Beispiele für Kupon- und Abzinsungsinstrumente!

8. Erklären Sie den Unterschied der Berechnung der Zinsen zwischen der Angabe eines Zinssatzes und eines Diskontsatzes!

9. Was versteht man unter „LIBOR" bzw. „LIBID"?

10. Welchen Vorteil bzw. Nachteil hat ein CD gegenüber einem Depotgeschäft?

11. Wer tritt normalerweise als Emittent eines Certificates of Deposit (CD) auf?
    a) Industrieunternehmen
    b) Staat
    c) Diskonthaus
    d) Investmentbanken
    e) Kreditinstitute
    f) Zentralbank

12. Die maximale Laufzeit von Certificates of Deposit (CDs) beträgt …
    a) 3 Jahre
    b) 6 Monate
    c) 12 Monate
    d) 5 Jahre

13. On Monday, 10 November, you give an O/N deposit. What is the value date?
    a) 13 November
    b) 11 November
    c) 12 November
    d) 10 November

14. An USD 5,000,000 CD originally issued for 181 days with a coupon of 6.15% is sold with 90 days remaining at 5.85%. What are the proceeds?
    a) USD 5,080,276.50
    b) USD 5,080,304.71
    c) USD 5,069,124.71
    d) USD 5,075,444.21

15. What is meant by an "eligible bill"?

16. What is true regarding commercial papers (CPs)?
    a) They are short dated securities.
    b) They are long dated securities.
    c) They are issued by banks.
    d) They are issued by companies with a low rating.

17. A 3-month (91 days) USD Bankers Acceptance is quoted at a rate of 3.20%. What is the true market yield on this instrument?
    a) 3.201%
    b) 3.226%
    c) 3.021%
    d) 3.262%

18. A USD bankers acceptance of 20 m was issued 55 days ago and has a remaining term of 35 days. You redeem the BA at a discount rate of 3.7%. How many USD do you receive?
    a) USD 19,928,055.56
    b) USD 20,041,111.11
    c) USD 20,071,944.44
    d) USD 19,958,888.89

19. Which instrument is issued through an auction?
    a) Bankers acceptance
    b) Commercial paper
    c) Certificate of deposit
    d) Treasury bill

20. Which of the following instruments is issued by corporates?
    a) CPs
    b) CDs
    c) BAs
    d) T-bills

13. Sie schließen am Montag, den 10. November ein O/N Depot ab. Wann ist der Valutatag (= Starttag)?
   a) 13. November
   b) 11. November
   c) 12. November
   d) 10. November

14. Folgendes Certificate of Deposit ist gegeben:
Volumen: USD 5 Mio., Laufzeit: 181 Tage, Kupon 6,15%.
Sie verkaufen das CD 90 Tage vor Fälligkeit zu 5,85%. Welcher Betrag wird realisiert?
   a) USD 5.080.276,50
   b) USD 5.080.304,71
   c) USD 5.069.124,71
   d) USD 5.075.444,21

15. Was versteht man unter einem „gezogenen Wechsel"?

16. Was trifft auf Commercial Papers zu?
   a) Sie haben kurze Laufzeiten.
   b) Sie haben lange Laufzeiten.
   c) Sie werden unter anderem von Banken emittiert.
   d) Sie werden unter anderem von Unternehmen mit niedriger Bonität emittiert.

17. Ein 3-Monats-(91 Tage)-USD Bankers Acceptance notiert bei einem Zinssatz von
3,20%. Wie hoch ist die Rendite dieses Instruments?
   a) 3,201%
   b) 3,226%
   c) 3,021%
   d) 3,262%

18. Ein Wechsel über USD 20 Mio. wurde vor 55 Tagen ausgestellt und hat eine Restlaufzeit von 35 Tagen. Sie lösen den Wechsel zu einem Diskontzinssatz von 3,7%
ein. Wie viel USD erhalten Sie?
   a) USD 19.928.055,56
   b) USD 20.041.111,11
   c) USD 20.071.944,44
   d) USD 19.958.888,89

19. Welches Instrument wird im Rahmen einer Auktion begeben?
   a) Bankers Acceptance
   b) Commercial Paper
   c) Certificate of Deposit
   d) Treasury Bill

20. Welches der folgenden Instrumente wird von Unternehmen emittiert?
   a) CPs
   b) CDs
   c) BAs
   d) T-Bills

21. Which of the following instruments are traded on a discount basis?
    a) BA
    b) CD
    c) USCP
    d) ECP
    e) T-bill
    f) Interbank Deposit
22. Which of the following yields the highest return?
    a) All have the same yield.
    b) US BA, remaining term of 60 days
    c) USCP, remaining term of 60 days
    d) T-bill 5%, remaining term of 60 days

21. Welche der folgenden Instrumente werden auf Diskontbasis quotiert?
    a) BA
    b) CD
    c) USCP
    d) ECP
    e) T-Bill
    f) Interbank-Depot

22. Welches dieser Geschäfte bringt die höchste Rendite?
    a) Alle Geschäfte bringen die gleiche Rendite.
    b) US BA, Restlaufzeit 60 Tage
    c) USCP, Restlaufzeit 60 Tage
    d) T-Bill 5%, Restlaufzeit 60 Tage

3. Short-term Interest Rate Derivatives

In this chapter you learn ...

- about uses, terminology and conventions concerning forward rate agreements.
- how the amount due is computed for forward rate agreements.
- which risks to consider when dealing with forward rate agreements.
- how forward rates are computed.
- about the connection between yield curve and forward rates.
- what is meant by money market futures.
- how money market futures are used.
- which conventions and contract specifications apply when dealing with money market futures.
- about the most important money market future contracts.
- about the role of exchange and clearing house when dealing with money market futures.
- which types of margin are used in the margin system.
- what is meant by open interest and how is it computed.
- about the three types of "basis".
- about the differences between forward rate agreements and money market futures.
- how money market futures are used for pricing und hedging forward rate agreements.
- how the hedge ratio is computed.
- what is meant by the convexity effect.
- which spread strategies are used for money market futures.

3.1. Forward Rate Agreement (FRA)

The forward, or future rate agreement, is a contract between two parties to **fix a future interest rate**. This contract defines the interest rate for a future period based on an agreed principal.

If on the agreed date (fixing date) the FRA rate differs from the current market rate (reference rate), a settlement payment depending on the difference must be paid by one of the contractors. The principal is not exchanged and there is no obligation by either party to borrow or lend capital.

The FRA can be used

- by market participants who wish to hedge against future interest rate risks by setting the future interest rate today **(Hedging)**.
- by market participants who want to make profits based on their expectations on the future development of interest rates **(Trading)**.
- by market participants who try to take advantage of the different prices of FRAs and other financial instruments, e.g. futures, by means of **arbitrage**.

3. Geldmarktderivate

In diesem Kapitel lernen Sie ...

- was man unter einem Forward Rate Agreement versteht.
- wozu ein Forward Rate Agreement verwendet wird.
- welche Terminologien bzw. Usancen bei Forward Rate Agreements verwendet werden.
- wie die Ausgleichszahlung bei Forward Rate Agreements berechnet wird.
- welche Risiken bei Forward Rate Agreements auftreten können.
- wie Forward-Sätze ermittelt werden.
- welcher Zusammenhang zwischen Zinskurve und Forward-Satz besteht.
- was man unter Geldmarktfutures versteht.
- wozu Geldmarktfutures verwendet werden.
- welche Usancen und Kontraktspezifikationen bei Geldmarktfutures verwendet werden.
- die wichtigsten Geldmarktfuture-Kontrakte kennen.
- welche Rolle die Börse und das Clearing House beim Handel mit Geldmarktfutures einnehmen.
- welche Arten von Margins im Margin-System verwendet werden.
- was man unter Open Interest versteht und wie dieses berechnet wird.
- welche drei Formen der „Basis" es gibt.
- wodurch sich Forward Rate Agreements und Geldmarktfutures unterscheiden.
- wie Geldmarktfutures zum Pricing und Hedging von Forward Rate Agreements verwendet werden.
- wie die Hedge Ratio ermittelt wird.
- was man unter Konvexitätseffekt versteht.
- welche Spread-Strategien bei Geldmarktfutures angewendet werden.

3.1. Forward Rate Agreement (FRA)

Ein Forward Rate Agreement ist ein **Zinstermingeschäft**. Es fixiert den Zinssatz für einen vereinbarten Nominalbetrag für eine bestimmte Periode in der Zukunft.

Am Beginn der vereinbarten Periode (Settlement-Tag) kommt es lediglich zu einer Vergütung der Differenz zwischen dem vereinbarten FRA-Zinssatz und dem am Fixing-Tag am Geldmarkt festgestellten gültigen Satz (Referenzzinssatz). Es besteht jedoch keine Verpflichtung, den vereinbarten Nominalbetrag zu liefern oder bereitzustellen.

Das FRA kann verwendet werden von Marktteilnehmern,

- um zukünftiges Zinsrisiko dadurch auszuschalten, dass der Zinssatz heute fixiert (gesichert) wird **(Hedging).**
- die mit ihrer Meinung über die zukünftige Zinsentwicklung verdienen möchten **(Trading).**
- die die unterschiedlichen Preise der FRAs und anderer Finanzinstrumente wie beispielsweise Futures durch **Arbitrage** ausnützen möchten.

FRAs are **over-the-counter (OTC)** products and are available for a variety of periods: starting from a few days to terms of several years. In practice, however, the FRA-market for 1-year FRAs offers the highest liquidity and is therefore also regarded as a money-market instrument.

The FRA is not an obligation to borrow or lend any capital in the future. At settlement date, the principal just serves as the basis to calculate the difference between the two interest rates, or rather the settlement payment that results from this difference

3.1.1. Terminology

Example

On 10th January the following FRA is dealt:
FRA 6/12 spot
Principal: EUR 100 m
FRA rate: 4½%

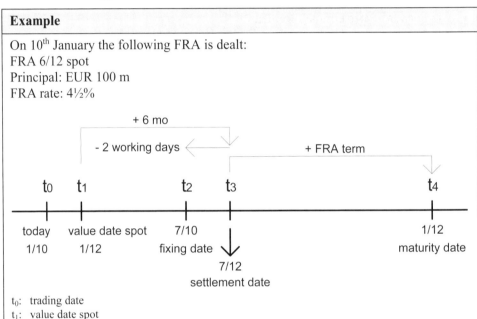

t_0: trading date
t_1: value date spot
t_2: fixing date: the difference between contract rate and reference rate is determined two working days before settlement date.
t_3: settlement date: the settlement payment is exchanged ("amount due")
t_4: maturity date (final maturity): defines the end of the FRA period, there are no more payments to be made, but the exact term of the FRA is determined; final maturity – settlement date = days of FRA term

---

FRA rate

The FRA rate is the interest rate stipulated in the contract, e.g. here 4½%.

FRA term

The FRA term is **the period from settlement date until maturity date**. For this period the interest rate has been fixed. E.g. the term of a 3/9 FRA is six months.

FRAs werden **„over the counter" (OTC)** gehandelt. Sie sind für eine Vielzahl von Perioden, beginnend bei wenigen Tagen bis zu einer Endlaufzeit von mehreren Jahren, verfügbar. In der Praxis hat der FRA-Markt bis zu einem Jahr Laufzeit die höchste Liquidität. FRAs werden daher auch als Money-Market-Instrument angesehen.

Ein FRA stellt keine Verpflichtung dar, in Zukunft Depots zu veranlagen oder aufzunehmen. Der Kapitalbetrag dient lediglich als Rechengröße, um die Zinsdifferenz bzw. die daraus resultierende Zahlung am Settlement-Tag zu berechnen.

3.1.1. Terminologie

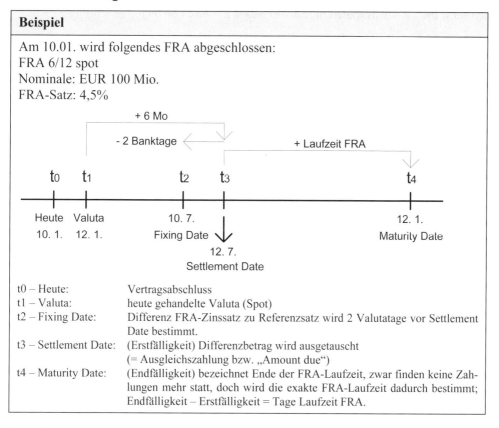

Beispiel

Am 10.01. wird folgendes FRA abgeschlossen:
FRA 6/12 spot
Nominale: EUR 100 Mio.
FRA-Satz: 4,5%

t0 – Heute:	Vertragsabschluss
t1 – Valuta:	heute gehandelte Valuta (Spot)
t2 – Fixing Date:	Differenz FRA-Zinssatz zu Referenzsatz wird 2 Valutatage vor Settlement Date bestimmt.
t3 – Settlement Date:	(Erstfälligkeit) Differenzbetrag wird ausgetauscht (= Ausgleichszahlung bzw. „Amount due")
t4 – Maturity Date:	(Endfälligkeit) bezeichnet Ende der FRA-Laufzeit, zwar finden keine Zahlungen mehr statt, doch wird die exakte FRA-Laufzeit dadurch bestimmt; Endfälligkeit – Erstfälligkeit = Tage Laufzeit FRA.

FRA-Zinssatz

Der FRA-Zinssatz ist der im Kontrakt vereinbarte Zinssatz, in diesem Beispiel 4,5%.

Laufzeit

Die Laufzeit eines FRAs ist die **Periode zwischen Settlement-Tag und Maturity-Tag.** Sie ist die Periode, für die der Zinssatz fixiert wurde. Daher ist beispielsweise die Laufzeit eines 3/9 FRAs sechs Monate. Die Zeit zwischen Valuta-Tag und Settlement-Tag wird als Vorlaufzeit bezeichnet (hier also drei Monate).

Reference rate

The reference rate is the rate which the FRA rate is compared to on the fixing date. The basis for the reference rate is agreed upon on the trade date. Usually for the main currencies (e.g. USD, GBP, CHF, JPY, AUD, etc.) the **LIBOR** calculated by BBA (British Bankers Association) is used. For the EUR it is mostly **EURIBOR**. For currencies where there is no LIBOR calculated local fixings are used (e.g. WIBOR for PLN, PRIBOR for CZK, etc.).

It has to be taken into account that all reference rates represent an **offer side** (LIBOR, EURIBOR, WIBOR, etc.) and are therefore a rate for taking money (as Market User), no matter if the FRA was traded in order to hedge a future borrowing or lending.

Fixing date

Usually the fixing date is **two working days before settlement date**. GBP FRAs are settled on the same-day (not at value date after two days) and constitute therefore an exception.

Amount due

The amount due is the only cash-flow that exists in an FRA and is **due on the settlement date**. The amount due is determined by the **difference between FRA rate and reference rate** multiplied by the amount of capital times the FRA term and is discounted to the settlement date (because the calculation would be due on maturity date).

The formula to calculate the settlement payment is:

$$AD = \frac{(REF - FRA) \times (\pm\, VOL) \times \dfrac{D}{B}}{1 + \left(REF \times \dfrac{D}{B} \right)}$$

AD   = amount due
REF = reference rate (e.g. LIBOR) in decimals
VOL = volume of the FRA (+ = buy; – = sell)
FRA = FRA rate in decimals
D   = number of days of the FRA term
B   = day basis of calculation

Referenzsatz

Der Referenzsatz ist jener Zinssatz, mit dem der vereinbarte FRA-Zinssatz beim Fixing verglichen wird. Der zu verwendende Referenzzinssatz wird bei Geschäftsabschluss vereinbart. Üblicherweise ist dies für die Hauptwährungen (z.B. USD, GBP, CHF, JPY, AUD usw.) der von der BBA (British Bankers Association) ermittelte **LIBOR.** Beim Euro ist der Referenzsatz meist **EURIBOR.** Für Währungen, bei denen kein LIBOR ermittelt wird, werden lokale Fixings verwendet (z.B. WIBOR für PLN, PRIBOR für CZK usw.).

Zu beachten ist, dass alle Referenzsätze einen **Briefsatz** repräsentieren (LIBOR, EURIBOR, WIBOR usw.) und somit den Zinssatz für Geldaufnahme (als Market User) darstellen, egal ob das FRA zur Absicherung einer zukünftigen Anlage oder Aufnahme dient.

Fixing-Tag

Der Fixing-Tag ist üblicherweise **zwei Banktage vor dem Settlement-Tag.** Eine Ausnahme stellt das **GBP** dar, das **tagesgleich** fixiert wird.

Ausgleichszahlung

Die Ausgleichszahlung ist der einzige Cashflow, der beim FRA anfällt, und zwar zum Zeitpunkt des Settlement Dates. Die Ausgleichszahlung ergibt sich aus der **Differenz zwischen FRA-Satz und Referenzsatz** mal Betragsvolumen mal FRA-Laufzeit. Da sie bereits **zum Beginn der FRA-Laufzeit zu bezahlen** ist (am Settlement-Tag), wird der Betrag abgezinst.

Formel für die Berechnung der Ausgleichszahlung:

$$AZ = \frac{(REF - FRA) * (\pm VOL) * \dfrac{T_{FRA}}{B}}{1 + \left(REF * \dfrac{T_{FRA}}{B} \right)}$$

AZ = Ausgleichszahlung
REF = Referenzsatz (z.B. LIBOR) in Dezimalen
VOL = Volumen FRA (+ = Kauf, – = Verkauf)
T_{FRA} = Anzahl der Tage im FRA
B = Berechnungsbasis
FRA = FRA-Zinssatz in Dezimalen

Example

You have sold the following FRA:
EUR 100 m FRA 3/9 at 4.50%
Days of FRA (interest period): 181
6-months LIBOR at fixing date: 4.75%
What is the amount due?

$$AD = \frac{(0.0475 - 0.045) \times -100,000,000 \times \dfrac{181}{360}}{1 + \left(0.0475 \times \dfrac{181}{360}\right)} = -122,762.63$$

You have to pay EUR 122,762.63 value settlement date.

FRA purchase (buy FRA)

The buyer of an FRA receives the amount due if on the fixing date the reference rate is higher than the FRA rate. If the reference rate is below the FRA rate the buyer has to pay the amount due. An FRA can be purchased in order to **speculate on rising interest rates** in the future or as a **hedge for a future short position in deposits** and thus a protection against rising interest rates.

FRA sale (sell FRA)

The seller of an FRA receives the amount due if on the fixing date the reference rate is lower than the FRA rate. If the reference rate is above the FRA rate the seller has to pay the amount due. An FRA can be sold in order to **speculate on falling interest rates** in the future or as a **hedge for a future long position in deposits** and thus a protection against falling interest rates. For example this is necessary, if you are **"over-borrowed"**. "Over-borrowed" means that a dealer or corporation has more money borrowed than lent (Liabilities are higher than assets = debit carryover). Therefore you have the risk of falling interest rates respectively a surplus of liquidity.

Quotation

FRA terms are usually labeled by a slash (3/9) or by a dot (3•6). The FRA terms most commonly used are terms of 3, 6, 9, or 12 months.

1/4	1/7	2/5	2/8	3/6	3/9	3/12
6/12	6/18	9/12	9/15	9/18	12/18	12/24

Usual FRA periods

As FRAs are OTC instruments the maturities and the periods of FRAs can be **freely agreed** upon by the counterparties. For the standard periods like 3, 6 and 12 months market liquidity is the highest. Generally also an FRA with a e.g. 5-months period (e.g. a 2/7 FRA) can be traded.

Beispiel

Sie haben folgendes FRA verkauft:
EUR 100 Mio. FRA 3/9 zu 4,50%
Laufzeit: 181 Tage
6-Monats-EURIBOR am Fixingtag: 4,75%
Wie hoch ist die Ausgleichszahlung?

$$AZ=\frac{\left(0,0475-0,045\right)*\left(-100.000.000\right)*\dfrac{181}{360}}{1+\left(0,0475*\dfrac{181}{360}\right)}=-122.762,63$$

Sie müssen **EUR 122.762,63** mit Valuta-Settlement-Tag zahlen.

Kauf FRA (FRA buy)

Der Käufer des FRA erhält eine Ausgleichszahlung, wenn der Referenzsatz am Fixing-Tag über dem vereinbarten FRA-Satz liegt. Liegt der Referenzsatz darunter, muss er die Ausgleichszahlung leisten. Somit kann ein FRA zur **Spekulation auf höhere Zinsen** verwendet werden oder zur **Absicherung** einer zukünftigen Refinanzierung (Passivgeschäft) **gegen steigende Zinsen.**

Verkauf FRA (FRA sell)

Der Verkäufer des FRA erhält eine Ausgleichszahlung, wenn der Referenzsatz am Fixing-Tag unter dem vereinbarten FRA-Satz liegt. Liegt der Referenzsatz darüber, muss er die Ausgleichszahlung leisten. Somit kann ein FRA zur **Spekulation auf niedrigere Zinsen** verwendet werden oder zur **Absicherung** einer zukünftigen Anlage (Aktivgeschäft) **gegen fallende Zinsen.** Beispielsweise ist dies notwendig, wenn man „over-borrowed" ist. Als **„over-borrowed"** bezeichnet man eine Situation, in der ein Händler bzw. ein Unternehmen mehr Geld genommen als gegeben hat (Passiva deutlich höher als Aktiva = Passivüberhang) und damit ein Risiko fallender Zinsen bzw. einen Überschuss an Liquidität hat.

Quotierung

Gebräuchlich ist, FRA-Perioden durch einen Schrägstrich (3/9) oder ein Malzeichen (3x6) zu kennzeichnen. Die gebräuchlichsten FRA-Perioden sind Laufzeiten für 3, 6, 9 oder 12 Monate, wie z.B.:

1/4	1/7	2/5	2/8	3/6	3/9	3/12
6/12	6/18	9/12	9/15	9/18	12/18	12/24

Übliche FRA-Perioden

Da FRAs OTC-Instrumente sind, können die Fälligkeiten und Laufzeiten von FRAs zwischen den beiden Vertragspartnern **frei vereinbart** werden. Für die Standardlaufzeiten – das sind drei, sechs und zwölf Monate – ist die Liquidität im Markt jedoch am höchsten. Grundsätzlich könnte jedoch auch ein FRA mit einer Laufzeit von z.B. fünf Monaten (2/7 FRA) vereinbart werden.

Regarding the settlement date you have the following categories:

- **Spot FRAs**
  the settlement date is exactly x full months after spot value
- **Broken dates**
  the settlement date is not exactly x full months after spot value
- **IMM FRAs**
  the settlement date is a future maturity, i.e. on an IMM date (International Monetary Market). The IMM dates are always the 3rd Wednesday in March, June, September and December. Therefore IMM FRAs are a special kind of broken dates.

Example

Trade date: Tue 24nd Mar 2009
Spot value: Thu 26th Mar 2009
What is the term of a "3/6 spot", of a "3/6 over the 9th" and of a "3/6 IMM" FRA?

3/6 spot FRA: settlement: Fri   26th Jun 2009
                        maturity: Mon 28th Sep 2009

3/6 over the 9th: settlement: Tue 9th Jun 2009
(= Broken Date) maturity: Wed 9th Sep 2009

3/6 IMM: settlement: Wed 17th Jun 2009 (3rd Wed in June)
                        maturity: Thu   17th Sep 2009

Excerpt from a Reuters page for EUR Spot FRAs:

1X4	2.129	2.149	COMMERZBANK	FFT	CBFT	10:13
2X5	2.205	2.225	COMMERZBANK	FFT	CBFT	10:36
3X6	2.249	2.269	COMMERZBANK	FFT	CBFT	10:36
4X7	2.240	2.260	ABN AMRO	AMS	ABNF	10:40
5X8	2.345	2.365	COMMERZBANK	FFT	CBFT	10:46
6X9	2.361	2.376	TULL FIN	LON	TULP	10:47
7X10	2.422	2.442	RABOBANK	UTR	RABO	10:47
8X11	2.496	2.516	RABOBANK	UTR	RABO	10:47
9X12	2.582	2.602	RABOBANK	UTR	RABO	10:47
12X15	2.79	2.81	TRADITION	LON		10:36
1X7	2.237	2.257	COMMERZBANK	FFT	CBFT	10:36
2X8	2.297	2.317	COMMERZBANK	FFT	CBFT	10:46
3X9	2.3000	2.3300	FINACOR	MUN	FING	10:47
4X10	2.342	2.362	RABOBANK	UTR	RABO	10:47
5X11	2.404	2.424	RABOBANK	UTR	RABO	10:47
6X12	2.494	2.509	TULL FIN	LON	TULP	10:47
9X15	2.715	2.725	SOC GENERALE	PAR		10:45

Bezüglich Settlement-Datum (= Laufzeitbeginn) werden folgende Kategorien unterschieden:

- **Spot FRAs**
  Der Settlement-Tag (= Laufzeitbeginn) liegt genau x volle Monate nach der aktuellen Spot Valuta.
- **Broken Dates**
  Der Settlement-Tag liegt nicht genau x volle Monate nach der aktuellen Spot Valuta.
- **IMM-FRAs**
  Der Settlement-Tag liegt auf einer Future-Fälligkeit, d.h. auf einem IMM-Date (International-Monetary-Market-Date). Die IMM-Dates sind jeweils der 3. Mittwoch in den Monaten März, Juni, September und Dezember. Somit sind IMM-FRAs Spezialfälle von Broken Dates.

Beispiel

Handelstag: Di 24.03.2009
Spot Valuta: Do 26.03.2009
Was ist die Laufzeit eines „3/6 Spot"-FRAs, „3/6 über den 9." und „3/6 IMM"-FRAs?

3/6 Spot FRA	Settlement	Fr. 26.06.2009
	Maturity	Mo. 28.09.2009
3/6 über den 9.	Settlement	Di. 09.06.2009
(= Broken Date)	Maturity	Mi. 09.09.2009
3/6 IMM-FRA	Settlement	Mi. 17.06.2009 (3. Mittwoch im Juni)
	Maturity	Do. 17.09.2009

Ausschnitt aus einer Reuters-Seite für EUR Spot-FRAs:

1X4	2.129	2.149	COMMERZBANK	FFT	CBFT	10:13
2X5	2.205	2.225	COMMERZBANK	FFT	CBFT	10:36
3X6	2.249	2.269	COMMERZBANK	FFT	CBFT	10:36
4X7	2.240	2.260	ABN AMRO	AMS	ABNF	10:40
5X8	2.345	2.365	COMMERZBANK	FFT	CBFT	10:46
6X9	2.361	2.376	TULL FIN	LON	TULP	10:47
7X10	2.422	2.442	RABOBANK	UTR	RABO	10:47
8X11	2.496	2.516	RABOBANK	UTR	RABO	10:47
9X12	2.582	2.602	RABOBANK	UTR	RABO	10:47
12X15	2.79	2.81	TRADITION	LON		10:36
1X7	2.237	2.257	COMMERZBANK	FFT	CBFT	10:36
2X8	2.297	2.317	COMMERZBANK	FFT	CBFT	10:46
3X9	2.3000	2.3300	FINACOR	MUN	FING	10:47
4X10	2.342	2.362	RABOBANK	UTR	RABO	10:47
5X11	2.404	2.424	RABOBANK	UTR	RABO	10:47
6X12	2.494	2.509	TULL FIN	LON	TULP	10:47
9X15	2.715	2.725	SOC GENERALE	PAR		10:45

Market liquidity and spreads

FRA-markets in USD, EUR and GBP are the most liquid ones.

As a rule:

- FRAs **with** MM futures-underlying → **low** spreads (e.g. EUR 6/12, quotation 3.43–3.45)
- FRAs **without** MM futures-underlying → **greater** spreads (e.g. HUF 6/12, quotation 8.05–8.15)

Regarding the maturity the **liquidity of IMM FRAs is the highest** followed by spot FRAs and broken dates. Therefore the spread for IMM FRAs is often only 1 BP whereas for broken dates spreads of 3–5 BP are common.

Standard documentation

The usual legal contract basis for FRAs were **FRABBA** terms, which are composed by British Bankers' Association (BBA) and are now mostly replaced by **ISDA**-Agreements.

Credit risk (Risk of Default) of an FRA

The FRA comprises no exchange of principal. Therefore, the only risk is the **non-fulfill-ment of the amount due** at settlement date **(replacement risk)**. The credit risk is thereby limited to the difference between FRA rate and the locked-in reference rate at settlement date.

The credit line (partner limit) used by an FRA is therefore usually between 1–5% p.a. of the principal amount (with regard to the term of the FRA-period), from spot until settlement date. In addition one should also take into account the following factors:

- **Period to settlement**
  the longer the period to settlement, the higher the risk that the reference rate differs strongly from the FRA rate which would lead to a higher amount due
- **FRA period**
  the longer the FRA period, the stronger the impact of the interest rate differential on the amount due
- **Volatility**
  the higher the statistical margin of deviation (= volatility), the higher the probability that the reference rate differs strongly from the FRA rate

Ideally limit-systems guarantee a permanent mark-to-market-valuation plus an add-on factor for the remaining time until settlement which can be calculated with the Value at Risk (VAR) approach.

Marktliquidität und Spreads

FRA-Märkte in USD, EUR und GBP haben die größte Liquidität.

In der Regel gilt:

- FRAs **mit** Futures-Unterlegung → **geringe** Spreads (z.B. Euro 6/12, Quotierung 3,43–3,45)
- FRAs **ohne** Futures-Unterlegung → **größere** Spreads (z.B. HUF 6/12, Quotierung 8,05–8,15)

Bezüglich Fälligkeit ist die **Liquidität bei IMM-FRAs am größten**, gefolgt von Spot-FRAs und Broken Dates. Dementsprechend beträgt der Spread bei IMM-FRAs oft nur 1 Basispunkt (BP), hingegen sind für Broken Dates auch Spreads von 3 bis 5 BP üblich.

Standarddokumentation

Die übliche rechtliche Vertragsgrundlage bei FRAs waren die **FRABBA**-Terms. Es sind dies Standardverträge, die von der British Bankers' Association (BBA) verfasst wurden. Aktuell wird FRABBA durch **ISDA**-Agreements (International Swaps and Derivatives Association) ersetzt.

Kreditrisiko (Ausfallsrisiko) bei FRAs

Das FRA beinhaltet keinen Austausch von Kapitalnominalbeträgen. Dementsprechend beschränkt sich das Kreditrisiko auf das **Wiederbeschaffungsrisiko**. Einziges mögliches Risiko ist die **Nichterfüllung der Ausgleichszahlung** zum Settlement-Tag. Somit besteht das Kreditrisiko vom Abschlusstag bis zur Erfüllung der Ausgleichszahlung, d.h. bis zum Settlement-Tag.

Die Limitbelastung für das Kreditrisiko (Partnerlimit) beträgt daher üblicherweise nur 1 bis 5% p.a. des Nominalbetrags, wobei bei Berechnung der Limitbelastung folgende Faktoren berücksichtigt werden sollten:

- **Vorlaufzeit**
  Je größer die Vorlaufzeit, desto höher das Risiko, dass der Referenzsatz stark vom vereinbarten FRA-Satz abweicht und es somit zu einer hohen Ausgleichszahlung kommt.
- **Laufzeit**
  Je länger die Laufzeit, desto stärker wirkt sich die Zinsdifferenz auf die Ausgleichszahlung aus.
- **Volatilität**
  Je höher die statistische Schwankungsbreite (= Volatilität), desto höher die Wahrscheinlichkeit, dass der Referenzsatz vom FRA-Satz stark abweicht.

Im Idealfall berücksichtigen Limitsysteme den aktuellen Marktwert des FRAs plus einen Add-on-Faktor für die verbleibende Zeit bis zum Settlement, der mit dem Value-at-Risk-Ansatz berechnet werden kann.

3.1.2. Hedging with FRAs

The main advantage of derivatives like FRAs is the **separation of liquidity and interest rate risk**. Thus the interest rate risk can be controlled more efficient, i.e. at more favourable prices (closer spreads) and by avoiding additional credit risk which would occur for controlling the interest rate risk with cash instruments.

When hedging cash positions with derivatives you have to take into account that you always **only hedge a reference rate** (e.g. LIBOR, EURIBOR, etc.). For the total result the spreads to the reference rate that have to be paid in the cash market have to be considered. For example you cannot assume that you can lend at LIBOR. For borrowings a premium on the LIBOR (**credit spread**) has to be considered.

Example

Your position shows that you have to refinance EUR 100 m from 3 to 6 months.
3/6 FRA: 3.46-50%
Your condition for refinancing: EURIBOR +25 BP
You are hedging your position with an FRA.
What is your result assuming that the 3-months EURIBOR in 3 months will be 4.25%?

You have the risk that the 3-months EURIBOR rises and therefore buy a 3/6 EUR FRA 100 m at 3.50% for hedging.
After 3 months you refinance at the current rate of 4.50% (EURIBOR 4.25 + 0.25 credit spread).
You receive a cash settlement of 0.75% (4.25% – 3.50%).
Thus your total result is 3.75% (4.50 – 0.75 = cash rate – amount due). The 3.75% can also be interpreted as: FRA rate + spread EURIBOR (= 3.50 + 0.25).

Example

Your cash position shows a liquidity overhang from 3 to 6 months. You are hedging the interest rate by a 3/6 FRA sale at 3.46%. What is your result, assuming that you can lend cash at EURIBOR - 5 BP?
The result will be **3.41%** (= FRA rate – spread EURIBOR = 3.46 – 0.05). The following table shows the result for different interest rate scenarios:

EURIBOR in 3 months	3.00%	4.00%	5.00%
Interest rate for lending (E – 5 BP)	2.95%	3.95%	4.95%
Amount due (FRA – E)	+0.46%	–0.54%	–1.54%
Result (lending + amount due)	3.41%	3.41%	3.41%

3.1.2. Anwendung von FRAs im Hedging

Der wesentliche Vorteil von Derivaten wie FRAs liegt in der **Trennung von Liquidität und Zinsrisiko.** Dadurch kann das Zinsrisiko effizient gesteuert werden, d.h. zu günstigen Preisen (engen Spreads) und unter Vermeidung von zusätzlichem Kreditrisiko, das bei einer Steuerung des Zinsrisikos mit Cash-Instrumenten anfallen würde.

Beim Hedging von Cash-Positionen mit Derivaten ist zu beachten, dass mit diesen **immer nur ein Referenzsatz** (z.B. LIBOR, EURIBOR usw.) **abgesichert** wird. In der Ergebnisrechnung müssen daher die im Cash-Markt zu zahlenden Spreads zum Referenzsatz berücksichtigt werden. Beispielsweise kann man nicht davon ausgehen, dass man zu LIBOR anlegen kann. Bei Refinanzierungen ist ein etwaiger Aufschlag auf den LIBOR **(Credit Spread)** zu berücksichtigen.

Beispiel

Ihre Position zeigt einen Refinanzierungsbedarf von EUR 100 Mio. von 3 auf 6 Monate.
3x6 FRA: 3,46–50%
Ihre Kondition für Refinanzierungen: EURIBOR +25 BP
Sie sichern sich über ein FRA ab. Wie lautet Ihr Ergebnis, wenn der 3-Monats-EURIBOR in 3 Monaten bei 4,25% liegt?

Sie haben das Risiko, dass der 3-Monats-EURIBOR steigt, und kaufen daher 100 Mio. 3x6 FRA zu 3,50% zur Absicherung.
Nach 3 Monaten refinanzieren Sie sich zum aktuellen Zinssatz von 4,50% (EURIBOR 4,25 + 0,25 Credit Spread).
Aus dem FRA erhalten Sie eine Ausgleichszahlung von 0,75% (4,25 – 3,50).
Somit ist das Gesamtergebnis 3,75% (4,50 – 0,75 = Cash-Satz – Ausgleichszahlung).
Die 3,75% können auch anders interpretiert werden: FRA-Satz plus Spread zum EURIBOR (= 3,50 + 0,25).

Beispiel

Ihre Cash-Position zeigt einen Liquiditätsüberhang von 3 auf 6 Monaten. Sie sichern den Zinssatz durch den Verkauf eines 3/6 FRAs zu 3,46% ab. Wie lautet Ihr Ergebnis, wenn Sie davon ausgehen, dass Sie Cash zu EURIBOR -5 BP anlegen können?
Das Ergebnis wird **3,41%** lauten (= FRA-Satz – Spread zu EURIBOR = 3,46 – 0,05).
In der Folge wird das Ergebnis bei unterschiedlichen Zinsszenarien dargestellt.

EURIBOR in 3 Monaten	3,00%	4,00%	5,00%
Zinssatz für Anlage (E – 5 BP)	2,95%	3,95%	4,95%
Ausgleichszahlung (FRAU – E)	+0,46%	–0,54%	–1,54%
Ergebnis (Anlage + AZ)	3,41%	3,41%	3,41%

Remaining risks when hedging with derivatives

- **LIBOR risk**

  As shown in the example, the result remains the same and is therefore independent of the LIBOR resp. EURIBOR level. But only assuming, that the cash transaction can be done exactly at LIBOR plus a certain spread. Thus you have the **risk that the market rate (at which you lend or borrow cash) does not comply with the LIBOR.** (e.g. LIBOR has been fixed at 11:00 a.m. at 3%, you make the refinancing at 1:00 p.m. and the market has changed to 3.05%).

- **Liquidity risk**

  Assuming that interest rates are unchanged, you still have the risk that the spread (at which you can lend or borrow cash) changes. In the example a credit spread of 25 BP is calculated (LIBOR +25 BP). You have the risk that this spread increases up to +35 BP, for example. Here liquidity risk is the **risk of higher refinancing costs** due to a widening of the credit spreads (e.g. because of a worsening of your own credit rating or because the market asks for higher premiums for the same credit ratings).

3.1.3. Determination of Forward Interest Rates

3.1.3.1. The principle of Forward Interest Rates

Forward interest rates can be derived from the **current yield curve** as you can always produce a forward deposit by means of two deposits with different terms. For example you can produce a forward borrowing from 6 to 12 months by borrowing for 12 months and lending for 6 months at the same time. The resulting interest rate depends on the costs resp. returns of the 2 deposits – and therefore on the yield curve. That interest rate (costs) of the two deposits can be alternatively called **Implied Rate**, **Break-even Rate** or **Forward-forward Rate**.

Example

Money market rates:
6 months: 4%
12 months: 4.5%
How can you produce today the interest rate for a borrowing from 6 to 12 months?

Answer: Borrowing for 12 months at 4.5% and lending for 6 months at 4% at the same time

---

Restrisiken beim Hedging mit Derivaten

- **LIBOR-Risiko**

  Im Beispiel oben wurde gezeigt, dass das Ergebnis unabhängig vom LIBOR- bzw. EU-RIBOR-Niveau stabil ist. Allerdings wurde dabei unterstellt, dass die Cash-Transaktion genau auf Basis des LIBOR plus einem bestimmten Spread durchgeführt werden kann. Somit besteht das **Risiko, dass der Marktsatz,** zu dem Sie die Anlage bzw. Aufnahme der zugrundeliegenden Cash-Position durchführen, **nicht dem LIBOR entspricht** (z.B. LIBOR wurde um 11.00 Uhr mit 3% gefixt, Sie führen die Refinanzierung um 13.00 Uhr durch, und der Marktsatz hat sich in 3,05% geändert).

- **Liquiditätsrisiko**

  Nehmen wir einmal an, dass die Zinsen unverändert sind, so verbleibt immer noch das Risiko, dass sich der Spread, zu dem Sie die Cash-Transaktion durchführen können, verändert hat. Im Beispiel sind Sie in Ihrer Kalkulation davon ausgegangen, dass Sie zu LIBOR +25 BP aufnehmen können. Ihr Risiko besteht nun in einer Erhöhung des Spreads z.B. auf +35 BP. Unter Liquiditätsrisiko versteht man hier also das **Risiko der Verteuerung der Refinanzierungskosten** aufgrund einer Ausweitung des Credit Spreads (z.B. wegen einer Verschlechterung der eigenen Bonität oder weil der Markt für gleiche Bonitäten höhere Aufschläge verlangt).

3.1.3. Ermittlung von Forward-Zinssätzen

3.1.3.1. Das Prinzip der Forward-Sätze

Der Preis von Forward-Zinssätzen leitet sich von der **aktuellen Zinskurve** ab. Dahinter steckt das Prinzip, dass mittels zweier Depots mit unterschiedlichen Laufzeiten ein Forward-Depot produziert werden kann. So kann beispielsweise durch Aufnahme auf zwölf Monate und gleichzeitige Anlage auf sechs Monate eine „Forward Aufnahme" von sechs auf zwölf Monate produziert werden. Der sich daraus ergebende Zinssatz hängt dabei von den Kosten bzw. Erträgen aus den beiden Geschäften – und somit von der Zinskurve – ab. Diesen Zinssatz (Kosten), den man sich über diese zwei Geschäfte dargestellt hat, bezeichnet man alternativ als **Implied Rate**, **Break-even Rate** oder **Forward-forward Rate**.

Beispiel
Geldmarktsätze: 6 Monate: 4% 12 Monate: 4,5% Durch welche Geschäfte kann der Zinssatz für eine Aufnahme von sechs bis zwölf Monaten schon heute produziert werden? Lösung: Aufnahme auf zwölf Monate zu 4,5% und gleichzeitige Anlage auf sechs Monate zu 4%.

Cash flows:

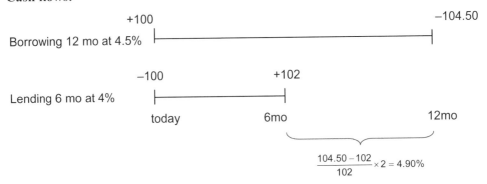

You have a positive cash flow of +102 after 6 months (= borrowing of 102) and a negative cash-flow of -104.50 after 12 months (= paying back the principle plus 2.5 interest rate). Interest of 2.5 for half a year based on a starting capital of 102 results in an interest rate of 4.90% p.a. (see above calculation). **Thus the forward interest rate is 4.90%.**

3.1.3.2. Highest and Lowest FRA Price Limits

The highest resp. lowest FRA price limits are determined by the **forward rates.** A future interest rate can be produced (as shown above) by means of two deposits (forward deposit). But it can also be produced by means of derivatives, e.g. FRAs. Both interest rates have to be linked to each other; otherwise it would be possible to profit from the price differences without any risk (= Arbitrage). The theoretical highest resp. lowest FRA price limits can be derived from the money market cash forward rates.

Determination of the highest FRA price limit

The question is: At what rate can a FRA sale position be closed in the cash market? The FRA price has to be lower than that synthetic cash price. Otherwise you could sell the FRA directly in the market and close the position by a synthetic FRA purchase in the cash market at the same time.

Example

Money market rates: 6 mo: 4.00–4.10% (180 days)
                      12 mo: 4.40–4.50% (360 days)

What is the highest FRA price limit of a 6/12 FRA with the given yield curve?

With a sold FRA you can fix a rate for a future lending. Therefore the FRA sale is equivalent to a future lending. Thus this interest rate position can be closed by fixing an interest rate for a future borrowing (= synthetic FRA purchase = borrowing 12 months + lending 6 months).

The highest FRA price limit is therefore defined by the price of a synthetic FRA purchase.

Cashflows:

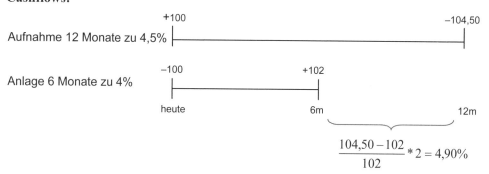

$$\frac{104,50-102}{102}*2=4,90\%$$

Aus den beiden Geschäften ergibt sich „heute" ein Netto-Cashflow von 0, in sechs Monaten ein positiver Cashflow von +102 und nach zwölf Monaten ein negativer Cashflow von -104,50. Das entspricht einer Kreditaufnahme von 102 nach sechs Monaten und der Rückzahlung des Kapitals plus 2,5 Zinsen nach zwölf Monaten. Ein Zinsbetrag von 2,5 für ein halbes Jahr bezogen auf ein Anfangskapital von 102 entspricht daher einem p.a.-Zinssatz von 4,9%. **Somit beträgt der Forward-Zinssatz 4,90%.**

3.1.3.2. Preisobergrenze und -untergrenze

Die Preisobergrenze bzw. -untergrenze des FRA-Marktes wird durch die **Forward-Sätze** bestimmt. Ein zukünftiger Zinssatz kann – wie oben dargestellt – durch zwei Depots produziert werden (Forward-Depot). Er kann aber auch derivativ fixiert werden, z.B. mit einem FRA. Die beiden Zinssätze müssen in einem bestimmten Zusammenhang zueinander stehen; ansonsten wäre es möglich, aus Preisdifferenzen einen risikolosen Ertrag zu erzielen (= Arbitrage). Aus den Forward-Sätzen des Cash-Marktes lassen sich daher die theoretische Preisobergrenze und -untergrenze ableiten.

Bestimmung der Preisobergrenze des FRA

Die Frage, die sich stellt, ist: Zu welchem Preis kann eine FRA-Verkaufsposition im Cash-Markt geschlossen werden? Der FRA-Preis muss dann unter diesem synthetischen Cash-Preis liegen. Läge er darüber, so könnte das FRA im Markt verkauft und gleichzeitig durch einen synthetischen FRA-Kauf im Cash-Markt mit Gewinn geschlossen werden.

Beispiel

Geldmarktsätze: 6 Mo: 4,00–4,10% (180 Tage)
12 Mo: 4,40–4,50% (360 Tage)
Wo liegt die Preisobergrenze eines 6/12 FRA bei gegebener Zinskurve?
Mit einem verkauften FRA kann der Zinssatz für eine zukünftige Anlage fixiert werden, somit entspricht ein FRA-Verkauf zinsmäßig einer zukünftigen Anlage. Diese Zinsposition kann daher durch die Fixierung eines Zinssatzes für eine zukünftige Aufnahme geschlossen werden (= synthetischer FRA-Kauf = Aufnahme 12 Monate + Anlage 6 Monate).
Die Preisobergrenze ist daher durch den Preis eines synthetischen FRA-Kaufs definiert.

Cash flows:

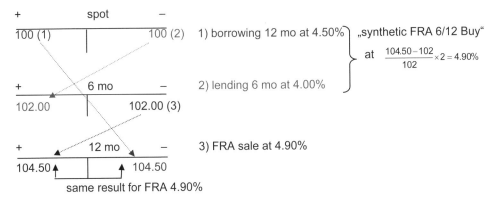

same result for FRA 4.90%

If the FRA can be sold above 4.90%, arbitrage is possible. Thus the **highest FRA price limit is 4.90%** and is equivalent to the price of a synthetic FRA purchase which can be produced by borrowing for the long period and lending for the short period (= take long + give short).

Note: You have a remaining risk for the cash lending at LIBOR in 6 months. In this example it is the risk at the FRA maturity date to give 6 months cash at LIBOR (= LIBOR risk). If you only get less, e.g. LIBOR -10 BP, your result is reduced.

Determination of the lowest FRA price limit

Here the question is: At what rate can an FRA long position be closed in the cash market? The FRA price has to be higher than that cash price. Otherwise you could buy the FRA directly in the market and close the position by a synthetic FRA sale in the cash market at the same time.

Example
Money market rates: 6 mo: 4.00–4.10% (180 days)   12 mo: 4.40–4.50% (360 days) What is the lowest FRA price limit of a 6/12 FRA with the given yield curve? With a bought FRA you can fix a rate for a future borrowing. Therefore the FRA purchase is equivalent to a future borrowing. Thus this interest rate position can be closed by fixing an interest rate for a future lending (= synthetic FRA sale = lending 12 months + borrowing 6 months). The lowest FRA price limit is therefore defined by the price of a synthetic FRA sale.

Cashflows:

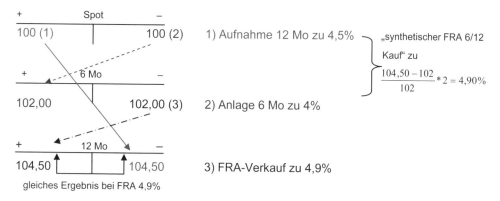

gleiches Ergebnis bei FRA 4,9%

Kann das FRA im Markt über 4,9% verkauft werden, so ist Arbitrage möglich. Somit liegt die **Preisobergrenze bei 4,9%** und entspricht dem Satz des synthetischen FRA-Kaufs, der durch eine Aufnahme für die lange Periode und die Anlage für die kurze Periode produziert werden kann (= lang nehmen + kurz geben).

Anmerkung: Es besteht hier das Restrisiko der Cash-Anlage in sechs Monaten zu LIBOR. In diesem Beispiel trägt der Arbitrageur das Risiko, bei FRA-Fälligkeit ein 6-Monats-Depot zu LIBOR zu geben (= LIBOR-Risiko). Liegen die tatsächlichen Erträge darunter, z.B. LIBOR -10 BP, verschlechtert sich sein Ergebnis.

Bestimmung der Preisuntergrenze des FRA

Wieder stellt sich die Frage: Ab welchem FRA-Satz kann ein risikoloser Ertrag erzielt werden, und zwar diesmal durch den Kauf des FRAs und die gleichzeitige Schließung im Cash-Markt durch den Verkauf eines „synthetischen FRAs" (= lang geben + kurz nehmen)?

Beispiel
Geldmarktsätze: 6 Mo: 4,00–4,10% (180 Tage)   12 Mo: 4,40–4,50% (360 Tage)   Wo liegt die Preisuntergrenze eines 6/12-FRAs bei gegebener Zinskurve?   Mit einem gekauften FRA kann der Zinssatz für eine zukünftige Aufnahme fixiert werden, somit entspricht ein FRA-Kauf zinsmäßig einer zukünftigen Aufnahme. Diese Zinsposition kann daher durch die Fixierung eines Zinssatzes für eine zukünftige Anlage geschlossen werden (= synthetischer FRA-Verkauf = Anlage 12 Monate + Aufnahme 6 Monate).   Die Preisuntergrenze ist daher durch den Preis eines synthetischen FRA-Verkaufs definiert.

Cash flows:

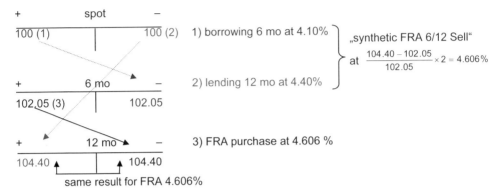

If the FRA can be bought below 4.606%, arbitrage is possible. Thus the **lowest FRA price limit is 4.606%** and is equivalent to the price of a synthetic FRA sale which can be produced by lending for the long period and borrowing for the short period (= give long + take short).

Note: You have a remaining risk for the cash borrowing at LIBOR in 6 months. In this example it is the risk at the FRA maturity date to take 6 months cash at LIBOR (= LIBOR risk). If you pay more, e.g. LIBOR + 10 BP, your result is reduced.

Consequences for the highest and lowest FRA price limits

The FRA market prices should always lie between the price limits which are determined by the cash rates. In the above example this would be 4.60% and 4.90%. If the market prices were outside this range, arbitrage would be possible. The position of the FRA price within this range shows the market participants' expectations. If the FRA rate is positioned just under the higher price limit, the market participants expect the rates to rise and therefore the demand for FRAs rises. Thus the FRA price rises though the cash rates are still unchanged, as these are mainly influenced by the liquidity situation resp. the central bank.

Analogically, if the FRA rate is positioned just above the lower price limit, the market participants expect the rates to fall.

Cashflows:

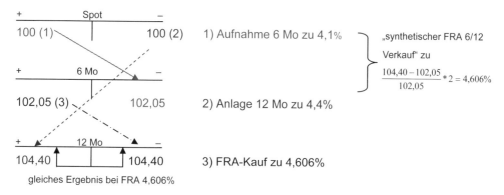

1) Aufnahme 6 Mo zu 4,1%

2) Anlage 12 Mo zu 4,4%

3) FRA-Kauf zu 4,606%

„synthetischer FRA 6/12 Verkauf" zu

$$\frac{104,40 - 102,05}{102,05} * 2 = 4,606\%$$

gleiches Ergebnis bei FRA 4,606%

Kann das FRA im Markt unter 4,606% gekauft werden, so ist Arbitrage möglich. Somit liegt die **Preisuntergrenze bei 4,606%** und entspricht dem Satz des synthetischen FRA-Verkaufs, der durch eine Anlage für die lange Periode und die Aufnahme für die kurze Laufzeit produziert werden kann (= lang geben + kurz nehmen).

Anmerkung: Es besteht hier das Restrisiko der Cash-Aufnahme in sechs Monaten zu LI-BOR. In diesem Beispiel trägt der Arbitrageur das Risiko, bei FRA-Fälligkeit ein 6-Mo-nats-Depot zu LIBOR zu nehmen (= LIBOR-Risiko). Liegen die tatsächlichen Kosten darüber, z.B. LIBOR +10 BP, verschlechtert sich sein Ergebnis.

Konsequenz aus der Preisobergrenze bzw. -untergrenze

Die FRA-Preise im Markt sollten innerhalb der durch die Cash-Sätze bestimmten Preis-grenzen liegen, also im obigen Beispiel zwischen 4,60 und 4,90. Lägen Sie außerhalb, so wäre Arbitrage möglich. An welchem Ende dieser Bandbreite der FRA-Satz liegt, spie-gelt die Erwartungshaltung der Marktteilnehmer wider. Liegt der FRA-Satz am oberen Ende, so deutet das darauf hin, dass im Markt in Erwartung steigender Zinsen ein Nach-frageüberhang nach FRAs besteht. Dadurch steigt der FRA-Preis, obwohl die Cash-Sätze vorerst noch unverändert geblieben sind, da diese hauptsächlich durch die Liquiditäts-situation bzw. die Notenbankpolitik bestimmt sind. Analog dazu deuten FRA-Preise am unteren Ende der theoretischen Bandbreite auf die Erwartung fallender Zinsen hin.

3.1.3.3. The FRA Formula

For calculating FRA prices and forward deposit rates you have the following formulae:

$$FRA_{bid} = \left\{ \left[\frac{1 + \left(\frac{r_{L(bid)} \cdot D_L}{B} \right)}{1 + \left(\frac{r_{S(offer)} \cdot D_S}{B} \right)} \right] - 1 \right\} \cdot \frac{B}{D_{FRA}}$$

$$FRA_{offer} = \left\{ \left[\frac{1 + \left(\frac{r_{L(offer)} \cdot D_L}{B} \right)}{1 + \left(\frac{r_{S(bid)} \cdot D_S}{B} \right)} \right] - 1 \right\} \cdot \frac{B}{D_{FRA}}$$

r_L =   interest rate, long-term
r_S =   interest rate, short-term
B =   day basis of calculation
D_L =   number of days, long-term
D_S =   number of days, short-term
D_{FRA} =   number of days, FRA

Example

Money market rates: 6 mo: 4.00 – 4.10% (180 days)
                           12 mo: 4.40 – 4.50% (360 days)

$$FRA_{offer} = \left[\frac{1 + \left(\frac{0.045 \cdot 360}{360} \right)}{1 + \left(\frac{0.04 \cdot 180}{360} \right)} - 1 \right] \cdot \frac{360}{180} = 4.90196\%$$

$$FRA_{bid} = \left[\frac{1 + \left(\frac{0.044 \cdot 360}{360} \right)}{1 + \left(\frac{0.041 \cdot 180}{360} \right)} - 1 \right] \cdot \frac{360}{180} = 4.60559\%$$

Compare the FRA prices to the results of the calculation of the higher and lower FRA price limits! You will notice that the lower price limit (4.606%) complies with the bid side and the higher price limit (4.902%) complies with the offer side.

3.1.3.3. Die FRA-Formel

Zur Berechnung von FRA-Preisen und von Forward-Depot-Preisen gelten folgende Formeln:

$$FRA_{Geld} = \left\{ \left[\frac{1 + \left(\dfrac{r_{L(Geld)} * T_L}{B} \right)}{1 + \left(\dfrac{r_{K(Brief)} * T_K}{B} \right)} \right] - 1 \right\} * \frac{B}{T_{FRA}}$$

$$FRA_{Brief} = \left\{ \left[\frac{1 + \left(\dfrac{r_{L(Brief)} * T_L}{B} \right)}{1 + \left(\dfrac{r_{K(Geld)} * T_K}{B} \right)} \right] - 1 \right\} * \frac{B}{T_{FRA}}$$

r_L = Zinssatz, langes Depot
r_K = Zinssatz, kurzes Depot
B = Tagesbasis
T_L = Anzahl der Tage, langes Depot
T_K = Anzahl der Tage, kurzes Depot
T_{FRA} = Anzahl der Tage, FRA

Beispiel

Geldmarktsätze: 6 Mo: 4,00–4,10% (180 Tage)
                 12 Mo: 4,40–4,50% (360 Tage)

$$FRA_{Geld} = \left[\frac{1 + \left(\dfrac{0,044 * 360}{360} \right)}{1 + \left(\dfrac{0,041 * 180}{360} \right)} - 1 \right] * \frac{360}{180} = 4,60559\,\%$$

$$FRA_{Brief} = \left[\frac{1 + \left(\dfrac{0,045 * 360}{360} \right)}{1 + \left(\dfrac{0,04 * 180}{360} \right)} - 1 \right] * \frac{360}{180} = 4,90196\,\%$$

Vergleichen Sie die FRA-Preise mit den Ergebnissen bei der Bestimmung der Preisober- bzw. -untergrenze. Sie werden feststellen, dass die Preisuntergrenze (4,606%) der Geldseite und die Preisobergrenze (4,902%) der Briefseite entspricht.

The Connection between Yield Curve and FRA Rates

As shown above, the FRA rates can be derived from the yield curve.

- The **steeper** the yield curve, the **higher** the FRA rates.
- The **flatter** the yield curve, the **lower** the FRA rates.
- For a **normal** yield curve FRA rates are **higher** than the interest rate level.
- For an **inverse** yield curve FRA rates are **lower** than the interest rate level.

3.1.3.4. Calculating FRA Rates through Fwd/Fwd Rates

FRA rates can be calculated from cash and futures rates as well as from forward/forward swaps.

Example

EUR/USD spot: 1.2000
3-months forward rate: 1.1970
3/6 forward/forward swap: 39–37 (90 days)
3/6 EUR FRA: 2.48–2.50% (90 days)
How can you compute the price for a 3/6 USD FRA purchase for 100 m USD synthetically?

The purchase of a 3/6 FRA is equivalent to the interest rate of a future borrowing. This can also be produced by buying the USD in 3 months and selling the USD in 6 months (=Fwd/Fwd FX swap sell and buy EUR/USD). The EUR side of the swap has to be closed with a purchase of a 3/6 EUR FRA. The rate for the period 3/6 can be derived from the USD Cash-Flows.

Cash flows:

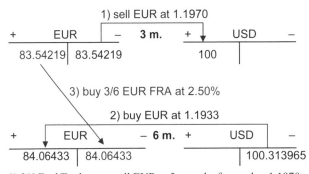

1) 3/6 Fwd/Fwd swap: sell EUR at 3-months forward at 1.1970
2) 3/6 Fwd/Fwd swap: buy EUR at 6-months forward at 1.1933 (1.1970 – 0.0037)
3) Buy 3/6 EUR FRA at 2.50%

Result: (100.313965 – 100) / 100.00 x 360/90 = 1.25586%
You can buy the 3/6 USD FRA synthetically at 1.2559%.

Note: In 3 months the short leg of the FX swap is delivered, i.e. you sell EUR and buy USD. These cash-flows have to be closed again, e.g. with a 3-months FX swap buy and sell EUR/USD.

Zusammenhang zwischen Zinskurve und Forward-Satz

Wie oben dargestellt, leiten sich die Forward-Sätze von der Zinskurve ab. Folgende Zusammenhänge gelten dabei immer:

- Je **steiler** die Zinskurve, desto **höher** die FRA-Sätze.
- Je **flacher** die Zinskurve, desto **niedriger** die FRA-Sätze.
- Bei **normaler** Zinskurve sind die FRA-Sätze **höher** als das Zinsniveau.
- Bei **inverser** Zinskurve sind die FRA-Sätze **niedriger** als das Zinsniveau.

3.1.3.4. Ermittlung von FRA-Sätzen aus Forward/Forward Swaps

FRA-Sätze können nicht nur aus Depot- und Futures-Sätzen, sondern auch aus Forward/Forward Swaps berechnet werden.

Beispiel
EUR/USD Spot: 1,2000 3-Monats-Terminkurs: 1,1970 3/6 Forward/Forward Swap: 39–37 (90 Tage) 3/6 EUR FRA: 2,48–2,50% (90 Tage) Wie können Sie den Preis eines gekauften 3/6 USD FRA für 100 Mio. USD synthetisch darstellen? Der Kauf eines 3/6 FRAs entspricht dem Zinssatz einer zukünftigen Refinanzierung. Diese kann auch durch Kauf der USD in drei Monaten und Verkauf in 6 Monaten produziert werden (= Fwd/Fwd FX-Swap sell & buy EUR/USD). Die EUR-Seite des Swaps muss dann mit dem Kauf eines 3/6-FRAs geschlossen werden. Aus den USD-Cashflows lässt sich dann der Zinssatz für die Periode 3/6 mit der einfachen Zinsformel ableiten.

Cashflows:

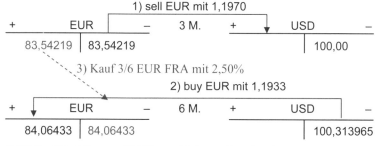

1) 3/6 Fwd/Fwd Swap: sell EUR per 3-Monats-Termin mit 1,1970
2) 3/6 Fwd/Fwd Swap: buy EUR per 6-Monats-Termin mit 1,1933 (1,1970 – 0,0037)
3) Kauf 3/6 EUR FRA mit 2,50%

Ergebnis: (100,313965 – 100,00) / 100,00 x 360/90 = 1,25586%
Den 3/6 USD FRA können Sie synthetisch mit 1,2559% kaufen.

Anmerkung: In drei Monaten wird der kurze Teil des FX-Swaps geliefert, d.h., Sie verkaufen EUR und erhalten USD. Diese Cashflows müssen dann wieder geschlossen werden, z.B. durch den Kauf und Verkauf eines 3-Monats-EUR/USD-FX-Swaps.

Formula for calculating FRA Rates from Fwd/Fwd Swaps

A spot FX swap is derived from the interest rates of the two currencies. Therefore you can also derive the interest rates of the two currencies from the FX swap prices.

As a Fwd/Fwd swap is a future FX swap, the interest rates are forward resp. FRA rates. According to this, the FRA rates can be calculated by means of an adapted formula for the calculation of interest rates out of FX swaps:

FRA base currency

$$FRA_B = \left\{ \left[\frac{\left(1 + FRA_Q \times \dfrac{D}{B_Q}\right) \times FWD_S}{FWD_L} \right] - 1 \right\} \times \frac{B_B}{D}$$

FRA quote currency

$$FRA_Q = \left\{ \left[\frac{\left(1 + FRA_B \times \dfrac{D}{B_B}\right) \times FWD_L}{FWD_S} \right] - 1 \right\} \times \frac{B_Q}{D}$$

FWD	=	forward FX rate
FRA_Q	=	FRA p. a. in decimals, quote currency
FRA_B	=	FRA p. a. in decimals, base currency
B_Q	=	basis quote currency (360 or 365)
B_B	=	basis base currency (360 or 365)
D	=	days
S	=	short period
L	=	long period

Excursus: With FRAs you can also "extend" the period of an FX Outright deal before maturity. This can be calculated with the normal forward rate formula (the spot rate is replaced by the forward rate and both deposit rates by the FRA rates):

$$O_{long} = O_{short} \times \frac{1 + \left(FRA_Q \times \dfrac{D}{B_Q}\right)}{1 + \left(FRA_B \times \dfrac{D}{B_B}\right)}$$

D	=	days
O_{long}	=	outright rate
O_{short}	=	spot rate
FRA_Q	=	FRA p. a. in decimals, quote currency
FRA_B	=	FRA p. a. in decimals, base currency
B_Q	=	basis quote curreny (360 or 365)
B_B	=	basis base currency (360 or 365)

Formel zur Errechnung von FRA-Sätzen aus Fwd/Fwd Swaps

Ein Spot-FX-Swap leitet sich aus den Zinssätzen der beiden beteiligten Währungen ab. Umgekehrt können auch die Zinssätze der beiden Währungen aus den Preisen eines FX-Swaps abgeleitet werden.

Da ein Fwd/Fwd-FX-Swap ein in der Zukunft beginnender FX-Swap ist, sind die analogen Zinssätze Forward- bzw. FRA-Sätze. Dementsprechend können die FRA-Sätze mittels einer adaptierten Formel für die Berechnung von Zinssätzen aus FX-Swaps berechnet werden.

FRA quotierte Währung

$$FRA_Q = \left\{ \left[\frac{\left(1 + FRA_G * \dfrac{T}{B_G}\right) * FWD_K}{FWD_L} \right] - 1 \right\} * \frac{B_Q}{T}$$

FRA Gegenwährung

$$FRA_G = \left\{ \left[\frac{\left(1 + FRA_Q * \dfrac{T}{B_Q}\right) * FWD_L}{FWD_K} \right] - 1 \right\} * \frac{B_G}{T}$$

FWD = Terminkurs
FRA = FRA-Satz in Dezimalen, z.B. 0,04
B = Basis (360 oder 365 Tage)
T = Tage
Q = quotierte Währung
G = Gegenwährung
K = kurze Periode
L = lange Periode

Exkurs: Mit FRAs kann auch die Laufzeit eines Termingeschäfts vorzeitig „verlängert" werden. Dafür nehmen wir die normale Terminkursformel und ersetzen den Kassakurs durch den Terminkurs und die beiden Deposätze durch FRA-Sätze:

$$TK_{lang} = TK_{kurz} * \frac{1 + \left(FRA_G * \dfrac{T}{B_G}\right)}{1 + \left(FRA_Q * \dfrac{T}{B_Q}\right)}$$

T = Anzahl der Tage
TK_{lang} = Terminkurs
TK_{kurz} = Spotkurs
FRA_Q = FRA p.a. in Dezimalen, quotierte Währung
FRA_G = FRA p.a. in Dezimalen, Gegenwährung
BQ = Berechnungsbasis für die quotierte Währung (360 oder 365)
BG = Berechnungsbasis für die Gegenwährung (360 oder 365)

3.2. Money Market Futures

Money market futures are **exchange-traded interest rate contracts**. Contrary to their counterpart in the OTC market – the FRA – the specifications of futures are **strongly standardised**. Usually, the underlying is a 3-month deposit, in some currencies also a 1-month deposit, that represents the interest rate of a future time period.

Money market futures can be used like FRAs. That is, to
- eliminate a future interest rate risk **(hedging)**
- speculate on interest rate trends **(trading)**
- to arbitrage between different markets **(arbitrage)**

Money market futures are standardised products, because they are traded in the exchange market. Thus, some specifications are already fixed by the particular exchange:
- contract volume
- maturity dates
- marginal price changes (tick size)
- value of a price change by one tick based on one contract (tick value)

For money market futures the most important exchanges are Euronext.Liffe (London), CME (Chicago) and SGX (Singapore) resp. Tiffe (Tokio).

Mostly, futures contracts can only be closed at the same exchange where the position has been opened. Some contracts can be sold or bought (and consequently closed), at different exchanges [e.g. a USD 3-months contract purchased in Chicago (CME) and sold in Singapore (Simex)]. Thus the contract can be traded 24 hours and not only during the trading hours at the particular exchange.

3.2.1. Conventions and Contract Specifications

Delivery dates

Delivery dates of money market futures are set by the futures exchange. For the core markets these are always the third Wednesday of the last month of the quarter (March, June, September, December). These delivery dates are called IMM-Dates (International Monetary Market-dates).

The delivery months have the following abbreviations:
- March → H
- June → M
- September → U
- December → Z

(*Note:* The abbreviations do not follow any logic.)

In addition, at most futures exchanges so-called **serial months** are traded. These are the maturities between the IMM dates. At the LIFFE for example, in addition to the IMM dates, 4 serial months are traded. Consequently, there are maturities for all following 6 months.

3.2. Geldmarktfutures

Geldmarktfutures sind **börsengehandelte Zinstermingeschäfte.** Im Unterschied zu ihrem Gegenstück im OTC-Markt – dem FRA – sind die Spezifikationen von Futures **stark standardisiert.** Als zugrundeliegendes Instrument dient meist ein 3-Monats-Depot, in einigen Währungen werden zusätzlich auch Futures auf ein 1-Monats-Depot gehandelt.

Geldmarktfutures können ähnlich wie ein FRA verwendet werden, um

- ein zukünftiges Zinsrisiko auszuschalten **(Hedging),**
- auf eine Zinsmeinung zu spekulieren **(Trading),**
- Preisunterschiede zwischen unterschiedlichen Märkten auszunutzen **(Arbitrage).**

Für börsengehandelte Produkte ist es typisch, dass die Spezifikationen standardisiert sind. Folgende Merkmale werden von der jeweiligen Börse vorgegeben:

- Volumsgröße eines Kontraktes
- Fälligkeitstermine
- minimale Preisbewegung (Tick Size)
- Wert der Preisänderung um einen Tick, bezogen auf einen Kontrakt (Tick Value)

Für Geldmarktfutures sind die wichtigsten Börsen Euronext.LIFFE (London), CME (Chicago) und SGX (Singapore) bzw. Tiffe (Tokio).

Futureskontrakte können im Normalfall nur an der gleichen Börse geschlossen werden, an der die Position eingegangen wurde. Einige Kontrakte können jedoch auch an unterschiedlichen Börsen gekauft und verkauft (z.B. der 3-Monats-Eurodollar-Kontrakt-Kauf in Chicago (CME) und Verkauf in Singapore (SGX)) und damit auch geschlossen werden. Dadurch kann der Kontrakt rund um die Uhr gehandelt werden und nicht nur während der Handelsstunden der jeweiligen Börse.

3.2.1. Usancen und Kontraktspezifikationen

Liefertage

Die Liefertage für Money Market Futures sind von der Börse vorgegeben. An den Hauptmärkten sind die Liefertage der jeweils dritte Mittwoch des letzten Monats im Quartal, d.h. März, Juni, September, Dezember. Diese Liefertage werden auch als **IMM-Dates** (International Monetary Market-Dates) bezeichnet.

Die Liefermonate werden mit folgenden Buchstaben abgekürzt:

- März   → H
- Juni   → M
- September → U
- Dezember → Z

(*Anmerkung:* Die Abkürzungen folgen keiner bestimmten Logik.)

Zusätzlich werden an den meisten Futuresbörsen auch noch die sogenannten **Serial Months** gehandelt. Darunter versteht man Fälligkeiten zwischen den IMM-Dates. An der LIFFE z.B. werden zusätzlich zu den IMM-Dates noch vier Serial Months gehandelt, sodass es in jedem der nächsten sechs Monate eine Fälligkeit gibt.

Example

Trade date: 4th April
Maturities:
May   (serial month)
June   (IMM)
July   (serial month)
August   (serial month)
September   (IMM)
October   (serial Month)
(After settlement of the May contract the next new serial month will be November.)

Front month is the contract with the next maturity. Contracts with a later maturity are called **Back months**. For the front month liquidity is usually the highest.

Last trading day

Last trading days of futures are determined by the exchanges and are usually **two days before delivery date** (an exception is GBP, where the theoretical delivery date is the last trading date, i.e. same-day fixing).

Quotation

The quotation for futures prices is: **100.00 minus interest rate**

Therefore a forward interest rate of 4.50 % p.a. (i.e. an interest rate for a future period) equals a futures price of 95.50 (= 100 – 4.50).

The consequences of this quoting convention are illustrated below:

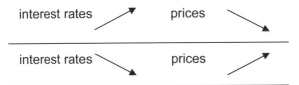

Example

If the interest rate rises from 4.50% to 5%, the future price will fall from 95.50 to 95.00. If the interest rate falls from 4.50% to 4%, the future price will rise from 95.50 to 96.00. With the quotation of an interest rate on the basis of 100, the buying/selling of a money market future has just the opposite effect to an FRA purchase/sale:

FRA PURCHASE   =   FUTURE SHORT
FRA SALE   =   FUTURE LONG

A future's quote of JUNE (M) 96.64/96.65 corresponds to an interest rate of 3.35%/3.36% p.a. for the term from the third Wednesday in June XY until the third Wednesday in September XY, in a specific currency.

Beispiel

Handelstag: 4. April
Fälligkeiten:
Mai   (Serial Month)
Juni   (IMM)
Juli   (Serial Month)
August   (Serial Month)
September   (IMM)
Oktober   (Serial Month)
(Nach dem Settlement des Mai-Kontraktes wird der November als neuer Serial Month
eingeführt.)

Unter **Front Month** versteht man den Kontrakt mit der nächsten Fälligkeit. Kontrakte
mit einer späteren Fälligkeit werden als **Back Months** bezeichnet. Für den Front Month
herrscht üblicherweise die weitaus höchste Liquidität.

Letzter Handelstag

Der letzte Handelstag ist von der Börse vorgegeben und liegt üblicherweise **zwei Werktage vor dem Liefertag** (Ausnahme ist z.B. GBP: Theoretischer Liefertag ist der letzte
Handelstag, also taggleich).

Quotierung

Die Quotierung bei Futures ist: **100,00 minus Zinssatz.**

   Somit entspricht ein sogenannter Forward-Zinssatz von 4,50% p.a. (also ein Zinssatz
für eine zukünftige Periode) einem Futurespreis von 95,50 (= 100 – 4,50).

   Die Konsequenzen dieser Usance bei der Quotierung veranschaulicht die Grafik:

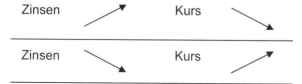

Beispiel

Steigt der Zinssatz von 4,50% auf 5%, so fällt der Futures-Preis von 95,50 auf 95,00.
Fällt der Zinssatz von 4,50% auf 4%, so steigt der Futures-Preis von 95,50 auf 96,00.
Durch die Quotierung 100 minus Zinssatz hat der Kauf/Verkauf eines Money Market
Futures die genau umgekehrte Wirkung eines FRAs.

KAUF FRA   =   VERKAUF FUTURE
VERKAUF FRA   =   KAUF FUTURE

Eine Futuresquotierung von JUNI (M) 96,64/96,65 entspricht somit einem Zinssatz
von 3,35/3,36% p.a. für eine 3-Monats-Laufzeit beginnend am dritten Mittwoch im
Juni.

Underlying

Usually, the underlying is a 3-months interbank deposit (e.g. Eurodollar, Euroyen, Euro Swiss Franc, EURIBOR). The fixing for these contracts is normally BBA LIBOR (resp. EURIBOR for EURIBOR futures). The term is always exactly 90 days for the 3-months futures period (resp. 30 days for a 1-month futures period). The fixed LIBOR resp. EURIBOR though is calculated on the exact number of days.

Volume of the contract

Not only the underlying but also the volume (principal) of a future contract is exactly specified. (see table below)

Futures purchase

as hedging operation: → protection **against falling** interest rates
as speculation: → speculation **on falling** interest rates

Futures sale

as hedging operation: → protection **against rising** interest rates
as speculation: → speculation **on rising** interest rates

Tick

A tick is the **marginal movement of the futures price**. For EUR, USD and JPY money market futures, a tick is usually half a basis point, i.e. a hundredth of 0.5 % (= 0.005 % or 0.00005), for GBP contracts it is 1 BP (see table below).

Tick value

The tick value is the **profit or loss** which occurs when the price changes by one tick. Also the tick value is specified by the exchange (e.g. USD 12.5 for the 3-months Eurodollar contract at LIFFE). The tick value can be determined in the following way:

$$\text{volume of the contract} \times \text{quantity of the tick} \times \frac{\text{term}}{360}$$

Example		
3-months Eurodollar	$1{,}000{,}000 \times 0.00005 \times \frac{90}{360}$	= USD 12.5
1-months LIBOR	$3{,}000{,}000 \times 0.000025 \times \frac{30}{360}$	= USD 6.25
3-months EURIBOR	$1{,}000{,}000 \times 0.00005 \times \frac{90}{360}$	= EUR 12.5
3-months short sterling	$500{,}000 \times 0.0001 \times \frac{90}{360}$	= GBP 12.5

Basisinstrument (Underlying)

Das Underlying ist üblicherweise ein 3-Monats-Interbank-Eurogeldmarktsatz (z.B. Eurodollar, Euroyen, Euro Swiss Franc, EURIBOR). Das Fixing erfolgt dann bei den meisten Kontrakten auch gegen den BBA LIBOR (bzw. gegen EURIBOR beim EURIBOR-Future). Zu beachten ist, dass beim Future immer 90 Tage für die 3-Monats-Laufzeit unterstellt wird (bzw. 30 Tage für 1 Monat). Der fixierte LIBOR bzw. EURIBOR gilt jedoch immer für die echten Tage.

Kontraktvolumen

Nicht nur das zugrundeliegende Instrument, sondern auch das Volumen (Nominale) eines Futureskontrakts ist genau definiert (siehe Tabelle).

Kauf Future

als Hedge-Geschäft → Sicherung **gegen fallende** Zinsen
als Spekulation → Spekulation **auf fallende** Zinsen

Verkauf Future

als Hedge-Geschäft → Sicherung **gegen steigende** Zinsen
als Spekulation → Spekulation **auf steigende** Zinsen

Tick

Als Tick bezeichnet man die **Mindestpreisbewegung eines Futureskontrakts**. Bei EUR, USD und JPY Futures ist das in der Regel ein halber Basispunkt, d.h. ein Hundertstel von 0,5% (= 0,005% oder 0,00005), bei CHF Kontrakten 1 BP.

Der Tickwert

Der Tickwert ist der **Gewinn bzw. Verlust**, der sich aus einer Preisbewegung um einen Tick für einen Kontrakt ergibt. Der Tickwert wird ebenfalls von der Börse spezifiziert (z.B. USD 12,5 beim 3-Monats-Eurodollar-Kontrakt an der LIFFE). Er kann jedoch auch folgendermaßen errechnet werden:

$$Kontraktgröße * Tickgröße * \frac{Laufzeit}{360}$$

Beispiel		
3-Monats-Eurodollar	$1.000.000 * 0,00005 * \frac{90}{360}$	= USD 12,5
1-Monats-LIBOR	$3.000.000 * 0,000025 * \frac{30}{360}$	= USD 6,25
3-Monats-EURIBOR	$1.000.000 * 0,00005 * \frac{90}{360}$	= EUR 12,5
3-Monats-Short-Sterling	$500.000 * 0,0001 * \frac{90}{360}$	= GBP 12,5

3.2.2. Main Markets of Money Market Futures

Cur-rency	Futures exchange	Contract volume	Underlying	Tick size	Tick value	BP value
EUR	EUREX	1,000,000	3-mo EURIBOR	0.5 BP	12.5 EUR	25 EUR
EUR	LIFFE	1,000,000	3-mo EURIBOR	0.5 BP	12.5 EUR	25 EUR
GBP	LIFFE	500,000	3-mo LIBOR (Short Sterling)	1 BP	12.5 GBP	12.5 GBP
JPY	LIFFE	100,000,000	3-mo TIBOR (Euroyen)	0.5 BP	1,250 JPY	2,500 JPY
CHF	LIFFE	1,000000	3-mo LIBOR (Euroswiss)	1 BP	25 CHF	25 CHF
USD	CME	1,000,000	3-mo LIBOR (Eurodollar)	0.5 BP*)	12.5 USD*)	25 USD
USD	CME	3,000,000	1-mo LIBOR	0.25 BP	6.25 USD	25 USD
USD	CME	1,000,000	13 weeks T-bill	0.5 BP	12.5 USD	25 USD

*) At the CME the tick size for the 3-month Eurodollar future can vary from 0.25 BP to 0.5 BP or 1 BP, depending on the delivery month.

Some contracts are traded at several exchanges, e.g.:
3-months Eurodollar: CME, Euronext.LIFFE and SGX
3-months Euroyen: CME, Euronext.LIFFE and SGX

Links:
- Eurex (Frankfurt, Zürich): www.eurexchange.com
- Euronext.Liffe (London): www.liffe.com
- CME (Chicago):   www.cme.com
- SGX (Singapore):   www.sgx.com

3.2.3. Exchange und Clearing House

The **exchange** specifies the conditions for the trading. It defines – among other things – which contracts are traded and their specifications.

     The settlement of the deals is carried out by the **clearing house** of the exchange.

3.2.2. Die wichtigsten Geldmarktfuture-Kontrakte

Währung	Börse	Kontrakt-Volumen	Underlying	Tickgröße	Tickwert	BP-Wert
EUR	EUREX	1.000.000	3-Mo-EURIBOR	0,5 BP	12,5 EUR	25 EUR
EUR	LIFFE	1.000.000	3-Mo-EURIBOR	0,5 BP	12,5 EUR	25 EUR
GBP	LIFFE	500.000	3-Mo-LIBOR (Short Sterling)	1 BP	12,5 GBP	12,5 GBP
JPY	LIFFE	100.000.000	3-Mo-TIBOR (Euroyen)	0,5 BP	1.250 JPY	2.500 JPY
CHF	LIFFE	1.000.000	3-Mo-LIBOR (Euroswiss)	1 BP	25 CHF	25 CHF
USD	CME	1.000.000	3-Mo-LIBOR (Eurodollar)	0,5 BP*)	12,5 USD*)	25 USD
USD	CME	3.000.000	1-Mo-LIBOR	0,25 BP	6,25 USD	25 USD
USD	CME	1.000.000	13-weeks-T-bill	0,5 BP	12,5 USD	12,5 USD

*) An der CME kann die Tickgröße beim 3-Monats-Eurodollar-Future zwischen 0,25 BP, 0,5 BP und 1 BP abhängig vom Liefermonat variieren.

Einige Kontrakte werden auch an mehreren Börsen gehandelt z.B.:
3-Monats-Eurodollar: CME, Euronext.LIFFE und SGX
3-Monats-Euroyen: CME, Euronext.LIFFE und SGX

Links:
- Eurex (Frankfurt, Zürich): www.eurexchange.com
- Euronext.Liffe (London): www.liffe.com
- CME (Chicago):   www.cme.com
- SGX (Singapore):   www.sgx.com

3.2.3. Die Rollen von Börse und Clearing House

Die **Börse** gibt die Rahmenbedingungen vor, unter denen der Handel stattfindet. Sie bestimmt unter anderem, welche Kontrakte gehandelt werden sowie die Spezifikationen der einzelnen Kontrakte.

Die Abwicklung der Geschäfte erfolgt durch das **Clearing House** der Futuresbörse.

The **clearing house** has the following **main functions:**
- It is counterparty for both the buyer and the seller in all traded contracts. Placing the clearing house between buyer and seller reduces the credit risk. To **reduce this risk** to a minimum, the clearing house deals solely with registered clearing members who for their part offer their services as brokers or clearers. In order to protect against default risk of exchange members, so-called **initial margins** and **variation margins** are calculated.
- Daily revaluation and accounting of variation margins for all open deals.
- Fixing of the initial margin; the initial margin depends on the market's volatility. Therefore it is adjusted regularly to the actual market conditions.

3.2.4. The Margin System

As mentioned above, margins are required when dealing with futures. They **reduce the credit risk** for the exchange to a minimum. They are demanded either "one-shot" and up-front in relation to the number of contracts (initial margin) or daily for the accrued profits and losses (variation margin).

Initial Margin

The initial margin is a **fixed amount**; differing by contract and currency, e.g. USD 350 for each 3-month eurodollar contract. The amount is fixed by the clearing house and changes in relation to the volatility of the markets. The initial margin **serves as an additional protection against default risk** in order to cover the potential loss of a market participant that could result from the daily price fluctuations. The initial margin is usually not paid in cash but **securities**. The returns of these securities belong to the market participant. The initial margin is returned to the market participant at expiry of the position or if the position is closed earlier.

Spread Margin

A spread margin is a **reduced initial margin due to simultaneous long and short positions** (in different periods), e.g. Eurodollar March long, 100 contracts and June short, 100 contracts. Instead of paying a margin of USD 350 for 200 contracts (total amount of contracts), i.e. USD 70,000, a reduced spread margin is applied, e.g. USD 250. New calculation 200 (total amount of contracts) x 250 = USD 50,000.

Span Margin

Some clearing houses calculate the **initial margin by means of a risk-based system with certain parameters**. This method is called span margin (Standardized Portfolio Analysis of Risk). Here the total risk of a position is calculated based on a series of risk factors. The result is converted by a specific ratio into a margin that is eventually charged.

Das **Clearing House** hat folgende **Hauptaufgaben:**
- Es wird zum Geschäftspartner in allen gehandelten Kontrakten. Die Platzierung des Clearing Houses zwischen dem Käufer und Verkäufer dient der **Reduzierung des Kreditrisikos.** Um dieses Risiko auf ein Minimum zu reduzieren, handelt das Clearing House nur mit registrierten Clearing-Mitgliedern, die ihrerseits ihre Dienste als Broker oder nur als Clearer anbieten. Um das Kreditrisiko des Clearing Houses so gering wie möglich zu halten, werden Einschüsse, sogenannte **Initial Margins**, und auch **Variation Margins** verlangt.
- Tägliche Bewertung und Abrechnung der Variation Margin für alle offenen Geschäfte.
- Festlegung der Initial Margin; die Höhe der Initial Margin hängt von der Volatilität des Marktes ab. Sie wird daher auch regelmäßig an die aktuellen Marktgegebenheiten angepasst.

3.2.4. Das Margin-System

Das Ziel des Margin-Systems ist die **Ausschließung des Kontrahentenrisikos (Kreditrisiko).** Dies erfolgt durch einen fixen Einschuss pro Kontrakt (Initial Margin) und zusätzlich durch die tägliche Abrechnung der angelaufenen Gewinne und Verluste (Variation Margin).

Initial Margin

Die Initial Margin ist eine **festgelegte Betragshöhe pro Kontrakt**, z.B. je 3-Monats-Eurodollar-Kontrakt USD 350. Die Höhe der Initial Margin ist für verschiedene Kontrakte unterschiedlich. Sie wird vom Clearing House festgesetzt bzw. entsprechend der Volatilität der Märkte verändert. Die Initial Margin dient als zusätzliche Ausfallsicherung, sodass der potenzielle Verlust eines Marktteilnehmers, der durch die täglichen Kursschwankungen eintreten könnte, gedeckt ist. Sie dient daher zur **Besicherung für potenzielle zukünftige Verluste.** Die Initial Margin wird üblicherweise nicht bar hinterlegt, sondern **in Form von Wertpapieren.** Die Erträge aus den Wertpapieren fallen weiterhin dem Marktteilnehmer zu. Die Initial Margin wird bei Auslaufen oder bei vorzeitigem Schließen einer Position an den Marktteilnehmer rückerstattet.

Spread Margin

Unter Spread Margin ist eine **reduzierte Initial Margin bei gleichzeitiger Long- und Short- Position** (in unterschiedlichen Perioden) zu verstehen, z.B. Eurodollar März long, 100 Kontrakte und Juni short, 100 Kontrakte. Um statt für 200 Kontrakte z.B. USD 350, also insgesamt USD 70.000 Einschuss zu veranlagen, gelangt eine reduzierte Spread Margin, z.B. USD 250, zur Anwendung, also 200 (Total-Kontrakte) × 250 = USD 50.000.

Span Margin

Von einigen Clearinghäusern wird die Initial Margin mittels eines **risikobasierten Systems mit festgelegten Parametern** berechnet. Diese Methode wird Span Margin genannt (Standardized Portfolio Analysis of Risk). Hier wird durch eine Reihe von Risikofaktoren das Gesamtrisiko einer Position ermittelt und durch einen bestimmten Aufteilungsschlüssel als Margin in Rechnung gestellt.

Variation margin (Margin Calls)

The variation margin is the **daily accounting of all accrued profits or losses**. Here the difference between closing price and purchase price (or the closing price of the day before) is determined daily, and thus, the real profits or losses are charged.

Example
5th of May 10:00 a.m., buy 100 June Eurodollar futures, price 96.60 (without initial margin) Closing price 5th of May: 96.65: Variation margin: 10 ticks x 12.5 tick value x 100 = USD 12,500 (credit) Closing price 6th of May: 96.57: Variation margin: 16 ticks x 12.5 tick value x 100 = USD 20,000 (charge) → Realised loss since the purchase = 6 x 12.5 x 100 = USD 7,500 (this equals the total sum of all margin calls)

Note: As the variation margin is paid cash, for the exact calculation of the total result of a futures position also the refinancing costs (resp. investment returns) have to be taken into account.

Settlement on the last Trading Date (EDSP)

While bond futures (e.g. US T-bonds, UK gilt, Euro-Bund) need to be settled by physical delivery of the underlying, the money market futures are settled cash on the last trading date. The "cash settlement" is based on the **EDSP** (Exchange Delivery Settlement Price) which is determined on the last trading day. Thus, the EDSP is **100 – fixing rate** (e.g. 3-months USD LIBOR). The settlement amount is calculated as the difference between the EDSP and the closing price of the day before. The result of a futures position is the **sum of the daily variation margins plus the settlement amount of the last trading day**.

Example
You are long 100 contracts 3-months June Eurodollar futures. Purchase price: 96.50 Yesterday closing price: 96.75 3-months BBA LIBOR today: 3.30% (= last trading date) What is the settlement amount? The EDSP is 96.70 (100 – 3.30). Settlement amount: (96.70 – 96.75) x 2 = -0.1 (10 ticks) 10 x 12.5 x 100 = USD -12,500 You have to pay **USD 12,500**.

Note: Of course the total result of this position is a profit. The remaining result has been taken into account for the daily variation margins.

Variation Margin (Margin Calls)

Die Variation Margin ist eine tägliche Abrechnung der aufgelaufenen Gewinne und Verluste. Hier wird täglich der Unterschied zwischen dem Vortagesschlusskurs und dem Tagesschlusskurs – also der tatsächlich angefallene Kursgewinn oder -verlust – in Rechnung gestellt.

Beispiel

5. Mai: 10.00 Uhr, Kauf 100 Kontrakte Eurodollar Juni, Kurs 96,60

Schlusskurs, 5. Mai: 96,65
Variation Margin: 10 Ticks × 12,5 Tickvalue × 100 = USD 12.500 (Gutschrift)
Schlusskurs, 6. Mai: 96, 57
Variation Margin 16 Ticks × 12,5 Tickvalue × 100 = USD 20.000 (Belastung)
→ Tatsächlicher Verlust seit Einstand = 6 × 12,5 × 100 = USD 7.500 (Das entspricht auch der Summe der Marginzahlungen.)

Anmerkung: Da die Variation Margins **in Cash ausgezahlt** werden, sind bei der exakten Berechnung des Gesamtergebnisses einer Futuresposition auch die Refinanzierungskosten (bzw. Veranlagungserträge) der Variation Margin zu berücksichtigen.

Methodik der Abrechnung am letzten Handelstag

Bei Money Market Futures erfolgt das Settlement als „Cash-Settlement" (im Gegensatz zu Kapitalmarkt-Futures wie z.B. US-T-Bond-Future oder Euro-Bund-Future, die physisch geliefert werden). Das „Cash-Settlement" basiert auf dem **EDSP (Exchange Delivery Settlement Price)**, der am letzten Handelstag ermittelt wird. Der EDSP ist **100 minus Fixing-Satz** (z.B. 3-Monats-USD-LIBOR). Der Settlement-Betrag errechnet sich dann als Differenz zwischen dem EDSP und dem Schlusskurs des Vortages. Das Ergebnis auf eine Futuresposition setzt sich also aus der **Summe der täglichen Variation Margins plus dem Settlement-Betrag am letzten Handelstag** zusammen.

Beispiel

Sie sind 100 Kontrakte 3-Monats-Juni-Eurodollar-Futures long.
Einstandskurs: 96,50
Gestriger Schlusskurs: 96,75
Heutiger 3-Monats-BBA LIBOR: 3,30% (= letzter Handelstag)
Wie hoch ist der Settlement-Betrag?

Der EDSP ist 96,70 (100 – 3,30).
Settlement Betrag: (96,70 – 96,75) × 2 = -0,1 (10 Ticks)
10 × 12,5 × 100 = USD -12.500
Sie müssen **USD 12.500** zahlen.

Anmerkung: Das Gesamtergebnis der Position ist natürlich ein Gewinn. Das restliche Ergebnis wurde jedoch bereits in der täglichen Abrechnung der Variation Margin berücksichtigt.

Closing a Futures Position

Each futures position can be closed by an appropriate, opposite futures position before or at the last trading date. The closing leads to the **elimination of the position and the related initial margin**. The profits and losses result from the daily variation margin payments (plus possible interest returns resp. payments).

Open interest and traded volume

These figures define the liquidity of contracts and periods. Generally the contract with the shortest period (front month) has the highest traded volume.

The sum of all open contracts is the **open interest**. A contract has both a buyer and a seller, so the two market players combine to make one contract. The open interest position that is reported each day represents the increase or decrease in the number of contracts for that day, and it is shown as a positive or negative number.

The higher the traded volume and the open interest, the more liquid the market. This has the advantage for the market participants that they can trade big volumes at close spreads anytime. An increase in open interest along with an increase in price is said to confirm an upward trend. Similarly, an increase in open interest along with a decrease in price confirms a downward trend. An increase or decrease in prices while open interest remains flat or declining may indicate a possible trend reversal.

Computing the open interest

The open interest is not, despite common opinion, the volume of the traded options or futures. See the following example:

Schließen einer Futuresposition

Jede Futuresposition kann vor bzw. am letzten Handelstag mit einer entgegengesetzten Futuresposition aufgelöst werden. Ein Schließen bewirkt die **Auflösung der Position und somit der damit verbundenen Initial Margin.** Der Gewinn bzw. Verlust ergibt sich aus der Summe der täglichen Margin-Zahlungen (plus etwaiger Zinserträge bzw. -aufwendungen).

Open Interest und Handelsvolumen

Diese Daten geben Aufschluss über die Liquidität in einzelnen Kontrakten und Laufzeiten. Das höchste Handelsvolumen weist üblicherweise der Kontrakt mit der kürzesten Laufzeit auf (Front Month).

Als **Open Interest** wird die Summe aller noch offenen Kontrakte bezeichnet. Daraus folgt: Wer einen Terminkontrakt kauft („long geht"), ohne zuvor über eine Verkaufsposition in diesem Kontrakt zu verfügen, erhöht das Open Interest immer dann um 1, wenn der Verkäufer gleichzeitig eine neue Verkaufsposition eingeht („short geht"). Wer umgekehrt einen Terminkontrakt verkauft („short"), ohne zuvor über eine Kaufposition in diesem Kontrakt zu verfügen, erhöht das Open Interest immer dann um 1, wenn der Käufer zugleich eine neue Kaufposition eingeht („long"). Gleiches gilt spiegelgleich auch für die Verringerung des Open Interest.

Anders ausgedrückt: Das Open Interest gibt an, **wie viele Positionen eines bestimmten Kontraktes noch von Marktteilnehmern gehalten werden, die nicht glattgestellt wurden.**

Je höher das Handelsvolumen und das Open Interest, desto liquider ist der Markt. Für die Marktteilnehmer bringt das den Vorteil, dass auch große Volumina jederzeit zu niedrigen Spreads gehandelt werden können. So deutet z.B. ein zunehmendes „Open Interest" bei gleichzeitig steigenden Umsätzen und steigenden Kursen auf künftig weitere Kurssteigerungen hin.

Berechnung Open Interest

Ein weit verbreitetes Missverständnis ist, dass das Open Interest für das Volumen der gehandelten Optionen und Futures gehalten wird. Dies ist nicht richtig, wie im folgenden Beispiel dargestellt wird:

Example			
Day	**Trading Activity**	**Open Interest**	**Volume per day**
1st May	A buys 1 option and B sells 1 option	1	1
2nd May	C buys 5 options and D sells 5 options	6	5
3rd May	A sells his one option and D buys 1 option	5	1
4th May	E buys 5 options from C, who sells his 5 options	5	5

Open interest = (all open long positions + all open short positions) / 2

1st May: A buys an option which leaves an open interest and creates trading volume of 1.

2nd May: C and D create trading volume of 5 and there are also 5 more options left open.

3rd May: A takes an offsetting position, therefore open interest is reduced by 1, volume 1.

4th May: E simply replaces C and therefore open interest does not change, trading volume increases by 5

Spezifikationen z.B. des 3-Monats-Eurodollar-Futures an der Euronext.LIFFE (Quelle: www.liffe.com)

Three Month Eurodollar Interest Rate Futures Contract

Unit of Trading	Interest rate on three month deposit of $1,000,000
Delivery Months	March, June, September, December and four serial months, such that 24 delivery months are available for trading, with the nearest six delivery months being consecutive calendar months
Quotation	100.000 minus rate of interest
Minimum Price Movement (Tick Size & Value)	0.005 ($12.50) for all delivery months
Last Trading Day	11.00 London time – Two London business days prior to the third Wednesday of the delivery month
Delivery Day	First business day following the Last Trading Day
Trading Hours	07.00 to 21.00 London time
Daily Settlement	Positions settled to nearest 0.005 20.00 London time

Beispiel			
Tag	**Geschäftsabschlüsse**	**Open Interest**	**Volumen pro Tag**
1. Mai	A kauft 1 Option und B verkauft 1 Option	1	1
2. Mai	C kauft 5 Optionen und D verkauft 5 Optionen	6	5
3. Mai	A verkauft eine Option und D kauft 1 Option	5	1
4. Mai	E kauft 5 Optionen von C, der seine 5 Optionen verkauft	5	5

Open Interest = (alle offenen Long-Positionen + alle offenen Short-Positionen) / 2

1. Mai: A kauft eine Option, was zu einem Open Interest und einem Volumen von 1 führt.
2. Mai: C und D erhöhen das Open Interest um 5, Volumen an diesem Tag: 5.
3. Mai: A schließt seine Position und reduziert somit das Open Interest um 1, Volumen 1.
4. Mai: E ersetzt einfach C, wodurch das Open Interest sich nicht verändert, Volumen an diesem Tag 5.

Spezifikationen z.B. des 3-Monats-Eurodollar-Futures an der Euronext.LIFFE (Quelle: www.liffe.com)

Three Month Eurodollar Interest Rate Futures Contract

Unit of Trading	Interest rate on three month deposit of $1,000,000
Delivery Months	March, June, September, December and four serial months, such that 24 delivery months are available for trading, with the nearest six delivery months being consecutive calendar months
Quotation	100.000 minus rate of interest
Minimum Price Movement (Tick Size & Value)	0.005 ($12.50) for all delivery months
Last Trading Day	11.00 London time – Two London business days prior to the third Wednesday of the delivery month
Delivery Day	First business day following the Last Trading Day
Trading Hours	07.00 to 21.00 London time
Daily Settlement	Positions settled to nearest 0.005 20.00 London time

Exchange Delivery Settlement Price (EDSP)

Based on the British Bankers' Association offered rate (BBA US$ LIBOR) for three month US $ deposits at 11:00 London time on the Last Trading Day. The settlement price will be 100.000 minus the BBA US$ LIBOR. Where the EDSP Rate is not an exact multiple of 0.001, it will be rounded to the nearest 0.001 or, where the EDSP Rate is an exact uneven multiple of 0.0005, to the nearest lower 0.001 (e.g. BBA US$ LIBOR of 1.53750 becomes 1.537).

Contract Standard:

Cash settlement based on the Exchange Delivery Settlement Price.

3.2.5. Futures Basis

In the Future markets three different types of basis are used

- "Basis" (or Simple Basis),
- "Theoretical Basis"
- "Net Basis" (or Value Basis)

They are all **differences between different rates**. The calculations are based on interest rates (and not on futures prices). Mind the algebraic signs (+/-)!

EXCURSUS: Convergence

In the Futures markets it is usually assumed that the cash rates converge towards the futures prices (as the forward rates are interpreted as an indication for the level of future cash rates).

Example
Convergence: Implied future rate: 3,50% Actual cash rate: 3,20% (Simple basis = 0,30%) Actual value day   6.10. December future expiry day: 15.12. Lead time future: 70 days (6.10.–15.12.)
Under the assumption of linear convergence, where will the cash rate on 15th of November be (40 days later)?
$3,20\% + ((0,30\%/70) \times 40) = 3,37\%$
The cash rate will be around 3,37% on this date.

Exchange Delivery Settlement Price (EDSP)

Based on the British Bankers' Association offered rate (BBA US$ LIBOR) for three month US$ deposits at 11:00 London time on the Last Trading Day. The settlement price will be 100.000 minus the BBA US$ LIBOR. Where the EDSP Rate is not an exact multiple of 0.001, it will be rounded to the nearest 0.001 or, where the EDSP Rate is an exact uneven multiple of 0.0005, to the nearest lower 0.001 (e.g. BBA US$ LIBOR of 1.53750 becomes 1.537).

Contract Standard

Cash-Settlement based on the Exchange Delivery Settlement Price.

3.2.5. Futures-Basis

Im Futuresmarkt gibt es drei verschiedene Formen der sogenannten „Basis".

- einfache Basis
- theoretische Basis
- Wert- bzw. Net-Basis

Bei dieser Basis handelt sich immer um **Differenzen zwischen definierten Preisen/Sätzen**. Unsere Berechnungen basieren auf Zinssätzen (nicht auf Futurespreisen). Bitte beachten Sie die mathematischen Vorzeichen (+/–)!

EXKURS: Konvergenz

Im Futuresmarkt wird üblicherweise angenommen, dass sich die Cash-Sätze den Futures-Preisen annähern (da die Forward-Preise als Indikation für zukünftige Cash-Sätze gesehen werden).

Beispiel
Konvergenz: Implizierter Futures-Satz: 3,50% Aktueller Cash-Satz: 3,20% (Einfache Basis = 0,30%) Valuta: 6.10. Dezember Future Fälligkeit: 15.12. Laufzeit Future: 70 Tage (6.10.–15.12.)
Wo wird der Cash-Satz am 15. November (40 Tage später), unter der Annahme linearer Konvergenz, sein?
$3,20\% + ((0,30\%/70) \times 40) = 3,37\%$
An diesem Tag wird der Cash-Satz ca. 3,37% sein.

Basis (Simple Basis)

The simple Basis is the **difference between the implied forward rate of the actual future price and the actual cash rate.**

Simple Basis = implied Future rate – cash rate

Rules

As in case of a positive yield curve the implied Future rate is usually higher then the actual cash rate, the simple basis is positive in times of a positive yield curve and negative in times of an inverse yield curve.

positive yield curve   →   **positive** simple basis
inverse yield curve   →   **negative** simple basis

This difference should tend towards zero on the last trading day for the futures contract, as the closing price for the contract is defined to be 100 minus Libor on the last trading day.

Example
GBP LIBOR: 5,32%   Future: 94,37 (5,63%)   Forward: 5,61%
Explanation: Simple Basis: Implied Future Rate – Cash Rate (5,63% – 5,32% = + 0,31%)

Theoretical Basis

The theoretical basis is the difference between the fair forward rate (derived from the actual cash rates) and the actual cash rate.

Theoretical Basis = fair forward rate – cash rate

Einfache Basis (Simple Basis)

Die einfache Basis ist die **Differenz zwischen dem implizierten Futures-Satz** (berechnet aus dem aktuellen Futures-Preis) **und dem aktuellen Cash-Satz.**

Einfache Basis = implizierter Futures-Satz – Cash-Satz

Regeln

Da bei einer normalen Zinskurve der implizierte Futures-Satz normalerweise höher als der aktuelle Cash-Satz ist, ist die einfache Basis bei einer normalen Zinskurve positiv und bei einer inversen Zinskurve negativ.

positive Zinskurve $\rightarrow$ einfache Basis **positiv**
inverse Zinskurve $\rightarrow$ einfache Basis **negativ**

Diese Differenz sollte am letzten Handelstag des entsprechenden Futures gegen null tendieren, da der Schlusspreis des Kontraktes als 100 minus LIBOR des letzten Handelstages definiert ist.

Beispiel

GBP LIBOR: 5,32%
Future: 94,37 (5,63%)
Forward: 5,61%

Erklärung:
Einfache Basis: implizierter Futures-Satz – Cash-Satz (5,63% – 5,32% = +0,31%)

Theoretische Basis

Die theoretische Basis ist die Differenz zwischen dem rechnerischen Forward-Satz (abgeleitet aus den aktuellen Cash-Sätzen) und dem aktuellen Cash-Satz.

Theoretische Basis = rechnerischer Forward-Satz – Cash-Satz

Rules (same as the simple basis)

As in case of a positive yield curve the forward is usually higher then the actual cash rate, the theoretical basis is positive in times of a positive yield curve and negative in times of an inverse yield curve.

positive yield curve $\rightarrow$ **positive** theoretical basis
inverse yield curve $\rightarrow$ **negative** theoretical basis

This difference depends on the exact calculation of the fair price and will also tend towards zero on the last trading day for the futures contract.

Example
GBP LIBOR: 5.32%
Future: 94.37 (5.63%)
Forward: 5.61%
Theoretic Basis: fair Forward rate – Cash rate (5.61% – 5.32% = + 0.29%)

Net Basis (Value Basis)

The net basis is the difference between the implied forward rate of the actual futures price in the market and the "fair" forward rate. If the value basis is temporarily large, arbitrageurs will trade in such a way as to reduce it.

Net Basis = implied future rate – fair forward rate

Rules

In case of a positive net basis, arbitrageurs will rather buy futures and hedge them with cash deposits.

In case of a negative net basis, arbitrageurs will rather sell the futures and hedge them with cash deposits

Example
GBP LIBOR: 5.32%
Future: 94.37 (5.63%)
Fwd/Fwd: 5.61%
Net Basis: implied Future rate – Forward rate (5.63% – 5.61%) = +0.02%

Regeln (wie bei der einfachen Basis)

Da bei einer normalen Zinskurve der rechnerische Forward-Satz normalerweise höher als der aktuelle Cash-Satz ist, ist die theoretische Basis bei einer normalen Zinskurve positiv und bei einer inversen Zinskurve negativ.

Positive Zinskurve $\rightarrow$ theoretische Basis **positiv**
Inverse Zinskurve $\rightarrow$ theoretische Basis **negativ**

Diese Differenz hängt von der exakten Berechnung des rechnerischen (fairen) Satzes ab und wird ebenfalls am letzten Handelstag des Futureskontrakes gegen null tendieren.

Beispiel

GBP LIBOR: 5,32%
Future: 94,37 (5,63%)
Forward: 5,61%

Theoretische Basis: rechnerischer Forward-Satz – aktueller Cash-Satz
$(5,61\% - 5,32\% = +0,29\%)$

Wert-Basis (Net-Basis)

Die Wert-Basis ist die Differenz zwischen dem implizierten Futures-Satz (aus dem aktuellen Futures-Preis) und dem rechnerischen Forward-Satz (abgeleitet aus den aktuellen Cash-Sätzen). Wenn die Wert-Basis zeitweise relativ hoch ist, sorgen Arbitrageure durch ihr Handeln wieder für eine Reduktion.

Wert-Basis = implizierter Futures-Satz – rechnerischem Forward-Satz

Regeln

Bei einer positiven Wert-Basis werden Arbitrageure eher Futures kaufen und diese mit Cash-Depots hedgen.

Im Falle einer negativen Wert-Basis werden Arbitrageure Futures eher verkaufen und ebenfalls mit Cash-Depots hedgen.

Beispiel

GBP LIBOR: 5,32%
Future: 94,37 (5,63%)
Forward: 5,61%

Wert-Basis: implizierter Futures-Satz – rechnerischer Forward-Satz $(5,63\% - 5,61\%)$
$= +0,02\%$

3.2.6. Comparison: Money Market Futures vs. FRA

Since money market futures and forward rate agreements have very similar effects, we compare these two instruments:

FRA	Money Market Futures
quotation = interest rate (e.g. 4.50 %)	quotation = 100 – interest rate (e.g. 95.50)
OTC product	product of exchange market
non-standard contracts	standard contracts
volume: unlimited (depending on dealer)	volume (e.g. EUR, USD 1 m) fixed, depending on currency
terms: unlimited (also broken dates)	terms: 1 or 3 months (often only specific months, as March, June, etc.)
spread: 1–4 points (main currencies)	spread: mostly 1 bp, sometimes ½ bp
small credit risk	no credit risk
small charge of capital	no charge of capital
reversal (doubled charge of the line, twice charge of capital, two FRAs in the books)	buying/selling possible: in the future's book only balanced, open positions
low back office requirements	a lot of back office work: margins must be booked daily
calculation of interest: real number of days	calculation of interest: always 30 or 90 days
difference between interest rates is discounted	if paid "flat", no discounting "front fee" by margins

3.2.7. Function of Futures for Pricing and Hedging FRAs

In practice, FRAs are priced via futures. Thus the market depth and the close quotes in the futures market can be utilized. For pricing FRAs via futures the contracts close to the FRA maturity are converted into an FRA rate, either by compound interest calculation (futures strip) or by interpolation.

3.2.7.1. Calculation of 3-months IMM FRAs

Easiest case: if the maturity and the period of the FRA match with the maturity of the future (like for a 3-months IMM FRA), the FRA rate can be derived directly from the future price.

3.2.6. Vergleich Geldmarktfutures – Forward Rate Agreements

Da Money Market Futures und FRAs fast identische Wirkungsweisen haben, finden Sie hier einen kurzen Vergleich:

FRA	Money Market Future
Quotierung = Zinssatz (z.B. 4,50%)	Quotierung = 100 – Zinssatz (z.B. 95,50)
OTC-Produkt	Börsenprodukt
keine Standardkontrakte	Standardkontrakte
Volumen, händlerspezifisch alles darstellbar	Volumen (z.B. CHF, USD 1 Mio.) je nach Währung fix definiert
Laufzeiten: alles darstellbar (auch Broken Dates)	Laufzeiten 1 bzw. 3 Monate (oft nur bestimmte Monate, wie März, Juni etc.)
Spread: 1–4 Punkte (Hauptwährungen)	Spread: meist 1 BP, eventuell auch ½ BP
Kreditrisiko gering	kein Kreditrisiko
geringe Eigenkapitalbelastung	keine Eigenkapitalbelastung
Schließung durch Reversal (doppelte Linienbelastung, zweimal Eigenkapitalkosten, zwei FRAs in den Büchern)	Kauf/Verkauf möglich: im Futurebuch nur saldierte offene Positionen
geringer Arbeitsaufwand im Backoffice	arbeitsaufwändig: durch Einschüsse, Margins – jeden Tag Buchungssätze
Zinsberechnung echte Tage	Zinsberechnung immer 30 bzw. 90 Tage
Zinsdifferenz wird abdiskontiert	wird „flat" ausbezahlt, nicht abdiskontiert → „front fee" durch Einschüsse

3.2.7. Anwendung von Futures zum Pricing und Hedging von FRAs

FRAs werden in der Praxis meistens über Futures gepriced. Dadurch werden die Markttiefe und die engen Quotierungen der liquiden Futures-Märkte genutzt. Dazu werden die Kontrakte herangezogen, die der FRA-Fälligkeit am nächsten liegen, und entweder mittels Zinseszinsrechnung (Futures-Strip) oder Interpolation in einen FRA-Zins umgerechnet.

3.2.7.1. Berechnung von 3-Monats-IMM-FRAs

Der einfachste Fall liegt vor, wenn Fälligkeit und Laufzeit des FRAs mit der Fälligkeit des Futures übereinstimmen, wie bei 3-Monats-IMM-FRAs. Dann kann der FRA-Satz direkt vom Futures-Preis abgeleitet werden.

Example					
Trade date: 13th April 20XX					
3-mo EURIBOR-Future		IMM FRA	FRA Price	Period FRA	FRA Days
JUN XX (M)	96,75 – 76	2 x 5	3,24 – 25	15.06. – 15.09.XX	92
SEP XX (U)	96,65 – 66	5 x 8	3,34 – 35	15.09. – 15.12.XX	91
DEC XX (Z)	96,50 – 51	8 x 11	3,49 – 50	15.12. – 15.03.XX+1	90

Note: For hedges futures vs. FRAs you should have to take into account the difference in days – for futures it is always 90 days, for the FRAs in this example 91 days.

3.2.7.2. Calculation of IMM FRAs with longer Periods (Futures Strips)

Longer periods can be produced out of a series of futures – so-called futures strip. The FRA rate is the effective rate of the 3-months periods, i.e. compound interest is taken into account.

Example					
Trade date: 13th April 20XX What is the bid rate of a 2/11 IMM FRA? The bid rate can be calculated through the purchase of the futures strip JUN, SEP and DEC. Thus in the first step you have to derive the single FRA rates from the 3-months periods:					
3-mo EURIBOR-Future		IMM FRA	FRA Price	Period FRA	FRA Days
JUN XX (M)	96,75 – 76	2 x 5	3,24 – 25	15.06. – 15.09.XX	92
SEP XX (U)	96,65 – 66	5 x 8	3,34 – 35	15.09. – 15.12.XX	91
DEC XX (Z)	96,50 – 51	8 x 11	3,49 – 50	15.12. – 15.03.XX+1	90
In the second step you calculate the price of the 2/11 IMM FRA with the effective rate formula:					

$$2 \times 11 \text{FRA} = \left[\left(1 + 0.0324 \times \frac{92}{360}\right) \times \left(1 + 0.0334 \times \frac{91}{360}\right) \times \left(1 + 0.0349 \times \frac{90}{360}\right) - 1 \right] \times \frac{360}{273} = 3.384\%$$

Beispiel				
Handelstag: 13. April 20XX				
3-Mo-EURIBOR-Future	**IMM-FRA**	**FRA-Preis**	**Laufzeit FRA**	**FRA-Tage**
JUN XX (M) 96,75 – **76**	2 x 5	**3,24** – 25	15.06. – 15.09.XX	92
SEP XX (U) 96,65 – **66**	5 x 8	**3,34** – 35	15.09. – 15.12.XX	91
DEC XX (Z) 96,50 – **51**	8 x 11	**3,49** – 50	15.12. – 15.03.XX+1	90

Anmerkung: Für Hedges Futures vs. FRAs wäre noch die Tagesdifferenz – bei Futures sind das immer 90 Tage, für die FRAs in diesem Beispiel 91 Tage – zu berücksichtigen.

3.2.7.2. Berechnung von IMM-FRAs mit längeren Laufzeiten (Futures Strips)

Längere Laufzeiten können aus der Serie von Futures – sogenannte Futures Strips – konstruiert werden. Der FRA-Satz errechnet sich aus dem Effektivzinssatz der einzelnen 3-Monats-Perioden, d.h., es werden bei der Berechnung auch die Zinseszinsen berücksichtigt.

Beispiel				
Handelstag: 13. April 20XX Was ist die Geldseite eines 2/11-IMM-FRAs? Die Geldseite kann durch den Kauf des Futures-Strip JUN, SEP und DEC konstruiert werden. Daher sind im ersten Schritt die FRA-Sätze für die einzelnen 3-Monats-Perioden abzuleiten:				
3-Mo-EURIBOR-Future	**IMM-FRA**	**FRA-Preis**	**Laufzeit FRA**	**FRA-Tage**
JUN XX (M) 96,75 – **76**	2 x 5	**3,24** – 25	15.06. – 15.09.XX	92
SEP XX (U) 96,65 – **66**	5 x 8	**3,34** – 35	15.09. – 15.12.XX	91
DEC XX (Z) 96,50 – **51**	8 x 11	**3,49** – 50	15.12. – 15.03.XX+1	90
Im zweiten Schritt wird mit der Effektivzinsformel der Preis des 2x11 IMM-FRAs berechnet: $$2x11\,FRA = \left[\left(1+0{,}0324 * \frac{92}{360}\right) * \left(1+0{,}0334 * \frac{91}{360}\right) * \left(1+0{,}0349 * \frac{90}{360}\right) - 1\right] * \frac{360}{273} = 3{,}384\%$$				

3.2.7.3. Calculation of non-IMM FRAs

If the period of the FRA does not start on an IMM date, the FRA rate is calculated approximately through an effective rate which is weighted with the period.

Example

Trade date: 13th April 20XX
Spot value: 15th April 20XX
What is the bid rate of a 3x9 spot FRA (184 days)?

3-mo EURIBOR-Future		IMM FRA	FRA Price	Period FRA	FRA Days
JUN XX (M)	96,75 – 76	2 x 5	3,24 – 25	15.06. – 15.09.XX	92
SEP XX (U)	96,65 – 66	5 x 8	3,34 – 35	15.09. – 15.12.XX	91
DEC XX (Z)	96,50 – 51	8 x 11	3,49 – 50	15.12. – 15.03.XX+1	90

For the calculation the FRA period is devided into the pro rate futures periods. The FRA rate is then produced by the effective rate of the individual periods:

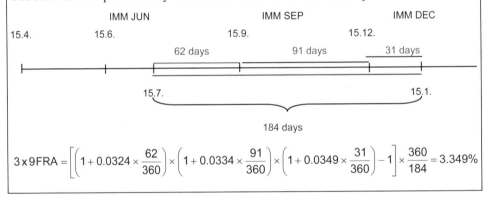

$$3\times9\,FRA = \left[\left(1+0.0324\times\frac{62}{360}\right)\times\left(1+0.0334\times\frac{91}{360}\right)\times\left(1+0.0349\times\frac{31}{360}\right)-1\right]\times\frac{360}{184}=3.349\%$$

3.2.7.4. Strip Hedging

If interest rate risk has to be managed for periods longer than the typical 3-month periods of futures, a series of futures (a so called **futures strip**) may be used. For instance, a 6-month interest rate risk may be hedged by buying or selling two consecutive future contracts.

3.2.7.3. Berechnung von Non-IMM-FRAs

Beginnt die Laufzeit des FRAs nicht an einem IMM-Date, so wird der FRA-Satz annä-
herungsweise durch einen laufzeitgewichteten Effektivzinssatz berechnet.

Beispiel				
Handelstag: 13. April 20XX Spot Valuta: 15. April 20XX Was ist die Geldseite eines 3x9 Spot FRAs (184 Tage)?				
3-Mo-EURIBOR-Future		**IMM-FRA**	**FRA-Preis**	**Laufzeit FRA**	**FRA-Tage**
JUN XX (M)	96,75 – 76	2 x 5	**3,24** – 25	15.06. – 15.09.XX	92
SEP XX (U)	96,65 – 66	5 x 8	**3,34** – 35	15.09. – 15.12.XX	91
DEC XX (Z)	96,50 – 51	8 x 11	**3,49** – 50	15.12. – 15.03.XX+1	90

Die FRA-Laufzeit wird bei der Berechnung in die anteiligen Futuresperioden unterteilt. Der Zinssatz ergibt sich dann wieder aus dem Effektivzinssatz der einzelnen Perioden:

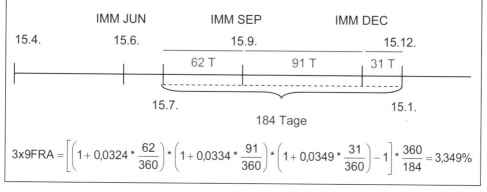

$$3x9FRA = \left[\left(1 + 0,0324 * \frac{62}{360}\right) * \left(1 + 0,0334 * \frac{91}{360}\right) * \left(1 + 0,0349 * \frac{31}{360}\right) - 1\right] * \frac{360}{184} = 3,349\%$$

3.2.7.4. Strip Hedging

Für den Fall, dass das Zinsrisiko über längere als die für Futures klassischen Zeiträume
gemanagt werden muss, können **Future Strips** verwendet werden. Beispielsweise kann
ein 6-Monats-Zinsrisiko über den Kauf bzw. Verkauf zweier aufeinanderfolgender Futureskontrakte abgesichert werden.

Example

Trading day: 13th March 20XX
The bank has an open 6x12 IMM-FRA position (sold with a price of 5.37%,
EUR 1,000,000) and hedges the position with the sale of a SEP XX and a DEC XX
future.

3-mo-EURIBOR-Future	IMM FRA	FRA Price	Period FRA	FRA Days
JUN XX (M)	95,15	3 x 6	4,85	15.06. – 15.09.XX	92
SEP XX (U)	94,82	6 x 9	5,18	15.09. – 15.12.XX	91
DEC XX (Z)	94,51	9 x 12	5,49	15.12. – 15.03.XX+1	90

After six months, we have the following situation.

3-mo-EURIBOR-Future	IMM FRA	FRA Price	Period FRA	FRA Days
SEP XX (U)	95,80	0 x 3	4,20	15.09. – 15.12.XX	91
DEC XX (Z)	95,05	3 x 6	4,95	15.12. – 15.03.XX+1	90
MAR XX+1 (H)	94,33	6 x 9	5,67	15.03. – 15.06.XX+1	92
JUN XX+1 (M)	93,65	9 x 12	6,35	15.06. – 15.09.XX+1	92

With a short glance one notices that short-term rates have remained stable while the interest yield curve has steepened as a whole. The 6-month rate is 4.60%. Therefore the bank receives a payment of

$((5.37\% – 4.60\%) \times 1,000,000 \times 181/360)/(1 + 4.60\% \times 181/360) = $ **EUR +3.784**.

The SEP XX Future costs the bank $(94.82 – 95.80) \times 100 \times 25 = $ **EUR -2.450**, the DEC XX future $(94.51 – 95.05) \times 100 \times 25 = $ **EUR -1,350**. Thus, we remain with a total result of **EUR -16.12**, which shows that the hedge worked out perfectly despite a change in the shape of the interest rate curve. The remaining difference is the consequence of the non-perfect hedge (see below) and rounding effects

3.2.7.5. Stack Hedging

In contrary to a strip hedge, where you trade a series of consecutive futures, for a stack hedge you only trade the **future with the closest delivery month**. Stack hedging is used when the futures which are needed for the hedge are not liquid enough (or are not traded at all). These futures are then replaced by futures with shorter periods and rolled-over at maturity.

Beispiel

Handelstag: 13. März 20XX
Die Bank hat eine offene 6x12 IMM-FRA-Position (verkauft mit Strike 5,37%, EUR 1.000.000) und hedget diese über den Verkauf eines SEP XX und eines DEC XX Futures.

3-Mo-EURIBOR-Future	IMM-FRA	FRA-Preis	Laufzeit FRA	FRA-Tage
JUN XX (M)	95,15	3 x 6	4,85	15.06. – 15.09.XX	92
SEP XX (U)	94,82	6 x 9	5,18	15.09. – 15.12.XX	91
DEC XX (Z)	94,51	9 x 12	5,49	15.12. – 15.03.XX+1	90

Nach sechs Monaten haben wir die folgende Situation:

3-Mo-EURIBOR-Future	IMM-FRA	FRA-Preis	Laufzeit FRA	FRA-Tage
SEP XX (U)	95,80	0 x 3	4,20	15.09. – 15.12.XX	91
DEC XX (Z)	95,05	3 x 6	4,95	15.12. – 15.03.XX+1	90
MAR XX+1 (H)	94,33	6 x 9	5,67	15.03. – 15.06.XX+1	92
JUN XX+1 (M)	93,65	9 x 12	6,35	15.06. – 15.09.XX+1	92

Mit geübtem Auge kann man erkennen, dass das kurze Zinsniveau in etwa dasselbe geblieben ist, während die Zinskurve als Ganzes steiler geworden ist. Der 6-Monats-Zins beträgt 4,60%. Damit erhält die Bank eine Zahlung von

$$((5,37\% - 4,60\%) \times 1.000.000 \times 181/360)/(1 + 4,60\% \times 181/360) = \textbf{EUR +3.784}.$$

Der SEP XX Future kostet die Bank $(94,82 - 95,80) \times 100 \times 25 = \textbf{EUR -2.450}$, der DEC XX Future $(94,51 - 95,05) \times 100 \times 25 = \textbf{EUR -1.350}$. Damit verbleibt ein Gesamtergebnis von **EUR -16,12**, der Hedge hat also trotz Zinskurvendrehung bestens funktioniert. Die verbleibende Differenz ergibt sich aus einer nicht perfekten Hedge Ratio (siehe unten) sowie Rundungsfehlern.

3.2.7.5. Stack Hedging

Im Unterschied zu einem Strip Hedge, bei dem die Serie der aufeinanderfolgenden Futures gehandelt wird, wird beim Stack Hedge nur der **Future mit dem nächstgelegenen Delivery Month gehandelt**. Stack Hedging wird angewendet, wenn die für einen Hedge benötigten Futures entweder nicht gehandelt werden oder nicht ausreichend liquide sind. Es werden dann diese Futures durch solche mit einer kürzeren Laufzeit ersetzt und bei Fälligkeit weitergerollt.

Stack hedging is based on the underlying assumption that the price of the shorter future develops the same way as the price of the longer future. This method of hedging contains substantial interest yield curve risk as this assumption is violated when the shape of the interest yield curve changes.

Example

In June, you want to hedge a short 9/15 FRA position of EUR 100 m with futures. For a strip hedge you would have to sell MAR and JUN contracts. As you deem both contracts too illiquid you trade a stack hedge.

Futures hedge:
You replace the illiquid MAR and JUN contracts by the liquid DEC contract which results in the following transactions:
sell 200 contracts 3-months EURIBOR DEC

Roll-over:
As soon as the liquidity of the MAR contract increases, you roll-over the DEC futures, i.e. you make the following transactions:
Buy back 200 contracts 3-months EURIBOR DEC
Sell 200 contracts 3-months EURIBOR MAR

3.2.7.6. Stubs and Tails

If starting and final dates of an interest position which should be hedged are non-IMM dates, this results in so called stubs and tails. This terms stand for the periods at the beginning (stub) and the end (tail) of the total period that cannot be directly covered with futures.

Example

Stub:

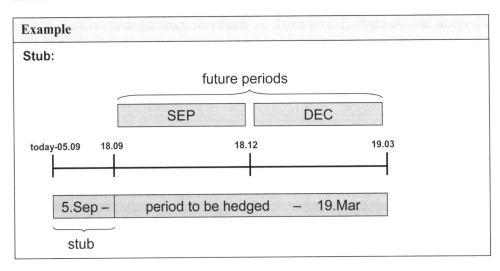

Beim Stack Hedging wird unterstellt, dass sich der Preis des kurzen Futures ähnlich wie jener des langen Futures entwickelt. Da vor allem bei einer Drehung der Zinskurve diese Annahme keineswegs erfüllt ist, beinhaltet diese Absicherungsmethode Zinskurvenrisiko. Ein Stack Hedge muss im Zeitablauf üblicherweise weitergerollt werden. Dies wird dann notwendig, wenn die Zinsanpassungen der abzusichernden Periode zu späteren Daten als der Termin des Stack Hedges sind.

Beispiel

Es ist Juni, und Sie wollen eine short 9x15 FRA-Postition über EUR 100 Mio. mit Futures hedgen. Für einen Strip Hedge müssten Sie MAR- als auch JUN-Kontrakte verkaufen Da Ihnen beide Kontrakte nicht ausreichend liquide erscheinen, führen Sie einen Stack Hedge durch:

Futures Hedge:
Sie ersetzen die illiquiden MAR- und JUN-Kontrakte durch den liquiden DEC-Kontrakt und führen daher folgende Transaktion durch:
Verkauf 200 Kontrakte 3-Monats-EURIBOR-DEC.

Roll-over:
Wenn sich die Liquidität des MAR-Kontraktes erhöht, rollen Sie die DEC-Futures weiter, d.h., Sie führen folgende Transaktionen durch:
Rückkauf 200 Kontrakte 3-Monats-EURIBOR-DEC.
Verkauf 200 Kontrakte 3-Monats-EURIBOR-MAR.

3.2.7.6. Stubs und Tails

Wenn die Start- und Endpunkte einer zu hedgenden Periode nicht mit den Daten für Future-Fälligkeiten eines Strip Hedges zusammenfallen, entstehen sogenannte Stubs und Tails. Diese Begriffe beschreiben die nicht direkt mit Futureperioden abgedeckten Teilperioden der zu hedgenden Periode vorne (Stub) und hinten (Tail). Dazu zwei Beispiele:

Beispiel

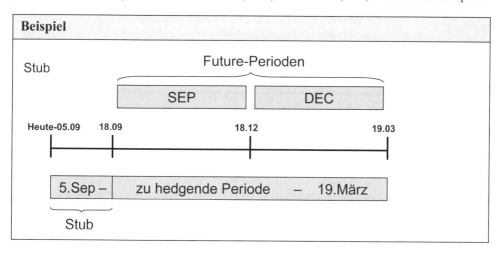

The period to be hedged ranges from Sep 5th to March 19th of the following year. The stub is the period between Sep 5th and Sep 18th, where the latter date is the last trading day for SEP futures. In this case a higher number of SEP futures will be bought or sold respectively in order to hedge the risk of the stub period.

Example

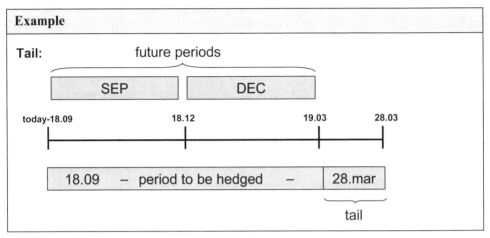

Here, the period to be hedged ranges from Sep 18th to Mar 28th of the following year. The tail is the period between Mar 19th, the maturity date of the DEC contract and Mar 28th. In this case a higher number of DEC futures will be bought or sold respectively in order to hedge the risk of the tail period.

3.2.7.7. Calculating the Hedge Ratio for FRA/Futures Hedge Positions

As the profit/loss of a future is always due today, i.e. with present value, one futures contract has more weight than an equivalent FRA. Therefore, when hedging, the futures volume has to be less than the FRA volume. For calculating the hedge ratio you have to discount the FRA volume for the FRA period (i.e. maturity date until spot).

$$\text{Hedge Ratio} = \frac{\text{Volume FRA}}{1 + i \times \dfrac{\text{period FRA}}{\text{basis}}}$$

Example

Hedge ratio for FRA/Futures Hedge:
You are long USD 100 DEC IMM 3/6 FRA (90 days) at 5.00% and want to hedge this position with the purchase of 100 DEC Eurodollar Futures.
How many futures do you have to buy? (interest rate 180 days: 5%)

$$HR = \frac{100}{1 + 0.05 \times \dfrac{180}{360}} = 97.56$$

The hedge ratio is 97.56, i.e. You have to buy 98 contracts (and are therefore slightly overhedged).

Die zu hedgende Periode reicht vom 5.9. bis zum 19.3. des nächsten Jahres. Der Stub ist die Periode zwischen dem 5.9. und dem 18.9., dem letzten Handelstag für den SEP-Future. In diesem Fall wird eine größere Anzahl von SEP-Futures ge- bzw. verkauft, um das zusätzliche Risiko der Stub-Periode zu hedgen.

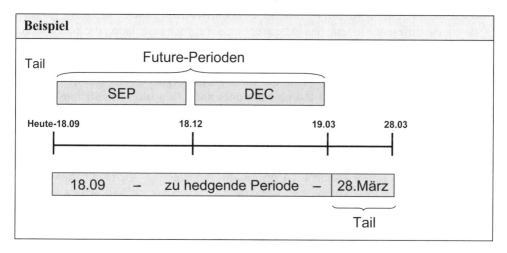

Beispiel

Die zu hedgende Periode reicht hier vom 18.9. bis zum 28.3. des nächsten Jahres. Der Tail ist die Periode zwischen dem 19.3., dem Laufzeitende des DEC-Kontrakts und dem 28.3. In diesem Fall wird eine größere Anzahl von DEC-Futures ge- bzw. verkauft, um das zusätzliche Risiko der Tail-Periode zu hedgen.

3.2.7.7. Ermittlung der Hedge Ratio von FRAs/Futures Hedgepositionen

Da der Gewinn/Verlust eines Futures immer sofort, d.h. barwertig anfällt, wiegt ein Futureskontrakt mehr als das laufzeit- und volumskonforme FRA. Daher muss bei einem Hedge nur ein geringeres Volumen an Futures gehandelt werden. Die **Hedge Ratio** wird ermittelt, indem das FRA-Volumen für die Gesamtlaufzeit (d.h. Maturity Date bis Spot) abgezinst wird.

$$\text{Hedge Ratio} = \frac{Volumen\ FRA}{1 + i * \dfrac{Gesamtlaufzeit\ FRA}{Basis}}$$

Beispiel

Hedge Ratio bei FRA/Futures-Hedge:
Sie sind long USD 100 DEC IMM 3x6 FRAs (90 Tage) zu 5% und wollen die Position durch den Kauf von DEC-Eurodollar Futures hedgen.
Wie viele Futures müssen Sie kaufen? (Zinsen 180 Tage: 5%)

Die Hedge Ratio beträgt 97,56, d.h., Sie werden 98 Kontrakte kaufen (und sind damit leicht überhedget).

The hedge ratio **depends on two factors**: The **total length of the FRA** and the **interest level**. The influence of the second factor is termed the "convexity effect". In the following, we will have a closer look at this effect and its consequences for FRA/future hedges before we will further describe the necessary dynamic adjustments of the hedge ratio.

Note: If the FRA term (usually 91 or 92 days) differs from the future term (always 90 days), the difference in term has to be accounted for when calculating the hedge ratio.

3.2.7.8. Significance of Convexity Effects on FRA / Futures Hegdes

Convexity effects arise whenever you are trading FRAs. This means that the **present value (mark-to-market) of an FRA position does not follow interest rate movements entirely linearly.** The same phenomenon can be observed with bonds: There, the term convexity is used to describe the estimation error that comes from calculating price changes linearly using the modified duration or the Present Value of a Basis Point concept.

Assume that you have a short FRA position. If the rates rise, the revaluation of this position will show a loss. The present value of this loss, however, will be less than expected as the (future) negative differential between forward and FRA rate is now discounted with a higher interest rate. On the contrary, the profit in case of lower interest rates will be higher than our guess as it is discounted at a lower interest rate. A short FRA position therefore has a **positive convexity**, i.e. when rates change the result will always be better than linearly estimated.

In analogy a long FRA position has a **negative convexity** as the profit in case of higher rates is discounted at a higher rate and the loss in case of lower rates is discounted with a lower rate.

When hedging cash positions with FRAs, these convexity effects are irrelevant as cash positions have the same convexity effects and therefore the convexity effects cancel each other out.

In contrast, money market futures do not have any convexity effects as the value of one BP is always the same, independent of the level of interest rates (mostly 25 EUR, USD, etc.). As price changes are adjusted daily through variation margins the BP value is also always the present value (no matter if the interest rate level is at 10% or 1%).

If you hedge a FRA with futures (for arbitrage futures vs. FRA) you have to take into account the convexity. The following example shows the effects:

Wie aus der Formel ersichtlich ist, ist die Hedge Ratio **von zwei Faktoren abhängig**: Der **Gesamtlaufzeit** und dem **Abzinsungsfaktor**. Der Einfluss des zweiten Faktors wird auch als „**Konvexitätseffekt**" beschrieben. Im Folgenden wird dieser Begriff näher erklärt und gezeigt, welche Auswirkungen die Konvexität bei FRA/Future-Hedges hat, bevor wir im Anschluss daran die notwendige dynamische Anpassung der Hedge Ratio weiter verfolgen.

Anmerkung: Weicht die Laufzeit des FRAs (meist 91 oder 92 Tage) von der Laufzeit des Futures (immer 90 Tage) ab, so wirkt sich auch dieser Laufzeitunterschied auf das Gewicht der FRA-Position aus und muss in der Hedge Ratio berücksichtigt werden.

3.2.7.8. Berücksichtigung von Konvexitätseffekten bei FRAs/Futures Hedges

Bei FRAs gibt es Konvexitätseffekte. Damit ist gemeint, dass der **Zusammenhang zwischen der Barwertentwicklung (mark-to-market) einer FRA-Position und dem entsprechenden Zinssatz nicht völlig linear** ist. Es handelt sich hierbei um dasselbe Phänomen wie bei Anleihen: Dort beschreibt der Begriff Konvexität den Schätzfehler, den man erhält, wenn man die Veränderung von Anleihepreisen linear über die Modified Duration schätzt.

Denken Sie z.B. an eine short FRA-Position. Wenn die Zinsen steigen, wird die Bewertung dieser Position einen Verlust ausweisen. Der Barwertverlust wird aber geringer ausfallen als über die reine Zinsdifferenz geschätzt, da ja der (zukünftige) Verlust jetzt mit einem höheren Zinssatz abgezinst wird. Umkehrt wird der Gewinn bei fallenden Zinsen höher ausfallen als geschätzt, da ja jetzt nur mit einem niedrigeren Zinssatz abgezinst werden muss. Eine short FRA-Position hat daher eine **positive Konvexität**, d.h., das Ergebnis ist bei einer Änderung der Zinsen immer leicht besser als über lineare Hochrechnung geschätzt.

Umgekehrt hat ein long FRA eine **negative Konvexität**, weil der Gewinn bei steigenden Zinsen mit einem höheren Zinssatz diskontiert werden muss bzw. der Verlust bei fallenden Zinsen mit einem niedrigeren Zinssatz.

Beim Hedging (bzw. Arbitrieren) von Cash-Positionen oder FRAs mit FRAs spielen diese Konvexitätseffekte keine Rolle, da die zugrundeliegende Cash-Position ebenso Konvexitätseffekte aufweist und sich die Wirkung in Summe neutralisiert.

Im Gegensatz dazu haben MM-Futures keine Konvexität, weil der Wert eines BP unabhängig vom Zinsniveau immer gleich ist. Da Preisänderungen täglich in Form der Variation Margin ausgeglichen werden, entspricht der BP-Wert also auch immer dem Barwert (egal ob das Zinsniveau bei 10% oder 1% ist).

Werden nun Futures für das Hedgen (bzw. Arbitrieren) von FRAs verwendet, ist die Konvexität zu berücksichtigen.

Example

FRA/futures Hedge:

You are long USD 1000 DEC IMM 3/6 FRA (90 days) at 5% and hedge this position with the purchase of 976 DEC Eurodollar Futures (the hedge ratio is calculated assuming a 6m rate of 5%: 1000/(1 + 5% x 180/360) ~ 976) at 95.00. The volume and the period for both are the same. You therefore expect a perfect hedge (no profit, no loss) except for rounding errors.
On the same day interest rates rise to 8%. What is your result now?

Fair price FRA at 8%:	Fair price future at 8%:
$3 \times 6 = \left[\dfrac{1+0.08\times\dfrac{180}{360}}{1+0.08\times\dfrac{90}{360}}-1\right]\times\dfrac{360}{90}=7.843\%$	Future $= 100 - 7,843 = 92,157$
Mark to Market FRA:	MTM future (= margin call)
$\dfrac{(0.07843-0.05)\times 1,000,000,000\times\dfrac{90}{360}}{1+0.08\times\dfrac{180}{360}}=6,834,135$	-284.3 BP x 25 x 976 = $-6,937,255$.

Thus the revaluation shows a **loss of USD 103,120** (6,834,135 − 6,937,255).

The loss for the future position was bigger than the profit for the FRA position. This is due to the fact that the profit of the FRA is a future value and has therefore to be discounted at a higher rate than the rate that was used calculating the hedge ratio. On the other hand, the variation margin has to be paid today. I.e. the total position has a negative convexity.

The hedge ratio is revealed by assuming a 6-months-interest of 5%:

1,000/(1 + 5% x 180/360) ~ 976.

As the hedge ratio depends on the period and the level of interest rates it has to be adjusted dynamically. Should rates rise, the hedge ratio falls (and vice versa).

Depending on the particular position, the hedge adjustment leads to profits or losses:

short FRA + short future:

rates rise → future falls → HR falls → futures has to be bought back → profit
rates fall → Y future rises → HR rises → further futures has to be sold → profit

long FRA + long future:

rates rise → future falls → HR falls → futures have to be sold again → loss
rates fall → future rises → HR rises → further futures have to be bought → loss

Beispiel

FRA/Futures Hedge

Sie sind long USD 1.000 DEC-IMM 3x6 FRAs (90 Tage) zu 5% und hedgen diese Position durch den Kauf von 976 DEC-Eurodollar Futures zu 95,00. Aufgrund des gleichen Volumens und der gleichen Laufzeit gehen Sie davon aus, dass Sie einen (bis auf die Rundungsungenauigkeiten der Hedge Ratio) perfekten Hedge durchgeführt haben (mit null Gewinn und Verlust). Am gleichen Tag steigen die Zinsen auf 8% flat. Was ist jetzt Ihr Ergebnis?

Fairer Preis FRA bei 8%	**Fairer Preis Future bei 8%**
$3x6 = \left[\dfrac{1 + 0{,}08 * \dfrac{180}{360}}{1 + 0{,}08 * \dfrac{90}{360}} - 1 \right] * \dfrac{360}{90} = 7{,}843\%$	Future $= 100 - 7{,}843 = 92{,}157$
Mark to Market FRA	MTM Future (= Margin Call)
$\dfrac{(0{,}07843 - 0{,}05)*1.000.000.000 * \dfrac{90}{360}}{1 + 0{,}08 * \dfrac{180}{360}} = 6.834.135$	$-284{,}3$ BP x 25 x 976 = $-6.937.255$

Somit zeigt die Bewertung einen Verlust von **USD 103.120** (6.834.135 – 6.937.255).

Der Verlust auf die Futuresposition war also größer als der Gewinn auf die FRA-Position. Der Grund liegt darin, dass der Gewinn des FRAs erst in der Zukunft anfällt und daher abgezinst werden muss (und zwar stärker als erwartet und über die Hedge Ratio berücksichtigt), die Variation Margin jedoch sofort anfällt, d.h., die Gesamtposition hat eine negative Konvexität.

Die Hedge Ratio ergibt sich bei Annahme eines 6-Monats-Zinses von 5%:

1.000/(1 + 5% x 180/360) ~ 976.

Da die Hedge Ratio von der Laufzeit und dem Zinsniveau abhängt, muss sie dynamisch angepasst werden. Steigen die Zinsen, fällt die Hedge Ratio und umgekehrt. Je nach Position führt die Anpassung des Hedges zu Gewinnen oder Verlusten:

short FRA + short Future:

Zinsen steigen → Future fällt → HR fällt → Futures müssen zurückgekauft werden → Gewinn

Zinsen fallen → Future steigt → HR steigt → weitere Futures müssen verkauft werden → Gewinn

long FRA + long Future:

Zinsen steigen → Future fällt → HR fällt → Futures müssen wieder verkauft werden → Verlust

Zinsen fallen → Future steigt → HR steigt → weitere Futures müssen gekauft werden → Verlust

Thus following rules can be defined for the convexity of futures/FRA (resp. cash) hedges:

- FRA short + future short → profit on position when rates change (positive convexity)
- FRA long + future long → loss on position when rates change (negative convexity)

Additionally to the interest rate level, the residual term represents the second dynamic influencing factor of the hedge ratio. As the residual term decreases the hedge ratio increases and more future contracts have to be bought or sold accordingly.

3.2.8. Spread Strategies

Generally, the simultaneous purchase and sale of futures contracts with different times to maturity and the same underlying is called an **intra-contract spread**.

Intra-Contract Spread Strategies

Calendar Spread / Time Spread / Spread

A **Calendar Spread** – often just referred to as a **Time Spread** or simply **"Spread"** in futures - is the **simultaneous purchase and sale of futures contracts** with different times to maturity and the same underlying. The spread is calculated as follows:

Spread   = + Price of short contract
          − Price of long contract

If the Spread is positive or negative depends on the prices of the contracts. Since the price of MM futures is mainly determined by the yield curve structure, a steep yield curve entails lower futures prices compared to the spot price. Thus the following rules hold:

- Steep yield curve   →   Spread positive
- Inverse yield curve   →   Spread negative

Like in options trading, spreads on futures are also traded separately.

The terminology used is:

Buy Spread = Buy short contract, sell long contract
Sell Spread = Sell short contract, buy long contract

Note: The terminology is usually geared towards the first/shortest contract, i.e. for a long futures strategy, the shortest contract is a long position.

Calendar Spreads carry considerably less risk than "pure" futures positions, since they depend on the relation between two contracts and not on the development of absolute values. Accordingly, stock exchanges demand usually lower margins for Spread deals.

Somit lassen sich folgende Regeln für die Konvexität bei Futures/FRA (bzw. Cash) Hedges zusammenfassen:

- FRA short + Future short → Position gewinnt bei Zinsänderung (positive Konvexität)
- FRA long + Future long → Position verliert bei Zinsänderungen (negative Konvexität)

Neben dem Zinsniveau ist die Laufzeit der zweite dynamische Einflussfaktor auf die Hedge Ratio. Mit sinkender Laufzeit steigt die Hedge Ratio und es müssen entsprechend mehr Futures ge- bzw. verkauft werden.

3.2.8. Spread-Strategien

Die Kombination von Kauf- und Verkaufskontrakten in unterschiedlichen Laufzeiten auf dasselbe Underlying (für den gleichen Kontrakt) wird im Futuresmarkt üblicherweise als **„Intra-Kontraktspread"** bezeichnet.

Intra-Kontraktspread-Strategien

Calendar Spread / Time Spread / Spread

Unter einem **Calendar Spread** bzw. **Time Spread** (oder einfach nur „**Spread**" bei Futures genannt) ist der **gleichzeitige Kauf und Verkauf eines Futures auf dasselbe Underlying**, jedoch mit unterschiedlichen Liefertagen zu verstehen. Als Spread wird dann folgende Differenz bezeichnet:

Spread = + Kurs des kurzen Kontraktes
            – Kurs des langen Kontraktes

Abhängig von den Preisen der unterschiedlichen Laufzeiten kann dieser Spread sowohl positiv als auch negativ sein. Da die Preise bei Geldmarktfutures zum Großteil von der Zinskurve abhängen und eine positive Zinskurve zu niedrigen Futurepreisen (im Vergleich zur Kassa) führt, gelten üblicherweise folgende Regeln:

- positive Zinskurve   →   Spread positiv
- negative Zinskurve   →   Spread negativ

Wie im Optionshandel hat sich auch im Futurehandel der separate Handel von Spreads durchgesetzt.

Dabei gilt folgende Terminologie:

Kauf Spread   = Kauf des kurzen Termins
                     Verkauf des langen Termins
Verkauf Spread = Verkauf des kurzen Termins
                     Kauf des langen Termins

Anmerkung: Die Terminologie richtet sich bei Futures-Strategien üblicherweise nach dem kürzesten Kontrakt, d.h., eine Futures-Strategie ist long, wenn auch der kürzeste Kontrakt long ist.

Calendar Spreads sind wesentlich risikoärmer als der reine Kauf bzw. Verkauf des Futures. Sie hängen nicht von der absoluten Wertentwicklung, sondern nur vom Verhältnis der Wertentwicklung der zwei Kontrakte ab. Dementsprechend werden von der Börse üblicherweise geringere Einschüsse als für reine Kauf- oder Verkaufspositionen verlangt.

Application

Buying a Spread makes sense when the buyer expects an inverse yield curve to flatten or a normal yield curve to steepen. Obviously, this expectation has to apply to the maturities of the Spread strategy. Selling a Spread makes sense when the seller expects a steep yield curve to flatten or a flat yield curve to become inverse.

Butterfly (Spread)

A **Butterfly Spread strategy** regarding futures involves **two (Calendar) Spreads with the same volume**. Buying a Butterfly equals buying a shorter Spread and selling a longer spread, whereby the longer future of the shorter Spread has the same maturity as the shorter future of the longer Spread.

Example
Buying a shorter Spread: Buying 100 JUN XX future contracts Selling 100 SEP XX future contracts
Selling a longer Spread: Selling 100 SEP XX future contracts Buying 100 DEC XX future contracts

The terminology used is therefore:
Buy Butterfly = Buy short contract, sell 2 x medium contracts, buy long contract
Sell Butterfly = Sell short contract, buy 2 x medium contracts, sell long contract

Application

A butterfly strategy has limited risk and limited profit and can be used to profit from stable yield curves as well as from changing yield curves.

Condor (Spread)

Similar to a Butterfly, a Condor involves a shorter Spread and a converse longer Spread, with the difference that the shorter contract of the longer Spread has a longer maturity than the longer contract of the shorter Spread.

Anwendung

Einen Spread zu kaufen macht Sinn, wenn der Käufer erwartet, dass eine inverse Zins-kurve flach wird oder dass eine flache oder normale Zinskurve steiler wird. Die **Erwar-tung zur Drehung der Zinskurve** muss natürlich diejenigen Laufzeiten betreffen, die dem Spread entsprechen. Einen Spread zu verkaufen macht Sinn, wenn man von einer flacher werdenden Normal-Zinskurve oder einer invers werdenden Zinskurve profitieren will.

Butterfly (Spread)

Eine **Futures-Butterfly-Strategie** beinhaltet den **Kauf und Verkauf von jeweils einem (Calendar) Spread mit demselben Volumen**. Der Kauf eines Butterflys entspricht dem Kauf eines (kurzen) Spreads und dem gleichzeitigen Verkauf eines längeren Spreads, wobei der längere Future des kurzen Spreads und der kürzere Future des längeren Spreads dieselbe Laufzeit haben.

Beispiel
Kauf eines Spreads: Kauf von 100 JUN XX Future-Kontrakten Verkauf von 100 SEP XX Future-Kontrakten
Verkauf eines Spreads: Verkauf von 100 SEP XX Future-Kontrakten Kauf von 100 DEC XX Future-Kontrakten

Es gilt daher folgende Terminologie:
Kauf Butterfly = Kauf eines „kurzen Futures", Verkauf zweier „mittlerer" Futures, Kauf eines „langen" Futures.
Verkauf Butterfly = Verkauf eines „kurzen Futures", Kauf zweier „mittlerer" Futures, Verkauf eines „langen" Futures.

Anwendung

Bei einer Butterfly-Strategie sind Gewinn- und Verlustmöglichkeiten beschränkt. But-terfly-Strategien können sowohl bei stabilen als auch bei sich ändernden Yield-Kurven eingesetzt werden.

Kondor (Spread)

Ähnlich wie bei einer Butterfly-Strategie werden hier ein kürzerer und ein längerer (Ca-lendar) Spread gegenläufig kombiniert. Der Unterschied ist, dass hier der kürzere Kon-trakt des längeren Spreads eine längere Laufzeit hat als der lange Kontrakt des kurzen Spreads.

Example

Buying a shorter Spread:
Buying 100 JUN XX future contracts
Selling 100 SEP XX future contracts

Selling a longer Spread:
Selling 100 DEC XX future contracts
Buying 100 MAR XX future contracts

The terminology used is therefore:

Buy Condor = Buy short contract, sell 2 x medium contracts with different maturities, buy long contract
Sell Butterfly = Sell short contract, buy 2 x medium contracts with different maturities, sell long contract

Application

A condor strategy has limited risk and limited profit and can be used to profit from stable yield curves as well as from changing yield curves.

Inter-Contract Spread

An Inter-Contract Spread is the **simultaneous purchase and sale of futures contracts** on different underlyings. Different times to maturity are not required.

Generally, Inter-Spreading pays attention to a proven correlation between two contracts and that the strategy is backed by a market opinion towards the price developments of the two futures. In contrast to Intra-Spreading, there is **no convention concerning terminology**.

Beispiel

Kauf eines Spreads:
Kauf von 100 JUN XX Future-Kontrakten
Verkauf von 100 XX SEP Future-Kontrakten

Verkauf eines Spreads:
Verkauf 100 XX DEC Future-Kontrakte
Kauf 100 MAR XX+1 Future-Kontrakte

Es gilt daher folgende Terminologie:

Kauf Kondor = Kauf eines „kurzen Futures", Verkauf zweier „mittlerer" Futures mit unterschiedlichen Laufzeiten, Kauf eines „langen" Futures.

Verkauf Kondor = Verkauf eines „kurzen Futures", Kauf zweier „mittlerer" Futures mit unterschiedlichen Laufzeiten, Verkauf eines „langen" Futures.

Anwendung

Bei einer Kondor-Strategie sind Gewinn- und Verlustmöglichkeiten beschränkt. Butterfly-Strategien können sowohl bei stabilen als auch bei sich ändernden Yield-Kurven eingesetzt werden.

Inter-Kontraktspread

Als Inter-Kontraktspread wird der **gleichzeitige Kauf und Verkauf von Futures mit unterschiedlichen Underlyings** bezeichnet. Anders als beim Intra-Kontraktspread sind unterschiedliche Liefertage nicht erforderlich.

Im Allgemeinen wird beim Inter-Spreading darauf geachtet, dass ein begründeter Wertzusammenhang zwischen den zwei Kontrakten besteht und dass hinter der Strategie eine entsprechende Marktmeinung über die zukünftigen Entwicklungen im Preisgefüge der zwei Futures steht.

Im Gegensatz zum Intra-Spreading gibt es beim Inter-Spreading **keine allgemeingültigen Usancen,** wann von einem gekauften/verkauften Spread bzw. positivem/negativem Spread gesprochen wird.

Summary

The forward, or future rate agreement, is a contract between two parties to fix a future interest rate. This contract defines the interest rate for a future period based on an agreed principal. If the FRA rate differs from the current market rate (reference rate) on the agreed date (fixing date), a settlement payment depending on the difference must be paid by one of the contractors. The principal is not exchanged and there is no obligation by either party to borrow or lend capital. FRAs are over-the-counter (OTC) products and are available for a variety of periods: starting from a few days to terms of several years. The FRA term is the period from settlement date until maturity date. The reference rate is the rate which the FRA rate is compared to on the fixing date. The basis for the reference rate is agreed upon on the trade date. Usually the fixing date is two working days before settlement date. GBP FRAs are settled on the same day (not at value date after 2 days) and therefore constitute an exception.

An FRA can be purchased in order to speculate on rising interest rates or as a hedge for a future short position in deposits and thus as a protection against rising interest rates. An FRA can be sold in order to speculate on falling interest rates or as a hedge for a future long position in deposits and thus as a protection against falling interest rates.

The FRA involves no exchange of principal. Therefore, the only risk is the non-fulfillment of the amount due at settlement date (replacement risk). The credit risk is thereby limited to the difference between FRA rate and the locked-in reference rate at settlement date. The credit line (partner limit) used by an FRA is therefore usually between 1–5% p.a. of the principal amount (with regard to the term of the FRA period) from spot until settlement date.

The main advantage of derivatives like FRAs is the separation of liquidity and interest rate risk. Thus the interest rate risk can be controlled more efficiently, i.e. at more favourable prices (closer spreads). Further, additional credit risk can be avoided which would occur when controlling the interest rate risk with cash instruments. When hedging cash positions with derivatives you have to take into account that you always only hedge a reference rate (e.g. LIBOR, EURIBOR, etc.).

Forward interest rates can be derived from the current yield curve as you can always produce a forward deposit by means of two deposits with different terms. The resulting interest rate depends on the costs resp. returns of the 2 deposits – and therefore on the yield curve. This interest rate (costs) of the two deposits can be alternatively called Implied Rate, Break-even Rate or Forward-forward Rate.

Money market futures are exchange-traded interest rate contracts. Money market futures can be used like FRAs to eliminate a future interest rate risk (hedging), to speculate on interest rate trends (trading) or to arbitrage between different markets (arbitrage)

Money market futures are standardised products, because they are traded in the exchange market. Thus, some specifications are already fixed by the particular exchange: contract volume, maturity dates, marginal price changes (tick size) and value of a price change by one tick based on one contract (tick value).

Zusammenfassung

Ein Forward Rate Agreement ist ein Zinstermingeschäft. Es fixiert den Zinssatz für einen vereinbarten Nominalbetrag für eine bestimmte Periode in der Zukunft. Am Beginn der vereinbarten Periode (Settlement-Tag) kommt es lediglich zu einer Vergütung der Differenz zwischen dem vereinbarten FRA-Zinssatz und dem am Fixing-Tag am Geldmarkt festgestellten gültigen Satz (Referenzzinssatz). Es besteht jedoch keine Verpflichtung, den vereinbarten Nominalbetrag zu liefern oder bereitzustellen. FRAs werden „over the counter" (OTC) gehandelt. Sie sind für eine Vielzahl von Perioden, beginnend bei wenigen Tagen bis zu einer Endlaufzeit von mehreren Jahren, verfügbar. Die Laufzeit eines FRAs ist die Periode zwischen Settlement-Tag und Maturity-Tag. Der Referenzsatz ist jener Zinssatz, mit dem der vereinbarte FRA-Zinssatz beim Fixing verglichen wird. Der zu verwendende Referenzzinssatz wird bei Geschäftsabschluss vereinbart. Der Fixing-Tag ist üblicherweise zwei Banktage vor dem Settlement-Tag. Eine Ausnahme bildet GBP, das tagesgleich fixiert wird.

Der Käufer eines FRAs kann ein FRA zur Spekulation auf höhere Zinsen oder zur Absicherung einer zukünftigen Refinanzierung (Passivgeschäft) gegen steigende Zinsen verwenden. Der Verkäufer eines FRAs kann ein FRA zur Spekulation auf niedrigere Zinsen oder zur Absicherung einer zukünftigen Anlage (Aktivgeschäft) gegen fallende Zinsen verwenden.

Das FRA beinhaltet keinen Austausch von Kapitalnominalbeträgen. Dementsprechend beschränkt sich das Kreditrisiko auf das Wiederbeschaffungsrisiko. Einziges mögliches Risiko ist die Nichterfüllung der Ausgleichszahlung zum Settlement-Tag. Somit besteht das Kreditrisiko vom Abschlusstag bis zur Erfüllung der Ausgleichszahlung, d.h. bis zum Settlement-Tag.

Der wesentliche Vorteil von Derivaten wie FRAs liegt in der Trennung von Liquidität und Zinsrisiko. Dadurch kann das Zinsrisiko effizient gesteuert werden. Beim Hedging von Cash-Positionen mit Derivaten ist zu beachten, dass mit diesen immer nur ein Referenzsatz (z.B. LIBOR, EURIBOR usw.) abgesichert wird.

Der Preis von Forward-Zinssätzen leitet sich von der aktuellen Zinskurve ab. Dahinter steckt das Prinzip, dass mittels zweier Depots mit unterschiedlichen Laufzeiten ein Forward-Depot produziert werden kann. Der sich daraus ergebende Zinssatz hängt dabei von den Kosten bzw. Erträgen aus den beiden Geschäften – und somit von der Zinskurve – ab. Diesen Zinssatz (Kosten), den man über diese zwei Geschäfte dargestellt hat, bezeichnet man alternativ als Implied Rate, Break-even Rate oder Forward-forward Rate.

Geldmarktfutures sind börsengehandelte Zinstermingeschäfte. Geldmarktfutures können ähnlich wie ein FRA verwendet werden, um ein zukünftiges Zinsrisiko auszuschalten (Hedging), auf eine Zinsmeinung zu spekulieren (Trading) oder Preisunterschiede zwischen unterschiedlichen Märkten auszunutzen (Arbitrage).

Für börsengehandelte Produkte ist es typisch, dass die Spezifikationen standardisiert sind. Folgende Merkmale werden von der jeweiligen Börse vorgegeben: Volumsgröße eines Kontraktes, Fälligkeitstermine, minimale Preisbewegung (Tick Size) und Wert der Preisänderung um einen Tick, bezogen auf einen Kontrakt (Tick Value).

Delivery dates of money market futures are set by the futures exchange. For the core markets these are always the third Wednesday of the last month of the quarter (March, June, September, December). These delivery dates are called IMM-dates (International money market dates). Last trading days of futures are determined by the exchanges and are usually two days before delivery date (an exception is GBP, where the theoretical delivery date is the last trading date, i.e. same-day fixing).

The quotation for futures prices is 100.00 minus interest rate.

A tick is the marginal movement of the futures price. The tick value is the profit or loss which occurs when the price changes by one tick.

The settlement of the deals is carried out by the clearing house of the exchange. The exchange specifies the conditions for the trading. It defines – among other things – which contracts are traded and their specifications.

Margins are required when dealing with futures. They reduce the credit risk for the exchange to a minimum. They are demanded either "one-shot" and up-front in relation to the number of contracts (initial margin) or daily for the accrued profits and losses (variation margin).

Each futures position can be closed by an appropriate opposite futures position before or at the last trading date. The closing leads to the elimination of the position and the related initial margin. The profits and losses result from the daily variation margin payments (plus possible interest returns resp. payments).

In the future markets three different types of basis are used: "Basis" (or Simple Basis), "Theoretical Basis" and "Net Basis" (or Value Basis).

If interest rate risk has to be managed for periods longer than the typical 3-month periods of futures, a series of futures (a so-called futures strip) may be used. Contrary to a strip hedge, where you trade a series of consecutive futures, for a stack hedge you only trade the future with the closest delivery month. Stack hegdes are used if the corresponding terms (needed for the hedge) are not liquid/available.

Generally, the simultaneous purchase and sale of futures contracts with different times to maturity and the same underlying is called an intra-contract spread. A Calendar Spread – often just referred to as a Time Spread or simply "Spread" in futures – is the simultaneous purchase and sale of futures contracts with different times to maturity and the same underlying. A Butterfly Spread strategy regarding futures involves two (Calendar) Spreads with the same volume.

An Inter-Contract Spread is the simultaneous purchase and sale of futures contracts on different underlyings. Different times to maturity are not required.

Die Liefertage für Money Market Futures sind von der Börse vorgegeben. An den Hauptmärkten sind die Liefertage der jeweils dritte Mittwoch des letzten Monats im Quartal, d.h. März, Juni, September, Dezember. Diese Liefertage werden auch als IMM-Dates bezeichnet. Der letzte Handelstag ist von der Börse vorgegeben und liegt üblicherweise zwei Werktage vor dem Liefertag (Ausnahme ist z.B. GBP: theoretischer Liefertag ist der letzte Handelstag, also taggleich).

Die Quotierung bei Futures ist 100,00 minus Zinssatz.

Als Tick bezeichnet man die Mindestpreisbewegung eines Futureskontrakts. Der Tickwert ist der Gewinn bzw. Verlust, der sich aus einer Preisbewegung um einen Tick für einen Kontrakt ergibt.

Die Börse gibt die Rahmenbedingungen vor, unter denen der Handel stattfindet. Sie bestimmt unter anderem, welche Kontrakte gehandelt werden sowie die Spezifikationen der einzelnen Kontrakte. Die Abwicklung der Geschäfte erfolgt durch das Clearing House der Futuresbörse.

Das Ziel des Margin-Systems ist die Ausschließung des Kontrahentenrisikos (Kreditrisiko). Dies erfolgt durch einen fixen Einschuss pro Kontrakt (Initial Margin) und zusätzlich durch die tägliche Abrechnung der angelaufenen Gewinne und Verluste (Variation Margin).

Jede Futuresposition kann vor bzw. am letzten Handelstag mit einer entgegengesetzten Futuresposition aufgelöst werden. Ein Schließen bewirkt die Auflösung der Position und somit der damit verbundenen Initial Margin. Der Gewinn bzw. Verlust ergibt sich aus der Summe der täglichen Margin-Zahlungen (plus etwaiger Zinserträge bzw. -aufwendungen).

Im Futuresmarkt gibt es drei verschiedene Formen der sogenannten „Basis“: einfache Basis, theoretische Basis und Wert- bzw. Net-Basis. Bei dieser Basis handelt sich immer um Differenzen zwischen definierten Preisen/Sätzen.

Für den Fall, dass das Zinsrisiko über längere als die für Futures klassischen Zeiträume gemanagt werden muss, können Future Strips verwendet werden. Im Unterschied zu einem Strip Hedge, bei dem die Serie der aufeinanderfolgenden Futures gehandelt wird, wird beim Stack Hedge nur der Future mit dem nächstgelegenen Delivery Month gehandelt. Stack Hedging wird angewendet, wenn die für einen Hedge benötigten Laufzeiten nicht handelbar/liquide sind.

Die Kombination von Kauf- und Verkaufskontrakten in unterschiedlichen Laufzeiten auf dasselbe Underlying (für den gleichen Kontrakt) wird im Futuresmarkt üblicherweise als „Intra-Kontraktspread“ bezeichnet. Unter einem Calendar Spread bzw. Time Spread (oder einfach nur „Spread“ bei Futures genannt) ist der gleichzeitige Kauf und Verkauf eines Futures auf dasselbe Underlying, jedoch mit unterschiedlichen Liefertagen zu verstehen. Eine Futures-Butterfly-Strategie beinhaltet den Kauf und Verkauf von jeweils einem (Calendar) Spread mit demselben Volumen.

Als Inter-Kontraktspread wird der gleichzeitige Kauf und Verkauf von Futures mit unterschiedlichen Underlyings bezeichnet. Anders als beim Intra-Kontraktspread sind unterschiedliche Liefertage nicht erforderlich.

3.3. Practice Questions

1. What is true regarding a Forward Rate Agreement?
    a) It swaps capital and interest.
    b) It is a contract on a futures exchange.
    c) It is a forward/forward cash rate.
    d) All answers are false.

2. Which of the following are characteristics of the FRA market?
    a) standardized contract dates
    b) OTC instrument
    c) Interest is paid at maturity.
    d) exchange of capital
    e) The settelement payment is directly related to the difference between interest rates.

3. When is the reference interest rate for a FRA settlement fixed?
    a) Maturity date
    b) Spot date
    c) Settlement date
    d) Fixing date

4. What is the time to maturity of a forward rate agreement?

5. FRABBA terms use a settlement formula under which the cash amount is paid at the beginning of the period in question. Which method is used?
    a) compounding the cash value of the interets differential
    b) discounting the cash value of the interest differential
    c) reinvesting the FRA settlement amount
    d) paying the difference between LIBOR and the FRA rate

6. You buy a 3/6 FRA at 9,62%. What is your motivation?
    a) to speculate on falling rates
    b) to protect against rising rates
    c) to protect against falling rates
    d) All answers are false.

7. If the short -term cash yield curve is positive, the forward cash yield curve is …
    a) positive
    b) flat
    c) negative
    d) positive, flat or negative

8. You have a 6-month liability which you can only cover for three months for balance sheet reasons. Which of the following would best cover the interest rate risk for the remaining three months?
    a) purchase of a 3/6 FRA
    b) sale of a 3/6 FRA
    c) purchase of a 0/6 FRA
    d) sale of a 0/6 FRA

9. Explain the connection between yield curve and forward rates!

3.3. Wiederholungsfragen

1. Was trifft auf ein Forward Rate Agreement zu?
   a) Es tauscht Kapital und Zinsen aus.
   b) Es ist ein Vertrag am Futures Exchange.
   c) Es ist ein Forward/Forward-Kassakurs.
   d) Alle Antworten sind falsch.

2. Was sind Charakteristika des FRA-Marktes?
   a) fixe Kontraktzeitpunkte
   b) OTC-Instrument
   c) endfällige Zinszahlungen
   d) Austausch von Kapital
   e) Die Ausgleichszahlung bewegt sich in direkter Relation zur Differenz der Zinssätze.

3. Wann wird der Referenzzinssatz für ein FRA-Settlement festgelegt?
   a) Maturity Date
   b) Spot Date
   c) Settlement Date
   d) Fixing Date

4. Welchen Zeitraum bezeichnet man als Laufzeit eines Forward Rate Agreements?

5. Was trifft auf das Settlement von FRAs zu?
   a) Die Zinsdifferenz wird aufgezinst.
   b) Die Zinsdifferenz wird abgezinst.
   c) Der FRA-Settlementbetrag wird reinvestiert.
   d) Die Differenz zwischen LIBOR- und FRA-Satz wird am Ende der Laufzeit gezahlt.

6. Sie kaufen ein 3/6 FRA zu 9,62%. Was ist Ihr Beweggrund?
   a) Spekulation auf fallende Zinsen
   b) Absicherung gegen steigende Zinsen
   c) Absicherung gegen fallende Zinsen
   d) Alle Antworten sind falsch.

7. Wenn die Geldmarktzinskurve positiv ist, dann ist die (Geldmarkt-)Forward-Kurve …
   a) positiv
   b) flach
   c) invers
   d) positiv, flach oder invers

8. Sie haben Geld für sechs Monate angelegt und für drei Monate aufgenommen. Wie können Sie Ihr Zinsrisiko absichern?
   a) Kauf 3/6 FRA
   b) Verkauf 3/6 FRA
   c) Kauf 0/6 FRA
   d) Verkauf 0/6 FRA

9. Erklären Sie den Zusammenhang zwischen Zinskurve und FRA-Sätzen!

10. You have made an FRA spread over USD 10,000,000, selling a 1/4 FRA and buying a 3/9 FRA. If you currently have a steep yield curve, which of the following developments would you prefer?
    a) a steepening of the yield curve
    b) a flattening of the yield curve
    c) a parallel downward shift
    d) insufficient information to decide

11. Which strategy is generated by the following position?
    buy 10 m 3/6 FRA
    sell 20 m 6/9 FRA
    buy 10 m 9/12 FRA
    a) butterfly
    b) condor
    c) strip
    d) stack

12. A customer sells a 6/9 USD 10,000,000 FRA at 5.50–55%. If rates rise to 6 5/16%– 6 7/16% at fixing date, what settlement is paid?
    a) The customer pays a settlement based on 93.75 bp.
    b) The customer receives a settlement based on 81.75 bp.
    c) The customer pays a settlement based on 81.75 bp.
    d) The customer receives a settlement based on 93.75 bp.

13. Which of the following statements is true regarding the credit risk of a FRA?
    a) It does not exist.
    b) It comprises the notional amount plus interest.
    c) It is limited to the amount due.
    d) It is applied against the limits from settlement date to maturity date.

14. Which interest rate does a 3-months eurodollar futures price of 92.25 imply?
    a) 7.75
    b) 8.75
    c) 7.25
    d) 8.50

15. Which of the following is true for a 3-months eurodollar futures contract?
    a) It is an exchange-traded product.
    b) It is an OTC instrument.
    c) The future is physically delivered.
    d) The specifications can be adapted to the wishes of the counterparty.

16. Which of the following functions are the responsibility of the clearing house attached to a futures exchange?
    a) It regulates floor practice.
    b) It acts as a counterparty to every trade.
    c) It provides price information.
    d) It introduces new contracts.
    e) It clears all the transactions of a futures exchange.

10. Sie sind einen FRA-Spread eingegangen und haben USD 10 Mio. 1/4 Monate verkauft und USD 10 Mio. 3/9 Monate gekauft. Wovon würden Sie am meisten profitieren, wenn eine steile Zinskurve vorhanden wäre?
    a) von einer steiler werdenden Zinskurve
    b) von einer flacher werdenden Zinskurve
    c) von einer Parallelverschiebung nach unten
    d) nicht genug Informationen, um zu entscheiden

11. Welcher Begriff passt zu folgender Position?
    Kauf 10 Mio. 3/6 FRA
    Verkauf 20 Mio. 6/9 FRA
    Kauf 10 Mio. 9/12 FRA
    a) Butterfly
    b) Kondor
    c) Strip
    d) Stack

12. Ein Kunde verkauft ein 10 Mio. 6/9 FRA mit der Quotierung 5,50–5,55. Die Zinssätze steigen auf 6 1/4–6 3/8% am Fixing Date. Welche Ausgleichszahlung findet statt?
    a) Der Kunde zahlt auf der Basis von 87,5 BP.
    b) Der Kunde zahlt auf der Basis von 75 BP.
    c) Der Kunde erhält eine Zahlung basierend auf 75 BP.
    d) Der Kunde erhält eine Zahlung basierend auf 87,5 BP.

13. Was stimmt bezogen auf das Ausfallsrisiko bei FRAs?
    a) Es existiert nicht.
    b) Es umfasst Nominalbetrag und Zinsen.
    c) Es umfasst nur die Ausgleichszahlung.
    d) Es wird vom Settlement Date bis zum Maturity Date den Limits angerechnet.

14. Welchen Zinssatz impliziert ein Preis von 92,25 für einen 3-Monats-Eurodollar-Future?
    a) 7,75
    b) 8,75
    c) 7,25
    d) 8,50

15. Welche der folgenden Eigenschaften treffen auf 3-Monats-Eurodollar-Future zu?
    a) Er ist ein börsengehandeltes Produkt.
    b) Er ist ein OTC-Instrument.
    c) Der Future wird physisch geliefert.
    d) Die Spezifikationen können an die Wünsche der Gegenpartei angepasst werden.

16. Welche der folgenden Funktionen erfüllt das Clearing House?
    a) Es reguliert die Usancen am Händlerparkett.
    b) Es agiert als Geschäftspartner in jedem Geschäft.
    c) Es stellt Preisinformationen zur Verfügung.
    d) Es führt neue Kontrakte ein.
    e) Es rechnet alle Geschäfte an einer Futuresbörse ab.

17. What is a tick?
   a) 1/10 of one percentage point
   b) one per cent of nominal value
   c) 1/100 of one per cent of nominal value
   d) minimum price movement of a futures contract

18. What is meant by open interest?

19. What is meant by "theoretical basis"?
   a) difference between the actual futures rate and the fair forward rate
   b) difference between the fair forward rate and the actual cash rate
   c) difference between the fair forward rate and the actual market rate
   d) All answers are false.

20. The simple basis is …
   a) the simplest method to calculate the futures price.
   b) the difference between the actual cash rate and the fair future price.
   c) the difference between the implied forward rate of the actual future price and the actual cash rate.
   d) There is no simple basis.

21. What is the value basis?

22. How is the initial margin on a futures contract calculated?
   a) revaluation against the weighted average price
   b) a fixed margin per contract
   c) revaluation against LIBOR fixing
   d) revaluation against the closing price on the exchange

23. How is the variation margin on a futures contract normally calculated?
   a) against LIBOR fixing
   b) as a fixed margin per contract
   c) against the weighted average price
   d) against the closing price on the exchange

24. What does the term "strip hedging" stand for?
   a) hedge of an interest rate swap using a cap
   b) hedging of a FRA using series of MM futures
   c) hedging of a series of MM futures using a FRA
   d) partial hedge of a FRA using a diminishing hedge position
   e) hedging of FRAs using futures with the next delivery month

25. What does the term "stack hedging" stand for?

17. Was ist ein Tick?
   a) 1/10 von 1 Prozent
   b) 1 Prozent des Nominalwertes
   c) 1/100 von einem Prozent des Nominalwertes
   d) Mindestpreisbewegung eines Futureskontraktes

18. Was bezeichnet man als Open Interest?

19. Was versteht man unter der „theoretischen Basis"?
   a) Differenz zwischen dem implizierten Futures-Satz und dem theoretischen Preis (aus fwd-fwd gerechnet)
   b) Differenz zwischen dem rechnerischen Forward-Satz und dem aktuellen Cash-Satz
   c) Differenz zwischen dem Forward-Satz gerechnet aus dem aktuellen Cash-Satz und dem aktuellen Marktpreis
   d) Alle Antworten sind falsch.

20. Die einfache Basis ist …
   a) die einfachste Methode den Futures-Preis zu berechnen.
   b) die Differenz zwischen dem aktuellen Cash-Satz und dem Futures-Preis gerechnet aus dem Forward-Satz.
   c) die Differenz zwischen dem Satz gerechnet aus dem Futures-Marktpreis und dem aktuellen Cash-Satz.
   d) Es gibt keine einfache Basis.

21. Was versteht man unter Wert-Basis?

22. Wie wird die Initial Margin auf einen Futureskontrakt berechnet?
   a) Bewertung gegen einen gewichteten Durchschnittspreis
   b) als fixer Einschuss pro Kontrakt
   c) Bewertung gegen das LIBOR-Fixing
   d) Bewertung gegen den Schlusspreis an der Börse

23. Wie wird die Variation Margin auf einen Futureskontrakt normalerweise berechnet?
   a) gegen das LIBOR-Fixing
   b) als fixer Einschuss pro Kontrakt
   c) gegen einen gewichteten Durchschnittspreis
   d) gegen den Schlusskurs an der Börse

24. Wofür steht der Begriff „Strip Hedging"?
   a) Absicherung eines Zinsswaps mit einem Cap
   b) Absicherung eines FRAs mit einer Serie von MM-Futures
   c) Absicherung einer Serie von MM-Futures mit einem FRA
   d) teilweise Absicherung eines FRAs mit einem immer kleiner werdenden Hedge
   e) Absicherung eines FRAs mittels Futures mit dem nächstgelegenen Delivery Month

25. Wofür steht der Begriff „Stack Hedging"?

26. You would like to hedge a bought FRA with a term of four months and the IMM settlement date of June 17th using futures. What do you have to consider?
    a) a stub and a tail
    b) a tail
    c) a stub
    d) All answers are false.

27. Which positions are subject to convexity effects?
    a) bought FRAs
    b) bought futures
    c) sold FRAs
    d) sold futures

28. What does the term hedge ratio mean when applied to the hedge of a FRA position using MM futures?
    a) ratio of futures volume to FRA volume
    b) ratio between the reference rate and the forward rate to be applied
    c) extent of the hedge against future interest rate movements
    d) ratio of the initial margin to the futures volume

29. What is an intra-contract spread?

30. What is an inter-contract spread?

31. You believe that a positive yield will steepen. Which futures position should you take?
    a) buy a near contract
    b) buy a far contract
    c) buy a near contract and buy a far contract
    d) sell a near contract and buy a far contract

32. You sold a MAR future and would like to roll over this position for three more months. What do you do?
    a) buy a butterfly
    b) buy a calendar spread
    c) sell a butterfly
    d) sell a calendar spread

26. Sie möchten einen gekauften FRA mit vier Monaten Laufzeit und dem IMM-Settle-
    ment-Datum 17.6. mit Futures hedgen. Was ist dabei zu berücksichtigen?
    a) ein Stub und ein Tail
    b) ein Tail
    c) ein Stub
    d) Alle Antworten sind falsch.

27. Bei welchen Positionen treten Konvexitätseffekte auf?
    a) gekaufte FRAs
    b) gekaufte Futures
    c) verkaufte FRAs
    d) verkaufte Futures

28. Worauf bezieht sich der Begriff Hedge Ratio bei der Absicherung einer FRA-Position
    mittels MM-Futures?
    a) Verhältnis des Futures-Volumens zum FRA-Volumen
    b) Verhältnis des Referenzzinssatzes zum anzuwendenden Forward-Satz
    c) Ausmaß der Absicherung gegen zukünftige Zinsschwankungen
    d) Verhältnis der an der Börse hinterlegten Sicherheit (Initial Margin) zum Fu-
       ture/Forward-Volumen

29. Was ist ein Intra-Kontraktspread?

30. Was ist ein Inter-Kontraktspread?

31. Sie glauben, dass eine positive Zinskurve steiler wird. Welche Futurespositionen soll-
    ten Sie nehmen?
    a) Kauf eines Kontraktes vorne
    b) Kauf eines Kontraktes hinten
    c) Kauf eines Kontraktes vorne und Verkauf eines Kontraktes hinten
    d) Verkauf eines Kontraktes vorne und Kauf eines Kontraktes hinten

32. Sie haben einen MAR-Futures verkauft und möchten diesen um drei Monate weiter-
    rollen. Was machen Sie nun?
    a) Kauf Butterfly
    b) Kauf Calendar Spread
    c) Verkauf Butterfly
    d) Verkauf Calendar Spread

4. Repurchase Agreements (Repos)

In this chapter you learn ...

- what a repurchase agreement is.
- about the three types in the repo market.
- what legal framework regarding legal status and risk and return on collateral has to be considered when dealing with repos
- which types of repos are used regarding the term.
- how repos are quoted.
- which terminology is used for repos.
- what is meant by a cash-driven and a security-driven repo.
- what is meant by general collateral and special collateral.
- about the most important market participants in the repo market.
- what an initial margin is and how it is calculated.
- what a variation margin is and how it is calculated.
- which three basic alternatives for custody of collateral exist.
- what is meant by the right of substitution.
- what is meant by sell/buy-backs/buy/sell-backs and how they are calculated.
- which frame contracts are used for repos and which regulations they contain.
- which risks occur in dealing with repos and how they can be reduced.
- which special types of repos are used.
- what is meant by a synthetic repo.
- what is meant by security lending.

4.1. Common Definition

4.1.1. Structure of Contract

A repo (**Sale and Repurchase agreement**) is a contract under which the seller

- commits to sell securities to the buyer (alternativ term: to repo out securities) and
- simultaneously commits to repurchase the same (or similar) securities from the buyer at a later date (maturity date), repaying the original sum of money plus a return for the use of that money over the term of the repo.

4. Repurchase Agreements (Repos)

In diesem Kapitel lernen Sie ...

- was man unter Repurchase Agreements versteht.
- welche drei Varianten im Repomarkt unterschieden werden.
- welche rechtlichen Grundlagen bezüglich rechtlichen und wirtschaftlichen Eigentums beim Abschluss eines Repos beachtet werden müssen.
- welche Arten von Repos bezüglich Laufzeit verwendet werden.
- wie Repos quotiert werden.
- welche Terminologien im Zusammenhang mit Repos verwendet werden.
- was man unter einem Cash-getriebenen bzw. Wertpapier-getriebenen Repo versteht.
- was man unter General Collateral bzw. Special Collateral versteht.
- die wichtigsten Marktteilnehmer im Repomarkt kennen.
- was man unter Initial Margin versteht und wie diese berechnet wird.
- was man unter Variation Margin versteht und wie diese berechnet wird.
- welche Möglichkeiten zur Verwahrung der Collaterals unterschieden werden.
- was man unter dem Recht zur Substitution versteht.
- was man unter Sell/Buy-Backs/Buy/Sell-Backs versteht und wie diese berechnet werden.
- welche Rahmenverträge bei Repos anwendbar sind und welche Regelungen diese enthalten.
- welche Risiken beim Repogeschäft auftreten können und wie diese reduziert werden können.
- welche Sonderformen von Repos verwendet werden.
- was man unter einem synthetischen Repo versteht.
- was man unter Security Lending versteht.

4.1. Allgemeines

4.1.1. Kontraktstruktur

Ein Repo (**Sale and Repurchase Agreement**) ist ein Vertrag, bei dem der Verkäufer

- Wertpapiere an den Käufer verkauft und
- sich gleichzeitig verpflichtet, dieselben (oder ähnliche) Wertpapiere zu einem späteren Zeitpunkt zurückzukaufen, wobei er den gleichen Preis wie beim ursprünglichen Verkauf zuzüglich Zinsen für den für die Laufzeit des Repos erhaltenen Cash-Betrag zahlt.

Repo steht also für Sale and Repurchase Agreement. Die deutsche Bezeichnung dafür ist **Pensionsgeschäft**, das auch als **befristete Überlassung von Wertpapieren** beschrieben werden kann.

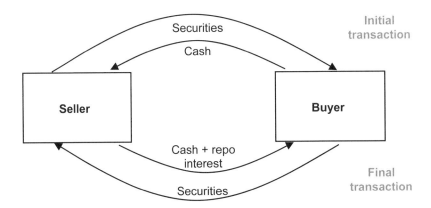

As the graphic shows, there are **two legs to a repo transaction:**

- On the value date, the repo seller sells securities (collateral) to the buyer for an agreed sum of money (initial transaction)
- At maturity, the seller
  - repurchases the securities for the original sum, and
  - pays a return for the use of the cash proceeds during the term of the repo.

Please note that the securities are only running through, i.e. at maturity the securities of the initial transaction are just delivered back.

Depending on which way you look at it, the repo is either

- a mechanism for borrowing/lending funds on a secured basis or
- a method of borrowing/lending securities against cash.

In the market, **three types** of repos are generally differentiated:

- **Classic repo (US-style repo)**
  Both transactions are conducted under the same frame contract.
- **Sell/buy-back (resp. buy/sell-back)**
  Economically sell/buy-backs have the same result as classic repos. Legally, however, both transactions in a sell/buy-back are conducted under two different contracts.
- **Security lending**
  Two securities are swapped for a certain period of time. It is also possible to lend one security without secured basis.

We shall focus the discussion on classic repos; in the sections for sell/buy-backs and security lending we will only explain the differences between the three types.

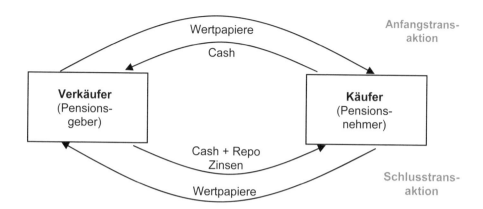

Wie die Grafik zeigt, besteht ein Repo aus **zwei Transaktionen:**

- Zum Valutadatum verkauft der Verkäufer die Wertpapiere (das Collateral) an den Käufer zu einem vereinbarten Betrag (Anfangstransaktion).
- Bei Fälligkeit
  - kauft der Verkäufer die Wertpapiere zum ursprünglichen Betrag wieder zurück und
  - zahlt an den Käufer Zinsen für den Cashbetrag, den er für die Laufzeit des Repos erhalten hat.

Beachten Sie, dass das Wertpapier dabei nur durchläuft, d.h., am Ende werden die Wertpapiere der Anfangstransaktion einfach wieder zurückgeliefert.

De facto sind Repos daher – je nachdem von welcher Seite man sie betrachtet – entweder

- ein wertpapierbesicherter Kredit (bzw. Anlage) oder
- eine Wertpapierleihe gegen Cash.

Im Markt werden grundsätzlich **drei Varianten** unterschieden:

- **Klassisches Repo** (US-style Repo)
  Bei dieser Art werden beide Transaktionen unter einem gemeinsamen Rahmenvertrag abgeschlossen.
- **Sell/Buy-Back** (bzw. Buy/Sell-Back)
  Wirtschaftlich führen Sell/Buy-Backs zum gleichen Ergebnis wie klassische Repos. In rechtlicher Hinsicht unterscheiden sie sich insofern, als jede der beiden Transaktionen einen rechtlich eigenständigen Vertrag darstellt.
- **Security Lending** (Wertpapierleihe)
  Hier werden zwei Wertpapiere für eine bestimmte Dauer getauscht. Auch die Leihe ohne Besicherung durch ein anderes Wertpapier ist möglich.

In der Folge konzentrieren wir uns auf die Darstellung von klassischen Repos. In den Abschnitten über Sell/Buy-Backs und Wertpapierleihe gehen wir dann nur noch auf die Unterschiede dazu ein.

4.1.2. Legal framework

4.1.2.1. Legal status

The collateral in a repo is not pledged but sold to the buyer (= gives cash). As a consequence the **collateral passes from the seller to the buyer**, i.e. legal title is transferred for the term of the repo.

If the collateral was only pledged, as in a secured loan, the buyer would not be allowed to liquidate the collateral immediately upon a default by the seller but would have to wait until insolvency proceedings were completed which could take a long time. Moreover, the buyer may have to defend his rights to the collateral in court against claims by other creditors.

In comparison with pledged collateral, collateral sold through a repo is therefore exposed to much less legal risk.

Transferring legal title to the collateral does also allows the buyer to use repo elsewhere, e.g. to cover a short position in securities or to enter into another repo.

Transferring legal title to collateral does not imply that repo is a sale and repurchase of identical securities, as the repo buyer will not necessarily be able to return securities with the same identification numbers (e.g. he has used them in another repo). This is why repo is defined as a sale and repurchase of "the same or similar securities" and thus, in some contracts, the buyer has the right to return substitute securities within certain broad parameters.

4.1.2.2. Risk and Return on Collateral

Although legal title to collateral in a repo is transferred to the buyer, the commitment of the seller to repurchase the collateral at the original value means that the risk and return on the collateral remain with the seller. Thus the **economic ownership stays with the seller.**

If the value of the collateral falls during the term of the repo – as a result of a fall in its price or because the issuer defaults – the seller repurchases it at its original (higher) value, so he makes a loss.

If the value of the collateral rises during the term of the repo, the seller repurchases the collateral at its original (lower) value, so he makes a profit.

Therefore, the seller retains all the economic risk on the collateral, even though the buyer becomes the legal owner during the term of the repo.

Since the seller retains all the risks on the collateral, he is also entitled to keep the return. In the case of repoed bonds, this includes the coupon interest which accrues over the term of a repo.

4.1.2. Rechtliche Grundlagen

4.1.2.1. Rechtliches Eigentum

Das Wertpapier dient im Repo als Besicherung (englisch: „collateral"). Zu diesem Zweck wird es jedoch nicht verpfändet, sondern an den Käufer (= Pensionsnehmer, Cashgeber) verkauft. **Im Repo wechselt also das rechtliche Eigentum** am Wertpapier für die Laufzeit des Repos.

Dies hat für den Käufer den Vorteil, dass er bei einem Ausfall des Partners (Default Event), keine Ansprüche auf das Wertpapier mehr geltend zu machen braucht, sondern bereits legaler Eigentümer des Wertpapieres ist. Er kann dadurch bei einem Default Event das Wertpapier sofort verkaufen.

Wäre die Sicherheit nur verpfändet – wie dies z.B. bei einem herkömmlichen Wertpapier-besicherten Kredit (Lombardkredit) der Fall ist –, so wäre der Käufer im Falle eines Default Events nicht automatisch berechtigt, die Wertpapiere sofort zu liquidieren, sondern müsste warten, bis das Insolvenzverfahren abgeschlossen wäre, was eine lange Zeit in Anspruch nehmen kann. Zusätzlich müsste der Schuldner möglicherweise seine Rechte erst gegen andere Gläubiger durchsetzen.

Verglichen mit einer Verpfändung von Wertpapieren ist ein Repo daher einem wesentlich geringeren Risiko ausgesetzt.

Der Übergang des rechtlichen Eigentums versetzt den Käufer in die Lage, das Collateral anderweitig zu verwenden, z.B. eine Short-Position im Wertpapier zu covern oder ein weiteres Repo damit einzugehen.

Der Transfer des rechtlichen Eigentums bedeutet jedoch nicht notwendigerweise, dass in einem Repo immer genau identische Wertpapiere verkauft und gekauft werden müssen. Möglicherweise ist der Käufer nicht in der Lage, ein Wertpapier mit genau derselben Wertpapiernummer zurückzuliefern (z.B. weil er es in einem anderen Repo verwendet hat). Darum ist ein Repo als Verkauf und Kauf von „denselben oder ähnlichen Wertpapieren" definiert. Es kann daher auch vereinbart werden, dass der Käufer in der Schlusstransaktion ersatzweise ähnliche, jedoch bestimmte Parameter erfüllende Wertpapiere zurückliefern darf.

4.1.2.2. Wirtschaftliches Eigentum

Obwohl das rechtliche Eigentum vom Verkäufer auf den Käufer übergeht, verbleiben die wirtschaftlichen Risiken beim ursprünglichen Verkäufer, da er sich ja verpflichtet, das Collateral zum gleichen Preis wieder zurückzukaufen. Man sagt daher: **Das wirtschaftliche Eigentum verbleibt beim Verkäufer.**

Fällt der Kurs der Anleihe (oder geht der Emittent gar bankrott), so muss er sie trotzdem zum ursprünglichen (höheren) Preis wieder zurücknehmen, er macht dadurch also einen Verlust. Steigt der Kurs der Anleihe hingegen, so macht er einen Gewinn, weil er sie ja zum niedrigeren Kurs der Anfangstransaktion wieder zurückerhält.

Da der Verkäufer das wirtschaftliche Risiko behält, steht ihm – als wirtschaftlichem Eigentümer – auch der Ertrag aus dem Collateral zu. Im Falle von Anleihen betrifft das die Kuponzinsen. Diese fallen in Form der Stückzinsen, die sich über die Repolaufzeit angesammelt haben, dem Verkäufer am Ende des Repos automatisch zu.

If a coupon is paid on a bond collateral during the term of a repo, it will actually be paid to the repo buyer, who is the legal owner during the term of the repo. However, under the terms of the repo contract, the buyer is required to make an equivalent cash payment to the seller. This payment is called a **manufactured dividend**.

4.1.3. Types of repos regarding the term

The value date (start date) for a repo transaction in a particular currency will typically be the same as the conventional value date in the interbank deposits market in the same currency, i.e. two working days after the trade date. Forward value dates are also available.

Regarding the **term**, the following types can be differentiated:

- **Open repo or demand repo**
  which is rolled over at the same rate until one of the counterparties decides to terminate the transaction.
- **Short-dated repo**
  which is for a term of less than one month (most commonly, on an overnight basis). According to an ISMA survey in 2004 this is the case for about 2/3 of all repos.
- **Term repo**
  which is negotiated for a fixed term longer than one month.

4.1.4. Quotation

Repos are quoted on a **p.a. basis** (like interbank deposits). The repo interest rate is **calculated according to the relevant money market convention**, i.e. act/360 resp. act/365 for GBP. The repo terminology, however, is based on the securities side of the deal.

The seller sells the securities in the initial transaction (sale and repurchase) and takes cash.

The buyer of the repo is the party that purchases the bond in the first leg and gives cash. This is also called a **reverse repo**.

Repo   → sell securities = take cash
Reverse repo → buy securities = give cash

According to this convention the bid rate is higher than the offer rate (e.g. 3.28–25%).

The market maker buys the bond at the bid rate (i.e. he lends money at the higher side of the quote) and sells it at the offer rate (i.e. borrows money on the lower side of the quote).

Note: Also the opposite quotation is possible (bid < offer). However, the market user will always take cash at the higher rate and give cash at the lower rate (and vice versa for the market maker). In this case you should first define if you take or give cash and if you act as market maker or market user. Then decide which rate is used after checking both sides of the quotation.

Findet jedoch während des Repos eine Kuponzahlung statt, so wird diese zuerst an den rechtlichen Eigentümer, d.h. den Käufer, gezahlt. Dieser ist jedoch verpflichtet, den Kupon sofort an den wirtschaftlichen Eigentümer (Verkäufer) weiterzuleiten. Diese Zahlung wird **manufactured dividend** genannt.

4.1.3. Arten von Repos

Das Valutadatum (Startdatum) entspricht üblicherweise der Konvention im Interbank-Depotmarkt für die entsprechende Währung, liegt also meist zwei Banktage nach dem Handelstag. Es sind jedoch auch Forward-Repos im Markt üblich.

Bezüglich der **Laufzeit** können folgende Arten unterschieden werden:

- **Open Repo** (auch Demand Repo)
  Dieses wird täglich zum gleichen Satz weitergerollt, bis es eine der beiden Parteien beendet, d.h., es läuft bis auf Weiteres.
- **Short dated Repo**
  Hiermit sind fix vereinbarte Laufzeiten bis zu einem Monat gemeint; nach einer Erhebung der ISMA in 2004 trifft das auf ca. 2/3 der Repos zu, ein Großteil davon wird auf Overnight-Basis abgeschlossen.
- **Term Repo**
  Fix vereinbarte Laufzeiten über einen Monat.

4.1.4. Quotierung

Repos werden **in Zinsen p.a.** (analog Interbank-Depots) quotiert. Die Repo-Zinsen werden **analog den entsprechenden Usancen im Geldmarkt** berechnet, also ACT/360 bzw. ACT/365 bei GBP. Im Repo-Markt ist die Terminologie im Gegensatz zu klassischen Interbank-Depots von der Wertpapierseite dominiert. Der Verkäufer im Repo verkauft die Anleihe in der Anfangstransaktion (sale and repurchase) und erhält dafür den Cashbetrag. Der Käufer im Repo hingegen kauft die Anleihe und gibt dafür Cash, er macht also eine umgekehrte Repotransaktion. Man spricht daher auch von einem **Reverse Repo.**

Repo   → Anleihe verkaufen (Pensionsgeber) = Cash nehmen
Reverse Repo → Anleihe kaufen (Pensionsnehmer)   = Cash geben

Durch diese Usance gibt es im Repo-Markt „englische Quotierungen" – d.h., die Geldseite ist höher als die Briefseite (z.B. 3,28–25).

Der Market Maker kauft auf der Geldseite seiner Quotierung die Anleihe (= gibt Cash auf der höheren Seite der Quotierung) und verkauft auf der von ihm quotierten Briefseite die Anleihe (= nimmt Cash auf dem niedrigeren Satz).

Anmerkung: Es kann auch vorkommen, dass – entgegen der beschriebenen Konvention – anders quotiert wird (Geld < Brief). Es wird jedoch immer der Market User auf dem höheren Satz Cash nehmen und auf dem niedrigeren Satz Cash geben (und umgekehrt für den Market Maker). In diesem Fall sollten Sie zuerst feststellen, ob Sie Cash nehmen oder geben und ob Sie als Market Maker oder Market User agieren. Entscheiden Sie erst dann, welcher Zinssatz zur Anwendung kommt, nachdem Sie beide Seiten der Quotierung betrachtet haben.

Example

You are quoted the following repo rates: 3.30–3.25%
On the bid side – as Market User – you can sell the bond and thus pay 3.30% for the cash you take. On the offer side you "buy" the bond and receive 3.25% on the cash you give to the seller.

4.2. Application of Repos

As already described, repo usually has two major uses:

- cash-driven: lending cash against securities
- security-driven: lending securities against cash

4.2.1. Cash-driven Repo

Today, this is the most common type. The repo is used as a money market instrument like a classic interbank deposit. Thus, the focus is on the cash. The main difference to interbank deposits is the **collateral**. For the borrower of cash this results in a lower refinancing rate. The lender of the cash can profit from the reduced credit risk.

Example

Classic repo – cash-driven

A bond trader holds EUR 10 m of 5 ½ German government bond due 14th August 2013. The actual clean price is 108.27. For the refinancing of the bond position he needs 10 m cash for 1 month (30 days), i.e. he repos out the bond. Spot value is 14th November and a repo trader quotes him 3.27–3.25% for one month.

The bond trader enters into the following repo:

Repo seller: bond trader
Repo buyer: repo trader
Collateral: 5 1/2% Fed. Republic of Germany 14th Aug. 2013 (ACT/ACT)
Clean price: 108.27
Accrued interest: 92 days
Accrued interest: 1.3863014 (5.5 x 92/365)
Dirty price: 109.6563014
Repo rate: 3.27%
Term: 30 days

Beispiel

Folgender Repo-Satz wird Ihnen quotiert: 3,30–3,25%
Auf der Geldseite können Sie – als Market User – die Anleihe verkaufen und zahlen
damit 3,30% für den erhaltenen Cash-Betrag (= genommenes Depot). Auf der Briefseite „kaufen" Sie die Anleihe und erhalten damit 3,25% für den gegebenen Cash-Betrag (= gegebenes Depot).

4.2. Anwendung von Repos

Wie bereits dargestellt, gibt es grundsätzlich zwei treibende Faktoren für Repos:

- Cash-getriebene: wertpapierbesicherter Kredit/Anlage
- Wertpapier-getriebene: Wertpapierleihe gegen Cash

4.2.1. Repo als wertpapierbesicherter Kredit (Cash-getrieben)

Das Cash-getriebene Repo ist heute die häufigste Anwendungsart. Das Repo wird hier
als Money-Market-Instrument wie ein normales Interbank-Depot verwendet. Im Vordergrund steht dabei also das Cash. Der wesentliche Unterschied zu Interbank-Depots besteht in der **zusätzlichen Besicherung durch das Collateral.** Für den Cashnehmer bedeutet das einen niedrigeren Finanzierungszinssatz. Der Cashgeber profitiert vom verringerten Kreditrisiko.

Beispiel

Klassisches Repo – Cash-getrieben

Ein Bondhändler hält EUR 10 Mio. 5 1/2% Deutsche Bundesanleihen 14.08.2013. Der
aktuelle Clean Price ist 108,27. Zur Refinanzierung der Anleiheposition braucht er
EUR 10 Mio. Cash für 1 Monat (30 Tage). Spot Valuta ist der 14. November, und ein
Repohändler quotiert ihm 3,27–3,25% für einen Monat.

Der Bondhändler schließt folgendes Repo ab:

Repo-Verkäufer:	Bondhändler
Repo-Käufer:	Repohändler
Collateral:	5 1/2% Bundesrepublik Deutschland 14.08.2013 (ACT/ACT)
Clean Price:	108,27
Stückzinstage:	92
Stückzinsen:	1,3863014 (5,5 x 92 / 365)
Dirty Price:	109,6563014 (CP plus Stückzinsen)
Reposatz:	3,27%
Laufzeit:	30 Tage

The bond trader needs exactly EUR 10 m (cash-driven). Instead he has to deliver collateral with a current market value of also EUR 10 m.

Initial transaction cash: EUR 10,000,000.00
Initial transaction bond: EUR 9,119,402.96 (10,000,000 / 109.6563014 / 100)

The bond trader sells the bond in the repo and takes the cash. Therefore he sells on the bid side at 3.27%.

Repo interest: EUR 27,250.00   (10,000,000 x 0.0327 x 30/360)
Final transaction cash: EUR 10,027,250.00 (10,000,000 + 27,250.00)
Final transaction bond: EUR 9,119,402.96

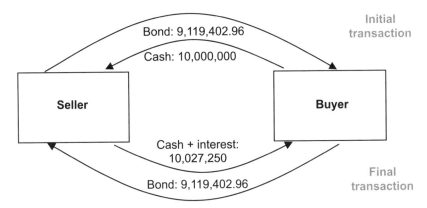

The graphic shows that in a cash-driven repo, the main difference to interbank deposits is the collateral. For the calculation of the nominal amount of the collateral one has to consider that the bond's market value (= dirty price) equals the borrowed cash amount. To the repo buyer it does not matter what bond is used as long as certain quality criteria are guaranteed. Therefore you also speak of a so-called general collateral (opposite to special collateral). At maturity the collateral is transferred back, the seller (cash borrower) pays back the cash amount plus repo interest to the buyer (cash lender).

Der Bondhändler braucht genau EUR 10 Mio. (Cash-getrieben). Dafür muss er Collateral mit einem aktuellen Marktwert von ebenfalls EUR 10 Mio. als Sicherheit liefern.

Anfangstransaktion Cash: EUR 10.000.000,00
Anfangstransaktion WP: EUR 9.119.402,96 (10.000.000 / (109,6563014 / 100))

Der Bondhändler verkauft die Anleihe im Repo und nimmt Cash. Er handelt daher auf der Geldseite zu 3,27%.

Repo-Zinsen: EUR 27.250,00   (10.000.000 x 0,0327 x 30/360)
Schlusstransaktion Cash: EUR 10.027.250,00 (10.000.000 + 27.250,00)
Schlusstransaktion WP: EUR 9.119.402,96

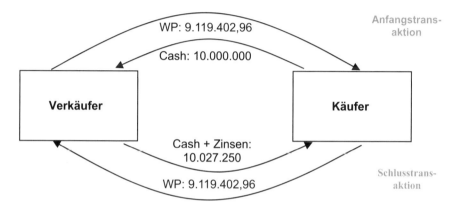

In der Grafik kann man erkennen, dass bei einem Cash-getriebenen Repo der einzige Unterschied zu einem Interbank Depot im Austausch des Collaterals liegt. Bei der Berechnung des Nominalbetrages des Collaterals ist nur das Prinzip zu beachten, dass der Marktwert des Wertpapiers (= Dirty Price) dem geliehenen Cashbetrag entspricht. Welches Wertpapier dazu verwendet wird, ist dem Pensionsnehmer egal, solange es bestimmte Qualitätskriterien erfüllt. Man spricht daher auch von einem sogenannten **General Collateral** (im Gegensatz zu einem **Special Collateral**). Am Ende der Laufzeit wird das Collateral zurückübertragen, und der Verkäufer (Cashnehmer) zahlt den Kapitalbetrag zuzüglich der Repozinsen an den Käufer (Cashgeber).

Zusammenfassend werden für ein Cash-getriebenes Repo also folgende Berechnungen benötigt:

Classic repo – cash-driven

Initial transaction:

Cash amount: specified

Bond nominal amount: $$\frac{\frac{\text{cash initial transaction}}{\text{dirty price}}}{100}$$

Final transaction:

Cash amount: $$\text{cash initial transaction} \times \left(1 + \text{repo rate} \times \frac{\text{days}}{\text{basis}}\right)$$

Bond nominal amount: nominal of the initial transaction

4.2.2. Security-driven Repo

Repos do not necessarily have to be cash-driven; they can also be used for a temporary security lending. Contrary to a normal security lending the collateral is no other security but cash.

Why is security lending needed? Assuming a bond trader expects the price of a certain bond to fall. In order to profit from that fall he will sell this bond (go short) and buy it back on a later date at a hopefully fallen price. When selling the bond he has to deliver the bond physically – but he does not have it yet. By means of a reverse repo he can borrow the bond for a certain period of time (= buy bond against cash value spot and simultaneously sell bond at a later date).

Example
Classic repo – security-driven A bond trader expects the German government bonds to fall. Therefore he goes short EUR 10 m of the 5 1/2% Federal Republic of Germany 14th August 2013. The actual clean price is 108.27. In order to cover the short position he enters into a 1-month reverse repo (30 days), i.e. he needs to reverse in the bond. Spot value is 14th November and a repo trader quotes him 3.27–3.25% for one month. Repo seller: repo trader Repo buyer: bond trader Collateral: 5 1/2% Fed. Republic of Germany 14th Aug. 2013 (ACT/ACT) Clean price: 108.27 Accrued interest: 92 days Accrued interest: 1.3863014 (5.5 x 92/365) Dirty price: 109.6563014 Repo rate: 3.25% Term: 30 days The bond trader needs exactly EUR 10 m of the bond nominal (security-driven). Instead he has to give cash to the extent of the current market value.

Klassisches Repo – Cash-getrieben:

Anfangstransaktion:

Cashbetrag: vorgegeben

WP-Nominale: $\dfrac{\text{Cash Anfangstransaktion}}{\left(\dfrac{\text{Dirty Price}}{100}\right)}$

Schlusstransaktion:

Cashbetrag: $\text{Cash Anfangstransaktion} \times \left(1 + \text{Repozins} * \dfrac{\text{Tage}}{\text{Basis}}\right)$

WP-Nominale: Nominale der Anfangstransaktion

4.2.2. Repo als Wertpapierleihe gegen Cash (Wertpapier-getrieben)

Betrachtet man ein Repo nicht von der Cash-Seite, sondern andersherum, so kann es auch zur vorübergehenden Leihe eines bestimmten Wertpapiers verwendet werden. Im Unterschied zur normalen Wertpapierleihe gibt der Pensionsnehmer kein anderes Wertpapier als Sicherheit, sondern Cash.

Wozu wird eine Wertpapierleihe benötigt? Betrachten wir einmal den Fall eines Bondhändlers. Angenommen er erwartet, dass der Kurs einer ganz bestimmten Anleihe fallen wird. Um davon zu profitieren, wird er diese Anleihe verkaufen (short gehen) und zu einem späteren Zeitpunkt – zu einem hoffentlich niedrigeren Kurs – wieder zurückkaufen. Beim Verkauf muss er die Anleihe, die er noch gar nicht hat, jedoch physisch liefern. Durch ein Reverse Repo kann er das Wertpapier vorübergehend leihen (= Kauf Anleihe gegen Cash in der Kassa und gleichzeitiger Verkauf zu einem späteren Termin).

Beispiel

Klassisches Repo – Wertpapier-getrieben

Ein Bondhändler erwartet, dass die deutschen Bundesanleihen im Preis fallen werden. Darum geht er EUR 10 Mio. 5 1/2% Bund 14.08.2013 short. Der aktuelle Clean Price ist 108,27. Um die Short-Position einzudecken, macht er ein Reverse Repo für 1 Monat (30 Tage), d.h., er kauft und verkauft. Spot Valuta ist der 14. November, und ein Repohändler quotiert ihm 3,27–3,25% für einen Monat.

Repo-Verkäufer: Repohändler
Repo-Käufer: Bondhändler
Collateral: 5 1/2% Bundesrepublik Deutschland 14.08.2013 (ACT/ACT)
Clean Price: 108,27
Stückzinstage: 92
Stückzinsen: 1,3863014 (5,5 x 92/365)
Dirty Price: 109,6563014 (= CP plus Stückzinsen)
Reposatz: 3,25%
Laufzeit: 30 Tage

Der Bondhändler braucht genau ein Nominale von EUR 10 Mio. des geshorteten Bund (Wertpapier-getrieben). Dafür muss er Cash im Ausmaß des aktuellen Marktwertes liefern.

Initial transaction cash: EUR 10,965,630.14 (10,000,000 x 109.65630137/100)
Initial transaction bond: EUR 10,000,000.00

The bond trader buys the bond in the repo and gives cash. Therefore he buys on the offer side at 3.25%.

Repo interest: EUR 29,698.58   (10,965,630.14 x 0.0325 x 30/360)
Final transaction cash: EUR 10,995,328.72 (10,965,630.14 + 29,698.58)
Final transaction bond: EUR 10,000,000.00

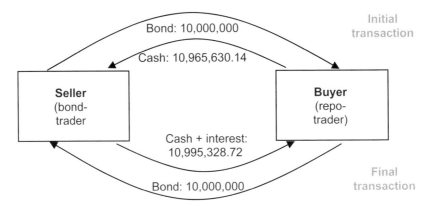

For a security-driven repo the basis is the bond nominal and not a specific cash amount. The initial cash amount then is the actual market value (dirty price) of the collateral. In the final transaction the collateral is transferred back, and for the cash amount repo interest is added to the initial amount.

Classic repo – security-driven

Initial transaction:

Cash amount: $\text{bond nominal} \times \dfrac{\text{dirty price}}{100}$

Bond nominal: specified

Final transaction:

Cash amount: $\text{cash initial transaction} \times \left(1 + \text{repo rate} \times \dfrac{\text{days}}{\text{basis}}\right)$

Bond nominal: nominal of the initial transaction

Anfangstransaktion Cash: EUR 10.965.630,14 (10.000.000 x 109,65630137/100)
Anfangstransaktion WP: EUR 10.000.000,00

Der Bondhändler kauft die Anleihe im Repo und gibt Cash. Als Market User handelt er daher auf der Briefseite zu 3,25%.

Repo-Zinsen: EUR 29.698,58 (10.965.630,14 x 0,0325 x 30/360)
Schlusstransaktion Cash: EUR 10.995.328,72 (10.965.630,14 + 29.698,58)
Schlusstransaktion WP: EUR 10.000.000,00

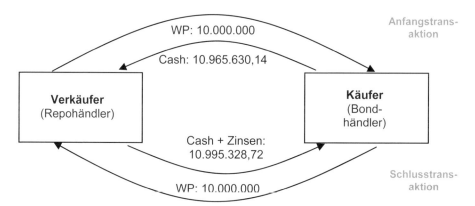

Bei einem Wertpapier-getriebenen Repo ist der Ausgangspunkt also das benötigte Wertpapier-Nominale und nicht ein bestimmter Cashbetrag. Der Anfangs-Cashbetrag ist dann einfach der aktuelle Marktwert (Dirty Price) des Collaterals. Wiederum wird in der Schlusstransaktion das Collateral zurückübertragen, und der Cashbetrag errechnet sich einfach aus dem Anfangsbetrag zuzüglich der Repozinsen.

Zusammenfassend werden für ein Wertpapier-getriebenes Repo also folgende Berechnungen benötigt:

Klassisches Repo – Wertpapier-getrieben

Anfangstransaktion:

Cashbetrag: $\text{WP Nominale} * \dfrac{\text{Dirty Price}}{100}$

WP-Nominale: vorgegeben

Schlusstransaktion:

Cashbetrag: $\text{Cash Anfangstransaktion} * \left(1 + \text{Repozins} * \dfrac{\text{Tage}}{\text{Basis}}\right)$

WP-Nominale: Nominale der Anfangstransaktion

4.3. General Collateral/Special Collateral

When describing the different typical applications, on the one hand the cash is the basis, on the other hand it is the security. Thus you can differentiate between repos with a **general collateral** (GC) or a **special collateral**.

4.3.1. General Collateral (GC)

For cash-driven repos the only reason for the collateral is the **securitisation for the lended cash amount**. The party giving the cash does not care which bond is used as long as certain **predetermined criteria** are satisfied. The repo can be regarded as a **loan on a secured basis**.

The interest rates of GC repos therefore tend towards other money market rates. Due to the collateral, repo rates are usually lower than rates for non-secured interbank deposits (i.e. LIBOR resp. EURIBOR).

Comparison EURIBOR rates vs. GC Repos (EUREPO):

	1 week	2 weeks	3 weeks	1 mth	2 mth	3 mth	6 mth	9 mth	12 mth
EURIBOR (Average 2003)	2.35	2.35	2.35	2.35	2.34	2.33	2.30	2.31	2.33
Eurepo (Average 2003)	2.33	2.33	2.32	2.30	2.28	2.26	2.21	2.21	2.24
Differenz	−0.02	−0.02	−0.03	−0.04	−0.06	−0.07	−0.09	−0.10	−0.09

Usually domestic **government bonds** are used as collateral. On www.isma.org or www.icma-group.org the European Repo Council publishes a list of issuers which have to be accepted as general collateral as long as a bond is not excluded by one counterpart before trading the repo.

General Collateral Conventions

Submitted for publication on www.isma.org on May 25, 2001

European repo council acceptable general collateral (GC) list

With effect from May 25, 2001 the security types set out in the following table were deemed by ISMA's (now: ICMA's) European Repo Council to be acceptable as collateral on general collateral (GC) repo and buy/sell transactions, unless specifically indicated otherwise prior to engaging in transactions.

4.3. General Collateral/Special Collateral

Bei den oben beschriebenen typischen Anwendungen ist einmal das Cash im Vordergrund gestanden und einmal ein bestimmtes Wertpapier. Dementsprechend wird zwischen Repos mit einem **General Collateral (GC)** und Repos mit einem **Special Collateral** unterschieden.

4.3.1. General Collateral (GC)

Bei Cash-getriebenen Repos ist der einzige Zweck des Collaterals eine **ausreichende Besicherung des geliehenen Cashbetrages**. Dem Cashgeber ist daher egal, welches Wertpapier dafür verwendet wird, solange **bestimmte Qualitätskriterien** erfüllt werden. Das Repo ist hier also als ein **wertpapierbesicherter Kredit** zu sehen.

Die Zinssätze von GC-Repos tendieren daher zu anderen Money-Market-Zinssätzen. Aufgrund der Besicherung liegen die Repo-Sätze typischerweise jedoch etwas unter den Zinssätzen für unbesicherte Interbank-Depots (also LIBOR bzw. EURIBOR).

Vergleich der EURIBOR-Sätze mit GC-Repos (EUREPO)

	1 week	2 weeks	3 weeks	1 mth	2 mth	3 mth	6 mth	9 mth	12 mth
EURIBOR (Durchschn. 2003)	2,35	2,35	2,35	2,35	2,34	2,33	2,30	2,31	2,33
EuRepo (Durchschn. 2003)	2,33	2,33	2,32	2,30	2,28	2,26	2,21	2,21	2,24
Differenz	−0,02	−0,02	−0,03	−0,04	−0,06	−0,07	−0,09	−0,10	−0,09

Üblicherweise werden Domestic Government Bonds, also **Staatsanleihen**, als Collateral verwendet. Das European Repo Council veröffentlicht auf www.icma-group.org eine Liste von Emittenten, die als General Collateral zu akzeptieren sind, sofern ein Papier nicht vor Abschluss des Repos von einer Partei explizit ausgeschlossen wurde.

General Collateral Conventions

Submitted for publication on www.isma.org on May 25, 2001

European Repo council acceptable general collateral (GC) list

With effect from May 25, 2001 the security types set out in the following table were deemed by ISMA's (now: ICMA's) European Repo Council to be acceptable as collateral on general collateral (GC) Repo and buy/sell transactions, unless specifically indicated otherwise prior to engaging in transactions.

Country of issuance	Currency	Details
Euro GC		
Austria	EUR	Government guaranteed bonds and bills
Belgium	EUR	Government guaranteed bonds and bills
Cyprus	EUR	Government guaranteed bonds and bills
Finland	EUR	Government guaranteed bonds and bills
France	EUR	*Bloomberg tickers* OATs, FRTR, BTANs, BTFs, FRTR (fixed coupon securities only), BTNS (fixed coupon securities only), BTF *Strips* FRTRR, FRTRS
Germany	EUR	*Bloomberg tickers* Unity — DBRUF Bund — DBR Bobl — OBL Treuhand — THA Schatz — BKO Bubill — BUBILL
Greece	EUR	Government guaranteed bonds and bills
Ireland	EUR	Government guaranteed bonds and bills
Italy	EUR	*Bloomberg tickers* CCT, BTP, BOT, CTZ, CCTS, BTPS, BOTS, ICTZ
Luxembourg	EUR	Government guaranteed bonds and bills
Malta	EUR	Government guaranteed bonds and bills
Netherlands	EUR	Government guaranteed bonds and bills
Slovenia	EUR	Government guaranteed bonds and bills
Portugal	EUR	Government guaranteed bonds and bills
Spain	EUR	Government guaranteed bonds and bills
Sterling GC		
United Kingdom	GBP	UK Treasury stock (UK Conversion stock)
Danish GC		
Kingdom of Denmark	DKK	DKK Government guaranteed bonds and bills (Danish mortgages are excluded)
Swedish GC		
Kingdom of Sweden	SEK	SEK Government guaranteed bonds and bills (Swedish mortgages are excluded)
Norwegian GC		
Kingdom of	NOK	Government guaranteed bonds and bills
Swiss GC		
Switzerland	CHF	Government guaranteed bonds and bills

Country of issuance	Currency	Details
Euro GC		
Austria	EUR	Government guaranteed bonds and bills
Belgium	EUR	Government guaranteed bonds and bills
Cyprus	EUR	Government guaranteed bonds and bills
Finland	EUR	Government guaranteed bonds and bills
France	EUR	Bloomberg tickers OATs, FRTR, BTANs, BTFs, FRTR (fixed coupon securities only), BTNS (fixed coupon securities only), BTF Strips FRTRR, FRTRS
Germany	EUR	*Bloomberg tickers* Unity — DBRUF Bund — DBR Bobl — OBL Treuhand — THA Schatz — BKO Bubill — BUBILL
Greece	EUR	Government guaranteed bonds and bills
Ireland	EUR	Government guaranteed bonds and bills
Italy	EUR	*Bloomberg tickers* CCT, BTP, BOT, CTZ, CCTS, BTPS, BOTS, ICTZ
Luxembourg	EUR	Government guaranteed bonds and bills
Malta	EUR	Government guaranteed bonds and bills
Netherlands	EUR	Government guaranteed bonds and bills
Slovenia	EUR	Government guaranteed bonds and bills
Portugal	EUR	Government guaranteed bonds and bills
Spain	EUR	Government guaranteed bonds and bills
Sterling GC		
United Kingdom	GBP	UK Treasury stock (UK Conversion stock)
Danish GC		
Kingdom of Denmark	DKK	DKK Government guaranteed bonds and bills (Danish mortgages are excluded)
Swedish GC		
Kingdom of Sweden	SEK	SEK Government guaranteed bonds and bills (Swedish mortgages are excluded)
Norwegian GC		
Kingdom of Norway	NOK	Government guaranteed bonds and bills
Swiss GC		
Switzerland	CHF	Government guaranteed bonds and bills

The current list can be downloaded from the following homepage: www.eurepo.org/eurepo/eurepogc.html.

EUREPO

Since the introduction of the Euro, the European repo markets have developed significantly, with more and more emphasis on cross border financing trades. This has led to an increasingly homogenous Euro-denominated General Collateral (GC) market.

Since 2002, the **benchmark for secured money market transactions (GC repos)** in the Euro zone is **EUREPO** (in analogy to the EURIBOR as the benchmark for unsecured interbank deposits).

Definition: "Eurepo is the rate at which one prime bank offers funds in euro to another prime bank if in exchange the former receives from the latter Eurepo GC as collateral."

The range of EUREPO quoted maturities is T/N, 1, 2 and 3 weeks and 1, 2, 3, 6, 9 and 12 months. **Daily, at 11:00 a.m. (CET), Moneyline Telerate** will process the EUREPO calculation as **the average of all quotes from the bank panel**, for each maturity, eliminating the highest and lowest 15% of all the quotes collected. The remaining rates will be averaged and rounded to two decimal places. The panel consists of first-class international banks (within and outside Europe, currently 34 banks).

4.3.2. Special Collateral

If the buyer in a repo transaction requires a specific security as collateral, then he needs to do a special repo. The essential purpose of repo in this context is the borrowing and lending of specific **securities against cash.** We also call this a **security-driven repo**.

Buyers of special repo often find themselves competing against each other for the same securities. In those situations, competition will force the buyers to offer cheap cash in exchange, and the repo rate on the collateral falls below the GC rate (in extreme situations the rate can even be negative); the security in question will be said to have "gone on special".

Securities can go on special for a number of reasons. In particular:

- A government bond that becomes the **cheapest-to-deliver (CTD)** against a bond futures contract is prone to go on special. Such bonds are strong contenders for delivery against maturing futures contracts. CTD is the most common reason for securities going special.
- **Benchmark bond issues** (e.g. government bonds with 2-, 3-, 5-, and 10-years maturities) are also prone to go on special because they are usually in demand by traders who tend to concentrate their activity in swaps, caps and other fixed income derivatives on those maturities.

Die aktuelle Liste kann unter folgendem Link heruntergeladen werden: www.eurepo.org/eurepo/eurepogc.html.

EUREPO

Seit der Einführung des Euro haben sich die europäischen Repomärkte deutlich weiterentwickelt. Zugleich hat die Bedeutung von Cross-Border-Transaktionen stark zugenommen und damit zu einem immer homogeneren Euro-denominierten General-Collateral-(GC)-Markt geführt. Daher wurde analog zum EURIBOR, der die Benchmark für unbesicherte Interbank-Depots darstellt, im Jahr 2002 **EUREPO als Benchmark für GC-Repos** eingeführt:

Definition: „Eurepo is the rate at which one prime bank offers funds in euro to another prime bank if in exchange the former receives from the latter Eurepo GC as collateral."

EUREPO wird für die Laufzeiten T/N, 1, 2, 3 Wochen und für 1, 2, 3, 6, 9 und 12 Monate ermittelt. Er wird **täglich um 11.00 (CET) von Reuters als Durchschnitt der Quotierungen der Panel-Banken errechnet**, wobei die höchsten und niedrigsten 15% aller Quotierungen nicht berücksichtigt werden. Das Panel setzt sich aus erstklassigen internationalen Banken (innerhalb und außerhalb Europas) zusammen (derzeit 34 Banken).

4.3.2. Special Collateral

Wenn ein Käufer in einem Repo (Pensionsnehmer) eine ganz bestimmte Anleihe als Collateral benötigt, muss er ein sogenanntes Special Repo machen. In diesem Fall ist das Repo daher als **Wertpapierleihe gegen Cash** anzusehen. Wir sprechen auch von einem **Wertpapier-getriebenen Repo**.

Käufer eines Special Repos stehen oft in Konkurrenz zu anderen Marktteilnehmern, die dieselbe Anleihe nachfragen. Besteht also ein Nachfrageüberhang nach einer bestimmten Anleihe, so wird die Konkurrenzsituation die Nachfrager dazu zwingen, den Verkäufern des Repos als Gegenleistung das Cash zu einem niedrigeren Satz anzubieten. Das führt dazu, dass Repo-Käufer für ein bestimmtes Collateral – je nach Nachfragesituation – Cash zu einem deutlich unter dem aktuellen Geldmarktsatz liegenden Zinssatz anbieten (in extremen Situationen kann er sogar negativ sein). Man sagt dann, dass die entsprechende Anleihe „special gegangen" ist (the security has gone special).

Anleihen können aus verschiedenen Gründen special gehen, die häufigsten sind folgende:

- Anleihen, die **cheapest-to-deliver (CTD)** in einem Bond-Futureskontrakt geworden sind, neigen dazu, special zu gehen, weil diese Anleihen die günstigste Möglichkeit darstellen, einen Futureskontrakt zu erfüllen. CTD ist der weitaus häufigste Grund, dass Anleihen special gehen.

- Auch sogenannte **Benchmark-Anleihen** (z.B. Staatsanleihen mit 2-, 3-, 5- oder 10-jähriger Laufzeit) neigen dazu, special zu gehen, weil sie häufig von Händlern nachgefragt werden, die dazu tendieren, ihre Aktivitäten in Swaps, Caps und anderen Zinsderivaten auf eben diese Laufzeiten zu konzentrieren.

4.4. Main Repo Market Participants

As shown above, repos can be done for different reasons. In the following, the most important repo market participants are described:

Bond trader

As shown in the above examples, there are two typical applications for bond traders:
- funding of long positions in securities – here a repo is a secured form of borrowing.
- funding of short positions in securities – here a repo is security lending against cash.

Investors

Risk averse investors, who have surplus cash to place in the money markets, have two main advantages:
- because repo is secured, it carries lower credit risk.
- it incurs lower capital charges than unsecured lending under regulations such as the EU Capital Adequacy Directive (CAD). (Providing repo is documented and counterparties can call variation margins.)

Instead, they are willing to accept a lower interest rate compared to unsecured investments like CDs or CPs.

Fund managers

Among the number of securities in a fund you often also find specials. These can be repoed out in order to acquire "cheap" cash. This additional liquidity can then be borrowed at higher rates in the money market which means additional income.

Repo Market Maker

The aim of the repo market makers is to earn the bid-offer spread, although in very mature markets this spread has become very close.

Central banks

Another important player in most countries is the central bank. Central banks use repo as a tool of domestic money market intervention, to control short-term interest rates on a regular basis, often every one to two weeks. The repo rate then serves additionally as an important signal for the future interest rate policy of the central bank.

For repos done by central banks you have to consider that the terminology is regarded at from the commercial banks' point of view:
- **Central bank repo:** the central bank adds liquidity to the money markets, they buy-and-sell securities (buy securities, give cash) in the repo market, i.e. actually not the central bank but the commercial banks do repo.

4.4. Marktteilnehmer im Repomarkt

Wie aus den bisherigen Ausführungen bereits hervorgeht, könnnen Repos aus den unterschiedlichsten Beweggründen abgeschlossen werden. In der Folge werden die wichtigsten Marktteilnehmer im Repomarkt beschrieben:

Wertpapierhändler

Wie in den obigen Beispielen gezeigt, gibt es zwei typische Anwendungsmöglichkeiten für Bond Trader:

- günstige Refinanzierung einer long Wertpapierposition – das Repo ist hier ein wertpapierbesicherter Kredit.
- Eindeckung einer Short-Position in Wertpapieren – hier ist das Repo eine Wertpapierleihe gegen Cash.

Investoren

Risikoaverse Investoren, die Cash im Geldmarkt anlegen möchten, haben vor allem zwei Vorteile:

- Sie erhalten durch das Collateral eine zusätzliche Sicherheit.
- Die Eigenkapitalunterlegung nach der Kapitaladäquanzrichtlinie (KAR) ist geringer (vorausgesetzt, es handelt sich um ein dokumentiertes Repo, bei dem auch eine Variation Margin zur Anwendung kommt).

Dafür sind sie bereit, einen – im Vergleich zu unbesicherten Anlagen wie CDs oder CPs – niedrigeren Zinssatz zu akzeptieren.

Fondsmanager

Häufig befinden sich unter den zahlreichen Wertpapieren in einem Fonds auch Specials. Diese können zur Beschaffung von günstigem Cash in Pension gegeben werden. Diese zusätzliche Liquidität kann dann zu höheren Sätzen im Geldmarkt wieder angelegt werden, wodurch ein Zusatzertrag geschaffen werden kann.

Repo Market Maker

Das Ziel der Market Maker ist, den Spread zwischen Geld und Brief zu verdienen, auch wenn dieser in den entwickelten, reifen Märkten bereits sehr eng geworden ist.

Zentralbanken

In vielen Ländern ist die Zentralbank ein wichtiger Marktteilnehmer. Sie benutzen Repos zur Feinsteuerung der kurzfristigen Liquidität, indem sie regelmäßige Repos – häufig im 1- oder 2-Wochen-Rhythmus – durchführen. Die Höhe des Repo-Satzes dient dabei zusätzlich als wichtiges Signal für die zukünftige Zinspolitik der Zentralbank.

Bei Repos von Zentralbanken ist zu beachten, dass die Terminologie aus Sicht der Geschäftsbanken angewendet wird:

- **Zentralbank Repo**
  Die Zentralbank führt dem Banksystem Liquidität zu, indem sie Wertpapiere kauft und Cash in den Markt gibt; d.h., eigentlich macht nicht die Zentralbank ein Repo, sondern die Geschäftsbanken.

- **Central bank reverse repo:** the central bank sells securities and thus drain liquidity from the money markets.

In the US, you have to be more careful with the terminology: here reverse repos are also called **"matched sale-purchase"** (MSP, "matched funding"). From the FED's point of view, securities are sold and bought and thereby liquidity is drained from the money markets.

In the US one speaks also of **"system repos"** resp. **"matched funding"** if repo is done in order to serve the money market policy. FED also does so-called "customer repos" where it acts for international central banks or supranational institutions who want to invest liquidity surplus.

4.5. Collateral Management

4.5.1. Initial Margin/Haircut

The collateral in a repo is intended to protect the buyer (cash lender) against default by the seller. The buyer therefore has to ensure that he has enough collateral. As shown in the above examples, typically, the collateral is valued at its current market price (i.e. dirty price). This may subsequently prove to be inadequate cover because:

- **Illiquid market**
  The market of the asset used as collateral may be illiquid, in which case, the buyer may find prices falling very fast as he starts to sell the collateral. Even liquid markets may become illiquid in a crisis.
- **Price volatility**
  The price of the asset used as collateral may be volatile. Even if the collateral was enough for today, a price decline tomorrow could lead to a deficit of collateral.

To build in some protection against valuation problems, the buyer may insist on buying the collateral at a discount to its current market value – i.e. the repo will be overcollateralised. The degree of overcollateralisation is called an **initial margin** or **haircut**.

In theory, the seller could seek similar protection by insisting that his collateral should be sold at a premium to its current market value which in practice is not common.

The amount of haircut can be **freely fixed** by the counterparts. Typical haircuts are 2% for European government bonds, at least 5% for equity and as much as 50% for emerging market debt. However, haircuts are unusual between repo professionals and on very short-term repo.

- **Zentralbank Reverse Repo**
  Die Zentralbank verkauft Wertpapiere und nimmt dadurch Liquidität aus dem Markt.

In den USA muss bei der Terminologie noch etwas mehr achtgegeben werden: Reverse Repos werden hier **„Matched Sale-Purchase"** (MSP, „Matched Funding") genannt. Aus Sicht der FED werden dabei Wertpapiere verkauft und gekauft, d.h., es wird somit Liquidität aus dem Markt genommen (FED signalisiert steigende Zinsen).

In den USA spricht man auch von **„System Repos"** bzw. **„Matched Funding",** wenn die Pensionsgeschäfte zur Verfolgung der Geldmarktpolitik durchgeführt werden. Die FED macht aber auch sogenannte **„Customer Repos",** also Kunden-Repos. Sie wird dabei hauptsächlich für ausländische Zentralbanken oder supranationale Institutionen tätig, die Liquiditätsüberschüsse anlegen wollen.

4.5. Collateral Management

4.5.1. Initial Margin/Haircut

Das Collateral in einem Repo dient dazu, den Käufer (Pensionsnehmer, Cashgeber) gegen Verluste bei einem Ausfall des Kontrahenten zu schützen. Daher muss sichergestellt werden, dass der Verkäufer einen ausreichenden Gegenwert an Wertpapieren zur Verfügung gestellt hat. Wie in den bisherigen Beispielen gezeigt wurde, wird daher bei Abschluss des Repos das Wertpapier grundsätzlich zum Marktwert bewertet (d.h., es wird der Dirty Price berücksichtigt). Diese Vorgangsweise allein mag jedoch aus folgenden Gründen keinen ausreichenden Schutz bieten:

- **Illiquider Markt**
  Wenn ein illiquides Wertpapier im Repo verwendet wird, kann es für den Pensionsnehmer schwierig werden, das Papier im Markt zum Bewertungskurs zu verkaufen. Bei größeren Positionen wird dabei allein durch die Verkaufsaktivitäten der Kurs des Collaterals zusätzlich gedrückt. Es ist auch unbedingt zu bedenken, dass in Krisensituationen selbst normalerweise liquide Titel, illiquide werden können.
- **Preisvolatilität**
  Der Preis des Collaterals kann sich ändern. Selbst wenn die Besicherung heute noch ausreichend wäre, könnte am nächsten Tag ein Kursrückgang schon zu einer Unterbesicherung führen.

Zum Schutz gegen diese Probleme werden bei Repos häufig Margins angewendet. Dabei verlangt der Cashgeber eine Überbesicherung, eine sogenannte Initial Margin – im Repomarkt auch **Haircut** genannt. Die Initial Margin schützt also den Käufer des Wertpapiers vor einem Preisverfall des Papiers in der Zeit zwischen dem Ausfall des Partners und der Veräußerung des Collaterals. Theoretisch könnte auch der Verkäufer des Wertpapiers eine Überbesicherung verlangen, was in der Praxis jedoch nicht üblich ist. Die Höhe des Haircuts ist zwischen den Kontrahenten **frei vereinbar**. Eine übliche Größenordnung ist dabei ca. 2% für europäische Staatsanleihen, mindestens 5% für Aktien und bis zu 50% für Emerging Markets. Zwischen professionellen Repomarktteilnehmern und für sehr kurze Laufzeiten ist die Anwendung von Haircuts jedoch eher unüblich.

Calculation of haircut

If an initial margin is agreed, the cash amount of the the initial transaction can be calculated in two different ways:

with fixed nominal:

$$\text{Method 1:} \quad \text{Cash}_{start} = \text{nominal} \times \frac{\text{dirty price}}{100} \times (1-\text{haircut})$$

or

$$\text{Method 2:} \quad \text{Cash}_{start} = \frac{\text{nominal} \times \dfrac{\text{dirty price}}{100}}{1+\text{haircut}}$$

Method 2 is recommended by ERC (European Repo Committee) in "Best Practice Guide to Repo Margining" and also complies to the regulations of PSA/ISMA Global Master Repurchase Agreement.

If you would like to calculate how much nominal of the collateral you have repo out against a given cash amount (e.g. for a cash-driven repo), you have the following formula:

with fixed cash:

$$\text{Nominal} = \frac{\text{Cash}_{start}}{\dfrac{\text{dirty price}}{100}} \times (1+\text{haircut})$$

Example

Classic repo with haircut:

Collateral: 5 1/2% Fed. Republic of Germany 14th August 2013
Dirty Price: 109.65
Haircut: 2%

Cash amount for fixed nominal (10,000,000):

$$\text{Cash}_{start} = \frac{10{,}000{,}000 \times \dfrac{109.65}{100}}{1+0.02} = 10{,}750{,}000$$

Nominal with fixed cash amount (10,000,000):

$$\text{Nominal} = \frac{10{,}000{,}000}{\dfrac{109.65}{100}} \times (1+0.02) = 9{,}302{,}325.58$$

Die Berechnung des Haircuts

Wird eine Initial Margin vereinbart, so kann der Cashbetrag der Anfangstransaktion auf zwei Arten ermittelt werden:

Bei fixiertem Nominale:

Methode 1: $\text{Cash}_{\text{start}} = \text{Nominale} * \dfrac{\text{Dirty Price}}{100} * (1 - \text{Haircut})$

oder

Methode 2: $\text{Cash}_{\text{start}} = \dfrac{\text{Nominale} \times * \dfrac{\text{Dirty Price}}{100}}{1 + \text{Haircut}}$

Die Anwendung der Methode 2 wird im „Best Practice Guide to Repo Margining" vom ERC (European Repo Committee) empfohlen und entspricht auch den Bestimmungen des PSA/ISMA Global Master Repurchase Agreement.

Wollen Sie berechnen, wie viel Nominale des Collaterals Sie für einen gegebenen Cashbetrag liefern müssen (z.B. bei einem Cash-getriebenen Repo), kommt folgende Formel zum Einsatz:

Bei fixiertem Cashbetrag:

$\text{Nominale} = \dfrac{\text{Cash}_{\text{start}}}{\dfrac{\text{Dirty Price}}{100}} * (1 + \text{Haircut})$

Beispiel

Klassisches Repo mit Haircut:

Collateral: 5 1/2% Bundesrepublik Deutschland 14.08.2013
Dirty Price: 109,65
Haircut: 2%

Cashbetrag bei fixiertem Nominale (10.000.000):

$\text{Cash}_{\text{start}} = \dfrac{10.000.000 \times \dfrac{109,65}{100}}{1 + 0,02} = 10.750.000$

Nominale bei fixiertem Cashbetrag (10.000.000):

$\text{Nominale} = \dfrac{10.000.000}{\dfrac{109,65}{100}} \times (1 + 0,02) = 9.302.325,58$

4.5.2. Variation Margin

Initial margins may prove inadequate if the price of the collateral falls more than expected. To maintain the intended balance between the collateral and cash in repo, variation margins are used. Variation margins are extra transfers of collateral or extra payments of cash, made during the term of the repo, to eliminate divergences between the agreed initial values of the collateral and the cash. These margin calls can be paid either in cash or securities:

- If the value of the collateral falls during the term of the repo, the buyer (=cash lender) can demand that seller provides either extra collateral, or refunds the excess cash.
- If the value of the collateral rises, the seller can demand that the buyer either returns the excess collateral or pays extra cash.

Note that the variation margins may be made by **either buyer or seller**, whereas initial margins are usually only made by the seller.

With general collaterals margin calls are paid in securities, whilst with specials they are paid in cash. In this case the margin call is a kind of redemption resp. increase of the lended cash amount and thus has to be considered in the final transaction (incl. interest). For the interest calculation of cash margins a reference rate should be defined. The European Repo Committee (ERC) recommends EONIA.

Variation margining may be used in conjunction with initial margins or on their own. Note that a once agreed initial margin has be maintained during the whole term of the repo.

Unlike initial margins, regulators require that variation margins should be used by **all types of market participants**, including professionals. Variation margins require that the collateral should be marked to market – i.e. revalued – at least daily for professional players.

Variation margins require **considerable operational resources**. In order to reduce the burden on the back office, it is standard practice to reduce the size and frequency of variation margin calls by defining so-called **trigger levels** resp. **margin threshold**. Margin calls are then only paid if an agreed minimum amount is exceeded. However, if this trigger level is exceeded, the whole margin call amount has to be paid, not only the amount exceeding the trigger.

4.5.2. Variation Margin

Bei Repos mit längerer Laufzeit reicht möglicherweise die Überbesicherung durch die Initial Margin nicht aus. Daher kommen Variation Margins zur Anwendung. Diese haben das Ziel, über die gesamte Laufzeit des Repos hinweg für eine ausreichende Besicherung zu sorgen. Dazu wird das Repo, d.h. sowohl das Collateral als auch der Cashbetrag inklusive angelaufener Zinsen, einer **regelmäßigen – üblicherweise täglichen – Mark-to-Market-Bewertung** unterzogen. Kommt es zu Abweichungen zwischen dem Wert des Collaterals und dem Cashbetrag, so kommt es zu Margin Calls, entweder in Cash oder in Wertpapieren:

- Fällt der Kurs des Collaterals, so kann der Käufer (= Cashgeber) zusätzliche Wertpapiere verlangen oder der Verkäufer zahlt den Cashüberhang zurück.
- Steigt der Kurs des Collaterals, so kann der Verkäufer einen Teil der Wertpapiere zurückfordern oder er bekommt zusätzliches Cash.

Beachten Sie, dass die Variation Margin – abhängig vom Kurs des Collaterals – **sowohl vom Käufer als auch vom Verkäufer zu leisten** ist (im Unterschied zur Initial Margin).

Bei General Collaterals erfolgen Margin Calls in Form von Wertpapieren, bei Specials hingegen in Cash. In diesem Fall wirkt die Margin wie eine vorzeitige Rückzahlung bzw. Erhöhung des geliehenen Cashbetrages und muss daher – inklusive Zinsen – in der Schlusstransaktion berücksichtigt werden. Zur Verzinsung von Cash Margins sollte ein Referenzsatz vereinbart werden. Vom European Repo Committee (ERC) wird EONIA empfohlen.

Eine Variation Margin kann zusätzlich zu einer etwaigen Initial Margin vereinbart werden (auch ohne Initial Margin möglich). Es ist zu beachten, dass eine einmal vereinbarte Initial Margin während der gesamten Laufzeit aufrechtzuerhalten ist.

Während die Initial Margin zwischen professionellen Marktteilnehmern eher unüblich ist, verlangt der Gesetzgeber, dass die Variation Margin **zwischen allen Marktteilnehmern angewendet** wird. Dabei wird eine zumindest tägliche Mark-to-Market-Bewertung verlangt.

Die Variation Margin führt daher zu einem **erheblichen Arbeitsaufwand**. Um den Aufwand des Backoffice so gering wie möglich zu halten, ist es Marktpraxis, die Häufigkeit der Margin Calls durch das Festlegen von sogenannten **Trigger Levels** bzw. **Margin Tresholds** zu reduzieren. Damit ist gemeint, dass der Margin Call erst stattfindet, wenn ein bilateral vereinbarter Mindestbetrag überschritten wird. Wird dieser Trigger Level überschritten, so muss jedoch der gesamte Margin-Betrag geleistet werden, und nicht nur der den Trigger Level übersteigende Betrag.

Example

Margin Call – GC repo (cash-driven)

A bond trader does the following repo. After ten days the price of the collateral falls to 107.00. What is the variation margin?

Volume: EUR 10,000,000 cash
Repo term: 30 days
Repo rate: 3.27%
Collateral: 5 1/2% Fed. Republic of Germany 14th Aug. 2013 (ACT/ACT)
Clean price: 108.27
Accrued interest: 92 days
Accrued interest: 1.3863014(5.5 x 92 / 365)
Dirty price: 109.6563014
Haircut: 2%

The bond trader needs exactly EUR 10 m (cash-driven). Instead he has to pay collateral with a current market value of also EUR 10 m plus 2% initial margin.

Initial transaction cash: EUR 10,000,000.00

Initial transaction bonds: EUR 9,301,791.02 $\left[\dfrac{10,000,000}{\dfrac{109.6563014}{100}} \times (1+0.02)\right]$

As this is a GC, in this case, the nominal amount could also have been rounded. Revaluation after 10 days: in the first step the current interest on the cash has to be calculated. Then, for the actual cash amount, the required bond nominal based on the actual dirty price has to be calculated. If a haircut has been agreed, it has to be maintained during the whole repo term.

Cash$_{day\ 10}$:   EUR 10,009,083.33 [(10,000,000 x (1 + 0.0327x10/360)]
Dirty Price$_{day\ 10}$: 108.5369863   [107+(5.5 x 102 / 365)]

equired bond nominal: EUR 9,406,254.35 $\left[\dfrac{10,009,083.33}{\dfrac{108.5369863}{100}} \times (1+0.02)\right]$

As originally the value of the collateral was less than now required, the seller has to settle the difference in securities.

Margin call: EUR 104,463.33 nominal (9,406,254.35 – 9,301,791.02)

Beispiel

Margin Call – GC Repo (Cash-getrieben)

Ein Bondhändler schließt folgendes Repo ab. Nach zehn Tagen fällt der Kurs des Collaterals auf 107,00. Welche Variation Margin fällt an?

Volumen: EUR 10.000.000 Cash
Laufzeit: 30 Tage
Reposatz: 3,27%
Collateral: 5 1/2% Bundesrepublik Deutschland 14.08.2013 (ACT/ACT)
Clean Price: 108,27
Stückzinstage: 92
Stückzinsen: 1,3863014 (5,5 x 92/365)
Dirty Price: 109,6563014
Haircut: 2%

Der Bondhändler braucht genau EUR 10 Mio. (Cash-getrieben). Dafür muss er Collateral mit einem aktuellen Marktwert von ebenfalls EUR 10 Mio. zuzüglich 2% Initial Margin liefern.

Anfangstransaktion Cash: EUR 10.000.000,00

$$\text{Anfangstransaktion: WPEUR } 9.301.791,02 \left[\frac{10.000.000}{\frac{109,6563014}{100}} \times (1+0,02) \right]$$

Da es sich um ein GC handelt, könnte hier der Nominalbetrag auch gerundet werden. Bewertung nach zehn Tagen: Im ersten Schritt müssen die angelaufenen Zinsen für das Cash ermittelt werden. Dann wird für den aktuellen Cashbetrag das benötigte Wertpapier-Nominale auf Basis des aktuellen Dirty Price ermittelt. Wurde ein Haircut vereinbart, so muss dieser während der gesamten Laufzeit aufrechterhalten werden!

$\text{Cash}_{\text{Tag 10}}$: EUR 10.009.083,33 [(10.000.000 x (1 + 0,0327 x 10/360)]
$\text{Dirty Price}_{\text{Tag 10}}$: 108,5369863 [107 + (5,5 x 102/365)]

$$\text{Benötigtes WP-Nominale: EUR } 9.406.254,35 \left[\frac{10.009.083,33}{\frac{108,5369863}{100}} \times (1+0,02) \right]$$

Da ursprünglich weniger Collateral geliefert wurde, als aktuell zur Aufrechterhaltung der Besicherung benötigt wird, muss der Verkäufer die Differenz in Anleihen nachschießen.

Margin Call: EUR 104.463,33 Nominale (9.406.254,35 – 9.301.791,02)

Note: For cash-driven GC repos variation margin is always paid in securities. Thus margins calls **do not have any impact on the final transaction.** Depending on the price movement of the collateral either the seller or the buyer has to pay the margin. If, for example, the price rises, the seller receives the collateral surplus from the buyer.

Example

Margin call – security-driven

A bond trader does the following repo. After ten days the price of the collateral falls to 107.00. What is the variation margin?

Volume:	EUR 10,000,000 nominal
Repo term:	30 days
Repo rate:	3.27%
Collateral:	5 1/2% Fed. Republic of Germany 14th Aug. 2013 (ACT/ACT)
Clean price:	108.27
Accrued interest:	92 days
Accrued interest:	1.3863014 (5.5 x 92/365)
Dirty price:	109.6563014
Haircut:	2%

The bond trader needs exactly EUR 10 m nominal (security-driven). Instead he has to pay cash (less 2% initial margin).

Initial transaction bonds: EUR 10,000,000.00

Initial transaction cash: EUR 10,750,617.78 $\left[\dfrac{10,000,000 \times \dfrac{109.6563014}{100}}{1+0.02}\right]$

Revaluation after ten days: with specials the variation margin is in cash. First, the securities are revalued (less haircut) and then compared to the actual cash amount (incl. interest).

Dirty price$_{day\ 10}$: 108.5369863 [107 + (5.5 x 102/365)]

MTM bonds (less haircut): EUR 10,640,881.01 $\left[\dfrac{10,000,000 \times \dfrac{108.5369863}{100}}{1+0.02}\right]$

Cash$_{day\ 10}$: EUR 10,760,382.92 [10,750,617.78 x (1 + 0.0327x10/360)]

As the cash amount exceeds the market value of the collateral, the seller (= cash borrower) has to pay back cash.

Margin call: EUR 119,501.91 cash (10,760,382.92 – 10,640,881.01)

Anmerkung: Bei Cash-getriebenen GC-Repos wird die Variation Margin immer in Wertpapieren geliefert. Daher haben Margin Calls **keinen Einfluss auf die Cash-Schlusstransaktion**. Je nach Kursentwicklung des Collaterals muss entweder der Verkäufer oder der Käufer die Margin leisten. Wäre z.B. der Kurs gestiegen, so hätte der Verkäufer das überschüssige Collateral vom Käufer zurückerhalten.

Beispiel

Margin Call – Wertpapier-getrieben

Ein Bondhändler schließt folgendes Repo ab. Nach zehn Tagen fällt der Kurs des Collaterals auf 107,00. Welche Variation Margin fällt an?

Volumen:	EUR 10.000.000 Nominale
Laufzeit:	30 Tage
Reposatz:	3,27%
Collateral:	5 1/2% Bundesrepublik Deutschland 14.08.2013 (ACT/ACT)
Clean Price:	108,27
Stückzinstage:	92
Stückzinsen:	1,3863014 (5,5 x 92/365)
Dirty Price:	109,6563014
Haircut:	2%

Der Bondhändler braucht Wertpapiere im Nominale von genau EUR 10 Mio. (Wertpapier-getrieben). Dafür liefert er Cash (abzüglich 2% Initial Margin).

Anfangstransaktion WP: EUR 10.000.000,00

$$\text{Anfangstransaktion Cash: EUR } 10.750.617,78 \left[\frac{10.000.000 \times \dfrac{109,6563014}{100}}{1+0,02} \right]$$

Bewertung nach 10 Tagen: Bei Specials fällt die Variation Margin in Cash an. Zuerst werden daher die Anleihen bewertet (abzügl. Haircut) und dann mit dem aktuellen Cashbetrag (inkl. Zinsen) verglichen.

Dirty Price$_{\text{Tag 10}}$: 108,5369863 [107 + (5,5 v 102 / 365)]

$$\text{MTM WP (abzügl. Haircut): EUR } 10.640.881,01 \left[\frac{10.000.000 \times \dfrac{108,5369863}{100}}{1+0,02} \right]$$

Cash$_{\text{Tag 10}}$: EUR 10.760.382,92 [10.750.617,78 × (1 + 0,0327 × 10 /360)]

Da der Cashbetrag den Marktwert des Collaterals übersteigt, muss der Cashnehmer (= Verkäufer) Cash zurückzahlen.

Margin Call: **EUR 119.501,91 Cash** (10.760.382,92 – 10.640.881,01)

If the margin is paid in cash, it has to be considered in the final transaction including interest.

Cash final transaction:

Initial amount:	10,750,617.78	
+ interest:	+ 29,295.43	$[10,750,617.78 \times (1 + 0.0327 \times 30/360)]$
+/– margin (here -):	– 119,501.91	see above
+/– interest on margin:	– 217.10	$[119,501.91 \times (1 + 0.0327 \times 20/360)]$
Final transaction:	**10,660,194.20**	

4.5.3. Custody of Collateral

A major issue in repo is, who has custody of the collateral. There are three basic alternatives:

- **Bilateral repo (delivery repo)**
  The buyer takes custody of the collateral from the seller. This is the **safest for the buyer**, given that the collateral is under his direct control. However, because collateral has to be transferred across settlement systems, it is also the **most expensive alternative**.

- **Hold-in-custody (HIC) repo:**
  The **seller retains custody** of the collateral on behalf of the buyer. This exposes the buyer to the **greatest credit risk**, as there could be difficulties in recovering the collateral from the seller, in the event that the seller defaults. In addition, an unscrupulous seller could use the same piece of collateral several times in parallel HIC repos. Of course, this is forbidden and is called **"double-dipping"**. However, because the collateral does not have to be transferred against settlement systems, HIC repo is the cheapest option and should reward the buyer with higher repo rate than delivery repo.

- **Tri-party repo:**
  The tri-party agent (custodian bank or international clearing organization) acts as an intermediary between the two parties of the repo (collateral provider and cash investor). But note that a tri-party agent does not play the role of a broker and does not match dealers with cash investors. The cash investors and the collateral providers hold balances and securities accounts on the books of a tri-party agent. The collateral is transferred into the custody of the buyer across these accounts. This means that the buyer of a repo controls the collateral, as in a delivery repo. However, because the transfer of collateral is handled internally by the custodian, tri-party repo should avoid the cost of using a settlement system. The seller pays a fee to the custodian, but this should be less than the cost of the settlement system, so a tri-party repo should be cheaper than a delivery repo. By taking custody of the collateral, the clearing banks provide a guarantee to the cash investor that the collateral is segregated and identifiable in case of default of the collateral provider. This reduces the legal risk faced by the cash investors. In addition, because the collateral is being held by an agent, counterparty risk is reduced.

> Wird die Margin in Cash gezahlt, muss sie auch inklusive Zinsen in der Schlusstransaktion berücksichtigt werden.
>
> Die Cash-Schlusstransaktion ergibt sich wie folgt:

Anfangsbetrag:	10.750.617,78	
+ Zinsen:	+ 29.295,43	$[10.750.617{,}78 \times (1 + 0{,}0327 \times 30 / 360)]$
+/– Margin (hier –):	– 119.501,91	siehe oben
+/– Zinsen für Margin:	– 217,10	$[119.501{,}91 \times (1 + 0{,}0327 \times 20 / 360)]$
Schlusstransaktion:	**10.660.194,20**	

4.5.3. Verwahrung des Collaterals

Eine bedeutende Frage bei Repos ist, wer das Collateral verwahrt. Grundsätzlich können dabei drei Möglichkeiten unterschieden werden:

- **Bilaterales Repo (Delivery Repo)**
  Die **Wertpapiere werden vom Verkäufer an den Käufer geliefert.** Hierbei handelt es sich um die **sicherste Art** von Repos, weil die Wertpapiere sich in der direkten Kontrolle des Käufers befinden. Allerdings ist es auch die **teuerste Form,** weil die Wertpapiere über ein Settlement-System transferiert werden müssen.

- **Hold-in-Custody (HIC) Repo**
  Der **Verkäufer behält die Wertpapiere** und verwahrt sie treuhändisch für den Käufer. Hierbei hat der Käufer das **größte Risiko,** da es bei einem Default Event zu Schwierigkeiten kommen kann, wenn er in den Besitz der Papiere kommen will. Außerdem könnte ein unseriöser Verkäufer dasselbe Papier in mehreren Repos verwenden. Diese – selbstverständlich verbotene – Vorgangsweise wird auch **„double dipping"** genannt.
  Da das Wertpapier bei einem HIC Repo den Besitzer überhaupt nicht wechselt und somit auch nicht transferiert werden muss, sind HIC Repos die **billigste Form** der Abwicklung. Der Käufer eines HIC Repos sollte – aufgrund des erhöhten Risikos – mit einem etwas höheren Zinssatz belohnt werden.

- **Tri-party Repo**
  Der Tri-Party Agent (verwahrende Bank oder internationale Clearing-Organisation) agiert als Intermediär zwischen den zwei Parteien eines Repos (Wertpapiergeber und Geldgeber). Zu beachten ist jedoch, dass der Tri-Party Agent nicht die Rolle eines Brokers einnimmt und nicht Händler und Geldgeber verbindet. Die Geldgeber und Wertpapiergeber halten Geld- und Wertpapierkonten beim Tri-Party Agenten. Das Wertpapier wird dabei vom Konto des Verkäufers (Wertpapiergeber) auf das Konto des Käufers (Geldgeber) übertragen. Das bedeutet, dass der Käufer direkte Kontrolle auf das Wertpapier hat – so wie bei einem bilateralen Repo. Da der Transfer beim Clearer (= Verwahrer, engl. „custodian") nur einen internen Übertrag bedeutet, kommt die Abwicklung jedoch günstiger. Die Gebühren werden dabei stets vom Verkäufer bezahlt, aber die Gebühren sollten geringer sein als die Kosten für ein Settlement-System. Somit sollte ein Tri-Party Repo billiger sein als ein bilaterales Repo. Der Clearer garantiert dem Geldgeber bei der Verwahrung des Collaterals, dass das Collateral abgesondert und eindeutig identifizierbar ist im Falle eines Ausfalls des Wertpapiergebers. Dies reduziert das rechtliche Risiko des Geldgebers. Zusätzlich wird durch die Verwahrung des Collaterals bei Tri-Party Agenten das Kontrahentenrisiko reduziert.

Therefore the benefits of cash investors are:

- no requirement to install repo settlement and monitoring systems,
- no requirement to take delivery of collateral, or to maintain an account at the clearing agency,
- independent monitoring of market movements and margin requirements,
- in the event of default, a tri-party agent that can implement default measures.

The main tri-party agents (clearing houses) are Euroclear, Clearstream (formerly Cedel), Bank of New York Mellon (BNYM) and JPMorgan Chase (JPMC). These clearing houses take custody of securities used as collateral in a tri-party repo transaction, they value the securities and make sure that the specified margin is applied, they settle the transaction on their books and they offer services to help dealers to optimize the use of their collateral. The responsibilities of the tri-party agent can include:

- the preparation of documentation,
- the setting-up of the repo account,
- monitoring of cash against purchased securities, both at inception and at maturity,
- the safekeeping of securities handed over as collateral,
- managing the substitution of securities, where this is required,
- monitoring the market value of the securities against the cash lent out in the repo,
- issuing margin calls to the borrower of cash.

The first tri-party repo deal took place in 1993 between the European Bank for Reconstruction and Development (EBRD) and Swiss Bank Corporation. Tri-party repo is the normal method of settlement in the US market. According to a survey made by ISMA in December 2003, only 11.2% is the proportion in Europe, but with an increasing trend.

Die Vorteile der Geldgeber sind also:

- keine Erfordernis einer Installation von Repo-Settlement- und Beobachtungs- bzw. Kontrollsystemen,
- keine Erfordernis, das Collateral entgegenzunehmen oder ein Konto bei der Clearing-Haus zu verwalten,
- unabhängige Kontrolle der Marktbewegungen und der erforderlichen Margin Calls,
- im Verzugsfall kann der Tri-party Agent die entsprechenden Maßnahmen setzen.

Die bedeutendsten Clearing-Häuser sind Euroclear, Clearstream (ehemals Cedel), Bank of New York Mellon (BNYM) und JPMorgan Chase (JPMC). Diese Clearing-Häuser nehmen die Sicherheiten in Verwahrung, die als Collateral im Tri-Party-Repo-Geschäft verwendet werden; sie bewerten die Wertpapiere und stellen sicher, dass die festgesetzte Margin angewendet wird, sie rechnen das Geschäft in ihren Büchern ab und bieten Händlern ein Service bei der Optimierung des verwendeten Collaterals an. Folgende Aufgaben können Clearing-Häuser erfüllen:

- die Erstellung der Dokumentation,
- die Einrichtung des Repo-Kontos,
- Kontrolle des Austauschs von Geld gegen die gekauften Wertpapiere am Beginn und am Ende der Laufzeit,
- sichere Aufbewahrung der als Collateral übertragenen Wertpapiere,
- Abwicklung des Austausches von Wertpapieren, wenn erforderlich,
- Beobachtung des Marktwerts der Wertpapiere gegenüber dem entsprechenden Geldwert, der verliehen wurde,
- Weitergabe der Margin Calls an den Entleiher des Geldes.

Das erste Tri-party-Repo-Geschäft wurde im Jahre 1993 zwischen der Europäischen Bank für Wiederaufbau und Entwicklung (EBWE) und dem Schweizerischen Bankverein (SBV) abgeschlossen. Tri-party Repos werden vor allem in den USA häufig angewendet. Nach einer Erhebung der ISMA im Dezember 2003 beträgt der Anteil in Europa nur 11,2%, jedoch mit stark steigender Tendenz.

4.5.4. Substitution

Sellers may be reluctant to use certain securities as collateral in longer-term repo, in case they need the securities for another purpose before the maturity of the repo. This concern will tend to reduce the terms for which seller will repo out certain assets or result in those assets being withheld from the repo market entirely.

A solution is for the repo seller to seek rights of substitution of collateral from the buyer. This **allows the seller to recall collateral during a repo and substitute alternative collateral of equivalent value and quality.** Rights of substitution may be limited to certain dates within the contract period, or the seller may only be allowed to substitute a limited number of times during the course of a contract.

Substitution rights are valuable to the seller, but they may be inconvenient for the buyer, for example, if the collateral has been used to settle a short date. If the seller exercises his right of substitution, the buyer will incur operational expenses in returning the original collateral and taking in new collateral. Accordingly, a buyer will expect to receive a **higher repo rate** on his cash in exchange for granting rights of substitution.

Example
Substitution
A bond trader does the following repo. After ten days the collateral is supposed to be substituted.

Volume: EUR 10,000,000 cash
Repo term: 30 days
Repo rate: 3.27%
Collateral: 5 1/2% Fed. Republic of Germany 14th Aug. 2013 (ACT/ACT)
Dirty price: 109.6563014
Haircut: 2%

Initial transaction cash: EUR 10,000,000.00

Final transaction bonds: EUR 9,301,791.02 $\left[\dfrac{10.000.000}{109.6563014\,/\,100} \times (1+0.02) \right]$

After ten days the collateral is supposed to be substituted by the following bond:

Collateral: 4 3/4 % BTF (France) 17th March 2011
Dirty price: 103.6581902

4.5.4. Substitution

Verkäufer sind zurückhaltend, wenn es darum geht, bestimmte Wertpapiere für länger laufende Repos zu verwenden, weil sie möglicherweise diese Wertpapiere anderweitig vor Ablauf der Repos benötigen. Das führt zu einer Verringerung der Laufzeit für Repos mit bestimmten Collaterals oder sogar dazu, dass diese Wertpapiere überhaupt nicht für Repos herangezogen werden.

Abhilfe bietet das Recht zur Substitution. Darunter versteht man das **Recht des Verkäufers, das Collateral während der Laufzeit vom Käufer zurückzuverlangen und durch ein anderes Wertpapier von ähnlicher oder besserer Qualität zu ersetzen.** Das Recht zur Substitution muss zwar explizit zwischen den Parteien vereinbart werden, ist aber durchaus nicht unüblich. Es ist naheliegend, dass Substitution **nur bei General Collaterals** Anwendung findet, da bei Specials der Verkäufer ja ehestmöglich durch ein General ersetzen würde. Das Recht zur Substitution kann auch auf einzelne Daten oder eine maximale Anzahl im Laufe des Repos beschränkt werden.

Substitution ist für den Verkäufer ein wertvolles Recht. So kann er es – z.B. falls das Collateral special geht – durch ein GC ersetzen und selbst vom Special profitieren. Im Gegensatz dazu kann die Substitution für den Käufer unangenehm werden, vor allem wenn er das Wertpapier zur Eindeckung einer Short-Position verwendet. Die Beschaffung eines Ersatzes, falls das Collateral substituiert wird, kann dann möglicherweise zu erheblichen Kosten führen. Daher wird der Käufer für die Gewährung eines Substitutionsrechts einen **Aufschlag auf den Reposatz** verlangen.

Beispiel

Substitution

Ein Bondhändler schließt folgendes Repo ab. Nach zehn Tagen soll das Collateral substituiert werden.

Volumen: EUR 10.000.000,00 Cash
Laufzeit: 30 Tage
Reposatz: 3,27%
Collateral: 5 1/2% Bundesrepublik Deutschland 14.08.2013 (ACT/ACT)
Dirty Price: 109,6563014
Haircut: 2%

Anfangstransaktion Cash: EUR 10.000.000,00

Anfangstransaktion WP: EUR 9.301.791,02 $\left[\dfrac{10.000.000}{109,6563014 / 100} \times (1+0,02) \right]$

Nach zehn Tagen soll das Collateral durch folgende Anleihe substituiert werden:

Collateral: 4 3/4% BTF (Frankreich) 17.03.2011
Dirty Price: 103,6581902

The buyer delivers back the original collateral (Bund) and substitutes it by the new one (BTF). The nominal is calculated in same way as for the initial transaction, i.e. first, the actual cash amount is determined (incl. interest).

$Cash_{day\ 10}$:   EUR 10,009,083.33 [(10,000,000 x (1+0.0327 x 10 / 360)]

Required BTF nominal: EUR 9,848,970.91 $\left[\dfrac{10,009,083.33}{103.6581902/100} \times (1+0.02) \right]$

For the substitution of the Bund a BTF nominal of EUR 9,848,970.91 has to be delivered.
The substitution has no impact on the final cash transaction.

4.6. Sell/Buy-Backs / Buy/Sell-Backs

As we mentioned before, the term repo is used to describe two types of transaction:

- Classic repo (US-style repo)
- Sell/buy-backs (resp- buy/sell-backs)

There is no significant economic difference between the two types of repo, only minor structural differences. Therefore classic repos and sell/buy-backs for the same maturity, amount and collateral should yield approximately the same return.

The really significant difference is in their legal status and in the way in which each type of repo is managed. For a sell/buy-back **two legally independent contracts** are concluded – a spot transaction and the opposite forward transaction with different prices. Thus the net cost of the repo is implicit in the difference between the start and the end proceeds, whereas in classic repo the proceeds are the same and the cost of repo is explicitly stated as a repo interest amount.

Due to the independence of the two contracts **neither variation margin nor substitution** can be made. Thus sell/buy-backs are **less safe and flexible than classic repos**.

Classic repos predominate in the US, the UK, France and Switzerland; sell/buy-backs predominate in Germany, Italy, Spain and most emerging markets.

Der Käufer liefert das ursprüngliche Collateral (Bund) zurück und ersetzt es durch das neue (BTF). Die Ermittlung des nötigen Nominales erfolgt analog der Berechnung für die Anfangstransaktion, d.h., es wird zuerst der aktuelle Cashbetrag (inkl. Zinsen) ermittelt.

$Cash_{Tag\ 10}$:   EUR 10.009.083,33 [(10.000.000 x (1 + 0,0327 x 10/360)]

Benötigtes BTF-Nom.: EUR 9.848.970,91 $\left[\dfrac{10.009.083,33}{103,6581902 / 100} \times (1 + 0,02) \right]$

Zur Substitution des Bund muss ein BTF-Nominale von EUR 9.848.970,91 geliefert werden.
An der Cash-Schlusstransaktion ändert sich durch die Substitution nichts.

4.6. Sell/Buy-Backs / Buy/Sell-Backs

Wie in der allgemeinen Definition von Pensionsgeschäften beschrieben, wird zwischen zwei Haupttypen unterschieden:

- Klassische Repos (US-style Repos)
- Sell/Buy-Backs (bzw. Buy/Sell-Backs)

Wirtschaftlich betrachtet besteht kein wesentlicher Unterschied zwischen den beiden Typen. Daher sollte der Zinssatz von klassischen Repos und Sell/Buy-Backs für die gleiche Laufzeit sehr ähnlich sein.

Der wesentliche Unterschied besteht in der rechtlichen Natur. Bei **Sell/Buy-Backs** werden **zwei rechtlich eigenständige Geschäfte** – ein Kassageschäft und ein gegenläufiges Termingeschäft – abgeschlossen. Für die beiden Geschäfte werden unterschiedliche Kurse vereinbart. Die Verzinsung ergibt sich dann implizit aus der Differenz zwischen den beiden Kursen, während bei Repos der Zinssatz explizit in der Vereinbarung angeführt wird.

Aufgrund der Eigenständigkeit der beiden Vereinbarungen können **keine Variation Margin** und **keine Substitution** vereinbart werden. Somit sind Sell/Buy-Backs **weniger sicher und flexibel als klassische Repos.**

Während klassische Repos in den USA, UK, Frankreich und der Schweiz dominieren, werden Sell/Buy-Backs häufig in Deutschland, Spanien, Italien und den meisten Emerging Markets angewendet.

Structure of sell/buy-backs:

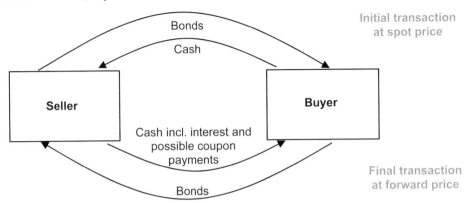

The structure is nearly the same as for classic repos. The main difference is that the **interest** (and possible coupon payments during the term of the repo plus interest) have to be considered **in the forward price of the final transaction.**

4.6.1. Comparison Classic Repo vs. Sell/Buy-Back

Classic repo	Sell/buy-back (undocumented)
Both transactions are concluded under one single contract	Two legally independent contracts
Documented: a written legal agreement (frame contract) evidences the rights and obligations of the counterparties	Traditionally undocumented, i.e. there is only one confirmation for the spot and the forward transaction
Same price for initial and final transaction; repo interest is paid separately	Different prices for initial and final transaction; the forward price includes both interest as well as possible coupon payments
The start proceeds should never be rounded	The start proceeds should never be rounded as they are the basis for the interest!
Initial margin/haircut and variation margin is allowed	Initial margin can be agreed; variation margin is not possible
Allows right of substitution: this encourages the counterparties to undertake longer-term transactions	Substitution is not possible
The buyer is obliged to pay the manufactured dividend to the seller on the same day he receives the coupon from the issuer	The buyer is obliged to pay the manufactured dividend to the seller at maturity. However, the buyer will have to add reinvestment interest to compensate the seller for the delay

Struktur von Sell/Buy-Backs:

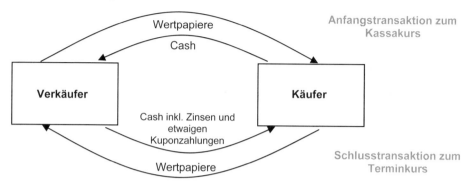

Die Struktur ähnelt stark der von klassischen Repos. Der Unterschied besteht hauptsächlich darin, dass die **Zinsen** (und etwaige Kuponzahlungen während der Laufzeit zuzüglich Zinsen) **im Terminkurs der Schlusstransaktion** berücksichtigt werden.

4.6.1. Vergleich klassische Repos vs. Sell/Buy-Backs

Klassisches Repo	Sell/Buy-Back (undokumentiert)
Beide Transaktionen werden unter einem einzigen Vertrag abgeschlossen.	Zwei rechtlich unabhängige Verträge.
Dokumentiert: In einer schriftlichen Vereinbarung (Rahmenvertrag) werden die Rechte und Pflichten der Parteien zusammengefasst.	Undokumentiert, d.h., es gibt nur jeweils eine Bestätigung für ein Kassageschäft und ein Termingeschäft.
Gleicher Kurs für die Anfangs- und Schlusstransaktion; die Repozinsen werden extra bezahlt.	Unterschiedliche Kurse für die Anfangs- und Schlusstransaktion; der Terminkurs enthält sowohl Zinsen also auch etwaige Kuponzahlungen.
Das Wertpapiernominale der Anfangstransaktion darf nie gerundet werden.	Die Beträge dürfen niemals gerundet werden, weil sich daraus ja die Zinsen ableiten!
Sowohl Initial also auch Variation Margin sind möglich.	Initial Margin kann vereinbart werden; Variation Margin ist nicht möglich.
Das Recht zur Substitution kann vereinbart werden; dadurch werden Verkäufer ermutigt, auch längere Laufzeiten abzuschließen.	Substitution ist nicht möglich.
Kuponzahlungen werden vom Käufer an den Verkäufer sofort weitergeleitet (manufactured dividend).	Der Käufer behält Kuponzahlungen und berücksichtigt sie inklusive Zinsen bei der Schlusstransaktion.

Originally, sell/buy-backs have always been undocumented, i.e. the frame contract solely referred to classic repos. Since November 1995, it has been possible to document sell/buy-backs under the PSA/ISMA Global Master Repurchase Agreement. Consequently, it is now possible to distinguish **three major types of repo**:

- **Classic repo** – always documented
- **Traditional sell/buy-back** – undocumented
- **Documented sell/buy-back** – always documented

Documented sell/buy-backs are more like classic repos in that they are single contracts and allow margins and rights of substitution. It is a common practice for sell/buy-backs to agree neither variation margins nor substitution rights. These two stipulations are managed within the so-called „**early termination and reprice**"-method (also called „early close-out" or „close and reprice"), in which the sell/buy-back is terminated and a new transaction is arranged for the remaining term to maturity at the original rates, but with the amount of cash or collateral changed. In a documented sell/buy-back divergences between the value of cash and collateral can be managed by the agreement of margin payments or by Repricing. Usually Repricing is used in sell/buy-backs for managing divergences between the value of cash and collateral.

4.6.2. Calculation of Sell/Buy-Backs

The quotation for sell/buy-backs is – like for classic repos – also in percent, however, in the confirmation both the clean prices for the initial and the final transaction are fixed which reflect the agreed interest rate.

Price initial transaction: clean price

Amount initial transaction: $\dfrac{dirty\ price}{100} \times nominal$

Amount final transaction: $initial\ transaction \times \left(1 + repo\ repo \times \dfrac{days}{basis} \right)$

Dirty price of the final transaction: $\dfrac{amount\ final\ transaction}{nominal}$

Price final transaction (cp): $dirty\ price_{start} - accrued\ interest$

Ursprünglich waren Sell/Buy-Backs immer undokumentiert, d.h., der Rahmenvertrag hat sich ausschließlich auf klassische Repos bezogen. Seit November 1995 umfasst das PSA/ISMA Global Master Repurchase Agreement auch Sell/Buy-Backs, wodurch heute **drei unterschiedliche Formen** unterschieden werden können:

- **klassisches Repo** – immer dokumentiert
- **traditionelles Sell/Buy-Back** – undokumentiert
- **dokumentiertes Sell/Buy-Back** – immer dokumentiert

Bei dokumentierten Sell/Buy-Backs bestehen kaum noch Unterschiede zu klassischen Repos. Derzeit ist es jedoch immer noch üblich, bei Sell/Buy-Backs weder Variation Margins nach Substitutionen zu vereinbaren. Inhaltlich können diese beiden Funktionalitäten über die sogenannte „**early termination and reprice**"-Methode dargestellt werden (auch „early close-out" bzw. „close and reprice" genannt). Dabei wird der Kontrakt vorzeitig beendet und gleichzeitig eine Ersatztransaktion für die Restlaufzeit zum ursprünglichen Zinssatz abgeschlossen. Dadurch ist der Effekt der gleiche wie bei einem Margin Call, d.h. der Wert des Collaterals wird an den Cashbetrag angepasst. Bei dokumentieren Sell/Buy-Backs können Abweichungen zwischen dem Wert des Collaterals und dem Cashbetrag sowohl durch Vereinbarung von Marginzahlungen, als auch durch Repricing ausgeglichen werden. In der Regel wird aber Repricing zum Ausgleich von Abweichungen verwendet.

4.6.2. Berechnung von Sell/Buy-Backs

Die Quotierung erfolgt zwar – wie bei klassischen Repos – auch in Prozent, in der Abschlussbestätigung werden jedoch die Clean Preise für die Anfangs- und Schlusstransaktion festgehalten, die genau den vereinbarten Zinssatz widerspiegeln.

Kurs Anfangstransaktion: Clean Price

Betrag der Anfangstransaktion: $\dfrac{\text{Dirty Price}}{100} \times \text{Nominale}$

Betrag der Schlusstransaktion: $\text{Anfangstransaktion} \times \left(1 + \text{RepoSatz} \times \dfrac{\text{Tage}}{\text{Basis}} \right)$

Dirty Price der Schlusstransaktion: $\dfrac{\text{Betrag Schlusstransaktion}}{\text{Nominale}}$

Kurs Schlusstransaktion (Clean P.): $\text{Dirty Price}_{\text{schluss}} - \text{Stückzinsen}$

Example

Buy/sell-back

A trader buys EUR 10 m Bund in a sell/buy-back.

Collateral: 5 1/2% Fed. Republic of Germany 14th Aug. 2013 (ACT/ACT)
Clean Price: 108.27
Accrued interest: 92 days
Accrued interest: 1.3863014(5.5 x 92/365)
Dirty price: 109.6563014
Repo rate: 3.27-3.25%
Repo term: 30 Tage

Initial transaction cash: EUR 10,965,630.14 [(10,000,000 x 109.65630137/100)]
Initial transaction bonds: EUR 10,000,000.00

The bond trader buys the bond in a repo and gives cash. As market user he trades on the offer side at 3.25%.

Final transaction cash: EUR 10,995,328.72 [10,965,630.14 x (1 + 0.0325 x 30/360)]
Final transaction bonds: EUR 10,000,000.00
Dirty price: 109.9532872
Accrued interest (122 days): 1.8383562
Clean price: 108.1149310

For this buy/sell-back transaction both the **spot price of 108.27** as well as the **forward price of 108.1149310** are confirmed (both clean prices).

NOTE: It is – contrary to classic repos – not allowed to round!

Structure:

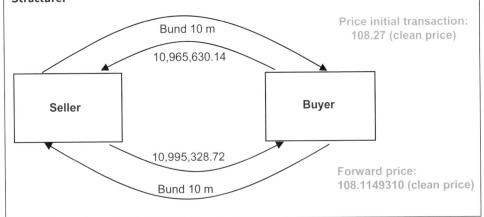

Beispiel

Buy/Sell-Back

Ein Händler kauft EUR 10 Mio. Bund in einem Buy/Sell-Back.

Collateral: 5 1/2% Bundesrepublik Deutschland 14.08.2013 (ACT/ACT)
Clean Price: 108,27
Stückzinstage: 92
Stückzinsen: 1,3863014 (5,5 × 92/365)
Dirty Price: 109,6563014
Reposatz: 3,27–3,25%
Laufzeit: 30 Tage

Anfangstransaktion Cash: EUR 10.965.630,14 [(10.000.000 × 109,65630137/100)]
Anfangstransaktion WP: EUR 10.000.000,00

Der Bondhändler kauft die Anleihe im Repo und gibt Cash. Als Market User handelt er daher auf der Briefseite zu 3,25%.

Schlusstransaktion Cash: EUR 10.995.328,72 [10.965.630,14 × (1 + 0,0325 x 30/360)]
Schlusstransaktion WP: EUR 10.000.000,00
Dirty Price: 109,9532872
Stückzinsen (122 Tage): 1,8383562
Clean Price: 108,1149310

Bei dieser Buy/Sell-Back-Transaktion werden also als **Kassakurs 108,27** und als **Terminkurs 108,1149310** bestätigt (beides Clean Preise).

ACHTUNG: Hier darf – im Unterschied zu klassischen Repos – nicht gerundet werden!

Struktur:

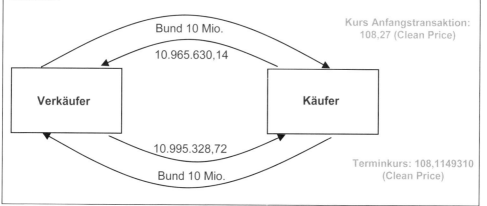

Example

Buy/sell-back
Calculation forward price with interim coupon payments

A trader buys EUR 10 m Bund in a sell/buy-back.

Collateral: 5% Fed. Republic of Germany
Clean price: 108.00
Accrued interest: 345 days
Accrued interest: 4.7260274   (5 x 345/365)
Dirty price: 112.7260274
Repo rate: 3.50%
Repo term: 30 days

Initial transaction cash: EUR 1,272,602.74 [(10,000,000 x 112.7260274/100)]
Initial transactions bonds: EUR 0,000,000.00

After 20 days the buyer (= cash lender) receives the coupon. He does not transfer the coupon to the seller but takes it into account for the final transaction – plus interest. The coupon payment equals an early redemption of the cash amount.

$Coupon_{day20}$:   EUR 500,000.00 (0.05 x 10,000,000)
$Interest_{day\ 20-30}$: EUR 486.11   (500,000 x 0.035 x 10/360)

Final transaction cash:
Initial amount: 11,272,602.74
Repo interest: 32,878.42
– Coupon: – 500,000.00
– Interest Coupon: – 486.11
                          _____
                          10,804,995.05

The dirty price of the final transaction is the result of dividing the cash amount by the bond nominal:

Dirty price: 108.0499505

For the forward price (clean price) the accrued interest have to be substracted.

Accrued interest (10 days):   0.1369863
Clean price: 107.9129642

The forward price for this transaction is 107.9129642.

Beispiel

Buy/Sell-Back
Berechnung Terminkurs bei zwischenzeitlicher Kuponzahlung

Ein Händler kauft EUR 10 Mio. Bund in einem Buy/Sell-Back.

Collateral: 5% Bundesrepublik Deutschland
Clean Price: 108,00
Stückzinstage: 345
Stückzinsen: 4,7260274 (5 × 345/365)
Dirty Price: 112,7260274
Reposatz: 3,50%
Laufzeit: 30 Tage

Anfangstransaktion Cash: EUR 11.272.602,74 [(10.000.000 × 112,7260274/100)]
Anfangstransaktion WP: EUR 10.000.000,00

Nach 20 Tagen erhält der Käufer (Cashgeber) den fälligen Kupon. Dieser leitet ihn nicht an den Verkäufer weiter, sondern bringt die Kuponzahlung zuzüglich Zinsen in der Schlusstransaktion zum Abzug. Die Kuponzahlung wirkt hier also wie eine vorzeitige Rückzahlung des Cashbetrages.

$Kupon_{Tag20}$:   EUR 500.000,00 (0,05 × 10.000.000)
$Zinsen_{Tag\,20\text{-}30}$: EUR 486,11   (500.000 × 0,035 × 10/360)

Somit ergibt sich folgende Schlusstransaktion Cash

Anfangsbetrag: 11.272.602,74
Repo-Zinsen: 32.878,42
– Kupon: – 500.000,00
– Zinsen Kupon: – 486,11
                      10.804.995,05

Der Dirty Price der Schlusstransaktion ergibt sich durch die Division des Cashbetrages durch das Wertpapier-Nominale.

Dirty Price: 108,0499505

Für den Terminkurs (Clean Price) müssen noch die Stückzinsen abgezogen werden.

Stückzinsen (10 Tage):   0,1369863
Clean Price: 107,9129642

Der Terminkurs bei dieser Transaktion ist 107,9129642.

Example

Buy/sell-back - close and reprice with collateral adjustment

A trader buys EUR 10 m Bund in a sell/buy-back. After ten days the price of the collateral falls to 105.00. Which transactions have to be made if close and reprice with collateral adjustment has been agreed?

Collateral:	5 1/2% Fed. Republic of Germany 14th Aug. 2013 (ACT/ACT)
Clean price:	108.27
Accrued interest:	92 days
Accrued interest:	1.3863014 (5.5 x 92/365)
Dirty price:	109.6563014
Repo rate:	3.25%
Repo term:	30 days

Initial transaction cash: EUR 10,965,630.14 [(10,000,000 x 109.65630137/100)]
Initial transaction bonds: EUR 10,000,000.00

Close and reprice means that the original deal is early terminated. Thus the buyer delivers back the bonds and receives the cash plus interest. At the same time a new deal is done at the amount of the outstanding cash amount. As payments are netted, there is actually only one delivery in securities.

Close:	closing of the original deal
Collateral:	EUR 10,000,000.00 from buyer to seller
Cash:	EUR 10,975,529.67 from seller to buyer
	[10,965,630.14 x (1+0.0325 x 10/360)]
Reprice:	new deal
Clean price:	105.00
Accrued interest (102 days):	1.5369863 [5.5 x 102/365]
Dirty price:	106.5369863
Cash:	EUR 10,975,529.67 from buyer to seller
Collateral:	EUR 10,302,083.86 from seller to buyer
	[10,975,529.67 / 1.065369863]

Thus, the seller has to deliver **EUR 302,083.86** additional collateral (nominal) to the buyer.

The new deal has the following specifications:

Initial transaction:

Clean price:	105.00
Dirty price:	106.5369863
Bond nominal:	EUR 10,302,083.86
Cash:	EUR 10,975,529.67

Beispiel

Buy/Sell-Back – Close and Reprice mit Collateral Anpassung

Ein Händler kauft EUR 10 Mio. Bund in einem Buy/Sell-Back. Nach zehn Tagen fällt der Kurs des Collaterals auf 105,00. Welche Transaktion findet statt, wenn Close and Reprice mit Collateral Anpassung vereinbart wurde?

Collateral: 5 1/2% Bundesrepublik Deutschland 14.08.2013 (ACT/ACT)
Clean Price: 108,27
Stückzinstage: 92
Stückzinsen: 1,3863014 (5,5 × 92/365)
Dirty Price: 109,6563014
Reposatz: 3,25%
Laufzeit: 30 Tage

Anfangstransaktion Cash: EUR 10.965.630,14 [(10.000.000 × 109,65630137/100)]
Anfangstransaktion WP: EUR 10.000.000,00

Beim Close and Reprice wird das ursprüngliche Geschäft frühzeitig beendet. Daher liefert der Käufer die Anleihen zurück und erhält das Cash zuzüglich angelaufener Zinsen zurück. Gleichzeitig wird ein neues Geschäft über den ausstehenden Cashbetrag abgeschlossen. Da die Zahlungen genettet werden, findet de facto nur eine Wertpapierlieferung statt.

Close: Schließung des ursprünglichen Geschäfts
Collateral: EUR 10.000.000,00 vom Käufer an den Verkäufer
Cash: EUR 10.975.529,67 vom Verkäufer an den Käufer
                    [10.965.630,14 x (1 + 0,0325 × 10/360)]

Reprice: neues Geschäft
Clean Price: 105,00
Stückzinsen (102 T): 1,5369863 [5,5 x 102/365]
Dirty Price: 106,5369863
Cash: EUR 10.975.529,67 vom Käufer an den Verkäufer
Collateral: EUR 10.302.083,86 vom Verkäufer an den Käufer
                    [10.975.529,67 / 1,065369863]

Der Verkäufer muss daher an den Käufer zusätzliches Collateral mit Nominale von **EUR 302.083,86** liefern.

Das neue Geschäft weist folgende Daten auf:

Anfangstransaktion
Clean Price: 105,00
Dirty Price: 106,5369863
WP-Nominale: EUR 10.302.083,86
Cash: EUR 10.975.529,67

Final transaction:

Cash:	EUR 10,995,346.50 [10,975,529.67 x (1+0.0325 x 20/360)
Bond nominal:	EUR 10,302,083.86
Dirty price:	106.7293447 [10,995,346.50 / 10,302,083.86]
Accrued interest (122 days):	1.8383562
Clean price:	104.8909885

The new deal is done at **105.00 (spot price)** and **104.8909885 (forward price)**.

4.7. Documentation – Frame Contracts

Repo depends on the ability of the buyer (= cash lender) to sell collateral in order to re-cover his cash in the event of a default by the seller. This depends on legal title to the collateral being successfully transferred to the buyer. However, transfer of legal title is not possible in all jurisdictions. Even in jurisdictions where this is possible, the transfer may be subject to conditions. The main problem is compounded by the number of jurisdictions potentially involved, which could be different for the repo seller, the buyer, the issuer of the collateral, the depository holding the collateral and the jurisdiction of the governing law chosen by the counterparties to the contract. Anyone using repo should take care to ensure that the contracts are legally enforceable in the event of a dispute.

A vital safeguard against legal difficulties is obviously to **document the agreed rights and obligations** of the counterparties. The main obstacle to documentation in the past has been cost, but this has been greatly reduced by the publication of **standard frame contracts**.

The most common frame contract in the repo market is the **TBMA/ISMA Global Master Repurchase Agreement** (TBMA/ISMA GMRA). TBMA (The Bond Market Association) is the US-American association of bond traders and the successor of the PSA (Public Securities Association). ISMA stands for International Securities Market Association. The ISMA merged in 2005 with the International Primary Market Association to form the ICMA (International Capital Market Association).

The first version has been published in 1992. A substantially revised version followed in 1995 (PSA/ISMA 1995) where sell/buy-backs have been added. The third and actual version has been published in 2000 (TBMA/ISMA 2000). The frame contract is regularly updated and a number of additions have been made. The GMRA is subject to **British law**, additionally there are national attachments.

One aim of ISMA is also to ensure the legal enforceability for as many countries as possible. For that purpose, at present, **legal opinions** for 30 countries are available.

Schlusstransaktion:

Cash:	EUR 10.995.346,50 [10.975.529,67 × (1 + 0,0325 × 20/360)]
WP-Nominale:	EUR 10.302.083,86
Dirty Price:	106,7293447 [10.995.346,50 / 10.302.083,86]
Stückzinsen (122 T):	1,8383562
Clean Price:	104,8909885

Das neue Geschäft wird also zu den Kursen von **105,00 (Kassa)** und **104,8909885 (Terminkurs)** abgeschlossen.

4.7. Dokumentation – Rahmenverträge

Repos beruhen auf der Möglichkeit des Käufers (= Cashgeber), sich im Falle der Nichterfüllung durch den Verkäufer (Default Event) durch den sofortigen Verkauf des Collaterals schadlos zu halten. Dazu ist die Übertragung des rechtlichen Eigentums an den Wertpapieren auf den Käufer nötig. Speziell bei grenzüberschreitenden Transaktionen kann dabei das Problem bestehen, dass eine Übertragung des Eigentums in manchen Ländern nicht möglich bzw. anerkannt ist. Selbst in Ländern, wo dies möglich ist, kann die Eigentumsübertragung an bestimmte Bedingungen gekoppelt sein. Problematisch ist vor allem, dass die beteiligten Parteien (Käufer, Verkäufer, Verwahrer usw.) jeweils einem anderen nationalen Recht unterliegen. Daher ist es für alle Marktteilnehmer von Interesse, die juristische Durchsetzbarkeit der Rechte zu überprüfen und sicherzustellen.

Ein wichtiges Mittel zur Vermeidung von rechtlichen Problemen ist eine **ausreichende Dokumentation der Rechte und Pflichten der Kontrahenten** und darüber, welches Recht anzuwenden ist. In der Vergangenheit war das Hauptproblem dabei der damit verbundene Aufwand und damit die Kosten. Diese Problematik wurde durch die **Verfassung von Standardrahmenverträgen** weitgehend entschärft.

Im Repomarkt ist der am häufigsten angewendete Rahmenvertrag das **TBMA/ISMA Global Master Repurchase Agreement** (TBMA/ISMA GMRA). TBMA (The Bond Market Association) ist die US-amerikanische Vereinigung der Bondhändler und ist die Nachfolgeorganisation der PSA (Public Securities Association). ISMA steht für International Securities Market Association. Diese verschmolz im Juli 2005 mit der International Primary Market Association (IPMA) zur International Capital Markets Association (ICMA). Das Kürzel ISMA wird weiterhin für das Master Agreement verwendet.

Die erste Version wurde 1992 veröffentlicht. 1995 erfolgte eine substantiell überarbeitete Version (PSA/ISMA 1995). Der wesentlichste Punkt war dabei die Ergänzung um Sell/Buy-Backs. Die dritte und aktuelle Version wurde 2000 veröffentlicht (TBMA/ISMA 2000). Der Rahmenvertrag wird ständig weiterentwickelt und durch zahlreiche Anhänge ergänzt. Der GMRA unterliegt **englischem Recht**, zusätzlich gibt es mehrere nationale Anhänge.

Ein Ziel der ISMA ist auch, die rechtliche Durchsetzbarkeit in möglichst vielen Ländern sicherzustellen. Dazu liegen derzeit Rechtsgutachten – sogenannte **Legal Opinions** – für 30 Länder vor.

The frame contract also defines the **events of default**. Here, some of them are roughly summarised:

- price is not paid
- securities are not delivered (optional)
- margin calls are not done (regulations regarding the margin maintanance)
- dividends resp. accrued interest due under a transaction are not paid
- insolvency

The occurrence of an event of default has the effect of accelerating outstanding transactions, converting delivery obligations in respect of securities to cash sums based on the market value of those securities (close-out) and then applying set-off. The defaulting party will be liable for the non-defaulting party's expenses in connection with the event of default, together with interest.

Except for certain cases of insolvency (where default arises automatically) the non-defaulting party can decide if these events have to be regarded as events of default which would then lead to the termination of the frame contract. If this party decides to treat the event as an event of default, it has to inform the other party **("note of default")**. The granting of a grace period is not necessary, i.e. the collateral can immediately be liquidated.

In the event of a close-out following the event of default, the non-defaulting party is allowed to **calculate the close-out amount** by reference to an actual sale or purchase price or the market value of the securities, in either case at any time during the **five dealing days following the occurrence of the event of default**. If, however, the non-defaulting party determines that it is not commercially reasonable to obtain quotations, it may instead determine the market value to be the "Net Value" of the securities. The "Net Value" is a fair market value reasonably determined by the non-defaulting party.

Where there has been a failure to deliver securities on the purchase or repurchase date and this event is not specified as a default event, or the non-defaulting party chooses not to give a default notice, the non-defaulting party is entitled to

- require the repayment of the (re)purchase price if it has paid it, or
- if it has a transaction exposure, require the payment of cash margin, or
- declare by written notice, that only that transaction shall be terminated

The complete frame contract including annexes and guidance notes can be downloaded at www.icma-group.org

Im Rahmenvertrag werden auch die **Ereignisse der Nichterfüllung** (Events of Default) angeführt. Einige davon werden hier grob zusammengefasst:

- Nichtzahlung des Kaufpreises
- Nichtlieferung der Wertpapiere (optional)
- Nichterfüllung der Margin-Zahlungen (Bestimmungen über die Aufrechterhaltung der Einschüsse)
- Nichtzahlung von Dividenden bzw. Stückzinsen im Rahmen einer Transaktion
- Insolvenzfall

Der Eintritt eines Ereignisses der Nichterfüllung hat die Wirkung, offene Transaktionen vorzeitig fällig zu stellen, Lieferverpflichtungen in Bezug auf Wertpapiere in Barbeträge auf Basis des Marktwerts der betreffenden Wertpapiere umzuwandeln und dann eine Aufrechnung vorzunehmen (Glattstellen bzw. Close-Out und Set-Off). Die nicht erfüllende Partei haftet für die Aufwendungen der nicht säumigen Partei.

Außer in bestimmten Insolvenzfällen (wo die Nichterfüllung automatisch erfolgt) liegt es **im Ermessen der nicht-säumigen Partei** zu entscheiden, ob diese Ereignisse als Ereignisse der Nichterfüllung behandelt werden sollen, die zur Beendigung des Rahmenvertrags führen. Wenn sie beschließt, ein Ereignis als Ereignis der Nichterfüllung zu behandeln, muss sie der anderen Partei eine entsprechende Mitteilung (**„Nichterfüllungsanzeige"**) zustellen. Das Setzen einer Nachfrist ist nicht nötig, d.h., das Collateral kann sofort liquidiert werden.

Zum Zwecke der Glattstellung (= Close-Out) bei Ereignissen der Nichterfüllung kann die nicht-säumige Partei den **Glattstellungsbetrag** anhand eines tatsächlichen Verkaufs- oder Kaufpreises oder anhand des Marktwerts der Wertpapiere, und zwar **jederzeit während der fünf Handelstage nach dem Eintritt des Ereignisses der Nichterfüllung feststellen**. Wenn die Marktkonditionen keine kaufmännisch sinnvolle Einholung von Kursstellungen erlaubt, hat die nicht-säumige Partei auch das Recht, einen „Nettowert" der Marktwerte zu bestimmen. Dieser Nettowert ist dabei ein angemessener Marktwert, der von der nicht-säumigen Partei ermittelt wird.

Werden Wertpapiere bei Kauf bzw. Verkauf nicht geliefert und ist dieses Event nicht als Nichterfüllungsereignis definiert bzw. wird das Event nicht als solches angezeigt, so hat die nicht-säumige Partei unter anderem das Recht,

- die Rückzahlung des (Rück-)Kaufpreises zu verlangen, sofern dieser bereits gezahlt wurde, oder
- die Zahlung eines Bareinschusses (Margin) zu verlangen, um ein Transaktionsexposure abzudecken, oder
- die Transaktion für beendet zu erklären.

Der vollständige Rahmenvertrag inklusive aller Anhänge kann unter www.icma-group.org heruntergeladen werden.

4.8. Risks

Repos offer a **double indemnity against credit risk:**

- Repo collateral provides protection against loss due to a default by a repo counterparty; if a repo counterparty fails, the non-defaulting buyer would sell the collateral and the non-defaulting seller would use the cash to buy new collateral.
- The repo counterparty provides protection against loss due to a default by the issuer of the collateral securities; if the issuer of the collateral fails, the seller has an obligation to repurchase the defaulted collateral at the original price, or provide new collateral.

For the counterparty that lends cash (= buyer), loss can only incur if both the seller as well as the issuer of the collateral simultaneously default. As long as there is limited correlation between the credit risk on the repo counterparty and the credit risk on the issuer of the collateral, making a simultaneous default unlikely, each repo counterparty has **two more or less independent sources of comfort** which significantly **reduces the credit risk exposure** through a repo. Especially when regarding the extreme case where the seller (= cash borrower) offers self-issued securities (correlation = 100%), the collateral does not provide any more comfort as in the event of default of the seller also the issuer of the collateral would default.

If the issuer of collateral fails, the buyer has merely to demand fresh collateral from the seller, what – due to margin calls - would happen automatically. Whereas, if the repo counterparty fails, the non-defaulting counterparty may be exposed to a variety of potential problems:

- **Legal risk**
  Eeven though the repo should transfer ownership of the collateral to the buyer, the buyer's rights to it may be challenged in court by the administrator of a defaulting counterparty, or by other creditors.
- **Operational risk**
  The collateral may turn out to be inadequate due to operational inefficiencies, e.g. inability to sell illiquid collateral, failure to call variation margins, inefficiency in collecting the collateral from a custodian, or a delay in identifying an event of default
- **Inconvenience**
  A default, even on a secured instrument like repo, will require the non-defaulting counterparty to monitor bankruptcy proceedings, to ensure that there are no legal challenges to the buyer's right to collateral; and it may have to pursue a claim if there is a shortfall in collateral

Because of the potential problems, the primary credit risk in a repo is typically on the repo counterparty, rather than on the collateral. The collateral provided through a repo should be regarded only as secondary protection against default by the counterparty.

4.8. Risiken

Repos bieten eine **doppelte Absicherung gegen das Kreditrisiko:**

- Das Collateral bietet eine Absicherung bei einem Ausfall des Kontrahenten. Der nicht ausfallende Käufer verkauft die Wertpapiere, um sich schadlos zu halten. Der nicht ausfallende Verkäufer benutzt das Cash, um sich neue Wertpapiere zu kaufen, falls der Käufer ausfällt.
- Der Verkäufer bietet auch Schutz gegen einen Verlust für den Käufer bei einem Ausfall des Emittenten, da er ja verpflichtet ist, das Papier zu einem fixierten Kurs wieder zurückzukaufen.

Für den Cashgeber kann es nur zu Verlusten kommen, wenn sowohl der Verkäufer als auch der Emittent des Collaterals gleichzeitig ausfallen. Der Cashgeber hat also **zwei Quellen der Besicherung**, wodurch das **gesamte Kreditrisiko deutlich reduziert** wird. Das Kreditrisiko ist dabei umso geringer, je geringer die Korrelation zwischen dem Cashnehmer und dem Collateral ist. Dies wird deutlich, wenn wir den Extremfall betrachten, bei dem der Cashnehmer von ihm selber emittierte Anleihen als Sicherheit anbietet. Da die Korrelation dann 100% beträgt, ergibt sich durch das Collateral keine zusätzliche Sicherheit, weil ja bei einem Ausfall des Cashnehmers gleichzeitig auch immer der Emittent des Collaterals ausfällt. Somit sollte deutlich geworden sein, dass eine niedrige Korrelation zwischen dem Cashnehmer und dem Collateral zu einem niedrigeren Kreditrisiko führt.

Wenn der Emittent des Collaterals ausfällt, muss der Käufer lediglich ein neues Collateral vom Cashnehmer verlangen, was ja im Rahmen der Margin Calls automatisch erfolgen würde. Wenn hingegen der Cashnehmer im Repo ausfällt, kann der Käufer einer Reihe von Problemen ausgesetzt sein:

- **Rechtliches Risiko**
  Obwohl im Repo das rechtliche Eigentum auf den Käufer übergehen sollte, kann es vorkommen, dass die Eigentumsübertragung vom Masseverwalter oder anderen Gläubigern angefochten wird.
- **Operationelle Risiken**
  Das Collateral kann sich aus operationellen Gründen als unzureichend herausstellen, z.B. wenn illiquide Papiere nicht zum Bewertungskurs verkauft werden können, Fehler bei der Verrechnung der Variation Margin passiert sind, die Beschaffung des Collaterals vom Custodian (Verwahrer) zu Verzögerungen führt oder wenn der Ausfall des Kontrahenten erst verspätet entdeckt wird.
- **Aufwand bei der Abwicklung**
  Auch bei einem besicherten Instrument wie dem Repo sollte die nicht ausfallende Partei die Insolvenzabwicklung genau verfolgen, um zu verhindern, dass andere Gläubiger das Collateral beanspruchen. Außerdem müssen die eigenen Forderungen geltend gemacht werden, falls das Collateral sich als unzureichend herausstellt.

Aufgrund dieser möglichen Probleme ist das primäre Risiko der Repo-Kontrahent. Das Collateral sollte nur als sekundäre Sicherheit bei einem Ausfall des Kontrahenten betrachtet werden.

Repo transactions are inherently safer than unsecured instruments, but they should not be used to do business with institutions who would otherwise be unacceptable counterparties for unsecured business. The appropriated way of taking extra risk to enhance returns on repos is to take riskier collateral from acceptable counterparties.

In summary, repos are **operationally intensive** and thus bear **operational risks**:

- The sale and repurchase, variation margins, rights of substitution and payments of manufactured dividends all involve transfers of securities and/or cash.
- In order to mark to market, professional systems and good price sources are required. Once made, margin calls have to be monitored until they arrive.
- Collateral has to be managed to avoid undue concentrations of particular securities in holdings of collateral.
- Documentation, tax and accounting implications have to be understood and monitored. All these activities require an efficient back office operation in terms of people and systems.

4.9. Special Types of Repos

Dollar repo

A dollar repo is a repo in which the buyer may return at maturity a security which is different, within agreed limits, from the original collateral.

Forward start repo

This is a repo where the start date is for value later than the normal settlement date for the security concerned.

Floating rate repo

In a floating rate repo, the repo rate is re-set at pre-determined intervals according o some benchmark, such as LIBOR. It is also common to use an overnight reference rate like EONIA.

Reverse to maturity repo

This is a reverse repo with the same maturity date as the security used as collateral.

Flex repo

In a flex repo the seller pays back the cash in instalments, following an exact repayment plan.

Open repo

An open repo can be terminated by both counterparties. A specific maturity date is not fixed.

Obwohl Repos ungleich sicherer als unbesicherte Instrumente sind, sollten Repos mit Kontrahenten, die ansonsten unakzeptabel wären, nur mit Vorsicht gemacht werden. Der bessere Weg, zusätzliches Risiko für höhere Erträge zu nehmen, wäre, schlechteres Collateral von ansonsten akzeptablen Kontrahenten zu nehmen.

Zusammenfassend ist zu sagen, dass Repos einen **hohen operationellen Aufwand** – und damit einhergehend **operationelle Risiken** – mit sich bringen:

- Der Kauf und Verkauf, Variation Margins, Substitution und die Zahlung der Manufactured Dividends führen zu einem Transfer von Cash und/oder Wertpapieren.
- Die laufende Mark-to-Market-Bewertung benötigt umfangreiche Systeme und zuverlässige Preisquellen. Fallen Margin Calls an, muss auch deren Eingang überwacht werden.
- Ein effizientes Collateral Management muss für die Vermeidung von unerwünschten Konzentrationsrisiken in einzelnen Collaterals sorgen.
- Für Fragen der Dokumentation, Steuer und Bilanzierung muss ausreichend geschultes Personal vorhanden sein.

4.9. Sonderformen von Repos

Dollar Repo

Ein Dollar Repo ist ein Repo, das dem Käufer erlaubt, unterschiedliche Papiere – von fixierter Qualität – in der Schlusstransaktion zurückzuliefern.

Forward Start Repo

Ein Forward Start Repo ist ein Repo, das nicht am normalen Value Date startet, sondern zu einem späteren Zeitpunkt.

Floating Rate Repo

Ein Floating Rate Repo hat üblicherweise fixierte Zinsanpassungstermine, an denen der Repo-Satz mit einer im Vorhinein fixierten Benchmark (z.B. LIBOR) angepasst wird. Üblich ist auch die Verwendung eines Overnight-Referenzsatzes, z.B. EONIA.

Reverse to Maturity Repo

Bei einem Reverse to Maturity Repo endet das Repo am gleichen Tag, an dem das Wertpapier getilgt wird.

Flex Repo

Bei einem Flex Repo wird das Cash, einem genauen Tilgungsplan folgend, in Raten zurückgezahlt.

Open Repo

Ein offenes Repo räumt sowohl dem Käufer wie auch dem Verkäufer das Recht ein, das Repo-Geschäft jederzeit zu beenden.

4.10. Synthetic Repo

A synthetic repo is a strategy that consists of more than one deal which then altogether have the same effect as a repo.

As we know, a reverse repo is the simultaneous purchase and later sale of a security. A **synthetic reverse repo**, for example, would be a sale of bond futures and, at the same time, purchase of deliverable bonds in the spot market. Out of this you can calculate the implicit interest rate for an investment – the so-called **implied repo rate**. Such a strategy is also called "cash-and-carry arbitrage". To make this arbitrage perfect, the synthetic repo position has to be hedged by a "real" repo, i.e. here the bond is sold and bought. If in this case, the implicit reverse repo rate for the investment was higher than the repo rate for the "real" repo, this would be a profit.

A **synthetic repo** would be produced the other way round: sell deliverable bonds in the spot market and buy bond futures. The short bond position had to be hedged by means of a "real" repo. In this case, it was a profit if the implied repo rate was lower than the reverse repo rate.

4.11. Security Lending

Security lending is the exchange of two securities for the term of the deal. This is sensible if the seller of the security does not need cash and wants to wait until his security turns **special**. With other words, securities lending is the exchange of two securities, where one is usually a special and the other a general collateral.

Quotation

The terminology in securities lending follows that in a classic repo but takes the viewpoint of the special. The "buyer" is therefore the party buying the special, and the seller is the party selling the special.

Since in securities lending no cash transfers take place, a premium (=**security lending fee**) in percentage p.a. based on the market value of the security is quoted instead of the repo rate. This fee has to be paid by the buyer (of the special).

The security lending fee is the **difference between a GC repo rate and the repo rate for the corresponding special**.

4.10. Synthetisches Repo

Unter einem synthetischen Repo versteht man eine Strategie, die aus mehreren Geschäften besteht, die zusammen den gleichen Effekt wie ein Repo haben.

Wie wir wissen, ist ein Reverse Repo der Kauf und gleichzeitige Verkauf eines Wertpapiers zu einem späteren Datum. Ein **synthetisches Reverse Repo** ist somit z.B. der Verkauf eines Bond Futures und der gleichzeitige Kauf einer lieferbaren Anleihe im Kassamarkt. Daraus kann der implizite Zinssatz für eine Veranlagung errechnet werden – die sogenannte **„Implied Repo Rate"**. Das ist genau jene Strategie, die auch **„Cash-and-Carry Arbitrage"** genannt wird. Um die Arbitrage perfekt zu machen, muss das synthetische Repo durch ein „echtes" Repo geschlossen werden, d.h., die Anleihe wird wieder verkauft und gekauft. Ist in diesem Fall der implizierte Reverse Repo-Zinssatz für die Anlage höher als der Repo-Satz im „echten Repo", ergibt sich für den Arbitrageur ein Gewinn.

Ein **synthetisches Repo** würde genau umgekehrt konstruiert werden: Verkauf der lieferbaren Anleihe in der Kassa und Kauf des Bond Futures. Die zwischenzeitliche Short-Anleiheposition müsste durch ein „echtes" Reverse Repo geschlossen werden. In diesem Fall würde sich ein Gewinn ergeben, wenn die Implied Repo Rate niedriger als der Zinssatz des Reverse Repos ist.

4.11. Security Lending

Beim Security Lending steht immer ein **Special** im Mittelpunkt. Der Verleiher des Specials erhält dabei ein General Collateral als Sicherheit. Als Preis für die Überlassung des Specials erhält er zusätzlich eine Prämie als Leihgebühr.

Quotierung

Beim Security Lending wird in der Terminologie die Sicht des Specials eingenommen. Mit Verkäufer ist der Verkäufer des Specials gemeint, der Käufer ist der Käufer des Specials.

Beim Security Lending wird kein Cash geborgt. Daher wird üblicherweise nicht der Repo-Satz quotiert, sondern eine Prämie (die **Security Lending Fee**) in % p.a., die vom Käufer (des Specials) zu bezahlen ist.

Die Security Lending Fee ergibt sich aus der **Differenz zwischen einem GC-Reposatz und dem Reposatz für das entsprechende Special**.

Example

GC repo rate:	3.00 %
Special rate:	2.25 %
Security lending fee:	0.75 %

If the premium did not equal the difference between GC and special, arbitrage would be possible:

Premium < difference, e.g. 0.5%:

Special lending	at 0.50%	(costs)
Repo (special)	at 2.25%	(= borrow cash at 2.25%)
Reverse repo GC	at 3.00%	(= lend cash at 3.00%)

Profit:	0.25%

Premium > difference, e.g. 1.0%:

Special lending	at 1.00%	(return)
Rev. repo (Special)	at 2.25%	(= lend cash at 2.25%)
Repo GC	at 3.00%	(= borrow cash at 3.00%)

Profit:	0.25%

Coupon payment

Coupon payments are treated analogue to classic repos, i.e. these coupon payments are transferred immediately to the original owner (seller).

Margins

Like in a classic repo, initial margin and margin calls can be required under securities lending.

Contrary to the classic repo, the **initial margin must be paid by the buyer of the special** because it is the securities lent which are driving the deal.

Margin calls are paid in the same way as in classic repo, but this generally by adjusting the amount of collateral rather than the amount of the security lent (= special), because the borrower has a need for that particular amount of that security.

Beispiel		
GC-Reposatz:	3,00%	
Special Satz:	2,25%	
Security Lending Fee:	0,75%	

Würde die Prämie nicht der Differenz zwischen GC und Special entsprechen, könnte Arbitrage betrieben werden:

Prämie < Differenz z.B. 0,5%:

Leihe des Special	zu 0,50%	(Kosten)
Repo (Special)	zu 2,25%	(= Cash nehmen zu 2,25%)
Reverse Repo GC	zu 3,00%	(= Cash geben zu 3,00%)
Gewinn	0,25%	

Prämie > Differenz z.B. 1%:

Verleihen des Special	zu 1,00%	(Ertrag)
Reverse Repo (Special)	zu 2,25%	(= Cash geben zu 2,25%)
Repo GC	zu 3,00%	(= Cash nehmen zu 3,00%)
Gewinn	0,25%	

Kuponzahlungen

Fallen während der Laufzeit bei einem der zwei Anleihen Kuponzahlungen an, so sind diese Kuponzahlungen – analog dem klassischen Repo – gleich an den ursprünglichen Besitzer weiterzuleiten.

Margins

Wie beim klassischen Repo können bei einem Security Lending sowohl Initial Margin als auch Margin Calls vereinbart werden.

Während die Initial Margin beim Repo jedoch vom Verkäufer der Anleihe zu leisten ist, ist beim Security Lending die **Initial Margin vom Käufer** (des Specials) **zu entrichten** (da der Markt vom Bedarf der Käufer angetrieben wird).

Bei den Margin Calls gelten die gleichen Bedingungen wie beim klassischen Repo. Die Anpassung an den aktuellen Marktwert wird dabei immer im General Collateral gemacht. Dies ist dadurch bedingt, dass der Käufer des Specials üblicherweise einen genau definierten Bedarf an diesem Papier hat.

Summary

A repo (sale and repurchase agreement) is a contract under which the seller commits to sell securities to the buyer (alternative term: to repo out securities) and simultaneously commits to repurchase the same (or similar) securities from the buyer at a later date (maturity date), repaying the original sum of money plus a return for the use of that money over the term of the repo.

In the market three types of repos are generally differentiated: classic repo (US-style repo), sell/buy-back (resp. buy/sell-back) and security lending.

The collateral is not pledged but sold to the buyer (=gives cash). As a consequence, the collateral passes from the seller to the buyer, i.e. legal title is transferred for the term of the repo. Although the legal title to collateral is transferred to the buyer, the commitment of the seller to repurchase the collateral at the original value means that the risk and return on the collateral remain with the seller. Thus, the economic ownership remains with the seller.

With regard to term, the following types can be differentiated: open repo (demand repo), short-dated repo and term repo.

Repos are quoted on a p.a. basis (like interbank deposits). The repo interest rate is calculated according to the relevant money market convention, i.e. act/360 resp. act/365 for GBP. The repo terminology, however, is based on the securities side of the deal. The seller sells the securities in the initial transaction (sale and repurchase) and takes cash. The buyer of the repo is the party that purchases the bond and gives cash. This is also called a reverse repo.

A repo takes two major forms: cash-driven (lending cash against securities) and security-driven (lending securities against cash).

The cash-driven repo is the most common type. This repo is used as a money market instrument like a classic interbank deposit. Thus, the focus is on cash. The main difference to interbank deposits is the collateral. For the borrower of cash this results in a lower refinancing rate. The lender of the cash can profit from the reduced credit risk. For the calculation of the nominal amount of the collateral one has to consider that the bond's market value (= dirty price) equals the borrowed cash amount. To the repo buyer it does not matter which bond is used as long as certain quality criteria are guaranteed. Therefore, you also speak of a so-called general collateral (in contrast to special collateral). At maturity the collateral is transferred back, the seller (cash borrower) pays back to the buyer the cash amount plus repo interest (cash lender).

Zusammenfassung

Ein Repo (Sale and Repurchase Agreement) ist ein Vertrag, bei dem der Verkäufer Wertpapiere an den Käufer verkauft und sich gleichzeitig verpflichtet, dieselben (oder ähnliche) Wertpapiere zu einem späteren Zeitpunkt zurückzukaufen, wobei er den gleichen Preis wie beim ursprünglichen Verkauf zuzüglich Zinsen für den, für die Laufzeit des Repos, erhaltenen Cash-Betrag zahlt. Die deutsche Bezeichnung dafür ist Pensionsgeschäft, das auch als befristete Überlassung von Wertpapieren beschrieben werden kann.

Grundsätzlich werden drei Varianten von Repos unterschieden: Klassisches Repo (US-style Repo), Sell/Buy-Back (bzw. Buy/Sell-Back) und Security Lending (Wertpapierleihe).

Das Wertpapier dient im Repo als Besicherung („collateral"). Zu diesem Zweck wird es jedoch nicht verpfändet, sondern an den Käufer (= Pensionsnehmer, Cashgeber) verkauft. Im Repo wechselt also das rechtliche Eigentum am Wertpapier für die Laufzeit des Repos. Obwohl das rechtliche Eigentum vom Verkäufer auf den Käufer übergeht, verbleiben die wirtschaftlichen Risiken beim ursprünglichen Verkäufer, da er sich ja verpflichtet, das Collateral zum gleichen Preis wieder zurückzukaufen. Man sagt daher: Das wirtschaftliche Eigentum verbleibt beim Verkäufer.

Bezüglich der Laufzeit können folgende drei Arten von Repos unterschieden werden: Open Repo (Demand Repo), Short dated Repo und Term Repo.

Repos werden in Zinsen p.a. (analog Interbank-Depots) quotiert. Die Repo-Zinsen werden analog den entsprechenden Usancen im Geldmarkt berechnet, also ACT/360 bzw. ACT/365 bei GBP. Der Verkäufer im Repo verkauft die Anleihe in der Anfangstransaktion (sale and repurchase) und erhält dafür den Cashbetrag. Der Käufer im Repo hingegen kauft die Anleihe und gibt dafür Cash, er macht also eine umgekehrte Repotransaktion. Man spricht daher auch von einem Reverse Repo.

Grundsätzlich gibt es zwei treibende Faktoren für Repos: Cash-getriebene (wertpapierbesicherte(r) Kredit/Anlage) und Wertpapier-getriebene (Wertpapierleihe gegen Cash).

Das Cash-getriebene Repo ist heute die häufigste Anwendungsart. Das Repo wird hier als Money-Market-Instrument wie ein normales Interbank-Depot verwendet. Im Vordergrund steht dabei also das Cash. Der wesentliche Unterschied zu Interbank-Depots besteht in der zusätzlichen Besicherung durch das Collateral. Für den Cashnehmer bedeutet das einen niedrigeren Finanzierungszinssatz. Der Cashgeber profitiert vom verringerten Kreditrisiko. Bei der Berechnung des Nominalbetrages des Collaterals ist nur das Prinzip zu beachten, dass der Marktwert des Wertpapiers (Dirty Price) dem geliehenen Cashbetrag entspricht. Welches Wertpapier dazu verwendet wird, ist dem Pensionsnehmer egal, solange es bestimmte Qualitätskriterien erfüllt. Man spricht daher auch von einem sogenannten General Collateral (im Gegensatz zu einem Special Collateral). Am Ende der Laufzeit wird das Collateral zurückübertragen, und der Verkäufer (Cashnehmer) zahlt den Kapitalbetrag zuzüglich der Repo-Zinsen an den Käufer (Cashgeber).

Repos do not necessarily have to be cash-driven; they can also be used for a temporary security lending. Contrary to normal security lending the collateral is no other security but cash. For a security-driven repo the basis is the bond nominal and not a specific cash amount. The initial cash amount, then, is the actual market value (dirty price) of the collateral. In the final transaction the collateral is transferred back, and for the cash amount repo interest is added to the initial amount.

When describing the different typical applications, on the one hand cash is the basis, on the other hand it is the security. Thus, you can differentiate between repos with a general collateral (GC) or a special collateral. For cash-driven repos the only reason for the collateral is the securitisation of the loaned cash amount. The party giving the cash does not care which bond is used as long as certain predetermined criteria are satisfied. The repo can be regarded as a loan on a secured basis. Usually government bonds are used as collateral. The European Repo Council publishes a list of issuers which have to be accepted as general collateral as long as a bond is not excluded by one counterparty before trading the repo. Since 2002, the benchmark for secured money market transactions (GC repos) in the euro zone is EUREPO (in analogy to the EURIBOR as the benchmark for unsecured interbank deposits). Daily, at 11:00 a.m. (CET), Moneyline Telerate will process the EUREPO calculation as the average of all quotes from the bank panel.

If the buyer in a repo transaction requires a specific security as collateral, then he needs to do a special repo. The purpose of a repo in this context is the borrowing and lending of specific securities against cash. This is also called a security-driven repo.

The main repo market participants are bond traders, investors, fund managers, repo market makers and central banks.

In theory, the seller could seek similar protection by insisting that his collateral should be sold at a premium to its current market value which in practice is not common. To build in some protection against valuation problems, the buyer may insist on buying the collateral at a discount to its current market value, i.e. the repo would be overcollateralised. The degree of overcollateralisation is called an initial margin or haircut. The collateral in a repo is intended to protect the buyer (cash lender) against default by the seller. The buyer therefore has to ensure that he has enough collateral.

Betrachtet man ein Repo nicht von der Cash-Seite, sondern andersherum, so kann es auch zur vorübergehenden Leihe eines bestimmten Wertpapiers verwendet werden. Im Unterschied zur normalen Wertpapierleihe gibt der Pensionsnehmer kein anderes Wertpapier als Sicherheit, sondern Cash. Bei einem Wertpapier-getriebenen Repo ist der Ausgangspunkt also das benötigte Wertpapier-Nominale und nicht ein bestimmter Cashbetrag. Der Anfangs-Cashbetrag ist dann einfach der aktuelle Marktwert (Dirty Price) des Collaterals. Wiederum wird in der Schlusstransaktion das Collateral zurückübertragen, und der Cashbetrag errechnet sich einfach aus dem Anfangsbetrag zuzüglich der Repozinsen.

Bei den typischen Anwendungen von Repos wird zwischen Repos mit einem General Collateral (GC) und Repos mit einem Special Collateral unterschieden. Bei Cash-getriebenen Repos ist der einzige Zweck des Collaterals eine ausreichende Besicherung des geliehenen Cashbetrages. Dem Cashgeber ist daher egal, welches Wertpapier dafür verwendet wird, solange bestimmte Qualitätskriterien erfüllt werden. Das Repo ist hier also als ein Wertpapier-besicherter Kredit zu sehen. Üblicherweise werden Government Bonds, also Staatsanleihen, als Collateral verwendet. Das European Repo Council veröffentlicht eine Liste von Emittenten, die als General Collateral zu akzeptieren sind, sofern ein Papier nicht vor Abschluss des Repos von einer Partei explizit ausgeschlossen wurde. Außerdem wurde analog zum EURIBOR, der die Benchmark für unbesicherte Interbank-Depots darstellt, im Jahr 2002 EUREPO als Benchmark für GC-Repos eingeführt. Eurepo wird täglich um 11.00 (CET) von Reuters als Durchschnitt der Quotierungen der Panel-Banken errechnet.

Wenn ein Käufer in einem Repo (Pensionsnehmer) eine ganz bestimmte Anleihe als Collateral benötigt, muss er ein sogenanntes Special Repo machen. In diesem Fall ist das Repo daher als Wertpapierleihe gegen Cash anzusehen. Wir sprechen auch von einem Wertpapier-getriebenen Repo.

Die wichtigsten Marktteilnehmer im Repomarkt sind Wertpapierhändler, Investoren, Fondsmanager, Repo Market Maker und Zentralbanken.

Das Collateral in einem Repo dient dazu, den Käufer (Pensionsnehmer, Cashgeber) gegen Verluste bei einem Ausfall des Kontrahenten zu schützen. Daher muss sichergestellt werden, dass der Verkäufer einen ausreichenden Gegenwert an Wertpapieren zur Verfügung gestellt hat. Das Wertpapier wird bei Abschluss des Repos grundsätzlich zum Marktwert bewertet (d.h., es wird der Dirty Price berücksichtigt). Diese Vorgangsweise bietet jedoch nicht immer einen ausreichenden Schutz (z.B. bei Verwendung illiquider Wertpapiere, Volatilität). Zum Schutz gegen diese Probleme werden bei Repos häufig Margins angewendet. Dabei verlangt der Cashgeber eine Überbesicherung, eine sogenannte Initial Margin – im Repomarkt auch Haircut genannt. Die Initial Margin schützt also den Käufer des Wertpapiers vor einem Preisverfall des Papiers in der Zeit zwischen dem Ausfall des Partners und der Veräußerung des Collaterals. Die Höhe des Haircuts ist zwischen den Kontrahenten frei vereinbar.

Initial margins may prove inadequate if the price of the collateral falls more than expected. To maintain the intended balance between the collateral and cash in a repo, variation margins are used. Variation margins are additional transfers of collateral or extra payments of cash, made during the term of the repo, to eliminate differences between the agreed initial values of the collateral and the cash.

With general collaterals margin calls are paid in securities, whilst with specials they are paid in cash. In this case, the margin call is a kind of redemption or increase of the loaned cash amount and thus has to be considered in the final transaction (incl. interest).

Variation margins may be used in conjunction with initial margins or on their own. Note that a once agreed an initial margin has to be maintained during the entire term of the repo.

Unlike initial margins, regulators require that variation margins should be used by all types of market participants, including professionals. Variation margins require that the collateral should be marked to market – i.e. revalued – at least daily for professional players.

A major issue is who has custody of the collateral. There are three basic alternatives: bilateral repo (delivery repo), hold-in-custody (HIC) repo and tri-party repo.

Sellers may be reluctant to use certain securities as collateral in longer-term repo in case they need the securities for another purpose before the maturity of the repo. A solution is for the repo seller to seek rights of substitution of collateral from the buyer. This allows the seller to recall collateral during a repo and substitute alternative collateral of equivalent value and quality. Rights of substitution may be limited to certain dates within the contract period, or the seller may only be allowed to substitute a limited number of times during the course of a contract.

There are two types of transaction: classic repo (US-style repo) and sell/buy-backs (or buy/sell-backs). There is no significant economic difference between the two types of repo, only minor structural differences. Therefore, classic repos and sell/buy-backs for the same maturity, amount and collateral should yield approximately the same return. The only significant difference is their legal status and in the way in which each type of repo is managed. For a sell/buy-back, two legally independent contracts are concluded – a spot transaction and the opposite forward transaction with different prices. Due to the independence of the two contracts, neither variation margin nor substitution can be used. Thus, sell/buy-backs are less safe and flexible than classic repos.

Originally, sell/buy-backs have always been undocumented, i.e. the frame contract referred only to classic repos.

Bei Repos mit längerer Laufzeit reicht möglicherweise die Überbesicherung durch die Initial Margin nicht aus. Daher kommen Variation Margins zur Anwendung. Diese haben das Ziel, über die gesamte Laufzeit des Repos hinweg für eine ausreichende Besicherung zu sorgen. Dazu wird das Repo, d.h. sowohl das Collateral als auch der Cashbetrag inklusive angelaufener Zinsen, einer regelmäßigen – üblicherweise täglichen – Mark-to-Market-Bewertung unterzogen. Kommt es zu Abweichungen zwischen dem Wert des Collaterals und dem Cashbetrag, so kommt es zu Margin Calls, entweder in Cash oder in Wertpapieren. Die Variation Margin ist – abhängig vom Kurs des Collaterals – entweder vom Käufer oder vom Verkäufer zu leisten (im Unterschied zur Initial Margin). Bei General Collaterals erfolgen Margin Calls in Form von Wertpapieren, bei Specials hingegen in Cash. Eine Variation Margin kann zusätzlich zu einer etwaigen Initial Margin vereinbart werden (auch ohne Initial Margin möglich). Es ist zu beachten, dass eine einmal vereinbarte Initial Margin während der gesamten Laufzeit aufrechtzuerhalten ist. Während die Initial Margin zwischen professionellen Marktteilnehmern eher unüblich ist, verlangt der Gesetzgeber, dass die Variation Margin zwischen allen Marktteilnehmern angewendet wird. Dabei wird eine zumindest tägliche Mark-to-Market-Bewertung verlangt.

Bei der Verwahrung des Collaterals können grundsätzlich drei Möglichkeiten unterschieden werden: bilaterales Repo (Delivery Repo), Hold-in-Custody (HIC) Repo und Tri-party Repo.

Wenn es darum geht, bestimmte Wertpapiere für länger laufende Repos zu verwenden, weil sie möglicherweise diese Wertpapiere anderweitig vor Ablauf der Repos benötigen, sind Verkäufer zurückhaltend. Daher gibt es die Möglichkeit, ein Recht zur Substitution zwischen den Parteien zu vereinbaren. Darunter versteht man das Recht des Verkäufers, das Collateral während der Laufzeit vom Käufer zurückzuverlangen und durch ein anderes Wertpapier von ähnlicher oder besserer Qualität zu ersetzen. Es ist naheliegend, dass Substitution nur bei General Collaterals Anwendung findet, da bei Specials der Verkäufer ja ehestmöglich durch ein General ersetzen würde. Für die Gewährung eines Substitutionsrechts wird der Käufer einen Aufschlag auf den Reposatz verlangen.

Bei Pensionsgeschäften wird zwischen zwei Haupttypen unterschieden: klassische Repos (US-style Repos) und Sell/Buy-Backs (bzw. Buy/Sell-Backs). Wirtschaftlich betrachtet besteht kein wesentlicher Unterschied zwischen den beiden Typen. Daher sollte der Zinssatz für klassische Repos und von Sell/Buy-Backs für die gleiche Laufzeit sehr ähnlich sein. Der wesentliche Unterschied besteht in der rechtlichen Natur. Bei Sell/Buy-Backs werden zwei rechtlich eigenständige Geschäfte – ein Kassageschäft und ein gegenläufiges Termingeschäft – abgeschlossen. Für die beiden Geschäfte werden unterschiedliche Kurse vereinbart. Die Verzinsung ergibt sich dann implizit aus der Differenz zwischen den beiden Kursen, während bei Repos der Zinssatz explizit in der Vereinbarung angeführt wird. Aufgrund der Eigenständigkeit der beiden Vereinbarungen können keine Variation Margin und keine Substitution vereinbart werden. Somit sind Sell/Buy-Backs weniger sicher und flexibel als klassische Repos. Die Struktur ähnelt stark der von klassischen Repos. Der Unterschied besteht hauptsächlich darin, dass die Zinsen (und etwaige Kuponzahlungen während der Laufzeit zuzüglich Zinsen) im Terminkurs der Schlusstransaktion berücksichtigt werden.

Since November 1995 it has been possible to document sell/buy-backs under the PSA/ISMA Global Master Repurchase Agreement. Consequently, it is now possible to distinguish three major types of repo: classic repo – always documented; traditional sell/buy-back – undocumented; and documented sell/buy-back – always documented. The quotation for sell/buy-backs is – as for classic repos – also in percent. However, in the confirmation both the clean prices for the initial and the final transaction are fixed which reflects the agreed interest rate.

A vital safeguard against legal difficulties is to document the agreed rights and obligations of the counterparties. In the past, the main obstacle to documentation has been cost, but this has been greatly reduced by the publication of standard frame contracts. The most common frame contract in the repo market is the TBMA/ISMA Global Master Repurchase Agreement (TBMA/ISMA GMRA). One aim of ISMA is to ensure the legal enforceability for as many countries as possible. The frame contract also defines the events of default: price is not paid, securities are not delivered (optional), margin calls are not done (regulations regarding the margin maintanance), dividends resp. accrued interest due under a transaction are not paid and insolvency.

For the counterparty that lends cash (= buyer), loss can only occur if both the seller as well as the issuer of the collateral default simultaneously. As long as there is limited correlation between the credit risk of the repo counterparty and the credit risk of the issuer of the collateral making a simultaneous default unlikely, each repo counterparty has two more or less independent sources of comfort which significantly reduce the credit risk exposure through a repo. Repos cause operational costs and thus operational risks.

There are also special types of repos: dollar repo, forward start repo, floating rate repo, reverse to maturity repo, flex repo and open repo.

A synthetic repo is a strategy that consists of more than one deal which then altogether have the same effect as a repo. Security lending is the exchange of two securities for the term of the deal. This is sensible if the seller of the security does not need cash and wants to wait until his security turns special.

Since in securities lending no cash transfers take place, a premium (=security lending fee) is quoted in percentage p.a. based on the market value of the security instead of the repo rate.

Ursprünglich waren Sell/Buy-Backs immer undokumentiert. Seit November 1995 umfasst das PSA/ISMA Global Master Repurchase Agreement auch Sell/Buy-Backs, wodurch heute drei unterschiedliche Formen unterschieden werden können: klassisches Repo – immer dokumentiert, traditionelles Sell/Buy-Back – undokumentiert, und dokumentiertes Sell/Buy-Back – immer dokumentiert. Die Quotierung erfolgt zwar – wie bei klassischen Repos – auch in Zinsen p.a., in der Abschlussbestätigung werden jedoch die Clean Preise für die Anfangs- und Schlusstransaktion festgehalten, die genau den vereinbarten Zinssatz widerspiegeln.

Ein wichtiges Mittel zur Vermeidung von rechtlichen Problemen ist eine ausreichende Dokumentation der Rechte und Pflichten der Kontrahenten und darüber, welches Recht anzuwenden ist. In der Vergangenheit war das Hauptproblem dabei der damit verbundene Aufwand und damit die Kosten. Diese Problematik wurde durch die Verfassung von Standardrahmenverträgen weitgehend entschärft. Der im Repomarkt am häufigsten angewendete Rahmenvertrag ist das TBMA/ISMA Global Master Repurchase Agreement (TBMA/ISMA GMRA), dessen aktuelle Version im Jahr 2000 veröffentlicht wurde. Der GMRA unterliegt englischem Recht. Ein Ziel der ISMA ist auch, die rechtliche Durchsetzbarkeit in möglichst vielen Ländern sicherzustellen. Zu den im Rahmenvertrag angeführten Ereignissen der Nichterfüllung (Events of Default) zählen die Nichtzahlung des Kaufpreises, die Nichtlieferung der Wertpapiere, die Nichterfüllung der Margin-Zahlungen, die Nichtzahlung von Dividenden bzw. Stückzinsen im Rahmen einer Transaktion und der Insolvenzfall.

Repos bieten einerseits eine Absicherung bei einem Ausfall des Kontrahenten und andererseits Schutz gegen einen Verlust für den Käufer bei einem Ausfall des Emittenten. Für den Cashgeber kann es daher nur zu Verlusten kommen, wenn sowohl der Verkäufer als auch der Emittent des Collaterals gleichzeitig ausfallen. Außerdem bringen Repos einen hohen operationellen Aufwand – und damit einhergehend operationelle Risiken – mit sich.

Neben den bekannten Arten von Repos gibt es auch noch Sonderformen von Repos: Dollar Repo, Forward Start Repo, Floating Rate Repo, Reverse to Maturity Repo, Flex Repo und Open Repo.

Unter einem synthetischen Repo versteht man eine Strategie, die aus mehreren Geschäften besteht, die zusammen den gleichen Effekt wie ein Repo haben.

Beim Security Lending steht immer ein Special im Mittelpunkt. Der Verleiher des Specials erhält dabei ein General Collateral als Sicherheit. Als Preis für die Überlassung des Specials erhält er zusätzlich eine Prämie als Leihgebühr.

4.12. Practice Questions

1. What is a repo?
   a) the sale of a bond with the obligation to buy the bond back later
   b) the purchase of a bond with the option to buy the bond back later
   c) the sale of a bond with the option to buy the bond back later
   d) the purchase of a bond with the obligation to buy the bond back later

2. A classic repo is characterised by counterparty credit. What is the second unique condition for a repo?
   a) bonds provide security for the loan
   b) standardized legal agreements
   c) the high creditworthiness of the sellers
   d) All answers are false.

3. Who has legal and economic title to the securities used in a repo transaction?
   a) buyer: legal and economic title
   b) seller: legal and economic title
   c) buyer: economic title; seller: legal title
   d) seller: eonomic title; buyer: legal title

4. What is meant by a sell/buy-back?
   a) the simultaneously buying of one bond and selling of another
   b) borrowing cash for repayment in future using bonds as collateral
   c) simultaneously going long on a bond and short on the bond future
   d) the buying of a bond now and the outright sale of the same bond to the original counterparty at a fixed date in the future

5. The current quote for an EUR repo (general collateral) is 3.02–3.05%. You want to buy the repo. Which statement is true?
   a) You pay 3.02% interest.
   b) You receive 3.05% interest.
   c) You receive 3.02% interest.
   d) You pay 3.05% interest.

6. In which case is the credit risk of a bought repo at the lowest level?
   a) The credit risk is equal in all cases.
   b) The rating of the repo counterparty is excellent.
   c) high haircuts
   d) the collateral is rated AAA

4.12. Wiederholungsfragen

1. Was ist ein Repo?
   a) Ein Repo ist der Verkauf einer Anleihe mit der Pflicht, die Anleihe zu einem späteren Zeitpunkt zurückzukaufen.
   b) Ein Repo ist der Kauf einer Anleihe mit der Option, die Anleihe zu einem späteren Zeitpunkt wieder zu verkaufen.
   c) Ein Repo ist der Verkauf einer Anleihe mit der Option, die Anleihe zu einem späteren Zeitpunkt zurückzukaufen.
   d) Ein Repo ist der Kauf einer Anleihe mit der Pflicht, die Anleihe zu einem späteren Zeitpunkt zurückzukaufen.

2. Ein Repo ist dadurch charakterisiert, dass es einen Kontrahentenkredit gibt. Was ist die zweite Besonderheit eines Repos?
   a) Der Kredit ist durch Wertpapiere besichert.
   b) standardisierte rechtliche Vereinbarungen
   c) die hohe Kreditwürdigkeit der Verkäufer
   d) Alle Antworten sind falsch.

3. Wer ist der rechtliche und wirtschaftliche Eigentümer von Wertpapieren, die in einem Pensionsgeschäft eingesetzt werden?
   a) Käufer: rechtlich und wirtschaftlich
   b) Verkäufer: rechtlich und wirtschaftlich
   c) Käufer: wirtschaftlich; Verkäufer: rechtlich
   d) Verkäufer: wirtschaftlich; Käufer: rechtlich

4. Was versteht man unter einem Sell/Buy-Back?
   a) gleichzeitiger Kauf und Verkauf einer Anleihe
   b) die mit Anleihen besicherte Geldaufnahme für zukünftige Zahlungen
   c) eine Long-Position in der Anleihe und eine gleichzeitige Short-Position im Anleihe-Future
   d) Kauf einer Anleihe heute und Verkauf derselben Anleihe zu einem fixierten Zeitpunkt an den ursprünglichen Verkäufer

5. Die aktuelle Quotierung für ein Repo in EUR ist 3,02–3,05%. Sie kaufen das Repo. Welche der folgenden Aussagen ist richtig?
   a) Sie zahlen 3,02%.
   b) Sie erhalten 3,05%.
   c) Sie erhalten 3,02%.
   d) Sie zahlen 3,05%.

6. Wann ist bei einem gekauften Repo das Kreditrisiko am geringsten?
   a) Das Kreditrisiko ist in allen Fällen gleich.
   b) bei exzellentem Rating des Repo-Partners
   c) bei hohen Haircuts
   d) bei AAA-Rating des Collaterals

7. Which of the following statements is true regarding open repos?
   a) Only the buyer can terminate the deal prematurely.
   b) Only the seller can terminate the deal prematurely.
   c) Either party can terminate the repo at any time.
   d) The seller of the repo closes a short bond position.

8. What is meant by the right of substitution?

9. How is a repo with an exactly defined term called?
   a) special
   b) term repo
   c) dollar repo
   d) classic repo

10. What is meant by a general collateral transaction?
    a) repo in which a bond is bought
    b) repo in which the repo rate is above the money market rate
    c) repo in which the repo rate is closely related to the marginal lending facility
    d) repo in which the repo rate is slightly below the money market rate

11. Which of the following statements regarding EUREPO is true?
    a) EUREPO is the benchmark of special repos.
    b) EUREPO is the benchmark of GC and special repos between prime banks.
    c) EUREPO is the benchmark of GC repos between prime banks.
    d) EUREPO is the benchmark of GC repos with low-rated banks.

12. What is the most common reason for bonds going special in the repo market?
    a) default
    b) tax
    c) the issuer's rating
    d) they are cheapest-to-deliver

13. How are margin calls paid in classic repos?
    a) Margin calls are never applied.
    b) in cash
    c) with securities
    d) They can be paid in cash or in securities.

14. Name and explain the three types of custody of collateral!

15. Which of the following is the correct definition of close and reprice?
    a) mark-to-market of an interest rate swap
    b) matched book dealing
    c) Fed reverse repo
    d) calculation of margin calls for sell/buy-backs

7. Welche Aussage stimmt bezogen auf Open Repos?
   a) Der Käufer kann das Geschäft jederzeit beenden.
   b) Der Verkäufer kann das Geschäft jederzeit beenden.
   c) Das Geschäft kann von beiden Partnern jederzeit beendet werden.
   d) Der Verkäufer der Anleihe schließt eine short Anleihe-Position.

8. Was versteht man unter dem Recht zur Substitution?

9. Wie heißt ein Repo mit genau definierter Laufzeit?
   a) Special
   b) Term Repo
   c) Dollar Repo
   d) klassisches Repo

10. Was versteht man unter einem General-Collateral-Geschäft?
    a) Repo, bei dem eine Anleihe gekauft wird.
    b) Repo, bei dem der Repo-Satz über dem Geldmarktsatz liegt.
    c) Repo, bei dem der Repo-Satz an die Spitzenrefinanzierungsfazilität gebunden ist.
    d) Repo, bei dem der Repo-Satz leicht unter dem Geldmarktsatz liegt.

11. Was trifft auf EUREPO zu?
    a) EUREPO ist die Benchmark für Special Repos.
    b) EUREPO ist die Benchmark für GC- und Special Repos zwischen erstklassigen Adressen.
    c) EUREPO ist die Benchmark für GC-Repos zwischen erstklassigen Adressen.
    d) EUREPO ist die Benchmark für GC-Repos zwischen Adressen mit niedrigem Rating.

12. Was ist die häufigste Ursache dafür, dass Anleihen special gehen?
    a) Nichterfüllung
    b) steuerliche Gründe
    c) Bonität des Emittenten
    d) Sie sind cheapest-to-deliver.

13. Wie sind Margin Calls bei klassischen Repos zu entrichten?
    a) Sie werden prinzipiell nicht vereinbart.
    b) in Cash
    c) in Wertpapieren
    d) Sie können je nach Vereinbarung in Cash oder in Wertpapieren entrichtet werden.

14. Nennen und erläutern Sie kurz die drei Möglichkeiten zur Verwahrung des Collaterals!

15. Welche der folgenden Definitionen beschreibt am besten Close and Reprice?
    a) Mark-to-Market eines Zinsswaps
    b) Matched Book Dealing
    c) Fed Reverse-Repo
    d) Berechnung des Margin Calls bei Sell/Buy-Back

16. Who pays the initial margin requirement in the repo market?
    a) the buyer of the bond
    b) the seller of the bond
    c) the seller and the buyer of the bond half-and-half
    d) neither the seller nor the buyer of the bond

17. Assuming that repo rates are lower than coupon rates, which statement related to the clean price in the final transaction of a sell/buy-back is correct?
    a) cannot be determined
    b) clean price in final transaction = clean price in initial transaction
    c) clean price in final transaction is higher than the clean price in the initial transaction
    d) clean price in final transaction is lower than the clean price in the initial transaction

18. Name at least three differences between a classic repo and an undocumented sell/buy-back!

19. How can you design a synthetic repo?
    a) buy specials and sell GCs
    b) buy bond and buy EONIA Swap
    c) sell bond spot and buy bond future
    d) buy bond spot and sell bond future

20. Which events are possible events of default as specified in the TBMA/ISMA Global Master Repurchase Agreement?
    a) failure to pay margin calls
    b) insolvency
    c) security goes on special
    d) failure to deliver securities
    e) delivery of the cheapest-to-deliver bond

16. Von wem wird im Repo-Markt die Initial Margin geleistet?
    a) vom Käufer der Anleihe
    b) vom Verkäufer der Anleihe
    c) zu gleichen Teilen von beiden Partnern
    d) weder vom Verkäufer noch vom Käufer

17. Welche Aussage bezogen auf den Schlusskurs (Clean Price) bei einem Sell/Buy-Back stimmt (Annahme: Repo-Zinsen sind niedriger als Kuponzinsen)?
    a) kann nicht bestimmt werden
    b) Clean Price Schlusstransaktion = Clean Price Anfangstransaktion
    c) Clean Price Schlusstransaktion ist höher Clean Price Anfangstransaktion
    d) Clean Price Schlusstransaktion ist niedriger Clean Price Anfangstransaktion

18. Nennen Sie mindestens drei Unterschiede zwischen einem klassischen Repo und einem undokumentierten Sell/Buy-Back!

19. Wie kann ein synthetisches Repo konstruiert werden?
    a) Kauf eines Specials + Verkauf eines GC
    b) Kauf Anleihe + Kauf EONIA-Swap
    c) Verkauf Bund in der Kassa + Kauf eines Bund Futures
    d) Kauf Bund in der Kassa + Verkauf eines Bund Futures

20. Welche der folgenden Ereignisse sind mögliche Ereignisse der Nichterfüllung innerhalb des TBMA/ISMA Global Master Repurchase Agreements?
    a) Nichterfüllung der Margin-Zahlungen
    b) Insolvenzfall
    c) gekauftes General Collateral geht special
    d) Nichtlieferung der Wertpapiere
    e) Lieferung einer cheapest-to-deliver Anleihe

5. Overnight Index Swaps (OIS)

In this chapter you learn ...
- what is meant by overnight index swaps.
- how the different swaps in the OIS markets are called.
- about the function of overnight index swaps and how they are calculated.
- how overnight index swaps are used.
- about the conventions for EONIA swaps.
- what is the difference between EONIA swap rates and EURIBOR.
- what is meant by SONIA, TOIS and Fed Funds Swap.
- what is meant by forward overnight index swap.

While normal IRS are generally utilised in the capital markets, especially for short-term interest rates there was still a derivative missing with which interest rate risks could be reduced and flexibility increased. This gap could be filled with the development of the overnight index swap markets which have become **more and more important in recent years**. This swap helps to vary interest rate positions on a short-term basis and to reduce the risk of varying overnight rates.

OIS Markets

Depending on the currency and the relevant overnight index the swaps are called differently:
- EUR: EONIA swap
- USD: Fed Funds swap
- GBP: SONIA swap
- CHF: TOIS

5.1. Function and Calculation

OIS are a **special kind of coupon swap**, i.e. a fixed interest rate is swapped against a floating interest rate. In opposition to a normal IRS the variable rate is an overnight rate. At the trading date, the fixed interest rate, the principal, and the length of the term are determined.

In a normal IRS the variable interest rate is paid in the end of the interest period. As for an OIS the interest period is only one day (resp. three days for weekends) this would mean that you have an interest payment every single day which would lead to very high back-office efforts.

5. Overnight Index Swaps (OIS)

In diesem Kapitel lernen Sie ...

- was man unter Overnight Index Swaps versteht.
- wie die unterschiedlichen Swaps in den OIS-Märkten genannt werden.
- wie Overnight Index Swaps funktionieren und berechnet werden.
- wozu Overnight Index Swaps verwendet werden.
- welche Konventionen beim EONIA-Swap verwendet werden.
- wodurch sich EONIA-Swap-Sätze im Vergleich zum EURIBOR unterscheiden.
- was man unter SONIA, TOIS und Fed Funds Swap versteht.
- was man unter Forward Overnight Index Swap versteht.

Während normale IRS typischerweise im Kapitalmarkt ihre Anwendung finden, hat im kurzfristigen Zinsbereich lange Zeit ein analoges, derivatives Instrument gefehlt, mit dessen Hilfe Zinsrisiken begrenzt und die Flexibilität erhöht werden kann. Diese Lücke wurde mit der Entwicklung der Overnight-Index-Swap-Märkte geschlossen, die **in den letzten Jahren im Geldmarkt enorm an Bedeutung gewonnen** haben. So bietet dieser Swap unter anderem die Möglichkeit, Zinsbindungen kurzfristig zu variieren und das Risiko schwankender Taggeldsätze zu minimieren.

OIS-Märkte

Je nach Währung und dem relevanten Overnight-Index werden die Swaps unterschiedlich genannt:

- EUR: EONIA-Swap
- USD: Fed Funds Swap
- GBP: SONIA Swap
- CHF: TOIS

5.1. Funktionsweise und Berechnung

OIS sind eine **Spezialform von Kuponswaps**, d.h., es wird ein fester gegen einen variablen Zinssatz getauscht. Im Unterschied zu normalen IRS ist der variable Zinssatz jedoch ein Overnight-Satz. Bei Geschäftsabschluss werden die Höhe des fixen Satzes, das Nominalvolumen und die Laufzeit vereinbart.

Bei normalen IRS wird der variable Zinssatz jeweils am Ende der Zinsbindungsperiode gezahlt. Da bei einem OIS die Zinsbindungsperiode jeweils nur ein Tag ist (bzw. drei Tage an Wochenenden) würde das bedeuten, dass jeden Tag eine Zahlung stattfindet, was zu einem sehr hohen Abwicklungsaufwand führen würde.

Therefore the variable interest in an OIS is only paid in the end of the period by the effective rate of the single fixings. Thus the effects of **compound interest** are taken into account.

As a result both the fixed and the variable rate payments are made in the end of the swap period. Both **payments are then netted**, i.e. only the **difference between the calculated variable rate and the fixed rate** based on the maturity and the notional amount is paid.

Formula to calculate the floating rate:

$$r = \left\{ \left[\prod_{i=d_1}^{d_e-1} \left(1 + \frac{r_i \cdot D_i}{360} \right) \right] - 1 \right\} \cdot \frac{360}{D}$$

r = floating rate including effects of compound interest
d_1 = start date of the OIS swap
d_e = maturity date
r_i = rate of overnight fixing (in per cent, divided by 100)
D_i = number of days for which r_i is valid (usually 1 day, weekends: 3 days)
D = days of OIS swap's term

Example

Two parties (A and B) complete an EONIA swap with an underlying of EUR 250 m: A is receiver of the fixed-rate of 3.20 % for a term of seven days (April 7th–14th)

Assume the following overnight rates:
Mon   April 7th:   3.12% (1 day)
Tue   April 8th:   3.10% (1 day)
Wed   April 9th:   3.15% (1 day)
Thu   April 10th:   3.15% (1 day)
Fri   April 11th:   3.13% (3 days)

Effective rate for all single EONIA fixings:

$$\left\{ \left[\left(1 + \frac{0.0312}{360} \right) \left(1 + \frac{0.031}{360} \right) \left(1 + \frac{0.0315}{360} \right) \left(1 + \frac{0.0315}{360} \right) \left(1 + \frac{0.0313 \cdot 3}{360} \right) \right] - 1 \right\} \cdot \frac{360}{7} = 3.13070\%$$

(Comparison: the arithmetic average = 3.13000)

Party A gets 3.20% for 7 days on EUR 250 m, i.e. EUR 155,555.56. At the same time, A pays 3.1307% for the same principal and the same term, i.e. EUR 152,186.81.

This means, A receives a settlement payment of EUR 3,368.75 from B, because only the difference between the two payments is exchanged (netting).

Note: Usually the effective rate is rounded to 5 decimals.

Daher wird bei OIS die variable Zinszahlung erst am Ende der Laufzeit in Form des Effektivzinssatzes der einzelnen Fixings gezahlt. Das bedeutet, dass bei der Berechnung der variablen Seite **auch Zinseszinsen berücksichtigt** werden.

Somit finden sowohl die Zahlung der variablen als auch der fixen Seite am Ende der Laufzeit statt, was dazu führt, dass **am Ende der Laufzeit nur eine Differenzzahlung** stattfindet, die aus dem **Unterschied zwischen dem ermittelten variablen Satz und dem Festsatz,** bezogen auf die Laufzeit und das Nominalvolumen, resultiert.

Berechnung des variablen Satzes:

$$r = \left\{ \left[\prod_{i=t_1}^{t_e-1} \left(1 + \frac{r_i * T_i}{360} \right) \right] - 1 \right\} * \frac{360}{T}$$

r   = zu ermittelnder variabler Satz unter Berücksichtigung von Zinseszinseffekten
t_1 = Startdatum des OIS-Swaps
t_e = Enddatum
r_i = Taggeld-Fixing-Satz (in Dezimalen)
T_i = Anzahl der Tage, für die r_i gültig ist (normalerweise 1 Tag, WE 3 Tage)
T   = Laufzeit des Swaps in Tagen

Beispiel

Berechnung der Differenzzahlung eines OIS-Swaps:
Zwei Parteien (A + B) schließen folgenden EONIA-Swap über EUR 250 Mio. ab. A ist Empfänger des Festsatzes in Höhe von 3,2% für eine Laufzeit von sieben Tagen (Mo 7.–14. April).

Folgende EONIA-Sätze werden während der Laufzeit fixiert:

Mo   7. April: 3,12% (1 Tag)
Di   8. April: 3,10% (1 Tag)
Mi   9. April: 3,15% (1 Tag)
Do 10. April: 3,15% (1 Tag)
Fr   11. April: 3,13% (3 Tage)

Effektivzinssatz aus den einzelnen EONIA-Fixings:

$$\left\{ \left[\left(1 + \frac{0,0312}{360} \right) * \left(1 + \frac{0,031}{360} \right) * \left(1 + \frac{0,0315}{360} \right) * \left(1 + \frac{0,0315}{360} \right) * \left(1 + \frac{0,0313 * 3}{360} \right) \right] - 1 \right\} * \frac{360}{7} = 3{,}13070\%$$

(zum Vergleich: arithmetisches Mittel = 3,13000)

A erhält 3,2% für sieben Tage auf EUR 250 Mio., also EUR 155.555,56, und zahlt 3,1307%, d.h. EUR 152.186,81.

Da die beiden Beträge genettet werden, findet nur eine Ausgleichszahlung von EUR 3.368,75 statt.

Anmerkung: Der Effektivzinssatz wird üblicherweise auf fünf Dezimalstellen gerundet.

5.2. Application

Hedging

OIS allow the **separated control of liquidity and interest rate risk**. Thus, when controlling the interest rate risk, you can profit from high liquidity and close spreads in the OIS market. At the same time the liquidity is adjusted only through short-term lending resp. borrowing of the liquidity overhang resp. gap. That way you stay flexible regarding the liquidity, i.e. you can avoid the ballooning of the balance sheet which would be the result of a number of long-term deposits. This **reduces the credit risk and – consequently – equity capital costs**.

Example

Controlling the interest rate risk with an OIS

You are responsible for controlling the short-term interest rate risk in your bank, and the following deals are done:

Day 1

loan to a customer, EUR 100 m for 3 months at 4.50%.

Regarding the liquidity you want to stay flexible and therefore take the liquidity by an overnight refinancing. As you receive a fixed rate out of the customer's credit, your interest rate risk is a rising o/n-rate. You hedge this risk through a purchase of a 3-months EONIA swap at 4.00% (= pay fixed and receive EONIA).

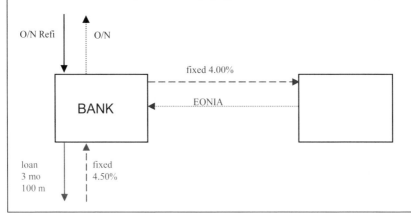

5.2. Anwendung

Hedging

OIS ermöglichen eine **getrennte Steuerung von Liquidität und Zinsrisiko**. Somit kann in der Zinsrisikosteuerung von der hohen Liquidität und den engen Spreads im OIS-Markt profitiert werden. Gleichzeitig erfolgt der Ausgleich der Liquidität nur durch kurzfristige Anlage des Liquiditätsüberhanges bzw. durch Aufnahme der Liquiditätslücke. Auf diese Weise bleibt man liquiditätsmäßig flexibel, d.h., es kann eine Aufblähung der Bilanz durch eine Vielzahl von längerfristigen Depotgeschäften vermieden werden, was zu einer **Verringerung des Kreditrisikos und somit der Eigenkapitalkosten** führt.

Beispiel

Steuerung des Zinsrisikos mit OIS

Sie sind verantwortlich für die Steuerung des kurzfristigen Zinsrisikos Ihrer Bank, und es finden folgende Geschäftsfälle statt:

Tag 1

Kredit an einen Kunden, EUR 100 Mio., drei Monate Laufzeit zu 4,50%.
Liquiditätsmäßig möchten Sie flexibel bleiben und besorgen sich die Liquidität durch eine Overnight-Refinanzierung. Da Sie aus dem Kundenkredit einen festen Zinssatz erhalten, besteht Ihr Zinsrisiko in einem Anstieg des O/N-Satzes. Dieses Risiko hedgen Sie durch den Kauf eines 3-Monats-EONIA-Swaps zu 4,00% (= fest zahlen und EONIA empfangen).

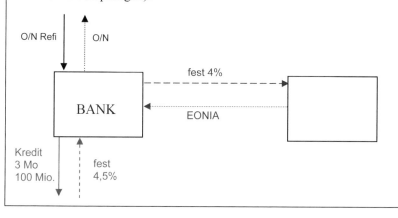

Day 2

Rates have risen and you take a customer's deposit, EUR 100 m for 3 months at 4.50%. On day 2 you pay back the o/n refinancing through the liquidity of the deposit. You have now refinanced the customer's loan through the customer's deposit and do not need any further interbank cash transactions. You close the EONIA swap by an opposite trade.

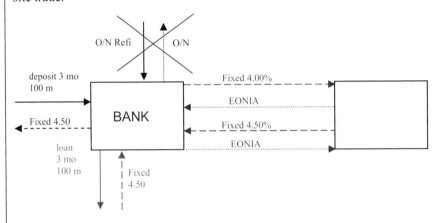

Result

Without EONIA swap the interest rate risk of the customer's loan could have only be closed by a 3-months interbank refinancing with the same period. On the other hand the liquidity overhang of the customer's deposit at day 2 would have to be closed by a 3-months interbank lending. Thus you would have had two interbank cash transactions in your books what, on the one hand, would have reduced your refinancing facilities, on the other hand it had increased your credit risk and equity capital costs.

By means of an EONIA swap you have **hedged your interest rate risk with a derivative**. Interbank cash transactions (o/n) have only been utilised to compensate the liquidity balance.

Trading (Speculation)

OIS can be utilised for **speculating on interest rate changes**. With OIS, for the first time, one can also speculate on overnight cash rate changes with derivatives. Contrary to forward instruments like FRA and futures, OIS positions do only have an **interest rate level risk, no interest rate curve risk**.

Tag 2

Die Zinsen sind gestiegen und Sie nehmen eine Kundeneinlage, EUR 100 Mio., drei Monate Laufzeit zu 4,5%, herein. Am Tag 2 zahlen Sie die O/N-Refinanzierung mit der Liquidität aus der Kundeneinlage zurück. Sie haben jetzt den Kundenkredit mit einer Kundeneinlage refinanziert und benötigen keine weiteren Interbank-Depotgeschäfte mehr. Den EONIA-Swap lösen Sie durch ein Gegengeschäft wieder auf.

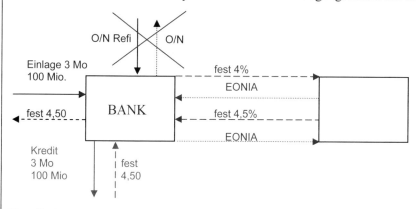

Resultat

Ohne EONIA-Swap hätte das Zinsrisiko aus dem Kundenkredit nur durch eine fristenkonforme 3-Monats-Interbank-Refinanzierung geschlossen werden können. Andererseits hätte der Liquiditätsüberschuss durch die Kundeneinlage am Tag 2 durch eine 3-Monats-Interbank-Anlage ausgeglichen werden müssen. Somit hätten Sie zwei Interbank-Depots in den Büchern, was einerseits eine Reduzierung Ihrer weiteren Refinanzierungsmöglichkeiten bedeutet hätte, andererseits zusätzliches Kreditrisiko und damit verbunden zusätzliche Eigenkapitalkosten.

Mithilfe der EONIA-Swaps haben Sie das **Zinsrisiko derivativ gehedged**. Interbank-Depots (O/N) haben Sie nur zum kurzfristigen Ausgleich des Liquiditätssaldos benutzt.

Trading (Spekulation)

OIS können auch zur **Spekulation auf Zinsänderungen** verwendet werden. Mit OIS kann nun erstmals auch derivativ auf Taggeldschwankungen spekuliert werden. Im Unterschied zu Forward-Instrumenten wie FRA und Futures unterliegt eine OIS-Position **keinem Zinskurvenrisiko**, sondern **nur** einem **Zinsniveaurisiko**.

Example

Comparison: 3-months OIS position vs. 3/6 FRA position

Market data:
3 mo: 3%
6 mo: 3.5%
3/6 FRA: 3.97%
You are expecting a rise in the 3-months rates and have the choice between the purchase of a 3-months OIS and the purchase of a 3/6 FRA.
Compare the two results when, on the same day, rates rise as follows:
3 mo: 4%
6 mo: 3.75%

Result FRA

The fair FRA price with the above interest rate curve would be 3.47%. The FRA price has fallen, although rates have risen as the interest rate curve has turned from steep to inverse. Thus the result is a **loss of 50 BP**.

Result OIS

The 3-months have risen from 3.00% to 4.00%. Thus the result is a **profit of 100 BP**.

Conclusion

The FRA rate does not only depend on the interest rate level, but mainly on the interest rate curve. Therefore the FRA price has fallen although rates have risen as the interest rate curve has turned from normal to inverse. The long FRA position bears a loss, despite the rate rise. In contrast an OIS does not have any interest rate curve risk; therefore the interest rate level rise produces directly a profit for the long OIS position.

Arbitrage

By buying and selling OIS with different periods forward positions can be produced. Possible differences in prices compared to other forward instruments (FRA, futures, forward IRS, forward deposits, fwd/fwd swaps) can be capitalised by arbitrage.

5.3. EONIA Swap Conventions

Period

As OIS are typical money market instruments, the terms vary from 2 days to 24 months.

Beispiel

Vergleich 3-Monats-OIS-Position mit 3/6 FRA-Position

Aktuelle Marktdaten:
3 Monate: 3%
6 Monate: 3,5%
3/6 FRA: 3,97%
Sie erwarten sich einen Anstieg der 3-Monats-Zinsen und haben die Wahl zwischen dem Kauf eines 3-Monats-OIS und dem Kauf eines 3/6 FRA.
Vergleichen Sie die beiden Ergebnisse, wenn die Zinsen am gleichen Tag wie folgt steigen:
3 Monate: 4%
6 Monate: 3,75%

Ergebnis FRA

Der faire Preis des FRA bei obiger Zinskurve liegt bei 3,47%. Der FRA ist gefallen, obwohl die Zinsen gestiegen sind, weil die Zinskurve von steil auf invers gedreht hat. Somit ist das Ergebnis ein **Verlust von 50 BP**.

Ergebnis OIS

Die 3-Monats-Zinsen sind von 3% auf 4% gestiegen, somit ist das Ergebnis ein **Gewinn von 100 BP**.

Zusammenfassung

Der FRA-Satz hängt nicht nur vom Zinsniveau, sondern hauptsächlich auch von der Zinskurve ab. Daher ist der Preis des FRA gefallen, obwohl die Zinsen gestiegen sind, weil die Zinskurve von normal auf invers gedreht hat. Die long FRA-Position hat somit trotz des Zinsanstiegs zu einem Verlust geführt. Im Gegensatz dazu unterliegt ein OIS keinem Zinskurvenrisiko, wodurch der Zinsniveauanstieg auch direkt zu einem Gewinn bei einer long OIS-Position führt.

Arbitrage

Durch den Kauf und Verkauf von OIS mit unterschiedlichen Laufzeiten können Forward-Positionen produziert werden. Etwaige Preisunterschiede zu anderen Forward-Instrumenten (FRA, Futures, Forward IRS, Forward Depots, Fwd/Fwd FX-Swaps) können durch Arbitrage ausgenutzt werden.

5.3. Konventionen EONIA-Swap

Laufzeit

EONIA-Swaps sind typische Geldmarktprodukte. Dementsprechend liegen die Laufzeiten zwischen 2 Tagen und 24 Monaten.

Start Date

For spot swaps the term usually starts **two working days after the trade date**. But there has also developed a very liquid forward EONIA swap market.

Date of Payment

Both the **variable and the fixed payment are netted**, there is a cash settlement in the amount of the difference between fixed and variable rate.

EONIA Fixing

EONIA = Euro Overnight Index Average. Contrary to EURIBOR or LIBOR, EONIA is traded as a **weighted average of all overnight unsecured lending transactions** under-taken in the interbank market, initiated within the euro area by the contributing banks. The bank panel which takes part in the EURIBOR fixing also takes part in the EONIA fixing (at the moment 43 banks). The EONIA rate is computed by the ECB at the **end of the day** who publishes the fixed rate between 6:45 and 7:00 p.m. CET via Reuters. The EONIA rate is fixed to three decimals and is calculated with the Euro-money market method (ACT/360).

Beispiel		
A EURIBOR panel bank has done the following unsecured o/n trades. What does it report for the EONIA fixing?		
amount	**rate**	**weighted rate**
EUR 100 m	2,17%	217,00
EUR 50 m	2,12%	106,00
EUR 300 m	2,18%	654,00
EUR 50 m	2,13%	106,50
EUR 500 m		**1.083,50**
Weighted average: 1,083.50 / 500 = 2.167% The bank reports **EUR 500 m at 2.167%** (rounded to 2 decimals).		

Startdatum

Bei Spot Swaps beginnt die Laufzeit **zwei Handelstage nach Abschluss**. Es hat sich jedoch auch ein sehr liquider Forward-EONIA-Swap-Markt entwickelt.

Zahlungsdatum

Sowohl die variable als auch die feste Zinszahlung finden **am Laufzeitende** statt. Da beide Zahlungen genettet werden, findet nur eine **Ausgleichszahlung in der Höhe der Differenz** zwischen dem Festsatz und dem variablen Satz statt.

EONIA-Fixing

EONIA steht für Euro Overnight Index Average. Im Unterschied zu EURIBOR oder LIBOR wird EONIA als **betragsgewichteter Durchschnitt der tatsächlich gehandelten, unbesicherten Overnight-Ausleihungen** ermittelt. Am EONIA-Fixing nehmen die gleichen Banken wie beim EURIBOR-Fixing Teil (derzeit 43 internationale Banken). Der EONIA-Satz wird von der EZB **am Tagesende ermittelt** und zwischen 18.45 und 19.00 Uhr CET über Reuters veröffentlicht. Die Berechnung erfolgt auf drei Dezimalstellen und entspricht der Euro-Geldmarktmethode (ACT/360).

Beispiel		
Eine EURIBOR Panel-Bank hat heute die angeführten unbesicherten Overnight-Geschäfte durchgeführt. Was meldet sie im EONIA-Fixing?		
Betrag	**Zinssatz**	**Gewichteter Zinssatz**
EUR 100 Mio.	2,17%	217,00
EUR 50 Mio.	2,12%	106,00
EUR 300 Mio.	2,18%	654,00
EUR 50 Mio.	2,13%	106,50
EUR 500 Mio.		**1.083,50**
Gewichteter Durchschnitt: 1.083,50 / 500 = 2,167% Die Bank meldet somit **EUR 500 Mio. zu einem Zinssatz von 2,17%** (gerundet auf zwei Dezimalstellen).		

5.4. EONIA swap rates compared to EURIBOR

If you compare the EONIA swap rates to the EURIBORs with the same term, the **swap rate lies usually below EURIBOR**. EURIBOR represents the rate at which first-class counterparties can borrow cash for a certain period (e.g. 12 months). Thus **EURIBOR** includes the **credit spread for these first-class counterparties**. On the contrary, the **EONIA swap rate** is the **rate without credit spread** as, at this rate, only interest rate payments are swapped, but no cash is lent. Therefore the OIS rates tend towards the cash bid rates. (Bid rate = rate at which the market maker is willing to take cash. Thus for the market maker the bid rate is the rate without credit risk.)

5.5. SONIA, TOIS and Fed Funds Swap

SONIA (Sterling Overnight Index Average)

SONIA was introduced by the Wholesale Markets Brokers' Association (WMBA) in March 1997. SONIA is the **weighted average rate to four decimal places of all unsecured sterling overnight cash transactions brokered in London** by WMBA member firms between midnight and 4.15 p.m. with all counterparties in a minimum deal size of GBP 25 million, published by 5.00 p.m. **on the day of calculation**. Data is available from the following sources: Telerate page 3937, Reuters SONIA 1, Bloomberg WMBA<GO>.

TOIS (Tom-Next Indexed Swap)

The TOIS is an **index of unsecured CHF T/N offered Money Market rates**. Payment Date is **Termination Date + 2 Zurich business days** (net of fixed and compound floating rate). The TOIS is fixed by 20 – 30 leading banks actively trading TOIS or are active in lending short term CHF funds in the interbank market at 11.00am (Zurich time). Data is available from the following sources: Telerate page 3450, Reuters TN/SWAP (RIC: CHFTOIS=).

Fed Funds Swap

The fed funds swap is an **OIS in USD** where a **fixed rate is swapped against the fed funds rate**. The federal funds rate (fed funds rate) is the rate for short-term cash borrowing in the US-American market. The target federal funds rate is set by the Federal Open Market Committee (FOMC). The fed funds swap is fixed against the so-called **fed funds effective rate** which is calculated daily by the FED and may vary around the target rate.

5.4. EONIA-Swap-Sätze im Vergleich zum EURIBOR

Vergleicht man die EONIA-Swap-Sätze mit den laufzeitkonformen EURIBORs, so bemerkt man, dass **im Normalfall der Swap-Satz unter dem EURIBOR-Satz** liegt. EURIBOR repräsentiert den Zinssatz, zu dem erstklassige Adressen für eine bestimmte Periode (z.B. 12 Monate) Geld aufnehmen können. Somit beinhaltet **EURIBOR** den **Credit Spread für** eben **diese erstklassigen Adressen.** Im Gegensatz dazu stellt der **EONIA-Swap-Satz** den **Zinssatz ohne Credit Spread** dar, weil zu diesem Satz nur die Zinszahlungen getauscht werden, nicht jedoch Geld geliehen wird. Daher tendieren die Sätze im OIS-Markt Richtung Geldseite im Cash-Markt. (Die Geldseite ist jener Satz, den der Market Maker für Geldaufnahme bereit ist zu bezahlen. Somit stellt die Geldseite für den Market Maker den Zinssatz ohne Kreditrisiko dar.)

5.5. SONIA, TOIS und Fed Funds Swap

SONIA (Sterling Overnight Index Average)

SONIA wurde im März 1997 von der Wholesale Markets Brokers Association (WMBA) eingeführt. SONIA ist der **gewichtete Durchschnittssatz (vier Dezimalstellen) für alle unbesicherten GBP-Overnight-Cash-Transaktionen,** die in London von WMBA-Mitgliedsbanken zwischen 0.00 und 16.15 Uhr, London-Zeit, mit allen Kontrahenten durchgeführt wurden (Mindestvolumen 25 Mio. GBP), und wird **am selben Tag** um 17.00 Uhr, London-Zeit, auf Telerate Seite 3937, Reuters SONIA 1 und Bloomberg WMBA<GO> veröffentlicht.

TOIS (Tom-Next Indexed Swap)

Der TOIS ist ein **Index aller unbesicherten CHF-T/N-Geldmarktsätze (Briefseite).** Die Zahlung erfolgt **zwei Züricher Geschäftstage nach Fälligkeit** (Netting des fixen und variablen Satzes). Der TOIS wird von 20 bis 30 führenden Banken gefixt, die aktiv TOIS handeln oder aktiv kurzfristige CHF-Gelder im Interbankenmarkt ausleihen (Fixing um 11.00 Uhr, Zürich-Zeit). TOIS wird veröffentlicht auf Telerate Seite 3450 und Reuters TN/SWAP (RIC: CHFTOIS=).

Fed Funds Swap

Der Fed Funds Swap ist ein **OIS im USD,** bei dem der **Festsatz gegen die Fed Funds Rate getauscht** wird. Der Federal Funds Satz (Fed Funds Satz) ist der Zinssatz am US-amerikanischen Geldmarkt für kurzfristige Geldaufnahmen. Der Fed Funds Satz wird vom Federal Open Market Committee (FOMC) als Target vorgegeben. Das Fixing der Fed Funds Swaps erfolgt gegen die sogenannte **Fed Funds Effective Rate,** die täglich von der FED berechnet wird und um die Target Rate schwanken kann.

5.6. Forward OIS

Through two OIS with different periods a forward OIS can be produced. The forward rate can be calculated with the FRA formula.

Example

Which forward rate is produced for the purchase of a 3/6 forward EONIA swap?
EONIA swap rates:
3 mo: 3.50–51% (91 days)
6 mo: 3.70–71% (183 days)
The purchase of the 3/6 forward EONIA swap can be produced by the purchase of a 6-months EONIA swap at 3.71% and the sale of a 3-months EONIA swap at 3.50% at the same.

$$
FWD\,EONIA = \left[\frac{1 + 0.0371 \times \dfrac{183}{360}}{1 + 0.035 \times \dfrac{91}{360}} - 1 \right] \times \frac{360}{92} = 3.883\%
$$

Summary

While normal IRS are generally used in the capital markets, especially for short-term interest rates an instrument was missing to reduce interest rate risks and increase flexibility. This gap was filled by overnight index swap markets which have become more and more important in recent years. This swap helps to vary interest rate positions on a short-term basis and to reduce the risk of varying overnight rates. Depending on the currency and the relevant overnight index, swaps are called differently: EUR – EONIA swap, USD – Fed Funds swap, GBP – SONIA swap, CHF – TOIS. OIS are a special kind of coupon swap, i.e. a fixed interest rate is swapped against a floating interest rate. In a normal IRS the variable interest rate is paid at the end of the interest period. As for an OIS, the interest period is only 1 day (resp. 3 days for weekends). This would lead to interest payments every single day resulting in very high back-office costs. Therefore, the variable interest in an OIS is only paid at the end of the period to the extent of the effective rate of the single fixings. Thus, the effects of compound interest are taken into account. As a result both the fixed and the variable rate payments are made at the end of the swap period. Both payments are then netted, i.e. only the difference between the calculated variable rate and the fixed rate based on the maturity and the notional amount is paid.

5.6. Forward OIS

Durch zwei OIS mit unterschiedlichen Laufzeiten kann ein Forward OIS produziert werden. Der Forward-Satz kann mit der FRA-Formel errechnet werden.

Beispiel

Welcher Forward-Satz ergibt sich für den Kauf eines 3/6 Forward-EONIA-Swap?
EONIA-Swap-Sätze:
3 Monate: 3,50–51% (91 Tage)
6 Monate: 3,70–71% (183 Tage)
Der Kauf eines 3/6 Forward-EONIA-Swaps kann durch den Kauf eines 6-Monats-EONIA-Swaps zu 3,71% und gleichzeitigen Verkauf eines 3-Monats-EONIA-Swaps zu 3,5% produziert werden.

$$\text{FWD EONIA} = \left[\frac{1 + 0,0371 * \dfrac{183}{360}}{1 + 0,035 * \dfrac{91}{360}} - 1 \right] * \frac{360}{92} = 3,883\%$$

Zusammenfassung

Während „normale" Zinsswapgeschäfte typischerweise im Kapitalmarkt ihre Anwendung finden, hat im kurzfristigen Zinsbereich lange Zeit ein analoges, derivatives Instrument gefehlt, mit dessen Hilfe Zinsrisiken begrenzt und die Flexibilität erhöht werden kann. Diese Lücke wurde mit der Entwicklung der Overnight-Index-Swap-Märkte geschlossen, die in den letzten Jahren im Geldmarkt enorm an Bedeutung gewonnen haben. So bietet dieser Swap unter anderem die Möglichkeit, Zinsbindungen kurzfristig zu variieren und das Risiko schwankender Taggeldsätze zu minimieren. Je nach Währung und dem relevanten Overnight-Index werden die Swaps unterschiedlich genannt: EUR – EONIA-Swap, USD – Fed Funds Swap, GBP – SONIA Swap, CHF – TOIS. OIS sind eine Spezialform von Kuponswaps, d.h., es wird ein fester gegen einen variablen Zinssatz getauscht. Im Unterschied zu normalen IRS ist der variable Zinssatz jedoch ein Overnight-Satz. Bei normalen IRS wird der variable Zinssatz jeweils am Ende der Zinsbindungsperiode gezahlt. Da bei einem OIS die Zinsbindungsperiode jeweils nur ein Tag ist (bzw. drei Tage an Wochenenden), würde das bedeuten, dass jeden Tag eine Zahlung stattfindet, was zu einem sehr hohen Abwicklungsaufwand führen würde. Daher wird bei OIS die variable Zinszahlung erst am Ende der Laufzeit in Form des Effektivzinssatzes der einzelnen Fixings gezahlt. Das bedeutet, dass bei der Berechnung der variablen Seite auch Zinseszinsen berücksichtigt werden. Somit finden sowohl die Zahlung der variablen als auch der fixen Seite am Ende der Laufzeit statt, was dazu führt, dass am Ende der Laufzeit nur eine Differenzzahlung stattfindet, die aus dem Unterschied zwischen dem ermittelten variablen Satz und dem Festsatz, bezogen auf die Laufzeit und das Nominalvolumen, resultiert.

OIS allow the separate control of liquidity and interest rate risk. Thus, when controlling the interest rate risk, you can profit from high liquidity and close spreads in the OIS market. At the same time, liquidity is adjusted only through short-term lending resp. borrowing of the liquidity overhang resp. gap. That way, you remain flexible regarding liquidity, i.e. you can avoid the ballooning of the balance sheet which would be the result of a number of long-term deposits. This reduces the credit risk and – consequently – equity capital costs. OIS can be used for speculating on interest rate changes. With OIS, for the first time, one can also speculate on overnight cash rate changes with derivatives. Contrary to forward instruments like FRA and futures, OIS positions only have an interest rate level risk, no interest rate curve risk. By buying and selling OIS with different periods forward positions can be produced. Possible differences in prices compared to other forward instruments (FRA, futures, forward IRS, forward deposits, fwd/fwd swaps) can be capitalised by arbitrage.

EONIA (Euro Overnight Index Average) is traded as a weighted average of all overnight unsecured lending transactions undertaken in the interbank market, initiated within the euro area by the contributing banks. The bank panel which takes part in the EURIBOR fixing also takes part in the EONIA fixing (at the moment 43 banks). The EONIA rate is computed by the ECB at the end of the day and published between 6:45 and 7:00 p.m. CET via Reuters. The EONIA rate is fixed to three decimals and is calculated with the euro money market method (ACT/360). The SONIA is the weighted average rate to four decimal places of all unsecured sterling overnight cash transactions brokered in London and published by 5.00 p.m. on the day of calculation. The TOIS is an index of unsecured CHF T/N offered money market rates. Payment date is termination date + 2 Zurich business days (net of fixed and compound floating rate). The fed funds swap is fixed against the so-called fed funds effective rate which is calculated daily by the FED and may vary around the target rate. The fed funds swap is an OIS in USD where a fixed rate is swapped against the fed funds rate.

5.7. Practice Questions

1. What are the advantages of overnight index swaps in contrast to normal interest rate swaps?
2. Which of the following statements regarding EONIA swaps is true?
    a) Two variable interest payments are exchanged.
    b) Two fixed interest payments are exchanged.
    c) It is available for terms of longer than one year.
    d) An overnight rate is exchanged against a fixed rate.

OIS ermöglichen eine getrennte Steuerung von Liquidität und Zinsrisiko. Somit kann in der Zinsrisikosteuerung von der hohen Liquidität und den engen Spreads im OIS-Markt profitiert werden. Gleichzeitig erfolgt der Ausgleich der Liquidität nur durch kurzfristige Anlage des Liquiditätsüberhanges bzw. durch Aufnahme der Liquiditätslücke. Auf diese Weise bleibt man liquiditätsmäßig flexibel, d.h., es kann eine Aufblähung der Bilanz durch eine Vielzahl von längerfristigen Depotgeschäften vermieden werden, was zu einer Verringerung des Kreditrisikos und somit der Eigenkapitalkosten führt. OIS können auch zur Spekulation auf Zinsänderungen verwendet werden. Mit OIS kann nun auch derivativ auf Taggeldschwankungen spekuliert werden. Im Unterschied zu Forward-Instrumenten wie FRA und Futures unterliegt eine OIS-Position keinem Zinskurvenrisiko, sondern nur einem Zinsniveaurisiko. Durch den Kauf und Verkauf von OIS mit unterschiedlichen Laufzeiten können Forward-Positionen produziert werden. Etwaige Preisunterschiede zu anderen Forward-Instrumenten (FRA, Futures, Forward IRS, Forward Depots, Fwd/Fwd FX-Swaps) können durch Arbitrage ausgenutzt werden.

EONIA steht für Euro Overnight Index Average. Im Unterschied zu EURIBOR oder LIBOR wird EONIA als betragsgewichteter Durchschnitt der tatsächlich gehandelten, unbesicherten Overnight-Ausleihungen ermittelt. Am EONIA-Fixing nehmen die gleichen Banken wie beim EURIBOR-Fixing teil (derzeit 43 internationale Banken, davon 36 Banken aus der Eurozone). Der EONIA-Satz wird von der EZB am Tagesende ermittelt und zwischen 18.45 und 19.00 Uhr CET über Reuters veröffentlicht. Die Berechnung erfolgt auf drei Dezimalstellen und entspricht der Euro-Geldmarktmethode (ACT/360). Der SONIA (Sterling Overnight Index Average) ist der gewichtete Durchschnittssatz (vier Dezimalstellen) für alle unbesicherten GBP-Overnight-Cash-Transaktionen und wird am selben Tag um 17.00 Uhr, London-Zeit, veröffentlicht. Der TOIS ist ein Index aller unbesicherten CHF-T/N-Geldmarktsätze (Briefseite). Die Zahlung erfolgt zwei Züricher Geschäftstage nach Fälligkeit (Netting des fixen und variablen Satzes). Der Fed Funds Swap ist ein OIS im USD, bei dem der Festsatz gegen die Fed Funds Rate getauscht wird. Das Fixing der Fed Funds Swaps erfolgt gegen die sogenannte Fed Funds Effective Rate, die täglich von der FED berechnet wird und um die Target Rate schwanken kann.

5.7. Wiederholungsfragen

1. Welche Vorteile bieten Overnight Index Swaps im Vergleich zu normalen Zinsswaps?
2. Welche Aussage trifft auf einen EONIA-Swap zu?
   a) Zwei variable Zinssätze werden getauscht.
   b) Zwei feste Zinssätze werden getauscht.
   c) Er wird für lange Laufzeiten ab einem Jahr gehandelt.
   d) Ein Overnight-Satz wird gegen einen festen Zinssatz getauscht.

3. On which date are EONIA swaps settled?
    a) according to the agreement of the counterparties
    b) maturity (same day)
    c) maturity + 1 day
    d) maturity + 2 days

4. When is the variable side of a EONIA swap paid?
    a) at every EONIA fixing
    b) at maturity without taking compound interest into account
    c) at maturity as a weighted average of the EONIA fixings
    d) at maturity as an effective interest rate of the EONIA fixings

5. You believe that the 3-month interest rates will fall within one months time. The current yield curve is steep and could even get steeper when rates are falling. What kind of position would you prefer?
    a) buy 3/6 FRA
    b) sell 3/6 FRA
    c) sell 3-month EONIA swap
    d) buy 3-month EONIA swap

6. You take cash from a customer for 1 month which you hedge via an overnight investment and the sale of an EONIA swap (1 month period). What is your remaining risk?
    a) the investment cannot be done at EONIA fixing rate
    b) falling interest rate level
    c) falling overnight rates
    d) default of the customer

7. Which of the following statements are true?
    a) 43 international banks, 36 of which from the euro area, take part in the EONIA fixing.
    b) The EONIA rate is fixed to two decimals.
    c) Only banks from the euro area take part in the EONIA fixing.
    d) The EONIA rate is fixed to three decimals.

8. In which currency is TOIS traded?
    a) JPY
    b) CAD
    c) USD
    d) CHF

9. What is exchanged in an USD-OIS?
    a) fixed rate against USD-LIBOR
    b) variable rate against Fed Funds Target of FOMC
    c) fixed rate against Fed Funds Effective Rate
    d) fixed rate against Fed Funds Target of FOMC

3. An welchem Tag findet beim EONIA die Ausgleichszahlung statt?
   a) nach Absprache der Beteiligten
   b) maturity (same day)
   c) maturity + 1 Tag
   d) maturity + 2 Tage

4. Wie wird die variable Seite bei einem EONIA-Swap gezahlt?
   a) bei jedem EONIA-Fixing
   b) am Laufzeitende ohne Berücksichtigung von Zinseszinsen
   c) am Laufzeitende als gewichteter Durchschnittszinssatz der EONIA-Fixings
   d) am Laufzeitende als Effektivzinssatz der EONIA-Fixings

5. Sie glauben, dass die 3-Monats-Zinsen innerhalb des nächsten Monats fallen werden. Die aktuelle Zinskurve ist steil und könnte bei einem Rückgang der Zinsen noch steiler werden. Welche Position werden Sie eingehen?
   a) Kauf 3/6 FRA
   b) Verkauf 3/6 FRA
   c) Verkauf 3-Monats-EONIA-Swap
   d) Kauf 3-Monats-EONIA-Swap

6. Sie erhalten von einem Kunden eine 1-Monats-Einlage, die Sie über eine Taggeld-Anlage und den Verkauf eines EONIA-Swaps (Laufzeit 1 Monat) absichern. Was ist Ihr Restrisiko?
   a) Die Anlage kann nicht zu EONIA-Fixing realisiert werden.
   b) Das Zinsniveau fällt.
   c) Die Taggeldzinsen fallen.
   d) Der Kunde fällt aus.

7. Welche der folgenden Aussagen sind richtig?
   a) Am EONIA-Fixing nehmen derzeit 43 internationale Banken, davon 36 Banken aus der Eurozone teil.
   b) Der EONIA wird auf zwei Nachkommastellen berechnet.
   c) Am EONIA-Fixing nehmen ausschließlich Banken der Eurozone teil.
   d) Der EONIA wird auf drei Nachkommastellen berechnet.

8. In welcher Währung wird der TOIS gehandelt?
   a) JPY
   b) CAD
   c) USD
   d) CHF

9. Was wird beim USD-OIS getauscht?
   a) fixer Satz gegen USD-LIBOR
   b) variabler Satz gegen Fed Funds Target von FOMC
   c) fixer Satz gegen Fed Funds Effective Rate
   d) fixer Satz gegen Fed Funds Target von FOMC

Part II: The Capital Market

Teil II: Der Kapitalmarkt

The capital market is made up of all relations between investors and capital acquirers. In a strict sense it is a market in which money is provided for periods longer than one year via shares, loans and fixed income instruments such as bonds. In primary markets, new stock or bond issues are sold to investors via a mechanism known as underwriting. In secondary markets, existing securities are sold and bought among investors or traders, usually on a securities exchange, over-the-counter, or elsewhere.

The economic importance of the capital market is to provide investors with long-term capital in the form of equity capital or debt capital and to provide creditors with variable (e.g. dividends) or fixed revenue (e.g. interest for debt capital). Trades are made in security markets (organised capital market) or in free (non-organised) capital markets.

The first chapter provides information on the basics of bond trading. First, the bond market and its features are decribed. Then, quotation and pricing as well as their influence factors are explained. Furthermore, this chapter deals with the calculation of price sensibilities and the concept of duration. At the end the reader will find information on rating agencies and rating grades.

Chapter 2 deals with interest rate swaps. After a short description of the historical development of interest rate swaps, the terminology of interest rate swaps and their application are explained. Afterwards, a special interest swap - the cross currency swap - and its functionality, conventions, terminology and application are described.

The third chapter gives information on interest rate options. After explaining the terminology of option deals the functionality and different types of interest rate options are described.

Included in the following exams:
- **ACI Dealing Certificate (only chapter 2 and 3)**
- **ACI Diploma**
- **ACI Operations Certificate**

Der Kapitalmarkt stellt die Verbindung der Beziehungen von Kapitalgebern (Anbieter von Kapital) und Kapitalnehmern (Nachfrager von Kapital) dar und ist im engeren Sinne der Markt für die mittel- und langfristige Kapitalbeschaffung durch Wertpapiererwerb (Beteiligungen, Aktien, Kredite, festverzinsliche Wertpapiere, z.B. Anleihen, Pfandbriefe). Unterscheidet man den Kapitalmarkt in einen Primär- und einen Sekundärmarkt, so lassen sich für den Primärmarkt eine Mittelbereitstellungs- und für den Sekundärmarkt eine Fungibilitätsfunktion erkennen.

Die wirtschaftliche Bedeutung des Kapitalmarktes liegt insbesondere darin, den Investoren langfristig Mittel in Form von Eigen- oder Fremdkapital zur Verfügung zu stellen und dass die Kapitalgeber hierfür einen variablen Ertrag (z.B. Dividende) oder einen festen Betrag (z.B. Fremdkapitalzinsen) erhalten. Der Handel erfolgt an Wertpapierbörsen (organisierter Kapitalmarkt) oder an freien (nicht organisierten) Kapitalmärkten.

Das erste Kapitel vermittelt dem Leser die Grundlagen des Handels mit Anleihen. Zu Beginn werden der Anleihenmarkt und seine Merkmale näher erläutert. Anschließend werden die Quotierung und die Preisfindung sowie deren Einflussfaktoren behandelt. Außerdem werden die Berechnung von Preissensibilitäten und das Konzept der Duration dargestellt. Abschließend wird näher auf die Ratingstufen und die Ratingagenturen eingegangen.

Das Kapitel 2 beschäftigt sich mit den Zinsswapgeschäften. Nach einer kurzen Darstellung der historischen Entwicklung von Zinsswapgeschäften werden die Terminologien im Zusammenhang mit Zinsswaps sowie deren Anwendung näher erläutert. Anschließend wird auf zwei spezielle Zinsswaps, nämlich Overnight Index Swaps und Cross Currency Swaps sowie deren Funktionsweise, Usancen bzw. Terminologien und Anwendung eingegangen.

Das dritte Kapitel vermittelt dem Leser die Grundlagen zum Themenbereich Zinsoptionen. Hier erfährt der Leser zunächst, welche Terminologien bei Optionsgeschäften verwendet werden. Anschließend wird speziell auf die Funktionsweise und Anwendung der verschiedenen Arten von Zinsoptionen eingegangen.

Prüfungsrelevant für:

- **ACI Dealing Certificate (nur Kapitel 2 und 3)**
- **ACI Diploma**
- **ACI Operations Certificate**

1. Bonds

In this chapter you learn ...
- what parts the financial market is composed of.
- which financial instruments are traded at the different markets.
- about the features of bonds and shares.
- which types of bonds are issued.
- about well-known bonds from all over the world.
- which abbreviations and conventions are used in the bond market.
- how bonds are quoted.
- about the influencing factors on the market price of a bond
- which methods are used for calculating the fair market price of a bond.
- how pricing works with the help of the zero curve.
- which methods are used for calculating price sensitivities.
- how the concept of duration works.
- which types of rates are differentiated.
- what is meant by rating.
- about the most important rating agencies.
- which rating grades are used by the rating agencies.

1.1. The Bond Market

In the bond market **bonds/debentures with medium- and long-term maturities are traded**. A bond/debenture is a negotiable debt. The issuer obliges himself to pay the owner a specific interest rate for an agreed period of time and to repay the principal on a specified settlement day (or on several settlement days). From the issuer's point of view bonds are debt capital, and the owner of the bond is the creditor. This is also the main difference to shares which securitise an investment in a company. Here, from the issuing company's point of view, the shares are equity capital. Therefore shares do not have any specific term and the interest (dividend) depends on the economical success.

1. Anleihen

In diesem Kapitel lernen Sie ...

- aus welchen Märkten sich der Finanzmarkt zusammensetzt.
- welche Finanzinstrumente auf den einzelnen Märkten gehandelt werden.
- welche Unterscheidungsmerkmale es zwischen Anleihen und Aktien gibt.
- welche Arten von Anleihen emittiert werden.
- bekannte Anleihen aus aller Welt kennen.
- welche Abkürzungen und Konventionen im Anleihenmarkt verwendet werden.
- wie Anleihen quotiert werden.
- welche Faktoren Einfluss auf den Marktpreis einer Anleihe haben.
- welche Methoden zur Berechnung des fairen Marktpreises einer Anleihe verwendet werden.
- wie das Pricing mithilfe der Zero-Kurve funktioniert.
- welche Methoden zur Berechnung der Preissensibilitäten verwendet werden.
- wie das Konzept der Duration funktioniert.
- welche Arten von Zinssätzen unterschieden werden.
- was man unter Rating versteht.
- die wichtigsten Ratingagenturen kennen.
- welche Ratingstufen von den Ratingagenturen verwendet werden.

1.1. Der Anleihenmarkt

Unter dem Anleihemarkt (auch Rentenmarkt) versteht man den **Handel mit Gläubiger-papieren mit mittel- und langfristigen Laufzeiten.** Anleihen sind **handelbare Wert-papiere, die eine Schuld verbriefen.** Der Emittent verpflichtet sich, dem Besitzer des Papiers einen spezifizierten Zinssatz für eine definierte Laufzeit zu zahlen und das gesamte Kapital zu einem angegebenen Stichtag (oder mehreren Stichtagen) zurückzuzahlen. Aus Sicht des Emittenten stellen Anleihen also Fremdkapital dar, der Inhaber der Anleihe ist Gläubiger. Darin besteht auch das wesentliche Unterscheidungsmerkmal zu Aktien, die Anteilspapiere sind, d.h., sie verbriefen eine Beteiligung an einem Unternehmen, wodurch Aktien aus Sicht des emittierenden Unternehmens Eigenkapital darstellen. Aktien haben daher auch keine bestimmte Laufzeit, und die Verzinsung (Dividende) hängt vom wirtschaftlichen Erfolg des Unternehmens ab.

Overview financial markets:

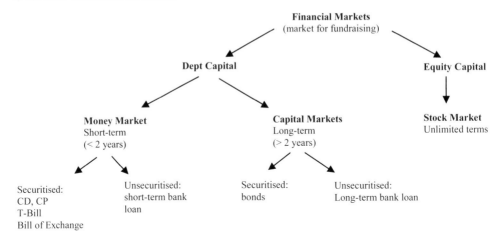

Note: Due to the many different criteria, there exist also other classifications. Capital Markets is often also a synonym for the bond market of the financial markets in common. This script focuses on the bond market and also uses the names capital market resp. fixed income.

For the issuer, bonds are a **very important instrument for fundraising**. Due to the securitisation and the tradability the issuer can find a number of potential investors, like private investors, banks, companies or investment funds.

The investors have the advantage that they can choose from a variety of investment opportunities, depending on their investment horizon and their "risk appetite".

1.1.1. Different Criteria for Bonds

Bonds can be divided along many different criteria:

I. Issuer
II. Primary market
III. Interest payment

I. Issuer

Bonds can be categorised in terms of their issuer into

- **Government bonds**
  The most important issuers are states which use bonds for **financing their national debts**. Because of the big volumina this market is very liquid and is therefore very important for the whole bond market. Due to the good ratings, government bonds are also regarded as benchmark for non-risk investments.

Übersicht Finanzmarkt:

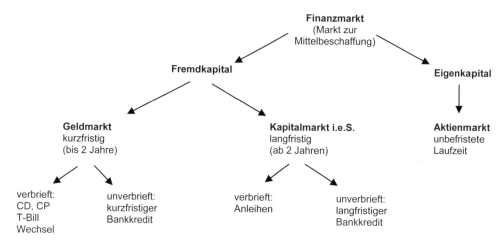

Anmerkung: Aufgrund der vielfältigen möglichen Unterscheidungskriterien sind in der Literatur auch andere Einteilungen zu finden. Auch der Begriff „Kapitalmarkt" wird oft als Synonym für den Wertpapiermarkt oder die Finanzmärkte im Allgemeinen verwendet. Dieses Kapitel beschränkt sich auf den Anleihenmarkt und verwendet dafür auch die Begriffe „Kapitalmarkt" bzw. „Fixed Income".

Anleihen stellen für die Emittenten ein **wichtiges Instrument zur Liquiditätsbeschaffung** dar. Durch die Verbriefung und Handelbarkeit kann ein Emittent eine große Anzahl von potenziellen Investoren ansprechen, wie z.B. Private, Banken, Unternehmen oder Investmentfonds.

Aus Sicht der Investoren ergibt sich am Anleihemarkt der Vorteil, dass sie je nach Investmenthorizont und Risikoneigung aus einer großen Auswahl von Anlagemöglichkeiten wählen können.

1.1.1. Unterscheidungskriterien

Anleihen unterliegen einer Vielzahl von Unterscheidungskriterien:

I. nach Emittent
II. nach Emissionsmarkt
III. nach Zinszahlung

I. nach Emittent

Je nach Emittent sind zu unterscheiden:

- **Staatsanleihen (Government Bonds)**
  Die bei weitem größten Emittenten sind Staaten, die Anleihen zur **Finanzierung der Staatsschuld** verwenden. Durch die großen Volumina ist der Markt sehr liquide und spielt daher eine wichtige Rolle im Anleihemarkt. Wegen der hohen Bonität werden Staatsanleihen auch als Benchmark für risikolose Geldanlagen angesehen.

- **Bank bonds**
  Banks use the bond market for **refinancing their loans to customers**.
- **Corporate bonds**
  The number of corporate issuances has been strongly increasing in recent years. For corporates, bonds are an **alternative to the common bank loan**.

II. Primary market

- **Domestic bonds**
  Bonds that are issued by the government, banks, or corporations in their **own, domestic market**, are called domestic bonds. Issuers have to follow the legal regulations. For example, in the US market every public bond issuance has to be registered at the SEC (US Securities and Exchange Commission) what can lead to significantly high costs. To avoid these costs so-called private placements are conducted, i.e. the bonds are sold to only one single investor or a small number of investors. Here only larger financial institutions come into question which reduces the bonds' tradability.
- **Foreign bonds**
  Bonds that are issued in the **domestic market by a foreign institution**; e.g. a bond that is issued by a US bank in Germany. Like domestic bonds also foreign bonds underly the specific local conditions. The US have by far the largest foreign bond market. Foreign bonds often carry typical names. A bond, issued by a foreign (e.g. British) issuer in the US is called Yankee. Further names are Bulldog (UK), Matador (Spain), Alpine (Switzerland) or Samurai (Japan).
- **Eurobonds or international bonds**
  Eurobonds are **issued and traded at the international markets** and are always in different currency than the currency of the country where the bonds are issued (e.g. JPY bond in Germany, USD bond in UK).
  Conditions under British law are common, but also US law and others are applied. Some years ago every single issuance had its own prospectus. Today standardised bonds are often issued within issuance programs (e.g. debt issuance program, medium term note program, commercial paper program). For these programs a sample documentation, a so-called sample prospectus, is written which shows the description of the issuer. The individual documentation for individual bonds belonging to such a program is reduced to additional writings. Thus the time for preparation and costs can be reduced significantly.

Due to the increasing deregulation of domestic markets the differentiation between domestic, foreign and eurobonds is becoming more and more obsolete.

- **Bankanleihen**
  Banken benutzen den Anleihemarkt zur **Refinanzierung der Kundenkredite.**
- **Unternehmensanleihen (Corporate Bonds)**
  Die Anzahl der Emissionen durch Unternehmen hat in den letzten Jahren stark zuge-
  nommen. Anleihen stellen für die Unternehmen dabei eine **Alternative zum klassi-
  schen Bankkredit** dar.

II. nach Emissionsmarkt

- **Inlandsanleihen (Domestic Bonds)**
  Anleihen, die **im Land des Emittenten begeben** werden, werden Inlandsanleihen genannt. Emittenten müssen dabei die gesetzlichen Vorschriften befolgen. So muss z.B.
  in den USA jede öffentlich aufgelegte Anleihe bei der SEC (US-Securities and Exchange Commission) registriert werden, was zu erheblichen Kosten führen kann. Um
  diese Kosten zu vermeiden, werden auch sogenannte Privatplatzierungen (Private
  Placements) durchgeführt, d.h., die Anleihen werden nur an einen einzigen oder eine
  kleine Anzahl von Investoren verkauft. Dabei kommen nur größere Finanzinstitutionen infrage, was die Handelbarkeit der Anleihen einschränkt.
- **Auslandsanleihen**
  Anleihen, die **im Ausland an lokale Investoren verkauft** werden, sind Auslandsanleihen, z.B. eine Anleihe, die von einer amerikanischen Bank in Deutschland emittiert
  wird. Diese Emissionen unterliegen ebenso wie Inlandsanleihen den jeweiligen lokalen Bestimmungen. Die USA sind mit Abstand der größte Markt für Auslandsanleihen. Ausländische Anleihen tragen oft typische Namen. So wird z.B. eine Anleihe eines ausländischen (z.B. britischen) Emittenten, die in den USA begeben wird, Yankee
  genannt. Weitere Bezeichnungen sind z.B. Bulldog (im UK-Markt), Matador (Spani-
  en), Alpine (Schweiz) oder Samurai (Japan).
- **Euroanleihen oder internationale Anleihen**
  Eurobonds sind Anleihen, die **für den internationalen Kapitalmarkt emittiert und
  gehandelt** werden. Sie werden jedoch nie in der Währung des Landes, wo sie emittiert
  wurden, begeben (z.B. JPY-Anleihe in Deutschland, USD-Anleihe in GB).
  Verbreitet ist die Erstellung der Anleihebedingungen unter englischem Recht, aber
  auch US-Recht und andere finden Verwendung. Vor einigen Jahren wurde noch fast
  für jede Emission ein eigener Prospekt erstellt. Heute werden standardisierte Anleihen
  häufig im Rahmen von Emissionsprogrammen begeben (z.B. Debt Issuance Programm, Medium Term Note Programm, Commercial Paper Programm). Für diese Programme wird eine Musterdokumentation, ein sog. Masterprospekt, erstellt, der die Beschreibung des Emittenten enthält. Die individuelle Dokumentation einzelner unter
  diesen Programmen gezogener Anleihen wird auf Ergänzungsschreiben, in denen die
  Konditionen der jeweiligen Ziehung festgelegt werden, reduziert. Dadurch können die
  Vorbereitungszeit und Kosten erheblich gesenkt werden.
  Die Deregulierung der Heimmärkte macht jedoch die Differenzierung in Inlands-,
  Auslands- und Euroanleihen zunehmend obsolet.

Die Deregulierung der Heimmärkte macht jedoch die Differenzierung in Inlands-, Aus-
lands- und Euroanleihen zunehmend obsolet.

III. Interest payments

There exist fixed-rate interest bonds on the one hand and floating-rate interest bonds (floating-rate notes, FRNs) on the other hand.

With **fixed-rate interest bonds**, the interest rate (in per cent of the nominal value) is fixed at the time of issue and does not change during the bond's term.

With **floating-rate interest bonds**, the interest rate is defined as a premium or discount to a specific reference/benchmark rate (e.g. LIBOR, EURIBOR). Due to possible changes of the reference rate, the interest payments may vary during the bond's term. The fixing of the interest rate for the next period is done at pre-defined dates.

Another criterion to distinct bonds is the frequency of the interest payments. The following types of bonds can be found in the market:

- With **zero-bonds**, no interest payments take place during the bond's term. With zero-bonds, no interest payments take place during the bond's term. Like the money market discount instruments (T-bill of exchange) zero bonds are issued under par and redeemed at face value. The whole interest payment (including compound interest) is done at maturity. The whole interest payment (including compound interest) is done at maturity.
- With **annual interest payments**, a payment has to be made annually.
- With **non-annual interest payments**, payments take place either quarterly or six-monthly.

Registered bonds/bearer bonds

A bond might be issued as either a registered or a bearer bond.

- **Registered bonds:** The current owner of the bond and every change of ownership is recorded in a central register. Coupon payments and redemption are booked on the account of the current owner.
- **Bearer bonds:** The current bearer of the bond is entitled to receive the interest payments and redemption. The current owner is not registered. Interest payments are made to the bearer of the interest coupons and the repayment is to be made to the bearer or sender of the bond.

Redemption

Usually, the issuer of a bond obliges himself to pay off the capital at a pre-set date and at a defined rate (usually at a rate of 100). If the whole bond is paid off at once it is called a **"bullet"**. If the bond is paid off gradually, it is called an **amortising bond** or a **"sinking fund"**. In the contract it is fixed that parts of the bond can be redeemed earlier at fixed dates and at a fixed rate.

The redemption plan can define a certain amount or the different redemption parts. You can also only define the amount and determine the different redemption parts by lot. Then you know what amount will be repaid earlier, but not to which investor.

In addition to the bonds mentioned above, there are the so-called **callable bonds**, where the issuer has the right to pay off the bond before maturity at a prior defined rate.

III. nach Zinszahlungen

Bei den Zinszahlungen wird zwischen Festzinsanleihen und variablen Anleihen (Floating Rate Notes, FRN) unterschieden.

Festzinsanleihen fixieren den Zinssatz (als Prozentsatz auf den Nominalwert) bereits bei Emission. Er verändert sich während der gesamten Laufzeit der Anleihe nicht.

Bei **variablen Anleihen** wird der Zinssatz als Auf- oder Abschlag zu einem definierten Referenzsatz oder Benchmark definiert (z.B. LIBOR, EURIBOR). Bedingt durch etwaige Veränderungen des Referenzsatzes variiert die Zinszahlung während der Laufzeit der Anleihe. Die Zinsanpassung für die nächste Zinsperiode erfolgt jeweils zu fixierten Tagen.

Ein zusätzliches Unterscheidungskriterium bei der Zinszahlung ist die Häufigkeit.

- Bei **Zero-Anleihen** werden keine Zinszahlungen während der gesamten Laufzeit geleistet. Ähnlich wie die Diskont-Instrumente am Geldmarkt (T-Bill oder Wechsel) werden die Zero-Bonds unter dem Nennwert ausgegeben und werden dann at par zurückbezahlt. Somit erfolgt die gesamte Zinszahlung (inklusive der angefallenen Zinseszinsen) am Ende der Laufzeit.
- Bei **jährlicher Zinszahlung** erfolgt die Auszahlung der Zinsen einmal jährlich.
- Bei **unterjähriger Zinszahlung** werden die Zinsen entweder halbjährlich oder vierteljährlich ausbezahlt.

Namensschuldverschreibung/Inhaberschuldverschreibung

Eine Anleihe kann als Inhaber- oder Namensschuldverschreibung emittiert werden.

- Eine **Namensschuldverschreibung** ist eine Anleihe, bei der der aktuelle Besitzer sowie jede Besitzänderung in einem Zentralregister aufgezeichnet wird. Zinszahlung und Rückzahlung erfolgen auf das Konto des aktuellen Besitzers.
- Eine **Inhaberschuldverschreibung** ist eine Anleihe, die den Überbringer berechtigt, Zins- und Rückzahlung zu erhalten. Der aktuelle Besitzer ist nicht dokumentiert, Zinszahlungen erfolgen an den Überbringer der Kuponabschnitte, die Rückzahlung erfolgt an den Überbringer oder Einsender der Schuldverschreibung.

Rückzahlung

Üblicherweise verpflichtet sich der Emittent einer Anleihe, das Kapital zu einem genau definierten Zeitpunkt und genau definierten Kurs (üblicherweise zum Kurs von 100) zu tilgen. Wird die gesamte Anleihe zu einem einzigen Datum getilgt, spricht man von **endfälligen Anleihen** oder auch **Bullet Redemption.** Wird die Anleihe in einzelnen Stufen zurückbezahlt, spricht man von einer **amortisierenden Anleihe** oder einem sogenannten **Sinking Fund.** Vertraglich ist festgelegt, dass Teile der Anleihe vorzeitig zu fix vereinbarten Zeitpunkten mit einem fixen Kurs getilgt werden.

Der Tilgungsplan kann eine Betragshöhe und die zu tilgenden Anleihenlose festlegen. Es kann aber auch nur die Betragshöhe vereinbart werden, und die zu tilgenden Anleihenlose werden mittels Auslosung ermittelt. Man weiß also, wann wie viel vorzeitig zurückgezahlt wird, jedoch nicht an welchen Investor.

Zusätzlich zu den oben erwähnten Anleihen gibt es auch noch sogenannte **Callable Bonds,** die den Emittenten dazu berechtigen, die Anleihe zu einem im Voraus fixierten Kurs vorzeitig zurückzuzahlen.

Convertible bonds

Convertible bonds are unsecured fixed-rate bonds that give the owner the **right** (but not the obligation) **to convert the bonds into shares** (under conditions that have been specified in advance). Usually, the **interest rate** for such convertible bonds is **below the interest rate for "normal" bonds**, since the owner has the right to convert the bond into shares.

1.1.2. EXCURSUS: Common Bonds and Their Abbreviations and Conventions

USA	T-Bill	Short-term US government bond on a discount basis
	T-Bond	US government bond with terms of more than 10 years
	T-Note	US government bond with terms of less than 10 years
Deutschland	Bobl	Bundesobligation, German government bond
	Bund	Bundesanleihe, German government bond
	OBL	Bundesobligation (Bobl), German government bond
	REX	German bonds with variable interest payments which are bound to a long-term benchmark
UK	Gilt	UK government bond
Japan	JGB	Japanese government bond
Frankreich	BTAN	Bon de trésor à taux fixe et intérêt annuel, short-term French government bond
	BTF	Bon de trésor à taux fixe et intérêt précompté, French government bond on a discount basis (~T-Bill)
	OAT	Obligation assimilable du Trésor, French government bond
	OATi	French government bond, linked to inflation
	TEC	French bonds with variable interest payments which are bound to a long-term benchmark
Italien	BTP	Buoni del Tresoro Poliennali, Italian government bonds > 1 year with fixed interest payment
	CCT	Certificati di Credito del Tresoro, Italian government bonds > 1 year with floating interest payment
	CTZ	Certificati di Credito del Tresoro „Zero Coupon", Italian government bonds > 1 year without interest coupon

Wandelanleihen

Wandelanleihen sind nicht besicherte Festzinsanleihen, die dem Besitzer das **Recht**, aber nicht die Pflicht geben, diese **Anleihen zu vorher fixierten Bedingungen in Aktien umzuwandeln.** Der **Zinssatz** für solche Wandelanleihen ist **normalerweise niedriger** als bei „normalen" Anleihen, da der Inhaber zusätzlich das Recht besitzt, die Anleihe in Aktien umzuwandeln.

1.1.2. EXKURS: Bekannte Anleihen aus aller Welt und ihre Abkürzungen und Konventionen

USA	T-Bill	kurzfristiges US-Staatspapier auf Diskontbasis
	T-Bond	US-Staatsanleihe mit einer Emissionslaufzeit von mehr als 10 Jahren
	T-Note	US-Staatsanleihe mit einer Emissionslaufzeit von weniger als 10 Jahren
Deutschland	Bobl	Bundesobligation, deutsche Staatsanleihe
	Bund	Bundesanleihe, deutsche Staatsanleihe
	OBL	Bundesobligation (Bobl), deutsche Staatsanleihe
	REX	deutsche Anleihen mit variabler Verzinsung, die an eine langfristige Benchmark gebunden ist
UK	Gilt	UK-Staatsanleihe
Japan	JGB	Japanische Staatsanleihe
Frankreich	BTAN	Bon de trésor à taux fixe et intérêt annuel, kurzfristige französische Staatsanleihe
	BTF	Bon de trésor à taux fixe et intérêt précompté, französisches Staatspapier auf Diskontbasis (~T-Bill)
	OAT	Obligation assimilable du Trésor, französische Staatsanleihe
	OATi	französische Staatsanleihe, die an die Inflation gebunden ist
	TEC	französische Anleihen mit variabler Verzinsung, die an eine langfristige Benchmark gebunden ist
Italien	BTP	Buoni del Tresoro Poliennali, mehrjährige italienische Staatsanleihen mit fixer Verzinsung
	CCT	Certificati di Credito del Tresoro, mehrjährige italienische Staatsanleihen mit variabler Verzinsung
	CTZ	Certificati di Credito del Tresoro „Zero Coupon", mehrjährige italienische Staatsanleihen ohne Zinskupon

Day counting in the capital markets

Country	Day Counting
Euro area	ACT/ACT
USA	ACT/ACT
UK	Gilts: s.a. ACT/ACT
Japan	30/360 or ACT/ACT
Switzerland	30/360 or 30E/360

Interest payments

Type	Interest payment
Eurobonds	annual
Government bonds	
Bund	annual
Treasury Note	semi-annual
UK / Gilts	semi-annual
Japan	semi-annual

1.1.3. Glossary Capital Market

ABS	Asset Backed Securities; a bond which is securitised by certain assets (e.g. loans, credit card outstandings, leasings etc.)
BBAIRS	British Bankers' Association Interest Rate Swaps, standard documentation by the British Bankers' Association for interest rate swaps
Bullet	Bond which repays 100% of the nominal at maturity
Callable Bond	Bond where the issuer has the right to repay earlier
Cedel	A clearing house, founded in Luxemburg, after the merger with Deutsche Bank Cedel had been absorbed in Clearstream
CGO	Central Gilt Office
CTD	Cheapest to deliver, the bond which is the "cheapest" at the moment regarding delivery in futures
DVP	Delivery versus Payment
Euroclear	One of the two largest security clearing houses, based in Brussels
Flat quotation	Bond quotation at dirty price (incl. accrued interest)
GNMA	Government National Mortgage Association (also called "Ginnie Mae"), a state agency in the US which buys mortgages from financial institutions, then securitises these mortgages and sells it to investors as bonds.

Berechnung der Tage im Kapitalmarkt

Land	Tageberechnung
Euroraum	ACT/ACT
USA	ACT/ACT
UK	Gilts: s.a. ACT/ACT
Japan	30/360 oder ACT/ACT
Schweiz	30/360 oder 30E/360

Zinszahlungen

Typ	Zinszahlung
Eurobonds	jährlich
Staatsanleihen	
Bund	jährlich
Treasury Note	halbjährlich
UK/Gilts	halbjährlich
Japan	halbjährlich

1.1.3. Glossar Kapitalmarkt

ABS	Asset Backed Securities; eine Anleihe, die durch bestimmte Aktiva (z.B. Kredite, Kreditkartenforderungen, Leasingfinanzierungen usw.) besichert ist
BBAIRS	British Bankers' Association Interest Rate Swaps, Standard-Dokumentation von der British Bankers' Association für Zinsswaps
Bullet	Anleihe, die zur Fälligkeit 100% Nominale zurückzahlt
Callable Bond	eine Anleihe, bei der der Emittent das Recht hat, die Anleihe vorzeitig zu tilgen
Cedel	ein in Luxemburg gegründetes Clearinghaus; nach der Fusion mit der Deutsche Börse Clearing AG ist Cedel in Clearstream aufgegangen
CGO	Central Gilt Office
CTD	Cheapest to deliver; die Anleihe, die derzeit am „billigsten" ist bezogen auf die Lieferung in Futures
DVP	Delivery versus Payment
Euroclear	eines der zwei größten Wertpapier-Clearinghäuser mit Sitz in Brüssel
Flat quotation	Bond Quotierung in Dirty Preis (inkl. Stückzinsen)
GNMA	Government National Mortgage Association, eine staatliche Agentur in den USA, die Hypothekarforderungen von Kreditinstituten ankauft, verbrieft und in Form von Anleihen an Investoren weiterverkauft. Die GNMA wird auch Ginnie Mae genannt.

Gross-Up	the obligation of an issuer to offset the withholding tax, if such a tax is introduced during the term of the bond, grossing-up clauses are frequently used in eurobonds
ISDA	International Securities and Derivatives Association
ISMA	International Securities Market Association
Conversion Price	Defined share price for the option of a convertible bond
MBS	Mortgage Backed Securities, an ABS kind with mortgages
Pari Passu	A clause which obliges the issuer to treat all investors the same
SEC	Securities and Exchange Commission (USA)
Step Up Bond	Bond with a rising coupon
Swappable Bond	The coupon of this bond is higher than the actual interest rate swap rate
Convertible Bond	A bond that gives the owner the right to convert the nominal into shares at a defined price

1.2. Quotation of Bonds

Face value

Every bond has a fixed face value. This face value serves

- as the basis for the interest payment
- as the basis to calculate the redemption value which can differ from the face value (if redemption value is 100, otherwise face value x fixed price).
- as the basis of the issuing price. If the current price of the bond is above (below) 100, the bond is said to be quoted at a premium (discount).

Quotation

Bond prices are usually quoted in **per cent of the face value**. For example, the bond's price of 101.50 for EUR government bonds corresponds to the price of EUR 101.50 per cent of the nominal value.

In the **eurobond market**, prices are usually quoted in **decimals** (e.g. 101.50), while in the US and in UK they are often quoted with fractions (e.g. 101½ or 101 16/32).

In the bond market, market makers quote both bid and offer on request: the **bid price** is the price they are willing to pay for bonds while the **offer price** is the price at which they are willing to sell the bonds.

Gross-Up	die Verpflichtung des Emittenten einer Anleihe, die Quellensteuer auszugleichen, falls eine solche während der Laufzeit im Heimland des Emittenten eingeführt wird; die Grossing-Up Clause wird häufig bei Euro-Bonds angewendet
ISDA	International Securities and Derivatives Association
ISMA	International Securities Market Association
Konversionspreis	definierter Aktienpreis für die Option in einer Wandelanleihe
MBS	Mortgage Backed Securities; eine ABS-Form mit Hypothekarkrediten
Pari Passu	Klausel, die den Emittenten verpflichtet, alle Gläubiger gleichzustellen
SEC	Securities and Exchange Commission (USA)
Step Up Bond	Anleihe mit ansteigenden Kupons
Swapable Bond	eine Anleihe, deren Kupon höher als der aktuelle Zinsswap-Festzins ist
Wandelanleihe	Convertible Bond; eine Anleihe, bei der der Käufer das Recht hat, das Nominale zu einem definierten Preis in Aktien umzuwandeln

1.2. Die Quotierung von Anleihen

Nominalwert

Jede Anleihe hat einen fixierten Nominalwert (Nennwert). Dieser Nominalwert ist

- die Basis der Zinszahlung,
- der Betrag der Rückzahlung (falls Tilgungskurs 100, ansonsten Nominalwert x fixiertem Kurs),
- die Basis des Emissionspreises: Dieser kann über oder unter dem Nominalwert liegen. Liegt er über dem Nominalwert, spricht man von **Agio**, liegt er unter dem Nominalwert, spricht man von einem **Disagio.**

Anleihepreis

Die Preisquotierung bei Anleihen erfolgt üblicherweise als **Prozentsatz vom Nominalwert.** Zum Beispiel entspricht ein Anleihepreis von 101,50 für EUR-Bundanleihen dem Preis von EUR 101,50 pro 100 EUR Nominalbetrag.

Im **Eurobond-Markt** werden die Preise üblicherweise in **Dezimalstellen** quotiert (z.B. 101,50), während in den USA und in UK häufiger in Brüchen quotiert wird (101 1/2 bzw. 101 16/32).

Auch im Anleihemarkt quotieren Market Maker auf Anfrage sowohl die Geld- als auch die Briefseite. Die **Geldseite** ist der Preis, den sie für Anleihen zu bezahlen bereit sind. Die **Briefseite** ist der Preis, den sie bei Verkauf der Anleihe verlangen. Die quotierten Preise sind sogenannte Clean Preise, d.h. der Preis der Anleihe ohne die sogenannten Stückzinsen.

Accrued interest

The owner of the bond receives the full amount of interest at coupon dates, even though he might not have possessed the bond during the whole period of interest. Therefore, when a bond is sold or bought, accrued interest has to be taken into account. Since comparing bond prices, that include accrued interest, is a complicated business, **bonds are usually quoted without accrued interest**. Nonetheless, the buyer of a bond has to pay the accrued interest to the seller when he purchases the bond.

The price without accrued interest is called0147 **clean price**. The price including accrued interest is called **dirty price**.

To calculate the accrued interest, one computes the interest on the face value for the elapsed days (taking into account the respective method of calculation). According to the ISMA conventions the calculation of the accrued interest days includes the start value of the interest period, but not the end value (= trade date of the bond).

Example

Dirty Price

A USD bond with a 7%-coupon (30/360 annual) and a time to maturity of 3½ years is sold at a price of 101.50 (= clean price). Since the last coupon date, 6 months (= 180 days) have elapsed.

$$\text{Dirty price} = 101.50 + 100 \times 0.07 \times \frac{180}{360} = 105.00$$

Therefore, the buyer of the coupon must pay a price of 105.00.

Example

Start/end value

A EUR-Bund, coupon 6.0% (ACT/ACT annual), had its last coupon payment on 12th January 2001. On 18th April Bank A sells the bond to Bank B. The accrued interest days based on ACT are calculated as follows:

	Period	**Days**
January	$12^{th} - 31^{st}$	20
February		28
March		31
April	$- 17^{th}$	16
	Total	**95**

The accrued interest, that Bank B has to pay, are **EUR 1.56164383.**

$$\left(0.06 \times \frac{95}{365}\right) \times 100$$

Stückzinsen

Bei Kuponauszahlung fließen die vollen Zinsen dem Besitzer der Anleihe zu, unabhängig davon, ob er diese Anleihe für die ganze Zinsperiode in seinem Besitz hatte. Daher müssen die abgegrenzten Zinsen bei Kauf und Verkauf berücksichtigt werden. Eine Berücksichtigung der angefallenen Stückzinsen in den Preisen würde die Vergleichbarkeit der Preise stark beeinträchtigen. Aus diesem Grund hat sich die Usance eingebürgert, **Anleihenpreise ohne die bisher angefallenen Stückzinsen zu quotieren**. Bei etwaigem Abschluss sind die bisher angefallenen Zinsen vom Käufer der Anleihe an den Verkäufer zu zahlen.

Den Preis ohne Stückzinsen nennt man **Clean Price**. Der Preis, der die angefallenen Zinsen mit berücksichtigt, ist der **Dirty Price**.

Die Berechnung der Stückzinsen kalkuliert die Zinsen auf den Nominalwert für die angefallenen Tage (unter Berücksichtigung der jeweiligen Zinsberechnungsmethode). Gemäß der ISMA-Konventionen wird die Beginnvaluta der Zinsperiode bei der Ermittlung der Stückzinstage inkludiert, die Endvaluta (= Handelstag der Anleihe) nicht.

Beispiel

Dirty Price

Eine USD-Anleihe mit 7%-Kupon (30/360 jährlich), Nominale 100 und einer Restlaufzeit von dreieinhalb Jahren, wird zum Preis von 101,50 (= Clean Price) verkauft. Seit dem letzten Zinszahlungstermin sind 180 Tage vergangen.

Dirty Price = $101{,}50 + 100 \times 0{,}07 \times \dfrac{180}{360} = 105{,}00$

Der Käufer der Anleihe muss also einen Preis von 105,00 zahlen.

Beispiel

Beginn-/Endvaluta

Ein EUR-Bund, Kupon 6% (ACT/ACT, jährlich), Nominale 100, hatte seine letzte Kuponzahlung am 12. Jänner. Am 18. April verkauft Bank A die Anleihe an Bank B. Die Stückzinstage auf Basis der ACT-Methode berechnen sich wie folgt:

	Zeitraum	Tage
Jänner	12.1.–31.1.	20
Februar		28
März		31
April	–17.4.	16
	Summe	**95**

Die Stückzinsen, die Bank B ablösen muss, betragen **EUR 1,56164383**.

$$\left(0{,}06 * \frac{95}{365}\right) * 100$$

1.3. Pricing of Bonds

1.3.1. Influencing Factors

The price of a fixed-rate interest bond corresponds to the price at which market participants are willing to buy or sell the bond. When speaking of the price of a bond, one usually refers to its market price. This market price is **influenced by the following factors**:

- the time to maturity of the bond
- the actual market yield of bonds with the same time to maturity
- the fixed interest rate of the bond
- the linked credit risk (credit quality of the issuer)
- the liquidity of the bond's secondary market

We will concentrate on the first three of these factors (time to maturity, yield, and coupon). We use government bonds for demonstration purposes, because here the influence
of both the premium for credit risks and a possible liquidity premium are reduced to a
minimum.

1.3.2. Calculation of Bond Prices

How can the fair bond price be determined? The answer is simple. If you buy a bond you
know that you will receive regular coupon payments during the bond's term and the nominal at maturity. Therefore, today, you are willing to pay the present value of these future
cash-flows. Thus the fair bond price is the **present value of all future cash-flows**.

Example

Following example: Assuming, a 5-year government bond which is issued today at a
price of 100 has a coupon of 6%. At a price of 100 a coupon of 6% equals an interest
rate of 6% for the nominal amount. Therefore, the market yield for 5-year government
bonds is 6%.

There is another government bond in the market with the same maturity which pays a
coupon of 7%. Which price are you willing to pay for this 7%-bond? Answer: you are
willing to pay as much as the interest on the nominal amount corresponds to the market
yield of 6%. We look at every single cash-flow and check how much we can pay for
it in order to have a return of 6%. The purchase of nominal EUR 100 m of the above
7%-bond has the following Cash-Flows:

	CF1	CF2	CF3	CF4	CF5	
Cash-Flow	+7	+7	+7	+7	+107	
Present value	+6.60	+6.23	+5.88	+5.54	+79.96	sum: 104.21

How many EUR can you pay today for a cash-flow of EUR 7 in one year to get a return
of 6%?

1.3. Die Preisfindung von Anleihen

1.3.1. Einflussfaktoren

Der Preis einer Festzinsanleihe ist jener, zu dem Marktteilnehmer bereit sind, diese Anleihe zu kaufen bzw. zu verkaufen. Wenn vom Preis der Anleihe gesprochen wird, ist damit üblicherweise der aktuelle Marktpreis gemeint. Dieser Marktpreis unterliegt folgenden **Haupteinflussfaktoren:**

- der Restlaufzeit der Anleihe
- der aktuellen marktüblichen Rendite für Anleihen mit gleicher Restlaufzeit
- dem in der Anleihe fixierten Zinssatz
- dem mit der Anleihe verbundenen Kreditrisiko (Bonität des Emittenten)
- der Liquidität des Sekundärmarktes für die Anleihe

Die folgenden Ausführungen gehen ausschließlich auf die drei ersten Einflussfaktoren (Restlaufzeit, Rendite und Kupon) ein. Die Erklärungen ziehen Staatsanleihen heran, da hier sowohl Kreditrisikoaufschlag als auch etwaige Liquiditätsaufschläge am geringsten sind.

1.3.2. Preisberechnung

Wie kann der faire Preis einer Anleihe bestimmt werden? Die Antwort ist einfach. Wenn Sie eine Anleihe kaufen, wissen Sie, dass Sie in regelmäßigen Abständen die Kuponzahlungen und am Ende der Laufzeit die Rückzahlung des Nominales erhalten werden. Daher werden Sie heute bereit sein, den Barwert der zukünftigen Cashflows zu bezahlen. Somit entspricht der faire Preis einer Anleihe den **diskontierten Cashflows.**

Beispiel

Ziehen wir dafür folgendes Beispiel heran: Angenommen der Kupon für 5-jährige Bundesanleihen, die heute zum Preis von 100 emittiert werden, ist 6%. Bei einem Preis von 100 entspricht ein Kupon von 6% auch einer Verzinsung des eingesetzten Kapitals von 6%. Wir sagen daher, die aktuelle Marktrendite für 5-jährige Bundesanleihen ist 6%.
Weiters gibt es im Markt eine Bundesanleihe mit genau der gleichen Restlaufzeit, die einen Kupon von 7% bezahlt. Welchen Preis werden wir bereit sein, für die 7%-ige Anleihe zu bezahlen? Die Lösung ist: Wir sind bereit, so viel zu bezahlen, dass die Verzinsung des eingesetzten Kapitals der aktuellen Marktrendite, also 6%, entspricht. Wir betrachten also jeden einzelnen Cashflow der Anleihe und fragen uns, wie viel wir heute dafür bezahlen können, um zu einer Verzinsung von 6% zu gelangen. Der Kauf von EUR 100 Nominale der 7%-igen Anleihe bringt folgende Cashflows:

	CF1	CF2	CF3	CF4	CF5	
Cashflow	+7	+7	+7	+7	+107	
Barwert	+6,60	+6,23	+5,88	+5,54	+ 79,96	Summe: 104,21

Wie viel EUR können wir heute für einen Cashflow von 7 EUR in einem Jahr bezahlen, um auf eine Verzinsung von 6% zu kommen?

Answer: the discounted amount, i.e. 7/(1+0.06) = EUR 6.60377. Analogically EUR 7 in 2 years are worth today 7/(1+0.06)^2 = EUR 6.22998, etc. If today, we pay the sum of the present values of all Cash-Flows, we will receive a return on the investment which equals the market yield.

1.3.2.1. General Formula for Pricing

Since the amount of capital is not necessarily paid back at maturity and the interest payments are not necessarily paid annually, a number of specialised formulae for pricing exist. For this reason, we present a general formula that takes into account different types of interest payments as well as different types of repayment arrangements.

First, we determine the Cash-Flows that result from a nominal amount of 100. Then, these cash-flows are discounted by the current yield.

$$P = \sum_{n=1}^{N} \frac{1}{(1+r)^n} \cdot CF_n$$

P = price
r = current yield, in decimals
n = ongoing period
N = total number of periods
CF_n = Cash-Flow (at a nominal of 100) at time n

Since pricing does not necessarily happen at coupon dates (result is a "broken" period at the beginning), therefore we have to generalise the formula again:

Clean Price (Moosmüller-method)

$$P_c = \left[\frac{CF_1}{1+r \times \frac{d}{B}} + \sum_{n=2}^{N} \frac{CF_n}{\left(1+r \times \frac{d}{B}\right) \times (1+r)^{n-1}} \right] - AI$$

Pc = clean price
d = days to the first cash-flow
AI = accrued interest
B = day base (360/ 365/ ACT)
CF_n = cash-flow (at a nominal of 100) at time n

Note: With "broken" periods there are different ways of calculation. In Germany, the **"Moosmüller-method"** is usually employed, i.e. the first **discounting** is calculated **linearly** $(1+r \times d/B)$; internationally, the **"ISMA-method"** is commonly used, which discounts cash-flows exponentially, i.e. $(1+r \times d/B)$ is replaced by $(1+r)^{d/B}$. The ISMA-method always leads to a higher result than the Moosmüller-method.

> Antwort: den mit 6% abgezinsten Betrag, also $7/(1+0,06)$ = EUR 6,60377. Analog dazu sind 7 EUR in 2 Jahren heute $7/(1+0,06)^2$ = EUR 6,22998 wert usw. Wenn wir heute die Summe der Barwerte der einzelnen Cashflows bezahlen, werden wir eine Verzinsung auf das eingesetzte Kapital erhalten, die der aktuellen Marktrendite entspricht.

1.3.2.1. Allgemeine Formel

Das Kapital wird nicht immer zur Gänze erst am Ende der Laufzeit zurückbezahlt. Auch die Zinsen werden nicht unbedingt jährlich bezahlt. Daher müssten für all diese Fälle spezielle Formeln zur Preisberechnung herangezogen werden. Aus diesem Grund gibt es eine allgemeine Formel, die sowohl unterschiedliche Zinszahlungsmodalitäten wie auch unterschiedliche Rückzahlungsvereinbarungen berücksichtigt.

Im ersten Schritt sind die Zahlungsströme (Cashflows), die sich bei einem Nominalbetrag von 100 ergeben, zu ermitteln. Dann werden diese Cashflows für ihre unterschiedliche Laufzeit mit der aktuellen Rendite abgezinst.

$$P = \sum_{n=1}^{N} \frac{1}{(1+r)^n} \times CF_n$$

P = Preis
r = aktuelle Rendite in Dezimalen für die Periode
n = fortlaufende Periode
N = Gesamtlaufzeit in Perioden
CF_n = Cashflow (auf Nominale 100) zum Zeitpunkt n

Zusätzlich ist zu bedenken, dass eine Preisberechnung nicht nur zu Kuponterminen erfolgt. Das bedeutet, es ergibt sich eine „gebrochene" Periode am Anfang. Daher verallgemeinert sich die Formel weiter:

Clean Preis („Moosmüller-Methode")

$$Pc = \left[\frac{CF_1}{1+r \times \frac{t}{B}} + \sum_{n=2}^{N} \frac{CF_n}{\left(1+r \times \frac{t}{B}\right) \times (1+r)^{n-1}} \right] - SZ$$

Pc = Clean Preis
t = Tage bis zum ersten Cashflow
SZ = Stückzinsen
B = Basis (360/365/ACT)
CF_n = Cashflow (auf Nominale 100) zum Zeitpunkt n

Anmerkung: Bei „gebrochenen" Perioden sind unterschiedliche Methoden möglich. In Deutschland ist die **„Moosmüller-Methode"** üblich, d.h., die erste **Abzinsung** erfolgt wie angegeben **linear** $(1+r \times t/B)$; international häufiger ist die **„ISMA-Methode"**, die **exponenziell abzinst**, d.h., $(1+r \times t/B)$ wird ersetzt durch $(1+r)^{t/B}$. Die ISMA-Methode führt immer zu einem etwas höheren Ergebnis als die Moosmüller-Methode.

1.3.2.2. Formula for "Bullet" Bonds with Annual Coupons

The common formula used in the pricing of a bullet bond is as follows:

$$PV = \frac{C}{1+r} + \frac{C}{(1+r)^2} + \ldots + \frac{C}{(1+r)^N} + \frac{Nom}{(1+r)^N}$$

or

$$PV = \left\{ \left(C \times \sum_{n=1}^{N} \frac{1}{(1+r)^n} \right) + \frac{1}{(1+r)^N} \right\} \times 100$$

PV = present value = fair bond price
C   = coupon, in decimals (6% = 0.06)
r   = current market yield, in decimals
n   = ongoing year
N   = total number of years
Nom = nominal = 100

Example

Calculate the price for a EUR government bond with a 7%-coupon, 5 years to maturity, and annual interest payments (the latest payment just took place). The current interest rate (yield) for government bonds with 5 years to maturity is 6%.

$$PV = \left\{ \left(0.07 \times \sum_{n=1}^{5} \frac{1}{(1+0.06)^n} \right) + \frac{1}{(1+0.06)^5} \right\} \times 100$$

$$= ((0.07 \times 4.21237) + 0.74726) \times 100 = 104.21$$

The fair price of this bond is 104.21.

1.3.2.2. Formel für endfällige ganzjährige Anleihen

Aus den oben angestellten Überlegungen können wir die Formel für die Anleiheberechnung ableiten:

$$PV = \frac{C}{1+r} + \frac{C}{(1+r)^2} + \dots + \frac{C}{(1+r)^N} + \frac{Nom}{(1+r)^N}$$

oder

$$PV = \left\{ \left(C \times \sum_{n=1}^{N} \frac{1}{(1+r)^n} \right) + \frac{1}{(1+r)^N} \right\} \times 100$$

PV = Barwert = fairer Kurs der Anleihe
C   = Kupon in Dezimalen, z.B. 6% = 0,06
r   = aktuelle Marktrendite in Dezimalen
n   = laufendes Jahr
N   = Laufzeit in Jahren
Nom = Nominale =100

Beispiel

Für eine Euro-Bundesanleihe mit 7%-Kupon, 5-jähriger Restlaufzeit und jährlicher Zinszahlung, wobei die letzte Zinszahlung gerade stattgefunden hat, soll der aktuelle Preis berechnet werden. Die aktuelle Verzinsung (Rendite) für 5-jährige Euro-Anleihen beträgt 6%.

$$PV = \left\{ \left(0,07 \times \sum_{n=1}^{5} \frac{1}{(1+0,06)^n} \right) + \frac{1}{(1+0,06)^5} \right\} \times 100$$

$$= \left((0,07 \times 4,21237) + 0,74726 \right) \times 100 = 104,21$$

Der faire Preis der Anleihe ist 104,21.

We demonstrate the calculation of the sum $\left(\sum_{n=1}^{5} \dfrac{1}{(1+0.06)^n} \right)$ in the following table:

Year	Discount factor
1	$\dfrac{1}{(1+0.06)^1} = 0.94340$
2	$\dfrac{1}{(1+0.06)^2} = 0.89000$
3	$\dfrac{1}{(1+0.06)^3} = 0.83962$
4	$\dfrac{1}{(1+0.06)^4} = 0.79209$
5	$\dfrac{1}{(1+0.06)^5} = 0.74726$
Sum:	**4.21237**

Market yield and bond price

If the market yield rises, the future cash-flow will be discounted at a higher interest rate which leads to a lower present value (and vice versa). Thus we have the following connection:

Interest rate ↗ → Price ↘

Interest rate ↘ → Price ↗

In other words: If a bond pays a coupon which is lower than the current market yield, an investor will only be willing to pay a price which is lower than 100 in order to compensate for the difference between the low coupon payments and the actual issuances. Is the coupon higher than the current yield the bond price will be above 100.

Die Summenberechnung $\left(\sum_{n=1}^{5} \dfrac{1}{(1+0{,}06)^n}\right)$ stellen wir am besten anhand einer kleinen Tabelle dar:

Jahr	Diskontfaktor
1	$\dfrac{1}{(1+0{,}06)^1} = 0{,}94340$
2	$\dfrac{1}{(1+0{,}06)^2} = 0{,}89000$
3	$\dfrac{1}{(1+0{,}06)^3} = 0{,}83962$
4	$\dfrac{1}{(1+0{,}06)^4} = 0{,}79209$
5	$\dfrac{1}{(1+0{,}06)^5} = 0{,}74726$
Summe:	**4,21237**

Zusammenhang zwischen Marktrendite und Anleihekurs

Steigt die Marktrendite, so wird der zukünftige Cashflow mit einem höheren Zinssatz diskontiert, woraus ein niedrigerer Barwert resultiert und umgekehrt. Somit gilt immer folgender Zusammenhang:

Zinsen ↗ → Kurs ↘

Zinsen ↘ → Kurs ↗

Mit anderen Worten: Zahlt eine Anleihe einen Kupon, der unter der aktuellen Marktrendite liegt, wird ein Investor nur einen Preis unter 100 zu bezahlen bereit sein, um die im Vergleich zu aktuellen Emissionen niedrigeren Kuponzahlungen auszugleichen. Liegt der Kupon über der aktuellen Rendite, so wird der Preis der Anleihe über 100 liegen.

1.3.2.3. Examples for Calculation

Example

"Bullet" bond at the coupon date

Bond: German government bond (Bund)
Coupon: 7% fixed
Time to maturity: 5 years
Interest payment: annual
Redemption: bullet
Current yield: 6.00%
Assumption: The latest interest payment has just been made.

1 Year	2 Cash-flow	3 Discounting	4 Present value (2x3)
1	7	$\dfrac{1}{(1+0.06)^1}=0.94340$	6.6038
2	7	$\dfrac{1}{(1+0.06)^2}=0.89000$	6.2300
3	7	$\dfrac{1}{(1+0.06)^3}=0.83962$	5.8773
4	7	$\dfrac{1}{(1+0.06)^4}=0.79209$	5.5447
5	107	$\dfrac{1}{(1+0.06)^5}=0.74726$	79.9566
		Sum:	**104.2124**

The calculated bond price is **104.2124**. As the latest interest payment has just been made, here, clean price = dirty price.

1.3.2.3. Rechenbeispiele

Beispiel

Endfällige Anleihe an einem Kupontermin

Anleihe:	German Government Bond (Bund)
Kupon:	7% fest
Laufzeit:	5 Jahre
Zinszahlung:	jährlich
Tilgung:	endfällig
aktuelle Rendite:	6%
Annahme:	Die letzte Zinszahlung hat gerade stattgefunden.

1 Jahr	2 Cashflow	3 Abzinsung (Diskontfaktor)	4 Barwert (2x3)
1	7	$\dfrac{1}{(1+0,06)^1} = 0,94340$	6,6038
2	7	$\dfrac{1}{(1+0,06)^2} = 0,89000$	6,2300
3	7	$\dfrac{1}{(1+0,06)^3} = 0,83962$	5,8773
4	7	$\dfrac{1}{(1+0,06)^4} = 0,79209$	5,5447
5	107	$\dfrac{1}{(1+0,06)^5} = 0,74726$	79,9566
		Summe:	**104,2124**

Der errechnete Kurs der Anleihe ist **104,2124.** Da die letzte Kuponzahlung soeben stattgefunden hat, entspricht der Clean Preis dem Dirty Preis.

Example

"Bullet" bond between coupon dates
Calculation with Moosmüller-method

Bond:	German government bond (Bund)
Coupon:	7% fixed
Time to maturity:	4 years, 270 days
Interest payment:	annual
Redemption:	bullet
Current yield:	6%

1 Year	2 Cash-flow	3 Discounting	4 Present value (2x3)
270 days	7	$\dfrac{1}{\left(1+0.06 \times \dfrac{270}{365}\right)} = 0.9575$	6.7025
1 year, 270 days	7	$\dfrac{1}{\left(1+0.06 \times \dfrac{270}{365}\right) \times (1+0.06)^1} = 0.9033$	6.3231
2 years, 270 days	7	$\dfrac{1}{\left(1+0.06 \times \dfrac{270}{365}\right) \times (1+0.06)^2} = 0.8522$	5.9652
3 years, 270 days	7	$\dfrac{1}{\left(1+0.06 \times \dfrac{270}{365}\right) \times (1+0.06)^3} = 0.8039$	5.6276
4 years, 270 days	107	$\dfrac{1}{\left(1+0.06 \times \dfrac{270}{365}\right) \times (1+0.06)^4} = 0.7584$	81.1522
	Sum (dirty price):		105.7706
	− Accrued interest: $\left(7 \times \dfrac{95}{365}\right)$		1.8219
	Price (clean price): with Moosmüller-method		**103.9487**

The sum of all discounted cash-flows is the dirty price. This amount has to be paid when buying the bond, i.e. clean price plus accrued interest. The **clean price** is quoted which is the result of the **dirty price minus accrued interest**.

Beispiel

Endfällige Anleihe zwischen den Kuponterminen
Berechnung nach Moosmüller

Anleihe:	German Government Bond (Bund)
Kupon:	7% fest
Laufzeit:	4 Jahre, 270 Tage
Zinszahlung:	jährlich
Tilgung:	endfällig
aktuelle Rendite:	6%

1 Jahr	2 Cashflow	3 Abzinsung (nach Moosmüller)	4 Barwert (2x3)
270 Tage	7	$\dfrac{1}{\left(1+0{,}06 \times \dfrac{270}{365}\right)} = 0{,}9575$	6,7025
1 Jahr, 270 Tage	7	$\dfrac{1}{\left(1+0{,}06 \times \dfrac{270}{365}\right) \times (1+0{,}06)^1} = 0{,}9033$	6,3231
2 Jahre, 270 Tage	7	$\dfrac{1}{\left(1+0{,}06 \times \dfrac{270}{365}\right) \times (1+0{,}06)^2} = 0{,}8522$	5,9652
3 Jahre, 270 Tage	7	$\dfrac{1}{\left(1+0{,}06 \times \dfrac{270}{365}\right) \times (1+0{,}06)^3} = 0{,}8039$	5,6276
4 Jahre, 270 Tage	107	$\dfrac{1}{\left(1+0{,}06 \times \dfrac{270}{365}\right) \times (1+0{,}06)^4} = 0{,}7584$	81,1522
		Summe (Dirty Price):	105,7706
		– Stückzinsen: $\left(7 \times \dfrac{95}{365}\right)$	1,8219
		Kurs (Clean Price) nach Moosmüller:	**103,9487**

Die Summe der abgezinsten Cashflows ergibt den Dirty Preis. Das ist jener Betrag, den man beim Kauf der Anleihe aufwenden muss, also Clean Preis zuzüglich Stück- kosten. Quotiert wird der **Clean Preis,** der sich aus dem **Dirty Preis abzüglich der anteiligen Stückzinsen** ergibt.

Example
Continuation: **same bond, calculation with ISMA-method**

Bond: German government bond (Bund)
Coupon: 7% fixed
Time to maturity: 4 years, 270 days
Interest payment: annual
Redemption: bullet
Current yield: 6%

1 Year	2 Cash-flow	3 Discounting	4 Present value (2x3)
270 days	7	$$\frac{1}{(1+0.06)^{\frac{270}{365}}} = 0{,}95781$$	6.7047
1 year, 270 days	7	$$\frac{1}{(1+0.06)^{\frac{270}{365}} \times (1+0.06)^1} = 0{,}90360$$	6.3252
2 years, 270 days	7	$$\frac{1}{(1+0.06)^{\frac{270}{365}} \times (1+0.06)^2} = 0{,}85245$$	5.9671
3 years, 270 days	7	$$\frac{1}{(1+0.06)^{\frac{270}{365}} \times (1+0.06)^3} = 0{,}80420$$	5.6294
4 years, 270 days	107	$$\frac{1}{(1+0.06)^{\frac{270}{365}} \times (1+0.06)^4} = 0{,}75868$$	81.1785
	Sum (dirty price):		105.8049
	– Accrued interest: $\left(7 \times \dfrac{95}{365}\right)$		1.8219
	Price (clean price): with ISMA-method		**103.9830**

With the ISMA-method the clean price is **103.9830**. Compared to the Moosmüller-calculation (103.9487) this price is by 0.0343 higher.

Beispiel			

Fortsetzung: Gleiche Anleihe, Preisberechnung nach ISMA

Anleihe:	German Government Bond (Bund)
Kupon:	7% fest
Laufzeit:	4 Jahre, 270 Tage
Zinszahlung:	jährlich
Tilgung:	endfällig
aktuelle Rendite:	6%

1 Jahr	2 Cashflow	3 Abzinsung (nach ISMA)	4 Barwert (2x3)
270 Tage	7	$\dfrac{1}{(1+0,06)^{\frac{270}{365}}} = 0,95781$	6,7047
1 Jahr, 270 Tage	7	$\dfrac{1}{(1+0,06)^{\frac{270}{365}} \times (1+0,06)^1} = 0,90360$	6,3252
2 Jahre, 270 Tage	7	$\dfrac{1}{(1+0,06)^{\frac{270}{365}} \times (1+0,06)^2} = 0,85245$	5,9671
3 Jahre, 270 Tage	7	$\dfrac{1}{(1+0,06)^{\frac{270}{365}} \times (1+0,06)^3} = 0,80420$	5,6294
4 Jahre, 270 Tage	107	$\dfrac{1}{(1+0,06)^{\frac{270}{365}} \times (1+0,06)^4} = 0,75868$	81,1785
		Summe (Dirty Price):	105,8049
		$- \text{Stückzinsen:} \left(7 \times \dfrac{95}{365} \right)$	1,8219
		Kurs (Clean Price) nach ISMA:	**103,9830**

Mit der ISMA-Methode erhält man einen Kurs von **103,9830.** Verglichen mit der Berechnung nach Moosmüller (103,9487) ist dieser Kurs also um 0,0343 höher.

Example

"Bullet" bond with semi-annual coupon

Coupon:	7% fixed
Time to maturity:	3 years
Interest payment:	semi-annually
Redemption:	bullet
Current yield:	6% SA (= 3% per period)
Assumption:	The latest interest payment just took place.

For coupon periods less than one year the number of interest periods increases. For the price calculation the particular cash-flow is discounted for the number of interest periods by the interest rate divided by the number of the yearly interest periods.

1 Year	2 Cash-flow	3 Discounting	4 Present value (2x3)
0.5	3.5	$\dfrac{1}{(1+0.03)^1} = 0.9708738$	3.3980583
1	3.5	$\dfrac{1}{(1+0.03)^2} = 0.9425959$	3.2990857
1.5	3.5	$\dfrac{1}{(1+0.03)^3} = 0.9151417$	3.2029958
2	3.5	$\dfrac{1}{(1+0.03)^4} = 0.8884871$	3.1097047
2.5	3.5	$\dfrac{1}{(1+0.03)^5} = 0.8626088$	3.0191308
3	103.5	$\dfrac{1}{(1+0.03)^6} = 0.8374843$	86.6796251
		Sum:	**102.7086**

Note: one could also convert the semi-annual rate into an annual rate ($1.03^2 - 1 = 6.09\%$) and then discount with the number of years, i.e. 0.5; 1; 1.5; etc.

Beispiel

Endfällige Anleihe mit halbjährigen Zinszahlungen

Kupon:	7% fest
Laufzeit:	3 Jahre
Zinszahlung:	halbjährlich
Tilgung:	endfällig
Aktuelle Rendite:	6% HJ (= 3% pro Periode)
Annahme:	Die letzte Zinszahlung hat gerade stattgefunden.

Unterjährige Zinszahlungen bedeuten, dass sich die Anzahl der Zinsperioden erhöht. Bei der Preisberechnung wird der jeweilige Cashflow für die Anzahl der Zinsperioden diskontiert, allerdings mit dem durch die Anzahl der jährlichen Zinsperioden dividierten Zinssatz.

1 Jahr	2 Cashflow	3 Abzinsung	4 Barwert (2x3)
0,5	3,5	$\dfrac{1}{(1+0,03)^1} = 0,9708738$	3,3980583
1	3,5	$\dfrac{1}{(1+0,03)^2} = 0,9425959$	3,2990857
1,5	3,5	$\dfrac{1}{(1+0,03)^3} = 0,9151417$	3,2029958
2	3,5	$\dfrac{1}{(1+0,03)^4} = 0,8884871$	3,1097047
2,5	3,5	$\dfrac{1}{(1+0,03)^5} = 0,8626088$	3,0191308
3	103,5	$\dfrac{1}{(1+0,03)^6} = 0,8374843$	86,6796251
		Summe:	**102,7086**

Anmerkung: Man könnte auch zuerst den halbjährigen Zinssatz auf einen Jahreszinssatz umrechnen ($1,03^2 - 1 = 6,09\%$) und dann mit der Anzahl der Jahre, d.h. mit 0,5; 1; 1,5; usw., abzinsen.

Example

Bond with partial redemption before maturity

Coupon:	7% fixed
Time to maturity:	5 years
Interest payment:	annual
Redemption:	50% after 3 years, rest: at end of term
Current yield:	6%
Assumption:	The latest interest payment just took place.

At first, the cash-flows have to be determined. In the years 1, 2 and 3 the coupon is paid for the whole nominal amount. In year 3 there is an additional partial redemption of 50. In the years 4 and 5 the coupon is only paid for 50 and is therefore only 3.5.

1 Year	2 Cash-flow	3 Discounting	4 Present value (2x3)
1	7	$\frac{1}{(1+0.06)^1}=0.94340$	6.6038
2	7	$\frac{1}{(1+0.06)^2}=0.89000$	6.2300
3	57	$\frac{1}{(1+0.06)^3}=0.83962$	47.8583
4	3.5	$\frac{1}{(1+0.06)^4}=0.79209$	2.7723
5	53.5	$\frac{1}{(1+0.06)^5}=0.74726$	39.9783
		Sum:	**103.4427**

1.3.2.4. Assumptions for the Traditional Bond Formula

When calculating the bond price with the traditional pricing formula (Moosmüller or IS-MA) we have discounted all cash-flows with the current market yield for comparable bonds. However, this method is not perfect. On closer examination one can see that two assumptions are made:

- **Flat yield curve: All future Cash-Flows are discounted with the same interest rate**, the market yield for the bond's maturity. However, we know that in practice in most cases different interest rates for different maturities are paid. Thus, for the calculation with the traditional bond formulae a flat yield curve is assumed.

Beispiel

Anleihe mit zwischenzeitlicher Teiltilgung

Kupon: 7% fest
Laufzeit: 5 Jahre
Zinszahlung: jährlich
Tilgung: 50% Tilgung nach 3 Jahren, Rest endfällig
Aktuelle Rendite: 6%
Annahme: Die letzte Zinszahlung hat gerade stattgefunden.

Zuerst sind die Cashflows zu bestimmen. In den Jahren 1, 2 und 3 wird der Kupon auf das volle Nominale gezahlt. Im Jahr 3 erfolgt zusätzlich eine Teiltilgung von 50. In den Jahren 4 und 5 wird der Kupon nur noch auf das ausstehende Kapital – also 50 – gezahlt und beträgt daher nur noch 3,5.

1 Jahr	2 Cashflow	3 Abzinsung	4 Barwert (2x3)
1	7	$\dfrac{1}{\left(1+0{,}06\right)^{1}} = 0{,}94340$	6,6038
2	7	$\dfrac{1}{\left(1+0{,}06\right)^{2}} = 0{,}89000$	6,2300
3	57	$\dfrac{1}{\left(1+0{,}06\right)^{3}} = 0{,}83962$	47,8583
4	3,5	$\dfrac{1}{\left(1+0{,}06\right)^{4}} = 0{,}79209$	2,7723
5	53,5	$\dfrac{1}{\left(1+0{,}06\right)^{5}} = 0{,}74726$	39,9783
		Summe:	**103,4427**

1.3.2.4. Annahmen der klassischen Anleihenformeln

Bei der Berechnung des Anleihepreises mit der klassischen Preisformel (Moosmüller oder ISMA) haben wir also alle Cashflows mit der aktuellen Marktrendite für vergleichbare Anlagen abgezinst. Diese Methode ist jedoch nicht perfekt. Bei einer genaueren Betrachtung fällt auf, dass dabei zwei Annahmen unterstellt werden:

- **Flache Zinskurve: Alle zukünftigen Cashflows werden mit dem gleichen Zinssatz,** nämlich der Marktrendite für die Endfälligkeit der Anleihe, **diskontiert.** Dies, obwohl wir wissen, dass in der Realität in den meisten Fällen unterschiedliche Zinssätze für verschiedene Laufzeiten bezahlt werden. Somit wird bei der Berechnung mit der klassischen Formel eine flache Zinskurve unterstellt.

- **Re-investment of the interest returns at the same interest rate:** When calculating the present value the question is: how much are we willing to pay today for a future cash-flow? We then discount the future cash-flow with the interest rate for a comparable alternative investment. The future value of this alternative investment should then be the same as the future Cash-Flow.

However, when calculating the present value with the formula $1/(1+r)^n$, you are assuming that **during the term of the bond the interest payments can always be invested at the same rate**. In practice interest rates are changing which makes it uncertain at which rate interest payments during the term can be re-invested. Even when assuming unchanged rates the re-investment at the same rate would only be possible for a flat yield curve. Thus, in practice, it is not sure if the investment of the present value results in the underlying future value.

1.3.2.5. Pricing with the Zero Curve

The calculation with the traditional formula does not give you any exact fair price but only a result which is true, assuming a flat yield curve and a re-investment of the coupon payments at the same rate (unrealistic scenario).

Theoretically, one should use a calculation based on the so-called **zero curve** that is already state-of-the-art in the swap market, but has not yet been fully accepted in the bond market.

With the zero bond method, **interest payments during the term of the bond are eliminated** so you do not have to make any assumptions concerning their re-investment. When calculating the bond price with the zero-curve, each cash-flow is treated like a cash-flow from a zero bond. This way, every single cash-flow is discounted with the particular zero rate for the particular period. Thus no flat yield curve is assumed anymore but the actual interest rates for the different periods are used.

The calculation of zero rates – bootstrapping

Where do the zero-rates come from? Talking about interest rates, they are normally the rates for coupon instruments (interest rate swaps, government bonds, etc.). One also calls them yields, par yields or yield to maturity. It is important to understand that the zero curve is derived from one of these other curves, i.e. the zero rates can be calculated from the interest rates of coupon instruments. This transaction is called **bootstrapping**. The zero curve concept is therefore a mathematical method which gives us an exact result and does not make any assumptions regarding the re-investment of the interest payments during the term.

How can these zero rates be calculated? First, the interest payments during the term are eliminated, or more precisely, they are hedged at the actual market rates. After this there are only two cash-flows left: the underlying amount in the beginning and the back payment at maturity. Thus we have a present value and a future value for which an interest rate can easily be computed.

- **Reinvestition der Zinserträge zum gleichen Zinssatz:** Beim Barwertkonzept gehen wir von der Frage aus: Wie viel sind wir heute bereit, für einen Cashflow in der Zukunft zu bezahlen? Wir zinsen dann den zukünftigen Cashflow mit dem Zinssatz einer vergleichbaren Alternativveranlagung ab. Der Endwert der Alternativveranlagung sollte dann genau gleich hoch sein wie der zukünftige Cashflow.

Bei der Berechnung des Barwertes mit der Formel $1/(1+r)^n$ wird allerdings unterstellt, dass **während der Laufzeit ausgezahlte Zinszahlungen immer zum gleichen Zinssatz wieder angelegt** werden können. In der Realität ändern sich die Zinsen jedoch, wodurch ungewiss ist, zu welchem Zinssatz zwischenzeitliche Zinszahlungen reinvestiert werden können. Selbst bei unveränderten Zinssätzen würde die Reinvestition nur bei einer flachen Zinskurve immer wieder zum gleichen Zinssatz durchgeführt werden können. Somit ist in der Realität ungewiss, ob die Anlage in Höhe des errechneten Barwertes tatsächlich den zugrundegelegten Endwert ergibt.

1.3.2.5. Pricing mit der Zero-Kurve

Die Berechnung mit den klassischen Formeln liefert also keinen exakten fairen Preis, sondern nur ein Ergebnis unter den (unrealistischen) Annahmen einer flachen Zinskurve und der Reinvestition der Kuponerträge zum gleichen Zinssatz.

Theoretisch richtig wäre eine Berechnung über die sogenannte **Zero-Kurve,** die im Swapmarkt State of the Art ist, sich aber am Anleihemarkt noch nicht ganz durchgesetzt hat.

Im Konzept der Zero-Kurve werden **zwischenzeitliche Zinszahlungen eliminiert,** wodurch auch keine Annahmen bezüglich deren Reinvestition getroffen werden müssen. Bei der Preisberechnung einer Anleihe über die Zero-Kurve wird also jeder einzelne Zahlungsstrom so behandelt, als käme die Zahlung aus einer Zero-Kupon-Anleihe. Es wird also jeder Zahlungsstrom mit dem entsprechenden Zero-Kupon-Zinssatz der entsprechenden Laufzeit abgezinst. Somit wird keine flache Zinskurve mehr unterstellt, sondern es werden die tatsächlichen Zinssätze der einzelnen Laufzeiten herangezogen.

Die Berechnung von Zero-Zinssätzen – Bootstrapping

Woher kommen nun die Zero-Kupon-Sätze? Spricht man von Zinsen, handelt es sich im Normalfall um Sätze von kupontragenden Instrumenten (Interest Rate Swaps, Bundesanleihen usw.). Man spricht auch von Renditen, Par Yields oder Yield to Maturity. Es ist wichtig zu verstehen, dass die Zero-Kurve eine von diesen Zinskurven abgeleitete Zinskurve ist, d.h., die Zero-Zinsen können aus den Zinssätzen von zinstragenden Instrumenten errechnet werden. Dieser Vorgang wird **Bootstrapping** genannt. Das Konzept der Zero-Kurve ist also eine mathematische Methode, die uns zu einem exakten Ergebnis bringt und somit keine Annahmen über die Wiederveranlagung der zwischenzeitlichen Zinszahlungen trifft.

Wie können nun diese Zero-Kupon-Sätze errechnet werden? Dabei werden in einem ersten Schritt die zwischenzeitlichen Kuponzahlungen eliminiert, oder besser gesagt, sie werden zu den aktuellen Marktsätzen abgesichert. Nach der Eliminierung der zwischenzeitlichen Kuponzahlungen verbleiben nur noch zwei Cashflows: der investierte Anfangsbetrag und die Rückzahlung am Laufzeitende. Somit haben wir einen Barwert und einen Endwert, aus denen sich der Zinssatz sehr leicht ermitteln lässt.

Unfortunately, the effective calculation is a bit more complex and is therefore a typical case for a spread sheet analysis. However, it is important to understand the underlying principle which should be demonstrated in the following example.

Example

From this yield curve the zero rates have to be derived.

Period	Yield
1 year	4.00%
2 years	4.50%
3 years	5.00%
4 years	5.50%
5 years	6.00%

1-year zero rate
With a term of 1 year, there is no interest payment during the term (annual payments assumed). Therefore, by definition the one-year zero rate (Z1) is the same as the one-year yield; i.e. here 4%.

2-year zero rate
At first, we look at the cash-flow which is produced when investing in a 2-year bond at a market rate of 4.5%:

	CF0	CF1	CF2
Cash-flow (bond)	−100	+4.50	+104.50

At time 0 we pay the price for the bond, the Cash-Flow is -100. After one year we receive a coupon payment over 4.50 and after 2 years another coupon payment plus 100 redemption.
In the next step we eliminate the coupon payment in one year over 4.50 (CF1). The question is: how much can we borrow today in order to pay back exactly 4.50 in one year? Answer: 4.50/(1+0.04) = **4.327**.

After the hedging we have the following new Cash-Flow:

	CF0	CF1	CF2	
Cash-flow (bond)	−100	+4.50	+104.50	
Cash-flow (hedge)	+ 4.327	−4.50		[4.50 / (1+0.04)]
Total:	−95.673		+104.50	

The zero rate can now be calculated from the present value −95.673 (CF0) and the future value +104.50 (CF2):

$$Z_n = \sqrt[n]{\frac{CF_n}{CF_0}} - 1 = \sqrt[2]{\frac{104.50}{95.673}} - 1 = 4.5113\%$$

Z_n = zero rate at time n
n = ongoing year
CF_n = Cash-Flow at time n

Die effektive Berechnung stellt sich leider etwas aufwändiger dar und ist ein typischer Fall für die Anwendung in einem Tabellenkalkulationsprogramm. Es ist jedoch wichtig, das dahinterstehende Prinzip zu verstehen, das anhand des folgenden Beispiels demonstriert werden soll.

Beispiel

Aus der angegebenen Renditestruktur-Kurve sollen die Zero-Sätze abgeleitet werden.

Laufzeit	Rendite
1 Jahr	4,00%
2 Jahre	4,50%
3 Jahre	5,00%
4 Jahre	5,50%
5 Jahre	6,00%

1-Jahres-Zero-Satz

Da bei einer Laufzeit von 1 Jahr (bei unterstellter jährlicher Zins-zahlung) während der Laufzeit keine Zinszahlung erfolgt, entspricht der 1-Jahres-Zerosatz (Z1) per definitionem der 1-jährigen Rendite, im Beispiel also 4%.

2-Jahres-Zero-Satz

Zunächst betrachten wir den Cashflow, der sich beim Investment in eine 2-jährige Anleihe zum Marktsatz von 4,5% ergibt:

	CF0	CF1	CF2
Cashflow (Anleihe)	–100	+4,50	+104,50

Zum Zeitpunkt 0 zahlen wir den Kaufpreis der Anleihe, der Cashflow ist also –100, nach einem Jahr erhalten wir eine Kuponzahlung von 4,50 und nach 2 Jahren eine weitere Kuponzahlung plus die Tilgung zu 100.

Im nächsten Schritt eliminieren wir die Kuponzahlung in einem Jahr von +4,50 (CF1). Das bedeutet, wir produzieren einen genau entgegengesetzten Cashflow. Dazu stellen wir uns die Frage: Wie viel können wir heute aufnehmen, um in einem Jahr genau 4,50 zurückzuzahlen? Die Lösung ist: 4,50/(1+0,04) = **4,327**.

Nach der Absicherung ergibt sich folgender neuer Cashflow:

	CF0	CF1	CF2	
Cashflow (Anleihe)	–100	+4,50	+104,50	
Cashflow (Absicherung)	+4,327	–4,50		[4,50/(1+0,04)]
Gesamt:	–95,673		+104,50	

Aus dem verbleibenden Barwert –95,673 (CF0) und Endwert +104,50 (CF2) kann nun der Zero-Satz einfach berechnet werden:

$$Z_n = \sqrt[n]{\frac{CF_n}{CF_0}} - 1 \quad = \sqrt[2]{\frac{104,50}{95,673}} - 1 = 4,5113\%$$

Z_n = Zero-Zins zum Zeitpunkt n
n = fortlaufendes Jahr
CF_n = Cashflow zum Zeitpunkt n

Thus for the 2nd year we have a zero rate at 4.5113%. This would be the rate for the period of 2 years after hedging all cash-flows during the term.
At the moment we have the following rates:

Period	Yield	Zero rate
1 year	4.00%	4.0000%
2 years	4.50%	4.5113%
3 years	5.00%	???
4 years	5.50%	
5 years	6.00%	

What is the zero rate for 3 years?

3-year zero rate

We use the same principle and, first, look at the cash-flows of a 3-year bond with the current market yield (5%):

	CF0	CF1	CF2	CF3
Cash-flow (bond)	−100	+5.00	+5.00	+105.00

Now we have to eliminate resp. hedge two Cash-Flows. Again the question is: how much can we borrow today in order to pay back exactly 5.00 after year 1 and year 2? Therefore we discount the cash-flows with the particular zero rates:

	CF0	CF1	CF2	CF3	
Cash-flow (bond)	−100	+5.00	+5.00	+105.00	
Cash-flow (hedge CF1)	+ 4.808	−5.00			$[5 / (1+0.04)]$
Cash-flow (hedge CF2)	+ 4.578		−5.00		$[5 / (1+0.045113)^2]$
Total	−90.6146485		+105.00		

$$Z_3 = \sqrt[3]{\frac{CF_3}{CF_0}} - 1 = \sqrt[3]{\frac{105.00}{90.6146485}} - 1 = 5.03409464\%$$

The 3-year zero rate is **5.0341%**.

4-year zero rate

	CF0	CF1	CF2	CF3	CF4	
CF (bond 4 years)	−100.00	+5.50	+5.50	+5.50	+105.50	
CF (hedge CF1)	+ 5.288	−5.50				$[5.5 / (1+0.04)]$
CF (hedge CF2)	+ 5.035		−5.50			$[5.5 / (1+0.045113)^2]$
CF (hedge CF3)	+ 4.746			−5.50		$[5.5 / (1+0.050341)^3]$
Total	−84.9296318			+105.50		

$$Z_4 = \sqrt[4]{\frac{CF_4}{CF_0}} - 1 = \sqrt[4]{\frac{105.50}{84.9296318}} - 1 = 5.57189196\%$$

The 4-year zero rate is **5.5719%**.

Somit erhalten wir einen Zero-Satz für 2 Jahre von 4,5113%. Das ist also jener Zinssatz, der sich nach Absicherung aller zwischenzeitlichen Cashflows für eine Laufzeit von 2 Jahren ergäbe.

Es ergibt sich also folgender Zwischenstand:

Laufzeit	Rendite	Zero-Satz
1 Jahr	4,00%	4,0000%
2 Jahre	4,50%	4,5113%
3 Jahre	5,00%	???
4 Jahre	5,50%	
5 Jahre	6,00%	

Welcher Zero-Satz errechnet sich für 3 Jahre?

3-Jahres-Zero-Satz

Wir wenden das gleiche Prinzip an und betrachten vorerst die Cashflows einer 3-jährigen Anleihe mit der aktuellen Marktrendite (= 5%).

	CF0	CF1	CF2	CF3
Cashflow (Anleihe)	−100	+5,00	+5,0	+105,00

Nun müssen wir zwei Cashflows eliminieren bzw. absichern. Wir stellen uns also wieder die Frage: Wie viel können wir heute aufnehmen, um nach Jahr 1 und Jahr 2 jeweils genau 5,00 zurückzuzahlen? Dabei diskontieren wir die Cashflows mit den jeweiligen Zero-Sätzen:

	CF0	CF1	CF2	CF3	
Cashflow (Anleihe)	−100	+5,00	+5,00	+105,00	
Cashflow (Absicherung CF1)	+ 4,808	−5,00			$[5/(1+0,04)]$
Cashflow (Absicherung CF2)	+ 4,578		−5,00		$[5/(1+0,045113)^2]$
Gesamt	−90,6146485			+105,00	

$$Z_3 = \sqrt[3]{\frac{CF_3}{CF_0}} - 1 \quad = \sqrt[3]{\frac{105,00}{90,6146485}} - 1 = \quad 5,03409464\%$$

Der 3-Jahres-Zero-Satz ist **5,0341%**.

4-Jahres-Zero-Satz

	CF0	CF1	CF2	CF3	CF4	
CF (Anleihe 4 Jahre)	−100,00	+5,50	+5,50	+5,50	+105,50	
CF (Absicherung CF1)	+ 5,288	−5,50				$[5,5/(1+0,04)]$
CF (Absicherung CF2)	+ 5,035		−5,50			$[5,5/(1+0,045113)^2]$
CF (Absicherung CF3)	+ 4,746			−5,50		$[5,5/(1+0,050341)^3]$
Gesamt	−84,9296318				+105,50	

$$Z_4 = \sqrt[4]{\frac{CF_4}{CF_0}} - 1 \quad = \sqrt[4]{\frac{105,50}{84,9296318}} - 1 = \quad 5,57189196\%$$

Der 4-Jahres-Zero-Satz ist **5,5719%**.

5-year zero rate

	CF0	CF1	CF2	CF3	CF4	CF5	
CF (bond 5 years)	−100.000	+6.00	+6.00	+6.00	+6.00	+106.00	
CF (hedge CF1)	+ 5.769	−6.00					$[6.0 / (1+0.04)]$
CF (hedge CF2)	+ 5.493		−6.00				$[6.0 / (1+0.045113)^2]$
CF (hedge CF3)	+ 5.178			−6.00			$[6.0 / (1+0.050341)^3]$
CF (hedge CF4)	+ 4.830				− 6.00		$[6.0 / (1+0.055719)^4]$
Total	−78.7294771					+106.00	

$$Z_5 = \sqrt[5]{\frac{CF_5}{CF_0}} - 1 = \sqrt[5]{\frac{106.00}{78.7294771}} - 1 = 6.12890899\%$$

The 5-year zero rate is **6.1289%**.

Result: zero rates derived from the yield curve

Period	yield	Zero-rate
1 year	4.00%	4.0000%
2 years	4.50%	4.5113%
3 years	5.00%	5.0341%
4 years	5.50%	5.5719%
5 years	6.00%	6.1289%

General formula for zero-calculation:

$$Z_N = \sqrt[N]{\frac{1+r_N}{1 - \sum_{n=1}^{N-1}\left(\frac{r_N}{(1+Z_n)^n}\right)}} - 1$$

r_N = bond yield for period n years in decimals
N = total period in years
Z_n = zero rate at time n in decimals
n = ongoing year

Note: Only recursive calculation is possible: to get the 5-year zero-rate you first have to calculate the zeros for the years 1 through 4.

Therefore the calculation without a spread sheet analysis is very complex.

Summary

- The zero curve is derived from the yield curve, i.e. from interest rates for coupon-instruments (e.g. IRS, government bonds, etc.)
- The zero curve includes the costs/returns for hedging the future cash-flows at actual market rates.
- The zero curve does not make any assumptions regarding the form of the curve and the re-investment of coupon payments during the bond term.

5-Jahres-Zero-Satz

	CF0	CF1	CF2	CF3	CF4	CF5	
CF (Anleihe 5 Jahre)	−100,00	+6,00	+6,00	+6,00	+6,00	+106,00	
CF (Absicherung CF1)	+5,769	−6,00					$[6,0/(1+0,04)]$
CF (Absicherung CF2)	+5,493		−6,00				$[6,0/(1+0,045113)^2]$
CF (Absicherung CF3)	+5,178			−6,00			$[6,0/(1+0,050341)^3]$
CF (Absicherung CF4)	+4,830				− 6,00		$[6,0/(1+0,055719)^4]$
Gesamt	−78,7294771					+106,00	

$$Z_5 = \sqrt[5]{\frac{CF_5}{CF_0}} - 1 \quad = \sqrt[5]{\frac{106,00}{78,7294771}} - 1 = \quad 6,12890899\%$$

Der 5-Jahres-Zero-Satz ist **6,1289%**.

Zusammenfassend errechnen sich folgende Zero-Sätze aus der Renditekurve:

Laufzeit	Rendite	Zero-Satz
1 Jahr	4,00%	4,0000%
2 Jahre	4,50%	4,5113%
3 Jahre	5,00%	5,0341%
4 Jahre	5,50%	5,5719%
5 Jahre	6,00%	6,1289%

Allgemeine Formel zur Zero-Berechnung:

$$Z_N = \sqrt[N]{\frac{1+r_N}{1 - \sum_{n=1}^{N-1} \left(\frac{r_N}{(1+Z_n)^n}\right)}} - 1$$

r_N = Anleiherendite für die Laufzeit n Jahre in Dezimalen
Z_n = Zero-Zins für die Laufzeit n Jahre in Dezimalen
N = betrachtete Gesamtlaufzeit in Jahren
n = fortlaufendes Jahr

Anmerkung: Eine Berechnung kann nur rekursiv erfolgen, d.h. zur Berechnung des Zero-Zinses für fünf Jahre müssen zuvor die Zeros für ein bis vier Jahre kalkuliert werden. Dadurch ist die Berechnung ohne Verwendung eines Tabellenkalkulationsprogrammes relativ aufwändig.

Zusammenfassung

• Die Zero-Kurve leitet sich von der Renditekurve ab, d.h. von Zinssätzen von kupontragenden Instrumenten (z.B. IRS, Bundesanleihen usw.).
• Die Zero-Kurve beinhaltet die Kosten/Erträge der Absicherung der zukünftigen Cashflows zu aktuellen Marktpreisen.
• Die Zero-Kurve trifft daher keine Annahmen bezüglich der Form der Zinskurve und der Reinvestition der zwischenzeitlichen Kuponzahlungen.

Comparison zero rates vs. yields

If you compare the yields to the zero rates in the above example you can see that the **zero rates are higher**. This is the case whenever you have a **normal yield curve**. With an **inverted yield curve zero rates are lower than the yields**, with a flat curve they are about the same.

	steep		inverted		flat	
	Yield	Zero	Yield	Zero	Yield	Zero
1 year	4.00%	4.00%	8.00%	8.00%	6.00%	6.00%
2 years	4.50%	4.51%	7.50%	7.48%	6.00%	6.00%
3 years	5.00%	5.03%	7.00%	6.95%	6.00%	6.00%
4 years	5.50%	5.57%	6.50%	6.42%	6.00%	6.00%
5 years	6.00%	**6.13%**	6.00%	**5.88%**	6.00%	**6.00%**

Example

Price of a EUR government bond with the following specifications:

Coupon: 7% fixed
Time to maturity: 5 years
Interest payment: annual
Redemption: bullet
Current yield: 6%
Assumption: The latest interest payment has just been made.

Year	Interest rate	Zero rate
1	4.00%	4.00%
2	4.50%	4.51%
3	5.00%	5.03%
4	5.50%	5.57%
5	6.00%	6.13%

Vergleich von Zero-Sätzen und Renditen

Vergleicht man beim obigen Beispiel die Rendite mit den davon abgeleiteten Zero-Sätzen, so fällt auf, dass die **Zero-Sätze höher** sind. Dies ist bei einer **normalen Zinskurve** immer der Fall. Bei einer **inversen Zinskurve** liegen die **Zero-Sätze unter den Renditen,** und bei einer flachen Kurve sind beide gleich.

	steil		invers		flach	
	Rendite	Zero	Rendite	Zero	Rendite	Zero
1 Jahr	4,00%	4,00%	8,00%	8,00%	6,00%	6,00%
2 Jahre	4,50%	4,51%	7,50%	7,48%	6,00%	6,00%
3 Jahre	5,00%	5,03%	7,00%	6,95%	6,00%	6,00%
4 Jahre	5,50%	5,57%	6,50%	6,42%	6,00%	6,00%
5 Jahre	6,00%	**6,13%**	6,00%	**5,88%**	6,00%	**6,00%**

Beispiel

Euro-Bundesanleihe mit folgender Spezifikation:

Kupon: 7% fest
Laufzeit: 5 Jahre
Zinszahlung: jährlich
Tilgung: endfällig
aktuelle Rendite: 6%
Annahme: Die letzte Zinszahlung hat gerade stattgefunden.

Jahr	Zinssatz	Zero-Zins
1	4,00%	4,00%
2	4,50%	4,51%
3	5,00%	5,03%
4	5,50%	5,57%
5	6,00%	6,13%

1 Year	2 Cash-flow	3 Zero rate	4 Discounting	5 Present value (2x4)
1	7	4,00%	$\dfrac{1}{(1+0,0400)^1} = 0,96154$	6,7308
2	7	4,51%	$\dfrac{1}{(1+0,0451)^2} = 0,91555$	6,4089
3	7	5,03%	$\dfrac{1}{(1+0,0503)^3} = 0,86310$	6,0417
4	7	5,57%	$\dfrac{1}{(1+0,0557)^4} = 0,80508$	5,6355
5	107	6,13%	$\dfrac{1}{(1+0,0613)^5} = 0,74269$	79,4681
			Sum:	104,2850

Taking into account the yield curve for the price calculation, you get a theoretical price difference for this example of approx. 7 basis points (cp. other example, 104.2124 to 104.2850).

1.4. Calculation of Price Sensitivities/The Concept of Duration

For dealers of short-term positions in bonds (trading book) it is useful to estimate how the bond's price changes when the interest rates change. For this purpose several concepts have been developed.

1.4.1. The Simple Duration (Macaulay Duration)

The concept of the simple duration was developed by Frederick R. Macaulay in 1938. If rates change you have two impacts on a bond position. On the one hand the bond price will change, on the other hand the coupon payments can be re-invested at a different rate. These two effects are always directly opposed. If, for example, rates rise, on the one hand the bond price falls, on the other hand the future coupon payments can be re-invested at a higher interest rate level and vice versa. The Macaulay duration describes **the time where these two effects compensate each other**. In other words, it is a time dimension in **years which indicates the period which is needed for a fixed-rate interest bond in order to exactly compensate the price and compound interest effects** which result from a change in rates. This model assumes, however, a **singular, parallel yield curve shift**.

1 Jahr	2 Cashflow	3 Zero-Zins	4 Abzinsung	5 Barwert (2x4)
1	7	4,00%	$\dfrac{1}{(1+0,0400)^1} = 0,96154$	6,7308
2	7	4,51%	$\dfrac{1}{(1+0,0451)^2} = 0,91555$	6,4089
3	7	5,03%	$\dfrac{1}{(1+0,0503)^3} = 0,86310$	6,0417
4	7	5,57%	$\dfrac{1}{(1+0,0557)^4} = 0,80508$	5,6355
5	107	6,13%	$\dfrac{1}{(1+0,0613)^5} = 0,74269$	79,4681
			Summe:	**104,2850**

Durch die Berücksichtigung der Zinskurve in der Preisberechnung entsteht ein theoretischer Preisunterschied von ca. sieben Basispunkten (vgl. im anderen Beispiel 104,2124 zu 104,2850).

1.4. Berechnung von Preissensibilitäten/Konzept der Duration

Für Händler, die kurzfristige Positionen in Anleihen eingehen, ist interessant, wie der Preis reagiert, wenn sich die Marktzinsen ändern. Dazu wurden verschiedene Konzepte entwickelt.

1.4.1. Die einfache Duration (Macaulay Duration)

Das Konzept der einfachen Duration wurde von Frederick R. Macaulay 1938 entwickelt. Ändern sich die Zinsen, so hat dies zwei Auswirkungen auf eine Anleiheposition. Zum einen wird sich der Kurs der Anleihe ändern, zum anderen können die Kuponzahlungen zu einem anderen Zinssatz reinvestiert werden. Diese beiden Effekte sind in der Wirkung immer entgegengesetzt. Steigen beispielsweise die Marktzinsen, so fällt einerseits der Kurs der Anleihe, andererseits können die zukünftigen Kuponzahlungen auf einem höheren Zinsniveau wieder angelegt werden und umgekehrt. Die Macaulay Duration beschreibt nun jenen Zeitpunkt, an dem sich diese beiden Effekte neutralisieren. Anders gesagt ist sie eine Zeitgröße in Jahren, die den **Zeitraum** angibt, **der bei einem festverzinslichen Wertpapier benötigt wird, damit sich die aus einer Zinsänderung ergebenden Kurs- und Zinseszinseffekte gerade ausgleichen.** Dieses Modell unterliegt jedoch der Einschränkung, dass nur eine **einmalige, parallele Verschiebung der Zinskurve** unterstellt wird.

$$D_{Macaulay} = \frac{\sum_{n=1}^{N} \dfrac{n \times CF_n}{(1+r)^n}}{\sum_{n=1}^{N} \dfrac{CF_n}{(1+r)^n}}$$

$D_{Macaulay}$ = Macaulay Duration
n   = ongoing year
N   = total number of years
CF_n = cash-flow (at a nominal of 100) at time n
r   = current yield in decimals

Example

Bond: 3 years
Coupon: 5%
Market yield: 5%
Price: 100.00

The Macaulay duration is 2.86 years. That means that after 2.86 years the price loss due to a rate rise is compensated by higher compound interest for the coupon payments and vice versa.

The following table shows the results at different times with and without interest rate changes:

| Year | CF | Price | Rates at 5% | | Rates at 6% | | |
			Coupon + compound interest	Price + interest	Price	Coupon + compound interest	Price + interest
1	5	100	5	105.00	98.17	5	103.17
2	5	100	5.0 + 0.25	110.25	99.06	5.0 + 0.30	109.36
2.86	5	100	4.3 + 0.44	114.99	99.86	4.3 + 0.53	114.99
3	5	100	5.0 + 0.51	115.51	100.00	5.0 + 0.56	115.56

After 2.86 years the price loss of the bond is compensated by higher compound interest. For both scenarios the result is 114.99. This conclusion, however, is only valid assuming that during the term there are no further interest rate changes.

1.4.2. Modified Duration

When speaking of duration one usually does not mean the Macaulay duration but the modified duration. It is said to be the **best known technique for the determination of price sensitivities**. It shows the leverage how the bond price reacts to a market rate movement.

$$D_{Macaulay} = \dfrac{\displaystyle\sum_{n=1}^{N} \dfrac{n \times CF_n}{(1+r)^n}}{\displaystyle\sum_{n=1}^{N} \dfrac{CF_n}{(1+r)^n}}$$

$D_{Macaulay}$ = Macaulay Duration
n = fortlaufendes Jahr
N = Gesamtlaufzeit in Jahren
CF_n = Cashflow (auf Nominale 100) zum Zeitpunkt n
r = aktuelle Rendite in Dezimalen

Beispiel

Anleihe: 3 Jahre
Kupon: 5%
Marktrendite: 5%
Kurs: 100,00

Die Berechnung der Macaulay Duration ergibt 2,86 Jahre. Das bedeutet, dass nach 2,86 Jahren der – durch eine Erhöhung des Zinssatzes verursachte – Kursverlust durch höhere Zinseszinsen auf die Kuponzahlungen kompensiert wird und umgekehrt.

Folgende Tabelle zeigt die Ergebnisse zu verschiedenen Zeitpunkten mit und ohne Zinsänderung:

Jahr	CF	Zinsen bei 5%			Zinsen bei 6%		
		Preis	Kupon + Zinseszinsen	Preis + Zinsen	Preis	Kupon + Zinseszinsen	Preis + Zinsen
1	5	100	5,0	105,00	98,17	5,0	103,17
2	5	100	5,0 + 0,25	110,25	99,06	5,0 + 0,30	109,36
2,86	5	100	4,3 + 0,44	114,99	99,86	4,3 + 0,53	114,99
3	5	100	5,0 + 0,51	115,51	100,00	5,0 + 0,56	115,56

Nach 2,86 Jahren wird der Kursverlust auf die Anleihe durch die höheren Zinseszinsen kompensiert. Bei beiden Szenarien ist das Gesamtergebnis 114,99. Diese Aussage ist allerdings nur unter der Annahme gültig, dass während der Laufzeit keine weiteren Zinsänderungen stattfinden.

1.4.2. Modified Duration (MD)

Wenn man von Duration spricht, meint man damit üblicherweise nicht die Macaulay Duration, sondern die Modified Duration. Sie ist die wohl **bekannteste Technik zur Ermittlung der Preissensitivität.** Sie zeigt den Hebel an, mit dem der Preis einer Anleihe auf eine Marktzinsänderung reagiert.

Modified Duration

$$MD = \frac{\displaystyle\sum_{n=1}^{N} n \times CF_n \times \frac{1}{(1+r)^n}}{\displaystyle\sum_{n=1}^{N} CF_n \times \frac{1}{(1+r)^n}} \times \frac{1}{(1+r)}$$

MD = modified duration
n   = ongoing year
N   = total number of years
CF_n = cash-flow (at a nominal of 100) at time n
r   = current yield in decimals

If you compare this formula one can realise that this formula is a modification of the Macaulay Duration:

$$MD = D_{Macaulay} \times \frac{1}{1+r}$$

On closer examination of the calculation you can look at the duration as the term-weighted present value of all cash-flows or, vice versa, as the PV-weighted average binding period.

Example
Calculate the Modified Duration for a 5-year "bullet" bond. The coupon is 7%, the current market yield is 6%.

1 Year	2 Cash-flow	3 Discounting	4 Present value of weighted cash-flow (1x2x3)	5 Present value of cash flow (2x4)
1	7	$\frac{1}{(1+0.06)^1} = 0.94340$	6.6038	6.6038
2	7	$\frac{1}{(1+0.06)^2} = 0.89000$	12.4600	6.2300
3	7	$\frac{1}{(1+0.06)^3} = 0.83962$	17.6320	5.8773
4	7	$\frac{1}{(1+0.06)^4} = 0.79209$	22.1786	5.5447
5	107	$\frac{1}{(1+0.06)^5} = 0.74726$	399.7831	79.9566
		Sum:	**458.6575**	**104.2124**

Modified Duration

$$MD = \frac{\sum_{n=1}^{N} \dfrac{n \times CF_n}{(1+r)^n}}{\sum_{n=1}^{N} \dfrac{CF_n}{(1+r)^n}} \times \frac{1}{1+r}$$

MD = Modified Duration
n   = fortlaufendes Jahr
N   = Gesamtlaufzeit in Jahren
CF_n = Cashflow (auf Nominale 100) zum Zeitpunkt n
r   = aktuelle Rendite in Dezimalen

Vergleicht man die Formel, so stellt man fest, dass sie eine Modifikation der Macaulay Duration ist:

$$MD = D_{Macaulay} \times \frac{1}{1+r}$$

Bei genauer Betrachtung der Berechnung kann man die Duration auch als laufzeitgewichteten Barwert der Cashflows oder, andersherum, als barwertgewichtete durchschnittliche Bindungsdauer bezeichnen.

Beispiel				
Berechnen Sie die Modified Duration einer fünfjährigen endfälligen Anleihe. Der Kupon beträgt 7% und die aktuelle Marktrendite 6%.				
1 **Jahr**	**2** **Cashflow**	**3** **Abzinsung**	**4** **Barwert gewichteter Cashflow** **(1x2x3)**	**5** **Barwert Cashflow** **(2x4)**
1	7	$\dfrac{1}{(1+0{,}06)^1} = 0{,}94340$	6,6038	6,6038
2	7	$\dfrac{1}{(1+0{,}06)^2} = 0{,}89000$	12,4600	6,2300
3	7	$\dfrac{1}{(1+0{,}06)^3} = 0{,}83962$	17,6320	5,8773
4	7	$\dfrac{1}{(1+0{,}06)^4} = 0{,}79209$	22,1786	5,5447
5	107	$\dfrac{1}{(1+0{,}06)^5} = 0{,}74726$	399,7831	79,9566
		Summe:	**458,6575**	**104,2124**

$$MD = \frac{458.6575}{104.2124} \times \frac{1}{(1+0.06)} = 4.15$$

The duration for this 5-year bond is 4.15. By means of the duration one can now estimate the price change of the bond when market rates change. Assuming the current bond price is 104.21. If this bond has a MD of 4.15, this means that if rates change by 1%, the bond price will change by 4.15%, i.e. by 4.32 (= 104.21 x 4.15%).

In combination with our rules concerning price changes in the wake of interest rate changes, we receive the following result:

- if interest rates rise by 1%, the price of the bond falls by 4.32 percentage points.
- if interest rates falls by 1%, the price of the bond rises by 4.32 percentage points.

$$CP = (-MD) \times P \times CY$$

CP = change of the bond price
MD = modified duration
P   = price of the bond (dirty price)
CY = change of the market yield in decimals (1% = 0.01)

Example

Specifications of a fixed-rate interest bond:

Current price   104.00
Modified duration   3.50
Current yield   6%

Estimate what will be the bond price if the market yield falls to 5.75% or rises to 6.75%?

5.75%: $CP = (-3.50) \times 104.00 \times (-0.0025) = (+)0.91$
If rates fall to 5.75% the price of the bond will rise to 104.91 (104.00 + 0.91).

6.75%: $CP = (-3.50) \times 104.00 \times (+0.0075) = (-)2.73$
If rates rise to 6.75% the price of the bond will fall to 101.27 (104.00 – 2.73).

1.4.2.1. Influencing Factors on the Modified Duration

The modified duration depends on:

- **Term of the bond:** the longer the term of the bond, the stronger the impact of rate changes on the bond price.
- **Coupon:** a high coupon means that parts of the bond are paid back earlier through coupon payments. Thus the modified duration is lower, i.e. a shorter average minimum lockup period. Therefore the price sensitivity for high coupon bonds is lower than for zero coupon bonds.

$$MD = \frac{458,6575}{104,2124} \times \frac{1}{(1+0,06)} = 4,15$$

Die Duration dieser fünfjährigen Anleihe beträgt also 4,15. Mithilfe der Duration kann nun die Preisänderung der Anleihe bei einer Änderung der Marktzinsen geschätzt werden. Angenommen, der aktuelle Preis der betrachteten Anleihe ist 104,21. Hat diese Anleihe nun eine MD von 4,15, so bedeutet das, dass sich bei einer Veränderung der Zinsen um 1 Prozentpunkt der Preis der Anleihe um 4,15% ändern wird, d.h. um 4,32 (= 104,21 x 4,15%).

Nach den bisher erarbeiteten Regeln über die Richtung der Kursänderung bei Anstieg und Rückgang der Zinsen bedeutet das:

- Steigen die Zinsen um 1%, so fällt der Kurs der Anleihe um 4,32 Prozentpunkte.
- Fallen die Zinsen um 1%, so steigt der Kurs der Anleihe um 4,32 Prozentpunkte.

$$VK = (-MD) \times K \times VR$$

VK = Veränderung im Kurs der Anleihe
MD = Modified Duration
K = Kurs der Anleihe (Dirty Price)
VR = Veränderung der Marktrendite in Dezimalen (1% = 0,01)

Beispiel

Spezifikationen Festzinsanleihe:

aktueller Kurs: 104,00
Modified Duration: 3,50
aktuelle Rendite: 6%

Schätzen Sie den Preis der Anleihe, wenn die Marktrendite auf 5,75% fällt bzw. auf 6,75% steigt.

5,75%: VK = (–3,50) x 104,00 x (–0,0025) = (+) 0,91
Fallen die Zinsen auf 5,75%, wird der Kurs auf **104,91** steigen (104 + 0,91).

6,75%: VK = (–3,50) x 104,00 x (+0,0075) = (–)2,73
Steigen die Zinsen auf 6,75%, wird der Kurs auf **101,27** fallen (104 – 2,73).

1.4.2.1. Einflussfaktoren

Die Höhe der Modified Duration ist abhängig von:

- der **Laufzeit der Anleihe:** Je länger eine Anleihe läuft, desto größer ist der Einfluss von Zinsänderungen auf den Preis.
- der **Kuponhöhe:** Ein hoher Kupon bedeutet, dass Teile der Anleihe in Form von Kuponzahlungen schon frühzeitig zurückgezahlt werden. Dadurch ergibt sich eine niedrigere MD, d.h. eine kürzere durchschnittliche Bindungsdauer. Somit ist die Preissensitivität von Hochzinsanleihen geringer als die von Zero-Kupon-Anleihen.

- **Market yield:** the cash-flows are discounted with the market yield. The higher the market yield, the lower the present value and thus the MD. Therefore the impact of a rate change by 1% is weaker on a high interest rate level than on a low one.

To sum up, we can state the following rules regarding price sensitivity of fixed-rate interest bonds:

High duration at (=high price sensitivity)	⇒	long term low coupon low market yield
Low duration at (=low price sensitivity)	⇒	short term high coupon high market yield

The following table shows the modified duration for a 10-year bond with different coupons and for different market yields:

	Coupon		
	0%	5%	10%
0%	10.00	8.50	7.75
Yield 5%	9.52	7.72	6.92
10%	9.09	6.96	6.14

All calculations with the modified duration assume a **flat yield curve** – like also for the bond price calculation with the traditional formula. Also for the determination of the price sensitivity the effect of the yield curve can be considered. Then you call it "**effective duration**". The impact of the yield curve on the duration, however, is not that strong, therefore here we set aside the calculation of the effective duration.

1.4.2.2. The Estimation Failure of the Duration – the Convexity

The concept of the duration assumes a **linear connection between the yield and the price change**, i.e. you are assuming that the change of the bond price is the same for rates rising by 1% and rates falling by 1%. In practice, when rates change, the bond price does not run on a straight line but on a curve.

- der **Marktrendite:** Die Cashflows werden mit der Marktrendite abgezinst. Je höher die Marktrendite ist, desto niedriger ist der Barwert und somit die MD. Somit wirkt sich bei einem hohen Zinsniveau die Änderung der Zinsen um einen Prozentpunkt weniger aus als bei einem niedrigen Zinsniveau.

Zusammenfassend können folgende **Regeln für die Preissensitivität von Festzinsanleihen** festlegt werden:

Hohe Duration (= hohe Preissensitivität) bei	➡	langer Laufzeit niedrigem Kupon niedriger Marktrendite
Niedrige Duration (= niedrige Preissensitivität) bei	➡	kurzer Laufzeit hohem Kupon hoher Marktrendite

Die folgende Tabelle zeigt die Modified Duration einer zehnjährigen Anleihe mit verschiedenen Kupons bei unterschiedlichen Marktrenditen:

Kupon

Rendite		0%	5%	10%
	0%	10,00	8,50	7,75
	5%	9,52	7,72	6,92
	10%	9,09	6,96	6,14

Alle Berechnungen der Modified Duration unterstellen wie bei der Preisberechnung von Anleihen mit den klassischen Formeln eine **flache Zinskurve.** Auch bei der Berechnung der Preissensitivität kann der Effekt der Zinskurve mitberücksichtigt werden. Man redet dann von einer „**Effective Duration".** Der Einfluss der Zinskurve auf die Duration ist jedoch nicht so groß, sodass an dieser Stelle auf die Berechnung der Effective Duration verzichtet wird.

1.4.2.2. Der Schätzfehler bei der Duration – die Konvexität

Das Konzept der Duration unterstellt einen **linearen Zusammenhang zwischen Rendite und Kursänderung,** d.h., es wird davon ausgegangen, dass die Preisänderung einer Anleihe sowohl bei einem Anstieg als auch einem Rückgang des Zinsniveaus um z.B. einen Prozentpunkt gleich hoch ist. In der Realität bewegt sich der Anleihekurs bei einer Änderung der Zinsen jedoch nicht entlang einer Geraden, sondern entlang einer Kurve.

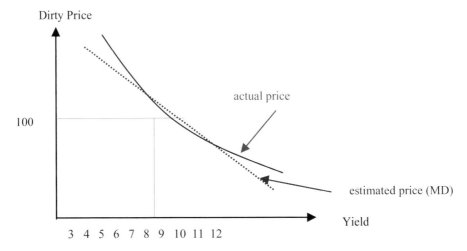

Dirty Price

100

3 4 5 6 7 8 9 10 11 12

actual price

estimated price (MD)

Yield

When applying the duration you therefore have an estimation failure. The **convexity** is the measure for this estimation failure resp. the non-linear (contorted) price-yield-curve. The larger the interest rate change, the more the actual price will diverge from the estimated price. Thus the duration gives satisfactory results only for relatively small rate changes.

As the yield itself is an input factor for the calculation of the duration, also the modified duration changes when the interest rate level moves. If the interest rate level rises, the duration falls and therefore the actual bond price fall will be smaller than originally estimated. On the contrary, the duration rises when yields fall and therefore the actual bond price rise will be higher than originally estimated.

Example

Bond: 10 years
Coupon: 6%
Yield: 5%
Price: 107.72
Modified duration: 7.52%

Compare the actual rate to the estimated rate when rates change by +/–1 percentage point.
When rates change by +/– 1 percentage point the estimated price change is 8.10 (107.72 x 7.52%).

Yield	4%	5%	6%
Estimated rate	115.82		99.62
Calculated rate	116.22	107.72	100.00
Difference	+ 0.40		+ 0.38

The example shows that for the owner of a bond the convexity effects are always positive, i.e. when rates fall the profit is higher and when rates rise the loss is lower than expected.

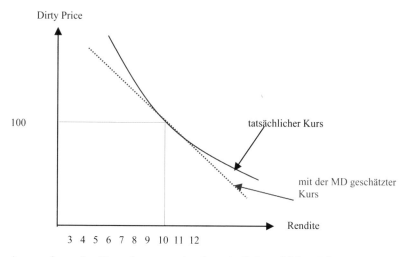

Bei der Anwendung der Duration entsteht also ein Schätzfehler. Die **Konvexität** ist der Maßstab für diesen Schätzfehler bzw. die Nicht-Linearität (oder Krümmung) der Kurs-Renditekurve. Je größer die Zinsänderung ist, desto weiter wird der tatsächliche Kurs von der Schätzung abweichen. Daher liefert die Duration nur für relativ kleine Zinsänderungen zufriedenstellende Ergebnisse.

Da die Rendite selbst ein Inputfaktor bei der Berechnung der Duration ist, ändert sich auch die Modified Duration, sobald sich das Zinsniveau ändert. Steigt das Zinsniveau, so fällt die Duration, wodurch der Kursrückgang kleiner als ursprünglich geschätzt ausfallen wird. Umgekehrt wird bei einem Renditerückgang die Duration steigen, wodurch der Preisanstieg der Anleihe die ursprüngliche Schätzung übertreffen wird.

Beispiel

Anleihe:	10 Jahre
Kupon:	6%
Rendite:	5%
Preis:	107,72
Modified Duration:	7,52

Vergleichen Sie die tatsächlichen Kurse mit den geschätzten Kursen bei einer Änderung der Zinsen um +/– 1 Prozentpunkt.

Die geschätzte Preisänderung bei einer Zinsänderung um +/– 1 Prozentpunkt ist 8,10 (107,72 x 7,52%).

Rendite	4%	5%	6%
Geschätzter Kurs	115,82		99,62
Errechneter Kurs	116,22	107,72	100,00
Differenz	+0,40		+0,38

Das Beispiel zeigt, dass für den Besitzer einer Anleihe die Konvexitätseffekte immer positiv sind, d.h., bei einem Zinsrückgang ist der Gewinn höher und bei einem Zinsanstieg der Verlust niedriger als erwartet.

Example
Modified Duration for a bond with partial redemption before maturity

Time to maturity: 5 years
Coupon: 7%
Current yield: 6%
Interest payment: annual
Redemption: 50% after 3 years, rest: end of term
Assumption: The latest interest payment just took place.

1 Year	2 Cash- flow	3 Discounting	4 Present value of weighted cash-flow (1x2x3)	5 Present value of cash-flow (2x3)
1	7	$\dfrac{1}{(1+0.06)^1}=0.94340$	6.6038	6.6038
2	7	$\dfrac{1}{(1+0.06)^2}=0.89000$	12.4600	6.2300
3	57	$\dfrac{1}{(1+0.06)^3}=0.83962$	143.5749	47.8583
4	3.5	$\dfrac{1}{(1+0.06)^4}=0.79209$	11.0893	2.7723
5	53.5	$\dfrac{1}{(1+0.06)^5}=0.74726$	199.8916	39.9783
		Sum:	**373.6195**	**103.4427**

$$MD = \frac{373.6195}{103.4427} \times \frac{1}{(1+0.06)} = 3.41$$

1.5. Types of interest rates

Knowing the interest rate does not tell you all about the real return on this investment. As we already know we need several additional information like the day counting, interest payment frequency, if interest is calculated on the start amount or future value (as for a discount rate), etc. Even if we are assuming that all these factors are unchanged we have to define more precisely what we mean when speaking about interest rates.

Beispiel

Modified Duration einer Anleihe mit vorzeitiger Tilgung:

Laufzeit:	5 Jahre
Kupon:	7%
Marktrendite:	6%
Zinszahlung:	jährlich
Tilgung:	50% Tilgung nach 3 Jahren, Rest endfällig
Annahme:	Die letzte Zinszahlung hat gerade stattgefunden.

1 Jahr	2 Cashflow	3 Abzinsung	4 Barwertgew. Cashflow (1x2x3)	5 Barwert Cashflow (2x3)
1	7	$\dfrac{1}{(1+0,06)^1} = 0,94340$	6,6038	6,6038
2	7	$\dfrac{1}{(1+0,06)^2} = 0,89000$	12,4600	6,2300
3	57	$\dfrac{1}{(1+0,06)^3} = 0,83962$	143,5749	47,8583
4	3,5	$\dfrac{1}{(1+0,06)^4} = 0,79209$	11,0893	2,7723
5	53,5	$\dfrac{1}{(1+0,06)^5} = 0,74726$	199,8916	39,9783
		Summe:	373,6195	103,4427

$$MD = \frac{373,6195}{103,4427} \times \frac{1}{(1+0,06)} = 3,41$$

1.5. Arten von Zinssätzen

Die bloße Kenntnis eines Zinssatzes verrät noch nicht alles über den Ertrag, den eine Anlage abwirft. Wie wir wissen, benötigen wir noch einige Zusatzinformationen wie die Tageberechnung, wie häufig die Zinszahlungen während eines Jahres stattfinden, ob die Zinsen vom Anfangsbetrag oder vom Endbetrag (wie bei einem Diskontsatz) berechnet werden und dergleichen. Doch selbst wenn wir annehmen, dass all diese Faktoren gleich sind, müssen wir bei der Angabe von Zinssätzen genauer spezifizieren, was wir damit meinen.

Coupon (Nominal Interest Rate)

Every interest rate defined in the conditions of a bond is called coupon. It is the basis for the yearly interest payments. These are always calculated on the basis of the nominal amount (100), and are therefore independent from the actual bond price. One is also speaking of the nominal interest rate. The coupon only determines the bond's cash-flows. But it does not give any exact information regarding the return on the invested amount as the bond is usually purchase at a price above or below 100.

Yield to maturity

The most common concept in order to determine the effective return of a bond is the yield to maturity (YTM) resp. effective interest rate. If you want to determine the YTM you have to reverse the bond price calculation: while for a price calculation you are looking for the bond price at a given market yield, for the YTM calculation the yield as result of a given bond price is determined. The YTM can also be called **internal rate of return (IRR)** of a cash-flow. If we refer to the YTM as y we can formally describe the dirty price of a bond (= present value of all cash-flows) with the following equation:

$$P_{dirty} = \frac{CF_1}{1+y} + \frac{CF_2}{(1+y)^2} + \dots + \frac{CF_N}{(1+y)^N}$$

P_{dirty} = dirty price (= present value of all cash-flows)
y   = yield to maturity (= IRR)
CF_n = cash-flow at time n
n   = ongoing year
N   = total number of years

If now the YTM for a given bond has to be calculated, both the dirty price and the cash-flows are known. Therefore the equation has only be solved for y. This is done by means of approximation procedures and can be done with programmable calculators or Excel quite easily.

Kupon (Nominalzinssatz)

Damit wird jener Zinssatz bezeichnet, der in den Anleihebedingungen festgelegt wird. Er wird verwendet, um die jährlichen Zinszahlungen zu berechnen. Diese werden dabei immer auf der Basis des Nominales – also 100 – berechnet, also unabhängig vom aktuellen Kurs der Anleihe. Man spricht daher auch von Nominalzinssatz. Durch den Kuponzinssatz wird also nur der Cashflow, den eine Anleihe liefert, bestimmt. Er sagt jedoch wenig über den Ertrag auf den investierten Betrag aus, da der Kauf einer Anleihe ja häufig zu einem Kurs über oder unter 100 erfolgt.

Yield to Maturity (Rendite)

Das am häufigsten verwendete Konzept, um den effektiven Ertrag einer Anleihe zu beschreiben, ist die Yield to Maturity (YTM) bzw. Rendite oder Effektivzinssatz. Zur YTM gelangt man, indem man die Preisberechnung einer Anleihe umkehrt: Während bei der Preisberechnung der Preis der Anleihe bei einer gegebenen Rendite gesucht wird, wird bei der YTM-Berechnung die Rendite ermittelt, die ein gegebener Anleihepreis bringt. Die YTM kann auch als **Internal Rate of Return** (IRR, interner Zinssatz) eines Cashflows bezeichnet werden.

Wenn wir die IRR als y bezeichnen, dann können wir formal den Dirty Price einer Anleihe (= Barwert der Cashflows) mit folgender Gleichung beschreiben:

$$P_{dirty} = \frac{CF_1}{1+y} + \frac{CF_2}{(1+y)^2} + ... + \frac{CF_N}{(1+y)^N}$$

P_{dirty} = Dirty Price (= Barwert der Cashflows)
y = Yield to Maturity (= interner Zinssatz IRR)
CF_n = Cashflow zum Zeitpunkt n
N = Gesamtlaufzeit in Jahren
n = laufendes Jahr

Soll nun die Yield to Maturity einer gegebenen Anleihe berechnet werden, so sind sowohl der Dirty Price als auch die Cashflows bekannt. Es muss die Gleichung daher nunmehr nach y aufgelöst werden. Das erfolgt mit Näherungsverfahren und ist bei Verwendung von programmierbaren Taschenrechnern oder Excel (Zielwertsuche) einfach durchzuführen.

Example

A 5-year bond with a coupon of 5% has a price of 84.44. What is the yield to maturity?

Cash-flows:

CF0	CF1	CF2	CF3	CF4	CF5
−84.44	+5	+5	+5	+5	+105

The question is: with which interest rate do the cash-flows CF1 through CF5 have to be discounted in order to receive the present value CF0? Therefore we set up the following equation:

$$84.44 = \frac{5}{1+y} + \frac{5}{(1+y)^2} + ... + \frac{105}{(1+y)^5}$$

This equation can only be solved by approximation (trial and error). In Excel we have used the function goal seek under Extras and get the solution $y = 9.00\%$.
If we buy this bond we have a yield of 9.00%.
You can verify this result by calculating the bond price for a given market yield of 9.00% with the traditional bond price formula:

year	YTM	CF	PV
1	9%	5	4.59
2	9%	5	4.21
3	9%	5	3.86
4	9%	5	3.54
5	9%	105	68.24
Sum:			**84.44**

When using the traditional bond price formulae the calculated values for price and yield show consistent results. For each way the same equation is solved in opposite directions (one time for the price, the other time for the yield).

Problems with the YTM

As the YTM applies the same method as the traditional bond price formulae, you have the same problem here: a **flat yield curve** is assumed.

Let us go back to the bond price calculation. We have seen that the fair bond price is the present value of all future cash-flows. For the precise calculation of the present values we have discounted every single cash-flow with the particular zero rate. Thus we have considered the yield curve for the precise calculation what led to a number of different interest rates. We have realised that this result had diverged from the price determined by the traditional formula.

Beispiel

Eine 5-jährige Anleihe mit einem Kupon von 5% kostet aktuell 84,44. Wie hoch ist die Rendite (Yield to Maturity)?

Cashflows:

CF0	CF1	CF2	CF3	CF4	CF5
−84,44	+5	+5	+5	+5	+105

Wir stellen uns also die Frage: Mit welchem Zinssatz müssen die Cashflows CF1 bis CF5 abgezinst werden, um zum Barwert CF0 zu gelangen? Dafür setzen wir folgende Gleichung an:

$$84,44 = \frac{5}{1+y} + \frac{5}{(1+y)^2} + ... + \frac{105}{(1+y)^5}$$

Diese Gleichung kann nun durch Näherung (also durch trial and error) gelöst werden. Wir haben dazu im Excel die Funktion Zielwertsuche unter Extras verwendet und kommen zur Lösung y = 9%.

Wenn wir diese Anleihe kaufen, erzielen wir eine Rendite von 9%.

Sie können das Ergebnis überprüfen, indem Sie den Preis der Anleihe bei einer gegebenen Marktrendite von 9% mit der klassischen Anleiheformel berechnen:

Jahr	YTM	CF	PV
1	9%	5	4,59
2	9%	5	4,21
3	9%	5	3,86
4	9%	5	3,54
5	9%	105	68,24
Summe:			**84,44**

Bei der Verwendung der klassischen Anleiheformeln liefern die errechneten Werte für Kurs und Rendite also konsistente Ergebnisse. Es wird dabei ja dieselbe Gleichung jeweils in umgekehrter Richtung aufgelöst (einmal nach dem Kurs, einmal nach der Rendite).

Probleme mit der YTM

Da die YTM die gleiche Methodik wie die klassischen Anleihenformeln verwendet, tritt hier auch die gleiche Problematik auf: Es wird eine **flache Zinskurve** unterstellt.

Denken wir zurück an die Preisberechnung einer Anleihe. Wir haben festgestellt, dass der faire Preis einer Anleihe der Barwert aller zukünftigen Cashflows ist. Bei der sauberen Berechnung der Barwerte haben wir jede einzelne Zahlung mit dem entsprechenden Zero-Satz abgezinst. Wir haben also die Zinsstrukturkurve bei der exakten Berechnung einfließen lassen, wodurch eine Anzahl von unterschiedlichen Zinssätzen zur Anwendung gekommen ist. Wir haben festgestellt, dass dieses Ergebnis vom Preis, der mit der klassischen Formel errechnet wurde, abgewichen ist.

In order to determine the return on an investment with a consistent interest rate the YTM is used. It is the rate with which all cash-flows have to be discounted to get the actual bond price. If the actual price equals the price determined by the zero curve, the YTM is a kind of nominal-weighted average of the yield curve. As most averages also the YTM has to be regarded critically. The following example is supposed to show the problem,

We would like to apply the yield to maturity in order to analyse two investment alternatives. Assuming you have the choice between two 5-year Bund notes.

Bond	Price
5%	85.21
10%	105.43

To find out which of the bonds is more attractive you have to calculate the YTM. For this purpose you have to take the cash-flows and determine the internal rate of return:

Bond	CF0	CF1	CF2	CF3	CF4	CF5	YTM
5%	−85.21	+5	+5	+5	+5	+105	8.78%
10%	−105.43	+10	+10	+10	+10	+110	8.62%

Obviously the 5% bond is more attractive as it has a higher YTM. Therefore it is self-evident that this bond is –relatively regarded – cheaper than the 10% bond. We want to verify this assumption and calculate the fair bond price with the current zero curve.

		5% bond		10% bond	
Year	Zero	CF	PV	CF	PV
1	5%	5	4,763	10	9,524
2	6%	5	4,450	10	8,900
3	7%	5	4,081	10	8,163
4	8%	5	3,675	10	7,350
5	9%	105	68,243	110	71,492
	Sum:		85,211		105,429
Comparison:		Market prices:	85,210		105,430

Against our first assumption both prices correspond exactly to the fair prices determined by the zero curve. So both bonds are priced fairly, i.e. equally attractive. Obviously the YTM does not tell the whole truth. What can be the reasons?

As we have learned for the calculation of the YTM only one interest rate is used for discounting the cash-flows. So a flat yield curve is assumed and it is further assumed that all interest payments can be re-invested at the YTM. In practice you usually have different rates for different periods.

Um nun umgekehrt den Ertrag eines Investments mit einem einheitlichen Zinssatz zu beschreiben, wird die Yield to Maturity verwendet. Sie ist jener Zinssatz, mit dem man alle Cashflows abzinsen muss, um zum aktuellen Preis der Anleihe zu gelangen. Entspricht nun der aktuelle Preis dem mit der Zero-Kurve ermittelten fairen Preis, so stellt die YTM eine Art betragsgewichteter Durchschnitt der Zinsstrukturkurve dar. Wie die meisten Durchschnitte ist daher auch die YTM kritisch zu hinterfragen. Das folgende Beispiel soll die Problematik darstellen.

Wir möchten die Yield to Maturity heranziehen, um zwei Anlagealternativen zu analysieren. Angenommen, Sie haben die Wahl zwischen zwei 5-jährigen Bund-Anleihen.

Bond	Preis
5%	85,21
10%	105,43

Um herauszufinden, welche Anleihe attraktiver ist, berechnen Sie die Yield to Maturity. Dazu nehmen Sie die Cashflows und ermitteln daraus den internen Zinssatz:

Bond	CF0	CF1	CF2	CF3	CF4	CF5	YTM
5%	−85,21	+5	+5	+5	+5	+105	8,78%
10%	−105,43	+10	+10	+10	+10	+110	8,62%

Offensichtlich ist die 5%-Anleihe attraktiver, da sie eine höhere Yield to Maturity bringt. Es ist daher naheliegend, dass diese Anleihe relativ gesehen billiger als die 10%ige ist. Wir wollen diese Annahme überprüfen und berechnen den fairen Preis der Anleihe mit der aktuellen Zero-Kurve.

Jahr	Zero	5%-Anleihe		10%-Anleihe	
		CF	PV	CF	PV
1	5%	5	4,763	10	9,524
2	6%	5	4,450	10	8,900
3	7%	5	4,081	10	8,163
4	8%	5	3,675	10	7,350
5	9%	105	68,243	110	71,492
	Summe:		**85,211**		**105,429**
Zum Vergleich:	Marktpreise:		85,210		105,430

Entgegen unserer ersten Annahme entsprechen beide Preise exakt den mit der Zero-Kurve berechneten fairen Preisen. Beide Anleihen sind also fair gepreist, d.h. gleich attraktiv. Offensichtlich liefert die YTM nicht die gesamte Wahrheit. Was sind die Gründe dafür?

Wie wir gesehen haben, wird bei der Berechnung der Yield to Maturity nur ein Zinssatz für das Abzinsen aller Cashflows verwendet. Es wird also eine flache Zinskurve unterstellt und weiters angenommen, dass alle Zinszahlungen zur YTM wieder angelegt werden können. In der Realität herrschen aber unterschiedliche Zinssätze für verschiedene Laufzeiten.

Let us have a look at bonds with different coupons: With a high coupon a (partial) redemption on the invested capital is done already during the term by means of higher coupon payments. With a steep interest rate curve these "early redemptions" would have to be discounted only with a lower short-term interest rate. When calculating the YTM, however, all cash-flows are discounted with an average (higher) rate what means that the result in this case looks worse than it actually is.

Summary

- The YTM only gives a consistent result when calculating bond prices with the traditional formula.
- Due to the simplification (flat interest rate curve and re-investment) bonds with different coupons fairly calculated with the zero curve have different YTM.
- The YTM is a nominal-weighted average interest rate.
- Like most averages the YTM does not give all information. An evaluation of an investment only on the basis of the YTM can lead to wrong results.

Par yield

We often apply yields, e.g. when we examine a yield curve or calculate a bond price with the current market yield. The chapter before, however, has shown that the concept of yield calculation can be a problem because bonds with different coupons have different yields. To solve this problem you usually use the so-called par yield when speaking of e.g. the market yield. The par yield is the **yield of a bond which is quoted at (or close) par**, i.e. the price is around 100. This way the problem of a "wrong" YTM calculation for bonds with prices ≠ 100 can be avoided.

Zero coupon rate

The zero rates have been discussed in detail in the chapter pricing with the zero curve. Summary:

- Zero rates are derived from the yield curve.
- The advantage of the zero rates is that there is no assumption made regarding the form of the yield curve or the re-investment of interest payments during the term.
- Zero rates take into account the costs/returns for the hedging of the interest payments during the term.

Betrachten wir einmal Anleihen mit unterschiedlichen Kupons: Bei einem hohen Kupon erfolgt eine (Teil-)Rückzahlung des eingesetzten Kapitals bereits während der Laufzeit in Form der erhöhten Kuponzahlungen. Bei einer steilen Zinskurve müssten diese „vorzeitigen Tilgungen" nur mit einem niedrigeren kurzfristigen Zinssatz diskontiert werden. Bei der Berechnung der YTM werden jedoch alle Cashflows mit dem durchschnittlichen (höheren) Satz abgezinst, was dazu führt, dass das Ergebnis in diesem Fall schlechter aussieht, als es tatsächlich ist.

Zusammenfassung

- Die YTM bringt nur bei der Anleihebewertung mit der klassischen Formel ein konsistentes Ergebnis.
- Aufgrund der Vereinfachung (flache Zinskurve und Reinvestition) haben mit der Zero-Kurve fair bewertete Anleihen mit unterschiedlichen Kupons unterschiedliche YTM.
- Die YTM ist ein betragsgewichteter durchschnittlicher Zinssatz.
- Wie die meisten Durchschnitte liefert die YTM nicht die ganze Information. Eine Beurteilung einer Investition nur auf Basis der YTM kann daher zu falschen Ergebnissen führen.

Par Yield

Wir verwenden häufig Renditen, z.B. wenn wir eine Renditestrukturkurve betrachten oder mit der aktuellen Marktrendite den Kurs einer Anleihe berechnen. Das vorangegangene Kapitel hat jedoch gezeigt, dass das Konzept der Renditeberechnung problematisch sein kann, weil Anleihen mit unterschiedlichen Kupons unterschiedliche Renditen aufweisen. Um diese Problematik zu minimieren, meint man üblicherweise die sogenannte Par Yield, wenn man z.B. von der Marktrendite spricht. Die Par Yield ist die **Rendite einer Anleihe, die zu (oder nahe) Par notiert**, d.h. deren Preis bei etwa 100 liegt. Damit wird das Problem der „falschen" YTM Berechnung bei Anleihen mit Kursen $\neq$ 100 vermieden.

Zero-Kupon-Satz

Das Thema der Zero-Sätze haben wir ausführlich im Kapitel Pricing mit der Zero-Kurve behandelt. Zusammenfassend soll hier erwähnt werden:

- Zero-Sätze werden von der Renditestrukturkurve abgeleitet.
- Der Vorteil beim Verwenden des Konzepts der Zero-Kurve liegt darin, dass keine Annahmen bezüglich der Form der Zinskurve und der Wiederveranlagung der zwischenzeitlichen Zinszahlungen getroffen werden müssen.
- Die Zero-Sätze berücksichtigen die Kosten bzw. Erträge für die Absicherung der zwischenzeitlichen Zinszahlungen.

1.6. Ratings

So far we have concentrated on government bonds or – more precisely – on government bonds with the best credit standing (e.g. no Russian bonds). We have been assuming that these bonds are an investment without any risk as these countries have best credit standings. When saying "without any risk" we are referring to the credit risk which is the risk of a loss which would occur if the counterparty defaulted. However, also banks and corporates issue bonds. So the investor has a wider choice of investment opportunities. However, the purchase of a bond also always includes a loan to the issuer. Before granting a loan you ideally should **examine the credit risk**. This examination is quite complex regarding time and money. Thus **standardised credit ratings** have been developed. These ratings classify credit users and bond issuers regarding their credit-worthiness with consistent methods. The rating gives **international investors true benchmarks as a basis for their investment decisions**. Thus **transparency and efficiency of the capital markets** are increased.

1.6.1. Rating grades

The credit ratings are done by international **rating agencies**. The most important agencies are Standard and Poor's, Moody's and Fitch IBCA. Individual ratings for short-term debts (e.g. Commercial Papers, Certificates of Deposits) and long-term debts (e.g. bonds) are defined.

   Short-term ratings refer to the debtor's ability to pay back short-term liabilities. It is necessary that the issuer has enough credit range for paying back bonds at maturity, called "back-up line of credit".

   For **long-term ratings** (bond ratings) the agencies have developed benchmarks for the different debtor groups, e.g. for sovereign governments, municipalities, banks and corporates.

1.6. Ratings

Bisher haben wir uns auf die Betrachtung von Staatsanleihen oder, im engeren Sinne, auf Anleihen von Staaten mit höchster Bonität (also z.B. keine Russland-Anleihen) beschränkt. Wir sind davon ausgegangen, dass diese risikolose Anlagen darstellen, da Staaten die höchste Bonität aufweisen. Wenn wir hier von risikolos sprechen, beziehen wir uns auf das Kreditrisiko, also das Risiko eines Verlustes, den wir aufgrund des Ausfalls des Schuldners erleiden. Anleihen werden jedoch auch von Banken und Industrieunternehmen begeben. Für den Investor bedeutet dies eine größere Auswahl an Anlagealternativen. Der Kauf einer Anleihe bedeutet jedoch auch immer, dass man einen Kredit an den Emittenten gibt. Einer Kreditvergabe sollte idealerweise eine eingehende **Prüfung des Kreditrisikos** vorangehen. Diese ist jedoch mit erheblichem Aufwand verbunden, sowohl was Zeit als auch was Kosten betrifft. Daher haben sich **standardisierte Bonitätsbeurteilungen**, sogenannte Ratings, durchgesetzt. Dabei handelt es sich um die bonitätsmäßige Einstufung von Kreditnehmern bzw. Anleiheschuldnern nach einheitlichen und konsistenten Verfahren. Das Rating gibt internationalen Investoren **gültige Maßstäbe als Grundlage für Investitionsentscheidungen**. Damit werden die **Transparenz und Effizienz des Kapitalmarktes** gesteigert.

1.6.1. Ratingstufen

Die Bonitätsbeurteilung wird von internationalen **Ratingagenturen** vorgenommen. Die wichtigsten Agenturen sind Standard & Poor's, Moody's und Fitch Ratings. Es werden eigene Ratings für kurzfristige Schulden (z.B. Commercial Papers, Certificates of Deposits) und langfristige Schulden (z.B. Anleihen) vergeben.

Kurzfristige Ratings beziehen sich hauptsächlich auf die Fähigkeit der Schuldner, ihre kurzfristigen Verbindlichkeiten zurückzuzahlen. Voraussetzung hierfür ist, dass der Emittent einen genügenden Kreditspielraum zur Einlösung fälliger Papiere nachweisen kann, eine sogenannte Backup Line of Credit (Vorsorgelinie).

Für **langfristige Ratings** (Bond Ratings) haben die Agenturen Maßstäbe für verschiedene Schuldnergruppen entwickelt, so z.B. für unabhängige Staaten (Sovereign Governments), Gemeinden (Municipalities), Banken und Industrieunternehmen (Corporates).

The different rating grades are marked with symbols.

CP-Ratings (short-term)		Bond-Ratings (long-term)			
S&P's	Moody's	S&P's	Moody's		
A-1	P-1	AAA	Aaa	Gruppe I	Investment Grade
A-2	P-2	AA	Aa		
A-3	P-3	A	A	Gruppe II	
B	(P = Prime)	BBB	Baa		
		BB	Ba	Gruppe III	non-Investment Grade (Speculative Grade, Junk Bonds)
C		B	B		
D		CCC	Caa		
		CC	Ca		
		C	C	Gruppe IV	
		D			

The bond ratings can be explained as follows:

- **Group I:** first-class addresses; these bonds have no risk for the investor.
- **Group II:** companies with a good through average standing; normally these bonds can be regarded as safe bond investments if the economical background holds steady.
- **Group III:** bonds with speculative character. The issuers are in economical resp. financial troubles; interest and redemption payments are not always guaranteed.
- **Group IV:** cash-strapped bonds

Issuers through rating BBB resp. Baa are called **investment grade**, i.e. they are regarded as a safe investment. Bonds with a worse rating are called **speculative grade**/non-investment grade or **junk bonds**.

1.6.2. Credit rating and yield

The basic principle in the financial markets is that **higher risk has to be awarded with a higher return**. Thus investors ask for a higher interest rate when the issuer's rating is bad. Therefore the yield of AAA (spoken "triple A") rated government bonds is the lowest. They are the interest rate for investments with the lowest credit risk and thus act as so-called **benchmark yields**. All bonds rated worse have to pay a premium to this benchmark. This premium is called **credit spread**.

Die einzelnen Bonitätsstufen werden mit Symbolen bezeichnet.

CP-Ratings (kurzfristig)		**Bond-Ratings** (langfristig)			
S&P's	Moody's	S&P's	Moody's		
A-1	P-1	AAA	Aaa	Gruppe I	Investment Grade
A-2	P-2	AA	Aa		
A-3	P-3	A	A	Gruppe II	
B	(P = Prime)	BBB	Baa		
		BB	Ba	Gruppe III	Non-Investment Grade (Speculative Grade, Junk Bonds)
C		B	B		
D		CCC	Caa		
		CC	Ca		
		C	C	Gruppe IV	
		D			

Die Bond-Ratings können wie folgt erläutert werden:

* **Gruppe I:**   allerbeste Adressen; diese Titel bieten dem Anleger eine risikolose Anlage.
* **Gruppe II:**   Unternehmen mit einem guten bis durchschnittlichen Marktstanding; diese Titel sind unter stabilen wirtschaftlichen Verhältnissen i.d.R. als sichere Wertpapieranlagen zu betrachten.
* **Gruppe III:**   Papiere mit spekulativem Charakter. Die Emittenten befinden sich in wirtschaftlichen bzw. finanziellen Schwierigkeiten; Zins- und Tilgungszahlungen sind nicht immer gewährleistet.
* **Gruppe IV:**   notleidende Titel

Emittenten bis zum Rating BBB bzw. Baa werden als **Investment Grade** bezeichnet, d.h., sie werden als sichere Anlage angesehen. Titel mit einem schlechteren Rating werden als **Speculative Grade / Non-Investment Grade** oder auch als **Junk Bonds** bezeichnet.

1.6.2. Bonität und Rendite

Das Grundprinzip in den Finanzmärkten ist, dass **höheres Risiko mit einem höheren Ertrag belohnt** werden muss. Dementsprechend verlangen Investoren einen umso höheren Zinssatz, je schlechter das Rating eines Emittenten ist. Somit ist die Rendite von AAA (sprich: „Triple A") gerateten Staatsanleihen am niedrigsten. Sie stellen also den Zinssatz für Anlagen mit dem geringsten Kreditrisiko dar und fungieren als sogenannte **Benchmark-Rendite.** Alle schlechter gerateten Anleihen müssen einen Aufschlag auf diese Benchmark zahlen. Dieser Aufschlag wird als **Credit Spread** bezeichnet.

1.6.3. Quotation of interest rates

The interest rate for bonds are not only quoted as a fixed rate (e.g. 5%) but also as a premium to the yields of government bonds, Interest Rate Swaps resp. EURIBOR or LIBOR.

Premium to the benchmark yield

The total yield is the result of the **interest rate without risk** plus the **credit spread** which depends on the issuer's credit standing. If now an investor compares bonds of different issuers (e.g. corporates) s/he is mainly interested in the premium to the investment without risk. Thus s/he can better evaluate if the credit spread as compensation for the credit risk is enough. If only the credit spreads are quoted, an investor can compare different issuers more easily.

The quotation of a 10-year USD bond of an A (spoken: "single A") rated US corporate could also be: 10-year Treasury bond +120 BP. If the 10-year Treasury bond quotes at e.g. 5.00%, the bond of the A-issuer would be traded at 6.20%. Attention has here to be paid to the interest convention of the benchmark, e.g. semi-annual payments for Treasury notes.

Premium to the Interest Rate Swap Rate

Instead of the government bond yields interest rate swap rates are often used as reference rate for the interest rate. Then the **credit spread** is the **difference to the IRS rate**. The reason for this is that in recent years the risk management systematics could be further developed. Here different risks can be controlled separately. Thus the accounting of profit and loss for the individual causer can be shown more transparently. In the case of bonds the risks involved are interest rate risk and credit risk. For the evaluation of the profit and loss not only the total result of the investment has to be regarded but also which part can be attributed to the interest rate risk and which part to the credit risk.

So far we had always defined government bonds as benchmark for the interest rate without risk. Looking at it closer, this is not very precise as the government bond yields are – like all loans – also composed of the actual interest rate without risk plus credit spread for the debtor country. What is the interest rate without risk in this consideration? It is the rate which can be fixed without any loan (i.e. without any liquidity), thus the interest rate swap rate.

The consequence is that it is becoming more and more common to define credit spreads not as difference to the particular government bond but as difference to the IRS rate.

1.6.3. Die Quotierung von Zinssätzen

Die Zinssätze von Anleihen werden nicht nur als fester Zinssatz (z.B. 5%) angegeben, sondern auch als Aufschlag auf die Rendite von Staatsanleihen, Interest-Rate-Swap-Satz bzw. EURIBOR oder LIBOR.

Aufschlag auf die Benchmark-Rendite

Die Gesamtrendite setzt sich also aus dem **risikolosen Zinssatz** und dem **Credit Spread**, der von der Bonität des Emittenten abhängt, zusammen. Vergleicht nun ein Investor Anleihen von verschiedenen Emittenten (z.B. Unternehmen), so interessiert ihn hauptsächlich der Aufschlag auf die risikolose Anlage. Somit kann er besser beurteilen, ob ihm der Credit Spread als Entschädigung für das Eingehen des Kreditrisikos auf den Emittenten reicht. Werden nur die Credit Spreads quotiert, kann ein Investor leichter verschiedene Emittenten miteinander vergleichen.

Die Quotierung einer 10-jährigen USD-Anleihe eines A (sprich: „Single A") gerateten US-Industrieunternehmens könnte beispielsweise auch lauten: 10-Jahres-Treasury Bond +120 BP. Wenn der zehnjährige T-Bond z.B. aktuell mit 5% rentiert, würde die Anleihe des A-gerateten Emittenten zu 6,2% gehandelt werden. Zu beachten sind hierbei die Konventionen der Benchmark, z.B. die halbjährlichen Zinszahlungen bei Treasury Notes.

Aufschlag auf den Interest-Rate-Swap-Satz

Häufig wird als Referenzsatz für den Zinssatz anstatt der Rendite für Staatsanleihen der Interest-Rate-Swap-Satz verwendet. Der **Credit Spread** ist dann also die **Differenz zum IRS-Satz.** Der Grund dafür liegt darin, dass in den letzten Jahren Fortschritte in der Systematik des Risikomanagements gemacht wurden. Dabei werden die verschiedenen Risiken separat gesteuert. Dadurch wird die Zuordnung des Erfolges zum jeweiligen Verursacher transparenter. Im Falle einer Anleihe sind die involvierten Risiken vor allem das Zinsänderungsrisiko und das Kreditrisiko. Bei der Beurteilung des Erfolges ist dabei nicht nur das Gesamtergebnis des Investments von Interesse, sondern auch, welcher Anteil davon auf das Eingehen von Zinsrisiko und welcher auf das Eingehen von Kreditrisiko zurückzuführen ist.

Bisher hatten wir als Benchmark für den risikolosen Zinssatz stets Staatsanleihen herangezogen. Bei genauer Betrachtung ist diese Vorgangsweise nicht ganz sauber, denn die Rendite für Staatsanleihen besteht wie alle Kreditvergaben aus dem aktuellen risikolosen Zinssatz zuzüglich Credit Spread für den Schuldnerstaat.

Was ist in dieser Systematik nun der risikolose Zinssatz? Dies ist jener Zinssatz, der ohne Vergabe eines Kredites (d.h. ohne Liquiditätseinsatz) fixiert werden kann, also der Interest-Rate-Swap-Satz.

Dies hat zur Folge, dass es immer üblicher wird, Credit Spreads nicht als Differenz zur jeweiligen Staatsanleihe zu definieren, sondern als Differenz zum IRS-Satz.

Example

Currently 5-year bonds from A rated German car suppliers are traded at a premium of 80 BP to the IRS rate. What are the costs for an issuer of this group when s/he wants to issue a 5-year fixed-rate interest bond?

First, s/he has to look where the actual 5-year IRS rate is. If it is at 4.5% s/he has to pay 5.3%.

Assuming an investor thinks the price of 80 BP is adequate but prefers a variable rate. This investor could conduct following transactions: purchase of the bond at IRS + 80 and payer swap at 4.50%.

The result is a variable investment at EURIBOR +80 BP. It is composed of the EURIBOR payments in the IRS plus the difference between the bond interest rate and the fixed rate in the IRS.

As with an IRS a fixed rate position can be transferred into a variable one, the quotation of IRS +80 BP corresponds to a variable interest rate of EURIBOR +80 BP.

The combination of a bond (asset) and an IRS is called **asset swap**. When quoting on an asset swap basis **EURIBOR + credit spread** is meant.

Note: Asset swaps are usually traded in packages, i.e. the seller of the bond is the partner for the swap at the same time. The bond is delivered – independent from the actual price – at 100 and the fixed rate in the swap equals the coupon of the bond. The variable payment in the swap is then not EURIBOR flat but EURIBOR + credit spread.

Credit spreads for government bonds

When looking at the historic yields of government bonds one can see that they are below the IRS rates, i.e. the **spread to the IRS is negative**. This means that government bonds on an asset swap basis usually quote at EURIBOR (resp. LIBOR) minus credit spread. The reason is that EURIBOR (resp. IRS) are the rates for first-class banks. As the credit standing of countries is higher than the credit standing of banks, the interest rate has to be lower than the interest rate for banks (EURIBOR).

Beispiel

5-jährige Anleihen von A-gerateten deutschen Autozulieferern werden derzeit mit einem Aufschlag von 80 BP auf den IRS-Satz gehandelt. Mit welchen Kosten muss ein Emittent dieser Gruppe rechnen, wenn er eine 5-jährige Festzinsanleihe emittieren möchte?

Im ersten Schritt muss er feststellen, wo aktuell der 5-jährige IRS-Satz liegt. Liegt er beispielsweise bei 4,5%, so muss er mit Kosten von 5,3% rechnen.

Angenommen, ein Investor findet den Preis von 80 BP für diesen Emittenten angemessen, bevorzugt jedoch einen variablen Zinssatz. Dieser Investor könnte folgende Transaktion durchführen: Kauf der Anleihe zu IRS +80 und Abschluss eines Festzinszahlerswaps zu 4,5%.

Das Ergebnis ist eine variable Anlage zu EURIBOR +80 BP. Es setzt sich zusammen aus den EURIBOR-Zahlungen im IRS plus der Differenz zwischen dem Anleihezinssatz und dem Festzins im IRS.

Da mit einem IRS eine Festzinsposition in eine variable gedreht werden kann, entspricht eine Quotierung von IRS +80 BP einem variablen Zinssatz von EURIBOR +80 BP.

Die Kombination einer Anleihe (Asset) mit einem IRS wird **Asset Swap** genannt. Mit einer Quotierung auf Asset-Swap-Basis meint man daher **EURIBOR + Credit Spread.**

Anmerkung: Asset Swaps werden üblicherweise im Package gehandelt, d.h., der Verkäufer der Anleihe ist gleichzeitig Partner im IRS. Die Anleihe wird dabei – unabhängig vom aktuellen Kurs – zu 100 geliefert, und der Festsatz im Swap entspricht dem Kupon der Anleihe. Die variable Zahlung im Swap ist dann nicht EURIBOR flat, sondern EURIBOR + Credit Spread.

Credit Spreads von Staatsanleihen

Betrachtet man die historischen Renditen von Staatsanleihen, so stellt man fest, dass sie unter den IRS-Sätzen liegen, d.h., dass der **Spread zum IRS negativ** ist. Das bedeutet, dass Staatsanleihen auf Asset-Swap-Basis üblicherweise zu EURIBOR (bzw. LIBOR) minus Credit Spread quotieren. Das lässt sich damit erklären, dass EURIBOR (bzw. IRS) dem Zinssatz für beste Bankadressen entspricht. Da die Bonität von Staaten höher als jene von Banken eingestuft wird, muss folglich auch der Zinssatz niedriger als jener der Banken (also EURIBOR) sein.

Summary

In the bond market bonds/debentures with medium and long-term maturities are traded. A bond is a negotiable debt. The issuer obliges himself to pay the owner a specific interest rate for an agreed period of time and to repay the principal on a specified settlement day (or on several settlement days). From the issuer's point of view, bonds are debt capital, and the creditor owns the bond. For the issuer, bonds are a very important instrument for fundraising.

Bonds can be divided according to many different criteria: issuer, primary market and interest payment. Bonds can be categorised in terms of their issuer into government bonds, bank bonds and corporate bonds. Furthermore, bonds can be categorised in terms of their primary market: domestic bonds, foreign bonds, Eurobonds or international bonds. For interest payment we differentiate between fixed-rate interest bonds and floating-rate interest bonds.

Usually, the issuer of a bond obliges himself to pay off the capital at a pre-set date and at a defined rate (usually at a rate of 100). If the whole bond is paid off at once it is called a "bullet". If the bond is paid off gradually, it is called an amortising bond or a "sinking fund".

In addition to the bonds mentioned above, there are the so-called callable bonds, where the issuer has the right to pay off the bond before maturity at a previously defined rate. Convertible bonds are unsecured fixed-rate bonds that give the owner the right (but not the obligation) to convert the bonds into shares (under conditions that have been specified in advance).

Every bond has a fixed face value. This face value serves as the basis for the interest payment and as the basis to calculate the redemption value which can differ from the face value. If the current price of the bond is above (below) 100, the bond is said to be quoted at a premium (discount).

Bond prices are usually quoted in per cent of the face value. In the bond market, market makers quote both bid and offer on request: the bid price is the price they are willing to pay for bonds while the offer price is the price at which they are willing to sell the bonds. In the eurobond market, prices are usually quoted in decimals (e.g. 101.50), while in the US and in UK they are often quoted with fractions (e.g. 101½ or 10116/32).

The owner of the bond receives the full amount of interest at coupon dates, even though he might not have possessed the bond during the whole period of interest. Therefore, when a bond is sold or bought, accrued interest has to be taken into account. Since comparing bond prices including accrued interest is a complicated business, bonds are usually quoted without accrued interest. Nonetheless, the buyer of a bond has to pay the accrued interest to the seller when he purchases the bond. The price without accrued interest is called "clean" price. The price including accrued interest is called "dirty" price.

The market price is influenced by the following factors: time to maturity of the bond, the actual market yield of bonds with the same time to maturity, the fixed interest rate of the bond, the linked credit risk and the liquidity of the bond's secondary market.

Zusammenfassung

Unter dem Anleihemarkt (auch Rentenmarkt) versteht man den Handel von Gläubigerpapieren mit mittel- und langfristigen Laufzeiten. Anleihen sind handelbare Wertpapiere, die eine Schuld verbriefen. Der Emittent verpflichtet sich, dem Besitzer des Papiers einen spezifizierten Zinssatz für eine definierte Laufzeit zu zahlen und das gesamte Kapital zu einem angegebenen Stichtag (oder mehreren Stichtagen) zurückzuzahlen. Anleihen stellen für die Emittenten ein wichtiges Instrument zur Liquiditätsbeschaffung dar.

Anleihen unterliegen einer Vielzahl von Unterscheidungskriterien: nach Emittent, nach Emissionsmarkt und nach Zinszahlung. Emittenten von Anleihen können der Staat, Banken und Unternehmen sein. Nach dem Emissionsmarkt kann man Inlandsanleihen, Auslandsanleihen und Euroanleihen bzw. internationale Anleihen unterscheiden. Bei der Zinszahlung wird zwischen Festzinsanleihen und variablen Anleihen unterschieden.

Üblicherweise verpflichtet sich der Emittent einer Anleihe, das Kapital zu einem genau definierten Zeitpunkt und genau definiertem Kurs (üblicherweise zum Kurs von 100) zu tilgen. Wird die gesamte Anleihe zu einem einzigen Datum getilgt, spricht man von endfälligen Anleihen oder auch Bullet Redemption. Wird die Anleihe in einzelnen Stufen zurückbezahlt, spricht man von einer amortisierenden Anleihe oder einem sogenannten Sinking Fund. Außerdem gibt es noch sogenannte Callable Bonds, die den Emittenten dazu berechtigen, die Anleihe zu einem im Voraus fixierten Kurs vorzeitig zurückzuzahlen.

Wandelanleihen sind nicht besicherte Festzinsanleihen, die dem Besitzer das Recht, aber nicht die Pflicht geben, diese Anleihen zu vorher fixierten Bedingungen in Aktien umzuwandeln.

Der Nominalwert (Nennwert) einer Anleihe ist die Basis der Zinszahlung, der Betrag der Rückzahlung und die Basis des Emissionspreises (dieser kann über oder unter dem Nominalwert liegen). Liegt er über dem Nominalwert, spricht man von Agio, liegt er unter dem Nominalwert, spricht man von einem Disagio.

Die Preisquotierung bei Anleihen erfolgt üblicherweise als Prozentsatz vom Nominalwert. Im Eurobond-Markt werden die Preise üblicherweise in Dezimalstellen quotiert (z.B. 101,50), während in den USA und in UK häufiger in Brüchen quotiert wird (101 1/2 bzw. 101 16/32). Auch im Anleihemarkt quotieren Market Maker auf Anfrage sowohl die Geld- als auch die Briefseite.

Bei Kuponauszahlung fließen die vollen Zinsen dem Besitzer der Anleihe zu, unabhängig davon, ob er diese Anleihe für die ganze Zinsperiode in seinem Besitz hatte. Daher müssen die abgegrenzten Zinsen bei Kauf und Verkauf berücksichtigt werden. Anleihenpreise werden üblicherweise ohne die bisher angefallenen Stückzinsen quotiert. Den Preis ohne Stückzinsen nennt man Clean Price. Der Preis, der die angefallenen Zinsen mitberücksichtigt, ist der Dirty Price.

Der aktuelle Marktpreis einer Anleihe wird von der Restlaufzeit der Anleihe, der aktuellen marktüblichen Rendite für Anleihen mit gleicher Restlaufzeit, dem in der Anleihe fixierten Zinssatz, dem mit der Anleihe verbundenen Kreditrisiko (Bonität des Emittenten) und der Liquidität des Sekundärmarktes für die Anleihe beeinflusst.

The fair bond price is the present value of all future cash-flows. The general formula takes into account different types of interest payments as well as different types of re-payment arrangements. With "broken" periods there are different ways of calculation. In Germany, the "Moosmüller method" is usually employed, i.e. the first discounting is calculated linearly. Internationally, the "ISMA method" is commonly used, which discounts cash-flows exponentially. The ISMA method always leads to a higher result than the Moosmüller method.

There is a connection between market yield and price of the bond: if the market yield rises, the future cash-flow will be discounted at a higher interest rate which leads to a lower present value and vice versa.

When calculating the bond price with the traditional pricing formula (Moosmüller or ISMA) all cash-flows are discounted with the current market yield for comparable bonds. However, this method is not perfect. On closer examination one can see that two assumptions are made: a flat yield curve or a re-investment of the interest returns at the same interest rate. Theoretically, one should use a calculation based on the so-called zero curve that is already state-of-the-art in the swap market, but has not yet been fully accepted in the bond market. With the zero bond method, interest payments during the term of the bond are eliminated so that no assumptions concerning its re-investment are made. When calculating the bond price with the zero-curve, each cash-flow is treated like a cash-flow from a zero bond. Thus, no flat yield curve is assumed but the actual interest rates for the different periods are used.

Talking about interest rates, they are normally the rates for coupon instruments (interest rate swaps, government bonds, etc.). One also calls them yields, par yields or yield to maturity. It is important to understand that the zero curve is derived from one of these other curves, i.e. the zero rates can be calculated from the interest rates of coupon instruments. This transaction is called bootstrapping.

For dealers of short-term positions in bonds (trading book) it is useful to estimate how bond prices change when interest rates change. For this purpose several concepts have been developed. The concept of the simple duration was developed by Frederick R. Macaulay in 1938. If rates change you have two impacts on a bond position. On the one hand, the bond price will change, on the other hand the coupon payments can be re-invested at a different rate. These two effects are always directly opposed. The Macaulay duration describes the time where these two effects cancel each other out. This model assumes, however, a singular parallel yield curve shift.

Der faire Preis einer Anleihe entspricht dem Barwert der zukünftigen Cashflows (diskontierte Cashflows). Dazu gibt es eine allgemeine Formel, die sowohl unterschiedliche Zinszahlungsmodalitäten wie auch unterschiedliche Rückzahlungsvereinbarungen berücksichtigt. Zusätzlich ist zu bedenken, dass eine Preisberechnung nicht nur zu Kuponterminen erfolgt. Das bedeutet, es ergibt sich eine „gebrochene" Periode am Anfang. Bei „gebrochenen" Perioden sind unterschiedliche Methoden möglich. In Deutschland ist die „Moosmüller-Methode" üblich, d.h., die erste Abzinsung erfolgt wie angegeben linear; international häufiger ist die „ISMA-Methode", die exponenziell abzinst. Die ISMA-Methode führt immer zu einem etwas höheren Ergebnis als die Moosmüller-Methode.

Der Zusammenhang zwischen Marktrendite und Anleihekurs lässt sich folgendermaßen erklären: Steigt die Marktrendite, so wird der zukünftige Cashflow mit einem höheren Zinssatz diskontiert, woraus ein niedrigerer Barwert (Anleihekurs) resultiert und umgekehrt. Bei der Berechnung des Anleihepreises mit der klassischen Preisformel (Moosmüller oder ISMA) werden alle Cashflows mit der aktuellen Marktrendite für vergleichbare Anlagen abgezinst. Diese Methode ist jedoch nicht perfekt. Bei einer genaueren Betrachtung fällt auf, dass dabei eine flache Zinskurve bzw. eine Reinvestition der Zinserträge zum gleichen Zinssatz unterstellt wird. Theoretisch richtig wäre eine Berechnung über die sogenannte Zero-Kurve, die im Swapmarkt State of the Art ist, sich aber am Anleihemarkt noch nicht ganz durchgesetzt hat. Im Konzept der Zero-Kurve werden zwischenzeitliche Zinszahlungen eliminiert, wodurch auch keine Annahmen bezüglich deren Reinvestition getroffen werden müssen. Bei der Preisberechnung einer Anleihe über die Zero-Kurve wird also jeder einzelne Zahlungsstrom so behandelt, als käme die Zahlung aus einer Zero-Kupon-Anleihe. Es wird also jeder Zahlungsstrom mit dem entsprechenden Zero-Kupon-Zinssatz der entsprechenden Laufzeit abgezinst. Somit wird keine flache Zinskurve mehr unterstellt, sondern es werden die tatsächlichen Zinssätze der einzelnen Laufzeiten herangezogen.

Spricht man von Zinsen, handelt es sich im Normalfall um Sätze von kupontragenden Instrumenten (Interest Rate Swaps, Bundesanleihen, usw.). Man spricht auch von Renditen, Par Yields oder Yield to Maturity. Es ist wichtig zu verstehen, dass die Zero-Kurve eine von diesen Zinskurven abgeleitete Zinskurve ist, d.h., die Zero-Zinsen können aus den Zinssätzen von zinstragenden Instrumenten errechnet werden. Dieser Vorgang wird Bootstrapping genannt.

Für Händler, die kurzfristige Positionen in Anleihen eingehen, ist interessant, wie der Preis reagiert, wenn sich die Marktzinsen ändern. Dazu wurden verschiedene Konzepte entwickelt. Das Konzept der einfachen Duration (Macaulay Duration) wurde von Frederick R. Macaulay 1938 entwickelt. Ändern sich die Zinsen, so hat dies zwei Auswirkungen auf eine Anleiheposition. Zum einen wird sich der Kurs der Anleihe ändern, zum anderen können die Kuponzahlungen zu einem anderen Zinssatz reinvestiert werden. Diese beiden Effekte sind in der Wirkung immer entgegengesetzt. Die Macaulay Duration beschreibt jenen Zeitpunkt, bei dem sich diese beiden Effekte neutralisieren. Dieses Modell unterliegt jedoch der Einschränkung, dass nur eine einmalige, parallele Verschiebung der Zinskurve unterstellt wird.

When speaking of duration one usually does not mean the Macaulay duration but the modified duration. This is probably the most widely used technique for determining price sensitivities. It shows how the bond price reacts to a market rate movement. The modified duration depends on the term of the bond, coupon and market yield. All calculations with the modified duration assume a flat yield curve – equal to bond price calculations with the traditional formula.

The concept of the duration assumes a linear connection between the yield and the price change. In practice, when rates change the bond price does not run on a straight line but on a curve. Therefore, when applying the duration you get an estimation mistake. Convexity is the measure for this estimation mistaker or non-linear (contorted) price-yield-curve.

We differentiate between different types of interest rates: coupon (nominal interest rate), yield to maturity, par yield and zero coupon rate. Every interest rate defined in the conditions of a bond is called coupon. It is the basis for the yearly interest payments. The most common concept to determine the effective return of a bond is the yield to maturity (YTM) or effective interest rate. When determining the YTM one has to reverse the bond price calculation: while for a price calculation you are looking for the bond price at a given market yield, for the YTM calculation the yield as result of a given bond price is determined. The par yield is the yield of a bond which is quoted at (or close) par, i.e. the price is around 100. Zero rates are derived from the yield curve and take into account the costs/returns for the hedging of the interest payments during the term.

However, the purchase of a bond also always includes a loan to the issuer. Before granting a loan you ideally should examine the credit risk. This examination is quite complex with regard to time and money. Thus, standardised credit ratings have been developed. These ratings classify credit users and bond issuers according to their credit-worthiness with consistent methods. The rating gives international investors benchmarks as a basis for their investment decisions. Credit ratings are done by international rating agencies. The most important agencies are Standard and Poor's, Moody's and Fitch IBCA. Individual ratings for short-term debts (e.g. commercial papers, certificates of deposits) and long-term debts (e.g. bonds) are defined. The bond-ratings are divided in different groups, from group I with first-class addresses (no risk for investor) to group IV with cash-strapped bonds.

Wenn man von Duration spricht, meint man damit üblicherweise nicht die Macaulay Duration, sondern die Modified Duration. Sie ist die wohl bekannteste Technik zur Ermittlung der Preissensitivität. Sie zeigt den Hebel an, mit dem der Preis einer Anleihe auf eine Marktzinsänderung reagiert. Die Höhe der Modified Duration ist abhängig von der Laufzeit der Anleihe, der Kuponhöhe und der Marktrendite. Alle Berechnungen der Modified Duration unterstellen wie bei der Preisberechnung von Anleihen mit den klassischen Formeln eine flache Zinskurve.

Das Konzept der Duration unterstellt einen linearen Zusammenhang zwischen Rendite und Kursänderung. In der Realität bewegt sich der Anleihekurs bei einer Änderung der Zinsen jedoch nicht entlang einer Geraden, sondern entlang einer Kurve. Bei der Anwendung der Duration entsteht also ein Schätzfehler. Der Maßstab für diesen Schätzfehler bzw. die Nicht-Linearität (oder Krümmung) der Kurs-Renditekurve wird als Konvexität bezeichnet.

Bei den Zinssätzen wird unterschieden zwischen Kupon (Nominalzinssatz), Yield to Maturity (Rendite), Par Yield und Zero-Kupon-Satz. Der Kupon (Nominalzinssatz) ist jener Zinssatz, der in den Anleihebedingungen festgelegt wird. Er wird verwendet, um die jährlichen Zinszahlungen zu berechnen. Das am häufigsten verwendete Konzept, um den effektiven Ertrag einer Anleihe zu beschreiben, ist die Yield to Maturity (YTM) bzw. die Rendite- oder der Effektivzinssatz. Zur YTM gelangt man, indem man die Preisberechnung einer Anleihe umkehrt: Während bei der Preisberechnung der Preis der Anleihe bei einer gegebenen Rendite gesucht wird, wird bei der YTM Berechnung die Rendite ermittelt, die ein gegebener Anleihepreis bringt. Die Par Yield ist die Rendite einer Anleihe, die zu (oder nahe) Par notiert, d.h. deren Preis bei etwa 100 liegt. Der Zero-Kupon-Satz wird von der Renditestrukturkurve abgeleitet und berücksichtigt die Kosten bzw. Erträge für die Absicherung der zwischenzeitlichen Zinszahlungen.

Der Kauf einer Anleihe bedeutet jedoch auch immer, dass man einen Kredit an den Emittenten gibt. Einer Kreditvergabe sollte idealerweise eine eingehende Prüfung des Kreditrisikos vorangehen. Diese ist jedoch mit erheblichem Aufwand verbunden, sowohl was Zeit als auch was Kosten betrifft. Daher haben sich standardisierte Bonitätsbeurteilungen, sogenannte Ratings, durchgesetzt. Dabei handelt es sich um die bonitätsmäßige Einstufung von Kreditnehmern bzw. Anleiheschuldnern nach einheitlichen und konsistenten Verfahren. Das Rating gibt internationalen Investoren gültige Maßstäbe als Grundlage für Investitionsentscheidungen. Die Bonitätsbeurteilung wird von internationalen Ratingagenturen vorgenommen. Die wichtigsten Agenturen sind Standard & Poor's, Moody's und Fitch Ratings. Es werden eigene Ratings für kurzfristige Schulden (z.B. Commercial Papers, Certificates of Deposits) und langfristige Schulden (z.B. Anleihen) vergeben. Die Bond-Ratings werden in vier verschiedene Gruppen eingeteilt, wobei zur Gruppe I allerbeste Adressen (risikolose Anlagen) und zur Gruppe IV notleidende Titel gehören.

The basic principle in financial markets is that higher risk has to be awarded with a higher return. Thus, investors ask for a higher interest rate when the issuer's rating is poor. Therefore, the yield of AAA (spoken "triple A") rated government bonds is the lowest. They are the interest rate for investments with the lowest credit risk and thus act as so-called benchmark yields. All bonds rated worse have to pay a premium to this benchmark. This premium is called credit spread.

1.7. Practice Questions

1. A company has the choice whether to issue bonds or shares. Which of the below statements decribes a major difference?
   a) Shares are more tax efficient.
   b) Shares have no maturity date.
   c) Shares are cheaper because they pay no interest.
   d) Shares can be issued in larger amounts.

2. Which statements are correct regarding differences between money markets and capital markets?
   a) There is a higher degree of regulation in the money markets.
   b) The volumes are higher in the money market.
   c) Rates in the money market are higher.
   d) The terms are longer in capital market.
   e) Loan equity is traded in the money markets, equity capital is traded in the capital markets.

3. Which institutions can issue bonds?

4. Explain the differences between registered bonds and bearer bonds!

5. What is meant by "ABS"?

6. What is an Eurobond?
   a) The bond is issued in EUR.
   b) The bond is issued in the eurozone.
   c) The bond is issued in the international market.
   d) The bond is issued in the eurozone by a foreign issuer.

7. Which of the following is NOT a foreign bond?
   a) Samurai
   b) Matador
   c) Yankee
   d) Maple Leaf

8. What is a zero coupon bond?
   a) a bond with zero yield
   b) a bond with a floating interest rate
   c) a bond with no interim payments
   d) a bond restricted to annual interest payments

Das Grundprinzip in den Finanzmärkten ist, dass höheres Risiko mit einem höheren Ertrag belohnt werden muss. Dementsprechend verlangen Investoren einen umso höheren Zinssatz, je schlechter das Rating eines Emittenten ist. Somit ist die Rendite von „Triple A"-gerateten Staatsanleihen am niedrigsten. Sie stellen also den Zinssatz für Anlagen mit dem geringsten Kreditrisiko dar und fungieren als sogenannte Benchmark-Rendite. Alle schlechter gerateten Anleihen müssen einen Aufschlag auf diese Benchmark zahlen. Dieser Aufschlag wird als Credit Spread bezeichnet.

1.7. Wiederholungsfragen

1. Ein Unternehmen steht vor der Wahl, Aktien oder Anleihen zu emittieren. Was ist der wesentliche Unterschied zwischen diesen beiden Finanzinstrumenten?
   a) Aktien sind steuerlich meistens günstiger.
   b) Aktien haben keine Laufzeit.
   c) Aktien sind billiger, weil sie keine Zinsen zahlen.
   d) Mit Aktien kann ein größeres Volumen aufgebracht werden.

2. In welchen Punkten unterscheidet sich der Geldmarkt vom Kapitalmarkt?
   a) Der Geldmarkt ist stärker reguliert.
   b) Die Volumina im Geldmarkt sind höher.
   c) Die Zinssätze im Geldmarkt sind höher.
   d) Die Laufzeiten im Kapitalmarkt sind länger.
   e) Im Geldmarkt wird Fremdkapital und im Kapitalmarkt Eigenkapital gehandelt.

3. Welche Insitutionen können als Emittenten von Anleihen auftreten?

4. Erklären Sie den Unterschied zwischen Namens- und Inhaberschuldverschreibung!

5. Was versteht man unter „ABS"?

6. Was versteht man unter einem Eurobond?
   a) eine auf Euro lautende Anleihe
   b) eine im Euroraum emittierte Anleihe
   c) eine Anleihe, die im internationalen Markt emittiert wird
   d) eine von einem ausländischen Emittenten im Euroraum emittierte Anleihe

7. Welches der folgenden Papiere ist KEINE ausländische Anleihe?
   a) Samurai
   b) Matador
   c) Yankee
   d) Maple Leaf

8. Was ist eine Nullkuponanleihe?
   a) Anleihe ohne Verzinsung
   b) Anleihe mit variabler Verzinsung
   c) Anleihe ohne Zinszahlungen während der Laufzeit
   d) Anleihe, die auf jährliche Zinszahlungen beschränkt ist

9. How is a bond called that redeems the full amount at maturity?
   a) bullet bond
   b) full bond
   c) zero bond
   d) amortising bond

10. Which of the following is typical of convertible bonds?
    a) They are bonds with a floating rate.
    b) They oblige the issuer to redeem the bond in another currency.
    c) They oblige the buyer to convert the bond into stock at fixed conditions.
    d) They give the buyer the right to convert the bond into stock at fixed conditions.

11. What is a Callable Bond?
    a) right of the issuer to repay the bond prior to maturity
    b) right of the investor to convert the bond into shares
    c) right of the investor to repay the bond prior to maturity at 100
    d) right of the issuer to repay the nominal value by shares at maturity

12. What is a dirty price?
    a) a price outside the market
    b) bond price including accrued interest
    c) repo price for a rarely accepted collateral
    d) repo price against a bond with a coupon payment during the repo term

13. What are the assumptions for the traditional bond formulae?

14. What is meant by "bootstrapping"?

15. What determines the price of a bond?
    a) the present value of the coupons discounted by the maturity
    b) the present value of the coupons and the principal divided by maturity
    c) the present value of the coupons discounted at the yield of maturity
    d) the present value of the coupons and the principal discounted at the yield to maturity

16. What does it mean if a bond is traded at premium?
    a) The price is higher than face value.
    b) The coupon is lower than the yield.
    c) The issuer has a first class rating.
    d) There is a higher risk of reinvestment.

17. A 5-year eurobond with a coupon of 5.5% trades at 95.00. What will the yield to maturity be?
    a) It is 5.5%.
    b) It is higher than 5.5%
    c) It is lower than 5.5%.
    d) You cannot tell.

18. On which factors does the modified duration depend?

9. Wie wird eine Anleihe bezeichnet, deren Tilgung zur Gänze am Laufzeitende erfolgt?
   a) Bullet Anleihe
   b) Full Anleihe
   c) Zero Anleihe
   d) amortisierende Anleihe

10. Was ist typisch für Wandelanleihen?
   a) Sie sind variabel verzinste Anleihen.
   b) Sie verpflichten den Emittenten, die Anleihe in einer anderen Währung zu tilgen.
   c) Sie verpflichten den Käufer, die Anleihe zu bestimmten Bedingungen in Aktien umzuwandeln.
   d) Sie geben dem Käufer das Recht, die Anleihe zu vorher fixierten Bedingungen in Aktien umzuwandeln.

11. Was trifft auf einen Callable Bond zu?
   a) Recht des Emittenten, die Anleihe vorzeitig zu tilgen
   b) Recht des Käufers, die Anleihe in Aktien umzutauschen
   c) Recht des Käufers, die Anleihe vorzeitig zu 100 zurückzugeben
   d) Recht des Emittenten, bei Fälligkeit Aktien im Nominalwert zurückzuzahlen

12. Was versteht man unter dem Dirty Price?
   a) Preis außerhalb des Marktes
   b) Anleihepreis inklusive aufgelaufener Stückzinsen
   c) Repo-Preis mit einer selten akzeptierten Sicherheit
   d) Repo-Preis gegen eine Anleihe mit einer Kuponzahlung während der Repolaufzeit

13. Welche Annahmen unterstellen die klassischen Anleihenformeln?

14. Was versteht man unter „Bootstrapping"?

15. Wodurch wird der Preis einer Anleihe bestimmt?
   a) durch den Barwert der mit der Laufzeit diskontierten Kuponzahlungen
   b) durch den Barwert der Kupons und des Nominales dividiert durch die Laufzeit
   c) durch den Barwert der mit der Laufzeitrendite diskontierten Kuponzahlungen
   d) durch den Barwert der mit der Laufzeitrendite diskontierten Zins- und Tilgungszahlungen

16. Was bedeutet es, wenn eine Anleihe mit einem Agio gehandelt wird?
   a) Preis ist höher als der Nominalwert.
   b) Kupon ist niedriger als die Rendite.
   c) Der Emittent genießt erstklassige Bonität.
   d) Es besteht ein höheres Reinvestitionsrisiko.

17. Ein 5-Jahres-Eurobond mit einem Kupon von 5,5% notiert bei 95,00. Was stimmt bezogen auf die Marktrendite bis zur Fälligkeit?
   a) Sie ist 5,5%.
   b) Sie ist höher als 5,5%.
   c) Sie ist niedriger als 5,5%.
   d) Sie haben nicht genug Informationen, um zu entscheiden.

18. Wovon hängt die Höhe der Modified Duration ab?

19. Which of the following statements regarding modified duration is true?
    a) It is stated in years.
    b) It estimates the price changes of a bond due to interest rate changes.
    c) It is the point in time at which a loss in a bonds price will be compensated by higher compound interest.
    d) It states exactly the change of the bond price if the change of interest rate is 1 per cent.

20. What is meant by convexity?
    a) estimation error of the modified duration
    b) difference between modified duration and effective duration
    c) difference between the term and the modified duration
    d) difference between modified duration und Macaulay duration

21. Which positions show the highest convexity effects?
    a) fixed rate positions, long-term
    b) fixed rate positions, short-term
    c) money market future
    d) FRN

22. Which statement is correct regarding the yield to maturity of a bond?
    a) The YTM is the par yield of a cash-flow.
    b) The YTM is the internal rate of return of cash-flows.
    c) The YTM is usually lower than the coupon.
    d) Bonds with the same term but different coupons have the same YTM if their price was calculated with the zero curve.

23. An AA rated bond is currently traded at IRS +10 BP. What is the yield of an A rated bond?
    a) It depends mainly on the term to maturity.
    b) below IRS +10 BP
    c) IRS +10 BP
    d) above IRS +10 BP

24. Which statements relating to the bond market are correct?
    a) You buy treasury bonds in order to gain high yields.
    b) You buy zero bonds in order to benefit from a falling interest rate.
    c) You buy a reverse floating rate note in order to benefit from falling interest rates.
    d) You buy junk bonds in order to gain high yields.
    e) You buy bonds with a high duration in order to gain high yields.
    f) You buy a high coupon bond with a short term to maturity in order to keep the interest rate sensitivity as small as possible.

19. Welche der folgenden Aussagen trifft auf die Modified Duration zu?
    a) Sie wird in Jahren angegeben.
    b) Sie schätzt die Preisänderung einer Anleihe bei Änderung der Zinsen.
    c) Sie gibt den Zeitpunkt an, zu dem Kursverluste auf eine Anleihe durch die höheren Zinseszinsen kompensiert werden.
    d) Sie gibt exakt an, um wie viel sich der Kurs einer Anleihe ändert, wenn sich das Zinsniveau um 1 Prozentpunkt ändert.

20. Was versteht man unter Konvexität?
    a) Schätzfehler der Modified Duration
    b) Differenz zwischen Modified Duration und Effective Duration
    c) Differenz zwischen der Laufzeit und der Modified Duration
    d) Differenz zwischen Modified Duration und Macaulay Duration

21. Bei welchen Positionen sind die Konvexitätseffekte am ausgeprägtesten?
    a) Fixzinspositionen mit langen Laufzeiten
    b) Fixzinspositionen mit kurzen Laufzeiten
    c) Money Market Future
    d) FRN

22. Was stimmt bezüglich Yield to Maturity einer Anleihe?
    a) Die YTM entspricht der Par Yield eines Cashflows.
    b) Die YTM ist der interne Zinssatz eines Cashflows.
    c) Die YTM ist zumeist niedriger als der Kupon.
    d) Die YTM ist für Anleihen mit gleicher Laufzeit gleich, wenn ihr Kurs mit der Zero-Methode ermittelt wurde.

23. Die Anleihe eines AA-gerateten Emittenten wird zu IRS +10 BP gehandelt. Wo liegt die Rendite eines Emittenten mit einem A-Rating?
    a) Das hängt hauptsächlich von der Laufzeit ab.
    b) niedriger als IRS +10 BP
    c) IRS +10 BP
    d) höher als IRS +10 BP

24. Welche der folgenden Überlegungen treffen auf den Anleihenmarkt zu?
    a) Um hohe Renditen zu erzielen, kaufen Sie Treasury Bonds.
    b) Um von fallenden Zinsen zu profitieren, kaufen Sie Zero Bonds.
    c) Um von fallenden Zinsen zu profitieren, kaufen Sie eine Reverse Floating Rate Note.
    d) Um hohe Renditen zu erzielen, kaufen Sie Junk Bonds.
    e) Um hohe Renditen zu erzielen, kaufen Sie Anleihen mit hoher Duration.
    f) Um von Zinsänderungen möglichst wenig betroffen zu sein, kaufen Sie Hochkuponanleihen mit kurzer Restlaufzeit.

2. Interest Rate Swaps

In this chapter you learn ...

- how financial swaps have developed over time.
- what is meant by an interest rate swap.
- about the different types of interest rate swaps.
- about the role of banks regarding swap transactions.
- which terminology and conventions are used regarding swap transactions.
- what is meant by an asset swap or liability swap.
- how pricing and mark-to-market revalutation of interest rate swaps are done.
- what is meant by Cross Currency Swap.
- how cross currency swaps are used.
- how a swap position is closed.

2.1. Development of Financial Swaps

The **World Bank and IBM** undertook one of the **first publicly known financial swaps** in August 1981. This deal demonstrates the background and the development of the swap market very well and is quoted often as the classic example.

In 1981, the USD rose against European currencies. Therefore, in order to take **advantage of the favourable exchange rates**, IBM was looking for the possibility to pay back pre-maturely its CHF and DEM liabilities (dating back to 1979) which it entered in order to finance USD investments on the US capital. However, a termination of these liabilities was not possible.

At the same time, the **World Bank was wanted to enter into liabilities in currencies that had low interest rates**. Because of its earlier use of the CHF capital market, no first class conditions were available – contrary to the situation in the USD capital market. The matching needs of IBM and World Bank made it possible to arrange a swap **deal from which both parties gained**.

2. Zinsswapgeschäfte

In diesem Kapitel lernen Sie ...

- wie sich Zinsswapgeschäfte historisch entwickelt haben.
- was man unter einem Zinsswap versteht.
- welche Arten von Zinsswaps unterschieden werden.
- welche Rollen Banken im Rahmen von Swapgeschäften spielen.
- welche Terminologien bzw. Usancen im Rahmen von Swapgeschäften verwendet werden.
- was man unter Asset Swap bzw. Liability Swap versteht.
- wie beim Pricing und bei der Mark-to-Market-Bewertung von Zinsswaps vorgegangen wird.
- was man unter einem Cross Currency Swap versteht.
- wozu Cross Currency Swaps verwendet werden.
- wie eine Swapposition geschlossen werden kann.

2.1. Entstehung von Zinsswapgeschäften

Eine der **ersten bekannten Swaptransaktionen** wurde im August 1981 **zwischen der Weltbank und IBM** abgeschlossen. Da sich anhand dieses Swapabschlusses die Hintergründe um die Entstehung des Swapmarktes gut aufzeigen lassen, ist er seither ein viel zitiertes und klassisches Beispiel.

1981 gewann der USD gegenüber den europäischen Währungen an Stärke. **IBM** suchte deshalb nach einer Möglichkeit, die seit 1979 bestehenden Verbindlichkeiten in CHF und DEM, die zur Finanzierung von USD-Investitionen am Kapitalmarkt eingegangen waren, vorzeitig zurückzuzahlen, um die **Währungsgewinne zu realisieren.** Eine vorzeitige Kündigung der Verbindlichkeiten war jedoch ausgeschlossen.

Zur selben Zeit war die **Weltbank** bestrebt, **Verbindlichkeiten in Niedrigzinswährungen** einzugehen. Aufgrund vorangegangener Beanspruchungen des CHF-Kapitalmarktes waren aber – im Gegensatz zum USD-Kapitalmarkt – keine erstklassigen Konditionen für sie durchsetzbar. Die sich gegenüberstehenden Bedürfnisse ermöglichten es IBM und der Weltbank, eine **Transaktion zum beiderseitigen Nutzen** abzuwickeln.

The following figure shows the different **Cash-flows**:

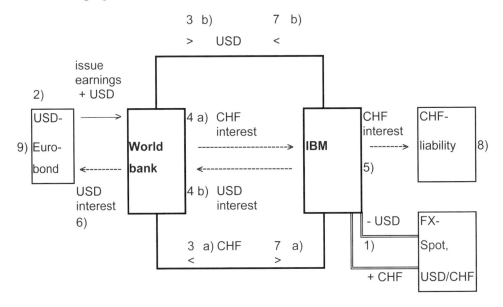

1) IBM buys CHF equal to the CHF liability against USD (the CHF from the original liability were exchanged into USD in 1979 just after the purchase)
2) The World Bank issues a USD Eurobond (conditions as arranged with IBM: principal and term correspond to the liability (see 1) - the spot deal USD/CHF)
3) IBM and the World Bank enter a cross currency swap with the following arrangements:
   a) IBM gives CHF from the FX deal to the World Bank and
   b receives an amount that comes from the World Bank's Eurobond. This amount is given in USD; the exchange rate is determined by the swap's conditions.
4) During the currency swap's term,
   a) IBM receives CHF interest from the World Bank and 5) services its CHF liability with it
   b) the World Bank receives USD interest from IBM and 6) services its USD Eurobond with it
   At the end of the swap term, in addition to the interest payments 4a), 4b), 5), and 6), other payments are made:
7) a) the World Bank pays back the CHF 3a) it received as initial transaction from IBM
   b) IBM pays back the USD 3b) it received as initial transaction from the World Bank
8) IBM uses the CHF from 7a) to pay off its own CHF liability
9) The World Bank pays off the Eurobond with the USD payment 7b)

In the same way, the World Bank and IBM treated the DEM liabilities with a USD/DEM currency swap. In this way, IBM eliminated the economic risk of having CHF and DEM in its balance sheet without any offsetting positions and realised a currency profit. The World Bank took advantage of its advantage regarding costs in the Euro-USD market and "transferred" this advantage into CHF and DEM. Thereby it got better interest conditions than if it had directly operated in the Swiss or German capital markets.

Ever since, currency swaps have developed into one of the **most important instruments in the financial market**.

Die folgende Abbildung stellt die verschiedenen **Zahlungsströme** dar:

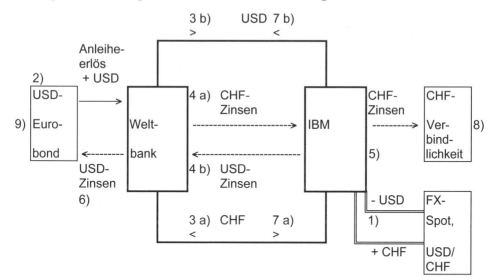

1) IBM kauft CHF in Höhe der CHF-Verbindlichkeit gegen USD (die ursprünglich aus der Verbindlichkeit stammenden CHF wurden 1979 nach Erhalt in USD konvertiert).
2) Die Weltbank emittierte einen USD-Eurobond (Ausstattung: Betrag und Laufzeit auf die CHF-Verbindlichkeit (siehe 1) – das Kassageschäft USD/CHF – von IBM abgestimmt).
3) IBM und die Weltbank schließen einen Währungsswap ab, indem folgende Zahlungen geleistet werden:
   a) IBM gibt die CHF aus dem Devisengeschäft der Weltbank und
   b) bekommt dafür von der Weltbank den zu dem im Währungsswap vereinbarten Tauschkurs fixierten Gegenwert in USD, der aus dem Weltbank-Eurobond stammt.
4) Während der Laufzeit des Währungsswaps
   a) erhält IBM von der Weltbank CHF-Zinsen und 5) bedient damit die CHF-Verbindlichkeit.
   b) erhält die Weltbank von IBM USD-Zinsen und 6) bedient damit den USD-Eurobond.
   Am Ende der Laufzeit des Währungsswaps fließen zusätzlich zu den Zinszahlungen 4 a), 4 b), 5) und 6) die folgenden Geldströme:
7) a   die Weltbank zahlt an IBM die am Starttag erhaltenen CHF 3 a) zurück.
   b) IBM zahlt im Gegenzug die am Starttag erhaltenen USD 3 b) an die Weltbank.
8) IBM verwendet die CHF aus 7 a), um die eigene CHF-Verbindlichkeit zu tilgen.
9) Die Weltbank tilgt mit der USD-Zahlung aus 7 b) den Eurobond.

Ebenso verfuhren die Weltbank und IBM im Währungsswap USD/DEM für die DEM-Verbindlichkeiten. Auf diese Weise entledigte sich IBM des wirtschaftlichen Risikos, CHF bzw. DEM ohne entsprechende Gegenpositionen in der Bilanz zu haben, und realisierte einen Währungsgewinn. Die Weltbank nutzte ihren Kostenvorteil auf dem EUR-USD-Bondmarkt, übernahm ihn in die CHF bzw. DEM und zahlte so Zinsen, die unter denen einer direkten Kapitalaufnahme am Schweizer bzw. deutschen Markt lagen.

Seit Anfang der 80er-Jahre wird der Begriff „Swap" – also Tauschgeschäft – neben der Sonderform der Devisentermingeschäfte auch für eine Gruppe weiterer Finanzinstrumente verwendet, die Zinsswaps. Die Zinsswaps (häufig auch nur „Swaps" genannt) haben sich seither zu den **wichtigsten Finanzinnovationen des Finanzmarktes** entwickelt.

2.2. Interest Rate Swap (IRS)

An interest rate swap is a contract between two parties (A and B) to **exchange different, specified interest payments in the same currency** during a term that is stated in the contract. The amount of the interest payment is calculated on the underlying principal and the interest rate of the respective interest period. The principal is not exchanged under an interest rate swap.

We differentiate between the following types of financial swaps:

- interest rate swaps
- currency swaps, cross currency swaps
- credit swaps and swaps of the second and third generation (which will not be discussed here)

The possible roles of banks in the swap business are explained in the following:

Public agent

The bank brokers a swap deal between two potential parties and supports them with its know-how during the negotiations of the contract. Legally, the bank is not involved in the contract and therefore does not take on any risk.

Anonymous agent

The bank takes the role of an intermediary between two parties ("A" and "C"). With both parties, the bank concludes a contract separately. Parties "A" and "C" do not enter a legal agreement. In this case, the risks of creditworthiness are taken over by the bank.

Active party

The swap is taken as an active position by the bank on its own risk, i.e. the bank takes on the credit risk as well as the market risk.

Counterparties

The two parties to a swap deal.

Fixed-rate payer

The fixed-rate payer of a swap is the party that pays a fix interest-rate. The fixed-rate payer is also called swap "buyer". The recipient of the fixed-rate interest is called fixed-rate receiver or swap "seller".

Floating-rate payer

The floating-rate payer of a swap is the party that pays a floating interest rate.

2.2. Zinsswap (Interest Rate Swap – IRS)

Ein Zinsswap ist ein Vertrag zwischen zwei Parteien (A und B) über den **Austausch unterschiedlicher, spezifizierter Zinszahlungen in einer Währung** während eines im Vertrag fixierten Zeitraums. Die Höhe der Zinszahlung ergibt sich aus dem der jeweiligen Zinsperiode zugrundeliegenden Zinssatz und Kapitalbetrag, auch „Notional Amount" genannt. Die Notional Amount wird beim Zinsswap nicht ausgetauscht.

Man unterscheidet folgende Arten von Zinsswaps:

- normale Zinsswaps (Interest Rate Swaps),
- Currency Swaps, Cross Currency Swaps und
- Kredit- und andere Swaps der zweiten und dritten Generation (auf die hier aber nicht eingegangen wird)

Banken spielen im Rahmen von Swapgeschäften unterschiedliche Rollen:

Offene Vermittlung

Die Bank als Arrangeur führt zwei potenzielle Swappartner zusammen und unterstützt mit ihrem Know-how die Vertragsverhandlungen. Am Swapvertrag selbst ist sie jedoch rechtlich nicht beteiligt – sie übernimmt also kein Risiko.

Anonyme Vermittlung

Die Bank stellt sich als Mittler zwischen zwei Partner (A und C) und schließt mit jedem der beiden Kontrahenten einen separaten Vertrag ab. Die Partner A und C stehen in keiner direkten rechtlichen Verbindung zueinander. Die Bonitätsrisiken trägt in diesem Fall die Bank.

Aktiver Partner

Der Swap wird von der Bank auf eigenes Risiko als Handelsposition übernommen, d.h., die Bank übernimmt neben dem Bonitätsrisiko auch das Marktpreisrisiko.

Counterparties/Kontrahenten

sind die beiden Vertragsparteien in einem Swapgeschäft.

Festzinszahler (Fixed Rate Payer)

ist der Partner in einem Swap, der einen Festzins zahlt. Man nennt den Festzinszahler auch „Swapkäufer". Im Gegenzug nennt man den Festzinsempfänger (Fixed Rate Receiver) auch „Swapverkäufer".

Zahler variabler Zinsen (Floating Rate Payer)

ist der Partner in einem Swap, der einen variablen Zinssatz zahlt.

2.2.1. Types of Interest Rate Swaps

Swaps can be differentiated with regard the types of interest payment:

- **Coupon swap** (also called fixed-rate interest swap)
  Exchange of a fixed against a floating interest rate

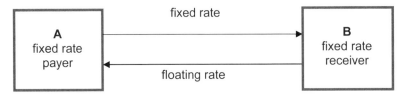

- **Basis swap**
  Exchange of two different, floating interest rates in the same currency.

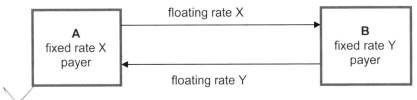

- **Cross Currency Interest Rate Swap**
  Exchange of two interest rates in different currencies

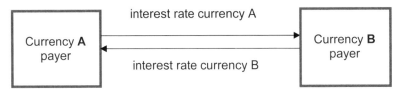

Coupon swaps

A coupon swap (also called fixed-rate interest swap, par swap, or plain vanilla swap) is a contract between two parties ("A" and "B") to **exchange a fixed-rate interest payment for a floating-rate interest payment**. It is calculated on the basis of a fixed principal for an agreed period of time.

2.2.2. Terminology and Conventions

Notional Amount

is the capital sum in the swap for calculating the interest rate (current trade amounts: 10 to 100 m per transaction – other amounts are possible).

Trade date

is the day, on which the two parties agree to conclude a swap.

2.2.1. Arten von Zinsswaps

Je nach Art der Zinsvereinbarung unterscheidet man:

- **Kuponswap** (auch Festzinsswap genannt)
  Austausch eines fixen gegen einen variablen Zinssatz

- **Basisswap**
  Austausch von zwei unterschiedlichen, variablen Zinssätzen in einer Währung

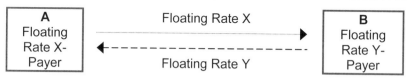

- **Cross Currency Interest Rate Swap**
  Austausch von zwei Zinssätzen in unterschiedlichen Währungen

Kuponswaps

Ein Kuponswap (auch Festzinsswap, Par Swap oder Plain Vanilla Swap genannt) ist ein Vertrag zwischen zwei Parteien (A und B) über den **Austausch einer fixen Zinszahlung gegen eine variable Zinszahlung,** berechnet auf einen fixierten Nominalbetrag für eine vereinbarte Laufzeit.

2.2.2. Terminologie und Usancen

Nominalbetrag (Notional Amount)

ist der der Zinsberechnung zugrundeliegende Kapitalbetrag im Swap (marktübliche Handelsbeträge: 10 bis 100 Mio. pro Geschäft – andere Beträge sind möglich).

Handelstag (Trade Date)

ist der Tag, an dem die zwei Parteien vereinbaren, einen Swap abzuschließen.

Settlement Date/Effective Date

is the day on which the interest calculation starts. We distinguish between

- **Spot Swaps**, for which value date is two bank days after the trade date (exception e.g. GBP on the same day).
- **Forward Swaps**, for which value date is on another date es the usual two bank days (exception see above).

Maturity Date

is the last day of maturity.

Example

USD fixed-rate interest swap with a term of 5 years, annual fixed-rate interest payments against 6-months-LIBOR.

Trading date: September 1st, 2009
Principal: USD 100,000,000
Deal: 5 years fixed, 5.2% annually
First LIBOR, fixed: 3.5%

LIBOR fixing	Beginning of the interest period	End of the interest period	Interest payments floating	fixed
September 1st, 2009	September 3rd, 2009	March 3rd, 2010	3.50%	–
February 27th, 2010	March 3rd, 2010	September 3rd, 2010	LIBOR	5.2%
September 1st, 2010	September 3rd, 2010	March 3rd, 2011	LIBOR	–
March 1st, 2011	March 3rd, 2011	September 5th, 2011	LIBOR	5.2%
September 1st, 2011	September 5th, 2011	March 5th, 2012	LIBOR	–
March 1st, 2012	March 5th, 2012	September 3rd, 2012	LIBOR	5.2%
August 30th, 2012	September 3rd, 2012	March 4th, 2013	LIBOR	–
February 28th, 2013	March 4th, 2013	September 3rd, 2013	LIBOR	5.2%
August 30th, 2013	September 3rd, 2013	March 3rd, 2014	LIBOR	–
February 27th, 2014	March 3rd, 2014	September 3rd, 2014	LIBOR	5.2%

Quotation

Fixed-rate interest swaps are usually quoted as a **fixed interest rate** for the term **on the basis of the reference rate** (e.g. LIBOR) without spread, i.e. flat.

In the example above, the quotation of the 5-year CHF swap against the 6-months CHF LIBOR would be 5.2%.

The quotation on the fixed-rate side can be done by a quotation of the interest rate (e.g. 5.2%) or by a quotation of the spread to the current yield of (usually) government bonds (usually for USD).

Starttag/Erstfälligkeit/Valuta (Settlement Date/Effective Date)

ist der Tag, an dem die Zinsberechnung für den Swap startet. Je nach Startdatum unterscheidet man:

- **Spot Swaps**, bei denen die Valuta üblicherweise zwei Bankarbeitstage nach dem Handelstag ist (Ausnahme z.B. GBP gleichtägig).
- **Forward Swaps**, bei denen die Valuta zu einem anderen Datum als die üblichen zwei Bankarbeitstage (Ausnahmen siehe oben) festgelegt wird.

Endfälligkeit (Maturity Date)

ist der letzte Tag der Laufzeit.

Beispiel

USD-Festzinsswaps mit 5 Jahren Laufzeit, Festzinszahlung jährlich gegen den 6-Monats-LIBOR.

Handelstag:	1. September 2009
Nominalbetrag:	USD 100.000.000
Abschluss:	5 Jahre fest, 5,2% jährlich
Erster LIBOR, gefixed:	3,5%

Zinsfixing für LIBOR	Start der Zinsperiode	Ende der Zinsperiode	Zinszahlungen variabel	fix
1. September 2009	3. September 2009	3. März 2010	3,5%	–
1. März 2010	3. März 2010	3. September 2010	LIBOR	5,2%
1. September 2010	3. September 2010	3. März 2011	LIBOR	–
1. März 2011	3. März 2011	5. September 2011	LIBOR	5,2%
1. September 2011	5. September 2011	5. März 2012	LIBOR	–
1. März 2012	5. März 2012	3. September 2012	LIBOR	5,2%
30. August 2012	3. September 2012	4. März 2013	LIBOR	–
28. Februar 2013	4. März 2013	3. September 2013	LIBOR	5,2%
30. August 2013	3. September 2013	3. März 2014	LIBOR	–
27. Februar 2014	3. März 2014	3. September 2014	LIBOR	5,2%

Quotierung

Festzinsswaps werden üblicherweise auf dem **Basis-Referenzzinssatz** (z.B. LIBOR) ohne Spread, d.h. flat, als **Festzinssatz** für die Laufzeit quotiert. Im vorliegenden Beispiel des 5-Jahres-USD-Swaps gegen 6-Monats-LIBOR würde die Quotierung also 5,2% lauten.

Die Quotierung der festen Seite kann durch eine Zinsquotierung (z.B. 5,2%) oder mit einem Spread zu der aktuellen Rendite (üblicherweise) von Staatspapieren (gängig in USD) erfolgen.

Example

A market maker's quotation for a 5-year USD fixed-rate swap against 3-months USD LIBOR would be:

5.00%-5.05%

The market maker is willing to pay a fixed interest rate of 5% for the swap. As fixed-rate receiver, he demands 5.05 % from the counterparty.
The market maker's quotation could also be the following:

5-years T bond + 20/25

In this case, the current yield of 5-year T-bonds had to be fixed first and then the quoted spread of 20 and 25 basis points is added. If we assume a current 5-year yield of 4.8% the following rates would be effective

5.00% (4.80% + 20 bp) – 5.05% (4.80% + 25 bp)

I. Floating-rate interest payments

Floating index

Usually the **money market reference rate** (LIBOR, EURIBOR, TIBOR), often a 3-months or 6-months index, but also individual solutions for each swap, i.e. 1-months, 12-months or other indices are also possible.

Reset Date/Fixing Date

On fixing date, the **interest rate is adjusted**, i.e. the interest rate for the following interest period is fixed. Usually, the fixing of swap rates takes place **two working days before the interest period starts** (exceptions: GBP same-day fixing); but it is also possible to fix the swap rate during the term which is then valid for the running term (in arrears).

Interest period

The length of an interest period normally equals the **floating rate index**, i.e. with a swap against a 3-months LIBOR the floating interest period is 3 months (but also concerning the structuring of interest periods, swaps are usually quite flexible).

Frequency of payments

Usually, payments are due at the **end of each interest period** (exception: EONIA Swap).

Calculation of interest payments

Usually, the interest payments are calculated according to the **currencies' money market conventions**.

Beispiel

Eine Quotierung eines Market Makers für einen 5-Jahres-USD-Festzinsswap gegen den 3-Monats-USD-LIBOR lautet:

5,00%–5,05%

Der Market Maker ist bereit, für den Swap einen Festzins von 5% zu zahlen. Als Festzinsempfänger verlangt er vom Swappartner 5,05%.

Die Quotierung des Market Makers könnte auch lauten:

5-Jahres-T-Bond + 20/25

In diesem Fall wäre zuerst die aktuelle Treasury Bond Rendite für 5 Jahre festzulegen und um den quotierten Aufschlag von 20 bzw. 25 Basispunkte zu erhöhen. Mit einer angenommenen aktuellen 5-Jahres-Rendite von 4,8% gelten daher:

5% (4,8% + 20 BP) – 5,05% (4,8% + 25 BP)

I. Variable Zinszahlungen

Variabler Index

Üblicherweise **Geldmarktreferenzsatz** (LIBOR, EURIBOR, TIBOR, PRIBOR etc.), häufig 3- oder 6-Monats-Index, jedoch für jeden Swap frei vereinbar, d.h auch 1-, 12-Monats- oder andere Indizes sind möglich. Im Euro-Swapmarkt ist der 6-Monats-EURIBOR Konvention, wenn nicht anderes vereinbart ist.

Zinsfixing-Tag (Reset Date/Fixing Date)

Zinsfixing-Tag ist der **Tag, an dem die Zinsanpassung stattfindet**, d.h. an dem der Zinssatz für eine Zinsperiode festgesetzt wird. Das Fixing bei Swaps erfolgt **in der Regel zwei Bankarbeitstage vor** (in advance) **dem Beginn jeder Zinsperiode** (Ausnahme: GBP tagggleich), kann aber als Sonderform auch während bzw. am Ende einer laufenden Zinsperiode mit Geltung für eben diese erfolgen (in arrears).

Zinsperiode

Die Länge der Zinsperiode entspricht normalerweise dem **variablen Index**, das heißt z.B., bei einem Swap gegen den 3-Monats-LIBOR ist üblicherweise die variable Zinsperiode drei Monate lang (auch die Gestaltung der Länge der Zinsperiode ist, wie generell im Swap, flexibel).

Zahlungsfrequenz

Üblicherweise erfolgen die Zahlungen **am Ende jeder Zinsperiode** (Ausnahme: z.B. EONIA-Swaps).

Zinszahlungsberechnung

Üblicherweise wird die Zinszahlung **analog den Usancen der entsprechenden Währung** für Geldmarktgeschäfte berechnet (Money Market Terms).

II. Fixed-rate interest payments

Fixed interest rate

The interest rate, agreed on the trading date, holds for the whole term of the swap.

Adjustment of interest rate

The interest rate is not adjusted.

Frequency of payments

The frequency of interest payments can be **freely arranged** (monthly, quarterly, six-monthly, annually, etc.). With EUR and CHF, annual payments are usual, with USD/GBP/JPY semi-annual payments are quite common.

Calculation of interest payments

The calculation of interest payments is analogously to the **practice on the respective capital markets**.

Netting

If, in a swap, interest payments between the counterparties flow on the same dates, only the **difference between the interest payments**, i.e. the net amount, is exchanged.

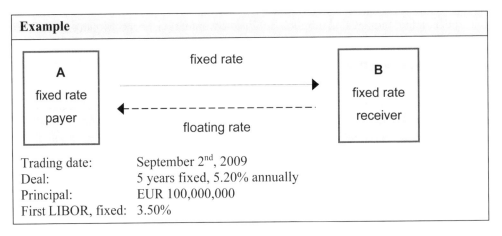

Example

Trading date: September 2nd, 2009
Deal: 5 years fixed, 5.20% annually
Principal: EUR 100,000,000
First LIBOR, fixed: 3.50%

II. Feste Zinszahlung

Festzins

Als Zinssatz gilt der bei Swapabschluss für die gesamte Swaplaufzeit fixierte Zins.

Zinsanpassung

Es erfolgt keine Zinsanpassung.

Zahlungsfrequenz

Die Zahlungsfrequenz ist **beim Abschluss frei vereinbar** (monatlich, vierteljährlich, halbjährlich, jährlich etc.). In den Währungen EUR und CHF erfolgt sie im Allgemeinen jährlich, in USD, GBP, JPY ist halbjährliche Zinszahlung üblich.

Zinszahlungsberechnung

Die Zinszahlungsberechnung entspricht den **Usancen des jeweiligen Kapitalmarktes.** Bei EUR-Zinsswaps gilt gemäß dem Model Code als Konvention 30/360, wenn nicht anderes vereinbart.

Netting

Fallen die sich im Swap gegenüberstehenden Zinszahlungsverpflichtungen von A an B und von B an A auf den gleichen Termin, fließt üblicherweise nur die **Differenz zwischen den beiden Zinszahlungen,** also der Nettobetrag.

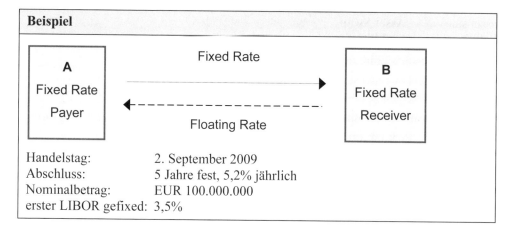

Beispiel

A
Fixed Rate
Payer

Fixed Rate →

Floating Rate ←

B
Fixed Rate
Receiver

Handelstag: 2. September 2009
Abschluss: 5 Jahre fest, 5,2% jährlich
Nominalbetrag: EUR 100.000.000
erster LIBOR gefixed: 3,5%

LIBOR fixing	Beginning of the interest period	End of the interest period	Interest payments floating	fixed
September 2nd, 2009	September 4th, 2009	March 4th, 2010	3.5%	
March 2nd, 2010	March 4th, 2010	September 6th, 2010	EURIBOR	5.2%
September 2nd, 2010	September 6th, 2010	March 4th, 2011	EURIBOR	–
.	.	.	.	.
.	.	.	.	.
.	.	.	.	.
February 28th, 2014	March 4th, 2014	September 4th, 2014	EURIBOR	5.2%

on March 4th, 2010	I) B pays A 3.5% for the first 6 months
on September 6th, 2010	I) B pays A LIBOR for the second 6 months
on September 6th, 2010	II) A pays B 5.2% for the first year
Cash-flow on September, 6th 2010:	I) – II) = net cash-flow
	if I) < II) A pays the difference to B
	if I) > II) B pays the difference to A

Asset swap and liability swap

The terms "asset swap" and "liability swap" are used according to the **side of the balance sheet** that is changed by the swap transaction:

asset side   **Asset Swap**
liability side   **Liability Swap**

From the investor's point of view, an **asset swap** is the swapping of a

- fixed interest rate investment into a floating rate investment (= fixed-rate payer swap)
- floating interest rate into a fixed rate investment (= fixed-rate receiver swap).

A **liability swap** deals with the re-financing side of the balance. It is a swap that turns a

- fixed into a floating refinancing (= fixed-rate receiver swap)
- floating into a fixed refinancing (= fixed-rate payer swap).

Swap Structures

Amortising/Step-Down Swap

In an amortising or a step-down swap the notional amount decreases gradually by a certain amount during the term. It is often used in a connection with a changing underlying transaction (e.g. a loan repaid over the term).

Accreting/Step-Up Swap

In an accreting or a step-up swap the notional amount increases gradually over the time.

Rollercoaster-Swap

In a rollercoaster swap the notional amount increases and decreases during the term at certain points in time. This irregular structure of the principal amount is fixed at the conclusion of the swap.

Zinsfixing für LIBOR	Start der Zinsperiode	Ende der Zinsperiode	Zinszahlungen variabel	fix
2. September 2009	4. September 2009	4. März 2010	3.5%	–
2. März 2010	4. März 2010	6. September 2010	EURIBOR	5,2%
2. September 2010	6. September 2010	4. März 2011	EURIBOR	–
.	.	.	.	.
.	.	.	.	.
.	.	.	.	.
28. Februar 2014	4. März 2014	4. September 2014	EURIBOR	5,2%

Am 4. März 2010   I) B zahlt an A 3,5% für die ersten sechs Monate.

Am 6. September 2010   I) B zahlt an A EURIBOR für die zweiten sechs Monate.

Am 6. September 2010   II) A zahlt an B 5,2% für ein Jahr.

Cashflow am 6. September 2010: I) – II) = Netto-Cashflow

                        Wenn I) < II): zahlt A Differenz an B.

                        Wenn I) > II): zahlt B Differenz an A.

Asset Swap und Liability Swap

Die Bezeichnungen Asset Swap und Liability Swap verwendet man zur **Kennzeichnung jener Seite der Bilanz**, die durch die Swaptransaktion verändert werden soll:

Aktivseite   **Asset Swap**   (auch Aktiv-Swap genannt)

Passivseite   **Liability Swap**   (auch Passiv-Swap genannt)

Ein **Asset Swap** ist also ein Swap aus der Sicht des Investors, der damit

- seine feste in eine variable Anlage (= Festzinszahler-Swap) oder
- seine variable in eine feste Anlage (= Festzinsempfänger-Swap) swapt.

Beim **Liability Swap** handelt es sich also um einen Swap unter Betrachtung der Refinanzierungsseite, durch den

- eine feste in eine variable Refinanzierung (= Festzinsempfänger-Swap) oder
- eine variable in eine feste Refinanzierung (= Festzinszahler-Swap) geswapt wird.

Swapstrukturen

Amortising/Step-Down Swap

Bei einem Amortising Swap or Step-Down Swap sinkt der Nominalbetrag regelmäßig um eine bestimmte Höhe während der Laufzeit. Hintergrund ist oft die Anpassung der Swap-Sensitivität an ein sich veränderndes Grundgeschäft (z.B. einen über die Laufzeit getilgten Kredit).

Accreting/Step-Up Swap

Bei einem Accreting Swap oder Step-Up Swap nimmt der Nominalbetrag über die Laufzeit zu.

Rollercoaster-Swap

Bei einem Rollercoaster Swap kann der Nominalbetrag während der Laufzeit zu bestimmten Zeitpunkten steigen oder sinken. Diese unregelmäßige Struktur des Nominalbetrages wird beim Abschluss des Swaps vertraglich geregelt.

2.2.3. Application

Example

Swap from floating into fixed refinancing:

Bank X has a floating refinancing in the market with the following conditions:
7 years at 6-months LIBOR + 0.25%

The bank expects interest rates to rise in 2 years. It decides to swaps the floating rate into a fixed rate. This can be done by re-paying the current liabilities and simultaneously borrowing money at a fixed interest rate. A pre-mature repayment is not possible or would be unprofitable for the bank because of the high additional costs for the contract termination.

Therefore, X completes a fixed-rate interest rate swap for the rest of the term (5 years) at market conditions:
5-years at 5.20% for the 6-months LIBOR.

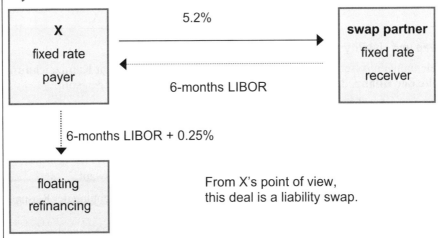

Under the interest rate swap, the 6-months LIBOR is just like a running position:

- X pays 6-months LIBOR +0.25 % for the floating refinancing.
- X receives 6-months LIBOR from the interest rate swap.

For X, the net interest payment from the two floating interest rates (0.25%) remains. The fixed interest rate from the swap has to be added.
Ignoring the effects of compound interest (annual fixed interest rate in contrast to a 6-months LIBOR) and the different basis of interest (30/360 compared to ACT/360), the effective costs are:

X pays	0.25%
X pays	5.20%
X pays	**5.45%**

2.2.3. Anwendung

Beispiel

Umstieg von einer variablen auf eine feste Refinanzierung:

Bank (Unternehmen) X hat eine variable Refinanzierung im Markt zu folgenden Konditionen abgeschlossen: sieben Jahre Laufzeit zu 6-Monats-LIBOR + 0,25%

Nach Ablauf von zwei Jahren erwarten die Zinsmanager einen Zinsanstieg. Man beschließt daher, die variable in eine feste Refinanzierung umzuwandeln. Dies könnte durch die Rückzahlung der bisherigen Verbindlichkeit und die gleichzeitige Neuaufnahme der Gelder zu einem Festzins erreicht werden. Eine vorzeitige Rückzahlung ist ausgeschlossen bzw. wäre durch anfallende Zusatzkosten für die Kündigung für die Bank unrentabel.

Daher schließt X einen Zinsswap (Festzinszahler-Swap) für die Restlaufzeit von 5 Jahren zu folgenen Marktkonditionen ab: fünf Jahre Laufzeit zu 5,2% gegen den 6-Monats-LIBOR.

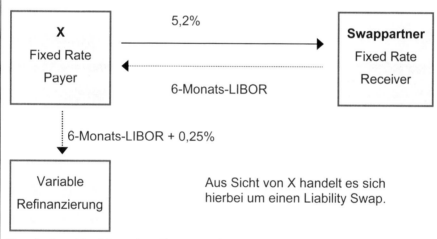

Durch den Abschluss des Zinsswaps ist der 6-Monats-LIBOR für X nur noch ein Durchleitposten:

- X zahlt 6-Monats-LIBOR +0,25% für die variable Refinanzierung.
- X erhält 6-Monats-LIBOR aus dem Zinsswap.

Die Nettozinszahlung aus den beiden variablen Zinssätzen für X in Höhe von 0,25% bleibt erhalten. Hinzu kommt der Festzins von 5,2% im Swap.

Lässt man nun den Zinseszinseffekt (jährliche Festzins- gegenüber halbjährlicher LIBOR-Zahlung) und die unterschiedliche Zinsbasis (ACT/ACT gegenüber ACT/360) außer Acht, verbleiben folgende effektive Kosten:

X zahlt	0,25%
X zahlt	5,20%
X zahlt	**5,45%**

Example

Swap from fixed to floating refinancing:

Bank X issued a fixed-rate interest bond 2 years ago: fixed interest rate is 4.75%, total term 7 years.

The bank decides to change the fixed-rate interest payment into a floating one, according to its expectations on the further development of interest rates.

This could be done by an additional floating refinancing and a fixed-rate interest investment. But this would lead to an unwanted extension of the balance sheet. Also, the costs of the spread between investment and refinancing must be taken into account. Because X wants to avoid these effects, the bank will use an interest rate swap (fixed-rate receiver swap).

Market conditions:
5-years at 5.20% for a 6-months LIBOR.
(From X's point of view, this is a liability swap, because the swap will leads to a change on the liability side of the balance.)

X could turn the fixed interest payments into floating ones by completing the swap.

The following are the effective interest costs for X:

X pays	4.75% for the fixed-rate interest bond
X receives	5.20% from the interest rate swap
X receives	0.45%

X pays 6-months LIBOR for the interest rate swap.

Often, the difference between the interest rates (here: 0.45%) is defined as the LIBOR spread. Ignoring compound interest and different basis of interest rates, X pays 6-months LIBOR – 0.45%.

In this example, the change in the market interest rates leads to 6-months LIBOR – 0.45 %. In other cases, the cost of refinancing ("LIBOR – x") can be achieved by exploiting the of advantages of capital markets through swaps.

Beispiel

Umstieg von einer festen auf eine variable Refinanzierung:

Bank (Unternehmen) X hat vor zwei Jahren eine Festzinsanleihe mit 4,75%, Gesamtlaufzeit sieben Jahre, emittiert.

Die Zinsmanager beschließen gemäß ihrer Zinsmeinung, die feste in eine variable
Zinszahlung umzuwandeln.

Dies könnte über eine zusätzliche variable Refinanzierung und eine Festzinsanlage realisiert werden. Dadurch erfolgt jedoch eine möglicherweise ungewollte Bilanzver-
längerung. Außerdem sind die Spreadkosten zwischen Anlage und Aufnahme zu berücksichtigen. Da dies im vorliegenden Fall nicht gewollt wird, setzt man einen Zinsswap (Festzinsempfänger-Swap) ein, um die Zinsmeinung umzusetzen.

Marktkonditionen:
5 Jahre Laufzeit zu 5,2% gegen den 6-Monats-LIBOR.
(Auch in diesem Fall spricht man von einem Liability Swap, da X eine Veränderung
der Zinsstruktur der Passivseite der Bilanz herbeiführt.)

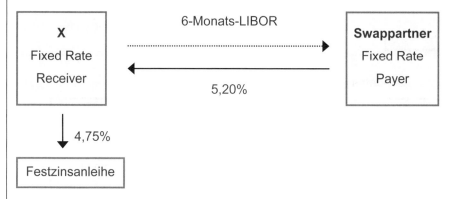

X konnte durch den Zinsswap die festen in variable Zinszahlungen drehen.

Der Zinsaufwand für X beträgt nun:

X zahlt	4,75%	für die Festzinsanleihe
X erhält	5,20%	aus dem Zinsswap
X erhält	0,45%	

X zahlt 6-Monats-LIBOR im Zinsswap.

Häufig wird die Zinsdifferenz (hier 0,45%) als LIBOR-Spread ausgedrückt. Lässt man
nun auch hier den Zinseszinseffekt und die unterschiedliche Zinsbasis außer Acht,
zahlt X den 6-Monats-LIBOR 0,45%.

Im vorliegenden Fall entsteht der 6-Monats-LIBOR – 0,45% – durch die Veränderung
der Marktzinssätze seit Emission der Festzinsanleihe. In anderen Fällen können Refinanzierungskosten von „LIBOR – x" durch die Nutzung von Kapitalmarktvorteilen
bzw. durch den Einsatz von Swaps erreicht werden.

Example

Swap from floating into fixed investment (loan):

Bank X gives a rollover credit (6-months LIBOR + 1%, 7-year term) to a company. At the same time, the bank has the possibility to issue a fixed-rate interest bond at 5.50% and a term of 7 years.

X wants to use the issue's liquidity for the credit but does not want to take on any interest rate risks. This cannot be achieved with the classic instruments of the balance sheet. By completing a fixed-rate receiver swap, X can use the issue's liquidity for the credit while simultaneously eliminating the interest rate risk.

In this case, a clear line between an asset swap and a liability swap cannot be drawn. In combination with the rollover credit the deal is an asset swap while in conjunction with the issue the same swap is a liability swap.

X completes an interest rate swap:
5.55% for 6-months LIBOR, 7-year term.

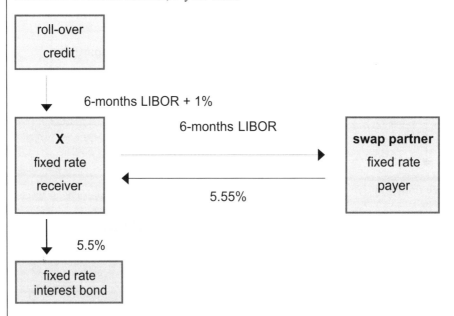

Because X pays and receives interest payments on both the floating and fixed side, it has virtually eliminated the interest rate risk.

The net interest income of the whole deal is:

+ (6-months LIBOR + 1%) – (6-months LIBOR)	=	1.00%
– (5.50%) + (5.55%)	=	0.05%
	=	1.05%*)

*) Ignoring arrangements for payments of fixed and floating rates of interest.

Beispiel

Umstieg von einer variablen auf eine feste Anlage (Forderung):

Bank (Unternehmen) X gibt einen Roll-over-Kredit 6-Monats-LIBOR + 1%, Laufzeit 7 Jahre, an ein Industrieunternehmen. Gleichzeitig hat X die Möglichkeit, eine 5,5% Festzinsanleihe, Laufzeit 7 Jahre, zu günstigen Konditionen zu emittieren.

X will die Liquidität aus der Emission für den Kredit verwenden, jedoch kein Zinsrisiko eingehen. Mit den klassischen Bilanzinstrumenten würde X an dieser Aufgabenstellung scheitern. Durch den Abschluss eines Festzinsempfänger-Swaps kann X die Liquidität aus der Emission für den Kredit verwenden und gleichzeitig das Zinsrisiko ausschalten.

In diesem Fall ist die Bezeichnung Asset- bzw. Liability Swap nicht mehr eindeutig: Der Swap in Verbindung mit dem Roll-over-Kredit ist ein Asset Swap (Aktiv-Swap), von der Emissionsseite betrachtet handelt es sich um einen Liability Swap.

X schließt einen Zinsswap ab:
5,55% gegen 6-Monats-LIBOR, Laufzeit 7 Jahre.

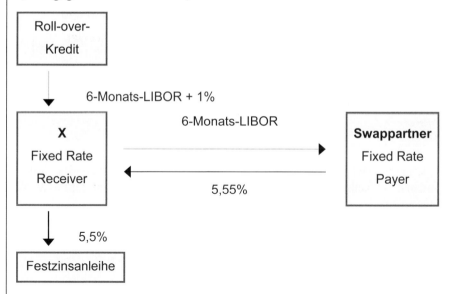

Da X sowohl auf der variablen als auch auf der Festzinsseite einen Zinseingang und Zinsausgang hat, ist das Zinsrisiko ausgeschaltet.

Der Zinsüberschuss aus dem Gesamtgeschäft beträgt:

$$+ \ (\text{6-Monats-LIBOR} + 1\%) - (\text{6-Monats-LIBOR}) \quad = \quad 1{,}00\%$$
$$- \ (5{,}5\%) + (5{,}55\%) \qquad\qquad\qquad\qquad\qquad = \quad 0{,}05\%$$
$$= \quad 1{,}05\%{*})$$

*) ohne Berücksichtigung der Zinsmodalitäten für variable und feste Zinszahlungen

Example

Swap from fixed into floating investment:

In times of high interest rates, X had completed a fixed-rate interest bond: 7.0 % fixed-rate interest bond, time to maturity: 5 years.

The bank assumes that the interest rates have already passed the trough and are going to rise again. The sale of the bond may not be possible for several reasons:

- The bond is part of the fixed assets and therefore cannot be sold.
- The market for this bond is not very liquid and the selling price is not attractive.
- The liquidity that results from the sale of the bond must be invested, and possible spreads and/or equity costs may occur.

X decides to go in for an asset swap: in this case a fixed-rate payer swap
5.20% for 6-months LIBOR, 5-year term

By completing the swap, X can realise a net interest income of 1.80% until maturity (assuming that the bank refinances at LIBOR +/- 0.0%, i.e. LIBOR flat, for the whole term of the swap).

Note: The term "coupon" swap for a fixed-rate interest swap may result from the above application: The earnings of the coupons go (partly) into the interest rate swap.

Arbitrage on credits with interest rate swaps

Interest rate swaps are often used to exploit the so-called comparative advantage. This term was coined by **David Ricardo**, who in the 19th century developed the **theory of comparative advantage for the international exchange of goods**. Applied to the financial market, the theory says that the exchange of different interest rates can be profitable for both parties if they encounter different conditions on the different markets. This is even true, if one of the parties has better conditions on both markets, i.e. has a lower fixed and floating interest rate.

Beispiel

Umstieg von einer festen auf eine variable Anlage:

In einer Hochzinsphase hat X eine Festzinsanleihe mit folgenden Konditionen gekauft: 7% Kupon p.a., Restlaufzeit per heute fünf Jahre.

Die Zinsmanager gehen davon aus, dass die Zinsen jetzt die Talsohle erreicht haben und nun wieder steigen. Der Verkauf der Anleihe kann aus verschiedenen Gründen für X unmöglich oder unrentabel sein:

- Die Anleihe ist Teil des Anlagevermögens und kann deshalb nicht verkauft werden.
- Der Markt für diese Anleihe ist nicht liquide, der Verkaufskurs nicht interessant.
- Die durch den Verkauf frei werdende Liquidität muss wieder angelegt werden, dadurch entstehen möglicherweise Spread- und/oder Eigenkapitalkosten.

X entschließt sich für einen Asset Swap: hier Festzinszahler-Swap 5,20% gegen den 6-Monats-LIBOR, Laufzeit fünf Jahre.

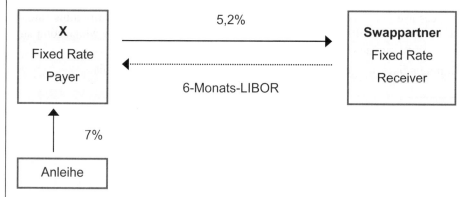

Durch den Abschluss des Swaps kann der Zinsüberschuss von 1,8% p.a. bis zur Endfälligkeit realisiert werden (Annahme: Die Bank refinanziert sich während der Swaplaufzeit zu LIBOR +/– 0,0%, d.h. zu LIBOR flat).

Anmerkung: Die für einen Festzinsswap verwendete Bezeichnung Kuponswap dürfte von dieser Anwendung kommen. Die Kuponerträge aus der Anleihe fließen (teilweise) in den Zinsswap.

Kreditarbitragen mit Zinsswaps

Bei Unternehmen (oder Banken) mit unterschiedlichen Ratings werden Zinsswaps öfter zur **Nutzung sogenannter komparativer Vorteile** eingesetzt. Diese Bezeichnung entstammt der **Theorie von David Ricardo,** der am Beginn des 19. Jahrhunderts das Prinzip der komparativen Vorteile für den internationalen Güteraustausch entwickelte. Angewendet auf den Finanzmarkt bedeutet dieses Prinzip, dass der Austausch von unterschiedlichen Zinssätzen für beide Partner profitabel sein kann, wenn die beiden Partner unterschiedliche Konditionen an den verschiedenen Märkten erhalten.

Example

Assume, that company X has an AAA rating company Y has an A-rating. Company X needs a variable refinancing for 5 years and company Y needs a fixed refinancing for 5 years.

	Company X	Company Y
Fixed interest rate	5.50%	6.25 %
Floating interest rate	LIBOR	LIBOR + 25 bp

If both companies refinance themselves according to their demand, the costs would be for:
Company X floating at LIBOR and for
Company Y fixed at 6.25%.

Alternatively, both companies may choose the opposite refinancing; i.e. company X refinances itself at a fixed rate of 5.50% while company Y chooses a floating rate of LIBOR +25 bp. Simultaneously, they arrange an interest rate swap by which company X gets a fixed rate and pays LIBOR (vice versa for company Y).

Assuming a fixed interest rate of 5.75%, the deal can be shown as this:

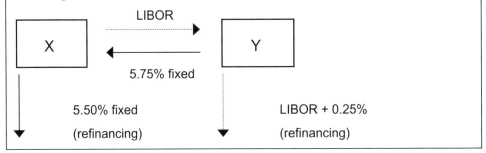

Result

X pays a fixed rate of 5.50% for its refinancing and receives a fixed rate of 5.75% from the swap: the profit on the fixed rate side is 0.25%. Since X has to pay LIBOR, the total cost is LIBOR -25 bp. This calculation takes the profit from the fixed side into account.

Beispiel

Unternehmen X verfügt über ein AAA-Rating, Unternehmen Y hat ein A-Rating. Unternehmen X braucht eine variable Refinanzierung für 5 Jahre, Unternehmen Y braucht eine feste Refinanzierung für 5 Jahre.

Die genannten Unternehmen haben derzeit folgende Konditionen an den unterschiedlichen Märkten:

	Unternehmen X	Unternehmen Y
Festzins	5,5%	6,25%
variabler Zins	LIBOR	LIBOR +25 BP

Refinanzieren sich beide Unternehmen konform ihres Bedarfes, so ergeben sich folgende Kosten:
Unternehmen X: variabel zu LIBOR
Unternehmen Y: fest zu 6,25%

Alternativ können die zwei Unternehmen jedoch auch die gegenteilige Refinanzierung wählen, d.h., Unternehmen X refinanziert sich fest zu 5,5% und Y refinanziert sich variabel zu LIBOR +25 BP. Parallel dazu wird ein Festzinsswap zwischen den zwei Unternehmen abgeschlossen, bei dem Unternehmen X einen festen Satz erhält und LIBOR bezahlt (vice versa aus der Sicht von Y).

Bei einem angenommenen Festsatz von 5,75% ergibt sich:

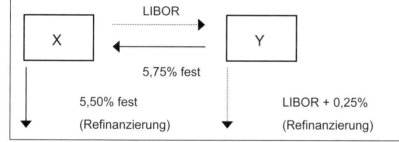

Ergebnis

X zahlt einen festen Satz von 5,5% für die Refinanzierung und erhält aus dem abgeschlossenen Zinsswap einen Festsatz von 5,75%. Dadurch ergibt sich ein Gewinn auf der festen Seite von 0,25%. Übrig bleibt ihm eine variable Zinszahlung von LIBOR, die unter Berücksichtigung vom Gewinn der festen Seite LIBOR –25 BP entspricht. Gegenüber der einfachen variablen Refinanzierung konnte unser AAA-Kunde die Refinanzierung um 25 BP verbilligen (LIBOR/LIBOR –25 BP).

Y pays a floating rate of LIBOR +25 bp for its refinancing and receives a floating rate of LIBOR from the swap: the loss on the floating side 25 bp. Since Y faces a fixed interest rate payment of 5.75%, it has locked in a fixed rate of 6.00% (5.75% from the swap +25 bp loss on the floating interest rate). Company Y could also reduce its refinancing costs by 25 bp (6.25% to 6.00%).

The total benefit from the interest rate swap is 0.50% and is a result of the different market conditions for the companies in the markets. In the market for floating rates, the difference between the conditions is 0.25% (X: LIBOR; Y: LIBOR + 0.25%), in the market for fixed rates the difference is 0.75% (X: 5.50%; Y: 6.25%). The total difference of 0.50% (0.75% – 0.25%) is the comparative advantage that is realised in the swap deal.

Note: In order to speak of a real arbitrage, one had to compare interest rates in the capital market, i.e. the conditions for both contractors over the whole term, for fixed- and floating-rates. In practice, the possible interbank refinancing in the money market is often used as the basis for the floating interest rates.

In the situation above, this would mean from Y's point of view that the company has access to an interbank refinancing at LIBOR +25 bp for the whole term. If the spread changes during the term, the basis for the calculation also changes.

2.2.4. Pricing and Mark to Market Revaluation of IRS

As shown in the example of comparative advantage, a swap deal can be of advantage for both counterparties. You assume that the price was "fair" when the deal was settled.

But when can one speak of a "fair" price?

Assumption: The market quote for a 5-year swap against 6-months LIBOR is 5.18-5.22% p.a. Therefore a swap settled at 5.20% is fair. Neither party A nor B is in a better situation than its partner at the trading date. This means, that the present value of the swap is 0.

If the market price for a 5-year swap changes during the day due to changes in supply and demand, to 5.23-5.27% p.a., the present value of a settled swap also changes.

To evaluate swaps at market interest rates (a "mark to market" evaluation) the variable cash-flows (floating rate payments) have to be compared to the fixed rate payments. In order to make cash flows of different times comparable, the present values of the cash flows are calculated (with zero rates).

Y zahlt einen variablen Zinssatz von LIBOR +25 BP für die variable Refinanzierung und erhält aus dem Zinsswap eine LIBOR-Zahlung.

Dadurch ergibt sich ein Verlust auf der variablen Seite von 25 BP. Zusätzlich leistet Y eine Festzinszahlung von 5,75% aus dem Zinsswap. Der feste Zinssatz, den Y sich damit sichern konnte, ist 6% (5,75% Zinsaufwand Zinsswap +25 BP Verlust auf variablen Zins). Auch Unternehmen Y konnte somit die Refinanzierungskosten um 25 BP (6,25%/6%) verbilligen.

Der Gesamtnutzen aus dem Zinsswap beträgt 0,50%. Er ergibt sich aus den unterschiedlichen Zugängen zu den verschiedenen Märkten: Auf der variablen Seite gibt es einen Unterschied von 0,25% (X: LIBOR; Y: LIBOR + 0,25%) für die beiden Marktteilnehmer, bei den festen Zinsen beträgt der Unterschied 0,75% (X: 5,50%; Y: 6,25%). Die Differenz von 0,50% (0,75% – 0,25%) ist der komparative Vorteil, der durch den Zinsswap ausgenutzt werden kann.

Anmerkung: Um von einer wirklichen Arbitrage reden zu können, müssten die Kapitalmarktzinsen, also die Konditionen für die Gesamtlaufzeit für beide Partner, für feste und variable Refinanzierungen verglichen werden.

In der Praxis werden oft die Interbank-Refinanzierungsmöglichkeiten auf dem Geldmarkt als Basis für die variablen Zinsen herangezogen. In der oben dargestellten Konstellation bedeutet dies jedoch aus Sicht des Unternehmens Y, dass für die Gesamtlaufzeit eine Interbank-Refinanzierung von LIBOR +25 BP realisiert werden kann. Ändert sich der Aufschlag während der Laufzeit, verändert sich auch die Kalkulationsbasis.

2.2.4. Pricing und Mark-to-Market-Bewertung von Zinsswaps

Wie im Beispiel über die Nutzung von „komparativen Kostenvorteilen" für zwei Kontrahenten gezeigt, haben beide Swappartner durch den Geschäftsabschluss einen Vorteil. Man geht davon aus, dass der Preis bei Vertragsabschluss „fair" war.

Doch wann ist der Preis für einen Swap „fair"?

Annahme: Die Marktquotierung für einen 5-Jahres-Swap gegen den 6-Monats-LIBOR lautet 5,18 – 5,22% p.a. Folglich ist ein Geschäftsabschluss bei 5,20% fair. Weder Swappartner A noch B haben zum Zeitpunkt des Abschlusses einen Vorteil gegenüber dem anderen Partner. Der Barwert des Swaps ist also 0,00.

Verändert sich jetzt im Laufe des Tages durch Angebot und Nachfrage der Preis für 5-Jahres-Swaps am Markt, z.B. auf 5,23 – 5,27% p.a., ändert sich der Barwert des abgeschlossenen Swaps.

Um einen Zinsswap „Mark-to-Market" bewerten zu können, ist das Ergebnis des Zinsswaps bei Schließung der Position zu aktuellen Marktpreisen zu berechnen. Es werden die Cashflows aus den variablen und festen Zinszahlungen gegenübergestellt und die Barwerte der Netto-Cashflows ermittelt. Für die Barwert-Rechnung werden Zero-Zinsen verwendet.

Example

Bank A has entered into a fixed rate receiver swap with Bank B, for EUR 100 m for 5 years. It receives 4,75% p.a. against 6-months EURIBOR. After 3 years Bank A wants to close the position and receives the following EUR IRS quotation from Bank C: 2-years IRS against 6-months EURIBOR 4.31–4.35%. The zero rates for 1 year are 4.50% and for 2 years 4.55%.

What is the MtM-value of the swap position?

The position of Bank A looks as follows:

Bank A closes the original swap deal by buying the 2-years IRS from Bank C (=fixed rate payer swap). It pays 4.35% and receives 6-months EURIBOR. As the variable interest payments run through, only the two fixed rate payments have to be considered for the calculation of the MtM value.

Calculation of the result:

Year	Original swap deal	Opposite deal	Result	Discount $(1/(1+r)^n)$	Present Value
1	+4,750,000	-4,350,000	+400,000	0.9569378	+382,775
2	+4,750,000	-4,350,000	+400,000	0.9148543	+365,942
Total					**+748,717**

The actual value of the 5-years EUR IRS is **EUR 748,717** (=Mark to Market result).

2.3. Cross Currency Swap

2.3.1. Terminology

Definition

A currency swap (or cross-currency swap) is a contract between two parties (A and B) to **exchange two different, specific interest payments in different currencies** (1 and 2) during a term that is fixed in the contract. The interest payments are calculated on the basis of the principals of the two currencies and the interest rate for the respective term of interest.

Under a currency swap, the principal is usually exchanged. For all the transactions an exchange rate is fixed for all transactions when the swap is entered.

Beispiel

Bank A hat einen EUR 100 Mio. Festzinsempfänger-Swap mit Bank B abgeschlossen, Laufzeit fünf Jahre. Sie erhält 4,75% p.a. gegen 6-Monats-EURIBOR. Nach drei Jahren möchte Bank A die Position schließen und erhält von Bank C folgende EUR-Zinsswap-Quotierung für einen 2-Jahres Swap gegen 6-Monats-EURIBOR 4,31 – 4,35%. Die Zero-Zinsen für 1 Jahr sind 4,5%, für zwei Jahre 4,55%.

Was ist der aktuelle Marktwert der Swapposition?

Die Position von Bank A sieht folgendermaßen aus:

Bank A schließt den ursprünglichen Swap, indem sie den 2-Jahres Swap von Bank C kauft (= Festzinszahlerswap). Sie zahlt 4,35% und erhält 6-Monats-EURIBOR. Da die variablen Zinszahlungen Durchlaufposten sind, müssen nur die beiden Festzinszahlungen zur Ermittlung des Marktwertes herangezogen werden.

Das Ergebnis errechnet sich wie folgt:

Jahr	Ursprungs-geschäft	Gegen-geschäft	Ergebnis	Abzinsung $(1/(1+r)^n)$	Barwert
1	+4.750.000	–4.350.000	+400.000	0,9569378	+382.775
2	+4.750.000	–4.350.000	+400.000	0,9148543	+365.942
Gesamt					**748.717**

Der aktuelle Wert der 5-Jahres EUR-Swap beträgt **EUR 748.717,00** (= Mark-to-Market-Ergebnis).

2.3. Cross Currency Swap

2.3.1. Terminologie

Definition

Ein Cross Currency Swap (auch Currency oder Währungsswap) ist ein Vertrag zwischen zwei Parteien (A und B) über den **Austausch von unterschiedlichen, spezifizierten Zinszahlungen in verschiedenen Währungen** (1 und 2) innerhalb eines im Vertrag fixierten Zeitraumes. Die Höhe der Zinszahlung errechnet sich aus dem der jeweiligen Zinsperiode zugrundeliegenden Zinssatz und Kapitalbetrag der Währung 1 bzw. 2.

Die Notional Amount wird beim Währungsswap in der Regel ausgetauscht. Für alle Währungstransaktionen wird bei Geschäftsabschluss ein Devisenkurs fixiert.

Basically, one can divide a currency swap into **three different transactions**:

- **Initial transaction:** Exchange of the principal in different currencies 1 and 2 (initial exchange)
- **Interest payment:** Exchange of interest payments in different currencies during the swap term.
- **Final transaction:** Re-exchange of the principal in 1 and 2 (final exchange).

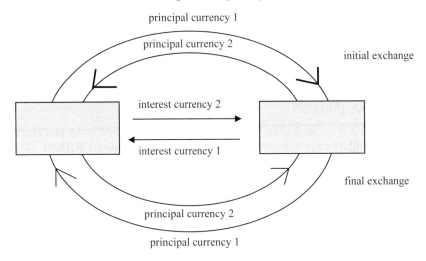

Cross currency swaps are closely related to FX swaps where only the principals are exchanged and no interest payments are made in the two currencies. The term of a currency swap is usually longer than 1 year.

Depending on the stipulated rate for the final exchange, one differentiates between "forward outright" and "par value" swap:

Forward outright: At a forward outright cross currency swap, a forward exchange rate, prevailing at the trading date, for the final exchange is fixed.

Par value: At a par value cross currency swap, the exchange rate for the initial exchange is the same as the exchange rate for the final exchange (one usually fixes the par value rate at the mid spot rate).

Note: As an exceptional case, the initial or final exchange (or both) may not take place at all.

For cross currency swaps, like for interest rate swaps, **exist several combinations** concerning the exchange of interest payments.

Üblicherweise lässt sich ein Currency- bzw. Cross Currency Swap in **drei Transaktionen** gliedern:

- **Anfangstransaktion:** Tausch der Kapitalbeträge in zwei unterschiedlichen Währungen 1 und 2 (Initial Exchange).
- **Zinstransaktion:** In der Zinstransaktion werden während der Laufzeit des Swaps Zinszahlungen in den zwei unterschiedlichen Währungen geleistet.
- **Schlusstransaktion:** Rücktausch der Kapitalbeträge in 1 und 2 (Final Exchange).

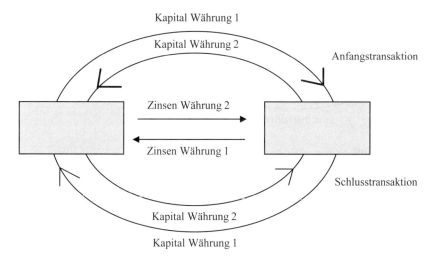

Currency Swaps sind eng verwandt mit Devisenswaps, bei denen jedoch nur der Kapitaltausch erfolgt und nicht der zusätzliche Tausch von Zinsen in den zwei Währungen. Die Laufzeit der Währungsswaps ist meist länger als 1 Jahr.

Je nach vereinbartem Kurs für die Schlusstransaktion unterscheidet man zwischen Forward Outright und Par Value.

Forward Outright: Bei einem Forward Outright Currency Swap wird für die Schlusstransaktion ein bei Geschäftsabschluss herrschender Terminkurs fixiert (ähnlich wie bei einem Devisenswap).

Par Value: Bei einem Par Value Currency Swap wird für die Anfangs- und Schlusstransaktion der gleiche Kurs fixiert (üblich ist der Kassamittekurs). Der Par Value Swap ist die übliche Variante.

Anmerkung: In Sonderfällen können die Anfangs-, die End- oder beide Transaktionen fehlen.

Vereinbarte Zinszahlungen gibt es auch bei den Währungsswaps, wie bei Zinsswaps, in allen **möglichen Kombinationen.**

Fixed against fixed

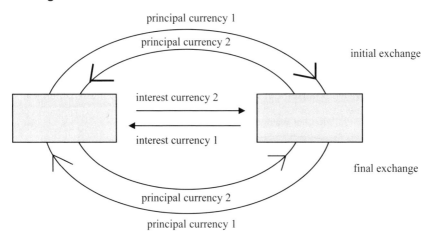

Fixed against floating

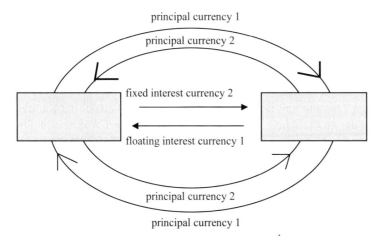

Fest gegen Fest

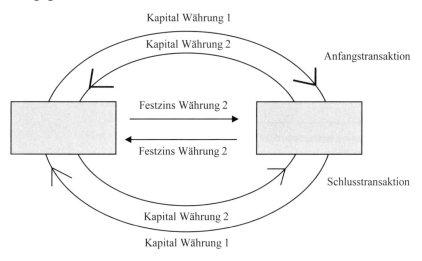

Fest gegen Variabel

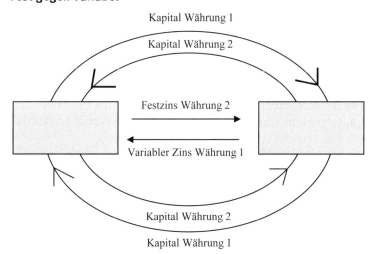

Floating against floating

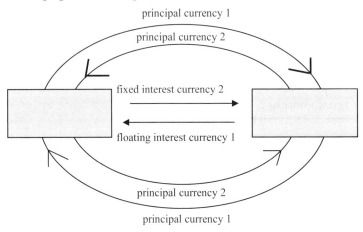

Cross currency swaps are used

- to hedge against interest rate risk and currency risk
- to exploit cost advantages resulting due to different spreads in the two capital markets involved (see 2.3.2. Application).

2.3.2. Application

Example
A Swiss bank X, with an A rating, needs USD 100 Mio for 5 years at a fixed rate and could refinance itself at 6.50 % in USD; the current yield in the capital market is 6.25 % (5 years).
X has the possibility to issue a 5-year bond in Swiss francs with an interest rate of 5.625%. The current rate in the capital market is CHF 5.50%.
The treasurer of bank X enters into a par value currency swap with an exchange of fixed interest rates:
6.25% in USD 5.50% in CHF
For both the initial and final exchange a USD/CHF rate of 1.4500 is fixed.

Variabel gegen Variabel

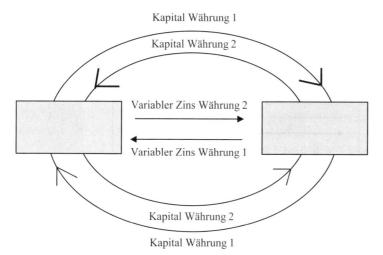

Kapital Währung 1

Kapital Währung 2

Variabler Zins Währung 2

Variabler Zins Währung 1

Kapital Währung 2

Kapital Währung 1

Currency- und Cross Currency Swaps werden unter anderem eingesetzt um,

- Zins- und Währungsrisiken abzusichern und
- Kostenvorteile, die durch unterschiedliche Spreads in zwei verschiedenen Kapitalmärkten auftreten, zu nutzen (siehe Punkt 2.3.2 Anwendung).

2.3.2. Anwendung

Beispiel
Eine Schweizer Bank (Unternehmen) X mit einem A-Rating benötigt USD 100 Mio. für fünf Jahre zu einem Festsatz und könnte sich derzeit bei einer aktuellen Kapitalmarktrendite von 6,25% (fünf Jahre) zu einem Zinssatz von 6,5% in USD refinanzieren.   In Schweizer Franken hat X die Möglichkeit, eine 5-Jahres-Festzinsemission zum Zinssatz von 5,625% zu begeben. Der aktuelle Kapitalmarktsatz beträgt in CHF 5,5%. Der Treasurer der Bank X schließt einen Par Value Currency Swap mit einem Austausch von festen Zinsen ab: 6,25% in USD   5,5% in CHF   Für die Anfangs- und Schlusstransaktion wird ein USD-CHF-Kurs von 1,4500 vereinbart.

From X's point of view the situation looks like this:

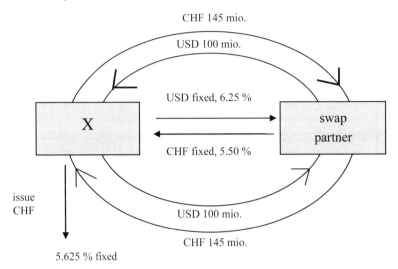

With the CHF-issue and the simultaneous currency swap, X could secure the needed USD 100 Mio. On the CHF side, a loss of 0.125% will be incurred (5.625% expenditure for the issue – 5.50% interest return on the swap). As for the USD, there is just an expenditure of 6.25% from the currency swap.

Theoretically, the total expenditure of the deal is:

6.250 % in USD
0.125 % in CHF

6.375 %

We do not go into the so-called conversion factors that are needed to transfer spreads from one currency to another. In this example we assume that 1/8% in CHF equals 1/8% in USD. Under the currency swap, X was able to raise the USD 1/8% cheaper than in a possible USD issue (6.50%).

Note: You have still to compare the advantages from the swap with the disadvantages, e.g. the required equity costs and the required limits.

Die Position für X stellt sich wie folgt dar:

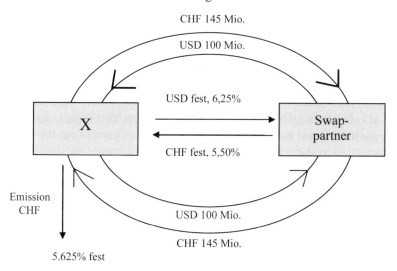

X konnte sich durch die CHF-Emission und den parallelen Abschluss des Currency Swaps die benötigten USD 100 Mio. sichern. In CHF wird ein Verlust von 0,125% realisiert (5,625% Zinsaufwand für Emission – 5,5% Zinsertrag im Currency Swap). In USD gibt es lediglich einen Zinsausgang aus dem Currency Swap in Höhe von 6,25%.

Der Gesamtzinsaufwand für X beträgt also theoretisch:

6,250% in USD
0,125% in CHF
6,375%

Auf sogenannte Conversion-Faktoren, die zur Umrechnung der Spreads von einer in die andere Währung zu berücksichtigen sind, soll hier nicht näher eingegangen werden. Das Beispiel unterstellt, dass 1/8% in CHF 1/8% in USD entspricht. Über die Konstruktion mit einem Währungsswap konnte sich X somit die USD um 1/8% günstiger beschaffen als mit einer USD-Emission (6,5%).

Anmerkung: Der Refinanzierungsvergünstigung sind die durch den Currency- bzw. Cross Currency Swap anfallenden Eigenkapitalkosten und die dazu notwendigen Partnerlimite entgegenzusetzen.

2.4. Reversal, Close Out and Assignment

There are three different ways of closing an open swap position:

- reversal
- closing-out
- assignment

Reversal

A reversal is the **most common way to close an interest rate swap**. In this case, the bank enters a **second, opposite interest rate swap** (usually with a third party) over the same principal and the same term as the original swap. Thereby, both interest rate swaps lead to fixed profits and losses in the future. Nevertheless, they are still in the balance sheet and must be taken into account when determining the respective limits and the equity cover.

Closing-out

A closing-out is an **early termination of the swap deal**. Both parties agree to eliminate the interest rate swap from their books. The outstanding cash flows are **marked-to-market**. Usually, one of the counterparties has to make a settlement payment. Since in a closing-out the swap is eliminated from the books, no receivables or liabilities have to be considered when the partner limits or the equity cover are determined.

Assignment

Transferring the swap to a third party can also close a swap deal. This new party must agree to accept the original swap on all the original conditions and must accept the swap's counterparty. Furthermore, the original counterparty must give his consent to the new partner. With an assignment, usually an **up-front payment** has to be made if the current market rates differ from the original rates of the interest rate swap.

2.4. Reversal, Close Out und Assignment

Eine Swapposition kann auf drei Arten geschlossen werden:

- Reversal
- Close Out
- Assignment

Reversal

Ein Reversal ist die **häufigste Art, einen Zinsswap zu schließen.** Die Bank schließt einen **zweiten gegenläufigen Zinsswap** (normalerweise mit einem anderen Partner) über den gleichen Betrag und die gleiche Laufzeit ab. Aus den Zinszahlungen entstehen somit in der Zukunft fixierte Gewinne oder Verluste. **Beide Zinsswaps bleiben jedoch erhalten** und sind bei der Ermittlung der jeweiligen Partnerlimite und Eigenkapitalunterlegungen zu berücksichtigen.

Close Out

Ein Closing Out ist das **vorzeitige Beenden eines Swapvertrages.** Beide Partner im Swap kommen überein, den Zinsswap aus ihren Büchern zu eliminieren und die **Differenz zum aktuellen Marktpreis,** zum heutigen Datum, **für die Gesamtlaufzeit des Swaps am selben Tag zu bezahlen.** Die Zahlung, die von einem der beiden Partner zu leisten ist, wird analog der Darstellung der Mark-to-Market-Bewertung berechnet. Da es durch ein Closing Out zu keinen zukünftigen Forderungen und Verbindlichkeiten durch diesen Swap kommen kann, ist das Geschäft auch bei den Partnerlimiten und der Eigenkapitalunterlegung nicht mehr zu berücksichtigen.

Assignment

Ein Swapgeschäft kann auch durch die **Weitergabe des Swaps an einen dritten Partner** geschlossen werden. Der neue Partner im Zinsswap muss jedoch bereit sein, diesen ursprünglichen Swap (mit allen Vereinbarungen) zu übernehmen und den Partner im Swapgeschäft zu akzeptieren. Auch der ursprüngliche Partner muss damit einverstanden sein, dass er jetzt einen neuen Partner in den Büchern hat. Üblicherweise fällt bei diesem Assignment eine **Up-Front-Zahlung** an, wenn sich die Marktsätze gegenüber den Ursprungssätzen verändert haben.

Summary

Since the beginning of the 80s the term "swap" is used for FX outright transactions and another group of financial instruments, namely interest rate swaps. Ever since, interest rate swaps have grown to become one of the most important instruments in the financial market. The World Bank and IBM undertook one of the first recorded swap transactions in August 1981.

An interest rate swap is a contract between two parties ("A" and "B") to exchange different specified interest payments in the same currency during a term that is stated in the contract. The amount of the interest payment is calculated on the underlying principal and the interest rate of the respective interest period. The principal is not exchanged under an interest rate swap. We differentiate between the following types of swaps: interest rate swaps, currency swaps, cross currency swaps and credit swaps, and swaps of the second and third generation.

Swaps can be classified with regard the types of interest payment: coupon swap, basis swap and cross currency interest swap. A coupon swap (also called fixed-rate interest swap, par swap, or plain vanilla swap) is a contract between two parties ("A" and "B") to exchange a fixed-rate interest payment for a floating-rate interest payment. A basis swap is the exchange of two different floating interest rates in the same currency. A cross currency interest rate swap is the exchange of two interest rates in different currencies.

Fixed-rate interest swaps are usually quoted as a fixed interest rate for the term on the basis of the reference rate (e.g. LIBOR) without spread, i.e. flat.

For floating interest rate payments, the interest rate is adjusted on fixing date, i.e. the interest rate for the following interest period is fixed. Usually, the fixing of swap rates takes place two working days before the interest period starts (exceptions: GBP same-day fixing). The frequency of interest payments can be set freely (monthly, quarterly, six-monthly, annually, etc.). With EUR and CHF annual payments are usual, with USD/GBP/JPY semi-annual payments are quite common. The calculation of interest payments is the same as the practice on the respective capital markets. If, in a swap, interest payments between the counterparties flow on the same date, only the difference between the interest payments, i.e. the net amount, is exchanged.

Zusammenfassung

Seit Anfang der 80er-Jahre wird der Begriff „Swap" – also Tauschgeschäft – neben der Sonderform der Devisentermingeschäfte auch für eine Gruppe weiterer Finanzinstrumente verwendet, die Zinsswaps. Die Zinsswaps (häufig auch nur „Swaps" genannt) haben sich seither zu den wichtigsten Innovationen des Finanzmarktes entwickelt. Die erste bekannte Swaptransaktion wurde im August 1981 zwischen der Weltbank und IBM abgeschlossen.

Ein Zinsswap ist ein Vertrag zwischen zwei Parteien über den Austausch unterschiedlicher, spezifizierter Zinszahlungen in einer Währung während eines im Vertrag fixierten Zeitraums. Die Höhe der Zinszahlung ergibt sich aus dem der jeweiligen Zinsperiode zugrundeliegenden Zinssatz und Kapitalbetrag, auch „Notional Amount" genannt. Die Notional Amount wird beim Zinsswap nicht ausgetauscht. Man unterscheidet folgende Arten von Zinsswaps: Zinsswaps (Interest Rate Swaps), FX-Swaps, Cross Currency Swaps und Kredit- und andere Swaps der zweiten und dritten Generation.

Je nach Art der Zinsvereinbarung unterscheidet man zwischen Kuponswap (Festzinsswap), Basisswap und Cross Currency Interest Rate Swap. Ein Kuponswap (auch Festzinsswap, Par Swap oder Plain Vanilla Swap genannt) ist ein Vertrag zwischen zwei Parteien über den Austausch einer fixen Zinszahlung gegen eine variable Zinszahlung, berechnet auf einen fixierten Nominalbetrag für eine vereinbarte Laufzeit. Bei einem Basisswap werden zwei unterschiedliche, variable Zinssätze in einer Währung ausgetauscht. Als Cross Currency Interest Rate Swap wird der Austausch von zwei Zinssätzen in unterschiedlichen Währungen bezeichnet.

Der Nominalbetrag (Notional Amount) ist der der Zinsberechnung zugrundeliegende Kapitalbetrag im Swap. Festzinsswaps werden üblicherweise auf der Basis Referenzzinssatz (z.B. LIBOR) ohne Spread, d.h. flat, als Festzinssatz für die Laufzeit quotiert. Die Quotierung der festen Seite kann durch eine Zinsquotierung (z.B. 5,2%) oder mit einem Spread zu der aktuellen Rendite (üblicherweise) von Staatspapieren (gängig in USD) erfolgen.

Bei der variablen Zinszahlung ist der Zinsfixing-Tag jener Tag, an dem die Zinsanpassung stattfindet, d.h. an dem der Zinssatz für eine Zinsperiode festgesetzt wird. Das Fixing bei Swaps erfolgt in der Regel zwei Bankarbeitstage vor dem Beginn jeder Zinsperiode (Ausnahme: GBP taggleich). Die Zinszahlungen erfolgen üblicherweise am Ende jeder Zinsperiode (Ausnahme: z.B. EONIA-Swaps). Üblicherweise wird die Zinszahlung analog den Usancen der entsprechenden Währung für Geldmarktgeschäfte berechnet (Money Market Terms). Bei der festen Zinszahlung ist die Zahlungsfrequenz beim Abschluss frei vereinbar (monatlich, vierteljährlich, halbjährlich, jährlich etc.). In den Währungen EUR und CHF erfolgt sie im Allgemeinen jährlich, in USD, GBP, JPY ist halbjährliche Zinszahlung üblich. Die Zinszahlungsberechnung entspricht den Usancen des jeweiligen Kapitalmarktes.

Fallen die sich im Swap gegenüberstehenden Zinszahlungsverpflichtungen auf den gleichen Termin, fließt üblicherweise nur die Differenz zwischen den beiden Zinszahlungen, also der Nettobetrag.

The terms "asset swap" and "liability swap" are used according to the side of the balance sheet that is changed by the swap transaction.

Interest rate swaps are often used to exploit the so-called comparative advantage. This term was coined by David Ricardo, who in the 19th century developed the theory of comparative advantage for the international exchange of goods. Applied to the financial market, the theory states that the exchange of different interest rates can be profitable for both parties if they encounter different conditions on the different markets.

To evaluate swaps at market interest rates (a "mark-to-market" evaluation) the variable cash-flows (floating rate payments) have to be compared to the fixed rate payments.

In order to make cash flows of different times comparable, the present values of the cash flows are calculated (with zero rates).

A currency swap (or cross-currency swap) is a contract between two parties (A and B) to exchange two different specific interest payments in different currencies (1 and 2) during a term that is fixed in the contract. The interest payments are calculated on the basis of the principals of the two currencies and the interest rate for the respective term of interest. Under a currency swap, the principal is usually exchanged. For all transactions an exchange rate is fixed for all transactions when the swap is entered. Cross-currency swaps are closely related to FX swaps where only the principals are exchanged and no interest payments are made in the two currencies. The term of a currency swap is usually longer than one year. Cross-currency swaps are used to hedge against interest rate risk and currency risk and to exploit cost advantages due to different spreads in the two capital markets involved.

There are three different ways of closing an open swap position: reversal, closing-out or assignment. A reversal is the most common way to close an interest rate swap. In this case, the bank enters a second, opposite interest rate swap (usually with a third party) over the same principal and the same term as the original swap. A closing-out is an early termination of the swap deal. Transferring the swap to a third party can also close a swap deal (assignment).

Zur Kennzeichnung jener Seite der Bilanz, die durch die Swaptransaktion verändert werden soll, werden die Bezeichnung Asset Swap (Aktiv-Swap) und Liability Swap (Passiv-Swap) verwendet.

Bei Unternehmen (oder Banken) mit unterschiedlichen Ratings werden Zinsswaps öfter zur Nutzung sogenannter komparativer Vorteile eingesetzt. Diese Bezeichnung entstammt der Theorie von David Ricardo, der am Beginn des 19. Jahrhunderts das Prinzip der komparativen Vorteile für den internationalen Güteraustausch entwickelte. Angewendet auf den Finanzmarkt bedeutet dieses Prinzip, dass der Austausch von unterschiedlichen Zinssätzen für beide Partner profitabel sein kann, wenn die beiden Partner unterschiedliche Konditionen an den verschiedenen Märkten erhalten.

Um einen Zinsswap „Mark-to-Market" bewerten zu können, ist das Ergebnis des Zinsswaps bei Schließung der Position zu aktuellen Marktpreisen zu berechnen. Es werden die Cashflows aus den variablen und festen Zinszahlungen gegenübergestellt und die Barwerte der Netto-Cashflows ermittelt. Für die Barwert-Rechnung werden Zero-Zinsen verwendet.

Ein Cross Currency Swap (auch Currency- oder Währungsswap) ist ein Vertrag zwischen zwei Parteien über den Austausch von unterschiedlichen, spezifizierten Zinszahlungen in verschiedenen Währungen innerhalb eines im Vertrag fixierten Zeitraumes. Die Notional Amount wird beim Währungsswap in der Regel ausgetauscht. Für alle Währungstransaktionen wird bei Geschäftsabschluss ein Devisenkurs fixiert. Currency Swaps sind eng verwandt mit Devisenswaps, bei denen jedoch nur der Kapitalaustausch erfolgt und nicht der zusätzliche Tausch von Zinsen in den zwei Währungen. Die Laufzeit der Währungsswaps ist meist länger als ein Jahr. Currency- und Cross Currency Swaps werden unter anderem eingesetzt, um Zins- und Währungsrisiken abzusichern und um Kostenvorteile, die durch unterschiedliche Spreads in zwei verschiedenen Kapitalmärkten auftreten, zu nutzen.

Eine Swapposition kann auf drei Arten geschlossen werden: Reversal, Close Out oder Assignment. Ein Reversal ist die häufigste Art, einen Zinsswap zu schließen. Hier schließt die Bank einen zweiten gegenläufigen Zinsswap (normalerweise mit einem anderen Partner) über den gleichen Betrag und die gleiche Laufzeit ab. Ein Closing Out ist das vorzeitige Beenden eines Swapvertrages. Beide Partner im Swap kommen überein, den Zinsswap aus ihren Büchern zu eliminieren und die Differenz zum aktuellen Marktpreis, zum heutigen Datum, für die Gesamtlaufzeit des Swaps am selben Tag zu bezahlen. Unter Assignment versteht man die Weitergabe des Swaps an einen dritten Partner.

2.5. Practice Questions

1. Explain the differences between public agent and anonymous agent!
2. In a standard interest rate swap the notional amount …
   a) does not change during the life of the swap.
   b) is calculated anew for every interest payment
   c) is exchanged as collateral at the beginning.
   d) is repaid in instalments at every exchange of interest
3. A bank agrees to pay fixed JPY in exchange for 6-month USD LIBOR in a 5-year contract. How is this swap called?
   a) FX swap
   b) basis swap
   c) coupon swap
   d) cross currency swap
4. Explain the differences between spot swaps and forward swaps!
5. Which of the following is NOT a basis or index swap?
   a) EURIBOR to USD-LIBOR
   b) 12-month USD-LIBOR to prime rate
   c) 3-month USD-LIBOR to 6-month USD-LIBOR
   d) 6-month USD-LIBOR to AUD fixed
6. Which of the following instruments is exchange-traded?
   a) FRA
   b) cross currency swap
   c) IRS
   d) futures
7. Which of the following types of bonds is often used as the basis for the pricing of asset swaps?
   a) junk bonds
   b) US treasuries
   c) convertible bonds
   d) collared FRNs
8. Which of the following constructions is a liability swap?
   a) swap of debt capital into equity
   b) swap of fixed interest income of a EUR bond into variable EUR payments
   c) swap of fixed interest income of a EUR bond into fixed USD interest income
   d) swap of fixed interest obligations of an issued EUR bond into variable EUR payments
9. Near the end of the trading day a swap market maker is the net receiver of a fixed rate in a 5-year USD fixed/floating swap. Which of the following is the most appropriate overnight hedge for this position?
   a) sell a FRA
   b) leave it open because bond prices are falling
   c) buy a long bond in the cash market
   d) sell a 5-year treasury note future

2.5. Wiederholungsfragen

1. Erklären Sie den Unterschied zwischen offener und anonymer Vermittlung von Banken!

2. Bei einem Standard-Zinsswap wird der zugrundeliegende Kapitalbetrag ...
   a) während der Swaplaufzeit nicht verändert.
   b) für jede Zinszahlung neu berechnet.
   c) zu Beginn als Sicherheit ausgetauscht.
   d) bei jedem Zinsaustausch aliquot bezahlt.

3. Sie schließen mit einer anderen Bank einen 5-Jahres-Swap ab, indem Sie fixe JPY gegen 6-Monats-USD-LIBOR tauschen. Wie nennt man diesen Swap?
   a) FX-Swap
   b) Basisswap
   c) Kuponswap
   d) Cross Currency Swap

4. Erklären Sie den Unterschied zwischen Spot Swaps und Forward Swaps!

5. Welches der folgenden Geschäfte ist kein Basis- oder Indexswap?
   a) EURIBOR gegen USD-LIBOR
   b) 12-Monats-USD-LIBOR gegen Prime Rate
   c) 3-Monats-USD-LIBOR gegen 6-Monats-USD-LIBOR
   d) 6-Monats-USD-LIBOR gegen AUD fixed

6. Welches der folgenden Instrumente ist börsengehandelt?
   a) FRA
   b) Cross Currency Swap
   c) IRS
   d) Futures

7. Welcher Anleihetyp dient oft als Basis für die Preisfestsetzung von Asset Swaps?
   a) Junk Bonds
   b) US-Treasuries
   c) Wandelschuldverschreibung
   d) Collared FRNs

8. Welche der angeführten Konstruktionen ist ein Liability Swap?
   a) Tausch von Fremdkapital in Eigenkapital
   b) Fixzinszahlungen aus einer EUR-Emission geswapt in variable EUR-Zinszahlungen
   c) Fixzinszahlungen aus einer EUR-Emission geswapt in fixe USD-Zinszahlungen
   d) Fixzinseingänge aus einem USD-Bond geswapt in variable USD-Zinsverpflichtungen

9. Knapp vor Ende des Handelstages ist ein Market Maker Festzinsempfänger in einem 5-Jahres-USD Festzinsempfänger-Swap. Was ist der geeignetste Overnight-Hedge?
   a) Verkauf eines FRA
   b) offen lassen, weil die Anleihenpreise fallen
   c) Kauf einer langfristigen Anleihe am Geldmarkt
   d) Verkauf eines 5-Jahres-Treasury-Note-Futures

10. You have the following interest rate swap: You pay fixed 10% and receive the 3-month LIBOR, remaining time 5 years. How could you close your interest position?
    a) borrow for 1 year and lend at 3-month LIBOR
    b) lend for 1 year and borrow for 1 year
    c) lend for 5 years and lend for 3 months
    d) lend for 5 years and borrow at 3-month LIBOR

11. How is a swap valued in a closing-out?
    a) against LIBOR
    b) at the reference rate
    c) marked-to-market
    d) at the purchase price

12. What are the three transactions of a cross currency swap?

13. Which of the following is an alternative description of a 5-year cross currency swap?
    a) a series of forward FX transactions
    b) a series of currency options at the same strike price
    c) a series of FRA at the same contract price
    d) A single long-term forward FX transaction

14. Which of the following is a characteristic of a forward outright currency swap?
    a) There is no exchange of principal.
    b) The exchange rate for the end transaction is fixed on maturity date.
    c) The exchange rate for the end transaction is fixed on start date.
    d) The same exchange rate is fixed for the start and end transactions.

15. What are the possibilities to close a swap?
    a) shut out
    b) closing out
    c) reversal
    d) roll over
    e) CAP

10. Sie haben folgenden Zinsswap: Sie zahlen 10% fix und erhalten den 3-Monats-LI-BOR, Restlaufzeit 5 Jahre. Mit welchen Transaktionen können Sie die Zinsposition schließen?
    a) Geld auf 1 Jahr geben und Geld zu 3-Monats-LIBOR geben
    b) Geld auf 1 Jahr geben und Geld auf 1 Jahr nehmen
    c) Geld auf 5 Jahre geben und Geld auf 3 Monate geben
    d) Geld auf 5 Jahre geben und Geld zu 3-Monats-LIBOR nehmen

11. Wie wird ein Swap beim Closing Out bewertet?
    a) gegen LIBOR
    b) zum Referenzsatz
    c) Mark-to-Market
    d) zum Anschaffungskurs

12. In welche drei Transaktionen lässt sich ein Cross Currency Swap gliedern?

13. Wie kann ein 5-Jahres-Cross-Currency-Swap alternativ beschrieben werden?
    a) Serie von Termin FX-Transaktionen
    b) Serie von Devisenoptionen zum selben Ausübungspreis
    c) Serie von FRAs zum selben FRA-Preis
    d) eine einzige langfristige Termin-FX-Transaktion

14. Was ist ein Charakteristikum eines Forward-Outright-Currency Swap?
    a) Es werden keine Kapitalbeträge ausgetauscht.
    b) Der Kurs der Schlusstransaktion wird am Fälligkeitstag fixiert.
    c) Der Kurs der Schlusstransaktion ist der Terminkurs bei Geschäftsabschluss.
    d) Für die Anfangs- und Schlusstransaktion wird der gleiche Kurs fixiert.

15. Mit welchen Möglichkeiten können Sie einen Swap schließen?
    a) Shut Out
    b) Closing Out
    c) Reversal
    d) Roll-over
    e) CAP

3. Interest Rate Options

In this chapter you learn ...

- what is meant by an interest rate option.
- about the differences between call and put options.
- what is meant by underlying and strike price.
- about the differences between American and European options.
- about the differences between options at, in and out of the money.
- about the components of the option premium.
- about the influences on the option premium.
- what is meant by a cap.
- how a cap is used.
- what is meant by a floor.
- how a floor is used.
- what is meant by a collar.
- how a collar is used.
- what is meant by futures options.
- how futures options are used.
- what is meant by bond options.
- how bond options are used.
- what is meant by swaptions.
- how swaptions are used.

3.1. Terminology

An **interest rate option** is an agreement between two parties. It grants one party (buyer) the right to buy (call option) or sell (put option) a financial instrument at a fixed price at a defined date (or during a defined period of time).

The buyer of an option does not have to exercise this right. For this right, the buyer pays a **certain price (premium)** to the option seller. On the other hand, the seller has no control on the possible exercise.

Call (option to buy)

With a call option the buyer gets the **right to buy a financial instrument at defined conditions**. The seller has the obligation to deliver this instrument at the agreed conditions if the buyer exercises the right to purchase.

Put (option to sell)

With a put option the buyer has the **right to sell a financial instrument at agreed conditions**. The seller has the obligation to receive this instrument at the agreed conditions if the buyer exercises his right to sell.

3. Zinsoptionen

In diesem Kapitel lernen Sie ...

- was man unter einer Zinsoption versteht.
- den Unterschied zwischen Call- und Put-Option kennen.
- was man unter Underlying und Strike-Preis versteht.
- den Unterschied zwischen Amerikanischer und Europäischer Option kennen.
- den Unterschied zwischen Optionen am, im und aus dem Geld kennen.
- woraus sich die Optionsprämie zusammensetzt.
- wovon die Optionsprämie beeinflusst wird.
- was man unter einem Cap versteht.
- wozu ein Cap verwendet wird.
- was man unter einem Floor versteht.
- wozu ein Floor verwendet wird.
- was man unter einem Collar versteht.
- wozu ein Collar verwendet wird.
- was man unter Optionen auf Futures versteht.
- wozu Optionen auf Futures verwendet werden.
- was man unter Bond-Optionen versteht.
- wozu Bond-Optionen verwendet werden.
- was man unter Swaptions versteht.
- wozu Swaptions verwendet werden.

3.1. Terminologie

Eine **Zinsoption** ist eine Vereinbarung zwischen zwei Parteien, die einer der beiden Parteien (dem Käufer) das Recht einräumt, ein Finanzinstrument zu einem vorher fixierten Preis zu einem bestimmten Datum (oder einer fixierten Zeitspanne) zu kaufen (Call-Option) oder zu verkaufen (Put-Option).

Der Käufer der Option geht jedoch im Optionskontrakt **keine Verpflichtung** ein, von diesem Recht Gebrauch zu machen. Für dieses Recht zahlt er dem Verkäufer einen Preis, nämlich die **Optionsprämie.** Der Verkäufer hat keine Möglichkeit zu entscheiden, ob das Optionsrecht ausgenutzt wird oder nicht.

Call (Kaufoption)

Eine Call-Option gibt dem Käufer das **Recht, zu definierten Konditionen ein Finanzinstrument zu kaufen.** Für den Verkäufer gilt die Verpflichtung, das zugrundeliegende Instrument zu den vorher vereinbarten Bedingungen zu liefern, wenn der Käufer sein Kaufrecht ausüben will.

Put (Verkaufsoption)

Eine Put-Option gibt dem Käufer das **Recht, zu definierten Konditionen ein Finanzinstrument zu verkaufen.** Für den Verkäufer ist damit die Option die Verpflichtung, das zugrundeliegende Instrument zu den vorher vereinbarten Bedingungen zu kaufen, wenn der Optionskäufer verkaufen will.

Underlying

The underlying instrument is the one, which is defined in the contract of the option. The underlying has to be delivered or bought at an agreed price or interest rate if the option is exercised.

Strike price/basis price

The strike price is the price that is **defined in the option's contract** if the option is exercised.

American option

An American option can be **exercised any time during the life of the option**.

European option

An European option can be **exercised only at expiry**.

At the money

If an option is "at the money" its **strike price** is almost the **same as the current market price**.

In the money

An option is "in the money" if the **strike price** is either **below (call option) or above (put option) the market price** of the underlying, i.e. "in this moment" one would exercise the option.

Out of the money

An option is "out of the money" if the **strike price** is either **above (call option) or below (put option) the market price** of the underlying, i.e. in this case one would not exercise the option.

Premium

The option's premium is the **price the buyer must pay to the seller**.

Intrinsic value

The option's intrinsic value is **part of the option's premium**. For an in the money option, it represents the amount by which the strike price is either below (call option) or above (put option) the price of the underlying.

Time value

The option's time value is part of the option's premium. It is influenced by

- the **life of the option**,
- by the expectations on the **volatility** of the underlying, and
- by the **ratio between market price and strike price**.

premium = intrinsic value + time value

Basisinstrument (Underlying)

Das Basisinstrument ist **das im Optionskontrakt definierte Instrument,** das bei Ausübung der Option mit dem vorher fixierten Preis oder Zinssatz zu liefern oder zu kaufen ist.

Strike-Preis/Ausübungspreis/Basispreis

Der Ausübungspreis ist der **im Optionskontrakt fixierte Preis bei Ausübung.**

Amerikanische Option

Eine amerikanische Option ist eine Option, die **an jedem Handelstag während ihrer Laufzeit ausgeübt** werden kann.

Europäische Option

Eine europäische Option ist eine Option, die **nur am letzten Tag ihrer Laufzeit ausgeübt** werden kann.

At the money/Am Geld

Eine Option „at the money" ist eine Option, deren **Strike-Preis** in etwa **dem Marktpreis des Underlying entspricht.**

In the money/Im Geld

Eine Option „in the money" ist eine Option, deren **Strike-Preis beim Call niedriger bzw. beim Put höher als der Marktpreis des Underlying** ist, d.h., die Option würde „jetzt" ausgeübt.

Out of money/Aus dem Geld

Eine Option „out of Money" ist eine Option, deren **Strike-Preis beim Call höher bzw. beim Put niedriger als der Marktpreis des Underlying** ist, d.h., die Option würde „im Moment" nicht ausgeübt.

Optionsprämie

Die Optionsprämie ist der **Preis,** den der Käufer dem Verkäufer bezahlt, **um das Optionsrecht zu erwerben.**

Innerer Wert

Der innere Wert einer Option ist ein **Teil der Optionsprämie.** Er ist der **Betrag, um den der Strike-Preis** einer In-the-money-Option beim Call unter bzw. beim Put **über dem Marktpreis des Underlying liegt.** Daher haben nur Optionen „in the money" einen inneren Wert.

Zeitwert

Der Zeitwert einer Option ist **Bestandteil der Optionsprämie.** Er wird von

- der **Laufzeit,**
- der von den Marktteilnehmern erwarteten **Volatilität** des Basiswertes und
- vom **Verhältnis Marktpreis zu Strike-Preis**

beeinflusst.

Optionsprämie = Innerer Wert + Zeitwert

3.2. Cap

A Cap is a **contract between two parties (OTC) over an interest rate ceiling** with regard to the principal.

If at certain dates (fixing dates) the agreed reference rate (usually LIBOR) is above the defined interest rate (strike price) **the seller has to settle the difference between reference rate and interest rate ceiling** and has to pay the buyer. If at the fixing dates the reference rate is below the strike price no payments are made.

Caps can be used by the buyer of the option as an **insurance against rising interest rates**. If you choose a floating refinancing expecting that interest rates will fall, then the Cap makes sure that the refinancing will not be more expensive than the rate fixed in the cap. On the other hand, the buyer takes full **advantage of the expected fall in the interest rates**.

Quotation

The quotation of Caps is usually done **on the basis of the premium**, which is a **single payment** when the contract is settled.

If a Cap for 100 Mio is quoted at 2.50%, the buyer of the option has to pay 2.5 Mio (100,000,000 x 0.025) once when the contract is settled.

Pricing

Technically, Caps can be seen as a **series of options on a series of FRAs on 3-month or 6-month interest rates**. Since an FRA is a forward on a future money market rate and an FRA purchase is a hedge against rising interest rates, a Cap represents a **series of options on FRA purchases**.

The FRA, or rather the series of FRAs, is therefore the underlying for the Cap and is important for determining whether an option is in the money, at the money, or out of the money. According to our rules for FRAs (forward rates) the yield curve is the main factor of influence when determining the future interest rates. The interest rate ceiling that is fixed by the contract has to be compared to the respective forward rates for each interest period (and not to the current money market rates) in order to determine the intrinsic value of the CAP.

Example		
6-month interest rate:	3.50%	days: 180
12-month interest rate:	3.75%	days: 360
6/12 forward rate:	3.93%	days: 180

Under a Cap with an interest rate ceiling of 3.75% the first term of interest would be in the money with 0.18% (3.93% – 3.75%).

3.2. Zinsobergrenze (Cap)

Ein Cap ist eine **vertragliche Vereinbarung zwischen zwei Parteien (OTC) über eine fixierte Zinsobergrenze**, bezogen auf einen zugrundeliegenden nominellen Kapitalbetrag.

Fixiert der festgelegte Referenzsatz (i.d.R. LIBOR bzw. EURIBOR) zu vorher definierten Zeitpunkten über der vertraglich fixierten Zinsobergrenze (Strike-Preis), so **zahlt der Verkäufer der Option dem Optionskäufer die Differenz zwischen Zinsobergrenze und Referenzsatz** aus. Fixiert der Referenzsatz zu einem der definierten Zeitpunkte unter dem Strike-Preis, so findet keine Zahlung zu diesem Termin statt.

Caps können damit für den Käufer der Option **Absicherungen gegen steigende Zinsen** darstellen. Wird eine variable Refinanzierung mit der Zinsmeinung in Anspruch genommen, dass die Zinsen eher fallen werden, ist der Cap die Versicherung, dass die Refinanzierung nicht teurer wird als die im Cap-Vertrag abgesicherte Basis. Andererseits kann auch voll **vom erwarteten Zinsrückgang profitiert** werden.

Quotierung

Die Quotierung von Caps erfolgt üblicherweise **über die Optionsprämie.** Sie stellt i.d.R. eine **Einmalzahlung** bei Abschluss des Geschäftes dar.

Wird für ein Cap-Programm von 100 Mio. eine Quotierung von 2,5% angegeben, so bedeutet dies, dass der Käufer der Option bei Abschluss des Geschäftes eine Einmalzahlung von 2,5 Mio. (100.000.000 × 0,025) leisten muss.

Preisfindung

Technisch gesehen ergeben Caps eine **Serie von Optionen mit zunehmend langer Vorlaufzeit auf 3- oder 6-Monats-Zinssätze.** Da ein FRA ein Termingeschäft auf einen zukünftigen Geldmarktsatz ist und ein FRA-Kauf die Absicherung gegen steigende Zinsen, ist ein Cap die **Serie der Optionen auf gekaufte FRAs** (sogenannte Caplets).

Der FRA oder besser die **Serie der FRAs** ist damit der **Basiswert des Caps** und ist auch bei der Bestimmung, ob die Option im Geld, am Geld oder aus dem Geld ist, heranzuziehen. Entsprechend unserer Regeln bei FRAs (Forward-Sätzen) ist die **Zinskurve** ein Haupteinflussfaktor bei der Bestimmung der Terminpreise. Die im Cap-Programm fixierte Zinsobergrenze muss für die Bestimmung des inneren Wertes mit den entsprechenden Forward-Sätzen für die einzelnen Zinsperioden und nicht mit den aktuellen Geldmarktsätzen verglichen werden.

Beispiel		
6-Monats-Zinssatz:	3,50%	180 Tage
12-Monats-Zinssatz:	3,75%	360 Tage
6/12-Forward-Satz:	3,93%	180 Tage

Bei einem Cap-Programm mit einer Zinsobergrenze von 3,75% wäre damit die erste Zinsperiode mit 0,18% (3,93% – 3,75%) im Geld.

Application

A bank needs a **fixed refinancing for 5 years** and has the possibility to borrow money at a fixed rate of 6.00% or at a floating rate of LIBOR. The treasurer in charge expects the interest rates to fall, but is not willing (or able) to take on the whole risk involved in a floating refinancing. He decides to buy a Cap with a strike price of 6.00% (interest rate ceiling) on the whole volume, for which he has to pay 2.50% premium.

First, one has to make the option's premium comparable over the years – since it is due only once.

Ignoring compound interest (for reasons of simplicity), the premium of 2.50% equals an annual cost of $0.50\% \times \left(\dfrac{2.50\%}{5}\right)$.

The following diagram shows the cost of refinancing for each period.

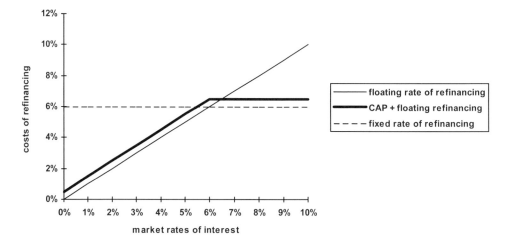

If the reference rate is below 6.00% the option expires. The bank just has to bear the cost of refinancing plus the annualised premium of the option. If the reference rate is exactly 6.00% the total cost of refinancing is 6.50% (6.00% LIBOR + 0.50% annualised premium). For example, if LIBOR is at 5.00%, the total cost is 5.50 % (5.00% LIBOR + 0.50% premium).

Assuming that LIBOR rises above 6.00% the option will be exercised and the **total cost of refinancing consists of the interest rate ceiling and the option's premium**. At an assumed LIBOR rate of 7.00% the effective refinancing cost is 7.00% but from the Cap one gets the difference of 1.00% (LIBOR – interest rate ceiling), so the total cost adds up to 6.50% (7.00% LIBOR – 1.00% settlement payment of the Cap + 0.50% annualised premium of the option). Even if the reference rate rises up to 10%, the total refinancing costs remain at 6.50% (10.00 % – 4.00% + 0.50%).

Thereby, an **asymmetric P & L profile** develops that is typical for options; it enables the buyer of the Cap to **hedge against rising interest rates**, whereas he still has an **"unlimited" profit potential if the interest rates fall**.

Anwendung

Bank (Unternehmen) A braucht eine **feste Refinanzierung auf fünf Jahre** und hat die Möglichkeit, das benötigte Geld zu einem festen Satz von 6% oder zu einem variablen LIBOR-Satz aufzunehmen. Der zuständige Treasurer vertritt die Marktmeinung, dass die Zinsen eher fallen werden, möchte jedoch nicht das volle Risiko einer variablen Refinanzierung übernehmen. Er beschließt, einen Cap mit einem Strike-Preis von 6% für das gesamte Volumen zu kaufen, für den er 2,5% Prämie zahlen muss.

Als erster Schritt muss zum Zwecke der Vergleichbarkeit die **Optionsprämie annualisiert** werden. Ohne Berücksichtigung der Zinseszinsen (zur Vereinfachung) ergibt die 2,5% Prämie p.a. Kosten von $0,50\% \times \left(\dfrac{2,50\%}{5}\right)$.

Die folgende Grafik zeigt die Refinanzierungskosten für die einzelnen Perioden an:

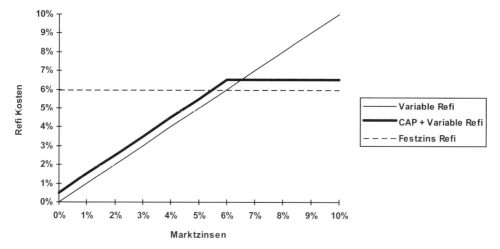

Liegt der Referenzsatz unter 6%, so verfällt die Option. Bank (Unternehmen) A hat also nur die Kosten der Refinanzierung zuzüglich der annualisierten Optionsprämie zu tragen. Liegt der Referenzsatz bei genau 6%, so sind die Gesamtkosten der Refinanzierung 6,5% (6% LIBOR + 0,5% annualisierte Optionsprämie). Liegt der LIBOR beispielsweise bei 5%, so betragen die Gesamtkosten 5,5% (5% LIBOR plus 0,5% Optionsprämie).

Angenommen der LIBOR steigt über 6%, so kann die Option ausgeübt werden. Die **Gesamtkosten der Refinanzierung** setzen sich aus der **Zinsobergrenze und der annualisierten Optionsprämie** zusammen. Bei 7% LIBOR kostet die effektive Refinanzierung zwar 7%, aus dem Cap wird jedoch die Differenz von 1% (LIBOR minus Zinsobergrenze) ausbezahlt, sodass sich Gesamtkosten von 6,5% (7% LIBOR – 1% Ausgleichszahlung Cap + 0,5% annualisierte Optionsprämie) ergeben. Auch im Falle von einem LIBOR von 10% bleiben die Gesamtkosten der Refinanzierung bei 6,5% (10% – 4% + 0,5%).

Damit ergibt sich ein für Optionen **typisches, asymmetrisches Gewinn-und-Verlust-Profil.** Zwar erlaubt es dem Cap-Käufer eine **Absicherung gegen einen Anstieg der Zinsen.** Andererseits bleibt **„unbeschränktes" Gewinnpotenzial bei fallenden Zinsen** bestehen.

426 • Interest Rate Options

3.3. Floor

A Floor is just the opposite of a Cap. A Floor is a **contract between two parties (OTC) over a defined interest rate lower limit** for a given principal.

If on certain dates (fixing dates) the agreed reference rate (usually LIBOR) is below the agreed interest rate (strike price), **the seller has to settle the difference between interest rate floor and reference rate** by paying the buyer. If on the fixing date the reference rate is above the strike price no payments are made.

Floors can be used by the buyer of the option as an **insurance against falling interest rates**. If one chooses a floating lending operation, expecting that interest rates will rise, then the Floor makes sure that the lending operation will achieve a minimum yield of the lower limit of the Floor. On the other hand, the buyer takes full **advantage of the expected rise in interest rates**.

Quotation

The quotation of Floors is usually done **on the basis of the premium**, which is a **single payment**, which is made when the contract is settled (just as with Caps).

Pricing

Technically, Floors can be seen as a **series of options on a strip of FRAs on 3-month or 6-month interest rates**. Since an FRA is a forward on a future money market rate and an FRA sale is a hedge against falling interest rates, a Floor is a series of options on FRA sales.

The FRA, or rather the **series of FRAs**, therefore is the **underlying for the Floor** and is important when determining whether an option is in the money, at the money, or out of the money. According to our rules for FRAs (forward rates) the **yield curve** is the main influence factor when determining the future interest rates. The interest rate floor that is fixed by the contract has to be compared to the respective forward rates for each interest period (and not to the current money market rates) in order to determine the intrinsic value of the Floor.

Example		
6-month interest rate:	3.50%	days: 180
12-month interest rate:	3.75%	days: 360
6/12 forward rate:	3.93%	days: 180
Under a Floor program with an interest rate lower limit of 3.75% the first term of interest would be out of the money with 0.18% (3.93% – 3.75%).		

3.3. Zinsuntergrenze (Floor)

Ein Floor ist das Gegenstück zu einem Cap. Er ist eine **vertragliche Vereinbarung zwischen zwei Parteien (OTC) über eine fixierte Zinsuntergrenze,** bezogen auf einen zugrundeliegenden nominellen Kapitalbetrag.

Liegt zu vorher definierten Zeitpunkten der festgelegte Referenzsatz (i.d.R. LIBOR bzw. EURIBOR) unter der vertraglich fixierten Zinsuntergrenze (Strike-Preis), so **zahlt der Verkäufer der Option dem Optionskäufer die Differenz zwischen Zinsuntergrenze und Referenzsatz** aus. Ist zu einem der definierten Zeitpunkte der Referenzsatz über dem Strike-Preis, so findet keine Zahlung zu diesem Termin statt.

Floors können damit für den Käufer der Option eine **Absicherung gegen fallende Zinsen** darstellen. Wird mit der Zinsmeinung, dass die Zinsen tendenziell eher steigen werden, eine variable Veranlagung getätigt, ist der Floor die Versicherung, dass die Veranlagung eine Mindestrendite, die der Zinsuntergrenze des Floors entspricht, erbringt. Andererseits kann jedoch voll vom **erwarteten Zinsanstieg profitiert** werden.

Quotierung

Die Quotierung von Floors erfolgt wie die Quotierung von Caps **über die Optionsprämie.** Sie ist eine **Einmalzahlung** bei Abschluss des Geschäftes.

Preisfindung

Technisch betrachtet ergeben Floors eine **Serie von Optionen mit zunehmend langer Vorlaufzeit auf üblicherweise 3- oder 6-Monats-Zinssätze.** Da ein FRA ein Termingeschäft auf einen zukünftigen Geldmarktsatz ist und ein FRA-Verkauf die Absicherung gegen fallende Zinsen, ist ein Floor die **Serie der Optionen auf verkaufte FRAs** (sogenannte Floorlets).

Der FRA oder besser die **Serie der FRAs** ist damit der **Basiswert des Floors** und muss auch bei der Bestimmung, ob die Option im Geld, am Geld oder aus dem Geld ist, herangezogen werden. Entsprechend unserer Regeln bei FRAs (Forward-Sätzen) ist die **Zinskurve** ein Haupteinflussfaktor bei der Bestimmung der Terminpreise. Die im Floor fixierte Zinsuntergrenze ist für die Bestimmung des inneren Wertes mit den entsprechenden Forward-Sätzen für die einzelnen Zinsperioden und nicht mit den aktuellen Geldmarktsätzen zu vergleichen.

Beispiel		
6-Monats-Zinssatz:	3,50%	180 Tage
12-Monats-Zinssatz:	3,75%	360 Tage
6/12-Forward-Satz:	3,93%	180 Tage
Bei einem Floor mit einer Zinsuntergrenze von 3,75%, wäre damit die erste Zinsperiode mit 0,18% (3,93% – 3,75%) aus dem Geld.		

Application

An insurance company wants to **lend money for 5 years** and has the possibility to lend at either a fixed rate of 6.5% or at LIBOR. The treasurer in charge expects the interest rates to rise, but is not willing (or able) to take on the whole risk involved in a floating lending operation. He decides to buy a Floor with a strike price of 3% (interest rate floor) on the whole volume, for which he pays a 2% premium.

First, one has to make the option's premium comparable over the years – since it is due only once. Ignoring compound interest (for reasons of simplicity) the premium of

2.00% equals an annual cost of 0.4% $\times \left(\dfrac{2,0\%}{5} \right)$.

The diagram below shows the earnings of the lending operation for each period:

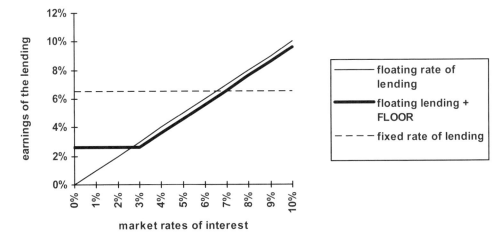

If the reference rate is above 3% the option expires. The insurance company is able to lend its liquidity at the prevailing market rate; the total earnings are figured out by LIBOR minus the annualised premium of the option. If the reference rate is exactly 3%, the total earnings from the lending operation are 2.6% (3% LIBOR – 0.4% annualised premium). If for example the LIBOR is at 5%, the total earnings are 4.6% (5% LIBOR – 0.4% premium of the option).

Assuming that LIBOR falls below 3% the option can be exercised and the **total earnings from the lending operation are computed as the floor interest rate minus the annualised premium of the option**. At an assumed LIBOR rate of 2%, the earnings from the investment are just 2 % but from the Floor the difference of 1% (interest rate floor minus LIBOR) is accrued, so the total earnings add up to 2.6% (2% LIBOR + 1% settlement payment – 0.4% annualised premium). Even if LIBOR is at 1.00 % the total earnings will still be 2.6% (1% + 2% – 0.4%).

Anwendung

Eine Versicherung möchte eine **5-Jahres-Veranlagung** tätigen und hat die Möglichkeit, das Geld zu einem festen Satz von 6,5% oder zu einem variablen LIBOR-Satz zu veranlagen. Der zuständige Treasurer vertritt die Marktmeinung, dass die Zinsen eher steigen werden, möchte jedoch nicht das volle Risiko einer variablen Veranlagung übernehmen. Er beschließt, einen Floor mit einem Strike-Preis von 3% für das gesamte Volumen zu kaufen, für den er 2% Prämie zahlen muss.

Als erster Schritt muss zum Zwecke der Vergleichbarkeit die **Optionsprämie annualisiert** werden. Ohne Berücksichtigung der Zinseszinsen ergeben die 2% Prämie p.a.

Kosten von $0,4\% \times \left(\dfrac{2,0\%}{5} \right)$.

Die Veranlagungserträge für die einzelnen Perioden lassen sich wie folgt grafisch darstellen:

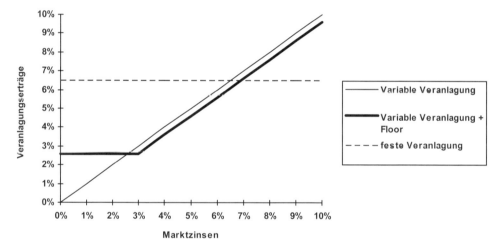

Liegt der Referenzsatz über 3%, so verfällt die Option. Unsere Versicherung kann also ihre Liquidität zum aktuellen Satz veranlagen. Der Gesamtertrag ergibt sich aus dem LIBOR abzüglich der annualisierten Optionsprämie. Liegt der Referenzsatz bei genau 3%, so sind die Gesamterträge der Veranlagung 2,6% (3% LIBOR – 0,4% annualisierte Optionsprämie). Liegt der LIBOR bei beispielsweise 5%, so betragen die Gesamterträge 4,6% (5% LIBOR – 0,4% Optionsprämie).

Angenommen der LIBOR fällt unter 3%, so kann die Option ausgeübt werden. Die **Gesamterträge der Veranlagung** setzen sich aus der **Zinsuntergrenze minus der annualisierten Optionsprämie** zusammen. Bei 2% LIBOR bringt die effektive Veranlagung zwar nur 2%, aus dem Floor wird jedoch die Differenz von 1% (Zinsuntergrenze minus LIBOR) ausbezahlt, sodass sich ein Gesamtertrag von 2,6% (2% LIBOR + 1% Ausgleichszahlung Floor – 0,4% annualisierte Optionsprämie) ergibt. Auch im Falle von einem LIBOR von 1% bleiben die Gesamterträge bei 2,6% (1% + 2% – 0,4%).

Thereby, an **asymmetric P & L profile**, as is typical for options, becomes evident; it enables the buyer of the Floor to **hedge against falling interest rates**, while he still has an **"unlimited" profit potential if the interest rates rise**.

Note: In general, every option that is used for **hedging** is bought in the belief that the option will expire. Only in such a case, the additional earnings, speculated for in the underlying deal, can be achieved. Although it can be argued that the option's premium was paid in this case for nothing (since the assurance was not needed), **the risk of the speculation could be limited by the option**.

3.4. Collar

A collar is a **combined purchased/sold cap and a sold/purchased floor**.

The **aim of a collar is to reduce the cost** (= premium) of the bought cap/floor by selling the floor/cap. If the cap's interest floor and the floor's interest ceiling are combine in a way that the two premiums are the same, the construction is called a **zero-cost collar**.

Pricing and Quotation

The price of a collar can be derived from the prices for caps and floors. The collar is usually **quoted in a "package"**. This means, that the **option premium is quoted in percentage for a collar** and not separately as two premiums for the used caps and floors.

Example
A collar constructed by a cap with a premium of 1.75% and a floor with a premium of 0.5% is directly quoted with a premium of 1.25%. Since the buyer of the cap simultaneously sells a floor both parties bear a counterparty risk in a collar.

Application

A treasurer borrowed money for 5 years at a floating rate that is LIBOR. Currently LIBOR is 5%. In order to hedge against rising interest rates the treasurer buys a cap at 6%. Since the premium of 3% (= 6% p.a.) seems too high for him he decides to reduce the cost by selling a floor at 4% for which he receives a premium of 3%.

So ergibt sich auch beim Floor ein **asymmetrisches Gewinn-und-Verlust-Profil,** das dem Floor-Käufer eine **Absicherung gegen ein Fallen der Zinsen** erlaubt. Andererseits bleibt ein **„unbeschränktes" Gewinnpotenzial beim Anstieg der Zinsen** bestehen. Die Versicherung wird also hoffen, dass der Floor nicht zum Tragen kommt.

Anmerkung: Generell wird jede Option als **Absicherung einer bestehenden Position** gekauft, in der Hoffnung, dass die Option verfallen wird. Nur dann können die Zusatzerträge, auf die in der Basisposition spekuliert wurde, auch wirklich eingefahren werden. Dem Argument, dass damit die Optionsprämie umsonst bezahlt wurde (da die Versicherung ja in diesem Falle nicht gebraucht wurde), ist entgegenzuhalten, dass **über die Option mit begrenztem Risiko spekuliert** werden konnte.

3.4. Collar

Ein Collar ist die **Kombination eines gekauften/verkauften Cap mit einem verkauften/gekauften Floor.**

Das **Ziel** eines Collars ist, die **Kosten** (= Prämie) für den gekauften Cap/Floor durch den Verkauf eines Floor/Cap zu **verringern.** Werden die Zinsobergrenze des Cap und die Zinsuntergrenze des Floor so kombiniert, dass sich gezahlte und erhaltene Prämie aufheben, so spricht man von einem **Zero-Cost-Collar.**

Preisfindung und Quotierung

Der Preis für den Collar ergibt sich aus den Cap- und Floor-Preisen. Bei Collars erfolgt die **Quotierung** meist **„im Package".** Das bedeutet, es wird eine **Optionsprämie** in Prozent **für eine bestimmte Collar-Kombination** quotiert und nicht zwei Prämien für Cap und Floor, die dann saldiert werden, quotiert.

Beispiel
Ein Collar aus einem Cap mit Prämie 1,75% und einem Floor mit 0,5% wird direkt mit einer Prämie von 1,25% quotiert. Da der Käufer des Caps auch den Floor verkauft, tragen im Gegensatz zum Cap bzw. Floor beim Collar zwei Parteien ein Kreditrisiko.

Anwendung

Ein Treasurer hat folgende variable Refinanzierung: 5 Jahre Laufzeit zu LIBOR mit aktuellen 5%. Um sich gegen steigende Zinsen abzusichern, kauft er einen Cap mit 6% Strike. Da ihm die Prämie für den Cap mit 3% (= 0,6% p.a.) zu hoch ist, entscheidet sich der Treasurer für einen Collar und verkauft einen Floor mit Strike 4% und 3% Prämie.

The following table shows the borrowing cost of the treasurer:

Premium p.a.		3%	4%	5%	6%	7%
p.a borrowing cost		–3%	–4%	–5%	–6%	–7%
Bought Cap 6%	–0.6%	/	/	/	/	+1%
Sold Floor 4%	+0.6%	–1%	/	/	/	/
Total Premium	0%	0%	0%	0%	0%	0%
Total result Borrowing cost		–4%	–4%	–5%	–6%	–6%

With the collar you save part or the entire premium but you forgo also to **profit from some advantages interest rate movements**. In our example, the treasurer has fixed his maximum borrowing rate at 6% and his minimum-borrowing rate at 4%. If interest rates fall below 4% he cannot profit from this development since he would have to pay in the floor.

3.5. Futures Options

A futures option gives the buyer the **right to buy (call) or sell (put) a future at a pre-defined price (= strike price)**.

Specifications

Futures options are **usually american-style options**, i.e. they can be **excersised anytime** (e.g. options on Euro-Bond-Future). Futures options are **standardised products** which derive their specifications from the underlying. Trading and clearing is executed via the exchange (e.g. EUREX).

The options' expiry months are the three next consecutive months and the following month from the cycle March, June, September and December. Thus, option **terms for 1, 2, 3 until 6 months** at max. are available.

If the options's expiry month and the delivery month of the future are not the same, the future following the options's expiry month has to be delivered.

Example
Purchase EUR-Bond-Future option in May, term 3 months. The options's expiry month is August. As there is no August future, the September future will be delivered in case of an expiry of the option.

Sein Refinanzierungsprofil stellt sich folgendermaßen dar:

Marktzins Prämie p.a.		3%	4%	5,0%	6%	7%
p.a Kosten Refi Markt		–3%	–4%	–5%	–6%	–7%
Gekaufter Cap 6%	–0,6%	/	/	/	/	+1%
Verkaufter Floor 4%	+0,6%	–1%	/	/	/	/
Summe Prämie	0,0%	0%	0%	0%	0%	0%
Gesamtergebnis Refinanzierungskosten		–4%	–4%	–5%	–6%	–6%

Mit einem Collar **spart** man zwar **per Saldo einen Teil oder die gesamte Prämie,** nimmt dafür jedoch zugleich in Kauf, **von vorteilhaften Zinsentwicklungen nicht voll profitieren** zu können.

Im vorliegenden Beispiel kann der Treasurer seine variable Refinanzierung auf eine Bandbreite von 4% bis 6% einschränken, nimmt jedoch einen Mindestzinssatz von 4% für die variable Refinanzierung in Kauf. Von stärker fallenden Zinsen kann er nicht profitieren, da er den Floor verkauft hat.

3.5. Optionen auf Futures

Eine Option auf einen Future gibt dem Käufer der Option das **Recht, zu einem im Vorhinein vereinbarten Preis (= Strike-Preis) den Future zu kaufen (Call) bzw. zu verkaufen (Put).**

Spezifikation

Optionen auf Futures sind **üblicherweise amerikanischen Typs.** Sie können **jederzeit ausgeübt** werden (z.B. Optionen auf Euro-Bond-Future). Optionen auf Futures sind **standardisierte Produkte,** die ihre Spezifikation aus dem Underlying ableiten. Handel und Clearing erfolgt über die Börse (z.B. EUREX).

Die Verfallmonate der Option sind die drei nächsten, aufeinanderfolgenden Monate sowie der darauf folgende Monat aus dem Zyklus März, Juni, September und Dezember. Das bedeutet, Optionen von **ein, zwei, drei bis maximal sechs Monaten Laufzeit** sind verfügbar.

Sind der Options-Verfallsmonat und der Fälligkeitsmonat des Futures nicht ident, ist der dem Verfallsmonat der Option nachgelagerte Future zu liefern.

Beispiel

Kauf EUR-Bond-Future-Option im Mai, Laufzeit 3 Monate. Der Options-Verfallsmonat ist August. Da es keinen August-Future gibt, wird der September-Future im Falle der Ausübung der Option geliefert.

Premium

Like for all other options, the **buyer of futures options has to pay a premium**. A special characteristic for futures options is that the seller has to pay a **margin to the exchange**. As for futures an initial margin and – if necessary – a variation margin have to be paid. Usually, margins are paid **through assets**. The margin is only relevant for the seller as only the seller might become a credit risk when at expiry he cannot deliver the underlying. After payment of the premium, the buyer is no credit risk for the exchange anymore.

Application

Futures options offer the opportunity to **hedge deposits against falling rates and loans against rising rates** without excluding profit potential from advantageous interest rate movements. As for all other options, the premium reduces the profit potential whereas the **loss is limited**.

Example

Hedging a bond portfolio with futures options

A company has 14 m Euro-Bonds in its books. The actual price is 95.50. The company wants to sell the bonds in 2 months and therefore hedge the risk of rising rates (= falling bond prices).

To hedge itself against rising rates the company can

- sell a Euro-Bond-Future or
- buy a put option on a Euro-Bond-Future

The company decides to buy an option on the Euro-Bond-Future, strike 95.50, premium: EUR 2,500.

At the delivery date of the option the September future is traded at
1) 92.00   2) 97.00

Option

	92.00	97.00
Future	955,000	0
Premium	–2,500	–2,500
Bond sale	0	970,000
Result	**952,500**	**967,500**

↑
fixed selling price

Futures

	92.00	97.00
Bond sale	920,000	970.000
Premium	0	0
Result	**920,000**	**970,000**

Prämie

Der **Käufer** hat für Futures-Optionen wie auch bei anderen Optionen eine **Prämie zu bezahlen.** Die Besonderheit an Futures-Optionen ist, dass der Verkäufer eine **Margin an die Börse** zu zahlen hat. Wie bei Futures sind ein Initial Margin und bei Bedarf eine Variation Margin einzuschießen. Margins werden üblicherweise **in Wertpapieren** geleistet. Die Margin ist nur vom **Verkäufer zu entrichten,** weil nur er ein Kreditrisiko darstellt, wenn er bei Ausübung der Option nicht erfüllen kann. Der Käufer stellt nach Zahlung der Prämie kein Kreditrisiko für die Börse dar.

Einsatzmöglichkeiten

Futures-Optionen bieten die Möglichkeit, **Aktivpositionen gegen fallende Zinsen und Passivpositionen gegen steigende Zinsen absichern** zu können, ohne dabei das Gewinnpotenzial günstiger Zinsentwicklungen auszuschließen. Wie auch bei anderen Optionen wird das Gewinnpotenzial um die Prämie geschmälert. Dafür bleibt das **Verlustpotenzial beschränkt.**

Beispiel

Absicherung Anleiheportfolio durch Futures-Optionen:

Ein Unternehmen hat 14 Mio. Euro-Bonds in seinen Büchern. Der aktuelle Kurs ist 95,50. Das Unternehmen möchte in zwei Monaten die Anleihen verkaufen und das Risiko steigender Zinsen (= sinkende Anleihepreise) absichern.

Um sich gegen steigende Zinsen abzusichern, kann es

- einen Euro-Bond-Future verkaufen oder
- eine Put-Option auf einen Euro-Bond-Future kaufen.

Das Unternehmen entscheidet sich, eine Option auf einen Euro-Bond-Future, Strike 95,50, zu kaufen, Prämie: EUR 2.500.

Am Liefertag der Option ist der September-Future bei
1) 92,00   2) 97,00

Option

	92,00	97,00
Future	955.000	0
Prämie	−2.500	−2.500
Anleihenverkauf	0	970.000
Ergebnis	**952.500**	**967.500**

↑
Fixer Einstandspreis

Futures

	92,00	97,00
Anleihenverkauf	920.000	970.000
Prämie	0	0
Ergebnis	**920.000**	**970.000**

Thanks to the option, the company can

- fix a **selling price at 95.25**. In the example the result is by EUR 32,500 better than without any hedging.
- **profit from falling interest rates**. The profit of the option position is exactely by EUR 2,500 (premium) lower than as for the pure futures trade.

3.6. Bond Options

The buyer of a bond option has the **right to buy (call) resp. sell (put) the underlying bond at expiry at a predefined price**. On the other hand, the seller has the obligation to deliver (call) resp. buy (put) the bond. The **seller** bears the **complete bond price risk**, the **buyer** might only lose the **premium**.

Premium

The premium and thus the value of a bond option depends on

- the chosen strike price
- the term
- the volatility
- the interest rate differential between money market and capital market.

The premium can either be quoted in **basis points** or can be computed with the **"futures style" method**. With the "futures style" method the premium is computed individually as a **percentage** depending on the risk of the whole options and futures portfolio.

Example

Application of bond options

A company wants to hedge a EUR bond portfolio due EUR 10 m against rising rates. Actual bond price 96.00, strike price 96.00, premium: 55 bp.

At the delivery date of the option the bond is traded at
1) 98,00   2) 93,00

	98,00	**93,00**
Option		9.600.000
Premium	−55.000	−55.000
Bond sale	9.800.000	
Result	**9.745.000**	**9.545.000**

Minimum selling price

Das Optionsgeschäft bedeutet für das Unternehmen, dass

- es einen **Einstandskurs von 95,25 fixiert.** Im Beispiel ist das Ergebnis um EUR 32.500 besser als ohne Absicherung.
- es **von fallenden Zinsen profitieren** kann. Der Gewinn im Optionsgeschäft ist exakt um die Prämie von EUR 2.500 niedriger als bei einem reinen Futuresgeschäft.

3.6. Bond-Optionen

Der Käufer einer Bondoption hat das **Recht, die zugrundeliegende Anleihe (= Underlying) am Fälligkeitstag zu einem im Vorhinein fixierten Preis zu kaufen (Call) bzw. zu verkaufen (Put).** Der Verkäufer hat dann die Pflicht, die Anleihe zu liefern (Call) bzw. zu übernehmen (Put). Der **Verkäufer** trägt das **volle Kursänderungsrisiko** der Anleihe, der **Käufer** nur das **Risiko des Verlustes der Prämie.**

Prämie

Die Prämie und damit der Wert einer Bond-Option hängt ab von

- dem gewählten Strike-Preis,
- der Laufzeit,
- der Volatilität,
- der Zinsdifferenz zwischen Geld- und Kapitalmarkt.

Prämien werden entweder in **Basispunkten** quotiert oder nach dem **„futures-style"-Verfahren** berechnet. Die Prämie wird bei einem „futures-style"-Verfahren als **Prozentsatz** in Abhängigkeit vom Risiko des Gesamtportfolios an Optionen und Futures individuell ermittelt.

Beispiel

Einsatz von Bond-Optionen:

Ein Unternehmen möchte ein EUR-Anleiheportfolio im Wert von EUR 10 Mio. gegen ansteigende Zinsen absichern. Aktueller Kurs in der Anleihe: 96,00. Strike-Preis der Option: 96,00. Prämie: 55 BP.

Bei Auslaufen der Option ist der Anleihepreis
1) 98,00   2) 93,00

	98,00	**93,00**
Option		9.600.000
Prämie	–55.000	–55.000
Anleihenverkauf	9.800.000	
Ergebnis	**9.745.000**	**9.545.000**

↑
Minimum Einstandspreis

Bond options vs. futures:

Corresponding to the last example, the company could have also sold 10 EUR-futures at 96.00.

The results would have been.

	98,00	93,00
Future (= bond) sale	9.600.000	9.600.000
Bond sale without hedging	9.800.000	9.300.000
Result	**−200.000**	**+300.000**

↑
better result

Comparison result at price 98.00

The hedge via option only costs the premium (EUR 55,000). With the futures trade the opportunity costs would be considerably higher (EUR 200,000).

Comparison result at price 93.00

With the option the company gains EUR 245,000 (= 9,545,000 – 9,300,000), while with the futures trade profit would be EUR 300,000.

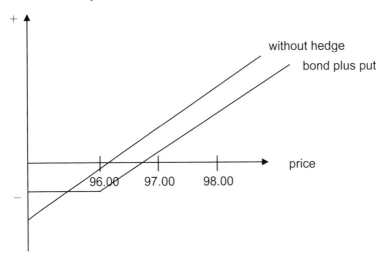

If the bond price rises, the result without hedging is better than the result of the option strategy. If the bond price falls, the result of the forward hedge is better than the result of the option strategy. The main character of an option strategy is that the biggest part of the profit potential is retained in a use without bearing the full risk of a decrease in price.

Bond-Optionen versus Futures:

Bauen wir auf dem Geschäftsfall des letzten Beispiels auf, hätte das Unternehmen auch 10 EUR-Futures zu 96,00 verkaufen können.

Die Ergebnisse wären:

	98,00	93,00
Future	9.600.000	9.600.000
Anleihenverkauf	9.800.000	9.300.000
Ergebnis	**−200.000**	**+300.000**

↑
besseres Ergebnis

Ergebnisvergleich Kurs 98,00

Die Absicherung durch die Option kostet nur den Verlust der Prämie (EUR 55.000). Beim Futures-Geschäft wären die Opportunitätskosten (= Verlust) mit EUR 200.000 deutlich höher.

Ergebnisvergleich Kurs 93,00

Bei der Option macht das Unternehmen EUR 245.000 Gewinn (= 9.545.000 − 9.300.000), während beim Futures-Geschäft der Gewinn EUR 300.000 beträgt.

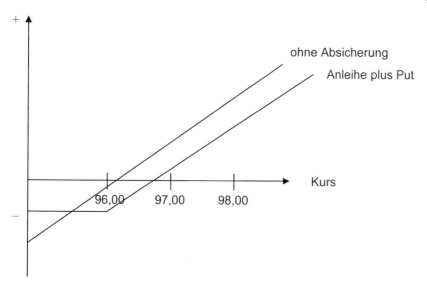

Steigt der Kurs der Anleihe, ist das Ergebnis ohne Absicherung besser als das Ergebnis mit der Optionsstrategie. Fällt der Kurs der Anleihe, ist das Ergebnis mit Absicherung mittels Future besser als das Ergebnis mit Optionen. **Das Wesen der Optionsstrategie ist, dass der größte Teil des Gewinnpotenzials bei einem Anstieg bewahrt wird, ohne jedoch das volle Risiko eines Kursrückgangs zu tragen.**

3.7. Swaptions

A swaption is a contract between two parties (OTC). It provides the buyer the **right to enter at an agreed date into an interest rate swap with defined term, interest rate and principal**.

In contrast to Caps and Floors, a swaption is an **option on a fixed interest rate at a certain date**. While under Caps and Floors a settlement payment has to be made at certain dates, a swaption offers **two possible forms of settlement**; **cash settlement** (settlement payment, with which the current present value of the swap is paid off) or **physical "delivery"** of a real interest rate swap.

For the option buyer, a call swaption bears the right to buy an interest rate swap at a fixed rate in the future (option on a **fixed-rate payer swap**, commonly known in the market as payer swaption).

For the buyer, a put swaption contains the right to sell an interest rate swap at a fixed rate in the future (option on a **fixed-rate receiver swap**, commonly known in the market as **receiver swaption**).

Swaptions are commonly **used in two business fields**:

- **during the offer phase in project financing:** with a swaption, the interest rates for refinancing, that may influence the project at an early stage, can be secured.
- **to secure assets and liabilities that are due in the future:** in case of non-congruence of interest rates, a swaption guarantees a fixed interest rate for lending or refinancing operations in the future.

Quotation

The quotation is done **on the basis of the premium**, which is a **single payment** when the contract is settled (just as with Caps and Floors).

Pricing

Since the **basic value** of a swaption is an **interest rate with a delayed starting date** (or rather a forward start swap), the agreed interest rate of the swaption has to be compared to the respective forward swap. Thus, the difference represents the intrinsic value, or the amount by which the swaption is in the money. Additional factors of influence are – as with all types of options – the time to expiry as well as the respective **volatility in the market**.

Example
Current 2-year swap rate: 4.25%   Current 7-year swap rate: 4.75%   Forward swap 2 + 5:   4.95% (without compound interest)
A payer swaption (option on a fixed-rate payer swap), starting in two years with a term of 5 year, strike price of 4.50 %, would be in the money with 0.45% (4.95% – 4.50%). A receiver swaption (option on a fixed-rate receiver swap), starting in 2 years with a term of 5 years at a strike price of 4.50%, would be out of the money with 0.45% (4.95% – 4.50%).

3.7. Swaptions

Eine Swaption ist eine vertragliche Vereinbarung zwischen zwei Parteien (OTC), die dem Käufer der Swaption das **Recht** gibt, **zu einem festgelegten Zeitpunkt in einen Zinsswap mit fixierter Laufzeit, Zinssatz und Nominalbetrag einzusteigen.**

Im Gegensatz zu Caps und Floors ist eine Swaption also eine **Option auf einen festen Zinssatz ab einem bestimmten Datum.** Während bei Caps und Floors eine Zinsausgleichszahlung zu den einzelnen Terminen stattfindet, gibt es bei Swaptions **beide Möglichkeiten des Settlements;** sowohl ein **Cash-Settlement** (Ausgleichszahlung, bei der der aktuelle Barwert des Swaps ausbezahlt wird) als auch die **physische Lieferung,** bei deren Ausübung ein echter Zinsswap „geliefert" wird, kann vereinbart werden.

Eine Call-Swaption bedeutet für den Käufer der Option das Recht, in der Zukunft einen Zinsswap zu einem fixierten Preis zu kaufen (Option auf einen **Festzinszahler-Swap,** marktüblich **Payer-Swaption** genannt).

Eine Put-Swaption bedeutet für den Käufer der Option das Recht, in der Zukunft einen Zinsswap zu einem fixierten Preis zu verkaufen (Option auf einen **Festzinsempfänger Swap,** marktüblich **Receiver-Swaption** genannt).

Swaptions finden ihre **typischen Anwendungen**

- **in der Angebotsphase bei Projektfinanzierungen:** Mit der Swaption können damit die das Projekt beeinflussenden Refinanzierungszinsen bereits bei Angebotslegung abgesichert werden.

- **zur Absicherung von in Zukunft fälligen Aktiva oder Passiva:** Bei Zinsinkongruenzen kann mit einer Swaption ein garantierter Zinssatz für die zukünftig fällige Veranlagung oder Refinanzierung dargestellt werden.

Quotierung

Die Quotierung von Swaptions erfolgt wie bei Caps und Floors **über die Optionsprämie,** die eine **Einmalzahlung** bei Abschluss des Geschäftes darstellt.

Preisfindung

Da der **Basiswert** bei einer Swaption ein **Zinsswap mit verzögertem Startdatum** ist (oder besser ein Forward-Start-Swap), ist der vereinbarte Zinssatz in der Swaption mit dem aktuellen Preis für entsprechende Forward-Swaps zu vergleichen. So ergibt sich als Differenz der innere Wert bzw. der Betrag, den die Swaption im Geld ist. Zusätzliche Einflussfaktoren sind – wie bei allen Optionstypen – auch die **Vorlaufzeit** und die entsprechende **Marktvolatilität.**

Beispiel
Aktueller 2-Jahres-Swap-Satz: 4,25%   Aktueller 7-Jahres-Swap-Satz: 4,75%   Forward-Swap 2 + 5:   4,95% (ohne Zinseszins)   Eine Payer-Swaption (Option auf Festzinszahler-Swap), startend in zwei Jahren mit einer Laufzeit von fünf Jahren zu einem Strike von 4,5%, wäre damit 0,45% im Geld (4,95% – 4,5%).   Eine Receiver-Swaption (Option auf Festzinsempfänger-Swap), startend in zwei Jahren mit einer Laufzeit von fünf Jahren zu einem Strike von 4,5%, wäre damit 0,45% aus dem Geld (4,95% – 4,5%).

Application

A bank has made a fixed-rate issue for 5 years. The treasurer in charge wants to keep the profit potential of falling interest rates, but also wants to secure a minimum interest rate of 6% for 5 more years. Therefore, he decides to buy a payer swaption (strike price is 6%) at a premium of 2% (option on a fixed-rate payer swap). An alternative forward rate swap would cost a fixed rate of 5.75%.

First, the single payment of the premium must be converted on the basis of the underlying's term. In this case, the premium of 2% must be split over the last 5 years of the term: this gives an annualised premium of 0.4% (ignoring the fact that the premium has to be paid at the trading date).

The following diagram shows the possible refinancing between years 5 and 10:

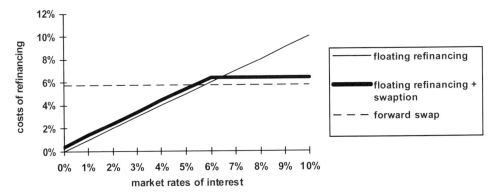

If the rate of the 5-year swap is below 6.00% in 5 years time, the expectations of the treasurer turned out to be true and he can take full advantage of the conditions of refinancing in the market.

His **costs of refinancing are made up of the current market rate minus the annualised premium**. In this case, he will not exercise the swaption. With an assumed 5-year rate of 5%, the refinancing costs (ignoring the credit margin) are 5.4% (5% market interest rate + 0.4% premium for the option).

If the market rate is above 6%, he will exercise the option and can enter a fixed-rate payer swap at 6%. Thereby, his costs of refinancing (without the credit's spread) will be 6.4%, no matter how high the effective market interest rates are going to be. Above a market rate of 6%, the basis of his refinancing costs is determined by adding strike price and annualised premium of the option.

Anwendung

Eine Bank hat eine Festzinsemission für fünf Jahre. Der Treasurer möchte das Potenzial fallender Zinsen behalten, sich jedoch einen Mindestzinssatz von 6% für weitere fünf Jahre sichern und beschließt daher, eine Payer-Swaption (Strike-Preis 6%) zu einer Prämie von 2% zu kaufen (Option auf Festzinszahler-Swap). Beim alternativen Abschluss eines Forward-Start-Swaps müsste er einen Festsatz von 5,75% bezahlen.

Als erster Schritt muss die Einmalprämie auf die Laufzeit des zugrundeliegenden Geschäftes aufgeteilt werden. Im vorliegenden Fall ist die Optionsprämie von 2% auf die hinteren fünf Jahre Laufzeit aufzuteilen. Das ergibt eine annualisierte Optionsprämie von 0,4% (ohne Berücksichtigung des Effektes, dass die Prämie bereits zum Zeitpunkt 0 zu zahlen ist).

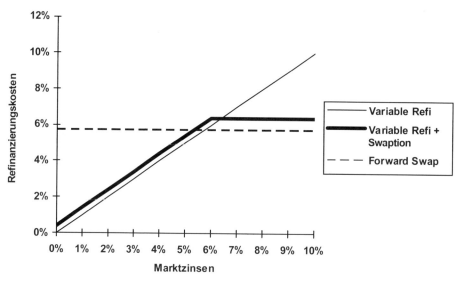

Liegt der 5-Jahres-Swap-Satz in 5 Jahren unter 6%, so greift die Idee des Treasurers, und er kann von den günstigen Refinanzierungsmöglichkeiten im Markt Gebrauch machen.

Seine **Refinanzierungskosten** setzen sich aus dem **aktuellen Marktsatz zuzüglich der annualisierten Prämie** zusammen. Die Swaption wird er in diesem Fall nicht ausüben. Bei einem angenommenen 5-Jahres-Satz von 5% ergeben sich (ohne Berücksichtigung seines Kreditaufschlages) somit Refinanzierungskosten von 5,4% (5% Marktsatz + 0,4% Optionsprämie).

Liegt der Marktsatz über 6%, so übt er seine Option aus und kann damit einen Festzinszahler-Swap zu 6% abschließen. Damit ergeben sich für ihn Refinanzierungskosten (ohne Kreditaufschlag) von 6,4% – unabhängig davon, wie hoch die effektiven Marktzinsen sind. Über den Marktsatz von 6% ergibt sich die Basis seiner Refinanzierungskosten durch die Addition von Strike-Preis und annualisierter Optionsprämie.

Summary

An interest rate option is an agreement between two parties. It grants one party (buyer) the right to buy (call option) or sell (put option) a financial instrument at a fixed price at a defined date (or during a defined period of time). The buyer of an option does not have to exercise this right. For this right, the buyer pays a certain price (premium) to the option seller. On the other hand, the seller has no control over the possible execution.

If an option is "at the money" its strike price is almost the same as the current market price. An option is "out of the money" if the strike price is "better" than the actual market price or in other words if the strike price is either above (call option) or below (put option) the market price of the underlying. An option is "in the money" if the strike price is "better" than the actual market price or in other words is either below (call option) or above (put option) the market price of the underlying.

A cap is a contract between two parties (OTC) over an interest rate ceiling with regard to the principal. If at certain dates (fixing dates) the agreed reference rate (usually LIBOR) is above the defined interest rate (strike price) the seller has to settle the difference between reference rate and interest rate ceiling and has to pay the buyer. If at the fixing dates the reference rate is below the strike price no payments are made.

The quotation of caps is usually done on the basis of the premium, which is a single payment when the contract is settled.

Caps can be used by the buyer of the option as an insurance against rising interest rates. On the other hand, the buyer takes full advantage of the expected fall in the interest rates. Thereby, an asymmetric P&L profile develops that is typical for options; it enables the buyer of the cap to hedge against rising interest rates, whereas he still has an "unlimited" profit potential if the interest rates fall.

A floor is just the opposite of a cap. A floor is a contract between two parties (OTC) over a defined interest rate lower limit for a given principal. If on certain dates (fixing dates) the agreed reference rate (usually LIBOR) is below the agreed interest rate (strike price), the seller has to settle the difference between interest rate floor and reference rate by paying the buyer. If on the fixing date the reference rate is above the strike price no payments are made.

Floors can be used by the buyer of the option as an insurance against falling interest rates. On the other hand, the buyer takes full advantage of the expected rise in interest rates.

The quotation of floors is usually done on the basis of the premium, which is a single payment to be made when the contract is settled (just as with caps).

Zusammenfassung

Eine Zinsoption ist eine Vereinbarung zwischen zwei Parteien, die einer der beiden Parteien (dem Käufer) das Recht einräumt, ein Finanzinstrument (Underlying) zu einem vorher fixierten Preis (Strike-Preis) zu einem bestimmten Datum (oder einer fixierten Zeitspanne) zu kaufen (Call-Option) oder zu verkaufen (Put-Option). Der Käufer der Option geht jedoch im Optionskontrakt keine Verpflichtung ein, von diesem Recht Gebrauch zu machen. Für dieses Recht zahlt er dem Verkäufer einen Preis, nämlich die Optionsprämie (Zeitwert + innerer Wert). Der Verkäufer hat keine Möglichkeit zu entscheiden, ob das Optionsrecht ausgenutzt wird oder nicht.

Eine Option „at the money" ist eine Option, deren Strike-Preis in etwa dem Marktpreis des Underlying entspricht. Eine Option „in the money" ist eine Option, deren Strike-Preis „besser" als der Marktpreis ist, d.h. beim Call niedriger bzw. beim Put höher als der Marktpreis des Underlyings. Eine Option „out of money" ist eine Option, deren Strike-Preis „schlechter" als der Marktpreis ist, d.h. beim Call höher bzw. beim Put niedriger als der Marktpreis des Underlyings.

Ein Cap ist eine vertragliche Vereinbarung zwischen zwei Parteien (OTC) über eine fixierte Zinsobergrenze, bezogen auf einen zugrundeliegenden nominellen Kapitalbetrag. Wird der festgelegte Referenzsatz (i.d.R. LIBOR bzw. EURIBOR) zu vorher definierten Zeitpunkten über der vertraglich fixierten Zinsobergrenze (Strike-Preis) „gefixt", so zahlt der Verkäufer der Option dem Optionskäufer die Differenz zwischen Zinsobergrenze und Referenzsatz aus. Ist zu einem der definierten Zeitpunkte der Referenzsatz unter dem Strike-Preis, so findet keine Zahlung zu diesem Termin statt.

Die Quotierung von Caps erfolgt üblicherweise über die Optionsprämie. Sie stellt i.d.R. eine Einmalzahlung bei Abschluss des Geschäftes dar.

Caps können für den Käufer der Option Absicherungen gegen steigende Zinsen darstellen. Andererseits kann auch voll vom erwarteten Zinsrückgang profitiert werden.

Technisch gesehen sind Caps eine Serie von Optionen auf gekaufte FRAs (sogenannte Caplets). Der FRA oder besser die Serie der FRAs ist damit der Basiswert des Caps. Es ergibt sich ein für Optionen typisches, asymmetrisches Gewinn-und-Verlust-Profil. Es erlaubt dem Cap-Käufer eine Absicherung gegen ein Steigen der Zinsen, andererseits bleibt „unbeschränktes" Gewinnpotenzial bei fallenden Zinsen bestehen.

Ein Floor ist das Gegenstück zu einem Cap. Er ist eine vertragliche Vereinbarung zwischen zwei Parteien (OTC) über eine fixierte Zinsuntergrenze, bezogen auf einen zugrundeliegenden nominellen Kapitalbetrag. Liegt zu vorher definierten Zeitpunkten der festgelegte Referenzsatz (i.d.R. LIBOR bzw. EURIBOR) unter der vertraglich fixierten Zinsuntergrenze (Strike-Preis), so zahlt der Verkäufer der Option dem Optionskäufer die Differenz zwischen Zinsuntergrenze und Referenzsatz aus. Ist zu einem der definierten Zeitpunkte der Referenzsatz über dem Strike-Preis, so findet keine Zahlung zu diesem Termin statt.

Floors können für den Käufer der Option eine Absicherung gegen fallende Zinsen darstellen, er behält jedoch weiter das Potenzial beim erwarteten Zinsanstieg.

Die Quotierung von Floors erfolgt wie die Quotierung von Caps über die Optionsprämie. Sie ist eine Einmalzahlung bei Abschluss des Geschäftes.

Thereby, an asymmetric P&L profile, as is typical for options, becomes evident; it enables the buyer of the floor to hedge against falling interest rates, while he still has an "unlimited" profit potential if the interest rates rise.

A collar is a combined purchased/sold cap and a sold/purchased floor. The aim of a collar is to reduce the cost (= premium) of the bought cap/floor by selling the floor/cap. If the cap's interest floor and the floor's interest ceiling are combined in a way that the two premiums are the same, the construction is called a zero-cost collar.

The price of a collar can be derived from the prices for caps and floors. The collar is usually quoted as a "package". This means, that the option premium is quoted in percentage for a collar and not separately as two premiums for the used caps and floors.

A futures option gives the buyer the right to buy (call) or sell (put) a future at a predefined price (= strike price). Futures options are usually American-style options, i.e. they can be excercised anytime (e.g. options on euro bond future). Futures options are standardised products which derive their specifications from the underlying. Trading and clearing is executed via the exchange (e.g. EUREX).

As for all other options, the buyer of futures options has to pay a premium. A special characteristic for futures options is that the seller has to pay a margin to the exchange. Therefore, futures options offer the chance to hedge deposits against falling rates and loans against rising rates without excluding profit potential from advantageous interest rate movements.

The buyer of a bond option has the right to buy (call) or sell (put) the underlying bond at expiry at a predefined price. On the other hand, the seller has the obligation to deliver (call) or buy (put) the bond. The seller bears the complete bond price risk, the buyer might only lose the premium.

A swaption is a contract between two parties (OTC). It provides the buyer with the right to enter at an agreed date into an interest rate swap with a defined term, interest rate and principal.

In contrast to caps and floors, a swaption is an option on a fixed interest rate at a certain date. While under caps and floors a settlement payment has to be made at certain dates, a swaption offers two possible forms of settlement; cash settlement (settlement payment, with which the current present value of the swap is paid off) or physical "delivery" of a real interest rate swap.

Technisch betrachtet ergeben Floors eine Serie von Optionen auf verkaufte FRAs (sogenannte Floorlets).

Auch beim Floor ergibt sich ein asymmetrisches Gewinn-und-Verlust-Profil, das dem Floor-Käufer eine Absicherung gegen ein Fallen der Zinsen erlaubt. Andererseits bleibt ein „unbeschränktes" Gewinnpotenzial beim Anstieg der Zinsen bestehen.

Ein Collar ist die Kombination eines gekauften/verkauften Cap mit einem verkauften/gekauften Floor. Das Ziel eines Collars ist, die Kosten (= Prämie) für den gekauften Cap/Floor durch den Verkauf eines Floor/Cap zu verringern. Werden die Zinsobergrenze des Cap und die Zinsuntergrenze des Floor so kombiniert, dass sich gezahlte und erhaltene Prämie aufheben, so spricht man von einem Zero-Cost-Collar.

Bei Collars erfolgt die Quotierung meist „im Package". Das bedeutet, es wird eine Optionsprämie in Prozent für eine bestimmte Collar-Kombination quotiert und nicht zwei Prämien für Cap und Floor, die dann saldiert werden.

Eine Option auf einen Future gibt dem Käufer der Option das Recht, zu einem im Vorhinein vereinbarten Preis (= Strike-Preis) den Future zu kaufen (Call) bzw. zu verkaufen (Put). Optionen auf Futures sind üblicherweise amerikanischen Typs. Sie können jederzeit ausgeübt werden (z.B. Optionen auf Euro-Bond-Future). Optionen auf Futures sind standardisierte Produkte, die ihre Spezifikation aus dem Underlying ableiten.

Der Käufer hat für Futures-Optionen wie auch bei anderen Optionen eine Prämie zu bezahlen. Die Besonderheit an Futures-Optionen ist, dass der Verkäufer eine Margin an die Börse zu zahlen hat.

Futures-Optionen bieten die Möglichkeit, Aktivpositionen gegen fallende Zinsen und Passivpositionen gegen steigende Zinsen absichern zu können, ohne dabei das Gewinnpotenzial günstiger Zinsentwicklungen auszuschließen.

Der Käufer einer Bond-Option hat das Recht, die zugrundeliegende Anleihe (= Underlying) am Fälligkeitstag zu einem im Vorhinein fixierten Preis zu kaufen (Call) bzw. zu verkaufen (Put). Der Verkäufer hat dann die Pflicht, die Anleihe zu liefern (Call) bzw. zu übernehmen (Put). Der Verkäufer trägt das volle Kursänderungsrisiko der Anleihe, der Käufer nur das Risiko des Verlustes der Prämie.

Prämien werden entweder in Basispunkten quotiert oder nach dem „futures-style"-Verfahren berechnet. Die Prämie wird bei einem „futures-style"-Verfahren als Prozentsatz in Abhängigkeit vom Risiko des Gesamtportfolios an Optionen und Futures individuell ermittelt.

Eine Swaption ist eine vertragliche Vereinbarung zwischen zwei Parteien (OTC), die dem Käufer der Swaption das Recht gibt, zu einem festgelegten Zeitpunkt in einen Zinsswap mit fixierter Laufzeit, Zinssatz und Nominalbetrag einzusteigen.

Im Gegensatz zu Caps und Floors ist eine Swaption also eine Option auf einen festen Zinssatz ab einem bestimmten Datum. Während bei Caps und Floors eine Zinsausgleichszahlung zu den einzelnen Terminen stattfindet, gibt es bei Swaptions beide Möglichkeiten des Settlements; sowohl ein Cash-Settlement (Ausgleichszahlung, bei der der aktuelle Barwert des Swaps ausbezahlt wird) als auch die physische Lieferung, bei deren Ausübung ein echter Zinsswap „geliefert" wird, kann vereinbart werden.

The quotation is done on the basis of the premium, which is a single payment when the contract is settled (just as with caps and floors).

Since the basic value of a swaption is an interest rate with a delayed starting date (or rather a forward start swap), the agreed interest rate of the swaption has to be compared to the respective forward swap.

3.8. Practice Questions

1. Explain the differences between American and European options!

2. What is meant by the intrinsic value of an option?

3. What has an influence on the time value of an option?

4. Company X sells a 3-month LIBOR floor at 8%. On the first maturity date the interest rate is 9%. Which of the following statements is true?
   a) Company X receives the premium and the rate differential.
   b) Company X pays the premium and the rate differential.
   c) Company X receives the premium and there are no further payments at the first maturity date.
   d) Company X receives the premium and pays the rate differential at the first maturity date.

5. You buy a series of caps on a notional of USD 50,000,000, based on the given data: premium 3.5%, strike 4%, 6-month LIBOR 3.8%, term of maturity 3 years. Which premium do you pay?
   a) USD 0
   b) USD 175,000
   c) USD 250,000
   d) USD 1,750,000

6. What is the intention when buying a cap?
   a) to hedge against falling interest rates
   b) to hedge against rising interest rates
   c) to profit from falling volatility
   d) to close out the option position of a short capped FRN

7. What risks does a seller of a cap face?
   a) rising foreign exchange rates
   b) falling inflation
   c) rising interest rates
   d) falling interest rates

8. Why would you buy a floor?
   a) in order to lock in your maximum borrowing rate
   b) in order to hedge your long futures position
   c) in order to hedge against rising interest rates
   d) in order to hedge against falling interest rates

Die Quotierung von Swaptions erfolgt wie bei Caps und Floors über die Optionsprämie, die eine Einmalzahlung bei Abschluss des Geschäftes darstellt.
Da der Basiswert bei einer Swaption ein Zinsswap mit verzögertem Startdatum ist (oder besser ein Forward-Start-Swap), ist der vereinbarte Zinssatz in der Swaption mit dem aktuellen Preis für entsprechende Forward-Swaps zu vergleichen.

3.8. Wiederholungsfragen

1. Erklären Sie den Unterschied zwischen amerikanischer und europäischer Option!
2. Was versteht man unter dem inneren Wert einer Option?
3. Wovon wird der Zeitwert einer Option beeinflusst?
4. Firma X verkauft einen 3-Monats-LIBOR Floor zu 8%. Am ersten Fälligkeitstag ist der LIBOR 9%. Welche der folgenden Aussagen ist richtig?
   a) Firma X erhält die Prämie und die Zinsdifferenz.
   b) Firma X zahlt die Prämie und die Zinsdifferenz.
   c) Firma X erhält die Prämie und keine weiteren Zahlungen finden statt.
   d) Firma X erhält die Prämie und zahlt die Zinsdifferenz.
5. Sie kaufen ein Cap über USD 50.000.000. Es gelten folgende Daten: Prämie 3,5%, Strike 4%, 6-Monats-LIBOR 3,8%, Laufzeit 3 Jahre. Wie viel Prämie bezahlen Sie?
   a) USD 0
   b) USD 175.000
   c) USD 250.000
   d) USD 1.750.000
6. Warum kauft ein Unternehmen einen CAP?
   a) um sich gegen fallende Zinsen abzusichern
   b) um sich gegen steigende Zinsen abzusichern
   c) um von der fallenden Volatilität zu profitieren
   d) um die Optionsposition einer short capped FRN-Position aufzulösen
7. Welche der folgenden Risiken trägt der Verkäufer eines Cap?
   a) steigender Wechselkurs
   b) fallende Inflation
   c) steigende Zinsen
   d) fallende Zinsen
8. Wozu kaufen Sie einen Floor?
   a) um eine Zinsobergrenze für einen Kredit zu fixieren
   b) um einen Futures-Kauf zu hedgen
   c) um sich gegen steigende Zinsen abzusichern
   d) um sich gegen fallende Zinsen abzusichern

9. Which of the following transactions can be used as protection against rising interest rates?
   a) long floor
   b) long cap
   c) short cap
   d) receiver swap

10. You bought a collar. What does this entail?
    a) You bought a cap and bought a floor.
    b) You sold a cap and bought a floor.
    c) You sold a cap and sold a floor.
    d) You bought a cap and sold a floor.

11. What is the purpose of collars?

12. What is a zero-cost collar?
    a) long cap and short floor at zero premium
    b) long cap and short floor at same strike
    c) long cap and long floor at zero premium
    d) long cap and long floor at same strike

13. How are collars quoted?

14. Which factors influence the premium and therefore the value of a bond option?

15. How is the premium of bond options quoted or computed?

16. Which three instruments protect a USD payer swap against a falling interest rate?
    a) long FRN
    b) long cap
    c) short bond
    d) long floor
    e) long payer swaption
    f) long receiver swaption
    g) receiver swap

17. How can you settle a swaption?

18. You have bought a payer swaption at 5.4%. What happens if you exercise the swaption?
    a) You pay 5.4% fixed for the swap.
    b) You receive 5.4% for the swap.
    c) The offer rate of the swap quote is below 5.4%.
    d) You pay 5.4% for the next floating interest rate period.

19. You have bought a payer swaption with a strike of 5.6%. The current quote for a comparable forward start swap is 6.00-6.10%. What is true for your swaption?
    a) It is at the money.
    b) It is in the money.
    c) It is out of the money.
    d) It is on the run.

9. Welches der folgenden Geschäfte dient als Absicherung gegen steigende Zinsen?
   a) Long Floor
   b) Long Cap
   c) Short Cap
   d) Festzinsempfänger-Swap

10. Was bedeutet der Kauf eines Collars?
    a) Kauf eines Cap und Kauf eines Floor
    b) Verkauf eines Cap und Kauf eines Floor
    c) Verkauf eines Cap und Verkauf eines Floor
    d) Kauf eines Cap und Verkauf eines Floor

11. Was ist das Ziel eines Collars?

12. Was ist ein Zero-Cost Collar?
    a) Long Cap und Short Floor ohne Kosten
    b) Long Cap und Short Floor zum selben Strike
    c) Long Cap und Long Floor ohne Kosten
    d) Long Cap und Long Floor zum selben Strike

13. Wie erfolgt die Quotierung von Collars?

14. Wovon hängt die Prämie und damit der Wert einer Bond-Option ab?

15. Wie wird die Prämie von Bond-Optionen quotiert bzw. berechnet?

16. Mit welchen drei der folgenden Instrumente lässt sich ein USD-Festzinszahler-Swap gegen fallende Zinsen absichern?
    a) long FRN
    b) Kauf Cap
    c) Short Bond
    d) Kauf Floor
    e) Kauf Payer-Swaption
    f) Kauf Receiver-Swaption
    g) Festzinsempfänger-Swap

17. Welche Möglichkeiten des Settlements gibt es bei Swaptions?

18. Sie haben eine Payer-Swaption zu 5,4% gekauft. Was passiert, wenn Sie die Swaption ausüben?
    a) Sie zahlen beim Swap 5,4% fix.
    b) Sie erhalten beim Swap 5,4%.
    c) Die Briefseite der Swapquotierung liegt unter 5,4%.
    d) Sie zahlen für die nächste variable Zinsperiode 5,4%.

19. Sie haben eine Payer-Swaption zu einem Strike von 5,6% gekauft. Der aktuelle Forward-Swap lautet 6,00–6,10%. Was trifft auf Ihre Swaption zu?
    a) Sie ist am Geld.
    b) Sie ist im Geld.
    c) Sie ist aus dem Geld.
    d) Sie ist verfallen.

20. Which right do you acquire if you buy a payer swaption?
    a) right to receive a fixed interest
    b) right to pay a fixed interest
    c) right to pay a floating interest
    d) right to receive a floating interest

21. The 2+5 forward start swap is quoted at 7.50-60%. What are the components of the premium of a time-identical receiver swaption with a strike of 7%?
    a) only intrinsic value
    b) only time value
    c) intrinsic value and time value
    d) It depends whether the receiver swaption was bought or sold.

20. Welches Recht erwerben Sie mit dem Kauf einer Payer-Swaption?
   a) Recht, Festzins zu erhalten
   b) Recht, Festzins zu zahlen
   c) Recht, variablen Zins zu zahlen
   d) Recht, variablen Zins zu erhalten

21. Der 2+5 Forward Start-Swap notiert bei 7,50–60%. Woraus besteht die Prämie einer laufzeitidenten Receiver-Swaption mit Strike 7%?
   a) nur aus dem inneren Wert
   b) nur aus dem Zeitwert
   c) aus innerem Wert und Zeitwert
   d) Es hängt davon ab, ob die Receiver-Swaption gekauft oder verkauft wurde.

PART III: Foreign Exchange, Options & Commodities

TEIL III: Foreign Exchange, Optionen & Rohstoffe

The Foreign Exchange Market is the place where supply of and demand for foreign exchange meet and where foreign exchange then is changed at an agreed exchange rate. Through the foreign exchange market the exchange of domestic money into foreign money is made possible and purchasing power changes from the domestic currency to the foreign currency. Global foreign exchange markets are characterized by foreign exchange trading. Next to financial institutions large industrial companies, private foreign exchange dealers, brokers and trading houses are the main participants on the foreign exchange market. Another important actor on the foreign exchange market are the central banks. The central banks can intervene in the market for (economic) political reasons, e.g. to rebalance the foreign exchange market.

The biggest part of foreign exchange trading is done off-market in interbank trading. In contrast to security markets, forex markets were hardly involved in foreign exchange trading and therefore largely eliminated. In Europe their function, ie, the setting of official exchange rates, is fulfilled by the reference rates. Online trading platforms such as electronic brokers or trading by telephone are used as a trading medium. The object of trading are foreign exchanges which are identified by their country of origin.

This part of the books is divided into three chapters: FX spot market, FX outrights or FX swaps and FX options.

The first chapter deals with the FX spot market. In addition to the normally used conventions in the spot market this chapter gives you information on the calculation of cross rates and the currency codes of the ACI member countries.

In the second chapter FX outrights and FX swaps are described. At the beginning the conventions, the price calculation and the quotation of FX outrights are explained. Furthermore, the conventions and risks of time options and non-deliverable forwards are described. Afterwards, this chapter deals with the conventions, quotation, valuation and risks of FX swaps. At the end of the chapter you will find information on the application of FX outrights and FX swaps.

The third chapter deals with interest rate options. It explains the terminology, the different types of options, the option premium, the profit and loss profiles or strategies for option deals and the risk factors with regard to interest rate options. Finally, "skew" and risk reversal are shortly described

In the finishing fourth chapter the trading with commodities is explained. At the beginning the most important traded commodities are described. Afterwards you will find information about the workings of trading with commodities on spot- and forward market. Furthermore the chapter deals with the conventions of commodites and explains at which stock exchanges these commodities can be traded. Moreover the role of stock exchange and clearing house as well as the margin system are explained. Finally, the different used financial instruments are illustrated theoretically as well as in practice in the form of application examples.

Included in the following exams:
- **ACI Dealing Certificate**
- **ACI Diploma**
- **ACI Operations Certificate**

Der Foreign Exchange Market (Devisenmarkt) ist der ökonomische Ort, an dem Devisenangebot und Devisennachfrage aufeinandertreffen und zum ausgehandelten Devisenkurs getauscht werden. Durch den Devisenmarkt wird der Tausch inländischen Geldes in ausländisches und umgekehrt ermöglicht und dadurch Kaufkraft von Inlandswährung in Auslandswährung umgewandelt. Die weltweiten Devisenmärkte werden insbesondere durch den Devisenhandel geprägt. Neben Kreditinstituten sind auch größere Industrieunternehmen, private Devisenhändler, Devisenmakler und Handelshäuser wesentliche Marktteilnehmer auf dem Devisenmarkt. Eine wichtige Gruppe von Akteuren auf dem Devisenmarkt sind die Zentralbanken. Diese können durch Devisenmarktinterventionen aus (wirtschafts-)politischen Gründen in den Markt eingreifen, um z.B. das Devisenmarktgleichgewicht wiederherzustellen.

Der allergrößte Teil des Devisenhandels vollzieht sich außerbörslich im Interbankenhandel. Devisenbörsen waren – anders als die Wertpapierbörsen – in den Devisenhandel kaum eingeschaltet und sind deshalb weitgehend abgeschafft worden. Ihre wesentlichste Funktion, die Ermittlung der amtlichen Devisenkurse, erfüllen in Europa seither Referenzwerte. Als Handelsmedium wurde vor allem der Online-Handel über Handelsplattformen wie dem elektronischen Makler EBS und der Telefonhandel forciert. Das Handelsobjekt sind Devisen, die eine ihr Herkunftsland repräsentierende Währungsbezeichnung besitzen.

Dieser Teil des Buches gliedert sich in drei Kapitel, und zwar in die Kapitel Kassadevisenmarkt, Devisentermingeschäfte bzw. Devisenswaps und Devisenoptionen.

Das erste Kapitel beschäftigt sich mit dem Kassadevisenmarkt. Neben den handelsüblichen Usancen im Kassamarkt und der Berechnung von Cross Rates bietet dieses Kapitel einen Überblick über die Währungscodes der ACI-Mitgliedsländer.

Im zweiten Kapitel wird auf die Devisentermingeschäfte bzw. Devisenswaps näher eingegangen. Zu Beginn werden die Usancen, die Preisberechnung sowie die Quotierung von Devisentermingeschäften dargestellt. Außerdem werden die Usancen und Risiken von Termingeschäften mit Laufzeitoption und Non-deliverable Forwards näher erläutert. In weiterer Folge werden die Usancen, Quotierung, Bewertung und Risiken von Devisenswaps näher beleuchtet. Am Ende des Kapitels werden abschließend die Einsatzmöglichkeiten von Devisentermingeschäften bzw. Devisenswaps dargestellt.

Das dritte Kapitel beschäftigt sich mit Devisenoptionen. Dabei wird auf die verwendeten Terminologien, die verschiedenen Arten von Optionen, die Optionsprämie, die Gewinn- und Verlustprofile bzw. Strategien bei Optionsgeschäften und auf die Risikokennzahlen im Zusammenhang mit Devisenoptionen eingegangen. Abschließend werden noch kurz der „Skew" und Risk Reversal erläutert.

Im abschließenden vierten Kapitel wird auf den Handel mit Rohstoffen näher eingegangen. Am Beginn werden die wichtigsten gehandelten Rohstoffe vorgestellt. Anschließend wird genauer auf die Funktionsweise des Handels mit Rohstoffen auf dem Kassa- und Terminmarkt eingegangen. Weiters wird erläutert, welche Konventionen für Rohstoffe gelten und an welchen Börsen diese gehandelt werden können. Außerdem wird die Rolle von Börse und Clearing House sowie das Margin-System näher erläutert. Abschließend werden die verschiedenen eingesetzten Produkte sowohl theoretisch als auch praktisch in Form von Anwendungsbeispielen dargestellt.

Prüfungsrelevant für:
- **ACI Dealing Certificate**
- **ACI Diploma**
- **ACI Operations Certificate**

1. FX Spot

In this chapter you learn ...

- what is meant by spot rate.
- how spot transactions are valued.
- what is meant by base currency and quote currency.
- about the difference between bid and offer rate.
- about the differences between market maker and market user.
- about the short cuts in Reuters conversations.
- about the features of brokers.
- which types of broker exist.
- what is meant by spread.
- what is meant by long, short and square position.
- about the differences between direct and indirect quotes.
- what is meant by big figure and pips.
- what is meant by cross rates.
- how cross rates are calculated.
- about the currency codes for ACI member countries.

A **spot FX transaction** is the **purchase or sale of one currency for another**, with delivery usually two days after the dealing date.

Below you can see a Reuters screen which shows spot rates for various currencies against the USD. The different expressions will be discussed in detail on the next pages.

```
                         Big figure        pips
1037 CCY PAGE NAME * REUTER SPOT RATES    * CCY HI*EURO*LO FXFX
1037 EUR CICZ CITIBANK      PRG 1.1507/10  * EUR  1.1566  1.1463
1037 GBP RBSH RBS_HK        HKG 1.6054/59  * GBP  1.6115  1.6043
1037 CHF NBP1 NBP           PAR 1.3156/61  * CHF  1.3188  1.3095
1037 JPY RBSH RBS_HK        HKG 116.97/98  * JPY  117.51  116.32
1037 AUD HSC1 HSBC BANKPLC LON 0.6452/57   * AUD  0.6498  0.6437
1037 CAD HSC1 HSBC BANKPLC LON 1.3879/89   * CAD  1.3937  1.3871
1037 DKK SEBA S E B         STO 6.4507/27  * DKK  6.4709  6.4272
1037 NOK DNBO DEN NORSKE    OSL 6.8320/70  * NOK  6.8555  6.8140
----------------------------------------------------------------
XAU AIGB 351.10/351.60 * ED3  1.20/ 1.30 * FED       * WGVS 30Y
XAG SGCT  4.84/ 4.86   * US30Y YTM  4.65 * 1.18- 1.18 *111.08/10

    Swift Code    quoting bank      bid rate      offer rate
```

1.1. Market conventions

The exchange rate at which the spot transaction is done is called the **"spot rate"**.

1. Kassadevisenmarkt (FX-Spot)

In diesem Kapitel lernen Sie ...

- was man unter Spot Rate versteht.
- wie Kassageschäfte valutiert werden.
- was man unter quotierter Währung und Gegenwährung versteht.
- den Unterschied zwischen Geld- und Briefquotierung kennen.
- den Unterschied zwischen Market Maker und Market User kennen.
- die Bedeutung der Abkürzungen, die in Reuters-Konversationen verwendet werden, kennen.
- die Eigenschaften eines Brokers kennen.
- die Arten von Brokern kennen.
- was man unter Spread versteht.
- was man unter Long-, Short- und Square-Position versteht.
- den Unterschied zwischen direkter und indirekter Quotierung kennen.
- was man unter Big Figure und Pips versteht.
- was man unter Cross Rates versteht.
- wie Cross Rates berechnet werden.
- die Währungscodes der ACI-Mitgliedsländer kennen.

Eine **Devisenkassa-Transaktion** ist der **Kauf oder Verkauf einer Währung gegen eine andere.** Dabei findet die Lieferung zwei Banktage nach Abschluss des Geschäftes statt.

Hier sehen Sie eine Reuters-Seite, auf der Kassakurse für einige Währungen gegen den USD angezeigt werden. Die verschiedenen Ausdrücke werden auf den folgenden Seiten noch genauer erklärt.

Big figure   Pips

```
1037 CCY PAGE NAME * REUTER SPOT RATES     * CCY HI*EURO*LO FXFX
1037 EUR CICZ CITIBANK      PRG 1.1507/10   * EUR  1.1566   1.1463
1037 GBP RBSH RBS_HK        HKG 1.6054/59   * GBP  1.6115   1.6043
1037 CHF NBP1 NBP           PAR 1.3156/61   * CHF  1.3188   1.3095
1037 JPY RBSH RBS_HK        HKG 116.97/98   * JPY  117.51   116.32
1037 AUD HSC1 HSBC BANKPLC  LON 0.6452/57   * AUD  0.6498   0.6437
1037 CAD HSC1 HSBC BANKPLC  LON 1.3879/89   * CAD  1.3937   1.3871
1037 DKK SEBA S E B         STO 6.4507/27   * DKK  6.4709   6.4272
1037 NOK DNBO DEN NORSKE    OSL 6.8320/70   * NOK  6.8555   6.8140
------------------------------------------------------------------
XAU AIGB 351.10/351.60 * ED3  1.20/ 1.30 * FED        * WGVS 30Y
XAG SGCT   4.84/ 4.86   * US30Y YTM  4.65 * 1.12- 1.18 *111.08/10
```

Swiftcode   Quotierende Bank   Geldkurs   Briefkurs

1.1. Usancen

Den Wechselkurs, zu dem die Kassatransaktion – auch Komptantgeschäft oder Spotgeschäft genannt – getätigt wird, bezeichnen wir auch als **Spot Rate** oder **Kassakurs**.

Value date of spot transactions

The delivery day of a spot transaction is called value date. **Business days** do not include Saturdays, Sundays or bank holidays in either of the countries of the two currencies involved. If the "normal" **value date** (two days after the dealing date) falls on a public holiday in one of the centres of the currencies involved, the next working day is taken as the value date for the transaction.

> **Example**
>
> A USD/JPY spot transaction – with dealing date on Wednesday the 4th of January – would normally have value date on Friday, the 6th of January. If however the 6th of January is a public holiday in Japan or in the US, the value date will be deferred to Monday the 9th of January.

Exceptions

- USD-CAD-transactions are often dealt on a so-called **"funds"-basis**. This means that **delivery will be done one working day after the dealing date.**
- FX markets in the **Middle East** are closed on Fridays but open on Saturdays. A USD-SAR transaction could therefore have a **split settlement** date, with the USD delivered on Friday and the SAR delivered on Saturday.
- Before implementation of the Euro the value date of **cross transactions** (FX spot deals not involving the USD) could have been deferred due to US public holidays. Since Euro implementation **US public holidays are more and more disregarded in value dates** of cross transactions.

Swiftcodes (ISO-Codes)

Each currency can be identified by a **three-letter code**. The first two letters refer to the name of the country. The third letter refers to the name of the currency. These codes are used by the Swift message system and have become **international accepted standards**. The major currencies and their swift codes are listed in point 1.3.

For some currencies **nicknames** are rather common among dealers. Of course the correct swift code should be used when confirming a trade.

Valutierung von Kassageschäften

Das Datum des Geschäftsabschlusses heißt **Handelstag.** Den Liefertag eines Geschäftes nennen wir **Valuta.** Das Valutadatum ist **zwei Banktage nach dem Handelstag.** Valutatage sind alle Wochentage, ausgenommen Samstage, Sonntage und Bankfeiertage in jenen Ländern, die am Kassageschäft beteiligt sind. Findet ein Kassageschäft z.B. am Freitag statt, setzt man als Liefertag (Valutatag) den Dienstag fest. Fällt der Valutatag auf einen gesetzlichen Bankfeiertag in einem der beiden Länder, so ergibt sich der nächste Werktag als Valutatag.

Beispiel

Eine EUR/USD-Transaktion findet am Mittwoch, den 4. Januar statt. Valutatag ist Freitag, der 6. Januar. Ist jedoch dieses Datum in Euroland oder den USA ein gesetzlicher Bankfeiertag, so wird für diese Transaktion als Valutatag Montag, der 9. Januar, herangezogen.

Ausnahmen

- USD-CAD-Transaktionen werden öfter auf einer sogenannten **Funds-Basis** durchgeführt. Das bedeutet, dass die **Valutierung bereits einen Tag nach Abschluss des Geschäftes** stattfindet.
- Im **Mittleren Osten** sind die Banken freitags geschlossen, jedoch samstags geöffnet. Im Fall von Transaktionen gegen USD ist eine sogenannte **Split-Valutierung möglich.** Die USD werden bereits am Freitag angeliefert, die Gegentransaktion findet jedoch erst am Samstag statt.
- Vor der Einführung des Euro war es gängige Marktpraxis, bei der Valutierung von **Cross-Geschäften** etwaige amerikanische Bankfeiertage zu berücksichtigen. Seit der Einführung des Euro werden bei der Bestimmung der Valuta von Cross-Geschäften in der Praxis **US-Feiertage immer mehr außer Acht gelassen.** Als Cross-Geschäfte im FX-Markt werden üblicherweise **Devisengeschäfte, bei denen der USD nicht vorkommt,** bezeichnet (z.B. EUR/CHF CAD/JPY).

Swiftcodes (ISO-Codes)

Jede Währung ist über einen **dreistelligen Buchstabencode** identifizierbar. Die ersten beiden Buchstaben bezeichnen den Namen des Landes, in dem die Währung Heimwährung ist. Der dritte Buchstabe kennzeichnet den Namen der Währung. Diese Codes finden im SWIFT-Übertragungssystem Anwendung und sind **international akzeptierte Standardcodes.** Die gängigsten Währungen sowie die entsprechenden Swiftcodes finden Sie im Kapitel 1.3.

Für einige Währungen haben sich im Handel **Spitznamen** etabliert. Allerdings sollte man den korrekten Swiftcode nennen, wenn man ein Geschäft bestätigt.

Example
GBP/USD:　Cable CHF:　　　Swissi SEK:　　　Stocki AUD:　　　Aussi, Ozzy NZD:　　　Kiwi

Base currency and quote currency

Spot rates are quoted as one unit of the base currency (= base currency) against a number of units of the quote currency (also variable currency or counter currency).

$$1 \text{ unit of base currency} = x \text{ units of quote currency}$$

When spot rates are quoted, the first currency always represents the base currency (base currency) and the second currency is the quote currency/variable currency.

Example		
	Base currency	**Quote currency/ Variable Currency**
EUR/USD	Euro	US-Dollar
USD/CZK	US-Dollar	Czech Crown
EUR/USD 0.9850		
If the spot rate quoted for EUR/USD is 0.9850, this means that one Euro is worth 0.9850 USD.		

Bid and offer rates

Spot rates are usually quoted in two rates

- the bid rate and
- the offer rate.

 EUR/USD 1.0850/1.0860 or
 EUR/USD 1.0850-60 or
 EUR/USD 50-60

The **bid rate** is the rate at which the bank quoting the price (the Market maker) is ready to buy the base currency from the market user (the counterpart asking for a price).

 The **offer rate** is the price at which the market maker will sell the base currency to the market user.

Beispiel

GBP/USD:	Cable
CHF:	Swissi
SEK:	Stocki
AUD:	Aussi, Ozzy
NZD:	Kiwi

Quotierte Währung (Basiswährung)/Gegenwährung (variable Währung)

Der Kassakurs drückt aus, wie viele Einheiten der Gegenwährung (variable Währung) eine Einheit der quotierten Währung (Basiswährung) wert ist.

$$1 \text{ Einheit der quotierten Währung} = X \text{ Einheiten der Gegenwährung}$$

Bei der Quotierung von Devisenkursen ist die erste Währung immer die quotierte Währung, die zweite Währung die Gegenwährung.

Beispiel

	Quotierte Währung/ Basiswährung	Gegenwährung/ variable Währung
EUR/USD	Euro	US-Dollar
USD/CZK	US-Dollar	Tschechische Kronen

EUR/USD 0,9850
Der Kassakurs 0,9850 für die Quotierung EUR/USD (Euro/US-Dollar) bedeutet z.B., dass man für 1 EUR 0,9850 USD erhält.

Geld- und Briefquotierung

Allgemein werden Wechselkurse in zwei Kursen angegeben:

- dem Geldkurs und
- dem Briefkurs.

EUR/USD	1,0850/1,0860 oder abgekürzt
EUR/USD	1,0850-60 oder
EUR/USD	50-60

Die **Geldseite** ist jener Kurs, zu dem der quotierende Händler (Market Maker, Preissteller) die quotierte Währung kauft. Sie ist zugleich auch der Kurs, zu dem der anfragende Händler (Market User, Preisnehmer) die quotierte Währung verkaufen kann.

Die **Briefseite** ist der Kurs, zu dem der Market Maker die quotierte Währung verkauft und damit auch der Kurs, zu dem der Market User die quotierte Währung kauft.

Market Maker			
Bid Rate:	buys base currency sells quote currency	Offer rate:	sells base currency buys quote currency

Market User			
Bid rate:	sells base currency buys quote currency	Offer rate:	buys base currency sells quote currency

If a dealer receives a call from another bank, in order to make a quote, he acts as the **Market Maker**. If the same dealer is calling another bank in order to ask for prices he acts as the market user.

The market maker has the risk of changing rates while quoting, so that afterwards he possibly cannot close his position without loss.

The **Market User** is the counterpart asking for prices. The market user may be a corporation, an institutional investor, a bank or the central bank.

In order not to be confused by the different dimensions (market maker/market user, bid/offer, base currency/quote currency) we suggest the following procedure:

I.   **Adjust the question to be answered for the base currency:**
     This means e.g. for a EUR/USD quotation and a question where USD are bought (or sold), the question should be adjusted to EUR to be sold (or bought).
II. **Adjust the question to be answered to Market User/Market Maker:**
     Market Maker (quoting bank) **buys** at **bid rate** and sells at **offer rate**.
     Market User (bank asking for a quote) buys at **offer rate** and sells at **bid rate**.

Example

You want to buy USD 10 m against EUR.
Four different banks quote you the following prices:
Bank A: 1.0830-40
Bank B: 1.0850-60
Bank C: 1.0800-10
Bank D: 1.0790-00
Where do you buy your USD?
I. The base currency is the EUR. You want to buy USD, meaning you sell EUR.
II. You ask for the rate. You act as **market user and sell EUR at the highest bid rate at 1.0850 to Bank B**.
Thus you buy USD 10 m at the rate of 1.0850 and **pay EUR 9,216,589.86 (10,000,000/1.0850).**

Market Maker (quotierender Händler, Preissteller)	
Geldkurs: Kauf der quotierten Währung Verkauf der Gegenwährung	Briefkurs: Verkauf der quotierten Währung Kauf der Gegenwährung

Market User (anfragender Händler, Preisnehmer)	
Geldkurs: Verkauf der quotierten Währung Kauf der Gegenwährung	Briefkurs: Kauf der quotierten Währung Verkauf der Gegenwährung

Die **quotierende Bank** agiert immer als **Market Maker.** Der Market Maker handelt immer zum **günstigeren Preis,** d.h., er kauft auf der Geldseite und verkauft auf der Briefseite. Allerdings trägt er bei der Quotierung auch das **Risiko sich ändernder Kurse,** sodass er nach Abschluss des Geschäftes die ihm entstandene Position möglicherweise nicht mehr ohne Verlust schließen kann.

Die **anfragende Bank** agiert immer als **Market User.** Der Market User handelt immer zum **ungünstigeren Preis,** d.h., er kauft auf der Briefseite und verkauft auf der Geldseite. Dies gilt für alle Marktteilnehmer, die neben Geschäftsbanken auch Zentralbanken, Industriekunden, institutionelle Investoren usw. sein können.

Um eindeutig zu klären, wer zu welchem Kurs was kauft oder verkauft, ist folgende Vorgangsweise hilfreich:

I. **Situation auf die quotierte Währung anpassen:**
Bei einer EUR/USD-Quotierung ist der Kauf von USD gleichbedeutend mit dem Verkauf von EUR.

II. **Situation auf Market Maker/Market User anpassen:**
Der **Market Maker** (quotierende Bank) **kauft** zum **Geldkurs** und **verkauft** zum **Briefkurs.**
Der **Market User** (Bank, die nach einem Preis fragt) **kauft** zum **Briefkurs** und **verkauft** zum **Geldkurs.**

Beispiel

Sie möchten USD 10 Mio. gegen EUR kaufen.
Sie bekommen von vier verschiedenen Banken folgende EUR/USD-Kurse quotiert:
Bank A: 1,0830-40
Bank B: 1,0850-60
Bank C: 1,0800-10
Bank D: 1,0790-00
I. Bei welcher Bank kaufen Sie Ihre USD?
II. Die quotierte Währung ist der EUR. Sie möchten USD kaufen, verkaufen also EUR.
Sie möchten EUR verkaufen. Sie agieren als **Market User** und **verkaufen** daher zum **Geldkurs. Bank B** stellt Ihnen den **höchsten Geldkurs,** d.h., Sie verkaufen EUR an Bank B mit 1,0850.
Sie können somit Ihre USD 10 Mio. zum Kurs von 1,0850 kaufen.
Sie erhalten USD 10 Mio. und zahlen **EUR 9.216.589,90** (10 Mio./1,0850)

Reuters Conversation

In the trade between the banks the communication is often made via electronic media, e.g. via Reuters Dealing. The dealer uses in the process a number of shortcuts.

Example

Here you can see a typical Reuters Conversation in the FX Spot Market:
#EUR USD 10
 12 14
#URS
 OK TO CONFIRM I BUY EUR 10 MIO AGAINST USD AT 1.1512
 MY EUR DIRECT PLS
#TO CONFIRM I SELL EUR 10 MIO AGAINST USD AT 1.1512
#MY USD TO CITI N.Y. PLS
#THKS VM AND BIBI
#END REMOTE

Explanation

A **hash (#)** at the beginning of a line marks your **own text**.

#EUR USD 10

This bank is asking for a rate for EUR 10 m against USD. Usually you do not tell if you want to buy or sell.

12 14

This bank is quoting the **pips** of bid and offer rate (Market Maker).As market participants normally know the big figure, it is left out when quoting so you can save time (FX Spot Market is the fastest market of the world!). In this case we assume that the regular rate is 1.1512-1.1514.

#URS

The asking bank deals and sells EUR 10 m at the bid rate (market user). At the same time it buys USD at 1.1512 (i.e. 10,000,000 x 1.1512 = 11,512,000 USD). **"URS" is a common abbreviation for "yours"** which means "I sell" (opposite "mine" for "I buy").

OK TO CONFIRM I BUY EUR 10 MIO AGAINST USD AT 1.1512
MY EUR DIRECT PLS

The quoting bank confirms the deal and gives payment instructions for the EUR it receives.

Reuters-Konversation

Im Handel zwischen Banken (Interbankhandel) erfolgt die Kommunikation häufig über elektronische Medien, z.B. über Reuters Dealing. Die Händler verwenden dabei eine Reihe von Abkürzungen.

Beispiel

Hier ein Beispiel einer typischen Reuters-Konversation im Kassamarkt:
#EUR USD 10
 12 14
#URS
 OK TO CONFIRM I BUY EUR 10 MIO AGAINST USD AT 1.1512
 MY EUR DIRECT PLS
#TO CONFIRM I SELL EUR 10 MIO AGAINST USD AT 1.1512
#MY USD TO CITI N.Y. PLS
#THKS VM AND BIBI
#END REMOTE

Erläuterungen

Eine **Raute (#)** am Beginn der Zeile kennzeichnet den **eigenen Text,** d.h. Zeilen ohne Raute sind jene des anderen Händlers.

#EUR USD 10

Diese Bank bittet um einen Preis für 10 Mio. EUR gegen USD. Ob gekauft oder verkauft werden soll, wird üblicherweise nicht mitgeteilt.

12 14

Diese Bank stellt einen Geld- und Briefkurs (Market Maker), quotiert aber nur die **Pips.** Da den Marktteilnehmern die aktuelle Big Figure bekannt ist, wird diese, um Zeit zu sparen (der Kassahandel ist der schnellste Markt der Welt), nicht explizit genannt. In unserem Fall gehen wir davon aus, dass der Preis 1,1512–1,1514 lautet.

#URS

Die anfragende Bank schließt ab und verkauft EUR 10 Mio. zum Geldkurs (Market User). Im Gegenzug kauft sie USD zu einem Kurs von 1,1512 (also EUR 10.000.000 x 1,1512 = 11.512.000 USD). „URS" ist in der Händlersprache die **Abkürzung von „Yours"** und heißt analog auf Deutsch **„an dich"** (Gegenteil „Mine", auf Deutsch „von dir").

OK TO CONFIRM I BUY EUR 10 MIO AGAINST USD AT 1.1512 MY EUR DIRECT PLS

Die quotierende Bank bestätigt das Geschäft und gibt die Zahlungsanweisung für die EUR an, die sie erhält.

#TO CONFIRM I SELL EUR 10 MIO AGAINST USD AT 1.1512
#MY USD TO CITI N.Y. PLS
#THKS VM AND BIBI
#END REMOTE

The asking bank confirms the deal as well and gives payment instructions for the USD it receives. The bank thanks for the deal; the conversation is ended.

Broker

Banks can not only trade directly with each other but also via broker. A broker acts as an **agent for the two counterparties** and receives a **brokerage** for his service. This brokerage **depends on the traded volume**, i.e. 10 USD brokerage per traded million EUR would be for 10 m: 10 x 10 = 100 EUR.

The broker's advantage is the **bigger market depth** compared to the one-to-one direct trading in the interbank market as with a broker you have a lot **more potential counterparties at the same time**. In contrary to his customers the broker never takes trading positions. You can distinguish between **voice brokers** and **electronic brokers resp. broking systems**.

A **voice broker** is a real human being who trades with banks **via open telephone line (or Reuters Conversation)**. He informs his customers about the actual quotes all the time. If a bank trades on a broker's price, a deal is done between this bank and the bank which quoted the price (if they both have enough limit for each other). The broker then **confirms the deal** with both of them and additionally **sends a written confirmation to both counterparts** as well.

An **electronic broker** resp. an electronic broking system works like a voice broker but the quotes and deals are done through a **special system**. The best known systems are **Reuters 3000** and **EBS**. Also these systems check if both banks have enough limit to deal with each other. The more banks with big limits have been put to the system, the better prices are for the user (bid/offer spread is smaller), the better his liquidity is. All banks log in with so-called **Dealing Codes, a code with four letters** (e.g. CITL = Citi London). If two counterparts trade in one of these systems you call it **"matching"**, i.e. the system checks the quotes of the dealing codes and matches them if it finds identical numbers. Then the system **prints a confirmation for both counterparties**.

Spread

The spread is the **difference between the bid and offer rates**.

#TO CONFIRM I SELL EUR 10 MIO AGAINST USD AT 1.1512
#MY USD TO CITI N.Y. PLS
#THKS VM AND BIBI
#END REMOTE

Die anfragende Bank bestätigt das Geschäft (ihre Seite = I sell) und gibt Zahlungsanweisung für die USD, die sie erhält. Sie bedankt sich; die Konversation ist beendet.

Broker

Banken können nicht nur untereinander (direkt) handeln, sondern auch Broker (Makler) dazwischenschalten. Ein Broker **vermittelt Geschäfte zwischen Banken (Geschäftspartnern)** und erhält dafür eine **Brokerage (Maklercourtage).** Diese ist **abhängig vom gehandelten Volumen,** z.B. 10 USD Brokerage pro gehandelter Mio. EUR ergibt bei einem Volumen von EUR 10 Mio. USD 100 USD (10 x 10).

Der Vorteil eines Brokers ist die **größere Markttiefe.** Während man beim direkten Interbankhandel immer nur eine begrenzte Anzahl an Banken gleichzeitig für einen Preis fragen kann, hat man über den Broker **gleichzeitig Zugriff auf eine große Zahl von potenziellen Kontrahenten.** Der Broker selbst geht – im Gegensatz zu seinen Kunden – keine eigene Position ein. Man unterscheidet sogenannte **Voice Broker** und **elektronische Broker bzw. Broking-Systeme.**

Ein **Voice Broker** ist ein Mensch aus Fleisch und Blut, der **per Telefonstandleitung (auch via Reuters-Konversation)** die Banken untereinander vermittelt. Er hält seine Kunden mit den aktuellen Quotierungen permanent auf dem Laufenden. Entschließt sich eine Bank, auf den beim Broker aktuell gültigen Kurs zu handeln, entsteht ein Geschäft zwischen dieser Bank und derjenigen, von der die Quotierung stammt (wenn beide Banken genügend Limit füreinander haben). Der Broker **bestätigt** dann beiden Banken **mündlich den Geschäftsabschluss** und sendet zusätzlich eine **schriftliche Bestätigung an beide Kontrahenten.**

Ein **elektronischer Broker** bzw. ein elektronisches Broking-System funktioniert wie ein Voice Broker, nur erfolgen die Quotierungen und Abschlüsse in einem **speziellen System.** Die bekanntesten dieser Systeme sind **Reuters 3000** und **EBS.** Zusätzlich **prüfen** diese Systeme **vor Abschluss die Limite der Banken** füreinander. Je mehr Banken mit höheren Limiten im elektronischen Broking-System eingepflegt sind, umso bessere („engere") Preise stehen dem Nutzer zur Verfügung, d.h. umso höher ist seine Liquidität. Die Kennung der Banken erfolgt durch einen **vierbuchstabigen** sogenannten **Dealing Code,** mit dem die Banken jeweils eingeloggt sind (z.B. CITL = Citi London). In Hinblick auf den Abschluss im elektronischen Broking-System spricht man auch von „**Matching**", d.h., das System überprüft die Quotierungen der einzelnen Dealing Codes und „matched" sie bei Übereinstimmung. Nach erfolgtem Abschluss erstellt das System eine **schriftliche Bestätigung für beide Kontrahenten.**

Spread

Als Spread bezeichnet man die Differenz zwischen dem Geldsatz und dem Briefsatz (auch **Geld-/Briefspanne).**

Quoted Currencies		
Currency Pair	**Buying Rate (Bid)**	**Selling Rate (Offer)**
USD/CHF	1.4720	1.4730
EUR/USD	1.0125	1.0130
USD/CZK	30.210	30.220
USD/NOK	7.4500	7.4800
CHF/JPY	86.760	86.800
USD/JPY	105.80	105.90
USD/SEK	6.7270	6.7300
GBP/USD	1.5585	1.5595
GBP/JPY	195.70	195.90

The rates shown are examples for the bid and offer rates for interbank spot deals. For customers, spreads are normally a little wider.

If USD/CHF is quoted 1.4720-30, the bid rate is the buying price quoted for the USD (or selling price for the CHF). The offer rate is the selling price for the USD (or the buying price for the CHF).

Long-, short-, square-position

Banks resp. dealers of foreign currency, have a long, short or square position in the different currencies.

- A **long position** in a currency means that the dealer has bought more of the currency than he has sold. If this position is taken purposely the dealer expects the currency to rise.
- Having sold more than bought the dealer speaks of a **short position** in a currency. The expectation will normally be that of a declining rate.
- A **square or a flat position** in one currency means that the dealer has bought and sold the same amount of currency and has no risk if the rates change.

Direct/indirect quote

In the international markets **most currencies are quoted against the USD**. In this case the USD is usually the base currency (e.g. USD/CHF, USD/NOK, USD/CZK, USD/PLN, USD/JPY, etc). However there are some exemptions to this rule: e.g. GBP/USD, EUR/USD, AUD/USD.

In the home market it is sometimes more convenient to reverse the quoting conventions. The method to quote CZK against CHF may in this case be in Prague different to Zurich.

Quotierte Währungen		
Währungspaar	**Geldkurs**	**Briefkurs**
USD/CHF	1,4720	1,4730
EUR/USD	1,0125	1,0130
USD/CZK	30,210	30,220
USD/NOK	7,4500	7,4800
CHF/JPY	86,760	86,800
USD/JPY	105,80	105,90
USD/SEK	6,7270	6,7300
GBP/USD	1,5585	1,5595
GBP/JPY	195,70	195,90

Diese Tabelle zeigt Beispiele für Ankaufs- und Verkaufskurse für Devisengeschäfte unter Banken für **Standardbeträge** (Interbankkurse). Je nach Währungspaar liegen die Standardbeträge zwischen ein und mehreren Millionen USD oder Gegenwert. Bei Geschäften mit Kunden ist die Spanne üblicherweise größer.

Wenn beispielsweise für USD gegen CHF ein Kurs von 1,4720-30 quotiert wird, handelt es sich beim ersten Kurs um den Ankaufskurs für USD (oder den Verkaufskurs für CHF), während der zweite Kurs dem Verkaufskurs für den USD (oder dem Ankaufskurs für CHF) entspricht (jeweils aus Sicht des Preisstellers bzw. Market Makers).

Long-, Short- und Square-Position

Banken bzw. Händler, die mit Fremdwährungen handeln, haben entweder eine Long-, Short- oder Square-Position in jeder einzelnen Währung.

- Kauft ein Händler mehr von einer Währung als er verkauft, so spricht man von einer **Long-Position** in dieser Währung. Er gewinnt bei steigenden Kursen und verliert bei fallenden Kursen. Bezieht der Händler diese Position bewusst, so geht er davon aus, dass der Kurs der betreffenden Währung steigen wird.
- Verkauft der Händler mehr von einer Währung als er gekauft hat, so spricht man von einer **Short-Position** in dieser Währung. Die Kursmeinung wird in diesem Fall üblicherweise ein Fallen des Kurses dieser Währung sein.
- Nimmt der Händler weder eine Long- noch eine Short-Position ein, so spricht man von einer **Square-** oder **Flat-Position** in einer Währung.

Direkte/Indirekte Quotierung

An den internationalen Finanzmärkten haben sich bestimmte Währungen als Basiswährung etabliert. Die **meisten Währungen** werden **gegen den US-Dollar quotiert** (USD/JPY, USD/CHF, USD/CZK usw.).

Vor allem bei Cross-Quotierungen (das sind Währungspaare, die den USD nicht enthalten) ist die Art der Quotierung nicht immer einheitlich. Im Heimatmarkt ist es oft praktikabler, umgekehrt zu quotieren. So kann die Methode der Quotierung für beispielsweise CZK gegen CHF in Prag (CHF/CZK) und Zürich (CZK/CHF) unterschiedlich sein.

Ist der Wert der quotierten Währung wesentlich niedriger als der der Gegenwährung, so wird der Kurs oft für 100 Einheiten angegeben.

- In a direct quote the home currency is the quote currency and the foreign currency is the base currency. Frequently the quote is done for 100 units of the quote currency. example:
  direct quote for CZK in Zurich: CZK/CHF 4.8075 (i.e. 100 CZK cost 4.8075 CHF)
  direct quote for CHF in Prague: CHF/CZK 20.800 (i.e. 1 CHF costs 20.800 CZK)

- In an indirect quote the home currency is the base currency and the foreign currency is the quote currency.
  example:
  indirect quote for CHF in Prague: CZK/CHF 4.8075
  indirect quote for CZK in Zurich: CHF/CZK 20.800

The indirect quote is the reciprocal value (1 divided by) of the direct quote. In order to get an indirect quote the following rules have to be observed:

The bid of the indirect quote is the reciprocal value of the offer rate of the direct quote.
The offer of the indirect quote is the reciprocal value of the bid rate of the direct quote.

Rates indirect quote	
Bid Rate	**Offer Rate**
$\dfrac{1}{\text{Offer}_{\text{direct}}}$	$\dfrac{1}{\text{Bid}_{\text{direct}}}$

Example

In New York the direct quote for GBP is:
GBP/USD 1.6200-1.6210
The corresponding indirect quote in New York may be computed:

USD/GBP, bid rate: $\dfrac{1}{1.6210}=0.6169$

USD/GBP, offer rate: $\dfrac{1}{1.6200}=0.6173$

- Bei einer **direkten Quotierung** ist die **Basiswährung (quotierte Währung)** die **Fremd-währung** und die **Heimwährung** die **Gegenwährung.**
  Beispiel:
  Direkte Quotierung für CZK in Zürich: CZK/CHF 4,8075 (100 CZK kosten 4,8075 CHF).
  Direkte Quotierung für CHF in Prag: CHF/CZK 20,800 (1 CHF kosten 20,800 CZK).

- Bei einer **indirekten Quotierung** ist die **Heimwährung** die **Basiswährung (quotierte Währung)** und die **Fremdwährung** die **Gegenwährung.**
  Die Quotierung EUR/USD ist also aus europäischer Sicht eine indirekte Quotierung und aus amerikanischer Sicht eine direkte Quotierung.
  Beispiel:
  Indirekte Quotierung für CHF in Prag: CZK/CHF 4,8075
  Indirekte Quotierung für CZK in Zürich: CHF/CZK 20,800

Die indirekte Quotierung entspricht dem reziproken Wert (1 dividiert durch den Ausgangs-wert) der direkten Quotierung. Um die indirekte Quotierung zu ermitteln, ist zu beachten:

Geldseite (indirekte Quotierung) = Reziprokwert der Briefseite (direkte Quotierung)
Briefseite (indirekte Quotierung) = Reziprokwert der Geldseite (direkte Quotierung)

Kurse indirekte Quotierung	
Geldseite	**Briefseite**
$\dfrac{1}{\text{Brief}_{\text{Direkt}}}$	$\dfrac{1}{\text{Geld}_{\text{Direkt}}}$

Beispiel

In Prag lautet die direkte Quotierung:
GBP/USD 1.6200-1.6210
Die entsprechende indirekte Quotierung in New York ist folgendermaßen zu berechnen:

USD/GBP, Geld: $\dfrac{1}{1.6210} = 0.6169$

USD/GBP, Brief: $\dfrac{1}{1.6200} = 0.6173$

Pips and Big Figure

An FX quote usually consists of **five digits**.

Example
EUR/USD 1.1510 USD/CHF 1.3160 AUD/USD 0.6455 USD/JPY 117.15 USD/CZK 27.323 etc.

The last two digits of the spot rate are the so-called **pips**. The rest of the spot quotation is called **big figure**.

Example

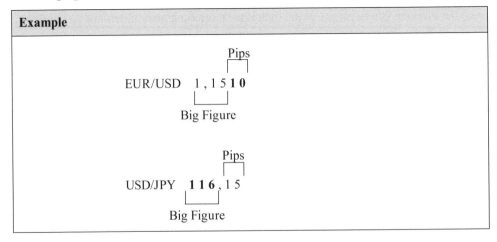

In general the pip is one hundredth of **one hundredth of a currency**

Example
USD 0.0001 EUR 0.0001 CHF 0.0001 However, some **exceptions** can be observed in the markets. For a USD/JPY quotation one pip is one hundredth of a JPY (JPY 0.01).

In day-to-day business, spot dealers assume that, every counterpart knows the big figure of the given quotation. Hence, **spot rates are often quoted only with their pips**. As this may be rather dangerous (especially in very volatile markets), the code of conduct recommends to indicate the big figure for every deal.

Pips und Big Figure

Eine FX-Quotierung besteht üblicherweise aus **fünf Stellen:**

Beispiel
EUR/USD 1.1510 AUD/USD 0.6455 USD/JPY 117.15 USD/CZK 27.323 etc.

Die letzten beiden Ziffern eines Kassakurses bezeichnet man als **Pips** oder Punkte. Die restlichen Ziffern der Kassakursquotierung bilden die sogenannte **Big Figure.**

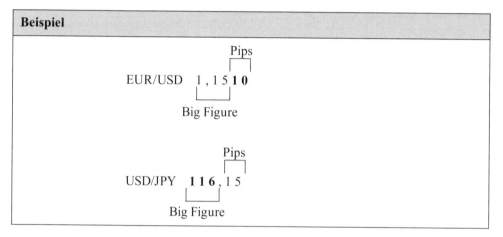

Beispiel

Allgemein ist **ein Pip ein Hundertstel vom Hundertstel einer Währung.**

Beispiel
USD 0,0001 EUR 0,0001 CHF 0,0001 Davon gibt es einige **Ausnahmen.** Werden beispielsweise Dollar gegen YEN quotiert, ist ein Pip das Hundertstel von einem YEN (JPY 0,01).

Im Tagesgeschäft gehen Kassahändler davon aus, dass jeder, mit dem sie zu tun haben, die aktuelle Big Figure der Hauptwährungen kennt. Daher werden **Kassageschäfte häufig nur unter Quotierung der Pips abgeschlossen.** Besonders in volatilen Märkten ist diese Gewohnheit nicht unproblematisch. Der ACI Model Code hält daher die Händler dazu an, bei jedem Geschäft die entsprechende Big Figure anzugeben.

1.2. Cross Rates

A cross rate is the **quote for a currency pair which does not include the USD** (e.g. EUR/CHF, GBP/JPY etc.).

In the professional spot markets most of the deals are done with the USD as the base currency. Since some years however, cross deals have increased in importance.

Every **cross rate** can be computed by **using the corresponding USD quotes**.

Example
Following rates are quoted in the market: USD/CHF: 1,4980-85 USD/NOK: 6,3272-92 What is the NOK/CHF-Cross-Rate?

Bid rate

In order to compute the NOK/CHF bid rate (at which we sell NOK against CHF) we have to do the following transactions:
(1)   We sell NOK 1 and buy USD 0.1580 (at 6.3292)
(2)   We sell USD 0.1580 and buy CHF 0.23668 (1.4980)

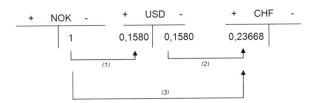

(3) Result: When selling NOK 1 you receive CHF 0.23668. Thus the bid rate NOK/CHF is **0.2367**.

Offer rate

In order to compute the NOK/CHF offer rate (at which we buy NOK against CHF) we have to do the following transactions:
(1)   We buy NOK 1 and sell USD 0.15805 (at 6.3272)
(2)   We buy USD 0.15805 and sell CHF 0.23683 (at 1.4985)

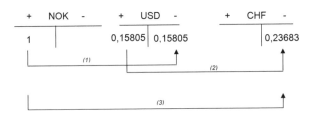

1.2. Cross Rates

Der professionelle Devisenhandel drückt die Kurse der verschiedenen Währungen üblicherweise gegenüber dem **US-Dollar** aus. Er dient als **Vehikel- oder Transaktionswährung.** Allerdings hat der Cross-Handel, also der Handel Währung gegen Währung, unter Ausschluss des USD in den letzten Jahren enorm an Wichtigkeit gewonnen.

Die Cross Rate zwischen zwei Währungen **kann aus zwei Währungspaaren über den Dollar errechnet** werden.

Beispiel

Folgende Sätze werden im Markt quotiert:
USD/CHF: 1,4980-85
USD/NOK: 6,3272-92
Was ist die NOK/CHF-Cross-Rate?

Geldseite

Um die Geldseite zu ermitteln, zu der auf den quotierten Kursen NOK gegen CHF verkauft werden können, sind folgende Transaktionen durchzuführen:
(1)   Verkauf NOK 1 gegen Kauf USD 0,1580 (zu 6,3292)
(2)   Verkauf USD 0,1580 gegen Kauf CHF 0,23668 (1,4980)

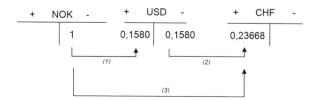

(3)   Ergebnis: Durch den Verkauf von 1 NOK erhalten wir 0,23668 CHF, d.h., der Geldkurs NOK/CHF ist **0,2367.**

Briefseite

Um die Briefseite zu ermitteln, zu der zu den quotierten Kursen NOK gegen CHF gekauft werden können, sind folgende Transaktionen durchzuführen:
(1)   Kauf 1 NOK gegen Verkauf 0,15805 USD (zu 6,3272)
(2)   Kauf 0,15805 USD gegen Verkauf 0,23683 CHF (1,4985)

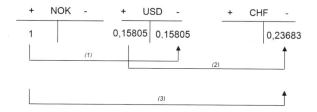

(3) Result: By buying NOK 1 you pay CHF 0.23683. Thus the NOK/CHF offer rate is **0.2368**.

Rules for calculating cross rates:

The simple case:
USD is the base currency for one currency pair and quote currency for the other currency pair **("cross-over")**.

Example
EUR/USD: 1.1500-10 USD/CHF: 1.4980-85 → you want to quote EUR/CHF. As EUR is the base currency and CHF the quote currency for the cross rate you do not have to change the quotes above. **EUR/CHF bid** → multiplication of bid rates: 1.1500 x 1.4980 = **1.7227** **EUR/CHF ask** → multiplication of ask rates: 1.1510 x 1.4985 = **1.7248** (If you had to quote CHF/EUR, you would have to calculate as stated above and then compute the reciprocal rate in the end.)

The complex case:
USD is the base currency resp. quote currency for **both currency pairs.**

Example
USD/CHF: 1.4980-85 USD/NOK: 6.3272-92 → you want to quote NOK/CHF

Step 1: Conversion USD/NOK in NOK/USD
In order to make NOK the base currency calculate the reciprocal quotation of USD/NOK (if you had to quote CHF/NOK you would have to compute the reciprocal value of USD/CHF).

NOK/USD bid: $\frac{1}{6.3292}$ = 0.15800   NOK/USD ask: $\frac{1}{6.3272}$ = 0.15805

Step 2: After Step 1 the currency is quoted "cross over" again. Thus you can proceed like in the above stated "simple case":

NOK/CHF bid → multiplication of the bid rates: 1.4980 x 0.15800 = **0.2367**
NOK/CHF ask → multiplication of ask rates: 1.4985 x 0.15805 = **0.2368**

(3) Ergebnis: Durch den Kauf von 1 NOK erhalten wir 0,23683 CHF, d.h., der Briefkurs NOK/CHF ist **0,2368**.

Regeln für das Berechnen von Cross Rates:

Der einfachste Fall:

Die Vehikelwährung (USD) ist bei dem einen Währungspaar die quotierte Währung, bei dem anderen die Gegenwährung (also **„USD über Kreuz"**).

Beispiel

EUR/USD: 1,1500-10
USD/CHF: 1,4980-85
Sie suchen den EUR/CHF-Kurs.
Da EUR die quotierte Währung und CHF die Gegenwährung der Cross Rate sein soll, können Sie die Quotierungen unverändert lassen.
EUR/CHF Geld → Multiplikation der Geldseiten: 1,1500 x 1,4980 = **1,7227**
EUR/CHF Brief → Multiplikation der Briefseiten: 1,1510 x 1,4985 = **1,7248**
(Wäre hier nach CHF/EUR gefragt, könnten Sie die Berechnungen wie oben durchführen und müssten dann zum Schluss den reziproken Kurs ermitteln.)

Der komplexere Fall:

Die Vehikelwährung (USD) ist bei beiden Währungspaaren die quotierte Währung bzw. bei beiden die Gegenwährung.

Beispiel

USD/CHF: 1,4980-85
USD/NOK: 6,3272-92
Sie suchen den NOK/CHF-Kurs.

Schritt 1: Umwandlung von USD/NOK in NOK/USD.
Um NOK zur quotierten Währung zu machen, ermitteln Sie die reziproke Quotierung von USD/NOK (wäre CHF/NOK gefragt, müssten Sie den reziproken USD/CHF-Kurs ermitteln).

NOK/USD Geld: $\dfrac{1}{6,3292} = 0,15800$ NOK/USD Brief: $\dfrac{1}{6,3272} = 0,15805$

Schritt 2: Durch den Schritt 1 ist die quotierte Währung wieder „über kreuz". Sie können somit wie im oben beschriebenen einfachsten Fall weiterverfahren:

NOK/CHF Geld → Multiplikation der Geldkurse: 1,4980 x 0,15800 = **0,2367**
NOK/CHF Brief → Multiplikation der Briefkurse: 1,4985 x 0,15805 = **0,2368**

1.3. Currency Codes

Three letter currency codes are used to represent currencies. In most cases, the **first two letters of the currency code** represent the **country** and the **last one represents the currency**.

CAD: CA stands for **Ca**nada and D for **D**ollar
JPY: JP stands for **Ja**pan and Y for **Y**en

The ISO (International Organization for Standardization) publishes a worldwide standard for currency codes (ISO 4217). Usually, these codes are used by SWIFT as well. Thus these currency codes are frequently called **ISO-Codes** or **SWIFT-Codes**.

Currency codes of ACI member countries

Europe		European Union		Asia Pacific	
Albania	ALL	Austria	EUR	Australia	AUD
Channel Islands	GBP	Belgium		China	CNY
Croatia	HRK	Bulgaria	BGN	Hong Kong	HKD
Czech Republic	CZK	Cyprus		India	INR
Denmark	DKK	Estonia		Indonesia	IDR
Georgia	GEL	Finland		Japan	JPY
Hungary	HUF	France		Korea (Republic of)	KRW
Iceland	ISK	Germany		Macau	MOP
Israel	ILS	Greece		Malaysia	MYR
Latvia	LVL	Ireland		Mongolia	MNT
Lithuania	LTL	Italy		New Zealand	NZD
Macedonia	MKD	Luxembourg		Pakistan	PKR
Monaco	EUR	Malta		Philippines	PHP
Norway	NOK	Netherlands		Singapore	SGD
Poland	PLN	Portugal		Sri Lanka	LKR
Russia	RUB	Romania	RON	Thailand	THB
Serbia	RSD	Slovakia			
Sweden	SEK	Slovenia			
Switzerland	CHF	Spain			
Turkey	TRY				
Ukraine	UAH	**Middle East and Africa**	BHD		
United Kingdom	GBP	Bahrain	EGP		
		Egypt	JOD		
Americas		Jordan	KES		
Argentina	ARS	Kenya	KWD		
Bahamas	BSD	Kuwait	LBP		
Canada	CAD	Lebanon	MUR		
Mexico	MXN	Mauritius	NGN		
USA	USD	Nigeria	ZAR		
		South Africa	TZS		
		Tanzania	TND		
		Tunisia	AED		
		United Arab Emirates			

1.3. Währungscodes

Währungen werden mit einem **3-stelligen Code** abgekürzt. Meist stehen die **ersten beiden Buchstaben** dabei für das **Land** und der **dritte Buchstabe** für die **Währung.**

> CAD: CA steht für **Ca**nada und D für **D**ollar.
> JPY: JP steht für **Ja**pan und Y für **Y**en.

Die ISO (International Organization for Standardization) ist für die weltweite Normierung der Codes zuständig (ISO 4217). Diese Codes werden auch von SWIFT verwendet. Daher werden die Währungsbezeichnungen auch **ISO-Codes** bzw. **SWIFT-Codes** genannt.

Währungscodes der ACI-Mitgliedsländer

Asien und pazifischer Raum		Europa		Europäische Union	
		Albanien	**ALL**	Belgien	**EUR**
Australien	**AUD**	Dänemark	**DKK**	Bulgarien	**BGN**
China	**CNY**	Georgien	**GEL**	Deutschland	
Hongkong	**HKD**	Großbritannien	**GBP**	Estland	
Indien	**INR**	Island	**ISK**	Finnland	
Indonesien	**IDR**	Israel	**ILS**	Frankreich	
Japan	**JPY**	Lettland	**LVL**	Griechenland	
Korea (Republic of)	**KRW**	Litauen	**LTL**	Irland	
Macao	**MOP**	Kanalinseln	**GBP**	Italien	
Malaysia	**MYR**	Kroatien	**HRK**	Luxemburg	
Mongolei	**MNT**	Mazedonien	**MKD**	Malta	
Neuseeland	**NZD**	Monaco	**EUR**	Niederlande	
Pakistan	**PKR**	Norwegen	**NOK**	Österreich	
Philippinen	**PHP**	Poland	**PLN**	Portugal	
Singapur	**SGD**	Russland	**RUB**	Rumänien	**RON**
Sri Lanka	**LKR**	Serbien	**RSD**	Slowakei	
Thailand	**THB**	Schweden	**SEK**	Slowenien	
		Schweiz	**CHF**	Spanien	
Naher Osten und		Tschechien	**CZK**	Zypern	
Afrika		Türkei	**TRY**		
Ägypten	**EGP**	Ungarn	**HUF**	**Nord- und Südame-**	**ARS**
Bahrain	**BHD**	Ukraine	**UAH**	**rika**	**BSD**
Jordan	**JOD**			Argentinien	**MXN**
Kenia	**KES**			Bahamas	**CAD**
Kuwait	**KWD**			Mexico	**USD**
Libanon	**LBP**			Kanada	
Mauritius	**MUR**			USA	
Nigeria	**NGN**				
Südafrika	**ZAR**				
Tansania	**TZS**				
Tunesien	**TND**				
Vereinigte Arabische					
Emirate	**AED**				

Summary

A spot FX transaction is the purchase or sale of one currency for another, with delivery usually two days after the dealing date. The delivery day of a spot transaction is called value date.

The exchange rate at which the spot transaction is done is called the "spot rate".

Spot rates are quoted as one unit of the base currency (= base currency) against a number of units of the quote currency (also variable currency or counter currency).

When spot rates are quoted, the first currency always represents the base currency (base currency) and the second currency is the quote currency/variable currency.

Spot rates are usually quoted in two rates, the bid rate and the offer rate. The bid rate is the rate at which the bank quoting the price (the market maker) is prepared to buy the base currency from the market user (the counterparty asking for a price). The offer rate is the price at which the market maker will sell the base currency to the market user.

Banks may not only trade directly with each other but also via a broker. A broker acts as an agent for the two counterparties and receives a brokerage fee for his service. A broker offers a deeper market compared to the one-to-one direct trading in the interbank market since with a broker you have many more potential counterparties. A voice broker is a real human being who trades with banks via open telephone line (or Reuters conversation). An electronic broker or an electronic broking system works like a voice broker but the quotes and deals are done through a special system. The best known systems are Reuters 3000 and EBS.

The spread is the difference between the bid and offer rates.

Banks or dealers of foreign currency have a long, short or square position in the different currencies.

In a direct quote, the home currency is the quote currency and the foreign currency is the base currency. In an indirect quote, the home currency is the base currency and the foreign currency is the quote currency.

An FX quote usually consists of five digits. The last two digits of the spot rate are the so-called pips. The rest of the spot quotation is called big figure.

A cross rate is the quote for a currency pair which does not include the USD (e.g. EUR/CHF, GBP/JPY etc.). In the professional spot markets most deals are done with the USD as the base currency. For some years, however, cross deals have gained in importance.

Three-letter currency codes are used to represent currencies. In most cases, the first two letters of the currency code represent the country and the last one represents the currency. These currency codes are often called ISO codes or SWIFT codes.

Zusammenfassung

Eine Devisenkassa-Transaktion ist der Kauf oder Verkauf einer Währung gegen eine andere. Das Datum des Geschäftsabschlusses heißt Handelstag. Den Liefertag eines Geschäftes nennen wir Valuta. Das Valutadatum ist zwei Banktage nach dem Handelstag. Den Wechselkurs, zu dem die Kassatransaktion – auch Komptantgeschäft oder Spotgeschäft genannt – getätigt wird, bezeichnen wir auch als Spot Rate oder Kassakurs. Der Kassakurs drückt aus, wie viele Einheiten der Gegenwährung (variable Währung) eine Einheit der quotierten Währung (Basiswährung) wert ist.

Die Geldseite ist jener Kurs, zu dem der quotierende Händler (Market Maker, Preissteller) die quotierte Währung kauft. Sie ist zugleich auch der Kurs, zu dem der anfragende Händler (Market User, Preisnehmer) die quotierte Währung verkaufen kann. Die Briefseite ist der Kurs, zu dem der Market Maker die quotierte Währung verkauft und damit auch der Kurs, zu dem der Market User die quotierte Währung kauft.

Banken können nicht nur untereinander (direkt) handeln, sondern auch Broker (Makler) dazwischenschalten. Ein Broker vermittelt Geschäfte zwischen Banken (Geschäftspartnern) und erhält dafür eine Brokerage (Maklercourtage). Diese ist abhängig vom gehandelten Volumen. Der Vorteil eines Brokers ist die größere Markttiefe. Ein Voice Broker ist ein Mensch aus Fleisch und Blut, der per Telefonstandleitung (auch via Reuters-Konversation) die Banken untereinander vermittelt. Ein elektronischer Broker bzw. ein elektronisches Broking-System funktioniert wie ein Voice Broker, nur erfolgen die Quotierungen und Abschlüsse in einem speziellen System. Die bekanntesten dieser Systeme sind Reuters 3000 und EBS.

Als Spread bezeichnet man die Differenz zwischen dem Geldsatz und dem Briefsatz (auch Geld-/Briefspanne).

Banken bzw. Händler, die mit Fremdwährungen handeln, haben entweder eine Long- (mehr gekauft als verkauft), Short- (mehr verkauft als gekauft) oder Square-Position (weder Long- noch Short-Position) in jeder einzelnen Währung.

Bei einer direkten Quotierung ist die Basiswährung (quotierte Währung) die Fremdwährung und die Heimwährung die Gegenwährung. Bei einer indirekten Quotierung ist die Heimwährung die Basiswährung (quotierte Währung) und die Fremdwährung die Gegenwährung. Die indirekte Quotierung entspricht dem reziproken Wert (1 dividiert durch den Ausgangswert) der direkten Quotierung.

Eine FX-Quotierung besteht üblicherweise aus fünf Stellen. Die letzten beiden Ziffern eines Kassakurses bezeichnet man als Pips oder Punkte. Die restlichen Ziffern der Kassakursquotierung bilden die sogenannte Big Figure.

Der professionelle Devisenhandel drückt die Kurse der verschiedenen Währungen üblicherweise gegenüber dem US-Dollar aus. Er dient als Vehikel- oder Transaktionswährung. Allerdings hat der Cross-Handel, also der Handel Währung gegen Währung, unter Ausschluss des USD in den letzten Jahren enorm an Wichtigkeit gewonnen. Die Cross Rate zwischen zwei Währungen kann aus zwei Währungspaaren über den Dollar errechnet werden.

Währungen werden mit einem dreistelligen Code abgekürzt. Meist stehen die ersten beiden Buchstaben dabei für das Land und der dritte Buchstabe für die Währung. Die Währungsbezeichnungen werden auch ISO-Codes bzw. SWIFT-Codes genannt.

1.4. Practice Questions

1. You buy EUR against USD. After how many bankdays does the delivery take place?
2. What is the correct value date of a spot transaction that was traded on Thursday, 17 December (ignoring holidays, if any)?
3. How is the quote currency also called?
   a) foreign currency
   b) variable currency
   c) base currency
   d) home currency
4. Which of the following statements is true for the currency pair CHF/JPY?
   a) CHF is the variable currency.
   b) CHF is the base currency.
   c) CHF is the base currency only in Europe.
   d) CHF is always the home currency.
5. What is the incentive for a bank to act as market maker?
   a) bid/offer spread
   b) better liquidity in the market
   c) information on flows
   d) All answers are true.
6. What is the main advantage of using a broker as opposed to direct interbank dealing?
7. Explain the differences between a voice broker and an electronic broker!
8. You deal with a voice broker. Who is your counterparty?
   a) clearinghouse
   b) broker himself
   c) quoting bank
   d) All answers are false.
9. You have bought USD/CHF. Which position do you have now?
   a) short position in USD
   b) long position in USD
   c) long position in CHF
   d) insufficient information to decide
10. As market user you need to buy USD against YEN. You receive the following quotes. Which is the best for you?
    a) 101.83-91
    b) 101.88-93
    c) 101.85-90
    d) 101.84-89
    e) 101.89-94
11. What is the big figure of a GBP/AUD quote of 2.5963?
12. What are the pips in a GBP/USD quote of 1.7970?
13. You buy spot DKK against USD at 7.0302 (USD/DKK). A bank quotes DKK/USD 0.14200-25 and you close the position. What is the result?
    a) a loss

1.4. Wiederholungsfragen

1. Sie kaufen EUR gegen USD. Nach wie vielen Bankarbeitstagen findet die Lieferung statt?

2. Welcher ist der korrekte Valutatag eines Kassageschäftes, das am Donnerstag, den 17. Dezember, abgeschlossen wurde (ohne Berücksichtigung von Feiertagen)?

3. Wie wird die quotierte Währung noch genannt?
   a) Gegenwährung
   b) Basiswährung
   c) variable Währung
   d) Heimwährung

4. Welche Aussage für das Währungspaar CHF/JPY ist richtig?
   a) Der CHF ist die Gegenwährung.
   b) Der CHF ist die quotierte Währung.
   c) Der CHF ist nur in Europa die quotierte Währung.
   d) Der CHF ist grundsätzlich die Heimwährung.

5. Was sind die Gründe für eine Bank, Market Maker zu sein?
   a) Die Bank verdient am Geld-/Brief-Spread.
   b) Die Bank verbessert die Liquidität im Markt.
   c) Die Bank erhält Informationen über die Flows im Markt.
   d) Alle Antworten sind richtig.

6. Welchen Vorteil hat eine Bank durch Zwischenschaltung eines Brokers im Vergleich zum direkten Interbankhandel?

7. Erklären Sie den Unterschied zwischen einem Voice Broker und einem elektronischen Broker!

8. Sie handeln bei einem Voice Broker. Wer ist Ihr Counterpart?
   a) das Clearinghouse
   b) der Broker selbst
   c) die quotierende Bank.
   d) Alle Antworten sind falsch.

9. Sie haben USD/CHF gekauft. Welche Position haben Sie?
   a) Short-Position in USD
   b) Long-Position in USD
   c) Long-Position in CHF
   d) nicht genügend Informationen, um diese Frage zu beantworten

10. Sie wollen bei einer Bank USD gegen YEN kaufen. Welche USD/JPY-Quotierung ist für Sie die beste?
    a) 101,83-91
    b) 101,88-93
    c) 101,85-90
    d) 101,84-89
    e) 101,89-94

11. Was ist die Big Figure von einer GBP/AUD-Quotierung von 2,5963?

12. Was sind die Pips bei einer GBP/USD-Quotierung von 1,7970?

13. Sie kaufen Kassa DKK gegen USD zu 7,0302 (USD/DKK). Eine Bank quotiert Ihnen DKK/USD 0,14200-25 und Sie schließen Ihre Position. Was ist Ihr Ergebnis?
    a) ein Verlust

    b) a profit

    c) neither profit or loss

    d) insufficient information to decide

14. You are long USD against CHF and you want to close your position. At which quotation do you make the biggest profit as market maker?

    a) 1.5040-45

    b) 1.5040-50

    c) 1.5042-47

    d) 1.5032-37

15. What is meant by "spread"?

16. Explain the differences between direct and indirect quote!

17. What is meant by "square or flat position"?

18. USD/CHF is quoted at 1.5890/1.5900 and USD/CAD is quoted at 1.4095-00. What is the CAD/CHF cross rate?

    a) 1.1270-81

    b) 1.1270-90

    c) 1.1273-75

    d) 1.2831-40

    e) 2.2405-81

    f) 1.1273-77

    g) 2.2397-19

19. A bank wants to sell SEK against JPY (spot rates: USD/JPY 135.17-32; USD/SEK 7.3140-60). Which SEK/JPY rate do you quote?

20. Which of the following ISO codes are correct?

    a) YEN

    b) SFR

    c) GBP

    d) CHF

    e) STG

21. Complete the following table!

Country	ISO Code
New Zealand	
Hungary	
Sweden	
Mexico	
Macedonia	
Australia	
Argentina	
South Africa	
Egypt	
Norway	
Poland	
Thailand	
Hong Kong	

    b) ein Gewinn

    c) ausgeglichenes Ergebnis

    d) nicht genügend Information, um zu entscheiden

14. Sie sind long USD gegen CHF und wollen Ihre Position schließen. Bei welcher Quotierung machen Sie als Market Maker den größten Gewinn?

    a) 1,5040-45

    b) 1,5040-50

    c) 1,5042-47

    d) 1,5032-37

15. Was versteht man unter „Spread"?

16. Erklären Sie den Unterschied zwischen direkter und indirekter Quotierung!

17. Was versteht man unter einer „Square-" oder „Flat-Position"?

18. USD/CHF quotiert bei 1,5890/1,5900 und USD/CAD quotiert bei 1,4095-00. Wo quotiert die CAD/CHF Cross Rate?

    a) 1,1270-81

    b) 1,1270-90

    c) 1,1273-75

    d) 1,2831-40

    e) 2,2405-81

    f) 1,1273-77

    g) 2,2397-19

19. Eine Bank möchte SEK gegen JPY verkaufen (Kassakurse: USD/JPY 135,17-32; USD/SEK 7,3140-60). Welchen SEK/JPY-Kurs quotieren Sie?

20. Welche ISO-Codes sind richtig?

    a) YEN

    b) SFR

    c) GBP

    d) CHF

    e) STG

21. Ergänzen Sie die folgende Tabelle!

Land	ISO-Code
Neuseeland	
Ungarn	
Schweden	
Mexiko	
Mazedonien	
Australien	
Argentinien	
Südafrika	
Ägypten	
Norwegen	
Polen	
Thailand	
Hongkong	

2. FX Outrights and FX Swaps

In this chapter you learn ...

- what is meant by an outright.
- which conventions are used for outright deals.
- what is meant by the Interest Rate Parity Theorem.
- how the price of outright deals is calculated.
- how the forward rate is calculated.
- what is meant by premium and discount.
- how forward rates are quoted.
- which factors may influence the forward rate.
- what is meant by time options.
- what is meant by non-deliverable forwards.
- which conventions are normally used for non-deliverable forwards.
- which risks may occur with non-deliverable forwards.
- what is meant by an FX swap.
- which conventions are normally used for FX swaps.
- how the risk of an FX swap is valued.
- what is meant by matched and mismatched principal FX swaps.
- what is meant by forward/forward swaps.
- which FX deals exist for value prior to spot.
- what is meant by Synthetic Agreement for Forward Exchange.
- how FX outrights and FX swaps can be used in practice.

2.1. FX Forward Outrights

An outright is an agreement between two counterparts to exchange currencies on a future date at a fixed rate.

2.1.1. Conventions and Terminology

Value date

The regular terms for outrights are the straight months (resp. weeks) up to 1 year e.g.: 1w, 2w, 3w, 1m, 2m, 3m, 4m...12m. **"Broken Dates"**, i.e. terms that differ from regular terms, are quoted on request. For the major currencies terms of up to 5 years are possible.

The term of an outright deal is measured starting with the spot value date.

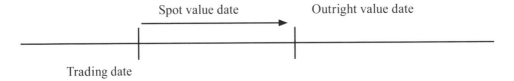

2. Devisentermingeschäfte und Devisenswaps

In diesem Kapitel lernen Sie ...

- was man unter einem Devisentermingeschäft versteht.
- welche Usancen bei Devisentermingeschäften üblich sind.
- was man unter der Zinsparitätentheorie versteht.
- wie der Preis für Devisentermingeschäfte berechnet wird.
- wie man den Terminkurs berechnen kann.
- was man unter Auf- bzw. Abschlag versteht.
- in welcher Form Terminkurse quotiert werden.
- welche Faktoren den Terminkurs beeinflussen.
- was man unter Time Options versteht.
- was man unter Non-deliverable Forwards versteht.
- welche Usancen bei Non-deliverable Forwards üblich sind.
- welche Risiken bei Non-deliverable Forwards auftreten können.
- was man unter einem Devisenswap versteht.
- welche Usancen bei Devisenswaps üblich sind.
- wie das Risiko eines Devisenswaps bewertet wird.
- was man unter Matched und Mismatched Principal FX-Swaps versteht.
- was man unter Forward/Forward Swaps versteht.
- welche Kassageschäfte mit Valuta vor dem Spotdatum es gibt.
- was man unter Synthetic Agreement for Forward Exchange versteht.
- wie Devisentermingeschäfte und -swaps in der Praxis sinnvoll eingesetzt werden können.

2.1. Devisentermingeschäft (FX-Outright)

Ein Devisentermingeschäft (FX-Outright) ist eine feste Vereinbarung zwischen zwei Parteien, eine Devisentransaktion zu einem fixierten Kurs mit einem späteren Datum als dem Kassavalutatag durchzuführen.

2.1.1. Usancen

Valuta

Devisenterminkurse werden standardmäßig für Laufzeiten von 1, 2, 3, 6 und 12 Monaten quotiert. **„Broken Dates"**, d.h. von diesen Standardlaufzeiten abweichende Termine, werden auf Anfrage ebenfalls quotiert. Für die Hauptwährungen sind auch Laufzeiten bis zu fünf Jahren oder mehr möglich.

Die Laufzeit für ein Devisentermingeschäft wird ab dem Valutatag des Spotgeschäfts gemessen.

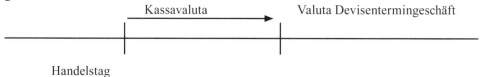

If the theoretical value date of an outright is a Saturday, Sunday or a bank holiday, the value date is deferred to the next working day.

Example

The value date of a 1-month outright, traded on Wednesday, the 22nd of October, would be the 24th of November. If the 24th of November is a Sunday, the value date will be the 25th of November.

EXCEPTION: End/End deal

For the so-called **end/end deals** (outrights with spot value dates on the last working day of a month), the value date of the outright is the **last working day**.

Example

The trading day of a one-month outright deal is Wednesday, the 29th of October. Value date of the spot deal would be Friday, the 31st of October. The value date of the outright deal is in this case Friday the 28th of November (last bank day in November).

Interest Rate Parity Theorem

The Interest Rate Parity Theorem explains the **relation between interest rate and exchange rate**. The foreign exchange market is balanced if the deposits in all currencies have the same expected yield. This parity of expected yields for deposits in two optional currencies, measured in the same currency, is called interest rate parity. According to this theorem the investor is indifferent concerning an investment in the home country and an investment in a foreign country.

The **"covered" Interest Rate Parity Theorem** is used for the case the currency risk of an asset was hedged in a foreign currency (for. ex. FX Swap).

In case the currency risk is not hedged, the so called **"uncovered" Interest Rate Parity Theorem** (for. ex. Carry Trades) is applied.

Fällt der Valutatag eines Devisentermingeschäftes auf einen Samstag, Sonntag oder einen Bankfeiertag, so ist der Valutatag der nächstgültige Handelstag.

Beispiel

Am Mittwoch, den 22. Oktober, wird ein 1-Monats-Termin gehandelt. Spot Valuta ist zwei Banktage nach dem Handelstag, d.h. am 24. Oktober. Das Valutadatum des Termingeschäfts ist genau ein Monat nach der Spot Valuta, d.h. ist der 24. November ein Samstag, wäre das Valutadatum der 25. November.

AUSNAHME: End/End-Geschäft

Ein End/End-Geschäft ist ein Devisentermingeschäft, bei dem die Valuta des Kassageschäftes auf den **letzten Handelstag eines Monats** fällt. Für diese Geschäfte ist die **Valuta** des Devisentermingeschäftes auch der **letzte Handelstag im Monat der Fälligkeit des Geschäftes.**

Beispiel

Ein 1-Monats-Devisentermingeschäft wird am Mittwoch, den 29. Oktober (Handelstag), abgeschlossen. Die Valuta eines Kassageschäftes wäre Freitag, der 31. Oktober. Die Valuta des Devisentermingeschäftes fällt somit auf Freitag, den 28. November (letzter Handelstag im November).

Zinsparitätentheorie

Im Zusammenhang mit Devisentermingeschäften wird häufig das Konzept der Zinsparitätentheorie genannt. Die Zinsparitätentheorie ist ein auf John Maynard Keynes zurückgehendes weit verbreitetes volkswirtschaftliches Modell und erklärt den **Zusammenhang zwischen Zinssatz und Wechselkurs.** Der Devisenmarkt befindet sich im Gleichgewicht, wenn die Anlagen in allen Währungen dieselbe erwartete Rendite bieten. Diese Gleichheit der erwarteten Renditen auf Anlagen in zwei beliebigen Währungen, gemessen in derselben Währung, bezeichnet man als **Zinsparität**. Das Vorliegen der Bedingung der Zinsparität hat eine Renditegleichheit von inländischen und ausländischen Kapitalanlagen zur Folge. Der Anleger ist somit bezüglich einer Anlage im Inland und einer Anlage im Ausland indifferent.

Die sogenannte **„gedeckte" Zinsparitätentheorie** deckt den Fall ab, in dem das Währungsrisiko einer Anlage in Fremdwährung abgesichert wurde (z.B. über FX-Swap).

Von der **„ungedeckten" Zinsparitätentheorie** spricht man, wenn das Währungsrisiko nicht abgesichert wurde (z.B. bei sogenannten Carry Trades).

2.1.2. Computing Outright Rates

Example

The table shows some examples of spot 12-month outright rates:

	EUR/USD	USD/CHF	EUR/GBP
Spot	1.0980	1.5000	0.6975
12 mth	1.0870	1.4720	0.7033

These examples demonstrate that the outright rates usually differ from the spot rate, but they are not a forecast for the spot rate at the end of the term. If, for example, the rate for a 12-month outright USD/CHF is 1.4720, this does not mean that the market expects a rate of 1.4720 in 12 month time.

The **difference between the outright rate and the spot rate** only reflects the **interest differential between the two currencies involved**. Would the outright rates not conform to the interest differential, arbitrage between the foreign exchange market and the euro deposit market would be possible.

Example

USD/CHF spot: 1.5000
USD 6-mth deposit rate: 6%
CHF 6-mth deposit rate: 2% (184 days).
A company is long USD/CHF value date 6 months and wants to hedge the FX-risk. There are two alternatives:
1. sell USD outright against CHF
or
2. sell USD spot against CHF and refinance USD for 6 months by means of an interbank deposit and invest CHF for 6 months by means of an interbank deposit.
The results of both alternatives must be the same. Otherwise the market participants would do arbitrage that means they would buy the cheaper alternative and close the position by selling the other one. Hence the difference would disappear very quickly.

2.1.2. Preisberechnung

<table>
<tr><td colspan="4">Beispiel</td></tr>
<tr><td colspan="4">

Die Tabelle zeigt einige Beispiele für Kassa- und Terminkurse:

	EUR/USD	USD/CHF	EUR/GBP
Spot	1.0980	1.5000	0.6975
12 Monate	1.0870	1.4720	0.7033

</td></tr>
</table>

Wechselkurse für Termingeschäfte unterscheiden sich zwar von den Kassakursen, sind aber keine Prognose für den Kassakurs am Ende der Laufzeit. Beträgt beispielsweise der Terminkurs für eine USD/CHF-Transaktion für 1 Monat 1,4720, so ist nicht davon auszugehen, dass der Markt den Kassakurs in einem Monat bei 1,4720 erwartet.

Der **Unterschied zwischen Terminkurs und Kassakurs** zweier Währungen trifft lediglich eine **Aussage über die unterschiedlichen Zinssätze** in diesen Währungen. Würden die Terminkurse nicht das wahre Zinsgefälle zwischen zwei Währungen widerspiegeln, so wäre es möglich, risikolosen Profit aus den Preisunterschieden zwischen dem Devisenmarkt und dem Geldmarkt zu erwirtschaften.

<table>
<tr><td>Beispiel</td></tr>
<tr><td>

Ein Schweizer Unternehmen erhält in 6 Monaten einen Eingang über USD 1 Mio. Da es CHF benötigt, will es den USD/CHF-Kurs absichern.

Aktuelle Marktdaten:

Kassakurs USD/CHF: 1,5000

CHF Zinssatz für 6 Monate (184 Tage):   2%

USD Zinssatz für 6 Monate (184 Tage):   6%

Terminkurs USD/CHF 6 Monate: 1,4703

Dem Unternehmen stehen folgende Möglichkeiten zur Absicherung offen:

1. Verkauf von USD 1 Mio. auf Termin gegen CHF zu 1,4703

oder

2. USD 1 Mio. in der Kassa gegen CHF zu 1,5000 verkaufen, die USD für sechs Monate aufnehmen und die CHF für sechs Monate veranlagen.

</td></tr>
</table>

If both alternatives produce the same result, the 6 months outright rate can be computed as shown below

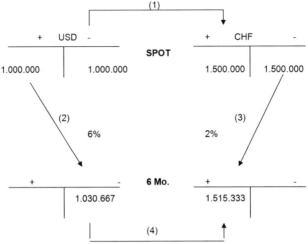

- Sell spot USD 1,000,000 against CHF at a rate of 1.5000 (1)
- Take 184 days USD deposit 1,000,000 at 6% (2)
- Give 184 days CHF deposit 1,500,000 at 2% (3)
- Computing the outright rate: 1,515,333/1,030,667 = 1.4702 (4)

The result of the second alternative with 1,4703 is equal with the outright rate. If it would be higher (e.g. 1,4750), the company will choose this alternative.

Formula for calculating the outright rate

The outright rate can be computed by using the stated formula, too

$$O = SPOT \times \frac{1 + \left(i_Q \times \dfrac{D}{B_Q} \right)}{1 + \left(i_B \times \dfrac{D}{B_B} \right)}$$

D = number of days
O = outright rate
SPOT = spot rate
i_B = interest rate p.a. in decimals, base currency
i_Q = interest rate p.a. in decimals, quote/variable currency
B_B = basis of term calculation for the base currency (360 or 365)
B_Q = basis of term calculation for the quote/variable currency (360 or 365)

For calculating the outright rate, you need

- the spot rate
- the exact days of the period
- the interest rate for both currencies.

In der folgenden Grafik wird das Ergebnis der zweiten Variante dargestellt:

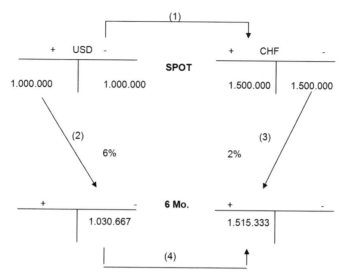

- Kassa Verkauf USD 1.000.000 zu 1,50 gegen CHF (1)
- Aufnahme USD 1.000.000 für 184 Tage zu 6% (2)
- Veranlagung CHF 1.500.000 für 184 Tage zu 2% (3)
- Berechnung des sich ergebenden Terminkurses: 1.515.333/1.030.667 = 1,4703 (4)

Das Ergebnis der zweiten Variante ist mit 1,4703 also gleich wie der Terminkurs. Wäre es höher (z.B. 1,4750), so würde das Unternehmen diese Variante wählen.

Formel zur Berechnung des Terminkurses

Der Devisenterminkurs kann daher über folgende Formel hergeleitet werden:

$$TK = KASSA \times \frac{1 + \left(r_G \times \dfrac{T}{B_G}\right)}{1 + \left(r_Q \times \dfrac{T}{B_Q}\right)}$$

T = Anzahl der Tage
TK = Terminkurs
KASSA = Spotkurs
r_Q = Zinssatz p.a. in Dezimalen, quotierte Währung
r_G = Zinssatz p.a. in Dezimalen, Gegenwährung
B_Q = Berechnungsbasis für die quotierte Währung (360 oder 365)
B_G = Berechnungsbasis für die Gegenwährung (360 oder 365)

Um den Terminkurs zu berechnen, benötigen wir:

- den Kassakurs,
- die exakten Tage der Terminperiode und
- den Zinssatz in jeder Währung.

Example

What is the 6-month outright rate of USD/CHF (184 days)?
USD/CHF spot: 1.5000
interest rates: USD (base currency)   6%
                  CHF (quote currency)   2%

$$O = 1.50 \times \frac{1 + \left(0.02 \times \dfrac{184}{360} \right)}{1 + \left(0.06 \times \dfrac{184}{360} \right)} = 1.4702$$

Premium/Discount

If the **outright rate is lower** than the spot rate, the base currency is at a **discount**.
If the **outright rate is higher** than the spot rate, the base currency is at a **premium**.

Rules for premium/discount

interest rate base currency < interest rate quote currency → premium
interest rate base currency > interest rate quote currency → discount

Computing outright rate in consideration of bid/offer rates

Since deposit rates are usually quoted with a spread the bid and the offer rate has to be taken into account when computing the bid resp. the offer rate of an outright

$$O_{Bid} = SPOT_{Bid} \times \frac{1 + \left(i_{BidQ} \times \dfrac{D}{B_Q} \right)}{1 + \left(i_{OfferB} \times \dfrac{D}{B_B} \right)}$$

$$O_{Offer} = SPOT_{Offer} \times \frac{1 + \left(i_{OfferQ} \times \dfrac{D}{B_Q} \right)}{1 + \left(i_{BidB} \times \dfrac{D}{B_B} \right)}$$

D   = number of days
O   = outright rate
SPOT = spot rate
i_B = interest rate p.a. in decimals, base currency
i_Q = interest rate p.a. in decimals, quote/variable currency
B_B = day basis of the base currency (360 or 365)
B_Q = day basis of the quote/variable currency (360 or 365)

Beispiel

Terminkurs für USD/CHF, sechs Monate (184 Tage)
Zinsen USD (quotierte Währung): 6%
Zinsen CHF (Gegenwährung):   2%
Spotkurs USD/CHF: 1,5000

$$TK = 1,50 \ x \ \frac{1 + \left(0,02 \ x \ \dfrac{184}{360}\right)}{1 + \left(0,06 \ x \ \dfrac{184}{360}\right)} = 1,4702$$

Aufschlag/Abschlag

Ist der **Terminkurs niedriger** als die aktuelle Kassa, ist die Währung im **Abschlag** (Abschlag = Discount = Deport).

Ist der **Terminkurs höher** als die aktuelle Kassa, ist die Währung im **Aufschlag** (Aufschlag = Premium = Report).

Regeln für Aufschlag/Abschlag

Zinssatz Gegenwährung > Zinssatz quotierte Währung → Aufschlag
Zinssatz Gegenwährung < Zinssatz quotierte Währung → Abschlag

Berücksichtigung von Geld- und Briefkursen

In der Praxis sind die Spreads zwischen den quotierten Geld- und Briefkursen bei der Preisermittlung des Terminkurses zu berücksichtigen.

Daraus ergeben sich folgende Formeln:

$$TK_{Geld} = KASSA_{Geld} \ x \ \frac{1 + \left(r_{GeldG} \ x \ \dfrac{T}{B_G}\right)}{1 + \left(r_{BriefQ} \ x \ \dfrac{T}{B_Q}\right)}$$

$$TK_{Brief} = KASSA_{Brief} \ x \ \frac{1 + \left(r_{BriefG} \ x \ \dfrac{T}{B_G}\right)}{1 + \left(r_{GeldQ} \ x \ \dfrac{T}{B_Q}\right)}$$

T = Anzahl der Tage
TK = Terminkurs
KASSA = Spotkurs
rQ = Zinssatz p.a. in Dezimalen, quotierte Währung
rG = Zinssatz p.a. in Dezimalen, Gegenwährung
BQ = Berechnungsbasis für die quotierte Währung (360 oder 365)
BG = Berechnungsbasis für die Gegenwährung (360 oder 365)

You receive the following quotes:

Example

USD/CHF: 1.5000-10
interest rate USD, 184 days: $5^7/_8$-6%
interest rate CHF, 184 days: 2-$2^1/_8$%

What is the quotation of a 6-months (184 days) outright USD/CHF?

Using these prices the quotation for a 6-months outright rate (USD/CHF) can be computed as follows:

$$\text{Outright rate}_{\text{Bid}} = 1.5000 \frac{1+\left(0.02 \cdot \frac{184}{360}\right)}{1+\left(0.06 \cdot \frac{184}{360}\right)} = 1.4702$$

$$\text{Outright rate}_{\text{Offer}} = 1.5010 \frac{1+\left(0.02125 \cdot \frac{184}{360}\right)}{1+\left(0.05875 \cdot \frac{184}{360}\right)} = 1.4731$$

The 6-months USD/CHF outright rate is 1.4702-31.

2.1.3. Quotation of Outright Rates

Outright forward FX transactions are usually quoted as **full forward exchange rate** to customers. In the interbank market outright forward FX transactions are quoted as **forward points** or full forward exchange rate. The **forward points** are also called **swap points**. By adding (premium) or subtracting (discount) these forward points from the spot rate you get the full forward exchange rate.

Two examples of Reuters pages are shown below:

EUR/USD-Swaps:

RIC	Bid	Ask	Srce	Time
EURON=	-0.385	-0.335	BAFX	12:46
EURTN=	-1.25	-1.21	RBSL	13:03
EURSN=	-0.41	-0.38	BOAF	12:46
EURSW=	-3.29	-3.24	RBSL	13:03
EUR2W=	-5.8	-5.7	DRE4	12:59
EUR1M=	-12.67	-12.42	INGX	13:03
EUR2M=	-23.66	-22.66	PBGR	13:03
EUR3M=	-33.05	-32.55	INGX	13:03
EUR4M=	-43.01	-42.61	RABN	13:02
EUR5M=	-53.04	-52.54	RABN	13:02
EUR6M=	-62.05	-61.65	SELV	13:03
EUR7M=	-71.2	-70.2	RZBA	13:03
EUR8M=	-80.6	-79.6	RZBA	13:03
EUR9M=	-89.20	-88.00	SELV	13:03
EUR10M=	-97.62	-96.37	DRE4	13:03
EUR11M=	-105.63	-104.38	DRE4	13:03
EUR1Y=	-112.60	-111.40	SELV	13:03
EUR2Y=	-177.5	-172.5		13:03
EUR3Y=	-215	-195		13:02
EUR4Y=	-219	-189		13:02
EUR5Y=	-214	-174		13:02
EUR10Y=	-191	-91		13:02

USD/CAD-Swap:

RIC	Bid	Ask	Srce	Time
CADON=	2.96	3.01	RBCM	06:09
CADTN=	2.70	2.80	RBCM	:
CADSN=	0.73	0.78	DRE4	06:00
CADSW=	5.25	5.55		05:59
CAD1M=	23.30	23.70		06:03
CAD2M=	48.70	49.50		06:09
CAD3M=	74.00	75.00		06:09
CAD6M=	154.50	157.00		06:09
CAD9M=	239.00	243.00		05:59
CAD1Y=	317.00	322.00		06:10
CAD2Y=	580	605	BAFX	05:44
CAD3Y=	790	830	BAFX	05:44
CAD4Y=	900	950	BAFX	05:44
CAD5Y=	1056	1093	CHNV	05:12
CAD7Y=	1258	1408	LTFX	06:17

Folgende Quotierungen gelten:

Beispiel

USD/CHF: 1,5000-10
Zinsen USD, 184 Tage: 5 7/8 - 6%
Zinsen CHF, 184 Tage: 2 - 2 1/8%

Aus diesen Preisen soll die Quotierung für einen 6-Monats-Devisenterminkurs (USD/CHF) abgeleitet werden.

$$= 1{,}5000 \times \frac{1 + \left(0{,}02 \times \dfrac{184}{360}\right)}{1 + \left(0{,}06 \times \dfrac{184}{360}\right)} = 1{,}4702$$

$$= 1{,}5010 \times \frac{1 + \left(0{,}02125 \times \dfrac{184}{360}\right)}{1 + \left(0{,}05875 \times \dfrac{184}{360}\right)} = 1{,}4731$$

Der 6-Monats-Devisenterminkurs ist 1,4702-31.

2.1.3. Quotierung von Terminkursen

Devisentermingeschäfte werden gegenüber Kunden üblicherweise als **vollständiger Terminkurs** quotiert. Im Interbankenhandel werden Devisentermingeschäfte in Form von **Swappunkten** oder als vollständiger Terminkurs quotiert. Zum Terminkurs gelangt man, indem man den Kassakurs um die Swappunkte ändert.

Diese Swappunkte werden auch **Forward-Points** oder **Swapstellen** genannt.

Sie finden hier zwei Beispiele von Reuters-Seiten:

EUR/USD-Swaps:

RIC	Bid	Ask	Srce	Time
EURON=	-0.385	-0.335	BAFX	12:46
EURTN=	-1.25	-1.21	RBSL	13:03
EURSN=	-0.41	-0.38	BOAF	12:46
EURSW=	-3.29	-3.24	RBSL	13:03
EUR2W=	-5.8	-5.7	DRE4	12:59
EUR1M=	-12.67	-12.42	INGX	13:03
EUR2M=	-23.66	-22.66	PBGR	13:03
EUR3M=	-33.05	-32.55	INGX	13:03
EUR4M=	-43.01	-42.61	RABN	13:02
EUR5M=	-53.04	-52.54	RABN	13:02
EUR6M=	-62.05	-61.65	SELV	13:03
EUR7M=	-71.2	-70.2	RZBA	13:03
EUR8M=	-80.6	-79.6	RZBA	13:03
EUR9M=	-89.20	-88.00	SELV	13:03
EUR10M=	-97.62	-96.37	DRE4	13:03
EUR11M=	-105.63	-104.38	DRE4	13:03
EUR1Y=	-112.60	-111.40	SELV	13:03
EUR2Y=	-177.5	-172.5		13:03
EUR3Y=	-215	-195		13:03
EUR4Y=	-219	-189		13:02
EUR5Y=	-214	-174		13:02
EUR10Y=	-191	-91		13:02

USD/CAD-Swap:

RIC	Bid	Ask	Srce	Time
CADON=	2.96	3.01	RBCM	06:09
CADTN=	2.70	2.80	RBCM	:
CADSN=	0.73	0.78	DRE4	06:00
CADSW=	5.25	5.55		05:59
CAD1M=	23.30	23.70		06:03
CAD2M=	48.70	49.50		06:09
CAD3M=	74.00	75.00		06:09
CAD6M=	154.50	157.00		06:09
CAD9M=	239.00	243.00		05:59
CAD1Y=	317.00	322.00		06:10
CAD2Y=	580	605	BAFX	05:44
CAD3Y=	790	830	BAFX	05:44
CAD4Y=	900	950	BAFX	05:44
CAD5Y=	1056	1093	CHNY	05:12
CAD7Y=	1258	1408	LTFX	06:17

Premium/Discount

Usually, traders do not state the algebraic sign when quoting swap points. There are two ways to find out whether the swap points are at a premium or at a discount.

Analysis of the interest rates

interest rate **base currency** < interest rate **quote currency** → premium
interest rate **base currency** > interest rate **quote currency** → discount

---

Example

Interest rates:
USD: 1.50%　　　EUR: 2.50%　　　CAD: 3.50%
Are the swap points of EUR/USD and USD/CAD at a premium or discount?
EUR/USD: EUR rate > USD rate → discount
USD/CAD: USD rate < CAD rate → premium

Analysis of the quotation

Forward points are quoted with bid and offer rates, just like spot rates. The market user sells at the bid rate and buys at the offer rate.

$$Bid \; > \; Offer \rightarrow Discount$$
$$Bid \; < \; Offer \rightarrow Premium$$

Note: Quotes near parity (+/-0) are usually quoted with plus and minus.

Example

The table shows the spot rates and swap points for several terms

	GBP/USD	EUR/USD
Spot	1.5930-1.5935	1.1805-1.1810
1 month	40-39	20-21
3 months	120-118	35-37
12 months	280-275	65-70

What are the outright rates of GBP/USD and EUR/USD?

GBP/USD: the **bid rate is higher than the offer** (e.g. 40-39 for 1 month). This means:

- GBP/USD is at a **discount**.
- The **forward points** have to be **subtracted**.

Aufschlag/Abschlag

Normalerweise wird das Vorzeichen bei der Quotierung von Swappunkten nicht angegeben. Es gibt zwei Möglichkeiten, um herauszufinden, ob es sich um einen Auf- bzw. einen Abschlag handelt.

Betrachtung der beiden Zinssätze

Zinssatz **quotierte** Währung < Zinssatz **Gegenwährung** → **Aufschlag**
Zinssatz **quotierte** Währung > Zinssatz **Gegenwährung** → **Abschlag**

Beispiel

Zinsen:
USD: 1,5%, EUR: 2,5%, CAD: 3,5%.
Sind die Swappunkte für EUR/USD und USD/CAD ein Auf- oder ein Abschlag?
EUR/USD: EUR Zinsen > USD Zinsen → Abschlag
USD/CAD: USD Zinsen < CAD Zinsen → Aufschlag

Betrachtung der Quotierung

Swappunkte werden, wie auch Kassakurse, mit Geld- und Briefseite quotiert. Der Market User verkauft zur Geldseite und kauft zur Briefseite.

$$\text{Geld} > \text{Brief} \;\rightarrow\; \text{Abschlag}$$
$$\text{Geld} < \text{Brief} \;\rightarrow\; \text{Aufschlag}$$

Anmerkung: Bei Quotierungen um pari (+/-0) wird üblicherweise mit Plus und Minus quotiert.

Beispiel

Die folgende Tabelle zeigt Devisenkurse:

	GBP/USD	**EUR/USD**
Spot	1,5930-1,5935	0,9805-0,9810
1 Monat	40-39	20-21
3 Monate	120-118	35-37
12 Monate	280-275	65-70

Die Kurstafel zeigt zwei Währungspaare, bei denen die Swappunkte für 1-, 3- und 12-Monats-Terminkurse zum Kassakurs gestellt sind. Im Fall der Quotierung GBP/USD sind die **Swappunkte auf der linken Seite höher als auf der rechten Seite** (z.B. 40-39 für den 1-Monats-Terminkurs).

Das bedeutet:

- Die **quotierte Währung (GBP) ist auf Termin weniger wert als in der Kasse** im Vergleich zur Gegenwährung (USD).
- Die Swappunkte müssen daher für dieses Währungspaar **vom Kassakurs abgezogen** werden.

GBP/USD rate	1-month	3-months	12-months
Spot rate	1.5930-1.5935	1.5930-1.5935	1.5930 -1.5935
Forward points (discount)	40-39	120-118	280-275
Outright rate	**1.5890-1.5896**	**1.5810-1.5817**	**1.5650-1.5660**

EUR/USD: the **bid rate is lower than the offer rate** (e.g. 20-21 for the 1-month term). This means:

- EUR/USD is at a **premium.**
- The **forward points** have to be **added** to the spot rate.

EUR/USD rate	1-month	3-month	12-month
Spot rate	1.1005-1.1010	1.1005-1.1010	1.1005-1.1010
Forward points (premium)	20-21	35-37	65-70
Outright forward rate	**1.1025-1.1031**	**1.1040-1.1047**	**1.1070-1.1080**

Which factors do influence the outright rate?

Since the outright rate consists of the spot rate plus or minus the swap points it changes if:

- the spot rate changes or
- the interest rate differential changes (i.e. the swap points change).

Example

The quotation for 3-month outright EUR/USD is 20/25 and changes to 50/55.
Knowing this we can conclude that:
- The interest rates in USD are higher than the interest rates in EUR (bid < offer → EUR is at a premium).
- The forward points increased as the interest differential increased. This could mean that either the interest rates for USD rose or that the EUR interest rates fell. Just by knowing the change in forward points we cannot conclude which of the two things actually happened.

Note: In the strict sense the increased forward points can also be caused by an increase of the spot price. However the influence is relatively low for short terms and is stronger for longer terms.

GBP/USD-Kurs	1-Monats-Termin	3-Monats-Termin	12-Monats-Termin
Kassakurs	1,5930-1,5935	1,5930-1,5935	1,5930-1,5935
Swappunkte/Abschlag	40-39	120-118	280-275
Outright-Terminkurs	1,5890-1,5896	1,5810-1,5817	1,5650-1,5660

Im Falle der Quotierung EUR/USD sind die **Swappunkte auf der linken Seite niedriger als auf der rechten Seite,** z.B. für ein 1 Monat 20-21. Das bedeutet:

- Der EUR/USD-Kurs ist auf Termin **höher** als in der Kassa.
- Die **Swappunkte** müssen daher zum Kassakurs **addiert** werden.

EUR/USD-Kurs	1-Monats-Termin	3-Monats-Termin	12-Monats-Termin
Kassakurs	0,9805-0,9810	0,9805-0,9810	0,9805-0,9810
Swappunkte/Aufschlag	20-21	35-37	65-70
Outright-Terminkurs	0,9825-0,9831	0,9840-0,9847	0,9870-0,9880

Welche Faktoren beeinflussen den Terminkurs?

Ein Terminkurs ändert sich immer, wenn

- sich der Kassakurs oder
- die Zinsdifferenz der beiden Währungen

ändert.

Beispiel

Für ein 3-Monats-Termingeschäft in EUR/USD werden die Swappunkte 20/25 quotiert. Wenn sie sich auf 50/55 ändern, ist aus dieser Information Folgendes zu schließen:
- Die Zinssätze in USD sind höher als die Zinssätze in EUR (Swappunkte auf der Geldseite tiefer → EUR im Aufschlag).
- Die Swappunkte haben sich erhöht, weil sich die Zinsdifferenz zwischen den beiden Währungen vergrößert hat. Das kann bedeuten, dass der Zinssatz für USD gestiegen ist oder der Zinssatz für EUR gefallen ist. Aus dieser Information ist nicht zu schließen, welcher der beiden Fälle eingetreten ist.

Anmerkung: Genau genommen könnte die Erhöhung der Swappunkte jedoch auch durch eine Erhöhung des Kassakurses ausgelöst worden sein. Dieser Einfluss ist jedoch relativ gering bei kurzen Laufzeiten und wird umso stärker, je länger die Laufzeit ist.

Computing discount/premium

The swap points can be computed by means of the swap formula, which is derived from the outright formula.

$$\text{Premium/discount} = \text{Spot} \times \left(\frac{1 + \left(r_G \times \dfrac{T}{B_G} \right)}{1 + \left(r_Q \times \dfrac{T}{B_Q} \right)} - 1 \right)$$

D = number of days
SPOT = spot rate
i_B = interest rate p.a. in decimals, base currency
i_Q = interest rate p.a. in decimals, quote/variable currency
B_B = basis of the base currency (360 or 365)
B_Q = basis of the quote/variable currency (360 or 365)

Example

Premium/discount
Interest rates: USD (base currency):   6%
                 CHF (quote currency):   2%
Spot rate: USD/CHF: 1.5000
What are the 6-month (184 days) swap points?

$$\text{Discount} = 1.50 \times \left(\frac{1 + \left(0.02 \times \dfrac{184}{360} \right)}{1 + \left(0.06 \times \dfrac{184}{360} \right)} - 1 \right) = -0{,}0298$$

6-months USD/CHF swap points are -298.

Taking bid/offer rates into account when computing swap points

Bid

$$\text{Premium/discount}_{Bid} = \text{SPOT}_{Mean} \times \left(\frac{1 + \left(i_{BidQ} \times \dfrac{D}{B_Q} \right)}{1 + \left(i_{OfferB} \times \dfrac{D}{B_B} \right)} - 1 \right)$$

Offer

$$\text{Premium/discount}_{Offer} = \text{SPOT}_{Mean} \times \left(\frac{1 + \left(i_{OfferQ} \times \dfrac{D}{B_Q} \right)}{1 + \left(i_{BidB} \times \dfrac{D}{B_B} \right)} - 1 \right)$$

Note: As only the premium/discount has to be computed, the calculation may be done with the **mean quotation** of the spot rate. Bid and offer for spot has almost no impact on the fair price.

Berechnung Aufschlag/Abschlag

Zur Berechnung der Auf- und Abschläge adaptieren wir die Terminkursformel wie folgt:

$$\text{Auf} - / \text{Abschlag} = \text{KASSA} \times \left(\frac{1 + \left(r_G \times \dfrac{T}{B_G} \right)}{1 + \left(r_Q \times \dfrac{T}{B_Q} \right)} - 1 \right)$$

T = Anzahl der Tage
KASSA = Spot Kurs
r_Q = Zinssatz p.a. in Dezimalen, quotierte Währung
r_G = Zinssatz p.a. in Dezimalen, Gegenwährung
B_Q = Tagesbasis für die quotierte Währung
B_G = Tagesbasis für die Gegenwährung

Beispiel

Termin Aufschlag/Abschlag für USD/CHF: 6 Monate (184 Tage)
Zinsen USD (quotierte Währung):   6%
Zinsen CHF (Gegenwährung):   2%
Spotkurs USD/CHF: 1,5000

$$\text{Abschlag} = 1{,}50 \times \left(\frac{1 + \left(0{,}02 \times \dfrac{184}{360} \right)}{1 + \left(0{,}06 \times \dfrac{184}{360} \right)} - 1 \right) = -0{,}0298$$

6-Monats-USD/CHF-Swappunkte sind -298.

Berücksichtigung von Geld- und Briefkursen bei der Berechnung von Aufschlägen/Abschlägen:

Geld

$$\text{Auf} - / \text{Abschlag}_{\text{Geld}} = \text{KASSA}_{\text{Mitte}} \times \left(\frac{1 + \left(r_{\text{GeldG}} \times \dfrac{T}{B_G} \right)}{1 + \left(r_{\text{BriefQ}} \times \dfrac{T}{B_Q} \right)} - 1 \right)$$

Brief

$$\text{Auf} - / \text{Abschlag}_{\text{Brief}} = \text{KASSA}_{\text{Mitte}} \times \left(\frac{1 + \left(r_{\text{BriefG}} \times \dfrac{T}{B_G} \right)}{1 + \left(r_{\text{GeldQ}} \times \dfrac{T}{B_Q} \right)} - 1 \right)$$

Anmerkung: Da hier nur Auf- und Abschläge berechnet werden, kann mit der **Kassamitte** operiert werden. Die Geld- und Briefseite hat kaum Einfluss auf das Ergebnis.

> **Example**
>
> USD/CHF   1.5000-10
> USD interest rate, 184 days   5 7/8-6%
> CHF interest rate, 184 days   2-2 1/8%
> What are the 6-month swap points and outright rates?

$$\text{BID} = 1.5005 \times \left(\frac{1 + \left(0.02 \times \dfrac{184}{360} \right)}{1 + \left(0.06 \times \dfrac{184}{360} \right)} - 1 \right) = -298$$

$$\text{Offer} = 1.5005 \times \left(\frac{1 + \left(0.02125 \times \dfrac{184}{360} \right)}{1 + \left(0.05875 \times \dfrac{184}{360} \right)} - 1 \right) = -279$$

Spot	1.5000	1.5010
swap (discount)	- 298	- 279
= outright rate	**1.4702**	**- 1.4731**

Why premium/discount is quoted?

There are a lot of reasons why outrights are quoted in terms of forward points:

- Forward points are mainly influenced by **interest rates**. Interest rates are not that volatile than spot rates. If outright rates would be quoted, they would have to be updated for every move in the spot rate.
- Customers, or market users, **compare the quotes of different Market Makers** and look at the spot rate only when they are ready to deal.
- In practical dealing the **FX-forward trading book is separated from the FX-spot trading book**. Thus forward points (FX swaps) are not quoted at the spot desk. Usually the FX-forward desk belongs to the money market department.
- Forward deals are most frequently used as a part of **FX swap transactions** in the interbank market. FX-swaps are dominated by the interest rate differential rather than the spot rate.

Calculation of forward rates for broken dates – linear interpolation

If you have to compute a forward rate for a certain period, you can also calculate this rate by linear interpolation of the two nearest forward rates.

Beispiel

Folgende Quotierungen gelten:
USD/CHF: 1,5000-10
Zinsen USD, 184 Tage: 5 7/8-6%
Zinsen CHF, 184 Tage: 2-2 1/8%

Aus diesen Preisen soll unsere Quotierung für den 6-Monats-Devisenterminkurs (USD/CHF) abgeleitet werden.

$$\text{Geld} = 1{,}5005 \times \left(\frac{1 + \left(0{,}02 \times \dfrac{184}{360}\right)}{1 + \left(0{,}06 \times \dfrac{184}{360}\right)} - 1 \right) = -298$$

$$\text{Brief} = 1{,}5005 \times \left(\frac{1 + \left(0{,}02125 \times \dfrac{184}{360}\right)}{1 + \left(0{,}05875 \times \dfrac{184}{360}\right)} - 1 \right) = -279$$

Unsere Quotierung würde damit folgendermaßen aussehen:

Spot	1,5000	1,5010
Swap	- 298	- 279
Terminkurs	**1,4702**	**1,4731**

Warum verwendet man eine Quotierung als Auf- oder Abschlag?

Es gibt eine Reihe von Gründen, Terminkurse als Swappunkte zu quotieren:

- Swappunkte hängen vorwiegend von den **Zinssätzen** ab. Sie ändern sich daher weniger häufig als der Kassakurs. Werden Outright-Kurse quotiert, müssen sie bei jeder Kassabewegung geändert werden.
- Kunden bzw. Preisnehmer **vergleichen die Terminkurse von unterschiedlichen Banken** und überlegen den Kassakurs erst, wenn sie bereit sind, zu handeln bzw. ein Geschäft abzuschließen.
- In der Praxis wird das **Terminbuch getrennt vom Kassabuch** geführt. Swappunkte für Outrights werden daher von einem eigenen Terminhändler quotiert, nicht von einem Kassahändler. Es kommt auch vor, dass die Swappunkte für Terminkurse von Money Market-Händlern quotiert werden, da ja die Swappunkte von den Zinssätzen im Geldmarkt abhängen.
- Die meisten Interbank-Termingeschäfte werden in Form von **Devisenswaps** durchgeführt, wo Swappunkte gehandelt werden.

Berechnung von Terminkursen bei Broken Dates – lineare Interpolation

Wenn Sie einen Terminkurs für eine bestimmte Laufzeit berechnen müssen, können Sie diesen Terminkurs auch durch lineare Interpolation der beiden nächstliegenden Terminkurse ermitteln.

Example

Market data:
Spot EUR/USD: 1.1500-10
6 months swap: 1.1438-40   180 days
9 months swap: 1.1380-82   270 days
You have to sell EUR 8 months forward (240 days).
What is the forward rate?

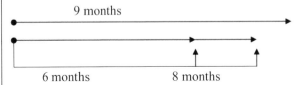

You know that the 8 months swap is between the 6 months and 9 months swaps. As you want to sell EUR, you have to concentrate on the bid rates.
The difference between the 6 months and 9 months swaps is 58 pips (1.1438 – 1.1380). If the EUR/USD forward curve runs linear you can assume that between the 6 and 9 months the discount per month has to be 19.3 pips (one third of 58). So you would have an estimated 8 months forward rate of 1.1399 (1.1380 – (-) 0.00193).

$$O = 1.1438 + \left[\frac{1.1380 - 1.1438}{270 - 180}\right] \cdot (240 - 180) = 1.1399$$

You can sell EUR at 1.1399 8 months forward.

Example

Of course you can use the linear interpolation also for swap points.
Market data:
Spot EUR/USD: 1.1500-10
6 months swap: 62-60   180 days
9 months swap: 120-118   270 days
You have to sell EUR 8 months forward (240 days).
What are the swap points?
You are looking for the bid rate of the 8 months swap.

$$\text{swap points} = -62 + \left[\frac{-120 - (-)62}{270 - 180}\right] \times (240 - 180) = -100.67$$

The discount for 8 months is -100.67 pips.

Beispiel

Es gelten folgende Marktdaten:
Spot EUR/USD: 1,1500-10
6-Monats-Swap: 1,1438-40   (180 Tage)
9-Monats-Swap: 1,1380-82   (270 Tage)
Sie wollen EUR auf Termin 8 Monate (240 Tage) verkaufen.
Wie lautet der Terminkurs?

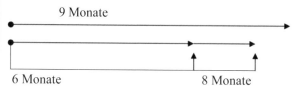

Sie wissen, dass der 8-Monats-Terminkurs zwischen dem 6-Monats- und dem 9-Monats-Terminkurs liegt. Da Sie EUR verkaufen wollen, betrachten Sie nur die Geldseiten.
Die Differenz zwischen dem 6-Monats- und dem 9-Monats-Termin beträgt 58 Pips (1,1438 – 1,1380). Wenn die EUR/USD-Terminkurve relativ linear verläuft, kann man davon ausgehen, dass zwischen den 6 und 9 Monaten pro Monat ca. 19,3 Pips (ein Drittel von 58) Terminabschlag anfallen. So würde sich ein geschätzter 8-Monats-Terminkurs von 1,1399 (1,1380 – (-)0,00193) ergeben.

$$TK = 1{,}1438 + \left[\frac{1{,}1380 - 1{,}1438}{270 - 180}\right] \times (240 - 180) = 1{,}1399$$

Sie können EUR auf 8 Monate mit einem Kurs von 1,1399 verkaufen.

Beispiel

Natürlich können Sie die lineare Interpolation auch für Swappunkte anwenden.
Es gelten folgende Marktdaten:
Spot EUR/USD: 1,1500-10
6-Monats-Swap: 62-60   (180 Tage)
9-Monats-Swap: 120-118   (270 Tage)
Sie wollen EUR auf Termin 8 Monate (240 Tage) verkaufen.
Wie hoch sind die Swappunkte?
Gesucht ist also die Geldseite des 8-Monats-Swaps.
Vorgehensweise analog wie oben:

$$Swap = -62 + \left[\frac{-120 - (-)62}{270 - 180}\right] \times (240 - 180) = -100{,}67$$

Der Abschlag für 8 Monate beträgt -100,67 Pips.

2.1.4. Cross Rates of Outrights

Forward cross rates are **outright rates of two currencies, where none of these two is USD**. Like spot transactions most of the outright deals are done against the USD. This means that liquidity in crosses is lower and the spreads are usually higher. Thus cross rates are frequently derived from quotes against the USD. If for example a bank likes to sell outright CHF against GBP, it would usually do the following transactions:

- sell CHF outright against USD
- sell USD outright against GBP

Example

The result of these transactions represents the GBP/CHF outright cross rate.

	USD/CHF	USD/AUD
Spot rate	1.3757/62	1.5930/35
3-month	125/120	115/110

What are the forward cross rates for CHF/AUD?
Step 1: determine the USD outright rates

	USD/CHF	USD/AUD
Spot	1.3757/62	1.5930/35
Swap points	-125/-120	-115/-110
Outright rate	1.3632/42	1.5815/25

Step 2: Knowing the outright rates, the same rules as used for spot crosses can be used.

Bid

(1) sell CHF 1 against USD 0.73303 (1.3642)
(2) sell USD 0.73303 against AUD 1.15929 (1.5815)

By selling 1 CHF you receive AUD 1.15929. Thus the **CHF/AUD bid rate is 1.1593**.

Offer

(1) Buy CHF 1 against USD 0.73357 (1.3632)
(2) Buy USD 0.73357 against AUD 1.16087 (1.5825)

By buying 1 CHF you receive AUD 1.16087. Thus the **CHF/AUD offer rate is 1.1609**.

2.1.4. Terminquotierungen von Cross-Kursen

Forward-Cross-Rates sind Terminkurse von **Währungspaaren, die keine USD enthalten.**
Wie bei Kassatransaktionen beinhalten die meisten großen Termintransaktionen zwischen
Banken einen Kauf oder Verkauf von USD. Große Termin-Cross-Käufe oder -Verkäufe sind
also eher selten. Um beispielsweise den Schweizer Franken (CHF) auf Termin gegen das
Pfund Sterling (GBP) zu verkaufen, würde eine Bank üblicherweise folgende Transaktio-
nen tätigen:

- Verkauf CHF gegen USD auf Termin
- Verkauf von USD auf Termin gegen GBP

Beispiel

Folgende Preise werden im Markt quotiert:

	USD/CHF	USD/AUD
Kassakurs	1,3757/62	1,5930/35
3 Monate	125/120	115/110

Wie lauten die Forward-Cross-Sätze (3 Monate) für CHF/AUD?
Schritt 1: Bestimmung der Terminkurse gegen den USD:

	USD/CHF	USD/AUD
Spot	1,3757/62	1,5930/35
Swappunkte	125/120	115/110
Outright-Kurs	1,3632/42	1,5815/25

Schritt 2: Berechnung der Crosses analog den Regeln für Kassa-Crosses:

Geldseite

(1) Verkauf von 1 CHF gegen 0,73303 USD (zu 1,3642)
(2) Verkauf von 0,73303 USD gegen 1,15929 AUD (zu 1,5815)

Somit konnten CHF gegen AUD über den USD zum Kurs von **1,1593** verkauft werden.

Briefseite

(1) Kauf 1 CHF gegen Verkauf 0,73357 USD (1,3632)
(2) Kauf USD 0,73357 gegen Verkauf 1,16087 AUD (1,5825)

Somit konnten CHF gegen AUD über den USD zum Kurs von **1,1609** gekauft werden.

2.1.5. Time Options

Contrary to traditional FX forward contracts the settlement of a time option is not on a specified day but – depending on the customer's choice – within a specified period of time. The term "option" therefore only relates to the **date of settlement**, not meaning that the customer has a choice to fulfill the contract or not (like with FX options).

Time options are **only traded by customers**, not in the interbank market. Customers use time options for hedging when the exact date of payment is not known. For this flexibility they have to accept an unfavourable rate compared to the rate of a traditional forward contract. (Professional market participants prefer traditional forward deals and compensate any differences in the date of settlement with FX swaps.)

2.1.5.1. Pricing of Time Options

Principle: you always quote the rate for the worst case scenario (for the bank) which is the most unfavourable settlement date.

Example
Time option when having **discounts**:   EUR/USD spot: 1.2050-55   3 mo swap: 45-43   4 mo swap: 62-60   What are the rates for a time option from 3 to 4 months?   Bid   Offer   3 mo   1.2005   **1.2012**   4 mo   **1.1988**   1.1995   You are quoting the two worst rates, i.e. **1.1988 – 1.2012**.   When having discounts: for the bid rate you take the discounts for the latest possible settlement, for the offer rate you calculate the discounts for the earliest possible settlement date.
Example
Time option when having **premiums**:   EUR/USD spot: 1.2050-55   3 mo swap: 43-45   4 mo swap: 60-62   What are the rates for a time option from 3 to 4 months?   Bid   Offer   3 mo   **1.2093**   1.2100   4 mo   1.2110   **1.2117**   You are quoting the two worst rates, i.e. **1.2093-1.2117**.   When having premiums: for the bid rate you take the premiums for the earliest possible settlement, for the offer rate you calculate the premiums for the latest possible settlement.

2.1.5. Termingeschäfte mit Laufzeitoption (Time Options)

Im Unterschied zu konventionellen Termingeschäften erfolgt die Erfüllung eines Termingeschäfts mit Laufzeitoption nicht an einem bestimmten Tag, sondern nach Wahl des Kunden innerhalb einer bei Abschluss festgelegten Periode. Der Ausdruck „Option" bezieht sich also ausschließlich auf den **Zeitpunkt der Erfüllung** des Termingeschäfts, nicht jedoch auf ein Wahlrecht, ob das Geschäft erfüllt wird oder nicht.

Time Options werden **ausschließlich von Kunden verwendet,** nicht jedoch im Interbankhandel. Kunden verwenden Time Options im Hedging, wenn der Zahlungszeitpunkt nicht genau bekannt ist, und nehmen für diese zusätzliche Flexibilität einen im Vergleich zu konventionellen Termingeschäften möglicherweise schlechteren Kurs in Kauf. (Professionelle Marktteilnehmer bevorzugen konventionelle Termingeschäfte und gleichen etwaige Unterschiede im effektiven Zahlungszeitpunkt mit FX-Swaps aus.)

2.1.5.1. Pricing von Termingeschäften mit Laufzeitoption

Prinzip: Es wird jeweils der Kurs für den – aus Banksicht – ungünstigsten Ausnutzungstermin, also ein Worst-Case-Kurs, quotiert.

Beispiel

Time Option bei **Abschlägen** auf Termin:

EUR/USD Spot: 1,2050-55
3 Mo Swap: 4-43
4 Mo Swap: 62-60

Welche Kurse ergeben sich für eine Time Option von 3 auf 4 Monate?

	Geldkurs	Briefkurs
3 Monate	1,2005	**1,2012**
4 Monate	**1,1988**	1,1995

Sie quotieren den jeweils schlechtesten Kurs, d.h. **1,1988-1,2012.**
Bei Abschlägen berücksichtigen Sie für die Geldseite also die Abschläge für die spätestmögliche Ausnutzung, für die Briefseite die Abschläge für die frühestmögliche Ausnutzung.

Beispiel

Time Option bei **Aufschlägen** auf Termin:

EUR/USD Spot: 1,2050-55
3-Monats-Swap: 43-45
4-Monats-Swap: 60-62

Welche Kurse ergeben sich für eine Time Option von 3 auf 4 Monate?

	Geldkurs	Briefkurs
3 Monate	**1,2093**	1,2100
4 Monate	1,2110	**1,2117**

Sie quotieren den jeweils schlechtesten Kurs, d.h. **1,2093-1,2117.**
Bei Aufschlägen berücksichtigen Sie für die Geldseite also die Aufschläge für die frühestmögliche Ausnutzung, für die Briefseite die Aufschläge für die spätestmögliche Ausnutzung.

2.1.5.2. Remaining Risk for Time Options

The time options pricing is based on the **most unfavourable settlement date**. Also the hedging of this position is done for this date. The bank assumes that at any other settlement date the result will be better. This assumption however is only correct when discounts do not turn into premiums and vice versa.

Example

Your customer sells a time option from 11 to 12 months.
EUR/USD spot: 1.2050-1.2055
11 mo swap: 220-222
12 mo swap: 235-237
Due to the premiums you are quoting the bid price for the shortest period, i.e. 1.2270. Also the hedge is done for 11 months.
You assume that your result will improve when your customer settles on a later date as then you could roll-over the hedging position with premiums.
After 11 months the EUR rates have risen and EUR/USD is quoted with **discounts**.
If the customer settles the deal on a later date, you have to roll-over your position with discounts which impairs your result.

The risk is a change from discount to premium (and vice versa). This risk cannot be hedged completely. It can only be reduced by limiting the period of the time option (e.g. max. one month).

2.1.6. Non-deliverable Forwards (NDF)

A Non-deliverable Forward (NDF) is a contract between two parties that **fixes the rate of exchange that will apply on a notional FX forward transaction**.

The NDF is to the FX forward market what the FRA is to the money markets: both are **agreements between parties to compensate each other for movements in a market rate**.

As with the FRA, the counterparties to an NDF do **not exchange the notional amount**, they simply pay each other a cash sum based on the difference between the NDF rate and a reference FX spot rate at the contract's maturity.

The NDF was developed in the 1990s to help investors into emerging markets manage their exposures to non-convertible currencies, or to currencies whose forward markets are restricted.

2.1.6.1. Terminology

NDF rate

The forward rate which is agreed on in the NDF (Outright rate).

Reference rate

is fixed on the fixing date. For most currencies there is an official fixing which is published on Telerate and Reuters. Usually this is a spot rate which is determined by a certain bank panel at a certain time.

2.1.5.2. Restrisiken bei Termingeschäften mit Laufzeitoption

Beim Pricing der Time Option wird vom jeweils **ungünstigsten Zeitpunkt der Erfüllung** ausgegangen. Das Hedging der Position erfolgt auf eben diesen Zeitpunkt. Man geht dabei davon aus, dass sich zu jedem anderen Erfüllungszeitpunkt das Ergebnis für die Bank verbessert. Diese Annahme trifft jedoch nur zu, wenn sich Aufschläge nicht in Abschläge verwandeln und umgekehrt.

Beispiel

Ihr Kunde verkauft eine EUR/USD Time Option von 11 auf 12 Monate.
EUR/USD Spot: 1,2050-1,2055
11-Monats-Swap: 220-222
12-Monats-Swap: 235-237
Aufgrund der Aufschläge quotieren Sie für die Geldseite den Preis der kürzesten Laufzeit, also 1,2270. Den Hedge führen Sie ebenfalls auf 11 Monate durch. Sie gehen dabei davon aus, dass sich Ihr Ergebnis verbessert, wenn der Kunde zu einem späteren Zeitpunkt ausübt, weil Sie die Hedgeposition dann mit Aufschlägen weiterrollen können.
Nach 11 Monaten sind die EUR-Zinsen gestiegen und EUR/USD quotiert nun im **Abschlag.** Wenn der Kunde nun erst später das Termingeschäft erfüllt, müssen Sie die Position mit Abschlägen weiterrollen, wodurch sich Ihr Ergebnis verschlechtert.

Das Risiko besteht also in einer Änderung von Abschlägen in Aufschlägen (und umgekehrt). Dieses Risiko kann nicht abgesichert werden. Es kann nur reduziert werden, indem man die Periode der Time Option beschränkt (z.B. maximal 1 Monat).

2.1.6. Non-deliverable Forward (NDF)

Ein Non-deliverable Forward (NDF) ist ein Kontrakt zwischen zwei Parteien, in dem ein **Devisenterminkurs für ein fiktives Devisentermingeschäft fixiert** wird.

Wie der FRA im Geldmarkt ist auch der NDF eine Vereinbarung, die es den beiden Kontrahenten ermöglicht, sich durch gegenseitige Kompensation **gegen unvorteilhafte Marktbewegungen absichern** zu können.

Wie auch beim FRA wird beim NDF **kein Kapital ausgetauscht,** es dient nur als Rechengröße. Bei Fälligkeit erfolgt ein Cash-Settlement, d.h., es wird eine Ausgleichzahlung über die Differenz zwischen NDF-Kurs und aktuellem Referenzkurs geleistet.

Der NDF entstand in den 1990ern, um auch Investoren in den Emerging Markets die Absicherung ihrer Währungspositionen zu ermöglichen, obwohl viele dieser Währungen nicht konvertibel sind oder in einigen Terminmärkten Restriktionen herrschen.

2.1.6.1. Usancen

NDF-Kurs

ist der Terminkurs, der im NDF festgelegt wird (entspricht dem Outright-Kurs).

Referenzkurs

ist der Kurs, der am Fixing Date zur Abrechnung des NDF festgelegt wird. Für die meisten Währungen gibt es offizielle Fixings, die auf Reuters veröffentlicht werden. Dies ist üb-

Compensation payment/Cash Settlement

The compensation payment is based on the difference between NDF rate and reference rate referring to the nominal amount and is usually settled cash in USD.

Fixing date

The day where the reference rate which is needed for the compensation payment is fixed.

Settlement date

The day where the cash settlement is conducted (= value date of the fixing date)

Buyer of an NDF

The buyer of an NDF is – like in a conventional FX forward transaction – the buyer of the base currency (only notional amount). For e.g. USD/BRL he would be USD buyer, i.e. he has got a long USD position and wants a rising USD/BRL rate (= weakening of BRL). Should the BRL fall until maturity and the USD/BRL rate rises above the NDF rate, the buyer receives a compensation payment from the seller.

Foreign companies with asset exposures in the non-convertible currency (or investors speculating on a depreciation of that currency) are natural buyers of NDFs on the hard currency.

Seller of an NDF

Along the lines of the buyer the seller of an NDF is the (fictitious) seller of the base currency, e.g. USD seller for USD/BRL, i.e. he participates in a falling USD/BRL rate (= rising BRL). Should the BRL rise until maturity and the USD/BRL fall below the NDF rate, the seller receives a compensation payment from the buyer.

Foreign companies with requirements for the non-convertible currency (or investors speculating on a rise in the value of that currency) are natural sellers of NDFs on the hard currency.

licherweise der aktuelle Kassakurs, der von einem bestimmten Bankengremium zu einem bestimmten Zeitpunkt festgelegt wird.

Ausgleichszahlung/Cash-Settlement

Die Ausgleichszahlung wird über die Differenz zwischen NDF-Kurs und Referenzkurs, bezogen auf das zugrundeliegende Kapital, berechnet. Die Ausgleichszahlung erfolgt üblicherweise in USD.

Fixing Date

ist der Tag, an dem der Referenzkurs fixiert wird. Er wird für die Berechnung der Ausgleichszahlung zugrundegelegt.

Settlement Date

ist der Tag, an dem die Ausgleichszahlung geleistet wird (= Spot Valuta am Fixing Date).

Käufer eines NDF

Der Käufer eines NDF ist – wie auch bei einem konventionellen Devisentermingeschäft – der Käufer der quotierten Währung (natürlich nur fiktiv). Beim Währungspaar USD/BRL (brasilianischer Real) z.B. wäre er USD-Käufer, d.h., er hat eine Long Position in USD und setzt auf einen steigenden USD/BRL-Kurs (= Abschwächung des BRL). Sollte der BRL bis zur Fälligkeit an Wert verlieren und steigt der USD/BRL-Kurs über den NDF-Kurs, erhält der Käufer vom Verkäufer eine Ausgleichszahlung.

Normalerweise sind Unternehmen, die Forderungen in der nicht-konvertiblen Währung haben, oder Spekulanten, die auf einen steigenden USD/BRL-Kurs setzen, Käufer von NDFs.

Verkäufer eines NDF

Analog zum Käufer ist der Verkäufer eines NDF der (fiktive) Verkäufer der quotierten Währung, z.B. USD-Verkäufer bei USD/BRL, d.h., er partizipiert an fallenden USD/BRL-Kursen (= Aufwertung des BRL).

Sollte der BRL bis zur Fälligkeit an Wert gewinnen und fällt der USD/BRL-Kurs unter den NDF-Kurs, erhält der Verkäufer vom Käufer eine Ausgleichszahlung. Unternehmen, die Verbindlichkeiten in der nicht-konvertiblen Währung haben oder auf einen fallenden USD/BRL-Kurs spekulieren, sind üblicherweise Verkäufer von NDFs.

Example

The Taiwan subsidiary of a multinational company plans to repatriate TWD 350 mio. at the year-end but expects the TWD to weaken substantially against the USD, so they would like to hedge the position. The central bank operates severe restrictions on the local FX forward market, so the parent company enters into a 12-months USD/TWD NDF.

Spot USD/TWD:　　　　　　　　　　33.75
12-months forward USD/TWD:　　33.20-33.27

The company has to hedge against a falling TWD (rising USD/TWD), i.e. it buys the 12-months NDF at 33.27. The NDF is settled after 12 months.

USD/TWD on fixing date:　　　　33.43
(published on Reuters page TFEMA at 11.00 a.m. Taipeh time)
As the fixing is above the NDF rate the company receives the compensation payment.
Calculation: $350,000,000/33.27 - 350,000,000/33.43 = 10,519,987.98$ USD $- 10,469,638.05$ USD $= \mathbf{50,349.93\ USD}$

The company receives 50,349.93 on the settlement date.
In this scenario the payment of USD 50,349.93 in favour of the company would have compensated the company for an equivalent loss on the underlying TWD 350 m repatriation. If the USD/TWD had fallen, the company would have been required to pay a compensation sum to the seller.

2.1.6.2. Risks for NDF

Market Risk

The market risk is the **risk of a loss due to market price changes**, here the currency rate. The market risk of a NDF is the same as with a traditional forward contract.

Credit Risk (Counterparty Risk)

The credit risk is the **risk of a loss due to a default of the counterparty**. With NDFs there is the risk that the counterpart does not pay the compensation payment. This kind of credit risk is called **replacement risk**. It is the same for NDFs as for traditional forward contracts.

Another kind of credit risk is the **settlement risk** which only occurs with exchange transactions. **If one party has already fulfilled its part of the contract, the other party fails to fulfill the remaining part.** As there is only a cash settlement for NDFs and no exchange of principal there is no settlement risk for NDFs.

Beispiel

Die Tochtergesellschaft eines internationalen Konzerns in Taiwan erhält in einem Jahr TWD 350 Mio. (Taiwan Dollars), die es dann in USD konvertieren möchte. Das Unternehmen befürchtet aber, dass sich der TWD gegenüber dem USD noch weiter abschwächt und kauft daher zur Absicherung einen USD/TWD-NDF auf 12 Monate (Offshore-Investoren ist es nicht erlaubt, konventionelle Devisentermingeschäfte im taiwanesischen Markt abzuschließen).

Spot USD/TWD: 33,75
12-Monats-Termin USD/TWD: 33,20-33,27

Das Unternehmen muss sich gegen einen fallenden TWD (steigenden USD/TWD-Kurs) absichern, d.h., es kauft einen 12-Monats-NDF mit 33,27. Nach 12 Monaten wird der NDF fällig.

USD/TWD am Fixing Date: 33,43

Da das Fixing über dem NDF-Kurs liegt, erhält das Unternehmen die Ausgleichszahlung:
(350.000.000/33,27) – (350.000.000/33,43) = USD 10.519.987,98 – USD 10.469.638,05 = **USD 50.349,93**

Das Unternehmen erhält am Settlement Date USD 50.349,93.
Diese Zahlung kompensiert exakt den Verlust, der dem Unternehmen durch die Konvertierung der TWD 350 Mio. entstanden wäre. Wäre der USD/TWD-Kurs gefallen, hätte das Unternehmen eine entsprechende Ausgleichszahlung an den Kontrahenten leisten müssen.

2.1.6.2. Risiken

Marktrisiko

Das Marktrisiko ist das **Risiko eines Verlustes aufgrund einer Änderung des Marktpreises,** hier also des Devisenkurses. Das Marktrisiko eines NDFs entspricht daher genau dem eines normalen FX-Outrights.

Kreditrisiko (Kontrahentenrisiko)

Das Kreditrisiko ist das **Risiko eines Verlustes aufgrund des Ausfalls des Kontrahenten.** Bei NDFs besteht das Risiko, dass der Kontrahent die Ausgleichszahlung nicht leistet, wenn er ausfällt. Diese Art des Kreditrisikos wird **Wiederbeschaffungsrisiko** genannt. Das Ausmaß des Wiederbeschaffungsrisikos von NDFs ist gleich dem von normalen FX-Outrights.

Eine weitere Form des Kreditrisikos ist das **Settlementrisiko,** das nur bei Tauschgeschäften auftritt. Es ist das **Risiko, dass man seinen Teil der Vereinbarung bereits geleistet hat und der Kontrahent ausfällt, bevor er seine Verpflichtung der Vereinbarung erfüllt.** Bei einem EUR/USD-Verkauf besteht beispielsweise das Risiko des Zeitpunktes der Durchführung der EUR-Zahlung bis zum Eingang des USD-Betrages, und zwar im vollen Volumen. Da bei NDFs nur eine Ausgleichszahlung stattfindet und kein Tausch der Währungen, gibt es bei NDFs auch kein Settlementrisiko.

Conversion Risk

Either way, the NDF effectively neutralises the underlying FX exposure. Although it does not cover the risk that the **company may be physically unable, in the event, to convert the underlying TWD into hard currency**.

Even when a conversion is possible it is not sure if it can be conducted at the fixing rate. Especially in times of crisis the fixing rate can differ from the market rate considerably.

2.2. FX Swaps

2.2.1. Terminology

An FX swap is a contract to buy an amount of the base currency at an agreed rate, and simultaneously resell the same amount of the base currency for a later value date to the same counterpart, also at an agreed rate (or vice versa).

Technically an FX swap is a **combination of a spot deal and a reverse outright deal**.

Example
EUR/USD Spot: 1.1548-52 12-mth swap:　　112-110 A dealer wants to sell an FX swap for EUR 10 m.

In FX swaps the term sell or buy refers to the **forward leg**. Since the dealer acts here as a market user he sells at the bid rate i.e. 112 (bid > ask → discount!).

In order to avoid misunderstandings it is advisable to say **"buy-and-sell"** instead of sell (and **sell-and-buy** instead of buy). Firstly the spot transaction is named and secondly the forward transaction is named.

Buy-and-sell here refers both to the EUR, which are bought spot and sold forward (it does not mean you buy EUR and sell USD!)

Spot basis

Both spot and forward transaction are agreed on the same spot basis, usually the current **mid rate** i.e. 1.1550.

If the mid rate is an uneven figure it is usually rounded to the nearest round lot, which lies within the current quote. E.g.: spot 1.1547 – 52 → spot basis: 1.1550

The parties in a swap can agree to use another rate instead of the spotbasis (e.g. bid rate or ask rate).

The spotbasis is usually fixed by the marketmaker and he should consider the rules above. It is not allowed to fix the spotbasis at a non-current market rate.

Konvertierungsrisiko

Grundsätzlich neutralisiert ein NDF das Marktrisiko der zugrundeliegenden FX-Position. Allerdings schützt er nicht davor, die betreffende Währung **bei Fälligkeit eventuell nicht am Kassamarkt in USD physisch konvertieren zu können** (aufgrund fehlender Liquidität oder neuer Restriktionen).

Selbst wenn eine Konvertierung möglich ist, stellt sich die Frage, ob diese auch zum gleichen Kurs wie das Fixing erfolgen kann. Gerade in Krisenzeiten kann der Fixingkurs erheblich vom tatsächlich im Markt erzielbaren Kassakurs abweichen.

2.2. Devisenswap (FX-Swap)

2.2.1. Usancen

Ein Devisenswap (FX-Swap) ist eine Vereinbarung zwischen zwei Parteien über eine Devisenkassatransaktion und ein gegenläufiges Devisentermingeschäft, über den üblicherweise selben Betrag in der quotierten Währung (Basiswährung).

Technisch gesehen ist ein FX-Swap also eine **Kombination von Kassa- und Termingeschäft.**

Beispiel

EUR/USD Kassa: 1,1548-52
12-Monats-Swappunkte: 112-110
Ein Händler möchte einen FX-Swap über 10 Mio. EUR verkaufen.

Bei FX-Swaps bezieht sich das Kaufen oder Verkaufen immer auf die **Termintransaktion.** Da der Händler in unserem Beispiel als Market User auftritt, verkauft er zur Geldseite, also mit 112 (Geld > Brief → Abschlag!).

Um Missverständnissen vorzubeugen, ist es üblich, **„kaufen und verkaufen"** anstatt verkaufen zu sagen (und **„verkaufen und kaufen"** anstatt kaufen). **Als Erstes wird die Kassatransaktion genannt, als Zweites die Transaktion auf Termin.**

Auch im deutschsprachigen Markt wird oft die englische Terminologie verwendet, d.h. für „kaufen und verkaufen" **„buy-and-sell"** und für „verkaufen und kaufen" **„sell-and-buy".** Buy-and-sell bezieht sich hier auf den EUR, der in der Kassa gekauft und auf Termin verkauft wird (es ist hier nicht gemeint: Er kauft EUR und verkauft USD!).

Kassabasis

Kassa- und Termintransaktion werden auf der gleichen Kassabasis gerechnet, dies ist normalerweise der aktuelle **Kassamittekurs,** hier 1,1550.

Sollte die Kassamitte ein ungerader Kurs sein, wird meistens zum nächsten geraden Kurs gerundet, z.B. Kassa 1,1547-52 → Kassabasis: 1,1550

Die Partner im Swap können jedoch auch vereinbaren, einen anderen Kurs als die Kassabasis zu verwenden (z.B. Geld- oder Briefkurs).

Üblicherweise fixiert der Market Maker die Kassabasis, er sollte sich dabei aber an die oben erwähnten Regeln halten. Es ist unstatthaft, eine Kassabasis zu einem nicht-aktuellen Marktkurs festzulegen.

Volume

In a regular FX swap the base currency's volume both for the spot and the forward transaction is the same, in the example EUR 10 m.

(However in the last years it became common to do FX swaps with uneven volumes as well. The reason is to avoid the residual FX risk)

Cash-flows

The dealer buys-and-sells EUR 10 m spot against 12 month at – 112, thus he

- buys spot EUR 10 m at 1.1550 and
- sells forward 12 month EUR 10 m at 1.1438

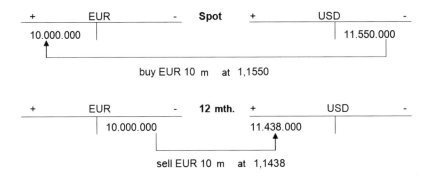

This figure can be interpreted in two ways:

- A pair of offsetting FX transactions for different value dates, concluded at the same time and on the same deal ticket with the same counterpart.
- Looked at vertically over time you are actually borrowing EUR for 12-month time and lending USD over the same period. The FX swap is a **pair of money market deals effected by means of FX transactions**.

Distinction between FX outrights and FX swaps

The difference between an outright and a FX swap is shown in the table below:

Outright	FX swap
buy outright	sell-and-buy (S/B) (= sell spot and buy forward)
or	or
sell outright	Buy-and-sell (B/S) (= buy spot and sell forward)

2.2.2. Quotation of FX swaps

FX swaps are quoted in **swap points** (or forward points).

Volumen

Bei einem regulären FX-Swap wird in der quotierten Währung immer der gleiche Betrag in der Spot und in der Termintransaktion gehandelt, in unserem Beispiel 10 Mio. EUR. Jedoch wurde es in den letzten Jahren üblich, FX-Swaps auch mit unterschiedlichen Beträgen zu handeln, um ein verbleibendes FX-Risiko zu vermeiden.

Cashflows

Der Händler führt folgenden FX-Swap durch: Buy-and-sell EUR 10 Mio. Spot gegen 12 Monate mit -112, das heißt, er

- kauft Spot EUR 10 Mio. mit 1,1550 und
- verkauft auf Termin 12 Monate EUR 10 Mio. mit 1,1438 (1,1550 – 0,0112)

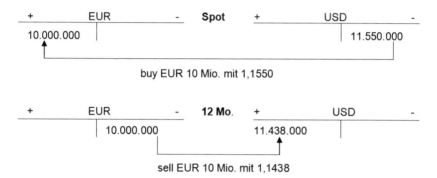

Diese Abbildung kann auf zwei Weisen interpretiert werden:

- Zwei FX-Transaktionen für verschiedene Valuten wurden zum selben Zeitpunkt auf demselben Deal Ticket mit demselben Kontrahenten durchgeführt.
- Unter Berücksichtigung der zeitlichen Abfolge erkennt man, dass die Cashflows einer Refinanzierung in EUR für 12 Monate und einer Anlage in USD für die gleiche Periode entsprechen. **Der FX-Swap entspricht also zwei Money-Market-Geschäften.**

Devisentermingeschäft/Devisenswap

Der Unterschied zwischen beiden Geschäftsarten kann wie folgt dargestellt werden:

Devisentermingeschäft	Devisenswap
Kauf auf Termin	Sell-and-buy (S/B) (= Verkauf Spot und Kauf Termin)
oder	oder
Verkauf auf Termin	Buy-and-sell (B/S) (= Kauf Spot und Verkauf Termin)

2.2.2. Quotierung

Swaps werden wie Terminkurse quotiert, d.h. in **Swappunkten** oder Forwardpunkten.

An example of a Reuters page is shown below:
EUR/USD swaps:

RIC	Bid	Ask	Srce	Time
EURON=	-0.385	-0.335	BAFX	12:46
EURTN=	-1.25	-1.21	RBSL	13:03
EURSN=	-0.41	-0.38	BOAF	12:46
EURSW=	-3.29	-3.24	RBSL	13:03
EUR2W=	-5.8	-5.7	DRE4	12:59
EUR1M=	-12.67	-12.42	INGX	13:03
EUR2M=	-23.66	-22.66	PBGR	13:03
EUR3M=	-33.05	-32.55	INGX	13:03
EUR4M=	-43.01	-42.61	RABN	13:02
EUR5M=	-53.04	-52.54	RABN	13:02
EUR6M=	-62.05	-61.65	SELV	13:03
EUR7M=	-71.2	-70.2	RZBA	13:03
EUR8M=	-80.6	-79.6	RZBA	13:03
EUR9M=	-89.20	-88.00	SELV	13:03
EUR10M=	-97.62	-96.37	DRE4	13:03
EUR11M=	-105.63	-104.38	DRE4	13:03
EUR1Y=	-112.60	-111.40	SELV	13:03
EUR2Y=	-177.5	-172.5		13:03
EUR3Y=	-215	-195		13:02
EUR4Y=	-219	-189		13:02
EUR5Y=	-214	-174		13:02
EUR10Y=	-191	-91		13:02

At the **bid rate** the **Market User sells** the swap i.e. he buys spot and sells forward **(buy-and-sell).**

At the **ask rate** the **Market User buys** the swap i.e. he sells spot and buys forward **(sell-and-buy).**

Example

EUR/USD spot: 1.1548-52
You ask a bank for the 6-mth EUR/USD swap and get the following quote:
6 month swap: 62.05-61.65
You buy and sell EUR 10 m. What are the transactions?
- you buy spot EUR 10 m against USD at 1.1550 (mid rate) and
- you sell 6 month forward EUR 10 m at 1.148795 against USD (= 1.1550 – 0.006205)

2.2.3. Mark to Market of FX swaps

The mark to market value of an FX swap is the sum of the present values of all cash flows which would occur if the swap were closed at the current market rate.

Example

EUR/USD spot: 1.1550
1 year swap: 112-110 (365 days)
1 year USD: 6%
1 year EUR: 7%

Hier das Beispiel einer Reuters-Seite:
EUR/USD-Swaps:

RIC	Bid	Ask	Srce	Time
EURON=	-0.385	-0.335	BAFX	12:46
EURTN=	-1.25	-1.21	RBSL	13:03
EURSN=	-0.41	-0.38	BOAF	12:46
EURSW=	-3.29	-3.24	RBSL	13:03
EUR2W=	-5.8	-5.7	DRE4	12:59
EUR1M=	-12.67	-12.42	INGX	13:03
EUR2M=	-23.66	-22.66	PBGR	13:03
EUR3M=	-33.05	-32.55	INGX	13:03
EUR4M=	-43.01	-42.61	RABN	13:02
EUR5M=	-53.04	-52.54	RABN	13:02
EUR6M=	-62.05	-61.65	SELV	13:03
EUR7M=	-71.2	-70.2	RZBA	13:03
EUR8M=	-80.6	-79.6	RZBA	13:03
EUR9M=	-89.20	-88.00	SELV	13:03
EUR10M=	-97.62	-96.37	DRE4	13:03
EUR11M=	-105.63	-104.38	DRE4	13:03
EUR1V=	-112.60	-111.40	SELV	13:03
EUR2V=	-177.5	-172.5		13:03
EUR3V=	-215	-195		13:02
EUR4V=	-219	-189		13:02
EUR5V=	-214	-174		13:02
EUR10V=	-191	-91		13:02

Zum **Geldkurs** verkauft der **Market User** den Swap, d.h., er kauft in der Kassa und verkauft auf Termin **(buy-and-sell)**.

Zum **Briefkurs** kauft der **Market User** den Swap, d.h., er verkauft in der Kassa und kauft auf Termin **(sell-and-buy)**.

Beispiel

EUR/USD Spot: 1,1548-52
Sie fragen eine Bank für den 6-Monats-EUR/USD-Swap und bekommen die folgende Quotierung:
6-Monats-Swap: 62,05 – 61,65
● Sie kaufen und verkaufen EUR 10 Mio. Welche Transaktionen werden durchgeführt?
● Sie kaufen in der Kassa EUR 10 Mio. gegen USD mit 1,1550 (Mittekurs)
● Sie verkaufen auf Termin 6 Monate EUR 10 Mio. gegen USD mit 1,148795 (= 1,1550 – 0,006205)

2.2.3. Mark-to-Market-Bewertung

Der Mark-to-Market-Wert eines FX-Swaps ist die Summe der Barwerte aller Cashflows, die entstehen würden, wenn der Swap zu aktuellen Kursen geschlossen würde.

Beispiel

EUR/USD Spot:	1,1550
1-Jahres-Swap:	112 – 110 (365 Tage)
1 Jahr USD-Zinsen:	6%
1 Jahr EUR-Zinsen:	7%

You speculate that EUR rates will fall today. Since this would lead to a fall in the swap points you sell/buy EUR 10 m spot against 1 year at -110 points.

Some hours later interest rates are still unchanged but EUR/USD surged to 1.2000 from 1.1550. This leads to an increase in the swap rate to -114.30. Since you bought at -110 you expect a loss of 4.3 pips i.e. USD 4,300 (10,000,000 x 0.00043).

The example illustrates the mark to market at the current swap of -114.30:

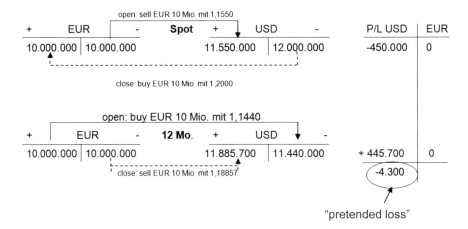

"pretended loss"

When closing the swap at the current rates you lose USD 450,000 spot and gain USD 445,700 forward. If the position is marked to market we are interested in the **present value**. Thus we have to discount the profit in 1 years time by the current USD rate of 6%.

$$present\ value = \frac{future\ value}{1 + rate \times \dfrac{days}{basis}}$$

$$present\ value = \frac{445,700}{1 + 0.06 \times \dfrac{365}{360}} = 420,141.40$$

The profits present value is just USD 420,141.40. Thus the total loss amounts to **USD 29,858.60** (420,141.40 – 450,000) instead of the expected loss of USD 4,300.

2.2.4. Residual FX Risk of FX Swaps (FX Tail)

The example above illustrates that the mark to market of FX swaps may change solely due to a change in the spot rate even if interest rates remain unchanged.

This may be surprising as we figured out earlier that FX swaps are actually comparable to two money market operations and that the FX risk of the spot leg is offset by the reverse forward leg. Strictly speaking this is not quite true.

Sie spekulieren darauf, dass die EUR-Zinsen heute fallen werden. Da dies zu einem Fallen der Swappunkte führen würde (Abschlag verringert sich), verkaufen und kaufen Sie EUR 10 Mio. Spot gegen 1 Jahr mit -110 Punkten („open").

Einige Stunden später sind die Zinssätze immer noch unverändert, aber EUR/USD steigt von 1,1550 auf 1,2000. Dies erhöht die Swappunkte auf -114,30 (Abschlag wird größer, „close"). Da Sie mit -110 Punkten gekauft haben, erwarten Sie einen Verlust von 4,3 Punkten, also 4.300 USD (10.000.000 x 0,00043).

Das Beispiel zeigt den Mark-to-Market-Wert beim aktuellen Swap von -114,30:

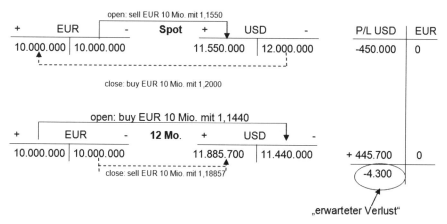

Wenn Sie die bestehende Swapposition zu aktuellen Kursen schließen, verlieren Sie in der Kassa 450.000 USD und verdienen auf Termin 445.700 USD. Wird diese Position Mark-to-Market bewertet, interessiert uns jedoch der **Barwert.** Daher müssen wir den Gewinn, der in einem Jahr anfällt, mit dem aktuellen USD-Zinssatz von 6% abzinsen:

$$Barwert = \frac{Endwert}{1 + Zins \times \dfrac{Tage}{Basis}}$$

$$Barwert = \frac{445.700}{1 + 0,06 \times \dfrac{365}{360}} = 420.141{,}40 \ USD$$

Der Barwert des Gewinns beträgt 420.141,40 USD. Daher ergibt sich ein **Gesamtverlust von 29.858,60 USD** (420.141,40 – 450.000) anstatt des erwarteten Verlustes von 4.300 USD.

2.2.4. FX-Risiko bei Devisenswaps (FX-Tail)

Das obige Beispiel zeigt, dass sich der Mark-to-Market-Wert eines FX-Swaps durchaus auch nur aufgrund einer Veränderung im Kassakurs ändern kann, sogar wenn die jeweiligen Zinssätze unverändert bleiben. Dies mag überraschend erscheinen, da wir ja zuvor gezeigt haben, dass FX-Swaps vergleichbar sind mit zwei Money-Market-Geschäften und dass das FX-Risiko in der Kassa durch das entgegengesetzte Termingeschäft ausgeglichen wird. Genau genommen ist dies nicht ganz richtig.

Changes in the spot rate have two effects on an FX swap position:

- A change in the spot rate leads to **profits and reverse losses at different points in time.** Since future cash flows have to be funded this may lead to additional profits or losses which is demonstrated in the example above.
- Since the **spot rate is a part of the swap formula a change in the spot rate will also cause a change in the forward points,** even if interest rates do not change. You can check this by applying the same interest rates to different spot rates in the swap formula.

General Rule for the residual FX risk

The FX position is the sum of the present value of all future Cash-Flows in the foreign currency.

The following example illustrates how the residual FX risk of FX swap can be identified.

Example
Follow-on of the mark-to-market example: EUR/USD spot: 1.1550 1 year swap: 112-110 (365 days) 1 year USD: 6% 1 year EUR: 7% You sold and bought EUR 10 m at -110. What is the residual FX risk (FX tail)?

In order to identify the spot risk we have to discount all cash flows of the foreign currency (USD). Afterwards we sum up the present values.

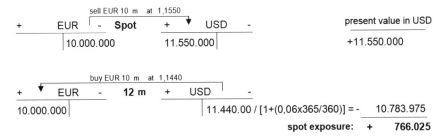

The given FX swap leads to an FX risk of USD + 766,025 i.e. EUR – 663,225. In order to hedge against the risk you should buy EUR 663,225 spot. The profit/loss on this hedge position offsets the profit/loss on the FX swap due to a spot change.

Check:

You bought EUR/USD 663,225 at 1.1550 (hedge of the residual spot risk)
EUR/USD goes up to 1.2000.
Profit on the hedge: 663,225 x (1.2000 – 1.1550) = **USD 29,845**
This profit offsets the loss suffered on the FX swap (see example above).

Veränderungen des Kassakurses haben zwei Effekte auf die FX-Swapposition:

- Eine Veränderung des Kassakurses führt zu **Gewinnen und Verlusten zu unterschiedlichen Zeitpunkten.** Da zukünftige Cashflows abgezinst werden müssen, kann dies zu zusätzlichen Gewinnen und Verlusten führen (wie im Beispiel oben dargestellt).
- Da der **Kassakurs ein Bestandteil der Swap-Formel ist,** verursacht eine **Änderung im Kassakurs auch eine Änderung der Swappunkte,** auch wenn die jeweiligen Zinssätze unverändert bleiben. Sie können dies überprüfen, indem Sie die gleichen Zinssätze mit unterschiedlichen Kassakursen in die Swap-Formel einsetzen.

Allgemeine Regel für das verbleibende FX-Risiko

Die FX-Position ist die Summe der Barwerte aller zukünftigen Cashflows in der Fremdwährung.

Das folgende Beispiel zeigt, wie das verbleibende FX-Risiko von FX-Swaps berechnet werden kann.

Beispiel
Weiterführung des Mark-to-Market-Beispiels (siehe oben):   EUR/USD Spot:　　　　　1,1550   1-Jahres-Swap:　　　　112-110 (365 Tage)   1-Jahres-USD-Zinssatz:　6%   1-Jahres-EUR-Zinssatz:　7%   Sie haben folgendes Geschäft abgeschlossen: Sell and buy 10 Mio. EUR mit -110.   Wie hoch ist das verbleibende FX-Risiko (FX-Tail)?

Um das Kassarisiko berechnen zu können, müssen alle Cashflows der Fremdwährung (USD) abgezinst werden. Anschließend addieren wir die Barwerte.

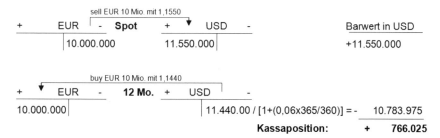

Der FX-Swap beinhaltet ein FX-Risiko von +766.025 USD, das sind -663.225 EUR. Um sich gegen das Risiko steigender EUR/USD-Kurse abzusichern, müssten Sie 663.225 EUR in der Kassa kaufen. Der Gewinn bzw. Verlust dieser Hedgeposition neutralisiert den Gewinn bzw. Verlust aus dem FX-Swap, wenn sich die Kassakurse ändern.

Check:

Sie haben EUR 663.225 gegen USD mit 1,1550 gekauft (Hedge des Kassarisikos).
EUR/USD steigt auf 1,2000.
Gewinn aus dem Hedge: 663.225 x (1,2000 – 1,1550) = **USD 29.845**
Dieser Gewinn neutralisiert den Verlust aus dem FX-Swap (siehe obiges Beispiel).

Calculation of the FX tail

The FX tail can be calculated with the following formula:

$$\text{FX tail} = \text{volume spot} + \frac{\text{volume forward}}{1 + r \times \dfrac{D}{B}}$$

For the above example the open USD FX position is calculated as follows:

$$\text{FX tail} = (+)11{,}550{,}000 + \frac{(-)11{,}440{,}000}{1 + 0.06 \times \dfrac{365}{360}} = (+)766{,}025$$

The FX position for this swap is + USD 766,025 and can be hedged by selling spot USD 766,025.

2.2.5. Effects of the Spot Basis on FX Swaps

FX swaps with the same principal amounts for the spot and forward transactions are also called Matched principal swaps and always have a FX Risk which can be hedged with a spot transaction. If the rate of the spot hedge equals the agreed spot rate the hedge will produce neither a profit nor a loss. Does it differ from the agreed rate, there will be either a profit or loss. Thus the **choice of the spot basis of Matched principal swaps does have a direct effect on the P/L of the position**.

Example

EUR/USD spot: 1.1545-55
1 year swap: 112-110 (365 days)
1 year USD rate: 6%
1 year EUR rate: 7%

You sell and buy 100 m EUR/USD (matched principal) at –110.
Hoes does your P/L change, if as spot basis you fix the a) bid, b) mid or c) offer rate?
In the first step we calculate the **FX tail**.
(Note: for the exact calculation one should rather calculate with the foreign currency volumes. For simplification reasons here we are calculating with EUR volumes.)

$$\text{FX tail} = (-)100{,}000{,}000 + \frac{(+)100{,}000{,}000}{1 + 0.07 \times \dfrac{365}{360}} = (-)6{,}626{,}897$$

For hedging purposes you should buy spot EUR 6,626,897 against USD at the actual offer rate 1.1555.

Result:

Spot basis:	hedge rate:	P/L in pips	P/L in USD
Bid 1.1545	1.1555	-10	USD 6,627
Mid 1.1550	1.1555	- 5	USD 3,313
Offer 1.1555	1.1555	0	USD 0

Berechnung des FX-Tails

Der FX-Tail kann mit folgender Formel berechnet werden:

$$FX - Tail = Volumen\ Spot + \frac{Volumen\ Termin}{1 + r \times \dfrac{T}{B}}$$

Angewendet auf das obige Beispiel errechnet sich die offene USD-FX-Position wie folgt:

$$FX - Tail = (+)11.550.000 + \frac{(-)11.440.000}{1 + 0,06 \times \dfrac{365}{360}} = (+)766.025$$

Die FX-Position bei diesem Swap ist + USD 766.025 und kann durch den Verkauf von USD 766.025 in der Kassa abgesichert werden.

2.2.5. Auswirkung der Kassabasis auf Devisenswaps

FX-Swaps mit gleichen Nominalbeträgen in der Spot- und Termintransaktion (sogenannte Matched Principal Swaps) weisen also immer auch ein FX-Risiko auf, das durch eine Kassatransaktion gehedged werden kann. Entspricht der Kurs des Kassahedges der vereinbarten Kassabasis, so ist diese Absicherung erfolgsneutral. Weicht er von der vereinbarten Kassabasis ab, entstehen Gewinne oder Verluste. Somit hat die **Wahl der Kassabasis von Matched Principal Swaps eine direkte Auswirkung auf die P/L der Position.**

Beispiel

EUR/USD Spot: 1,1545-55
1-Jahres-Swap: 112-110 (365 Tage)
1 Jahr USD-Zinsen: 6%
1 Jahr EUR-Zinsen: 7%

Sie verkaufen und kaufen 100 Mio. EUR/USD (Matched Principal) zu -110. Wie verändert sich Ihre P/L, wenn Sie als Kassabasis den a) Geld-, b) Mittel- oder c) Briefkurs vereinbaren?

Im ersten Schritt berechnen wir den **FX-Tail** (*Anmerkung:* für die exakte Berechnung müsste jeweils mit den Werten der Fremdwährung gerechnet werden. Zur Vereinfachung rechnen wir hier mit EUR-Werten.):

$$FX - Tail = (-)100.000.000 + \frac{(+)100.000.000}{1 + 0,07 \times \dfrac{365}{360}} = (-)6.626.897$$

Zur Absicherung müssten also in der Kassa EUR 6.626.897 gegen USD zum aktuellen Briefkurs von 1,1555 gekauft werden.

Ergebnis:

Kassabasis:	Hedgekurs:	P/L in Pips	P/L in USD
Geld 1,1545	1,1555	-10	USD 6.627
Mitte 1,1550	1,1555	-5	USD 3.313
Brief 1,1555	1,1555	0	USD 0

2.2.6. Matched and Mismatched Principal FX Swaps

Matched principal swaps are **FX swaps where the base currency is traded for the same volumes in the spot and in the forward transaction**. With FX swaps you trade interest rate risks. With matched principal swaps the FX risk occurs as an unwanted side effect which is usually hedged by a FX spot trade.

The effect of the spot basis on the P/L can be summarized as follows:

	Buy & Sell	Sell & Buy
High spot basis:	profit	loss
Low spot basis:	loss	profit

Reason: the **present value of the forward transaction is always lower than the one of the spot transaction**. Therefore with an e.g. buy-and sell swap you have to sell additionally in the spot market. Is the rate of the spot basis lower than the actual FX rate, there will be a loss.

The FX risk for both parties are exactly contrary. As both want to hedge their FX risk, one has to buy spot and the other has to sell spot. Thus both have the problem of potential risks if the hedge transaction can only be conducted with an unfavourable rate compared to the spot basis.

Therefore it became common practice to trade **FX swaps with different principal amounts in the spot and forward transaction (so-called mismatched principal FX swaps)**. Here the forward volume equals the compounded spot volume. Thus the present value of the forward transaction equals the volume of the spot transaction, the **FX risk is zero**.

Example

EUR/USD spot: 1.1545-55
1 year swap: 112-110 (365 days)
1 year USD rate: 6%
1 year EUR rate: 7%

You are trading a mismatched principal swap for EUR 10 m. Which amount is traded in the forward transaction?

The volume of the forward transaction equals the volume of the spot transaction:

$$\text{volume forward} = 100,000,000 \times \left(1 + 0.07 \times \frac{365}{360}\right) = 107,097,222.22$$

2.2.6. Matched und Mismatched Principal FX-Swaps

Unter **Matched Principal FX-Swaps** versteht man FX-Swaps, die über das **gleiche Volumen der quotierten Währung (oder der Gegenwährung) sowohl für die Kassa- als auch Termintransaktion** abgeschlossen werden. FX-Swaps werden üblicherweise verwendet, um Zinsrisiken zu handeln. Das FX-Risiko tritt dabei bei Matched Swaps als eine unerwünschte Nebenwirkung auf, das üblicherweise durch FX-Kassageschäfte geschlossen wird.

Die Auswirkung einer Veränderung des FX-Kurses auf die P/L eines Matched Principal FX-Swaps kann wie folgt zusammengefasst werden:

	Buy & Sell	Sell & Buy
Kassakurs steigt:	Gewinn	Verlust
Kassakurs fällt:	Verlust	Gewinn

Begründung: Der **Barwert der Termintransaktion ist immer niedriger als die Kassatransaktion.** Somit muss z.B. bei einem B/S-Swap zusätzlich in der Kassa verkauft werden, bzw. verlieren wir bei einem Kursrückgang, wenn diese Transaktion nicht zusätzlich gemacht wird.

Das FX-Risiko ist für die beiden Partner im Swap genau gegenläufig. Da beide danach trachten, das FX-Risiko abzusichern, muss einer in der Kassa kaufen und der andere verkaufen. Somit haben auch beide das Problem von potenziellen Verlusten, falls die Hedgetransaktion nur zu einem schlechteren Kurs als die Kassabasis durchgeführt werden kann.

Daher ist es in letzter Zeit üblich geworden, **FX-Swaps mit unterschiedlichen Beträgen in der Kassa- und Termintransaktion (Mismatched Principal FX-Swaps) zu handeln.** Dabei wird die Termintransaktion über das Volumen des aufgezinsten Kassavolumens vereinbart. Man spricht daher auch von **FX-Swaps mit Zinsdeckung.** Somit entspricht der Barwert der Termintransaktion genau dem der Kassatransaktion, wodurch das **FX-Risiko null** ist.

Beispiel

EUR/USD Spot: 1,1545-55
1-Jahres-Swap: 112-110 (365 Tage)
1 Jahr USD-Zinsen: 6%
1 Jahr EUR-Zinsen: 7%
Sie handeln einen Mismatched Principal Swap über EUR 100 Mio.
Welchen Betrag vereinbaren Sie für die Termintransaktion?
Die Termintransaktion ist der aufgezinste Betrag der Kassa-transaktion:

$$\text{Termin Volumen} = 100.000.000 \times \left(1 + 0,07 \times \frac{365}{360}\right) = 107.097.222,22$$

2.2.7. Forward/Forward Swaps

A forward/forward swap is an FX swap that starts in the **future**.

Contrary to a plain FX-swap where a spot and reverse forward transaction are combined, both FX-transactions in the forward/forward swap are **forward transactions**.

You can also describe a forward/forward swap as two different FX swaps.

A 3/6 forward/forward swap means:

- buy 3 months swap   (= sell spot, buy forward) and
- sell 6 months swap   (= buy spot, sell forward)

As both spot-transactions offset each other (if done at same spot rate and same volumes), the result of both transactions will be as follows:

- buy base currency 3 months forward (= sell spot, buy forward)
- sell base currency 6 months forward (= buy spot, sell forward)

Example

USD/CHF spot: 1.5000
3 month forward: 1.4925
6 month forward: 1.4862
You sell and buy USD 10 m 3 month against 6 month:

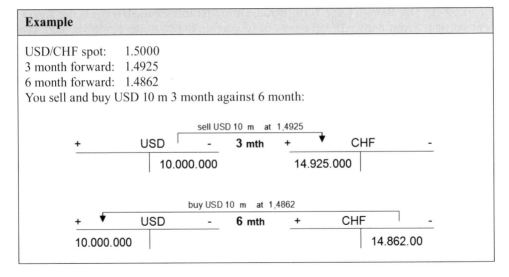

Construction of forward/forward swaps

Like spot start swaps fwd/fwd swaps are quoted in **forward points** rather than in FX forward rates. The fwd/fwd swap points are the margin between the near forward transaction and the far forward transaction. The price can be derived by **combining two reverse spot start swaps**.

Example

USD/CHF spot: 1.5000
3 month swap: 75-73
6 month swap: 140-38
Construct the following fwd/fwd swap:
sell and buy (S/B) USD 10 m 3 against 6 month.

2.2.7. Forward/Forward Swaps

Ein Forward/Forward FX-Swap ist ein Swap, der erst in der **Zukunft** beginnt. Er besteht aus einem Termingeschäft mit kurzer Laufzeit und einem gegenläufigen Termingeschäft mit langer Laufzeit. Ein Forward/Forward FX-Swap unterscheidet sich von einem normalen FX-Swap nur darin, dass die **kurze Transaktion** nicht aus einem Kassageschäft, sondern aus einem **Termingeschäft** besteht.

Den Forward/Forward Swap kann man auch als zwei einzelne Swapgeschäfte darstellen. Im Fall eines verkauften 3/6 Forward/Forward Swap bedeutet das:

- 3-Monats-Swap kaufen   (= Kassa verkaufen, auf Termin kaufen).
- 6-Monats-Swap verkaufen   (= Kassa kaufen, auf Termin verkaufen).

Da sich die Kassatransaktionen der beiden Geschäfte saldieren (bei gleicher Kassabasis sowohl betrags- als auch ergebnismäßig), ist das Resultat beider Transaktionen folgendes:

- Kauf der quotierten Währung auf 3-Monats-Termin sowie
- Verkauf der quotierten Währung per 6 Monate

Beispiel

USD/CHF Spot: 1,5000
3-Monats-Terminkurs: 1,4925
6-Monats-Terminkurs: 1,4862
Sie schließen folgendes Geschäft ab:

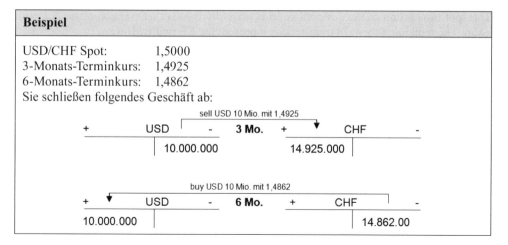

Konstruktion von Forward/Forward Swaps

Wie auch Spot Start FX-Swaps werden Forward/Forward Swaps in **Swappunkten** und nicht als Terminkurse quotiert. Die Forward/Forward-Swappunkte sind die Differenz zwischen der kurzen und der langen Termintransaktion. Der Preis kann durch die **Kombination zweier Spot Start FX-Swaps** ermittelt werden.

Beispiel

USD/CHF Spotkurs: 1.5000
Swap 3 Monate: 75-73
Swap 6 Monate: 140-38
Gesucht ist der folgende Forward/Forward Swap:
Verkauf und Kauf (V/K) USD 10 Mio. 3 gegen 6 Monate.

The fwd/fwd can be produced by effecting two reverse spot start FX swaps.
(1) buy-and-sell (B/S) 3 month at –75
(2) sell-and-buy (S/B) 6 month at –138

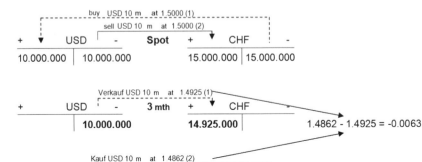

The spot transaction of the 3 month swap is offset by the spot transaction of the 6 month swap. The remaining forward transactions represent the 3/6 fwd/fwd swap:

You sold 3 month at 1.4925 and bought 6 month at 1.4862.
  The forward points are the margin between these two rates:
  3/6 fwd/fwd points = -63 (= 1.4862 – 1.4925)

Calculation rule for forward/forward swaps

Since you can construct fwd/fwd swaps from spot start swaps the price of fwd/fwd swaps can be derived from the spot start swaps as well.

The stated rules can be applied in order to compute fwd/fwd prices:
  bid rate: bid long term – ask short term
  ask rate: ask long term – bid short term

Example

USD/CHF spot: 1.5000
3 month swap: 75-73
6 month swap: 140-38
What is the price of the 3/6 fwd/fwd swap?

bid rate: bid long term:	-140	**ask** rate: ask long term:	-138
- ask short term:	- -73	- bid short term:	- -75
3/6 fwd/fwd bid:	**-67**	3/6 fwd/fwd ask:	**-63**

The 3/6 fwd/fwd swap points are 67-63.

Der Forward/Forward Swap kann mit zwei gegenläufigen FX-Swaps dargestellt werden:
(1) Kauf und Verkauf (K/V) 3 Monate mit -75
(2) Verkauf und Kauf (V/K) 6 Monate mit -138

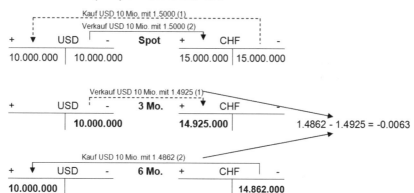

Die Kassatransaktion des 3-Monats-Swaps wird durch die Kassatransaktion des 6-Monats-Swaps ausgeglichen. Die verbleibenden Termintransaktionen ergeben den 3/6 Forward/Forward Swap:

Sie verkaufen 3 Monate mit 1,4925 und kaufen 6 Monate mit 1,4862.
   Die Swappunkte sind die Differenz zwischen diesen beiden Kursen:
   3/6 Forward/Forward Punkte = -63 (= 1.4862 – 1.4925)

Für Forward/Forward Swaps gilt: Da man einen Forward/Forward Swap durch Spot Start Swaps darstellen kann, kann auch der Preis eines Forward/Forward Swaps durch die Preise der Spot Start Swaps ermittelt werden.

Hier gelten folgende Regeln:
Geldseite: Geld lang minus Brief kurz
              (d.h., Aufschlag wird abgezogen und Abschlag addiert)
Briefseite: Brief lang minus Geld kurz
              (d.h., Aufschlag wird abgezogen und Abschlag addiert)

Beispiel

USD/CHF Spot: 1,5000
3-Monats-Swap: 75-73
6-Monats-Swap: 140-38
Was ist der Preis eines 3/6 Forward/Forward Swaps?

Geldseite:	Geld lang:	-140	Briefseite:	Brief lang:	-138
	- Brief kurz:	- -73		- Geld kurz:	- -75
3/6 Fwd/Fwd **Geld:**		**-67**	3/6 Fwd/Fwd **Brief:**		**-63**

Die 3/6 Forward/Forward Swappunkte sind 67-63.

"Spot Basis" of forward/forward swaps

In a forward/forward swap, the agreed rate for the short leg is not the current spot rate but the appropriate **forward mid rate** for the start date of the fwd/fwd swap.

Example

USD/CHF spot: 1.5000
3 month swap: 75-73
3/6 fwd/fwd: 67-63
You sell and buy USD/CHF 3 against 6 month fwd/fwd.
Which rates do you agree?

As a market user you S/B on the ask rate (- 63).
The forward mid rate is 1.4926.
You sell 3 month at **1.4926** (1.5000 – 0.0074) and
you buy 6 month at **1.4863** (1.4926 – 0.0063)

2.2.8. Short dated FX Swaps – FX Deals for Value prior to Spot

Usually FX swaps start value date spot (e.g. spot against 1 week, 1 month etc.). However, there are also swaps which start prior to value spot. There are two regular terms:

- O/N: starts today and ends tomorrow
- Tom/Next: starts tomorrow and ends the day after tomorrow (i.e. spot)

The figure below shows an example of a Reuters page for EUR/USD swaps:

RIC	Bid	Ask	Srce Time
EURON=	-0.385	-0.335	BAFX 12:46
EURTN=	-1.25	-1.21	RBSL 13:03
EURSN=	-0.41	-0.38	BOAF 12:46
EURSW=	-3.29	-3.24	RBSL 13:03
EUR2W=	-5.8	-5.7	DRE4 12:59
EUR1M=	-12.67	-12.42	INGX 13:03
EUR2M=	-23.66	-22.66	PBGR 13:03
EUR3M=	-33.05	-32.55	INGX 13:03
EUR4M=	-43.01	-42.61	RABN 13:02

„Spot-Basis" von Forward/Forward Swaps

Beim Forward/Forward Swap ist die angesetzte „Kassabasis" nicht der aktuelle Kassakurs, sondern der entsprechende **Terminkurs** (auch hier wie im normalen FX-Swap, falls nicht anders vereinbart, die Mitte) für die kurze Laufzeit des Forward/Forward Swaps.

Beispiel

USD/CHF Spot: 1,5000
3-Monats-Swap: 75-73
3/6 Fwd/Fwd: 67-63
Sie haben folgendes Geschäft abgeschlossen:
Sell and buy USD/CHF 3 gegen 6 Monate Forward/Forward.
Welche Kurse werden vereinbart?

Als Market User verkaufen und kaufen Sie mit der Briefseite (-63).
Der Terminmittelkurs liegt bei 1,4926.
Sie verkaufen 3 Monate mit **1,4926** (1,5000 – 0,0074) und Sie kaufen 6 Monate mit **1,4863** (1,4926 – 0,0063).

2.2.8. Kurze Devisenswaps – Kassageschäfte mit Valuta vor dem Spotdatum

Normalerweise starten FX-Swaps mit Valuta Spot (z.B. Spot gegen 1 Woche, 1 Monat, etc.). Es gibt aber auch Swaps, die vor dem Spotdatum starten. Hier sind zwei zu nennen:

- O/N (Overnight): startet heute und endet morgen.
- T/N (Tom(orrow)/Next): startet morgen und endet übermorgen (d.h. Spot).

Die Grafik zeigt das Beispiel einer Reuters-Seite für EUR/USD-Swaps:

RIC	Bid	Ask	Srce	Time
EURON=	-0.385	-0.335	BAFX	12:46
EURTN=	-1.25	-1.21	RBSL	13:03
EURSN=	-0.41	-0.38	BOAF	12:46
EURSW=	-3.29	-3.24	RBSL	13:03
EUR2W=	-5.8	-5.7	DRE4	12:59
EUR1M=	-12.67	-12.42	INGX	13:03
EUR2M=	-23.66	-22.66	PBGR	13:03
EUR3M=	-33.05	-32.55	INGX	13:03
EUR4M=	-43.01	-42.61	RABN	13:02

Producing an FX transaction value tomorrow

Using this short-dated swaps you can produce "forward" FX deals for value date prior to spot e.g. value tomorrow or even value today.

Example

Market data:
GBP/USD: 1.5800–1.5810
Tom/Next: 1.5–1.4
You want to sell GBP/USD for value tomorrow. Which rate can you produce?

In order to produce an FX deal for value tomorrow you do the following deals:

• Sell GBP/USD spot at 1.5800 and (1)
• Sell-and-buy GBP/USD tom/next at –1.4 (2)

Since the spot basis has to be agreed (assumption: mid-rate 1.5805), a bought T/N swap can be priced through the following rates:
Sell value tomorrow: 1.5805
Buy value spot: 1.58036 (1.5805 – 0.00014)

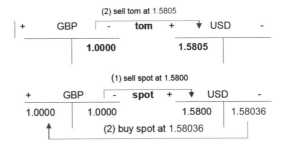

The rate of the resulting sale of GBP/USD value tomorrow is 1.58014:
Tomorrow: 1.5805 USD
Spot: –0,00036 USD (the difference between the USD spot transactions)
Total: 1.58014

As shown in the figure, the T/N swap should be traded on the opposite side (buy T/N swap) of the spot transaction (sell spot). The effect that the T/N swap is traded on a spot basis different than the spot transaction is irrelevant for pricing. The discount of the T/N swap leads here to higher price.

Rule for computing FX rates for value tomorrow

In order to compute the price of FX-deals for value tomorrow apply the following rule:

bid rate spot	offer rate spot
– offer rate T/N swap	– bid rate T/N swap
= bid rate value tomorrow	= offer rate value tomorrow

Kassageschäfte Valuta morgen

Soll ein FX-Geschäft mit Valuta einen Tag nach Handelsabschluss „produziert" werden, so muss das entsprechende Spot-Kassageschäft (zur Spot Valuta) mit einem T/N-Swap kombiniert werden.

Beispiel

Folgende Sätze werden im Markt quotiert:
GBP/USD: 1,5800–1,5810
T/N Swap: 1,5-1,4
Wie ist die Geldseite für Cable (GBP/USD) Valuta morgen?

Zur Ermittlung der Geldseite (zu der man auf den quotierten Kursen GBP per Valuta morgen verkaufen kann) sind folgende Transaktionen durchzuführen:

● Verkauf GBP/USD per Valuta Spot (Kurs 1,5800) (1)
● Kauf T/N Swap mit einem Abschlag von 1,4 (Verkauf GBP per Valuta morgen, Kauf GBP per Valuta Spot) (2)

Da für den Swap die Kassabasis festzulegen ist (Annahme hier 1,5805), gelten folgende Kurse für den gekauften T/N-Swap:
Verkauf Valuta Morgen: 1,5805
Kauf Valuta Spot: 1,58036 (1,5805 – 0,00014)

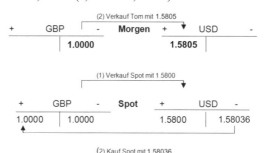

Per Valuta morgen konnte ein Kurs von **1,58014** produziert werden (= 1,5800 – (–)0,00014).
Morgen: 1,5805 USD
Spot: –0,00036 USD (das Saldo aus den USD-Spot-Transaktionen)
Gesamt: 1,58014 USD

Wie aus der Darstellung ersichtlich, muss der T/N-Swap auf der Gegenseite (hier Kauf T/N Swap) der Spot-Transaktion (hier Verkauf Spot) gehandelt werden. Für die Preisermittlung ist der Effekt, dass der Swap auf einer anderen Kassabasis als die Spot-Transaktion gehandelt wird, unerheblich. Der Abschlag des T/N-Swaps führt hier zu einer Erhöhung des Kurses.

Regeln für Kassageschäfte Valuta morgen

Um Kurse Valuta morgen zu berechnen, gilt folgende Regel:

	Geldseite Spot		Briefseite Spot
–	Briefseite T/N-Swap	–	Geldseite T/N-Swap
=	Geldseite Valuta Morgen	=	Briefseite Valuta Morgen

Alternative rule for computing FX rates for value tomorrow

reverse side and sign of tom/next swap points and add them to the spot rate (value spot)

Example		
Follow-on:		
What is the rate of GBP/USD value tomorrow?		
Spot:	1.5800	1.5810
Reversed swap:	+0.00014	+0.00015
GBP/USD value tom	**1.58014**	**1.58115**

Producing an FX transaction for value today

To price an FX deal for value today you have to trade FX spot combined with two short-dated swaps: T/N and O/N swap.

Example
Market data:
GBP/USD: 1.5800-1.5810
O/N: 1.8-1.7
Tom/Next: 1.5-1.4
You want to sell GBP/USD value today. Which rate can you produce?
In order to produce an FX deal for value today you do the following deals:
Bid rate
In order to produce the bid rate of an FX deal for value today you do the following deals:
● sell GBP/USD spot at 1.5800 (1)
● sell-and-buy GBP/USD tom/next at –1.4 (2)
● sell-and-buy GBP/USD O/N at –1.7 (3)

Rule for computing FX rates for value today

In order to compute the price of FX-deals for value today apply the following rule:

bid rate spot	offer rate spot
– offer rate T/N swap	– bid rate T/N swap
– offer rate O/N swap	– bid rate O/N swap
= **bid rate value today**	= **offer rate value today**

Alternative Regel für Kassageschäfte Valuta morgen

Seite und Vorzeichen der T/N-Swappunkte umdrehen und zum Kassakurs (Valuta Spot) addieren.

Beispiel

Für obiges Beispiel ergibt sich also eine Quotierung von:		
Kassakurs	1,5800	1,5810
– Swap T/N (Geld/Brief verdreht)	+ 0,00014	+ 0,00015
= Kurs per Valuta morgen	**1,58014**	**1,58115**

Kassageschäfte Valuta heute

Soll ein FX-Geschäft mit Valuta heute „produziert" werden, so muss das entsprechende Spot-Kassageschäft (zur Spot Valuta) mit einem T/N und einem O/N Swap kombiniert werden.

Beispiel

Folgende Sätze werden im Markt quotiert:

GBP/USD:	1,5800–1,5810
T/N:	1,5–1,4
O/N:	1,8–1,7

Aus diesen Kursen ist die Quotierung für ein GBP/USD FX-Geschäft mit Valuta heute abzuleiten.

Geldseite

Zur Ermittlung der Geldseite (zu der man auf den quotierten Kursen GBP per Valuta heute verkaufen kann), sind folgende Transaktionen durchzuführen:

- Verkauf GBP/USD per Valuta Spot (Kurs 1,5800)
- Kauf T/N-Swap mit einem Abschlag von 1,4 (Verkauf GBP per Valuta morgen, Kauf GBP per Valuta Spot)
- Kauf O/N-Swap mit einem Abschlag von 1,7 (Kauf GBP per Valuta morgen, Verkauf GBP per Valuta heute)

Regeln für Kassageschäfte Valuta heute

Um Kurse Valuta heute zu berechnen, gilt folgende Regel:

Geldseite Spot	Briefseite Spot
– Briefseite T/N-Swap	– Geldseite T/N-Swap
– Briefseite O/N-Swap	– Geldseite O/N-Swap
= Geldseite Valuta Heute	**= Briefseite Valuta Heute**

Alternative rule for computing FX rates for value today

**Reverse side and sign of tom/next and O/N swap points and
add them to the spot rate (value spot)**

Example		
Follow-on of the above example:		
	bid	offer
Spot rate:	1.5800	1.5810
– O/N swap:	+ 0.00017	+ 0.00018
– T/N swap:	+ 0.00014	+ 0.00015
GBP/USD value today	**1.58031**	**1.58133**

2.2.9. EXCURSUS: Synthetic Agreement for Forward Exchange (SAFE)

A SAFE (Synthetic Agreement for Forward Exchange), since 1987 governed by the BBA (British Bankers' Association) is a synthetic agreement for an FX swap. The purpose of SAFEs is the fixing of future swap rates resp. outright prices, without settlement risk (as with all traditional FX swaps).

There are two kinds of SAFEs:

ERA (Exchange Rate Agreement)

Launched by Barclays Bank in 1987, agreement between two parties to level off the difference between an agreed, future swap rate and the actual swap rate prevailing two days before the start of the swap term (cash settlement as for FRAs)

FXA (Forward Exchange Agreement)

Launched by Midland Bank some weeks later in 1987. In FXAs, the difference between an agreed outright price and the spot price at the beginning of the swap period are leveled off additionally.

2.3. Applications of FX Outrights and FX Swaps

2.3.1. Using FX Swaps for Hedging an Outright deal

FX swaps can be used to **transfer the value date of FX transaction to a later or an earlier date**. By that means a spot deal's value date may be postponed to a future date or an outright trades value date may be brought forward towards the spot date.

FX outrights concluded with customers are usually hedged by a **combination of a spot deal and an FX swap** rather than by means of a single interbank FX outright. The advantage of this practice (compared to a single outright deal) is the **higher liquidity in the markets for FX swaps and spot** compared to the outright markets.

Alternative Regeln für Kassageschäfte Valuta heute

**Seite und Vorzeichen der T/N- und O/N-Swappunkte umdrehen
und zum Kassakurs (Valuta Spot) addieren.**

Beispiel		
Für obiges Beispiel ergibt sich also eine Quotierung von:		
	Geld	Brief
Kassakurs	1,5800	1,5810
– Swap T/N	+ 0,00014	+ 0,00015
– O/N Swap	+ 0,00017	+ 0,00018
= GBP/USD per Valuta heute	**1,58031**	**1,58133**

2.2.9. EXKURS: Synthetic Agreement for Forward Exchange (SAFE)

Ein SAFE (Synthetic Agreement for Forward Exchange), seit 1987 von der BBA (British Bankers' Association) geregelt, ist eine synthetische Vereinbarung über einen FX-Swap. Der Zweck von SAFEs ist die Festsetzung von zukünftigen Swapsätzen bzw. Outrightkursen unter Vermeidung der normalen Erfüllungsrisiken (Settlementrisiko), wie sie sonst bei traditionellen FX-Swaps bestehen.

Es gibt zwei verschiedene Arten:

ERA (Exchange Rate Agreement)

ERA wurde 1987 von der Barclays Bank eingeführt und ist eine Vereinbarung zwischen zwei Parteien, die Differenz zwischen einem vereinbarten zukünftigen Swapsatz und dem zwei Tage vor Beginn der Swaplaufzeit tatsächlich herrschenden Swapsatz auszugleichen (Ausgleichszahlung wie bei FRA).

FXA (Forward Exchange Agreement)

FXA wurde ebenfalls 1987 einige Wochen später von der Midland Bank eingeführt. Beim FXA wird zusätzlich die Differenz zwischen einem vereinbarten Outright-Kurs und dem vor Beginn der Swapperiode geltenden Kassakurs ausgeglichen.

2.3. Einsatzmöglichkeiten

2.3.1. Der Devisenswap als Absicherung von Termingeschäften

Devisenswaps (FX-Swaps) können dazu dienen, eine **Fälligkeit auf ein früheres oder späteres Datum zu verschieben.** So kann die Valuta eines Kassageschäftes auf ein zukünftiges Datum verschoben oder die Valuta eines Termingeschäftes auf die aktuelle Kassavaluta vorgezogen werden.

Kundentermingeschäfte werden üblicherweise durch die **Kombination eines Kassageschäftes mit einem FX-Swap** gehedgt (nicht durch ein einzelnes Interbank-Termingeschäft). Der Vorteil dieser Vorgehensweise ergibt sich aus der **höheren Liquidität der Kassa- und Swapmärkte** verglichen mit den reinen Terminmärkten.

Example

USD/CHF spot: 1.5000
3 month swap: -75
You bought from a customer USD/CHF 1 m outright 3 month at 1.4925. How can you cover the risk?

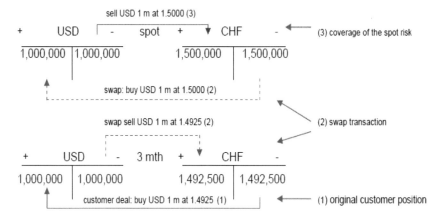

1) Original position: you bought USD 1 m from the customer.
2) Transfer the value date to the spot date by means of an FX swap
   you buy-and-sell USD/CHF spot against 3 month.
3) Cover the FX risk by selling USD 1 m spot.

Beispiel

USD/CHF Spot: 1,5000
3-Monats-Swap: -75
Sie haben von einem Kunden 1 Mio. USD/CHF auf Termin 3 Monate mit 1,4925 gekauft.
Wie können Sie das Risiko absichern?

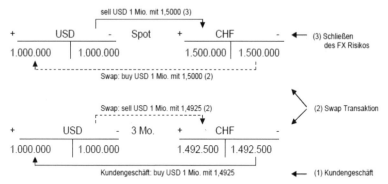

(1) Ursprüngliche Position: Sie haben 1 Mio. USD von Ihrem Kunden gekauft.
(2) Verschieben der Valuta auf das Spotdatum durch einen FX-Swap: Sie kaufen und
     verkaufen USD/CHF Spot gegen 3 Monate.
(3) Absicherung des FX-Risikos durch den Verkauf von 1 Mio. USD in der Kassa.

2.3.2. Arbitrage between Deposits and FX Swaps

The FX swap rate of two currencies has to correspond to the actual spot rate and the interest differential of the two currencies. If this is not the case, arbitrage between spot, outright and deposit markets is possible.

Example

Spot rate	USD/CHF:	1.5000	
Interest rates	USD:	4%	180 days
	CHF:	2%	180 days
FX swap	USD/CHF:	155-153	180 days

The "fair" outright rate should be:

$$-147 = 1.50 \times \left(\frac{1 + \left(0.02 \times \frac{180}{360}\right)}{1 + \left(0.04 \times \frac{180}{360}\right)} - 1 \right)$$

As the quoted discount is higher than the theoretical value we decide to buy the swap (i.e. sell-and-buy) at -153 and to close the position with deposit transactions (i.e. at -147).

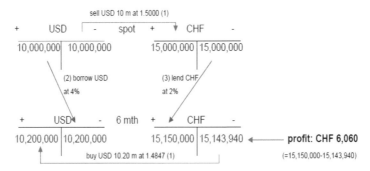

Result: The FX swap (1) is hedged by means of interbank deposits (2) + (3). The **remaining profit is CHF 6,060**.

Note: In practice, bid/offer spreads, equity costs and limits have to be taken into account.

2.3.2. Arbitrage zwischen Depots und Termingeschäften

Der Terminkurs zweier Währungen muss dem aktuellen Kassakurs und der Zinsdifferenz zwischen den beiden Währungen entsprechen. Ist dies nicht der Fall, so ergeben sich Arbitragemöglichkeiten zwischen dem Kassa- und Terminmarkt auf der einen und dem Depotmarkt auf der anderen Seite.

Beispiel

Spot USD/CHF: 1,5000
6-Monats-USD Zinsen: 4%   (180 Tage)
6-Monats-CHF Zinsen: 2%   (180 Tage)
USD/CHF FX-Swap 6 Monate: 155-53   (180 Tage)

Der faire Terminkurs ist:
$$-147 = 1{,}50 \times \left[\frac{1 + \left(0{,}02 \times \dfrac{180}{360} \right)}{1 + \left(0{,}04 \times \dfrac{180}{360} \right)} - 1 \right]$$

Da der quotierte Abschlag höher ist als der rechnerische Wert, entscheiden wir uns, den Swap mit -153 zu kaufen (d.h. sell and buy) und die Position mit Depotgeschäften zu schließen (d.h. synthetisch mit -147).

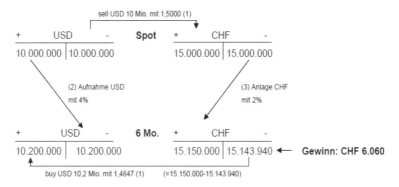

Ergebnis: Der FX-Swap (1) wird mit Depotgeschäften abgesichert (2) + (3). Der verbleibende **Gewinn ist 6.060 CHF.**

Anmerkung: In der Praxis sind noch etwaige Geld- und Briefspannen sowie Eigenkapitalkosten und Linienbelastungen dem Gewinn gegenüberzustellen.

2.3.3. Computing the Interest Rate from Spot and Forward Rate

FX swaps are often employed if an existing asset (liability) in one currency shall be transformed into an asset (liability) in another currency for a specified period. As FX swaps are off balance products a bank's cash liquidity position can be managed very efficiently.

Example

A customer placed CHF 15,000,000 at the given terms with you.

Interest rate   CHF: 1.75%
Term   180 days
Spot rate   USD/CHF: 1.5000
FX swap   USD/CHF: 155-153 (180 days)

You do need USD liquidity rather than CHF.
How can you transform CHF into USD?

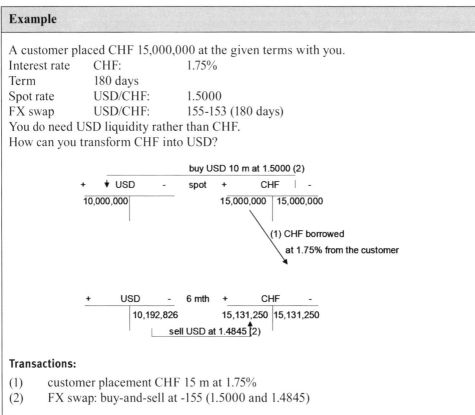

Transactions:

(1)   customer placement CHF 15 m at 1.75%
(2)   FX swap: buy-and-sell at -155 (1.5000 and 1.4845)

Result:

You produced a synthetic USD borrowing operation by using the FX swap. The CHF liquidity is transformed into USD liquidity, i.e. you receive USD 10,000,000 value spot and have to pay back 10,192,826 in 180 days time. This is an interest rate of **3,85652%** [(10,192,826-10,000,000)/10,000,000 x 360/180].

A trader might be interested in, which effective rate arises for the synthetic USD borrowing from these transactions. You can use the following formulas to compute the rate.

2.3.3. Berechnung des Zinssatzes aus Kassa- und Terminkurs

FX-Swaps werden oft dazu genutzt, eine Forderung (Verpflichtung) der einen Währung in eine Forderung (Verpflichtung) in einer anderen Währung für eine bestimmte Laufzeit zu tauschen. Da FX-Swaps Off-Balance-Instrumente sind, kann die Bank ihre Liquiditätsposition sehr effizient steuern.

Beispiel

Ein Kunde hat CHF 15 Mio. zu den angegebenen Konditionen bei Ihnen angelegt.

Zinssatz CHF:	1,75% (180 Tage)
Spot USD/CHF:	1,5000
FX-Swap USD/CHF:	155-153 (180 Tage)

Sie benötigen jedoch USD-Liquidität anstatt CHF-Liquidität.
Wie können Sie die CHF in USD umwandeln?

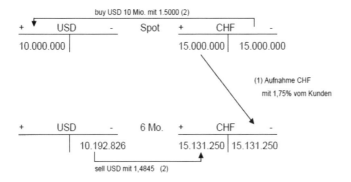

Transaktionen:

(1) Kundengeschäft: Aufnahme CHF 15 Mio. mit 1,75%
(2) FX-Swap: Buy and sell mit -155 (1,5000 und 1,4845)

Ergebnis:

Sie haben sich eine USD-Aufnahme synthetisch durch den FX-Swap dargestellt. Die CHF-Liquidität wurde in USD-Liquidität getauscht, d.h., Sie erhalten USD 10.000.000 Valuta Spot und müssen in 180 Tagen 10.192.826 USD zurückzahlen. Dies entspricht einem Zinssatz von **3,85652%** [(10.192.826 – 10.000.000)/10.000.000 x 360/180].

Einen Händler mag es interessieren, welcher effektive Zinssatz sich aus der synthetischen USD-Aufnahme ergibt. Sie können dazu folgende Formeln verwenden:

Interest rate calculation out of FX swaps:

rate of the base currency   **rate of the quote currency**

$$i_B = \left\{ \frac{\left(1 + \left(i_Q \times \frac{D}{B_Q}\right)\right) \times S}{O} - 1 \right\} \times \frac{B_B}{D}$$

$$i_Q = \left\{ \frac{\left(1 + \left(i_B \times \frac{D}{B_B}\right)\right) \times O}{S} - 1 \right\} \times \frac{B_Q}{D}$$

i_B = interest rate of base currency
i_Q = interest rate of quote currency
O = outright
S = spot rate
D = days
B_B = day basis of base currency for calculation
B_Q = day basis of quote/variable currency for calculation

Example

Follow-on:
A customer placed CHF 15,000,000 at the given terms with you.
Interest rate CHF: 1.75% (180 day)
Spot rate USD/CHF: 1.5000
FX swap: USD/CHF: 155-153 (180 days)
You do need USD liquidity rather than CHF.
Which synthetic USD rate can you produce?
In order to swap the CHF deposit into a synthetic USD deposit you have to buy-and-sell
USD/CHF at –155. Thus you buy USD/CHF spot at 1.50 and sell forward at 1.4845.
Computing the rate of the base currency (USD):

$$i_Q = \left\{ \frac{\left(1 + \left(0.0175 \times \frac{180}{360}\right)\right) \times 1.5000}{1.4845} - 1 \right\} \times \frac{360}{180} = 3.8565\%$$

By swapping CHF into USD you get a synthetic USD deposit at **3.8565%.**

Berechnung des Zinssatzes aus FX-Swaps:

Zinssatz quotierte Währung

$$r_Q = \left\{ \frac{\left[1 + \left(r_G \times \dfrac{T}{B_G}\right)\right] \times \text{KASSA}}{\text{TK}} - 1 \right\} \times \frac{B_Q}{T}$$

Zinssatz Gegenwährung

$$r_G = \left\{ \frac{\left[1 + \left(r_Q \times \dfrac{T}{B_Q}\right)\right] \times \text{TK}}{\text{KASSA}} - 1 \right\} \times \frac{B_G}{T}$$

T = Anzahl der Tage
TK = Terminkurs
KASSA = Spotkurs
rQ = Zinssatz p.a. in Dezimalen, quotierte Währung
rG = Zinssatz p.a. in Dezimalen, Gegenwährung
BQ = Berechnungsbasis für die quotierte Währung (360 oder 365)
BG = Berechnungsbasis für die Gegenwährung (360 oder 365)

Beispiel

Weiterführung des obigen Beispiels:
Ein Kunde hat Ihnen CHF 15 Mio. zu den angegebenen Konditionen gegeben.
Zinssatz CHF: 1.75%   (180 Tage)
Spot USD/CHF: 1,5000
FX-Swap USD/CHF: 155-153 (180 Tage)
Sie benötigen jedoch USD Liquidität anstatt CHF Liquidität.
Wie können Sie die CHF in USD umwandeln?
Um das CHF-Depot in ein synthetisches USD-Depot zu swappen, müssen Sie folgende
Transaktion durchführen: Buy and sell USD/CHF mit -155. Daher kaufen Sie USD/CHF
mit 1,5000 und verkaufen auf Termin mit 1,4845.

$$r_Q = \left\{ \frac{\left[1 + \left(0{,}0175 \times \dfrac{180}{360}\right)\right] \times 1{,}5000}{1{,}4845} - 1 \right\} \times \frac{360}{180} = 3{,}8565\,\%$$

Indem Sie die CHF in USD swappen, erhalten Sie einen synthetischen USD-Zinssatz von
3,8565%.

2.3.4. Prolongation of FX Forward Deals

The economical background for the prolongation of FX forward deals is based on the **use of forward deals as hedging instruments**. If the settlement of the underlying contract (e.g. delivery problems, delayed finalisation), the forward deal has to be prolonged in order to fix the hedge rate until the final settlement of the underlying contract.

Forward deals can be rolled-over by FX swaps at maturity. Due to the difference between the original forward rate and the actual spot rate of the FX swap Cash-Flows are created on the date of the original maturity. To avoid these cash-flows customers often ask for a **prolongation at a historic rate** instead of trading an FX swap at actual rates.

Prolongation at Actual Rates ("Best practice")

Therefore it is recommended to settle the original deal and then trade an FX swap for the remaining period which is only possible at actual rates. The difference between actual spot rate and original forward rate leads to **financing costs resp. investment revenues**.

Should the forward deal have a **negative market value** (from the customer's point of view), the bank has a **credit risk** for this amount. This risk has to be taken into account for the credit line.

Prolongation at Historic Rates

The prolongation of forward deals at historic rates has got **some additional risks** and is therefore regarded critically by several associations (e.g. ACI).

Following items have to be considered:

* There can be a concealment of profits and losses.
* There can be additional credit risks.

Prolongations at historic rates should therefore **only be conducted in exceptional cases**; the bank has to ensure that a complete documentation (reason for the prolongation, approval of management, etc.) is made.

2.3.4. Prolongation von Termingeschäften

Der wirtschaftliche Hintergrund für die Verlängerung von Devisentermingeschäften beruht auf dem **Einsatz von Termingeschäften als Absicherungsinstrument.** Wenn die Erfüllung des durch den Devisenterminkontrakt abgesicherten Geschäftes verzögert wird (z.B. durch Lieferprobleme, verspätete Fertigstellung), entsteht oft der Wunsch, das Devisentermingeschäft zu verlängern, um den Kurs bis zur endgültigen Erfüllung des abgesicherten Geschäftes zu fixieren. Fällige Devisentermingeschäfte können mit FX-Swaps weitergerollt werden. Aufgrund von Kursunterschieden zwischen dem ursprünglichen Termingeschäft und der Kassabasis des FX-Swaps kommt es dabei jedoch zu Cashflows zum Zeitpunkt der ursprünglichen Fälligkeit. Zur Vermeidung dieser Cashflows besteht bei den Kunden oft der Wunsch, die **Prolongation auf „alter Kursbasis"** durchzuführen, anstatt einen FX-Swap auf aktueller Kursbasis abzuschließen.

Prolongation auf aktueller Kursbasis („Best Practice")

Aus den genannten Gründen wird empfohlen, das Ursprungsgeschäft zu erfüllen und anschließend einen FX-Swap für die verbleibende Zeit abzuschließen. Dieser kann nur auf aktueller Kursbasis erfolgen. Der Unterschied zwischen dem aktuellen Kassakurs und dem alten Terminkurs führt daher zu **Finanzierungskosten bzw. Veranlagungserträgen.**

Hat das Termingeschäft bei Abschluss der Prolongation einen **negativen Marktwert** (aus Sicht des Kunden), stellt dieser Betrag ein **Kreditrisiko** dar. Dieses muss in der Kreditlinie Deckung finden.

Prolongation auf alter Kursbasis

Die Verlängerung von Devisentermingeschäften auf historischen Kursen ist mit **zusätzlichen Risiken** behaftet und wird deshalb von vielen Vereinigungen (z.B. ACI) kritisch betrachtet.

Folgende Punkte sind zu beachten:

- Es kann zu einer Gewinn- bzw. Verlustverschleierung kommen.
- Es können zusätzliche Kreditrisiken entstehen.

Prolongationen auf alter Kursbasis sollten daher **nur in Ausnahmefällen und unter Einhaltung einer genauen Dokumentation auf der Bankenseite** (Grund für die Verlängerung, Genehmigung durch den Vorgesetzten usw.) vorgenommen werden.

Example

6 months ago your customer has sold EUR 5 m against USD at 1.1440 as 6-months forward to hedge his USD outgoing payments. The deal is due today. Because of a delay of delivery he wants to prolong the deal at historic rates for another 6 months (180 days).

Actual spot EUR/USD: 1.2000
6-mo EUR/USD swap: 80/78
6-mo EUR rate: 2.50% (180 days)
6-mo USD rate: 1.20% (180 days)

What will be the rate for a prolongation at historic rates?

As the customer does not fulfill the contract at maturity you have to roll-over your original hedge transaction with an FX swap:

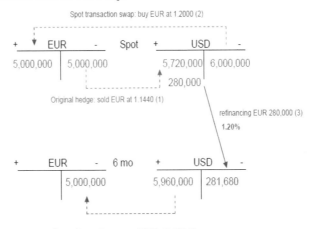

(1) Original hedge: sold EUR/USD 5 m at 1.1440
(2) FX swap: B/S EUR 5 m at 1.2000 und 1.1920
(3) refinancing of the difference: 280,000 USD at 1.20%

For the new maturity you have the following effective rate:
5,678,320 (= 5,960,000 – 281,680)/5,000,000 = **1.135664**
The discount for the new period will be **83.36 points.**

Credit Risk

Compared to the original maturity the forward deal had a **negative market value** for the customer in the amount of **USD 280,000** [5,000,000 x (1.1440 – 1.2000)].

The bank has to take this amount into account additionally to the credit line for the traditional forward deal. As the bank has to finance this amount, the customer's particular credit margin has to be added to the interbank rate for the calculation of the new forward rate.

Beispiel

Ihr Kunde hat vor 6 Monaten zur Absicherung eines USD-Zahlungsausganges 5 Mio. EUR gegen USD zu einem Terminkurs von 1,1440 auf 6-Monats-Termin verkauft. Das Geschäft ist heute fällig. Aufgrund von Lieferverzögerungen möchte er es aber auf der alten Kursbasis um 6 Monate (180 Tage) verlängern.

Aktueller Kassakurs: 1,2000
6-Monats-EUR/USD-Swap: 80/78
6-Monats-EUR-Zinsen: 2,50%   (180 Tage)
6-Monats-USD-Zinsen: 1,20%   (180 Tage)

Was ist der Kurs für eine Prolongation auf alter Basis?

Da der Kunde den Kontrakt bei Fälligkeit nicht erfüllt, müssen Sie Ihre ursprüngliche Hedgetransaktion mit einem FX-Swap weiterrollen:

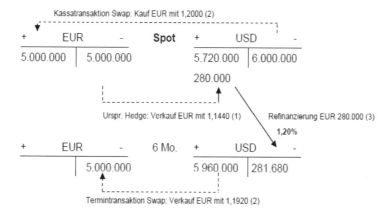

Ursprünglicher Hedge: Verkauf EUR/USD 5 Mio. zu 1,1440
FX-Swap: B/S EUR 5 Mio. zu 1,2000 und 1,1920
Refinanzierung der Kursdifferenz: 280.000 USD mit 1,20%

Zur neuen Fälligkeit ergibt sich folgender effektiver Kurs: 5.678.320 (= 5.960.000 − 281.680)/5.000.000 = **1,135664**
Der Abschlag beträgt also **83,36 Punkte.**

Kreditrisiko

Zur **ursprünglichen Fälligkeit** hatte das Termingeschäft für den Kunden einen **negativen Marktwert von USD 280.000** [5.000.000 x (1,1440 − 1,2000)]. Für die Bank bedeutet dies, dass dieser Betrag zusätzlich zur Linienbelastung eines normalen Termingeschäfts für die Restlaufzeit in der Kreditlinie berücksichtigt werden muss. Da die Bank diesen Betrag tatsächlich refinanzieren muss, sollte bei der Berechnung des neuen Terminkurses nicht nur der Interbank-Zinssatz, sondern zusätzlich die entsprechende Kreditmarge des Kunden berücksichtigt werden.

Calculation for the Prolongation at Historic Rates

Bid side forward deal (customer has sold):

$$O_{new} = O_{old} + swap_{bid} + \left[\left(O_{old} - spot \right) \times r_Q \times \frac{D}{B_Q} \right]$$

Offer side forward deal (customer has bought):

$$O_{new} = O_{old} + swap_{offer} + \left[\left(O_{old} - spot \right) \times r_Q \times \frac{D}{B_Q} \right]$$

D   = number of days
O   = outright
Spot = actual spot rate
r_Q = interest rate p.a. in decimals, quote currency
B_Q = calculation basis, quote currency (360 or 365)

Example

Matured forward deal: customer sells EUR/USD at 1.1440
Actual EUR/USD spot: 1.2000
6-mo EUR/USD swap: 80/78
6-mo USD rate: 1.20% (180 days)
What is the calculational rate for a prolongation of 180 days at historic rates?

$$O_{new} = 1.1440 + (-)0.0080 + \left[\left(1.1440 - 1.2000 \right) \times 0.012 \times \frac{180}{360} \right] = 1.135664$$

Due to the refinancing costs of the difference in rates the discount increases from -80 to **-83.36 points**.

Summary

An outright is an agreement between two counterparties to exchange currencies on a future date at a fixed rate. The regular terms for outrights are months (or weeks) up to 1 year, eg, 1w, 2w, 3w, 1m, 2m, 3m, 4m...12m. For the major currencies terms of up to 5 years are possible. The term of an outright deal is measured starting with the spot value date.
When talking about FX outrights, the Interest Rate Parity Theorem of John Maynard Keynes is often mentioned. It explains the relation between interest rate and exchange rate. The foreign exchange market is balanced if deposits in all currencies have the same expected yield. This parity of expected yields for deposits in any two currencies, measured in the same currency, is called interest rate parity.
Outright rates usually differ from the spot rate, but they are not a predictor for the spot rate at the end of the term. The difference between the outright rate and the spot rate only reflects the interest differences between the two currencies involved. Were outright rates not to conform to the interest differences, arbitrage between the foreign exchange market and the euro deposit market would be possible.

Berechnung des Prolongationskurses auf alter Basis

Geldseitiges Termingeschäft (Kunde hat verkauft):

$$TK_{neu} = TK_{alt} + Swap_{Geld} + \left[(TK_{alt} - Spot) \times r_G \times \frac{T}{B_G} \right]$$

Briefseitige Termingeschäft (Kunde hat gekauft):

$$TK_{neu} = TK_{alt} + Swap_{Brief} + \left[(TK_{alt} - Spot) \times r_G \times \frac{T}{B_G} \right]$$

T = Anzahl der Tage
TK = Terminkurs
Spot = aktueller Spotkurs
rG = Zinssatz p.a. in Dezimalen, Gegenwährung
BG = Berechnungsbasis für die Gegenwährung (360 oder 365)

Beispiel

Fälliges Termingeschäft: Kunde verkauft EUR/USD zu 1,1440
Aktueller EUR/USD-Kurs: 1,2000
6-Monats-EUR/USD-Swap: 80/78
6-Monats-USD-Zinsen: 1,20%   (180 Tage)
Was ist der rechnerische Kurs für eine Prolongation von 180 Tagen auf alter Basis?

$$TK_{neu} = 1,1440 + (-)0,0080 + \left[(1,1440 - 1,20) \times 0,012 \times \frac{180}{360} \right] = 1,135664$$

Aufgrund der Refinanzierungskosten der Kursdifferenz erhöht sich der Abschlag von -80 auf **-83,36 Punkte.**

Zusammenfassung

Ein Devisentermingeschäft (FX-Outright) ist eine feste Vereinbarung zwischen zwei Parteien, eine Devisentransaktion zu einem fixierten Kurs mit einem späteren Datum als dem Kassavalutatag durchzuführen. Devisenterminkurse werden standardmäßig für Laufzeiten von 1, 2, 3, 6 und 12 Monaten quotiert. Für die Hauptwährungen sind auch Laufzeiten bis zu fünf Jahren oder mehr möglich. Die Laufzeit für ein Devisentermingeschäft wird ab dem Valutatag des Spotgeschäfts gemessen.
Im Zusammenhang mit Devisentermingeschäften wird auch häufig das Konzept der Zinsparitätentheorie genannt. Die Zinsparitätentheorie ist ein auf John Maynard Keynes zurückgehendes weit verbreitetes volkswirtschaftliches Modell und erklärt den Zusammenhang zwischen Zinssatz und Wechselkurs. Der Devisenmarkt befindet sich im Gleichgewicht, wenn die Anlagen in allen Währungen dieselbe erwartete Rendite bieten. Diese Gleichheit der erwarteten Renditen auf Anlagen in zwei beliebigen Währungen, gemessen in derselben Währung, bezeichnet man als Zinsparität.
Wechselkurse für Termingeschäfte unterscheiden sich zwar von den Kassakursen, sind aber keine Prognose für den Kassakurs am Ende der Laufzeit. Der Unterschied zwischen Terminkurs und Kassakurs zweier Währungen trifft lediglich eine Aussage über die unterschiedlichen Zinssätze in diesen Währungen. Um den Terminkurs zu berechnen, be-

In order to calculate the outright rate, you need the spot rate, the number of days and the interest rates for both currencies. If the outright rate is lower than the spot rate, the base currency is at a discount. If the outright rate is higher than the spot rate, the base currency is at a premium.

Outright forward FX transactions are usually quoted to customers as full forward exchange rate. In the interbank market, outright forward FX transactions are quoted as forward points or full forward exchange rate. The forward points are also called swap points. By adding (premium) or subtracting (discount) these forward points from the spot rate you get the full forward exchange rate.

Since the outright rate consists of the spot rate plus or minus the swap points it changes if the spot rate changes or the interest rate difference changes (i.e. the swap points change). In a strict sense, an increase in forward points can also be caused by an increase of the spot price. This influence is relatively small for short terms and stronger for longer terms. Outrights are quoted in terms of forward points, because forward points are mainly influenced by interest rates and are not as volatile as spot rates. Furthermore, the FX forward trading book is separate from the FX spot trading book and forward deals are most often used as part of FX swap transactions in the interbank market. FX swaps are dominated by the interest rate difference rather than the spot rate.

Forward cross rates are outright rates of two currencies, where none of these is USD. Like spot transactions, most of the outright deals are done against the USD.

Contrary to traditional FX forward contracts the settlement of a time option is not on a specified day but – depending on the customer's choice – within a specified period of time. The term "option" therefore only relates to the date of settlement, not meaning that the customer has a choice to fulfill the contract or not (like with FX options). Time options are only traded by customers, not in the interbank market.

A Non-deliverable Forward (NDF) is a contract between two parties that fixes the rate of exchange that will apply to a notional FX forward transaction. The NDF is to the FX forward market what the FRA is to the money market: both are agreements between parties to compensate each other for movements in a market rate. As with the FRA, the counterparties to an NDF do not exchange the notional amount, they simply pay each other a cash sum based on the difference between the NDF rate and a reference FX spot rate at the contract's maturity.

The following risks can occur at NDFs: market risk (risk of a loss due to market price changes, here the currency rate), credit risk (risk of a loss due to a default of the counterparty, counterparty does not pay the compensation payment), settlement risk (when one party has already fulfilled its part of the contract and the other party fails to fulfill the remaining part) and conversion risk (company may be physically unable to convert the underlying TWD into hard currency).

An FX swap is a contract to buy an amount of the base currency at an agreed rate, and simultaneously resell the same amount of the base currency for a later value date to the same counterparty, also at an agreed rate. Technically, an FX swap is a combination of a spot deal and a reverse outright deal.

Both spot and forward transaction are agreed on the same spot basis, usually the current mid rate. In a regular FX swap the base currency's volume is the same both for the spot and the forward transaction. The mark-to-market value of an FX swap is the sum of the present values of all cashflows which would occur if the swap were closed at the current market rate.

nötigen wir den Kassakurs, die exakten Tage der Terminperiode und den Zinssatz in jeder Währung. Ist der Terminkurs niedriger als die aktuelle Kassa, ist die Währung im Abschlag (Abschlag = Discount = Deport). Ist der Terminkurs höher als die aktuelle Kassa, ist die Währung im Aufschlag (Aufschlag = Premium = Report).

Devisentermingeschäfte werden gegenüber Kunden üblicherweise als vollständiger Terminkurs quotiert. Im Interbankenhandel werden Devisentermingeschäfte in Form von Swappunkten oder als vollständiger Terminkurs quotiert. Zum Terminkurs gelangt man, indem man den Kassakurs um die Swappunkte ändert. Natürlich muss vor der Quotierung feststehen, ob die Swappunkte zu addieren oder vom Kassakurs zu subtrahieren sind. Die genaue Kenntnis der betreffenden Zinssätze lässt den Schluss zu, ob der Terminkurs höher oder niedriger als der Kassakurs sein wird. Zusätzlich zeigt auch die reine Quotierung der Swappunkte, ob man sie vom Kassakurs abziehen oder hinzuzählen muss.

Ein Terminkurs ändert sich immer, wenn sich die Zinsdifferenz der beiden Währungen ändert. Genau genommen könnte die Erhöhung der Swappunkte jedoch auch durch eine Erhöhung des Kassakurses ausgelöst worden sein. Dieser Einfluss ist jedoch relativ gering bei kurzen Laufzeiten und wird umso stärker, je länger die Laufzeit ist.

Terminkurse werden häufig als Swappunkte quotiert, da Swappunkte vorwiegend von den Zinssätzen abhängen und sie sich daher weniger häufig ändern als der Kassakurs. Außerdem wird in der Praxis das Terminbuch getrennt vom Kassabuch geführt und die meisten Interbank-Termingeschäfte werden in Form von Devisenswaps durchgeführt, wo Swappunkte gehandelt werden.

Forward-Cross-Rates sind Terminkurse von Währungspaaren, die keine USD enthalten (z.B. GBP/CHF-Terminkurs). Die Terminkurse für Nicht-Dollar-Währungen kann man daher kalkulieren, indem man den USD als „Vehikelwährung" für die Berechnung beider Terminkurse heranzieht.

Im Unterschied zu konventionellen Termingeschäften erfolgt die Erfüllung eines Termingeschäfts mit Laufzeitoption (Time Options) nicht an einem bestimmten Tag, sondern nach Wahl des Kunden innerhalb einer bei Abschluss festgelegten Periode. Der Ausdruck „Option" bezieht sich also ausschließlich auf den Zeitpunkt der Erfüllung des Termingeschäfts, nicht jedoch auf ein Wahlrecht, ob das Geschäft erfüllt wird oder nicht. Time Options werden ausschließlich von Kunden verwendet, nicht jedoch im Interbankhandel.

Ein Non-deliverable Forward (NDF) ist ein Kontrakt zwischen zwei Parteien, in dem ein Devisenterminkurs für ein fiktives Devisentermingeschäft fixiert wird. Wie der FRA im Geldmarkt ist auch der NDF eine Vereinbarung, die es den beiden Kontrahenten ermöglicht, sich durch gegenseitige Kompensation gegen unvorteilhafte Marktbewegungen absichern zu können. Wie auch beim FRA wird beim NDF kein Kapital ausgetauscht, es dient nur als Rechengröße. Bei Fälligkeit erfolgt ein Cash-Settlement, d.h., es wird eine Ausgleichzahlung über die Differenz zwischen NDF-Kurs und aktuellem Referenzkurs geleistet.

Bei einem NDF können folgende Risiken auftreten: Marktrisiko (Risiko eines Verlustes aufgrund einer Änderung des Marktpreises, hier also des Devisenkurses), Kreditrisiko (Risiko eines Verlustes aufgrund des Ausfalls des Kontrahenten, hier die Nichtleistung der Ausgleichszahlung), Settlementrisiko (Risiko, dass man seinen Teil der Vereinbarung bereits geleistet hat und der Kontrahent ausfällt, bevor er seine Verpflichtung aus der Vereinbarung erfüllt) und Konvertierungsrisiko (Risiko, bei Fälligkeit eventuell nicht am Kassamarkt in USD physisch konvertieren zu können).

Matched principal swaps are FX swaps where the base currency is traded for the same volumes in the spot and in the forward transaction.

A forward/forward swap is an FX swap that starts in the future. As opposed to a plain FX swap where a spot and reverse forward transaction are combined, both FX transactions in the forward/forward swap are forward transactions.

Usually FX swaps start at value date spot (eg, spot against 1 week, 1 month etc.). However, there are also swaps which start prior to value spot. There are two regular terms: O/N (Overnight): starts today and ends tomorrow and T/N (Tomorrow)/Next): starts tomorrow and ends the day after tomorrow (ie, spot).

There are different ways of using FX outrights and FX swaps. FX Swaps can be used to transfer the value date of FX transaction to a later or earlier date.

The FX swap rate of two currencies has to correspond to the actual spot rate and the interest differential of the two currencies. If this is not the case, arbitrage between spot, outright and deposit markets is possible. FX swaps are often employed if an existing asset (liability) in one currency shall be transformed into an asset (liability) in another currency for a specified period. As FX swaps are off-balance products, a bank's cash liquidity position can be managed very efficiently.

Often, FX forward deals are used as hedging instruments. If the settlement of the underlying contract is for some reason delayed (eg, due to delivery problems, delayed finalisation), the forward deal has to be prolonged in order to fix the hedge rate until the final settlement of the underlying contract. Forward deals can be rolled-over by FX swaps at maturity. Due to the difference between the original forward rate and the actual spot rate of the FX swap cashflows are created on the date of the original maturity. To avoid these cash-flows customers often ask for a prolongation at a historic rate instead of trading an FX swap at actual rates. The prolongation of forward deals at historic rates incurs some additional risks and is therefore frowned upon by many professional bodies (eg, ACI). Prolongations at historic rates should therefore only be conducted in exceptional cases; the bank has to ensure that is comprehensive documentation (reason for the prolongation, approval of management, etc).

Ein Devisenswap (FX-Swap) ist eine Vereinbarung zwischen zwei Parteien über eine Devisenkassatransaktion und ein gegenläufiges Devisentermingeschäft, über den üblicherweise selben Betrag in der quotierten Währung (Basiswährung). Technisch gesehen ist ein FX-Swap also eine Kombination von Kassa- und Termingeschäft.

Kassa- und Termintransaktion werden auf der gleichen Kassabasis gerechnet, normalerweise auf Basis des aktuellen Kassamittekurses. Bei einem regulären FX-Swap wird in der quotierten Währung immer der gleiche Betrag in der Spot-, FX- und in der Termintransaktion gehandelt, Swaps werden wie Terminkurse quotiert, d.h. in Swappunkten oder Forwardpunkten. Der Mark-to-Market-Wert eines FX-Swaps ist die Summe der Barwerte aller Cashflows, die entstehen würden, wenn der Swap zu aktuellen Kursen geschlossen würde.

Unter Matched Principal FX-Swaps versteht man FX-Swaps, die über das gleiche Volumen der quotierten Währung (oder der Gegenwährung) sowohl für die Kassa- als auch Termintransaktion abgeschlossen werden.

Ein Forward/Forward FX-Swap ist ein Swap, der erst in der Zukunft beginnt. Er besteht aus einem Termingeschäft mit kurzer Laufzeit und einem gegenläufigen Termingeschäft mit längerer Laufzeit.

Normalerweise starten FX-Swaps mit Valuta Spot (z.B. Spot gegen 1 Woche, 1 Monat, etc.). Es gibt aber auch Swaps, die vor dem Spotdatum starten. Hier sind zwei zu nennen: O/N (Overnight): startet heute und endet morgen; und T/N (Tom(orrow)/Next): startet morgen und endet übermorgen (d.h. Spot).

Für den Einsatz von Devisentermingeschäften und -swaps gibt eine Reihe von Möglichkeiten: Devisenswaps (FX-Swaps) können dazu dienen, eine Fälligkeit auf ein früheres oder späteres Datum zu verschieben.

Entspricht der Terminkurs zweier Währungen nicht dem aktuellen Kassakurs und der Zinsdifferenz zwischen den beiden Währungen, ergeben sich Arbitragemöglichkeiten zwischen dem Kassa- und Terminmarkt auf der einen Seite und dem Depotmarkt auf der anderen Seite. FX-Swaps werden auch oft dazu genutzt, eine Forderung (Verpflichtung) der einen Währung in eine Forderung (Verpflichtung) in einer anderen Währung für eine bestimmte Laufzeit zu tauschen. Da FX-Swaps Off-Balance-Instrumente sind, kann die Bank ihre Liquiditätsposition in den einzelnen Währungen sehr effizient steuern.

Häufig wird auch die Verlängerung von Devisentermingeschäften als Absicherungsinstrument eingesetzt. Wenn die Erfüllung des durch den Devisenterminkontrakt abgesicherten Geschäftes verzögert wird (z.B. durch Lieferprobleme, verspätete Fertigstellung), entsteht oft der Wunsch, das Devisentermingeschäft zu verlängern, um den Kurs bis zur endgültigen Erfüllung des abgesicherten Geschäftes zu fixieren. Fällige Devisentermingeschäfte können mit FX-Swaps weitergerollt werden. Aufgrund von Kursunterschieden zwischen dem ursprünglichen Termingeschäft und der Kassabasis des FX-Swaps kommt es dabei jedoch zu Cashflows zum Zeitpunkt der ursprünglichen Fälligkeit. Zur Vermeidung dieser Cashflows besteht bei den Kunden oft der Wunsch, die Prolongation auf „alter Kursbasis" durchzuführen, anstatt einen FX-Swap auf aktueller Kursbasis abzuschließen. Die Verlängerung von Devisentermingeschäften auf historischen Kursen ist mit zusätzlichen Risiken behaftet und wird deshalb von vielen Vereinigungen (z.B. ACI) kritisch betrachtet. Prolongationen auf alter Kursbasis sollten daher nur in Ausnahmefällen und unter Einhaltung einer genauen Dokumentation auf der Bankenseite vorgenommen werden.

2.4. Practice Questions

1. What is the delivery date for a 1-month forward currency deal that was traded on Thursday, 26 April?
   a) 26 May
   b) 31 May
   c) 30 May
   d) 1 June
   e) 27 May

2. Which of the following is true with respect to a currency that is at a forward discount?
   a) It is more expensive forward than spot.
   b) It is the same price forward and spot.
   c) It has a lower interest rate than the counter currency.
   d) insufficient information to decide
   e) It is cheaper forward than spot.

3. 6-month forward GBP/USD is quoted at 115-112. USD interest rates fall by 0.25% and GBP rates remain unchanged. Which of the following would you expect?
   a) arbitrage is possible
   b) decrease in forward points
   c) insufficient information to decide
   d) increase in forward points
   e) forward prices remain unchanged
   f) You quote at a premium.

4. Which relationship does the Interest Rate Parity Theorem explain?

5. What is meant by "covered" and "uncovered" interest rate parity?

6. How are outright forward FX transactions usually quoted to customers and in the interbank market?

7. Does a time option win or lose over time?
   a) not enough information
   b) win
   c) lose
   d) bought time options always win over time

8. What causes the tail risk in a FX forward book?
   a) premiums and discounts
   b) the different market conventions calculating the interest rates
   c) changes of the spot price
   d) the spot basis

9. Why are forward rates, as a rule, only quoted as premium or discount?
   a) Because then the quotes are shorter.
   b) Because interest rates are extremely volatile
   c) Because this method shows a higher level of accuracy.
   d) Because the premium/discount does not change as quickly as the forward rates.
   e) Because a change in the spot rate does not change the forward rate.
   f) Because the forward rates have no influence on forward exchange transactions

2.4. Wiederholungsfragen

1. Wann ist der Valutatag eines 1-Monats-Devisentermingeschäfts, das am Donnerstag, den 26. April, gehandelt wurde?
    a) 26. Mai
    b) 31. Mai
    c) 30. Mai
    d) 1. Juni
    e) 27. Mai
2. Welche Aussage trifft auf eine Währung im Deport zu?
    a) Sie ist auf Termin teurer als in der Kassa.
    b) Sie hat den gleichen Preis auf Termin wie in der Kassa.
    c) Sie hat einen niedrigeren Zinssatz als die Gegenwährung.
    d) nicht genügend Information, um die Frage zu beantworten.
    e) Sie ist auf Termin billiger als in der Kassa.
3. Die 6-Monats-Swappunkte GBP/USD quotieren bei 115-112. Die USD-Zinssätze fallen um 1/4% und die GBP-Zinsen bleiben unverändert. Was würden Sie erwarten?
    a) Es ist nun Arbitrage möglich.
    b) Fallen der Swappunkte
    c) nicht genug Information, um zu entscheiden
    d) Ansteigen der Swappunkte
    e) unveränderte Forward-Preise
    f) Sie notieren nun im Aufschlag.
4. Welchen Zusammenhang erklärt die Zinsparitätentheorie?
5. Was versteht man unter einer „gedeckten" bzw. „ungedeckten" Zinsparität?
6. In welcher Form werden Devisentermingeschäfte gegenüber Kunden bzw. im Inter-bankenhandel üblicherweise quotiert?
7. Gewinnt oder verliert eine Time Option bei Zeitablauf?
    a) nicht ausreichend Informationen vorhanden
    b) gewinnt
    c) verliert
    d) Gekaufte Time Options gewinnen immer bei Zeitablauf.
8. Wodurch wird das Tail-Risiko im Terminbuch verursacht?
    a) Auf- und Abschläge
    b) unterschiedliche Zinsusancen
    c) Veränderungen in der Kassa
    d) Kassabasis
9. Weshalb wird in der Regel bei der Quotierung von Terminkursen nur der Auf-/Abschlag quotiert?
    a) Weil die Quotierung kürzer ist.
    b) Weil die Zinsen sehr volatil sind.
    c) Weil diese Methode eine höhere Genauigkeit aufweist.
    d) Weil sich die Auf-/Abschläge nicht so schnell wie der Terminkurs ändern.
    e) Weil einer Änderung des Kassakurses den Terminkurs nicht verändert.
    f) Weil der Terminkurs keinen Einfluss auf die Transaktionen beim Devisentermingeschäft hat.

10. USD/JPY is 137.50-60, with four-month forward points of 75-73. What does this indicate?
   a) JPY interest rates are higher than USD interest rates.
   b) USD interest rates are very high at the short end.
   c) USD interest rates are the same as JPY interest rates.
   d) impossible to answer the question without additional information
   e) USD interest rates are higher than JPY interest rates.

11. What would be the spot basis of a bought USD/CHF FX swap if USD/CHF is quoted spot
1.5245-55?

12. Which of the following transactions is an FX swap?
   a) buy spot and sell outright
   b) buy spot and buy outright
   c) sell spot and sell outright
   d) buy a deposit in one currency and sell a deposit in another currency

13. If a dealer buys and sells 1-month USD/CHF, what is he doing?
   a) change USD temporarily into CHF involving FX risk for the principal amount
   b) change USD temporarily into CHF without involving FX risk
   c) change CHF temporarily into USD without involving FX risk
   d) change CHF temporarily into USD involving FX risk for the principal amount

14. Your customer bought EUR/USD from you. You hedged the FX risk by means of a spot
deal. Which additional transaction should you conclude?
   a) buy EUR/USD outright
   b) buy and sell EUR/USD
   c) sell and buy EUR/USD
   d) sell EUR/USD outright

15. What is true reagarding foreign exchange deals undertaken at non-current (historic)
rates?
   a) They should be undertaken at the dealer's discretion.
   b) They should be undertaken at the customer's request.
   c) They should be undertaken only under the specific authority of senior management.
   d) They should be undertaken in the event of rolling on a forward outright deal.

16. What information can be derived from an FX swap quotation?
   a) future interest rate development
   b) options price
   c) interest rate difference between the currencies
   d) future development of spot rates

17. Your customer has sold 9-month EUR/USD outright. 3 months later, the customer lets
you know that he will need USD in 3 months already. Which transaction do you suggest
to the customer (from the customer's point of view)?
   a) buy FX swap (3 months)
   b) buy FX swap (6 months)
   c) sell FX swap (3 months)
   d) sell FX swap (6 months)
   e) sell FX swap (9 months)

10. USD/JPY quotiert bei 137,50-60. Die 4-Monats-Swappunkte betragen 75-73. Was schließen Sie daraus?
   a) JPY-Zinssätze sind höher als USD-Zinssätze.
   b) USD-Zinssätze sind extrem hoch am kurzen Ende.
   c) USD-Zinssätze sind genauso hoch wie die JPY-Zinssätze.
   d) Es ist ohne Zusatzinformation keine Aussage möglich.
   e) USD-Zinssätze sind höher als JPY-Zinssätze.

11. Was wäre bei der folgenden Kassaquotierung eine marktübliche Kassabasis für einen gekauften USD/CHF-FX-Swap? Kassa USD/CHF: 1,5245-55

12. Welche der folgenden Devisentransaktionen ist ein FX-Swap?
   a) Kauf in der Kassa und Verkauf auf Termin
   b) Kauf in der Kassa und Kauf auf Termin
   c) Verkauf in der Kassa und Verkauf auf Termin
   d) ein Depot in einer Währung nehmen und in einer anderen Währung geben

13. Was haben Sie getan, wenn Sie einen USD/CHF-FX-Swap gekauft und verkauft haben?
   a) USD-Bestand vorübergehend in CHF getauscht mit FX-Risiko auf den Nominalbetrag
   b) USD-Bestand vorübergehend in CHF getauscht ohne FX-Risiko
   c) CHF-Bestand vorübergehend in USD getauscht ohne FX-Risiko
   d) CHF-Bestand vorübergehend in USD getauscht mit FX-Risiko auf den Nominalbetrag

14. Ein Kunde hat von Ihnen EUR/USD auf Termin gekauft. Sie haben das FX-Risiko durch ein Kassageschäft gehedgt. Welche Transaktion müssen Sie noch machen?
   a) EUR/USD auf Termin kaufen
   b) Buy and sell EUR/USD
   c) Sell and buy EUR/USD
   d) EUR/USD auf Termin verkaufen

15. Was trifft bei FX-Geschäften zu nicht-aktuellen (historischen) Kursen zu?
   a) Sie sollen nach Ermessen des Händlers abgeschlossen werden.
   b) Sie sollen auf Vorschlag des Kunden abgeschlossen werden.
   c) Sie sollen nur nach spezieller Genehmigung durch die Vorgesetzten abgeschlossen werden.
   d) Sie sollen aufgrund eines Rolling-on eines Outright-Geschäftes abgeschlossen werden.

16. Worüber gibt die Quotierung eines FX-Swaps Auskunft?
   a) zukünftige Zinsentwicklung
   b) Optionspreis
   c) Zinsunterschied zwischen den Währungen
   d) zukünftige Entwicklung der Kassakurse

17. Ihr Kunde hat EUR/USD mit neun Monaten Laufzeit verkauft. Drei Monate später teilt Ihnen Ihre Kunde mit, dass er bereits in drei Monaten die USD wieder benötigt. Welche Transaktionen schlagen Sie Ihrem Kunden vor (aus Sicht des Kunden)?
   a) Kauf FX-Swap (3 Monate)
   b) Kauf FX-Swap (6 Monate)
   c) Verkauf FX-Swap (3 Monate)
   d) Verkauf FX-Swap (6 Monate)
   e) Verkauf FX-Swap (9 Monate)

18. You buy a 6-month matched principal FX Swap EUR/USD (EUR 10 m) at the given market data: EUR/USD 1.4250; swap 30/28. What are the resulting cashflows?
    a) EUR spot -7,017,543.86; 6 months +7,031,359.86
    b) EUR spot -10,000,000.00; 6 months +10,000,000.00
    c) USD spot -10,000,000.00; 6 months +10,000,000.00
    d) USD spot +14,250,000.00; 6 months -14,222,000.00

19. What is a non-deliverable forward (NDF)?
    a) FX forward contract in default
    b) FX forward contract settled through CLS
    c) FX forward contract involving a currency subject to exchange controls
    d) FX forward contract settled net in one currency

20. A non-deliverable Forward (NDF) is …
    a) a cash-settled forward outright.
    b) a cash-settled FX swap.
    c) is only possible for convertible currencies.
    d) is only possible for non-convertible currencies.

21. As a buyer of an NDF …
    a) You are the buyer of the variable currency.
    b) You speculate on a rising price of the underlying.
    c) You receive the underlying on the settlement date.
    d) You will receive or pay the amount due, depending on the spot rate at maturity.

22. How is the amount due of NDFs calculated?

23. You buy EUR/USD value tomorrow. Which two statements are correct?
    EUR/USD Spot: 1.0625-30; Swaps: O/N: 1.1-1.3; Tom/next: 1.4-1.6; S/N: 1.8-2.0
    a) You add the ask side of tom/next swap to spot rate in order to calculate the price.
    b) You subtract the ask side of tom/next swap from the spot rate in order to calculate the price.
    c) You subtract the bid side of tom/next swap from the spot rate in order to calculate the price.
    d) You buy EUR spot and sell the EUR/USD tom/next swap.
    e) You trade the tom/next swap at a discount of 1.4.
    f) You trade the tom/next swap at a premium of 1.6.
    g) You sell EUR spot and sell the EUR/USD tom/next swap.

24. What is meant by SAFE?

25. Why do customers often wish to prolongate a forward deal at historic rates?

18. Sie kaufen einen 6-Monats-Matched-Principal-Swap über EUR 10 Mio. bei folgenden Marktdaten: EUR/USD 1,4250; Swap 30/28. Was sind die daraus resultierenden Cashflows?

    a) EUR Spot -7.017.543,86; 6 Monate +7.031.359,86

    b) EUR Spot -10.000.000,00; 6 Monate +10.000.000,00

    c) USD Spot -10.000.000,00; 6 Monate +10.000.000,00

    d) USD Spot +14.250.000,00; 6 Monate -14.222.000,00

19. Was ist ein Non-deliverable Forward (NDF)?

    a) ein normales Devisentermingeschäft

    b) ein Devisentermingeschäft, das durch CLS gesettled wird

    c) ein Devisentermingeschäft, bei dem eine Währung Kontrollen unterworfen ist

    d) ein Devisentermingeschäft, das Cash in einer Währung gesettled wird

20. Ein Non-deliverable Forward (NDF) ist …

    a) ein bar abgewickeltes Termingeschäft.

    b) ein bar abgewickelter FX-Swap.

    c) nur für konvertible Währungen möglich.

    d) nur für nicht konvertible Währungen möglich.

21. Als Käufer eines NDF …

    a) sind Sie Käufer der Gegenwährung.

    b) spekulieren Sie auf einen steigenden Kurs des Underlyings.

    c) erhalten Sie zum Settlement Date den Basiswert geliefert.

    d) werden Sie abhängig vom Kassakurs bei Fälligkeit eine Ausgleichszahlung erhalten bzw. zahlen.

22. Wie wird die Ausgleichszahlung eines NDFs berechnet?

23. Welche Aussagen treffen zu, wenn Sie EUR/USD mit Valuta morgen kaufen wollen? EUR/USD Spot: 1,0625-30; Swaps: O/N: 1,1-1,3; Tom/next: 1,4-1,6; S/N 1,8-2,0

    a) Sie addieren zur Preisbestimmung die Tom/next-Punkte der Briefseite zum Kassakurs.

    b) Sie ziehen zur Preisbestimmung die Tom/next-Punkte der Briefseite zum Kassakurs ab.

    c) Sie ziehen zur Preisbestimmung die Tom/next-Punkte der Geldseite zum Kassakurs ab.

    d) Sie kaufen EUR in der Kassa und verkaufen einen EUR/USD Tom/next-Swap.

    e) Sie handeln den Tom/next-Swap zu einem Abschlag von 1,4.

    f) Sie handeln den Tom/next-Swap zu einem Aufschlag von 1,6.

    g) Sie verkaufen EUR in der Kassa und verkaufen einen EUR/USD Tom/next-Swap.

24. Was versteht man unter SAFE?

25. Warum besteht bei Kunden oft der Wunsch, die Prolongation eines Termingeschäftes auf „alter Kursbasis" durchzuführen?

3. FX Options

In this chapter you learn ...

- what is meant by an option.
- what is the difference between call and put options.
- which terminology is used in option contracts.
- what is meant by European-style, American-style and Bermudian options.
- when an option is at, in or out of the money.
- about the four basic positions for buying and selling options.
- how options can be used for hedging and speculation.
- which exotic options are traded.
- what is meant by barrier options.
- what ismeant by the intrinsic value and the time value of an option and which factors influence these.
- what is meant by volatility.
- how premiums are quoted.
- how a fair option price can be calculated.
- which profit and loss profiles are used for trading with options.
- which strategies are used for trading with options.
- what are the best-known option pricing models.
- what is meant by call/put parity.
- how to measure factors that influence the option price during the term.
- what is meant by "skew" and risk reversal.

3.1. FX Options

Ever since the mid-eighties currency options have become an additional liquid instrument in the FX market.

An FX option gives the option buyer the **right to buy** (call option) **or sell** (put option)

- a defined **currency amount**
- at an agreed **rate** (strike price) and
- at expiry **date**.

This means that the holder has the right to exercise the option if this gives him an advantage compared to the actual market rates.

A **Call** option gives the right to **buy**, a Put option gives the right to **sell** a currency. The seller of the option receives a premium for giving this right to the buyer. This premium has to be paid on the day the option is traded.

The seller of an option has the obligation to buy (or to sell) a defined currency amount at an agreed rate at expiry date. For this obligation he receives a premium.

3. Devisenoptionen

In diesem Kapitel lernen Sie ...

- was man unter einer Option versteht.
- den Unterschied zwischen Call- und Put-Optionen kennen.
- welche Terminologien in Optionskontrakten verwendet werden.
- was man unter europäischen, amerikanischen und Bermudian Optionen versteht.
- wann eine Option am, in oder aus dem Geld ist.
- welche vier Grundpositionen beim Kauf bzw. Verkauf von Optionen möglich sind.
- wie Optionen zur Absicherung bzw. Spekulation verwendet werden können.
- welche exotischen Optionen gehandelt werden.
- was man unter Barrier Optionen versteht.
- was man unter dem inneren Wert und dem Zeitwert einer Option versteht und welche Faktoren diese beeinflussen.
- was man unter Volatilität versteht.
- in welcher Form Prämien quotiert werden.
- wie ein fairer Optionspreis berechnet werden kann.
- welche Gewinn- und Verlustprofile beim Handel mit Optionen verwendet werden.
- welche Strategien beim Handel mit Optionen verwendet werden.
- die bekanntesten Optionspreismodelle kennen.
- was man unter Call-/Put-Parität versteht.
- wie Faktoren, die den Optionspreis während der Laufzeit beeinflussen, gemessen werden können.
- was man unter „Skew" und Risk Reversal versteht.

3.1. Devisenoptionen (FX-Optionen)

Seit Mitte der 80er-Jahre ergänzen Devisenoptionen (FX-Optionen, Währungsoptionen) die bisher im Devisenhandel verfügbaren Instrumente von Kassa- und Devisentermingeschäften.

Eine Option gibt dem Inhaber das **Recht,**

- einen bestimmten **Wert** (Basiswert, Underlying)
- zu einem bestimmten **Preis** (Basispreis, Strike) und
- bis zu einem bestimmten **Zeitpunkt** (Verfalltag, Expiry Date)

zu kaufen (Call, Kaufoption) bzw. **zu verkaufen** (Put, Verkaufsoption).

Es steht also das Recht, den Basiswert zu kaufen bzw. zu verkaufen, im Mittelpunkt. Darin besteht der wesentliche Unterschied zu einem Termingeschäft, bei dem der fixe Kauf bzw. Verkauf vereinbart wird. Bei Devisenoptionen ist der Basiswert ein Währungspaar (z.B. EUR/USD).

Eine **Call**-Option berechtigt also den Inhaber zum **Kauf**, eine **Put**-Option zum **Verkauf** einer Währung. Für das Einräumen des Wahlrechtes verlangt der Verkäufer der Option eine einmalige Gebühr (Prämie), die bei Abschluss (d.h. mit Valuta Spot) fällig wird.

Der Verkäufer einer Option (auch Stillhalter) verpflichtet sich daher, einen bestimmten Betrag einer Währung zum vereinbarten Preis zu kaufen bzw. zu verkaufen, falls der Inhaber der Option diese ausübt.

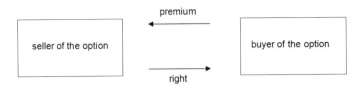

Example

Call EUR/USD: 10 m
Strike: 1.2500
Expiry date: 25th September
Premium: 3 USD Ct.
Explanation:
Call: deal type
EUR/USD: underlying: the instrument, the buyer of the option has the right to buy 10 m: volume of the base currency (the buyer of the call has the right to buy 10 mio EUR)
Strike 1.25: at this price the buyer of the call has the right – but not the obligation – to buy the underlying
expiry date: the last day on which the option seller accepts the exercise of the option
premium: price the buyer has to pay to the seller of the option (3 USD Ct. per EUR)

3.1.1. Terminology

Datas in the option contract:

- **trading date:** day when the option is dealt.
- **Premium payment date:** day when the option premium has to be paid, usually value two days.
- **Exercise date:** day when the option buyer exercises the option
- **Expiration date:** last day on which the option seller accepts the exercise of the option.
- **Settlement date:** day on which the underlying is deliverd. For American options is two bank days after exercise date and for European options two bank days after the expiry date.

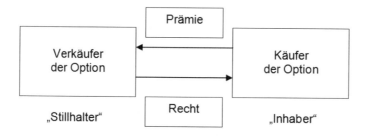

```
                        Prämie

  Verkäufer                              Käufer
  der Option                             der Option

     „Stillhalter"        Recht          „Inhaber"
```

Beispiel

Call EUR/USD: 10 Mio.
Strike: 1,2500
Verfalltag: 25. September
Prämie: 3 USD Cent

Erklärung:
Call: Optionsart
EUR/USD: Basiswert bzw. Underlying: jenes Instrument, das der Käufer des Calls kaufen kann, aber nicht muss. Bei Devisenoptionen bezieht sich das Recht immer auf die quotierte Währung (hier EUR). Im vorliegenden Beispiel hat also der Käufer des Calls das Recht, EUR zu kaufen (d.h. USD zu verkaufen).
10 Mio.: Bei Devisenoptionen bezieht sich das Volumen auf die quotierte Währung, d.h., der Käufer des Calls hat das Recht, EUR 10 Mio. zu kaufen.
Strike: 1,25: Ausübungspreis bzw. Basispreis: Kurs, zu dem der Käufer des Calls das Underlying kaufen darf, aber nicht muss.
Verfalltag: auch Expiry Date: letzter Tag, an dem der Optionskäufer sein Recht ausüben darf.
Prämie: Preis, den der Käufer der Option an den Verkäufer zahlt, hier 3 USD Cent pro EUR.

3.1.1. Terminologie

Daten im Optionskontrakt:
- **Handelstag:** der Tag, an dem der Optionskontrakt abgeschlossen wurde.
- **Premium payment date, Prämienvaluta:** der Tag, an dem die Prämie fällig ist, üblicherweise zwei Banktage nach dem Handelstag
- **Exercise Date (Ausübungstag):** das Datum, an dem der Käufer die Option ausübt.
- **Expiration Date (Verfalltag, Fälligkeitstag):** der letzte Tag, an dem der Käufer die Option ausüben darf. Bei europäischen Optionen entspricht das Exercise Date dem Expiration Date, während bei amerikanischen Optionen das Exercise Date vor dem Expiration Date liegen kann.
- **Settlement Date (Liefertag):** der Tag, an dem der Basiswert geliefert wird. Der Liefertag ist sowohl bei europäischen als auch bei amerikanischen Optionen zwei Banktage nach der Ausübung.

Standard Options

An **European-style** option is an option that can only be exercised on the expiry date.

An **American-style** option is an option that can be exercised at any trading day during the life of the option (usually with exchange traded options).

A **Bermudan** style option can only be exercised at certain dates during the option period. It is a mixture of European and American style option.

In-the-money (ITM)/ at-the-money (ATM)/ out-of-the money (OTM)

An option **at-the-money (ATM)** has a strike price around the actual market rate. If the strike price is compared to the spot rate, the option is called at-the-money spot. By comparing the strike with the outright rate, the option is called at-the-money forward.

An option is **in-the-money (ITM)** if the strike is "better" than the market rate. For a Call this means that the strike is below the market rate. The Put is in-the-money if the strike is higher than the market rate.

An option is **out-of-the-money (OTM)** if the market rate is "better" than the strike rate. For a Call out-of-the-money this means a lower market rate than the strike. A Put is out-of-the-money if the market rate is higher than the strike.

OTC/exchange-traded options

FX Options are almost exclusively traded **OTC ("over the counter")**. In opposition to exchange traded options where only standardized periods and strikes can be traded there are no restrictions in the OTC market. In practice OTC options have stood up to exchange traded options because the original deals have to be regarded individually.

3.1.2. The Four Basic Positions

	LONG BUY/HOLD	SHORT SELL/WRITE
PUT	RIGHT to SELL	OBLIGATION to BUY
CALL	RIGHT to BUY	OBLIGATION to SELL

Europäische-/amerikanische-/Bermudian-Optionen

Eine **europäische** oder European-style Option kann vom Käufer nur an einem Tag – dem Expiration Date (Verfalltag) – ausgeübt werden. Devisenoptionen sind praktisch immer europäische Optionen.

Eine **amerikanische** oder American-style Option kann jederzeit während der Handelszeiten bis zum Expiration Date (Verfallsdatum) ausgeübt werden. Diese Art ist bei Aktienoptionen üblich. Der Preis einer amerikanischen Option entspricht dem einer vergleichbaren europäischen Option, da europäische Optionen während der Laufzeit zwar nicht ausgeübt, aber jederzeit verkauft werden können.

Eine **Bermudian** oder Bermudian-style Option kann nur zu bestimmten, im Voraus definierten Terminen während der Laufzeit der Option ausgeübt werden. Sie ist also eine Mischform aus europäischer und amerikanischer Option.

Am Geld/Im Geld/Aus dem Geld

Eine Option ist **am Geld** (at the money, ATM), wenn ihr Ausübungspreis gleich oder nahezu gleich dem aktuellen Kurs ist.

Methodisch richtig und üblich ist dabei der Vergleich mit dem Terminkurs für die entsprechende Fälligkeit. Man spricht daher auch von at-the-money-forward. Manchmal wird der Strike jedoch auch mit dem Kassakurs verglichen. Man spricht dann von at-the-money-spot.

Im Geld (in the money, ITM) ist eine Option, wenn der Strike „besser" als der aktuelle Marktpreis des Basiswertes ist, d.h., wenn die Option für den Käufer einen Vorteil darstellt. Das bedeutet für einen Call, dass der Strike unter dem aktuellen Marktkurs liegt. Bei einem Put ist die Option im Geld, wenn der Strike über dem aktuellen Marktpreis liegt.

Aus dem Geld (out of the money, OTM) ist eine Option, wenn der Strike „schlechter" als der aktuelle Marktpreis ist. Das bedeutet für einen Call, dass der Strike über dem aktuellen Marktkurs liegt. Ein Put mit Strike unter dem aktuellen Marktpreis ist aus dem Geld.

OTC/Börsengehandelte Optionen

Bei Devisenoptionen handelt es sich fast ausschließlich um **OTC-(„over the counter")-**Optionen. Im Gegensatz zu börsengehandelten Optionen, wo nur standardisierte Laufzeiten und Strikes handelbar sind, sind im OTC-Markt keine Einschränkungen gegeben.

In der Praxis haben sich im FX- und Zinsmarkt die OTC gegenüber den börsengehandelten Optionen durchgesetzt, da die abzusichernden Grundgeschäfte keine einheitlichen Spezifikationen haben und somit individuell betrachtet werden müssen.

3.1.2. Die vier Grundpositionen

Aus der Kombination von Call bzw. Put und Kauf bzw. Verkauf ergeben sich vier mögliche Grundpositionen, die in der Tabelle zusammengefasst sind.

	LONG KAUFEN/BUY HOLD	SHORT VERKAUFEN/SELL SCHREIBEN/WRITE
CALL	RECHT zu KAUFEN	PFLICHT zu VERKAUFEN
PUT	RECHT zu VERKAUFEN	PFLICHT zu KAUFEN

3.1.2.1. Long Call

By buying a Call option you acquire the right to buy an agreed amount of a currency at the expiry date. If the market rate on the expiry date is lower than the agreed price, the option will not be exercised and the currency can be bought at the current market rate. During the term of the option you can also profit from low market rates by buying the currency at any time at 'low' rates.

3.1.2.2. Short Call

By **selling a Call option** the seller has the obligation to sell the currency at the strike price at expiry, if the buyer decides to exercise. For undertaking this risk the seller receives a premium.

3.1.2.3. Long Put

By **buying a Put option** you buy the right to sell the currency at the agreed price at expiry. In case of a higher rate at expiry the buyer of the option does not exercise and may sell at the higher market rate. Possible higher rates during the term can be locked in by selling (outright) the currency.

3.1.2.4. Short Put

The **seller of a Put option** takes on the obligation to buy the currency at the agreed price at expiry; if the buyer of the option decides to exercise. For taking this risk the seller receives a premium.

General rule: the Call in the base currency is at the same time always the Put in the quote currency (and vice versa), e.g. a EUR Call is at the same time a USD Put (the right to buy EUR equals the right to sell USD).

3.1.2.5. Application of options

Options can be used for hedging and for speculation. In the following the four basis positions are explained:

Long Call

Option for the importer, who has to buy the foreign currency (*Note*: USD Call → EUR Put!), hedging instrument against rising FX rates; hedging a short position; trading a long position with limited risk.

3.1.2.1. Long Call

Mit dem **Kauf eines Calls** erwirbt man das Recht, den vereinbarten Betrag einer Währung zum Ausübungspreis zu beziehen. Der Inhaber eines EUR/USD-Calls hat also das Recht, EUR/USD zum Strike-Preis zu kaufen, d.h. EUR zu kaufen und USD zu verkaufen.

3.1.2.2. Short Call

Mit dem **Verkauf eines Calls** verpflichtet sich der Verkäufer, den vereinbarten Betrag einer Währung zum vereinbarten Ausübungspreis zu liefern, sofern der Käufer der Option diese ausübt. Für die Übernahme dieses Risikos erhält der Verkäufer eine Prämie.

3.1.2.3. Long Put

Mit dem **Kauf eines Puts** erwirbt man das Recht, den vereinbarten Betrag einer Währung zum vereinbarten Ausübungspreis zu verkaufen. Der Inhaber eines EUR/USD Puts hat also das Recht, EUR/USD zum Strike-Preis zu verkaufen, d.h. EUR zu verkaufen und USD zu kaufen.

3.1.2.4. Short Put

Mit dem **Verkauf eines Puts** hingegen verpflichtet sich der Verkäufer, den vereinbarten Betrag einer Währung zum vereinbarten Ausübungspreis zu übernehmen, sofern der Käufer der Option dies verlangt. Für die Übernahme des Risikos erhält der Verkäufer eine Prämie.

Generell gilt: Der Call in der quotierten Währung ist immer gleichzeitig der Put in der Gegenwährung (und umgekehrt), z.B. ein EUR-Call ist gleichzeitig ein USD-Put (das Recht, EUR zu kaufen, entspricht dem Recht, USD zu verkaufen).

3.1.2.5. Anwendung von Optionen

Optionen können sowohl zur Absicherung (Hedging) als auch zur Positionsnahme (Spekulation) verwendet werden. Im Folgenden sind typische Anwendungen für die vier Grundpositionen dargestellt:

Long Call

Hedger: sichert sich gegen einen steigenden Kurs ab:

Beispiel
Ein europäischer Exporteur in die USA erhält USD in 6 Monaten. Er hat also das Risiko eines steigenden EUR/USD-Kurses (= fallender USD). Durch den Kauf eines EUR/USD-Call sichert er sich das Recht, zum Strike-Preis EUR/USD zu kaufen (= USD zu verkaufen). Liegt EUR/USD bei Fälligkeit über dem Strike, so übt er die Option aus, liegt der Kurs darunter, so lässt er die Option verfallen und kauft EUR/USD zum niedrigeren Kassakurs.

Long Put

Option for the exporter who hast to sell the foreign currency (*Note*: USD Put → EUR Call!), hedging instrument against falling FX rates; hedge against a long spot position; trading short position.

Short Call

By selling a Call against a long position, the option premium reduces the average buying price. This strategy however gives no hedge against declining rates and cuts the profit potential in case of higher rates.

Short Put

A company being short a currency can bring down the average price by selling Puts, e.g. a travel agency which needs foreign currency day-to-day.

Spekulant: spekuliert auf steigenden Kurs:

Beispiel

Ein Händler kauft eine EUR/USD-Call, Strike 1,2500 zu 3 Ct.
Ist EUR/USD am Verfalltag über dem Strike, z.B. bei 1,3000, so übt er aus und kauft zu 1,2500. Wenn er die EUR zum aktuellen Kurs von 1,3000 wieder verkauft, gewinnt er 5 Cent. Unter Berücksichtigung der bezahlten Prämie ist sein Ergebnis 2 Cent.

Der Inhaber einer Call-Option hat immer unbeschränktes Gewinnpotenzial, wogegen der mögliche Verlust auf die Prämie beschränkt ist.

Long Put

Hedger: sichert sich gegen einen fallenden Kurs ab:

Beispiel

Ein europäischer Importeur, der Waren aus den USA bezieht, sichert sich durch den Kauf eines EUR/USD-Put gegen einen fallenden EUR/USD-Kurs (= steigender USD) ab.

Spekulant: spekuliert auf fallenden Kurs:

Verkaufte Optionen sind niemals zur Absicherung geeignet, da sie eine Verpflichtung und kein Recht darstellen!

Short Call

Folgende Anwendung ist dennoch üblich:
Covered Call Writing: Ein Unternehmen, das eine Long-Position im Basiswert hält (z.B. EUR/USD Long-Position), verpflichtet sich durch den Verkauf eines Call, zum Strike-Preis zu verkaufen (d.h. die Long-Position zu schließen). Es behält dabei das Risiko fallender Kurse und kann an Kursanstiegen nur bis zum Strike-Preis partizipieren. Dafür erhält es die Prämie. Das Schreiben einer Call-Option gegen eine bestehende Long-Position im Basiswert wird auch Covered Call Writing genannt.
Spekulant: spekuliert darauf, dass die Option nicht ausgeübt wird, d.h., dass der Kurs nicht über den Strike-Preis steigt. Das Gewinnpotenzial ist auf die Prämie beschränkt, das Verlustpotenzial substantiell.

Short Put

Covered Put Writing: Ein Unternehmen, das EUR/USD kaufen muss, kann durch das Schreiben von EUR/USD-Puts den Einstandskurs durch die Prämieneinnahmen verbilligen. Liegt der Kassakurs bei Fälligkeit unter dem Strike, so muss es die EUR/USD zum Strike beziehen. Es kann also nicht an Kursen unter dem Strike partizipieren und ist auch nicht gegen einen Kursanstieg abgesichert.
Spekulant: spekuliert darauf, dass die Option nicht ausgeübt wird,

General rule: the Call in the base currency is at the same time always the Put in the quote currency (and vice versa), e.g. a EUR Call is at the same time a USD Put (the right to buy EUR equals the right to sell USD).

3.1.3. Exotic Options

In recent years additional to European and American style options a number of different variations of options have been developed. These mutations are called exotic options. Below the most important exotic options are described.

3.1.3.1. Asian Option (Average Rate Option, ARO)

These are options, which refer to the **average rate of the underlying exchange rate that exist during the life of the option**. This average will be used to determine the intrinsic value of the option by comparison with the predetermined fixed strike. If the option is a call option and the average rate exceeds the strike, the buyer will receive a Cash-Flow (i.e. the difference between the average rate and the strike). For a put option, the average must be below the strike.

3.1.3.2. Compound Option

A Compound option is an **option on an option**: the buyer has the right to buy a plain vanilla call or put option with a predetermined strike at a predetermined date and at a predetermined price (i.e. the options premium).

3.1.3.3. Barrier Options (Trigger Options)

These options are standard options with an **additional barrier (trigger) level**. The options right ceases to exist (respectively starts to exist) once the spot rate reaches the barrier level. As barrier options might expire prematurely (respectively they might never start to exist), these options are always cheaper than plain vanilla options.

Basically there are two types:

Knock-out options

A knock-out option is a **standard option, which expires worthless if a formerly specified exchange rate (barrier, trigger) is dealt in the spot market before expiration**. In the knock-out option the spot rate moves towards "out-of-the-money" in order to reach the "out-strike", i.e. the option is OTM when the barrier is hit.

Example
Spot: 1.2000   **down & out call**: call strike 1.2000 outstrike 1.1500   the option expires if spot falls below 1.1500   **up & out put:** put strike 1.2000 outstrike 1.2500   the option expires if spot rises over 1.2500

d.h., dass der Kurs nicht unter den Strike-Preis fällt. Das Gewinnpotenzial ist auf die Prämie beschränkt, das Verlustpotenzial substanziell (aber nicht unbeschränkt, da maximales Verlustpotenzial = aktueller Kurs – Prämie).

3.1.3. Exotische Optionen

In den letzten Jahren wurden zusätzlich zu den europäischen und amerikanischen Optionen eine Vielzahl von Varianten entwickelt, für die der Überbegriff „exotische Optionen" verwendet wird. In der Folge werden die wichtigsten exotischen Optionen kurz beschrieben.

3.1.3.1. Asian Option (Average Rate Option)

Eine Asian Option unterscheidet sich nicht durch den Zeitpunkt, sondern durch die **Art der Ausübung.** Bei einer Asian Option erfolgt **am Ende der Laufzeit eine Ausgleichszahlung** basierend auf der Differenz zwischen dem Strike-Preis und einem durchschnittlichen Kurs des Basiswertes. Zur Berechnung des Durchschnittskurses werden bei Abschluss bestimmte Termine bzw. Intervalle vereinbart. Die ARO ist in der Regel billiger als eine Standardoption und wird bei Verfall „cash gesettled".

3.1.3.2. Compound Option

Eine Compound Option ist eine **Option auf eine Option.** Somit gibt sie dem Käufer das Recht, eine Standardoption zu einem im Voraus bestimmten Preis und Zeitpunkt zu kaufen. Je mehr Prämie am Anfang bezahlt wird, desto größer ist die Wahrscheinlichkeit, dass die Strike-Prämie in the money enden und zu entsprechend kleineren Gesamtkosten führen wird. Falls die Compound Option ausgeübt wird, funktioniert die erworbene Option wie eine Standardoption.

3.1.3.3. Barrier Optionen (Trigger Optionen)

Diese Optionen beinhalten im Unterschied zu Standardoptionen noch ein **zusätzliches Kursniveau** (den sogenannten Barrier bzw. Trigger). Je nach Optionsart wird die Option bei Erreichen des Barriers gültig oder ungültig. Barrier Optionen sind immer billiger als Standardoptionen, da ja die Möglichkeit besteht, dass das Optionsrecht vorzeitig erlischt bzw. gar nicht erst entsteht.

Es gibt grundsätzlich zwei Arten von Barrier Optionen:

Knock-out-Optionen

Eine Knock-out-Option ist eine **Standardoption, die sofort verfällt, wenn der Wechselkurs während der Laufzeit der Option den Barrier („Outstrike") erreicht.** Bei Knock-out-Optionen liegt der Outstrike aus dem Geld, d.h., die Option hört auf zu existieren, wenn der Outstrike erreicht wird.

Beispiel

Spot: 1,2000
Down & out Call: Call Strike 1,2000 Outstrike 1,1500
Die Option verfällt, wenn Spot unter 1,1500 fällt.
Up & out Put: Put Strike 1,2000 Outstrike 1,2500
Die Option verfällt, wenn Spot über 1,2500 steigt.

Barrier options where the spot rate moves towards "in-the-money" in order to reach the out-strike are called **reverse knock-out** option or **kick-out option**.

Example
Spot: 1.2000 **up & out call**: call strike 1.2000 outstrike 1.2500 the option expires if spot rises above 1.2500 **down & out put:** put strike 1.2000 outstrike 1.1500 the option expires if spot falls below 1.1500

Knock-in options

A knock-in option is a **standard option, which only starts to exist if a formerly speci-fied exchange rate (barrier, trigger) is dealt in the spot market before expiration**. In the knock-in option the spot rate moves towards "out-of-the-money" in order to reach the "in-strike", i.e. the option is OTM when the barrier is hit.

Example
spot: 1.2000 **down & in call**: call strike 1.2000 instrike 1.1500 the option appears if spot falls below 1.1500 **up & in put:** put strike 1.2000 instrike 1.2500 the option appears if spot rises over 1.2500

Barrier options where the spot rate moves towards "in-the-money" in order to reach the in-strike are called **reverse knock-in option** or **kick-in option**.

Example
Spot: 1.2000 **up & in call**: call strike 1.2000 instrike 1.2500 the option appears if spot rises above 1.2500 **down & in put:** put strike 1.2000 instrike 1.1500 the option apears if spot falls below 1.1500

Variants of barrier options

Double knock-out options (**double knock-in** options) have two barrier levels. They expire worthless (start to exist) if one of them is reached in the spot market.

Usually the barrier level is valid during the whole life of barrier options. However, there are some variants where the barrier is just valid at the expiry date or during a predetermined period.

Barrier Optionen, bei denen der Outstrike Richtung im Geld liegt, werden **Reverse-Knockout-** oder auch **Kick-out-**Optionen genannt.

Beispiel

Spot: 1,2000
Up & out Call: Call Strike 1,2000 Outstrike 1,2500
Die Option verfällt, wenn Spot über 1,2500 steigt.
Down & out Put: Put Strike 1,2000 Outstrike 1,1500
Die Option verfällt, wenn Spot unter 1,1500 fällt.

Knock-in-Optionen

Eine Knock-in-Option ist eine **Standardoption, bei der das Optionsrecht erst zu existieren beginnt, wenn der Wechselkurs während der Laufzeit der Option den Barrier ("Instrike") erreicht.** Bei Knock-in-Optionen liegt der Instrike aus dem Geld, d.h., die Option ist aus dem Geld, wenn der Instrike erreicht wird.

Beispiel

Spot: 1,2000
Down & in Call: Call Strike 1,2000 Instrike 1,1500
Die Option entsteht erst, wenn Spot unter 1,1500 fällt.
Up & in Put: Put Strike 1,2000 Instrike 1,2500
Die Option entsteht erst, wenn Spot über 1,2500 steigt.

Barrier Optionen, bei denen der Instrike Richtung im Geld liegt, werden **Reverse-Knockin-** oder auch **Kick-in-**Optionen genannt.

Beispiel

Spot: 1,2000
Up & in Call: Call Strike 1,2000 Instrike 1,2500
Die Option entsteht erst, wenn Spot über 1,2500 steigt.
Down & in Put: Put Strike 1,2000 Outstrike 1,1500
Die Option entsteht erst, wenn Spot unter 1,1500 fällt.

Varianten zu Barrier Optionen

Double-Knock-out-Optionen bzw. **Double-Knock-in-Optionen** haben zwei Barriers. Es genügt das Erreichen eines der beiden Barriers, damit die Option verfällt bzw. zu existieren beginnt.

Im Normalfall ist der Barrier während der gesamten Laufzeit der Option gültig. Es gibt jedoch auch Varianten, bei denen der Barrier nur am Verfalltag oder auch nur innerhalb einer bestimmten Periode während der Laufzeit gültig ist.

3.1.3.4. Digital Options

A digital option is a transaction where a **specified amount** will be paid if the spot rate is above the strike at expiry for calls (or below the strike for puts). Usually the intervention path of spot between the trade date and expiry is irrelevant and the determining factor whether or not the spot is above or below the strike at the time of expiry. However, there are some variants where the strike is valid during the whole life of the option.

One Touch/No Touch Options

One touch is a transaction where a specified amount will be paid only if **spot rate is dealt at the touchstrike or an exceeding exchange rate before expiration**. One touch is also called "lock-in" or "touch digital". No touch options will pay a specified amount if spot rate is not dealt at the touchstrike. They are also called "lock-out"

Double No Touch (Range Binary)

A transaction where a specific amount will be paid only if spot is not dealt at, or at **levels** exceeding the predefined two exchange rates before expiration.

3.1.4. The Option Premium

These factors influence the price of the option:

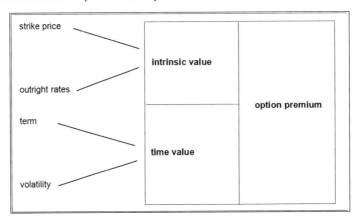

If an option has an **intrinsic value** this means that the strike price is "better" than the outright rate. All Calls with lower strikes than the outright rate and all Puts with higher strikes than the outright rate have an intrinsic value (ITM).

The option premium however is always higher than the intrinsic value. This difference is the **time value**. It is highest for

- longer option periods
- higher expected fluctuations of the underlying.

The option premium is also influenced by the **moneyness** of the option (ratio Strike and outright rate). Moneyness is a description of an option relating its strike price to the price of its underlying asset. Moneyness describes the intrinsic value of an option in its current state, which means that this business ratio describes how closely an option is in the money, out of

3.1.3.4. Digitale Optionen

Bei digitalen Optionen wird ein **fixierter Betrag** bezahlt, falls der Kassakurs am Verfalltag über bzw. unter einem bestimmten Kurs (Touchstrike) liegt. Im Standardfall ist das Erreichen des Touchstrikes während der Laufzeit irrelevant. Auch hier gibt es jedoch wieder eine Reihe von Varianten, bei denen der Touchstrike üblicherweise während der gesamten Laufzeit gültig ist.

One-touch-/No-touch-Optionen

Eine One-touch-Option (auch lock-in oder touch digital) zahlt einen bestimmten Betrag, falls ein **fixierter Kurs während der Laufzeit erreicht** wird. Das Gegenteil ist die No-touch-Option (auch lock-out), die einen bestimmten Betrag zahlt, falls der Touchstrike während der Laufzeit nicht erreicht wird.

Double-No-touch (Range Binary)

Eine Double-No-touch-Option zahlt einen bestimmten Betrag, falls der Kassakurs während der Laufzeit **eine bestimmte Bandbreite nicht verlässt,** d.h., falls keiner von zwei Touchstrikes erreicht wird.

3.1.4. Die Optionsprämie

Einflussfaktoren auf den Optionspreis:

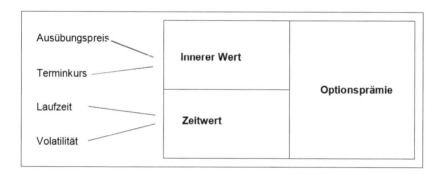

Der **innere Wert** einer Option ist jener Wert, um den der Strike besser als der aktuelle Terminkurs ist, d.h. jener Wert, den die Option im Geld ist. Somit haben nur Optionen im Geld einen inneren Wert. Daher kann der innere Wert nicht negativ, d.h. kleiner als 0 sein.

Die Prämie einer Option ist jedoch immer höher als der innere Wert. Diese Differenz ist der sogenannte **Zeitwert.** Er ist umso höher je

- länger die Laufzeit der Option und
- je höher die erwartete Schwankung des Basiswertes ist.

Der Optionspreis wird auch von der **Moneyness** der Option (Verhältnis Strike und Terminkurs) beeinflusst. Die Moneyness ist eine Kennzahl, die quasi die „Lage" (den aktuellen Börsenkurs) einer Option (oft auch eines Optionsscheines) in Bezug zum Geld (Basiskurs) beschreibt. Genauer gesagt, wird durch die Kennzahl beschrieben, wie nah im Geld, am Geld oder aus dem Geld der Optionsschein notiert. Dadurch wird bei Calls der gegenwär-

the money or at the money. Options at the money have a moneyness of 1, while a moneyness higher 1 indicates options in the money and a moneyness lower 1 indicates options out of the money.

The **volatility** is the measure for the variability or the **price range of the exchange rates or underlying prices**. There can be differentiated between historical and implied volatility. The **historical volatility** is calculated out of historical data and is mainly used for risk management calculations. For calculating actual option prices the **implied volatility** is needed. This volatility is a measure for the market participants' expectations concerning the future price range of the underlying. In the professional FX options market, traders only trade the volatility as it is the only number which is up to the trader's opinion.

Example	
GBP/USD Spot:	1.7000
Outright:	1.6800
Premium GBP Put Strike 1.7000:	3 Cent
Intrinsic value GBP Put:	2 Cent
Time value GBP Put:	1 Cent

Premium Quotations

Option premiums are quoted either in **per cent of the base currency** or in **BP of the quote currency**.

Example
GBP/USD Put, Strike 1.7000, premium 3 Ct.
If you buy the Put with contract volume of GBP 5.0 m you pay a premium of USD 150,000 (= 5 m x 0.03 USD)
GBP/USD Put, Strike 1.7000, premium 2%.
If you buy the Put with contract volume of GBP 5.0 m you pay a premium of GBP 100,000 (= 5 m x 0.02)

Reuters page with FX options volatilities:

	EUR/USD	USD/YEN	EUR/YEN	GBP/USD	AUD/USD	USD/CAD
ON	-	-	-	-	-	-
1WK	11.10-12.00		10.50-12.0	7.75 -8.75	10.00-10.75	8.0 -9.0
2WK	-	-	-	-	-	-
1M	10.50-10.70	10.60-11.00	9.80 -10.10	7.70 -7.95	9.80 -10.10	8.15 -8.40
2M	10.45-10.70	-	9.50 -9.80	7.75 -8.05	9.90 -10.15	7.55 -7.80
3M	10.50-10.65	10.00-10.50	9.40 -9.70	8.00 -8.20	9.85 -10.15	7.50 -7.70
6M	10.40-10.55	9.45 -9.60	9.20 -9.50	8.05 -8.30	9.90 -10.15	7.25 -7.55
1Y	10.45-10.55	9.25 -9.40	9.20 -9.45	8.15 -8.40	9.90 -10.15	7.20 -7.40

Interpretation of Volatility

The fair option price is calculated – generally speaking – by a **statistic model**. The main factor is the volatility as a measure for the fluctuation resp. uncertainty. Statistically volatility equals the annualized standard deviation (sigma). Also for risk management calculations the standard deviation is a main factor.

tige Underlying-Kurs durch den Strike-Preis dividiert bzw. bei Puts umgekehrt der Strike-Preis durch den Underlying-Kurs dividiert. Dadurch haben Optionsscheine, die am Geld stehen, eine Moneyness von 1, während Werte größer als 1 auf Optionsscheine hinweisen, die im Geld notieren, und Werte kleiner als 1 auf Optionsscheine, die aus dem Geld notieren.

Das **Maß für die Schwankung** ist die sogenannte **Volatilität.** Zur Bestimmung des Optionspreises wird die zukünftig erwartete Schwankung – die **implizite Volatilität** – verwendet. Davon unterscheidet man die **historische Volatilität.** Das ist die aus vergangenen Marktdaten errechnete Schwankung (statistisch: Standardabweichung) des Basiswertes. Diese wird vor allem in der Risikorechnung verwendet, nicht jedoch für die Berechnung von Optionspreisen.

Beispiel

GBP/USD Kassa:	1,7000
Terminkurs:	1,6800
Prämie GBP-Put Strike 1,7000:	3 Cent
Innerer Wert GBP-Put:	2 Cent
Zeitwert GBP-Put:	1 Cent

Prämienquotierung

Optionsprämien werden nicht nur in der **Gegenwährung,** sondern auch in **Prozent vom Volumen** quotiert. In diesem Fall ist die Prämie in der quotierten Währung zu bezahlen.

Beispiel

GBP/USD-Put, Strike 1,7000 hat eine Prämie von 3 Cent.
Wenn Sie den Put über ein Volumen von 5 Mio. GBP kaufen, zahlen Sie eine Prämie von USD 150.000 (= 5 Mio. x 0,03 USD).

GBP/USD-Put, Strike 1,7000 hat eine Prämie von 2%.
Wenn Sie den Put über ein Volumen von 5 Mio. GBP kaufen, zahlen Sie eine Prämie von GBP 100.000 (= 5 Mio. x 0,02).

Reuters-Seite mit FX-Options-Volatilitäten:

	EUR/USD	USD/YEN	EUR/YEN	GBP/USD	AUD/USD	USD/CAD
ON	-	-	-	-	-	-
1WK	11.10-12.00		10.50-12.0	7.75 -8.75	10.00-10.75	8.0 -9.0
2WK	-	-	-	-	-	-
1M	10.50-10.70	10.60-11.00	9.80 -10.10	7.70 -7.95	9.80 -10.10	8.15 -8.40
2M	10.45-10.70	-	9.50 -9.80	7.75 -8.05	9.90 -10.15	7.55 -7.80
3M	10.50-10.65	10.00-10.50	9.40 -9.70	8.00 -8.20	9.85 -10.15	7.50 -7.70
6M	10.40-10.55	9.45 -9.60	9.20 -9.50	8.05 -8.30	9.90 -10.15	7.25 -7.55
1V	10.45-10.55	9.25 -9.40	9.20 -9.45	8.15 -8.40	9.90 -10.15	7.20 -7.40

Interpretation der Volatilität

Der faire Optionspreis wird allgemein mittels eines **statistischen Modells** errechnet. Der wesentliche Einflussfaktor ist dabei die Volatilität als Maßzahl für die Schwankung bzw. die Unsicherheit. In der Statistik entspricht die Volatilität der annualisierten Standardabweichung (Sigma). Auch in der Risikomessung ist die Standardabweichung ein zentraler Faktor. Wie kann nun die Standardabweichung interpretiert werden?

How can the standard deviation be interpreted? A standard deviation is the range where 2/3 (exactly 68.26%) of all values (e.g. EUR/USD rates) can be found. In other words one could say that with a probability of 68.26% the value (e.g. EUR/USD rate) will not change more than one standard deviation. The term "annualized" means that the deviation refers to the period of one year, the so-called holding period is 1 year.

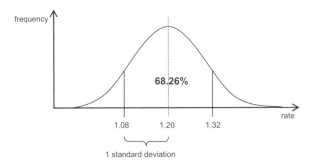

In the above example the annualized standard deviation is 0.12 resp. 10%, i.e. 68.26% of all values can be found within the interval from +/- 0.12 resp. 10% for the period of one year.

The volatility (meaning the annualized standard deviation) can be transformed into another holding period by multiplying it by the square root of the holding period (resp. dividing it when the holding period is reduced).

Example

Your risk manager tells you that the EUR/USD volatility is 10%. As the implied volatility is an annualized standard deviation, this means that the market expects that EUR/USD will not change more than 10% with a probability of 68.26% within one year.
What is the standard deviation from one day to the next day (i.e. holding period 1 day)?
In order to transform the holding period from 1 year (252 trading days) to 1 day the volatility has to be devided by the square root of the holding period:

$$Vol\,1D = \frac{Vola\,1year}{\sqrt{252}} \qquad Vola\,1D = \frac{10\%}{\sqrt{252}} = 0.00629941$$

Interpretation: The market expects that the EUR/USD fluctuation from one trading day to the other will not be more than 0.63% with a probability of 68.26%.
What is the standard deviation for a holding period of 10 trading days?
In order to scale the 1 day-volatility up to a 10 days-volatility it has to be multiplied by the square root out of 10:

$$Vola\,10D = Vola\,1D \times \sqrt{10} \qquad Vola\,10T = 0.63\% \times \sqrt{10} = 2.00\%$$

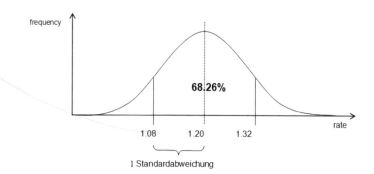

Eine Standardabweichung ist jener Bereich, in dem ca. 2/3 (genau 68,26%) aller beobachteten Werte (z.B. EUR/USD-Kurse) liegen. Anders könnte man auch sagen, dass mit einer Wahrscheinlichkeit von 68,26% der Wert (z.B. EUR/USD-Kurs) sich um nicht mehr als eine Standardabweichung verändern wird. Der Ausdruck „annualisiert" bedeutet dabei, dass sich die Abweichung auf eine Jahresperiode bezieht. Man sagt auch, die Haltedauer ist ein Jahr.

Im obigen Beispiel beträgt die annualisierte Standardabweichung 0,12 bzw. 10%. Dies würde bedeuten, dass 68,26% aller Werte innerhalb eines Jahres im Intervall von +/-0,12 bzw. 10% liegen werden.

Die Volatilität, also die annualisierte Standardabweichung, kann auf eine andere Haltedauer umgerechnet werden, indem sie mit der Wurzel der Haltedauer multipliziert wird (bzw. dividiert bei einer Verkürzung der Haltedauer).

Beispiel

Ihr Risikomanager sagt Ihnen, dass die EUR/USD Vola 10% ist. Da die implizite Vola eine annualisierte Standardabweichung ist, bedeutet das, dass der Markt erwartet, dass sich EUR/USD mit einer Wahrscheinlichkeit von 68,26% um nicht mehr als 10% innerhalb eines Jahres verändern wird.

Wie hoch ist die Standardabweichung von einem Tag auf den nächsten (d.h. Haltedauer ein Tag)?

Um die Haltedauer von einem Jahr (252 Handelstage) auf einen (Handels-)Tag umzurechnen, muss die Vola durch die Wurzel der Haltedauer dividiert werden.

$$Vola\,1T = \frac{Vola\,1Jahr}{\sqrt{252}} \qquad Vola\,1T = \frac{10\%}{\sqrt{252}} = 0,00629941$$

Interpretation: Der Markt erwartet, dass die Kursbewegung von EUR/USD von einem Tag auf den nächsten mit einer Wahrscheinlichkeit von 68,26% nicht größer als 0,63% sein wird.

Wie hoch ist die Standardabweichung für eine Haltedauer von zehn (Handels-)Tagen?

Um die Ein-Tages-Vola auf eine Zehn-Tages-Vola zu skalieren, muss sie mit der Wurzel aus 10 multipliziert werden.

$$Vola\,1T = Vola\,1T \times \sqrt{10} \qquad Vola\,1T = 0,63\% \times \sqrt{10} = 2,00\%$$

3.1.5. Profit and Loss Profiles

3.1.5.1. Call

Long Call

Long Call with strike A and break-even B (strike + premium)

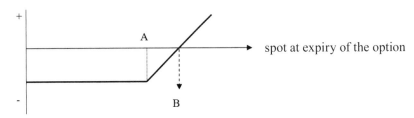

→ **Loss** if spot < Strike + Premium
→ **Profit** if spot > Strike + Premium

The break-even is reached, if the spot rate is at the strike plus premium on expiration day. The maximum loss is the premium.

Between point A and point B, exercising the option is profitable but not enough to cover the cost of the premium, therefore you make a loss.

Example

Buy EUR Call USD Put: Strike 1.0200. premium: 1 Cent (USD 0.01).
P&L in USD with the following EUR/USD Spot values at expiry:

Spot at expiry	1.000	1.0100	1.0250	1.0300	1.0400	1.0500
Long Call	0	0	+0.005	+0.01	+0.02	+0.03
Premium	-0.01	-0.01	-0.01	-0.01	-0.01	-0.01
Total	-0.01	-0.01	-0.005	0	+0.01	+0.02

The higher spot is at expiry, the bigger is the inner value. Premium is the same at every rate (0.01 USD), it is paid immediately when traded. The maximum loss is 0.01 USD (premium), the potential profit is theoretically unlimited.

3.1.5. Gewinn- und Verlustprofile

3.1.5.1. Call

Long Call

Long Call zum Strike A und Break-even B (Strike + Prämie)

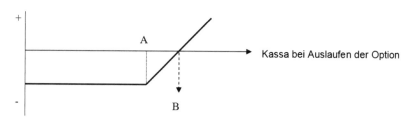

→ **Verlust,** wenn Kassa < Strike + Prämie
→ **Gewinn,** wenn Kassa > Strike + Prämie

Die Gewinnzone ist erreicht, wenn der Kassakurs am Verfalltag über dem Strike liegt und der Prämienaufwand verdient wird. Der maximale Verlust ist die Prämie.

Zwischen den Punkten A und B wird zwar durch das Ausüben der Option ein Gewinn erzielt, er reicht jedoch nicht aus, um die gesamten Prämienkosten abzudecken, um damit im Gesamtergebnis die Gewinnzone zu erreichen.

Beispiel

Kauf EUR-Call USD-Put: Strike 1,2000, Prämie: 1 Cent (USD 0,01).
GuV in USD bei angenommenen EUR/USD-Kassakursen am Verfalltag:

Kassakurs am Verfalltag	**1,1800**	**1,1900**	**1,2000**	**1,2100**	**1,2200**	**1,2300**
Ergebnis Long Call	0,00	0,00	0,00	+0,01	+0,02	+0,03
Prämie	-0,01	-0,01	-0,01	-0,01	-0,01	-0,01
Gesamt	-0,01	-0,01	-0,01	0	+0,01	+0,02

Je höher der Kassakurs am Verfalltag liegt, desto größer ist auch der innere Wert der Option. Die Prämie ist bei jedem angenommenen Kassakurs gleich (USD 0,01), sie wird sofort bei Abschluss an den Verkäufer gezahlt. Der maximale Verlust dieser Optionsposition beträgt USD 0,01 (Prämie), das Gewinnpotenzial ist prinzipiell unbegrenzt.

Short Call

Short Call with strike A and break-even B (strike + premium)

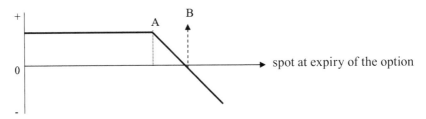

→ **Loss** if spot > Strike + Premium
→ **Profit** if spot < Strike + Premium

At expiry the seller of the option makes a profit as long as the spot price stays below the strike price plus premium. The potential loss is theoretically unlimited.

The maximum gain is the premium. Between point A and B the spot rate is above the strike price, but the seller gains more from the premium as he loses from the option.

Example

Sell EUR Call USD Put: Strike 1.0200, premium: 1 Cent (0.01 USD).
P&L in USD with the following EUR/USD Spot prices at expiration day:

Spot at expiry	1.000	1.0100	1.0250	1.0300	1.0400	1.0500
Long Call	0	0	-0.005	-0.01	-0.02	-0.03
Premium	+0.01	+0.01	+0.01	+0.01	+0.01	+0.01
Total	+0.01	+0.01	+0.005	0	-0.01	-0.02

The higher spot is at expiry, the bigger is the loss. Premium is the same at every rate (0.01 USD), it is paid immediately when traded. The maximum profit is 0.01 USD (premium), the potential loss is theoretically unlimited.

Short Call

Short Call zum Strike A und Break-even B (Strike + Prämie)

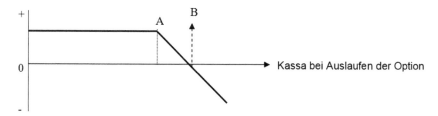

→ **Verlust**, wenn Kassa > Strike + Prämie
→ **Gewinn,** wenn Kassa < Strike + Prämie

Solange der Kassakurs am Verfalltag unter dem Strike zuzüglich der erhaltenen Prämie liegt, bleibt der Verkäufer der Option in der Gewinnzone. Der Verlust kann theoretisch ins Unendliche gehen.

Der maximale Gewinn ist die Prämie. Zwischen den Punkten A und B liegt der Kassapreis über dem Strike, aber der Verkäufer verdient aus der Prämie noch mehr, als er in der Option verliert.

Beispiel

Verkauf EUR-Call USD-Put: Strike 1,2000, Prämie: 1 Cent (0,01 USD).
GuV in USD bei folgenden EUR/USD-Kassakursen am Verfalltag:

Kassakurs am Verfalltag	1,1800	1,1900	1,2000	1,2100	1,2200	1,2300
Ergebnis Short Call	0,00	0,00	0,00	-0,01	-0,02	-0,03
Prämie	+0,01	+0,01	+0,01	+0,01	+0,01	+0,01
Gesamt	+0,01	+0,01	+0,01	0	-0,01	-0,02

Je höher der Kassakurs am Verfalltag liegt, desto größer ist auch der Verlust aus der Option. Die Prämie ist bei jedem angenommenen Kassakurs gleich (0,01 USD), sie wird sofort bei Abschluss vom Käufer gezahlt. Der maximale Gewinn dieser Optionsposition beträgt 0,01 USD (Prämie), das Verlustpotenzial ist prinzipiell unbegrenzt.

3.1.5.2. Put

Long Put

Long Put with Strike A and break-even B (strike – premium)

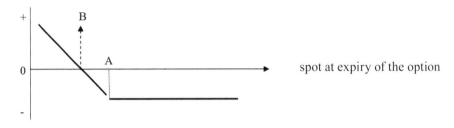

spot at expiry of the option

→ **Loss** if spot > Strike – Premium
→ **Profit** if spot < Strike – Premium

The break-even is reached if the spot price at expiry is at the strike price minus premium. The maximum loss is the premium. Between Point A and B the spot price is below the strike price but the buyer of the option gains less from exercising the option than he has paid for it. Anyway the buyer reduces his premium costs.

Example

Buy EUR Put USD Call: Strike 1.0200, premium: 1 Cent (0.01 USD).
P&L in USD with the following EUR/USD spot prices at expiry:

Spot at expiry	0.9900	1.0000	1.0100	1.0150	1.0200	1.0300
Long Put	+0.03	+0.02	+0.01	+0.005	0	0
premium	-0.01	-0.01	-0.01	-0.01	-0.01	-0.01
total	+0.02	+0.01	0	-0.005	-0.01	-0.01

The lower spot is at expiry, the bigger is the inner value. Premium is the same at every rate (0.01 USD), it is paid immediately when traded. The maximum loss is 0.01 USD (premium), the potential profit is theoretically unlimited (up to the value of the strike).

Remark: In the ACI exams the potential profits (losses) of long (short) positions are termed to be "substantial"!

3.1.5.2. Put

Long Put zum Strike A und Break-even B (Strike – Prämie)

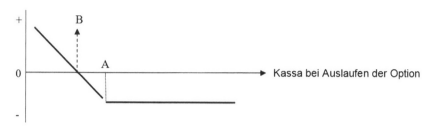

→ **Verlust,** wenn Kassa > Strike – Prämie
→ **Gewinn,** wenn Kassa < Strike – Prämie

Die Gewinnzone ist erreicht, wenn der Kassakurs am Verfalltag unter dem Strike liegt und der Prämienaufwand verdient wird. Der maximale Verlust ist die Prämie. Zwischen den Punkten A und B liegt der Kassapreis unter dem Strike, aber der Käufer verdient durch Ausüben der Option weniger, als er Prämie bezahlt hat. Immerhin reduziert der Käufer die Prämienkosten.

Beispiel

Kauf EUR-Put USD-Call: Strike 1,2000, Prämie: 1 Cent (0,01 USD).
GuV in USD bei folgenden EUR/USD-Kassakursen am Verfalltag:

Kassakurs am Verfalltag	1,1700	1,1800	1,1900	1,2000	1,2100	1,2200
Ergebnis Long Put	+0,03	+0,02	+0,01	0,00	0,00	0,00
Prämie	-0,01	-0,01	-0,01	-0,01	-0,01	-0,01
Gesamt	+0,02	+0,01	0	-0,01	-0,01	-0,01

Je niedriger der Kassakurs am Verfalltag liegt, desto größer ist auch der Gewinn aus der Option. Die Prämie ist bei jedem angenommenen Kassakurs gleich (0,01 USD), sie wird sofort bei Abschluss an den Verkäufer gezahlt. Der maximale Verlust dieser Optionsposition beträgt 0,01 USD (Prämie), das Gewinnpotenzial ist (bis zum Wert des Strikes) unbegrenzt.

Hinweis: Bei den ACI-Prüfungen wird das Gewinnpotenzial von Long-Positionen und das Verlustpotenzial von Short-Positionen als „substanziell" bezeichnet!

Short Put

Short Put with Strike A and break-even B (strike – premium)

→ **Loss** if spot < Strike – Premium
→ **Profit** if spot > Strike – Premium

For the seller the option is profitable until the spot price at expiration is below the strike price. In this case the gain from the premium is less than the loss from the option exercise buy the buyer of the option. The loss is theoretically limited by a spot price with zero. But because a short Put option is from the risk orientated sight a long position in the underlying (= risk of falling prices) and long FX-positions have unlimited risk, the risk of short Put positions is also unlimited.

The maximum gain is the premium. Between Point A and B the spot price is below the strike but the seller gains more from the premium as he loses from the option.

Example
Sell EUR Put USD Call: Strike 1.0200, premium: 1 Cent (0.01 USD). P&L in USD with the following EUR/USD spot prices at expiry:

Spot at expiry	0.9900	1.0000	1.0100	1.0150	1.0200	1.0300
Short Put	-0.03	-0.02	-0.01	-0.005	0	0
Premium	+0.01	+0.01	+0.01	+0.01	+0.01	+0.01
Total	-0.02	-0.01	0	+0.005	+0.01	+0.01

The lower spot is at expiry, the bigger is the loss. Premium is the same at every rate (0.01 USD), it is paid immediately when traded. The maximum profit is 0.01 USD (premium), the potential loss is theoretically unlimited (up to the value of the strike).

The tables show that the results for buyers and sellers are inverted.

Short Put

Short Put zum Strike A und Break-even B (Strike – Prämie)

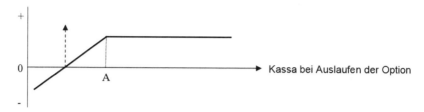

→ Verlust bei Kassa < Strike – Prämie
→ **Gewinn** bei Kassa > Strike – Prämie

Der Verkäufer bleibt so lange in der Gewinnzone, bis der Kassakurs am Verfalltag so weit unter dem Strike liegt, dass die Prämie niedriger als der Verlust aus der Optionsposition wird. Der Verlust ist streng theoretisch auf einen Kassakurs gleich null beschränkt.

Da aber ein Short Put vom Risiko her einer Long-Position im Underlying entspricht (= Risiko fallender Kurse) und niemand von einem begrenzten Risiko, z.B. bei einer EUR/USD-Long-Position, spricht, kann auch das Verlustrisiko eines Short Put als unbeschränkt bezeichnet werden. Maximaler Gewinn ist die Prämie. Zwischen den Punkten A und B liegt der Kassapreis unter dem Strike, aber der Verkäufer verdient aus der Prämie noch mehr, als er in der Option verliert.

Beispiel

Verkauf EUR-Put USD-Call: Strike 1,2000, Prämie: 1 Ct. (0,01 USD).
GuV in USD bei folgenden EUR/USD Kassakursen am Verfalltag:

Kassakurs am Verfalltag	1,1700	1,1800	1,1900	1,2000	1,2100	1,2200
Ergebnis Short Put	-0,03	-0,02	-0,01	0,00	0,00	0,00
Prämie	+0,01	+0,01	+0,01	+0,01	+0,01	+0,01
Gesamt	-0,02	-0,01	0	+0,01	+0,01	+0,01

Je niedriger der Kassakurs am Verfalltag liegt, desto größer ist auch der Verlust aus der Option. Die Prämie ist bei jedem angenommenen Kassakurs gleich (0,01 USD), sie wird sofort bei Abschluss vom Käufer gezahlt. Der maximale Gewinn dieser Optionsposition beträgt 0,01 USD (Prämie), das Verlustpotenzial ist (bis zum Wert des Strikes) unbegrenzt.

Die Tabellen zeigen, dass die Ergebnisse für Käufer und Verkäufer genau spiegelverkehrt sind.

3.1.6. Strategies

3.1.6.1. Straddle

A Straddle is the purchase resp. the sale of a Call and a Put with the **same strike**.

	Long Straddle	**Short Straddle**
Purchase/sale	purchase Call, purchase Put	sale Call, sale Put
Strikes	same, mostly ATM	same, mostly ATM
Maturity	same	same

Why is a Straddle used?

A **Long Straddle** gains with exchange-rate fluctuations (= volatility) independent of the direction. Because the position is purchased ATM a Long Straddle is an aggressive position. If the underlying does not fluctuate much the relatively high premium is lost.

A **Short Straddle** is used if low volatilities are expected. If the expected volatility is met, the premium is earned, if there are stronger fluctuations than expected the loss is proportional higher the higher the fluctuations are.

Long Straddle

Long Call and long Put, same term, same strike, normally ATM.

Short Straddle

Short Call and short Put, same term, same strike, normally ATM.

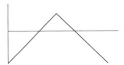

3.1.6.2 Strangle

A Strangle is the purchase resp. the sale of a Call and a Put with **different strike prices**.

	Long Strangle	**Short Strangle**
Purchase/sale	buy Call, buy Put	sell Call, sell Put
Strikes	different, OTM	different, OTM
Maturity	same	same

Why are Strangles dealt?

The **Long Strangle** gains if there are strong exchange rate fluctuations independent of the direction. In comparison to the Straddle the maximum loss is smaller, because the options are purchased OTM. Because of the OTM purchase of the option the leverage-effect of the Strangle is higher compared to the Straddle.

The **Short Strangle** gains if there are no strong exchange rate fluctuations. The effects are contrary to the Long Strangle.

3.1.6. Strategien

3.1.6.1. Straddle

Ein Straddle besteht aus einem Call und einem Put mit **gleichen Strikes.**

	Long Straddle	**Short Straddle**
Kauf/Verkauf	Kauf Call + Kauf Put	Verkauf Call + Verkauf Put
Strikes	ident, meist ATM	ident, meist ATM
Laufzeiten	ident	ident

Warum handelt man einen Straddle?

Ein **Long Straddle** verdient auf Kursschwankungen (= Volatilität), unabhängig von der Richtung. Wegen des Kaufs von Optionen am Geld ist ein Long Straddle eine aggressive Position. Bewegt sich das Underlying nicht so stark wie erwartet, geht die (relativ hohe, da doppelte) Prämie jedoch verloren.

Beim **Short Straddle** erwartet man niedrige Volatilitäten. Tritt die Volatilitätserwartung ein, verdient man die Prämie, bei starken Schwankungen verliert man aber entsprechend mehr.

Long Straddle

Kauf Call und Kauf Put, gleiche Laufzeit, gleicher Strike, üblicherweise ATM.

Short Straddle

Verkauf Call und Verkauf Put, gleiche Laufzeit, gleicher Strike, üblicherweise ATM.

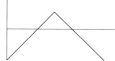

3.1.6.2. Strangle

Ein Strangle besteht aus einem Call und einem Put mit **unterschiedlichen Strikes.**

	Long Strangle	**Short Strangle**
Kauf/Verkauf	Kauf Call + Kauf Put	Verkauf Call + Verkauf Put
Strikes	verschieden, OTM	verschieden, OTM
Laufzeiten	ident	ident

Warum handelt man einen Strangle?

Der **Long Strangle** verdient auf sehr starke Kursschwankungen (= Volatilität), unabhängig von der Richtung. Im Verhältnis zum Straddle ist der Maximalverlust geringer, weil die Optionen aus dem Geld gekauft wurden, dafür ist die Verlustzone für die Maximalverluste größer. Durch den Kauf der OTM-Optionen ist der Leverage-Effekt beim Strangle in der Gewinnzone höher als beim Straddle.

Beim **Short Strangle** erwartet man niedrigere Volatilitäten. Die Auswirkungen sind dem Long Strangle entgegengesetzt.

Long Strangle

Long Call and long Put, same term, different strikes, usually OTM.

Short Strangle

Short Call and short Put, same term, different strikes, usually OTM.

3.1.6.3 Butterfly

A butterfly consists of a straddle and an opposite strangle.

	Long Butterfly	Short Butterfly
Long/short	short straddle + long strangle	long straddle + short strangle
Strikes	see straddle, strangle	see straddle, strangle
Maturity	same	same

Why are Butterflies dealt?

A **Short Butterfly** position gains if there are strong exchange rate fluctuations independent of the direction. In comparison with a long strangle or straddle position, the maximum gain of the position is limited as the butterfly position includes a short strangle to reduce the positions total premium

The **Long Butterfly** position yields a profit if there are little to none exchange rate fluctuations. The loss potential is limited, as opposed to short strangle or straddle positions.

Long Butterfly

Short Straddle and Long Strangle, same maturity.

Short Butterfly

Long Straddle and Short Strangle, same maturity.

3.1.6.5. Condor

A Condor consists of a two strangles – one is bought and the other is sold, i.e. a buy/write option strategy.

Long Strangle

Kauf Call und Kauf Put, gleiche Laufzeit, unterschiedliche Strikes, üblicherweise OTM.

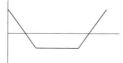

Short Strangle

Verkauf Call und Verkauf Put, gleiche Laufzeit, unterschiedliche Strikes, üblicherweise OTM.

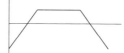

3.1.6.3. Butterfly

Ein Butterfly besteht aus einem Straddle und einem gegenläufigen Strangle.

Long/Short	**Long Butterfly**	**Short Butterfly**
Long/Short	Short Straddle + Long Strangle	Long Straddle + Short Strangle
Strikes	siehe Straddle, Strangle	siehe Straddle, Strangle
Laufzeiten	ident	ident

Warum handelt man einen Butterfly?

Der **Short Butterfly** verdient auf sehr starke Kursschwankungen, unabhängig von der Richtung. Im Gegensatz zu einem gekauften Strangle oder Straddle ist der Maximalgewinn begrenzt, da zwecks Prämienersparnis ein Strangle verkauft wird.

Beim **Long Butterfly** erwartet man wenig Änderung in den Kursen. Hier hat man den Vorteil, dass der Maximalverlust im Gegensatz zu verkauftem Strangle oder Straddle begrenzt ist.

Long Butterfly

Verkauf Straddle und Kauf Strangle, gleiche Laufzeit.

Short Butterfly

Kauf Straddle und Verkauf Strangle, gleiche Laufzeit.

3.1.6.5. Condor

Ein Condor besteht aus einem gekauften und einem verkauften Strangle. Damit ist der Condor eine weitere Kauf/Verkauf-Strategie.

	Long Condor	**Short Condor**
Long/short	long strangle (far OTM)+ short strangle (OTM)	short strangle (far OTM) + long strangle (OTM)
Strikes	different OTM	different OTM
Maturity	same	same

Why deal a Condor?

A **Long Condor** position is profitable if there are small fluctuations regardless of the direction. In contrast to Strangle the maximum profit and the maximum loss are limited. For trading a long condor constant exchange rates should be assumed. The risk of strong fluctuations is lower in comparison to Straddle, Strangle and Butterfly.

In a **Short Condor** position the expectation is towards strong fluctuation of exchange rates. Again, the risk compared to Straddle or Strangle is lower due to the premiums from the sale of the far OTM strangles.

Long Condor

long strangle (far OTM) and short strangle (OTM), same maturity

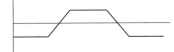

Short Condor

short strangle (far OTM) and long strangle (OTM), same maturity

3.1.6.5. Spread

A Spread is the purchase (sale) of an option and the sale (purchase) of another option at the same time. Contrary to the Straddle or Strangle this strategy is a

- **buy and sell** strategy
- strategy with **only one option type**

	Vertical spread	**Horizontal spread *)**	**Diagonal spread *)**
Purchase/sale	buy/sell Call or buy/sell Put	buy/sell Call or buy/sell Put	buy/sell Call or buy/sell Put
Strikes	different, one ITM, the other OTM	same	different, one ITM, the other OTM
Maturity	same	different	different

*) not often used in practice

The most usual Spread-Strategy is the vertical Spread. There is differentiated between **Bull and Bear Spreads**.

	Long Condor	**Short Condor**
Long/Short	Long Strangle(far OTM)+ Short Strangle (OTM)	Short Strangle (far OTM) + Long Strangle (OTM)
Strikes	verschieden OTM	verschieden OTM
Laufzeiten	ident	ident

Warum handelt man einen Condor?

Bei einem **Long Condor** verdient man auf kleine Kursschwankungen, unabhängig von der Richtung. Im Gegensatz zu einem Strangle ist sowohl der maximale Gewinn, als auch der maximale Verlust begrenzt. Bei einem Long Condor sollte von gleichbleibenden Kursen ausgegangen werden. Das Risiko bei größeren Schwankungen ist jedoch begrenzt und verglichen mit einem Straddle/Strangle/Butterfly geringer.

Beim **Short Condor** ist die Kurserwartung stark schwankende Kurse. Auch hier ist das Risiko verglichen mit einem Straddle/Strangle geringer, da durch den Verkauf des far OTM Strangles Prämien erhalten wurden.

Long Condor

Kauf Strangle (far OTM) und Verkauf Strangle (OTM), gleiche Laufzeit

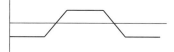

Short Condor

Verkauf Strangle (far OTM) und Kauf Strangle (OTM), gleiche Laufzeit

3.1.6.5. Spread

Ein Spread ist der Kauf (Verkauf) einer Option bei gleichzeitigem Verkauf (Kauf) einer anderen Option. Im Gegensatz zu Straddle oder Strangle handelt es sich um eine

- **Kauf- und Verkaufs-**Strategie
- Strategie, bei der **nur ein Optionstyp** verwendet wird.

	Vertikaler Spread	**Horizontaler Spread*)**	**Diagonaler Spread*)**
Kauf/Verkauf	Kauf/Verkauf Call oder Kauf/Verkauf Put	Kauf/Verkauf Call oder Kauf/Verkauf Put	Kauf/Verkauf Call oder Kauf/Verkauf Put
Strikes	verschieden, einer ITM, einer OTM	ident	verschieden, einer ITM, einer OTM
Laufzeiten	ident	verschieden	verschieden

*) in der Praxis selten verwendet

Die üblichste Spread-Strategie ist der vertikale Spread. Man unterscheidet **Bull** und **Bear Spreads.**

Bull Spread

Bull Spreads are usually formed with Call options, with one Call purchased in or ATM and one Call sold OTM.

If a Bull spread is traded with Put options, one Put is written ITM and the other Put is purchased OTM.

Example
Long Call ITM basis A, short Call OTM basis B, same term. 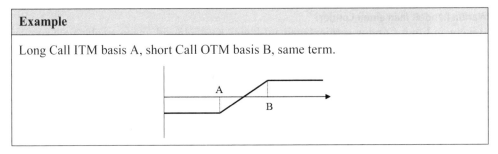

Bear Spread

A bear Spread is usually formed with a purchased Put in or ATM and a Put, which is sold OTM.

As well Bear Spreads can be constructed with Call options (sell ITM Call plus buy OTM Call).

Example
Long Put ITM basis A, short Put OTM basis B, same term. 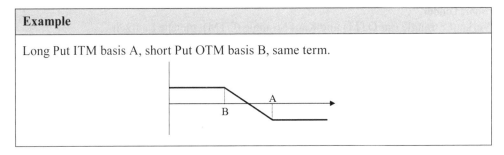

3.1.7. Option Pricing Models

The option market started to boom with the development of option pricing models. These models determine the price of an option as a function of variables like market data, volatility, strike price, term and interest rates. The main principle in option pricing is the calculation of the "fair option price", i.e. the price where no arbitrage is possible.

The best-known valuation model in option markets is the **Black/Scholes model**, published in 1973 by F. Black and M. Scholes and originally used for pricing share options.

Generally the following assumptions are made:

- The stock prices are subject to a log-normal distribution.
- During the option period no dividends are allowed.
- The annualised, riskless interest rate is constant during the option period.
- Markets are efficient, the hedge portfolio can be traded continuously.
- Options are European-style.
- Volatility remains constant during the option period.

Bull Spread

Bull Spreads werden üblicherweise aus Call-Optionen gebildet, wobei ein Call ITM oder ATM gekauft wird und ein Call OTM verkauft wird.

Wird ein Bull Spread über Puts gehandelt, wird der Put ITM geschrieben und der Put OTM gekauft.

Beispiel

Kauf Call ITM Basis A, Verkauf Call OTM Basis B, gleiche Laufzeit.

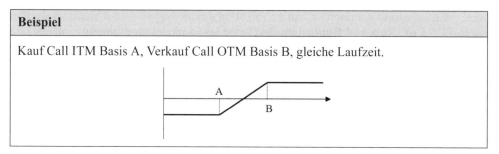

Bear Spread

Bei einem Bear Spread wird üblicherweise ein Put ITM oder ATM gekauft und ein Put OTM verkauft.

Bear Spreads können auch über Calls dargestellt werden (Verkauf ITM-Call plus Kauf OTM-Call).

Beispiel

Kauf Put ITM Basis A, Verkauf Put OTM Basis B, gleiche Laufzeit.

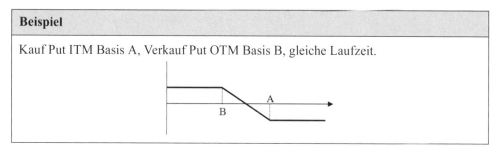

3.1.7. Optionspreismodelle

Der größte Durchbruch in der Optionstheorie war die Entwicklung von Optionspreismodellen. Diese Modelle bestimmen den Preis einer Option als Funktion von beobachtbaren Variablen wie Basiswert, Volatilität, Ausübungspreis, Laufzeit und Zinssatz. Das Grundprinzip im Optionspricing ist die Berechnung des „fairen Optionspreises". Darunter kann man jenen Preis verstehen, bei dem keine Arbitrage möglich ist.

Die bekannteste Bewertungsmethode ist das **Black & Scholes-Modell,** 1973 von F. Black und M. Scholes publiziert und ursprünglich für die Bewertung von Aktienoptionen entwickelt.

Generell werden beim Black & Scholes-Modell folgende Annahmen unterstellt:

- Die Aktienkurse unterliegen einer Log-Normalverteilung.
- Während der Laufzeit der Optionen dürfen keine Ausschüttungen erfolgen.
- Der annualisierte, risikolose Zinssatz ist während der Laufzeit konstant.
- Es existieren effiziente Märkte, sodass das Hedgeportfolio kontinuierlich gebildet werden kann.
- Es handelt sich um europäische Optionen.
- Die Volatilität bleibt während der Laufzeit der Option konstant.

The main difference between FX and share options is that the **foreign currency interest rates have to be integrated in the Black-Scholes model** as continuous dividend payments. For FX options the option price is influenced by the interest rates in both currencies.

The differences in the assumptions and in the valuation formula of the Black & Scholes model were published in an essay by Mark B. Garman and Steven W. Kohlhagen (December 1982). The **Garman-Kohlhagen valuation model** still is – even if slight modifications were done – the most common FX option valuation model.

In 1979 **Cox, Ross and Rubinstein** developed also a model for evaluating interest rate options. In contrary to the Garman-Kohlhagen and the Black-Scholes model the Cox, Ross and Rubinstein model assumes a discrete random variable, i.e. it does not assume a normal distribution like the other two models but a **binomial distribution.**

With the binomial distribution two different points of time are regarded, which are the points of beginning and end of a period resp. a time interval. Regarding the fixed, actual rate it is required that the rate at the end of the period can have exactly two different values, either a maximum or minimum value.

EXCURSUS: The option price formula

The price of a Call is the following:

$$CALL = \frac{1}{\left(1 + r_Q \times \dfrac{T}{B_Q}\right)} \times \left\{ [O \times N(d_1)] - S \times N(d_2) \right\}$$

$$\text{With: } d_1 = \frac{\ln\left(\dfrac{O}{S}\right) + \left(0{,}5 \times V^2 \times T\right)}{V \times T^{\frac{1}{2}}}$$

$$d_2 = d_1 - V \times T^{0.5}$$

S = strike
O = outright
V = volatility
T = term of the option (in% of a year)
I_B = interest rate p.a. in decimals, base currency
N(..) = cumulative normal distribution
B = day base (360 or 365)

3.1.8. Call/Put-Parity

The Call/Put-Parity describes the **relation between the price of a call and the price of an identical put** (i.e. same strike, same maturity). The possibility to rebuild every Call or Put position with a combination out of underlying and put resp. call is called call/put-parity.

Der Hauptunterschied zwischen Devisenoptionen und Aktienoptionen besteht darin, dass bei Devisenoptionen statt der üblichen kontinuierlichen Dividendenzahlung die **Fremdwährungszinsen in das Black & Scholes-Modell integriert** werden müssen. Für Devisenoptionen fließt also nicht ein risikoloser Zinssatz in die Bewertung ein, sondern der Optionspreis wird von der Höhe der Zinssätze in beiden Währungen beeinflusst.

In einem Artikel veröffentlichten Mark B. Garman und Steven W. Kohlhagen die Unterschiede in den Annahmen und der Bewertungsformel des Black & Scholes-Modells zwischen Devisen- und Aktienoptionen im Dezember 1982. Das **Garman/Kohlhagen-Modell** ist, wenn auch mit leichten Modifikationen, auch heute noch das am weitesten verbreitete Bewertungsmodell für Devisenoptionen.

1979 entwickelten auch noch Cox, Ross und Rubinstein ein Modell zur Bewertung von Zinsoptionen. Im Gegensatz zum Garman/Kohlhagen- und Black & Scholes-Modell unterstellt das **Cox-Ross-Rubinstein-Modell** eine diskrete Zufallsgröße, d.h., es unterstellt keine Normalverteilung zur Beschreibung der Kursentwicklung wie die beiden anderen Modelle, sondern eine **Binomialverteilung.**

Bei der Binomialverteilung werden jeweils zwei Zeitpunkte, nämlich der Anfangs- und Endpunkt einer Periode bzw. eines Zeitintervalls, betrachtet. Ausgehend von dem festen, aktuellen Kurs wird hierbei gefordert, dass der Kurs am Ende der Periode genau zwei Werte annehmen kann, entweder einen Maximalwert oder einen Minimalwert.

EXKURS: Die Optionspreis-Formel

Der Preis einer Call-Devisenoption errechnet sich wie folgt:

$$CALL = \frac{1}{\left(1 + r_Q \times \frac{T}{B_Q}\right)} \times \left\{\left[O \times N(d_1)\right] - S \times N(d_2)\right\}$$

$$\text{Dabei gilt:} \quad d_1 = \frac{\ln\left(\frac{O}{S}\right) + \left(0,5 \times V^2 \times T\right)}{V \times T^{\frac{1}{2}}}$$

$$d_2 = d_1 - V \times T^{0,5}$$

S = Strike
O = Outright
V = Volatilität
T = Laufzeit der Option (in Prozent eines Jahreswertes)
r_Q = Zinssatz p.a. in Dezimalen, quotierte Währung
N() = kumulative Normalverteilung
B_q = Berechnungsbasis, quotierte Währung

3.1.8. Call/Put-Parität

Die Call/Put-Parität beschreibt den **Zusammenhang zwischen dem Preis eines Calls und dem Preis eines sonst identen Puts** (d.h. gleicher Strike, gleiche Laufzeit). Durch diesen Zusammenhang kann aus einem Call durch die Kombination mit dem Basiswert eine synthetische Put-Position produziert werden (und umgekehrt).

Diagrams of Synthetic Options Positions

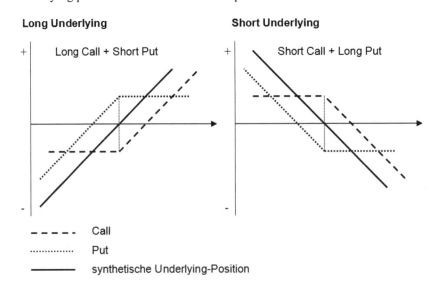

There are the following connections for describing **synthetical option positions**:

Long Put	+	Buy Outright	=	**Long Call**
Long Call	+	Sell Outright	=	**Long Put**
Short Put	+	Sell Outright	=	**Short Call**
Short Call	+	Buy Outright	=	**Short Put**

Diagrams of Synthetic Underlying Positions

Also underlying positions can be rebuilt with options.

Grafische Darstellung von synthetischen Optionspositionen

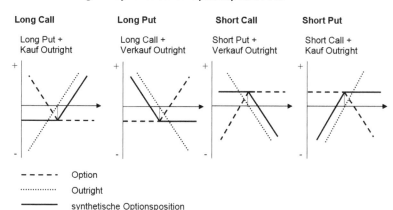

Es gelten also folgende Zusammenhänge, um **synthetische Optionspositionen** darzustellen:

Long Put	+	Kauf Outright	=	**Long Call**
Long Call	+	Verkauf Outright	=	**Long Put**
Short Put	+	Verkauf Outright	=	**Short Call**
Short Call	+	Kauf Outright	=	**Short Put**

Grafische Darstellung von synthetischen Underlyingpositionen

Underlying-Positionen können auch über Optionen nachgebildet werden.

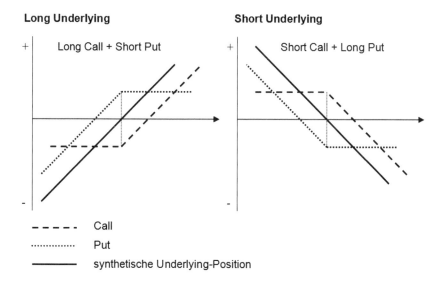

Es gelten demnach folgende Zusammenhänge, um eine Underlying-Position synthetisch abzubilden:

Short Put	+	Long Call	=	**Long Underlying**
Short Call	+	Long Put	=	**Short Underlying**

There are the following connections for describing a synthetical underlying position:

Short Put   +   Long Call   =   **Long Underlying**
Short Call +   Long Put   =   **Short Underlying**

The call/put-parity can be used for option price calculations. If the parity is not kept arbitrage will be possible.

Generally you have the following rules:

$$\text{Call} = \text{Put} + \frac{(O - S)}{\left(1 + \left(r_G \times \dfrac{T}{B_G}\right)\right)} \qquad\qquad \text{Put} = \text{Call} + \frac{(S - O)}{\left(1 + \left(r_G \times \dfrac{T}{B_G}\right)\right)}$$

O = outright
S = strike
rG = interest rate variable currency
T = days
BG = day basis variable currency (360 or 365)

The put price can be derived from arbitrage considerations. With a call and selling the underlying you can build a risk profile that is the same as for a put. Note: it has to be a European style option.

Example

You are looking for a price for a USD Put CHF Call 1.4600.
Premium USD Call 1.4600:   0.0552
Spot: 1.4500
Outright: 1.4714
Interest rate quote currency: 2.50%
Period: 90 days
Base: 360

$$putprice = 0.0552 + \frac{(1.46 - 1.4714)}{1 + 0.025x\dfrac{90}{360}} = 0.043870807 = 0.0439 CHF$$

If the market price of the Put with Strike 1.4600 is, e.g. 0.0450, a risk-free profit can be realised by selling the Put, selling the outright and buying the Call.

Spot rate at expiry	Premium	1.3000	1.4000	1.5000	1.6000
Sell put 1.46	+0.0450	-0.1600	-0.0600	–	–
Sell outright at 1.4714	-0.0552	+0.1714	+ 0.0714	-0.0286	-0.1286
Buy call 1.46		–	–	+0.0400	+0.1400
Total premium	-0.0102				
Total premium incl. interests	-0.0103	-0.0103	-0.0103	-0.0103	-0.0103
Total		**+ 0.0011**	**+ 0.0011**	**+0.0011**	**+0.0011**

Die Call/Put-Parität kann zur Preisbestimmung von Optionen herangezogen werden. Wird die Beziehung nicht eingehalten, ist Arbitrage möglich.

Grundsätzlich gelten folgende Regeln:

$$\text{Call} = \text{Put} + \frac{(O - S)}{\left(1 + \left(r_G \times \dfrac{T}{B_G}\right)\right)} \qquad \text{Put} = \text{Call} + \frac{(S - O)}{\left(1 + \left(r_G \times \dfrac{T}{B_G}\right)\right)}$$

O = Outright (Terminkurs)
S = Strike
rG = Zinssatz Gegenwährung
T = Tage
BG = Basis Gegenwährung (360 od. 365)

Der Preis des Puts kann allein aus Arbitrageüberlegungen abgeleitet werden. Durch den Verkauf des Basiswertes und eines Calls kann ein Gewinnprofil erstellt werden, das sich genauso auswirkt wie ein Put. Voraussetzung hierzu ist jedoch, dass es sich um eine europäische Option handelt.

Beispiel

Es wird der Preis eines USD Put CHF Call 1,4600 gesucht.
Preis USD Call 1,4600: 0,0552
Kassa: 1,4500
Outright: 1,4714
Zinssatz Gegenwährung: 2,50%
Laufzeit: 90 Tage
Berechnungsmethode: 360

$$\text{PreisPut} = 0,0552 + \frac{(1,46 - 1,4714)}{1 + 0,025 * \dfrac{90}{360}} = 0,043870807 = 0,0439 \; CHF$$

Liegt der Marktpreis des Puts mit Strike 1,4600 beispielsweise bei 0,0450, kann über den Verkauf des Puts und den gleichzeitigen Verkauf auf Termin und Kauf des Calls ein risikoloser Gewinn realisiert werden.

Kassa beim Auslaufen der Position	Prämie	1,3000	1,4000	1,5000	1,6000
Verkauf Put 1,4600	+ 0,0450	- 0,1600	- 0,0600	0	0
Verkauf Termin zu 1,4714		+ 0,1714	+ 0,0714	- 0,0286	- 0,1286
Kauf Call 1,4600	- 0,0552	0	0	+ 0,0400	+ 0,1400
Summe Prämie	- 0,0102				
Summe Prämien inkl. Zinsen	- 0,0103	- 0,0103	- 0,0103	- 0,0103	- 0,0103
Gesamt		**+ 0,0011**	**+ 0,0011**	**+ 0,0011**	**+ 0,0011**

As the theoretic Put price is 11 BP cheaper than the market price, these 11 BP can be arbitraged.

Note: The options premium has to be paid in the beginning of the option period, the results from option and outright turn up in the end of the option period. Therefore the (in this case) paid premium has to be compounded for the option period.

As the result of 11 BP turns up in the end of the option period, it has to be discounted for today.

3.2. Risk Factors

The profit and loss results described so far always assume that the option is held till expiry. On the following pages we describe the factors influencing the options position **during the term of the option**.

3.2.1. Delta and Delta Hedging

If the underlying price increases, the Call price increases too. The Delta of a Call shows by how much the Call price increases if the underlying increases.

$$\text{DELTA} = \frac{\text{Change in option price}}{\text{Change in underlying}}$$

The Delta shows the **change in the option price once there is a small change in the underlying**. Mathematically the Delta is the first derivation of the option price formula by the underlying. As the Call changes in the same direction as the underlying, the Delta of a Call is positive. By similar reasoning, the Delta of a Put is negative.

The Delta of an option has values in the range of **-1 and +1** (resp. -100% and +100%).

- OTM options: absolute delta from 0 to 0,5
- ITM options: absolute delta from 0,5 to 1
- ATM options: absolute delta is approx. 0,5

A Call with a Delta of 1, implies that the option price increases by 1 unit. A Delta of 0, means that there is no change in the option price if the underlying price changes.

For the different option types the following Deltas can be observed:

Delta sign	Call	Put
Long options	(+)	(−)
Short options	(−)	(+)

Example
A Delta of +0.5 (50%) for a GBP/USD Call means that if GBP/USD increases by 1 Cent, the Call price increases by 0.5 Cent.

Da der theoretische Put-Preis um 11 Punkte billiger ist als der im Markt quotierte Preis, können diese 11 Basispunkte jederzeit arbitriert werden.

Anmerkung: Die Optionsprämie ist zu Beginn der Laufzeit zu zahlen, die Ergebnisse der Option und des Termingeschäftes fallen dagegen erst am Ende der Laufzeit an. Daher muss die (in diesem Fall) bezahlte Prämie auf die Laufzeit der Option aufgezinst werden.

3.2. Risikokennzahlen

Die bisherigen Ausführungen beziehen sich nur auf die Situation bei Auslaufen der Option. Im Folgenden soll versucht werden, die Faktoren zu beschreiben, die den Optionspreis **während der Laufzeit** (d.h. vor Auslaufen der Option) beeinflussen, und es soll gezeigt werden, wie diese Faktoren gemessen werden können.

3.2.1. Delta und Delta Hedging

Der Preis eines Calls steigt (fällt), wenn der zugrundeliegende Basiswert steigt (fällt). Der Preis eines Puts steigt (fällt), wenn der zugrundeliegende Basiswert fällt (steigt). Um zu wissen, um wie viel der Preis steigt oder fällt, bedient man sich des **Delta-Wertes**.

$$DELTA = \frac{\ddot{A}nderung\ des\ Optionpreises}{\ddot{A}nderung\ des\ Basiswertes}$$

Das Delta misst die **Änderung des Optionspreises unter der Annahme einer kleinen Änderung im Basiswert.** Mathematisch gesehen ist dieser Delta-Wert die erste Ableitung der Optionspreisfunktion nach dem Basiswert. Da sich der Preis des Calls mit dem gleichen Vorzeichen entwickelt wie der Basiswert, ist das Delta des Calls positiv. Analog kommt man zum Schluss, dass das Delta eines Puts negativ sein muss.

Das Delta kann Werte **zwischen -1 und +1** (bzw. -100% und +100%) annehmen.

Grundsätzlich gilt:

- OTM-Optionen: absolutes Delta von 0 bis 0,5
- ITM-Optionen: absolutes Delta von 0,5 bis 1
- ATM-Optionen: Delta von ca. 0,5

Ein Call mit einem Delta von 1 heißt, dass sich der Wert des Calls um eine Einheit erhöht, wenn sich der Preis des Underlyings um eine Einheit erhöht. Ein Delta von 0 bedeutet, dass der Optionspreis sich nicht verändert, wenn der Basiswert sich verändert. Eine Kassaposition beispielsweise hat ein Delta von +1.

Das Delta wird auch häufig **„Ausübungswahrscheinlichkeit"** genannt, d.h., das Delta gibt darüber Auskunft, wie hoch heute die Wahrscheinlichkeit ist, dass die Option am Fälligkeitstag ausgeübt wird.

Delta-Vorzeichen	Call	Put
Long Optionen	(+)	(−)
Short Optionen	(−)	(+)

Beispiel

Ein Delta von +0,5 (50%) bei einem Call zeigt an, dass der Optionspreis 50% der Kassabewegung mitmacht. Steigt beispielsweise der Kassakurs GBP/USD um 1 Cent, so steigt der Call-Preis um 0,5 Cent.

Delta Hedging

Delta plays also an important role in hedging. Delta Hedging is the **hedging of an option position by a position in the underlying**. The gain/loss of the option is offset by the loss/gain in the underlying. The amount of the underlying is calculated by multiplying Delta with the number of option contracts.

In order to Delta-hedge a long Call or short Put you sell the underlying, for a short Call and long Put you buy the underlying.

Example

You have bought a USD Call/ CHF Put USD 1,000,000, Strike 1.3600. The Delta is 0.5. What is your Delta-hedge?
1. Options position: long USD call
2. With a long Call you are long the underlying, amount = volume x delta, i.e. 1,000,000 x 0.5 = USD 500,000.
3. So you are long spot USD 500,000.
4. Therefore you have to sell USD 500,000 in the spot market.

Therefore:

	Call		Put	
	long/buy	short/sell	long/buy	short/sell
Underlying:	**long**	**short**	**short**	**long**
Delta Hedge:	**sell**	**buy**	**buy**	**sell**

3.2.2. Gamma

As the Delta shows the change in the option price for a small change in the underlying, it can only serve as a snapshot calculation. The next question is, how Delta changes if the price of the underlying changes. This factor is called **Gamma**.

$$Gamma = \frac{Change\ in\ delta}{Change\ in\ underlying}$$

Since Gamma measures the change of Delta it is strongest where Delta is most volatile. This is at-the-money and with short time to maturity. Is Delta near 0 or (+/-) 1, a change in the underlying does not influence considerably the Delta position since the option stays still deep out-of-the-money or in-the-money. The Gamma shows the **expected change in Delta for a small change in the price of the underlying**.

Delta can be compared to the speed and Gamma to the acceleration. Gamma can also be taken as a measure of stability of the Delta.

Delta Hedging
Delta spielt auch im Rahmen des Risikomanagements bei Optionen eine bedeutende Rolle. Delta Hedging ist die **Absicherung einer Optionsposition mit einer Kassaposition.** Der Verlust/Gewinn der Optionsposition wird durch den Gewinn/Verlust der Kassaposition ausgeglichen. Der Betrag in der Kassaposition wird über das Delta ermittelt, indem das Gesamtvolumen des Optionsgeschäftes mit dem Delta multipliziert wird.

Es wird das Risiko abgesichert, das mit einer gewissen Wahrscheinlichkeit (Delta) durch die Ausübung der Option am Fälligkeitstag entsteht.

Bei einem Long Call und Short Put sind Sie long im Underlying, d.h., Sie müssen im Hedge in der Kassa verkaufen. Bei einem Short Call und Long Put sind Sie short im Underlying, d.h., Sie müssen im Hedge kaufen.

Beispiel

Sie haben einen USD Call CHF Put über USD 1.000.000 mit Strike 1,3600 gekauft. Das Delta Ihrer Position ist 0,5. Wie sieht Ihr Delta-Hedge aus?
1. Optionsposition: long USD Call
2. Bei long Call Positionen sind Sie long im Underlying, und zwar in Höhe von Volumen x Delta, d.h. 1.000.000 x 0,5 = USD 500.000. Sie sind also long USD 500.000 in der Kassa.
3. Als Hedge müssen Sie also USD 500.000 in der Kassa verkaufen.

Grundsätzlich gilt:

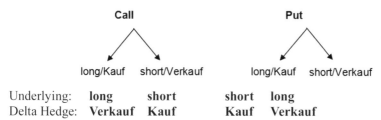

	Call			**Put**	
	long/Kauf	short/Verkauf		long/Kauf	short/Verkauf
Underlying:	**long**	**short**	**short**	**long**	
Delta Hedge:	**Verkauf**	**Kauf**	**Kauf**	**Verkauf**	

3.2.2. Gamma

Das Delta misst die Änderung des Optionspreises bei einer kleinen Änderung des Basiswertes. Daher ist es nur als Momentaufnahme interpretierbar. Das Delta verändert sich, wenn sich der Ausübungspreis ändert. Diese Kenngröße wird **Gamma** genannt.

$$GAMMA = \frac{\ddot{A}nderung\ im\ Delta}{\ddot{A}nderung\ des\ Basiswertes}$$

Das Gamma zeigt **die erwartete Änderung im Delta bei einer kleinen Änderung im Basiswert.** Bildlich gesehen entspricht das Delta der Geschwindigkeit, während das Gamma die Beschleunigung zeigen soll. Das Gamma kann auch als Kenngröße, die die Stabilität vom Delta bemisst, verstanden werden.

Da Gamma die Änderungsrate des Deltas ist, wirkt Gamma dort am stärksten, wo sich das Delta am schnellsten verändert. Das ist bei Optionen am Geld und mit kurzer Laufzeit der Fall.

Bei einem Delta von nahe 0 oder (+/-) 1 hat eine Veränderung des Wechselkurses keine besonderen Auswirkungen auf die Deltaposition, weil die Option weiter tief aus bzw. im Geld bleibt.

Gamma sign	Call	Put
Long options	(+)	(+)
Short options	(−)	(−)

Gamma has the strongest effect for

- **ATM** options and
- Options with a **short** period.

3.2.3. Theta

The longer the term, the more expensive the option. Therefore the price of an option has to decrease with the lapse of time (all other factors being stable).

$$THETA \ = \ \frac{change \ in \ option \ price}{time \ decay}$$

Theta is strongest for at-the-money and short-term options. Theta is for short time to maturities very strong (= time decay very high). If the life of the option is reduced by one day it will have little influence on the option price if the remaining time is one year. If though the remaining term is very short, the time value of the option deteriorates very quickly. In case of one day to maturity the whole time value is gone at the following day.

For deep in-the-money options the premium consists mainly of the intrinsic value, for deep out-of-the-money value a symbolic premium is paid. In both cases the time value of the option is very low and changes in the time to maturity have negligible influence on the option price.

The **change in the option price with the passage of time** is Called Theta. A positive Theta means, that the value of the option position is getting better as time goes on. A negative Theta means that with time passage, the position value decreases.

Theta sign	Call	Put
Long options (premium paid)	(−)	(−)
Short options (premium received)	(+)	(+)

Theta has the strongest effect for

- **ATM** options and
- Options with a **short** period

3.2.4. Vega (Kappa)

One of the most important influencing factors on the option price is the **volatility**. The question in risk measurement is, how much a change in volatility implies a change in the option price. This change is called Vega (or Kappa).

$$Kappa = \frac{Change \ in \ option \ price}{Change \ in \ volatility}$$

A **positive Vega** (long option) tells us that the option position is improving in value if volatility increases. A **negative Vega** (short option) means that we are losing in our option val-

Gamma-Vorzeichen	Call	Put
Long Optionen	(+)	(+)
Short Optionen	(–)	(–)

Gamma wirkt also am stärksten bei

- **ATM**-Optionen und
- Optionen mit **kurzer** Laufzeit

3.2.3. Theta

Optionen sind umso teurer, je länger ihre Laufzeit ist. Dies führt dazu, dass der Preis der Option über die Zeit bis zum Fälligkeitstag abnimmt, wenn sich die sonstigen Faktoren nicht verändern.

$$THETA = \frac{\ddot{A}nderung\ des\ Optionspreises}{Verk\ddot{u}rzung\ der\ Laufzeit}$$

Die **Änderung des Optionspreises im Zeitablauf** wird mit der Kennzahl Theta gemessen. Ein positives Theta sagt aus, dass sich der Wert der Optionsposition im Zeitablauf verbessert (verkaufte Optionen → Prämie erhalten), ein negatives Theta bedeutet, dass im Zeitablauf der Positionswert schlechter wird (gekaufte Optionen → Prämie gezahlt).

Wie auch Gamma ist Theta am stärksten für Optionen am Geld und mit kurzen Laufzeiten. Bei kurzen Laufzeiten ist Theta sehr stark (= Zeitwertverfall sehr groß). Eine Verkürzung der Optionslaufzeit um einen Tag wird nur einen sehr geringen Einfluss auf den Preis einer Option mit einer Gesamtlaufzeit von einem Jahr haben. Ist die Optionslaufzeit jedoch sehr kurz, so verfällt der Zeitwert der Option sehr schnell; bei einer Option mit einem Tag Restlaufzeit ist am nächsten Tag der gesamte Zeitwert verfallen.

Ist die Option tief im Geld, so besteht die Prämie hauptsächlich aus dem inneren Wert, bei Optionen tief aus dem Geld wird nur eine sehr niedrige „Anstandsprämie" bezahlt. In beiden Fällen ist der Zeitwert der Option sehr gering und der Einfluss der Laufzeit auf den Optionspreis niedrig.

Die Vorzeichen beim Theta verhalten sich genau umgekehrt wie beim Gamma.

Theta-Vorzeichen	Call	Put
Long Optionen	(–)	(–)
Short Optionen	(+)	(+)

Theta wirkt also am stärksten bei

- **ATM**-Optionen und
- Optionen mit **kurzer** Laufzeit

3.2.4. Vega (Kappa)

Einer der wichtigsten Einflussfaktoren der Optionspreise ist die **Volatilität.** Für die Risikomessung ergibt sich die Frage, wie eine Änderung der Volatilität den Optionspreis verändert. Diese Veränderung wird über die Kennzahl Vega (auch Kappa genannt) gemessen.

$$VEGA(Kappa) = \frac{\ddot{A}nderung\ des\ Optionspreises}{\ddot{A}nderung\ der\ Volatilit\ddot{a}t}$$

Ein **positives Vega** sagt aus, dass die Optionsposition sich verbessert, wenn die Volatilität im Markt ansteigt. Ein **negatives Vega** bedeutet, dass die Optionsposition bei steigender

uation as the volatility decreases. Higher volatilities lead to higher Call and Put premiums. For the seller of options this means that he is losing money and that the buyer of options is gaining money if volatility increases. For deep in-the-money options the premium consists mainly of the intrinsic value. Since the intrinsic value does not change if the volatility changes, a change of the volatility does not influence the option price strongly in this case.

Also deep out the money options are hardly influenced by volatility changes since the low premium will not change if the insecurity in the markets rise.

Vega sign	Call	Put
Long options	(+)	(+)
Short options	(−)	(−)

Vega has the strongest effect for

- **ATM** options and
- options with a **long** period

Option strategies are often described by their volatility view. According to this, volatility is "bought" or "sold". Buying volatility means that you profit from an increase in volatility; to sell volatility means that you profit from a decline in volatility. If volatility is the only undetermined measure in the option pricing formula, most option strategies may be reduced to views about the volatility.

3.2.5. Epsilon (Rho)

As shown in the section on option pricing, interest rates (of both currencies) have an influence on the option price. The epsilon of FX options shows the **influence of a change in interest differential on the option premium**.

$$EPSILON \ (RHO) \ = \ \frac{Change \ in \ option \ price}{Change \ in \ interest \ rate}$$

Price change	Call	Put
Base interest rate ↗	(−)	(+)
Base interest rate ↘	(+)	(−)
Variable interest rate ↗	(+)	(−)
Variable interest rate ↘	(−)	(+)

Epsilon (Rho) has the strongest effect for

- **ITM** options and
- Options with **long** periods

Epsilon (Rho) is not unambiguous, as sometimes it is calculated with interest rate of base currency, sometimes with interest rate of quoted currency and sometimes on interest difference.

Volatilität schlechter wird. Steigende Volatilität führt dazu, dass sowohl Put- als auch Call-Prämien teurer werden. Für den Verkäufer der Option bedeutet das somit eine Verschlechterung seiner Position, für den Käufer eine Verbesserung seiner Position.

Die Prämie, die ein Optionskäufer für eine Option zu zahlen hat, ist umso höher, je länger die Laufzeit dieser Option ist. Dadurch hat eine gegebene Volatilitätsänderung (z.B. 1%) einen stärkeren Einfluss auf Optionen mit längerer Laufzeit verglichen mit Optionen mit kurzer Laufzeit.

Für Optionen, die sehr stark im Geld sind, ist die Optionsprämie fast ausschließlich der innere Wert. Da sich der innere Wert nicht verändert, wenn sich die Volatilität verändert, hat eine Änderung der Volatilität kaum Einfluss auf den Optionspreis. Bei Optionen sehr weit aus dem Geld ist die zu zahlende Prämie sehr gering. Auch hier wird sich diese „Anstandsprämie" kaum verändern, wenn sich die Unsicherheit im Markt verändert.

Vega-Vorzeichen	Call	Put
Long Optionen	(+)	(+)
Short Optionen	(–)	(–)

Vega (Kappa) wirkt also am stärksten bei

- **ATM**-Optionen und
- Optionen mit **langer** Laufzeit.

Im Markt werden Optionsstrategien auch sehr oft nur durch die zugrundeliegende Volatilitätserwartung gehandelt. So wird Volatilität „gekauft" oder „verkauft". Volatilität kaufen heißt, dass von einem Anstieg der Volatilität profitiert wird. Volatilität verkaufen heißt, dass man von einem Rückgang der Volatilität profitiert. Da die Volatilität die einzige Größe in der Optionsformel ist, die nicht bestimmt ist, sondern zukünftige Erwartungen widerspiegelt, sind die meisten Optionsstrategien auf Volatilitätserwartungen zurückzuführen.

3.2.5. Epsilon (Rho)

Auch die Zinsen (in beiden Währungen) beeinflussen die Optionspreise. Die Kennzahl Epsilon drückt bei Devisenoptionen aus, **wie sich der Wert der Option** (oder des Optionsportefeuilles) **verändert, wenn sich die Zinsen verändern.**

$$EPSILON(Rho) = \frac{\text{Änderung des Optionspreises}}{\text{Änderung des Zinssatzes}}$$

Vega-Vorzeichen	Call	Put
Zinssatz quot. Whg. ↗	(–)	(+)
Zinssatz quot. Whg. ↘	(+)	(–)
Zinssatz Gegenwhg. ↗	(+)	(–)
Zinssatz Gegenwhg. ↘	(–)	(+)

Epsilon (Rho) wirkt am stärksten bei

- **ITM**-Optionen und
- Optionen mit **langer** Laufzeit.

Diese Kennzahl wird manchmal auf den Zinssatz der ersten Währung, manchmal auf den Zinssatz der zweiten Währung und manchmal auf die Zinsdifferenz dargestellt. **Daher ist sie nicht eindeutig!**

3.3. Skew and Risk Reversal

3.3.1. The "Skew" of Implied Volatility ("Smile Curve")

"Skew" means that the market quotes **different implied volatilities** for different strike prices.

The reason for this "skew" is that options with certain strikes might be favoured in the market. Market participants will always buy options which earn the maximum profit when markets move as expected. If the market expects a rate rise, OTM calls (i.e. options with higher strikes) will be favoured, if the market expects the rate to fall, OTM puts (i.e. options with lower strikes) will be favoured.

Therefore – when believing in **rising** rates and thus due to increasing demand– the implied volatilities for higher strikes will be higher than for lower strikes. As in the interbank options market only OTM options ("low deltas") are traded, in this case the low delta calls (regarding the base currency) are favoured compared to the low delta puts ("calls over puts").

If the market expects rates to **fall**, the demand for lower strikes will increase ("puts over calls").

If the market participants expect stronger fluctuations in prices **in both directions**, both higher strikes (low delta calls) and lower strikes (low delta puts) will be favoured with no particular preference for one or the other direction.

If **hardly any fluctuations** are expected, market participants are not willing to pay premiums for far-away strikes, low delta calls and puts are not interesting.

Illustration of typical volatility curves for different market expectations:

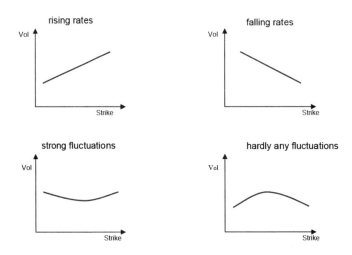

In practice you can often also find combinations of these volatility curves.

3.3. Skew und Risk Reversal

3.3.1. Der „Skew" der impliziten Volatilität („Smile Curve")

Unter „Skew" versteht man, dass für verschiedene Strike-Preise **unterschiedliche implizite Volatilitäten im Markt** quotiert werden.

Der Grund liegt in der unterschiedlichen Nachfragesituation für Optionen mit bestimmten Strike-Preisen. Die Marktteilnehmer werden jeweils jene Option kaufen, mit der sie bei Eintreten ihrer Erwartung einen maximalen Gewinn erzielen können. Bei einem erwarteten Kursanstieg des Basiswertes sind dies OTM-Calls (d.h. Optionen mit hohen Strikes), bei einem Kursrückgang OTM-Puts (d.h. Optionen mit niedrigen Strikes).

Glaubt der Markt an **steigende Kurse** des Währungspaares, so werden die Strikes, die über dem aktuellen Niveau liegen, gefragter sein als die niedrigeren. Aufgrund der Nachfrage liegen hier die impliziten Volatilitäten höher als bei den niedrigeren Strikes. Da im Interbank-Optionshandel grundsätzlich nur OTM-Optionen („low deltas") gehandelt werden, sind in diesem Fall die low delta Calls (bezogen auf die quotierte Währung) gefragter als die low delta Puts („Calls over Puts").

Erwartet der Markt **fallende Kurse**, so steigt die Nachfrage nach Strikes, die unter dem aktuellen Niveau liegen („Puts over Calls").

Gehen die Marktteilnehmer von **stärkeren Schwankungen** in beide Richtungen – vom aktuellen Niveau aus gesehen – aus, werden sowohl die höheren (low delta Calls) als auch die niedrigeren Strikes (low delta Puts) begehrt sein. Der Markt bevorzugt hier keine der beiden Seiten.

Werden **kaum Kursschwankungen** erwartet, sind die Marktteilnehmer nicht bereit, Prämien für weiter vom aktuellen Niveau entfernte Strikes aufzuwenden; das Interesse an low delta Optionen (Calls und Puts) fällt.

Nachfolgend finden Sie die grafische Darstellung der typischen Volakurven bei unterschiedlicher Marktmeinung:

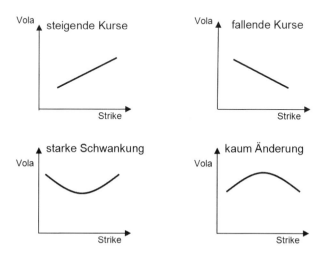

Generell findet man in der Praxis auch immer wieder Mischformen dieser typischen Volatilitätskurven.

The reason for the favouring and thus higher implied volatilities for certain strikes lies in the impact of the gamma-curve on the position.

When trading on certain price moves one should always go with an **ascending gamma-curve**, i.e. gamma should increase when reaching expected spot levels, not decrease. Gamma expresses by how much Delta changes when the underlying rate changes. Gamma is highest for ATM options.

For example a long call has a positive delta and profits from a rise of the underlying rate. Additionally the positive gamma of the long position leads to an increasing delta when rates rise (acceleration of profits). An OTM call moves in "ATM-direction" when rates rise. Thus gamma increases and the acceleration gets even stronger, i.e. you have an ascending gamma-curve.

Therefore:

When expecting **rising** rates → **buy** options with **higher** strikes (OTM calls)

When expecting **falling** rates → **buy** options with **lower** strikes (OTM puts)

3.3.2. Risk Reversal

These different expectations can be traded in the interbank options market. The quotation of a **risk reversal** expresses whether calls („upside") or puts („downside") are favoured. The quotation shows whether the market participants expect an upward move, a downward move or no particular move in one direction (viewed from the actual level).

A risk reversal is a **spread strategy**, i.e. one option is bought and another one is sold. It is always a (OTM) call and a (OTM) put, i.e. either one buys the call and sells the put or sells the call and buys the put. Usually both options have the same delta, e.g. 25%.

The quotation is in volatility. But not the whole volatility for each option is traded but only the difference (spread) between both volatilities.

Example
A quotation for a EUR/USD risk reversal might be: 3-monats R/R 25 delta 0.5 – 0.8 calls over First one can easily see that the 25 delta calls are favoured and thus have to be calculated with a higher implied volatility. The spread 0.5-0.8 is a bid and offer quotation (based on the favoured option), i.e. if one sells the call and buys the put, the volatility of the call lies 0.5% above the volatility of the put. If one buys the call and sells the put, the volatility of the call lies 0.8% above the volatility of the put.

Der Grund für die Favorisierung und damit für die höheren impliziten Volatilitäten für bestimmte Strikes liegt in der Auswirkung der Gamma-Kurve auf die Position.

Beim „Trading auf Kursbewegungen" sollte man sich immer auf einer **ansteigenden Gamma-Kurve** bewegen, d.h., das Gamma sollte bei der erwarteten Spot-Bewegung ansteigen und nicht abfallen. Das Gamma drückt aus, um wie viel sich das Delta bei einer Änderung des Kurses des Basiswertes ändert und ist bei ATM-Optionen am höchsten.

Beispielsweise hat eine Long-Call-Position ein positives Delta und profitiert daher von einem Anstieg des Kurses des Underlyings. Zusätzlich führt das positive Gamma der Long-Position dazu, dass das Delta bei einem Kursanstieg des Underlyings weiter ansteigt, wodurch sich die Gewinne beschleunigen. Eine OTM-Call-Option geht bei einem Anstieg des Underlyings „in Richtung ATM", wodurch das Gamma steigt und sich die Beschleunigung sogar noch erhöht, d.h., man befindet sich auf einer ansteigenden Gamma-Kurve.

Daher gilt grundsätzlich:

Bei Erwartung **steigender** Kurse → **Kauf** von Optionen mit **höherem** Strike (OTM-Calls).

Bei Erwartung **fallender** Kurse → **Kauf** von Optionen mit **niedrigerem** Strike (OTM-Puts).

3.3.2. Risk Reversal

Diese verschiedenen Markterwartungen sind auch im Interbank-Optionsmarkt handelbar. Ein **Risk Reversal** drückt in seiner Quotierung aus, ob die Calls („upside") oder die Puts („downside") stärker nachgefragt („gefavoured") werden. Daran kann man erkennen, ob der Markt eine Bewegung nach oben (vom aktuellen Niveau her betrachtet), nach unten oder in keine eindeutige Richtung erwartet.

Bei einem Risk Reversal handelt es sich um eine **Spread-Strategie**, d.h., eine Option wird gekauft und eine andere verkauft. Dabei handelt es sich immer um einen (OTM)-Call und einen (OTM)-Put, d.h., entweder kauft man den Call und verkauft den Put, oder man verkauft den Call und kauft den Put. Üblicherweise haben beide Optionen das gleiche Delta, z.B. 25%.

Die Quotierung erfolgt in Volatilität. Allerdings wird nicht die Volatilität der einzelnen Optionen selbst angezeigt, sondern lediglich der Unterschied („Spread") zwischen beiden.

Beispiel

Eine Quotierung für ein Risk Reversal für EUR/USD könnte lauten:
3-Monats-R/R 25 Delta 0,5 – 0,8 Calls over.
An dieser Quotierung erkennt man zunächst, dass die 25 Delta Calls „gefavoured" sind, also begehrter sind als die 25 Delta Puts und damit auch mit einer höheren impliziten Volatilität gerechnet werden müssen. Um wie viel höher, zeigt der Spread: 0,5 – 0,8 ist eine Geld- und Briefquotierung aus Sicht der nachgefragten Option, d.h., verkauft man den Call und kauft den Put, liegt die Volatilität des Calls um 0,5% über der des Puts, kauft man den Call und verkauft den Put, liegt die Volatilität um 0,8% über der des Puts.

For our example volatilities would be (starting from a volatility level of 11.0%):

Sell risk reversal at +0.5
→ sell call 25 delta at vol 11.5%
→ buy put 25 delta at vol 11.0%

Buy risk reversal at +0.8
→ buy call 25 delta at vol 11.8%
→ sell put 25 delta at vol 11.0%

Summary

An FX option gives the option buyer the right to buy (call option) or sell (put option) a defined currency amount at an agreed rate (strike price) and at expiry date. The seller of an option has the obligation to buy (or to sell) a defined currency amount at an agreed rate at expiry date. For this obligation he receives a premium.

A European-style option is an option that can only be exercised on the expiry date. An American-style option is an option that can be exercised at any trading day during the life of the option (usually with exchange-traded options). A Bermudan-style option can only be exercised at certain dates during the option period. It is a mix of European and American style options.

An option at-the-money (ATM) has a strike price around the actual market rate. An option is in-the-money (ITM) if the strike is "better" than the market rate. An option is out-of-the-money (OTM) if the market rate is "better" than the strike rate.

FX options are almost exclusively traded OTC ("over the counter"). As opposed to exchange-traded options where only standardized periods and strikes can be traded there are no restrictions in the OTC market.

By combining call or put and buy or sell one gets four basic positions: long call (buy call), short call (sell call), long put (buy put) and short put (sell put).

In recent years further to European- and American-style options a number of different variants of options have been developed. These mutations are called exotic options.

Asian options refer to the average rate of the underlying exchange rate that exist during the life of the option. A compound option is an option on an option: the buyer has the right to buy a plain vanilla call or put option with a predetermined strike at a predetermined date and at a predetermined price (i.e. the options premium).

Barrier options (trigger options) are standard options with an additional barrier (trigger) level. The options right ceases to exist (respectively starts to exist) once the spot rate reaches the barrier level. As barrier options might expire prematurely (respectively they might never start to exist), these options are always cheaper than plain vanilla options. A knock-out option is a standard option, which expires worthless if a formerly specified exchange rate (barrier, trigger) is dealt in the spot market before expiration. In the knock-in option the spot rate moves towards "out-of-the-money" in order to reach the "instrike", i.e. the option is OTM when the barrier is hit. A knock-in option is a standard option, which only starts to exist if a formerly specified exchange rate (barrier, trigger) is dealt in the spot market before expiration.

A digital option is a transaction where a specified amount will be paid if the spot rate is above the strike at expiry for calls (or below the strike for puts). Usually the interven-

Für unser Beispiel würde demnach – bei einem angenommenen Volatilitätsniveau von 11% – gelten:

Verkauf Risk Reversal mit +0,5
→ Verkauf Call 25 Delta mit Vola 11,5%
→ Kauf Put 25 Delta mit Vola 11%

Kauf Risk Reversal mit +0,8
→ Kauf Call 25 Delta mit Vola 11,8%
→ Verkauf Put 25 Delta mit Vola 11%

Zusammenfassung

Eine Option gibt dem Käufer das Recht, einen bestimmten Wert (Basiswert, Underlying) zu einem bestimmten Preis (Basispreis, Strike) und bis zu einem bestimmten Zeitpunkt (Verfalltag, Expiry Date) zu kaufen (Call, Kaufoption) bzw. zu verkaufen (Put, Verkaufsoption). Für das Einräumen des Wahlrechtes verlangt der Verkäufer der Option eine einmalige Gebühr (Prämie), die bei Abschluss (d.h. mit Valuta Spot) fällig wird.

Eine europäische oder European-style Option kann vom Käufer nur an einem Tag – dem Expiration date (Verfalltag) – ausgeübt werden. Eine amerikanische oder American-style Option kann jederzeit während der Handelszeiten bis zum Expiration Date (Verfallsdatum) ausgeübt werden. Eine Bermudian oder Bermudian-style Option kann nur an bestimmten, im Voraus definierten Terminen während der Laufzeit der Option ausgeübt werden. Sie ist also eine Mischform aus europäischer und amerikanischer Option.

Eine Option ist am Geld (at the money, ATM), wenn ihr Ausübungspreis gleich oder nahezu gleich dem aktuellen Kurs ist. Im Geld (in the money, ITM) ist eine Option, wenn der Strike „besser" als der aktuelle Marktpreis des Basiswertes ist, d.h., wenn die Option für den Käufer einen Vorteil darstellt. Aus dem Geld (out of the money, OTM) ist eine Option, wenn der Strike „schlechter" als der aktuelle Marktpreis ist.

Bei Devisenoptionen handelt es sich fast ausschließlich um OTC („over the counter")-Optionen. Im Gegensatz zu börsengehandelten Optionen, wo nur standardisierte Laufzeiten und Strikes handelbar sind, sind im OTC-Markt keine Einschränkungen gegeben. Aus der Kombination von Call bzw. Put und Kauf bzw. Verkauf ergeben sich vier mögliche Grundpositionen: Long Call (Kauf eines Calls), Short Call (Verkauf eines Calls), Long Put (Kauf eines Puts) und Short Put (Verkauf eines Puts).

In den letzten Jahren wurden zusätzlich zu den europäischen und amerikanischen Optionen eine Vielzahl von Varianten entwickelt, für die der Überbegriff „exotische Optionen" verwendet wird. Eine Asian Option unterscheidet sich nicht durch den Zeitpunkt, sondern durch die Art der Ausübung. Bei einer Asian Option erfolgt am Ende der Laufzeit eine Ausgleichszahlung basierend auf der Differenz zwischen dem Strike-Preis und einem durchschnittlichen Kurs des Basiswertes. Eine Compound Option ist eine Option auf eine Option. Somit gibt sie dem Käufer das Recht, eine Standardoption zu einem im Voraus bestimmten Preis und Zeitpunkt zu kaufen.

Barrier Optionen (Trigger Optionen) beinhalten im Unterschied zu Standardoptionen noch ein zusätzliches Kursniveau. Je nach Optionsart (Knock-out-Option bzw. Knock-in-Option) wird die Option bei Erreichen des Barriers gültig oder ungültig. Eine Knock-out-Option ist eine Standardoption, die sofort verfällt, wenn der Wechselkurs während der Laufzeit der Option den Barrier („Outstrike") erreicht. Eine Knock-in-Option ist eine Standardoption, bei der das Optionsrecht erst zu existieren beginnt, wenn der Wechselkurs während der Laufzeit der Option den Barrier („Instrike") erreicht.

Bei digitalen Optionen wird ein fixierter Betrag bezahlt, falls der Kassakurs am Verfalltag über bzw. unter einem bestimmten Kurs (Touchstrike) liegt. Im Standardfall ist

tion path of spot between the trade date and expiry is irrelevant and the determining factor whether or not the spot is above or below the strike at the time of expiry. However, there are some variants where the strike is valid during the whole life of the option. A one-touch option is a transaction where a specified amount will be paid only if spot rate is dealt at the touchstrike or an exceeding exchange rate before expiration. A double no-touch option is a transaction where a specific amount will be paid only if spot is not dealt at, or at levels exceeding the predefined two exchange rates before expiration.

These factors influence the price of the option: strike price, outright rate, term and volatility. If an option has an intrinsic value this means that the strike price is "better" than the outright rate. All calls with lower strikes than the outright rate and all puts with higher strikes than the outright rate have an intrinsic value (ITM). The option premium however is always higher than the intrinsic value. This difference is the time value. It is highest for longer option periods and higher expected fluctuations of the underlying.

The fair option price is calculated – generally speaking – using a statistical model. The main factor is the volatility as a measure for the fluctuation or uncertainty. Statistically, volatility equals the annualized standard deviation (sigma). Also for risk management calculations the standard deviation is a main factor. The volatility is the measure for the variability or the price range of the exchange rates or underlying prices. One may differentiate between historical and implied volatility. The historical volatility is calculated baes on historical data and is mainly used for risk management calculations. For calculating actual option prices the implied volatility is needed. This volatility is a measure of the market participants' expectations concerning the future price range of the underlying. In the professional FX options market, traders only trade the volatility as it is the only number which is up to the trader's opinion. Option premiums are quoted either in per cent of the base currency or in BP of the quote currency.

There are different strategies for trading with options: straddle, strangle, butterfly and spread.

A straddle is the purchase or the sale of a call and a put with the same strike. A long straddle gains with strong exchange-rate fluctuations independent of the direction. A short straddle is used if low fluctuations are expected.

A strangle is the purchase or the sale of a call and a put with different strike prices. The long strangle gains if there are strong exchange rate fluctuations independent of the direction. The short strangle gains if there are no strong exchange rate fluctuations.

A butterfly consists of a straddle and an opposite strangle. A short butterfly position gains if there are strong exchange rate fluctuations independent of the direction. The long butterfly position yields a profit if there are little to none exchange rate fluctuations.

A spread is the purchase (sale) of an option and the sale (purchase) of another option at the same time. As opposed to the straddle or strangle, this strategy is a buy and sell strategy or a strategy with only one option type. The most common spread strategy is the vertical spread. There are bull and bear spreads.

The option market started to boom with the development of option pricing models. These models determine the price of an option as a function of variables such as market data, volatility, strike price, term and interest rates. The main principle in option pricing is the calculation of the "fair option price", ie, the price where no arbitrage is possible. The best-known valuation model in option markets is the Black/Scholes Model. The differences in the assumptions and in the valuation formula of the Black Scholes Model were published

das Erreichen des Touchstrikes während der Laufzeit irrelevant. Auch hier gibt es jedoch wieder eine Reihe von Varianten, bei denen der Touchstrike üblicherweise während der gesamten Laufzeit gültig ist. Eine One-touch-Option (auch lock-in oder touch digital) zahlt einen bestimmten Betrag, falls ein fixierter Kurs während der Laufzeit erreicht wird. Eine Double-No-touch-Option zahlt einen bestimmten Betrag, falls der Kassakurs während der Laufzeit eine bestimmte Bandbreite nicht verlässt, d.h. falls keiner von zwei Touchstrikes erreicht wird.

Folgende Faktoren haben Einfluss auf den Optionspreis: Ausübungspreis, Terminkurs, Laufzeit und Volatilität. Der innere Wert einer Option ist jener Wert, um den der Strike besser als der aktuelle Terminkurs ist, d.h. jener Wert, den die Option im Geld ist. Somit haben nur Optionen im Geld einen inneren Wert. Daher kann der innere Wert nicht negativ, d.h. kleiner als 0 sein. Die Prämie einer Option ist jedoch immer höher als der innere Wert. Diese Differenz ist der sogenannte Zeitwert. Er ist umso höher, je länger die Laufzeit der Option und je höher die erwartete Schwankung des Basiswertes ist.

Der faire Optionspreis wird allgemein mittels eines statistischen Modells errechnet. Der wesentliche Einflussfaktor ist dabei die Volatilität als Maßzahl für die Schwankung bzw. die Unsicherheit. In der Statistik entspricht die Volatilität der annualisierten Standardabweichung (Sigma). Auch in der Risikomessung ist die Standardabweichung ein zentraler Faktor. Zur Bestimmung des Optionspreises wird die zukünftig erwartete Schwankung – die implizite Volatilität – verwendet. In der Risikomessung wird üblicherweise die historische Volatilität verwendet. Das ist die aus vergangenen Marktdaten errechnete Schwankung (statistisch: Standardabweichung) des Basiswertes. Optionsprämien werden nicht nur in der Gegenwährung, sondern auch in Prozent vom Volumen quotiert. In diesem Fall ist die Prämie in der quotierten Währung zu bezahlen.

Bei den Strategien wird zwischen Straddle, Strangle, Butterfly und Spread unterschieden.

Ein Straddle besteht aus einem Call und einem Put mit gleichen Strikes. Ein Long Straddle verdient auf Kursschwankungen unabhängig von der Richtung. Beim Short Straddle erwartet man geringe Kursschwankungen. Tritt die Erwartung ein, verdient man die Prämie, bei starken Schwankungen verliert man aber entsprechend mehr.

Ein Strangle besteht aus einem Call und einem Put mit unterschiedlichen Strikes. Der Long Strangle verdient auf sehr starke Kursschwankungen, unabhängig von der Richtung. Beim Short Strangle erwartet man geringe Kursschwankungen. Die Auswirkungen sind dem Long Strangle entgegengesetzt.

Ein Butterfly besteht aus einem Straddle und einem gegenläufigen Strangle. Der Short Butterfly verdient auf sehr starke Kursschwankungen, unabhängig von der Richtung. Im Gegensatz zu einem gekauften Strangle oder Straddle ist der Maximalgewinn begrenzt, da zwecks Prämienersparnis ein Strangle verkauft wird. Beim Long Butterfly erwartet man wenig Änderung in den Kursen.

Ein Spread ist der Kauf (Verkauf) einer Option bei gleichzeitigem Verkauf (Kauf) einer anderen Option. Im Gegensatz zu Straddle oder Strangle handelt es sich um eine Kauf- und Verkauf-Strategie bzw. eine Strategie, bei der nur ein Optionstyp verwendet wird. Die üblichste Spread-Strategie ist der vertikale Spread. Man unterscheidet Bull und Bear Spreads.

Der größte Durchbruch in der Optionstheorie war die Entwicklung von Optionspreismodellen. Diese Modelle bestimmen den Preis einer Option als Funktion von beobachtbaren

in an essay by Mark B. Garman and Steven W. Kohlhagen (December 1982). The Garman-Kohlhagen valuation model is still – even if slight modifications were done – the most common FX option valuation model. In 1979 Cox, Ross and Rubinstein developed a model for evaluating interest rate options. In contrast to the Garman-Kohlhagen Model and the Black-Scholes Model, the Cox, Ross and Rubinstein Model assumes a discrete random variable, i.e. it does not assume a normal distribution like the other two models but a binomial distribution.

The call/put parity describes the relation between the price of a call and the price of an identical put (i.e. same strike, same maturity). The possibility to rebuild every call or put position with a combination of underlying and put or call is called call/put parity.

The risk factors are delta and delta hedging, gamma, theta, vega (kappa) and epsilon (rho).

The delta shows the change in the option price once there is a small change in the underlying. Delta plays also an important role in hedging. Delta hedging is the hedging of an option position by a position in the underlying. The next question is: how does delta change if the price of the underlying changes. This factor is called gamma. Theta shows that the longer the term, the more expensive the option. Therefore, the price of an option has to decrease with the lapse of time (all other factors being stable). One of the most important influencing factors on the option price is the volatility. The question in risk measurement is how much a change in volatility implies a change in the option price. This change is called vega (or kappa). The epsilon of FX options shows the influence of a change in interest difference on the option premium.

"Skew" means that the market quotes different implied volatilities for different strike prices.

A risk reversal is a spread strategy, ie, one option is bought and another one is sold. It is always an (OTM) call and an (OTM) put, ie, either one buys the call and sells the put or sells the call and buys the put. The quotation is in volatility. The quotation of a risk reversal expresses whether calls ("upside") or puts ("downside") are favoured.

Variablen wie Basiswert, Volatilität, Ausübungspreis, Laufzeit und Zinssatz. Das Grundprinzip im Optionspricing ist die Berechnung des „fairen Optionspreises". Darunter kann
man jenen Preis verstehen, bei dem keine Arbitrage möglich ist. Die bekannteste Bewertungsmethode ist das Black & Scholes-Modell. In einem Artikel veröffentlichten Mark B.
Garman und Steven W. Kohlhagen die Unterschiede in den Annahmen und der Bewertungsformel des Black & Scholes-Modells zwischen Devisen- und Aktienoptionen im
Dezember 1982. Das Garman/Kohlhagen-Modell ist, wenn auch mit leichten Modifikationen, auch heute noch das am weitesten verbreitete Bewertungsmodell für Devisenoptionen. 1979 entwickelten auch noch Cox, Ross und Rubinstein ein Modell zur Bewertung
von Zinsoptionen. Im Gegensatz zum Garman/Kohlhagen- und Black & Scholes-Modell
unterstellt das Cox-Ross-Rubinstein-Modell eine diskrete Zufallsgröße, d.h., es unterstellt keine Normalverteilung zur Beschreibung der Kursentwicklung wie die beiden anderen Modelle, sondern eine Binomialverteilung.

Die Call/Put-Parität beschreibt den Zusammenhang zwischen dem Preis eines Calls und
dem Preis eines sonst identen Puts (d.h. gleicher Strike, gleiche Laufzeit). Durch diesen
Zusammenhang kann aus einem Call durch die Kombination mit dem Basiswert eine
synthetische Put-Position produziert werden (und umgekehrt).

Zu den Risikokennzahlen zählen: Delta, Gamma, Theta, Vega (Kappa) und Epsilon
(Rho). Das Delta misst die Änderung des Optionspreises unter der Annahme einer kleinen Änderung im Basiswert. Das Delta wird auch häufig „Ausübungswahrscheinlichkeit" genannt, d.h., das Delta gibt darüber Auskunft, wie hoch heute die Wahrscheinlichkeit ist, dass die Option am Fälligkeitstag ausgeübt wird. Delta spielt auch im Rahmen
des Risikomanagements bei Optionen eine bedeutende Rolle. Delta Hedging ist die Absicherung einer Optionsposition mit einer Kassaposition. Das Gamma zeigt die erwartete Änderung im Delta bei einer kleinen Änderung im Basiswert. Die Änderung des Optionspreises im Zeitablauf wird mit der Kennzahl Theta gemessen. Einer der wichtigsten
Einflussfaktoren der Optionspreise ist die Volatilität. Für die Risikomessung ergibt sich
die Frage, wie eine Änderung der Volatilität den Optionspreis verändert. Diese Veränderung wird über die Kennzahl Vega (auch Kappa genannt) gemessen. Auch die Zinsen
(in beiden Währungen) beeinflussen die Optionspreise. Die Kennzahl Epsilon drückt bei
Devisenoptionen aus, wie sich der Wert der Option (oder des Optionsportefeuilles) verändert, wenn sich die Zinsen verändern.

Unter „Skew" versteht man, dass für verschiedene Strike-Preise unterschiedliche implizite Volatilitäten im Markt quotiert werden.

Bei einem Risk Reversal handelt es sich um eine Spread-Strategie, d.h. eine Option wird
gekauft und eine andere verkauft. Ein Risk Reversal drückt in seiner Quotierung aus, ob
die Calls („upside") oder die Puts („downside") stärker nachgefragt („gefavoured") werden. Daran kann man erkennen, ob der Markt eine Bewegung nach oben (vom aktuellen
Niveau her betrachtet), nach unten oder in keine eindeutige Richtung erwartet.

3.4. Practice Questions

1. The buyer of a GBP/USD call exercises the option. What does this imply with regard to the seller of the option?
    a) He sells USD.
    b) He buys GBP.
    c) He gets the premium back from the buyer.
    d) He sells GBP.
2. Which statement concerning the buyer of a put is correct?
    a) has zero risk
    b) has limited risk
    c) has positive market expectations
    d) has unlimited (or substantial) risk
    e) All answers are false.
3. What is the intrinsic value of an option?
    a) premium plus time value
    b) price of the option
    c) premium invested at the reference interest rate
    d) depends on the remaining time to expiry
    e) difference between the strike price and the current market price of the underlying
4. Who pays the option premium?
    a) purchaser of the option
    b) clearing house
    c) broker
    d) seller of a call option
    e) seller of a put option
5. The price of the underlying is 120. The premium for a put 119 is 1.5. What is the correct time value?
6. How would you call an USD put/GBP call option with a strike of 1.6690 and a current GBP/USD forward rate of 1.6670?
    a) in the money
    b) at the money
    c) out of the money
    d) exotic option
7. Which of the statements regarding the strike price are true?
    a) The higher the strike price, the lower the call premium.
    b) The higher the strike price, the higher the call premium.
    c) The higher the strike price, the lower the put premium.
    d) The higher the strike price, the higher the put premium.
8. Which statement is correct with regard to an American-style option?
    a) The buyer can exercise at any time during the life of the option.
    b) The buyer can only exercise in the US.
    c) The buyer can only sell at maturity.
    d) The buyer can only exercise at maturity.
9. Which of the following statements is correct with regard to a European-style option?
    a) The buyer can only exercise at maturity.

3.4. Wiederholungsfragen

1. Der Käufer eines Calls GBP/USD übt die Option aus. Was bedeutet das für den Verkäufer der Option?
   a) Er verkauft USD.
   b) Er kauft GBP.
   c) Er bekommt die Prämie vom Käufer zurück.
   d) Er verkauft GBP.

2. Was trifft auf den Käufer einer Put-Option zu?
   a) Er hat kein Risiko.
   b) Er hat ein begrenztes Risiko.
   c) Er hat eine positive Markterwartung.
   d) Er hat ein unbegrenztes (bzw. substanzielles) Risiko.
   e) Keine der Möglichkeiten trifft zu.

3. Was ist der innere Wert einer Option?
   a) die Prämie plus dem Zeitwert
   b) der Preis, den Sie dafür zahlen
   c) die zum Referenzzinssatz veranlagte Prämie
   d) Er hängt von der Restlaufzeit der Option ab.
   e) die Differenz zwischen Strike und Marktpreis des Basisinstruments

4. Wer bezahlt die Optionsprämie?
   a) Optionskäufer
   b) Clearing House
   c) Broker
   d) Stillhalter eines Calls
   e) Stillhalter eines Puts

5. Der Basiswert notiert bei 120. Die Prämie für einen Put 119 ist 1,5. Wie hoch ist der Zeitwert?

6. Sie haben eine USD-Put/GBP-Call-Option mit einem Ausübungspreis von 1,6690 gekauft. Der GBP/USD-Terminkurs ist 1.6670. Wie bezeichnet man diese Option?
   a) im Geld
   b) am Geld
   c) aus dem Geld
   d) exotische Option

7. Welche der folgenden Aussagen sind richtig bezogen auf den Ausübungspreis einer Option?
   a) Je höher der Ausübungspreis, desto niedriger die Prämie des Call.
   b) Je höher der Ausübungspreis, desto höher die Prämie des Call.
   c) Je höher der Ausübungspreis, desto niedriger die Prämie des Put.
   d) Je höher der Ausübungspreis, desto höher die Prämie des Put.

8. Was trifft auf eine amerikanische Option zu?
   a) Der Käufer kann während der gesamten Laufzeit ausüben.
   b) Der Käufer kann nur in den USA ausüben.
   c) Der Käufer kann nur bei Fälligkeit verkaufen.
   d) Der Käufer kann nur bei Fälligkeit ausüben.

9. Was trifft auf eine europäische Option zu?
   a) Sie kann vom Käufer nur bei Fälligkeit ausgeübt werden.

    b) The buyer can exercise at any time during the life of the option.

    c) The contract is subject to European law.

    d) The option can only be dealt with a European counterparty.

10. What is meant by a Bermudian option?

11. What is the risk profile of a writer of a call option?

    a) limited loss potential and unlimited profit potential

    b) limited loss potential and limited profit potential

    c) unlimited loss potential and unlimited profit potential

    d) unlimited loss potential and limited profit potential

12. You think that the market is bullish. What will you do?

    a) buy a call at the money

    b) sell a put at the money

    c) buy a put at the money

    d) sell a call at the money

13. You want to profit from a rise in volatility. Which position would you take?

    a) You sell a straddle.

    b) You buy a butterfly.

    c) You buy a straddle.

    d) You sell put options.

    e) You sell a butterfly.

    f) You sell call options.

14. What is a risk reversal?

    a) long call plus short underlying

    b) long call and short put with same absolute delta, different strikes and same term

    c) option strategy in which the other counterparty bears all risks

    d) long call and long put with different strikes and same term

15. What expectations of volatility does a trader have if he chooses a short strangle position?

    a) He buys volatility because he expects volatility to fall.

    b) He thinks volatility will increase slightly.

    c) He thinks volatility will fall slightly.

    d) He is sure that volatility will increase sharply.

    e) Volatility is irrelevant to this strategy.

16. Which of the following does NOT directly determine an option's fair value?

    a) current market price of the underlying instrument

    b) time to maturity

    c) volatility

    d) market expectations as to future trends

17. A knock in option is a/an …

    a) barrier option

    b) compound option

    c) Asian option

    d) rainbow option

18. What is meant by the moneyness of an option?

19. What is true regarding the premiums of barrier options?

    a) They are paid if the exchange rate reaches the barrier point.

    b) They are lower than for a corresponding standard option.

   b) Sie kann vom Käufer jederzeit ausgeübt werden.

   c) Sie unterliegt europäischem Recht.

   d) Sie kann nur mit einem europäischen Partner abgeschlossen werden.

10. Was versteht man unter einen Bermudian Option?

11. Welches Risikoprofil hat der Stillhalter einer Call-Option?

   a) limitiertes Verlustpotenzial und unbegrenztes Gewinnpotenzial

   b) begrenztes Verlustpotenzial und begrenztes Gewinnpotenzial

   c) unbegrenztes Verlustpotenzial und unbegrenztes Gewinnpotenzial

   d) unbegrenztes Verlustpotenzial und begrenztes Gewinnpotenzial

12. Sie glauben, dass der Markt bullish ist. Was werden Sie tun?

   a) Sie kaufen einen Call at the money.

   b) Sie verkaufen einen Put at the money.

   c) Sie kaufen einen Put at the money.

   d) Sie verkaufen einen Call at the money.

13. Sie wollen von steigender Volatilität profitieren. Welche Position gehen Sie ein?

   a) Sie verkaufen einen Straddle.

   b) Sie kaufen einen Butterfly.

   c) Sie kaufen einen Straddle.

   d) Sie verkaufen Put-Optionen.

   e) Sie verkaufen einen Butterfly.

   f) Sie verkaufen Call-Optionen.

14. Was ist ein Risk Reversal?

   a) Long Call plus Short Underlying

   b) Long Call und Short Put mit gleichem absolutem Delta, unterschiedlichen Strikes und gleicher Laufzeit

   c) Optionsstrategie, bei der die Gegenpartei alle Risiken trägt

   d) Long Call und Long Put mit unterschiedlichen Strikes und gleicher Laufzeit

15. Welche Erwartungen hinsichtlich der Volatilität hat ein Händler, wenn er einen Short Strangle eingeht?

   a) Er kauft Volatilität, weil sie fällt.

   b) Er glaubt, dass die Volatilität steigen wird.

   c) Er glaubt, dass die Volatilität fallen wird.

   d) Er ist sicher, dass die Volatilität dramatisch steigen wird.

   e) Bei dieser Strategie spielt Volatilität keine Rolle.

16. Welcher dieser Faktoren hat KEINEN direkten Einfluss auf den Wert einer Option?

   a) Preis des Basisinstruments

   b) Restlaufzeit

   c) Volatilität

   d) Markterwartungen über zukünftige Trends

17. Eine Knock-in Option ist eine …

   a) Barrier Option

   b) Compound Option

   c) Asian Option

   d) Rainbow Option

18. Was versteht man unter Moneyness einer Option?

19. Was trifft auf die Prämien für Barrier Options zu?

   a) Sie werden bei Erreichen des Barrier Points bezahlt.

c) They are higher than for a corresponding standard option.

d) They are the same as for a corresponing standard option.

20. What is an Asian option?

a) an option that is subject to Asian law

b) an option that the buyer can exercise at any time during the life of the contract

c) an option that can only be dealt with an Asian counterparty

d) an option that is exercised at maturity at the average rate within the option period

21. What is delta?

a) second derivation of the option price formula

b) exotic option

c) change in the option price if the option expires

d) change in the option price in relation to a change in the price of the underlying

22. In which of the following ranges does the delta of a long put option lie?

a) between -1 and 0

b) between 0 and 1

c) between -0.5 and 0.5

d) between minus infinity and infinity

e) between -1 and 1

23. Which risk factor indicates the change of the option's delta due to a change in spot?

a) theta

b) delta hedge

c) rho

d) gamma

e) epsilon

f) kappa

g) vega

24. Which risk factor shows the price change of an option which is due to a change in volatility?

a) vega

b) gamma

c) delta

d) epsilon

e) theta

25. Which options have a high vega?

a) at the money options

b) deep in the money options

c) deep out of the money options

d) zero cost options

26. Theta is derived from the option pricing model. What does theta express?

a) time decay

b) change in the option value relative to a change in the option delta

c) change in the option value relative to a change in the volatility

d) change in the option value relative to a change in interest rates

27. Which relationship does epsilon/rho describe?

b) Sie sind niedriger als für Standardoptionen.

c) Sie sind teurer als für Standardoptionen.

d) Sie sind gleich wie für Standardoptionen.

20. Was ist eine Asian Option?

a) eine Option, die asiatischem Recht unterliegt

b) eine Option, die der Käufer jederzeit während der Laufzeit der Option ausüben kann

c) eine Option, die man nur mit einem asiatischen Vertragspartner handeln kann

d) eine Option, die bei Fälligkeit zum Durchschnittskurs aus allen Tagen der Optionslaufzeit ausgeübt wird

21. Was ist Delta?

a) zweite Ableitung nach dem Optionspreis

b) exotische Option

c) Veränderung des Optionspreises im Zeitverlauf

d) Veränderung des Optionspreises bei Änderung des Preises im Underlying

22. Wo liegt das Delta einer Long-Put-Option?

a) zwischen -1 und 0

b) zwischen 0 und 1

c) zwischen -0,5 und 0,5

d) zwischen minus unendlich und unendlich

e) zwischen -1 und 1

23. Wie heißt die Änderungsrate des Optionsdeltas?

a) Theta

b) Delta Hedge

c) Rho

d) Gamma

e) Epsilon

f) Kappa

g) Vega

24. Welche Kennzahl drückt die Preisänderung einer Option bei einer Änderung der Volatilität aus?

a) Vega

b) Gamma

c) Delta

d) Epsilon

e) Theta

25. Welche Optionen haben ein hohes Vega?

a) Optionen am Geld

b) Optionen tief im Geld

c) Optionen tief aus dem Geld

d) Zero-cost-Optionen

26. Theta ist eine Kennzahl des Optionspreismodells. Wofür steht Theta?

a) Zeitwertverfall einer Option

b) Änderung des Optionspreises im Verhältnis zur Änderung des Deltas

c) Änderung des Optionspreises im Verhältnis zur Änderung der Volatilität

d) Änderung des Optionspreises im Verhältnis zur Änderung der Zinssätze

    a) time decay and option value
    b) volatility and option value
    c) liquidity and option value
    d) interest rate changes and option value
28. What is called volatility?
    a) variance
    b) vega
    c) normal distribution
    d) standard deviation
29. What are the differences between the Cox-Ross-Rubinstein Model and the Garman/Kohlhagen and Black & Scholes Model?
30. What does the Black/Scholes Model assume regarding volatility?
    a) varies arbitrarily
    b) decreases exponentially
    c) varies intervally
    d) remains constant

27. Welchen Zusammenhang beschreibt Epsilon/Rho?
    a) Zeitablauf und Optionswert
    b) Volatilität und Optionswert
    c) Liquidität und Optionswert
    d) Zinsänderung und Optionswert
28. Was wird als Volatilität bezeichnet?
    a) die Varianz
    b) das Vega
    c) die Normalverteilung
    d) die Standardabweichung
29. Wodurch unterscheidet sich das Cox-Ross-Rubinstein-Modell vom Garman/Kohlhagen- und Black & Scholes-Modell?
30. Was ist die Annahme des Black/Scholes-Modells in Bezug auf die Volatilität?
    a) schwankt willkürlich
    b) nimmt exponenziell ab
    c) schwankt in Intervallen
    d) bleibt konstant

4. Commodities

In this chapter you learn …

- why hedging commodity risks becomes more and more important and what the advantages of hedging are.
- more about the most important traded commodities on the spot and forward markets, specifically energy, precious metals, industrial metals and agricultural products.
- at which stock exchanges the different commodities are traded.
- which factors play a role when deciding between purchasing physical products as opposed to making forward transactions.
- how trading commodities on the spot market works.
- how trading commodities on the forward market works.
- which conventions apply when trading different commodities.
- which role the stock exchange and the clearing house play in commodity trading.
- how the margin system works in commodity trading.
- what is meant by open interest and how it is calculated.
- which different financial instruments (futures, swaps, options) are used in commodity trading and how they work.
- what is meant by metal lending/borrowing and how it works.
- using examples, how each financial instrument can be used in practice.

Today, many companies are hedging interest rate risks and FX risks quite effectively, but still pay little attention to hedging commodity risks. Considering the relevance and impact of commodity risk on business performance, neither the quantification of commodity risks nor the use of available hedging instruments is developed in an appropriate way within most companies.

However, high volatility of commodity prices in the year 2008 led companies to focus more on the topic of commodity risk. An active commodity price and risk management can bring about the following **advantages**:

- Via hedging one can calculate with fixed prices and thereby decrease planning uncertainties.
- With the help of hedging, companies are able to offer fixed long-term prices.
- Using an active risk management, risks can be measured and therefore better controlled.
- An advanced risk management system can help improve the rating of the company.

Despite the rapid development of financial markets (especially stock and bond markets), commodity trading still plays an important role in the global economy. There are various reasons for this. Most notably, commodity markets are connected directly to the real economy and therefore commodities turned out to be **stable assets in times of rising inflation** or during banking and financial crises.

4. Rohstoffe

In diesem Kapitel lernen Sie ...

- warum die Absicherung von Rohstoffrisiken immer mehr an Bedeutung gewinnt und welche Vorteile dies bringt.
- die wichtigsten auf den Kassa- und Terminmärkten gehandelten Rohstoffe aus den Bereichen Energie, Edelmetalle, Industriemetalle und Agrargüter kennen.
- an welchen Börsen die einzelnen Rohstoffe gehandelt werden.
- welche Faktoren bei der Entscheidung zwischen physischem Besitz und dem Erwerb in Form von Termingeschäften eine Rolle spielen.
- wie der Handel mit Rohstoffen auf dem Kassamarkt funktioniert.
- wie der Handel mit Rohstoffen auf dem Terminmarkt funktioniert.
- welche Konventionen für den Handel mit den einzelnen Rohstoffen gelten.
- welche Rolle die Börse und das Clearing House beim Rohstoffhandel spielen.
- wie das Margin-System beim Rohstoffhandel funktioniert.
- was man unter Open Interest versteht und wie dieses berechnet wird.
- welche verschiedenen Produkte (Futures, Swaps, Optionen) im Rohstoffhandel eingesetzt werden und deren Funktionsweise.
- was man unter Metallleihe/-kredit versteht und wie diese funktionieren.
- anhand von Beispielen, wie die einzelnen Produkte konkret in der Praxis eingesetzt werden können.

Während sich heute bereits viele Unternehmen gegen Zinsrisiken und Währungsrisiken mit Erfolg absichern, wird der Absicherung von Rohstoffrisiken nach wie vor wenig Aufmerksamkeit geschenkt. Weder die Quantifizierung der Risiken noch der Einsatz der verfügbaren Sicherungsinstrumente sind damit derzeit bei den Unternehmen so entwickelt, wie es die Relevanz dieses Risikos auf das Unternehmensergebnis implizieren würde.

Die extremen Preisschwankungen im Jahr 2008 haben jedoch dazu geführt, dass das Thema Rohstoffrisiken bei Unternehmen verstärkt im Fokus steht. Ein aktives Preis- und Risikomanagement der Rohstoffrisiken kann zu folgenden **Vorteilen** bei Unternehmen führen:

- Durch die Absicherung kann mit festen Preisen kalkuliert werden und damit die Planungssicherheit erhöht werden.
- Durch Absicherungsmaßnahmen können die Unternehmen langfristige Festpreise anbieten.
- Durch ein aktives Risikomanagement sind die Risiken erkennbar und damit besser zu steuern.
- Ein entwickeltes Risikomanagementsystem kann ein Beitrag zur Verbesserung des Unternehmensratings sein.

Trotz rasanter Entwicklung der Finanzmärkte (vor allem der Aktien- und Anleihemärkte) spielt der Rohstoffhandel immer noch eine wichtige Rolle in der globalen Wirtschaft. Die Gründe dafür sind vielfältig. Rohstoffmärkte sind vor allem direkt mit dem realwirtschaftlichen Zyklus verbunden und haben sich daher als **stabilere Vermögenswerte bei steigender Inflation** und in Banken- oder Finanzkrisen erwiesen.

4.1. Overview

Commodities are natural resources, which are extracted by primary production (without pre-processing). Commodities have an asset value and are used either as a **store of value** ("pure assets" like gold) or as **expendable goods** by the processing industry.

Not all commodities are traded on international markets. However, markets cover the most commonly used and sought-after **energy commodities, industrial metals, agricultural products and precious metals**.

Classification of Commodities

Energy	Precious Metals	Industrial Metals	Agricultural Products
Oil	Gold	Ferrous Metals (Iron, Steel)	Crops (Corn, Sugar, Coffee, Cocoa)
Gas	Silver		
Electricity	Platinum	Non-ferrous Metals (Aluminium, Copper, Nickel, Zinc)	Livestock (Pigs, Cattle)

The most common traded commodity is oil and its derivatives (heating oil, petrol). Another heavily traded good are the so-called soft commodities (agricultural products) such as coffee, wheat, corn, rice, soybean, cocoa, orange juice concentrate and sugar; followed by precious metals such as gold, silver and platinum, as well as industrial metals like aluminium, nickel, copper, lead, iron and steel. These days, one can even trade electricity and biofuel on international commodity markets.

Energy Commodities

Energy commodities are pivotal for economic development. Due to their important role for economic production, they have a significant influence on the price of other commodities. The most commonly traded energy commodities are **crude oil, gas and electricity**.

Metal Markets

Metal markets can be divided into two main categories: **precious metals** (mainly used as a store of value) and **industrial metals** (mainly used in industrial production).

Precious Metals

Trading precious metals has a very long tradition. Similar to the financial markets in general, there has been an important development of derivative instruments besides the spot market. The most heavily traded metal is **gold** followed by **silver**, **platinum** and **palladium**.

Industrial Metals

According to their iron content, industrial metals can be divided into two categories: **non-ferrous metals** and **ferrous metals**. Non-ferrous metals include for example **aluminium, copper, nickel and zinc**. Ferrous metals comprise **iron ore, iron scrap** and

4.1. Überblick

Rohstoffe sind natürliche Ressourcen, die durch Primärproduktion (ohne Vorbearbeitung) gewonnen werden. Rohstoffe haben einen Vermögenswert und werden als **Wertaufbewahrungsmittel** („pure assets" wie Gold) oder als **Verbrauchsgüter** von der verarbeitenden Industrie benutzt.

Nicht alle Rohstoffe werden auf den internationalen Märkten gehandelt. Die Märkte umfassen vor allem die am meisten verbrauchten und nachgefragten **Energierohstoffe, Industriemetalle, Agrargüter und Edelmetalle.**

Klassifikation Rohstoffe

Energie	Edelmetalle	Industriemetalle	Agrargüter
Öl	Gold	Eisenmetalle (Eisen, Stahl)	Landwirtschaftliche Produkte (Mais, Zucker, Kaffee, Kakao)
Gas	Silber		
Strom	Platin	Nicht-Eisenmetalle (Aluminium, Kupfer, Nickel, Zink)	Vieh (Scheine, Rinder)

Die meistgehandelten Rohstoffe sind Erdöl und seine Derivate wie Heizöl und Benzin. Danach kommen auch die sogenannten Weichwaren (Agrarprodukte) wie Kaffee, Weizen, Mais, Reis, Sojabohnen, Kakao, Orangensaftkonzentrat und Zucker. Andere sehr häufig gehandelte Waren sind Edelmetalle wie Gold, Silber und Platin sowie Industriemetalle: Aluminium, Nickel, Kupfer, Blei und Stahl und Eisen. Strom und Biokraftstoffe können heutzutage auch auf den internationalen Rohstoffbörsen gehandelt werden.

Energierohstoffe

Energierohstoffe sind für die wirtschaftliche Entwicklung entscheidend. Aufgrund ihrer bedeutenden Rolle für die Produktion haben die Energiemärkte einen sehr starken Einfluss auf Preise anderer Rohstoffe. Die meistgehandelten Energierohstoffe sind **Erdöl, Erdgas und Strom**.

Die Metallmärkte umfassen generell zwei Hauptkategorien: **Edelmetalle** (genutzt vor allem als Wertaufbewahrungsmittel) und **Industriemetalle** (verwendet vor allem in der Industrieproduktion).

Edelmetalle

Der Handel mit Edelmetallen (englisch: precious metals) hat eine lange Tradition. Ebenso wie in den Finanzmärkten hat sich neben dem Kassamarkt eine Reihe von derivativen Instrumenten entwickelt. Das meistgehandelte Metall ist dabei **Gold,** gefolgt von **Silber, Platin und Palladium.**

Industriemetalle

Je nach Eisengehalt werden die Industriemetalle in zwei Kategorien unterteilt: **Nichteisenmetalle** (engl. *non-ferrous metals*) und **Eisenmetalle** (*ferrous metals*). Nichteisenme-

steel. The most traded metals are aluminium, lead, copper, nickel and zinc. These metals are mainly used in production and construction industries and their price development is often used as a leading indicator of the general economic development.

Agricultural Products

These commodities include **agrarian goods** such as cotton, corn, sugar, wheat, rape, coffee and cocoa, as well as **livestock** (pigs, cattle). There is one thing agricultural products have in common: they are mainly produced in poor countries and are imported by rich, developed countries. The soft commodity market is used both for speculation and by industrial companies for hedging purchasing and selling prices.

4.2. Markets

4.2.1. Spot Market

Physical trading on spot markets takes place directly between producers, intermediaries and consumers. For this purpose there is no real need for standardised exchanges or financial markets. For investors, trading commodities on the spot market is very expensive due to **high transportation and storage costs**. Therefore, most of the trade volume happens on the futures market (with the exception of precious metals).

When trading commodities either on the spot market or on the futures market, other factors besides the cost factor must be taken into account. These factors are for example: storage suitability, scarcity and development of stock levels, reproduction time, production costs and weather.

On physical spot markets, one can trade all kinds of commodities in different compositions, qualities and quantities and in many different locations.

Energy

Oil

Most of oil trading is done on future markets, but there is also the "real" trade with immediate physical delivery, reasons for the latter being the short-term supply of the physical good, taking advantage of price changes and certain demand developments. Physical delivery is usually taken within 2 weeks, that is, "on the spot".

Oil spot trading is not conducted on ordinary exchanges, but world-wide directly at big **oil ports**, where the oil can be easily transported to and from. Major ports include **New York, Houston/Texas, Rotterdam, Singapore and the Persian Gulf.** In the future, big Chinese ports such as Dalian can be expected to gain in importance.

When trading oil physically at oil ports, additional costs for transportation and storage have to be taken into account.

talle sind zum Beispiel **Aluminium, Kupfer, Nickel und Zink**. Eisenmetalle sind **Eisenerz, Eisenschrott und Stahl**. Die meistgehandelten Metalle sind Aluminium, Blei, Kupfer, Nickel und Zink. Sie werden vor allem von den produzierenden und Bauindustrien nachgefragt und ihre Preisentwicklung dient manchmal als Frühindikator für die wirtschaftliche Konjunktur.

Agrargüter

Die Agrargüter umfassen sowohl **landwirtschaftliche Produkte**, wie Baumwolle, Mais, Zucker, Weizen, Raps, Kaffee und Kakao, als auch **Vieh** (Schweine, Rinder). Häufig haben die Agrargüter eines gemein: Sie kommen meist aus armen Produktionsländern und werden von reichen Ländern importiert. Agrargüterprodukte werden sowohl als Spekulations- als auch als Absicherungsinstrument für Absatzpreise und Einkaufspreise von der Industrie verwendet.

4.2. Märkte

4.2.1. Kassamarkt (Spotmarkt)

Der physische Handel auf den Spotmärkten erfolgt direkt zwischen Produzenten, Zwischenhändlern und Verbrauchern, wobei keine Börsen oder Finanzmärkte notwendig sind. Für Anleger ist der Handel am Kassamarkt mit **hohen Transport- und Lagerkosten** verbunden, deshalb wird ein großer Teil des Handelsvolumens in Rohstoffen auf dem Terminmarkt abgewickelt (eine Ausnahme sind die Edelmetalle).

Neben dem Kostenfaktor spielen aber auch noch andere Faktoren (Lagerfähigkeit des Rohstoffes, Knappheit bzw. Entwicklung der Lagerbestände, Reproduktionszeit, Produktionskosten und Wetter) in wechselnder Intensität eine Rolle, die den physischen Besitz gegenüber einem Erwerb in Form von Termingeschäften attraktiver erscheinen lassen.

Auf dem physischen Markt (Spotmarkt) werden alle Sorten von Rohstoffen in verschiedenen Zusammensetzungen, Qualitäten und Mengen an vielen Orten gehandelt.

Energie

Öl

Neben dem Handel mit Öl auf den Terminbörsen gibt es auch einen „realen" Handel mit der physischen Ware. Gründe hierfür sind die kurzfristige Bereitstellung der physischen Ware, das Ausnutzen von Preisveränderungen sowie bestimmte Nachfrageentwicklungen. Dabei wird der physische Rohstoff direkt, meist innerhalb von zwei Wochen, „on the spot" verschoben.

Der Spothandel mit Öl erfolgt nicht an den Börsen, sondern an den großen **Ölhäfen** weltweit. Hier kann die Ware direkt ab- und antransportiert werden. Die wichtigsten Ölhäfen weltweit befinden sich in **New York, Houston/Texas, Rotterdam, Singapur und im Persischen Golf**. In Zukunft werden sicher auch die großen Häfen Chinas, wie der Hafen von Dalian, mehr an Bedeutung gewinnen.

Zu beachten ist, dass beim physischen Handel an den Ölhäfen noch Kosten, wie Transport- und Lagerkosten, hinzukommen.

Gas/Electricity

The point of trading on the spot market is to optimise the production/consumption portfolio. Buying and selling bids on the spot market are determined by short-term marginal costs, therefore only variable costs such as fuel costs are relevant for short-term production decisions. There are some energy exchanges with physical spot markets, for example: **European Energy Exchange (EEX) in Leipzig, Amsterdam Power Exchange, EPEX Spot in Paris, New York Mercantile Exchange and NordPool in Oslo**; The EEX-Spotmarkt (EEX Power Spot) was merged in 2009 into the new company EPEX Spot SE with headquarters in Paris and Leipzig. It is owned by the French Powernext SA and the EEX AG (50% each). On the spot market one can trade electricity for Germany, France, Austria and Switzerland. Additionally, the EEX offers spot trading for gas in the area of GASPOOL (former GUD and BEB) and NCG (Net Connect Germany, former EGT) and the spot trade of EU emission allowances (EUA).

Precious Metals

Precious metals are not only traded on global future markets, but also on spot markets. For gold, silver and platinum there are therefore not only changing future prices (i.e. COMEX) but also constantly changing spot prices.

The spot price of gold is defined as the price of gold for **immediate delivery**. When people are talking about the gold price in general, they mean the **spot price** of gold, which is quoted in **US-Dollars per ounce**.

In the world of finance, the spot price of precious metals is very important because it acts as a **reference price** for financial instruments, especially in **derivatives markets** (i.e. CFD, Options, Certificates, etc.). In contrast to precious metals, the reference prices of other commodities are basically the future prices.

Gold

For the gold spot price there are three main markets world-wide:

Trade in Tokyo: The spot price for physical delivery is quoted on the Tocom Futures Exchange.

Trade in London: The ten biggest members of the London Bullion Market Association (LBMA) quote bid and ask prices for gold.

Trade in New York: What is known as the "New York gold price" is the standard contract on US-Gold-Futures listed on COMEX (contract size of 100 ounces).

Silver

The most important trading platform for **silver bars** is the **London Bullion Market Association (LBMA)**. Only silver bars from refineries and mints are admitted, they have to fulfil certain quality criteria. The international seal of approval "good-delivery" guarantees traits such as fineness and weight, which are embossed on the bar. These bars with Good-Delivery status are traded and accepted worldwide. Further important physical markets are **New York** and **Zurich**.

Gas/Strom

Am Spotmarkt geht es darum, das Erzeugungs-/Verbrauchsportfolio meist für den nächsten Tag zu optimieren. Die Kauf- und Verkaufsgebote auf dem Spotmarkt erfolgen zu **kurzfristigen Grenzkosten**, nur die variablen Kosten wie etwa Brennstoffkosten sind für die kurzfristige Produktionsentscheidung relevant. Beispiele für Energiebörsen mit einem physischen Spotmarkt sind die **European Energy Exchange (EEX) in Leipzig, die Amsterdam Power Exchange, die EPEX Spot in Paris, die New York Mercantile Exchange sowie NordPool in Oslo**. Der EEX-Spotmarkt (EEX Power Spot) wurde 2009 in das neue Unternehmen EPEX Spot SE mit Sitz in Paris und Leipzig überführt. Dieses gehört zu jeweils 50 % der französischen Powernext SA und der EEX AG. Am Spotmarkt kann Strom für Deutschland, Frankreich, Österreich und die Schweiz gehandelt werden. Die EEX bietet darüber hinaus den Spothandel für Erdgas in den Marktgebieten GASPOOL (vormals GUD und BEB) und NCG (Net Connect Germany, vormals EGT) und für europäische Emissionsberechtigungen (sogenannte EU Allowances – EUA) an.

Edelmetalle

Edelmetalle werden weltweit nicht nur an den Warenterminbörsen, sondern auch an den Spotmärkten gehandelt. Für Gold, Silber und Platin gibt es neben den Future-Kursen (z.B. der COMEX) auch sich ständig ändernde Spot-Kursdaten.

Als Spotpreis wird der Preis für Gold zur **sofortigen Lieferung** („auf den Punkt" = engl. „spot") bezeichnet. Wenn allgemein vom Goldpreis gesprochen wird, dann ist immer der **Spotpreis** gemeint. Der Spotpreis wird in **US-Dollar pro Feinunze** angegeben.

Diese Spotkurse gelten in der Investmentwelt, besonders im derivativen Wertpapiergeschäft, als **Referenzkurse für z.B. CFDs (Contract for Difference), Zertifikate**, wodurch sich die Edelmetalle maßgeblich von den anderen Rohstoffen unterscheiden, bei denen grundsätzlich die jeweiligen Notierungen der Futures als Referenzkurse herangezogen werden.

Gold

Der Spotpreis von Gold kann weltweit in **drei Märkte** unterteilt werden:

- Handel in **Tokio**: Preise für physisches Gold werden auf der Tocom Futures Exchange notiert.
- Handel in **London**: Die zehn größten Mitglieder der London Bullion Market Association (LBMA) notieren Goldpreise sowohl für den Ankauf als auch für den Verkauf.
- Handel in **New York**: Der Standardvertrag für US-Gold-Futures, der 100-Unzen-Comex-Vertrag, wird auch „New-York-Goldpreis" genannt.

Silber

Für den physischen Markt (Silber in **Barrenform**) ist die **London Bullion Market Association (LBMA)** die wichtigste Handelsplattform weltweit. Zum Handel sind nur Barren von Affinerien und Münzprägeanstalten zugelassen, die bestimmte Qualitätsanforderungen erfüllen. Das internationale Gütesiegel „good delivery" (deutsch: „in guter Auslieferung") garantiert die aufgeprägten oder eingestanzten Merkmale wie Feinheit und Gewicht. Silberbarren mit Good-Delivery-Status werden weltweit akzeptiert und gehandelt. Weitere Marktplätze für den physischen Handel sind **New York** und **Zürich**.

Platinum

Besides future markets, there is also a spot market for immediate physical delivery of platinum. The most important quotations of platinum are the daily fixings of **the London Platinum & Palladium Market (LPPM)**. With regard to annual production, platinum is **the scarcest of the big three precious metals.** Compared to the annual mine production of silver, which is approximately 20,000 tons, and gold, which is approximately 2,500 tons, the production of platinum is only approximately 200 tons per year. Although the annual production of platinum is less than one tenth of the gold production, gold currently (May 2012) trades at higher prices. Experts argue that platinum demand is becoming more and more sensitive to economic development due to its use in industry, whereas gold is considered a crisis currency. This explains the outperformance of gold in times of a financial crisis.

Platinum is traded primarily on NYMEX in **New York** and on TOCOM in **Tokyo**. The contract size on NYMEX for platinum is 50 ounces (1 ounce = 31.1034768 g) and the price is quoted in US-dollar per ounce. In Tokyo the contract comprises 500 g of platinum and the price is quoted in JPY per gram.

Industrial Metals

The most important trading platforms are the **London Metal Exchange (LME)** and the **New York Mercantile Exchange (NYMEX)**. Traded contracts are opened on a daily basis with a time to maturity of three months. In addition to that, there is a spot price for immediate delivery and a price for contracts with a term to maturity of up to 27 months.

Agricultural Goods

These goods are primarily traded on future markets in the form of contracts; there is no trade on spot markets.

4.2.2. The Futures Market

Most of commodity trading is done on the futures market. Not only producers, wholesalers and their clients can increase their planning certainty by fixing future prices today, but also market participants, who wish to avoid physical delivery, can use the futures market for investment.

Originally, future and option transactions were executed by producers and consumers in order to hedge price risks.

The futures market consists of **OTC transactions** (forwards, swaps and options) and **standardised contracts** (futures and options), which are traded on organised exchanges. Commodity trade is executed mostly in the form of futures contracts on the biggest futures exchanges located in the USA and UK.

In the beginning, traded goods were mostly agricultural products (cereals, corn, wheat, cattle, etc.). The first futures exchange was the **Chicago Board of Trade (CBOT)**, which was founded in 1848. Afterwards many other international commodity exchanges were created such as the Chicago Mercantile Exchange (CME), the New York Mercantile Exchange (NYMEX), the London Metal Exchange (LME), etc., which also facilitate energy commodities, precious metals and industrial metals trading.

Platin

Auch beim Platin gibt es neben den Future-Märkten einen eigenen Spotmarkt für die sofortige Auslieferung. Die am **London Platin & Palladium Market (LPPM)** täglich festgesetzten Fixing-Kurse finden dabei große Beachtung. Platin ist im Hinblick auf die jährliche Fördermenge **das seltenste unter den drei großen Edelmetallen**. Während die jährliche Minenproduktion von Silber bei 20.000 Tonnen und die von Gold bei 2.500 Tonnen liegt, werden pro Jahr nur etwa 200 Tonnen Platin produziert. Obwohl die Fördermenge von Platin um ein Vielfaches geringer ist, erzielt Gold an den Börsen momentan (Stand: Mai 2012) einen höheren Preis. Experten führen dies darauf zurück, dass die Nachfrage nach Platin mehr und mehr von der konjunkturellen Situation abhängt, wohingegen Gold als Krisenwährung gilt, wodurch die Outperformance von Gold in Krisenzeiten nachvollziehbar ist.

Platin wird an der NYMEX in **New York** und der TOCOM in **Tokio** gehandelt. An der NYMEX beträgt die Kontraktgröße für den Platinpreis 50 Unzen (1 Unze = 31,1034768 g) und der Preis wird in US-$ pro Unze notiert. In Tokio beträgt die Kontraktgröße 500 g und der Platinpreis wird in Yen je Gramm angegeben.

Industriemetalle

Die wichtigsten Handelsplätze für Industriemetalle sind die **London Metal Exchange (LME)** und die **New York Mercantile Exchange (NYMEX)**. Die gehandelten Kontrakte werden auf täglicher Basis für jeweils drei Monate neu eröffnet. Zusätzlich wird ein Spotpreis für unmittelbare Lieferungen und längere Termine mit einer Laufzeit von bis zu 27 Monaten angeboten.

Agrargüter

Agrargüter werden überwiegend **an Terminbörsen in Form von Kontrakten** gehandelt. Ein Handel mit Agrargütern auf den Spotmärkten findet nicht statt.

4.2.2. Terminmarkt

Der Handel mit Rohstoffen erfolgt hauptsächlich auf den Terminmärkten. Somit wird die Planungssicherheit sowohl für die Produzenten, Großhändler und ihre Kunden erhöht, in dem sie sich die zukünftigen Preise heute fixieren können, als auch für Anleger, die die physische Lieferung vermeiden wollen, deren Hauptmotiv die Werterhaltung ihres Vermögens ist.

Termin- und Optionsgeschäfte wurden ursprünglich von Produzenten und Verbrauchern nur genutzt, um sich gegen Preisrisiken abzusichern.

Der Terminmarkt umfasst sowohl **OTC-Geschäfte** (Forwards, Swaps und Optionen) als auch **standardisierte Kontrakte** (Futures und Optionen) auf organisierten Börsen. Die Rohstoffe werden zum größten Teil in Form von **Future-Kontrakten** an den weltweit größten Warenterminbörsen in den USA und im Vereinigten Königreich gehandelt.

Ursprünglich umfasste der internationale Rohstoffhandel hauptsächlich die Agrarprodukte wie Getreide, Mais, Weizen, Vieh usw. 1848 wurde die **erste Terminbörse für Rohstoffe** geschaffen – die **Chicago Board of Trade (CBOT)**. Danach entstanden viele internationale Rohstoffbörsen, wie die Chicago Mercantile Exchange (CME), die New York Mercantile Exchange (NYMEX) und die London Metal Exchange (LME), auf denen auch Energierohstoffe, Edel- und Industriemetalle gehandelt werden können.

The most important international exchanges for the individual commodities are:

Commodity	Exchange
Energy	
WTI Crude Oil	NYMEX
Brent Crude Oil	ICE Futures
Gasoil	ICE Futures
Heating Oil	NYMEX
Unleaded Petrol	NYMEX
Natural Gas	NYMEX
Electricity	EEX
Industrial Metals	
Copper	LME, NYMEX
Aluminium	LME
Nickel	LME
Zinc	LME
Lead	LME
Precious Metals	
Gold	NYMEX
Silver	NYMEX
Agrarian Goods	
Corn	CBOT
Chicago Wheat	CBOT
Sugar	ICE Futures U.S.
Soybeans	CBOT
Cotton	ICE Futures U.S.
Coffee	ICE Futures U.S.
Kansas Wheat	KCBT
Cocoa	ICE Futures U.S.
Livestock	
Live Cattle	CME
Lean Hogs	CME
Feeder Cattle	CME

Für die einzelnen Rohstoffe sind die wichtigsten internationalen Börsen:

Rohstoff	Börse
Energie	
WTI-Erdöl	NYMEX
Brent-Erdöl	ICE Futures
Gasöl	ICE Futures
Heizöl	NYMEX
Bleifreies Benzin	NYMEX
Erdgas	NYMEX
Strom	EEX
Industriemetalle	
Kupfer	LME, NYMEX
Aluminium	LME
Nickel	LME
Zink	LME
Blei	LME
Edelmetalle	
Gold	NYMEX
Silber	NYMEX
Agrargüter	
Mais	CBOT
Chicago-Weizen	CBOT
Zucker	ICE Futures U.S.
Sojabohnen	CBOT
Baumwolle	ICE Futures U.S.
Kaffee	ICE Futures U.S.
Kansas-Weizen	KCBT
Kakao	ICE Futures U.S.
Lebendvieh	
Lebendrind	CME
Mageres Schwein	CME
Mastrind	CME

Energy Commodities

The London-based **ICE Futures** (formerly "International Petroleum Exchange", IPE) is the biggest futures exchange for options and futures contracts on crude oil, natural gas and electricity. It is also the trading platform for the Europe-wide popular Brent crude oil.

Commodity	Exchange	Contract Size	Trading Symbol
WTI Crude Oil	NYMEX, ICE	1000 (bbl) (42,000 US gal)	CL (NYMEX), WTI (ICE)
Brent Crude	ICE	1000 bbl	B
Natural Gas	NYMEX	10,000 million British thermal units (mmBtu).	NG
Heating Oil	NYMEX	1000 bbl	HO
Gasoil	ICE	100 tons	G

The **European Energy Exchange (EEX)** is the largest energy exchange in Continental Europe; handling **electricity futures and options, CO_2 certificates, coal and natural gas** trading. The EEX futures market caters to the German and French energy markets and therefore plays an important role in Continental European energy trading. The futures contract on the average price on EPEX-spot-market (Phelix) is settled in cash and is quoted in EUR per MWh.

Metals

Precious Metals

These are the **ISO Codes of the most important precious metals**:

Precious Metal	ISO Code
Gold	XAU
Silver	XAG
Platinum	XPT
Palladium	XPD

The London **gold fixing** is done by the „**London Bullion Market Association**" (**LBMA**) twice a day. The five fixing participants meet on every London banking day at **10.30** and **15.30**. The participating banks are: Bank of Nova Scotia – Scotia Mocatta, HSBC London, Deutsche Bank AG London, Société Générale London and Barclays Capital London.

Energierohstoffe

Die **ICE Futures** (früher „International Petroleum Exchange", IPE) mit Sitz in **London** ist die größte Terminbörse für Optionen und Futures auf Erdöl, Erdgas und elektrische Energie in Europa. Die Börse ist Handelsplattform für die in Europa führende Ölsorte Brent.

Rohstoff	Börse	Kontraktgröße	Handelssymbol
WTI Crude Oil	NYMEX, ICE	1.000 (bbl) (42,000 US gal)	CL (NYMEX), WTI (ICE)
Brent Crude	ICE	1.000 bbl	B
Natural Gas	NYMEX	10.000 million British thermal units (mmBtu)	NG
Heating Oil	NYMEX	1.000 bbl	HO
Gasoil	ICE	100 Tonnen	G

Die **European Energy Exchange (EEX)** ist die größte Energiebörse in Kontinentaleuropa. An der EEX werden **Strom-Futures und -Optionen, CO_2-Zertifikate, Kohle und Erdgas** gehandelt. Der EEX-Terminmarkt umfasst den deutschen und den französischen Strommarkt und hält damit eine zentrale Position im kontinentaleuropäischen Stromhandel. Ein Futures-Kontrakt auf den zukünftigen Durchschnittspreis am EPEX-Spotmarkt (Phelix) wird gegen Bargeld erfüllt (Cash Settlement) und quotiert in EUR pro MWh.

Metalle

Edelmetalle

Im Folgenden sind Beispiele für **Quotierungen der wichtigsten Edelmetalle** dargestellt:

Edelmetall	ISO Code
Gold	XAU
Silber	XAG
Platin	XPT
Palladium	XPD

Die **„London Bullion Market Association" (LBMA)** führt zweimal täglich ein **Goldfixing** durch. Die fünf Fixing-Teilnehmer treffen einander an jedem Londoner Banktag um **10:30** und **15:00 Uhr**. Die Fixing-Banken sind: Bank of Nova Scotia – Scotia Mocatta, HSBC London, Deutsche Bank AG London, Société Générale London und Barclays Capital London.

There are two functions of the fixing:

- **Execution of transactions at the fixing rate:** Customers can place their orders at participating banks whose representatives then determine the price in a transparent process matching supply and demand.
- **Benchmark:** The London gold fixing acts as a reference rate for the settlement of derivative instruments (i.e., options, swaps), which are settled in cash.

Industrial Metals

The most important trading platform regarding industrial metals is the **London Metal Exchange (LME)**. More than two thirds of the worlds' non-ferrous metal futures and options are traded on the LME. The metal prices, which are derived from the daily trade on LME, are considered as the global benchmark for the metal spot market worldwide. Other important non-ferrous metals trading exchanges are NYMEX, TOCOM (Tokyo Commodity Exchange), OME (Osaka Mercantile Exchange) and SFE (Shanghai Futures Exchange).

The following table shows some sample **quotations and contract sizes for the most important metal futures traded on LME:**

Industrial Metals	Code	Contract Size
Aluminium	AH	25 t
Aluminium Alloy	AA	20 t
Lead	PB	25 t
Copper	CA	25 t
Nickel	NI	6 t
Zinc	ZS	25 t

4.3. The Role of Exchange and Clearing House

The exchange provides the **framework** and **conditions** for trading. Among other things it determines which contracts are traded and their specifications.

The execution and settlement process of the operations is carried out by the futures exchange **clearing house**.

The **main functions** of the clearing house are:

- It acts as the **counterparty** for all traded contracts. The clearing house acting as an intermediary between buyer and seller **reduces credit** risk. In order to reduce risks to a minimum, the clearing house trades only with registered clearing members, who in turn offer their services as brokers or clearers to third parties. Furthermore, the clearing houses demand **initial margins** and/or **variation margins**.

Das Fixing erfüllt zwei Funktionen:

- **Durchführung von Geschäften zum Fixingkurs:** Kunden können Orders bei den Fixingmitgliedern platzieren. Deren Repräsentanten ermitteln dann in einem transparenten Prozess den Kurs, bei dem sich die Kauf- und Verkaufsaufträge ausgleichen.
- **Benchmark:** Das London Gold Fixing wird als Basis zur Abrechnung von derivativen Instrumenten (z.B. Optionen, Swaps) herangezogen, bei denen eine Barabrechnung (Cash Settlement) vereinbart wurde.

Industriemetalle

Die **London Metal Exchange (LME)** ist eine der wichtigsten Börsen für Industriemetalle. Es werden mehr als zwei Drittel der weltweiten Nichteisenmetall-Futures und -Optionen an der LME gehandelt. Die abgeleiteten Preise aus dem täglichen Handel an der LME gelten als globale Benchmark für die physischen Metallmärkte. Andere wichtige internationale Börsen für Nichteisenmetalle sind die NYMEX, TOCOM (Tokyo Commodity Exchange), OME (Osaka Mercantile Exchange) und SFE (Shanghai Futures Exchange).

Im Folgenden werden Beispiele für **Quotierungen und Kontraktspezifikationen der wichtigsten Metallfutures** an der LME dargestellt:

Industriemetalle	Code	Kontraktgröße
Aluminium	AH	25 t
Aluminiumlegierung	AA	20 t
Blei	PB	25 t
Kupfer	CA	25 t
Nickel	NI	6 t
Zink	ZS	25 t

4.3. Die Rollen von Börse und Clearing House

Die Börse gibt die **Rahmenbedingungen** vor, unter denen der Handel stattfindet. Sie bestimmt unter anderem, welche Kontrakte gehandelt werden, sowie die Spezifikationen der einzelnen Kontrakte.

Die Abwicklung der Geschäfte erfolgt durch das **Clearing House** der Futuresbörse.

Das Clearing House hat folgende **Hauptaufgaben**:

- Es wird zum **Geschäftspartner** in allen gehandelten Kontrakten. Die Platzierung des Clearing House zwischen Käufer und Verkäufer dient der **Reduzierung des Kreditrisikos**. Um dieses Risiko auf ein Minimum zu reduzieren, handelt das Clearing House nur mit registrierten Clearing-Mitgliedern, die ihrerseits ihre Dienste als Broker oder nur als Clearer anbieten. Um das Kreditrisiko des Clearing House so gering wie möglich zu halten, werden Einschüsse, sogenannte **Initial Margins**, und auch **Variation Margins** verlangt.

- **Daily valuation and settlement** of variation margins of all open transactions.
- **Initial margins** are set depending on market volatility and therefore revised regularly. The Margin System

4.3.1. The Margin System

The main purpose of the margin system is the **elimination of counterparty risk (credit risk)**. This is done via the provision of an initial margin and a variation or maintenance margin (set according to a daily evaluation and settlement of accrued profits and losses) for each contract.

Initial Margin

The initial margin is **defined individually on a contract-by-contract basis**. The amount is determined by the clearing house and adapted to market circumstances according to volatility. The initial margin serves as an over-collateralisation in order to cover the market participants' potential losses, which can occur due to daily price fluctuations. It is therefore used for **collateralisation of potential future losses**.

Usually, the initial margin is not provided in cash, but **in the form of securities.** The returns from these securities belong to the market participant. If a contract expires or is closed out before maturity, the initial margin will be returned to the customer.

Spread Margin

A spread margin leads to **a reduced initial margin because the market participant holds at the same time long and short positions of the same underlying** (with differing maturities), i.e., 100 contracts of coffee futures March long and 100 contracts June short).

Instead of depositing USD 350 per contract for 200 contracts, which would result in a margin payment of USD 70,000, the market participant has to provide only a reduced spread margin, for instance USD 250 per contract, leading to a margin payment of 200 (total contracts) * 250 = USD 50,000.

Span Margin

Some clearing houses calculate the **initial margin with the help of risk-based systems with defined parameters**. This method is called span margin (Standardised Portfolio Analysis of Risk). The total risk of a particular position is determined through the calculation of certain risk factors and then charged as margin payment according to a set allocation key.

Variation or Maintenance Margin (Margin Calls)

The variation or maintenance margin is the **daily settlement of accumulated profits and losses**. Each trading day, the clearing house charges the difference between the closing prices of the present day and the day before. This amount equals the effective accumulated profit or loss.

- **Tägliche Bewertung und Abrechnung** der Variation Margin für alle offenen Geschäfte.
- **Festlegung der Initial Margin**; die Höhe der Initial Margin hängt von der Volatilität des Marktes ab. Sie wird daher auch regelmäßig an die aktuellen Marktgegebenheiten angepasst.

4.3.1. Das Margin-System

Das Ziel des Margin-Systems ist die **Ausschließung des Kontrahentenrisikos (Kreditrisiko)**. Dies erfolgt durch einen fixen Einschuss pro Kontrakt (Initial Margin) und zusätzlich durch die tägliche Abrechnung der angelaufenen Gewinne und Verluste (Variation bzw. Maintenance Margin).

Initial Margin

Die Initial Margin ist eine **festgelegte Betragshöhe pro Kontrakt**. Die Höhe der Initial Margin ist für verschiedene Kontrakte unterschiedlich. Sie wird vom Clearing House festgesetzt bzw. entsprechend der Volatilität der Märkte verändert. Die Initial Margin dient als zusätzliche Ausfallsicherung, so dass der potenzielle Verlust eines Marktteilnehmers, der durch die täglichen Kursschwankungen eintreten könnte, gedeckt ist. Sie dient daher zur **Besicherung für potenzielle zukünftige Verluste**.

Die Initial Margin wird **üblicherweise** nicht bar hinterlegt, sondern **in Form von Wertpapieren**. Die Erträge aus den Wertpapieren fallen weiterhin dem Marktteilnehmer zu. Die Initial Margin wird bei Auslaufen oder bei vorzeitigem Schließen einer Position an den Marktteilnehmer rückerstattet.

Spread Margin

Unter Spread Margin ist eine **reduzierte Initial Margin bei gleichzeitiger Long und Short Position** (in unterschiedlichen Perioden) zu verstehen, z.B. Kaffee-Future März long, 100 Kontrakte und Juni short, 100 Kontrakte.

Statt für 200 Kontrakte z.B. USD 350, also insgesamt USD 70.000 Einschuss anzulegen, gelangt eine reduzierte Spread Margin, z.B. USD 250, zur Anwendung, also 200 (Totalkontrakte) * 250 = USD 50.000.

Span Margin

Von einigen Clearinghäusern wird die **Initial Margin mittels eines risikobasierten Systems mit festgelegten Parametern berechnet**. Diese Methode wird Span Margin genannt (Standardized Portfolio Analysis of Risk). Hier wird durch eine Reihe von Risikofaktoren das Gesamtrisiko einer Position ermittelt und durch einen bestimmten Aufteilungsschlüssel als Margin in Rechnung gestellt.

Variation bzw. Maintenance Margin (Margin Calls)

Die Variation bzw. Maintenance Margin ist eine **tägliche Abrechnung der aufgelaufenen Gewinne und Verluste**. Hier wird täglich der Unterschied zwischen dem Vortagesschlusskurs und dem Tagesschlusskurs – also der tatsächlich angefallene Kursgewinn oder -verlust – in Rechnung gestellt.

4.3.2. Methodology of settlement on the last trading day

At expiry the **buyer** of a commodity future (long) gets the **entitlement for reception** and the **seller** (short) receives the **entitlement to deliver** the underlying goods against payment in cash. This implies that, if someone holds an open position until the expiration date, he will have to **fulfil the contract in specie**. A precise list of futures contracts can be found in printed contract forms and product calendars, in which the exchange defines the settlement procedures. In these documents the exchange states specifically when there is a requirement of physical delivery.

If there is no requirement of physical delivery, the contract is settled in cash (**"cash settlement"**). Thereby, the future price at expiry is set equal to the spot price of the underlying asset and officially used as the final settlement price of the future contract. The total result of a futures position consists of the **aggregated sum of daily variation margins plus the settlement amount of the last trading day**.

Example

You are long 10 contracts nickel future.

Purchase Price:	17,220 USD/t
Closing price yesterday:	18,150 USD/t

What is your total result?

Settlement Amount: $(18,150 - 17,220) = 930$
$10 * 930 = $ USD 9,300
You receive **USD 9,300**.

Closing of Futures Positions

Each open position can be closed out before or on the last trading day by entering into the contrarian position. This "reversal" leads to the closure of the position and therefore to the restitution of the initial margin. The total **profit or loss** equals the **sum of daily margin payments** (including potential interest income or expenses).

4.3.3. Open Interest and Volume of Trade

These figures provide information about the **liquidity of the particular contracts with differing maturities**. Usually, the contract with the shortest term (front month) has the highest trading volume.

Open interest is a figure measuring the **amount of all currently open contracts**, meaning: if someone buys ("long") a futures contract without holding a short position in the same contract, open interest is increased by one, provided that the seller enters into a new selling position ("short") at the same time. The same is true for the opposite: if someone sells

4.3.2. Methodik der Abrechnung am letzten Handelstag

Der **Käufer** eines Commodity Future (Long) erhält mit Laufzeitende die **Empfangsberechtigung**, der **Verkäufer** (Short) die **Überlieferungsberechtigung** für die kontrahierte Ware gegen Entgelt. Das bedeutet, wer Kontrakte der eben bezeichneten Art kauft oder verkauft und sie bis zum Ende der Laufzeit behält, wird notwendig auf **Erfüllung in natura** in Anspruch genommen. In den börslich festgeschriebenen Kontraktformularen und dem Produktkalender, die beide dem Marktpublikum offen zur Einsicht vorliegen, findet man eine präzise Auflistung, welche Futures im Einzelnen wann zu ihrer Vollendung eine physische Lieferung verlangen.

Wird keine physische Lieferung verlangt, erfolgt das Settlement als „**Cash Settlement**". Dabei wird am Schluss des letzten Handelstags im fälligen Termin der Future-Kurs gleich dem dann herrschenden Kassapreis („spot price") der Wertbezugsbasis („underlying asset") gesetzt und offiziell als Schlussabrechnungspreis („final settlement price") des Futures ausgewiesen. Das Ergebnis auf eine Futures-Position setzt sich also aus der **Summe der täglichen Variation Margins und dem Settlement-Betrag am letzten Handelstag** zusammen.

Beispiel

Sie sind 10 Kontrakte Nickel-Futures long.
Einstandskurs: 17.220 USD/t
gestriger Schlusskurs: 18.150 USD/t
Wie hoch ist das Gesamtergebnis?

Settlement-Betrag: (18.150 – 17.220) = 930
10 * 930 = USD 9.300
Sie bekommen **USD 9.300**.

Schließen einer Futuresposition

Jede Futuresposition kann vor dem bzw. am letzten Handelstag mit einer entgegengesetzten Futuresposition aufgelöst werden. Ein Schließen bewirkt die Auflösung der Position und somit der damit verbundenen Initial Margin. Der **Gewinn bzw. Verlust** ergibt sich aus der **Summe der täglichen Margin-Zahlungen** (zuzüglich etwaiger Zinserträge bzw. -aufwendungen).

4.3.3. Open Interest und Handelsvolumen

Diese Daten geben Aufschluss über die **Liquidität in einzelnen Kontrakten und Laufzeiten**. Das höchste Handelsvolumen weist üblicherweise der Kontrakt mit der kürzesten Laufzeit auf (Front Month).

Als Open Interest wird die **Summe aller noch offenen Kontrakte** bezeichnet. Daraus folgt: Wer einen Terminkontrakt kauft („long geht"), ohne zuvor über eine Verkaufsposition in diesem Kontrakt zu verfügen, erhöht das Open Interest immer dann um eins, wenn der Verkäufer gleichzeitig eine neue Verkaufsposition eingeht („short geht"). Wer umgekehrt einen Terminkontrakt verkauft („short"), ohne zuvor über eine Kaufposition

a futures contract, the open interest is increased by one, provided that the buyer is entering into a new long position at the same time. The same holds true vice versa, when considering a decrease of open interest.

In other words: The open interest states **how many positions of a specific contract are held by market participants, and have NOT been closed out yet**.

The higher the trading volume and the open interest, the more liquid is the market. The advantage of highly liquid markets is that market participants can trade huge volumes at relatively low spreads. Therefore, an increasing open interest together with increasing trading volume and increasing prices indicates that the price will probably continue to rise.

Calculating Open Interest

There is a common misunderstanding, that open interest measures the volume of the traded options and futures. That is not true, as explained in the following example:

Beispiel			
Day	**Transactions**	**Open Interest**	**Volume Per Day**
May 1	A buys 1 option and B sells 1 option	1	1
May 2	C buys 5 options and D sells 5 options	6	5
May 3	A sells 1 option and D buys 1 option	5	1
May 4	E buys 5 options from C, who is selling his 5 options	5	5

Open Interest =
(All open long positions + All open short positions) / 2

May 1: A buys 1 option, resulting in an open interest and a volume of 1.
May 2: The transaction between C and D increases the open interest by 5, with a volume of 5.
May 3: A closes his position and thus the open interest is reduced by 1, volume 1.
May 4: E simply replaces C, what has no effect on open interest, the volume is 5 contracts.

in diesem Kontrakt zu verfügen, erhöht das Open Interest immer dann um eins, wenn der Käufer zugleich eine neue Kaufposition eingeht („long"). Gleiches gilt spiegelbildlich auch für die Verringerung des Open Interest.

Anders ausgedrückt: Das Open Interest gibt an, **wie viele Positionen eines bestimmten Kontraktes noch von Marktteilnehmern gehalten werden, die nicht glattgestellt wurden.**

Je höher das Handelsvolumen und das Open Interest, desto liquider ist der Markt. Für die Marktteilnehmer bringt das den Vorteil, dass auch große Volumina jederzeit zu niedrigen Spreads gehandelt werden können. So deutet z.B. ein zunehmendes „Open Interest" bei gleichzeitig steigenden Umsätzen und steigenden Kursen auf künftige weitere Kurssteigerungen hin.

Berechnung Open Interest

Ein geläufiges Missverständnis ist, dass das Open Interest für das Volumen der gehandelten Optionen und Futures gehalten wird. Dies ist nicht richtig, wie im folgenden Beispiel dargestellt:

Beispiel			
Tag	Geschäftsabschlüsse	Open Interest	Volumen pro Tag
1. Mai	A kauft 1 Option und B verkauft 1 Option	1	1
2. Mai	C kauft 5 Optionen und D verkauft 5 Optionen	6	5
3. Mai	A verkauft eine Option und D kauft 1 Option	5	1
4. Mai	E kauft 5 Optionen von C, der seine 5 Optionen verkauft	5	5

Open Interest =
(alle offenen Long-Positionen + alle offenen Short-Positionen) / 2

1. Mai: A kauft eine Option, was zu einem Open Interest und einem Volumen von 1 führt.

2. Mai: C und D erhöhen das Open Interest um 5, Volumen an diesem Tag 5

3. Mai: A schließt seine Position und reduziert somit das Open Interest um 1, Volumen 1

4. Mai: E ersetzt einfach C, wodurch das Open Interest sich nicht verändert, Volumen an diesem Tag 5.

4.4. Products

4.4.1. Futures

A commodity future is a **standardised contract**, where the buyer (seller) is obliged to **receive (deliver) the commodity at a certain price on a certain date in the future**. There are different contract specifications depending on the commodity itself and the exchange where the contracts are traded. The specifications include: value of underlying, contract size, quality, maturity date and price.

There is one big difference between financial futures and commodity futures. Financial products are used exclusively for investment purposes (cash settlement only), whereas **commodities** are also used as goods (**cash as well as physical settlement**). The main function of commodity future trading is risk management. For hedging commodity price risks companies can approach their bank, which will act in the futures market on their behalf.

Long Future = Hedging against rising prices / Speculation on rising prices
Short Future = Hedging against falling prices / Speculation on falling prices

Settlement and Delivery

Commodity futures require the **physical delivery** of the underlying at the end of the term. However, only a few future contracts lead to physical delivery, because the majority of future contracts is **closed out or rolled over before expiry**.

Rolling of Future Contracts

To avoid physical delivery at the end of the term (for hedging or speculative purposes), most futures positions are closed out at current market prices just before expiration. If a trader is willing to maintain his futures position, he can roll it over by closing the existing position and trading a new contract with a later maturity date. In doing so, the **price difference between the existing and the new contract leads to a profit or loss** (rolling profit or loss). Since short-term contracts are rolled over into subsequent contracts, market participants influence future prices. Most traders roll their positions over to contracts with the next-shortest maturity. Therefore, the **liquidity of the short-dated futures is rather high**. The future contracts with the shortest maturity dates are used as indicators for the future price development (such as the Brent Oil Future Contract on ICE in London).

Depending whether the expiring contract is cheaper or more expensive than the new contract, there are **two structures** in the futures market:

Contango

Contango is the premium, when the price of the new contract is higher than the price of the current one. This means: **future price > spot price.** The structure of a contango is an indicator for an **ascending futures curve**.

4.4. Produkte

4.4.1. Futures

Ein Rohstoff-Future (commodity future) ist ein **standardisierter Vertrag**, mit dem sich der Käufer (Verkäufer) verpflichtet, einen **Rohstoff zu einem bestimmten Preis zu einem bestimmten Zeitpunkt in der Zukunft abzunehmen (zu liefern)**. Je nach Rohstoff und Börse können die Kontraktspezifikationen eines Future abweichen: Basiswert, Kontraktgröße, Qualität, Fälligkeitstermin und Preis.

Der Hauptunterschied zwischen Finanz- und Rohstoff-Future ist, dass die Finanzprodukte reine Anlageprodukte sind, während **Rohstoffe sowohl Anlage- als auch Verbrauchsgüter** sein können. Futures auf Rohstoffe sind weithin zum Zweck des Risikomanagement gehandelt. Für eine Rohstoffpreissicherung können die Unternehmen sich an die Bank wenden, die den Futureshandel in ihrem Namen auf einer Börse durchführt.

Long Future = Absicherung gegen steigende Preise / Spekulation auf steigende Preise
Short Future = Absicherung gegen fallende Preise / Spekulation auf fallende Preise

Settlement und Lieferung

Die Rohstoff-Futures setzten eine **physische Lieferung** des Basiswertes am Ende der Laufzeit voraus. Jedoch führen wenige Futures-Kontrakte zu einer physischen Lieferung. Die meisten Futures werden **kurz vor dem Auslaufen aufgelöst/weitergerollt**.

Rollen von Futures-Kontrakten

Um die physische Lieferung bei Endfälligkeit (zwecks Absicherung oder Spekulation) zu vermeiden, werden die Futures-Positionen kurz vor dem Auslaufen zu den aktuellen Marktpreisen aufgelöst. Wenn der Händler seine Futuresposition beibehalten will, kann er sie weiterrollen, indem er die bestehende Position schließt und einen neuen Kontrakt mit späterem Fälligkeitstermin handelt. Dabei stellt die **Preisdifferenz zwischen dem bestehenden und dem neuen Kontrakt einen Gewinn oder einen Verlust** (Rollertrag bzw. Rollverlust) dar. Da der bald auslaufende Kontrakt in den nachfolgenden Kontrakt gerollt wird, beeinflussen die Marktteilnehmer die Preisbildung der Futures. Die meisten Händler wollen auf den nächsten kürzeren Kontrakt rollieren, was zu einer **hohen Liquidität für die kürzeren Termingeschäfte** führt. So wird zum Beispiel als Benchmark für die Entwicklung der Ölpreise der kürzeste Brent-Öl-Futureskontrakt am ICE in London herangezogen.

Je nachdem, ob der neue oder der auslaufende Kontrakt teurer oder billiger ist, existieren am Terminmarkt **zwei Strukturen**:

Contango

Ein Contango ist der **Aufschlag**, bei dem der Kurs des neuen Kontraktes höher als der des bestehenden Kontraktes quotiert, d.h. **Terminkurs > Kassakurs**. Die Contango-Struktur ist ein Indikator für eine **steigende Terminkurve**.

Example

Rollover Loss - Contango

Your client bought 100 contracts of MAR-Copper-Future at 7,401 USD per tonne (contract size 25 t). Three months later the JUN-Future is quoted at 7,801 USD per tonne and the MAR-Future is 7,501 USD.   What are the costs if the client is rolling over his position?

In order to roll over the long future position, the client has to sell the old MAR-contract and buy a new JUN-contract. The results (per tonne) can be calculated: + 7,501 – 7,801 = - 300 USD. The calculation shows a loss of 25 * 300 = 7,500 USD per contract, which leads to the total rollover loss of 750,000 USD for 100 contracts.

Example

Rollover Profit – Contango

Your client entered a short position on the MAR-Copper-Future. In order to roll over his position shortly before expiry, he buys the MAR-contract at 7,501 and sells the JUN-contract at 7,801. Therefore he generates a rollover profit of 300 * 25 * 100 = 750,000 USD.

Backwardation

Backwardation is the discount, when the new contract is cheaper than the current one. This means: **future price < spot price**. The structure of backwardation is an indicator of a declining futures curve.

Example

Rollover Profit – Backwardation

Your client bought 100 contracts of the MAR-Copper-Future at 7,401 USD per tonne. Three months later the JUN-Future is quoted at 7,001   USD per tonne and the MAR-contract is quoted at 7,301 USD. What are the costs, if the client is willing to roll over his position?

In order to roll over his long position in futures, the client has to sell the old MAR-contract and buy a new JUN-contract. The result can be seen in the following calculation: + 7,301 – 7,001 = + 300 USD (per tonne). Therefore, the profit per contract is: 25 * 300 = 7,500 USD, which leads to a total rollover profit of 750,000 USD for 100 contracts.

Example

Rollover Loss – Backwardation

Your client has a short position on the MAR-Copper-Future. To roll over his short position shortly before expiry, he buys the MAR-contract at 7,301 USD and sells the JUN-contract at 7,001 USD. The total rollover result is a loss of 750,000 USD.

Beispiel

Rollverlust bei Contango

Ihr Kunde kauft 100 Kontrakte von MAR-Kupfer-Future zu einem Preis von 7.401 USD per Tonne (Kontraktgröße 25 t). Nach drei Monaten notiert der JUN-Future zu 7.801 USD per Tonne und der MAR-Kontrakt ist 7.501. Wie hoch sind die Kosten, wenn der Kunde kurz vor Fälligkeit seine Position weiterrollen will?

Um die Long-Futures-Position weiterzurollen, muss der Kunde den alten MAR-Kontrakt verkaufen und einen neuen JUN-Kontrakt kaufen. Daraus ergibt sich folgende Rechnung (pro Tonne): + 7.501 − 7.801 = - 300 USD. Pro Kontrakt ergibt sich ein Verlust von 25 * 300 = 7.500 USD oder insgesamt ein Rollverlust von 750.000 USD für 100 Kontrakte.

Beispiel

Rollertrag bei Contango

Der Kunde hat eine Short-Position auf MAR-Kupfer-Future. Um seine Position kurz vor Fälligkeit weiterzurollen, kauft er den MAR-Kontrakt zu 7.501 und verkauft den JUN-Kontrakt zu 7.801. Daraus profitiert er von einem Rollertrag von 300 * 25 * 100 = 750.000 USD.

Backwardation

Backwardation nennt man den **Abschlag**, zu dem der neue Kontrakt günstiger am Markt zu kaufen ist, d.h. **Terminkurs < Kassakurs**. Bei Backwardation ist eine **fallende Terminkurve** zu erwarten.

Beispiel

Rollertrag bei Backwardation

Ihr Kunde kauft 100 Kontrakte von MAR-Kupfer-Future zu einem Preis von 7.401 USD per Tonne. Nach drei Monaten notiert der JUN-Future zu 7.001 USD per Tonne und der MAR-Kontrakt quotiert 7.301. Wie hoch sind die Kosten, wenn der Kunde kurz vor Fälligkeit seine Position weiterrollen will?

Um die Long-Futures-Position weiterzurollen, muss der Kunde den alten MAR-Kontrakt verkaufen und einen neuen JUN-Kontrakt kaufen. Daraus ergibt sich folgende Rechnung (pro Tonne): + 7.301 − 7.001 = + 300 USD. Per Kontrakt ergibt sich ein Gewinn von 25 * 300 = 7.500 USD oder insgesamt ein Rollgewinn von 750.000 USD für 100 Kontrakte.

Beispiel

Rollverlust bei Backwardation

Der Kunde hat eine Short-Position auf MAR Kupfer Future. Um seine Position kurz vor Fälligkeit weiterzurollen, kauft er den MAR-Kontrakt zu 7.301 und verkauft den JUN-Kontrakt zu 7.001. Daraus verliert er 750.000 USD.

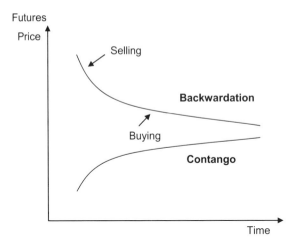

4.4.2. Swaps

Hedging by means of futures/forwards requires liquidity, which is paid into a margin account. Therefore, many companies use swaps for hedging in order to **avoid having to set aside cash**. In commodity markets, the same types of swaps as in the interest rate and foreign exchange markets can be found.

Example
Hedging by commodity swaps

Hedging by commodity swaps

Companies that process commodities have to procure large amounts of resources on a regular (monthly) basis. At the same time the company has already sold their finished products (for which the resources are needed) at a fixed price.

In order to hedge against increasing commodity prices and to achieve a stable sales margin, the company buys a swap. The resulting cash flows are shown in the following figure:

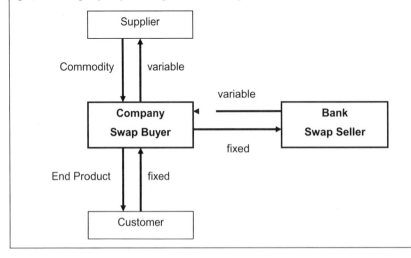

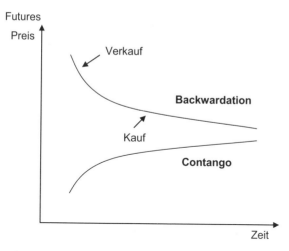

4.4.2. Swaps

Die Preissicherung mittels Futures/Forwards bindet Liquidität durch die Einzahlungen auf das Marginkonto. Aus diesem Grund greifen Unternehmen oft zu Swaps, die **kein Bargeld binden**. Bei Rohstoffen werden die gleichen Arten von Swaps wie im Zins- und FX-Bereich verwendet.

Beispiel

Absicherung mit Rohstoff-Swap

Ein rohstoffverarbeitendes Unternehmen muss regelmäßig (monatlich) einen bestimmten Rohstoff in großen Mengen beschaffen. Gleichzeitig hat es schon seine Absatzmenge (für die der Rohstoff benötigt wird) zu einem fixen Preis verkauft.

Um sich gegen steigende Rohstoffpreise abzusichern und eine stabile Absatzmarge zu erzielen, kauft das Unternehmen einen Swap. Die Cashflows können so dargestellt werden:

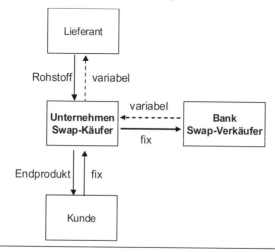

During the term of the swap transaction there are balancing payments, depending on the difference between fixed price and market price. If the fixed price is higher than the market price, the customer has to pay compensation and vice versa. Hence the customer is **fixing the purchasing price** and **hedging against market volatility**.

Conventions

Commodity	Fixing	Maximum Maturity	Currency
Aluminium		10 years	
Lead		5 years	
Copper		8 years	
Nickel		8 years	
Zinc	each working day	8 years	EUR, USD
Tin		6 years	
Crude Oil		20 years	
Jet Fuel		6 years	
Diesel		6 years	
Natural Gas		3 years	
Coal	each Friday	5 years	
Electricity	each working day	5 years	EUR

4.4.3. Options

An option grants its holder the right to **buy** (call option) or **sell** (put option)

- a specific asset (underlying),
- at a specific price (strike),
- until a specific date (expiration date).

An option focuses on the **right** to buy or sell the underlying. That is the big difference compared to future transactions, where the involved parties agree upon the fixed purchase or sale.

Call options grant the holder the right to **buy,** and **put** options grant the holder the right to **sell** the underlying. For granting the buyer the choice of exercising the option, the seller demands a fee (premium), which has to be paid on conclusion (that is spot valuta) of the option contract.

The seller (also called writer) of an option is obliged to buy or sell a specific amount of a specified underlying at a given price, if the holder of the option decides to exercise it.

Während der Laufzeit vom Swap-Geschäft erfolgt auf monatlicher Basis eine Ausgleichszahlung, je nachdem, ob der durchschnittliche Marktpreis höher oder niedriger als der vereinbarte Fixpreis ist. Wenn der Fixpreis höher als der Marktpreis ist, zahlt der Kunde an die Bank und vice versa. Somit hat er seinen **Einkaufspreis fixiert** und sich **gegen Marktvolatilitäten abgesichert**.

Konventionen

Rohstoff	Fixing	maximale Laufzeit	Währungen
Aluminium	jeden Werktag	10 Jahre	EUR, USD
Blei		5 Jahre	
Kupfer		8 Jahre	
Nickel		8 Jahre	
Zink		8 Jahre	
Zinn		6 Jahre	
Rohöl		20 Jahre	
Düsentreibstoff		6 Jahre	
Diesel		6 Jahre	
Erdgas		3 Jahre	
Kohle	jeden Freitag	5 Jahre	
Strom	jeden Werktag	5 Jahre	EUR

4.4.3. Optionen

Eine Option gibt dem Inhaber das **Recht**,

- einen bestimmten **Wert** (Basiswert, Underlying)
- zu einem bestimmten **Preis** (Basispreis, Strike) und
- bis zu einem bestimmten **Zeitpunkt** (Verfalltag, Expiry Date)

zu **kaufen** (Call, Kaufoption) bzw. zu **verkaufen** (Put, Verkaufsoption).

Es steht also das Recht, den Basiswert zu kaufen bzw. zu verkaufen, im Mittelpunkt. Darin besteht der wesentliche Unterschied zu einem Termingeschäft, bei dem der fixe Kauf bzw. Verkauf vereinbart wird.

Eine **Call**-Option berechtigt also den Inhaber zum **Kauf**, eine **Put**-Option zum **Verkauf** des Basiswertes. Für das Einräumen des Wahlrechtes verlangt der Verkäufer der Option eine einmalige Gebühr (Prämie), die bei Abschluss (d.h. mit Valuta Spot) fällig wird.

Der Verkäufer einer Option (auch Stillhalter) verpflichtet sich daher, einen bestimmten Betrag eines definierten Underlying zum vereinbarten Preis zu kaufen bzw. zu verkaufen, falls der Inhaber der Option diese ausübt.

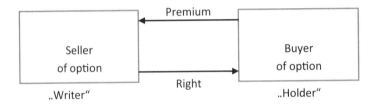

	Example
	In the following, you find an option contract in short form and an explanation of the data:

Call on diesel
Strike: 920 per tonne
Expiration day: 25th September
Premium: 30 USD

Explanation: |

Call: type of option
Diesel: Underlying:
                the instrument or asset, which the buyer of the call may buy but is not obliged to
Strike 920:   exercise price or base price:
                the rate at which the buyer of the call may buy the underlying but is not obliged to
Expiration day: the last day on which the buyer of the option has the right to exercise
Premium: the price the option buyer is paying to the seller, here 30 USD per unit

Data in option contracts

- **Dealing day**: day on which the option contract is concluded.
- **Premium payment date, premium valuta:** day on which the premium has to be paid, usually two banking days after the dealing day
- **Exercise date**: date on which the buyer may exercise the option.
- **Expiration date (maturity date)**: the last day on which the buyer has the chance to exercise the option. In the case of European options, the exercise date is equivalent to the expiration date, whereas American options can be exercised before expiration date as well.
- **Settlement date (delivery day)**: the day on which the underlying has to be delivered. The settlement day is usually two banking days after the exercise of the option both for American and European options.

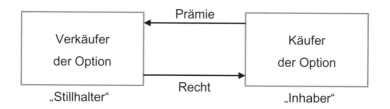

```
                    Prämie
┌─────────────────┐ ◄─────── ┌─────────────────┐
│   Verkäufer     │          │    Käufer       │
│                 │          │                 │
│   der Option    │ ───────► │   der Option    │
└─────────────────┘  Recht   └─────────────────┘
   „Stillhalter"                  „Inhaber"
```

Beispiel

Hier ist ein Optionskontrakt in Kurzform angegeben.
Die einzelnen Daten werden in der Folge erläutert:

Call auf Diesel
Strike: 920 pro Tonne
Verfalltag: 25. September
Prämie: 30 USD

Erklärung:
Call:	Optionsart
Diesel:	Basiswert bzw. Underlying: jenes Instrument, welches der Käufer des Call kaufen kann, aber nicht muss.
Strike 920:	Ausübungspreis bzw. Basispreis: Kurs, zu dem der Käufer des Call das Underlying kaufen darf, aber nicht muss
Verfalltag:	auch Expiry Date: letzter Tag, an dem der Optionskäufer sein Recht ausüben darf
Prämie:	Preis, den der Käufer der Option an den Verkäufer zahlt, hier 30 USD pro Einheit

---

Daten im Optionskontrakt

- **Handelstag:** der Tag, an dem der Optionskontrakt abgeschlossen wurde.
- **Premium Payment Date, Prämienvaluta:** der Tag, an dem die Prämie fällig ist, üblicherweise zwei Banktage nach dem Handelstag.
- **Exercise Date (Ausübungstag):** das Datum, an dem der Käufer die Option ausübt.
- **Expiration Date (Verfalltag, Fälligkeitstag):** der letzte Tag, an dem der Käufer die Option ausüben darf. Bei europäischen Optionen entspricht das Exercise Date dem Expiration Date, während bei amerikanischen Optionen das Exercise Date vor dem Expiration Date liegen kann.
- **Settlement Date (Liefertag):** der Tag, an dem der Basiswert geliefert wird. Der Liefertag ist sowohl bei europäischen als auch bei amerikanischen Optionen zwei Banktage nach der Ausübung.

European / American / Bermudian Options

A **European** or European-style option can be exercised by the buyer only on one specific day – expiration date.

An **American** or American-style option can be exercised at any time during the trading hours until the expiration date. This is the usual type of stock options. The price of American options is almost equivalent to the price of a comparable European option. Although they cannot be exercised before expiration date, they can be sold at any time.

A **Bermudian** or Bermudian-style option can be exercised only on specific dates of the term, which are set in advance. Therefore, it is a kind of hybrid between American and European options.

At the money / in the money / out of the money

An option is said to be **at the money** (ATM), if its strike price equals or is very near the actual price.

Methodically correct is the commonly practiced comparison of the strike price with the future price of the same maturity. This leads to the expression: the option is **at-the-money-forward**. Sometimes, however, the strike price is compared to the current spot price. Then, the option would be **at-the-money-spot**.

An option is **in the money** (ITM), if the strike price is "better" than the current market price of the underlying and thus granting the buyer an advantage. This means that the strike price is lower than the spot price considering a call option and vice versa considering a put option.

An option is **out of the money** (OTM), if the strike price is "worse" than the current market price. A call option is out of the money, if the strike price is above the current market price; and a put option is out of the money, if the strike price is lower than the actual market price.

The 4 Basic Option Positions

Long Call
Long call with strike A and break-even B (strike + premium)

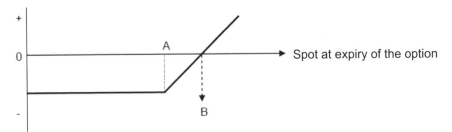

→ **Loss**, if Price < Strike + Premium
→ **Profit**, if Price > Strike + Premium

Europäische/amerikanische/Bermudian Optionen

Eine **europäische** oder European-style Option kann vom Käufer nur an einem Tag – dem Expiration Date (Verfalltag) – ausgeübt werden.

Eine **amerikanische** oder American-style Option kann jederzeit während der Handelszeiten bis zum Expiration Date (Verfallsdatum) ausgeübt werden. Diese Art ist bei Aktienoptionen üblich. Der Preis einer amerikanischen Option entspricht dem einer vergleichbaren europäischen Option, da europäische Optionen während der Laufzeit zwar nicht ausgeübt, aber jederzeit verkauft werden können.

Eine **Bermudian** oder Bermudian-style Option kann nur an bestimmten, im Voraus definierten Terminen während der Laufzeit der Option ausgeübt werden. Sie ist also eine Mischform aus europäischer und amerikanischer Option.

Am Geld/im Geld/aus dem Geld

Eine Option ist **am Geld** (at the money, ATM), wenn ihr Ausübungspreis gleich oder nahezu gleich dem aktuellen Kurs ist.

Methodisch richtig und üblich ist dabei der Vergleich mit dem Terminkurs für die entsprechende Fälligkeit. Man spricht daher auch von at-the-money-forward. Manchmal wird der Strike jedoch auch mit dem Kassakurs verglichen. Man spricht dann von at-the-money-spot.

Im Geld (in the money, ITM) ist eine Option, wenn der Strike „besser" als der aktuelle Marktpreis des Basiswertes ist, d.h. wenn die Option für den Käufer einen Vorteil darstellt. Das bedeutet für einen Call, dass der Strike unter dem aktuellen Marktkurs liegt. Bei einem Put ist die Option im Geld, wenn der Strike über dem aktuellen Marktpreis liegt.

Aus dem Geld (out of the money, OTM) ist eine Option, wenn der Strike „schlechter" als der aktuelle Marktpreis ist. Das bedeutet für einen Call, dass der Strike über dem aktuellen Marktkurs liegt. Ein Put mit Strike unter dem aktuellen Marktpreis ist aus dem Geld.

Die vier Grundpositionen bei Optionen

Long Call

Long Call zum Strike A und Break-even B (Strike + Prämie)

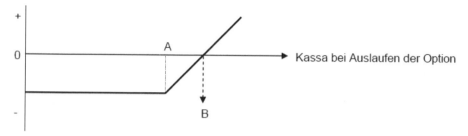

➜ **Verlust**, wenn Preis < Strike + Prämie
➜ **Gewinn**, wenn Preis > Strike + Prämie

The buyer of a call option (long call) makes a profit, if the spot price at expiration day is higher than the strike price and if the difference is also higher than the costs of the premium. The maximum loss is limited to the amount of the premium.

Between point A and point B the exercise of the option generates some profits, but these profits are not big enough to cover the expenses of the premium and therefore lead to an overall net loss.

Example

Purchase call diesel: strike 920.00 USD/t, premium: 30.00 USD
    Profit & loss in USD with assumed diesel prices at expiration day:

Price at expiration day	880,00	900,00	920,00	940,00	960,00
Result long call	0,00	0,00	0,00	+20,00	+40,00
Premium	-30,00	-30,00	-30,00	-30,00	-30,00
Total	-30,00	-30,00	-30,00	-10,00	+10,00

The higher the spot price on expiration day, the higher will be the intrinsic value of the option. The premium paid remains always the same (30,00 USD). On conclusion the premium is paid to the seller. The maximum loss of this particular option position is 30,00 USD (premium), whereas the potential profits are infinite.

Short Call

Short call with strike A and break-even B (strike + premium)

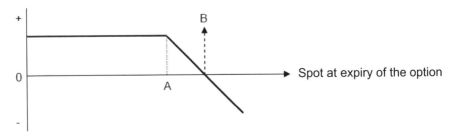

→ **Loss**, if Price > Strike + Premium
→ **Profit**, if Price < Strike + Premium

As long as the price at expiration day is lower than the strike price plus the obtained premium, the seller of the option generates a profit. The maximum loss is theoretically infinite.

The maximum profit is limited to the amount of the premium. Between point A and point B the price lies above the strike price, but the seller earns more via the premium than he loses by exercising the option.

Die Gewinnzone ist erreicht, wenn der Kassakurs am Verfalltag über dem Strike liegt und der Prämienaufwand verdient wird. Der maximale Verlust ist die Prämie.

Zwischen den Punkten A und B wird zwar durch das Ausüben der Option ein Gewinn erzielt, er reicht jedoch nicht aus, um die gesamten Prämienkosten abzudecken, um damit im Gesamtergebnis die Gewinnzone zu erreichen.

Beispiel

Kauf Call Diesel: Strike 920,00 USD/t, Prämie: 30,00 USD
   GuV in USD bei angenommenen Dieselpreisen am Verfalltag:

Preis am Verfalltag	880,00	900,00	920,00	940,00	960,00
Ergebnis Long Call	0,00	0,00	0,00	+20,00	+40,00
Prämie	–30,00	–30,00	–30,00	–30,00	–30,00
Gesamt	–30,00	–30,00	–30,00	–10,00	+10,00

Je höher der Kassakurs am Verfalltag liegt, desto größer ist auch der innere Wert der Option. Die Prämie ist bei jedem angenommenen

Kassakurs gleich (30,00 USD), sie wird sofort bei Abschluss an den Verkäufer gezahlt. Der maximale Verlust dieser Optionsposition beträgt 30,00 USD (Prämie), das Gewinnpotenzial ist unbegrenzt.

Short Call

Short Call zum Strike A und Break-even B (Strike + Prämie)

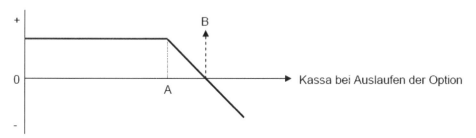

→ **Verlust**, wenn Preis > Strike + Prämie
→ **Gewinn**, wenn Preis < Strike + Prämie

Solange der Preis am Verfalltag unter dem Strike zuzüglich der erhaltenen Prämie liegt, bleibt der Verkäufer der Option in der Gewinnzone. Der Verlust kann theoretisch ins Unendliche gehen.

Der maximale Gewinn ist die Prämie. Zwischen den Punkten A und B liegt der Preis über dem Strike, aber der Verkäufer verdient aus der Prämie noch mehr, als er in der Option verliert.

Beispiel

Selling call diesel: strike 920.00 USD/t, premium: 30.00 USD
    Profit & loss with assumed diesel prices at expiration day:

Price at expiration day	880.00	900.00	920.00	940.00	960.00
Result short call	0.00	0.00	0.00	-20.00	-40.00
Premium	+30.00	+30.00	+30.00	+30.00	+30.00
Total	+30.00	+30.00	+30.00	+10.00	-10.00

The higher the price on expiration day, the higher the loss of the option position. The premium remains the same (30.00 USD); it does not depend on spot prices and is paid immediately on conclusion of the option contract. The maximum profit is limited to 30.00 USD (premium) and the potential loss is infinite.

Long Put

Long put with strike A and break-even B (strike – premium)

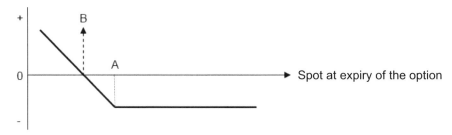

→ **Loss**, if Price > Strike - Premium
→ **Profit**, if Price < Strike - Premium

The buyer of a put option (long put) earns a profit, if the spot price at expiration day is lower than the strike price and if this difference is larger than the premium costs. The maximum loss is limited to the amount of the premium. Between point A and point B, the buyer makes a profit by exercising the option, but not enough to offset the expenses for the premium. However, it is possible for the buyer to reduce premium costs.

Example

Purchase put on diesel: Strike 920.00 USD/t, premium: 30.00 USD
    Profit & loss in USD with assumed diesel prices at expiration day:

Beispiel

Verkauf Call auf Diesel: Strike 920,00 USD/t, Prämie: 30,00 USD
  GuV in USD bei angenommenen Dieselpreisen am Verfalltag:

Preise am Verfalltag	880,00	900,00	920,00	940,00	960,00
Ergebnis Short Call	0,00	0,00	0,00	−20,00	−40,00
Prämie	+30,00	+30,00	+30,00	+30,00	+30,00
Gesamt	+30,00	+30,00	+30,00	+10,00	−10,00

Je höher der Preis am Verfalltag liegt, desto größer ist auch der Verlust aus der Option. Die Prämie ist bei jedem angenommenen Preis gleich (30,00 USD), sie wird sofort bei Abschluss vom Käufer gezahlt. Der maximale Gewinn dieser Optionsposition beträgt 30,00 USD (Prämie), das Verlustpotenzial ist unbegrenzt.

Long Put

Long Put zum Strike A und Break-even B (Strike – Prämie)

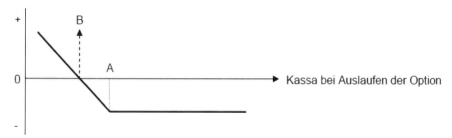

→ **Verlust**: wenn Preis > Strike – Prämie
→ **Gewinn:** wenn Preis < Strike – Prämie

Die Gewinnzone ist erreicht, wenn der Preis am Verfalltag unter dem Strike liegt und der Prämienaufwand verdient wird. Der maximale Verlust ist die Prämie. Zwischen den Punkten A und B liegt der Preis unter dem Strike, aber der Käufer verdient durch Ausüben der Option weniger, als er Prämie bezahlt hat. Immerhin reduziert der Käufer die Prämienkosten.

Beispiel

Verkauf Call auf Diesel: Strike 920,00 USD/t, Prämie: 30,00 USD
  GuV in USD bei angenommenen Dieselpreisen am Verfalltag:

Price at expiration day	880.00	900.00	920.00	940.00	960.00
Result long put	+40.00	+20.00	0.00	0.00	0.00
Premium	-30.00	-30.00	-30.00	-30.00	-30.00
Total	+10.00	-10.00	-30.00	-30.00	-30.00

The lower the price at expiration day, the higher will be the profit of the option position. The premium does not depend on the assumed price movement and remains always the same (30.00 USD). It has to be paid to the seller on conclusion of the option contract. The maximum loss is limited to the amount of the premium (30.00 USD) and the potential profit is infinite.

Short Put
Short put with strike A and break-even B (strike - premium)

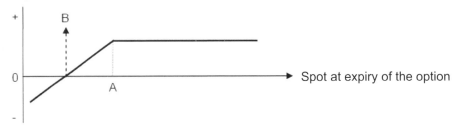

→ **Loss**, if Price < Strike - Premium
→ **Profit**, if Price > Strike - Premium

The seller remains in the profit zone until the price at expiration day is lower than the strike price and the loss at exercising the option exceeds the premium. The maximum loss is theoretically limited to a situation when the underlying has the price of zero.

Since a short put position is similar to a long position in the underlying (= risk of falling prices) and nobody talks about limited risk with regard to short positions, the risk is said to be substantial. The maximum profit is limited to the amount of the premium. Between point A and point B, the seller makes a loss when the buyer exercises the option, but these losses are smaller than the premium.

Example
Sale put on diesel: strike 920.00 USD/t, premium: 30.00 USD

Profit & loss with assumed diesel prices at expiration day:

Price at expiration day	880.00	900.00	920.00	940.00	960.00
Resultlong put	-40.00	-20.00	0.00	0.00	0.00
Premium	+30.00	+30.00	+30.00	+30.00	+30.00
Total	-10.00	+10.00	+30.00	+30.00	+30.00

Preise am Verfalltag	880,00	900,00	920,00	940,00	960,00
Ergebnis Long Put	+40,00	+20,00	0,00	0,00	0,00
Prämie	–30,00	–30,00	–30,00	–30,00	–30,00
Gesamt	+10,00	–10,00	–30,00	–30,00	–30,00

Je niedriger der Preis am Verfalltag liegt, desto größer ist auch der Gewinn aus der Option. Die Prämie ist bei jedem angenommenen Preis gleich (30,00 USD), sie wird sofort bei Abschluss an den Verkäufer gezahlt. Der maximale Verlust dieser Optionsposition beträgt 30,00 USD (Prämie), das Gewinnpotenzial ist substanziell.

Short Put

Short Put zum Strike A und Break-even B (Strike – Prämie)

→ **Verlust:** bei Preis < Strike – Prämie
→ **Gewinn:** bei Preis > Strike – Prämie

Der Verkäufer bleibt so lange in der Gewinnzone, bis der Preis am Verfalltag so weit unter dem Strike liegt, dass die Prämie niedriger als der Verlust aus der Optionsposition wird. Der Verlust ist streng theoretisch auf einen Preis gleich null beschränkt.

Da aber ein Short Put vom Risiko her einer Long-Position im Underlying entspricht (= Risiko fallender Preise) und niemand von einem begrenzten Risiko bei einer Short-Position spricht, kann auch das Verlustrisiko eines Short Put als substanziell bezeichnet werden. Maximaler Gewinn ist die Prämie. Zwischen den Punkten A und B liegt der Preis unter dem Strike, aber der Verkäufer verdient aus der Prämie noch mehr, als er in der Option verliert.

Beispiel

Verkauf Call auf Diesel: Strike 920,00 USD/t, Prämie: 30,00 USD
   GuV in USD bei angenommenen Dieselpreisen am Verfalltag:

Preise am Verfalltag	880,00	900,00	920,00	940,00	960,00
Ergebnis Short Put	–40,00	–20,00	0,00	0,00	0,00
Prämie	+30,00	+30,00	+30,00	+30,00	+30,00
Gesamt	–10,00	+10,00	+30,00	+30,00	+30,00

The lower the price on expiration day, the higher will be the loss of the option position. The premium remains the same (30.00 USD), it does not depend on spot prices and is paid immediately on conclusion of the option contract. The maximum profit is limited to 30.00 USD (premium) and the potential loss is infinite.

4.4.4. Metal Loan (Lending/Borrowing)

A market for metal lending (especially gold lending) has been developing since the 1980s. Investors (as well as central banks) would lend their gold holdings (especially to producers such as mining companies). Producers sell the gold on the spot market and use the obtained money to finance their production. The borrowed gold will be paid back later on by selling the gold the mining companies produces. Producers thus get access to relatively **cheap funding** and lenders obtain **yields** in the form of a lending fee on **gold, which does not pay interest per se**.

Gold Forward Offered Rate / Gold Lease Rate

The **"rate" at which dealers lend gold against USD,** is also called gold forward offered rate (GOFO) or gold lease rate.

The following example shows how the gold lease rate is determined by certain variables:

Example

Gold price spot   400.00
Future price 1 year   404.00 (360 days)
USD interest 1 year   1.50% (360 days)
 	
An investor could carry out the following transactions in order to generate additional returns:
• Selling gold on spot market at USD 400.00
• Investing these USD 400.00 at 1.5% for one year; after one year the investor gets back USD 406.00 [400 * (1 + 0.015 * 360 / 360)]
• Buying gold future 1 year at USD 404.00
 	
Result:
After one year the investor gets a risk-free return of 2 USD (406 - 404).
     This corresponds to an interest yield of 0.50% p.a. (2/400) on his gold holdings.
     If the investor lends his gold instead of undertaking the transactions described above, he should expect exactly the same yield, this means that he demands 0.5% p.a. for lending gold under the assumed circumstances. This leads to the conclusion that the rate of gold (gold lease rate) in this particular market setting is 0.5%.
     As demonstrated in this example, the rate at which gold can be borrowed can be deduced from the difference between the yield on an USD asset and the premium/discount of the gold future.

Je niedriger der Preis am Verfalltag liegt, desto größer ist auch der Verlust aus der Option. Die Prämie ist bei jedem angenommenen Preis gleich (30,00 USD), sie wird sofort bei Abschluss vom Käufer gezahlt. Der maximale Gewinn dieser Optionsposition beträgt 30,00 USD (Prämie), das Verlustpotenzial ist substanziell.

4.4.4. Metallleihe/-kredit (lending/borrowing)

Seit den Achtzigerjahren hat sich ein Markt für die Metallleihe (v.a. die Goldleihe) entwickelt. Hintergrund dabei ist, dass Investoren (aber auch Notenbanken) ihre Goldbestände verleihen (vor allem an Produzenten, z.B. an Minen). Die Produzenten verkaufen das Gold am Kassamarkt und verwenden das dadurch erhaltene Geld zur Finanzierung der Produktion. Der Goldkredit wird später durch das geförderte Gold wieder zurückgezahlt. Die Produzenten profitieren dabei von einer **günstigen Finanzierung** und die Verleiher erhalten durch die Leihgebühr einen **Ertrag auf die an sich zinslose Anlage in Gold**.

Gold Forward Offered Rate/Gold Lease Rate

Den bei diesen Leihtransaktionen angewendeten **„Zinssatz", zu dem Dealer Gold gegen USD verleihen**, nennt man auch Gold Forward Offered Rate (GOFO) oder Gold Lease Rate. Wodurch die Höhe der Gold Lease Rate bestimmt wird, soll am folgenden Beispiel demonstriert werden:

Beispiel	
Goldpreis-Spot	400,00
Terminkurs 1 Jahr	404,00(360 Tage)
USD Zinsen 1 Jahr	1,50 %(360 Tage)

Ein Anleger könnte folgende Transaktionen durchführen, um einen Zusatzertrag zu erwirtschaften:
- Verkauf Gold in der Kassa zu USD 400,00
- Anlage der USD 400,00 auf ein Jahr zu 1,5 %: dadurch erhält er nach einem Jahr USD 406,00 zurück [400 x (1 + 0,015 * 360/360)]
- Kauf Gold auf Termin 1 Jahr zu USD 404,00

Ergebnis:
Der Anleger hat nach einem Jahr einen Ertrag von 2 USD (406 – 404).

Das entspricht einer Verzinsung für seinen Goldbestand von 0,50 % p.a. (2/400).

Wenn der Anleger nun das Gold verleiht, anstatt die o.a. Transaktionen durchzuführen, sollte er den gleichen Ertrag erwarten können, d.h. er wird bei den angegebenen Marktdaten für die Verleihung des Goldes ebenfalls 0,5 % p.a. verlangen, d.h. der Zinssatz für Gold (die Gold Lease Rate) beträgt bei der obigen Marktkonstellation 0,5 %.

Wie im Beispiel demonstriert, ergibt sich also der Satz, zu dem Gold verliehen wird, aus der Differenz zwischen dem Zinssatz für eine Veranlagung des USD-Betrages und dem Aufschlag/Abschlag im Goldterminmarkt.

Formula for Calculating the Lease Rate

Lease Rate = LIBOR – Contango denominated in percent p.a.
respectively
Lease Rate = LIBOR + Backwardation denominated in percent p.a.

Example

Gold spot	400.00
Future 180 days	402.10
USD 180 days	1.30%

What is the lease rate?
Contango denominated in percent p.a. = (402.10 – 400.00) / 400 * 360/180 = 1.05%
Lease Rate = Libor – Contango
Lease Rate = 1.30% – 1.05% = 0.25%

Example of Lease Rates for Gold: (Contango/Premium)

	Gold	Premium	Libor	Lease rate
Spot	400.00	in % p.a.	in % p.a.	in % p.a.
90 days	400.75	0.75%	1.00%	0.25%
180 days	402.10	1.05%	1.20%	0.15%
360 days	404.00	1.00%	1.50%	0.50%

Example of Lease Rates for Platinum: (Backwardation/Discount)

	Platinum	Discount	Libor	Lease rate
Spot	840.00	in % p.a.	in % p.a.	in % p.a.
90 days	836.00	-1.90%	1.00%	2.90%
180 days	830.00	-2.38%	1.20%	3.58%
360 days	815.00	-2.98%	1.50%	4.48%

The higher the backwardation respectively the lower the contango, the higher is the lease rate.

4.5. Application Examples

4.5.1. Example Future

A stainless steel producer (nickel processing company) has a stock of 60 tonnes of nickel, which was bought at a price of 17,000 USD/t. Due to an assumed fall in nickel prices the company wants to hedge its exposure. Therefore, the producer carries out the following transactions on the LME:

- Selling of 10 nickel contracts (contract size 6 t) at the price of 17,220 USD/t
- Maturity: 1 month

Regel zur Ermittlung der Lease Rate

Lease Rate = LIBOR – Contango in Prozent p.a.

bzw.

Lease Rate = LIBOR + Backwardation in Prozent p.a.

Beispiel
Goldpreis-Spot 400,00   Terminkurs 180 Tage 402,10   USD Zinsen 180 Tage 1,30 %   Wie hoch ist die Lease Rate?   Contango in Prozent p.a. = (402,10 – 400,00) / 400 * 360/180 = 1,05 %   Lease Rate = Libor – Contango   Lease Rate = 1,30 % – 1,05 % = 0,25 %

Lease Rates am Beispiel Gold: (mit Contango/Aufschlag)

	Gold	**Aufschlag**	**Libor**	**Lease rate**
Spot	400,00	in % p.a.	in % p.a.	in % p.a.
90 Tage	400,75	0,75 %	1,00 %	0,25 %
180 Tage	402,10	1,05 %	1,20 %	0,15 %
360 Tage	404,00	1,00 %	1,50 %	0,50 %

Lease Rates am Beispiel Platin: (mit Backwardation/Abschlag)

	Platin	**Abschlag**	**Libor**	**Lease rate**
Spot	840,00	in % p.a.	in % p.a.	in % p.a.
90 Tage	836,00	–1,90 %	1,00 %	2,90 %
180 Tage	830,00	–2,38 %	1,20 %	3,58 %
360 Tage	815,00	–2,98 %	1,50 %	4,48 %

Die Lease Rate ist also umso höher, je höher die Backwardation bzw. je niedrigerer der Contango ist.

4.5. Anwendungsbeispiele

4.5.1. Beispiel Future

Ein Edelstahlhersteller (nickelverarbeitende Firma) hat einen Lagerbestand an Nickel von 60 Tonnen, der zu einem Preis von 17.000 USD/t eingekauft wurde und der auf Grund der Annahme von fallenden Nickelpreisen gegen einen Wertverfall abgesichert werden soll. Aus diesem Grund schließt er folgendes Geschäft an der LME ab:

- Verkauf von 10 Nickelkontrakten (Kontraktgröße 6 t) zum Preis von 17.220 USD/t
- Fälligkeit: ein Monat

At expiration day, the price of the future is 16,000 USD/t. Hence the company earns 1,220 USD/t (17,220 – 16,000) and successfully hedged its stock against falling prices. The initial purchase price of 17,000 USD/t was reduced by 1,220 USD by using futures (purchase price + hedging result = 15,780 USD/t)

4.5.2. Example Swap

A battery producer (lead processing company) attempts to fix purchasing prices. The company assumes a demand of 600 t of lead per month. Therefore the company enters a swap on lead on the LME in January 20XX

- Hedged volume: 600 t
- Price: 2,175 EUR/month
- Time frame: February 20XX until July 20XX

During the term of the hedge transaction the average price of the commodity on the relevant exchange is calculated on a monthly basis and compared to the stipulated fixed price (2,175 EUR/month). This difference (positive or negative) is multiplied by the amount of the commodity per month and thus results in cash flow payments in one direction or the other (i.e. from bank to customer or vice versa).

Result per 1 t:

	FEB	MAR	APR	MAY	JUN	JUL
Market price	2,300	2,100	2,250	2,300	2,400	2,500
Swap fix	-2,175	-2.,175	-2,175	-2,175	-2,175	-2,175
Swap variable	2,300	2,100	2,250	2,300	2,400	2,500
Result swap	**125**	**-75**	**75**	**125**	**225**	**325**
Purchase at market prices	-2,300	-2,100	-2,250	-2,300	-2,400	-2,500
Total result	**-2,175**	**-2,175**	**-2,175**	**-2,175**	**-2,175**	**-2,175**

4.5.3. Examples Options

Hedging with a Long Call

Example

A galvanising plant receives orders at fixed prices, while having to buy zinc on the market. The company expects the zinc price to decline, but still does not want to take the risk of increasing prices. Therefore, the company decides to hedge the price risk by buying a call option.

In order to hedge against rising purchasing prices, it buys a call with the strike price of 1,450 USD/t (price ceiling) and a premium of 55 USD.

Bei Fälligkeit des Futures ist der Preis bei 16.000 USD/t. Das Unternehmen verdient damit 1.220 USD/t (17.220 – 16.000) und konnte damit seinen Lagerbestand gegen fallende Preise absichern. Da sein Einstandspreis 17.000 USD/t war, wird der Einstandspreis über den Einsatz der Futures um 1.220 USD verbessert (Einstandspreis inkl. Absicherung damit 15.780 USD/t).

4.5.2. Beispiel Swap

Ein Batteriehersteller (bleiverarbeitendes Unternehmen) möchte seinen Einkaufspreis fixieren. Das Unternehmen rechnet mit einem monatlichen Bedarf von 600 t Blei. Aus diesem Grund wird im Januar 20XX folgender Swap auf Blei an der LME abgeschlossen:

- Sicherungsmenge: 600 t
- Preis: 2.175 EUR/mt
- Zeitraum: Februar 20XX bis Juli 20xx

Im Verlauf des Sicherungsgeschäfts wird auf monatlicher Basis der durchschnittliche Rohstoffpreis an der relevanten Börse ermittelt und mit dem vereinbarten Fixpreis (2.175 EUR/mt) verglichen. Die resultierende (positive oder negative) Differenz wird mit der Monatsrohstoffmenge multipliziert und ergibt so den Zahlungsstrom in die eine oder andere Richtung (d.h. von der Bank an den Kunden und umgekehrt).

Darstellung Ergebnis pro 1 t:

	FEB	MAR	APR	MAI	JUN	JUL
Marktpreis	2.300	2.100	2.250	2.300	2.400	2.500
Swap fest	–2.175	–2.175	–2.175	–2.175	–2.175	–2.175
Swap variabel	2.300	2.100	2.250	2.300	2.400	2.500
Ergebnis Swap	**125**	**–75**	**75**	**125**	**225**	**325**
Einkauf zu Marktpreis	–2.300	–2.100	–2.250	–2.300	–2.400	–2.500
Gesamtergebnis	**–2.175**	**–2.175**	**–2.175**	**–2.175**	**–2.175**	**–2.175**

4.5.3. Beispiele Optionen

Absicherung mit Long Call

> **Beispiel**
>
> Eine Verzinkerei hat Auftragseingänge zu Fixpreisen und muss sicham Markt Zink kaufen. Das Unternehmen erwartet fallende Zinkpreise, möchte/kann das Risiko von steigenden Preisen jedoch nicht eingehen. Das Unternehmen beschließt, die Absicherung mit einem gekauften Call zu machen.
>
> Um sich gegen steigende Einkaufspreise abzusichern, kauft es einen Call mit einem Strike von 1.450 USD/t (Preisobergrenze) und einer Prämie von 55 USD.

Price of zinc in USD	Pre-miu	1,250	1,300	1,350	1,400	1,450	1,500	1,550
Costs purchase zinc per t		-1,250	-1,300	-1,350	-1,400	-1,450	-1,500	-1,550
Result long call at 1,450 USD/t	-55	---	---	---	---	---	+50	+100
Total premium	-55	-55	-55	-55	-55	-55	-55	-55
Total costs per t in USD		- 1,305	- 1,355	- 1,355	-1,455	-1,505	-1,505	-1,505

By purchasing a call option the company has to pay the premium, but is able to fully profit from an advantageous price development (minus the premium). In the example given above, the company is able to lock in a maximum purchasing price at 1,505 USD/t and profit in case of falling prices as well.

Hedging with a Zero Cost Call

Example
A galvanising plant receives orders at fixed prices, while having to buy zinc on the market. The company expects the zinc price to decline slightly, but still does not want to take the risk of increasing prices.Since hedging by buying a call option would be too expensive, the company decides to engage in the following strategy: In order to hedge against rising purchasing prices, it buys a call with the strike price of 1,450 USD/t (maximum price limit) and a premium of 55 USD and at the same time it sells a put with the strike price of 1,350 USD/t (bottom price limit) and a premium of 55 USD.

Price of zinc in USD	Premi-um	1,300	1,350	1,400	1,450	1,500
Costs purchase zinc per t		-1,300	-1,350	-1,400	-1,450	-1,500
Result long call 1,450 USD/t	-55	---	---	---	---	+50
Result short put 1,350 USD/t	+55	-50	---	---	---	---
Total premium	0	0	0	0	0	0
Total costs per t in USD		- 1,350	-1,350	-1,400	-1,450	-1,450

By using a zero cost call the company saves the premium payment, but at the same time foregoes the chance to fully profit from advantageous price movements. In the example given, the company is able to limit its purchasing prices to a bandwidth of 1,350 USD/t to 1,450 USD/t, but has to accept a fixed minimum price of 1,350 USD/t. It cannot profit from further falling prices, because it sold the put option.

Zinkpreise in USD	Prämie	1.250	1.300	1.350	1.400	1.450	1.500	1.550
Kosten Einkauf Zink pro t		−1.250	−1.300	−1.350	−1.400	−1.450	−1.500	−1.550
Ergebnis Long Call 1.450 USD/t	−55	---	---	---	---	---	+50	+100
Summe Prämie	−55	−55	−55	−55	−55	−55	−55	−55
Gesamtkosten pro t in USD		**−1.305**	**−1.355**	**−1.355**	**−1.455**	**−1.505**	**−1.505**	**−1.505**

Mit einem Kauf des Call zahlt das Unternehmen die Optionsprämie, kann jedoch von vorteilhaften Preisentwicklungen voll (abzüglich bezahlter Prämie) profitieren. Im Beispiel kann das Unternehmen seinen Einkaufpreis mit maximal 1.505 fixieren und von den erwarteten fallenden Preisen profitieren.

Absicherung mit Zero Cost Call

Beispiel

Eine Verzinkerei hat Auftragseingänge zu Fixpreisen und muss sich am Markt Zink kaufen. Das Unternehmen erwartet leicht fallende Zinkpreise, möchte/kann das Risiko von steigenden Preisen jedoch nicht eingehen. Da die Absicherung mit einem gekauften Call zu teuer ist, entschließt sich das Unternehmen für die folgende Strategie:

Um sich gegen steigende Einkaufspreise abzusichern, kauft es einen Call mit einem Strike von 1.450 USD/t (Preisobergrenze) und einer Prämie von 55 USD und verkauft einen Put mit einem Strike von 1.350 USD/t (Preisuntergrenze) und einer Prämie von 55 USD.

Zinkpreise in USD		1.300	1.350	1.400	1.450	1.500
Kosten Einkauf Zink pro t		−1.300	−1.350	−1.400	−1.450	−1.500
Ergebnis Long Call 1.450 USD/t	−55	---	---	---	---	+50
Ergebnis Short Put 1.350 USD/t	+55	−50	---	---	---	---
Summe Prämie	0	0	0	0	0	0
Gesamtkosten pro t in USD		**−1.350**	**−1.350**	**−1.400**	**−1.450**	**−1.450**

Mit einem Zero Cost Call spart das Unternehmen die Optionspämie, nimmt dafür jedoch zugleich in Kauf, von vorteilhaften Preisentwicklungen nicht voll profitieren zu können. Im Beispiel kann das Unternehmen seine Einkaufpreise auf eine Bandbreite von 1.350 USD/t bis 1.450 USD/t einschränken, nimmt jedoch einen Mindestpreis von 1.350 USD/t in Kauf. Von stärker fallenden Preisen kann das Unternehmen nicht profitieren, da es den Put verkauft hat.

Hedging with a Long Put

> **Example**
>
> A galvanising plant has a relatively large stock of zinc; selling prices are variable, adapting to current market prices. The company expects the price of zinc to rise, but it does not want to take the risk of decreasing prices.
>
> In order to hedge against declining selling prices, it buys a put with the strike price of 1,350 USD/t (bottom price limit) and a premium of 55 USD.

Price of zinc in USD	Pre-miu	1,300	1,350	1,400	1,450	1,500
Revenue sale zinc per t		+1.300	+1.350	+1.400	+1.450	+1.500
Result purchase put 1,350 USD/t	-55	+50	---	---	---	---
Total premium	-55	-55	-55	-55	-55	-55
Total revenue per t in USD		**+1,295**	**+1,295**	**+1,345**	**+1,395**	**+1,445**

For the put the company has to pay the premium of 55 USD, but then is able to fully profit from advantageous price movements. In the given example, the company is able to limit the selling price to a minimum of 1,295 and fully profit from an expected price rise.

Hedging with a Zero Cost Put

> **Example**
>
> A galvanising plant has a relatively large stock of zinc; selling prices are variable, adapting to current market prices. The company expects the price of zinc to rise, but it does not want to take the risk of decreasing prices. Since buying a put option would be too expensive, the company decides to engage in the following strategy:
>
> In order to hedge against decreasing selling prices, it buys a put with the strike price of 1,350 USD/t (bottom price limit) and a premium of 55 USD and at the same time sells a call with the strike price of 1,450 USD/t (upper price limit) and a premium of 55 USD.

Price of zinc in USD	Pre-miu	1,300	1,350	1,400		1,500
Revenue sale zinc per t		+1,300	+1,350		+1,450	
Result sale call 1,450 USD/t	+55	---	---		---	
Result purchase put 1,350 USD/t	-55	+50	---		---	
Total premium	0	0	0		0	
Total revenue per t in USD		**+1,350**	**+1,350**	**+1,400**		**+1,450**

Absicherung mit Long Put

> **Beispiel**
>
> Eine Verzinkerei hat einen relativ großen Lagerbestand an Zink, die Verkaufspreise sind variabel und passen sich den aktuellen Zinspreisen am Markt an. Das Unternehmen erwartet steigende Zinkpreise und kann oder will das Risiko von fallenden Preisen nicht eingehen.
>
> Um sich gegen fallende Verkaufspreise abzusichern, kauft es einen Put mit einem Strike von 1.350 USD/t (Preisuntergrenze) und einer Prämie von 55 USD.

Zinkpreise in USD		1.300	1.350	1.400	1.450	1.500
Ertrag Verkauf Zink pro t		+1.300	+1.350	+1.400	+1.450	+1.500
Ergebnis Kauf Put 1.350 USD/t	–55	+50	---	---	---	---
Summe Prämie	–55	–55	–55	–55	–55	–55
Gesamtertrag pro t in USD		**+1.295**	**+1.295**	**+1.345**	**+1.395**	**+1.445**

Mit dem gekauften Put zahlt das Unternehmen die Prämie von 55 USD, kann aber dafür von vorteilhaften Preisentwicklungen voll profitieren. Im Beispiel kann das Unternehmen seine Verkaufspreise mit mindestens 1.295 fixieren und voll (abzüglich Prämie) vom erwarteten Anstieg der Preise profitieren.

Absicherung mit Zero Cost Put

> **Beispiel**
>
> Eine Verzinkerei hat einen relativ großen Lagerbestand an Zink, die Verkaufspreise sind variabel und passen sich den aktuellen Zinspreisen am Markt an. Das Unternehmen erwartet steigende Zinkpreise und kann oder will das Risiko von fallenden Preisen nicht eingehen. Da die Absicherung mit einem Put zu teuer erscheint, entschließt sich das Unternehmen für folgende Strategie:
>
> Um sich gegen fallende Verkaufspreise abzusichern, kauft es einen Put mit einem Strike von 1.350 USD/t (Preisuntergrenze) und einer Prämie von 55 USD und verkauft einen Call mit einem Strike von 1.450 USD/t (Preisobergrenze) und einer Prämie von 55 USD.

Zinkpreise in USD	Prämie	1.300	1.350	1.400	1.450	1.500
Ertrag Verkauf Zink pro t		+1.300	+1.350	+1.400	+1.450	+1.500
Ergebnis Verkauf Call 1.450 USD/t	+55	---	---	---	---	–50
Ergebnis Kauf Put 1.350 USD/t	–55	+50	---	---	---	---
Summe Prämie	0	0	0	0	0	0
Gesamtertrag pro t in USD		**+1.350**	**+1.350**	**+1.400**	**+1.450**	**+1.450**

By using a zero cost put the company saves the premium payment, but thereby foregoes profits from advantageous price movements. In the given example, the company is able to limit its selling prices to a bandwidth of 1,350 USD/t to 1,450 USD/t, but has to accept a fixed maximum price of 1,450 USD/t. It cannot profit from further increasing prices, because it sold the put option.

Summary

Today, many companies hedge interest rate risks and FX risks quite effectively, but still very little attention is drawn to hedging commodity risks. However, high commodity price volatility in the year 2008 led companies to focus more on the topic of commodity risk. Active price and management of commodity risks offers many advantages to companies. Commodities are natural resources, which are extracted by primary production (without pre-processing). Not all commodities are traded on international markets. However, markets cover the most commonly used and demanded energy commodities, industrial metals, agricultural products and precious metals. The most traded energy commodities are crude oil, natural gas and electricity. The most traded precious metal is gold, followed by silver, platinum and palladium. Depending on the iron content, industrial metals can be divided into two categories: non-ferrous metals and ferrous metals. Non-ferrous metals comprise for example aluminium, copper, nickel and zinc. Ferrous metals comprise iron ore, iron scrap and steel. Agricultural products include cotton, corn, wheat, rape, coffee and cocoa, as well as livestock (pigs, cattle).

Physical trade on spot markets happens directly between producers, intermediaries and consumers without recourse to standardised exchanges or financial markets. For investors, however, trading commodities on the spot market is very expensive due to high transportation and storage costs. Therefore, most of the trade volume take place on the futures market (with the exception of precious metals). On physical spot markets, one can trade all kinds of commodities of different compositions, qualities and quantities in many different locations.

Spot trade with oil is not conducted on ordinary exchanges, but directly at the big oil ports worldwide. The most important oil ports are located in New York, Houston/Texas, Rotterdam, Singapore and in the Persian Gulf.

The goal of trading gas and electricity on the spot market is the optimization of the portfolio of production and consumption mostly for the following day. There are some energy exchanges with physical spot markets, for example: the European Energy Exchange (EEX) in Leipzig, the Amsterdam Power Exchange, the EPEX Spot in Paris, the New York Mercantile Exchange and NordPool in Oslo.

Precious metals are not only traded on global future markets, but on spot markets as well. The spot price of gold is defined as the price of gold for immediate delivery. When mentioning the gold price in general, this means the spot price of gold, which is quoted in US-Dollars per ounce. There are three main markets in the world for the spot price of gold: Tokyo, London and New York.

Mit dem Zero Cost Put spart das Unternehmen die gesamte Prämie, nimmt dafür jedoch zugleich in Kauf, von vorteilhaften Preisentwicklungen nicht voll profitieren zu können. Im Beispiel kann das Unternehmen seine Verkaufspreise auf eine Bandbreite von 1.350 USD/t bis 1.450 USD/t einschränken, nimmt jedoch einen Höchstpreis von 1.450 USD/t in Kauf. Von stärker steigenden Preisen kann das Unternehmen nicht profitieren, da es den Call verkauft hat.

Zusammenfassung

Während sich heute bereits viele Unternehmen gegen Zinsrisiken und Währungsrisiken mit Erfolg absichern, wird der Absicherung von Rohstoffrisiken nach wie vor wenig Aufmerksamkeit geschenkt. Die extremen Preisschwankungen im Jahr 2008 haben jedoch dazu geführt, dass das Thema Rohstoffrisiken bei Unternehmen verstärkt im Fokus steht. Ein aktives Preis- und Risikomanagement der Rohstoffrisiken bringt viele Vorteile für Unternehmen mit sich. Rohstoffe sind natürliche Ressourcen, die durch Primärproduktion (ohne Vorbearbeitung) gewonnen werden. Nicht alle Rohstoffe werden auf den internationalen Märkten gehandelt. Die Märkte umfassen vor allem die am meisten verbrauchten und nachgefragten Energierohstoffe, Industriemetalle, Agrargüter und Edelmetalle. Die meistgehandelten Energierohstoffe sind Erdöl, Erdgas und Strom. Das meistgehandelte Edelmetall ist Gold, gefolgt von Silber, Platin und Palladium. Je nach Eisengchalt werden die Industriemetalle in zwei Kategorien unterteilt: Nichteisenmetalle (engl. non-ferrous metals) und Eisenmetalle (ferrous metals). Nichteisenmetalle sind zum Beispiel Aluminium, Kupfer, Nickel und Zink. Eisenmetalle sind Eisenerz, Eisenschrott und Stahl. Die Agrargüter umfassen sowohl landwirtschaftliche Produkte, wie Baumwolle, Mais, Zucker, Weizen, Raps, Kaffee und Kakao, als auch Vieh (Schweine, Rinder).

Der physische Handel auf den Spotmärkten erfolgt direkt zwischen Produzenten, Zwischenhändlern und Verbrauchern, wobei keine Börsen oder Finanzmärkte notwendig sind. Für Anleger ist der Handel am Kassamarkt mit hohen Transport- und Lagerkosten verbunden, deshalb wird ein großer Teil des Handelsvolumens in Rohstoffen auf dem Terminmarkt abgewickelt (eine Ausnahme sind die Edelmetalle). Auf dem physischen Markt (Spotmarkt) werden alle Sorten von Rohstoffen in verschiedenen Zusammensetzungen, Qualitäten und Mengen an vielen Orten gehandelt.

Der Spothandel mit Öl erfolgt nicht an den Börsen, sondern an den großen Ölhäfen weltweit. Die wichtigsten Ölhäfen weltweit befinden sich in New York, Houston/Texas, Rotterdam, Singapur und im Persischen Golf.

Am Spotmarkt für Gas/Strom geht es darum, das Erzeugungs-/Verbrauchsportfolio meist für den nächsten Tag zu optimieren. Beispiele für Energiebörsen mit einem physischen Spotmarkt sind die European Energy Exchange (EEX) in Leipzig, die Amsterdam Power Exchange, die EPEX Spot in Paris, die New York Mercantile Exchange sowie NordPool in Oslo.

Edelmetalle werden weltweit nicht nur an den Warenterminbörsen, sondern auch an den Spotmärkten gehandelt. Als Spotpreis wird der Preis für Gold zur sofortigen Lieferung bezeichnet. Wenn allgemein vom Goldpreis gesprochen wird, dann ist immer der Spotpreis gemeint. Der Spotpreis wird in US-Dollar pro Feinunze angegeben.

The most important trading platform for silver bars is the London Bullion Market Association (LBMA). Further important markets for the physical trade are New York and Zurich.

Although the annual production of platinum is less than one tenth of the gold production, gold currently (May 2012) trades at higher prices. Platinum is traded primarily on NYMEX in New York and on TOCOM in Tokyo.

The most important trading platforms for industrial metals are the London Metal Exchange (LME) and the New York Mercantile Exchange (NYMEX).

Agricultural goods are primarily traded on future markets in the form of contracts, and NOT on spot markets.

The future market comprises OTC transactions (forwards, swaps and options) and standardised contracts (futures and options), which are traded on organised exchanges. Commodities are traded mostly in the form of future contracts on the biggest future exchanges located in the USA and UK.

The London-based ICE Futures (formerly International Petroleum Exchange, IPE) is the biggest futures exchange for options and future contracts on crude oil, natural gas and electricity. It is also the trading platform for the European Brent crude oil. The European Energy Exchange (EEX) is the largest energy exchange in continental Europe. On the EEX the trade of electricity futures and options, CO_2 certificates, coal and natural gas takes place.

The London gold fixing is done by the „London Bullion Market Association" (LBMA) twice a day. There are five fixing participants meeting on every London banking day at 10.30 and 15.30. The fixing has two purposes: execution of transactions at fixing rate and benchmarking.

The most important trading platform for industrial metals is the London Metal Exchange (LME). More than two thirds of the worlds' non-ferrous metal futures and options are traded on LME.

The exchange provides the framework and the conditions for trade. Execution and settlement are carried out by the clearing house of the futures exchange. Therefore, the placement of the clearing house between buyer and seller reduces credit risk. The clearing houses demand initial margins and variation margins, which further reduce credit risks. The initial margin is a defined amount per contract. Usually, the initial margin is not provided in cash, but in the form of securities in order to compensate for potential future losses. The variation margin is the daily settlement of accumulated profits and losses.

At expiry the buyer of a commodity future (long) gets the entitlement for reception and the seller (short) receives the entitlement to deliver the underlying goods against payment in cash. If there is no requirement of physical delivery, the contract is settled in cash ("cash settlement"). The total result of a future position consists of the aggregated sum of daily variation margins plus the settlement amount of the last trading day. Every open position can be closed out before or on the last trading day by entering into the contrarian position.

Der Spotpreis von Gold kann weltweit in drei Märkte unterteilt werden: Tokio, London und New York.

Für den physischen Markt von Silber (in Barrenform) ist die London Bullion Market Association (LBMA) die wichtigste Handelsplattform weltweit. Weitere Marktplätze für den physischen Handel sind New York und Zürich.

Platin ist im Hinblick auf die jährliche Fördermenge das seltenste unter den drei großen Edelmetallen, dennoch wird Gold aktuell (Mai 2012) zu höheren Preisen gehandelt. Platin wird an der NYMEX in New York und der TOCOM in Tokio gehandelt.

Die wichtigsten Handelsplätze für Industriemetalle sind die London Metal Exchange (LME) und die New York Mercantile Exchange (NYMEX).

Agrargüter werden überwiegend an Terminbörsen in Form von Kontrakten gehandelt. Ein Handel mit Agrargütern auf den Spotmärkten findet nicht statt.

Der Terminmarkt umfasst sowohl OTC-Geschäfte (Forwards, Swaps und Optionen) als auch standardisierte Kontrakte (Futures und Optionen) auf organisierten Börsen. Die Rohstoffe werden zum größten Teil in Form von Future-Kontrakten an den weltweit größten Warenterminbörsen in den USA und UK gehandelt.

Die ICE Futures mit Sitz in London ist die größte Terminbörse für Optionen und Futures auf Erdöl, Erdgas und elektrische Energie in Europa. Die Börse ist Handelsplattform für die in Europa führende Ölsorte Brent. Die European Energy Exchange (EEX) ist die größte Energiebörse in Kontinentaleuropa. An der EEX werden Strom-Futures und -Optionen, CO_2-Zertifikate, Kohle und Erdgas gehandelt.

Die „London Bullion Market Association" (LBMA) führt zweimal täglich ein Goldfixing durch. Die fünf Fixing-Teilnehmer treffen einander an jedem Londoner Banktag um 10:30 und 15:00 Uhr. Das Fixing erfüllt zwei Funktionen: Durchführung von Geschäften zum Fixingkurs und als Benchmark.

Die London Metal Exchange (LME) ist eine der wichtigsten Börsen für Industriemetalle. Es werden mehr als zwei Drittel der weltweiten Nichteisenmetall-Futures und -Optionen an der LME gehandelt.

Die Börse gibt die Rahmenbedingungen vor, unter denen der Handel stattfindet. Die Abwicklung der Geschäfte erfolgt durch das Clearing House der Futuresbörse. Dies dient der Reduzierung des Kreditrisikos. Um das Kreditrisiko des Clearing House so gering wie möglich zu halten, werden Einschüsse, sogenannte Initial Margins und Variation Margins, verlangt. Die Initial Margin ist eine festgelegte Betragshöhe pro Kontrakt. Sie wird üblicherweise nicht bar hinterlegt, sondern in Form von Wertpapieren und dient zur Besicherung für potenzielle zukünftige Verluste. Die Variation Margin ist eine tägliche Abrechnung der aufgelaufenen Gewinne und Verluste.

Der Käufer eines Commodity Future (Long) erhält mit Laufzeitende die Empfangsberechtigung, der Verkäufer (Short) die Überlieferungsberechtigung für die kontrahierte Ware gegen Entgelt. Wird keine physische Lieferung verlangt, erfolgt das Settlement als Settlement". Das Ergebnis auf eine Futuresposition setzt sich aus der Summe der täglichen Variation Margins und dem Settlement-Betrag am letzten Handelstag zusammen. Jede Futuresposition kann vor dem bzw. am letzten Handelstag mit einer entgegengesetzten Futuresposition aufgelöst werden.

Open interest is a figure measuring the amount of currently open contracts. The open interest therefore states how many positions of a specific contract are held by market participants, which were not closed out yet.

A commodity future is a standardised contract, where the buyer (seller) is obliged to receive (deliver) the commodity at a certain price on a certain date in the future.

Most futures positions are closed out or rolled over just before expiration. Depending on whether the expiring contract is cheaper or more expensive than the new contract, there are two structures available in the futures market: contango and backwardation. Contango is the premium, when the price of the new contract is higher than the price of the current one, meaning: future price > spot price. Backwardation is the discount, when the new contract is cheaper than the current one, meaning: future price < spot price.

Hedging by means of futures/forwards requires liquidity tied up in margin payments. Therefore, many companies use swaps for hedging in order to avoid tying up cash. In commodity markets the same types of swaps can be found as in the interest rate and foreign exchange markets. This holds true for options as well.

A market for metal lending (especially gold lending) has been developing since the 1980s. Producers sell gold on the spot market and use the obtained money to finance their production. Thus, producers get access to relatively cheap funding and lenders obtain yields in the form of a lending fee on gold, which does not pay interest per se. The "rate" at which dealers lend gold against USD, is also called gold forward offered rate (GOFO) or gold lease rate.

4.6. Practice Questions

1. Which of the following commodities are NOT traded on international stock exchanges?
    a) gemstones
    b) energy resources
    c) industrial metals
    d) agricultural products
    e) precious metals
2. Which country is the biggest producer of agricultural products?
    a) India
    b) USA
    c) Brazil
    d) China
3. Apart from the cost factor, which of the following factors play an important role when choosing between physical property and buying in form of a forward transaction in a commodity purchase?
    a) economic cycle
    b) scarcity /development of inventory

„CasAls Open Interest wird die Summe aller noch offenen Kontrakte bezeichnet. Das Open Interest gibt also an, wie viele Positionen eines bestimmten Kontraktes noch von Marktteilnehmern gehalten werden, die nicht glattgestellt wurden.

Ein Rohstoff-Future (commodity future) ist ein standardisierter Vertrag, bei dem sich der Käufer (Verkäufer) verpflichtet, einen Rohstoff zu einem bestimmten Preis zu einem bestimmten Zeitpunkt in der Zukunft abzunehmen (zu liefern).

Die meisten Futures werden kurz vor dem Auslaufen aufgelöst/weitergerollt. Je nachdem, ob der neue oder der auslaufende Kontrakt teurer oder billiger ist, existieren am Terminmarkt zwei Strukturen: Contango und Backwardation. Ein Contango ist der Aufschlag, bei dem der Kurs des neuen Kontrakts höher als der des bestehenden Kontraktes quotiert, d.h. Terminkurs > Kassakurs. Backwardation nennt man den Abschlag, zu dem der neue Kontrakt günstiger am Markt zu kaufen ist, d.h. Terminkurs < Kassakurs.

Die Preissicherung mittels Futures/Forwards bindet Liquidität durch die Einzahlungen auf das Marginkonto. Aus diesem Grund greifen Unternehmen oft zu Swaps, die kein Bargeld binden. Bei Rohstoffen werden die gleichen Arten von Swaps wie im Zins- und FX-Bereich verwendet. Auch bei den Optionen werden die gleichen Arten wie im FX-Bereich verwendet.

Seit den Achtzigerjahren hat sich ein Markt für die Metallleihe (v.a. die Goldleihe) entwickelt. Die Produzenten verkaufen das Gold am Kassamarkt und verwenden das dadurch erhaltene Geld zur Finanzierung der Produktion. Die Produzenten profitieren dabei von einer günstigen Finanzierung und die Verleiher erhalten durch die Leihgebühr einen Ertrag auf die an sich zinslose Anlage in Gold. Den bei diesen Leihtransaktionen angewendeten „Zinssatz", zu dem Dealer Gold gegen USD verleihen, nennt man auch Gold Forward Offered Rate (GOFO) oder Gold Lease Rate.

4.6. Wiederholungsfragen

1. Welcher der folgenden Rohstoffe wird **nicht** auf den internationalen Börsen gehandelt?
    a) Edelsteine
    b) Energierohstoffe
    c) Industriemetalle
    d) Agrargüter
    e) Edelmetalle

2. Welches Land ist der größte Produzent von Agrargütern?
    a) Indien
    b) USA
    c) Brasilien
    d) China

3. Welche der folgenden Faktoren spielen beim Kauf von Rohstoffen neben dem Kostenfaktor eine entscheidende Rolle bei der Wahl zwischen physischem Besitz und dem Erwerb in Form von Termingeschäften?
    a) Konjunktur
    b) Knappheit bzw. Entwicklung der Lagerbestände

    c) reproduction time

    d) commodity attrition

    e) production costs

4. In trading which commodity are arbitrage (spot against forward market) opportunities the worst?

    a) electricity

    b) orange juice

    c) copper

    d) gold

5. Which two ports are the most important spot trading centres for oil?

    a) New York

    b) Houston

    c) Amsterdam

    d) Abu-Dhabi

6. Which of the following statements regarding the gas/electricity spot market is false?

    a) Variable costs are only relevant for short-term production decisions.

    b) The purpose of the spot market is to optimize the production/consumption portfolio for the next day.

    c) Fixed costs are only relevant for short-term production decisions.

    d) The purchase and sale quotations on the spot market are impacted by short-term marginal costs.

7. Which of the following statements regarding precious metals is true?

    a) Future prices are considered as reference rate in derivative securities transactions.

    b) Precious metals are only traded on forward markets.

    c) The spot price of gold is quoted in US-Dollar per kilogramme.

    d) Spot prices are considered as reference rate in derivative securities transactions.

8. Which of the following statements is true with regard to platinum trading?

    a) Apart from the future markets there is no separate spot market for spot delivery.

    b) Approximately 50 times more silver than platinum is produced yearly.

    c) The most important daily fixing is on the New York Platinum & Palladium Market.

    d) The most important physical trading centres are New York (NYMEX) and Tokyo (TOCOM).

9. What determines the interest rate for precious metals?

    a) the difference between USD interest rate and forward report

    b) the difference between forward report and deport

    c) the sum of forward report and deport

    d) There are no interest rates for precious metals.

    e) The interest rate is fixed by LBMA.

10. What is meant by the gold forward offered rate (GOFO)?

    a) the rate at which dealers will lend gold against GBP

    b) the difference between spot price and forward price

    c) the rate at which dealers will lend gold against USD

    d) the calculation basis for the cash settlement of derivative instruments

c) Reproduktionszeit

d) Rohstoffverschleiß

e) Produktionskosten

4. Bei welchem Rohstoff ist die Arbitrage (Spot- gegen Terminmarkt) am schlechtesten durchführbar?

a) Strom

b) Orangensaft

c) Kupfer

d) Gold

5. Welche zwei Häfen zählen zu den wichtigsten Spothandelsplätzen für Öl?

a) New York

b) b) Houston

c) c) Amsterdam

d) d) Abu-Dhabi

6. Welche der folgenden Aussagen über den Gas/Strom-Spotmarkt ist falsch?

a) Für die kurzfristige Produktionsentscheidung sind nur die variablen Kosten relevant.

b) Am Spotmarkt geht es darum, das Erzeugungs-/Verbrauchsportfolio für den nächsten Tag zu optimieren.

c) Für die kurzfristige Produktionsentscheidung sind nur die Fixkosten relevant.

d) Die Kauf- und Verkaufsgebote auf dem Spotmarkt erfolgen zu kurzfristigen Grenzkosten.

7. Welche der folgenden Aussagen über Edelmetalle ist richtig?

a) Die Futurepreise gelten im derivativen Wertpapiergeschäft als Referenzkurs.

b) Edelmetalle werden ausschließlich auf den Terminmärkten gehandelt.

c) Der Spotpreis für Gold wird in US-Dollar pro Kilogramm angegeben.

d) Die Spotpreise gelten im derivativen Wertpapiergeschäft als Referenzkurs.

8. Welche der folgenden Aussagen über den Platinhandel ist richtig?

a) Neben den Future-Märkten gibt es keinen eigenen Spotmarkt für die sofortige Auslieferung.

b) Es wird ca. 50 Mal mehr Silber als Platin pro Jahr produziert.

c) Das wichtigste Fixing findet täglich am New York Platin & Palladium Market statt.

d) Die wichtigsten physischen Handelsplätze sind New York (NYMEX) und Tokio (TOCOM).

9. Wodurch wird der Zinssatz für Edelmetalle bestimmt?

a) Differenz zwischen dem USD-Zinssatz und dem Terminaufschlag

b) Differenz zwischen Terminaufschlag und -abschlag

c) Summe aus Terminaufschlag und -abschlag

d) Für Metalle gibt es keine Zinsen.

e) Der Zinssatz wird durch die LBMA festgesetzt.

10. Was wird als Gold Forward Offered Rate (GOFO) bezeichnet?

a) Zinssatz, zu dem Dealer Gold gegen GBP verleihen

b) Differenz zwischen Kassa- und Terminkurs

c) Zinssatz, zu dem Dealer Gold gegen USD verleihen

d) Basis zur Abrechnung von derivativen Instrumenten

11. What is the gold lease rate for 180 days?

    USD LIBOR: 180 days 1.5% / gold prices: spot 400; forward (180 days) 402
    a) 1.00%
    b) 0.50%
    c) 2.00%
    d) 2.50%

12. You are holding 1,000 ounces of gold in bullion form. Which three transactions can you use to gain a profit on your long gold position?

    USD interest rate: 360 days 2%; gold prices: spot 400, forward (360 days) 404
    a) sell 1,000 oz gold spot at 400
    b) invest USD 400,000 for 360 days at 2%
    c) buy 1,000 oz gold 360 days forward at 404
    d) refinance USD 400,000 for 360 days at 2%
    e) sell 1,000 oz gold 360 days forward at 404

11. Wie hoch ist die Gold Lease Rate für 180 Tage?
    USD LIBOR: 180 Tage 1,5 %/Goldkurse: spot 400; Termin (180 Tage) 402
    a) 1,00 %
    b) 0,50 %
    c) 2,00 %
    d) 2,50 %

12. Sie halten 1.000 Unzen Gold in Barren. Durch welche drei Transaktionen können Sie einen Ertrag auf Ihre Gold-Long-Position erzielen?
    USD-Zinsen: 360 Tage 2 %/Goldkurse: spot 400; Termin (360 Tage) 404
    a) Verkauf 1.000 oz Gold spot zu 400
    b) Anlage USD 400.000 für 360 Tage zu 2 %
    c) Kauf 1.000 oz Gold auf Termin 360 Tage zu 404
    d) Refinanzierung USD 400.000 für 360 Tage zu 2 %
    e) Verkauf 1.000 oz Gold auf Termin 360 Tage zu 404

PART IV: The Settlement Process

TEIL IV: Der Settlementprozess

The first chapter of this part deals with the operational risk and its importance as well as the basics of the settlement process. The settlement process of an FX deal consists of the following stages: deal capture, trade entry, confirmation, netting, settlement and nostro reconciliation. Each stage is explained in detail in chapters two to six.

The deal capture marks the beginning of the settlement process. The entry of the trade data affects the general ledger, the payment and risk system and the nostro reconciliation process. The deal capture is followed by the confirmation. All trades, external and internal, must be confirmed either by issuing a confirmation or by responding to a bank's confirmation. Usually, confirmations are exchanged via S.W.I.F.T. or via bilateral netting systems on trade date. The next stage is the netting of the deal. Netting is an agreed offsetting of positions or obligations by trading partners or participants of a netting system. Settlement is the exchange of payments between counterparties on value date. All payments are exchanged through nostro accounts where the nostro banks get payment instructions on the day before settlement date in order to know the received and payed amounts. The clearing and settlement process comprises three stages: authorising and initiating the payment, transmitting and exchanging payment instructions and settlement between banks involved. The reconciliation of nostro accounts is the final stage of the settlement process. The main objective of nostro reconciliation is to ensure optimal liquidity management in order to avoid idle balances and high overdraft costs.

The accouting department is also involved in the settlement process. Accounting ensures FX transactions are properly recorded in the balance sheet and income statement. After a trade is executed the data is captured in subsidiary accounts that flow through to the general ledger at the end of each day. Accounting tasks and best practice are explained in chapter 7.

With regard to the settlement process there is also the problem of money laundering, which is described in chapter 8. Money laundering is the process by which illegally obtained money is given the appearance of having originated from a legitimate source. Money laundering comprises three stages: placement, layering and integration.

Finally, in chapter 9, we list examples for settlement risk. The failures of Bankhaus Herstatt, the Bank of Credit and Commercial International (BCCI) and the Barings Crisis are described.

Included in the following exams:
- **ACI Dealing Certificate**
- **ACI Operations Certificate**

Das erste Kapitel dieses Teiles widmet sich dem operationalen Risiko und seiner Bedeutung sowie den Grundlagen des Settlementprozesses. Der Settlementprozess eines FX-Geschäftes besteht aus folgenden Schritten: Erfassung des Geschäftes, Eingabe des Geschäftes durch das Backoffice, Bestätigung des Geschäftes, Netting, Settlement und Abgleich der Nostrokonten. Die einzelnen Schritte werden in den folgenden Kapiteln 2 bis 6 ausführlich dargestellt.

Am Beginn des Settlementprozesses steht die Erfassung des abgeschlossenen Geschäftes. Die Eingabe der Geschäftsdaten betrifft das Hauptbuch, das Zahlungs- und Risikosystem sowie alle Aufgaben zum Abgleich der Konten. Anschließend folgt der Bestätigungsprozess. Alle Geschäfte, auch interne Transaktionen, müssen bestätigt werden, entweder indem die Bank selbst eine Bestätigung ausstellt oder auf eine Bestätigung einer anderen Bank antwortet. Üblicherweise erfolgt der Bestätigungsprozess über S.W.I.F.T. oder bilaterale Nettingvereinbarungen am Handelstag. Der nächste Schritt ist das Netting des Geschäftes. Netting bedeutet, dass man die gegenseitigen Positionen oder Verpflichtungen von Geschäftspartnern oder Teilnehmern eines Systems aufrechnet. Settlement ist der Austausch von Zahlungen zwischen den Parteien am Valutatag. Das Settlement erfolgt über Nostrokonten, wobei die Nostrobanken am Tag vor dem Settlement-Tag Zahlungsinstruktionen erhalten, aus denen die zu leistenden und erhaltenden Zahlungen hervorgehen. Der Clearing- und Settlementprozess erfolgt in drei Stufen: Bewilligung und Freigabe der Zahlung, Übertragung und Austausch der Zahlungsanweisungen und Zahlungsausgleich zwischen den Banken. Am Ende des Clearing- und Settlementprozesses steht der Abgleich der Nostrokonten. Der Zweck des Abgleichs besteht darin, ein optimales Liquiditätsmanagement zu haben, sodass sowohl Liquiditätsüberschüsse als auch Liquiditätsengpässe vermieden werden.

Im Settlementprozess ist auch die Buchhaltung involviert. Die Buchhaltung verarbeitet die FX-Transaktionen in die Bilanzkonten sowie in die G&V. Nach Abschluss des Geschäftes werden die Daten in Unterkonten erfasst, die am Ende jedes Tages ins Hauptbuch zusammengeführt werden. Die Aufgaben der Buchhaltung sowie die Anforderungen an die Buchhaltung werden im Kapitel 7 näher erläutert.

Im Zusammenhang mit dem Settlementprozess ist auch das Problem der Geldwäsche relevant, das in Kapitel 8 behandelt wird. Geldwäsche ist der Prozess, illegale Gelder über Transaktionen in Geld mit dem Anschein legaler Herkunft zu verwandeln. Der Prozess der Geldwäsche bzw. die notwendige Kontrolle besteht aus drei Stufen: Anlage des Geldes, Entflechtung des Geldes und Integration in den legalen Wirtschaftskreislauf.

Abschließend werden in Kapitel 9 Beispiele für Fälle, in denen Settlementrisiken schlagend geworden sind, vorgestellt. Dabei wird auf den Zusammenbruch des Bankhauses Herstatt, auf die Bank of Credit and Commercial International und auf die Barings-Krise näher eingegangen.

Prüfungsrelevant für:

- **ACI Dealing Certificate**
- **ACI Operations Certificate**

1. Introduction

In this chapter you learn ...
- why the challenges in risk management have increased.
- what is meant by operational risk.
- about the typical losses incurred by operational risks.
- what is meant by systemic risk.
- which measures should be implemented to contain operational risk in FX trading.
- about back office duties in the settlement process.
- about the operational flow of an FX deal.

The increasing convergence of different markets, a tremendous rise of trading volume (approx. USD 5 trillion per day in the G-10 countries) and the introduction of new and complex FX- and money market products have **required risk management to improve**.

While many efforts have been undertaken to measure market and credit risk the determination of **operational risk** meets many obstacles because it is **very difficult to calculate** probabilities for losses due to operational errors (i.e.: failure of computer systems)

1.1. The Importance of Operational Risk

Operational risk is the risk of incurring interest charges or other penalties for misdirecting or otherwise failing to make settlement payments on time owing to an error or technical failure.

Typical losses incurred by operational risks are

- compensation payments for delayed or failed settlement
- wrong portfolio decisions due to misleading position management
- costs for investigating queries
- costs for negotiating a resolution with counterparty

If operational risk entail **liquidity and credit problems** for other counterparties operational failures can lead to **systemic risk**. Systemic risk is the risk that the failure of one participant in a transfer system, or in financial markets generally, to meet its required obligations when due will cause other participants or financial institutions to be unable to meet their obligations when due.

1.2. General Provisions to limit Operational Risk

The following measures should be implemented if operational risk in FX-trading should be contained:

- **Segregation of Back and Front Office Duties:** An appropriate segregation between key areas within operations should be ensured. Reporting lines of trading and operations should be independent from each other. The failure to separate back and front office duties lead to the failure of Barings Bank and Daiwa.

1. Grundlagen

In diesem Kapitel lernen Sie ...

- warum die Herausforderungen an das Risikomanagement gestiegen sind.
- was man unter operationalem Risiko versteht.
- welche typischen Verluste eintreten, wenn operationale Risiken schlagend werden.
- was man unter Systemrisiko versteht.
- welche Maßnahmen unbedingt notwendig sind, um operationale Risiken im FX-Handel besser kontrollieren bzw. begrenzen zu können.
- welche Funktionen das Backoffice im Rahmen des Settlementprozesses erfüllt.
- welche Schritte bei der Abwicklung eines FX-Geschäftes durchlaufen werden.

Mit der zunehmenden Vernetzung zwischen den unterschiedlichen Märkten, einem gewaltigen Anstieg im Handelsvolumen (ca. USD 5 Trillionen pro Tag in den G10-Staaten) und der Einführung neuer, komplexer Produkte auf den FX- und Geldmärkten sind auch die **Herausforderungen an das Risikomanagement gestiegen.**

Während für die Quantifizierung von Markt- und Kreditrisiko große Anstrengungen unternommen werden, fällt eine genaue **Bestimmung operationaler Risiken relativ schwer,** weil es problematisch ist, Wahrscheinlichkeiten für das Eintreten von Verlusten aufgrund operationaler Fehler (z.B. Absturz des Computersystems) zu errechnen.

1.1. Die Bedeutung des operationalen Risikos

Operationales Risiko ist das Risiko, Zinsen oder andere Gebühren zahlen zu müssen, weil durch Irrtum oder technisches Versagen eine zur Erfüllung eines Geschäftes geleistete Zahlung fehlgeleitet wird oder auf eine andere Weise nicht rechtzeitig zustande kommt.

Typische Verluste, wenn operationale Risiken schlagend werden, sind

- Kompensationszahlungen für ein verspätetes Settlement,
- eine falsche Portfolioentscheidung basierend auf einer falschen Position,
- Kosten für Untersuchungen der Vorfälle,
- Kosten für Verhandlungen mit der anderen Partei zur Schlichtung von Differenzen.

Im Zusammenhang mit operationalem Risiko muss auch das **Systemrisiko** genannt werden. Dabei handelt es sich um das Risiko, dass ein Marktteilnehmer seinen Verpflichtungen bei Fälligkeit nicht nachkommen kann (z.B. verspätete Zahlungsanweisung, Zahlungsunfähigkeit) und dadurch andere Marktteilnehmer bei Fälligkeit ebenfalls nicht erfüllen können. Dadurch können erhebliche **Liquiditäts- und Kreditprobleme** am Markt entstehen.

1.2. Maßnahmen zur Begrenzung des operationalen Risikos

Um operationale Risiken im FX-Handel besser kontrollieren zu können, sollten folgende Punkte beachtet werden:

- **Trennung von Back- und Frontoffice-Aktivitäten:** Auch innerhalb des Backoffice sollten die wichtigsten Funktionen getrennt wahrgenommen werden. Das Backoffice muss unabhängig vom Handel an die Geschäftsführung berichten. Die fehlende Tren-

- **Trading and Back Office should understand the various duties of the other department.** Traders should know the latest developments in settlement and the procedures of the settlement process. Particularly, they should have a good understanding of SSIs, the confirmation process and the importance of correct trade data capture. Similarly, operations should have comprehensive knowledge of traded products in order to understand and monitor better the risk related to each product.
- **Management must fully understand operational risk** in order to make appropriate changes or invest in technology to help mitigate these risks
- **A bank should have proper procedures in place for introducing new products**. These procedures should ensure that the bank is capable to price, value and settle the new types of transactions and to monitor the risks associated with the product launch.
- **A bank should have a sophisticated Model Signoff procedure**. Models may be used to evaluate risks and determine prices of products. If models are employed two kinds of model risk have to be considered. Direct and indirect model risks. Direct model risks occur when models are used to manage a bank's own positions and accounts. Indirect model risks occur when models are used in support of sales and advisory work and counterparty reporting.
  Because operation is usually most strongly involved in using models, the operations personnel should be integrally involved in any model signoff and implementation. A smooth and effective implementation of the new system is eased if the personnel concerned is properly trained and informed in advance.
  Each system should have access controls that only allow use by authorized individuals. Model changes should be confined to particularly trained technical staff. System access and entitlements should be periodically reviewed and adjusted if necessary.
- **A clear quantifiable operation performance measurement** should be established. Reports concerning the development and quality of operational procedures should be delivered to the management.
- A bank should **record all counterparty conversations** including conversations between operations of the bank and the counterparty. Tapes should be **retained for at least two months**.
- Every market participant should have a sophisticated, **independent audit unit** that ensures a proper functioning of controls already in place and report problems to the management.
- **Back office is responsible for retaining adequate records of all transactions, and supporting documentation for the financial statements.** The retention of data should be based on tax, regulatory and legal issues. The records can be maintained on paper, electronic or magnetic media. Proper measures against theft and destruction have to be implemented. In case of computer-based data storage the compatibility of programs and media should be guaranteed.
- **Contingency plans** should be developed and tested to cover both the long- and short-term incapacitation of a site, the failure of a system or the failure of a communication link between systems. Otherwise financial repercussions could follow.
- Banks should develop **various disaster recovery plans** that ensure that the bank can still complete its daily business if disaster strikes. The plans should be tested on a regular basis to gauge their validity and to measure the staff's readiness for dealing with emergency situations.

nung von Back- und Frontoffice war der Grund, dass ein Händler die Barings Bank ruinieren konnte.

- **Handel und Backoffice müssen die verschiedenen gegenseitigen Aufgaben kennen.** Die Händler müssen von den laufenden, neuen Entwicklungen in der Abwicklung wissen und die Bedeutung der einzelnen Schritte kennen, z.B. Verwendung von SSIs, korrekte Dateneingabe, richtige Bestätigungen. Andererseits muss auch im Backoffice ein ausreichendes Wissen über die gehandelten Produkte vorhanden sein, damit die Risiken besser erkannt werden können und geeignete Vorkehrungen getroffen werden können.

- **Operationale Risiken müssen vom Management verstanden werden,** damit Investitionen zur Verringerung des operationalen Risikos getätigt werden können.

- **Eine Bank sollte ein geeignetes Verfahren zur Einführung neuer Produkte haben.** Dadurch soll erreicht werden, dass die Bank das Pricing, die Bewertung und das Settlement der neuen Produkte durchführen kann und imstande ist, die mit dem neuen Produkt verbundenen Risiken zu überwachen und zu kontrollieren.

- **Es müssen umfassende Einführungsverfahren für neue Modelle vorhanden sein.** Die Verwendung von Modellen hilft bei der Bewertung von Risiken und dem Pricing von Produkten. Bei der Verwendung von Modellen unterscheidet man zwischen direkten und indirekten Modellrisiken. Direkte Modellrisiken betreffen Fehler bei der Positions- und Kontenführung, indirekte Modellrisiken beziehen sich auf Probleme beim Treasury Support, bei der Kundenberatung oder Berichten an den Partner.
  Da das Backoffice üblicherweise am stärksten mit Modellen arbeitet, sollte es bereits im Auswahlverfahren als Tester eingebunden werden. Bei der Einführung eines neuen Modells müssen alle Betroffenen über Änderungen informiert und geschult werden. Zugang zum System sollten nur autorisierte Personen im Handel und Backoffice haben. Änderungen an den Modellen dürfen nur von speziell dafür vorgesehenem technischem Personal durchgeführt werden. Die Zutritts- und Zugriffsberechtigungen sollten regelmäßig auf ihre Zweckmäßigkeit überprüft werden.

- **Es sollte eine quantifizierte Leistungsmessung der Backoffice-Aktivitäten implementiert werden.** Berichte über die Entwicklung der operationalen Abläufe und deren Qualität sollen an das Management geliefert werden.

- **Gespräche** zwischen Händlern und Backoffices sollen **auf Band aufgezeichnet** werden und **ausreichend lange** (mindestens zwei Monate wird von den Codes of Conduct empfohlen) **aufbewahrt** werden.

- Jeder Marktteilnehmer sollte eine **unabhängige Revisionseinheit** haben, die als Kontrollorgan wirkt und dem Management über Missstände berichtet.

- **Das Backoffice trägt die Verantwortung für eine vollständige Erfassung und Aufbewahrung der Geschäftsfälle und der dazugehörigen Dokumentation.** Die Aufbewahrung hat nach steuerlichen und rechtlichen Gesichtspunkten zu erfolgen. Dokumente können auf Papier, elektronischen oder magnetischen Datenträgern abgelegt werden. Für jedes Speichermedium sind adäquate Schutzvorrichtungen gegen Zerstörung oder Diebstahl einzurichten. Im Falle computergestützter Aufbewahrung ist auf die Kompatibilität der Speichermedien und Programme zu achten.
  Es müssen Notfallpläne für kurz- und langfristige Systemausfälle im Handel und Backoffice ausgearbeitet und getestet werden, da ansonsten große finanzielle Risiken entstehen.

- **Each employee must know whom to contact in a state of emergency.** Contingency contact lists with names, telephone numbers and tasks should be distributed to all employees.
- **All trading and associated support systems should be backed up.** Alternative sites should be maintained that can confirm and settle the bank's transactions.
- **Alternative communication channels for confirmations and settlement** with nostro banks should be established, e.g.: fax, telex. If trades are done via telephone, traders must be provided with mobile phones or other means (e.g.: cellular phones) to ensure an uninterrupted trading.

1.3. Back Office Duties

The main duties of the back office include:

- processing of transactions in the system
- recording of the transactions in the books
- making of payments
- timely confirmation of all trades
- timely settlement of transactions

If back office duties are assigned a **strict segregation of duties** between back office and front office as well as within key tasks of the back office should be ensured.

The following core competences should be fulfilled by different members of the back office unless deemed necessary by the bank's senior management.

▸ Data entry and data verification
▸ Data entry and confirmation
▸ Data entry and supervisory functions
▸ Generation of settlement instruction and release of payments
▸ Settlement and nostro reconciliation

1.4. The Operational Flow of an FX Deal

An FX-deal comprises the following stages:

- deal capture
- trade entry
- confirmation
- netting
- settlement
- nostro reconciliation

The following two points should be tied up in the settlement process:

- close cooperation with accounting
- appropriate feedback measures should be included in the settlement process in order to identify and resolve any exceptions quickly.

- **Es sind mögliche Katastrophenszenarien zu entwickeln und geeignete Pläne für die Vorgehensweisen im Ernstfall festzulegen.** Die Pläne sind regelmäßig auf ihre Tauglichkeit zu überprüfen.
- **Jeder Mitarbeiter muss wissen, wen er im Ernstfall zu kontaktieren hat.** Dazu sind Telefonlisten und Ablaufpläne zur Information ständig aufzulegen und zu aktualisieren.
- Es sollen **Ausweichquartiere mit entsprechenden Backup-Systemen** organisiert werden, von denen aus im Krisenfall gehandelt werden kann.
- Es sollen **alternative Kommunikationswege zu Nostrobanken vorhanden sein, z.B. Fax oder Telex.** Auch Handelssysteme müssen ein entsprechendes Backup haben. Wird über Telefon gehandelt, dann müssen z.B. Mobiltelefone für den Fall, dass die Telefonanlage ausfällt, zur Verfügung stehen.

1.3. Die Aufgaben des Backoffice

Im Rahmen des Settlementprozesses erfüllt das Backoffice folgende Funktionen:

- Verarbeitung der Transaktionen im System
- Aufzeichnung der Transaktionen in den Büchern
- Durchführung der Zahlungen
- pünktliche Bestätigung aller Geschäfte
- Erfüllung der Transaktionen zum vereinbarten Zeitpunkt

Bei den Aufgaben des Backoffice ist immer auf eine **genaue Aufgabentrennung** zu achten. Es müssen nicht nur Front- und Backoffice-Aktivitäten getrennt werden, sondern auch innerhalb des Backoffice Kernkompetenzen von unterschiedlichen Personen erfüllt werden.

Folgende Tätigkeiten sollten, so die Geschäftsleitung keine andere Notwendigkeit sieht, immer getrennt ausgeführt werden:

- Dateneingabe und -verifizierung
- Dateneingabe und Bestätigung
- Dateneingabe und Aufsichtsfunktionen
- Erstellung von Settlementanweisungen und Freigabe der Zahlung
- Settlement und Abstimmung der (Nostro-)Konten

1.4. Der operationale Ablauf eines FX-Geschäftes

Bei der Abwicklung eines FX-Geschäftes werden folgende Schritte durchlaufen:

- Erfassung des Geschäftes
- Eingabe des Geschäftes durch das Backoffice
- Bestätigung des Geschäftes
- Netting
- Settlement
- Abgleich der Nostrokonten

Während des Settlementprozesses ist

- eine enge Zusammenarbeit mit der Buchhaltung erforderlich.
- ein kontinuierliches Feedback-System zu etablieren, das Abweichungen und Fehler sofort erkennen lässt, sodass notwendige Korrekturmaßnahmen ergriffen werden können.

The figure below illustrates the FX process flow:

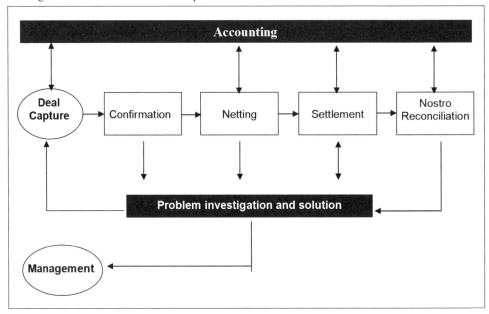

Summary

The increasing convergence of different markets, a tremendous rise of trading volume (approx. USD 5 trillion per day in the G-10 countries) and the introduction of new and complex FX and money market products place an increasing burden on risk management.

Operational risk is the risk of incurring interest charges or other penalties for misdirecting or otherwise failing to make settlement payments on time owing to an error or technical failure.

If operational risk entails liquidity and credit problems for other counterparties, operational failures can lead to systemic risk. Systemic risk is the risk that the failure of one participant in a transfer system, or in financial markets generally, to meet its required obligations when due will cause other participants or financial institutions to be unable to meet their obligations when due.

Measures to contain operational risk in FX trading include: segregation of back and front office duties, established procedures for introducing new products, sophisticated model sign-off procedures, quantifiable operational performance measurement, recording all counterparty conversations, sophisticated, independent audit unit, contingency plans, disaster recovery plans and alternative communication channels for confirmation and settlement.

Der **operationale Ablauf eines FX-Geschäftes** kann folgendermaßen dargestellt werden:

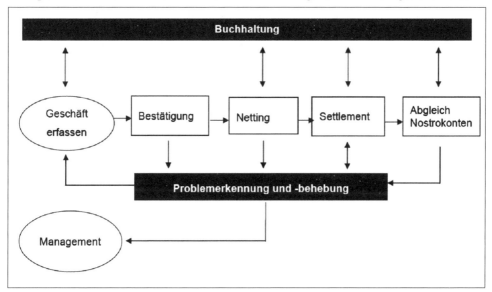

Zusammenfassung

Mit der zunehmenden Vernetzung zwischen den unterschiedlichen Märkten, einem gewaltigen Anstieg im Handelsvolumen (ca. USD 5 Trillionen pro Tag in den G10-Staaten) und der Einführung neuer, komplexer Produkte auf den FX- und Geldmärkten sind auch die Herausforderungen an das Risikomanagement gestiegen.

Operationales Risiko ist das Risiko, Zinsen oder andere Gebühren zahlen zu müssen, weil durch Irrtum oder technisches Versagen eine zur Erfüllung eines Geschäftes geleistete Zahlung fehlgeleitet wird oder auf eine andere Weise nicht rechtzeitig zustande kommt.

Im Zusammenhang mit operationalem Risiko muss auch das Systemrisiko genannt werden. Dabei handelt es sich um das Risiko, dass ein Marktteilnehmer seinen Verpflichtungen bei Fälligkeit nicht nachkommen kann (z.B. verspätete Zahlungsanweisung, Zahlungsunfähigkeit) und dadurch andere Marktteilnehmer bei Fälligkeit ebenfalls nicht erfüllen können.

Um operationale Risiken im FX-Handel besser kontrollieren zu können, sollten beispielsweise folgende Maßnahmen ergriffen werden: Trennung von Back- und Frontoffice-Aktivitäten, geeignetes Verfahren zur Einführung neuer Produkte, umfassende Einführungsverfahren für neue Modelle, Implementierung einer quantifizierten Leistungsmessung der Backoffice-Aktivitäten, Aufzeichnung von Gesprächen zwischen Händlern und Backoffices auf Band und ausreichend lange Aufbewahrung der Bänder, unabhängige Revisionseinheit, alternative Kommunikationswege zu Nostrobanken (z.B. Fax oder Telex), Organisation von Ausweichquartieren mit entsprechenden Backup-Systemen und Entwicklung von möglichen Katastrophenszenarien und Festlegung geeigneter Vorgehensweisen im Ernstfall.

The main duties of the back office include: processing transactions in the system, recording transactions in the books, making of payments, timely confirmation of all trades, timely settlement of transactions

When assigning back office duties, a strict segregation of duties between back office and front office as well as within key tasks of the back office must be ensured.

An FX deal comprises the following stages: deal capture, trade entry, confirmation, netting, settlement, nostro reconciliation.

1.5. Practice Questions

1. What are the reasons for the increasing challenges on risk management?
2. The failure of which of the following operational controls was mainly responsible for the Barings crisis?
   a) model sign-off and implementation
   b) contingency plans
   c) taping of conversations between counterparties
   d) segregation of front/back office
3. What is meant by operational risk?
4. What are typical losses incurred by operational risks?
5. What is meant by systemic risk?
6. Which of the following statements is true?
   a) The segregation of duties between back and front office can be abolished by the national supervisory bodies, if requested.
   b) The segregation of duties between back and front office has to be strictly maintained.
   c) Back office functions must be consolidated and located in the main trading centre of the bank.
   d) Senior management can allow traders to settle a deal if standard settlement instructions are in place for the underlying instrument.
7. Name at least five measures which should be implemented to contain operational risk in FX trading!
8. Why should a bank have proper procedures in place for introducing new products?
9. Explain the differences between direct and indirect model risks!
10. In which form should the back office record all transactions and support documentation for the financial statements?
11. What are the main duties of the back office in the settlement process?
12. Which core competences should be fulfilled by different members of the back office?
13. Which of the following describes the correct order of the settlement?
    a) trade entry, confirmation, nostro reconcilitation, netting, settlement
    b) trade entry, confirmation, netting, settlement, nostro reconcilitation
    c) netting, trade entry, settlement, confirmation, nostro reconcilitation
    d) confirmation, netting, trade entry, settlement, nostro reconcilitation
    e) trade entry, confirmation, settlement, nostro reconcilitation, netting

Im Rahmen des Settlementprozesses erfüllt das Backoffice folgende Funktionen: Verarbeitung der Transaktionen im System, Aufzeichnung der Transaktionen in den Büchern, Durchführung der Zahlungen, pünktliche Bestätigungen aller Geschäfte und Erfüllung der Transaktionen zum vereinbarten Zeitpunkt. Bei den Aufgaben des Backoffice ist immer auf eine genaue Aufgabentrennung zu achten. Es müssen nicht nur Front- und Backoffice-Aktivitäten getrennt werden, sondern auch innerhalb des Backoffice Kernkompetenzen von unterschiedlichen Personen erfüllt werden.

Bei der Abwicklung eines FX-Geschäftes werden folgende Schritte durchlaufen: Erfassung des Geschäftes, Eingabe des Geschäftes durch das Backoffice, Bestätigung des Geschäftes, Netting, Settlement und Abgleich der Nostrokonten

1.5. Wiederholungsfragen

1. Aus welchen Gründen sind die Herausforderungen an das Risikomanagement gestiegen?
2. Welcher Kontrollmechanismus hat bei der Barings Bank versagt?
   a) Modellgenehmigung
   b) Notfallplan
   c) Bandaufzeichnungen von Gesprächen
   d) Trennung Front- und Backoffice
3. Was versteht man unter operationalem Risiko?
4. Was sind typische Verluste, wenn operationale Risiken schlagend werden?
5. Was versteht man unter Systemrisiko?
6. Welche der folgenden Aussagen ist richtig?
   a) Eine inhaltliche Trennung von Front- und Backoffice kann von nationalen Aufsichtsbehörden auf Ansuchen aufgehoben werden.
   b) Eine inhaltliche Trennung von Front- und Backoffice ist zwingend notwendig.
   c) Backoffice-Funktionen müssen an jenem Ort zusammengefasst werden, wo der größte Handelsumsatz erfolgt.
   d) Die Geschäftsleitung kann bei Produkten, bei denen es Standard Settlement Instructions gibt, das Settlement dem Handel überlassen.
7. Nennen Sie mindestens fünf Maßnahmen zur besseren Kontrolle der operationalen Risiken im FX-Handel!
8. Wozu sollte eine Bank ein geeignetes Verfahren zur Einführung neuer Produkte haben?
9. Erklären Sie den Unterschied zwischen direkten und indirekten Modellrisiken!
10. In welcher Form sollte das Backoffice Geschäftsfälle und die dazugehörige Dokumentation erfassen bzw. aufbewahren?
11. Welche Funktionen erfüllt das Backoffice im Rahmen des Settlementprozesses?
12. Welche Tätigkeiten sollten immer getrennt ausgeführt werden?
13. Welche der folgenden Aufzählungen beschreibt den Settlementprozess in richtiger Reihenfolge?
    a) Geschäftseingabe, Bestätigung, Abgleich Nostrokonten, Netting, Settlement
    b) Geschäftseingabe, Bestätigung, Netting, Settlement, Abgleich Nostrokonten
    c) Netting, Geschäftseingabe, Settlement, Bestätigung, Abgleich Nostrokonten
    d) Bestätigung, Netting, Geschäftseingabe, Settlement, Abgleich Nostrokonten
    e) Geschäfteingabe, Bestätigung, Settlement, Abgleich Nostrokonten, Netting

2. Deal Capture

In this chapter you learn ...

- how a deal can be transacted.
- what is meant by "switching".
- about the two ways of capturing a deal.
- which information is normally involved in a dealing ticket.
- when all internal and external deals should be entered.
- about the purpose of straight-through processing.
- what is meant by "bulk trades".
- what issues should be considered for bulk trades.
- about the purpose of the use of an online credit system.
- what should be considered when using Standard Settlement Instructions.
- what should be considered for all third party payments.
- what should be considered for amendments to transaction details.
- about the duties of the Society for Worldwide-Interbank Financial Telecommunications (S.W.I.F.T).
- about the functional basis of S.W.I.F.T.
- how S.W.I.F.T. tries to ensure that messages are neither duplicated nor manipulated
- how the S.W.I.F.T. message types are composed.
- about the most important S.W.I.F.T. message types and their meanings.

2.1. Task Description

The **deal capture** is at the beginning of the settlement process. The entry of the trade data affects the general ledger, the payment and risk system and the nostro reconciliation process. A deal can be transacted

- directly between two counterparties or
- through a broker.

Note, that if you deal through a broker, the **name of the counterparty is disclosed only after the deal has been executed**. Thus, if credit lines turn out to be full or any other problems foil the deal with the counterparty, the broker will try to find a suitable counterparty to sit between the original counterparties. This practice is known as **"switching"**.

There are **two ways to capture a deal:**

- **electronically:** The front office enters the deal into the electronic dealing system (e.g.: Reuters 2000, EBS). If "straight-through processing" is established in a bank, all back

2. Der Geschäftserfassungsprozess

In diesem Kapitel lernen Sie ...

- in welcher Form der Geschäftsabschluss erfolgen kann.
- was man unter „Switching" versteht.
- welche zwei Möglichkeiten es bei der Eingabe des Geschäftes gibt.
- welche Informationen typischerweise auf einem Ticket erfasst werden.
- wann alle internen und externen Geschäfte zu erfassen sind.
- welchen Zweck die Verwendung einer automatischen Durchlaufverarbeitung erfüllt.
- was man unter „bulk trades" versteht.
- was bei bulk trades besonders zu beachten ist.
- welchen Zweck die Verwendung eines Online-Kreditsystems erfüllt.
- was bei der Verwendung von Standard Settlement Instructions zu beachten ist.
- was bei Zahlungsanweisungen an Dritte zu beachten ist.
- was bei Änderungen von Geschäftsdetails zu beachten ist.
- welche Aufgaben die Society for Worldwide Interbank Financial Telecommunication (S.W.I.F.T) hat.
- auf welcher Basis S.W.I.F.T. funktioniert.
- welche Sicherheiten gegen Manipulation und Duplizierungen von Nachrichten in S.W.I.F.T. vorgesehen sind.
- wie sich die dreistelligen Codes der S.W.I.F.T.-Message-Types zusammensetzen.
- die wichtigsten S.W.I.F.T.-Message-Types und deren Bedeutung kennen.

2.1. Aufgaben des Geschäftserfassungsprozesses

Die **Erfassung des abgeschlossenen Geschäftes** steht am Anfang des Settlementprozesses. Die Eingabe der Geschäftsdaten betrifft das Hauptbuch, das Zahlungs- und Risikosystem sowie alle Aufgaben zum Abgleich der Konten.

Der **Geschäftsabschluss** kann entweder

- direkt zwischen den Parteien oder
- über einen Broker

erfolgen.

Bei Geschäften über Broker ist zu beachten, dass der **Name des Geschäftspartners erst nach Abschluss des Geschäfts bekanntgegeben** wird. Sollten Probleme mit Partnerlimits auftreten, so kann der Broker einen geeigneten Partner zwischen die ursprünglichen Partner schalten. Diese Vorgehensweise nennt man **„Switching".**

Bei der Eingabe des Geschäftes gibt es zwei Möglichkeiten:

- Das Geschäft wird vom Frontoffice in ein **elektronisches Handelssystem** (z.B. Reuters 2000-2, EBS) eingegeben. Besondere Bedeutung kommt einer automatisch durchlaufenden Verarbeitung („straight-through processing") zu, bei der die sonst vom Backoffice durchgeführten Eingaben automatisch im System geändert werden, wenn das Geschäft eingegeben wird.

office work is automatically executed by the system and no manual input by the back office is required.

- **The trader writes a ticket.** This can be hand-written or computer-based. It is signed by the trader and passed to the back office where the trade data are captured.

A **dealing ticket** typically involves the following **data**:

- trade data
- time of trade
- settlement date
- counterparty
- financial instrument traded
- amount
- price/rate
- netting indicators
- settlement instructions (sometimes)

2.2. Best Practices – Deal Capture

BP1

All internal and external trades should be entered **immediately** and be accessible for both trading and operations.

Inaccurate or incomplete data entry can affect the following interrelated systems:

- credit limits
- intra-day P&L
- trader positions
- confirmation processing
- settlement
- general ledger

BP2

Where front office and back office use separate systems all deals, amendments, adjustments and cancellations should be **automatically fed from one system to the other**. Ideally the transaction data should also be carried straight through for **posting to the general ledger**.

Straight-through processing allows regular updating of credit information, generating money transfer instructions, feeding nostro reconciliation systems and eliminates particularly potential errors associated with multiple data entry by back and front office staff. Though straight-through processing **reduces operational risk** it may increase settlement risk since it becomes very difficult, if not impossible, to stop the settlement of a deal. Particularly payment instructions could become irrevocable at an early stage of the settlement process.

BP3

Credit lines should be updated as soon as deals are captured. A bank should establish **online credit systems** to calculate and **aggregate exposures globally on an individual basis**. All information should be made accessible to risk managers and trading.

- Der Händler erfasst **schriftlich** (handschriftlich oder computergestützt) **auf einem Ticket** das Geschäft, bestätigt es durch seine Unterschrift und gibt das Ticket an das Backoffice weiter, das die Daten eingibt.

Folgende Informationen werden auf einem **Ticket** typischerweise erfasst:

- Handelstag
- Uhrzeit
- Settlement Date
- Partner
- Art und Umfang des Geschäftes
- Preis
- Netting-Indikatoren
- Settlementanweisungen (fakultativ)

2.2. Anforderungen an den Geschäftserfassungsprozess

A1

Alle internen und externen Geschäfte sind **sofort nach Abschluss zu erfassen** und sollen sowohl für den Handel als auch das Backoffice zugreifbar sein.

Eine falsche oder verzögerte Eingabe kann auf folgende Bereiche Auswirkungen haben:

- Kreditlimits
- Intraday G&V
- Position des Händlers
- Bestätigungsvorgang
- Settlement
- Hauptbuch

A2

Werden im Handel und im Backoffice zwei verschiedene Systeme verwendet, so sollten alle Details und Änderungen (Zusätze, Stornierungen) von Geschäften **automatisch von einem System in das andere geleitet werden.** Idealerweise sollten die Daten auch **direkt in das Hauptbuch** gehen.

Eine **automatische Durchlaufverarbeitung („straight-through processing")** ermöglicht das Erstellen aktueller Kreditinformationen, löst Geldtransaktionen aus, aktualisiert die Aufzeichnungen über Nostrokonten und verringert vor allem die Fehlerquellen, die mehrfache händische Eingaben in sich bergen. Die Durchlaufverarbeitung **reduziert zwar das operationale Risiko, kann aber das Erfüllungs- bzw. Settlementrisiko erhöhen,** weil einmal eingeleitete Verfahren nicht mehr oder nur sehr schwierig gestoppt werden können. So kann ein Zahlungsauftrag zu einem sehr frühen Zeitpunkt unwiderruflich werden, obwohl er noch nicht abgewickelt worden ist.

A3

Die Kreditlinien sollten aktualisiert werden, sobald ein Geschäft eingegeben worden ist. Die Bank sollte ein **Online-Kreditsystem** installieren, das eine **aggregierte, globale Risikoposition pro Partner** berechnet. Diese Informationen müssen dem Handel und dem Risikomanager sofort zur Verfügung stehen.

Online credit systems help to

- keep the credit limits with counterparties, especially if the bank trades with them on an aggregate basis
- assess the creditworthiness of a counterparty and to adjust the limits if necessary
- avoid deals with counterparties whose limits are almost filled

BP4

Trading and operational practices should be established with all counterparties.

In particular, **bulk trades** should be **confirmed as soon as possible and not later than the end of the trade date.** All trade types, regardless of maturity (Spot; forwards; Tom/next; etc.) must be reported. If bulk trades are not properly allocated some credit risk may remain. Bulk or block trades are **large volume transactions that are split into smaller amounts** and allocated to specific customer accounts. This kind of deals is usually executed by fund managers.

BP5

Standard Settlement Instructions (SSIs) should be in place for all counterparties. SSIs usually exist in the interbank market, for institutional investors and for corporate customers. If no SSIs are in place, the back office should be responsible for obtaining and verifying the instructions. SSIs allow for complete and efficient deal capture. A standardized format enables the bank to take full advantage of straight through processing. Settlement instructions must be obtained for all spot deals. Because forward deals are not settled immediately, the back office may contact the counterparty at a later date for settlement instructions. Generally, the deal's financial details are best confirmed on trade date. In the case of "bulk trades" operations need to receive settlement instructions as soon as possible.

The following guidelines should be followed when using SSIs:

- If a bank changes its SSIs it should **inform the counterparties as soon as possible**. If both counterparties are subscribers to **SWIFT SSI/FX Directory**, changes can be directly transmitted via S.W.I.F.T. (Code MT 293). If one counterparty is not a member of S.W.I.F.T. network, SSI changes should be notified by **registered letter**. **S.W.I.F.T Broadcast is not an acceptable means** for establishing, cancelling or amending SSIs. A mutually agreed period of notice for changing SSIs should be given to each counterparty. Typically this will be between 10 working days and one month. If SSIs for nostro accounts are changed a notification period of 5 to 6 weeks is usually established.
- Institutions should update their records promptly when **changes to SSIs** are received from their counterparties.
- All outstanding deals, including maturing forwards, should be settled in accordance with the SSI in force at their value date unless otherwise and explicitly agreed by the parties at the time at which any change to an existing SSI is agreed. The old SSI should be reconfirmed at the date of change or before settlement.
- SSIs should be in the S.W.I.F.T. or ISO format in order to facilitate processing. Alternatively, SSIs can be **established by post, telex or fax**.
- If SSIs are not established operations must contact the counterparty to obtain settlement instructions and update the deal record according to the information received.

Mit einem Online-Kreditsystem soll ermöglicht werden, dass

- bei Geschäften mit einem Partner an verschiedenen Orten die Limits insgesamt eingehalten werden.
- im Frontoffice die Kreditlimite leichter eingehalten werden können.
- die Kreditwürdigkeit des Partners besser eingeschätzt werden kann und Limits angepasst werden können.

A4

Mit allen Partnern soll eine **Handels- und Abwicklungspraxis** festgelegt werden. Speziell im Fall von **„bulk trades"** sollte die Bank von den Kunden eine **Bestätigung bis zum Ende des Handelstages** erhalten. „Bulk trades" sind **großvolumige Transaktionen,** die von Fondsmanagern getätigt werden.

Die einzelne **große Transaktion wird in kleinere Transaktionen geteilt („split")** und vom Fondsmanager den einzelnen Kunden nach Bedarf zugeordnet. Fondsmanager sollen angehalten werden, alle Informationen über „bulk trades" am Handelstag weiterzuleiten, damit das **Kreditrisikomanagement aktualisiert** werden kann. Dabei sind alle Geschäfte, unabhängig von der Laufzeit (Spot, Tom/next, Forward), zu berücksichtigen.

A5

Jeder Marktteilnehmer sollte für seine Partner **Standard Settlement Instructions (SSIs)** erstellen. Im Interbankhandel sowie beim Handel mit institutionellen Kunden und Firmenkunden existieren üblicherweise Standard Settlement Instructions (SSIs) zur Abwicklung von Geschäften. Sind keine SSIs vorhanden, so ist das Backoffice für die Beschaffung und Überprüfung der Settlement-Instruktionen verantwortlich.

SSIs ermöglichen eine effiziente Erfassung der Handelsdaten. Durch die Schaffung standardisierter Formate wird auch eine Durchlaufverarbeitung erleichtert, die Fehler beim Settlement reduzieren hilft.

Folgende Punkte sind bei SSIs zu beachten:

- Wenn eine Bank SSIs ändert, dann sind die **Partner möglichst frühzeitig davon** zu **informieren.** Teilnehmer am SWIFT-Netzwerk können über das **SSI/FX-Directory Service** in automatisierter Form direkt auf SSIs zugreifen bzw. neue SSIs bekanntgeben (Code MT 293). Alternativ können die Änderungen auch mittels **eingeschriebenem Brief** mitgeteilt werden. **S.W.I.F.T. Broadcast** ist **nicht geeignet,** Änderungen von SSIs bekanntzugeben. Partner sind zehn Tage bis ein Monat im Vorhinein zu informieren. Änderungen der SSIs für Nostrokonten werden üblicherweise fünf bis sechs Wochen vor Umstellung bekanntgegeben.
- Sobald eine Bank von einem Partner **Änderungen der SSIs** erhält, sind diese **so rasch wie möglich zu berücksichtigen.**
- Werden SSIs für Termingeschäfte geändert, so soll die Bank die Settlementbedingungen für jene Geschäfte, die bereits abgeschlossen, aber noch nicht geliefert wurden, bestätigen.
- SSIs sollen im SWIFT- oder ISO-Format erstellt werden, um die Verarbeitung zu erleichtern. Ist der Partner **nicht im SWIFT-Netzwerk** integriert, so erfolgt die **Bestätigung per Post, Fax oder Telex.**
- Existieren mit einem Partner keine SSIs, so muss das Backoffice auf die Settlementanweisungen des Partners warten oder jene vom Handel übermittelten umsetzen.

BP6

Extra diligence and reviews of payment instructions should be in place for all third-party payments.

Extra diligence for third-party deals is necessary because the **bank does not know the validity of a third-party**. There should be clean guidelines for traders when requests for third-party payments can be accepted.

In case of third-party payments, the bank should seek to be **relieved from any liability for fraudulent activities of the third party**. Appropriate measures to ensure the identity and reliability of the third party include the requirement of SSIs, the requirement of authenticated S.W.I.F.T messages and telephone calls by an independent party in order to check the identity.

BP7

Amendments to transaction details should be conducted in a controlled manner that include front as well as back office in the process. Particular **care should be taken for amendments to FX swap transactions, after settlement of the near leg**.

While trading initiates and executes deals and takes positions, the back office records and confirms the deals. This segregation of duties is one of the key control mechanism of any bank.

Amendments to deals can be initiated by the trading or operations department. If the back office is responsible for amending the deal it should obtain supporting documentation and receive prior written authorization from trading before processing the amendments or cancellations. **Exception reports**, listing amendments and cancellations should be made available to the trading and operations management on a regular basis.

Amendments to swap transactions may present difficulties if the near leg has settled because offsetting deals have been already entered into. Thus, also the offsetting currency and interest rate positions must be amended if the incorrectly captured deal is corrected, leading to an accurate P&L.

2.3. EXCURSUS: The Society for World-wide-Interbank Financial Telecommunications (S.W.I.F.T.)

Overview

In 1973 European and US-banks founded S.W.I.F.T. in order to improve **communication between financial market participants by using modern technology and standardized processes**.

In November 2008, the S.W.I.F.T. network included **more than 8700 members from over 209 countries**. Besides 2,600 banks, brokers, exchanges and clearing houses take part as sub-members in S.W.I.F.T. In 2008, around 3 billion messages were transferred via S.W.I.F.T. The daily volume transferred hovers currently around USD 2 trillion.

Bei Kassageschäften müssen Settlementangelegenheiten sofort erledigt werden. Bei Termingeschäften können Settlementanweisungen später eingeholt werden, weil die Erfüllung zu einem späteren Zeitpunkt anfällt. Generell wird jedoch empfohlen, **alle finanziellen Details sofort** zu **dokumentieren**. Bei „bulk trades" muss das Backoffice versuchen, möglichst rasch die Settlementbedingungen für die „splits" zu erhalten.

A6

Für Zahlungsanweisungen an Dritte sollten **besondere Sorgfalt- und Prüfungsvorschriften** vorhanden sein.

Der Grund für die erhöhten Sorgfaltspflichten liegt darin, dass die **Gültigkeit der dritten Partei nicht bekannt** ist. Für Händler sollten klare Richtlinien existieren, wann solche Zahlungsanweisungen zu akzeptieren sind.

Im Fall von Zahlungen an Dritte hat die Bank auf eine **Haftungsbefreiung gegen Betrug durch den Auftraggeber** zu achten. Die Abwicklung über SWIFT und mittels SSIs sowie Kontrollanrufe durch einen unabhängigen Dritten bieten Sicherheit über die Identität und Seriosität der dritten Partei.

A7

Müssen fehlerhafte Aufzeichnungen über Geschäfte korrigiert werden, dann sind sowohl der Handel als auch das Backoffice an diesem Prozess zu beteiligen. Auf **besondere Sorgfalt** ist **bei FX-Swaps** zu achten, wenn das **erste Geschäft bereits gesettled** wurde.

Während der Handel die Geschäfte abschließt und Positionen fährt, zeichnet das Backoffice die Geschäfte auf und bestätigt sie. Diese Aufgabentrennung ist einer der wichtigsten Kontrollmechanismen in einer Bank.

Änderungen an Geschäftsdetails können sowohl vom Handel als auch vom Backoffice ausgehen. Werden sie vom Backoffice initiiert, so soll es sich einerseits unterstützendes Material vom Handel besorgen und andererseits eine schriftliche Bestätigung des Handels einholen, bevor die Änderungen ins System eingegeben werden. Die Änderungen sind in sogenannten **„Exception Reports"** regelmäßig an das Backoffice und Handelsmanagement zu melden.

Im Fall von FX-Swaps, wo bereits das erste Geschäft geliefert wurde (und damit kein Fehler, z.B. falscher Spotkurs, behoben werden kann), muss bei Änderungen mit besonderer Vorsicht agiert werden, weil die Devisen- bzw. Zinsposition zum Schließen des Geschäfts geändert werden muss.

2.3. EXKURS: Die Society for Worldwide Interbank Financial Telecommunication (S.W.I.F.T.)

Allgemeines

S.W.I.F.T. wurde 1973 von europäischen und US-amerikanischen Banken mit dem Ziel gegründet, die **Kommunikation zwischen den Teilnehmern auf den Finanzmärkten durch den Einsatz moderner Technologien und standardisierter Abläufe zu verbessern.**

Im November 2008 hatte das S.W.I.F.T.-Netzwerk insgesamt **mehr als 8.700 Teilnehmer in 209 Ländern.** Neben über 2.600 Banken nehmen unter anderem Clearing-Organisationen, Broker und Börsen als Sub-Mitglieder teil. 2008 wurden über 3 Mrd. Messages über S.W.I.F.T. geschickt.

The **advantages** of automated and standardized process flows are more efficiency, fewer errors and misunderstandings as well as more transparent information and management.

The mechanics of S.W.I.F.T.

The S.W.I.F.T. system is based on **standardized and encrypted three-digit codes** (Message Types-MTs). Furthermore only authorized users can enter the S.W.I.F.T. network and access is controlled through a **Smart Card System**.

This way

- no unauthorized person can use the network
- the sender and receiver can clearly be identified
- the confidentiality of information is secured and
- data can not be manipulated

S.W.I.F.T. tries to ensure that messages are neither duplicated nor manipulated by setting the following measures:

- **Bilateral Key Exchange:** Before authenticated messages (especially of category 1 and 2) are sent bilateral keys are exchanged between the parties by exchanging MTs 960 to 963. Through the bilateral key exchanges an unequivocal identification can be attached to each of the following messages.
- **Input and Output Sequence Numbers (ISNs and OSNs):** The S.W.I.F.T. systems puts to every message a number in order to avoid duplication of messages. If a message has to be sent again (e.g. the transmission was interrupted because of a line defect), S.W.I.F.T. adds to the ISN/OSN concerned the supplement PDM ("possible duplicated message") or PDE ("possibly duplicated emission"). This code alerts participants of possibly existing messages.
- **Two-level system:** Members of S.W.I.F.T. have access to GPA (General Progress Applications) where general information like S.W.I.F.T. Broadcast is available and an access code to FIN (Financial Application on S.W.I.F.T.). The access code is either electronically stored on a smart card which can be read by the system or has to be entered manually for each level.

S.W.I.F.T offers also the **informal communication system S.W.I.F.T. Broadcast**. This system is often used to exchange general information such as SSIs (MT 293) or by clearinghouses to deliver customer information (MT 599). S.W.I.F.T. Broadcast **should not be used to exchange information including any trades**.

The structure and meaning of S.W.I.F.T. MTs

S.W.I.F.T. codes consist of three digits. The composition of the codes follows a systematic structure.

- **1st digit: Category** (Market/Product)
- **2nd digit: Group** (General function of message)
- **3rd digit: Type** (Specific function of message)

S.W.I.F.T. is **used particularly for standardized and relatively simple trades**. The most often used MTs are: 103, 201-210, 300, 305, 520-523, 530-533, and 950.

Die **Vorteile** eines automatisierten und standardisierten Ablaufs sind eine erhöhte Effizienz, weniger Fehler und Missverständnisse sowie mehr und transparentere Information für das Management.

Funktionsweise von S.W.I.F.T.

S.W.I.F.T. funktioniert auf der Basis **standardisierter, verschlüsselter dreistelliger Transfercodes (Message Types – MTs).** Weiters können nur berechtigte Teilnehmer über ein **Smart-Card-System** in das S.W.I.F.T.-Netzwerk einsteigen. Auf diese Weise soll garantiert werden, dass

- keine unautorisierten Personen das Netzwerk benützen können,
- die Absender und Empfänger klar identifiziert werden können,
- Vertraulichkeit der Übermittlungen gewährleistet wird und
- keine Manipulationen vorgenommen werden können.

Folgende Sicherheiten gegen Manipulation und Duplizierungen von Nachrichten sind in S.W.I.F.T. vorgesehen:

- **Bilateral Key Exchange:** Bevor codierte Nachrichten (besonders Gruppe 1 und 2) gesendet werden, wird über die MTs 960 bis 963 ein Schlüssel definiert, der dem nachfolgenden MT eine **eindeutige Identifikation** zuordnet.
- **Input und Output Sequence Numbers (ISNs und OSNs):** Dabei handelt es sich um eine **fortlaufende Nummerierung der Nachrichten** durch das S.W.I.F.T.-System. Damit werden **Mehrfachtransaktionen unterbunden.** Sollte eine Nachricht noch einmal gesendet worden sein (weil z.B. ein Leitungsdefekt bei der ersten Übertragung auftrat), so kennzeichnet das S.W.I.F.T.-System die ISNS/OSN mit dem Zusatz PDM („possibly duplicated message") oder PDE („possibly duplicated emission"). Auf diese Weise werden die Teilnehmer darauf aufmerksam gemacht, dass die Nachricht vielleicht schon existiert.
- **Zweistufensystem:** Wer an S.W.I.F.T. teilnimmt, hat einen **Zutritt zur GPA (General Program Applications),** wo alle allgemeinen Informationen wie S.W.I.F.T. Broadcast oder eine Zutrittsberechtigung zum FIN (Financial Application on S.W.I.F.T.) zur Verfügung stehen. Die Zutrittscodes sind entweder auf einer Karte gespeichert und werden vom System abgelesen oder werden händisch für jede Stufe eingegeben.

S.W.I.F.T. ermöglicht auch die **Kommunikation über das formlose S.W.I.F.T. Broadcast-System.** Diese Form der Kommunikation soll jedoch **für offizielle Geschäfte nicht gewählt** werden. Oft werden jedoch allgemeine Informationen über dieses System gesendet, wie zum Beispiel SSIs (MT 293) oder Informationen von Clearinghäusern an ihre Kunden (MT 599).

Die Struktur und Bedeutung von S.W.I.F.T.-MTs

Der dreistellige Code der Message Types setzt sich folgendermaßen zusammen:

   1. Stelle: Kategorie (Markt/Produkt)
   2. Stelle: Gruppe (allgemeine Funktion der Mitteilung)
   3. Stelle: Typ (spezielle Funktion der Mitteilung)

S.W.I.F.T. wird **besonders für standardisierte und relativ einfache Geschäftsfälle** verwendet. Häufig verwendete MTs sind 103, 201-210, 300, 305, 520-523, 530-533 und 950.

S.W.I.F.T. is of relatively little significance for rather complex OTC derivative products (e.g. IRS) because individual arrangements require more flexible ways of documentation.

S.W.I.F.T. defines **ten categories** (1st digit), which cover the following markets and products respectively

I.   Customer payments and Checks
II.   Financial Institution Transfer
III.   Foreign Exchange, Money Market and Derivatives
IV.   Collections and Cash Letters
V.   Securities Market
VI.   Precious Metals and Syndications
VII.   Documentary Credits and Guarantees
VIII. Travellers Cheques
IX.   Cash Management and Customer Status
X.   N9n Common Group

Note: Category 9 MTs deals among others with netting and nostro reconciliation. Messages from the common group (90 to 99) have the same meaning across all categories. For example, 95 means that each MT with the last two digits 95 is a query in the category determined by the variable first digit.

The following table sums up the most important and commonly used Message Types:

Relativ selten werden S.W.I.F.T.-Codes in komplexeren OTC-Derivativgeschäften (z.B. Zinsswaps) eingesetzt, da aufgrund geschäftsindividueller Vereinbarungen andere Formen der Dokumentation besser entsprechen.

Es gibt **zehn Kategorien von Message Types,** die sich folgendermaßen zusammenfassen lassen (die Ziffer steht jeweils an erster Stelle):

I.   Kundenzahlungen und Schecks
II.   Transfer zwischen Finanzinstitutionen
III.   FX, Geldmarkt und Derivate
IV.   Überweisungen, Zahlungseinzug
V.   Wertpapiermarkt
VI.   Edelmetalle und Syndizierung
VII.   Dokumentenakkreditiv und Garantien
VIII. Reiseschecks
IX.   Cash Management und Kundenstatus
X.   N9n Allgemeine Standardinformationen

Anmerkung: In Kategorie 9 behandeln die MTs unter anderem Netting und den Abgleich der Nostrokonten. Die allgemeinen Standardinformationen (n90 bis n99) sind MTs, die für alle Kategorien denselben Inhalt haben. n95 bedeutet z.B., dass jeder MT mit den letzten beiden Ziffern 95 eine Anfrage darstellt, die sich auf jene Kategorie bezieht, die mit der variablen ersten Stelle belegt wird.

The following table sums up the most important and commonly used Message Types:

Category	Function	MT	Meaning
1 Customer Payments & Cheques	Customer Payments	101 102 103 104	Request for Transfer Mass Payment Transfer Customer Transfer Customer Direct Debit
	Cheques	110 111 112	Advice of Cheque Request for Stop Payment of a Cheque Status of a Request for Stop Payment for a Cheque
2 Financial Institution Transfer		200 201 202 203 204 205 210	Financial Institution Transfer for Its Own Account Multiple Financial Institution Transfer for Its Own A/C General Financial Institution Transfer Multiple General Financial Institution Transfer Financial Markets Direct Debit Message Financial Institution Transfer Execution Notice to Receive
3 Foreign Exchange, Money Markets & Derivatives	Foreign Exchange	300 303 304 305	Foreign Exchange Confirmation Forex/Currency Option Allocation Instruction Advice/Instruction of a Third Party Deal Foreign Currency Option Confirmation
	Loan/Deposit Message	320 324 330 335 350	Fixed Loan/Deposit Confirmation Liquidation Notice for Fixed Loan/Deposit Call/Notice Loan/Deposit Confirmation Advice of a Call/Notice Loan/Deposit Interest Rate Change Advice of Loan/Deposit Interest Payment
	Forward Rate Agreement	340 341	Forward Rate Agreement Confirmation Forward Rate Agreement Settlement Confirmation
	IRS (very seldomly used)	360 361 362 364	Single Currency Interest Rate Swap Cross Currency Interest Rate Swap Interest Rate Reset/Advice of Payment IRS termination

Abschließend präsentieren wir eine Liste der wichtigsten S.W.I.F.T.-MTs mit ihren Bedeutungen:

Kategorie	Funktion	MT	Inhalt
1 Kundenzah- lungsverkehr	Kunden- zahlungen	101	Zahlungsaufforderung
		102	Sammelzahlungsüberweisung
		103	Kundenüberweisung
		104	Kundenlastschrift
	Schecks	110	Avisierung eines Schecks
		111	Aufforderung zum Sperren eines Schecks
		112	Status einer MT 111 (Aufforderung zum Sperren eines Schecks)
2 Transfer zwischen Finanzinstitu- tionen		200	Transfer einer Finanzinstitution für eigene Rechnung
		201	Zusammenfassung mehrerer MT 200
		202	Allgemeiner Transfer zwischen Finanzinstitutionen
		203	Zusammenfassung mehrerer MT 202
		204	Lastschriftmitteilung auf Finanzmärkten
		205	Durchführung einer Überweisung
		210	Empfangsnachricht
3 Kassa-, Geldmarkt und Derivative	Kassa (FX)	300	FX-Bestätigung
		303	FX-Option-Ausübungsanweisung
		304	Ankündigung/-weisung eines Geschäftes mit Dritten
		305	FX-Option-Bestätigung
		320	Festzinskredit/festes Depot Bestätigung
		330	Bestätigung für Kredit/Depot mit Kündigungsfrist
		350	Aviso einer Zinszahlung auf Kredit/Depot
	FRAs	340	FRA-Bestätigung
		341	FRA-Setttlement-Bestätigung
	Zinsswaps (sehr selten verwen- det)	360	Bestätigung für Zinsswap in einer Währung
		361	Bestätigung für Cross Currency IRS
		362	IRS Reset-/Zahlungsankündigung
		364	IRS vorzeitig Beendigung oder teilweise Auflösung

Kategorie	Funktion	MT	Inhalt
5 Securities Markets	Securities	500	Order to buy
		501	Order to sell
		502	Order to buy or sell
		510	Confirmation of Purchase or Sale
		512	Securities Trade Confirmation
		513	Client Advice of Execution
		515	Client Confirmation of Purchase or Sale
		516	Securities Loan Confirmation
		517	Trade Confirmation Affirmation
		518	Market – Side Securities Trade Confirmation
		519	Advice of Execution
		526	General Securities Lending/Borrowing Message
		530	Confirmation of Receipt Free
		559	Paying Agent's Claim
		581	Collateral Adjustment Message
		582	Reimbursement Claim or Advice

Kategorie	Funktion	MT	Inhalt
5 Wertpapier- markt	Wertpapiere	500	Registrierungsinformation
		501	Bestätigung einer Registrierungsinformation
		502	Order zu Kauf oder Verkauf
		510	Registrierungsstatus
		513	Kundenaviso einer Ausübung
		515	Bestätigung von Kauf/Verkauf an Kunden
		516	Wertpapierleihe Bestätigung
		517	Rückbestätigung eines Geschäftes
		518	Rückbestätigung von Kunden (zu MT 515)
		519	Änderung Kundendetails
		526	Nachricht – allgemeines Security
		530	Lending/Borrowing
		559	Bestätigung MT 520
		581	Forderung der Zahlstelle
		582	Nachricht zur Anpassung der Besicherung Anspruch oder Aviso auf/von Rückerstattung

Kategorie	Funktion	MT	Inhalt
9 Cash Management & Customer Status	Advice	900 910	Confirmation of Debt Confirmation of Credit
	Balance Reporting	920 940 941 942	Request Message Customer Statement Message Balance Report Interim Transaction Report
	Nostro State- ments	950	Statement Message
	Bilateral Key Changes	960 961 962 963 964 965 966 967	Request for Service Initiation Message Initiation Response Message Key Service Message Key Acknowledgement Message Error Message Error in Key Service Message Discontinue Service Message Discontinuation Acknowledgement Message
	Netting	970 971 972 973	Netting Statement Netting Balance Report Netting Interim Statement Netting Request Message Standards General Information
Standards General Information	Common Group	n90 n91 n92 n93 n95 n96 n98 n99	Advice of Charges, Interest and Other Adjustments Request for Payment of Charges, Interest&Other Expenses Request for Cancellation Information Service Message Queries Answers Proprietary Free Format

Kategorie	Funktion	MT	Inhalt
9 Cash Management und Kundenstatus	Aviso	900	Bestätigung von Lastschrift
		910	Bestätigung einer Gutschrift
	Saldo- ausweis	920	Aufforderung, ein MT 240, 941, 942 oder 950 zu senden
		940	Kontoauszug des Kunden
		941	Saldoausweis
		942	Transaktionen Zwischenbericht
	Nostro- Angaben	950	Nostrokontoauszug-Nachricht
Cash Management und Kundenstatus	Bilateral Key Ex- change	960	Antrag zum Auslösen des Prozesses
		961	Antwort auf Auslösung
		962	Key Service Message
		963	Key Acknowledgement Message
		964	Fehlermeldung
		965	Fehler in MT 962
		966	Abbruch MT 962
		967	Abbruch MT 963
	Netting	970	Netting-Auszug
		971	Netting-Saldobericht
		972	Netting-Zwischenbericht
		973	Netting-Aufforderung (MT 971 oder 972 zu senden)
Standards für allgemeine Informationen	Allgemeine Gruppe	n90	Aviso Gebühren-, Zins- oder andere Anpassungen
		n91	Aufforderung zur Zahlung von Gebühren, Zin- sen u.Ä.
		n92	Aufforderung zur Stornierung
		n95	Anfragen
		n96	Antworten
		n98	In eigener Sache
		n99	Freies Format

Summary

The deal capture is at the beginning of the settlement process. A deal can be transacted directly between two counterparties or through a broker.

If you deal through a broker, the name of the counterparty is disclosed only after the deal has been executed. Thus, if credit lines turn out to be used up or any other problems foil the deal with the counterparty, the broker will try to find a suitable counterparty to sit between the original counterparties. This practice is known as "switching".

There are two ways to capture a deal, electronically or with the trader writing a ticket. A dealing ticket typically involves the following data: trade data, time of trade, settlement date, counterparty, financial instrument traded, amount, price/rate, netting indicators and settlement instructions (sometimes).

All internal and external trades should be entered immediately and be accessible for both trading and operations.

Where front office and back office use separate systems, all deals, amendments, adjustments and cancellations should be automatically fed from one system to the other.

Credit lines should be updated as soon as deals are captured. A bank should establish on-line credit systems to calculate and aggregate exposures globally on an individual basis.

Trading and operational practices should be established with all counterparties. In particular, bulk trades should be confirmed as soon as possible and no later than the end of the trade date. Bulk or block trades are large volume transactions that are split into smaller amounts and allocated to specific customer accounts.

Standard Settlement Instructions (SSIs) should be in place for all counterparties.

Extra diligence and reviews of payment instructions should be in place for all third-party payments.

While trading initiates and executes deals and takes positions, the back office records and confirms the deals. This segregation of duties is one of the key control mechanisms of any bank.

Amendments to transaction details should be conducted in a controlled manner including both front and back office. Particular care should be taken for amendments to FX swap transactions, after settlement of the near leg.

In 1973 European and US banks founded S.W.I.F.T. in order to improve communication between financial market participants by using modern technology and standardized processes.

The advantages of automated and standardized process flows are more efficiency, fewer errors and misunderstandings as well as more transparent information and management. The S.W.I.F.T. system is based on standardized and encrypted three-digit codes (Message Types, MTs). S.W.I.F.T. defines ten categories of S.W.I.F.T. message types. S.W.I.F.T. codes consist of three digits. The composition of the codes follows a systematic structure: category (market/product); group (general function of message); type (specific function of message)

Zusammenfassung

Die Erfassung des abgeschlossenen Geschäftes steht am Anfang des Settlementprozesses. Der Geschäftsabschluss kann entweder direkt zwischen den Parteien oder über einen Broker erfolgen.

Bei Geschäften über Broker ist zu beachten, dass der Name des Geschäftspartners erst nach Abschluss des Geschäfts bekanntgegeben wird. Sollten Probleme mit Partnerlimits auftreten, so kann der Broker einen geeigneten Partner zwischen die ursprünglichen Partner schalten. Diese Vorgehensweise nennt man „Switching".

Bei der Eingabe des Geschäftes wird das Geschäft entweder vom Frontoffice in ein elektronisches Handelssystem eingegeben oder vom Händler schriftlich auf einem Ticket erfasst. Folgende Informationen werden auf einem Ticket typischerweise erfasst: Handelstag, Uhrzeit, Settlement Date, Partner, Art und Umfang des Geschäftes, Preis, Netting-Indikatoren und Settlementanweisungen (fakultativ).

Alle internen und externen Geschäfte sind sofort nach Abschluss zu erfassen.

Werden im Handel und im Backoffice zwei verschiedene Systeme verwendet, so sollten alle Details und Änderungen (Zusätze, Stornierungen) von Geschäften automatisch von einem System in das andere geleitet werden.

Die Kreditlinien sollten aktualisiert werden, sobald ein Geschäft eingegeben worden ist. Die Bank sollte ein Online-Kreditsystem installieren, das eine aggregierte, globale Risikoposition pro Partner berechnet.

Mit allen Partnern soll eine Handels- und Abwicklungspraxis festgelegt werden. Speziell im Fall von „bulk trades" sollte die Bank von den Kunden eine Bestätigung bis zum Ende des Handelstages erhalten. „Bulk trades" sind großvolumige Transaktionen, die von Fondsmanagern getätigt werden.

Jeder Marktteilnehmer sollte für seine Partner Standard Settlement Instructions (SSIs) erstellen.

Für Zahlungsanweisungen an Dritte sollten besondere Sorgfalts- und Prüfungsvorschriften vorhanden sein.

Müssen fehlerhafte Aufzeichnungen über Geschäfte korrigiert werden, dann sind sowohl der Handel als auch das Backoffice an diesem Prozess zu beteiligen. Auf besondere Sorgfalt ist bei FX-Swaps zu achten, wenn das erste Geschäft bereits gesettled wurde.

Während der Handel die Geschäfte abschließt und Positionen fährt, zeichnet das Backoffice die Geschäfte auf und bestätigt sie. Diese Aufgabentrennung ist einer der wichtigsten Kontrollmechanismen in einer Bank.

S.W.I.F.T. wurde 1973 von europäischen und US-amerikanischen Banken mit dem Ziel gegründet, die Kommunikation zwischen den Teilnehmern auf den Finanzmärkten durch den Einsatz moderner Technologien und standardisierter Abläufe zu verbessern.

Die Vorteile eines automatisierten und standardisierten Ablaufs sind eine erhöhte Effizienz, weniger Fehler und Missverständnisse sowie mehr und transparentere Information für das Management.

S.W.I.F.T. funktioniert auf der Basis standardisierter, verschlüsselter, dreistelliger Transfercodes (Message Types – MTs). Es gibt zehn Kategorien von S.W.I.F.T.-Message Types. Der dreistellige Code der Message Types setzt sich folgendermaßen zusammen: Kategorie (Markt/Produkt), Gruppe (allgemeine Funktion der Mitteilung), Typ (spezielle Funktion der Mitteilung).

S.W.I.F.T. tries to ensure that messages are neither duplicated nor manipulated by setting the following measures: Bilateral Key Exchange, Input and Output Sequence Numbers (ISNs and OSNs) and Two-level system.
S.W.I.F.T also offers the informal communication system S.W.I.F.T. Broadcast. S.W.I.F.T. Broadcast should not be used to exchange information including any trades.

2.4. Practice questions

1. What should be considered when dealing through a broker?
2. What is meant by "switching"?
3. What are the two ways of capturing a deal?
4. Which information is normally involved in a dealing ticket?
5. What is the aim of an online credit system?
6. How should fund manager deal with "bulk trades"?
7. What is the preferred method of notification for changes to SSI?
    a) telephone
    b) paper mail
    c) Reuters dealing
    d) S.W.I.F.T. broadcast
8. When should internal and external deals be captured in the systems?
    a) within 1 hour after the transaction
    b) on the trading day
    c) within 24 hours after the transaction
    d) immediately
9. Which of the following can be affected by a delayed trade entry?
    (i) credit limits
    (ii) position keeping
    (iii) P+L
        a) only (i) and (ii)
        b) only (ii) and (iii)
        c) (i), (ii) and (iii)
        d) only (i) and (iii)
10. Why should be particular care be taken for amendments to FX swap transactions after settlement of the near leg?
11. What does S.W.I.F.T. stand for?
    a) Society for World-wide-interbank Financial Transactions
    b) Society for World-wide-interbank Financial Transfers
    c) Society for World-wide-interbank Financial Telecommunications
    d) Society for World-wide-international Financial Telecommunications
12. How does S.W.I.F.T. try to ensure that messages are neither duplicated nor manipulated?
13. How is the three-digit code of S.W.I.F.T. message types composed?
14. Which of the following S.W.I.F.T. message formats would you use in a foreign exchange confirmation and a fixed money market confirmation, respectively?
    a) MT 300, MT 950
    b) MT 400, MT 950
    c) MT 300, MT 320

In S.W.I.F.T. sind folgende Sicherheiten gegen Manipulation und Duplizierung von Nachrichten vorgesehen: Bilateral Key Exchange, Input und Output Sequence Numbers (ISNs und OSNs) und Zweistufensystem.

S.W.I.F.T. ermöglicht auch die Kommunikation über das formlose S.W.I.F.T. Broadcast-System. Diese Form der Kommunikation soll jedoch für offizielle Geschäfte nicht gewählt werden.

2.4. Wiederholungsfragen

1. Was ist bei Geschäften über Broker zu beachten?
2. Was versteht man unter „Switching"?
3. Welche zwei Möglichkeiten bezüglich der Eingabe eines Geschäftes gibt es?
4. Welche Informationen werden typischerweise auf einem Ticket erfasst?
5. Wozu dient der Einsatz eines Online-Kreditsystems?
6. Wie sollten Fondsmanager bei „bulk trades" am besten vorgehen?
7. Was ist die bevorzugte Methode, um Änderungen der SSIs mitzuteilen?
   a) Telefon
   b) Brief
   c) Reuters-Dealing
   d) S.W.I.F.T. Broadcast
8. Wann sollten alle externen und internen Geschäfte im Handelssystem erfasst sein?
   a) nach einer Stunde
   b) am Tag der Transaktion
   c) nach 24 Stunden
   d) sofort
9. Welche der folgenden Auswirkungen kann eine verzögerte Geschäftseingabe haben?
   (i)   verfälschte Kreditlimits
   (ii) unvollständige Positionsführung
   (iii) falsche G&V
       a) nur (i) und (ii)
       b) nur (ii) und (iii)
       c) (i), (ii) und (iii)
       d) nur (i) und (iii)
10. Warum sollte bei FX-Swaps, wo bereits das erste Geschäft geliefert wurde, bei Änderungen von Geschäftsdetails mit besonderer Vorsicht agiert werden?
11. Wofür steht die Abkürzung S.W.I.F.T.?
   a) Society for Worldwide Interbank Financial Transactions
   b) Society for Worldwide Interbank Financial Transfers
   c) Society for Worldwide Interbank Financial Telecommunication
   d) Society for Worldwide International Financial Telecommunication
12. Welche Sicherheiten gegen Manipulation und Duplizierung von Nachrichten sind in S.W.I.F.T. vorgesehen?
13. Wie setzt sich der dreistellige Code der S.W.I.F.T.-Message-Types zusammen?
14. Welche der folgenden S.W.I.F.T.-Botschaften würden Sie verwenden, um ein FX- und ein Festzins-Geldmarktgeschäft zu bestätigen?
   a) MT 300, MT 950
   b) MT 400, MT 950

d) MT 200, MT 103

15. When would you use a S.W.I.F.T. message MT 103?
    a) customer transfer
    b) foreign exchange confirmation
    c) multiple general financial institution transfer
    d) general financial institution transfer

16. When would you use a S.W.I.F.T. message MT 950?
    a) error message
    b) netting interim statement
    c) customer statement message
    d) nostro account statement message

17. Which S.W.I.F.T. format is common to all categories?
    a) Nn9
    b) 99n
    c) N9n
    d) 9Nn

18. In which category does S.W.I.F.T. sum up customer payments?
    a) category 2
    b) category 9
    c) category 3
    d) category 1

19. Which of the following S.W.I.F.T. MTs go together?
    a) MT 335
    b) MT 300
    c) MT 330
    d) MT 305

20. When would you use a S.W.I.F.T. Message MT 202?
    a) customer transfer
    b) general financial institution transfer
    c) multiple general financial institution transfer
    d) foreign exchange confirmation

21. Which of the following MTs refers to FRAs?
    a) 360
    b) 300
    c) 320
    d) 340

   c) MT 300, MT 320

   d) MT 200, MT 103

15. Wann wird eine S.W.I.F.T.-Botschaft MT 103 verwendet?

   a) Kundenüberweisung

   b) FX-Bestätigung

   c) mehrere Transfers zwischen Finanzinstitutionen

   d) allgemeiner Transfer zwischen Finanzinstitutionen

16. Wann wird eine S.W.I.F.T.-Botschaft MT 950 verwendet?

   a) Fehlermeldung

   b) Netting-Zwischenbericht

   c) Kontoauszug des Kunden

   d) Nachricht über Nostrokontoauszug

17. Welches S.W.I.F.T.-Format gilt für alle Kategorien?

   a) Nn9

   b) 99n

   c) N9n

   d) 9Nn

18. In welcher Kategorie ist der Kundenzahlungsverkehr zusammengefasst?

   a) Kategorie 2

   b) Kategorie 9

   c) Kategorie 3

   d) Kategorie 1

19. Welche der folgenden S.W.I.F.T.-MTs passen zusammen?

   a) MT 335

   b) MT 300

   c) MT 330

   d) MT 305

20. Wann würden Sie nur eine SWIFT-Nachricht MT 202 verwenden?

   a) Kundenüberweisung

   b) allgemeine Geldinstitutüberweisung

   c) Empfangsnachricht

   d) Lastschriftmitteilung auf Finanzmärkten

21. Welcher der folgenden MTs bezieht sich auf FRAs?

   a) 360

   b) 300

   c) 320

   d) 340

3. Confirmation Process

In this chapter you learn ...
- about the tasks and goals of the confirmation process.
- which data should be included in a confirmation.
- about the types of confirmations for FX deals.
- when deals should be confirmed.
- which deals and transactions should be confirmed.
- what should be considered if there is an error or deviation in the confirmation process.
- what should be considered at a "name switch".
- why standardized escalation procedures should be established to resolve any unconfirmed or disputed deals.
- why an electronic confirmation matching and tracking systems should be adopted as standard operation procedures.

3.1. Task Description

All trades, external and internal, must be confirmed either by issuing a confirmation or by responding to a bank's confirmation. Usually, confirmations are exchanged via S.W.I.F.T. or via bilateral netting systems on trade date.

The confirmation shall ensure that both banks involved in the deal record the trade data correctly and identically. Deals executed via electronic trading or matching systems have to be confirmed the same way as any other deal because the system checks only if the trade data was entered correctly by the own trading department but does not deliver any information if the counterparty correctly recorded the trade. Thus, Reuters-2000 logs should not be used as methods of confirmation.

The bilateral confirmation process should be completed before the settlement of the trade takes place. The **tasks of the confirmation process should be exclusively assigned to the Back-Office and be independent from trading**.

A confirmation should include the following **data** (data that **should correspond in a MT 300 is in bold letters**):

- **counterparties**
- nostro banks
- broker (if applicable)
- **trade date**
- **value date**
- **amount/currencies in the quoted as well as variable currency**
- buyer/seller
- **exchange rate/interest rate**
- **settlement instructions**

The confirmation process varies from bank to bank depending on the counterparty and the degree of automation in the bank.

3. Der Bestätigungsprozess

In diesem Kapitel lernen Sie ...

- welche Aufgabe bzw. welchen Zweck der Bestätigungsprozess erfüllt.
- welche Daten in einer Bestätigung enthalten sind.
- welche Arten von Bestätigungen es im FX-Geschäft gibt.
- wann Geschäfte spätestens bestätigt werden sollten.
- welche Geschäfte bzw. Transaktionen zu bestätigen sind.
- was bei Fehlern bzw. Abweichungen im Bestätigungsprozess zu beachten ist.
- was bei einem „name switch" zu beachten ist.
- warum ein standardisiertes Verfahren zur Lösung unbestätigter oder umstrittener Geschäfte im Bestätigungsprozess installiert werden sollte.
- warum ein elektronisches System zum Abgleich und zur Nachverfolgung von Bestätigungen installiert werden sollte.

3.1. Aufgaben des Bestätigungsprozesses

Alle Geschäfte, auch interne **Transaktionen, müssen bestätigt werden,** entweder indem die Bank selbst eine Bestätigung ausstellt oder auf eine Bestätigung einer anderen Bank antwortet. Üblicherweise erfolgt der Bestätigungsprozess über S.W.I.F.T. oder bilaterale Nettingvereinbarungen am Handelstag.

Der Sinn der Bestätigung liegt darin, die richtige und übereinstimmende Aufzeichnung des Geschäftes bei beiden an der Transaktion beteiligten Banken zu sichern. Daher sind auch Geschäfte, die über elektronische Handelssysteme laufen, nochmals zu bestätigen, weil im System nur überprüft werden kann, ob das Geschäft im Handel der eigenen Bank richtig und vollständig eingegeben wurde, aber keine Auskunft über die korrekte Erfassung des Geschäftes seitens des Partners vorliegt. Daher sollen z.B. Reuters-2000-logs nicht als primäre Form der Bestätigung verwendet werden.

Die gegenseitige Bestätigung des Geschäftes sollte **vor dem Settlement des Geschäftes** abgeschlossen werden. Weiters sollen die Aufgaben **alleine dem** Backoffice **zugeordnet und unabhängig vom Handel** sein.

Folgende Daten sind in einer Bestätigung enthalten (fett hervorgehoben sind jene Punkte, die in einem MT 300 übereinstimmen müssen):

- **die im Geschäft involvierten Parteien**
- Nostrobanken
- Broker (wenn vorhanden)
- **Handelstag**
- **Valuta**
- **Betrag und Name der gehandelten Währungen**
- Rolle der Parteien im Geschäft (Käufer/Verkäufer)
- **Wechselkurs**
- **Settlementanweisungen**

Der Prozessablauf im Rahmen der Bestätigung kann unterschiedliche Formen annehmen, abhängig vom Partner und dem Ausmaß der Automatisierung in der Bank.

There are three ways to confirm an FX-deal:

- **telephone/oral:** This type of confirmation is **gradually phased out**. Though some markets explicitly support phone confirmation (oral deal checks) the risk of misunderstandings is well understood. Thus, every oral confirmation must be followed by a written confirmation. Phone confirmations alone are an insufficient means to confirm an FX-deal.
- **written: Though Fax, mail and telex are accepted ways to confirm a deal**, the use of fax confirmation is strongly discouraged because of the risks involved. These include unauthorised replication or a misdirected transmission due to a wrong fax-number. Sending a confirmation by mail is an improper mean to confirm an FX-deal (particularly spot deals) since the confirmation may arrive after settlement, thus barring an early discovery of errors - a precondition for a low-cost, time-efficient confirmation process.
- **automated:** Increasingly, banks rely on automated confirmation processes (**S.W.I.F.T., TRAM, BART, ACS**). The counterparties send their deal information to the central information system, which then notifies both parties of a match or a problem in case the deal information does not match.

The back office is responsible for monitoring all unconfirmed trades and reporting them to the trading department. Additionally, counterparties should be contacted in order to resolve any differences. If problems turn out to be more complicated tape recordings or logs of electronic systems can be referred to for resolving the discrepancy. Once the error has been corrected, a new confirmation is issued. It serves as proof that both counterparties have the deal consistently registered.

Confirmations should be issued **quickly, accurately and correctly**. Therefore, confirmations should be exchanged in an **electronic format**, preferably S.W.I.F.T., or through an electronic matching system (e.g. ACS).

3.2. Best Practices – Confirmation Process

BP1

A bank should make every effort to send confirmations within **one to three hours after deals are executed**. Confirmations should be formatted based on trade data captured in the bank's system that is responsible to issuing payment instructions and for settling trades. Counterparties should either send out their own confirmations or affirm the confirmations they receive on a timely basis.

Prompt confirmations are an integral part for an orderly functioning of the marketplace to **minimize risk and prevent fraud**. All FX-spot and forward transactions should be confirmed within 3 hours of execution of the transaction. Costumer trades should also be confirmed within 3 hours, but not later than the end of the trading day. If deals remain unconfirmed additional **credit risks** (missing information leads to errors in MIS) and **legal risks** (the enforceability of deals is not sure) may arise.

BP2

A bank should include their own settlement instructions as well as the settlement instructions of its counterparty on confirmations. Each counterparty should check the set-

Es gibt drei Arten von Bestätigungen im FX-Geschäft:

- **Telefonisch/mündlich:** Diese Form wird immer stärker zurückgedrängt. Obwohl mündliche Bestätigungen in manchen Märkten dezidiert gefördert werden (siehe London Code of Conduct), sind sie **alleine nicht ausreichend** (bestimmt auch der London Code of Conduct), weil zu viele Missverständnisse auftreten können. Auf jeden Fall hat noch eine schriftliche Bestätigung zu folgen.
- **Schriftlich:** Immer **im Anschluss an mündliche Bestätigungen. Fax, Telex oder Post** sind möglich. Faxbestätigungen sind besonders problematisch, weil sie leicht an falsche Adressaten kommen können (z.B. durch eine falsche Nummer) und die einfache Reproduzierbarkeit betrügerische Aktivitäten erleichtert. Eine Bestätigung auf dem Postweg ist für FX-Geschäfte ungeeignet, da die Bestätigung möglicherweise nach dem Settlement Date eintrifft. Dadurch können Fehler nicht rechtzeitig entdeckt werden. Um Kosten und Zeit zu sparen, ist es aber besonders wichtig, Fehler rasch zu erkennen.
- **Automatisiert:** In zunehmendem Maße wird versucht, die Bestätigung von Geschäften zu automatisieren (**S.W.I.F.T., TRAM, BART, ACS**). Die Partner schicken ihre Bestätigungen an ein elektronisches Bestätigungssystem, das den Abgleich der Daten vornimmt und Abweichungen bzw. die Übereinstimmung an die Partner zurückmeldet.

Das Backoffice muss im Falle unbestätigter Geschäfte den Handel informieren. Zusätzlich ist der Partner zu kontaktieren, um eventuelle Diskrepanzen abzuklären. Sollte es notwendig sein, kann auf Tonbandaufzeichnungen und logs der elektronischen Systeme zurückgegriffen werden, um Unklarheiten zu beseitigen. Nachdem der Fehler behoben worden ist, wird eine neue Bestätigung, dass das Geschäft in beiden Systemen konsistent registriert worden ist, ausgestellt.

Bestätigungen sollten **rasch, genau** und **richtig ausgestellt** werden.

Deshalb sollte auf **elektronische Formen der Bestätigung** zurückgegriffen werden, insbesondere auf S.W.I.F.T. oder ein elektronisches Matching-System (z.B. ACS).

3.2. Anforderungen an den Bestätigungsprozess

A1

Jede Bank sollte alle Anstrengungen unternehmen, ein Geschäft **ein bis drei Stunden nach Durchführung** zu bestätigen. Das Format der Bestätigungen soll auf dem System, das zur Datenerfassung und dem Settlement verwendet wird, beruhen. Die Geschäftspartner sollen ihre eigenen Bestätigungen aussenden oder den Erhalt der Bestätigungen zeitgerecht zurückmelden.

Ein prompter Bestätigungsprozess ist für einen funktionierenden Handel unbedingt erforderlich, damit **Risiken minimiert** und **Betrugsversuche unterbunden** werden können. Kassa- und Termintransaktionen sollen bis drei Stunden nach Abschluss bestätigt werden, Kundengeschäfte innerhalb von drei Stunden, spätestens bis Tagesende. Bleiben Geschäfte unbestätigt, dann entsteht sowohl **Kreditrisiko** (indem Fehler im MIS nicht erkannt werden, weil Informationen fehlen) als auch ein **rechtliches Risiko** (weil die Durchsetzbarkeit der Ansprüche nicht gesichert ist).

A2

Die Bank sollte ihre Settlementanweisungen und **jene der Gegenpartei auf der schriftlichen Bestätigung vermerken.** Jede Partei sollte die Settlementanweisungen systematisch

tlement instructions systematically and review if they coincide with those agreed upon trade capture.

Confirmations based on Master Agreements should be checked the same way as any other. Generally, settlement instructions should be agreed upon before trade settlement. In case of derivatives, like IRS, it should be noted that transactions are settled at different dates or that there are several settlement dates (e.g. interest payments in an IRS)

BP3

All transactions, even those that will be netted, should be confirmed individually.

It is necessary to confirm all transactions under a netting agreement because in case of netting problems or errors the single payments have to be identified. It is important to know which transactions can be added or are to be removed from netting since each change of the netting amount entails a change of credit and settlement risk. A distorted credit or settlement risk position may lead to additional costs.

BP4

All "split" trades should be confirmed by the end of the day on trade date.

In case of so-called "bulk trades" banks should request fund managers to quickly pass names and amounts so that the credit risk system can be adjusted as soon as possible.

BP5

Any **exception or error** detected in the confirmation should be **resolved on the day it is discovered**.

Since errors that are not rectified immediately may lead to a distorted impression of the risk position, unexpected, missing or erroneous confirmations should be investigated and resolved immediately.

BP6

Broker confirmations should **clearly indicate if a broker did a name switch**.

This is an essential point if only brokers issue confirmations for a deal (typically if both counterparties reside in the same country) because the broker's confirmations serve as evidence for the counterparties that the deal was successfully finalized.

BP7

Brokers' advice may be used to review trade information.

Brokers' advices do not suit for confirmation purposes because the deal was done between the counterparties and not with the broker. Thus, direct and timely confirmations should be exchanged between the counterparties. If a bank does not receive a confirmation from the counterparty, it should ensure to its own satisfaction that its counterparty is bound to, and in agreement with, the terms of the deal as documented in the broker advice. If necessary the bank should rely a legal counsel.

BP8

Standardized escalation procedures should be established to **resolve any unconfirmed or disputed deals**. Banks should institute measures how to deal with counterparties that do not confirm transactions.

prüfen und die Übereinstimmung mit dem im Geschäft vereinbartem Vorgehen kontrollieren.

Auch Bestätigungen, die auf Rahmenverträgen beruhen, sollen überprüft werden. Auf jeden Fall sollen die Settlementanweisungen geklärt sein, bevor eine Zahlungsanweisung gegeben wird. Bei Derivaten, insbesondere IRS, ist zu beachten, dass das Settlement zu verschiedenen Zeitpunkten und mehrmals stattfinden kann.

A3

Alle Transaktionen, auch jene, die „genettet" werden, sind zu bestätigen.

Dieser Punkt ist deshalb wichtig, weil im Falle eines Fehlers beim Netting der Umfang der aus dem Netting herauszunehmenden Transaktion genau bestimmt werden können muss. Änderungen im Rahmen des Nettings führen zu einer Neubestimmung des Kredit- und Settlementrisikos und können zu zusätzlichen Kosten führen.

A4

Es sind alle Split-Geschäfte bis zum Ende des Geschäftstages zu bestätigen.

Im Fall von sogenannten „bulk trades" durch Fondsmanager sollten die Banken auf eine rasche Bekanntgabe der Namen und der zugewiesenen Beträge bestehen, damit das Kreditrisiko angepasst werden kann.

A5

Jeder **Fehler** und **jede Abweichung** im Bestätigungsprozess sollen **an dem Tag behoben werden, an dem er/sie entdeckt wurde.**

Jeder fehlerhaften oder nicht erwarteten Bestätigung ist nachzugehen, weil ohne Korrekturen ein falsches Bild über die Risikosituation entsteht.

A6

Alle Bestätigungen von Brokern sollen **klar anzeigen, falls ein „name switch" durchgeführt wurde.**

Dieser Punkt ist besonders dann wichtig, wenn nur der Broker Bestätigungen über das abgeschlossene Geschäft ausstellt (typischerweise bei Geschäften zwischen zwei Parteien mit Sitz im selben Land) und diese Bestätigung als einziger Nachweis für den Geschäftspartner gilt.

A7

Die Anweisungen von Brokern sollen verwendet werden, um Informationen über das Geschäft zu überprüfen.

Die **Verständigungen von Brokern sind als Bestätigung des Geschäftes nicht geeignet,** weil nicht mit dem Broker, sondern einer anderen Bank das Geschäft gemacht wurde. Deshalb sollen auf jeden Fall mit dem auf der Anweisung genannten Geschäftspartner Bestätigungen ausgetauscht werden. Erhält eine Bank keine Rückbestätigung, dann soll sie, auch unter Beiziehung eines Rechtsbeistandes, überprüfen, ob die in der Anweisung genannte Partei an das Geschäft und an die durch den Broker genannten Bedingungen gebunden ist.

A8

Es sollte ein **standardisiertes Verfahren zur Lösung unbestätigter oder umstrittener Geschäfte** existieren. Banken sollen Maßnahmen festlegen, wie mit Parteien, die Transaktionen nicht bestätigen, umzugehen ist.

Unconfirmed deals may indicate problems in the counterparty's settlement process or that the counterparty does not recognize the trade. Therefore, unconfirmed deals should be addressed immediately in order to avoid difficulties for the bank's trading operations.

The following issues should be noted:

- If the back office receives a confirmation for a deal that has not been captured in the bank's system, the trader and senior trader should be informed the following day and the counterparty be contacted.
- Senior management, sales and trading should be regularly notified of counterparties with whom exist settlement problems. This way, trading can reduce risks and management may review customer relationships. Standard procedures should be in place to effectively handle trade with nonconforming counterparties.
- Periodic statements of unconfirmed deals should be provided to the trading department and the non-confirming counterparties in order to heighten risk awareness of these deals. In the case of forward transactions, these reminders are sometimes even issued if the forward deal was confirmed. On internal reports, a mark-to-market result of the deal may be added.

BP9

Electronic confirmation matching and tracking systems should be adopted as standard operation procedures.

Auto confirmation and automated confirmation tracking (follow-up systems) help to

- reduce market risks and input errors
- minimize settlement expenses and compensation payments
- process larger volumes
- check periodically if confirmations were re-affirmed
- identify counterparties that did not confirm
- reduce operational costs
- escalate non-confirmation
- increase the STP (straight-through processing) rate

Summary

All trades, external and internal, must be confirmed either by issuing a confirmation or by responding to a bank's confirmation. The bilateral confirmation process should be completed before the settlement of the trade takes place. The tasks of the confirmation process should be exclusively assigned to the back office and be independent from trading.

A confirmation should include the following data: counterparties, nostro banks, broker (if applicable), trade date, value date, amount/currencies in the quoted as well as variable currency, buyer/seller, exchange rate/interest rate and settlement instructions.

There are three ways to confirm an FX deal: telephone/oral, written or automated.

Werden Geschäfte nicht bestätigt, so kann das auf Probleme im Settlement des Partners hinweisen oder bedeuten, dass das Geschäft nicht anerkannt wird. Deshalb sind unbestätigte Geschäfte so rasch wie möglich zu klären, damit die Handelsaktivitäten der Bank nicht beeinträchtigt werden.

Folgende Punkte sind zu beachten:

● Erhält das Backoffice eine Bestätigung, ohne dass eine interne Aufzeichnung vorliegt, müssen der Händler und der Chefhändler am nächsten Tag nach dem Handelstag informiert und die andere Partei kontaktiert werden.

● Es sind dem Handel und der Geschäftsleitung in regelmäßigen Abständen Berichte zu übermitteln, in denen jene Geschäftspartner genannt werden, mit denen Probleme im Settlement bestehen. So können im Handel Risiken vermindert und seitens des Management Kundenbeziehungen überprüft werden. Es sollten Vorgehensweisen beschlossen werden, wie mit Kunden, die nicht bestätigen, umzugehen ist (Erinnerung durch Betreuer, Einstellung des Handels).

● Sowohl der eigene Handel als auch die Geschäftspartner sollen in periodischen Abständen über nicht bestätigte Geschäfte informiert werden, damit das Risiko aus diesen Geschäften sichtbar gemacht wird. Das gilt speziell für Termingeschäfte, wo Bestätigungen manchmal erst nach einiger Zeit ausgetauscht werden. In internen Berichten kann dem Handel auch das Mark-to-Market-Ergebnis des Geschäftes vorgelegt werden.

A9

Ein elektronisches System zum Abgleich und zur Nachverfolgung von Bestätigungen sollte als Standard etabliert werden.

Mithilfe elektronischer Systeme zum Abgleich und zur Nachbearbeitung von Bestätigungen können

● Marktrisiken und Eingabefehler reduziert werden,
● Settlementkosten und Kompensationszahlungen minimiert werden,
● größere Volumina rascher verarbeitet werden,
● in regelmäßigen Abständen Geschäfte auf eine Gegenbestätigung geprüft und säumige Parteien identifiziert werden,
● operationale Kosten gesenkt werden sowie
● die STP (straight-through processing)-Rate erhöht werden.

Zusammenfassung

Alle Geschäfte, auch interne Transaktionen, müssen bestätigt werden, entweder indem die Bank selbst eine Bestätigung ausstellt oder auf eine Bestätigung einer anderen Bank antwortet. Die gegenseitige Bestätigung des Geschäftes sollte vor dem Settlement des Geschäftes abgeschlossen werden. Weiters sollen die Aufgaben alleine dem Backoffice zugeordnet und unabhängig vom Handel sein.

Folgende Daten sind in einer Bestätigung enthalten: die im Geschäft involvierten Parteien, Nostrobanken, Broker (wenn vorhanden), Handelstag, Valuta, Betrag und Name der gehandelten Währungen, Rolle der Parteien im Geschäft (Käufer/Verkäufer), Wechselkurs und Settlementanweisungen.

Es gibt drei Arten von Bestätigungen im FX-Geschäft: telefonisch/mündlich, schriftlich oder automatisiert.

The back office is responsible for monitoring all unconfirmed trades and reporting them to the trading department. Additionally, counterparties should be contacted in order to resolve any differences. If problems turn out to be more complicated, tape recordings or logs of electronic systems can be referred to for resolving the discrepancy. Once the error has been corrected, a new confirmation is issued. It serves as proof that both counterparties have registered the deal consistently.

Confirmations should be issued quickly, accurately and correctly.

A bank should make every effort to send confirmations within one to three hours after deals are executed.

A bank should include their own settlement instructions as well as the settlement instructions of its counterparty on written confirmations.

All transactions, even those that will be netted, should be confirmed individually.

All "split" trades should be confirmed by the end of the day on trade date.

Any exception or error detected in the confirmation should be resolved on the day it is discovered.

Broker confirmations should clearly indicate if a broker did a name switch.

Brokers' advices are not suitable for confirmation purposes because the deal was done between the counterparties and not with the broker.

Standardized escalation procedures should be established to resolve any unconfirmed or disputed deals. Electronic confirmation matching and tracking systems should be adopted as standard operation procedures.

3.3. Practice Questions

1. Which of the following shows the correct order of preference for methods of confirmation transmission, from most to least preferred?
   a) S.W.I.F.T., fax
   b) paper mail, telex
   c) fax, S.W.I.F.T.
   d) telex, paper mail
2. Which of the following statements is true with regard to confirmations?
   a) They must be sent out if the deals are not standardized.
   b) They must be sent out immediately after the deal is done.
   c) They must be sent out by electronic media only, e.g. fax, telex.
   d) They must be sent out as quickly as possible after the deal is done and addressed to the settlements department of the counterparty bank.
3. Which data should be included in a confirmation?
4. Which are the three types of confirmation for FX deals?
5. Which of the following statements is true?
   a) Banks should make every effort to send confirmations within half an hour.
   b) Banks should make every effort to send confirmations within 12 hours.

Das Backoffice muss im Falle unbestätigter Geschäfte den Handel informieren. Zusätzlich ist der Partner zu kontaktieren, um eventuelle Diskrepanzen abzuklären. Sollte es notwendig sein, kann auf Tonbandaufzeichnungen und logs der elektronischen Systeme zurückgegriffen werden, um Unklarheiten zu beseitigen. Nachdem der Fehler behoben worden ist, wird eine neue Bestätigung ausgestellt.

Bestätigungen sollten rasch, genau und richtig ausgestellt werden.

Obwohl mündliche Bestätigungen in manchen Märkten dezidiert gefördert werden, sind sie alleine nicht ausreichend, weil zu viele Missverständnisse auftreten können. Auf jeden Fall hat noch eine schriftliche Bestätigung zu folgen.

Jede Bank sollte alle Anstrengungen unternehmen, ein Geschäft ein bis drei Stunden nach Durchführung zu bestätigen.

Die Bank sollte ihre Settlementanweisungen und jene der Gegenpartei auf der schriftlichen Bestätigung vermerken.

Alle Transaktionen, auch jene, die „genettet" werden, sind zu bestätigen.

Es sind alle Split-Geschäfte bis zum Ende des Geschäftstages zu bestätigen.

Jeder Fehler und jede Abweichung im Bestätigungsprozess sollen an dem Tag behoben werden, an dem er/sie entdeckt wurde.

Alle Bestätigungen von Brokern sollen klar anzeigen, falls ein „name switch" durchgeführt wurde.

Die Verständigungen von Brokern sind als Bestätigung des Geschäftes nicht geeignet, weil nicht mit dem Broker, sondern einer anderen Bank das Geschäft gemacht wurde.

Es sollte ein standardisiertes Verfahren zur Lösung unbestätigter oder umstrittener Geschäfte existieren. Außerdem sollte ein elektronisches System zum Abgleich und zur Nachverfolgung von Bestätigungen als Standard etabliert werden.

3.3. Wiederholungsfragen

1. Welche der folgenden Verfahren sind, in richtiger Reihenfolge, die am meisten und am wenigsten bevorzugten Methoden, Bestätigungen zu übertragen?
   a) S.W.I.F.T., Fax
   b) Post, Telex
   c) Fax, S.W.I.F.T.
   d) Telex, Post
2. Was trifft auf Bestätigungen zu?
   a) Sie dürfen nur bei unüblichen Geschäften ausgetauscht werden.
   b) Sie müssen sofort nach dem Geschäftsabschluss ausgestellt werden.
   c) Sie dürfen nur mit elektronischen Medien wie Fax oder Telex gesendet werden.
   d) Sie müssen so schnell wie möglich erstellt und an das Settlement der Partnerbank gesendet werden.
3. Welche Daten sind in einer Bestätigung enthalten?
4. Welche drei Arten von Bestätigungen im FX-Geschäft gibt es?
5. Welche der folgenden Aussagen ist richtig?
   a) Banken sollten alle Anstrengungen unternehmen, ein Geschäft eine halbe Stunde nach Durchführung zu bestätigen.
   b) Banken sollten alle Anstrengungen unternehmen, ein Geschäft zwölf Stunden nach Durchführung zu bestätigen.

    c) Banks should make every effort to send confirmations within 24 hours.
    d) Banks should make every effort to send confirmations within 3 hours.
6. In which period of time should an error in the confirmation process be resolved?
    a) within 12 hours of discovery
    b) within 3 hours of discovery
    c) within 24 hours of discovery
    d) on the day it is discovered
7. Why are brokers' advices not suitable for confirmation purposes?
8. Which other functions are carried out by the bank department responsible for sending out confirmations?
    a) calculating positions
    b) settling trades
    c) calculating market risk
    d) issuing payment instructions
9. Which of the following statements could be described as best practice?
    a) Internal confirmations should be subject to the same procedures as external confirmations.
    b) Client control procedures should be relaxed for internal transactions.
    c) Internal transactions should not be confirmed as there is no credit risk involved.
    d) Chasers on internal confirmations should be sent less frequently than those for external confirmations.
10. Confirmations for which deals can be made later than three hours after transaction?
    a) customer deals
    b) FX spot
    c) FX forward
    d) All answers are false.
11. Which deals cannot be confirmed via S.W.I.F.T.?
    a) options
    b) NDFs
    c) FRAs
    d) IRS
12. Which of the following measures increase the STP rate?
    a) Implementation of CLS
    b) daily reconciliation of nostro accounts
    c) internal counterparty and country limits
    d) automatic processing of confirmations via S.W.I.F.T.
13. Why should electronic confirmation matching and tracking systems be adopted as standard operation procedures?

c) Banken sollten alle Anstrengungen unternehmen, ein Geschäft 24 Stunden nach Durchführung zu bestätigen.

d) Banken sollten alle Anstrengungen unternehmen, ein Geschäft drei Stunden nach Durchführung zu bestätigen.

6. Bis wann ist jede Abweichung im Bestätigungsprozess zu beheben?
   a) bis zwölf Stunden nach Auftreten
   b) bis drei Stunden nach Auftreten
   c) bis 24 Stunden nach Auftreten
   d) an dem Tag, an dem sie entdeckt wurde

7. Warum sind Verständigungen von Brokern nicht als Bestätigung des Geschäftes geeignet?

8. Welche Aufgaben soll jene Abteilung der Bank erfüllen, die auch Bestätigungen ausstellt?
   a) Berechnung der Positionen
   b) Settlement der Geschäfte
   c) Berechnung des Marktrisikos
   d) Ausstellen der Zahlungsanweisung

9. Welche der folgenden Aussagen ist bestmögliche Praxis?
   a) Bestätigungen für interne Geschäfte sollen denselben Anforderungen unterliegen wie jene für externe Geschäfte.
   b) Kundenüberprüfungsverfahren sollen für interne Verfahren gelockert werden.
   c) Interne Transaktionen müssen nicht bestätigt werden, da kein Kreditrisiko vorliegt.
   d) Nachforschungen bei Bestätigungen interner Geschäfte können weniger intensiv sein als bei externen Geschäften.

10. Für welche Geschäfte kann die Bestätigung später als nach drei Stunden erfolgen?
    a) Kundengeschäfte
    b) FX-Spot
    c) FX-Forward
    d) Alle Antworten sind falsch.

11. Welche Geschäfte können nicht mit S.W.I.F.T. bestätigt werden?
    a) Optionen
    b) NDFs
    c) FRAs
    d) IRS

12. Welche Maßnahme führt zu einer erhöhten STP-Rate?
    a) Einsatz von CLS
    b) tägliche Abstimmung der Nostrokonten
    c) interne Kontrahenten- und Länderlimits
    d) automatischer Abgleich der Bestätigungen über S.W.I.F.T.

13. Warum sollte ein elektronisches System zum Abgleich und zur Nachverfolgung von Bestätigungen als Standard etabliert werden?

4. Netting

In this chapter you learn ...

- what is meant by netting.
- about the back office tasks with regard to netting.
- which different types of netting can be distinguished.
- which master agreements are relevant for netting.
- about the advantages of netting agreements.
- which considerations should be made before making a netting agreement.
- what should be considered when setting up master agreements.
- why online payment netting systems should be installed.
- when to schedule the cut-off for confirming netted trades.
- about the G-10 recommendations (Lamfalussy Report) for the design of a multilateral cross-border and multi-currency netting and settlement scheme.
- about the most widely known bilateral netting services FX-Net and S.W.I.F.T Accord and their features.

4.1. Task Description

Netting is an agreed **offsetting of positions or obligations** by trading partners or participants of a netting system. The netting reduces a large number of individual positions or obligations to a smaller number of positions or obligations.

The main reasons for netting are the **reductions of credit and settlement risk**, lower transaction costs, lower fees for nostro accounts due to fewer payments a reduced debiting of credit lines.

The **tasks of the back office** in the netting process include:

- confirmation of netted amounts on the day before settlement-date
- confirmation of netting transactions on settlement-date
- investigation and resolution of disputes

Netting can be distinguished by

- type and volume of included payments
- the number of participants and the arrangements of the netting system

The first group involves Netting by novation and Close-out Netting.

Netting by novation

In this case existing contractual **obligations are satisfied or discharged by means of their replacement by new obligations**. Existing contracts are cancelled and replaced by one **new contract**. Since all payments are immediately included in the netting contract, the administrative work is relatively high.

4. Netting

In diesem Kapitel lernen Sie ...

- was man unter Netting versteht.
- welche Aufgaben für das Backoffice bezüglich Netting anfallen.
- welche Arten von Netting unterschieden werden.
- welche Rahmenverträge für das Netting relevant sind.
- welche Vorteile Nettingvereinbarungen haben.
- welche Überlegungen vor Eingehen einer Nettingvereinbarung angestellt werden sollen.
- was bei der Gestaltung von Rahmenverträgen zu beachten ist.
- warum Online-Payment-Nettingsysteme installiert werden sollten.
- wann der Cut-off zur Bestätigung von „genetteten" Geschäften angesetzt werden sollte.
- welche Empfehlungen die G10 zur Gestaltung eines multilateralen Mehrwährungsnettoabwicklungssystems im sogenannten Lamfalussy Report geben.
- die bekanntesten bilateralen Nettingdienste FX-Net und S.W.I.F.T. Accord sowie deren Eigenschaften kennen.

4.1. Aufgaben des Nettings

Unter Netting versteht man die vereinbarte **Aufrechnung von gegenseitigen Positionen oder Verpflichtungen** von Geschäftspartnern oder Teilnehmern eines Systems. Das Netting verringert eine große Zahl von Einzelpositionen oder -verpflichtungen auf eine kleinere Zahl.

Die wesentlichen Gründe für das Netting sind die **Reduzierung des Kredit- und Settlementrisikos** sowie die geringe Linienbelastung, geringere Transaktionskosten und günstigere Konten für die Nostrokonten, weil weniger Zahlungen anfallen.

Für das Backoffice fallen folgende Aufgaben an:

- Bestätigung des Nettingbetrages am Handelstag
- Bestätigung der genetteten Beträge am Tag vor dem Settlement Date
- Untersuchung und Lösung von Streitfällen

Beim Netting unterscheidet man bezüglich:

- Art und Umfang der inkludierten Zahlungsströme
- Anzahl der Teilnehmer am und Ausgestaltung des Nettingsystems

Zur ersten Gruppe zählen das Novations-Netting und das Close-out Netting.

Novations-Netting

Darunter versteht man die **Erfüllung bestehender vertraglicher Verpflichtungen mit schuldbefreiender Wirkung mittels Ersatz durch neue Verpflichtungen.** Beim Novations-Netting werden die einzelnen Schuldverhältnisse **in** einem **Schuldumwandlungsvertrag** erfasst. Da die Ansprüche und Verpflichtungen **immer schon zum** Entstehungszeitpunkt **saldiert** werden, entsteht beim Novations-Netting ein relativ hoher technischer Verwaltungsaufwand.

The advantage of netting by novation is that **all claims are legally enforceable if the counterparty goes bankrupt** and no "cherry-picking" can take place.

Close-out netting

In practice, close-out netting is the preferred method. It is an agreement to **settle all contracted but not yet due liabilities and claims on an institution by one single payment**, immediately upon the occurrence of a list of defined events, such as the appointment of a liquidator to that institution. The settlement amount is determined by marking to market all open payments.

In case of OTC derivatives, close-out netting can be used for **addressing counterparty risk** if

- the deals were concluded with one counterparty and
- the deals meet the netting criteria of the banking supervisory authorities.

The second group comprises bilateral and multilateral netting.

Bilateral payment netting

It is a legally binding agreement between two counterparties about the **netting of amounts in the same currency for settlement of the same day** under two or more trades. The counterparties agree to settle all trades by making or receiving a single payment or settlement-date. This procedure reduces costs and settlement risk. S.W.I.F.T. Accord and FX-net are bilateral netting services.

Multilateral Netting

In a multilateral netting system, **each bank in the system settles its overall net position in one currency** with respect to all the other members of the system. In order to avoid settlement problems, multilateral netting systems exist only for the most important and liquid currencies. All transactions outside the netting agreement still carry full credit risk.

Multilateral netting works through a **clearing house** (settlement agent), which receives payment instructions from the members and is responsible for calculating netting amounts correctly.

The following settlement matrix illustrates the mechanics of multilateral netting

Sending bank	Receiving bank				Sum of obligations (o)
	A	**B**	**C**	**D**	
A	0	90	40	80	210
B	70	0	0	0	70
C	0	50	0	20	70
D	10	30	60	0	100
Sum of claims (c)	80	170	100	100	450
					-450
Net positions (o–c)	-130	100	30	0	0

Der Vorteil des Novations-Netting liegt darin, dass **im Falle der Zahlungsunfähigkeit eines Unternehmens alle vom Nettingkontrakt abgedeckten Zahlungen durchsetzbar** sind. Damit wird die Gefahr, dass im Konkursverfahren nur die profitablen Transaktionen durchgeführt werden, ausgeschaltet.

Close-out Netting

In der Praxis wird dem Close-out Netting (Liquidations-Netting) der Vorzug gegeben. Hier werden **erst bei Eintritt bestimmter Ereignisse (Kündigung oder Insolvenz) alle offenen Forderungen und Verbindlichkeiten aus Finanzgeschäften zum Marktwert zu einer Position saldiert.** Der Ausgleichsanspruch in Höhe des ermittelten Netto-Marktwertes steht jener Partei zu, aus deren Sicht der Saldo positiv ist.

Mit dem Liquidations-Netting wird die **Verrechnung von Adressausfallsrisiken bei OTC-Derivaten** in allen Währungen ermöglicht, sofern

- die Geschäfte mit einem Partner abgeschlossen wurden und
- die Geschäfte nach den Vorschriften der Bankaufsicht für Aufrechnungsvereinbarungen anerkannt sind.

In der zweiten Gruppe unterscheidet man bilaterales und multilaterales Netting.

Bilaterales Payment Netting

Beim bilateralen Payment Netting werden **alle Geschäfte zwischen zwei Parteien in einer Währung gegeneinander aufgerechnet und der Saldo transferiert.** Auf diese Weise sollen Kosten und Risiken reduziert werden. Das bilaterale Payment Netting findet für Geschäfte mit der gleichen Valuta statt. FX-Net und S.W.I.F.T. Accord sind Beispiele für bilaterale Nettingsysteme.

Multilaterales Netting

Beim multilateralen Netting werden Zahlungsströme in einer Währung saldiert, wobei die **Zahlungen von allen am multilateralen Nettingsystem beteiligten Unternehmen berücksichtigt** werden. Multilaterale Nettingsysteme konzentrieren sich in der Regel auf die wichtigsten Währungen, um Probleme bei der Abwicklung zu vermeiden. Daher bleibt für alle außerhalb des Systems getätigten Transaktionen das Erfüllungsrisiko offen.

Im Zentrum des multilateralen Nettings steht ein **Clearing House,** über das alle Zahlungsanweisungen laufen und in dessen Verantwortung es liegt, die Nettingbeträge korrekt zu berechnen.

Die Funktionsweise des multilateralen Nettings kann man anhand einer Settlement-Matrix illustrieren:

Sendende Bank	Empfangende Bank				Summe der Verbindlichkeiten (V)
	A	**B**	**C**	**D**	
A	0	90	40	80	210
B	70	0	0	0	70
C	0	50	0	20	70
D	10	30	60	0	100
Summe der Forderungen (F)	80	170	100	100	450
					-450
Nettingposition (V–F)	-130	100	30	0	0

All-important Master Agreements deal with netting. **IFEMA** (International Foreign Exchange Master Agreement) for the FX-market and ICOM (International Currency Options Market) for FX-options allow for netting by novation and payment netting. Closeout netting provisions exist under the condition that closeout netting is allowed under local jurisdictions. IFEMA and ICOM were moulded to **FEOMA** (Foreign Exchange and Option Master Agreement), which covers netting on the same terms as IFEMA and ICOM. The **ISDA Master Agreement** enables counterparties to **include all FX-products** (Spot, forward, options) under one global cross-product closeout netting agreement. ISDA deals with payment netting only and does not provide for novation netting. The main snag in the ISDA agreement is that products with **different conventions are summed up and can be netted under one agreement**.

At the end, two tables should outline the **advantages** and the **considerations** for both bilateral and multilateral netting.

Advantages

Bilateral Netting	Multilateral Netting
<ul><li>settlement exposures can be reduced by up to 50%.</li><li>variety of methods available</li><li>no additional credit risk</li><li>more efficient settlement due to<ul><li>reduced number of payment instructions</li><li>fewer reconciliations</li><li>reduced funds paid out</li></ul></li></ul>	<ul><li>settlement exposure can be reduced up to 90%.</li><li>settlement exposure is transferred to clearing house</li><li>duration of settlement risk is reduced to 24 hours or less</li><li>more efficient settlement due to<ul><li>reduced number of payment instructions</li><li>fewer reconciliations</li><li>reduced funds paid out</li></ul></li></ul>

Considerations

Bilateral Netting	Multilateral Netting
<ul><li>modification of internal risk management systems → costs</li><li>cost and complexity of operations systems linkage to netting system</li><li>willingness ability of counterparty to net</li><li>compatibility with netting methods used by counterparties</li></ul>	<ul><li>collateral requirements and associated costs</li><li>clearing house limits</li><li>integration/modification of internal risk management systems</li><li>risk management procedures controlled by clearing house</li><li>currencies and transactions available for netting</li><li>loss allocation procedures</li></ul>

Die wichtigsten Rahmenverträge regeln auch das Netting. Das **IFEMA** (International Foreign Exchange Master Agreement) für den FX-Markt und ICOM (International Currency Options Market) für FX-Optionen sehen Novations-Netting und Payment Netting vor. Das Close-out Netting wird unter der Voraussetzung geregelt, dass Close-out Netting unter dem anzuwendenden Recht erlaubt ist. Das IFEMA und ICOM wurden zum **FEOMA** (Foreign Exchange and Options Master Agreement) verschmolzen, das dieselben Regelungen wie IFEMA und ICOM enthält.

Das ISDA Master Agreement fasst alle FX-Produkte (Kassa, Termingeschäfte, Optionen) unter eine Close-out-Nettingvereinbarung zusammen. ISDA sieht den Fall des Payment Nettings vor, regelt aber nicht Novations-Netting. Das Kernproblem beim **ISDA Master Agreement** ist, dass **verschiedene Produkte mit unterschiedlichen Konventionen genettet** werden können.

In der folgenden Aufstellung sollen abschließend die **Vorteile von Nettingvereinbarungen** illustriert und den **Überlegungen** gegenübergestellt werden, die **vor Eingehen einer Nettingvereinbarung** angestellt werden sollen.

Vorteile von Nettingvereinbarungen

Bilaterales Netting	Multilaterales Netting

• Das Settlementrisiko kann betragsmäßig bis zu 50% reduziert werden.
 • Es können verschiedene Methoden verwendet werden.
 • Kein zusätzliches Kreditrisiko
 • Vereinfachung des Settlements, weil
   – es weniger Zahlungsanweisungen gibt,
   – der Abgleich der Nostrokonten weniger oft durchzuführen ist,
   – geringere Beträge transferiert werden.
	• Das Settlementrisiko kann betragsmäßig bis zu 90% reduziert werden.
	 • Die offene Währungsposition wird zum Clearing House transferiert.
	 • Das Settlementrisiko wird auf 24 Stunden und weniger verkürzt.
	 • Vereinfachung des Settlements, weil
	   – es weniger Zahlungsanweisungen gibt,
	   – der Abgleich der Nostrokonten weniger oft durchzuführen ist,
	   – geringere Beträge transferiert werden.

Überlegungen vor Eingehen einer Nettingvereinbarung

Bilaterales Netting	Multilaterales Netting
• Anpassung des internen Risikomanagementsystems → Kosten • Kosten und Komplexität einer automatisierten Schnittstelle zum Nettingsystem • Wille und Fähigkeit anderer Parteien zum Netting • Kompatibilität der Nettingmethoden	• Kosten, die mit der Bereitstellung von Sicherheiten verbunden sind • Clearing-House-Limits • Integration und Anpassung des Risikomanagementsystems • Risikomanagementsystem des Clearing House • Währungen und Transaktionen, die „genettet" werden können • Verlust- bzw. Ausfallshaftung beim Clearing House

Generally, netting agreements are of use for **banks with few trading centres** and a limited number of counterparties for most of the transactions. Typically, this is the case for **Market Makers**.

4.2. Best Practices – Netting

BP1

A **valid Master Agreement** should be signed with each counterparty. The Master Agreement should contain payment netting and closeout netting clauses to protect against counterparty default.

Netting agreements allow banks to **reduce operational and credit risk**. ISDA, FEOMA, ICOM and IFEMA provide for netting agreements.

Master Agreements should contain the following features:

- appropriate events of default (e.g. insolvency, bankruptcy)
- conditions under witch with netting is applicable
- method to calculate the netting amount
- a clause that states that if a default occurs the netting amount includes all payments receivable and payable and that only a single net obligation is settled
- optional clause to support payment netting

Generally, master agreements provide legal certainty and the proper settlement of netting. Furthermore, in the case of default claims are easier enforceable and unjustified demands can more easily be refused.

A master agreement becomes valid with the **signatures of both counterparties**. Each bank should confer with local counsel to ensure the enforceability of netting provisions under local jurisdictions. If there are any discrepancies the counterparty should consider to what extent it is willing to compromise.

BP2

Online payment netting systems should be used to calculate net payments in each currency. On-line bank software should be purchased to ensure proper calculation.

Incorrect calculations of netting amounts lead to an inaccurate amount of credit risk and may damage counterparty relationship. If electronic netting systems are used, both counterparties enter deal information into the trade capture system, the system confirms the trade, calculates the net amount on a currency by currency basis for each party and notifies counterparties immediately of any discrepancies.

The introduction of multilateral netting and Payment vs. payment (PVP) may be further steps to **reduce settlement risk**.

BP3

Final amounts should be confirmed bilaterally at some predetermined cut-off time with the counterparty if they are not done electronically.

Netting ist besonders für **Banken mit wenigen Standorten und einer begrenzten Anzahl von Gegenparteien,** mit denen viele gegenläufige Geschäfte abgeschlossen werden, interessant. Diese Punkte treffen besonders auf **Market Maker** zu.

4.2. Anforderungen an das Netting

A1

Ein **gültiger Rahmenvertrag** soll mit jedem Geschäftspartner abgeschlossen werden. Der Rahmenvertrag soll Bestimmungen für das Payment Netting und das Close-out Netting enthalten, die im Falle des Konkurses des Geschäftspartners Schutz geben.

Mithilfe von Nettingvereinbarungen können Banken ihr **operationales Risiko und** ihr **Kreditrisiko verringern.** Folgende Rahmenverträge existieren: ISDA, IFEMA (für Kassa und Terminmarkt) und ICOM für FX-Optionen.

Folgende Punkte sind in Rahmenverträgen zu vereinbaren:

- Gründe für Zahlungsunfähigkeit, besonders Konkurs oder Ausgleich
- Bedingungen, unter denen Netting angewendet werden kann
- Verfahren, wie der Nettingbetrag zu errechnen ist
- eine Klausel, die bestimmt, dass alle offenen Forderungen und Verpflichtungen im Falle der Zahlungsunfähigkeit einer Partei zur Berechnung des Ausgleichsbetrages herangezogen und zu einer Zahlung zusammengefasst werden
- Option zur Verwendung von Payment Netting

Generell geben Rahmenverträge die rechtliche Sicherheit einer geordneten Abwicklung des Nettings und die Möglichkeit, Ansprüche im Falle der Zahlungsunfähigkeit des Partners (richtig) durchsetzen bzw. ungerechtfertigte Ansprüche abwehren zu können.

Der Rahmenvertrag wird **mit der Unterschrift beider Parteien gültig.** Jede Bank sollte sich vergewissern, ob die Bestimmungen mit der lokalen Rechtslage übereinstimmen und die Beeinträchtigung ihrer Interessen durch Abweichungen überprüfen.

A2

Es sollten **Online-Payment-Nettingsysteme zur Berechnung des Ausgleichsbetrages** je Währung installiert werden und die geeignete Software angeschafft werden.

Fehler bei der Errechnung von Nettingbeträgen führen zu einer falschen Risikoeinschätzung und können Kundenbeziehungen belasten. Elektronische Nettingsysteme bestätigen den Geschäftspartnern die Transaktion, ermitteln pro Währung den Nettingbetrag und melden sofort Abweichungen zurück.

Die Einführung multilateralen Nettings (= Payment Netting, das mehrere Partner umfasst) und von Payment vs. Payment sind als weitere Schritte zur **Reduzierung von Settlementrisiko** zu fördern.

A3

Wenn kein elektronisches Nettingsystem verwendet wird, sollen die Geschäftspartner die **ermittelten Nettingbeträge einander bis zu einem zuvor vereinbarten Zeitpunkt bestätigen,** um mögliche Fehler zu beheben.

BP4

The **cut-off for confirming** netted trades should be **as late as possible**. Credit system functions should be in place to accurately reflect the effect of netting.

A late cut-off should allow to include trades for **same-day settlement** to the netting amount. Credit systems adjusted to netting requirements **ensure a correct presentation of the risk position and line usage**. Deals that miss the netting cut-off should be settled gross and reflected as much for credit purposes.

BP5

Management should ensure that **credit and documentation policies** are consistent with operation practices. Credit systems can reflect netting only if documentation exists to support netting and a netting agreement has been signed between the bank and the counterparty, ensuring net settlement.

If documentations or operational practices do not coincide with those outlined in the agreements, the bank cannot benefit from netting (e.g. if netting is not incorporated in the trading systems) or meets unexpected risks (e.g. if netting is carried out without legal basis). Thus, it is important to establish proper operation procedures including

- cut-off times
- SSIs and
- agreed methods of confirmation/affirmation

Proposal of the G-10 for the design of a multilateral cross-border and multi-currency netting and settlement scheme (Lamfalussy Report):

1. Netting systems should have a **well-founded basis under all national jurisdictions**.
2. Netting scheme participants should have a **clear understanding of the impact of the particular scheme on each of the financial risks** affected by the netting process. They should be particularly aware of the deadline for irrevocable payment instructions.
3. Netting systems should have **clearly defined procedures for the management of credit and liquidity risks**.
4. Multilateral netting schemes should be capable of **ensuring daily settlements in the event that the largest single net-debtor defaults**.
5. Multilateral netting schemes should have **objective and publicly disclosed guidelines** for admission.
6. All netting schemes should ensure the **technical reliability** of the system and the availability of **back-up facilities**.

4.3. Main Netting Services

Bilateral netting services

FX-Net and **S.W.I.F.T. Accord** are the best-known bilateral netting services.

FX-Net

FX-Net was founded in 1986 and is owned by FX-Net Ltd. a consortium of 14 global banks. The system is operated by EBS Dealings Resources Inc., and based on a **completely automated netting process** supported by S.W.I.F.T. MTs

A4

Das **Cut-off zur Bestätigung von „genetteten" Geschäften** soll **so spät wie möglich** angesetzt werden. Das Kreditrisikosystem soll die Nettingeffekte exakt berücksichtigen.

Ein spätes Cut-off soll ermöglichen, noch **taggleiche Geschäfte in das Netting aufzunehmen.** Ein auf das Netting abgestimmtes Kreditrisikosystem ermöglicht die **aktuelle Abbildung der Risiken und Limitbelastung.** Geschäfte, die nach dem Cut-off getätigt werden, sind mit dem vollständigen Betrag zu erfassen und brutto zu erfüllen.

A5

Das Management muss für die **Einführung eines geeigneten Kreditrisikosystems und Dokumentationswesens** sorgen, das den operativen Anforderungen des Handels Rechnung trägt. Das Kreditrisikosystem kann Netting nur dann berücksichtigen, wenn zwischen der Bank und dem Partner eine Nettingvereinbarung und -dokumentation existiert und das Settlement auf Nettozahlung basiert.

Wenn die Dokumentation und die Systeme andere Anforderungen erfüllen, als durch Vereinbarungen festgelegt wurde, kann die Bank Vorteile des Nettings nicht nutzen (z.B. wenn Netting nicht im Handelssystem berücksichtigt ist) oder auf unerwartete Risiken treffen (z.B.: Netting wird ohne fixe rechtliche Grundlage durchgeführt).

Daher ist es wichtig, die operationalen Strukturen zu schaffen. Dazu zählen

- Bestimmung des Cut-off
- SSIs und
- Festlegen des Bestätigungsprozesses

Die Empfehlungen der G10 zur Gestaltung eines multilateralen Mehrwährungsnetto-Abwicklungssystems aus dem sogenannten Lamfalussy Report

1. Die verwendeten Nettingsysteme müssen auf einer **fundierten rechtlichen Basis** stehen.
2. Die Teilnehmer am Nettingsystem müssen die **Funktionsweise des Systems und die damit verbundenen Risiken verstehen.** Besonders bezüglich der Zeitpunkte, wenn eine Anweisung unwiderruflich ist.
3. Die Nettingsysteme müssen ein **klares System zum Management von Kredit- und Liquiditätsrisiken** haben.
4. Multilaterale Nettingsysteme müssen garantieren, dass zumindest der **Ausfall des Partners mit der größten Position das Settlement eines Tages nicht beeinträchtigt.**
5. Multilaterale Nettingsysteme müssen **klare Richtlinien** haben, zu denen Institutionen am System teilnehmen können.
6. Alle Nettingsysteme müssen die **technische Funktionsfähigkeit sicherstellen** sowie entsprechende **Notfalleinrichtungen** zur Verfügung haben.

4.3. Die wichtigsten Nettingdienste

Bilaterale Nettingdienste

Zu den bekanntesten bilateralen Nettingdiensten zählen **FX-Net** und **S.W.I.F.T. Accord.**

FX-Net

FX-Net wurde 1986 gegründet und ist im Besitz von FXNet Ltd., einem Konsortium von 14 weltweit aktiven Großbanken. Das System wird von EBS Dealing Resources, Inc. be-

The FX-net system consists of **two stages**:

I. Deal capture
Trade capture occurs via an electronic interface. Through several internal electronic instructions FX-Net creates a "MAC" (matched and confirmed) status (MT300).

II. Settlement
At the pre-determined cut-off time FX-Net exchanges automatically confirmations, settlement instructions and payment messages for the **netted amounts** to the counterparties (S.W.I.F.T. MT 202 and 210). Additionally, a MT 950 is generated in order to assist in the **reconciliation process**.

The **key factors** of FX-Net are:

- individually agreed cut-off times, for payments and receipts
- two confirmations: real-time for trade; on value date for net amount

S.W.I.F.T. Accord

S.W.I.F.T. Account is a **netting scheme integrated in the S.W.I.F.T. system**. All payment instructions of participants are **separately stored and matched at the agreed cut-off time**. Accord includes also transaction with counterparties that are not members of Accord. Accord provides the participants with a comprehensive documentation about confirmation and netting status. Reports can be required at any time.

Key features of S.W.I.F.T. Accord are:

- coverage of FX, money market and derivatives
- only authenticated S.W.I.F.T. messages are used
- only one counterparty of the deal needs to be participant of Accord in order to start the netting process

Summary

Netting is the agreed offsetting of positions or obligations by trading partners or participants of a netting system. Netting distills a large number of individual positions or obligations to a smaller number of positions or obligations.

The main reasons for netting are the reductions of credit and settlement risk, lower transaction costs, lower fees for nostro accounts due to fewer payments and reduced debiting of credit lines.

According to the type and volume of included payments we distinguish between novation and close-out netting. In case of netting by novation, existing contractual obligations are satisfied or discharged by means of their replacement by new obligations. Existing contracts are cancelled and replaced by one new contract. In practice, close-out netting is the preferred method. It is an agreement to settle all contracted but not yet due liabilities and claims on an institution by one single payment, immediately upon the occurrence of a list of defined events, such as the appointment of a liquidator to that institution.

trieben und basiert auf einem **voll automatisierten Nettingprozess** mithilfe von S.W.I.F.T. MT-Codes.

Das System von FX-Net funktioniert zweistufig:

I. Geschäftserfassung

Über den Austausch mehrerer elektronischer Anweisungen bestätigen die Parteien das Geschäft, indem sie die Transaktion eingeben und dem Geschäft zuordnen. Der Schritt endet mit dem „MAC"(matched and confirmed)-Status (S.W.I.F.T. MT 300).

II. Settlement

Zu den von den Parteien vereinbarten Cut-off-Zeiten **bestätigt** das FX-Net-System die Nettobeträge und sendet die Zahlungsanweisungen bzw. -benachrichtigungen an die betroffenen Parteien (S.W.I.F.T. MT 202 und 210). Weiters wird eine MT 950 Statement Message generiert, die für den **Abgleich der Nostrokonten** bedeutend ist.

Die **Kernpunkte** von FX-Net sind

- individuell vereinbarte Cut-off-Zeiten, selbst für zu leistende und empfangene Zahlungen,
- zwei Bestätigungen: Echtzeit für das Geschäft; am Valutatag für den Nettobetrag.

S.W.I.F.T. Accord

S.W.I.F.T. Accord ist eine **in das S.W.I.F.T.-System integrierte Nettingfunktion**. Alle Zahlungsnachrichten von an Accord teilnehmenden Banken werden **separat abgespeichert** und **zur vereinbarten Buchungsschlusszeit saldiert**. Beim Netting werden auch Transaktionen mit Teilnehmern berücksichtigt, die nicht am Accord teilnehmen, aber über S.W.I.F.T. ihre Geschäfte abwickeln. Die umfangreichen Dokumentationen über den Status der Bestätigungen und der Nettingpositionen werden nur an die Teilnehmer von Accord gesendet, wobei S.W.I.F.T. bereit ist, diesen Dienst zu jedem gewünschten Zeitpunkt anzubieten.

Die **Kernpunkte** von S.W.I.F.T. Accord sind:

- Es umfasst FX- und Geldmarkt sowie Derivative.
- Es werden nur speziell codierte S.W.I.F.T.-MTs verarbeitet.
- Es muss nur ein Teilnehmer am Geschäft Accord-Mitglied sein, damit Netting stattfindet.

Zusammenfassung

Unter Netting versteht man die vereinbarte Aufrechnung von gegenseitigen Positionen oder Verpflichtungen von Geschäftspartnern oder Teilnehmern eines Systems. Das Netting verringert eine große Zahl von Einzelpositionen oder -verpflichtungen auf eine kleinere Zahl.

Die wesentlichen Gründe für das Netting sind die Reduzierung des Kredit- und Settlementrisikos sowie die geringe Linienbelastung, geringere Transaktionskosten und günstigere Konten für die Nostrokonten, weil weniger Zahlungen anfallen.

Nach Art und Umfang der inkludierten Zahlungsströme unterscheidet man zwischen Novations-Netting und Close-out Netting. Unter Novations-Netting versteht man die Erfüllung bestehender vertraglicher Verpflichtungen mit schuldbefreiender Wirkung mittels Ersatz durch neue Verpflichtungen. Beim Novations-Netting werden die einzelnen Schuldverhältnisse in einem Schuldumwandlungsvertrag erfasst. In der Praxis wird dem

According to the number of participants and the arrangements of the netting system we distinguish between bilateral and multilateral netting. Bilateral payment netting is a legally binding agreement between two counterparties about the netting of amounts in the same currency for settlement of the same day under two or more trades. In a multilateral netting system, each bank in the system settles its overall net position in one currency with respect to all the other members of the system. Multilateral netting works through a clearing house (settlement agent), which receives payment instructions from the members and is responsible for calculating netting amounts correctly.

Important master agreements deal with netting. IFEMA (International Foreign Exchange Master Agreement) for the FX market and ICOM (International Currency Options Market) for FX options allow for netting by novation and payment netting. Close-out netting provisions exist where allowed under local jurisdiction.

Online payment netting systems should be used to calculate net payments in each currency.

Final amounts should be confirmed bilaterally at some predetermined cut-off time with the counterparty if they are not done electronically.

The cut-off for confirming netted trades should be as late as possible.

Management should ensure that credit and documentation policies are consistent with operation practices.

FX-Net and S.W.I.F.T. Accord are the best-known bilateral netting services.

FX-Net is based on a completely automated netting process supported by S.W.I.F.T. MTs. The key factors of FX-Net are: individually agreed cut-off times for payments and receipts and two confirmations: real-time for trade; on value date for net amount

S.W.I.F.T. Account is a netting scheme integrated into the S.W.I.F.T. system. All payment instructions of participants are separately stored and matched at the agreed cut-off time.

4.4. Practice Questions

1. Which of the following statements best describes the main advantage of a netting agreement?
   a) It reduces the settlement risk.
   b) It eliminates all delivery risk.
   c) It reduces all FX positional and credit risk.
   d) It eliminates all FX positional risk.
2. What is the difference between novations netting and close-out netting?

Close-out Netting (Liquidations-Netting) der Vorzug gegeben. Hier werden erst bei Eintritt bestimmter Ereignisse (Kündigung oder Insolvenz) alle offenen Forderungen und Verbindlichkeiten aus Finanzgeschäften zum Marktwert zu einer Position saldiert.

Nach Anzahl der Teilnehmer am und Ausgestaltung des Nettingsystems unterscheidet man zwischen bilateralem Payment Netting und multilateralem Netting. Beim bilateralen Payment Netting werden alle Geschäfte zwischen zwei Parteien in einer Währung gegeneinander aufgerechnet und der Saldo transferiert. Beim multilateralen Netting werden Zahlungsströme in einer Währung saldiert, wobei die Zahlungen von allen am multilateralen Nettingsystem beteiligten Unternehmen berücksichtigt werden. Im Zentrum des multilateralen Nettings steht ein Clearing House, über das alle Zahlungsanweisungen laufen und in dessen Verantwortung es liegt, die Nettingbeträge korrekt zu berechnen.

Die wichtigsten Rahmenverträge regeln auch das Netting. Das IFEMA (International Foreign Exchange Master Agreement) für den FX-Markt und ICOM (International Currency Options Market) für FX-Optionen sehen Novations-Netting und Payment Netting vor. Das Close-out Netting wird unter der Voraussetzung geregelt, dass Close-out Netting unter dem anzuwendenden Recht erlaubt ist.

Ein gültiger Rahmenvertrag soll mit jedem Geschäftspartner abgeschlossen werden. Der Rahmenvertrag soll Bestimmungen für das Payment Netting und das Close-out Netting enthalten, die Schutz im Falle des Konkurses des Geschäftspartners geben.

Es sollten Online-Payment-Nettingsysteme zur Berechnung des Ausgleichsbetrages je Währung installiert werden und die geeignete Software angeschafft werden.

Wenn kein elektronisches Nettingsystem verwendet wird, sollen die Geschäftspartner die ermittelten Nettingbeträge einander bis zu einem zuvor vereinbarten Zeitpunkt bestätigen, um mögliche Fehler zu beheben.

Das Cut-off zur Bestätigung von „genetteten" Geschäften soll so spät wie möglich angesetzt werden.

Das Management muss für die Einführung eines geeigneten Kreditrisikosystems und Dokumentationswesens sorgen, das den operativen Anforderungen des Handels Rechnung trägt.

Zu den bekanntesten bilateralen Nettingdiensten zählen FX-Net und S.W.I.F.T. Accord.

FX-Net basiert auf einem voll automatisierten Nettingprozess mithilfe von S.W.I.F.T. MT-Codes. Die Kernpunkte von FX-Net sind individuell vereinbarte Cut-off-Zeiten, selbst für zu leistende und empfangene Zahlungen und zwei Bestätigungen (Echtzeit für das Geschäft; am Valutatag für den Nettobetrag).

S.W.I.F.T. Accord ist eine in das S.W.I.F.T.-System integrierte Nettingfunktion. Alle Zahlungsnachrichten von an Accord teilnehmenden Banken werden separat abgespeichert und zur vereinbarten Buchungsschlusszeit saldiert.

4.4. Wiederholungsfragen

1. Welche der folgenden Aussagen beschreibt den größten Vorteil von (Liquidations-)Nettingvereinbarungen?
   a) Es reduziert das Settlementrisiko.
   b) Es schaltet das gesamte Lieferrisiko aus.
   c) Es reduziert alle FX- und Kreditrisiken.
   d) Es schaltet das FX-Risiko komplett aus.
2. Erklären Sie den Unterschied zwischen Novations-Netting und Close-out Netting!

3. What is the difference between bilateral and multilateral netting?
4. Name two advantages for each bilateral and multilateral netting!
5. What is true regarding bilateral netting services in FX settlement such as FX-Net?
   a) one net payment at the beginning of the day
   b) one net payment for each currency, day and instrument
   c) one net payment for each currency, counterparty and day
   d) multiple settlements for each currency, counterparty and day
6. Which of the following are back office tasks in the course of the netting process?
   a) adjustment of trader limits
   b) confirmation of netted transactions
   c) investigation of disputes
   d) confirmation of netted amounts
7. Which document includes six recommendations for the design of a multi-currency net settlement system?
   a) de Silguy Report
   b) Noel Report
   c) Lamfalussy Report
   d) Duisenberg Report
8. Which points should be agreed in master agreements?
9. When should be the cut-off for the confirmation of netted trades?
   a) as late as possible
   b) it depends on the trade
   c) several times a day
   d) as soon as possible
10. Which of the following master agreements does not contain a close-out netting clause?
    a) TBA/ISMA
    b) IFEMA
    c) ISDA
    d) ICOM
11. Which of the following statements concerning multilateral netting is true?
    a) Multilateral netting is a form of close-out netting.
    b) Payments between two counterparties in different countries are netted.
    c) Payments between several counterparties in one currency are netted.
    d) Only payments between domestic counterparties can be netted.
12. Why does netting simplify settlement?
    a) because fewer payment instructions need to be issued
    b) because fewer confirmations need to be sent
    c) because smaller amounts need to be transferred
    d) because nostro accounts need to be reconciled less often
13. You have a bilateral EUR/USD netting agreement with Bank A and make the following deal with bank A: sell EUR/USD 10 m, buy EUR/USD 8 m, buy EUR/GBP 4 m.
    What is the payment according to the netting agreement?
    a) You receive USD 2 m.
    b) You receive EUR 2 m.

3. Erklären Sie den Unterschied zwischen bilateralem und multilateralem Netting!
4. Nennen Sie je zwei Vorteile von bilateralem und multilateralem Netting!
5. Was trifft auf bilaterale Nettingdienste im FX-Settlement, wie z.B. FX-Net, zu?
   a) eine Nettozahlung am Anfang des Tages
   b) eine Nettozahlung pro Währung, Tag und Instrument
   c) eine Nettozahlung pro Währung, Partei und Tag
   d) mehrfache Settlements pro Währung, Partei und Tag
6. Welche der folgenden Aufgaben werden im Rahmen von Netting vom Backoffice erfüllt?
   a) Anpassung der Händlerlimite
   b) Bestätigung des Nettingbetrages
   c) Untersuchung von Streitfällen
   d) Bestätigung der genetteten Beträge
7. In welchem Dokument werden sechs Empfehlungen zur Gestaltung eines multilateralen Mehrwährungsnettoabwicklungssystems gegeben?
   a) de Silguy-Bericht
   b) Noel-Bericht
   c) Lamfalussy-Bericht
   d) Duisenberg-Bericht
8. Welche Punkte sind in Rahmenverträgen zu vereinbaren?
9. Wann soll der letztmögliche Zeitpunkt zur Bestätigung genetteter Beträge sein?
   a) so spät wie möglich
   b) abhängig vom Geschäft
   c) mehrmals täglich
   d) so früh wie möglich
10. Welcher der folgenden Rahmenverträge enthält KEINE Bestimmungen zum Close-out Netting?
    a) TBA/ISMA
    b) IFEMA
    c) ISDA
    d) ICOM
11. Welche der folgenden Aussagen trifft auf das multilaterale Netting zu?
    a) Multilaterales Netting ist eine Form des Close-out Nettings.
    b) Es werden die Zahlungen mit einem Partner in mehreren Währung saldiert.
    c) Es werden die Zahlungen an und von mehreren Partnern in einer Währung saldiert.
    d) Es können nur Zahlungen zwischen Parteien aus demselben Land saldiert werden.
12. Warum vereinfacht Netting das Settlement?
    a) weil es weniger Zahlungsanweisungen gibt
    b) weil weniger Bestätigungen geschickt werden müssen
    c) da geringere Beträge transferiert werden müssen
    d) da die Nostrokonten weniger oft abgestimmt werden müssen
13. Sie haben mit Bank A eine bilaterale EUR/USD-Nettingvereinbarung und schließen mit Bank A folgende Geschäfte ab: Verkauf EUR/USD 10 Mio., Kauf EUR/USD 8 Mio., Kauf EUR/GBP 4 Mio.
    Welche Zahlung findet gemäß der Nettingvereinbarung statt?
    a) Sie erhalten USD 2 Mio.
    b) Sie erhalten EUR 2 Mio.

c) You pay EUR 2 m.
d) There is no EUR settlement.

14. What is the special feature of the netting clauses in the ISDA Master Agreement?
    a) It contains no payment netting clause.
    b) It only contains a clause for netting by novations.
    c) It only contains a close-out clause.
    d) It is a cross-product netting agreement for all FX products with different market practices.

15. Which of the following statements concerning bilateral netting services are true?
    a) FX-Net sends two confirmations.
    b) S.W.I.F.T. Accord makes possible netting for transactions at the FX market, money market and for derivatives.
    c) Netting at S.W.I.F.T. Accord can only be made for payments between two Accord-members.
    d) The FX-Net-System confirms the gross amounts at the cutt-off dates and sends payment instructions.
    e) FX-Net makes it possible to agree individual cut-offs between the participants.

c) Sie bezahlen EUR 2 Mio.

d) Es kommt zu keinem EUR-Settlement.

14. Was ist das Besondere an den Nettingbestimmungen im ISDA-Rahmenvertrag?

a) Payment Netting wird nicht berücksichtigt.

b) Sie regeln nur das Novations-Netting.

c) Es enthält nur eine Bestimmung zum Close-out Netting.

d) Es fasst alle FX-Produkte mit verschiedenen Konventionen unter einer Nettingvereinbarung zusammen.

15. Welche der folgenden Aussagen bezüglich bilateraler Nettingdienste sind richtig?

a) FX-Net sendet zwei Bestätigungen.

b) S.W.I.F.T. Accord ermöglicht Netting für Transaktionen am FX-Markt, Geldmarkt und für Derivate.

c) Netting bei S.W.I.F.T. Accord kann nur für Zahlungen zwischen zwei Accord-Mitgliedern stattfinden.

d) Das FX-Net-System bestätigt zu den Cut-off-Terminen die Bruttobeträge und sendet die Zahlungsanweisungen.

e) FX-Net ermöglicht die Vereinbarung individueller Nettingschlusszeiten (Cut-offs) zwischen den Teilnehmern.

5. Clearing and Settlement in Payment Systems

In this chapter you learn ...

- what is meant by settlement.
- what is meant by nostro and vostro accounts.
- about the stages of the clearing and settlement process.
- which criteria to use to distinguished between clearing houses.
- what is meant by settlement risk.
- which types of settlement risk can occur.
- about the options to reduce settlement risks.
- which risks can occur at payment systems.
- which net payment systems are used in the eurozone and what their characteristics are.
- more about the Eurozone settlement process in net payment systems .
- about best practice in clearing and settlement.
- more about the settlement of securities.
- which models are used at the settlement of securities.
- more about the characteristics of the most important national payment systems.
- more about the characteristics of cross-border payment systems for the euro.

5.1. Task description

Settlement is the **exchange of payments between counterparties on value date**. All payments are exchanged through nostro accounts. **Nostro accounts** are denominated in the currency of the country where they are located. A **vostro account** is denominated in the domestic currency of the bank that runs the account on behalf of the foreign bank. Thus, each nostro account is also a vostro account. For example, if a German Bank A settles all in USD trades through its USD account that it holds with the US-Bank B, this account is a nostro account for Bank A and a vostro account for Bank B. A bank may use more than one nostro account abroad for the payment or receipt of a currency although a sophisticated cash management will then be required to avoid overdrafts and/or excessive balances.

The clearing and settlement process comprises **three stages**:

1. Authorising and initiating the payment
2. Transmitting and exchanging payment instructions
3. Settlement between banks involved

Settlement can be undertaken on a **bilateral basis or via a clearinghouse**. If a clearinghouse is placed between the counterparties, nostro accounts with the clearinghouse replace the system of nostro/vostro accounts.

5. Clearing und Settlement in Zahlungssystemen

In diesem Kapitel lernen Sie ...

- was man unter Settlement versteht.
- was man unter Nostro- bzw. Vostrokonto versteht.
- in welchen Stufen der Clearing- und Settlementprozess erfolgt.
- nach welchen Kriterien Clearinghäuser eingeteilt werden können.
- was man unter Settlementrisiko versteht.
- welche Arten von Settlementrisiken auftreten können.
- welche Möglichkeiten zur Einschränkung der Settlementrisiken zur Verfügung stehen.
- welche weiteren Risiken bei Zahlungssystemen auftreten können.
- welche Nettozahlungssysteme im Euroraum verwendet werden und deren Charakteristika.
- wie der Settlementprozess in diesen Nettozahlungssystemen im Euroraum abläuft.
- welche Anforderungen an das Clearing und Settlement bestehen.
- wie das Settlement von Wertpapiergeschäften abläuft.
- welche Modelle beim Settlement von Wertpapiergeschäften verwendet werden.
- die Charakteristika der wichtigsten nationalen Zahlungssysteme kennen.
- die Charakteristika eines grenzüberschreitenden Zahlungssystems für den Euro kennen.

5.1. Aufgaben des Clearing und Settlement

Settlement ist der **Austausch von Zahlungen zwischen den Parteien am Valutatag.** Das Settlement erfolgt über **Nostrokonten,** wobei die Nostrobanken am Tag vor dem Settlement-Tag Zahlungsinstruktionen erhalten, aus denen die zu leistenden und erhaltenden Zahlungen hervorgehen. Die Nostrokonten werden in den Heimwährungen jener Länder geführt, wo die Bank Geschäfte macht. Im Gegensatz dazu stehen **Vostrokonten.** Dabei handelt es sich um Konten in der Heimwährung einer Bank, die sie für andere Banken führt. Wenn beispielsweise Bank A aus Deutschland bei Bank B in den USA ein USD-Konto einrichtet, über das alle Zahlungsströme laufen, dann ist das Konto aus Sicht von Bank A ein Nostrokonto und aus der Sicht von Bank B ein Vostrokonto. Daher ist ein Nostrokonto immer ein Vostrokonto für jene Bank, bei der das Konto eingerichtet ist. Banken führen für eine Währung manchmal auch mehrere Nostrokonten, wobei dann darauf zu achten ist, dass weder Überschüsse ungenützt bleiben noch Konten überzogen werden.

Der Clearing- und Settlementprozess erfolgt in **drei Stufen:**

1. Bewilligung und Freigabe der Zahlung
2. Übertragung und Austausch der Zahlungsanweisungen
3. Zahlungsausgleich zwischen den Banken

Das Settlement kann über **bilaterale Vereinbarungen zwischen zwei Parteien oder über Dritte** erfolgen. Wird ein Clearing House zwischengeschaltet, so wird das verzweigte System von länderspezifisch eingerichteten Nostro-/Vostrokonten durch einzelne Devisenkonten beim Clearing House ersetzt, über die alle Transaktionen abgewickelt werden.

5.1.1. Clearing Houses

Clearing Houses can be distinguished by three criteria:

- **Owners**
  Central banks or private institutions. The best-known private sector clearinghouses are Euroclear, Cedel, EBA-Clearing and EAF. CLS Bank will start in the near future. It emerged from ECHO, Multinet and CLS Services.

- **Settlement system**
  Net versus Gross: While in a gross settlement system each transaction is settled by its full amount, a net settlement system settles only a net balance. Net settlement systems can be designed as:
  Sequential or Simultaneous Settlement systems: Simultaneous settlement is the settlement of payment obligations in different currencies at the same time. A simultaneous system does not pay out any currencies to any participant before all participants pay in all the currencies they owe. Sequential settlement systems would pay out some currencies to one or more participants before all relevant participants pay in al the currencies they owe.

- **Operational area**
  Cross border/domestic/regional

5.1.2. Risks in Clearing and Payment Systems

Settlement risk

Settlement risk is the risk that a **payment has been instructed irrevocably before the currency bought is received**. Settlement risk equals the full amount purchased and has to be added to credit risk. Settlement risk should be updated once or twice a day and a minimum and maximum exposure should be determined. The **minimum exposure** includes all trades for which the bank can no longer unilaterally revoke the payment instruction and all overdue amounts. The **maximum exposure** includes additionally all amounts that might not have been received. This additional risk arises because banks are often informed by their nostro banks with a delay of 1 or 2 days about incoming payments.

There are three **types of settlement risk**:

- **Liquidity risk**
  Liquidity risk is the risk that a counterparty (or participant in a settlement system) will not settle an obligation for full value when due. As a result, the counterparty (or several partners in the settlement system) is forced to quickly borrow funds in the market. This may lead to a liquidity squeeze and increased costs.

- **Delivery risk (principal risk)**
  Risk that one party of a foreign exchange transaction will pay the currency it sold but not receive the currency it bought. This risk increases if settlement takes place between time zones as the bankruptcy of Bankhaus Herstatt illustrated.

- **Replacement risk**
  The risk that a counterparty will fail to perform on the settlement date, leaving the other counterparty with an open or unhedged position that has to be replaced at currently

5.1.1. Clearinghäuser

Clearinghäuser können nach drei Punkten unterschieden werden:

- **Eigentümer**
  Zentralbanken oder private Institutionen. Die bekanntesten privaten Clearinghäuser sind EBA-Clearing, EAF, Euroclear, Cedel. Als Zusammenschluss von ECHO, Multinet und CLS Services enstand die CLS Bank.
- **Abwicklungssystem**
  Nettobeträge vs. Bruttobeträge: Während bei Bruttoabwicklungssystemen jede Transaktion gesettled wird, erfolgt bei Nettoabwicklungen nur die Begleichung eines Saldos. Dabei kann man wieder unterscheiden:
  Gestaffelte vs. simultane Abwicklung: Bei einer simultanen Abwicklung werden Beträge an Teilnehmer des Systems nur dann ausgezahlt, wenn alle Teilnehmer ihren Verpflichtungen in allen Währungen gegenüber dem Clearing House nachgekommen sind. Bei der gestaffelten Abwicklung erfolgt das Settlement von verschiedenen Währungen zu verschiedenen Zeitpunkten. Das bedeutet, es ist nicht notwendig, dass die Verpflichtungen in allen Währungen erfüllt sind, bevor die Auszahlung einzelner Beträge beginnt.
- **Wirkungsbereich**
  grenzüberschreitend oder regional.

5.1.2. Risiko im Clearing und Zahlungsverkehr

Settlementrisiko

Settlementrisiko bedeutet, dass die **Zahlung unwiderruflich angewiesen** wurde und der **Gegenbetrag in der anderen Währung noch nicht erhalten** wurde. Offene Zahlungen sollen dem bestehenden Kreditrisiko voll hinzugerechnet werden. Risikoberechnungen sollten ein- bis zweimal am Tag aktualisiert und das **Mindest- und Höchstrisiko** ermittelt werden. Das Mindestrisiko umfasst alle unwiderruflich angewiesenen Zahlungen und alle festgestellten Zahlungsausfälle. Das Höchstrisiko umfasst zusätzlich Zahlungen, die möglicherweise nicht termingemäß eingegangen sind. Dieses zusätzliche Risiko entsteht dadurch, dass Banken von ihren Nostrobanken mit ein bis zwei Tagen Verspätung über den Eingang informiert werden.

Es gibt drei **Arten von Settlementrisiken:**

- **Liquiditätsrisiko**
  Risiko, dass ein Geschäftspartner (oder ein Teilnehmer am Abwicklungssystem) eine Verpflichtung zum Fälligkeitsdatum nicht vollständig begleicht. Dadurch müssen der Partner (oder mehrere Partner im Abwicklungssystem) kurzfristig Geld beschaffen, was zu Engpässen und erhöhten Kosten führen kann.
- **Erfüllungsrisiko**
  Risiko, dass im Rahmen einer FX-Transaktion eine Zahlung geleistet wird, ohne eine Gegenzahlung zu erhalten. Dieses Risiko ist in jenen Fällen höher, wo aufgrund unterschiedlicher Zeitzonen eine Bank vorzeitig erfüllen muss, wie im Fall des Zusammenbruchs des Bankhauses Herstatt illustriert wurde.
- **Wiederbeschaffungsrisiko**
  Risiko, dass eine Partei durch die unpünktliche Erfüllung oder Nichterfüllung einer Verpflichtung eine offene Position mit geringerem Gewinn zu aktuellen Marktpreisen

unfavourable market prices. In fact, replacement risk is a consequence of liquidity and delivery risk.

There are several ways to **contain settlement risks**:

- **Introduction of simultaneous settlement**
  This way, delivery risk can be eliminated though liquidity risk remains.
- **Payment/receipt relationship**
  System payment vs. Payment (PVP). This is a mechanism that ensures that a final transfer of one currency occurs if and only if a final transfer of the other currency takes place.
- **Introduction of a Guaranteed Refund System**
  This is a system where counterparties are guaranteed that any settlement they make will be cancelled or returned if their counterparties fail to pay what they owe. This system should be established only with simultaneous settlement because sequential settlement would demand a rather costly and complicated system for meeting liquidity requirements and payment guarantees.
- **Introduction of a Guaranteed Receipt System**
  In this case, counterparties are guaranteed that if they fulfil their settlement obligations they will receive on time what they are owed. Also a Guaranteed refund system should be designed as simultaneous settlement system because the clearing house could benefit from the self-collateralising nature of FX-settlements (i.e. if Bank B does not fulfil its USD payments and has a EUR credit, the clearing house could sell the EUR against USD in order to settle Bank B's USD obligations and pays only the remaining EUR to Bank B).
- **Restricting membership of the payment system**
  Membership is restricted to institutions that meet certain criteria. (e.g. minimum rating standards)
- **Establishment of bilateral and system-wide intra-day limits**
  Bilateral receiver limits are set by each bank in the system on every other individual bank in the system. If the net position exceeds the limit the last payment to the counterparty is queued until the limit will be free again. By setting bilateral net receiver limits a bank can control counterparty risk according to its risk assessment. **System-wide net sender debit limits** place a limit on the aggregate net debit of a participant that it may have with the rest of the members as a whole.
  The successful operations of a limit system requires
  – Real time gross settlement (RTGS) and a
  – a full collateralisation of the limits for the case of default.
- **Loss-/Liquidity sharing agreements**
  The idea is that any shortfall due to default of a participant is shared and covered together by all solvent members in order to ensure settlement. All systems suppose that the defaulting partners stayed within the limits.

schließen muss. Das Wiederbeschaffungsrisiko ist de facto eine Konsequenz des Liquiditäts- und Erfüllungsrisikos.

Es gibt folgende Möglichkeiten, diese **Risiken einzuschränken:**

- **Einführung einer simultanen Abwicklung**
  Auf diese Weise kann theoretisch das Erfüllungsrisiko ausgeschaltet werden, das Liquiditätsrisiko bleibt bestehen.
- **Verknüpfung von Zahlung und Gegenleistung**
  System Zahlung gegen Zahlung (Payment versus Payment). Es handelt sich dabei um einen Mechanismus, der sicherstellt, dass die endgültige Übertragung eines Betrages in einer Währung erst und nur dann erfolgt, wenn auch die endgültige Übertragung in der anderen Währung erfolgt ist.
- **Einführung eines Systems mit Rückzahlungsgarantie**
  Den Teilnehmern wird garantiert, dass alle Zahlungen, die sie zur Erfüllung von Geschäften geleistet haben, storniert oder erstattet werden, wenn ihre Gegenparteien nicht erfüllen. Rückzahlungsgarantien sollten nur in Kombination mit simultaner Abwicklung etabliert werden, weil im Falle einer gestaffelten Abwicklung ein relativ aufwendiges System der Liquiditäts- und Zahlungssicherung notwendig wird.
- **Einführung eines Systems mit Empfangsgarantie**
  Dabei handelt es sich um eine Vereinbarung, dass Parteien die ihnen zustehenden Beträge erhalten, unter der Bedingung, dass sie ihre Abwicklungsverpflichtungen erfüllt haben. Auch in diesem Fall ist die simultane Abwicklung zu bevorzugen, weil im Notfall das Clearing House auf Zahlungsansprüche aus einer anderen Währung zurückgreifen kann, wenn Zahlungsverpflichtungen in einer Währung nicht nachgekommen wird (d.h. Bank B kommt ihren USD-Verpflichtungen nicht nach und hat Ansprüche auf EUR. Nun kann das Clearing House die EUR Ansprüche gegen USD verkaufen und die Verpflichtung von Bank B erfüllen. Bank B erhält dann nur noch den Restbetrag).
- **Einschränkung des Teilnehmerkreises**
  Es dürfen nur Institute teilnehmen, die ein bestimmtes Rating oder andere Qualifikationskriterien erfüllen.
- **Etablierung von bilateralen und systemweiten Intraday Limits**
  Die **bilateralen** Limits beziehen sich auf die offene Position, die ein Clearing-Teilnehmer mit einer Gegenpartei maximal haben möchte. Übersteigt die Nettozahlerposition an einen Kontrahenten einen gewissen Wert, dann wird die letzte Zahlung in eine Warteschlange gereiht, bis im Limit wieder Platz ist. Durch die Festsetzung von bilateralen Nettoempfängerlimits („net receiver limits") kann eine Bank je nach Einschätzung der Kreditwürdigkeit der anderen Teilnehmer ihr Risiko abstecken. **Systemweite Limits** beschränken üblicherweise die Nettozahlungsverpflichtung einer Bank, die sich aus allen Transaktionen mit den Teilnehmern am Zahlungssystem ergeben.
  Damit ein Limitsystem funktioniert, müssen zwei Voraussetzungen gegeben sein:
  - Das Zahlungssystem muss auf Echtzeitverarbeitung beruhen (RTGS).
  - Die eingeräumten Limits müssen für den Fall der Zahlungsunfähigkeit eines Partners entsprechend besichert sein.
- **Verlust- und Liquiditätsbeteiligung**
  Es geht darum, dass der durch den Ausfall eines Teilnehmers entstandene Verlust bzw. Liquiditätsengpass von den anderen Teilnehmern solidarisch getragen wird und somit das Settlement durchgeführt werden kann. Die Systeme unterstellen dabei, dass ein Partner nicht erfüllt, obwohl alle Limite eingehalten wurden.

There are three possible formulae for sharing out the shortfall:
- Equal shares: This solution is the easiest to calculate but the least fair because relationships are not taken into account
- Pro-rata sharing according to actual bilateral exposures
- Pro-rata sharing according to bilateral limits: This is probably the most equitable method of sharing out the loss because the shares are allocated according to the limits each bank had with the failed counterparty. This way, individual risk assessments are taken into account (i.e. the bigger the limit, the bigger the share)

None of the above methods can eliminate settlement risk but can only alleviate the consequences of the risk. Additionally, liquidity risk can always pose a big problem if a bank needs to cover open positions unexpectedly at short notice. (particularly in Guaranteed refund systems because despite the refund of payments the expected currency will not be received)

- **Recalculation of settlement amounts**
  Some clearinghouses recalculate the net positions if one counterparty fails to pay. In this case the net positions are recalculated excluding the transactions with the defaulting counterparty. The central banks of the G-10 reject this method because unexpected and short-term changes of expected payments/receipts may trigger a liquidity shortfall with solvent banks that may cause instability in the markets ($\rightarrow$ systemic risk)

- **Real-time Gross Settlement (RTGS)**
  In RTGS-systems, individual payments are settled across the settlement accounts of commercial banks at the central bank as soon as the payment instruction was received. This means that the receiving bank knows that the amount involved has already been settled if it receives a payment statement. RTGS eliminates delivery (principal) risk (except the payment has been queued due to liquidity problems). Well-known RTGS are Fedwire (USD), TARGET (EUR) or SIC (CHF).

- Though delivery risk can be almost eliminated, RTGS-systems need to set precautions against liquidity risk. **Three ways** evolved in the market:
  - Provide no additional liquidity: If the bank's balance is not sufficient the payment is queued or rejected until the account is sufficiently funded. This solution is chosen by SIC.
  - Limited overdrafts: Under special conditions banks receive an intra-day credit at a reference rate. Fedwire charges for overdrafts interests on the level of the overdrafts through the day.
  - Repo facility: Central banks provide liquidity against short-term, highly liquid assets. Securities are automatically reversed at the end of the business day.

Es gibt drei Modelle:
- Verteilung zu gleichen Teilen
- Diese Lösung ist am einfachsten zu kalkulieren, geht aber auf Kosten einer fairen Verteilung der Lasten.
- Verteilung anteilig zu den aktuellen bilateralen Positionen
- Verteilung anteilig zu den eingeräumten bilateralen Limits. Diese Variante dürfte am besten sein, da sie die Lasten gemessen am von den „überlebenden" Banken geschätzten Risiko verteilt. Das heißt, je größer das eingeräumte Limit, desto höher der Anteil an der Verlustverteilung.

Mit keinem Modell gelingt es, das Settlementrisiko auszuschalten, sondern lediglich die Auswirkungen eines eintretenden Risikos abzuschwächen. Außerdem ist nicht garantiert, dass Banken nicht trotzdem in Liquiditätsengpässe kommen (besonders bei Systemen mit Rückzahlungsgarantie, weil trotz allem die benötigte Währung nicht erhalten wird), wenn sie kurzfristig und unerwartet eine Verlustdeckung vornehmen müssen.

- **Neukalkulation der Settlementbeträge (Rückabwicklung)**
  Manche Clearinghäuser kalkulieren die Settlementbeträge neu, wenn ein Teilnehmer am System ausfällt. Dabei werden die Nettopositionen ohne Berücksichtigung der Transaktionen des insolventen Teilnehmers neu berechnet. Diese Lösung wird von den Zentralbanken der G10 abgelehnt, da durch unerwartete und kurzfristige Änderungen in den Zahlungsverpflichtungen auch die solventen Teilnehmer in Schwierigkeiten geraten könnten (→ Systemrisiko).

- **Abwicklung der Zahlung über Echtzeit-Bruttoabwicklungssysteme („Real Time Gross Settlement" – RTGS)**
  Bei diesen Systemen werden alle Zahlungen der Banken über bei der Zentralbank eingerichtete Konten gesettlet, sobald die Zahlungsanweisung eingelangt ist. Das heißt, eine begünstigte Bank kann sicher sein, dass sie bereits bei Erhalt einer Zahlungsnachricht den Gegenwert am Konto gutgeschrieben erhalten hat. Damit wird das Erfüllungsrisiko zum großen Teil eliminiert (außer die Zahlung wird aufgrund mangelnder Liquidität nach hinten gereiht). Bekannte RTGS sind das Fedwire System (USA), TARGET (EU) oder SIC (in der Schweiz).

- Obwohl das Erfüllungsrisiko eliminiert wird, erfordern RTGS Vorkehrungen gegen Liquiditätsknappheit, wobei sich **drei Ansätze** entwickelt haben:
  - Keine Liquiditätsspielräume: Wenn der Saldo einer Bank für eine Zahlung nicht ausreicht, dann wird die Zahlung so lange rückgereiht oder storniert, bis das Settlementkonto ausreichend ausgestattet ist. Diese Lösung wählt SIC.
  - Begrenzter Überziehungsrahmen: Dieses Prinzip ermöglicht, unter bestimmten Bedingungen eine gewisse Kreditlinie in Anspruch nehmen zu können. Fedwire verrechnet den Taggeldsatz für unbesicherte Geldbereitstellung.
  - Einrichtung einer Intraday Repo-Fazilität: Die Zentralbank stellt Liquidität kurzfristig gegen hochliquide Sicherheiten von Banken bereit, wobei die Wertpapiere am Ende des Handelstages wieder retourniert werden.

Further questions to be resolved in RTGS-systems are:
- Optimisation of payment traffic and cash management
- Conditions for direct membership in a RTGS-system
- New settlement procedures: Regular gross settlement instead of end-of-day net settlement

The main advantage of Real-time gross settlement systems is the **possibility to settle large-volume, time critical payments**. Further advantages include
- earlier finality of payments
- reduction of liquidity, system and credit risk.

Other risks

- **Legal risks**
  If payment systems transfer only a net amount there is the risk that if one participant of the system fails the liquidator of the company does not accept the netting agreement but insists on gross settlement of payments outstanding. If net settlement is replaced by gross settlement the solvent banks bear the following risks: They have to pay their obligations on time but receive their claims belatedly. They do not receive their claims only lately but also do not know how much of the outstanding claims will be satisfied. Generally, the existing liquidity plan becomes obsolete
- **Technical risks**
  This risk describes mainly the potential breakdown of the payments system. Proper back-up facilities and emergency plans have to be in place.
- **Fraud**
  This can take the form of deliberately wrong payment instructions or manipulated authenticated messages.
- **Human error**

5.1.3. Net payment systems in the EURO

EBA-Clearing

The **European Banking Association** provides the EBA-Clearing service, a cross-border clearing system for the Euro, which is **open from 7:30 a.m. until 4:00 p.m.**

Main characteristics of EBA-Clearing (Euro 1 System):

- Net settlement
- No unwinding: Payment instructions already processed can not be revoked
- If two counterparties want to unwind an already processed deal they have to send new payment instructions to EBA-Clearing to have the deal settled, i.e. cancelled.

Andere im Rahmen eines RTGS zu lösende Fragen sind:
- Optimierung des Zahlungsverkehrs-Management, insbesondere der Cashflows
- Bedingungen für eine direkte Teilnahme an einem RTGS
- Neue Abwicklungsmodalitäten für die Zentralbanken und Geschäftsbanken: Statt einer Nettozahlung am Ende des Tages wird jede Zahlung geleistet.

Der wesentliche Vorteil von Echtzeit-Bruttoabwicklungssystemen liegt in der **Möglichkeit, zeitkritische, großvolumige Zahlungen taggleich zu begleichen.**
Weitere Vorteile sind:
- Frühere Endgültigkeit der Zahlungen
- Reduzierung von Liquiditäts-, System- und Kreditrisiko

Weitere Risiken

- **Rechtliche Risiken**
  Im Rahmen von Zahlungssystemen, die nur Nettobeträge transferieren, besteht die Gefahr, dass im Rahmen des Ausfalls eines Partners der Masseverwalter der insolventen Bank die Nettingvereinbarung nicht akzeptiert und die Zahlungen auf Bruttobasis begleichen möchte. Ist dieses Vorhaben erfolgreich, dann hat dies negative Auswirkungen auf die solventen Teilnehmer: Sie müssen ihren Verpflichtungen in voller Höhe nachkommen und erhalten, wenn überhaupt, ihre Ansprüche verspätet. Ihre gesamte Liquiditätsplanung wird obsolet.

- **Technische Risiken**
  Darunter versteht man den Ausfall des Zahlungssystems. Es müssen entsprechende Sicherungseinrichtungen vorhanden sein.

- **Betrug**
  Es werden bewusst falsche Anweisungen gegeben oder authentische Anweisungen manipuliert.

- **Menschliches Versagen**

5.1.3. Nettozahlungssysteme im Euroraum

EBA-Clearing

Das EBA-Clearing wird von der **European Banking Association** bereitgestellt und ist als grenzüberschreitendes Euro-Clearing konzipiert. Das EBA-Clearing ist **von 7.30 bis 16.00 Uhr geöffnet**.

Charakteristika des EBA-Clearing (EURO 1 System):

- Netto-Settlement
- Keine Rückabwicklung: Eine Zahlungsanweisung kann nach Verarbeitung nicht widerrufen werden.
- Rückabwicklungen müssen zwischen den beiden Parteien direkt vereinbart werden und in Form neuer Zahlungsanweisungen an das EBA-Clearing abgewickelt werden.

- Each participant extends to each other participant a mandatory limit of EUR 5 million. The bilateral limits are limited to EUR 30 million per participant (limits are on a net basis!)
- Bilateral limits for the next business day can be changed until 6:00 p.m. the preceding day.
- The total of a participant's debit and credit cap may not exceed EUR 1 billion. The debit cap of a participant is the sum of the limits received from the other participants. The credit cap is the sum of limits given to the other participants.
- If the multilateral limit (EUR 1 billion) is exceeded the payment is queued.
- EBA has set up a collateral pool of EUR 1 billion at the ECB.

The settlement process in the EBA-Clearing

- The settlement process is initiated by the bilateral exchange of S.W.I.F.T. messages between the banks involved. The balances are advised to the ECB and EBA-Clearing.
- The payment is sent via **TARGET** and takes place at the settlement accounts established by the banks at the ECB.
- EBA-Clearing informs the ECB who is a net creditor/debtor in the Clearing and receives the payment confirmation from the ECB.
- Upon receipt of all confirmations, EBA-Clearing notifies all participants that the settlement operations are completed.

Ideally, settlement is completed until 4:30 p.m. The early closing time of EBA-Clearing should enable all participants to settle smoothly via TARGET.

EAF-2 (Elektronische Abrechnung Frankfurt)

The EAF settlement is operated by the **Landeszentralbank Hessen**. The organizational structure is basically the same as in EBA-Clearing, i.e. there is no unwinding after processing, payment instructions, payment exceeding limits are queued and bilateral as well as multilateral netting can be undertaken. The payments are settled via **TARGET**.

Differences to EBA-Clearing

- Operating hours: 7:00 a.m. to 4:00 p.m.
- EAF-2 settles EUR-payments only within Germany. Since there exists remote access, participants do not need to be physically present in the German market
- Participants provide a total liquidity of EUR 1.8 billion as collateral

The settlement process in EAF-2

The settlement is structured in two phases:

Phase 1 – Delivery phase

From 7:00 a.m. to 4:00 p.m. payments are **continually settled on a bilateral or multilateral basis**, depending on the instructions of the participants. The transferable amount is either limited by the Clearing-House limit or **sender limits**. Sender limits are set by the participants individually for each counterparty.

- Die Teilnehmer müssen sich untereinander ein bilaterales Mindestlimit von EUR 5 Mio. einräumen. Maximal darf das Limit EUR 30 Mio. pro Gegenpartei betragen (alle Limite beruhen auf Nettobasis).
- Bilaterale Limits für den nächsten Tag können bis 18.00 Uhr geändert werden.
- Die Summe aller eingeräumten Limits (credits) und erhaltener Limits (debits) ist auf je EUR 1 Mrd. beschränkt. Wird dieses multilaterale Limit durch eine Zahlung überschritten, dann wird die Zahlung gereiht, bis das Limit wieder erfüllt wird.
- EBA hat einen Pool an Sicherheiten im Wert von EUR 1 Mrd. bei der EZB hinterlegt.

Der Settlementprozess im EBA-Clearing

- Der Settlementprozess wird durch den bilateralen Austausch von S.W.I.F.T.-Nachrichten zwischen den Banken eingeleitet. Die Salden werden der EZB und EBA-Clearing avisiert.
- Der Zahlungsverkehr erfolgt über **TARGET** an die Zahlungsausgleichkonten bei der EZB.
- EBA-Clearing meldet der EZB, wer die Begünstigten beim Clearing sind, und erhält von der EZB die Zahlungsbestätigungen.
- EBA-Clearing verständigt alle Mitglieder nach Durchführung über den Abschluss des Settlements.

Idealtypisch ist der Abrechnungsprozess bis 16.30 Uhr beendet. Der frühere Schließungszeitpunkt von EBA-Clearing soll den reibungslosen Ablauf des Settlements über TARGET ermöglichen.

EAF-2 (Elektronische Abrechnung Frankfurt)

Das Abwicklungssystem über EAF wird von der **Landeszentralbank Hessen** betrieben und ist auf denselben Fundamenten wie das EBA-Clearing gebaut. Das heißt, es ist auch bilaterales wie multilaterales Netting möglich, es gibt keine Rückabwicklung von Zahlungen, nachdem die Anweisung verarbeitet wurde, und bei Überschreiten der Limite wird die Zahlung gereiht. Die Zahlungsabwicklung erfolgt auch über **TARGET.**

Unterschiede zum EBA-Clearing

- Öffnungszeiten: 7.00 bis 16.00 Uhr
- Es sind nur Eurozahlungen in Deutschland möglich, jedoch ist ein Fernzugriff eingerichtet, d.h., es ist keine physische Präsenz in Deutschland erforderlich, um an EAF teilzunehmen.
- Die Gesamtsicherheit auf dem Liquiditätssammelkonto beträgt EUR 1,8 Mrd. und wird von den Teilnehmern bereitgestellt.

Der Settlementprozess im EAF-2

Das Settlement im EAF erfolgt in zwei Phasen:

Phase 1 – Einlieferungsphase

Von 7.00 bis 16.00 Uhr werden die **Zahlungen kontinuierlich bilateral oder multilateral abgerechnet,** wobei jeder Teilnehmer im Vorhinein bestimmt, mit welchem Partner multilateral bzw. bilateral gesettled wird. Die Höhe der Zahlung ist durch die Deckung im Rahmen des Liquiditätssammelkontos oder sogenannter **Senderhöchstbeträge** begrenzt. Senderhöchstbeträge sind von den Teilnehmern bestimmte Obergrenzen für den Liquiditätsabfluss.

Phase 2 – Settlement phase

It takes place between 4:00 and 4:30 p.m. and is designed as a two-stage **multilateral netting** process. In stage 1 liquidity from the Bundesbank accounts of participants can be used to cover any shortage though participants can limit access to them.

If there are any debits left open after stage 1, the participants have 30 minutes to provide additional liquidity. If there remain any balances after stage 2 the payments are returned to the sender like in a gross settlement system.

Generally, EAF treats all payments as final. Consequently, the payments are at the disposal of the receiving bank throughout the day and can be used to cover short positions, but only within the EAF-2 system.

EAF-2 tries to **link the advantages of net and gross settlement** by

- providing early finality
- reducing credit, system and liquidity risk
- absorbing little liquidity.

Note: There are two more national net settlement systems for the Euro that operate only within the domestic market. PNS (Paris Net Settlement) in France and CAMARA (Cámara de Compensación de Madrid) in Spain.

5.2. Best Practices – Clearing and Settlement

BP1

Nostro balance **projections** should be made **on a real-time basis** and should incorporate the latest trades, cancellations and amendments.

Nostro balances should be calculated exactly in order to ensure efficient cash management that avoids any overdraft costs.

BP2

Banks should send electronic messages concerning expected receipts to their nostro banks.

With the receipt of an **electronic message advising of expected receipts**, nostro banks can identify payments that are directed to an incorrect account and can correct payment errors on a timely basis. Some nostro-banks attach the transaction reference number from the incoming message to the outgoing nostro statement.

Banks should consider a nostro bank's ability to process electronic messages in its decision to which nostro bank to use.

BP3

A bank should establish an **automated interface to their nostro banks** to enable on-line cancellations and amendments of payment instructions.

If a bank establishes an automated real-time system with its nostro bank

Phase 2 – Ausgleichsphase

Sie findet von 16.00 bis 16.30 Uhr statt. Dabei erfolgt in zwei Schritten **multilaterales Netting**. Im ersten multilateralen Netting wird zur Deckung von Sollsalden auch auf die Liquidität der Teilnehmer bei der Bundesbank zurückgegriffen, wobei die Teilnehmer den Zugriff begrenzen können.

Sollten nach der ersten multilateralen Abrechnung noch offene Salden vorhanden sein, haben die betroffenen Teilnehmer 30 Minuten Zeit, um auf die Bundesbankkonten eine entsprechende Deckung bereitzustellen. Bleibt dann noch ein Saldo offen, werden Zahlungen als nicht ausgeführt an den sendenden Teilnehmer, wie in einem Bruttoabwicklungssystem, retourniert.

Generell sind alle verrechneten Zahlungen als endgültig zu betrachten. Daher stehen den Empfängerbanken die fortlaufenden Zahlungen während des Tages zur Verfügung, wobei diese Zahlungen nur innerhalb von EAF wieder als Deckung verwendet werden können.

EAF-2 versucht durch die **Verbindung von Elementen des Netto- und Bruttosettlements** die Vorteile beider Systeme zu vereinen, indem

- eine frühe Endgültigkeit der Zahlungen erreicht wird,
- Kredit-, System- und Liquiditätsrisiken stark verringert werden und
- der Liquiditätsbedarf reduziert wird.

Anmerkung: Weitere nationale Nettogroßbetragszahlungssysteme im Euroraum sind PNS (Paris Net Settlement) in Frankreich und CAMARA (Cámara de Compensación de Madrid) in Spanien.

5.2. Anforderungen an das Clearing und Settlement

A1

Die **Prognosen** für die Salden der Nostrokonten sollen **auf Echtzeitbasis** erstellt werden und die jüngsten Handelsdaten, Zusätze und Geschäftsanullierungen berücksichtigen.

Die Salden der Nostrokonten sollen genau errechnet werden, damit das Cash Management der Bank perfekt funktioniert, d.h. insbesondere keine Kontokorrentzinsen zu zahlen sind.

A2

Banken sollen ihren Nostrobanken über elektronische Medien mitteilen, welche Zahlungseingänge zu erwarten sind.

Indem Banken an die Nostrobanken **Zahlungseingangsprognosen** senden, können schon frühzeitig Fehler im Settlement erkannt und falsche Zahlungseingänge korrigiert werden. Nostrobanken weisen oft die Nummer der elektronischen Nachricht dem Auszug des Nostrokontos zu.

Banken sollen Nostrobanken auch unter dem Gesichtspunkt wählen, ob sie die technischen Voraussetzungen zur Verarbeitung elektronischer Zahlungsprognosen haben.

A3

Banken sollen eine **automatische Schnittstelle zu Nostrobanken** einrichten, damit Zahlungsanweisungen online abgeändert oder widerrufen werden können.

Besteht zwischen der Bank und der Nostrobank ein **automatisiertes Echtzeitsystem,** so können

- flawed payment instructions can be corrected,
- last-minute amendments due to counterparty wishes can be processed,
- Payment instructions can be cancelled if there is some evidence that the counterparty may not fulfil, later deadlines for payment instructions can be established.

BP4

Management should achieve the **latest possible cut-off time for cancellation and alteration for payment instructions** to nostro banks as well as the earliest possible cut-off time for confirmation of final receipts.

The proper setting of cut-off times enables the bank to solve problems that surface lately in the settlement process and to identify early final as well as failed receipts. Nonreceipts of payments may indicate a (serious) problem at the counterparty. Ideally, a cancellation should be possible until the opening of the domestic large-value payments system on settlement-date, and confirmation should be sent immediately after the final receipt to the large-value payment system.

In practice, many payments can be cancelled until one or two days before settlement-date because domestic payments systems allow for sending payment instructions one to three days in advance. In netting systems, payment instructions become often irrevocable as soon as they are keyed into the system.

BP5

The **back office** should ensure credit supporting appropriately **updates settlement exposure** resulting from projected cash-flow movements and should include any failed receipts from previous transactions.

BP6

The senior management should fully understand the settlement process. Credit and risk managers should know all internal procedures of settlement.

Management, credit and risk management, and trading as well as back office must be fully aware of the timing of key events in the settlement process. These are:

- Time when payment instructions are recorded
- Time when a payment instruction becomes irrevocable
- Time when the confirmation of the counterparty is received with finality

BP7

Operations should understand the **procedures for crisis situations affecting settlement**. It should know who to notify if payments must be cancelled as if settlement procedures must be changed.

Crisis management should comprise the following measures:

- Availability of contact lists with the names of nostro bank staff
- Training and understanding of alternative settlement procedures
- Simulated exercises of crisis situations such as war, break-down of settlement-processing system or counterparty bankruptcy

- fehlerhafte Zahlungsanweisungen korrigiert werden,
- Änderungswünsche des Kunden, die im letzten Moment auftreten, berücksichtigt werden und
- Fristen für Abänderungen von Zahlungsanweisungen auf einen späteren Termin verlegt werden. Zahlungen können so noch storniert werden, wenn die berechtigte Annahme besteht, dass die Gegenpartei nicht erfüllt.

A4

Das Management soll mit den Nostrobanken eine **möglichst späte Frist für letzte Änderungen oder den Widerruf von Zahlungsanweisungen** vereinbaren, für die Bestätigung der endgültig erhaltenen Beträge jedoch den frühest möglichen.

Mit diesen Vereinbarungen soll den Banken einerseits ermöglicht werden, Probleme, die im Settlementprozess spät auftauchen, noch lösen zu können und andererseits potenzielle Risiken rasch zu erkennen, wenn Zahlungen nicht in gewünschter Form eingehen. Fehlende Zahlungseingänge können auch ein Hinweis auf Probleme beim Geschäftspartner sein.

Der Widerruf soll idealerweise bis zur Öffnung des inländischen Großbetragszahlungssystems am Abwicklungstag möglich sein, die Bestätigung sofort nach Endgültigkeit im inländischen Großbetragszahlungssystems festgestellt werden.

In der Praxis können Zahlungen aber oft nur ein bis zwei Tage vor der Valuta bei der Korrespondenzbank storniert werden, weil die inländischen Zahlungssysteme die Möglichkeit einräumen, ein bis drei Tage im Voraus einen Zahlungsauftrag einzugeben. Bei Nettingsystemen sind Zahlungsaufträge oft unwiderruflich, sobald sie im System eingegeben sind.

A5

Das **Backoffice** soll sicherstellen, dass im Kreditwesen das **Settlementrisiko** aufgrund erwarteter Zahlungsströme und offener Zahlungseingänge **aktualisiert** wird.

A6

Die Geschäftsleitung muss den Settlementprozess verstehen. Kredit- und Risikomanager sollen die internen Abläufe des Settlements kennen.

Geschäftsleitung, Kredit- und Risikomanagement, Handel und Backoffice sollen sich der Zeitpunkte für die wichtigsten Settlementaktionen bewusst sein. Das sind:

- Zeitpunkt, zu dem Zahlungsanweisungen aufgezeichnet werden,
- Zeitpunkt, ab dem eine Zahlungsanweisung unwiderruflich ist und
- Zeitpunkt, zu dem der endgültige Zahlungseingang der anderen Partei bestätigt wird.

A7

Das Backoffice muss die **Mechanismen zur Beilegung von das Settlement betreffenden Krisensituationen** kennen. Es muss wissen, wer im Falle von Zahlungswiderruf oder geänderten Settlementanweisungen zu kontaktieren ist.

Folgende Maßnahmen sollten getroffen werden:

- Listen mit Kontaktpersonen in Nostrobanken müssen verfügbar sein.
- Das Personal muss in alternativen Settlementmethoden geschult sein.
- Krisenszenarien wie Krieg, Zusammenbruch des Settlementsystems oder Zahlungsunfähigkeit eines Partners sollen durchgespielt werden.

5.3. Settlement of Securities

In case of securities settlement the securities as well as the cash transaction must be settled. Thus, one additional dimension has to be considered.

The counterparties in a security deal bear the same risks as in an FX-deal though principal and replacement risk must be considered additionally in the security leg of the trade.

Delivery versus Payment (DVP)

DVP is a mechanism that ensures that the final transfer of one asset occurs if and only if the final transfer of another asset(s) occur. Assets could include monetary assets (such as foreign exchange), securities or other financial instruments.

There are **three DVP-models** that deal differently with the settlement of the cash and security settlement:

	Gross securities settlement	**Net securities settlement**
Gross cash settlement	Model A	no models
Net cash settlement	Model B	Model C

Model A

All transactions are settled on a **gross basis**. Cash and securities settlement is done simultaneously, requiring a RTGS (**Real-Time Gross Settlement System**) for cash payments. This purest form of DVP is implemented by the Fedwire system.

Model B

Securities are settled on a **real-time gross basis** while the **cash amount** is **settled net at the end of the day**. Since securities are delivered before the cash amount is settled, this model is not a "pure" DVP. In fact, the existence of payment guarantees to the sellers of the securities eliminate principal risk.

Model C

Both transactions, cash and securities, are settled net at the end of the day. Settlement takes place only if all debtors have sufficient balances with the clearing agent.

5.4. Cross-border payment systems

The stability of domestic payments systems is the prerequisite for a working FX-market because most FX-deals involve cross-border payments. In the case of cross-border payments banks instruct their nostro banks to settle the deal (= pay the amount) through the domestic payments system. The **most important payments systems** are CHIPS (Clearing House Interbank Payment System) and Fedwire for USD, CHAPS (Clearing House Automated Payment System) for GBP, FEYCS (Foreign Exchange Yen Clearing System) and BOJ-Net (Bank of Japan-Financial Network System) for JPY and TARGET (Trans-European Automated Real-Time Gross Settlement Express Transfer System) for EUR.

5.3. Das Settlement von Wertpapiergeschäften

Das Settlement von Wertpapieren muss sowohl das Settlement des Wertpapiers als auch die Cash-Transaktion regeln. Bei Wertpapiergeschäften unterliegen die beteiligten Parteien denselben Risiken, wobei sich das Erfüllungs- und Wiederbeschaffungsrisiko sinngemäß auf die Wertpapiergeschäfte ausdehnt.

Lieferung gegen Zahlung (Delivery vs. Payment – DVP)

DVP ist ein Mechanismus, der sicherstellt, dass die endgültige Übertragung des einen Vermögenswerts erst und nur dann erfolgt, wenn die endgültige Übertragung des oder der anderen Vermögenswerte(s) stattfindet. Bei den Vermögenswerten kann es sich um monetäre Aktiva (z.B. Devisen), Wertpapiere oder sonstige Finanzinstrumente handeln.

Es gibt **drei Modelle des DVP,** die sich bei der Abwicklung unterscheiden:

	Wertpapier-Settlement brutto	**Wertpapier-Settlement netto**
Cash-Settlement brutto	Modell A	keine Modelle
Cash-Settlement netto	Modell B	Modell C

Modell A

Es werden **alle Transaktionen brutto abgewickelt,** wobei Cash und Wertpapier gleichzeitig gesettled werden. Damit diese reinste Form des DVP funktionieren kann, ist ein **Echtzeit-Bruttoabwicklungssystem** für die Cashzahlung erforderlich. Unter dieses Modell fällt das Fedwire System.

Modell B

Das **Settlement von Wertpapieren erfolgt kontinuierlich auf Bruttobasis,** während der **Cashbetrag am Tagesende als Nettobetrag bezahlt** wird. Genau genommen handelt es sich dabei um kein DVP, weil das Wertpapier früher geliefert wird als die Zahlung. Indem den Wertpapierverkäufern eine Zahlungsgarantie gegeben wird, kann das Erfüllungsrisiko de facto eliminiert werden.

Modell C

Alle Wertpapiere und Cashbeträge werden am Ende des Tages netto geliefert, unter der Voraussetzung, dass alle Teilnehmer ausreichende Salden auf ihren Konten haben.

5.4. Grenzüberschreitender Zahlungsverkehr

Da gerade im FX-Markt ein Großteil der Zahlungen grenzüberschreitend abgewickelt werden, müssen die nationalen Zahlungssysteme große Stabilität haben. Im grenzüberschreitenden Zahlungsverkehr weisen die Banken ihre ausländischen Nostrobanken an, die entsprechenden Zahlungen über die inländischen Zahlungssysteme abzuwickeln. Die **wichtigsten Zahlungssysteme** sind das CHIPS (Clearing House Interbank Payment System) und Fedwire für USD, das CHAPS (Clearing House Automated Payment System) für GBP, FEYCS (Foreign Exchange Yen Clearing System) und BOJ-Net (Bank of Japan – Financial Network System) für JPY und TARGET (Trans-European Automated Real-Time Gross Settlement Express Transfer System) für EUR.

The following table shows the key data concerning the major payment systems:

	BOJ	CHAPS	CHIPS	Fedwire	FEYCS	SIC	TARGET
Settlement (gross/net)	gross	gross	net	gross	net gross	gross	gross
Operation hours (local time)	9:00 a.m. – 5:00 p.m. from end 2000: 9:00 a.m. – 7:00 p.m.	8:30 a.m. – 4:45 p.m.	12:30 a.m. – 4:30 p.m.	12:30 a.m. – 6:30 p.m.	9:00 a.m. – 1:45 p.m. 9:00 a.m. – 5:00 p.m. from end 2000: 9:00 a.m. – 7:00 p.m.	6:00 p.m. till 14:15 p.m. the follow-ing day	7:00 a.m. – 6:00 p.m.
Cut-off for inter-na-tional pay-ments	3:00 p.m. from end 2000: 4:00 p.m.	noon	4:30 p.m.	6:00 p.m.	10:30 a.m.	8:00 a.m.	6:00 p.m.
Cut-off for third-party payments	3:00 p.m. from end 2000: 4:00 p.m.	no rule	see above	see above	see above	3:00 p.m.	5:00 p.m.
Currency	JPY	GBP	USD	USD	JPY	CHF	EUR

TARGET/TARGET2 – Example for a cross-border payment system

TARGET is the **real-time gross settlement system** (RTGS) for the EUR and started to op-erate on 4th January 1999. It consists of 15 national RTGS-systems and the payment mech-anism of the ECB (EPM). TARGET was scheduled to be replaced by TARGET2 until Sep-tember 2008.

TARGET members send their payment instructions in the national message format to the national RTGS. This way, they initiate the settlement process. Afterwards, TARGET settles the transactions and sends back a payments statement in the national format.

Following **RTGS-systems** are used in the Eurozone:

Belgium	ELLIPS
Germany	ELS
Finland	BOF-RGTS
France	TBF
Ireland	IRIS
Italy	LIPS-Gross
Luxembourg	LIPS-Gross
Netherlands	TOP
Austria	ARTIS
Portugal	SPGT
Spain	SLBE

EU members that do not participate in the EUR take also part in TARGET. Their central banks though have to provide collateral **daily until 8:00 a.m to ensure sufficient liquidity**.

Die Kerndaten der wichtigsten nationalen Zahlungssysteme:

	BOJ	CHAPS	CHIPS	Fedwire	FEYCS	SIC	TARGET
Abwicklung (brutto/netto)	brutto	brutto	netto	brutto	netto brutto	brutto	brutto
Betriebszeiten (Lokalzeit)	9:00 – 19:00	8.30 – 15.45	0:30 – 16:30 (CET)	0:30 – 18:30 (CET)	9:00 – 13:45 9:00 – 19:00	18:00 – 16:15 nächsten Tages	7:00 – 18:00
Cut-off-Zeit für internationale Zahlungen	15:00	12:00	16:30	18:00	10:30	8:00	18:00
Cut-off-Zeit für Zahlungsanweisungen an Dritte	siehe oben	keine Regelung	siehe oben	siehe oben	siehe oben	15:00	17:00
Währung	JPY	GBP	USD	USD	JPY	CHF	EUR

TARGET/TARGET2 – Beispiel für ein grenzübergreifendes Zahlungssystem

TARGET ist das **Echtzeit-Bruttoanzahlungssystem** (RTGS) für den EURO und nahm am 04.01.1999 seinen Betrieb auf. TARGET setzt sich aus 15 nationalen RTGS-Systemen und dem Zahlungsverkehrsmechanismus der EZB (EPM) zusammen, die untereinander verknüpft sind. Bis September 2008 hat TARGET2 das bestehende System abgelöst.

Die Teilnehmer an TARGET leiten grenzüberschreitende Zahlungen ein, indem sie Zahlungsaufträge im nationalen Nachrichtenformat in das nationale RTGS-System leiten. TARGET wickelt die Transaktion ab und sendet eine Zahlungsnachricht im nationalen Format zurück.

Folgende **RTGS-Systeme** sind im EUR-Raum in Verwendung:

Belgien	ELLIPS
Deutschland	ELS
Finnland	BOF-RGTS
Frankreich	TBF
Irland	IRIS
Italien	LIPS-Gross
Luxemburg	LIPS-Gross
Niederlande	TOP
Österreich	ARTIS
Portugal	SPGT
Spanien	SLBE

Jene EU-Staaten, die außerhalb der Eurozone geblieben sind, nehmen ebenfalls an TARGET teil, die Zentralbanken müssen **jedoch täglich bis 8.00 Uhr MEZ Liquiditätssicherheiten** liefern.

Country	RTGS	Collateral
Denmark	DEBES	€ 1 billion
Sweden	ERA	€ 1 billion
Great-Britain	CHAPS-Euro	€ 3 billions

Opening hours of TARGET are from 7:00 a.m. to 6:00 p.m., Frankfurt time. Cut-off for third-party payments is 5:00 p.m. Third parties are considered as all account holders in the books of the receiving and/or the sending bank. If unexpected payments are received in TARGET they have to be returned until cut off time the same day in order to avoid fines.

TARGET does not operate on New Year's Day, Good Friday, Easter Monday, 1 May, Christmas Day and 26 December. Operating hours of national RTGS-systems can be freely chosen but should be adapted to TARGET opening hours.

TARGET does **not impose any net-debit limits**. Since TARGET is based on a DVP mechanism, participants must provide sufficient liquidity to the central banks prior to any dealing through the system. Liquidity can be provided by Tier-one and Tier-two assets:

- **Tier one assets** consist of marketable debt instruments fulfilling uniform Monetary Union-wide eligibility criteria by the ECB.
- **Tier two assets** consist of additional assets, marketable and non-marketable, which are of particular importance for national financial markets and banking systems and for which eligibility criteria is established, subject to the minimum eligibility criteria established by the ECB. The specific eligibility criteria for tier two applied by the respective national central banks are subject to approval by the ECB.

Criteria	Tier one	Tier two
Type of asset	– ECB debt certificates – other marketable debt instruments (excluding "hybrid" instruments)	– marketable debt instruments – non-marketable debt instruments – equities traded on a regulated market
Settlement procedures	instruments must be centrally deposited in book-entry form with national central banks or a CSD fulfilling ECB minimum standards	assets must be easily accessible to the national central bank, which has included them in its tier, two list.
Type of issuer	– ESCB – public sector – private sector – international and supra-national institutions	– public sector – private sector (special ECB authorization)

Land	RTGS	Sicherheiten
Dänemark	DEBES	€ 1 Mrd.
Schweden	ERA	€ 1 Mrd.
Großbritannien	CHAPS-Euro	€ 3 Mrd.

TARGET ist jeden Werktag von 7.00 bis 18.00 Uhr (MEZ) offen, wobei der Annahmeschluss für Kundenzahlungen 17.00 Uhr ist. Unter Kundenzahlungen fallen alle Zahlungen, die nicht Interbank sind (d.h. von/auf Konten erfolgen, die bei den Banken von Dritten eingerichtet wurden). Werden unerwartete Zahlungen festgestellt, sind diese bis zum Cut-off jenes Tages zu retournieren, an dem die Zahlung eingegangen ist.

TARGET ist an folgenden Tagen nicht geöffnet: 1.1., Karfreitag, Ostermontag, 1. Mai, 25.12. und am 26.12. Die Öffnungszeiten nationaler RTGS sollten daran angepasst werden.

TARGET legt **keine Netto-Debitlimite als Kreditobergrenze** fest. Da TARGET auf einem DVP-Mechanismus beruht, müssen die Teilnehmer bereits im Vorhinein entsprechende Sicherheiten bei den Zentralbanken bereitstellen, damit die Zahlungen in Zentralbankgeld erfolgen können. Man unterscheidet dabei zwischen „Kategorie 1"- und „Kategorie 2"-Sicherheiten.

- Zur **Kategorie 1** zählen marktfähige Schuldtitel, die von der EZB festgelegte einheitliche und im gesamten Euro-Währungsraum geltende Zulassungskriterien erfüllen.
- Zur **Kategorie 2** zählen weitere marktfähige und nicht-marktfähige Sicherheiten, die für die nationalen Finanzmärkte und Bankensysteme von besonderer Bedeutung sind und für die nationale Zentralbanken die Zulassungskriterien auf Basis von EZB-Mindeststandards festlegen. Die von den nationalen Zentralbanken angewandten spezifischen Zulassungskriterien für Kategorie-2-Sicherheiten bedürfen der Zustimmung der EZB.

Kriterien	Kategorie 1	Kategorie 2
Art der Sicherheit	– EZB-Schuldverschreibungen – sonstige marktfähige Schuldtitel (außer „hybriden" Sicherheiten)	– marktfähige Schuldtitel – nicht-marktfähige Schuldtitel – an einem geregelten Markt gehandelte Aktien
Abwicklungsverfahren	Die Sicherheiten müssen zentral in girosammelverwahrfähiger Form bei nationalen Zentralbanken oder einer zentralen Wertpapierverwahrstelle hinterlegt werden, die den EZB-Mindeststandards entspricht.	Die Sicherheiten müssen der nationalen Zentralbank, die sie in ihr Kategorie-2-Verzeichnis aufgenommen hat, leicht zugänglich sein.
Emittenten	– ESZB – öffentliche Hand – privater Sektor gemäß OWAG-Richtlinie – internationale und supranationale Institutionen	– öffentliche Hand – privater Sektor (besondere Zustimmung der EZB)

Credit standard	the issuer (guarantor) must be deemed financially sound by the ECB	the issuer/debtor (guarantor) must be deemed financially sound by the national central bank which has included the assets in its tier two list.
Place of establishment of the issuer (or guarantor)	EEA (except international or supranational institutions)	Euro area
Location of asset	Euro area	Euro area
Currency	Euro or EUR-currencies	Euro or other EEA or widely traded currencies can be accepted subject to ECB approval
Cross-border use	Yes	Yes

If a bank cannot cover the intra-day credit facility at the settlement account of the national central bank it may use the ECB's **marginal lending facility** to obtain overnight liquidity. For this purpose the ECB provides liquidity through overnight repos or overnight Pfandbriefe. The marginal lending facility serves as interest rate ceiling for the overnight rate. The ECB offers also a **deposit facility** to banks with a liquidity surplus. The deposit facility generally marks the interest rate floor for overnight rates. Applications for the marginal lending facility must be sent not later than 6:00 p.m. to ECB while the deadline for a request to the deposit facility is 6:30 p.m., except the last two days of the maintenance period, where applications can be sent until 7:00 p.m. The ECB sets the facility rate daily according to its monetary policy goals and can change the conditions at its discretion.

The ECB treats any uncovered position on the settlement account automatically as an application to draw on the marginal lending facility. The ECB has the right to fine banks that do not fulfil the marginal facility requirement.

Summary

Settlement is the exchange of payments between counterparties on value date. All payments are exchanged through nostro accounts. Nostro accounts are denominated in the currency of the country where they are located. A vostro account is denominated in the domestic currency of the bank that runs the account on behalf of the foreign bank. Thus, each nostro account is also a vostro account.

The clearing and settlement process comprises three stages: authorising and initiating the payment, transmitting and exchanging payment instructions and settlement between banks involved. Settlement can be undertaken on a bilateral basis or via a clearing house.

Bonitätsanforderung	Der Emittent (Garant) muss von der EZB als bonitätsmäßig einwandfrei eingestuft worden sein.	Der Emittent/Schuldner (Garant) muss von der nationalen Zentralbank, die die Sicherheit in ihr Kategorie-2-Verzeichnis aufgenommen hat, als bonitätsmäßig einwandfrei eingestuft worden sein.
Sitz des Emittenten (oder des Garanten)	EWR (ausgenommen internationale oder supranationale Institutionen)	Euro-Währungsraum
Hinterlegung der Sicherheit	Euro-Währungsraum	Euro-Währungsraum
Währung	Euro oder EUR-Währungen	Euro oder EUR-Währungen
Grenzüberschreitende Nutzung	Ja	Ja

Erfüllt eine Bank den Innertags-Sollsaldo auf ihrem Zahlungsausgleichskonto bei der nationalen Zentralbank nicht, so muss sie die **Spitzenrefinanzierungsfazilität** der EZB beanspruchen. Dabei handelt es sich um ein **Instrument vorübergehender Liquiditätsbereitstellung durch die EZB** in Form von Overnight-Repos bzw. Overnight-Pfandbriefen. Für diese Geschäfte legt die EZB einen Zinssatz fest, der im Allgemeinen eine Obergrenze für den Tagesgeldsatz darstellt und zu dem die Banken ihre offenen Positionen am Ende des Tages refinanzieren können. Die EZB stellt den Banken auch eine **Einlagefazilität** für freie Liquidität zur Verfügung. Sie stellt in der Regel die Untergrenze für den Tagesgeldsatz dar. Anträge zur Spitzenrefinanzierungsfazilität sind bis 18.00 Uhr an die nationale Zentralbank zu richten. Anträge für die Einlagefazilität bis 18.30 Uhr, mit Ausnahme der letzten zwei Tage der Erfüllungsperiode der Mindestreserve. Für diesen Tag wurde der letzte Antragszeitpunkt auf 19.00 Uhr festgelegt. Die EZB hat das Recht, die Bedingungen der Fazilität gemäß geldpolitischen Überlegungen jederzeit zu ändern oder auch auszusetzen.

Bleibt nach Abschluss der Konten ein Sollsaldo auf dem Zahlungsausgleichskonto, so wird das automatisch als Antrag der Bank auf Inanspruchnahme der Spitzenfinanzierungsfazilität betrachtet. Wird die Spitzenrefinanzierungsfazilität nicht erfüllt, so kann die EZB die Bank mit einer Strafe belegen.

Zusammenfassung

Settlement ist der Austausch von Zahlungen zwischen den Parteien am Valutatag. Das Settlement erfolgt über Nostrokonten, wobei die Nostrobanken am Tag vor dem Settlement-Tag Zahlungsinstruktionen erhalten, aus denen die zu leistenden und erhaltenden Zahlungen hervorgehen. Die Nostrokonten werden in den Heimwährungen jener Länder geführt, wo die Bank Geschäfte macht. Im Gegensatz dazu stehen Vostrokonten. Dabei handelt es sich um Konten in der Heimwährung einer Bank, die sie für andere Banken führt.

Der Clearing- und Settlementprozess erfolgt in drei Stufen: Bewilligung und Freigabe der Zahlung, Übertragung und Austausch der Zahlungsanweisungen und Zahlungsausgleich zwischen den Banken. Das Settlement kann über bilaterale Vereinbarungen zwischen zwei Parteien oder über Dritte erfolgen.

Clearing houses can be distinguished by three criteria: owners (central banks or private institutions), settlement system (net versus gross, sequential or simultaneous settlement systems), operational area (cross border/domestic/regional).

Settlement risk is the risk that a payment has been instructed irrevocably before the currency bought is received. There are three types of settlement risk: liquidity risk (risk that a counterparty or participant in a settlement system will not settle an obligation for full value when due), delivery risk (risk that one party of a foreign exchange transaction will pay the currency it sold but not receive the currency it bought) and replacement risk (risk that a counterparty will fail to perform on the settlement date, leaving the other counterparty with an open or unhedged position that has to be replaced at currently unfavourable market prices).

There are several ways to contain settlement risks: introduction of simultaneous settlement, payment/receipt relationship, introduction of a guaranteed refund system, introduction of a guaranteed receipt system, restricting membership of the payment system, establishment of bilateral and system-wide intra-day limits, loss/liquidity sharing agreements, recalculation of settlement amounts and real-time gross settlement (RTGS).

Furthermore, there are legal risks, technical risks (breakdown of the payments system), fraud (wrong payment instructions or manipulated authenticated messages) or human error.

The European Banking Association provides the EBA-Clearing service, a cross-border clearing system for the euro, which is open from 7:30 a.m. until 4:00 p.m. The main characteristics of EBA-Clearing are: net settlement, no unwinding, mandatory limit of EUR 5 million, changing the bilateral limits for the next business until 6:00 p.m., multilateral limit (EUR 1 billion) is exceeded the payment is queue, collateral pool of EUR 1 billion at the ECB. The settlement process is initiated by the bilateral exchange of S.W.I.F.T. messages between the banks involved. The balances are advised to the ECB and EBA-Clearing. The payment is sent via TARGET and takes place at the settlement accounts established by the banks at the ECB. EBA-Clearing informs the ECB who is a net creditor/debtor in the Clearing and receives the payment confirmation from the ECB. Upon receipt of all confirmations, EBA-Clearing notifies all participants that the settlement operations are completed. Ideally, settlement is completed until 4:30 p.m. The early closing time of EBA-Clearing should enable all participants to settle smoothly via TARGET.

The EAF settlement is operated by the Landeszentralbank Hessen. The organisational structure is basically the same as in EBA-Clearing, i.e. there is no unwinding after processing, payment instructions, payment exceeding limits are queued and bilateral as well as multilateral netting can be undertaken. The payments are settled via TARGET.

The settlement is structured in two phases: delivery phase and settlement phase. From 7:00 a.m. to 4:00 p.m. payments are continually settled on a bilateral or multilateral basis, depending on the instructions of the participants. The settlement phase takes place between 4:00 and 4:30 p.m. and is designed as a two-stage multilateral netting process. In stage 1 liquidity from the Bundesbank accounts of participants can be used to cover any shortage though participants can limit access to them. If there are any debits left open after stage 1, the participants have 30 minutes to provide additional liquidity. If there remain any balances after stage 2 the payments are returned to the sender like in a gross settlement system.

In case of securities settlement, the securities as well as the cash transaction must be settled. Thus, one additional dimension has to be considered. The counterparties in a secu-

Clearinghäuser können hinsichtlich Eigentümer (Zentralbanken oder private Institutionen), Abwicklungssystem (Nettobeträge vs. Bruttobeträge, gestaffelte vs. simultane Abwicklung) und Wirkungsbereich (grenzüberschreitend oder regional) unterschieden werden.

Settlementrisiko bedeutet, dass die Zahlung unwiderruflich angewiesen wurde und der Gegenbetrag in der anderen Währung noch nicht erhalten wurde. Es gibt drei Arten von Settlementrisiken: Liquiditätsrisiko (Risiko, dass ein Geschäftspartner oder ein Teilnehmer am Abwicklungssystem eine Verpflichtung zum Fälligkeitsdatum nicht vollständig begleicht), Erfüllungsrisiko (Risiko, dass im Rahmen einer FX-Transaktion eine Zahlung geleistet wird, ohne eine Gegenzahlung zu erhalten) und Wiederbeschaffungsrisiko (Risiko, dass eine Partei durch die unpünktliche Erfüllung oder Nichterfüllung einer Verpflichtung eine offene Position mit geringerem Gewinn zu aktuellen Marktpreisen schließen muss).

Um diese Risiken einzuschränken, gibt es folgende Möglichkeiten: Einführung einer simultanen Abwicklung, Verknüpfung von Zahlung und Gegenleistung, Einführung eines Systems mit Rückzahlungsgarantie, Einführung eines Systems mit Empfangsgarantie, Einschränkung des Teilnehmerkreises, Etablierung von bilateralen und systemweiten Intraday Limits, Verlust- und Liquiditätsbeteiligung, Neukalkulation der Settlementbeträge (Rückabwicklung) und Abwicklung der Zahlung über ein Echtzeit-Bruttoabwicklungssystem („Real Time Gross Settlement" – RTGS).

Außerdem können auch rechtliche Risiken, technische Risiken (Ausfall des Zahlungssystems), Betrug (bewusst falsche Anweisungen oder Manipulation authentischer Anweisungen) oder menschliches Versagen auftreten.

Das EBA-Clearing wird von der European Banking Association bereitgestellt und ist als grenzüberschreitendes Euro-Clearing konzipiert. Das EBA-Clearing ist von 7.30 bis 16.00 geöffnet. Das EBA-Clearing weist folgende Charakteristika auf: Netto-Settlement, keine Rückabwicklung, Rückabwicklungen zwischen den beiden Parteien direkt vereinbart, bilaterales Mindestlimit von EUR 5 Mio., Änderung der bilateralen Limits für den nächsten Tag bis 18.00 Uhr, Summe aller eingeräumter Limits (credits) und erhaltener Limits (debits) ist auf je EUR 1 Mrd. beschränkt und Pool an Sicherheiten im Wert von EUR 1 Mrd. bei der EZB. Der Settlementprozess wird durch den bilateralen Austausch von S.W.I.F.T.-Nachrichten zwischen den Banken eingeleitet. Die Salden werden der EZB und dem EBA-Clearing avisiert. Der Zahlungsverkehr erfolgt über TARGET an die Zahlungsausgleichkonten bei der EZB. EBA-Clearing meldet der EZB, wer die Begünstigten beim Clearing sind und erhält von der EZB die Zahlungsbestätigungen. EBA-Clearing verständigt alle Mitglieder nach Durchführung über den Abschluss des Settlements. Idealtypisch ist der Abrechnungsprozess bis 16.30 Uhr beendet.

Das Abwicklungssystem EAF-2 wird von der Landeszentralbank Hessen betrieben und ist auf denselben Fundamenten wie das EBA-Clearing gebaut. Das heißt, es ist auch bilaterales wie multilaterales Netting möglich, es gibt keine Rückabwicklung von Zahlungen, nachdem die Anweisung verarbeitet wurde, und bei Überschreiten der Limite wird die Zahlung gereiht. Die Zahlungsabwicklung erfolgt auch über TARGET. Das Settlement im EAF erfolgt in zwei Phasen, nämlich der Einlieferungsphase und der Ausgleichsphase. Von 7.00 bis 16.00 Uhr werden die Zahlungen kontinuierlich bilateral oder multilateral abgerechnet, wobei jeder Teilnehmer im Vorhinein bestimmt, mit welchem Partner multilateral bzw. bilateral gesettled wird. Die Ausgleichphase findet von 16.00 bis

rity deal bear the same risks as in an FX deal though principal and replacement risk must be considered additionally in the security leg of the trade.

DVP is a mechanism that ensures that the final transfer of one asset occurs if and only if the final transfer of another asset(s) occur. Assets could include monetary assets (such as foreign exchange), securities or other financial instruments. There are three DVP-models that deal differently with the settlement of the cash and security settlement. At Model A all transactions are settled on a gross basis. At Model B securities are settled on a real-time gross basis while the cash amount is settled net at the end of the day. At Model C both transactions, cash and securities, are settled net at the end of the day.

The stability of domestic payments systems is a prerequisite for a working FX market because most FX deals involve cross-border payments. In case of cross-border payments, banks instruct their nostro banks to settle the deal (= pay the amount) through the domestic payments system. The most important payments systems are CHIPS (Clearing House Interbank Payment System) and Fedwire for USD, CHAPS (Clearing House Automated Payment System) for GBP, FEYCS (Foreign Exchange Yen Clearing System) and BOJ-Net (Bank of Japan-Financial Network System) for JPY and TARGET (Trans-European Automated Real-Time Gross Settlement Express Transfer System) for EUR.

TARGET is the real-time gross settlement system (RTGS) for the EUR and started to operate on 4th January 1999. It consists of 15 national RTGS-systems and the payment mechanism of the ECB (EPM). TARGET was scheduled to be replaced by TARGET2 until September 2008. TARGET members send their payment instructions in the national message format to the national RTGS. This way, they initiate the settlement process. Afterwards, TARGET settles the transactions and sends back a payment statement in the national format.

EU members that do not participate in the EUR take also part in TARGET. Their central banks have to provide collateral daily until 8:00 a.m to ensure sufficient liquidity. Opening hours of TARGET are from 7:00 a.m. to 6:00 p.m., Frankfurt time. Cut-off for third-party payments is 5:00 p.m. Third parties are considered as all account holders in the books of the receiving and/or the sending bank. If unexpected payments are received in TARGET they have to be returned until cut-off time the same day in order to avoid fines.

16.30 Uhr statt. Dabei erfolgt in zwei Schritten multilaterales Netting. Im ersten multilateralen Netting wird zur Deckung von Sollsalden auch auf die Liquidität der Teilnehmer bei der Bundesbank zurückgegriffen, wobei die Teilnehmer den Zugriff begrenzen können. Sollten nach der ersten multilateralen Abrechnung noch offene Salden vorhanden sein, haben die betroffenen Teilnehmer 30 Minuten Zeit, um auf den Bundesbankkonten eine entsprechende Deckung bereitzustellen. Bleibt dann noch ein Saldo offen, werden Zahlungen als nicht ausgeführt an den sendenden Teilnehmer, wie in einem Bruttoabwicklungssystem, retourniert.

Das Settlement von Wertpapieren muss sowohl das Settlement des Wertpapiers als auch die Cash-Transaktion regeln. Bei Wertpapiergeschäften unterliegen die beteiligten Parteien denselben Risiken, wobei sich das Erfüllungs- und Wiederbeschaffungsrisiko sinngemäß auf die Wertpapiergeschäfte ausdehnt.

DVP ist ein Mechanismus, der sicherstellt, dass die endgültige Übertragung des einen Vermögenswerts erst und nur dann erfolgt, wenn die endgültige Übertragung des oder der anderen Vermögenswerte(s) stattfindet. Es gibt drei Modelle des DVP, die sich bei der Abwicklung unterscheiden. Bei Modell A werden alle Transaktionen brutto abgewickelt, wobei Cash und Wertpapier gleichzeitig gesettled werden. Bei Modell B erfolgt das Settlement von Wertpapieren kontinuierlich auf Bruttobasis, während der Cashbetrag am Tagesende als Nettobetrag bezahlt wird. Bei Modell C werden alle Wertpapiere und Cashbeträge am Ende des Tages netto geliefert, unter der Voraussetzung, dass alle Teilnehmer ausreichende Salden auf ihren Konten haben.

Da gerade im FX-Markt ein Großteil der Zahlungen grenzüberschreitend abgewickelt wird, müssen die nationalen Zahlungssysteme große Stabilität haben. Im grenzüberschreitenden Zahlungsverkehr weisen die Banken ihre ausländischen Nostrobanken an, die entsprechenden Zahlungen über die inländischen Zahlungssysteme abzuwickeln. Die wichtigsten Zahlungssysteme sind das CHIPS (Clearing House Interbank Payment System) und Fedwire für USD, das CHAPS (Clearing House Automated Payment System) für GBP, FEYCS (Foreign Exchange Yen Clearing System) und BOJ-Net (Bank of Japan – Financial Network System) für JPY und TARGET (Trans-European Automated Real-Time Gross Settlement Express Transfer System)für EUR.

TARGET ist das Echtzeit-Bruttoanzahlungssystem (RTGS) für den EURO und nahm am 04.01.1999 seinen Betrieb auf. TARGET setzt sich aus 15 nationalen RTGS-Systemen und dem Zahlungsverkehrsmechanismus der EZB (EPM) zusammen, die untereinander verknüpft sind. Bis September 2008 hat TARGET2 das bestehende System abgelöst. Die Teilnehmer an TARGET leiten grenzüberschreitende Zahlungen ein, indem sie Zahlungsaufträge im nationalen Nachrichtenformat in das nationale RTGS-System leiten. TARGET wickelt die Transaktion ab und sendet eine Zahlungsnachricht im nationalen Format zurück.

Jene EU-Staaten, die außerhalb der Eurozone geblieben sind, nehmen ebenfalls an TARGET teil, die Zentralbanken müssen jedoch täglich bis 8.00 Uhr MEZ Liquiditätssicherheiten liefern. TARGET ist jeden Werktag von 7.00 bis 18.00 Uhr (MEZ) offen, wobei der Annahmeschluss für Kundenzahlungen 17.00 Uhr ist. Unter Kundenzahlungen fallen alle Zahlungen, die nicht Interbank sind (d.h. von/auf Konten erfolgen, die bei den Banken von Dritten eingerichtet wurden). Werden unerwartete Zahlungen festgestellt, sind diese bis zum Cut-off jenes Tages zu retournieren, an dem die Zahlung eingegangen ist. TARGET legt keine Netto-Debitlimite als Kreditobergrenze fest. Da TARGET auf einem

TARGET does not impose any net-debit limits. Since TARGET is based on a DVP mechanism, participants must provide sufficient liquidity to the central banks prior to any dealing through the system.

5.5. Practice Questions

1. What does it mean if a payment instruction includes the term "clearing"?
   a) Deals are settled through the local clearing system of the country of the base currency.
   b) Deals are settled as previously agreed between the two parties.
   c) The deal is settled through the local clearing system of the currency concerned.
   d) Deals are settled by crediting or debiting the account a counterparty runs in his book in the name of the other counterparty.
2. What is meant by nostro and vostro accounts?
3. What are the three stages of the clearing and settlement process?
4. Which of the following is NOT a proper way to settle payments?
   a) multilateral, net
   b) multilateral, gross
   c) bilateral, net
   d) third party, gross
5. What are the criteria for distinguishing clearing houses?
6. What is the difference between simultaneous and sequential settlement?
   a) Simultaneous settlement works only on a net basis.
   b) Sequential settlement works only on a gross basis.
   c) Simultaneous settlement pays before all obligations of the system members are met.
   d) Sequential settlement settles payments at different times.
7. The CLS Bank is used by banks for the settlement of FX transactions. Why was the CLS bank founded?
   a) in order to eliminate settlement risk
   b) in order to speed up cross-border payments
   c) in order to optimise the banks' liquidity management
   d) because G20 and the BIS have published a corresponding guideline
8. What is meant by settlement risk?
9. Which of the following are settlement risks?
   a) liquidity risk
   b) replacement risk
   c) basis risk
   d) principal risk
10. Name at least five options for the reduction of settlement risks!
11. Name other risks which can occur in the settlement process!
12. Name at least four characteristics of EBA-Clearing!
13. Describe shortly the settlement process in EBA-Clearing!
14. What are the differences between EBA-Clearing and EAF-2!
15. Describe shortly the settlement process in EAF-2!

DVP-Mechanismus beruht, müssen die Teilnehmer bereits im Vorhinein entsprechende Sicherheiten bei den Zentralbanken bereitstellen, damit die Zahlungen in Zentralbankgeld erfolgen können.

5.5. Wiederholungsfragen

1. Was bedeutet bei einer Zahlungsanweisung „Clearing"?
   a) Das Settlement erfolgt über CLS.
   b) Bestehende Settlementanweisungen gelten in der ursprünglich vereinbarten Form.
   c) Das Settlement erfolgt über das heimische Clearing-System der betroffenen Währung.
   d) Das Settlement erfolgt durch Belastung oder Kreditierung jenes Kontos, das der Partner bei der Bank eingerichtet hat.
2. Was versteht man unter Nostro- bzw. Vostrokonten?
3. In welchen drei Stufen erfolgt der Clearing- und Settlementprozess?
4. In welcher Form kann das Settlement von Zahlungen NICHT erfolgen?
   a) multilateral, netto
   b) multilateral, brutto
   c) bilateral, netto
   d) über Dritte, brutto
5. Nach welchen Kriterien können Clearinghäuser unterschieden werden?
6. Wodurch unterscheidet sich die gestaffelte von der simultanen Abwicklung?
   a) Simultane Abwicklung kann nur auf Bruttobasis erfolgen.
   b) Gestaffelte Abwicklung kann nur auf Nettobasis erfolgen.
   c) Bei der simultanen Abwicklung werden Zahlungen vor der kompletten Erfüllung aller Verpflichtungen geleistet.
   d) Bei der gestaffelten Abwicklung werden Zahlungen zu unterschiedlichen Zeitpunkten geleistet.
7. Die CLS-Bank wird von den Banken zur Abwicklung ihrer Devisentransaktionen genutzt. Warum wurde diese Bank gegründet?
   a) zur Minimierung der Abwicklungsrisiken
   b) zur Beschleunigung grenzüberschreitender Zahlungen
   c) zur effizienteren Steuerung der Bankenliquidität
   d) weil die G 20 und die BIZ eine entsprechende Richtlinie erlassen haben
8. Was versteht man unter Settlementrisiko?
9. Welche der folgenden Risiken sind Settlementrisiken?
   a) Liquiditätsrisiko
   b) Wiederbeschaffungsrisiko
   c) Basisrisiko
   d) Erfüllungsrisiko
10. Nennen Sie mindestens fünf Möglichkeiten zur Einschränkung der Settlementrisiken!
11. Nennen Sie weitere Risiken, die im Rahmen des Settlementprozesses auftreten können!
12. Nennen Sie mindestens vier Charakteristika des EBA-Clearings!
13. Beschreiben Sie kurz den Settlementprozess im EBA-Clearing!
14. Nennen Sie die Unterschiede zwischen EBA-Clearing und EAF-2!
15. Beschreiben Sie kurz den Settlementprozess in EAF-2!

16. What is the name of the RTGS system for GBP?
    a) Fedwire
    b) CHAPS
    c) CHIPS
    d) TARGET

17. Which of the following best describes the main benefit of a RTGS payment system?
    a) reduced costs due to implementation of less labour-intensive working practices
    b) reduced market risk due to smaller open positions
    c) reduced costs due to fewer payments passing through nostro accounts
    d) final settlement of interbank funds transfers on a continuous, trade-by-trade basis throughout the day

18. What does it mean if an RTGS does not provide additional liquidity?
    a) There is a liquidity shortage in the RTGS.
    b) Interest on the basis of the day-to-day cost is charged for each overdraft of the settlement account.
    c) No additional liquidity is provided without collateral.
    d) A payment is only settled if the sending bank has sufficient funds in the account.

19. Which of the following payment systems is used by the European Central Bank and the national central banks in Europe?
    a) TARGET
    b) EAF
    c) CLS
    d) S.W.I.F.T.

20. What statement is true given that banks send messages informing nostro banks about expected receipts?
    a) Nostro reconcilitation is simplified.
    b) The settlement process is speeded up.
    c) Nostro banks can correct payment errors at an early stage.
    d) Cut-off time for receipts can be fixed at an earlier time.

21. What does DVP stand for?
    a) Delivery vs. Purchase
    b) Discount vs. Payment
    c) Delivery vs. Payment
    d) Discount vs. Purchase

22. Which of the following models is NOT used for delivery versus payment?
    a) net settlement of securities and cash
    b) gross settlement of securities and cash
    c) net settlement of securities, gross settlement of cash
    d) gross settlement of securities, net settlement of cash

23. CHIPS is the commonly used name for the domestic clearing system in which of the following centres?
    a) Hong Kong
    b) London
    c) Frankfurt
    d) New York

16. Wie heißt das Echzeit-Bruttoabwicklungssystem für GBP?
    a) Fedwire
    b) CHAPS
    c) CHIPS
    d) TARGET

17. Welche der folgenden Aussagen beschreibt am besten den größten Vorteil von Echtzeit-Bruttoabwicklungssystemen?
    a) geringere Arbeitskosten
    b) geringeres Marktrisiko aufgrund kleinerer offener Positionen
    c) geringere Kosten für das Nostrokonto aufgrund weniger Überweisungen
    d) endgültiges Settlement von Interbankzahlungen für jedes Geschäft auf kontinuierlicher Basis über den ganzen Tag

18. Was bedeutet es, wenn im Rahmen eines RTGS keine Liquiditätsspielräume existieren?
    a) Es ist nicht genug Liquidität im Zahlungssystem.
    b) Für jede Überziehung des Settlementkontos sind Taggeldzinsen zu zahlen.
    c) Es wird keine zusätzliche Liquidität ohne Sicherheiten zur Verfügung gestellt.
    d) Eine Zahlung findet nur dann statt, wenn ausreichend Liquidität am Konto vorhanden ist.

19. Welches Zahlungssystem verwenden die Europäische Zentralbank und die nationalen Zentralbanken in Europa?
    a) TARGET
    b) EAF
    c) CLS
    d) S.W.I.F.T.

20. Da Banken ihren Nostrobanken Prognosen über Zahlungseingänge übermitteln, ist welche Aussage zutreffend?
    a) Es wird der Abgleich der Nostrokonten vereinfacht.
    b) Es wird der Settlementprozess beschleunigt.
    c) Es ist die Nostrobank über die Liquidität der Bankkonten informiert.
    d) Es können erhaltene Beträge möglichst spät abgeglichen werden.

21. Was heißt DVP?
    a) Delivery vs. Purchase
    b) Discount vs. Payment
    c) Delivery vs. Payment
    d) Discount vs. Purchase

22. Welches der folgenden Modelle findet man bei Lieferung gegen Zahlung NICHT?
    a) Netto-Wertpapier-Settlement, Netto-Cash-Settlement
    b) Brutto-Wertpapier-Settlement, Brutto-Cash-Settlement
    c) Netto-Wertpapier-Settlement, Brutto-Cash-Settlement
    d) Brutto-Wertpapier-Settlement, Netto-Cash-Settlement

23. CHIPS ist die Abkürzung für das inländische Zahlungssystem in welchem der folgenden Finanzzentren?
    a) Hongkong
    b) London
    c) Frankfurt
    d) New York

24. If an unexpected CHAPS payment has been received, what is the deadline for returning the payment to the sender without incurring charges?
   a) CHAPS cut-off on the next day
   b) 12:00 (midday) the next day
   c) within 24 hours of receiving the payment
   d) CHAPS cut-off on the same day

25. What is the cut-off time for third-party payments in TARGET?
   a) 5 p.m., local time
   b) 4.30 p.m., local time
   c) 6 p.m., local time
   d) 3 p.m., local time

26. Which of the following statements are true?
   a) SIC closes at 6 p.m.
   b) TARGET is the payment system for the EUR.
   c) JPY settlement via FEYCS has to be done on a gross basis.
   d) JPY settlement via FEYCS can be done on a gross or on a net basis.
   e) CHAPS does not have a specified cut-off for third-party payment instructions.

27. What are the operating hours (in local time) of TARGET?
   a) 7 a.m. – 6 p.m.
   b) 9 a.m. – 7 p.m.
   c) 8.30 a.m. – 3.45 p.m.
   d) 12.30 p.m. – 4.30 p.m.

24. Bis zu welchem Zeitpunkt sind über CHAPS empfangene, unerwartete Zahlungen an den Absender zu retournieren, ohne Gebühren zahlen zu müssen?
    a) Buchungsschluss von CHAPS am nächsten Tag
    b) 12.00 Uhr nächster Tag
    c) innerhalb von 24 Stunden nach Erhalt der Zahlung
    d) Buchungsschluss von CHAPS am selben Tag

25. Bis wann werden Zahlungsanweisungen an Dritte in TARGET akzeptiert?
    a) 17.00 Uhr Ortszeit
    b) 16.30 Uhr Ortszeit
    c) 18.00 Uhr Ortszeit
    d) 15.00 Uhr Ortszeit

26. Welche der folgenden Aussagen sind richtig?
    a) SIC schließt um 18.00 Uhr.
    b) TARGET ist das Zahlungssystem für den EUR.
    c) JPY-Settlement über FEYCS muss auf Bruttobasis erfolgen.
    d) JPY-Settlement über FEYCS kann sowohl auf Netto- als auch auf Bruttobasis erfolgen.
    e) In CHAPS gibt es keine Regelung für das Cut-off betreffend Zahlungsanweisungen an Dritte.

27. Was sind die Betriebszeiten (Ortszeit) von TARGET?
    a) 07.00–18.00 Uhr
    b) 09.00–19.00 Uhr
    c) 08.30–15.45 Uhr
    d) 00.30–16.30 Uhr

6. Reconciliation of Nostro Accounts

In this chapter you learn ...
- when nostro accounts should be reconciled.
- about the objectives of nostro account reconcilitation.
- about the two stages of nostro reconcilitation.
- when the reconcilitation of nostro accounts should be completed.
- how to handle failed payments.
- why reconcilitation should be automated.
- when payment of interest and penalties should be made.
- why it is important to require all other nostro account users to comply with the same operational standards

6.1. Task Description

The reconciliation of nostro accounts is the final stage of the settlement process. A bank should begin reconciliation **as soon as it receives notification from their nostro banks** that payments are received. If possible, reconciliation should be performed before the close of the currency's payments system enabling the bank to detect any problems in cash settlement and resolve them on settlement date. Typically however, a bank does not receive notification from its nostro banks until one day after settlement, which does not allow them to correct any payment error on settlement date.

The main objective of nostro reconciliation is to ensure **optimal liquidity management** in order to avoid idle balances and high overdraft costs.

Nostro reconciliation comprises **two stages**:

- The day before value day, the **back office determines all incoming and outgoing payments as well as the netting amounts**. This allows the bank to accurately fund its nostro accounts.
- After settlement, **expected Cash-Flows are compared to actual cash movements**. If any differences are detected the back office must contact the nostro bank or counterparty to resolve the difference. Typical causes for differences are wrong trade data capture, erroneous settlement instructions or that the nostro bank made an error. The counterparty that did the mistake has either to pay good value or compensation.

6.2. Best Practices – Nostro Reconciliation

BP1

Full reconciliation should be completed **as early as possible**. Banks should establish capabilities for intra-day processing of nostro confirmations of receipts, thereby allowing the reconciliation process to start before the end of the day. The sooner reconciliations are performed the better can a bank fund its nostro accounts and spot possible problems. The latest date for reconciliation should be the **day following settlement date**.

6. Abgleich (Reconciliation) der Nostrokonten

In diesem Kapitel lernen Sie ...

- wann der Abgleich der Nostrokonten durchgeführt wird.
- worin der Zweck des Abgleichs der Nostrokonten besteht.
- in welchen Phasen der Abgleich der Nostrokonten in der Praxis abläuft.
- wann der Abgleich der Nostrokonten abgeschlossen sein soll.
- wie man mit fehlenden Zahlungen umgehen soll.
- warum der Abgleich automatisiert werden sollte.
- wann Strafzahlungen und Verzugszinsen zu bezahlen sind.
- warum es wichtig ist, von allen Bereichen, die Nostrokonten verwenden, dieselben operationalen Standards zu verlangen.

6.1. Aufgaben der Reconciliation

Der Abgleich der Nostrokonten steht am Schluss des Settlementprozesses. Der Abgleich beginnt, **sobald die Bank von ihrer Nostrobank über Zahlungseingänge/-ausgänge informiert wird.** Im Idealfall sollte der Abgleich erfolgen, bevor das Zahlungssystem schließt. Da aber Banken üblicherweise erst am Tag nach dem Settlement von Nostrobanken informiert werden, besteht keine Möglichkeit, schon am Settlement-Tag eventuell auftretende Fehler zu klären.

Der Zweck des Abgleichs besteht darin, ein **optimales Liquiditätsmanagement** zu haben, sodass sowohl Liquiditätsüberschüsse (mit Zinsentgang) als auch Liquiditätsengpässe (mit hohen Überzugszinsen) vermieden werden.

Der Abgleich der Nostrokonten umfasst **zwei Phasen:**

- Am Valuta vorliegenden Tag werden die zu **erwartenden Zahlungseingänge und -ausgänge bestimmt bzw. die Nettingbeträge für die Nostrokonten ermittelt.** Auf diese Weise kann die Bank ihre Nostrokonten mit der notwendigen Liquidität ausstatten.
- Nach dem Settlement werden die **tatsächlichen Geldflüsse mit den ursprünglichen Prognosen verglichen.** Werden Abweichungen festgestellt, so werden die Ursachen ermittelt und die Abweichungen behoben. Typische Fehlerquellen sind falsch erfasste Handelsdaten, fehlerhafte Settlementinstruktionen oder Fehlverhalten der Nostrobanken. Jener Partner, auf dessen Seite der Fehler liegt, muss entweder eine Zahlung mit guter Valuta oder eine Kompensationszahlung leisten.

6.2. Anforderungen an die Reconciliation

A1

Der Abgleich soll **so früh wie möglich abgeschlossen** werden. Es sollten Systeme installiert werden, mit denen die Intraday-Verarbeitung von Nostro-Empfangsbestätigungen und damit ein Abgleich der Konten möglich ist. Je früher der Abgleich stattfindet, umso besser kann die Bank das Nostrokonto adäquat ausstatten und Probleme erkennen. Der **späteste Termin** zum Abgleich ist der **Tag nach dem Settlement Date.**

BP2

A bank should be capable of receiving automated feeds of nostro statements and implement **automated nostro reconciliation systems**.

The access to the bank's as well as to the nostro bank's settlement data should be automated. Automated reconciliation compares confirmed payments and receipts from the nostro bank against expected cash movements from the back office. In case of a **"ledger credit"** less funds were paid than expected, i.e. a payment has probably not been paid. A **"ledger debit"** means that more funds were paid than received, i.e. a payment has probably not been received yet. In any case, escalation procedures should be initiated and in place if differences are detected.

BP3

Management should establish procedures for detecting nonreceipts of payments and for notifying appropriate parties of their occurrences. Escalation **procedures** should be in place **for dealing with counterparties who fail to make payments**.

Missing payments should be prioritised by currency, amount and counterparty rating at any other internal classification criteria.

Follow-up **procedures for tracking down nonreceipts** should be established. Outstanding payments from counterparties should be reported to credit management, trading and senior management in order to possibly review limits or to limit the trading relationship. Recurring failures to settle on time as well as regular overdrafts of nostro accounts may indicate that the counterparty is an increased credit risk.

Generally, the payment of interest and penalties should be prompt.

BP4

The bank should **require all other users of its nostro account to comply with the same operational standards** as foreign exchange users.

This principle is important if other departments (e.g. fixed income, emerging markets, derivatives) also use nostro accounts. Without consistent standards, it would be then very difficult to establish a systematic and efficient settlement.

Summary

The reconciliation of nostro accounts is the final stage of the settlement process. A bank should begin reconciliation as soon as it receives notification from their nostro banks that payments have been received. The main objective of nostro reconciliation is to ensure optimal liquidity management in order to avoid idle balances and high overdraft costs.

Nostro reconciliation comprises two stages. The day before value day, the back office determines all incoming and outgoing payments as well as the netting amounts. After settlement, expected cashflows are compared with actual cash movements.

Full reconciliation should be completed as early as possible.

A bank should be capable of receiving automated feeds of nostro statements and implement automated nostro reconciliation systems.

Management should establish procedures for detecting nonreceipt of payments and for notifying the relevant parties. Escalation procedures should be in place for dealing with counterparties who fail to make payments.

A2

Es sollte ein **automatisches Abgleichsystem** eingeführt werden und die **automatische Übertragung von Zahlungsbestätigungen der Nostrobank** möglich sein.

Der Zugriff auf eigene Settlementdaten und jene der Nostrobank soll automatisiert sein. Automatische Reconciliation vergleicht bestätigte und bei der Nostrobank eingegangene Zahlungen mit den im Backoffice erwarteten Zahlungen. Bei einer **„Buchgutschrift"** wurde weniger als erwartet bezahlt, d.h., wahrscheinlich wurde eine Zahlung nicht geleistet. Bei einer **„Buchlastschrift"** ist wahrscheinlich eine Zahlung nicht eingegangen. Im Falle von Abweichungen sollte ein Krisenmanagement existieren.

A3

Das Management soll Verfahren etablieren, mit deren Hilfe möglichst früh fehlende Zahlungen entdeckt und damit die betroffenen Parteien kontaktiert werden können. Es sollten **Maßnahmen für das Verhalten gegenüber Partnern** vorhanden sein, **die nicht bezahlen.**

Fehlende Zahlungen sind nach Währung, Betrag und Kreditrating des Partners oder anderer interner Kriterien zu reihen.

Ein **Verfahren zur Verfolgung fehlender Zahlungseingänge** sollte entwickelt werden. Offene Zahlungseingänge sind dem Kreditmanagement, dem Handel und der Geschäftsleitung zu melden, um eventuell die Limits oder die gesamte Geschäftsbeziehung zum Partner zu prüfen. Regelmäßige Überziehungen des Nostrokontos sind ein Anzeichen, dass die Gegenpartei ein erhöhtes Kreditrisiko darstellt.

Strafzahlungen oder Verzugszinsen sind sofort zu bezahlen.

A4

Die Bank soll **von allen Bereichen, die Nostrokonten verwenden, dieselben operationalen Standards verlangen.**

Dieser Grundsatz ist dann wichtig, wenn neben dem FX-Bereich auch andere Abteilungen Emerging Markets, Derivate, Bonds oder Nostrokonten verwenden. Ohne einheitliche Standards ist es schwer, ein systematisches und effizientes Settlement zu schaffen.

Zusammenfassung

Der Abgleich der Nostrokonten steht am Schluss des Settlementprozesses. Der Abgleich beginnt, sobald die Bank von ihrer Nostrobank über Zahlungseingänge/-ausgänge informiert wird. Der Zweck des Abgleichs besteht darin, ein optimales Liquiditätsmanagement zu haben, sodass sowohl Liquiditätsüberschüsse (mit Zinsentgang) als auch Liquiditätsengpässe (mit hohen Überzugszinsen) vermieden werden.

Der Abgleich der Nostrokonten umfasst zwei Phasen. Am Valuta vorliegenden Tag werden die zu erwartenden Zahlungseingänge und -ausgänge bestimmt bzw. die Nettingbeträge für die Nostrokonten ermittelt. Nach dem Settlement werden die tatsächlichen Geldflüsse mit den ursprünglichen Prognosen verglichen.

Der Abgleich soll so früh wie möglich abgeschlossen werden.

Es sollte ein automatisches Abgleichsystem eingeführt werden und die automatische Übertragung von Zahlungsbestätigungen der Nostrobank möglich sein.

Ein Verfahren zur Verfolgung fehlender Zahlungseingänge sollte entwickelt werden. Außerdem sollten Maßnahmen für das Verhalten gegenüber Partnern vorhanden sein, die nicht bezahlen. Strafzahlungen oder Verzugszinsen sind sofort zu bezahlen.

The bank should require all other users of its nostro account to comply with the same operational standards as foreign exchange users.

6.3. Practice Questions

1. What is a nostro account?
   a) a money laundering account
   b) a minimum reserve account with the ECB
   c) an account in the home currency with the correspondent bank
   d) an account with the correspondent bank in the domestic currency of the country where the correspondent bank is located
2. When does reconciliation of the nostro accounts begin?
3. Which of the following best describes the main objective of the nostro reconcilitation function?
   a) to ensure that all receipts of foreign currency are made on time
   b) to ensure effective cash management
   c) the reduce the amounts paid in respect of interest rate claims on late payments
   d) to ensure that expected cash movements tally with the actual movements of currency
4. Which of the following best describes the overall benefits of good cash management?
   a) no overdraft charges
   b) reduced costs
   c) increased interest income
   d) maximized returns on credit balances and minimized risk of overdraft interest charges
5. Explain shortly the two stages of reconciliation of the nostro accounts!
6. Which of the following statements concerning reconciliation of nostro accounts are true?
   a) The day before value date all expected payments should be determined.
   b) The latest due to for the reconcilitation is two days after the settlement date.
   c) Reconciliations should be completed as late as possible.
   d) Capabilities should be established for intra-day processing of confirmations of nostro receipts.
   e) All users of nostro accounts should comply with the same operational standards.
7. What is the most likely cause of an outstanding ledger credit discovered during the reconciliation process?
   a) non-receipt of funds
   b) duplicated payment
   c) failed payment
   d) unexpected receipt of funds
8. You pay USD in a money market transaction with a Spanish bank. Whom will you instruct for payment transaction?
   a) ECB
   b) US correspondent bank
   c) reserve bank Hessen
   d) Spanish correspondent bank

Die Bank soll von allen Bereichen, die Nostrokonten verwenden, dieselben operationalen Standards verlangen.

6.3. Wiederholungsfragen

1. Was ist ein Nostrokonto?
   a) Konto für Geldwäsche
   b) Mindestreservekonto bei der EZB
   c) Konto bei einer Korrespondenzbank im Ausland in der Heimwährung
   d) Konto bei einer Korrespondenzbank im Ausland in der Währung des Landes der Korrespondenzbank
2. Wann beginnt der Abgleich der Nostrokonten?
3. Was ist das Hauptziel des Abgleichs der Nostrokonten?
   a) sicherstellen, dass alle Fremdwährungszahlungen rechtzeitig bezahlt werden
   b) Sicherstellen eines effizienten Cash Managements
   c) Pönalezahlungen für verspätete Zahlungen zu reduzieren
   d) sicherstellen, dass die erwarteten mit den tatsächlichen Geldflüssen übereinstimmen
4. Welcher der folgenden Punkte beschreibt am besten den allgemeinen Vorteil eines guten Cash Managements?
   a) keine Verzugszinsen
   b) reduzierte Kosten
   c) gesteigertes Zinseinkommen
   d) maximale Erträge auf Habensaldo und minimales Risiko von Überziehungszinsen
5. Beschreiben Sie kurz die zwei Phasen beim Abgleich der Nostrokonten!
6. Welche Aussagen treffen auf den Abgleich von Nostrokonten zu?
   a) Am Tag vor der Valuta sollen die erwarteten Zahlungsaus- und -eingänge ermittelt werden.
   b) Der späteste Termin zum Abgleich ist zwei Tage nach dem Settlement Date.
   c) Der Abgleich soll möglichst spät abgeschlossen werden.
   d) Es sollen Systeme installiert werden, die einen Intraday-Abgleich ermöglichen.
   e) Alle Bereiche, die Nostrokonten verwenden, sollen dieselben operationalen Standards verwenden.
7. Was ist die wahrscheinlichste Ursache für eine Bankgutschrift, die beim Abgleich der Nostrokonten entdeckt wird?
   a) keine Zahlung erhalten
   b) doppelte Zahlung geleistet
   c) eine Zahlung nicht geleistet
   d) unerwarteter Zahlungseingang
8. Sie zahlen USD im Rahmen eines Geldmarktgeschäfts mit einer spanischen Bank. Wen werden Sie mit der Zahlungsabwicklung beauftragen?
   a) EZB
   b) US-Korrespondenzbank
   c) Landeszentralbank Hessen
   d) Spanische Korrespondenzbank

9. When should payment of interest and penalties be made?
   a) prompt
   b) at least after 7 days
   c) at least after 30 days
   d) as agreed
10. Why is it important to require all other users of ones nostro account to comply with the same operational standards?

9. Wann sind Strafzahlungen oder Verzugszinsen zu bezahlen?
   a) sofort
   b) spätestens nach sieben Tagen
   c) spätestens nach 30 Tagen
   d) nach Vereinbarung
10. Warum ist es wichtig, dass eine Bank von allen Bereichen, die Nostrokonten verwenden, dieselben operationalen Standards verlangt?

7. Accounting and Financial Control

In this chapter you learn ...
- about accounting tasks with regard to FX transactions.
- how reconciliation between general ledger and back office and trade should be made.
- what should be considered at the daily mark–to-market revaluation.
- how rates and prices should be fed.

7.1. Task Description

Accounting ensures FX-transactions are properly recorded to the balance sheet and income statement. After a trade is executed the data is captured in subsidiary accounts that flow through to the **general ledger** at the end of each day. If this process takes place directly in the trading system, the back office has to verify the P&L figures. Sometimes P&L figures are calculated by the back office as well as by trading. An independent party subsequently verifies the figures. On the next day the financial management verifies the data and passes it to senior management for further analysis.

All positions in the general ledger are **marked-to-market**. Once the position is closed out, realized gains or losses are calculated and reported. **Cash-Flow** movements on settlement date are **calculated** by the **back office** and posted to the general ledger. If there occur any capture errors all entries to sub-ledgers and general ledgers must be corrected.

In order to ensure that sub-ledgers reconcile to general ledger accounts a monthly check of all subsystem accounts and an independent unit undertakes general ledger accounts.

7.2. Best Practices – Accounting and Financial Control

BP1

Systematic reconciliation of the general ledger to the back office and of front office to the back office should be done daily.

Discrepancies have to be resolved immediately after detection. Senior management should be notified of accounting discrepancies to review and update control procedures as needed.

BP2

Daily Profit & Loss and position reconciliations should take place between trading and back office. This control is imperative when all deal entries and adjustments are not passed electronically between front and back office. Differences can refer to positions or market parameters (i.e. prices, rates)

BP3

Positions should be marked-to-market on a daily basis. In less liquid markets banks should obtain independent valuations from other sources.

7. Buchhaltung

In diesem Kapitel lernen Sie ...

- welche Aufgaben die Buchhaltung bei der Verarbeitung von FX-Transaktionen übernimmt.
- wie der Abgleich zwischen Hauptbuch und Backoffice sowie Handel erfolgen sollte.
- was bei der täglichen Mark-to-Market-Bewertung zu beachten ist.
- in welcher Form die Daten importiert werden sollen.

7.1. Aufgaben der Buchhaltung

Die Buchhaltung verarbeitet die FX-Transaktionen in die Bilanzkonten sowie in die G&V. Nach Abschluss des Geschäftes werden die Daten in Unterkonten erfasst, die am Ende jeden Tages **ins Hauptbuch zusammengeführt** werden. Dieser Prozess kann im Handelssystem selbst erfolgen, wobei dann das Backoffice die G&V-Zahlen überprüft. Es können aber auch vom Handel und Backoffice je eine Aufstellung ermittelt werden, die dann von einer unabhängigen Stelle überprüft werden. Das Finanzmanagement überprüft am nächsten Tag die Zahlen und legt sie dem Management vor.

Im Hauptbuch werden die **Positionen kontinuierlich Mark-to-Market bewertet,** bis die Position geschlossen wird. Dann wird der Gewinn bzw. Verlust festgeschrieben.

Die am **Settlement Date** stattfindenden **Cashflows** werden vom **Backoffice berechnet** und direkt in das Hauptbuch übernommen. Wurden bei der Geschäftserfassung Fehler gemacht, die sich auf die Cashflows auswirken, so sind die Korrekturen im Hauptbuch wie in den Unterbüchern durchzuführen.

Um die Abstimmung zwischen Hauptbuch und Unterbüchern zu gewährleisten, wird **einmal im Monat die Konsistenz der Aufzeichnungen in den einzelnen Büchern kontrolliert.**

7.2. Anforderungen an die Buchhaltung

A1

Der Abgleich zwischen Hauptbuch und Backoffice sowie Handel soll in systematischer Form erfolgen, damit das Hauptbuch die aktuelle Lage der Bank korrekt widerspiegelt.

Abweichungen sind sofort nach Entdecken zu beheben. Die Geschäftsleitung ist von Abweichungen zu informieren und hat gegebenenfalls verbesserte Kontrollmechanismen zu installieren.

A2

Die Positionen und die G&V sind jeden Tag zwischen Backoffice und Handel abzugleichen. Diese Kontrolle ist besonders dann erforderlich, wenn keine direkte elektronische Verarbeitung zwischen Handel und Backoffice besteht. Abweichungen können aufgrund unterschiedlicher Positionen oder falsch eingegebener Daten entstehen.

A3

Positionen sind täglich Mark-to-Market zu bewerten. In wenig liquiden Märkten sollten unabhängige Bewertungen durch andere Quellen herangezogen werden.

The following points should be considered, of positions are marked-to-market:

- End of day rates and prices that are used for position valuations should be periodically checked to an independent source, such as market rates screens, other dealers, and broker quotations.
- At least once a month, the bank should check the model's valuation for consistency with other dealer's valuations.
- In illiquid markets (e.g. exotic options), a bank should seek to obtain quotes from other counterparties in the market.
- Management should be aware to the additional risks in illiquid markets and know the procedures to evaluate these positions.

BP4

Trade prices should be independently reviewed to ensure **reasonableness within the market prices** that existed on trade date. This way, capture errors and deals at non-current rates may be detected and unduly enrichment of any counterparty be eliminated.

BP5

Rates and prices should be fed electronically from source systems. Establishing electronic links help to eliminate errors associated with collecting and re-keying the required rates and prices.

Summary

Accounting ensures FX transactions are properly recorded in the balance sheet and income statement. After a trade is executed the data is captured in subsidiary accounts that flow through to the general ledger at the end of each day.

All positions in the general ledger are marked-to-market. Once the position is closed out, realized gains or losses are calculated and reported. Cashflow movements on settlement date are calculated by the back office and posted to the general ledger.

In order to ensure that sub-ledgers reconcile to general ledger accounts a monthly check of all subsystem accounts should be undertaken.

Systematic reconciliation of the general ledger to the back office and of front office to the back office should be done on a daily basis.

Daily Profit & Loss and position reconciliations should take place between trading and back office.

Positions should be marked-to-market on a daily basis.

Trade prices should be independently reviewed to ensure plausibility with market prices on trade date.

Rates and prices should be fed electronically from source systems.

Bei der Mark-to-Market-Bewertung sind folgende Punkte zu beachten:

- Die vom Handel am Tagesende herangezogenen Preise bzw. Zinssätze zur Bewertung der Positionen sind über dritte Quellen (z.B. Handelsschirme, Quotierungen anderer Händler oder Broker) auf ihre Gültigkeit zu prüfen.
- Zumindest einmal im Monat sollte die Bank die Plausibilität der Bewertungen durch ihr Modell prüfen.
- In illiquiden Märkten (z.B. exotischen Optionen) sollte man versuchen, durch Quotierungen von Dritten einen Anhaltspunkt für die Preise zu erhalten.
- Das Management muss sich der Probleme bei der Bewertung illiquider Produkte bewusst sein.

A4

Die gehandelten Preise sind dahingehend zu prüfen, ob sie in der am Handelstag vorhandenen **Preisbandbreite** gelegen sind. Damit sollen Eingabefehler und Geschäfte zu nicht-aktuellen Kursen erkannt werden.

A5

Die Preise und Zinssätze sollen elektronisch von der Datenquelle importiert werden.
Auf diese Weise sollen Fehler bei der Positionsbewertung ausgeschlossen werden, wenn von verschiedenen Systemen Daten als Bewertungsgrundlage herangezogen werden.

Zusammenfassung

Die Buchhaltung verarbeitet die FX-Transaktionen in die Bilanzkonten sowie in die G&V. Nach Abschluss des Geschäftes werden die Daten in Unterkonten erfasst, die am Ende jeden Tages ins Hauptbuch zusammengeführt werden.

Im Hauptbuch werden die Positionen kontinuierlich Mark-to-Market bewertet, bis die Position geschlossen wird. Dann wird der Gewinn bzw. Verlust festgeschrieben. Die am Settlement Date stattfindenden Cashflows werden vom Backoffice berechnet und direkt in das Hauptbuch übernommen.

Um die Abstimmung zwischen Hauptbuch und Unterbüchern zu gewährleisten, wird einmal im Monat die Konsistenz der Aufzeichnungen in den einzelnen Büchern kontrolliert.

Der Abgleich zwischen Hauptbuch und Backoffice sowie Handel soll in systematischer Form erfolgen, damit das Hauptbuch die aktuelle Lage der Bank korrekt widerspiegelt.

Die Positionen und die G&V sind jeden Tag zwischen Backoffice und Handel abzugleichen.

Positionen sind täglich Mark-to-Market zu bewerten.

Die gehandelten Preise sind dahingehend zu prüfen, ob sie in der am Handelstag vorhandenen Preisbandbreite gelegen sind.

Die Preise und Zinssätze sollen elektronisch von der Datenquelle importiert werden, um Fehler zu vermeiden.

7.3. Practice Questions

1. What are accounting tasks with regard to FX transactions?
2. What should be done to ensure that the general ledger has no accounting discrepancies?
3. Which of the following should the accounting department take into consideration when marking a position to market?
   a) Positions should be marked-to-market on a daily basis.
   b) All mentioned points should be considered.
   c) In illiquid markets, independent valuations from other sources should be obtained.
   d) Results of models should be checked at least once a month for consistency.
4. Why should the traded prices be checked by the back office?
   (i)   to ensure that the marked-to-market result is not falsified
   (ii) to identify a transaction with non-current rates
   (iii) for evaluating the performance of the dealer
      a) (ii) and (iii)
      b) (i) and (iii)
      c) (i) and (ii)
      d) only (ii)
      e) All answers are false.
5. How should rates and prices be fed?

7.3. Wiederholungsfragen

1. Welche Aufgaben übernimmt die Buchhaltung bei der Verarbeitung von FX-Transaktionen?

2. Was sollte gemacht werden, damit das Hauptbuch die aktuelle Lage der Bank korrekt widerspiegelt?

3. Was ist beim Mark-to-Market von Positionen in der Buchhaltung zu beachten?
   a) Das Mark-to-Market ist täglich durchzuführen.
   b) Alle angeführten Punkte sind zu beachten.
   c) Bei illiquiden Märkten sollen auch dritte Quellen zur Preisfindung herangezogen werden.
   d) Die Bewertungen der Modelle sollen einmal im Monat auf ihre Plausibilität überprüft werden.

4. Warum sollten die gehandelten Preise im Backoffice überprüft werden?
   (i)   damit das Mark-to-Market-Ergebnis nicht verfälscht wird.
   (ii)   um ein Geschäft zu nicht-aktuellen Kursen zu erkennen.
   (iii) um die Leistung der Händler zu bewerten.
        a) (ii) und (iii)
        b) (i) und (iii)
        c) (i) und (ii)
        d) nur (ii)
        e) Alle Antworten sind falsch.

5. In welcher Form sollten die Daten importiert werden?

8. Money Laundering

In this chapter you learn ...
- what is meant by money laundering.
- about the three stages of money laundering.
- what anti-money laundering measures are recommended by different organisations.
- why an unambiguous identification of the customer is important.
- what measures are necessary to identify the customer.
- which increased diligence should be applied.
- which countries and organisations are members of Financial Action Task Force on Money Laundering (FATF).

Money laundering is the process by which illegally obtained money is given the appearance of having originated from a legitimate source.

Money laundering comprises **three stages**:

- placement
- layering
- integration

In the first stage legal **ways to place illegal money** (e.g. drug trafficking, weapon sales) are looked for. The "black money" is placed in deposits, real estate or other yield-bearing assets. After, the origin of the **money is tried to be disguised by a network of complex transactions**. In the last stage, the **illegal money is integrated** in the legal economy as proceeds from legal business (e.g. sale of real estate).

8.1. Measures against money laundering

The problem of money laundering attracted the attention of many institutions so that there exist many guidelines and recommendations for how to contain money laundering. The first step was the UN convention against Illicit Traffic in Narcotic Drugs and Psychotropic Substances ("**Vienna Convention**") in 1988, followed by the **principles of Prevention of Criminal Use of the Banking System for the Purpose of Money Laundering** issued by the BIS the same year. The most comprehensive catalogue was developed by the **Financial Action Task Force on Money Laundering (FATF)** in 1990. The FATF was founded **1989 on a G-7 summit** and is an inter-governmental body associated with the OECD. The FATF drafted **40 recommendations** (last edition 1996) that deal with

- the role of national legal systems
- the role of financial systems
- the strengthening of international co-operation

in combating money laundering. In the following paragraphs only the recommendations concerning the role of the financial system whose intentions are also reflected in the BIS principles and Codes of Conduct, shall be further analysed.

Customer identification

Financial institutions **should not keep anonymous accounts or accounts in obviously fictitious names**. The counterparty should be identified on the basis of an official and reliable

8. Geldwäsche

In diesem Kapitel lernen Sie ...

- was man unter Geldwäsche versteht.
- aus welchen drei Stufen der Geldwäscheprozess besteht.
- welche Maßnahmen gegen Geldwäsche von verschiedenen Organisationen empfohlen werden.
- warum eine eindeutige Identifikation des Kunden von großer Bedeutung ist.
- welche Maßnahmen zur Identifikation des Kunden notwendig sind.
- welche erweiterten Sorgfaltspflichten unbedingt einzuhalten sind.
- welche Länder bzw. Organisationen Mitglied der Financial Action Task Force on Money Laundering (FATF) sind.

Geldwäsche ist der Prozess, illegale Gelder über Transaktionen in Geld mit dem Anschein legaler Herkunft zu verwandeln.

Im Wesentlichen besteht dieser Prozess aus **drei Stufen:**

- Anlage des Geldes
- Entflechtung des Geldes
- Integration in den legalen Wirtschaftskreislauf

Im ersten Schritt werden **Anlageobjckte** (z.B. Immobilien, Depots) gesucht, in die Schwarzgelder investiert werden können. Anschließend wird durch ein Netzwerk von Finanztransaktionen versucht, den **Ursprung des Geldes nicht länger nachvollziehbar** zu machen. Im dritten Schritt erfolgt die **„Reinigung" der Gelder,** indem aus den mit den illegalen Geldern getätigten Investitionen legale Einkünfte (z.B. Verkauf Immobilien) generiert werden.

8.1. Maßnahmen gegen Geldwäsche

Das Problem Geldwäsche wurde von vielen Seiten erkannt und so entstanden eine Reihe von Maßnahmenkatalogen und Empfehlungen gegen Geldwäsche. Die ersten Bemühungen waren die UN-Konvention gegen den illegalen Handel mit Narkotika und psychotropen Substanzen (**„Wiener Konvention"**) aus dem Jahr 1988 und die **Prinzipien der Bank für Internationalen Zahlungsausgleich.** Das umfangreichste Werk erstellte 1990 die **Financial Action Task Force on Money Laundering (FATF),** eine **1989 auf dem G7-Gipfel gegründete Organisation.** Die FATF formulierte **40 Empfehlungen,** die sich mit

- der Rolle der nationalen Rechtssysteme,
- der Rolle der Finanzinstitutionen und
- der Rolle der internationalen Zusammenarbeit

im Kampf gegen Geldwäsche auseinandersetzen. Im Folgenden sollen nur die Empfehlungen für das Verhalten der Finanzinstitute erläutert werden, die sinngemäß auch in den BIZ-Empfehlungen und den Ausführungen der Codes of Conduct Niederschlag gefunden haben.

Eindeutige Identifikation des Kunden

Es sollten **keine anonymen oder auf offensichtlich fiktiven Namen lautende Konten** geführt werden. Finanzinstitutionen sollten Kunden anhand offizieller und verlässlicher Aus-

identifying document. The identity of clients, either occasional or usual, should be recorded when establishing business relations or conducting transactions. Due diligence is particularly required if

- accounts on passbooks are opened
- a fiduciary transaction is entered into
- a safe deposit box is rented
- large cash transactions are performed

In case of **legal entities**, banks should if necessary, verify the legal existence and structure of the customer (e.g. obtain a proof of incorporation from public register) or verify that any person purporting to act on behalf of the customer is so authorized and identify that person.

Further recommendations include:

- Financial institutions should take **reasonable measures to obtain information about the true identity of the person** on whose behalf an account is opened or a transaction conducted if there are any doubts as to whether these clients or customers are acting on their own behalf, for example, in the case of domiciliary companies (i.e. institutions, corporations, foundations, trusts, etc. that do not conduct any commercial or manufacturing business or any other form of commercial operation in the country where their registered office is located).
- Financial institutions should **maintain, for at least five years, all necessary records on transactions**, both domestic or international, to enable them to comply swiftly with information requests from the competent authorities. Such records must be sufficient to permit reconstruction of individual transactions (including the amounts and types of currency involved if any) so as to provide, if necessary, evidence for prosecution of criminal behaviour.
- Financial institutions should **keep records on customer identification** (e.g. copies or records of official identification documents like passports, identity cards, driving licences or similar documents), account files and business correspondence for at least five years after the account is closed. These documents should be available to domestic competent authorities in the context of relevant criminal prosecutions and investigations.

Increased Diligence

- Financial institutions should **pay special attention to all complex, unusual large transactions**, and all unusual patterns of transactions, which have no apparent economic or visible lawful purpose. The background and purpose of such transactions should, as far as possible, be examined, the findings established in writing, and be available to help supervisors, auditors and law enforcement agencies.
- If financial institutions **suspect that funds stem from a criminal activity**, they should be **required to report promptly their suspicions to the competent authorities**.
- Financial institutions should develop **programs against money laundering**. These programs should include, as a minimum:
  - the development of internal policies, procedures and controls, including the designation of compliance officers at management level, and adequate screening procedures to ensure high standards when hiring employees;
  - an ongoing employee training programme;
  - an audit function to test the system.

weispapiere identifizieren und die Identität ihrer Gelegenheits- bzw. Stammkunden aufzeichnen, wenn Geschäftsbeziehungen hergestellt werden. Besondere Sorgfalt ist bei der

- Eröffnung von Konten oder Sparbüchern,
- Abwicklung von Treuhandgeschäften,
- Miete von Schließfächern und
- Durchführung bedeutender Bargeschäfte

anzuwenden.

Bei **juristischen Personen** müssen Finanzinstitutionen die juristische Existenz des Kunden überprüfen (z.B. Prüfung, ob im Handelsregister eingetragen) oder sich der Vollmacht der im Namen der juristischen Person handelnden Person versichern.

- Finanzinstitute sollen **angemessene Maßnahmen** ergreifen, um die **wirkliche Identität der Personen,** in deren Namen ein Konto eröffnet wurde oder ein Geschäft abgewickelt wurde („Geschäft mit einer dritten Partei"), **festzustellen,** wenn Zweifel bestehen, ob diese Kunden wirklich im eigenen Namen handeln (z.B. Unternehmen wie Stiftungen oder Gesellschaften, die in dem Land, in dem sich ihr Sitz befindet, keine gewerblichen, industriellen oder sonstigen Handelsgeschäfte ausüben).
- **Aufzeichnungen über Geschäfte** (z.B. involvierte Devisenbeträge und Währungen) im In- und Ausland sollten **mindestens fünf Jahre aufbewahrt** werden. Die Aufzeichnungen sollten so beschaffen sein, dass auf behördliche Anfrage individuelle Geschäfte rekonstruiert werden und gegebenenfalls als Beweismaterial eingesetzt werden können.
- **Aufzeichnungen über die Identität des Kunden** (z.B. Reisepass, Personalausweis), Kontoauszüge und Geschäftskorrespondenz sollen mindestens fünf Jahre nach der Schließung des Kontos aufbewahrt werden.

Erweiterte Sorgfaltspflichten

- Alle **komplexen, ungewöhnlich bedeutenden Geschäfte** sowie alle **unüblichen Geschäftsschemen,** die keinen klar ersichtlichen wirtschaftlichen oder gesetzmäßigen Zweck verfolgen, sind gegebenenfalls auf ihren **Hintergrund zu untersuchen** und die Geschäfte zu dokumentieren.
- Finanzinstitute, die den Verdacht haben, dass **Kapital aus einer strafbaren Handlung** stammen könnte, sollten diesen **Verdacht den Behörden melden.**
- Finanzinstitute sollen **Programme zur Bekämpfung der Geldwäsche** entwickeln, die folgende Punkte umfassen:
  - Entwicklung interner Politiken, Verfahren und Kontrollen, einschließlich der Bestimmung von Personen auf Führungsebene, die für die Einhaltung der Verfahren sorgen, und geeigneter Verfahren, die bei der Personenauswahl höchste Ansprüche gewährleisten.
  - Weiter- und Fortbildungsprogramm für Mitarbeiter
  - Interne Revisionsstelle zur Überprüfung der Wirksamkeit des Systems

Scope

The FATF states explicitly that the recommendations should not followed by the **banking sector** only but also by all **other financial institutions**, such as brokers or money exchange booths.

EXCURSUS: Members of FATF

The FATF comprises **34 countries** and **two international organisations**:

Countries	International Organisations
Argentina	European Commission
Australia	Gulf Cooperation Council
Austria	
Belgium	
Brasil	
Canada	
China	
Denmark	
Germany	
Finland	
France	
Greece	
Hong Kong	
Iceland	
India	
Ireland	
Italy	
Japan	
Luxembourg	
Mexico	
Netherlands	
New Zealand	
Norway	
Portugal	
Republic of Korea	
Russia	
Singapore	
South Africa	
Spain	
Sweden	
Switzerland	
Turkey	
United Kingdom	
United States	

Wirkungsbereich

Die FATF sieht explizit vor, dass ihre Empfehlungen über den **Bankensektor** hinaus auch **alle anderen Finanzinstitute** umfassen soll. Dazu zählen z.B. Broker oder Wechselstuben.

EXKURS: Mitglieder des FATF

Zu der FATF zählen aktuell **34 Länder** und **zwei internationale Organisationen:**

Länder	Internationale Organisationen
Argentinien	Europäische Kommission
Australien	Kooperationsrat der Golfstaaten
Belgien	
Brasilien	
China	
Dänemark	
Deutschland	
Finnland	
Frankreich	
Griechenland	
Großbritannien	
Hongkong	
Indien	
Irland	
Island	
Italien	
Japan	
Kanada	
Luxemburg	
Mexico	
Neuseeland	
Niederlande	
Norwegen	
Österreich	
Portugal	
Republik Korea	
Russland	
Schweden	
Schweiz	
Singapur	
Spanien	
Südafrika	
Türkei	
Vereinigte Staaten	

Summary

Money laundering is the process by which illegally obtained money is given the appearance of having originated from a legitimate source.

Money laundering comprises three stages: placement, layering and integration.

The first step against mone laundering was the UN convention against Illicit Traffic in Narcotic Drugs and Psychotropic Substances ("Vienna Convention") in 1988. The most comprehensive catalogue was developed by the Financial Action Task Force on Money Laundering (FATF) in 1990. The FATF was founded 1989 on a G-7 summit. The FATF comprises 34 countries and two international organisations. The FATF has drafted 40 recommendations dealing with the role of national legal systems, the role of financial systems and the strengthening of international co-operation.

Financial institutions should not keep anonymous accounts or accounts in obviously fictitious names. In case of legal entities, banks should verify the legal existence and structure of the customer (e.g. obtain proof of incorporation from a public register) or verify that any person purporting to act on behalf of the customer is so authorized and identify that person.

Financial institutions should pay special attention to all complex, unusually large transactions, and all unusual patterns of transactions, which have no apparent economic or lawful purpose. If financial institutions suspect that funds stem from criminal activity, they should be required to report promptly their suspicions to the relevant authorities.

The FATF states explicitly that recommendations should be observed not only by the banking sector but by all other financial institutions such as brokers.

8.2. Practice Questions

1. Which of the following best defines money laundering?
   a) the discovery of illicit earnings
   b) the production of counterfeit money
   c) the process of transferring illegal money abroad
   d) the process of converting illegal money into legitimate money through a network of transactions
2. In which order, first to last, do the three stages of money laundering take place?
   a) placement, layering, integration
   b) layering, integration, placement
   c) integration, placement, layering
   d) placement, integration, layering
3. Which of the following is the stage in the money laundering process when illegal money is fed into the economic system?
   a) integration
   b) clearing
   c) layering
   d) placement
4. Which UN convention deals with the problem of money laundering?

Zusammenfassung

Geldwäsche ist der Prozess, illegale Gelder über Transaktionen in Geld mit dem Anschein legaler Herkunft zu verwandeln.

Im Wesentlichen besteht dieser Prozess aus drei Stufen: Anlage des Geldes, Entflechtung des Geldes und Integration in den legalen Wirtschaftskreislauf.

Die ersten Bemühungen, Maßnahmenkataloge gegen Geldwäsche zu entwickeln, waren die UN-Konvention gegen den illegalen Handel mit Narkotika und psychotropen Substanzen („Wiener Konvention") aus dem Jahr 1988 und die Prinzipien der Bank für Internationalen Zahlungsausgleich. Das umfangreichste Werk erstellte 1990 die Financial Action Task Force on Money Laundering (FATF), eine 1989 auf dem G7-Gipfel gegründete Organisation. Zu der FATF zählen aktuell 34 Länder und zwei internationale Organisationen. Die FATF formulierte 40 Empfehlungen, die sich mit der Rolle der nationalen Rechtssysteme, der Rolle der Finanzinstitutionen und der Rolle der internationalen Zusammenarbeit auseinandersetzen.

Es sollten keine anonymen oder auf offensichtlich fiktiven Namen lautende Konten geführt werden. Bei juristischen Personen müssen Finanzinstitutionen die juristische Existenz des Kunden überprüfen (z.B. Prüfung, ob im Handelsregister eingetragen) oder sich der Vollmacht der im Namen der juristischen Person handelnden Person versichern.

Alle komplexen, ungewöhnlich bedeutenden Geschäfte sowie alle unüblichen Geschäftsschemen, die keinen klar ersichtlichen wirtschaftlichen oder gesetzmäßigen Zweck verfolgen, sind gegebenenfalls auf ihren Hintergrund zu untersuchen und die Geschäfte zu dokumentieren.

Die FATF sieht explizit vor, dass ihre Empfehlungen über den Bankensektor hinaus auch alle anderen Finanzinstitute umfassen soll.

8.2. Wiederholungsfragen

1. Welche Definition trifft auf Geldwäsche zu?
   a) Aufdecken von Schwarzgeldern
   b) Produktion von Falschgeld
   c) Prozess, illegale Gelder ins Ausland zu transferieren
   d) Prozess, illegale Gelder über Transaktionen in Geld mit scheinbar legaler Herkunft umzuwandeln
2. In welcher Reihenfolge findet der Prozess der Geldwäsche statt?
   a) Anlage des Geldes, Verschleierung, Integration
   b) Verschleierung, Integration, Anlage des Geldes
   c) Integration, Anlage des Geldes, Verschleierung
   d) Anlage des Geldes, Integration, Verschleierung
3. Mit welchem Schritt wird im Rahmen der Geldwäsche das illegale Geld in den Wirtschaftskreislauf gebracht?
   a) Integration
   b) Clearing
   c) Entflechtung
   d) Anlage
4. Welche UN-Konvention befasst sich mit dem Problem der Geldwäsche?

5. You have been asked to process a deal for a foundation that does not run any commercial operation in the country where the registered office is located. What should you do?
   a) refuse the deal
   b) process the deal
   c) contact the FATF
   d) take measures to identify the background of the foundation
6. What does FATF stand for?
7. Which of the following topics is NOT covered by the 40 FATF recommendations?
   a) role of financial institutions
   b) role of international co-operation
   c) establishment of an international drug enforcement body
   d) role of national legal systems
8. Which of the following types of payment normally demands extra diligence and review procedures?
   a) a variation margin payment to your futures clearer
   b) a payment being made to a third party
   c) value tomorrow USD payment
   d) value spot JPY payment
9. Which of the following transactions can be used for money laundering activities?
   a) fiduciary transactions
   b) purchase of real estate
   c) opening name accounts
   d) large cash deals
10. Which institutions should observe the FATF recommendations?
11. Which of the following countries are NOT member of the FATF?
    a) Iceland
    b) Austria
    c) Finland
    d) Uruguay
    e) New Zealand
    f) Turkey
    g) Ukraine
    h) Poland
12. Which points should a a financial institute's anti-money laundering program include?

5. Es soll ein Geschäft für eine Stiftung durchgeführt werden, von der keine Geschäftstätigkeit im Land ihres Sitzes bekannt ist. Was würden Sie tun?
    a) Geschäft ablehnen
    b) Geschäft durchführen
    c) sich bei der FATF erkundigen
    d) Maßnahmen zur Identifikation des Kunden ergreifen
6. Wofür steht die Abkürzung FATF?
7. Welches Gebiet wird von den 40 Empfehlungen gegen Geldwäsche der FATF NICHT geregelt?
    a) Rolle der Finanzinstitutionen
    b) Internationale Zusammenarbeit
    c) Einrichtung einer internationalen Drogenbehörde
    d) Gestaltung nationaler Rechtssysteme
8. Welche der folgenden Transaktionen sollte normalerweise zu zusätzlichen Überprüfungen führen?
    a) Zahlung einer Variation Margin
    b) Zahlung an dritte Parteien
    c) USD-Geschäft mit Valuta morgen
    d) JPY-Spot-Zahlung
9. Welche der folgenden Transaktionen eignen sich zur Geldwäsche?
    a) Treuhandgeschäfte
    b) Immobilienkauf
    c) Eröffnung von Namenskonten
    d) Bargeschäfte
10. Welche Institutionen sollen die Empfehlungen der FATF beachten?
11. Welche der folgenden Länder sind NICHT Mitglied der FATF?
    a) Island
    b) Österreich
    c) Finnland
    d) Uruguay
    e) Neuseeland
    f) Türkei
    g) Ukraine
    h) Polen
12. Welche Punkte sollte ein Programm zur Bekämpfung von Geldwäsche eines Finanzinstituts enthalten?

9. Examples for Settlement Risk

In this chapter you learn ...
- which risks have become apparent by the failure of Bankhaus Herstatt.
- which two problems were highlighted by the appointment of a liquidator for BCCI.
- about the impacts of the Barings Bank breakdown.
- about the learnings of the Barings crisis.

9.1. The Failure of Bankhaus Herstatt

The failure of Bankhaus Herstatt on **26 June 1974** illustrated the existence of credit, liquidity and replacement risk in the settlement process. Many counterparties had **already irrevocably paid Deutsche Mark** to Herstatt when the Bundesaufsichtsamt für Kreditwesen ordered the bank into **liquidation** in the afternoon of June 26. Since the German Interbank payment system was already closed the payments could not be revoked while the correspondent banks to stopped paying USD from Herstatt's account. This left the counterparties with credit and **liquidity risk for FX-spot deals** and additionally with **replacement risk for FX-forward trades**.

9.2. Bank of Credit and Commercial International (BCCI)

The **appointment of a liquidator** for BCCI on **5 July 1991** highlighted **two problems** in the settlement process:

- The existence of bilateral credit limit systems
- The right time to close down a bankrupt bank

An institution had delivered the GBP in a GBP/USD transaction but lost the USD amount because the USD payment was queued in the **CHIPS system due to full bilateral credit limits**. Because of this delay the correspondence bank could still cancel the payment instruction and wait for the liquidator's instructions.

Similarly, a Japanese bank lost the principal amount in a USD/JPY deal because it had already delivered the JPY when BCCI was put under supervision. The key problem was that under Luxembourg Law the appointment of a liquidator could take only place within the normal business day of the Court. Therefore, it was not possible to wait with the closedown of the bank until all relevant deals were settled.

The problem to close a bank without causing settlement will worsen because payment systems intend to have overlapping operating hours, thus creating a situation where at no time all payment systems are closed.

9. Beispiele für Settlementrisiko

In diesem Kapitel lernen Sie ...

- welche Risiken beim Zusammenbruch des Bankhauses Herstatt schlagend wurden.
- welche zwei Problemfelder im Settlement die Bestellung eines Liquidators für BCCI deutlich machte.
- welche Auswirkungen der Zusammenbruch der Barings Bank hatte.
- welche Lehren aus der Barings-Krise gezogen werden konnten.

9.1. Zusammenbruch des Bankhauses Herstatt

Der Zusammenbruch des Bankhauses Herstatt am **26. Juni 1974** illustrierte anhand von **USD/DEM-Kassa- und Termingeschäften,** wie Kredit-, Liquiditäts- und Wiederbeschaffungsrisiko im Rahmen des Settlements zum Problem werden können. Viele Banken hatten bereits ihre DEM-Zahlungen unwiderruflich angewiesen, als am Nachmittag des 26. Juni die Herstatt Bank ihre **Geschäftstätigkeit einstellte** und ein **Konkursverfahren** über sie von der Bankaufsicht angeordnet wurde. Da das deutsche Interbank-Zahlungsverkehrssystem bereits geschlossen war, konnten die ausgewiesenen Zahlungen an Herstatt nicht mehr rückgängig gemacht werden, während die Korrespondenzbank von Herstatt alle USD-Transaktionen einstellte. Dadurch wurden für die **geleisteten DEM-Zahlungen Kredit- und Liquiditätsrisiko** schlagend und bei den **offenen Termingeschäften** das **Wiederbeschaffungsrisiko** wirksam.

9.2. Bank of Credit and Commercial International (BCCI)

Die **Bestellung eines Liquidators** für BCCI am **5. Juli 1991** machte **zwei Problemfelder im Settlement** deutlich:

- Kreditlimitsysteme im Zahlungssystem und
- den richtigen Zeitpunkt zur Schließung einer insolventen Bank zu finden

Ein Institut erfüllte seine Verpflichtung aus einer GBP/USD-Transaktion, musste aber den Ausfall des USD-Betrages hinnehmen, weil der Zahlungsauftrag der amerikanischen Korrespondenzbank von BCCI aufgrund eines **bilateralen Kreditlimits im CHIPS-System** so lange warten musste, dass die Korrespondenzbank zeitgemäß stornieren konnte, die Anweisungen des Konkursverwalters von BCCI in London abzuwarten.

Ähnlich erging es einer japanischen Bank, die ihre JPY-Verpflichtung in einem USD/JPY-Kontrakt erfüllte, aber keine USD erhielt, weil zwischenzeitlich BCCI unter die Verwaltung der Aufsichtsbehörde gestellt wurde. Der Kern des Problems war, dass der Konkursverwalter nach luxemburgischem Recht nur während der üblichen Geschäftszeiten des Gerichts bestellt werden konnte.

Dieser Aspekt wird sich noch verschlimmern, da die Zahlungssysteme darauf achten, immer überlappend geöffnet zu sein, sodass immer ein Zahlungssystem geöffnet sein wird.

9.3. Barings Crisis

At the end of February 1995 Barings Bank collapsed and a bank that was member of the ECU Clearing wanted to revoke its payment. The bank learnt that the rules of EUR clearing did not permit this and could not reverse the transaction. At the end of the day the bank had an **overall debt position** in the system. It had to cover this position by borrowing from a long bank, so enabling the settlement between the participating banks.

This example demonstrates that clearing participants must have a thorough **understanding of the rules of the clearing system** (e.g. cut-off times) and that rather **minor events can put the settlement at risk** (only 1% of the payments had to do with Barings). If the bank had not covered its debt position the end-of-day settlement would have been frustrated since the ECU-Clearing was based on a PVP mechanism.

Summary

Crisis	Problem	Risk
Bankhaus Herstatt	Payments systems open and close at different times in different time zones	Credit risk Liquidity risk Replacement risk
BCCI	Limit systems in netting services 24-hour trading	Credit risk Replacement risk
Barings Bank	Netting services in a clearing system	Liquidity risk

9.4. Practice Questions

1. Which risks have become apparent by the failure of Bankhaus Herstatt in 1974?
2. Which two problems were highlighted by the appointment of a liquidator for BCCI on 5 July 1991?
3. What are the impacts of the Barings Bank failure in February 1995 for a member bank of ECU-Clearing?
4. What are the learnings of the Barings crisis?

9.3. Barings-Krise

Ende Februar 1995 brach die Barings Bank zusammen und eine am ECU-Clearing beteiligte Bank wollte ihre Zahlung widerrufen. Da dies aber im Rahmen des Clearings nicht mehr möglich war, kam die Bank in eine **Nettoschuldnerposition,** die sie nur durch rasche kurzfristige Kreditaufnahmen decken konnte. Ansonsten hätten keine Zahlungen zwischen den Clearing-Teilnehmern erfolgen können.

Dieser Vorfall zeigt einerseits, dass die **Teilnehmer am Clearing die genauen Vorschriften** (z.B. Buchungsschluss) **kennen** müssen, und andererseits, wie **relativ kleine Ereignisse** (die Clearingzahlungen hatten zu weniger als 1% mit Barings zu tun) **das gesamte Settlement gefährden** können. Hätte die betroffene Bank ihren Liquiditätsengpass nicht durch die kurzfristige Geldaufnahme noch decken können, hätte das gesamte Clearing aufgrund eines PVP-Systems nicht funktioniert.

Zusammenfassung

Bank	Problem	Risiko
Bankhaus Herstatt	Zahlungsverkehrssysteme öffnen und schließen zu unterschiedlichen Zeiten	Liquiditätsrisiko Kreditrisiko Wiederbeschaffungsrisiko
BCCI	Limitsysteme bei Nettozahlungssystemen	Kreditrisiko Wiederbeschaffungsrisiko
	24-Stunden-Handel	
Barings Bank	Nettingdienste beim Clearing	Liquiditätsrisiko

9.4. Wiederholungsfragen

1. Welche Risiken wurden beim Zusammenbruch des Bankhauses Herstatt für die geleisteten DEM-Zahlungen und bei den offenen Termingeschäften schlagend?
2. Welche zwei Problemfelder im Settlement machte die Bestellung eines Liquidators für BCCI am 5. Juli 1991 deutlich?
3. Welche Auswirkungen hatte der Zusammenbruch der Barings Bank Ende Februar 1995 für eine am ECU-Clearing beteiligte Bank?
4. Welche Lehren konnten aus der Barings-Krise gezogen werden?

PART V: The Model Code – International Code of Conduct for Financial Markets

TEIL V: Der Model Code – Internationaler Verhaltenskodex für die Finanzmärkte

A common aim of all codes of conduct is to promote efficient market practices by encouraging high standards of conduct and professionalism. Yet, the largely unregulated global foreign exchange market thrived and expanded for decades in the major international centres without any written code or guidelines on market practice or conduct.

The situation lasted until the early 1970's when the "O'Brien Letter" was issued to authorised banks in London by the Bank of England. This short, but timely and useful, first circular dealt with a number of dealing issues and provided much needed clarification and recommendations on some market practices and conventions, which were expanded upon in later editions. From 1980, the emergence of new markets and instruments such as financial futures, interest rate swaps, options and other derivatives employed by treasury and capital markets dealers further underlined the urgency of the situation.

Therefore, in May 2000 the Model Code was launched at ACI's International Congress in Paris. The Model Code has been compiled in response to an urgent international need amongst dealers and brokers operating in the OTC foreign exchange, money and derivatives markets. The Committee for Professionalism (CFP) of ACI – The Financial Markets Association has become increasingly aware of this need through regular contact with its membership of over 24,000 dealers, brokers, mid and back office staff in over 80 countries.

The Model consists of eleven chapters. The subjects range from business hours, personal conduct issues, back office, payments and confirmations, disputes/differences/mediation/compliance, authorisation, documentation/telephone taping, broker and brokerage via dealing practice and risk management through to market terminology and definitions.

The Model Code has been distributed in over 100 countries. Already, the regulators in 17 countries have adopted the Model Code in whole or in part with ongoing discussions taking place in an additional 35 countries. There is a growing demand for both the hard and soft copies.

Included in the following exams:
- **ACI Dealing Certificate**
- **ACI Operations Certificate**

Eine gemeinsame Aufgabe aller Codes of Conduct ist die Förderung effizienter Marktpraktiken durch hohe Verhaltens- und Professionalitätsstandards. Dennoch expandierte der weitgehend unregulierte globale Devisenmarkt über Jahrzehnte in den großen Finanzzentren, ohne dass es hierfür einen geschriebenen Kodex oder schriftliche Richtlinien für die Praktiken und das Verhalten auf diesem Markt gab.

Diese Situation bestand bis Anfang der 70er-Jahre, als die Bank of England autorisierten Banken in London den „O'Brien Letter" übergab, der sich mit einer Reihe von handelsrelevanten Fragen befasste und eine dringend nötige Klarstellung und Empfehlungen für eine Reihe von Marktpraktiken und Konventionen lieferte. Seit 1980 unterstreicht das Aufkommen neuer Märkte und die Anwendung neuer Instrumente, wie beispielsweise Financial Futures, Zinsswaps, Optionen und anderer Derivate, durch Devisen- und Kapitalmarkthändler den dringende Handlungsbedarf auf diesem Gebiet.

Daher wurde im Mai 2000 auf dem Internationalen ACI-Kongress in Paris erstmals ein einheitlicher Model Code eingeführt, der einen neuen Ansatz zur Verankerung von Marktpraxis und Verhaltensregeln für die globalen OTC-Devisen-, Geld- und Derivatemärkte darstellt. Dem Committee for Professionalism (CfP) von ACI – The Financial Markets Association – wurde diese Notwendigkeit durch seine regelmäßigen Kontakte mit den ihm angehörenden über 24.000 Händlern, Brokern sowie im Middle- und Backoffice-Bereich Beschäftigten in über 80 Ländern zunehmend bewusst.

Der Model Code umfasst einen weiten Geltungsbereich, der sich unter anderem auf Over-the-Counter-Märkte und Produkte, die von den Treasury-Abteilungen internationaler Banken gehandelt wurden, erstreckt. Aufgrund der Vielfalt von Märkten und Produkten, die heute von Banken gehandelt werden, ergeben sich zwangsläufig Überschneidungen in Bereichen, für die bereits eigene individuelle oder lokale Marktcodes existieren. Der Model Code legt großes Gewicht auf das Verhalten und die Praxis in dem kritischen Bereich des Quotierens von Handelspreisen und dem Abschluss von Geschäften. Gleichgütig, für welches Geschäft eine Quotierung gilt, muss in jedem Fall derselbe hohe Qualitätsmaßstab an Handelspraxis und Integrität gewahrt bleiben.

Der Model Code besteht aus elf Kapiteln. Die Themenbereiche reichen von Handelszeiten, persönlichem Verhalten, Backoffice, Zahlungen und Bestätigungen, Konflikten/Differenzen/Vermittlung/Erfüllung/Autorisierung/Dokumentation/Telefonaufzeichnungen, Brokern und Provisionen über Handelspraxis und Risikomanagement bis hin zu Marktterminologie und Definitionen.

Der Model Code wurde in mehr als 100 Ländern vertrieben. In 17 Ländern haben die Regulierungsstellen den Model Code bereits vollständig oder teilweise übernommen, in weiteren 35 Ländern wird dies derzeit diskutiert. Die Nachfrage sowohl nach der gedruckten als auch nach der elektronischen Fassung wächst kontinuierlich.

Prüfungsrelevant für:

- **ACI Dealing Certificate**
- **ACI Operations Certificate**

1. General facts about the Model Code

In this chapter you learn ...
- who has developed the Model Code.
- how the Model Code is structured.
- which financial instruments are included in the Model Code.
- which points are usually covered in standardised legal frameworks.
- about the main frame contracts.
- about the key aspects of internal trading activity surveillance.
- about the minimum requirements for FX deals.

The Model Code consists of **11 chapters** that deal systematically with all trading-related matters and market terminology.

1.1. History and aims

In May 2000, the **Committee for Professionalism (CfP) of the ACI** presented the new **Model Code** aiming to establish a world-wide code of conduct in the foreign exchange and money markets. The Model Code is based on the latest version of the ACI Code of Conduct and strives to embrace all main provisions of the recognised local Codes of Conduct.

The following Codes of Conduct were considered:

- ACI Code of Conduct (revised 1998)
- The Guidelines for Foreign Exchange Trading Activities (1995)
- The London Code of Conduct (revised by the FSA in 1999)
- The French Code of Conduct (1999)
- The Singapore Guide to Conduct and Market Practices for Treasury Activity (revised 1998)
- The Code of Conduct of the Tokyo Foreign Exchange Market Committee (1998)

1.2. Scope

The Model Code covers the following OTC and off-balance-sheet instruments:

- FX Spot and forward
- FX Options
- Money market deals
- Interest rate options
- FRAs
- Interest rate and Cross Currency Swaps
- Gold and precious metals

1.3. Documentation

Over time the international dealing business has developed a **standardised legal framework** for different products with the aim of creating a **uniform arrangement and documentation of all deals** and to ensure the smooth settlement of deals.

1. Allgemeines zum Model Code

In diesem Kapitel lernen Sie ...

- von wem der Model Code entwickelt wurde.
- wie der Model Code aufgebaut ist.
- welche Finanzinstrumente der Model Code umfasst.
- welche Punkte üblicherweise in Rahmenverträgen geregelt werden.
- die wichtigsten Standardverträge kennen.
- die wesentlichen Prüfungsschwerpunkte der internen Revision kennen.
- welche Mindestanforderungen an das Betreiben von Handelsgeschäften bestehen.

Der Model Code ist in **elf Kapitel** gegliedert, die sich systematisch mit Bereichen des Handels befassen und die Marktterminologie beschreiben.

1.1. Entwicklung und Ziele

Im Mai 2000 präsentierte das **Committee for Professonalism (CfP) des ACI** erstmals den **Model Code** mit dem Ziel, einen weltweit akzeptierten Verhaltenskodex im Geld- und Devisenhandel zu etablieren. Die Bestimmungen und Ausführungen der wichtigsten Codes of Conduct in der jeweiligen Letztfassung wurden zusammengeführt und zu einem einheitlichen Regelwerk geformt.

Folgende Codes bildeten dabei die Grundlage:

- ACI Code of Conduct (Fassung 1998)
- The Guidelines for Foreign Exchange Trading Activities (1995)
- The London Code of Conduct (1999)
- The French Code of Conduct (1999)
- The Singapore Guide to Conduct and Market Practices for Treasury Activity (1998)
- The Code of Conduct of the Tokyo Foreign Exchange Market Committee (1998)

1.2. Wirkungsbereich

Der Model Code gilt für folgende OTC (Over the Counter) und außerbilanzielle Geschäfte bzw. Instrumente:

- FX-Spot und Forward
- FX-Optionen
- Geldmarktgeschäfte
- Zinsoptionen
- FRAs
- Zins- und Cross Currency Swap
- Gold und Edelmetalle

1.3. Dokumentation

Im internationalen Handel haben sich **Rahmenverträge bzw. standardisierte Verträge** für die verschiedenen Produkte entwickelt. Zweck dieser Rahmenverträge ist die **einheitliche Gestaltung und Dokumentation aller Geschäfte**, um eine reibungslose Abwicklung zu gewährleisten.

Standardised legal frameworks usually cover the following points:

- Contents of contract: Definition of instruments or the group of instruments that are covered by the standardised contract
- Payments: When is interest on arrears payable; who pays taxes, fees and duties; settlement of money flows?
- Bank days: What is the delivery date, on which days can delivery not be made due to holidays?
- Reference rate: Fixing of the reference rate; what to do if the reference rate is not available; rounding of the reference rate
- Interest calculation: Determining interest calculation methods
- Termination: Reasons for premature cancellation of contracts, e.g. non-compliance, non-payments, and payment arrears
- Redemption: Claims in case of cancellation
- Final payment: Refund modalities for outstanding amounts
- Cover: Proceedings for covering the deals; rules governing when securities can be called upon
- Other: Presentation of business reports; contract changes; transfer of rights and duties to third parties; non-exercise, closing-out
- Appendix: Costs; opening of accounts; booking; settlement methods, business methods, closing confirmation

Deals are additionally confirmed with a closing paper that includes data on the trading date, value date, reference rate, volume, currency, term, interest fixing and account numbers applicable to the partners in the deal.

The main frame contracts

Product		Master Agreement
FRA		FRABBA (FRA British Bankers Association)
		German Master Agreement
		ISDA (International Swaps and Derivatives Association)
Interest Rate Swap		
		ISDA (International Swaps and Derivatives Association)
Cross Currency Swap		BBAIRS (British Bankers Association IRS)
		German Master Agreement
Cap/Floor		
FX Spot		
FX Swap		IFEMA
FX Outright		FEOMA
FX Options		ICOM
Repo		TBMA *)/ISMA GMRA **)
		German Master Agreement

*) TBMA (The Bond Market Association): former PSA (until 09/1997)

Rahmenverträge regeln üblicherweise folgende Punkte:

- Vertragszweck: Bestimmung der Instrumente oder der Instrumentengruppe, auf die der Rahmenvertrag zutrifft.
- Zahlungen: Wann fallen z.B. Verzugszinsen an, wer zahlt etwaige Steuern, Gebühren und Abgaben, Saldierung der Zahlungsströme?
- Bankarbeitstage: An welchen Tagen wird geliefert bzw. an welchen Tagen wird nicht geliefert?
- Basissatz: Mitteilung vom Basissatz; Vorgangsweise, wenn der Basissatz nicht zur Verfügung steht; Rundung der Basissätze
- Zinsberechnung: Bestimmung der Zinsberechnungsmethoden
- Beendigung: Gründe für die vorzeitige Kündigung: z.B. Nichterfüllung, Nichtzahlung, Verzug
- Schadenersatz: Ansprüche im Falle der Kündigung
- Abschlusszahlung: Rückerstattungsmodalitäten von ausstehenden Beträgen
- Deckung: Vorgangsweise bei Unterlegung der Geschäfte; Regelungen, wann die Sicherheiten verwendet werden dürfen
- Sonstiges: Vorlage der Geschäftsberichte; Änderungen des Vertrages; Übertragung der Rechte und Pflichten, Nichtausübung; Closing Out
- Anhang: Kosten; Kontoeröffnung; Buchung; Abrechnungsmethoden; Geschäftsarten; Schlussbestätigung

Einzelabschlüsse werden nur noch mit einem Schlusszettel bestätigt, auf dem für beide Partner Handelstag, Valutatag, Basissatz, Volumen, Währung, Laufzeit, Zinsfestsetzung und Kontoverbindungen des Geschäfts dokumentiert sind.

Die wichtigsten Standardverträge

Produkt	Rahmenvertrag
FRA	FRABBA (FRA British Bankers Association) Deutscher Rahmenvertrag ISDA (International Swaps and Derivatives Association)
Interest Rate Swap	
Cross Currency Swap	ISDA (International Swaps and Derivatives Association) BBAIRS (British Bankers Association IRS)
Cap/Floor	Deutscher Rahmenvertrag
FX-Spot	
FX-Swap	IFEMA
FX-Outright	FEOMA
FX-Optionen	ICOM
Repo	TBMA *)/ISMA GMRA **) Deutscher Rahmenvertrag

*) TBMA (The Bond Market Association): vormals PSA (bis 09/1997)

**) GMRA = General Master Repurchase Agreement

) GMRA = General Master Repurchase Agreement

The fact that 19 payment systems exist for the Euro prompted the **EBF (European Banking Federation)** to publish recommendations regarding the routing of Euro payments for same day value between clearing banks. The recommendations were drawn up by the so-called Heathrow Group, a group of 30 member banks within the EBF.

1.4. Key Aspects of Internal Surveillance of Trading Activities

The following chapter outlines the important points that should be checked by internal surveillance. The listed questions serve as examples, though many more questions can be formulated.

- **Structure and operation of deals**
  - Does documentation of the current organisational structure exist?
  - Are there written and explicit working instructions?
  - Do up-to-date job descriptions exist?
  - Is there a functional separation of dealing and settlement?

- **Blank and contractual affairs**
  - Is any minimum information for each deal required?
  - Has the law department or anyone else reviewed the signed standardised contracts regarding their legal validity?

- **Conclusion of deals**
  - Are dealing rates systematically monitored and reviewed as to their plausibility?
  - Is there a defined procedure if deals are concluded at non-current market rates?

- **Evaluation**
  - Are evaluation prices defined by authorities that are independent of the dealing section?
  - Do the instruments included in the trading books refer to the same market risk?
  - Are the structures of complex instruments correctly resolved?
  - Are internal deals concluded at market rates?
  - Is there a clear distinction between real and fictitious deals?
  - Does an unambiguous assignment to hedging and trading deals exist?

- **Risk management**
  - Is the risk measurement system in use documented?
  - Do written risk limits exist?
  - Is the market risk measured by an authority that is independent of the dealing section?
  - Has a documented procedure for the implementation of new products been established?
  - Does a consistent system for pricing, evaluation and risk measurement exist?
  - Are counterparty limits currently described and checked at the right time?
  - Are all products included in the counterparty limit?

Die **EBF (European Banking Federation)** veröffentlichte zusätzlich Richtlinien, wie zwischen den Clearing-Banken EUR-Zahlungen abgewickelt werden sollten, insbesondere unter dem Blickwinkel, dass 19 Zahlungssysteme für den EUR existieren. Die Richtlinien wurden von der sogenannten Heathrow-Group verfasst, einer Gruppe von 30 Banken innerhalb der EBF.

1.4. Prüfungsschwerpunkte der internen Revision für Handelsaktivitäten

Im folgenden Kapitel werden die wesentlichen Punkte, die von der internen Revision zu prüfen sind, skizziert. Die angeführten Fragen verstehen sich als Beispiele und erheben keinen Anspruch auf Vollständigkeit.

- **Ablauf- und Aufbauorganisation des Handels**
  - Gibt es eine aktuelle Dokumentation der Organisationsstruktur?
  - Gibt es schriftliche und explizite Arbeitsanweisungen?
  - Existieren aktuelle Arbeitsplatzbeschreibungen?
  - Gibt es eine funktionale Trennung der Handels- und Abwicklungsbereiche?

- **Formular- und Vertragswesen**
  - Existieren interne Anforderungen für die Mindestangaben bei Einzelgeschäftsabschlüssen?
  - Wurden die unterschriebenen Rahmenverträge von der Rechtsabteilung oder sonstigen Stellen auf ihre Rechtsgültigkeit überprüft?

- **Einzelgeschäftsabschlüsse**
  - Gibt es systemmäßige Überprüfungen der Plausibilität der Abschlusskurse?
  - Existiert eine vorgegebene Vorgangsweise bei Geschäftsabschlüssen mit marktunüblichen Preisen?

- **Bewertung**
  - Erfolgt die Festlegung der Bewertungspreise von einer vom Handel unabhängigen Stelle?
  - Beziehen sich die in den Handelsbüchern enthaltenen Instrumente auf das gleiche Marktrisiko?
  - Werden die Strukturen von komplexen Instrumenten richtig aufgelöst?
  - Erfolgen die internen Geschäftsabschlüsse zu marktüblichen Preisen?
  - Gibt es klare und definierte Abgrenzungen zwischen realen und fiktiven Geschäften?
  - Ist die Zuordnung zu Hedging- und Trading-Geschäften eindeutig?

- **Risikomanagement**
  - Gibt es eine aktuelle Dokumentation der verwendeten Systematik der Risikomessung?
  - Existieren schriftliche Risikolimite?
  - Wird das Marktrisiko von einer vom Handel unabhängigen Instanz gemessen?
  - Gibt es eine dokumentierte Vorgangsweise bei der Implementierung von neuen Produkten?
  - Gibt es eine einheitliche Systematik bei Pricing, Bewertung und Risikomessung?
  - Existiert eine zeitnahe Darstellung und Kontrolle der Kontrahentenlimite?
  - Sind alle Produkte im Kontrahentenlimit enthalten?

   – Is there a documented procedure in case counterparty limits are exceeded?

- **Other**
  - Does the internal reporting system incorporate current information concerning market and counterparty risk?
  - Are concluded deals correctly and systematically reported to the official authorities?

1.5. Minimum Requirements for FX Deals

Regarding the trading book, the German Federal Supervisory Authority for Credit Affairs took the initiative in October 1995 and released **organisational minimum requirements**. In the same way, the total responsibility of a bank's management board is interpreted by bank laws in many other countries. This means that trading losses due to a lack of organisation can straightaway be deemed a violation of due diligence.

   The basic idea behind the minimum requirement is to assure that the trading department of a bank is technically and professionally able to run a **conclusive and controllable risk management system** that follows the latest scientific findings in business administration.

   Minimum requirements focus on the following areas:

a) A framework that must be established by the management
b) Risk management requirements
c) Organisation of trading activities

a) A framework that must be established by the management

The management must be able to judge the trading risks and must be informed once a month about the bank's risk position. Within the management **one senior manager should be in charge of trading activities**. He or she should receive daily reports on the various risk positions.

   The management cannot delegate the following tasks:

- Limiting total risk
- Written documentation of frameworks
- (products, markets, counterparties, documentation, limits, proceedings in case of exceeding the limit, risk management techniques, personal and technical equipment, internal monitoring and surveillance, internal accounting, worker responsibility)
- Qualification and behaviour of employees (employees in the risk controlling department and management must have extensive product knowledge and have to understand the handling of risks in detail); dealing; settlement; accounting; supervision; surveillance and organisation; obligation to report major manipulations to the supervisory authorities.

b) Risk management requirements

Risk controlling has to assess the loss potential of all deals. Moreover, a risk management system which is able to **handle the loss potential** must be established.

   A risk system should meet the following requirements:

- All business areas of a bank have to be covered

– Gibt es eine dokumentierte Vorgangsweise beim Überschreiten der Kontrahentenlimite?

- **Sonstiges**
  – Enthält das interne Berichtswesen aktuelle Informationen über Markt- und Kontrahentenrisiken?
  – Werden die getätigten Geschäfte in den Meldungen gegenüber den offiziellen Stellen richtig und systematisch dargestellt?

1.5. Mindestanforderungen an das Betreiben von Handelsgeschäften

Im Oktober 1995 hat das deutsche Bundesaufsichtsamt für das Kreditwesen Initiative ergriffen und für das Handelsbuch **organisatorische Mindestanforderungen** erlassen. In diesem Sinne wird auch in anderen Ländern die Gesamtverantwortung der Geschäftsleitung einer Bank durch die Bankgesetzgebung interpretiert. Das bedeutet, dass Verluste im Handel aufgrund mangelhafter Organisation als Verletzung der Sorgfaltspflicht verstanden werden.

Die Mindestanforderungen stellen sicher, dass ein Institut für die Geschäftssparte Handel fachlich und technisch in der Lage ist, ein dem letzten Stand der Bankbetriebswirtschaftslehre entsprechendes **organisiertes, nachvollziehbares und kontrollierbares Risikomanagement** zu betreiben.

Im Einzelnen konzentrieren sich die Mindestanforderungen auf:

a) Rahmenbedingungen, welche die Geschäftsleitung vorgeben muss
b) Anforderungen an das Risikomanagement
c) Organisation der Handelstätigkeit

a) Rahmenbedingungen, welche die Geschäftsleitung vorgeben muss

Der Gesamtvorstand muss den Risikogehalt der Handelsgeschäfte beurteilen können. Einmal im Monat wird er über die Risikoposition der Bank informiert. In der Geschäftsleitung ist ein „**Handelsvorstand**" zu nominieren. Er wird täglich über den Risikogehalt der Geschäfte unterrichtet.

Nicht delegierbare Aufgaben der Geschäftsleitung sind:

- Begrenzung des Gesamtrisikos
- schriftliche Festlegung der Rahmenbedingungen (Produkte, Märkte, Kontrahenten, Dokumentation, Limits, Reaktion bei Limitüberschreitung, Risikomessverfahren, personelle und technische Ausstattung, interne Kontrolle und Überwachung, internes Rechnungswesen, Mitarbeiterverantwortung)
- Qualifikation und Verhalten der Mitarbeiter (umfassende Produkt- und Steuerungskenntnisse sind für Mitarbeiter im Risikocontrolling und Management erforderlich), Handeln, Abwicklung, Rechnungswesen, Überwachung, Revision und Organisation; Meldepflicht wesentlicher Manipulationen an die Aufsichtsbehörde

b) Anforderungen an das Risikomanagement

Das **Risikocontrolling** muss das Verlustpotenzial aller Handelsgeschäfte erheben. Darüber hinaus ist ein Risikomanagement zur **Steuerung des Verlustpotenzials** einzurichten.

Folgende Anforderungen werden an das Risikosystem gestellt:

- Alle Geschäftsbereiche der Bank sind zu erfassen.

- The method has to be described in detail and must be subject to continuous improvement
- With the help of worst-case scenarios loss potentials should be assessed and presented to the management

The **Capital Adequacy Directive** moulds these requirements for risk management of banks into a tangible framework.

c) Organisation of trading activities

Here, the chief principle is the strict functional separation into the following areas.

Management

				Senior manager in charge of trading

SETTLEMENT	TRADING

ACCOUNTING	SUPERVISION (Risk controlling)	SURVEILLANCE

Trading, at least, should be functionally separated from other areas. This separation has also to be ensured in PC programs. Guidelines for trading and risk handling must be set by an independent authority.

These rules of conduct listed in the minimum requirements are also covered by the ACI Code of Conduct.

Summary

The Model Code consists of 11 chapters and was presented by the Committee for Professionalism (CfP) of the ACI, aiming to establish a world-wide code of conduct in the foreign exchange and money markets. The Model Code covers the following OTC and off-balance-sheet instruments: FX spot and forward, FX options, money market deals, interest rate options, FRAs, interest rate and cross currency swaps, and gold and precious metals.

Over time, international traders have developed a standardised legal framework for different products with the aim of creating a uniform arrangement and documentation of all deals and to ensure the smooth settlement of deals. The fact that 19 payment systems exist for the euro prompted the EBF (European Banking Federation) to publish recommendations regarding the routing of euro payments for same-day value between clearing banks.

Regarding the trading book, the German Federal Supervisory Authority for Credit Affairs went ahead in October 1995 and released organisational minimum requirements. Minimum requirements focus on the following areas: a framework that must be established by the management, risk management requirements and organisation of trading activities.

Within management one senior manager should be in charge of trading activities. He or she should receive daily reports on the various risk positions. Risk controlling has to assess the loss potential of all deals. Moreover, a risk management system which is able to handle the loss potential must be established. Trading must be functionally separated from other areas.

- Die Methodik ist detailliert zu dokumentieren und fortlaufend weiter zu verbessern.
- Zur Auslotung des Verlustpotenzials sind Worst-Case-Szenarien zu skizzieren und die Ergebnisse der Geschäftsleitung nahezubringen.

Die **Kapitaladäquanzrichtlinie** gibt den Anforderungen an das Risikomanagement einer Bank eine konkrete Form.

c) Organisation der Handelstätigkeit

Oberster Grundsatz ist die funktionale Trennung folgender Bereiche:

Gesamtvorstand

					HANDELS-VORSTAND

ABWICKLUNG	HANDEL

BUCHHALTUNG	ÜBERWACHUNG (Risikocontrolling)	REVISION

Mindestanforderung ist die **funktionale Trennung des Handels von den anderen Bereichen.** Diese Trennung ist auch in den EDV-Programmen sicherzustellen. Vorgaben an Handel und Risikosteuerung sind von einer unabhängigen Stelle einzugeben.

Die Mindestanforderungen als Verhaltensregeln des Handels sind im Model Code des ACI festgehalten.

Zusammenfassung

Der Model Code ist in elf Kapitel gegliedert und wurde im Mai 2000 vom Committee for Professonalism (CfP) des ACI erstmals mit dem Ziel, einen weltweit akzeptierten Verhaltenskodex im Geld- und Devisenhandel zu etablieren, präsentiert. Der Model Code gilt für folgende Finanzinstrumente: FX-Spot und Forward, FX-Optionen, Geldmarktgeschäfte, Zinsoptionen, FRAs, Zins- und Cross Currency Swap und Gold und Edelmetalle.

Im internationalen Handel haben sich Rahmenverträge bzw. standardisierte Verträge für die verschiedenen Produkte mit dem Zweck einer einheitlichen Gestaltung und Dokumentation aller Geschäfte zur Gewährleistung einer reibungslosen Abwicklung entwickelt. Die EBF (European Banking Federation) veröffentlichte zusätzlich Richtlinien, wie zwischen den Clearing-Banken EUR-Zahlungen abgewickelt werden sollten.

Im Oktober 1995 hat das deutsche Bundesaufsichtsamt für das Kreditwesen Initiative ergriffen und für das Handelsbuch organisatorische Mindestanforderungen erlassen. Im Einzelnen konzentrieren sich die Mindestanforderungen auf Rahmenbedingungen, welche die Geschäftsleitung vorgeben muss, Anforderungen an das Risikomanagement und die Organisation der Handelstätigkeit.

In der Geschäftsleitung ist ein „Handelsvorstand" zu nominieren, der täglich über den Risikogehalt der Geschäfte unterrichtet wird. Das Risikocontrolling muss das Verlustpotenzial aller Handelsgeschäfte erheben. Darüber hinaus ist ein Risikomanagement zur Steuerung des Verlustpotenzials einzurichten. Mindestanforderung bei der Organisation der Handelstätigkeit ist die funktionale Trennung des Handels von den anderen Bereichen.

1.6. Practice Questions

1. Which of the following statements is FALSE?
    a) The Model Code consists of 11 chapters.
    b) The ACI Model Code is published by the CfP of ACI.
    c) The ACI Model Code sets out the practicalities of dealing in each and every financial instrument.
    d) The ACI Model Code is not legally binding.
    e) The ACI Model Code sets out the manner and spirit in which FX and money market business should be conducted.
2. Which financial instruments are covered by the Model Code?
    a) FX spot
    b) Repos
    c) T-bonds
    d) CDs
    e) Cross currency swaps
3. Institutions should make every effort to enter internationally recognised agreements. On which terms and conditions should FX options be based?
    a) ICOM, FEOMA
    b) BBAIRS, ISDA
    c) FRABBA, ICOM
    d) ISDA, FRABBA
4. Institutions should make every effort to enter internationally recognised agreements. On which terms and conditions should interest rate swaps be based?
    a) BBAIRS, ISDA
    b) FRABBA, ICOM
    c) ISDA, FRABBA
    d) ICOM, FEOMA
5. What is the aim of standardised legal frameworks in international trading?
6. Which points are usually covered in standardised legal frameworks?
7. What should be made sure by the organisational minimum requirements published by the German Federal Supervisory Authority for Credit Affairs in October 1995?
8. What are the management's duties in risk management?
    a) risk management requirements
    b) review of limits, policies and procedures
    c) approval of limit excesses and risk exposures
    d) All answers are true.
9. What are the requirements for the risk management of a bank?
10. Who is responsible for checking the activities of the trading staff at banks and brokers?
    a) dealer
    b) management
    c) central bank
    d) ACI

1.6. Wiederholungsfragen

1. Welche der folgenden Aussagen ist FALSCH?
   a) Der Model Code ist in elf Kapitel gegliedert.
   b) Der ACI Model Code wird vom CfP des ACI veröffentlicht.
   c) Der ACI Model Code definiert alle Usancen von jedem Finanzinstrument.
   d) Der ACI Model Code versucht nicht, die rechtlichen Angelegenheiten jedes Finanzinstruments zu behandeln.
   e) Der ACI Model Code definiert die Art und Einstellung, mit der im FX- und Geldmarkt Geschäfte gemacht werden sollen.
2. Welche Instrumente werden vom Model Code behandelt?
   a) FX-Kassa
   b) Repos
   c) T-Bonds
   d) CDs
   e) Cross Currency Swaps
3. Institutionen sollen sich bei Geschäften so gut wie möglich an internationale Rahmenverträge halten. Welche Verträge können für FX-Optionen herangezogen werden?
   a) ICOM, FEOMA
   b) BBAIRS, ISDA
   c) FRABBA, ICOM
   d) ISDA, FRABBA
4. Institutionen sollen sich bei Geschäften so gut wie möglich an internationale Rahmenverträge halten. Welche Verträge können für Zinsswaps herangezogen werden?
   a) BBAIRS, ISDA
   b) FRABBA, ICOM
   c) ISDA, FRABBA
   d) ICOM, FEOMA
5. Welchen Zweck haben Rahmenverträge bzw. standardisierte Verträge im internationalen Handel?
6. Welche Punkte werden üblicherweise in Rahmenverträgen geregelt?
7. Was stellen die im Oktober 1995 vom deutschen Bundesaufsichtsamt für das Kreditwesen erlassenen organisatorischen Mindestanforderungen für das Betreiben von Handelsgeschäften sicher?
8. Welche der folgenden Aufgaben sollte die Geschäftsleitung im Rahmen des Risikomanagements übernehmen?
   a) Errichtung der Rahmenbedingungen für das Risikomanagement
   b) Überprüfung von Limits, Methoden und Abläufen
   c) Zustimmung zu Limitüberschreitungen und Risikopositionen
   d) Alle Antworten sind richtig.
9. Welche Anforderungen werden an das Risikomanagement einer Bank gestellt?
10. Wem unterliegt die Kontrolle der Aktivitäten des Personals im Handel bei Banken und Brokern?
    a) Händler
    b) Management
    c) Notenbank
    d) ACI

11. What does the Model Code recommend regarding separation of back and front office?
    a) It is not necessary.
    b) A separation is only necessary for derivatives dealing.
    c) A separation in content is absolutely essential, a physical separation is recommended.
    d) Back office functions must be centralised.

11. Was ist der Standpunkt des Model Codes zur Trennung von Back- und Frontoffice?
    a) Es ist nicht notwendig.
    b) Eine Trennung ist nur im Derivativgeschäft erforderlich.
    c) Eine inhaltliche Trennung ist immer notwendig, eine räumliche empfehlenswert.
    d) Backoffice-Funktionen müssen zentral zusammengefasst sein.

2. Business hours

In this chapter you learn ...

- about the recommendations of the Model Code for trading after normal hours.
- what should be considered when installing answerphones in the trading room.
- what should be considered at 24 hours trade.
- about the official opening and closing times in the currency markets.
- what the Model Code recommends concerning bank holidays.
- about the Model Code recommendations for stop-loss orders.
- what should be considered at position parking.
- about the Model Code recommendations for market disruptions.

2.1. After hours/24 hours and off-premises dealing

Deals transacted after normal hours or from off premises should **only be undertaken with the express approval of management** who should issue clear written guidelines to their staff on the kinds of deals which are permitted and the limits applicable to such trades, specifying their normal trading hours.

Management should also list the names of the dealers authorised to deal off premises or after hours transactions and stipulate the procedure for the prompt reporting and recording thereof. Where **answer phone equipment** is used for instant reporting and recording, it should be installed and located in such a way that reported transactions could not subsequently be erased without senior management approval. The use of mobile phones within the dealing room, except when used in an emergency, is not considered good practice.

It would be prudent to have an **unofficial close for each trading day** against which end of day positions can be monitored or revalued, thus avoiding problems with determining intraday and overnight limits.

2.2. Market opening and closing

Trades transacted prior to 5:00 AM Sydney time, whether direct or via a broker, are done so under conditions not considered to be normal market conditions or market hours. Thus the official range in currency markets will be set from **5:00 AM Sydney time on Monday morning**, all year round. The recognised closing time for the currency markets is **on Friday 5:00 PM New York time** all year round.

2.3. New bank holidays/special holidays/market disruption

New bank holidays or non-business/clearing days may be announced by the authorities in various centres. Such announcements of a non-business/clearing day ("unscheduled holiday") may be made within a very short time period preceding the originally agreed settlement date. In order to ensure a smooth and efficient functioning of the market, and bearing in mind these holidays are often unforeseen, clear market practice and procedures should be in place.

2. Handelszeiten

> **In diesem Kapitel lernen Sie ...**
>
> - welche Empfehlungen der Model Code für den Handel außerhalb der regulären Geschäftszeiten bzw. Banken gibt.
> - was bei der Installation von Telefonanrufbeantwortern im Handelsraum zu beachten ist.
> - was beim 24-Stunden-Handel zu beachten ist.
> - wann die offizielle Beginn- und Schlusszeit für Währungsmärkte ist.
> - welche Vorgangsweise der Model Code bei Bankfeiertagen empfiehlt.
> - welche Empfehlungen der Model Code zu Stop-Loss-Orders gibt.
> - was bei Position Parking zu beachten ist.
> - welche Vorgangsweise der Model Code bei Marktunterbrechungen empfiehlt.

2.1. Handel außerhalb der regulären Geschäftszeiten bzw. Bank/ 24-Stunden-Handel

Sollten von einem Händler Transaktionen außerhalb der Geschäftszeiten und/oder in Räumlichkeiten außerhalb der Bank getätigt werden, bedarf dies der **ausdrücklichen Genehmigung des Managements.** Für die Dokumentation und Bestätigung dieser Geschäfte sind Regeln und Vorkehrungen aufzustellen. Dazu gehört unter anderem die Verpflichtung, Bestätigungen der Geschäfte sofort an geeignete Personen in der Bank zu senden sowie die Geschäftspartner über jene Personen zu informieren, die außerhalb der Geschäftsräumlichkeiten Geschäfte machen dürfen.

Im Handelsraum können **Telefonanrufbeantworter** installiert werden, auf die Händler die Bedingungen der Geschäfte, die sie außerhalb des Handelsraumes machen, sprechen können. Entsprechende **Sicherheitsvorkehrungen** sind zu treffen, damit die Aufzeichnungen nicht ohne Zustimmung der Geschäftsleitung gelöscht werden können.

Um Probleme mit der Behandlung von Risikolimiten (speziell dem Intraday und Overnightlimit) zu vermeiden, sollte ein **interner, inoffizieller Handelsschluss für jeden Tag** festgelegt werden, an dem die Positionen überprüft und bewertet werden.

2.2. Beginn und Ende der Handelswoche

Jedes Geschäft, das direkt oder über einen Broker vor 5.00 Uhr früh, Sydney-Zeit, abgeschlossen wurde, wurde außerhalb der Handelszeiten und unter nicht marktüblichen Umständen geschlossen. Daher ist die offizielle Beginnzeit für Währungsmärkte **Montagmorgen 5.00 Uhr, Sydney-Zeit**. Die offizielle Schlusszeit ist **Freitag, 17.00 Uhr, New-Yorker-Zeit.**

2.3. Neue Bankfeiertage/Spezielle Feiertage/Marktstörungen

Neue Bankfeiertage oder geschäftsfreie Tage bzw. Tage für Verrechnungsprozesse werden möglicherweise von den Behörden in den verschiedenen Zentren festgelegt. Die Bekanntgabe von solchen geschäftsfreien Tagen bzw. Tagen für Verrechnungsprozesse („Unscheduled Holiday") kann eventuell auch erst sehr kurz vor dem ursprünglichen Abwicklungstag erfolgen. Zur Sicherung der reibungslosen und effizienten Funktion des Marktes und angesichts der Tatsache, dass diese geschäftsfreien Tage häufig unvorhersehbar fixiert werden, sollten eine klare Marktpolitik und Verfahrensregelungen vorhanden sein.

In the event of a country or a state declaring a new national bank holiday or any other occurrence which would prevent settlement of banking transactions on a specific date, the following procedures are accepted as market practice for adjusting the settlement date of outstanding currency transactions maturing on that date:

- The affected parties should agree to adjust the exchange rate according to the prevailing relevant forward mid-rate
- Value dates in foreign exchange transactions will not be split other than in cases where both parties agree or, where local practice allows for split delivery such as in certain Islamic countries.
- The affected parties should agree to adjust the exchange rate according to the prevailing relevant forward mid-rate

2.4. Stop-loss orders

The terms under which such orders are accepted should be **explicitly identified and agreed between the parties concerned**, specifying any time validity or constraints, and be within any management criteria on such orders. Any dealer handling such an order must have adequate lines of communication with the counterparty for use in the event of an extreme price/rate movement or other unusual situation.

In accepting a stop-loss order, an institution assumes an obligation to make every reasonable effort to execute the order promptly ("best effort basis"). However, there is **no fixed-price guarantee** to the counterparty unless otherwise agreed by both parties in writing.

Should a dispute arise between institutions as to whether an order should have been executed, it should be borne in mind that whichever source is used to verify the market range, a completely accurate record may be difficult to obtain. Brokers can only be used as an information source, since a broking company represents only a trading range seen from within the institution, which may not be indicative of the entire market range. Therefore, information form all important and relevant sources should be canvassed and treated with discretion and professional caution.

2.5. Position parking

Management should not allow the parking of deals or positions with a counterparty and with the understanding to repatriate the dealing position at a given moment and at historical rates. Position parking can either lead to a **distorted risk position** or be abused for tax avoiding activities.

2.6. Market disruption

There are instances where the parties are prevented from performing their obligation under a transaction due to an event, which was not foreseeable at the time the transaction was entered into and which is beyond the parties' control. These include: capital controls, illegality or impossibility of performance, acts of God, illiquidity, etc.

Where there are instances of general market disruption caused by sudden events such as extreme weather or other unforeseen developments, **local regulators or central banks may intervene** with the publication of applicable procedures including interest rates to be implemented to cover interrupted settlement.

Für den Fall neu eingeführter Bankfeiertage oder anderer öffentlicher Feiertage, die eine Abwicklung des Geschäftes nicht zulassen, sind die folgenden Verfahren anzuwenden, um den Abwicklungstag ausstehender und an diesem Tag fällig werdender Devisengeschäfte entsprechend anzupassen:

- Im Falle von „Unscheduled Holidays" ist es marktübliche Praxis, Geschäfte, die an einem Bankfeiertag fällig sind, bis zum nächsten Geschäftstag zu verlängern, sofern nicht gegenteilige, bilaterale Vereinbarungen für solche Situationen von den beiden Parteien getroffen wurden.
- Es gibt kein Splitting der Valuta bei Devisengeschäften, es sei denn, dies wird von beiden Parteien so vereinbart, oder lokale Gepflogenheiten, beispielsweise in islamischen Ländern, lassen eine getrennte Abwicklung der beiden Währungsbeträge zu.
- Die betroffenen Parteien sollten vereinbaren, dass der Wechselkurs an den aktuell maßgeblichen Devisentermin-Mittekurs angepasst wird.

2.4. Stop-Loss-Orders

Für eine Stop-Loss-Order müssen die **Bedingungen für diese Anweisung exakt festgelegt** sein. Beide Parteien (Händler und Kunde) müssen darin übereinstimmen. Jeder Händler muss für den Notfall Möglichkeiten haben, mit dem Kunden zu kommunizieren, um im Falle außergewöhnlicher Kursbewegungen oder anderer ungewöhnlicher Situationen rückzufragen.

Akzeptiert eine Institution eine Stop-Loss-Order, muss sie jede Anstrengung unternehmen, um sie prompt zu erledigen („Best effort basis"). Der Auftraggeber darf jedoch eine Stop-Loss-Order **nicht als Fixpreis-Garantie auffassen**, sofern nicht schriftlich etwas anderes zwischen den beiden Parteien vereinbart wurde.

Sollte ein Streit zwischen Partnern darüber entstehen, ob das Limit erreicht wurde, sollte man unabhängig davon, welche Quelle zur Überprüfung der Bandbreite genutzt wird, berücksichtigen, dass es schwierig ist, genaue Daten zu erhalten. Broker können nur als Informationsquelle herangezogen werden, da Broker lediglich ihre individuelle Bandbreite der Quotierungen nennen können, die jedoch nicht die gesamten Marktbewegungen widerspiegeln. Daher sollten alle wichtigen und anerkannten Informationsquellen geprüft und die erhaltenen Informationen mit Augenmaß und professioneller Vorsicht behandelt werden.

2.5. Position Parking

Das **Management sollte verbieten,** dass Positionen bei einer anderen Partei mit der Absicht, dieses Geschäft zu einem späteren Zeitpunkt zu historischen Kursen in die Bücher rückzuführen, geparkt werden. Position Parking führt zu einer **verfälschten Darstellung der Risikoposition.**

2.6. Marktunterbrechungen

In gewissen Fällen können die Parteien aufgrund von Ereignissen, die zum Zeitpunkt des Geschäftsabschlusses nicht vorhersehbar waren und nicht in ihrer Kontrolle liegen, an der Erfüllung ihrer geschäftlichen Verpflichtungen gehindert werden. Dazu zählen: Kapitalkontrolle, Rechtswidrigkeit oder Unmöglichkeit der Leistungserfüllung, höhere Gewalt, Illiquidität usw.

In Fällen allgemeiner Marktunterbrechungen aufgrund von plötzlichen Ereignissen, wie z.B. extremen Wetterbedingungen oder sonstigen unvorhergesehenen Entwicklungen, können **lokale Aufsichtsbehörden oder Zentralbanken** durch Ankündigung entsprechender Maßnahmen, einschließlich der Änderung von Zinssätzen, **eingreifen,** um damit die weitere Abwicklung der Geschäfte zu gewährleisten.

Summary

Deals transacted after normal hours or from off-premises should only be undertaken with the express approval of management which should issue clear written guidelines to their staff on the kinds of deals which are permitted and the limits applicable to such trades, specifying their normal trading hours. Where answerphone equipment is used for instant reporting and recording, it should be installed and located in such a way that reported transactions could not subsequently be erased without senior management approval. It is prudent to have an unofficial close for each trading day against which end-of-day positions can be monitored or revalued, thus avoiding problems with determining intraday and overnight limits.

The official range in currency markets is set from 5:00 AM Sydney time on Monday morning, all year round. The recognised closing time for the currency markets is on Friday 5:00 PM New York time all year round.

In the event of a country or a state declaring a new national bank holiday, the new value date will be the first common business day (for both currencies of the contract) following the original value date.

The terms under which such orders are accepted should be explicitly identified and agreed between the parties concerned, specifying any time validity or constraints, and be within any management criteria on such orders. In accepting a stop-loss/profit order, an institution assumes an obligation to make every reasonable effort to execute the order quickly at the established price. However, the specified rate order does not necessarily provide a fixed-price guarantee to the counterparty.

Management should not allow the parking of deals or positions with a counterparty because it can either lead to a distorted risk position or be abused for tax avoiding activities. There are instances (eg, capital controls, illegality or impossibility of performance, acts of God, illiquidity, etc.). where market participants are prevented from fulfilling their part of the deal. In cases of general market disruption caused by sudden events such as extreme weather or other unforeseen developments, local regulators or central banks may intervene by publishing applicable procedures including interest rates to be implemented to cover interrupted settlement.

2.7. Practice Questions

1. What conditions should be fulfilled for trading outside normal business hours?
   a) Guidelines regarding people allowed to trade and thecorresponding limits are in force and known to the dealers.
   b) An approval system for taking up and confirming deals outside of normal business hours is installed.
   c) Trading in places other than the provided rooms should only be allowed with permission of management.
   d) All answers are true.
2. Which statement regarding trading outside the bank is true?
   a) It is recommended to react fast to market changes.
   b) Deals can be done in the rooms of a friendly broker.
   c) If there is a part ownership of more than 10% of the broker, a dealer can make deals up to USD 10m in the room of the broker.
   d) It is recommended to install an answerphone on which the conventions of deals done outside the trading room are to be recorded.

Zusammenfassung

Sollten von einem Händler Transaktionen außerhalb der Geschäftszeiten und/oder in Räumlichkeiten außerhalb der Bank getätigt werden, bedarf dies der ausdrücklichen Genehmigung des Managements. Bei der Installation von Telefonanrufbeantwortern sind entsprechende Sicherheitsvorkehrungen zu treffen, damit die Aufzeichnungen nicht ohne Zustimmung der Geschäftsleitung gelöscht werden können. Außerdem sollte zur Vermeidung von Problemen mit Risikolimiten ein interner, inoffizieller Handelsschluss für jeden Tag festgelegt werden, an dem die Positionen überprüft und bewertet werden.

Die offizielle Beginnzeit für Währungsmärkte ist Montagmorgen 5.00 Uhr, Sydney-Zeit und die offizielle Schlusszeit ist Freitag, 17.00 Uhr, New-Yorker-Zeit.

Für den Fall neu eingeführter Bankfeiertage oder anderer öffentlicher Feiertage, die ein Settlement des Geschäftes nicht zulassen, gilt der nächste gemeinsame Banktag (für beide gehandelten Währungen) nach der ursprünglichen Valuta als neue Valuta.

Für eine Stop-Loss-Order müssen die Bedingungen für diese Anweisung exakt festgelegt sein. Akzeptiert eine Institution eine Stop-Loss-Order, muss sie jede Anstrengung unternehmen, um sie beim vereinbarten Preis auszuführen. Der Auftraggeber darf jedoch eine Stop-Loss-Order nicht als Fixpreis-Garantie ansehen.

Das Management sollte Position Parking verbieten, da dies zu einer verfälschten Darstellung der Risikoposition führt.

In gewissen Fällen (z.B. Kapitalkontrolle, Illiquidität, höhere Gewalt usw.) können die Parteien an der Erfüllung ihrer geschäftlichen Verpflichtungen gehindert werden. In Fällen allgemeiner Marktunterbrechungen können lokale Aufsichtsbehörden oder Zentralbanken durch Ankündigung entsprechender Maßnahmen eingreifen, um damit die weitere Abwicklung der Geschäfte zu gewährleisten.

2.7. Wiederholungsfragen

1. Welche Bedingungen müssen erfüllt sein, damit Handel außerhalb der Geschäftszeiten erlaubt wird?
   a) Die Richtlinien betreffend die zum Handel berechtigten Personen und Limits sind in Kraft und den Händlern bekannt.
   b) Ein Kontrollsystem zur prompten Aufnahme und Bestätigung der Transaktionen außerhalb der gewöhnlichen Handelszeiten ist installiert.
   c) Handel in anderen als in der Bank vorgesehenen Räumlichkeiten soll nur nach vorheriger Genehmigung durch das Management erfolgen.
   d) Alle Antworten sind richtig.
2. Welche Aussage bezüglich Handelsaktivitäten außerhalb der Bank ist richtig?
   a) Es ist ratsam, weil es hilft, schnell auf Marktänderungen zu reagieren.
   b) Geschäfte können in den Räumlichkeiten befreundeter Broker abgeschlossen werden.
   c) Wenn eine Beteiligung von mehr als 10% beim Broker besteht, kann ein Händler aus den Handelsräumlichkeiten des Brokers Geschäfte bis USD 10 Mio. machen.
   d) Es ist ratsam, Telefonanrufbeantworter zu installieren, worauf die Händler die Bedingungen der Geschäfte sprechen, die sie außerhalb der Handelsräumlichkeiten abschließen.

3. What should financial institutions do in any case to avoid problems with determining intraday and overnight limits?
4. Which day is the new valuta day if a country or a state declares a new national bank holiday?
5. What is the official opening and closing time for currency markets?
6. You accept a stop-loss-order from a customer. What do you have to do?
    a) Tell the counterparty that you never accept this kind of deal.
    b) Tell the counterparty that this kind of deal is only possible in the stockmarket.
    c) Ensure that your counterparty understands the terms under which your bank accepts the order and that the counterparty can be contacted in the event of unusual situations.
    d) Tell the counterparty that this kind of deal can only be accepted with the approval of the head dealer.
7. Is a stop-loss-order a fixed-price guarantee?
8. What is meant by "position parking"?
9. What does the Model Code recommend for "position parking"?
10. Which of the following events would constitute an event of market disruption under the Model Code?
    a) terrorist attack on a financial centre
    b) failure of SWIFT
    c) market intervention by the central banks
    d) illiquidity
    e) imposition of capital controls
    f) extreme weather
    g) extreme fluctuations of interest rates
11. Which of the following statements is true?
    a) In cases of general market disruption, local regulators or central banks may intervene with the publication of applicable procedures including interest rates.
    b) In cases of general market disruption, local regulators or central banks may intervene with the publication of applicable procedures excluding interest rates.
    c) In cases of general market disruption, local regulators or central banks are not allowed to intervene with the publication of applicable procedures including interest rates in order to avoid distortion of competition.
    d) All answers are false.

3. Was sollten Finanzinstitutionen, die 24-Stunden-Handel betreiben, auf jeden Fall festlegen, um Probleme mit der Behandlung von Risikolimiten zu vermeiden?

4. Welcher Tag gilt als die neue Valuta für den Fall neu eingeführter Bankfeiertage oder anderer öffentlicher Feiertage?

5. Welche Zeitpunkte gelten als offizielle Beginn- und Schlusszeit für Währungsmärkte?

6. Wie sind Stop-Loss-Orders von Kunden zu behandeln?

   a) Stop-Loss-Orders von Kunden dürfen nicht angenommen werden.

   b) Stop-Loss-Orders von Kunden sind nur am Aktienmarkt möglich.

   c) Stop-Loss-Orders von Kunden sollten nur angenommen werden, wenn der Kunde die Bedingungen kennt und erreichbar ist.

   d) Stop-Loss-Orders von Kunden dürfen nur nach ausdrücklicher Rücksprache mit Ihrem Chefhändler angenommen werden.

7. Kann man eine Stop-Loss-Order als Fixpreis-Garantie ansehen?

8. Was versteht man unter „Position Parking"?

9. Welche Empfehlung gibt der Model Code zu „Position Parking" ab?

10. Welche dieser Ereignisse stellen Ereignisse der Marktunterbrechung im Sinne des Model Codes dar?

    a) Terroranschlag an einem Finanzplatz

    b) Fehler von SWIFT

    c) Marktintervention der Zentralbanken

    d) Illiquidität

    e) Auferlegung einer Kapitalkontrolle

    f) extreme Wetterbedingungen

    g) extreme Zinsbewegungen

11. Welche der folgenden Aussagen ist richtig?

    a) In Fällen allgemeiner Marktunterbrechungen aufgrund von plötzlichen Ereignissen können Zentralbanken durch Änderung der Zinssätze eingreifen.

    b) In Fällen allgemeiner Marktunterbrechungen aufgrund von plötzlichen Ereignissen können Zentralbanken durch Ankündigung entsprechender Maßnahmen eingreifen. Eine Änderung der Zinssätze ist aber verboten.

    c) In Fällen allgemeiner Marktunterbrechungen dürfen weder lokale Aufsichtsbehörden noch Zentralbanken in den Markt eingreifen, da es sonst zu einer Wettbewerbsverzerrung kommen würde.

    d) Keine dieser Antworten ist richtig.

3. Personal Conduct Issues

In this chapter you learn ...
- what management should do to prevent the use of drugs and illegal substances.
- about the Model Code recommendations concerning entertainment and gifts.
- about the Model Code position on gambling and betting between market participants.
- about the Model Code recommendations regarding money laundering and fraud.
- about the Model Code recommendations on dealing for personal account.
- about the Model Code recommendations regarding confidentiality.
- what should be done about misinformation and rumours.

3.1. Drugs and abused substances

Management should take all reasonable steps to educate themselves and their staff about possible signs and effects of the use of drugs and other abused substances. **Policies should be developed and clearly announced** for dealing with individuals who are found to be substance abusers. Any members of staff dependent on such substances may well be impaired and are likely to be vulnerable to outside inducement to conduct business not necessarily in the best interest of the firm or the market generally.

3.2. Entertainment and gifts

Neither management nor employees should offer inducements to conduct business, or solicit them from the personnel of other institutions. However, it is recognised that gifts and entertainment may be offered in the normal course of business; such gifts or entertainment should not be excessive in value or frequency.

Management should:

- monitor the form, frequency and cost of entertainment/gifts that the dealers receive
- have a clearly articulated policy towards the giving/receipt thereof and establish procedures for dealing with gifts judged to be excessive but which cannot be declined without causing offence
- ensure the transparency of all entertainments received or provided

Entertainment should neither be offered nor accepted where it is underwritten but not attended by the host.

3.3. Gambling/betting between market participants

Gambling or betting amongst market participants has obvious dangers and **should be strongly discouraged**. Where it is allowed the management should have a clearly defined written policy on the control of this activity.

3.4. Money laundering/know your counterparty

All banks are reminded of the need to "know their customer" and to take all necessary steps to satisfy themselves that their transactions are not used to facilitate money laundering.

3. Persönliches Verhalten

In diesem Kapitel lernen Sie ...

- wie das Management dem Gebrauch von verbotenen Substanzen vorbeugen soll.
- welche Empfehlungen der Model Code zu Bewirtung und Geschenkannahme gibt.
- wie mit Glücksspielen und Wetten umgegangen werden soll.
- was der Model Code bezüglich Geldwäsche und Betrug empfiehlt.
- welche Empfehlungen der Model Code für den Handel auf eigene Rechnung gibt.
- was der Model Code bezüglich Vertraulichkeit empfiehlt.
- wie mit Fehlinformationen und Gerüchten umgegangen werden soll.

3.1. Verbotene Substanzen

Das Management sollte alle vernünftigen Schritte setzen, um sich und die Mitarbeiter über die Anzeichen und Auswirkungen von Drogenkonsum, inklusive Alkohol und Medikamente, zu informieren. Es sollten **Vorgehensweisen** zum Umgang mit Mitarbeitern, die Drogen missbrauchen, **entwickelt und intern veröffentlicht** werden. Generell sind alle Mitarbeiter, die von solchen Substanzen abhängig sind, anfällig für Anreize von außen, die meistens nicht zum Vorteil der Firma oder des Marktes sind.

3.2. Bewirtung und Geschenkannahme

Weder das Management noch Händler sollen bei anderen Institutionen für Geschäfte werben. Geschenke und Einladungen dürfen im Geschäftsleben angenommen werden, solange sie nicht zu wertvoll sind oder zu häufig vorkommen.

Das Management soll:

- Art, Häufigkeit und Wert der Geschenke und Einladungen an die Händler beobachten.
- Richtlinien erlassen, welche Geschenke angenommen bzw. verschenkt werden dürfen und wie mit wertvollen Geschenken umzugehen ist, die aus Gründen der Höflichkeit nicht zurückgegeben werden können.
- Bei den angenommenen und verteilten Geschenken sollte Transparenz sichergestellt sein.

Es sollen **keine Einladungen** ausgesprochen oder akzeptiert werden, **die man als Gastgeber nicht besucht.**

3.3. Glücksspiele und Wetten

Glücksspiele und Wetten sollten unter Marktteilnehmern **nicht erlaubt** sein. Wird es trotzdem gestattet, sind unter allen Umständen Richtlinien zu erlassen, auf deren Einhaltung genau zu achten ist.

3.4. Geldwäsche

Für Banken ist wichtig, die Kunden zu kennen und sich zu versichern, dass deren Geschäfte nicht genutzt werden, um Geld zu waschen.

As part of the international effort to combat such activities, and in particular drugs-related laundering, the Central Bank governors of the G10 countries endorsed, in November 1988, a statement of best practice entitled "The Basle Statement of Principles". The G-7 in July 1989 promoted the creation of the Financial Action Task Force (FATF). Firms should adopt **appropriate procedures consistent with this G-10 governors statement and the FATF recommendations**, and also familiarise themselves with their legal responsibilities in this matter. Only senior management should decide whether to undertake business with institutions dealing on behalf of clients on a discretionary management basis.

Dealers should be aware of any suspicious transactions and should report any such to the compliance officer or the appointed officer who is charged with responsibility for money laundering issues. Also brokers should be aware of money laundering issues and be vigilant at all times where suspicious transactions are concerned.

3.5. Fraud

Attempts at fraud occur almost daily and many are meticulously planned. Great vigilance is required by all staff, particularly so when calls are received on an ordinary telephone line. It is strongly recommended that the **details of all telephone deals which do not include pre-agreed standard settlement instructions should be confirmed by telex or similar means** by the recipient seeking an answer-back to ensure the deal is genuine. Particular care should be taken before paying away funds in favour of a third party. In the event of any suspicious circumstances staff must notify management without delay.

3.6. Dealing for personal account

Where dealing for personal account is allowed, management should ensure that **adequate safeguards** and **clear, written directions** are established to prevent abuse or insider dealing in any form. These safeguards should also reflect the need to maintain confidentiality with respect to non-public price sensitive information and to ensure that no action is taken by employees which might adversely affect interests of the firm's clients or counterparties.

The management should establish guidelines concerning:

- Personal investments by traders
- Investments by traders on behalf of the trader's family, other members of personnel and management
- Instruments and products closely related to the ones in which the trader deals for the institution, avoiding conflict of interests
- Full disclosure and transparency of trades for personal account, particularly where day trading for personal account is allowed. This should ensure that the trader gives full attention to the institution's business.

Traders should recognise that they too have a responsibility to identify and avoid conflicts of interest.

3.7. Confidentiality

Confidentiality is essential for the preservation of a reputable and efficient market place. Dealers and brokers share equal responsibility for maintaining confidentiality and without

Als Teil der internationalen Bemühungen, derartige Aktivitäten – speziell das Waschen von Drogengeldern – zu bekämpfen, gab der Basler Ausschuss (gegründet von den Notenbanken der G10-Länder) 1988 das „Basel Statement Of Principles" heraus. Im Juli 1989 schuf die G7 die Financial Action Task Force zur Bekämpfung der Geldwäsche. Jede Firma ist angehalten, **Prozeduren** zu entwickeln, die mit den **Empfehlungen der G10 bzw. G7** konform gehen, und die **gesetzlichen Bestimmungen** zu beachten. Es soll im Ermessen der Geschäftsleitung liegen, ob mit Institutionen gehandelt wird, die für Dritte tätig werden.

Händler sollen sich ihrer Verpflichtung bewusst sein, alle verdächtigen Transaktionen an den Verantwortlichen für Geldwäsche zu melden. Ebenso sollen Broker auf Verdachtsmomente achten und diese anzeigen.

3.5. Betrug

Betrugsversuche gibt es fast täglich. Viele davon werden peinlich genau geplant. Die große Aufmerksamkeit aller Mitarbeiter ist nötig, vor allem wenn Gespräche nicht über die Standardtelefonleitungen hereinkommen. Es wird dringend empfohlen, dass alle **Details eines Geschäftes über Telefon,** die nicht vereinbarte Standardkonditionen (d.h. SSI) beinhalten, vom Geschäftspartner **schriftlich per Telex oder einem ähnlichen Medium bestätigt** werden, um zu sehen, ob das Geschäft in Ordnung ist. Besondere Vorsicht ist geboten, wenn Geldflüsse zugunsten einer dritten Partei getätigt werden. Auf jeden Fall haben Händler alle verdächtigen Vorkommnisse sofort an das Management zu melden.

3.6. Handel auf eigene Rechnung

Das Management hat festzulegen, ob Händler für ihr eigenes Konto Geschäfte abschließen dürfen. Wo dies erlaubt ist, sollten **ausreichende Kontrollen** und eine **klare, schriftliche Anleitung zur Geschäftsabwicklung** vorhanden sein, um Missbrauch auszuschließen. Damit soll die Vertraulichkeit sensibler, nicht-öffentlicher Informationen gewährleistet sein, sowie Insidergeschäfte verhindert und Handlungen unterbunden werden, welche die Interessen der Firma oder der Kunden beeinträchtigen können.

Die Richtlinien des Managements sollten folgende Punkte behandeln:

- persönliche Investitionen des Händlers
- Investitionen des Händlers für Familien- oder andere Firmenangehörige, inklusive Management
- Instrumente, die zum Eigenhandel erlaubt sind, um Interessenkonflikte mit dem Tagesgeschäft zu vermeiden
- Transparente Offenlegung aller auf eigene Rechnung gemachten Geschäfte, besonders wenn der Handel auf eigene Rechnung während des Handelstages erlaubt ist. So soll gewährleistet sein, dass die Interessen der Bank über den persönlichen Interessen stehen.

Händler haben die Verantwortung, Interessenkonflikte zu erkennen und weitgehend zu vermeiden.

3.7. Vertraulichkeit

Vertraulichkeit ist essenziell für den Ruf und die Effizienz eines Marktes. Händler und Makler sind in gleichem Maße dafür verantwortlich. Ohne die ausdrückliche Erlaubnis des Geschäftspartners dürfen keine Informationen über ausgeführte oder sich anbahnende Ge-

explicit permission from the parties involved, they should not disclose or discuss any information relating to deals transacted or in the process of being arranged except to or with the counterparties involved. Care should be taken over the use of open loudspeakers to ensure that no breaches of confidentiality occur. Dealers and brokers should also exercise great care if confidential issues are discussed in the public places where conversations can be overheard.

Individual dealers or brokers **should not visit each other's dealing rooms except with the ex-press permission of the management of both parties**. Dealers should not deal from within a broker's office nor should brokers arrange deals outside their own offices. A dealer should not place an order with a broker to find out the name of a counterparty in order to make direct contact to conclude the deal.

Brokers **should never forward banks' names before a deal is closed**. A dealer should not, in any way, pressure a broker by inducement, threat or promise, for information which would be improper for him to divulge. Pressure includes any statement to the effect of, or which could be taken as implying, that a failure to cooperate would lead to a reduction in business.

Dealers should resist any pressure from corporate clients to divulge confidential information. Nor should the corporate dealer exert such pressure.

Any breaches in confidentiality should be investigated immediately according to proper documented procedure.

Confidential information must never be used for personal gain. If the principle of confidentiality is compromised, management must take immediate action in accordance with documented procedures.

3.8. Misinformation and rumours

Dealers and brokers should not relay any information which they know to be false and should take great care when discussing unsubstantiated information which they suspect to be inaccurate and could be damaging to a third party.

Summary

Management should take all reasonable steps to educate themselves and their staff about possible signs and effects of the use of drugs and other illegal substances. Policies should be developed and published for dealing with individuals who are found to be substance abusers.

Neither management nor employees should offer inducements to win business, or solicit them from the personnel of other institutions. Entertainment should neither be offered nor accepted where it is underwritten but not attended by the host.

Gambling or betting amongst market participants has obvious dangers and should be strongly discouraged. Where it is allowed, management should have a clearly defined written policy on the control of this activity.

All banks are reminded of the need to "know their customer" and to take all necessary steps to satisfy themselves that their transactions are not used to facilitate money laundering.

Firms should adopt appropriate procedures consistent with the G-10 governors statement and FATF recommendations, and also familiarise themselves with their legal responsibil-

schäfte weitergegeben werden. Beim Gebrauch von Telefonlautsprechern sollte ganz besonders auf die Vertraulichkeit Bedacht genommen werden.

Händler dürfen die **Räume anderer Händler nur mit Genehmigung des Managements aufsuchen.** Händler sollen nicht in den Räumlichkeiten von Brokern Geschäfte abschließen, und Broker sollen keine Geschäfte außerhalb ihrer Büros tätigen. Es ist nicht mit der Ethik eines Händlers vereinbar, ein Geschäft über einen Broker zu initiieren, um den Namen der anderen Partei herauszufinden und das Geschäft direkt mit dem Partner zu machen.

Broker sollten die **Namen von Banken niemals weitergeben, bevor das Geschäft abgeschlossen ist.** Händler sollen keinen Druck auf Broker ausüben, um vertrauliche Informationen zu erhalten. Dazu zählt auch die explizite oder implizite Drohung, den Geschäftsumfang reduzieren zu wollen. Banken sollen Broker nicht auffordern, Details über Transaktionen mit Dritten weiterzugeben. Händler sollen dem Druck durch Kunden standhalten, vertrauliche Informationen weiterzugeben. Auch Kundenhändler sollen keinen Druck ausüben, um an Informationen zu kommen.

Vertrauliche Informationen dürfen nicht zum persönlichen Vorteil genutzt werden. Für den Fall, dass der Grundsatz der Vertraulichkeit verletzt wird, hat das Management sofort Maßnahmen gemäß einer dokumentierten Vorgehensweise zu ergreifen.

3.8. Fehlinformationen und Gerüchte

Händler und Broker sollen keine Informationen verbreiten, die falsch sind. Informationen, die ungenau sind oder einem Dritten schaden könnten, sind nur mit großer Vorsicht zu diskutieren.

Zusammenfassung

Das Management soll alle vernünftigen Schritte setzen, um sich und die Mitarbeiter über die Anzeichen und Auswirkungen von Drogenkonsum, inklusive Alkohol und Medikamente, zu informieren. Es sollten Vorgehensweisen zum Umgang mit Mitarbeitern, die Drogen missbrauchen, entwickelt und intern veröffentlicht werden.

Weder das Management noch Händler sollen bei anderen Institutionen für Geschäfte werben. Geschenke und Einladungen dürfen im Geschäftsleben angenommen werden, solange sie nicht zu wertvoll sind oder zu häufig vorkommen. Es sollen keine Einladungen ausgesprochen oder akzeptiert werden, die man als Gastgeber nicht besucht.

Glücksspiele und Wetten sollten unter Marktteilnehmern nicht erlaubt sein. Wird es trotzdem gestattet, sind unter allen Umständen Richtlinien zu erlassen, auf deren Einhaltung genau zu achten ist.

Für Banken ist wichtig, die Kunden zu kennen und sich zu versichern, dass deren Geschäfte nicht genutzt werden, um Geld zu waschen. Jede Firma ist angehalten, Prozeduren zu entwickeln, die mit den Empfehlungen der G10 bzw. G7 konform gehen, und die gesetzlichen Bestimmungen zu beachten. Es soll im Ermessen der Geschäftsleitung liegen, ob mit Institutionen gehandelt wird, die für Dritte tätig werden.

Zur Vermeidung von Betrugsfällen wird dringend empfohlen, dass alle Details eines Geschäftes über Telefon, die nicht vereinbarte Standardkonditionen (d.h. SSI) beinhalten, vom Geschäftspartner schriftlich per Telex oder einem ähnlichen Medium bestätigt werden, um zu sehen, ob das Geschäft in Ordnung ist.

ities in this matter. Only senior management should decide whether to undertake business with institutions dealing on behalf of clients on a discretionary management basis.

In order to avoid fraud it is strongly recommended that the details of all telephone deals which do not include pre-agreed standard settlement instructions should be confirmed by telex or similar means by the recipient seeking an answer-back to ensure the deal is genuine.

Where dealing for personal account is allowed, management should ensure that adequate safeguards and clear written directives are established to prevent abuse or insider dealing in any form.

Confidentiality is essential for the preservation of a reputable and efficient market place. Dealers and brokers share equal responsibility for maintaining confidentiality and without explicit permission from the parties involved. Dealers should resist any pressure from corporate clients to divulge confidential information. Brokers should never forward banks' names before a deal is closed. Individual dealers or brokers should not visit each other's dealing rooms except with the express permission of both parties' management. Dealers and brokers should not relay any information which they know to be false and should take great care when discussing unsubstantiated information which they suspect to be inaccurate and could be damaging to a third party.

3.9. Practice Questions

1. Which measures must management take where dealing for personal account is permitted?
   a) No special safeguards are necessary.
   b) The deal should be forbidden.
   c) Counterparty limits should be increased.
   d) It should ensure that adequate safeguards are set up to prevent abuse.
2. Which of the following is considered good practice in the foreign exchange and money markets?
   a) Dealers conclude transactions on the brokers premises.
   b) Brokers disclose counterparty names before closing a money market deal.
   c) Brokers press for market information by threatening, explicitly or otherwise, a reduction in business.
   d) All answers are incorrect.
3. Which of the following measures is of no use in curbing fraud?
   a) installing loud-speakers in the trading room
   b) Details of telephone deals which do not include SSI should be confirmed by the recipient immediately by telex or similar means, for return confirmation to ensure the deal is genuine.
   c) instilling greater vigilance in the staff by keeping them up-to-date on current fraud cases
   d) positively identifying the counterparty when receiving calls on an ordinary telephone line

Das Management hat festzulegen, ob Händler für ihr eigenes Konto Geschäfte abschließen dürfen. Wo dies erlaubt ist, sollten ausreichende Kontrollen und eine klare, schriftliche Anleitung zur Geschäftsabwicklung vorhanden sein, um Missbrauch auszuschließen.

Vertraulichkeit ist essenziell für den Ruf und die Effizienz eines Marktes. Ohne die ausdrückliche Erlaubnis des Geschäftspartners dürfen keine Informationen über ausgeführte oder sich anbahnende Geschäfte weitergegeben werden. Händler dürfen die Räume anderer Händler nur mit Genehmigung des Managements aufsuchen. Händler sollen nicht in den Räumlichkeiten von Brokern Geschäfte abschließen, und Broker sollen keine Geschäfte außerhalb ihrer Büros tätigen. Broker sollen die Namen von Banken niemals weitergeben, bevor das Geschäft abgeschlossen ist. Händler sollen keinen Druck auf Broker ausüben, um vertrauliche Informationen zu erhalten.

Händler und Broker sollen keine Informationen verbreiten, die falsch sind. Informationen, die ungenau sind oder einem Dritten schaden könnten, sind nur mit großer Vorsicht weiterzugeben.

3.9. Wiederholungsfragen

1. Welche Maßnahmen muss das Management setzen, falls der Handel auf eigene Rechnung gestattet wird?
   a) keine speziellen Sicherheitsvorkehrungen
   b) das Geschäft auf jeden Fall verbieten
   c) das Partnerlimit erhöhen
   d) adäquate Sicherheitsvorkehrungen gegen Missbrauch festlegen und klare Handlungsrichtlinien vorgeben

2. Welche der folgenden Aktivitäten ist mit einem ordnungsgemäßen Verhalten von Händlern vereinbar?
   a) Händler dürfen in den Räumlichkeiten anderer Händler Geschäfte abschließen.
   b) Broker dürfen am Geldmarkt Namen schon vor dem Abschluss eines Geschäftes nennen.
   c) Broker dürfen unter expliziter oder impliziter Androhung von Geschäftsentzug gezwungen werden, Marktinformationen weiterzugeben.
   d) Keine dieser Aktivitäten ist erlaubt.

3. Welche der folgenden Maßnahmen von Banken ist ungeeignet, Betrugsversuche zu unterbinden?
   a) Installation von Lautsprechern im Handelsraum
   b) Details von Telefongeschäften, die nicht auf SSI beruhen, sollen sofort mit Telex oder ähnlichen Medien bestätigt werden und eine Rückbestätigung der Echtheit des Geschäftes verlangt werden.
   c) das Personal am laufenden Stand über Betrugsfälle halten
   d) aktive Schritte zur Ermittlung der Identität des Geschäftspartners, wenn ein Anruf auf einer normalen Telefonleitung kommt.

4. An FX dealer has been invited to visit his brokers' dealing room after lunch. What should he do?
   a) decline the invitation
   b) accept the invitation
   c) visit the brokers' dealing room and thereafter report to management
   d) conclude all his deals there in order to save telephone costs

5. What does the Financial Action Task Force recommend for preventing attempts of fraud?

6. What is the Model Code position concerning gambling or betting amongst market participants?
   a) should be strongly discouraged
   b) can be allowed if it is monitored by the management
   c) should be forbidden
   d) has obvious dangers, but it is nevertheless usual practice and without restrictions exercisable

7. Which of the following statements is true?
   a) Financial markets are generally responsive to news on related developments.
   b) Dealers and brokers should not relay any information which they know to be false.
   c) Dealers and brokers should take great care when discussing unsubstantiated information which they suspect to be inaccurate and could be damaging to a third party.
   d) All answers are true.

4. Nach dem Mittagessen wird der FX-Händler von seinem Broker in dessen Räumlichkeiten eingeladen. Was soll er tun?
   a) Er sollte die Einladung ablehnen.
   b) Es ist ein Akt der Höflichkeit, die Einladung anzunehmen.
   c) Er sollte den Broker besuchen und danach dem Management berichten.
   d) Er sollte alle Geschäfte beim Broker abschließen, um Telefonkosten zu sparen.

5. Welche Empfehlungen gibt die Financial Action Task Force zur Bekämpfung der Geldwäsche ab?

6. Welchen Standpunkt vertritt der Model Code zu Glücksspielen und Wetten zwischen Marktteilnehmern?
   a) ist strengstens zu unterbinden
   b) kann erlaubt werden, wenn die Geschäftsleitung diese Aktivitäten überwacht
   c) sollte verboten werden
   d) bringt zwar offensichtliche Gefahren mit sich, ist aber trotzdem handelsübliche Praxis und ohne Einschränkungen anwendbar

7. Welche der folgenden Aussagen ist richtig?
   a) Die Finanzmärkte reagieren im Allgemeinen sehr sensibel auf Nachrichten aus ihrem Umfeld.
   b) Der Model Code verlangt von Händlern und Brokern, dass sie niemals Informationen weitergeben, deren Unrichtigkeit ihnen bekannt ist.
   c) Händler und Broker sollten insbesondere dann Sorge tragen, wenn sie über unbegründete Informationen reden, die ihres Erachtens unwahr sind und Dritten schaden könnten.
   d) Alle Antworten sind richtig.

4. Back Office, Payments and Confirmations

In this chapter you learn ...
- how back and front office should be separated.
- when and in which style written confirmations should be made.
- which information should be included in a written confirmation.
- when and in which style verbal confirmations should be made.
- what the Model Code recommends regarding payment and settlement instructions.
- what should be considered for netting.

4.1. Back office location and segregation of duties/reporting

The organisational structure of market participants should ensure a **strict segregation of duties and reporting lines** as well as independent risk management controls between front and back office staff. Where the middle office has a control or administrative function a similar segregation of duties and reporting should apply.

The issue of a **physical segregation of back and front office is a matter for the management to decide** in the light of essential controls and regulatory requirements. If international banks want to centralise all back office operations in the same centre (usually near the head office) the approval of the regulatory authorities in the centres involved is required. The incentive and compensation plans for back and middle office personnel should be independent from the financial performance of the traders.

If back office duties are assigned, then a strict segregation of duties between back office and front office, as well as within key tasks of the back office, should be ensured.

4.2. Written confirmations

The issue and checking of confirmations is a **back office** responsibility which should be carried out independently from those who initiate deals. Confirmations must be sent out **as quickly as possible** (preferably by electronic means) after a deal has been done and should be addressed to the back office or settlement department of the counterparty bank. The format and content of a confirmation will vary according to the instrument dealt in and reference should be made to any applicable terms and conditions published in order to ascertain the correct content and format for any particular instrument.

As a minimum, however, all confirmations should include the following information:

- Date of transaction
- By which means effected (Broker, phone, telex, dealing system, etc.)
- Name and Location of Counterparty
- Rate, Amount and Currency
- Type and Side of Deal
- Value Date, Maturity Date and all other relevant dates (e.g. Exercise Date)
- Standard Terms/Conditions applicable (e.g. FRABBA, BBAIRS, ICOM, etc.)
- All other important, relevant information

4. Backoffice, Zahlungen und Bestätigungen

In diesem Kapitel lernen Sie ...

- wie Back- und Frontoffice funktional getrennt werden sollen.
- wann und in welcher Form schriftliche Bestätigungen zu erstellen sind.
- welche Informationen eine schriftliche Bestätigung enthalten sollte.
- wann und in welcher Form mündliche Bestätigungen durchzuführen sind.
- welche Empfehlungen der Model Code zu Zahlungs- und Abwicklungsinstruktionen gibt.
- was beim Netting zu beachten ist.

4.1. Sitz des Backoffice, Funktionstrennung, Berichtslinien

Die **inhaltlichen Aufgaben** von Handel und Backoffice sowie die Berichtslinien sind **strikt voneinander zu trennen.** Nimmt das Middle-Office Kontroll- oder Administrativfunktionen wahr, ist auch hier auf eine entsprechende Funktionstrennung zu achten.

Eine **räumliche Trennung** von Back- und Frontoffice ist eine **Entscheidung des Managements.** Wird die Trennung aufgehoben, sind **geeignete Kontrollen** einzurichten. Werden die Backoffice-Aktivitäten internationaler Banken an einem Sitz zusammengefasst (üblicherweise nahe bei der Zentrale), dann ist die Zustimmung der Aufsichtsbehörden in den Handelszentren einzuholen.

Das Entlohnungssystem des Backoffice soll völlig von dem der Händler abgekoppelt sein.

4.2. Schriftliches Bestätigungsverfahren

Die Ausstellung und Überprüfung der Bestätigungen ist eine Aufgabe des **Backoffice.** Diese Arbeit sollte unabhängig von denen, die das Geschäft abgeschlossen haben, erfolgen.

Bestätigungen sind **so schnell wie möglich** zu erstellen und auf sicherem Weg, bevorzugt über elektronische Medien, an das Backoffice oder die Abwicklung des Geschäftspartners zu schicken. Der Inhalt dieser Bestätigung variiert von Geschäft zu Geschäft, jedoch soll auf Rahmenvereinbarungen hingewiesen werden, damit Inhalt und Format korrekt sind.

Auf jeden Fall müssen folgende Informationen enthalten sein:

- Datum der Transaktion
- verwendetes System (Makler, Telefon, Telex, Handelssystem)
- Name und Adresse des Geschäftspartners
- Kurs, Betrag und Währung
- Art und Seite (Kauf/Verkauf) des Geschäfts
- Wertstellungsdatum, Ablaufdatum und alle anderen wichtigen Daten (z.B. Ausübungstag)
- angewandte Standardkonditionen (z.B. FRABBA, BBAIRS, ISDA, ICOM, ...)
- alle sonstigen wichtigen Informationen

Upon receipt, all confirmations must immediately be thoroughly checked and appropriate action taken to rectify any differences. If the counterparty's confirmation is considered incorrect, the counterparty must immediately be informed. A new confirmation must be requested from and provided by the bank whose original confirmation was incorrect. Any bank failing to receive a confirmation must query the matter with the back office (or the management) of the counterparty. Where transactions are arranged through a broker, the broker should send a confirmation to each counterparty by fax or other acceptable electronic means.

In the **derivatives markets** it is perfectly acceptable that only one party of the deal sends out a confirmation if the two principals have agreed. The other counterparty has to check the confirmation promptly and should respond to the issuer agreeing or querying the terms. The issuer of the confirmation should have procedures in place for chasing a response if one is not forthcoming within a few hours of the confirmation being sent.

The practice of sending two confirmations (an initial one by telex, followed by a written confirmation) is discouraged since the late arrival of the second confirmation could cause confusion and uncertainty.

Many automated dealing systems produce confirmations automatically. Provided these are verified by the back office, no additional confirmation need be sent.

4.3. Verbal deal checks

Many dealers now request regular verbal or telex deal checks from brokers prior to the exchange and checking of a written or electronically dispatched confirmation. Their use can be an important means of helping reduce the number and size of differences, particularly when **dealing through brokers or for deals involving foreign counterparties**. The practice of intra-deal checks is strongly recommended. Verbal confirmations are particularly useful in **active and volatile markets** (e.g. FX spot) and **deals with short settlement period**.

It is for each firm to agree with their brokers (or counterparties) whether or not it wishes to be provided with this service and if so, how many such checks a day it requires. If a single check is thought to be sufficient, this should be undertaken towards or at the end of the trading day. Where it is not possible for the broker to send a full confirmation immediately, (e.g. during night time), the principal should verbally reconfirm with the broker all the completed transactions.

There should always be an acknowledgment between the parties on completion of the check that all deals have been agreed or, if not, that any identified discrepancies are resolved as a matter of urgency. Where a dispute results in an open risk position for one counterparty the position should be immediately closed out in the market, without inference that either party is wrong, pending final resolution of the dispute. Such action shall be seen as an act of prudence to eliminate the risk of further loss resulting from the dispute and shall not be construed as an admission of liability by that party. Where an error or difference is first highlighted by either party, lack of response should not be construed as acknowledgment.

4.4. Payments and settlement instructions

Instructions should be passed as quickly as possible to facilitate prompt settlement. The **use of standardised payment instructions** between counterparties who trade regularly with

Alle Bestätigungen sollen so schnell wie möglich genau geprüft werden. Im Falle von Differenzen ist der Geschäftspartner sofort und bevorzugt schriftlich auf elektronischem Wege zu informieren. Dann muss eine neue Bestätigung angefordert werden, die von der anderen Seite auch zur Verfügung gestellt werden muss.

Bei Geschäften über einen Makler hat dieser beiden Seiten eine Bestätigung auszustellen.

Bei **Derivaten** ist es durchaus üblich, dass nur eine Partei eine Bestätigung schickt. Die andere Partei muss prompt antworten und die Zustimmung geben bzw. Einsprüche geltend machen. Jene Partei, welche die Bestätigung ausstellt, muss ein Vorgehen entwickeln, um nach wenigen Stunden fehlende Rückmeldungen anzufordern.

Die Praxis, einer elektronischen Bestätigung eine schriftliche (auf dem Postweg) folgen zu lassen, wird nicht empfohlen, da dadurch Unklarheiten entstehen können, wenn die zweite Bestätigung möglicherweise erst nach dem Settlement-Tag eintrifft.

Werden Bestätigungen automatisch im Handelssystem erstellt, dann müssen keine weiteren Bestätigungen versendet werden, wenn die automatischen Bestätigungen durch das Backoffice verifiziert wurden.

4.3. Mündliches Bestätigungsverfahren

Viele Händler verlangen eine mündliche Bestätigung oder eine Bestätigung durch Telex vor einem Austausch und einer Überprüfung von geschriebenen oder elektronisch übermittelten Bestätigungen. Dies hilft, vor allem bei **Geschäften über Makler oder mit ausländischen Geschäftspartnern,** die Fehler zu reduzieren. Mündliche Bestätigungen sind besonders in **schnelllebigen Märkten,** wie z.B. FX-Spot, oder bei **Geschäften mit kurzer Settlementperiode** (z.B. taggleiche Valuta) nützlich.

Jede Firma sollte mit ihren Maklern aushandeln, ob und wenn ja, wie oft pro Tag dieser Dienst angeboten wird. Bei nur einer Überprüfung pro Tag wird empfohlen, dies eher gegen Ende des Geschäftstages durchzuführen. Kann ein Broker nicht sofort eine vollständige Bestätigung schicken (z.B. in der Nacht), dann soll die Bank mit dem Broker alle Geschäfte mündlich rückbestätigen.

Die Gegenparteien sollen sich bewusst sein, dass die Überprüfungen erst dann abgeschlossen sind, wenn beide Partner dem Geschäft zustimmen und Diskrepanzen geklärt sind. Jeder Streitfall ist rasch einer Lösung zuzuführen. Sollte aus der offenen Position ein Risiko entstehen, so soll das Geschäft, unabhängig vom Ergebnis der Schlichtung, sofort am Markt geschlossen werden. Wird eine Geschäftspartei auf einen Fehler oder eine Abweichung hingewiesen und antwortet nicht darauf, so kann die fehlende Antwort nicht als Zustimmung gewertet werden.

4.4. Zahlungs- und Abwicklungsinstruktionen

Anweisungen sollten prompt weitergegeben werden, um eine schnelle Abwicklung zu gewährleisten. Der **Gebrauch standardisierter Zahlungsbedingungen (Standard Settle-**

each other is recommended as their use can make a significant contribution to reducing both the incidence and size of differences arising from the mistaken settlement of funds. SSIs should be established either via authenticated SWIFT message or confirmed letter, and not by SWIFT broadcast.

In some foreign exchange and currency deposit markets, it is not customary for brokers to pass payment instructions where both counterparties are based in the same country as the broker, but the counterparties must themselves exchange instructions without delay.

Whether dealing directly or through a broker, principals should ensure that alterations to original payment instructions, including the paying agent where this has been specifically requested, should be immediately notified to the counterparty, or where a broker has been used and at least one of the principals is in another country, to the broker also.

This notification should be supported by written, telex or similar confirmation of the new instructions, receipt of which should be acknowledged by the counterparty concerned. Failure to inform the broker of a change in instructions could clearly place the liability for any ensuing difference with the principal.

Where the beneficiary of a transaction is a third party, it is the management's responsibility to ensure that appropriate authentication controls are in place for the payment to be executed.

Where differences or costs occur resulting from a broker's error on payment instructions, the broker's liability should be limited. This should reflect the broker's limited possibilities to rectify any payments that have gone astray.

4.5. Netting

Market participants should aim to reduce credit risk by establishing **bilateral currency netting agreements**. The potential of multilateral netting agreements should be investigated. It is strongly recommended that all participants are familiar with the following publications:

- Reducing Foreign Exchange Settlement Risk (New York FX Committee, 1994)
- The Supervisory Recognition of Netting for Capital Adequacy Purposes (BIS, 1993)
- The G-10 Central Banks Report of the Committee on Interbank Netting Schemes (1990)

Summary

The organisational structure of market participants should ensure a strict segregation of duties and reporting lines as well as independent risk management controls for front and back office staff. The issue of a physical segregation of back and front office is a matter for the management to decide in light of essential controls and regulatory requirements.

The issuing and checking of confirmations is a back office responsibility which should be carried out independently from those who initiate deals. Confirmations must be sent out as quickly as possible (preferably by electronic means) after a deal has been done and should be addressed to the back office or settlement department of the counterparty bank.

Upon receipt, all confirmations must be immediately checked thoroughly and appropriate action must be taken to clarify any differences. If the counterparty's confirmation is considered incorrect, the counterparty must be informed immediately.

ment Instructions – SSI) zwischen Parteien, die regelmäßig miteinander Geschäfte abschließen, wird dringend empfohlen. Sie dient der Verringerung möglicher Differenzen. SSI sollen über eine authentisierte S.W.I.F.T.-Botschaft oder einen eingeschriebenen Brief übermittelt werden. S.W.I.F.T. Broadcast eignet sich nicht zur Verbreitung von SSI.

In manchen FX- und Depotmärkten erteilt der Broker keine Zahlungsanweisungen, wenn beide Parteien im Land des Brokers sitzen. Die Anweisungen müssen dann unverzüglich zwischen den Parteien direkt ausgetauscht werden.

Bei direkten Geschäften und Geschäften mittels Makler haben die Auftraggeber darauf zu achten, dass Abweichungen von den ursprünglichen Zahlungsbedingungen, insbesondere Abweichungen von der Zahlungsstelle, den Geschäftspartnern unverzüglich bekanntgegeben werden. Wurde ein Broker zwischengeschaltet, so ist dieser zu informieren, wenn der Geschäftspartner im Ausland sitzt. Die Verständigung soll von einer schriftlichen Ausführung der neuen Bedingungen begleitet werden. Der Erhalt der neuen Anweisungen ist von der anderen Partei zu bestätigen. Wird der Broker nicht über geänderte Zahlungsbedingungen informiert, so trägt der Auftraggeber die Kosten möglicher Abweichungen.

Ist der Begünstigte einer Transaktion eine dritte Partei, dann hat das Management dafür zu sorgen, dass ausreichende Kontrollen für eine Zahlungsabwicklung existieren.

Kommt es zu Streitfällen, weil der Broker Zahlungsanweisungen falsch ausgestellt hat, ist bei der Bestimmung der Haftung des Brokers darauf zu achten, in welchem Ausmaß der Fehler direkt auf sein Verhalten zurückzuführen war.

4.5. Netting

Die Marktteilnehmer sollten darauf bedacht sein, Settlement- und Kreditrisiken durch **bilaterale Nettingvereinbarungen** zu reduzieren. Der Einsatz und das Potenzial multilateraler Nettingvereinbarungen soll untersucht werden.

Die Marktteilnehmer sollen mit folgenden Publikationen vertraut sein:

- Reducing Foreign Exchange Settlement Risk (New York FX Committee, 1994)
- The Supervisory Recognition of Netting for Capital Adequacy Purposes (BIZ, 1993)
- The G10 Central Banks Report of the Committee on Interbank Netting Schemes (1990)

Zusammenfassung

Die inhaltlichen Aufgaben von Handel und Backoffice sowie die Berichtslinien sind strikt voneinander zu trennen. Eine räumliche Trennung von Back- und Frontoffice ist eine Entscheidung des Managements. Wird die Trennung aufgehoben, sind geeignete Kontrollen einzurichten.

Die Ausstellung und Überprüfung der Bestätigungen ist eine Aufgabe des Backoffice. Bestätigungen sind so schnell wie möglich zu erstellen und auf sicherem Weg, bevorzugt über elektronische Medien, an das Backoffice oder die Abwicklung des Geschäftspartners zu schicken.

Alle Bestätigungen sollen so schnell wie möglich genau geprüft werden. Im Falle von Differenzen ist der Geschäftspartner sofort und bevorzugt schriftlich auf elektronischem Wege zu informieren.

Viele Händler verlangen eine mündliche Bestätigung oder eine Bestätigung durch Telex vor einem Austausch und einer Überprüfung von geschriebenen oder elektronisch übermittelten Bestätigungen. Dies hilft, vor allem bei Geschäften über Makler oder mit aus-

Many dealers now request regular verbal or telex deal checks from brokers prior to the exchange and checking of a written or electronically dispatched confirmation. Their use can be an important means of helping reduce the number and size of differences, particularly when dealing through brokers or for deals involving foreign counterparties. Verbal confirmations are particularly useful in active and volatile markets (eg, FX spot) and deals with short settlement periods.

Instructions should be passed on as quickly as possible to facilitate prompt settlement. The use of standardised payment instructions between counterparties who trade regularly with each other is recommended as their use can make a significant contribution to reducing both the incidence and size of differences arising from the mistaken settlement of funds. SSIs should be established either via authenticated SWIFT message or confirmed letter, and not by SWIFT broadcast.

Market participants should aim to reduce credit risk by establishing bilateral currency netting agreements.

4.6. Practice questions

1. What is the Model Code stance concerning the segregation of back and front office functions?
   a) It is not necessary.
   b) A strict segregation of duties is necessary, a physical segregation is recommended.
   c) Segregation is only necessary in derivatives dealing.
   d) Back office functions should be centralised.
2. You concluded a deal with bank A over the telephone at 10 a.m. this morning. What happens now?
   a) You write a ticket to inform your settlement department and update your position blotter.
   b) Your bank will confirm the deal by telephone at 6 p.m. on the same day.
   c) All answers are false.
   d) Your bank will confirm the deal by telex at 6 p.m. on the same day.
3. Which statement is true regarding confirmations?
   a) Confirmations must be sent out immediately after the deal is done.
   b) Confirmations must be sent out if the deals are not standardized.
   c) Confirmations must be sent out as quickly as possible after the deal is done and addressed to the settlements department of the counterparty bank.
   d) Confirmations must be sent out by electronic media only, e.g. fax, telex.
4. Which information does a written confirmation contain?
5. Which of the following statements concerning confirmations is FALSE?
   a) Confirmations must be exchanged between the settlement departments as quickly as possible.
   b) Confirmations must be checked as quickly as possible.
   c) The partner must be informed immediately if there are any mistakes in the confirmation.
   d) Incorrect confirmations need not be corrected.

ländischen Geschäftspartnern, die Fehler zu reduzieren. Mündliche Bestätigungen sind besonders in schnelllebigen Märkten, wie z.B. FX-Spot, oder bei Geschäften mit kurzer Settlementperiode (z.B. taggleiche Valuta) nützlich.

Anweisungen sollten prompt weitergegeben werden, um eine schnelle Abwicklung zu gewährleisten. Der Gebrauch standardisierter Zahlungsbedingungen (Standard Settlement Instructions – SSI) zwischen Parteien, die regelmäßig miteinander Geschäfte abschließen, wird dringend empfohlen. Sie dient der Verringerung möglicher Differenzen. SSI sollen über eine authentisierte S.W.I.F.T.-Botschaft oder einen eingeschriebenen Brief übermittelt werden. S.W.I.F.T. Broadcast eignet sich nicht zur Verbreitung von SSI.

Die Marktteilnehmer sollen darauf bedacht sein, Settlement- und Kreditrisiken durch bilaterale Nettingvereinbarungen zu reduzieren.

4.6. Wiederholungsfragen

1. Was ist der Standpunkt des Model Codes zur Trennung von Back- und Frontoffice?
   a) Es ist nicht notwendig.
   b) Eine inhaltliche Trennung ist immer notwendig, eine räumliche empfehlenswert.
   c) Eine Trennung ist nur im Derivativgeschäft erforderlich.
   d) Backoffice-Funktionen müssen zentral zusammengefasst sein.
2. Sie haben ein Geschäft mit Bank A per Telefon um 10.00 Uhr vormittags abgeschlossen. Was passiert nun?
   a) Sie senden ein Fax an Ihre Settlement-Abteilung und aktualisieren Ihre Position.
   b) Ihre Bank bestätigt um 6.00 Uhr abends telefonisch Ihr Geschäft.
   c) Ihre Bank bestätigt die Geschäfte gesammelt am Beginn des nächsten Handelstages.
   d) Ihre Bank bestätigt das Geschäft um 6.00 Uhr abends auf elektronischem Wege.
3. Welche der folgenden Aussagen zum Thema Bestätigungen ist richtig?
   a) Bestätigungen müssen sofort nach dem Geschäftsabschluss ausgestellt werden.
   b) Bestätigungen dürfen nur bei unüblichen Geschäften ausgetauscht werden.
   c) Bestätigungen müssen so schnell wie möglich erstellt und an das Settlement der Partnerbank gesendet werden.
   d) Bestätigungen dürfen nur mit elektronischen Medien wie Fax oder Telex gesendet werden.
4. Welche Informationen sollte eine schriftliche Bestätigung enthalten?
5. Welche der folgenden Aussagen betreffend Bestätigungen ist FALSCH?
   a) Bestätigungen sind zwischen den Settlementabteilungen so schnell wie möglich auszutauschen.
   b) Bestätigungen sind so schnell wie möglich zu kontrollieren.
   c) Fehler in Bestätigungen müssen sofort angezeigt werden.
   d) Falsche Bestätigungen müssen nicht berichtigt werden.

6. Which medium is not qualified for establishing SSI?
   a) S.W.I.F.T. Broadcast
   b) S.W.I.F.T. MT
   c) confirmed letter
   d) All three possibilities are qualified.
7. When can a broker consider a deal done?
   a) if a good price is quoted
   b) if both parties have established credit lines for each other
   c) if the dealer acknowledges the deal verbally
   d) if he puts a name and an amount to the quote
8. Why should market participants establish netting agreements?

6. Welches Medium ist ungeeignet, SSI zu übermitteln?
    a) S.W.I.F.T. Broadcast
    b) S.W.I.F.T. MT
    c) eingeschriebener Brief
    d) Alle drei Möglichkeiten sind geeignet.
7. Wann kann ein Broker ein Geschäft als abgeschlossen betrachten?
    a) wenn ein guter Preis vorliegt
    b) wenn die beiden Parteien Kreditlinien bei ihm eingerichtet haben
    c) wenn der Händler den Abschluss zumindest mündlich zur Kenntnis nimmt
    d) wenn er dem Händler Namen und Preis des Interessenten nennt
8. Wozu sollten Marktteilnehmer Nettingvereinbarungen treffen?

5. Disputes, Differences, Mediation, Compliance

In this chapter you learn ...
- how to handle disputes.
- what should be done in case of differences between principals.
- about the Model Code recommendations regarding differences with brokers and use of points.
- how to handle complaints.

5.1. Disputes and mediation

Where disputes arise, it is essential that the management of the parties involved take prompt action to resolve or settle the issue **quickly and fairly with a high degree of integrity and mutual respect**. Where disputes cannot be resolved between the parties and where all normal channels have been exhausted, the Chairman and members of the Committee for Professionalism are ready to assist in resolving such disputes through the **"Expert Determination Service"** lined out in the Model Code.

The Expert Determination Service

- is available for members and non-members of the ACI
- can be referred to in cases related to over-the-counter instruments dealt with in the Model Code
- deals with disputes related to market practice or conduct as set out in the Model Code, but excluding legal disputes

Where there are local restrictions in force or where differences exist between the Model Code and a similar document issued by the Regulatory Authority governing the conduct of those transacting business in the financial markets in the centre of which it is responsible, the terms of the local Code of Conduct shall apply for transactions between institutions in that centre. However, where differences exist involving transactions between two institutions in separately regulated centres, the terms of the Model Code shall apply.

The **vast majority of disputes** arise from:

- failure of dealers to use clear, unambiguous terminology or
- failure of back office staff to check promptly and accurately the counterparty's confirmation.

5.2. Differences between principals

If all the procedures recommended in the Model Code are adhered to, the incidence and size of differences should be reduced and those mistakes which do occur should be identified and corrected promptly. Nevertheless, mistakes and disputes will arise from time to time, both between banks when dealing directly with each other or between a bank and a broker. Disputes should be routinely **referred to senior management** for resolution, thereby transforming the dispute from an individual trader to trader or trader to broker issue to an inter-institutional issue.

5. Konflikte, Differenzen, Vermittlung, Erfüllung

In diesem Kapitel lernen Sie ...

● wie mit Konfliktfällen umgegangen werden soll.
● was zu tun ist, wenn es zu Differenzen zwischen Marktteilnehmern kommt.
● welche Empfehlungen der Model Code zu Differenzen mit Brokern und der Anwendung von Punktesystemen gibt.
● wie mit Beschwerden umgegangen werden soll.

5.1. Konflikte und Vermittlung

Konflikte sind **durch das Management mit Integrität und mit gegenseitigem Respekt fair und rasch zu lösen.** Sollte es zu keiner Einigung kommen, so sind der Vorsitzende und die Mitglieder des CfP auf Ansuchen bereit, in Konfliktfällen in Form des **„Expert Determination Service"** zu vermitteln.

Das Schlichtungsverfahren kann beansprucht werden:

● von Mitgliedern und Nichtmitgliedern des ACI;
● wenn der Streitfall ein vom Model Code abgedecktes OTC-Instrument betrifft;
● wenn sich der Streitfall auf eine Marktpraxis oder ein anderes im Model Code behandeltes Thema bezieht und nicht bei Gericht anhängig ist.

Der Model Code versteht sich in lokalen Märkten nachrangig gegenüber nationalen Codes of Conduct oder ähnlichen Regulativen. Sollte jedoch ein Streitfall zwischen zwei Institutionen vorliegen, die unterschiedlichen Regulativen unterliegen (d.h. in zwei verschiedenen Handelszentren tätig sind), dann wird der Model Code angewendet.

Die meisten **Probleme** entstehen entweder, weil

● die Händler eine unklare Terminologie benutzen oder
● das Backoffice die Bestätigung des Kontrahenten nicht sofort und ungenau kontrolliert.

5.2. Differenzen zwischen Marktteilnehmern

Sollten alle oben angeführten Maßnahmen durchgeführt werden, ist die Gefahr von Differenzen stark vermindert, und die Fehler, die noch entstehen, können leichter korrigiert werden. Trotzdem kann es immer wieder zu Unstimmigkeiten zwischen zwei Banken oder zwischen einer Bank und einem Makler kommen. Diese sollten als Regel **immer dem Management zugeleitet** werden. Damit wird aus Problemen zwischen Personen ein Problem zwischen Firmen.

Wo es um Betragshöhen, Währungen, Wertdaten (oder andere Faktoren, die bedingen, dass eine Partei eine offene Position hat) geht, wird dringend empfohlen, diese **Position** – möglichst nach Absprache mit der Gegenpartei – zu **schließen.** Diese Aktion sollte als Beitrag zur Risikominderung gesehen werden und darf nicht als Schuldeingeständnis gewertet werden.

Where a dispute involves the amount, currency, value date(s), (or any other factor which means that one of the two parties concerned has an "open" or "unmatched" position), it is strongly recommended that action should immediately be taken by one of the parties concerned (preferably with the agreement of the other) **to "square off" or "neutralise" the position**. Such action shall be seen as an act of prudence to eliminate the risk of further loss resulting from the dispute and shall not be construed as an admission of liability by that party.

Where difference payments arise because of errors in the payment of funds, principals should not benefit from undue enrichment by retaining the funds. All parties involved directly or indirectly, erroneous or otherwise in the settlement of the transaction should make every effort to achieve an equitable solution.

5.3. Differences with brokers and use of "points"

Where a broker quotes a firm or unqualified price and is subsequently unable to substantiate the quote when the deal is proposed, the bank proposing the trade is fully entitled to hold the broker to the price (so-called **"Stuffing"**). The broker must make good the difference between the price quoted and the price at which the business is concluded.

Where differences arise, the following guidelines for compensation should apply:

- Disputes should be routinely referred to senior management for resolution, thereby transforming the dispute from an individual trader to broker issue to an inter-institutional issue. All compensation should take the form of a bank cheque or wire transfer in the name of the institution or of adjustment to brokerage bills.
- All such transactions should be fully documented by each firm. It is bad practice to refuse a broker's cheque or reduction in the brokerage bill for the amount concerned and to insist on a name at the original price.

The CfP is **not in favour of the settlement of differences by points**, but recognises that in those financial markets where the regulatory authority controls all participants in that market, this practice, properly regulated by the appropriate authority, is acceptable.

Example

Example for "Settlement of differences by points"

Starting situation
Suppose a broker quotes EUR/USD at 1.2430-35. Bank A hits the 30 bid for EUR 10m. However, before the broker could let Bank A know, the price has been withdrawn by the market maker. The market for EUR/USD has now moved to 1.2425-30.

Best Practice
The broker delivers at 1.2425 and pays the difference of 50 points (i.e. 5 points per 1m EUR), that is USD 5,000, to Bank A in cash. This should be accepted by Bank A.

Settlement of differences by points
If Bank A insists on the original deal (this practice is sometimes referred to as "stuffing" the broker), the broker would have to find a Bank C, to whom he could sell at EUR at 1.2430 and compensate Bank C with USD 5,000 for the difference to the market rate, or arrange a deal for Bank B where it earns a profit of USD 5,000, thus offsetting the "negative points" from the first deal.

Liegt der Grund für eine Zahlungsdifferenz darin, dass eine Zahlung falsch angewiesen wurde, sollte die irrtümlich begünstigte Partei es unterlassen, davon zu profitieren. Alle beteiligten Parteien sollten zusammenarbeiten, um eine ausgewogene Lösung zu erreichen.

5.3. Differenzen mit Brokern und Anwendung von Punktesystemen

Banken haben das Recht, einen Broker für den gestellten Preis zur Verantwortung zu ziehen, selbst dann, wenn der Broker den Preis nicht mehr halten kann (**„Stuffing"**). Der Broker muss dann die Differenz bzw. den Verlust aus dem ursprünglich quotierten Preis und dem Preis, zu dem abgeschlossen wurde, ersetzen.

Differenzen zwischen Broker und Bank sollen nach folgenden Grundsätzen abgewickelt werden:

- Die Lösung soll auf Ebene der Geschäftsführung gesucht werden, um aus einem individuellen Streitfall einen institutionellen zu machen. Zahlungen sollen in Form eines Bankschecks, einer Überweisung oder einer Reduzierung der Brokerrechnung erfolgen.
- Alle mit dem Streitfall verbundenen Transaktionen sollen vollständig dokumentiert werden. Es ist unstatthaft, die Zahlung durch Bankscheck oder Reduzierung der Brokerrechnung abzulehnen und auf einen Namen zum vereinbarten Preis zu bestehen.

Das Committee for Professionalism **unterstützt nicht die Praxis des „Settlement of Differences by Points"**. Das CfP sieht jedoch diese Usance in jenen Märkten als akzeptable Praxis, wenn die Marktteilnehmer als auch der Prozess des „Settlement by Points" einer Aufsichtsbehörde unterliegen.

Beispiel

Beispiel für „Settlement of differences by points"

Ausgangssituation
Ein Broker quotiert EUR/USD 1.2430-35. Bank A akzeptiert EUR 10 Mio. zu verkaufen. Allerdings hat der Market Maker die Quotierung bereits zurückgezogen, der Broker hat Bank A diesbezüglich zu spät informiert. Der Preis für EUR/USD steht inzwischen bei 1.2425-30.

Best Practice
Der Broker verkauft die EUR 10 Mio. zu 1.2425 und zahlt die Differenz von 50 Punkten (d.h. 5 Punkte pro EUR 1 Mio.) an Bank A. Diese Abwicklung sollte von Bank A akzeptiert werden.

Settlement of differences by points
Sollte Bank A darauf bestehen, die Transaktion zum ursprünglichen Preis durchzuführen (diese Vorgehensweise wird „Stuffing of the broker" genannt), müsste der Broker eine Bank C finden, an die er EUR 10 Mio. zu 1.2430 verkaufen kann und die er für die Preisdifferenz mit USD 5,000 entschädigen kann. Oder er arrangiert alternativ einen Deal für Bank B, bei dem diese USD 5,000 verdienen und die originalen Transaktionen durchführen kann.

5.4. Compliance and Complaints

Compliance with the Model Code should ensure the **highest standards of integrity and fair dealing** in the international OTC market. Management should ensure that all complaints are fairly and independently investigated, whenever practicable, by employees or representatives who were not directly involved in the disputed transaction.

If any principal or broking firm believes that an institution has breached the letter or spirit of the Model Code it should seek to settle it **amicably**. If an amicable solution is not possible the counterparty subject to the complaint should make the complainant aware that it can bring the matter to the attention of the CFP of the ACI.

Summary

Where disputes with counterparts arise, it is essential that the management of the parties involved take prompt action to resolve or settle the issue quickly and fairly with a high degree of integrity and mutual respect. Where disputes cannot be resolved between the parties, the chairman and members of the Committee for Professionalism are ready to assist in resolving such disputes through the "Expert Determination Service". The vast majority of disputes arise from failure of dealers to use clear, unambiguous terminology or failure of back office staff to check promptly and accurately the counterparty's confirmation.

Where a dispute involves the amount, currency, value date(s), (or any other factor resulting in one of the two parties concerned having an "open" or "unmatched" position), it is strongly recommended that action should be taken immediately by one of the parties concerned to "square off" or "neutralise" the position. Where difference payments arise because of errors in the payment of funds, principals should not benefit from undue enrichment by retaining the funds.

Where a broker quotes a firm or unqualified price and is subsequently unable to substantiate the quote when the deal is proposed, the bank proposing the trade is fully entitled to hold the broker to the price (so-called "stuffing"). The broker must make good the difference between the price quoted and the price at which the business is concluded.

The CfP is not in favour of the settlement of differences by points, but recognises that in those financial markets where the regulatory authority controls all participants in that market, this practice, properly regulated by the appropriate authority, is acceptable.

5.5. Practice Questions

1. Under which circumstances will the CfP mediate in disputes?
    a) The counterparties have exhausted all efforts in trying to resolve the dispute themselves and the instrument concerned is covered by the Model Code.
    b) The counterparties have exhausted all efforts in trying to resolve the dispute themselves and the counterparties are of English origin.
    c) The counterparties have exhausted all efforts in trying to resolve the dispute themselves and the amount disputed is higher than USD 10m.
    d) The counterparties accept the CfPs decision as final and the amount disputed is higher than USD 10 m.

5.4. Erfüllung und Beschwerden

Die Erfüllung der Vorschriften des Model Codes sollten ein **hohes Maß an Integrität und Fairness** im Handel gewährleisten. Im Falle von Beschwerden soll das Management für eine faire Untersuchung sorgen, die, sofern praktikabel, von Personen, die nicht direkt in den Streitfall involviert sind, durchzuführen ist.

Grundsätzlich sollen Banken und Broker Vorfälle, die dem Inhalt und Geist des Model Codes nicht entsprechen, auf **freundschaftliche Art** lösen. Ist dies nicht möglich, soll jene Institution, die beschuldigt wird, den Model Code zu verletzen, den Beschwerdeführer auf die Möglichkeit, den Fall dem CfP zuweisen zu können, hinweisen.

> **Zusammenfassung**
>
> Konflikte mit anderen Marktteilnehmern sind durch das Management mit Integrität und mit gegenseitigem Respekt fair und rasch zu lösen. Sollte es zu keiner Einigung kommen, so sind der Vorsitzende und die Mitglieder des CfP auf Ansuchen bereit, in Konfliktfällen in Form des „Expert Determination Service" zu vermitteln. Die meisten Probleme entstehen entweder, weil die Händler eine unklare Terminologie benutzen oder das Backoffice die Bestätigung des Kontrahenten nicht sofort und ungenau kontrolliert.
>
> Wo es um Betragshöhen, Währungen, Wertdaten (oder andere Faktoren, die bedingen, dass eine Partei eine offene Position hat) geht, wird dringend empfohlen, diese Position – möglichst nach Absprache mit der Gegenpartei – zu schließen. Liegt der Grund für eine Zahlungsdifferenz darin, dass eine Zahlung falsch angewiesen wurde, sollte die irrtümlich begünstigte Partei es unterlassen, davon zu profitieren.
>
> Banken haben das Recht, einen Broker für den gestellten Preis zur Verantwortung zu ziehen, selbst dann, wenn der Broker den Preis nicht mehr halten kann („Stuffing"). Der Broker muss dann die Differenz bzw. den Verlust aus dem ursprünglich quotierten Preis und dem Preis, zu dem abgeschlossen wurde, ersetzen.
>
> Das Committee for Professionalism unterstützt nicht die Praxis des „Settlement of Differences by Points". Das CfP sieht jedoch diese Usance in jenen Märkten als akzeptable Praxis, wenn die Marktteilnehmer als auch der Prozess des „Settlement by Points" einer Aufsichtsbehörde unterliegen.

5.5. Wiederholungsfragen

1. Unter welchen Voraussetzungen schlichtet das CfP Konflikte?
   a) Die Parteien haben alle anderen Möglichkeiten ausgeschöpft. Das Instrument fällt unter den Model Code.
   b) Die Parteien haben alle anderen Möglichkeiten ausgeschöpft. Die Streitparteien sind englische Banken.
   c) Die Parteien haben alle anderen Möglichkeiten ausgeschöpft. Der Streitwert übersteigt USD 10 Mio.
   d) Die Parteien erklären sich bereit, die Entscheidungen des CfP zu akzeptieren. Der Streitwert übersteigt USD 10 Mio.

2. Which of the following is a major source of disputes in the trading environment?
   a) the establishment of proprietary trading
   b) vague guidelines for the acceptance of gifts
   c) use of unclear terminology by dealers
   d) dealers having no academic education
3. Which of the following applies if a broker cannot substantiate his quotation and a difference is payable to the principal?
   a) The settlement of the difference should be acceptable to the principal, who should not insist that the deal is contracted at the original rate.
   b) The settlement of the difference will be payable on the spot date in the absence of prior arrangements.
   c) The settlement of the difference will be determined by closing the deal at the next available price and a cheque will be sent to the principal setting out the details of the deal.
   d) All answers are true.
4. What are the principles for handling the differences between broker and bank?
5. What does the Model Code recommend for "Settlement of Differences by Points"?

2. Was ist gemäß den Erfahrungen des CfP die häufigste Ursache für Probleme im Handel?
   a) wenn der Handel auf eigene Rechnung erlaubt ist
   b) wenn keine Richtlinien für die Annahme von Geschenken vorliegen
   c) wenn die Händler eine unklare Terminologie benützen
   d) wenn die Händler keinen Universitätsabschluss haben

3. Was trifft zu, wenn ein Broker seine Quotierung nicht halten kann und er an die Bank eine Differenzzahlung leisten muss?
   a) Dann soll die Bank das Geschäft akzeptieren und nicht darauf bestehen, dass zum ursprünglichen Preis abgeschlossen wird.
   b) Dann hat das Settlement am Spot Date zu erfolgen, wenn keine andere Vereinbarung getroffen wurde.
   c) Die Bank soll das Geschäft zum nächsten Preis akzeptieren. Die Differenz wird vom Broker per Scheck beglichen.
   d) Alle Antworten sind richtig.

4. Nach welchen Grundsätzen sollten Differenzen zwischen Broker und Bank abgewickelt werden?

5. Welche Empfehlung gibt der Model Code zur Praxis des „Settlement of Differences by Points" ab?

6. Authorisation, Documentation, Telephone Taping

In this chapter you learn ...
- about the Model Code recommendations concerning authorisation and responsibility for dealing.
- about the Model Code recommendations concerning terms and documentation.
- about the details of proper dealing procedures.
- what should be observed when taping telephone conversations.
- what should be observed when using mobile devices for transactions.

6.1. Authorisation and responsibility for dealing

Control of the activities of all personnel engaged in dealing (both dealers and back office) in both banking and broking firms is the **responsibility of the management** of such organisations. Management should clearly set out, **in writing, the authorisations and responsibilities within which dealing** (and support staff) **should operate**.

These might include:

- General dealing policy including reporting procedures
- Persons authorised to deal
- Instruments to be dealt in
- Limits on open positions
- Confirmation and settlement procedures
- Relationships with brokers/banks
- Other relevant guidance as considered appropriate

It is the management's responsibility to ensure that all employees are adequately trained and are aware of their own and their firm's responsibilities.

6.2. Terms and documentation

Documentation should be **completed and exchanged as soon as possible** after a deal is done, and the use, wherever possible, of **standard terms and conditions** to facilitate this process is recommended strongly. Standard terms and conditions have been issued by various authorities for many instruments. When using such agreements, any proposed modifications or choices offered in the agreement must clearly be stated before dealing.

Dealers and brokers should make it clear whether or not they propose to use standard terms and where changes are proposed, these should be made clear. If the changes are substantial, these amendments should be negotiated and agreed before the consummation of the deal. For instruments where standard terms do not exist, particular care and attention should be paid to negotiation of terms and documentation.

In more complex transactions like swaps, dealers should regard themselves as bound to deal at the point where commercial terms of the transaction are agreed. Making swaps transactions subject to agreement on documentation is considered bad practice. Every effort should be made to finalise documentation as quickly as possible.

6. Autorisierung, Dokumentation, Telefonaufzeichnungen

In diesem Kapitel lernen Sie ...

- welche Empfehlungen der Model Code zur Autorisierung und Verantwortung für Handelsaktivitäten gibt.
- was der Model Code bezüglich Vertragsbedingungen und Dokumentation empfiehlt.
- wie qualifizierte Geschäftsbedingungen aussehen.
- wie mit Bandaufnahmen umgegangen werden soll.
- was bei der Verwendung mobiler Endgeräte bei Transaktionen zu beachten ist.

6.1. Autorisierung und Verantwortung für Handelsaktivitäten

Die Kontrolle der Aktivitäten aller an einem Handelsgeschäft beteiligten Personen (Händler und Backoffice), sowohl in Banken als auch bei Brokern, obliegt der **Verantwortung des jeweiligen Managements.** Die Geschäftsleitung soll **in klarer, schriftlicher Form die Kompetenzen und Verantwortlichkeiten definieren,** die dem Handel und dem Backoffice zufallen. Das Management soll auch im Kundengeschäft eindeutige Regelungen erlassen, zu welchen Transaktionen jeder Händler berechtigt ist.

Die Richtlinien des Managements sollten folgende Punkte enthalten:

- allgemeiner Handelsablauf inklusive Berichtsstruktur
- zum Handel berechtigte Personen
- gehandelte Instrumente
- Limitstruktur
- Bestätigungs- und Settlementprozess
- Beziehung zu Brokern und Banken
- andere relevante Punkte

Außerdem soll das Management sicherstellen, dass alle Mitarbeiter ausreichend qualifiziert sind und sich ihrer Verantwortungsbereiche bewusst sind.

6.2. Vertragsbedingungen und Dokumentation

Die **Dokumentation** sollte **so schnell wie möglich fertiggestellt und ausgetauscht** werden. Der **Gebrauch von Standardbedingungen,** die von verschiedenen Behörden herausgegeben werden, wird dringend empfohlen. Änderungen dieser Standardbedingungen müssen vor Geschäftsabschluss bekanntgegeben werden.

Bei Produkten, die vom Model Code behandelt werden, sollten Händler und Broker klarmachen, ob sie zu Standardbedingungen abschließen möchten oder nicht. Substanzielle Abweichungen zu den Standardbedingungen sollten vor Geschäftsabschluss verhandelt und festgelegt werden.

Bei Produkten, bei denen keine Standarddokumentationen existieren, ist größter Wert auf das Aushandeln aller Bedingungen und die Dokumentation zu legen. Bei komplexeren Transaktionen, wie z.B. Swaps, haben sich Händler an das Geschäft gebunden zu fühlen, sobald diese Bedingungen festgelegt wurden. Swapgeschäfte an die Dokumentation zu binden ist unstatthaft. Es sollte jede Anstrengung unternommen werden, die Dokumentation so schnell wie möglich abzuschließen.

6.3. Qualifying and preliminary dealing procedure

Both **dealers and brokers should state clearly at the outset, prior to a transaction being executed, any qualifying conditions to which it will be subject.** These include: where the price is quoted subject to the necessary credit approval; finding a counterparty for matching deals, or the ability to execute an associated transaction. If a dealer's ability to conclude a transaction is constrained by, for example, opening hours in other centres, this should be made known to brokers and potential counterparties at an early stage and before names are changed.

6.4. Telephone taping and recording of electronic text messages

Experience has shown that recourse to tapes proves invaluable to the speedy resolution of differences. The use of recording equipment in the offices of banks and brokers is strongly recommended. **All conversations** undertaken by dealers and brokers **should be recorded** together with back office telephone lines used by those responsible for confirming deals or passing payment or other instructions. When initially installing tape equipment or taking on new clients or counterparties, firms should inform their counterparties and clients that conversations will be recorded.

Tapes and other records should be **kept for at least two months**. Firms dealing in longer term interest rate swaps, FRAs or similar instruments where errors may only be found on the date that the first movement of funds is due to take place, may consider it prudent to retain tapes relevant to these transactions for longer periods.

Management should ensure that the use of recording equipment complies with local legislation including laws on data protection, privacy and human rights. There should be a clear written policy on whether and to what extent telephone conversations are to be taped and electronic text messages to be recorded and how long tapes and other records are kept. This policy should be reviewed regularly by management. The guidelines on taping telephone conversations and recording electronic text messages should impose controls to ensure that tapes and other recordings are not deliberately or inadvertently deleted. Management should ensure that access to tapes, whether in use or in store, is strictly controlled so that they cannot be tampered with.

6.5. Use of mobile devices for transacting business

Management should have a **clear written policy** regarding the use of these devices by trading, sales and settlement staff.

The policy guidelines should stipulate amongst other monitor and control measures:

- whether privately and/or company owned devices can be used inside the dealing room and back office to transact, advise or confirm transactions
- whether privately and/or company owned devices be allowed inside the dealing room
- terms, conditions and under which circumstances the use of such devices can be authorized by management
- procedures to allow an end-to-end transaction audit trail, including where appropriate, call back or answer phone facilities and controls

6.3. Qualifizierte Geschäftsbedingungen

Sowohl **Makler als auch Händler legen vor der Transaktion deutlich fest, unter welchen Bedingungen sie Geschäfte abwickeln.** Dazu gehört auch, ob Preise freibleibend oder unter der Bedingung von Kreditmöglichkeit Gegen- oder Absicherungsgeschäften genannt werden. Sollte die Möglichkeit, ein Geschäft abzuschließen, von anderen Möglichkeiten, wie z.B. den Handelszeiten in anderen Finanzzentren abhängen, muss auch dieses unverzüglich Brokern oder potenziellen Gegenparteien bekanntgegeben werden, noch bevor Namen ausgetauscht werden.

6.4. Bandaufnahmen und Speicherung von elektronischen Nachrichten

Es hat sich herausgestellt, dass Bandaufnahmen unerlässlich sind, um Differenzen schnell ausräumen zu können. Der Gebrauch von Tonbandgeräten wird dringend empfohlen. **Alle Gespräche** zwischen Händlern und Kunden sowie alle Gespräche mit dem Backoffice-Bereich sind **aufzuzeichnen.** Bei der Neuinstallierung von Aufzeichnungsgeräten sowie neuen Kunden müssen die Gesprächspartner darüber informiert werden, dass die Gespräche aufgezeichnet werden.

Alle Bänder sollen **mindestens zwei Monate aufbewahrt** werden. Gesprächsaufzeichnungen über längerfristige Geschäfte, z.B. Zinsswaps, FRAs oder ähnliche Produkte, bei denen sich Fehler erst dann bemerkbar machen, wenn die erste Geldbewegung stattfindet, sollten mindestens so lange verwahrt werden, bis die erste Transaktion aus diesem Geschäft erfolgt.

Das Management sollte sicherstellen, dass bei Gesprächsaufzeichnungen nicht gegen die lokalen Gesetze inklusive Datenschutz, Privatsphäre und Menschenrechte verstoßen wird. Es sollten klare, schriftliche Richtlinien erstellt werden, die regeln, ob und in welchem Ausmaß Telefongespräche aufgezeichnet und elektronische Nachrichten gespeichert werden und wie lange die Bänder behalten werden. Diese Richtlinien sollten regelmäßig vom Management überprüft werden.

Die Richtlinien für die Aufzeichnung von Gesprächen und die Speicherung von elektronischen Nachrichten sollten auch Kontrollmechanismen beinhalten, die sicherstellen, dass die Bänder nicht absichtlich oder unabsichtlich gelöscht werden. Außerdem sollte der Zugang zu den Bändern so gestaltet sein, dass eine nachträgliche Veränderung der Bänder ausgeschlossen werden kann.

6.5. Verwendung mobiler Endgeräte bei Transaktionen

Für die Verwendung von mobilen Endgeräten (z.B. Handys, Personal Digital Assistants etc.) in den Bereichen Handel, Vertrieb und Abwicklung sollte die Geschäftsleitung **klare, schriftliche Leitlinien** ausarbeiten.

Diese Leitlinien sollten folgende Regelungen enthalten:

- Verwendung privater und/oder firmeneigener mobiler Endgeräte im Handelsraum und im Backoffice, um Geschäfte abzuschließen und zu bestätigen oder um Beratungsgespräche zu führen
- Zulassung von privaten und/oder firmeneigenen mobilen Endgeräten innerhalb des Handelsraums
- Bestimmungen und Bedingungen für die Fälle, in denen diese Geräte von der Geschäftsleitung zugelassen werden
- Verfahren, die einen Audit Trail für die gesamte Transaktion ermöglichen, gegebenenfalls einschließlich Rückruf- und Anrufbeantworterfunktionen

The use of wireless communication devices within the front or back offices for official business, except in an emergency or disaster recovery situation or specifically approved by senior management is **not considered good practice**.

Summary

Controlling the activities of all personnel engaged in dealing (both dealers and back office) in both banking and broking firms is the responsibility of the management of such organisations. Management should clearly set out, in writing, the authorisations and responsibilities within which dealing (and support) staff should operate.

Documentation should be completed and exchanged as soon as possible after a deal is done, and the use, wherever possible, of standard terms and conditions to facilitate this process is recommended strongly. When using such agreements, any proposed modifications or choices offered in the agreement must clearly be stated before dealing. For instruments where standard terms do not exist, particular care and attention should be paid to negotiations of terms and documentation.

Both dealers and brokers should state clearly at the outset, prior to a transaction being executed, any qualifying conditions to which it will be subject. These include: where the price is quoted subject to the necessary credit approval; finding a counterparty for matching deals, or the ability to execute an associated transaction.

Experience has shown that recourse to tapes proves invaluable to the speedy resolution of differences. The use of recording equipment in the offices of banks and brokers is strongly recommended. All conversations undertaken by dealers and brokers should be recorded together with back office telephone lines used by those responsible for confirming deals or passing payment or other instructions. Tapes should be kept for at least two months.

Management should have a clear written policy regarding the use of these devices by trading, sales and settlement staff. The use of wireless communication devices within the front or back offices for official business, except in an emergency or disaster recovery situation or specifically approved by senior management is not considered good practice.

6.6. Practice questions

1. Which points should be clearly set out by the management for checking the authorisations and responsibilities within which dealing and support staff?
2. The Model Code recommends that all recordings of dealing conversations should be kept. For which period they should be kept?
   a) not at all
   b) at least one month
   c) at least two months
   d) at least three months
3. What are the recommendations of the Model Code concerning use of standard conditions?
4. At what time latest should terms and conditions be publiehsed announced?
   a) before switching the names
   b) before fixing the price of the swap spot transaction
   c) after checking the credit limit
   d) before getting the confirmation

Die Verwendung mobiler Endgeräte im Front- oder Backoffice zur Durchführung von Transaktionen gilt als **schlechter Stil.** Ausgenommen davon sind Fälle, in denen ein Notfall oder eine Disaster-Recovery-Situation besteht oder eine ausdrückliche Genehmigung der Geschäftsleitung vorliegt.

Zusammenfassung

Die Kontrolle der Aktivitäten aller an einem Handelsgeschäft beteiligten Personen (Händler und Backoffice), sowohl in Banken als auch bei Brokern, obliegt der Verantwortung des jeweiligen Managements. Die Geschäftsleitung soll in klarer, schriftlicher Form die Kompetenzen und Verantwortlichkeiten definieren, die dem Handel und dem Backoffice zufallen. Außerdem soll das Management sicherstellen, dass alle Mitarbeiter ausreichend qualifiziert sind und sich ihrer Verantwortungsbereiche bewusst sind.

Die Dokumentation sollte so schnell wie möglich fertiggestellt und ausgetauscht werden. Der Gebrauch von Standardbedingungen, die von verschiedenen Behörden herausgegeben werden, wird dringend empfohlen. Änderungen dieser Standardbedingungen müssen vor Geschäftsabschluss bekanntgegeben werden. Bei Produkten, bei denen keine Standarddokumentationen existieren, ist größter Wert auf das Aushandeln aller Bedingungen und die Dokumentation zu legen.

Sowohl Makler als auch Händler legen vor der Transaktion deutlich fest, unter welchen Bedingungen sie Geschäfte abwickeln. Dazu gehört auch, ob Preise freibleibend oder unter der Bedingung von Kreditmöglichkeit Gegen- oder Absicherungsgeschäften genannt werden.

Es hat sich herausgestellt, dass Bandaufnahmen unerlässlich sind, um Differenzen schnell ausräumen zu können. Der Gebrauch von Tonbandgeräten wird dringend empfohlen. Alle Gespräche zwischen Händlern und Kunden sowie alle Gespräche mit dem Backoffice-Bereich sind aufzuzeichnen. Alle Bänder sollen mindestens zwei Monate aufbewahrt werden.

Für die Verwendung von mobilen Endgeräten (z.B. Handys, Personal Digital Assistants etc.) in den Bereichen Handel, Vertrieb und Abwicklung sollte die Geschäftsleitung klare, schriftliche Leitlinien ausarbeiten. Die Verwendung mobiler Endgeräte im Front- oder Backoffice zur Durchführung von Transaktionen gilt als schlechter Stil. Ausgenommen davon sind Fälle, in denen ein Notfall oder eine Disaster-Recovery-Situation besteht oder eine ausdrückliche Genehmigung der Geschäftsleitung vorliegt.

6.6. Wiederholungsfragen

1. Welche Punkte sollten die Richtlinien des Managements zur Kontrolle der Aktivitäten aller an einem Handelsgeschäft beteiligten Personen enthalten?
2. Im Model Code wird empfohlen, alle Aufzeichnungen in Zusammenhang mit einem Handelsgeschäft aufzuheben. Wie lange sollen die Aufzeichnungen aufgehoben werden?
   a) gar nicht
   b) mindestens ein Monat
   c) mindestens zwei Monate
   d) mindestens drei Monate

5. Which points should be included in the guidelines for the use of mobile devices?
6. The use of wireless communication devices within the front or back offices for official business is not considered good practice except ...
    a) in an emergency.
    b) in volatile markets.
    c) when quoting for information only.
    d) in a disaster recovery situation.
    e) where it is specifically approved by the senior management.

3. Welche Empfehlungen gibt der Model Code bezüglich Gebrauch von Standardbedingungen?

4. Bis zu welchem Zeitpunkt sollen qualifizierte Geschäftsbedingungen bekanntgegeben werden?
   a) vor Austausch der Namen
   b) bis zur Fixierung des Kurses der Swap-Kassatransaktion
   c) nach Prüfung der Kreditlimits
   d) bis zum Eintreffen der Bestätigung

5. Welche Punkte sollten die Leitlinien zur Verwendung mobiler Endgeräte enthalten?

6. Der Model Code sieht die Verwendung mobiler Endgeräte im Front- oder Backoffice zur Durchführung von Transaktionen als schlechten Stil. Ausgenommen davon sind Fälle, in denen …
   a) ein Notfall vorliegt.
   b) in volatilen Märkten gehandelt wird.
   c) Preise nur zur Information quotiert werden.
   d) eine Disaster-Recovery-Situation vorliegt.
   e) eine ausdrückliche Genehmigung der Geschäftsleitung vorliegt.

7. Brokers and Brokerage

In this chapter you learn ...
- about the role of brokers and the relationship between dealer and broker.
- about the Model Code recommendations concerning commission and brokerage.
- what should be observed for electronic broking.
- in which cases names can be passed on by brokers.
- what is meant by switching and when it is used.

7.1. The role of brokers and dealer/broker relationship

Brokers act as **intermediaries or arrangers of deals** and should aim to agree mutually acceptable terms between principals. Brokers are **forbidden to act in any discretionary fund management capacity**.

Senior management of both trading institutions and brokerage firms should assume an active role in overseeing the trader-broker relationship. Management should **establish the terms under which brokerage service is to be rendered**, agree that any aspect of the relationship can be reviewed by either party at any time, and be available to intercede in disputes as they arise. The management of both institutions should ensure that their staffs are aware of and in compliance with internal policies governing the trader-broker relationship.

Ultimately, the senior management is responsible for the choice of the broker. Additionally it should periodically monitor the patterns of broker usage and be alert to possible undue concentration of business.

Management should impress upon their employees the need to **respect the interests of all the institutions** served by their firm.

7.2. Commission/brokerage

In countries where brokers' charges are freely negotiable, such charges **should be agreed only by directors or senior management** on each side and recorded **in writing**. Any deviation from previously agreed brokerage arrangements should be expressly approved by both parties and clearly recorded in writing. Brokers normally quote dealing **prices excluding commission/brokerage charges**.

Failure to pay brokerage bills promptly is not considered good practice as in some jurisdictions overdue payments are treated as a deduction from capital base for regulatory purposes, thus putting the broker at a disadvantage.

7.3. Electronic broking

Transactions executed through an electronic broking system should be handled in accordance with the provisions of individual vendor's Dealing Rule Book and with all documents and agreements relating to a customer's utilisation of the services. The vendor's dealing book should stipulate clearly the **procedure and responsibilities** that apply in the event of:

- communication breakdown at the point of the consummation of trades
- off-market discrepancies
- software inadequacies or limitations ("Bugs")

7. Broker und Provisionen

In diesem Kapitel lernen Sie ...

- die Rolle der Broker und das Verhältnis zwischen Händler und Broker kennen.
- welche Empfehlungen der Model Code zu Kommission/Provision gibt.
- was beim elektronischen Broking zu beachten ist.
- in welchen Fällen Namen durch Broker weitergegeben werden dürfen.
- was man unter Switching versteht und wann es angewendet wird.

7.1. Die Rolle der Broker und das Verhältnis zwischen Händler und Broker

Ein Broker wirkt als **Intermediär zwischen zwei Kontraktparteien** und soll die Übereinstimmung zwischen den Geschäftspartnern herbeiführen. Broker dürfen **keine Eigenpositionen** handeln.

Die Geschäftsleitungen von Bank und Broker sollen die Beziehung zwischen Händler und Broker überwachen und die kommerziellen **Bedingungen für die Zusammenarbeit festlegen.** Weiters soll zwischen den Geschäftsführungen vereinbart werden, dass alle Aspekte des Abkommens von beiden Parteien jederzeit überprüft werden können und Problemfälle auf Geschäftsleitungsebene behandelt werden. Das Management von Banken und Brokern hat darauf zu achten, dass die internen Vorschriften im Umgang mit dem Broker bzw. der Bank den Mitarbeitern bekannt sind und eingehalten werden.

Die Geschäftsleitung der Bank soll die Entscheidung über die Auswahl des Brokers treffen und in regelmäßigen Abständen überprüfen, ob es nicht zu unangebrachten Geschäftskonzentrationen mit einzelnen Brokern kommt.

Die Geschäftsleitung des Brokers hat darauf zu achten, dass die Mitarbeiter die **Interessen aller Kunden im selben Ausmaß berücksichtigen.**

7.2. Kommission/Provision

In Ländern, in denen Maklergebühren frei vereinbar sind, sollten solche Gebühren nur **vom Topmanagement oder von Direktoren festgelegt** werden. Dies sollte **schriftlich** geschehen. Jede Abweichung von diesen Gebühren muss im Einvernehmen mit dem Geschäftspartner und schriftlich erfolgen. Makler nennen **üblicherweise Preise ohne Provision oder Maklergebühr.**

Es ist unstatthaft, Brokergebühren nicht sofort zu bezahlen, da in einigen Rechtsprechungen überfällige Zahlungen von der Eigenkapitalbasis in Abzug gebracht werden und somit den Broker benachteiligen.

7.3. Elektronisches Broking

Alle über ein elektronisches Brokingsystem abgewickelten Transaktionen müssen mit dem individuellen Handelsregelbuch und allen Dokumenten und Vereinbarungen bezüglich der Verwendung dieser Dienstleistung durch den Kunden in Einklang stehen. Es sollten für folgende Fälle **klare Vorgehensweisen und Verantwortlichkeiten** definiert sein:

- Systemabsturz während eines Geschäftsabschlusses
- Eingabe marktferner Preise
- Softwaremängel oder -einschränkungen (sogenannte Bugs)

Electronic broking includes an **increased potential for systemic risk** particularly due to erroneous price or "big figure" inputting. It is unethical to consummate deals at rates outside current market prices when it is obvious that the counterparty has made a mistake.

Any abuse of the electronic system is deemed unethical and should be strongly discouraged by management. These include:

- Inputting of bid/offer prices well out of range of the current market spread, seeking profitable off market deals by exploiting big figure decimal errors in the confusion of sudden volatility.
- Sudden temporary withdrawal of a specific credit limit or limits in a tactical manipulation to mislead the market

Management of banks should institute control measures to prevent unauthorised access to any electronic broking system and ensure that dealers have a full comprehension of the system involved. To this end, dealers should read and understand the relevant operational manuals.

7.4. Passing of names by brokers

Brokers **should not divulge the names of principals prematurely**, and certainly not until satisfied that both sides display a serious intention to transact. Principals and brokers should, at all times, treat the details of transactions as absolutely confidential to the parties involved.

Bank dealers should, wherever possible, give brokers prior indication of counterparties with whom, for whatever reason, they would be unwilling to do business (referring as necessary to particular markets or instruments). At the same time, brokers should take full account of the best interests and the precise instructions of the client. In some instruments, dealers may also wish to give brokers guidance on the extent of their price differentiation across broad categories of counterparties.

In all transactions, brokers should aim to achieve **a mutual and immediate exchange of names**. However, this will not always be possible. There will be times when one principal's name proves unacceptable to another; and the broker will quite properly decline to divulge by whom it was refused. This may sometimes result in the principal whose name has been rejected feeling that the broker may in fact have quoted a price or rate which it could not in fact substantiate.

In certain centres, in such cases, either the Central Bank or some other neutral body, may be prepared to establish with the reluctant counterparty that it did have business to do at the quoted price and the reasons why the name was turned down so that the aggrieved party can be assured the original quote was valid without, of course, revealing the proposed counterparty's name. An example guideline here is Article 82 of the London Code of the FSA.

In the deposit markets, it is accepted that principals dealing through a broker have the right to turn down a name wishing to take deposits: this could therefore require pre-disclosure of the name before closing the deal. Once a lender (or buyer) has asked the key question "who pays?" or "whose paper is it?", it is considered committed to do business at the price quoted with the name or with an alternative acceptable name if offered immediately. The name of a lender (or buyer in respect of CD's) shall be disclosed only after the borrower's (or issuer's) name has been accepted by the lender (or buyer).

Elektronisches Broking beinhaltet ein **erhöhtes Systemrisiko,** insbesondere durch die Eingabe eines falschen Preises oder einer falschen „Big Figure". Da Fehler leicht passieren können, ist es unstatthaft, ein Geschäft zu einem marktfernen Preis abzuschließen.

Jeder Missbrauch des elektronischen Systems ist unethisch und vom Management zu unterbinden. Dazu zählen insbesondere:

- Eingabe von marktunüblichen Geld/Brief-Spreads, um „Big Figure"-Dezimalfehler, die aus Unsicherheit aufgrund hoher Volatilität entstehen, gewinnbringend zu nützen.
- Plötzlicher, vorübergehender Rückzug von einem oder mehreren Kreditlimits in manipulativer Absicht, d.h., um den Markt in die Irre zu führen.

Das Management hat Kontrollmechanismen zu installieren, die eine missbräuchliche Verwendung elektronischer Brokersysteme verhindern und gewährleisten sollen, dass die betroffenen Händler das System beherrschen. Zu diesem Zweck sollen Händler die Benutzerhandbücher lesen und verstehen.

7.4. Weitergabe von Namen durch Broker

Makler dürfen die **Namen ihres Auftraggebers nicht vor Abschluss des Handels,** auf jeden Fall nicht bevor beide Seiten ernsthafte Absichten gezeigt haben, **bekanntgeben.** Bekanntgegebene Namen müssen von beiden Seiten als vertraulich behandelt werden. Händler sollten, wenn möglich, den Maklern mitteilen, mit welchen Kunden sie – eventuell nur für bestimmte Instrumente und Märkte – keine Geschäfte abwickeln wollen.

Broker sollen die Interessen der Parteien bestens vertreten und ihren Anweisungen genauestens folgen. Bei manchen Instrumenten können Händler ihren Brokern eine Preisdifferenzierung nach Kundengruppen vorgeben.

Bei allen Transaktionen hat der Makler auf einen **schnellen Austausch der Namen** zu drängen. Das ist aber nicht immer möglich. Es gibt Fälle, in denen der Name einer Partei für die andere nicht akzeptabel ist, woraufhin der Broker zu Recht den Namen der ablehnenden Partei nicht bekanntgibt. Dies kann den abgelehnten Marktteilnehmer zum Glauben veranlassen, dass der Broker einen Preis angeboten hat, den er in der Realität nicht bedienen konnte.

In einigen Zentren ist die Zentralbank bereit (z.B. gemäß § 82 London Code der FSA), mit der ablehnenden Partei in Verbindung zu treten und festzustellen, dass sie – die Zentralbank – das Geschäft zu dem angebotenen Preis abwickeln will. Gleichzeitig erfragt sie die Gründe der Ablehnung. Damit hat die abgelehnte Partei die Gewissheit, dass die ursprüngliche Quotierung gültig war, ohne dass dabei der Name der vorgesehenen Partei offengelegt wird.

Im Depotmarkt ist es akzeptiert, dass Kunden, die durch einen Makler abschließen, gewisse Namen ablehnen können. Das führt dazu, dass der Name vor Abschluss offenbart werden muss. Sobald der Verkäufer (Käufer) von CDs nach dem Namen der anderen Partei fragt, ist er verpflichtet, zu dem quotierten Preis abzuschließen bzw. einen anderen akzeptablen Namen anzuerkennen, wenn er sofort angeboten wird. Der Name des Geldgebers sollte erst dann bekanntgegeben werden, wenn der Kreditnehmer vom Geldgeber akzeptiert worden ist.

The proposed **borrower may decline the lender's name** when,

- in the case of short date deposits, the borrower is not prepared to repay the deposit prior to advice of receipt of the funds from his correspondent bank
- he has no lending line for the placer of the funds and does not wish to be embarrassed by being unable to reciprocate
- the borrower is prohibited by management from entering into any transaction with the lending institution

Additionally, in the case of instruments like CDs, where the seller may not be the same entity as the issuer, the broker shall first disclose the issuer's name to the potential buyer. Once a buyer has asked "Whose paper is it?", the buyer is considered committed to deal at the price quoted. Once the buyer asks "Who sells?", he is considered committed with the particular seller in question (or an alternative acceptable name immediately shown to the buyer by the broker). The name of the buyer shall be disclosed only after the seller's name has been accepted by the buyer. The seller has the right to refuse the particular buyer so long as it is prepared to accept, at that time, sums up to the same amount and at the same price from an alternative acceptable name immediately shown to it by the broker.

7.5. Name substitution/switching by brokers

Switching is acceptable practice if the **circumstances justify** it and if it is **approved by the parties whose names are substituted**. In spot exchange, brokers typically do not reveal the names of counterparties until the amount and exchange rate are agreed upon. It is therefore possible that, after these details are agreed, the name of one counterparty may prove unacceptable to the other due to unavailability of a credit line. In these circumstances, it is accepted market practice that brokers will attempt to substitute a third name to stand between the two original counterparties to clear the transaction.

Because the two offsetting transactions will utilise credit lines and because they are often executed at an exchange rate that is off-market due to the time it takes to arrange name substitution, such activities should be **identified as switching transactions and they should be monitored and controlled**.

If requested by a broker to clear a transaction through name switching, a dealer must ensure that such activities have the prior approval of senior management, that he or she has the authority to switch names and that any such transactions are executed within policy guidelines. Finally, a dealer must not seek nor accept favours from the broker for switching names.

Summary

Brokers act as intermediaries or arrangers of deals and should aim to arrived at terms acceptable to both principals. Brokers are forbidden to act in any discretionary fund management capacity. Management should establish the terms under which brokerage service is to be rendered, agree that any aspect of the relationship can be reviewed by either party at any time, and be available to intercede in disputes as they arise.

In countries where brokers' charges are freely negotiable, such charges should be agreed only by directors or senior management on each side and recorded in writing. Brokers normally quote dealing prices excluding commission/brokerage charges. Failure to pay

Der Geldnehmer kann den **Namen des Geldgebers ablehnen,** wenn

- er bei „Short Dates" das Depot nicht zurückzahlen kann, bevor er eine Empfangsbestätigung von seiner Korrespondenzbank erhalten hat.
- keine Kreditlinie für den Partner hat und vermeiden will, ein Reziprok-Geschäft ablehnen zu müssen.
- der Händler von der Geschäftsleitung keine Erlaubnis hat, Geld vom potenziellen Kontrahenten zu nehmen.

Bei Instrumenten, bei denen der Aussteller nicht dem Verkäufer entsprechen muss (z.B. CDs), sollte der Broker den Namen des Ausstellers dem potenziellen Käufer bekanntgeben. Sobald die interessierte Partei nach dem Aussteller fragt („Whose paper is it?"), ist sie auch an die Quotierung gebunden.

Fragt der Käufer nach dem Namen („Who sells/pays?"), muss er den Namen (oder eine sofort vom Broker angezeigte akzeptable Alternative) akzeptieren.

Der Name des Käufers wird dem Käufer erst nach Abschluss des Geschäftes genannt. Der Verkäufer kann den Käufer nur ablehnen, wenn er an einen vom Broker sofort genannten akzeptierbaren Namen zum selben Preis denselben Betrag verkauft.

7.5. Ersatz/Tausch von Namen durch Broker (Switching)

Switching ist akzeptabel, wenn dies **nach den gegebenen Umständen gerechtfertigt** ist und wenn der **Tausch von dazu befugten Personen genehmigt** wurde.

Typischerweise werden im FX-Markt die Namen der Parteien vom Broker nicht genannt, bevor Volumen und Kurs bestimmt wurden. Sollte sich dann herausstellen, dass ein Name aufgrund ausgefüllter Kreditlinien nicht akzeptierbar ist, kann der Broker eine dritte Partei zwischenschalten, um das Geschäft zu ermöglichen. Switching soll vom Broker angezeigt werden.

Da beim Switching sowohl Kreditlinien beansprucht werden als auch die dabei verwendeten Kurse oft nicht mehr im Markt sind (aufgrund der zeitlichen Verzögerung, herbeigeführt durch die Suche nach einem dritten Namen), sollten diese **Aktivitäten überprüft, kontrolliert und als Switching-Transaktionen ausgewiesen** werden.

Wenn ein Broker ein Geschäft durch Switching durchführen will, muss der Händler sicher sein, dass er für diese Geschäfte die Zustimmung des Managements hat und diese Geschäfte in die vorgegebenen Richtlinien fallen. Ein Händler darf für Switching weder den Broker um Zuwendungen bitten noch welche von diesem akzeptieren.

Zusammenfassung

Ein Broker wirkt als Intermediär zwischen zwei Kontraktparteien und soll die Übereinstimmung zwischen den Geschäftspartnern herbeiführen. Broker dürfen keine Eigenpositionen handeln. Die Geschäftsleitungen von Bank und Broker sollen die Beziehung zwischen Händler und Broker überwachen und die kommerziellen Bedingungen für die Zusammenarbeit festlegen.

In Ländern, in denen Maklergebühren frei vereinbar sind, sollten solche Gebühren nur vom Topmanagement oder von Direktoren schriftlich festgelegt werden. Makler nennen Preise üblicherweise ohne Provision oder Maklergebühr. Es ist unstatthaft, Brokergebühren nicht sofort zu bezahlen, da in einigen Rechtsprechungen überfällige Zahlungen von der Eigenkapitalbasis in Abzug gebracht werden und somit den Broker benachteiligen.

brokerage bills promptly is not considered good practice as in some jurisdictions overdue payments are treated as a deduction from capital base for regulatory purposes, thus putting the broker at a disadvantage.

Transactions executed through an electronic broking system should be handled in accordance with the provisions of the individual vendor's Dealing Rule Book and with all documents and agreements relating to a customer's use of the services. Electronic broking entails an increased potential for systemic risk especially due to erroneous price or "big figure" inputting. It is unethical to consummate deals at rates outside current market prices when it is obvious that the counterparty has made a mistake.

Brokers should not divulge the names of principals prematurely, and certainly not until satisfied that both sides display a serious intention to transact. Principals and brokers should, at all times, treat the details of transactions as absolutely confidential to the parties involved.

In all transactions, brokers should aim to achieve a mutual and immediate exchange of names. In the deposit markets, it is accepted that principals dealing through a broker have the right to turn down a name wishing to take deposits. Once a lender (or buyer) has asked the key question "who pays?" or "whose paper is it?", he is considered committed to do business at the price quoted with the name or with an alternative acceptable name if offered immediately. The name of a lender (or buyer in respect of CD's) shall be disclosed only after the borrower's (or issuer's) name has been accepted by the lender (or buyer).

Switching is acceptable practice if the circumstances justify it and if it is approved by the parties whose names are substituted. Because the two offsetting transactions will utilise credit lines and because they are often executed at an exchange rate that is off-market due to the time it takes to arrange name substitution, such activities should be identified as switching transactions and they should be monitored and controlled.

7.6. Practice questions

1. Describe the role of brokers between two principals!
2. Are brokers allowed to deal for personal account?
3. Which of the following transactions within electronic broking systems are strongly discouraged by the ACI Model Code?
   a) exploiting big figure decimal errors in the confusion of sudden volatility
   b) inputting bids and offers well out of range of the current market spread
   c) sudden temporary withdrawal of a specific credit limit in an attempt to mislead the market
   d) All answers are true.
4. For which cases should the vendor's dealing book clearly stipulate the procedure and responsibilities?
5. Which of the following statements concerning electronic broking is FALSE?
   a) Brokers should not key into the system prices for amounts that they do not intend to offer.
   b) If the connection is lost the deal is automatically cancelled.
   c) If the connection is lost the counterparty should be contacted immediately in order to clarify the deal.
   d) An accidentally inputted deal can be nullified if the rate is way off the prevailing market price and the acting bank contacts the counterparty involved immediately to cancel the deal.

Alle über ein elektronisches Brokingsystem abgewickelten Transaktionen müssen mit dem individuellen Handelsregelbuch und allen Dokumenten und Vereinbarungen bezüglich der Verwendung dieser Dienstleistung durch den Kunden in Einklang stehen. Elektronisches Broking beinhaltet ein erhöhtes Systemrisiko, insbesondere durch die Eingabe eines falschen Preises oder einer falschen „Big Figure". Da Fehler leicht passieren können, ist es unstatthaft, ein Geschäft zu einem marktfernen Preis abzuschließen. Jeder Missbrauch des elektronischen Systems ist unethisch und vom Management zu unterbinden.

Makler dürfen die Namen ihres Auftraggebers nicht vor Abschluss des Geschäftes, auf jeden Fall nicht bevor beide Seiten ernsthafte Absichten gezeigt haben, bekanntgeben. Bekanntgegebene Namen müssen von beiden Seiten vertraulich behandelt werden. Bei allen Transaktionen hat der Makler auf einen schnellen Austausch der Namen zu drängen. Im Depotmarkt ist es akzeptiert, dass Kunden, die durch einen Makler abschließen, gewisse Namen ablehnen können. Bei Instrumenten, bei denen der Aussteller nicht dem Verkäufer entsprechen muss (z.B. CDs), soll der Broker den Namen des Ausstellers dem potenziellen Käufer bekanntgeben. Sobald die interessierte Partei nach dem Aussteller fragt, ist sie auch an die Quotierung gebunden. Fragt der Käufer nach dem Namen, muss er den Namen (oder eine sofort vom Broker angezeigte akzeptable Alternative) akzeptieren.

Switching ist akzeptabel, wenn dies nach den gegebenen Umständen gerechtfertigt ist und wenn der Tausch von dazu befugten Personen genehmigt wurde. Switching soll vom Broker angezeigt werden. Da beim Switching sowohl Kreditlinien beansprucht werden als auch die dabei verwendeten Kurse oft nicht mehr im Markt sind, sollten diese Aktivitäten überprüft, kontrolliert und als Switching-Transaktionen ausgewiesen werden.

7.6. Wiederholungsfragen

1. Beschreiben Sie die Rolle des Brokers beim Abschluss eines Kontrakts zwischen zwei Geschäftsparteien!
2. Sind Broker auch berechtigt, Eigenpositionen zu handeln?
3. Welche der folgenden Handlungen innerhalb elektronischer Brokersysteme sind laut Model Code abzulehnen?
   a) Ausnützen von Big-Figure-Irrtümern bei plötzlich einsetzender hoher Volatilität
   b) Eingabe von Kaufs- und Verkaufspreisen, die deutlich außerhalb der Bandbreite des aktuellen Marktes liegen
   c) plötzlicher und zeitweiliger Widerruf eines spezifischen Kreditlimits als taktische Manipulation zur Irreführung des Marktes
   d) Alle Antworten sind richtig.
4. Für welche Fälle sollten klare Vorgehensweisen und Verantwortlichkeiten in Bezug auf elektronisches Broking definiert sein?
5. Welche Aussage bezüglich des elektronischen Brokerings ist FALSCH?
   a) Broker sollen keine Preise für Beträge eingeben, die sie nicht akzeptieren wollen.
   b) Sollte die Verbindung abbrechen, gilt das Geschäft automatisch als nicht abgeschlossen.
   c) Sollte die Verbindung abbrechen, ist der Geschäftspartner sofort zu kontaktieren, um das Geschäft abzuklären.
   d) Wird ein Geschäft unbeabsichtigt abgeschlossen, so ist es ungültig, wenn der Preis weit aus dem Markt ist und die Bank sofort den Partner kontaktiert.

6. What does the Model Code recommend concerning commission and brokerage?
7. How do brokers normally quote dealing prices?
   a) according to commission negotiated
   b) including brokerage charges
   c) excluding commission
   d) including VAT
8. Which of the following statements is true?
   a) Brokers should only reveal the identity of a counterparty to a deal if they know the counterparty very well.
   b) Broker should reveal the identity of a counterparty to any deal in all mentioned cases.
   c) Broker should not reveal the identity of a counterparty to any deal unless expressly authorized to do so by the counterparty.
   d) Brokers should only reveal the identity of counterparty if they are forced to do so.
9. What can bank A do, if bank A is declined by bank B because of a problem with the name?
10. In which market can customers dealing with a broker decline certain names? What is the consequence?
11. Under what circumstances can a borrower decline a lender's name in the money market?
    a) if the lender is not the issuer of the CD
    b) never
    c) if the lender has a low rating
    d) if he has no credit line in place to reciprocate the deal.
12. You want to buy a CD and get a quotation of 5.20% from your broker. You ask: *Whose paper is it?* Which of the following statements is true?
    a) You must accept the name.
    b) You have bought at 5.20%.
    c) The names are switched.
    d) If you accept the name, you must buy at 5.20%.
13. Under which circumstances is switching an acceptable practice?
14. Why should switching activities be monitored and controlled?

6. Welche Empfehlung gibt der Model Code zu Maklerprovisionen ab?
7. Wie quotieren Makler üblicherweise?
   a) abhängig von der Maklerprovision
   b) inklusive Maklerprovision
   c) exklusive Maklerprovision
   d) inklusive Umsatzsteuer
8. Welche der folgenden Aussagen ist richtig?
   a) Broker sollen nur die Namen jener Banken anzeigen, die sie gut kennen.
   b) Broker können, unabhängig von den Intentionen der Parteien, so viele Namen wie möglich im Markt anzeigen.
   c) Broker sollen nur die Namen jener Banken anzeigen, die ernsthafte Absichten haben zu handeln.
   d) Broker sollten nur jene Namen von Banken anzeigen, die gute Provisionen bringen.
9. Was kann Bank A tun, wenn Bank A von Bank B abgelehnt wird, weil es ein Problem mit dem Namen gibt?
10. In welchem Markt können Kunden, die durch einen Makler abschließen, gewisse Namen ablehnen? Wohin führt dies?
11. Wann kann der Geldnehmer den Namen des Geldgebers bei Geldmarktgeschäften ablehnen?
    a) wenn der Geldgeber nicht der Aussteller des CD ist
    b) niemals
    c) wenn der Geldgeber ein schlechtes Rating hat
    d) wenn er keine Kreditlinie für ein Reziprok-Geschäft hat
12. Sie wollen ein CD kaufen und erhalten von Ihrem Broker eine Quotierung von 5,20%. Sie fragen: *Whose paper is it?* Welche der folgenden Aussagen ist richtig?
    a) Sie müssen den Namen akzeptieren.
    b) Sie haben zu 5,20% gekauft.
    c) Die Namen werden ausgetauscht.
    d) Sie müssen, so Sie den Namen akzeptieren, zu 5,20% kaufen.
13. Unter welchen Voraussetzungen ist Switching akzeptabel?
14. Warum sollten die Switching-Aktivitäten überprüft und kontrolliert werden?

8. Dealing Practice

In this chapter you learn ...

- about the Model Code recommendations concerning dealing at non-current rates.
- what should be observed at consummation of a deal.
- about the Model Code recommendations concerning firm quotation.
- about the Model Code recommendations concerning qualification and reference.
- about the Model Code recommendations dealing with unidenitfied principals.
- about the Model Code recommendations Internet/online trading.

8.1. Dealing at non-current rates

Deals at non-market rates **should generally be avoided**. Where, however, the use of non-current rates may be necessary, they should only be entered into with the prior express permission of senior management, who should ensure that proper controls are in place for the monitoring and reporting of such transactions to avoid losses, fraud, tax evasion, and unauthorised extension of credit.

Where, however, the use of non-current market rates may be necessary (as in swaps market or in certain transactions with corporate clients), they should be entered into with the **prior express permission of senior management**, who should ensure that proper controls are in place for the **monitoring and reporting of such transactions** to avoid the abovementioned problems.

Cash flow implications should be taken into account in the pricing. Spot rates should be fixed immediately within the current spread, to reflect current rates at the time the transaction was done.

In order to avoid misunderstandings it is recommended that not only the last two digits (Pips), but also the digit before ("Big Figure") should be included in all outright and spot FX quotations. In case of disputes in foreign exchange quotations, it is highly unethical for one party to hold another to an erroneously agreed rate where the quotation is demonstrably and verifiably a "Big Figure" or more off the prevailing market rate.

8.2. Consummation of a deal

Dealers should regard themselves as **bound to a deal once a price and any other key commercial terms have been agreed**. However, **holding brokers unreasonably to a price is viewed as unprofessional** and should be discouraged by management. Where prices are qualified as being indicative or subject to negotiation of commercial terms, dealers should normally treat themselves as bound to a deal to a point where terms have been agreed without qualifications. **Verbal agreements are considered binding**. The **subsequent confirmation is regarded as evidence of the deal**, but **should not override terms agreed verbally**. The practice of making a transaction "subject to documentation" is **not regarded as good practice**. In order to minimise the likelihood of disputes arising once documentation is prepared, firms should make every effort to agree all material points quickly during the verbal negotiation of terms and should agree any remaining details as soon as possible. Where brokers are involved, it is their responsibility to **ensure the principal providing the price or rate is made aware immediately it has been dealt upon**. As a general rule, a deal should only be regarded as having been done where the broker's contact is positively acknowledged by the dealer.

A broker should never assume a deal is done without some form of verbal acknowledgement from the dealer. Where a broker puts a specific proposition to a dealer for a price (e.g.

8. Handelspraxis

In diesem Kapitel lernen Sie ...

- welche Empfehlungen der Model Code für den Handel zu nicht-aktuellen Kursen gibt.
- was bei der Durchführung eines Geschäfts zu beachten ist.
- welche Empfehlungen der Model Code zur festen Quotierung gibt.
- welche Empfehlungen der Model Code zu Qualifikation und Referenz gibt.
- was der Model Code bezüglich Handel mit nicht-identifizierten Personen empfiehlt.
- was der Model Code bezüglich Internet-/Online-Handel empfiehlt.

8.1. Handel zu nicht-aktuellen Kursen

Diese Geschäfte sind **grundsätzlich zu vermeiden,** da sie zur Verschleierung von Gewinnen bzw. Verlusten sowie zu Betrug, Steuerhinterziehung oder einer ungenehmigten Ausweitung von Kreditlinien verwendet werden können. Wo solche Geschäfte aus verschiedenen Gründen trotzdem notwendig sind, dürfen sie nur mit vorheriger Genehmigung eines Vorgesetzten getätigt werden.

Sollte die Verwendung von nicht-aktuellen Kursen notwendig sein (z.B. im Swapmarkt oder bei speziellen Kundentransaktionen), sollte dies **nur nach ausdrücklicher Genehmigung der Geschäftsleitung** geschehen. Die Geschäftsleitung hat Sorge zu tragen, dass ein **geeignetes Überwachungs- und Berichtswesen** für Geschäfte mit historischen Kursen existiert.

Cashflow-Auswirkungen sollen beim Pricing berücksichtigt werden. Kassakurse sollten sofort innerhalb des Spreads fixiert werden, damit die aktuellen Kurse zur Zeit der Transaktion widergespiegelt werden.

Um Missverständnissen vorzubeugen, wird empfohlen, nicht nur die beiden letzten Stellen (Pips), sondern auch die vor diesen stehende Ziffer („Big Figure") in sämtlichen Quotierungen für Devisentermin- und Devisenkassageschäfte anzugeben.

Bei Streitigkeiten über Quotierungen für Devisengeschäfte gilt es als in höchstem Maße unethisch, wenn eine Partei gegenüber der anderen Partei an einem irrtümlicherweise vereinbarten Kurs festhält, wenn die Quotierung eindeutig und nachweislich um eine „Big Figure" oder noch stärker vom gültigen Marktkurs abwich.

8.2. Durchführung eines Geschäfts

Händler haben sich **an einen Deal gebunden** zu fühlen, **sobald der Preis und andere wichtige Bedingungen festgelegt worden sind.** Auf der anderen Seite ist es **unstatthaft,** einen **Makler in unzumutbarer Weise an einen Preis zu binden.** Wenn Preise als freibleibend qualifiziert wurden, sollten Händler sich dann an den Deal gebunden fühlen, wenn alle anderen Bedingungen festgelegt wurden. **Mündliche Vereinbarungen sind bindend.** Die folgende **schriftliche Bestätigung gilt als Beweis für das Geschäft.** Sie **ändert aber nicht die mündlichen Absprachen.** Ein Geschäft **von der Dokumentation abhängig zu machen** ist **unstatthaft.** Um die Wahrscheinlichkeit von Unstimmigkeiten zu senken, haben alle Beteiligten darauf zu achten, dass alle wichtigen Bedingungen mündlich vereinbart werden. Eventuell fehlende Details sollten so schnell wie möglich geklärt werden.

Broker sollen **die quotierende Partei unverzüglich informieren,** wenn auf ihrem Preis gehandelt wurde. Ein Geschäft gilt dann als abgeschlossen, wenn der Händler seine mündli-

specifying an amount and a name for which the quote is required), the dealer can reasonably expect to be told almost immediately by the broker whether the price has been hit or not.

In interbank trading, irrespective of whether direct or through a broker, a deal should be concluded upon verbal agreement. In cases where a dealer is calling "off" at the same instant as the broker is hitting a price, a transaction should be concluded. In such cases the broker should immediately inform the dealer that the deal is done and the name of the counterparty to the deal concerned. Conversely, in cases of a broker withdrawing at the same instant as a dealer is hitting a price, no transaction should be concluded. In such cases, the broker should immediately notify the dealer that no transaction has been concluded ("nothing done").

In cases where a **price being quoted by a broker is hit simultaneously by several banks** for a total amount greater than what the price concerned is valid for, the broker should apportion the amount the **price is valid for proportionally among the banks concerned** in accordance with the amount hit by each. In such cases, brokers should not be held to any obligation to deal in standard trading units of currency; however they should immediately inform all the relevant banks that apportionment will be carried out.

Under no circumstances should brokerage firms inform dealers that a deal has been concluded when in fact it has not.

8.3. Dealing quotations – firmness, qualification, reference

All market participants have a **duty to make absolutely clear whether the prices they are quoting are firm or merely indicative**. Prices quoted by brokers should be taken to be firm in marketable amounts unless otherwise qualified. A dealer quoting a firm price (or rate), either through a broker or directly to a potential counterparty, is committed to deal at that price (or rate) in a marketable amount provided the counterparty name is acceptable.

When dealing in fast moving markets (e.g. spot, FX, or currency options) a dealer has to assume that a price given by a broker is good only for a short length of time – typically a matter of seconds. However, if adopted when dealing in generally less hectic markets, this practice would offer room for misunderstandings about how quickly a price is deemed to lapse. The onus is on dealers in such circumstances to satisfy themselves that their prices have been taken off unless a **time limit** is placed by the dealer on his interest at the outset (e.g. price is firm for one minute). Otherwise, the **dealer should feel bound to deal with an acceptable name at the quoted rate in a marketable amount**.

Brokers should make every effort to assist dealers by checking with them from time to time whether their interest at a particular price or rate is still current. What constitutes a marketable amount varies from market to market, but will generally be familiar to those operating in that market. A broker, if quoting on the basis of small amounts or particular names, should qualify the quotation accordingly. Where dealers are proposing to deal in unfamiliar markets through a broker, it is recommended that they first ask brokers what amounts are sufficient to validate normal quotations. If their interest is in a smaller amount, this should be specified by the dealer when initially requesting or offering a price to the broker.

A dealer remains committed to a price quoted by a broker until one of the following situations occurs:

- The price was dealt on.
- The deal was cancelled.
- His quote is superseded by a better bid/offer.
- The broker closes the transaction in that currency with another counterparty at a price other than that originally proposed.

che Zustimmung gegeben hat. Stellt der Broker dem Händler mit bestimmten Zusätzen (d.h. Volumen und Namen), dann kann der Händler erwarten, dass der Broker sofort angibt, ob das Geschäft abgeschlossen wird oder nicht.

Im Interbankenhandel gilt das Geschäft als abgeschlossen, wenn eine mündliche Zusage vorliegt. Widerruft ein Händler einen Preis, während der Broker zuschlägt, so gilt das Geschäft, und der Broker hat den Händler zu informieren, mit wem das Geschäft abgeschlossen wurde. Widerruft der Broker, während der Händler zuschlägt, gilt das Geschäft als nicht gemacht und der Händler ist entsprechend zu informieren („nothing done").

Wird ein von Brokern **quotierter Preis von mehreren Kunden gleichzeitig genommen** und wird dadurch die Nachfrage größer als das Angebot, so soll der Broker den möglichen Betrag **proportional zu den gewünschten Beträgen aufteilen.** Der Broker kann nicht angehalten werden, Standardbeträge zuzuteilen, wenn sie zu groß sind. Jedoch soll der Broker sofort alle betroffenen Händler über die Zuteilung informieren.

Unter keinen Umständen darf ein Broker einen Händler informieren, dass ein Geschäft abgeschlossen wurde, wenn in Wahrheit keines gemacht worden ist.

8.3. Feste Quotierung, Qualifikation, Referenz

Alle Marktteilnehmer haben die **Pflicht, eindeutig festzulegen, ob die von ihnen genannten Preise fix oder freibleibend sind.** Falls dies nicht eindeutig festgestellt wird, gelten sie als bindend. Ein Händler, der einen fixen Preis oder Zinssatz stellt, ist verpflichtet, einen Deal über einen marktüblichen Betrag abzuschließen, sobald sein Geschäftspartner dics wünscht.

In sich schnell ändernden Märkten (z.B. Spot, Währungsoptionen) muss sich der Anfrager bewusst sein, dass der Preis nur für eine sehr kurze Zeitspanne, manchmal nur Sekunden, gilt. Diese Praxis kann aber in weniger hektischen Märkten (z.B. Forwards, Depots) zu Missverständnissen führen. Sollte **kein Zeitlimit** (z.B. firm für eine Minute) für den Preis festgelegt werden, liegt die **Last, Preise als nicht mehr bindend zu erklären, beim Händler.** Ansonsten ist der Händler verpflichtet, einen **marktüblichen Deal mit einem akzeptierbaren Namen** abzuschließen.

Makler sollten den Händlern helfen, indem sie von Zeit zu Zeit nachfragen, ob gewisse Preise oder Zinssätze noch gelten. Was als marktüblicher Deal gilt, ist von Markt zu Markt verschieden, aber den Marktteilnehmern normalerweise bekannt.

Quotiert ein Broker kleine Volumina bzw. spezielle Namen, sollte er dies anzeigen. Händlern, die sich über Broker in unbekannten Märkten engagieren wollen, wird empfohlen, zuerst die marktüblichen Volumina vom Broker zu erfragen. Möchten Händler einen geringeren als den Standardbetrag über Broker handeln, sollten sie diesen Wunsch zu Beginn der Anfrage äußern.

Händler sind an über Broker quotierte Preise so lange gebunden, bis einer der folgenden Fälle eintritt:

- Es wird auf den Kursen gehandelt.
- Der Händler widerruft.
- Seine Quotierung wird durch eine bessere Quotierung ersetzt.
- Der Broker hat eine andere Transaktion in derselben Währung mit einer anderen Partei zu einem anderen Preis abgeschlossen.

In the last two cases, the broker should consider the original bid/offer no longer valid unless reinstated by the dealer (that is, the broker places the bid/offer "under reference").

In the **swap market**, considerable use is made of **"indicative interest" quotations**. When arranging a swap an unconditional firm rate will only be given where a principal deals directly with a client or when such a principal has received a client's name or their rating from a broker. A principal who quotes a rate or spread as "firm subject to credit" is bound to deal at the quoted rate or spread if the name is consistent with a category of counterparty previously identified for this purpose.

The only exception is where the particular name cannot be done, for example, if the **principal has reached its credit limit for that name**, in which case the principal will correctly reject the transaction. It is **not an acceptable practice for a principal to revise a rate which was "firm subject to credit" once the name of the counterparty has been disclosed**. Brokers and principals should work together to establish a range of institutions for whom the principal's rate is firm subject to credit.

8.4. Dealing with unidentified principals

The recent increase in the volume of OTC transactions conducted through institutional fund managers and investment dealers/advisors has resulted in a substantial number of deals where the principal counterparties are not known at the time of transaction.

While the Model Code acknowledges the wish for anonymity in some cases, it recommends for the Compliance, Legal and Credit functions to have full knowledge of the principal's identity **at least prior to the execution** of a transaction, in order that credit risk, "Know Your Customer", anti-money laundering and potential fraud issues can be addressed. Where prior identification of the ultimate counterparty is difficult, for instance in case of a bulk transaction for later allocation to the principals of that agent, parties **should agree in writing that the result of such an allocation is confirmed as soon as possible after conclusion of the trade**.

Management of financial institutions should be continually aware of closely linked risks, particularly in respect of credit risk and money laundering, and should have appropriate written policies in place to safeguard this confidentiality internally. Furthermore, dealer firms should be aware that any disclosure of customer information to third parties is prohibited by law in most jurisdictions.

8.5. Internet/Online trading

Where Internet facilities are established by a bank for a client, the **conditions and controls should be comprehensively stated in the Bank rulebook**. There should be **appropriate security** in place governing access, authentication and identification of personnel who are authorised to use the facility. The **"know your customer" and money laundering provisions** should be meticulously followed.

Summary

Deals at non-market rates should generally be avoided in order to avoid losses, fraud, tax evasion and unauthorised extension of credit. Where, however, the use of non-current market rates may be necessary (as in the swap market or in certain transactions with corporate clients), they should be entered into with the prior express permission of senior management.

In den letzten beiden Fällen muss der Makler davon ausgehen, dass der Preis des Händlers nicht länger gilt und wiederbestätigt werden muss, d.h., der Broker muss den Preis „under reference" stellen.

Im **Swapmarkt** werden **oft freibleibende Preise** genannt. Eine fixe Preiszusage wird nur gegeben, wenn der Name oder die Bonität des Geschäftspartners bekannt ist bzw. eine Bank direkt mit dem Kunden handelt. Wird ein Preis oder ein Spread im Swapmarkt „Subject to Credit" quotiert, ist der Händler an den Preis gebunden, wenn der Name aus einer vorher definierten Gruppe von Gegenparteien stammt.

Die **einzige Möglichkeit abzulehnen** ergibt sich, wenn das **Kreditlimit für die Gegenpartei überschritten** wird. Eine **Änderung der Preise nach Preisgabe des Namens ist unstatthaft.** Broker und Händler sollten zusammen eine Liste jener Namen erstellen, bei denen Quotierungen an ein Kreditlimit gebunden sind.

8.4. Handel mit nicht-identifizierten Personen

Die jüngste Volumenzunahme bei außerbörslichen Handelsgeschäften, die über Fondsmanager bzw. Investmenthändler abgewickelt werden, hat zu einem erheblichen Anteil an Deals geführt, bei denen die Geschäftsparteien zum Zeitpunkt des Geschäftsabschlusses nicht bekannt sind.

Obwohl der Model Code den Wunsch nach Anonymität in einigen Fällen anerkennt, empfiehlt er, dass zumindest vor Durchführung der Transaktion die volle Identität der Gegenpartei bekannt ist, um Probleme in den Bereichen Kreditrisiko, „Kenne deinen Kunden", Geldwäsche und Betrug besser handhaben zu können. Ist die Identifikation der Gegenpartei vor Durchführung der Transaktion in der Praxis schwierig, beispielsweise im Falle einer Bulk Transaktion mit einer späteren Verrechnung an die Auftraggeber des Händlers, sollten die Parteien schriftlich vereinbaren, dass das Ergebnis der Verrechnung so bald wie möglich nach Eingabe des Geschäfts bestätigt wird.

Die Geschäftsleitung von auf dieser Basis tätigen Finanzinstituten muss sich der damit verbundenen Risiken, insbesondere im Hinblick auf Kreditrisiko und Geldwäsche, stets bewusst sein und für schriftlich festgelegte Regeln im Zusammenhang mit derartigen Geschäften sorgen. Zusätzlich sollten sich die Finanzinstitute im Klaren sein, dass jegliche Bekanntgabe von Kundeninformationen an dritte Parteien in den meisten Rechtssystemen gesetzlich verboten ist.

8.5. Internet/Online-Handel

Werden dem Kunden Leistungen angeboten, die auf dem Internet basieren, sind **Bedingungen und Kontrollen in einem bankinternen Regelbuch** zu dokumentieren. **Geeignete Sicherheitsmaßnahmen** sollen eingerichtet werden, die Zugang, Berechtigung und Identifikation des autorisierten Personals überprüfen. Alle **Bestimmungen bezüglich Geldwäsche und des Prinzips „Kenne deinen Kunden"** sind besonders genau zu beachten.

Zusammenfassung

Geschäfte zu nicht-aktuellen Kursen sind grundsätzlich zu vermeiden, da sie zur Verschleierung von Gewinnen bzw. Verlusten sowie zu Betrug, Steuerhinterziehung oder einer ungenehmigten Ausweitung von Kreditlinien verwendet werden können. Sollte die Verwendung von nicht-aktuellen Kursen trotzdem notwendig sein (z.B. im Swapmarkt oder bei speziellen Kundentransaktionen), sollte dies nur nach ausdrücklicher Genehmigung der Geschäftsleitung geschehen.

Dealers should regard themselves as bound to a deal once a price and any other key commercial terms have been agreed. However, holding brokers unreasonably to a price is viewed as unprofessional and should be discouraged by management.

Verbal agreements are considered binding. The subsequent confirmation is regarded as evidence of the deal, but should not override terms agreed verbally. The practice of making a transaction "subject to documentation" is not regarded as good practice.

In interbank trading, irrespective of whether direct or through a broker, a deal should be concluded upon verbal agreement. In cases where a price being quoted by a broker is hit simultaneously by several banks for a total amount greater than what the price concerned is valid for, the broker should apportion the amount the price is valid for proportionally among the banks concerned in accordance with the amount hit by each.

All market participants have a duty to make absolutely clear whether the prices they are quoting are firm or merely indicative. The onus is on dealers in such circumstances to satisfy themselves that their prices have been taken off unless a time limit is placed by the dealer on his interest at the outset (eg, price is firm for one minute). Otherwise, the dealer should feel bound to deal with an acceptable name at the quoted rate in a marketable amount.

In the swap market, frequent use is made of "indicative interest" quotations. When arranging a swap an unconditional firm rate will only be given where a principal deals directly with a client or when such a principal has received a client's name or their rating from a broker.

The only exception is where the particular name cannot be used, for example, if the principal has reached their credit limit for that name, in which case the principal will correctly reject the transaction. It is not an acceptable practice for a principal to revise a rate which was "firm subject to credit" once the name of the counterparty has been disclosed.

If transactions are conducted through funds managers/investment dealers, traders should undertake all efforts to identify the principal counterparties as soon as possible following a deal.

Where nternet facilities are established by a bank for a client, the conditions and controls should be comprehensively stated in the bank rulebook. The "know your customer" and money laundering provisions should be meticulously followed.

8.6. Practice Questions

1. What is true regarding foreign exchange deals undertaken at non-current historic rates?
   a) They should be undertaken at the customer's request.
   b) They should be undertaken at the dealer's discretion.
   c) They should be undertaken only under the specific authority of senior management.
   d) They should be undertaken in the event of rolling-on a forward outright deal.
2. Why should deals at non-market rates generally be avoided?
3. 90 days ago a client opened a forward contract to sell EUR 1 m against USD at 1.0580. Today, upon maturity of this contract, the client informs the bank that he wishes to extend the delivery date by 30 days. The prevailing EUR/USD spot rate is 1.0350. What are the appropriate steps?
   a) Forward contract must not be extended at non-current rates.
   b) Extend the contract after you have received permission from management; use the current swap points without any modification.

Händler haben sich an einen Deal gebunden zu fühlen, sobald der Preis und andere wichtige Bedingungen festgelegt worden sind. Auf der anderen Seite ist es unstatthaft, einen Makler in unzumutbarer Weise an einen Preis zu binden. Mündliche Vereinbarungen sind bindend. Die folgende schriftliche Bestätigung gilt als Beweis für das Geschäft. Sie ändert aber nicht die mündlichen Absprachen. Ein Geschäft von der Dokumentation abhängig zu machen ist unstatthaft. Broker sollen die quotierende Partei unverzüglich informieren, wenn auf ihrem Preis gehandelt wurde. Im Interbankhandel gilt das Geschäft als abgeschlossen, wenn eine mündliche Zusage vorliegt. Wird ein von Brokern quotierter Preis von mehreren Kunden gleichzeitig genommen und wird dadurch die Nachfrage größer als das Angebot, so soll der Broker den möglichen Betrag proportional zu den gewünschten Beträgen aufteilen.

Alle Marktteilnehmer haben die Pflicht, eindeutig festzulegen, ob die von ihnen genannten Preise fix oder freibleibend sind. Falls dies nicht eindeutig festgestellt wird, gelten sie als bindend. Sollte kein Zeitlimit (z.B. firm für eine Minute) für den Preis festgelegt werden, liegt die Last, Preise als nicht mehr bindend zu erklären, beim Händler. Ansonsten ist der Händler verpflichtet, einen marktüblichen Deal mit einem akzeptierbaren Namen abzuschließen.

Im Swapmarkt werden oft freibleibende Preise genannt. Eine fixe Preiszusage wird nur gegeben, wenn der Name oder die Bonität des Geschäftspartners bekannt ist bzw. eine Bank direkt mit dem Kunden handelt.

Die einzige Möglichkeit abzulehnen ergibt sich, wenn das Kreditlimit für die Gegenpartei überschritten wird. Eine Änderung der Preise nach Preisgabe des Namens ist unstatthaft.

Handeln Banken mit Fondsmanagern, entsteht das Problem, dass der Händler bei Geschäftsabschluss nicht weiß, mit welcher Gegenpartei er das Geschäft abgeschlossen hat. Händler sollten daher bestrebt sein, so rasch wie möglich die Namen zu ermitteln.

Werden dem Kunden Leistungen angeboten, die auf dem Internet basieren, sind Bedingungen und Kontrollen in einem bankinternen Regelbuch zu dokumentieren. Alle Bestimmungen bezüglich Geldwäsche und des Prinzips „Kenne deinen Kunden" sind besonders genau zu beachten.

8.6. Wiederholungsfragen

1. Was trifft auf FX-Geschäfte zu nicht-aktuellen Kursen zu?
   a) Sie sollen auf Vorschlag des Kunden abgeschlossen werden.
   b) Sie sollen nach Ermessen des Händlers abgeschlossen werden.
   c) Sie sollen nur nach spezieller Genehmigung durch die Vorgesetzten abgeschlossen werden.
   d) Sie sollen aufgrund eines Rolling-on eines Outright-Geschäftes abgeschlossen werden.
2. Warum sollten Geschäfte zu nicht-aktuellen Kursen grundsätzlich vermieden werden?
3. Ein Kunde hat vor 90 Tagen EUR 1 Mio. zu 1,0580 auf Termin gegen USD verkauft. Der Kontrakt läuft heute aus und der Kunde möchte den Kontrakt um 30 Tage verlängern. Der aktuelle Kassakurs ist 1,0350. Wie wäre die richtige Vorgangsweise?
   a) Terminkontrakte dürfen nie zu historischen Kursen rolliert werden.
   b) Genehmigung des Vorgesetzten einholen und zum aktuellen Swap verlängern, da die Kursdifferenz keinen Einfluss hat.

    c) Extend the contract after you have received permission from management; worsen the swap points by the cost of carry.

    d) Extend the contract after you have received permission from management; improve the swap points by the cost of carry.

4. Which of the following statements is correct due to the Model Code?
    a) Verbal agreements are considered binding.
    b) Only written agreements are considered binding.
    c) The written confirmation might override terms agreed verbally.
    d) All answers are false.

5. What happens in interbank trading if a dealer calls off at the same time as the broker hits the price?
    a) No transaction is concluded.
    b) A transaction should be concluded.
    c) The dealer has the choice whether to conclude the transaction or leave it.
    d) The broker decides whether the transaction is concluded or not.

6. What does the Model Code recommend for cases where a price being quoted by a broker is hit simultaneously by several banks for a total amount greater than what the price concerned is valid for?

7. When do market participants have a duty to make it clear whether their prices are firm or merely indicative?
    a) only if they are dealing with brokers
    b) only if the amount is not marketable
    c) only when dealing in fast-moving markets
    d) at all times
    e) only when trading derivatives

8. Name four cases where a dealer does not remain committed to a price quoted by a broker!

9. In the swap market, frequent use is made of "indicative interest" quotations. In which cases are firm quotations given?

10. What are the recommendations of the Model Code for dealing with unidentified principals?

11. What measures are necessary when a bank establishes internet facilities for a client?

12. Which of the following statements concerning online trading is true?
    a) The rules concerning "know your customer" are not relevant for online trading.
    b) All rules concerning "know your customer" and "money laundering" should be strictly adhered to in online trading.
    c) The Model Code does not give any recommendations concerning online trading.
    d) All answers are true.

c) Genehmigung des Vorgesetzten einholen und die Swappunkte um den Zinsnachteil aus der Kursdifferenz verschlechtern.

d) Genehmigung des Vorgesetzten einholen und die Swappunkte um den Zinsvorteil aus der Kursdifferenz verbessern.

4. Welche der folgenden Aussagen ist laut Model Code richtig?

a) Mündliche Vereinbarungen gelten als verbindlich.

b) Ausschließlich schriftliche Vereinbarungen gelten als verbindlich.

c) Die schriftliche Bestätigung darf die mündlich vereinbarten Konditionen außer Kraft setzen.

d) Alle Aussagen sind falsch.

5. Was geschieht im Interbankenhandel, falls ein Händler eine Quotierung zur selben Zeit, zu der ein Broker zuschlägt, widerruft?

a) Es findet kein Geschäft statt.

b) Das Geschäft soll abgeschlossen werden.

c) Der Händler entscheidet, ob das Geschäft abgeschlossen wird oder nicht.

d) Der Broker entscheidet, ob das Geschäft abgeschlossen wird oder nicht.

6. Welche Vorgangsweise empfiehlt der Model Code für den Fall, dass ein quotierter Preis von mehreren Kunden gleichzeitig genommen und dadurch die Nachfrage größer als das Angebot wird?

7. Wann haben Händler die Verpflichtung klarzumachen, ob Preise fix oder freibleibend sind?

a) nur wenn sie mit Broker handeln

b) nur wenn der Betrag marktunüblich ist

c) nur wenn sie in schnelllebigen Märkten handeln

d) immer

e) nur bei Derivaten

8. Nennen Sie vier Fälle, die zu einem Ende der Bindung des Händlers an über Broker quotierte Preise führen!

9. Im Swapmarkt werden oft freibleibende Preise genannt. In welchen Fällen werden fixe Preiszusagen gegeben?

10. Welche Empfehlungen gibt der Model Code zum Handel mit nicht identifizierten Personen ab?

11. Welche Maßnahmen sind notwendig, wenn dem Kunden Leistungen angeboten werden, die auf dem Internet basieren?

12. Welche der folgenden Aussagen bezüglich Online-Handel ist richtig?

a) Das Prinzip „Kenne Deinen Kunden" spielt im Online-Handel keine Rolle.

b) Alle Bestimmungen bezüglich Geldwäsche und des Prinzips „Kenne Deinen Kunden" sind im Online-Handel besonders genau zu beachten.

c) Der Model Code gibt zum Online-Handel keine Empfehlungen ab.

d) Alle Antworten sind richtig.

9. Dealing Practice for Specific Transactions

In this chapter you learn ...
- how deals using a "connected broker" are done.
- what should be condiered for assignment and transfer.
- what should be condiered for repos and stock lending.

9.1. Deals using a "connected broker"

Brokers should **advise their clients of the names of any principals** (i.e. banks and other financial institutions) **that hold a share/investment with the brokerage firm or have management responsibilities**. With increasing diversification of broker firms and groups it is increasingly important that principals know with certainty the broking legal entity in any transaction.

9.2. Assignment and Transfer

Brokers and principals assigning or transferring a swap to a third party must ensure that

- **principals** are aware that they are ultimately **responsible for assessing the creditworthiness of the counterparty** and
- their **staff are well trained in the practices** of the market place and are aware of the firm's business responsibilities.

Principals who enter into any wholesale market transaction with the intention of shortly afterwards assigning or transferring the deal to a third party should **make clear their intention to do so from the outset**. It is recommended that the confirmation sent by the principal should specify any intent to assign and give details of the procedure that will be used. When a principal is intending to execute such a transfer it **must obtain the consent of the transferee before releasing its name**. The transferee has an obligation to give the principal intending to transfer sufficient information to enable the transaction to be concluded in accordance with the principles of best practices.

9.3. Repos and stock lending

In the case of sale and repurchase agreements or stock lending or lending transactions, proper documentation including **written agreement of key terms and conditions** should be in place prior to the consummation of any trades. Legal opinion on the enforceability of the contract should be obtained.

Summary

Brokers should advise their clients of the names of any principals (ie, banks and other financial institutions) that hold a share/investment with the brokerage firm or have management responsibilities.
Brokers and principals assigning or transferring a swap to a third party must ensure that principals are aware that they are ultimately responsible for assessing the creditworthi-

9. Handelspraxis für spezielle Transaktionen

In diesem Kapitel lernen Sie ...
- wie Geschäfte über „verbundene Broker" ablaufen.
- was bei Abtretungen und Übertragungen zu beachten ist.
- was bei Wertpapierpensionsgeschäften zu beachten ist.

9.1. Geschäfte über „verbundene Broker"

Broker sollten ihren **Kunden alle Beteiligungsverhältnisse von und an Auftraggebern** (d.h. Banken und anderen Finanzinstitutionen) **anzeigen.** Dabei kann es sich um Investitionsbeteiligungen, Aktien oder Verflechtungen im Management handeln. Mit der zunehmenden Diversifikation der Makler ist es besonders wichtig, dass die Geschäftsparteien wissen, welche Rechtspersönlichkeit der Broker hat.

9.2. Abtretungen und Übertragungen

Bei der Abtretung oder Übertragung eines Swaps an eine dritte Partei müssen der Broker und die abtretende/übertragende Partei Folgendes beachten:

- Die **Banken** sind **für die Einschätzung der Kreditwürdigkeit der Gegenpartei verantwortlich.**
- Die **Mitarbeiter** müssen **gut ausgebildet** und mit den **Marktusancen des Produktes vertraut** sein.

Schließt eine Partei einen Swap mit der Absicht ab, diesen bald an eine dritte Partei abzutreten oder zu übertragen, so soll sie diese **Absicht schon bei den Verhandlungen klarmachen.** Es ist empfehlenswert, auf der Bestätigung die Absicht und die Abwicklung der Abtretung zu dokumentieren. Bevor die übertragende Partei das Assignment oder die Übertragung durchführt, soll sie die **Zustimmung des Übernehmers einholen,** seinen Namen bekanntgeben zu dürfen. Der Übernehmer hat die Pflicht, dem Übertragenden alle notwendigen Informationen zur Abwicklung gemäß den Prinzipien der bestmöglichen Praxis zur Verfügung zu stellen.

9.3. Repos und Wertpapierleihe

Bei Wertpapierpensionsgeschäften sollte eine **schriftliche Dokumentation** mit den wichtigsten Vertragsbedingungen vorhanden sein, bevor ein Geschäft abgeschlossen wird. Es ist empfehlenswert, eine Rechtsmeinung zur Durchsetzbarkeit des Vertrages einzuholen.

Zusammenfassung

Broker sollten ihren Kunden alle Beteiligungsverhältnisse von und an Auftraggebern (d.h. Banken und anderen Finanzinstitutionen) anzeigen. Dabei kann es sich um Investitionsbeteiligungen, Aktien oder Verflechtungen im Management handeln.
Broker und Geschäftsparteien, die ein Swapgeschäft an einen Dritten abtreten oder übertragen, müssen sicherstellen, dass den Parteien bewusst ist, dass sie letztendlich die Verantwortung für die Bewertung der Kreditwürdigkeit eines Geschäftspartners tragen und

ness of the counterparty and their staff are well-trained in the practices of the market place and are aware of the firm's business responsibilities.

Principals who enter into any wholesale market transaction with the intention of shortly after-wards assigning or transferring the deal to a third party should make clear their intention to do so from the outset.

In the case of sale and repurchase agreements or stock lending or lending transactions, proper documentation including written agreement of key terms and conditions should be in place prior to the consummation of any trades.

9.4. Practice Questions

1. What should you do as a broker if your owner is a bank and you want to make a deal with your counterparty?
    a) You should advise the other counterparty of the connection.
    b) You are not obligated to reveal the connection in the professional market.
    c) You are not obligated to reveal the connection provided a Chinese Wall is installed.
    d) All answers are false.
2. Brokers and principals assigning or transferring a swap to a third party must ensure that…
    a) principals are aware that they are ultimately responsible for assessing the creditworthiness of a counterparty.
    b) their staff is well-trained in the practices of the marketplace and aware of the firms business responsibilities.
    c) they make clear their intention to do so when initially negotiating the deal.
    d) All answers are true.
3. What should be done by the transferee before the assignment or transfer is transacted?
4. What should be in place prior to the consummation of any trades of repos?

dass ihre Mitarbeiter mit den Praktiken des Marktplatzes gut vertraut und sich der geschäftlichen Verantwortung des Unternehmens bewusst sind.

Schließt eine Partei einen Swap mit der Absicht ab, diesen bald an eine dritte Partei abzutreten oder zu übertragen, so soll sie diese Absicht schon bei den Verhandlungen klarmachen.

Bei Wertpapierpensionsgeschäften sollte eine schriftliche Dokumentation mit den wichtigsten Vertragsbedingungen vorhanden sein, bevor ein Geschäft abgeschlossen wird.

9.4. Wiederholungsfragen

1. Was müssen Sie als Broker-Unternehmen tun, wenn Ihre Eigentümer eine Bank ist und Sie ein Geschäft mit einem Geschäftspartner abschließen wollen?
   a) Sie sollten die Verbindung dem Geschäftspartner offenlegen.
   b) Sie sind nicht zur Offenlegung der Verbindung im professionellen Markt verpflichtet.
   c) Sie sind nicht zur Offenlegung der Verbindung verpflichtet, vorausgesetzt, eine Chinese Wall ist installiert.
   d) Alle Antworten sind falsch.
2. Was müssen Broker und Geschäftsparteien, die ein Swapgeschäft an einen Dritten abtreten oder übertragen, laut Model Code sicherstellen?
   a) dass den Parteien bewusst ist, dass sie letztendlich die Verantwortung für die Bewertung der Kreditwürdigkcit eines Geschäftspartners tragen.
   b) dass ihre Mitarbeiter mit den Praktiken des Marktplatzes gut vertraut und sich der geschäftlichen Verantwortung des Unternehmens bewusst sind.
   c) dass sie ihre Absicht, das Swapgeschäft abtreten oder übertragen zu wollen, gleich zu Beginn der Geschäftsverhandlungen klar zum Ausdruck bringen.
   d) Alle Antworten sind richtig.
3. Was sollte von der übertragenden Partei eingeholt werden, bevor sie das Assignment oder die Übertragung durchführt?
4. Was sollte bei einem Wertpapierpensionsgeschäft unbedingt vor Abschluss eines Geschäftes vorhanden sein?

10. Guidelines for Risk Management

In this chapter you learn ...
- which general risk management principles should be considered regarding organisation, customers and standards of conduct and ethics.
- which special guidelines should be observed when dealing with corporate or commercial clients.

10.1. General Risk Management Principles for Dealing Business

Promote the highest standard of conduct and ethics
- Honour, honesty and integrity to be the underlying principles of trading practices
- Establish, implement and enforce both The Model Code for trading and the rules and procedures of one's own institution
- Demand the highest ethical standards

Ensure senior management involvement and supervision
- Establishment, recommendation and regular review by senior management of risk management framework authorities, limits and policies
- Approval by Board of Directors is required
- Accountability of senior management for risk management

Organisational structure should ensure independent risk management and controls
- Provide independent monitoring to ensure compliance with risk management framework
- Ensure segregation of duties between the front, middle and back office activities
- Undertake regular internal audits independent of trading and risk management functions to ensure timely identification of internal control weaknesses
- Maintain clear and open communication channels between all levels of staff and across functions

Embed thoroughly professional management in all administrative processes
- Implement policies to ensure principles of quality are embedded in all processes
- Aim to minimise deal input cycles, errors and down time
- Regularly review internal processes to identify and rectify weaknesses, disconnections and failures
- Reduce time-wasting and resource inefficiencies while improving work environment

Provide appropriate systems and operational support
- Ensure appropriate systems for timely documentation, processing and reporting
- Have a technology policy to plan systemically for adequate systems support
- Have a contingency site ready for backup
- Ensure awareness and responsibility for identifying inconsistencies and weaknesses

10. Richtlinien zum Risikomanagement

In diesem Kapitel lernen Sie ...

- welche Regeln beim Risikomanagement von Geschäftsabschlüssen bezüglich Organisation, Kunden und Veranlagungsstandards zu beachten sind.
- welche speziellen Regeln für Geschäftsabschlüsse mit Firmen- bzw. Geschäftskunden zu beachten sind.

10.1 Allgemeine Regeln zum Risikomanagement bei Geschäftsabschlüssen

Förderung des höchsten Verhaltensstandards

- Die Handelspraxis soll von Ehrenhaftigkeit, Ehrlichkeit und Integrität geleitet sein.
- Händler sollen sowohl den Model Code als auch die bankinternen Handelsregeln einhalten.
- Es sind die höchsten ethischen Standards einzuhalten.

Einbeziehung der Geschäftsleitung und Überwachung gewährleisten

- Der Rahmen für das Risikomanagement soll von der Geschäftsleitung erstellt und regelmäßig auf seine Aktualität überprüft werden.
- Zustimmung seitens des Aufsichtsrats ist notwendig.
- Die Geschäftsleitung trägt die volle Verantwortung für das Risikomanagement.

Die Organisationsstruktur sorgt für eine unabhängige Kontrolle des Risikomanagements

- unabhängige Überwachung der Rahmenbedingungen des Risikomanagements
- Trennung der Aktivitäten zwischen Front-, Middle- und Backoffice
- regelmäßige interne Überprüfungen der internen Kontrollmechanismen
- Schaffung offener Kommunikationskanäle zwischen allen Ebenen

Sicherstellen von absoluter Professionalität des Managements in allen administrativen Prozessen

- Einrichtung von Verfahren, die hohe professionelle Standards in den Prozessen sicherstellen
- Minimierung des Geschäftseingabezyklus, der Fehler und Todzeiten
- Regelmäßige Überprüfung interner Prozesse auf Schwächen, Fehler und Unterbrechungen
- Reduktion ineffizienter Ressourcennutzung und Verbesserung des Arbeitsumfeldes

Verwendung geeigneter Systeme und operationale Unterstützung

- Gewährleistung geeigneter Systeme zur zeitgerechten Dokumentation, Verarbeitung und Berichterstattung
- Pläne zur adäquaten und strukturierten Systemunterstützung
- für Notfälle soll es eine vollständig getestete Backup-Lösung geben.
- Das Bewusstsein zur Identifikation von Inkonsistenzen und Schwächen sollte immer vorhanden sein.

Ensure timely and accurate risk management

- Trading positions to be regularly marked to market by function which is independent from trading
- Frequency of position valuation to be determined by market volatility, volume and the institution's risk profile
- Valuations to be verified against independent sources where possible
- Ensure robust process for evaluating off-market transactions
- Measure risks using approved methodologies based on generally accepted statistical practices and approved confidence intervals
- Market models to be validated before implementation

Control market risk exposure by assessing maximum likely exposure under various market conditions

- Assess impact on the institution's earnings, liquidity and capital position, especially under adverse conditions
- Where possible, regularly evaluate risk positions under stress scenarios
- Continually update volatility measures
- Promote most accurate possible measurements of risk

Always recognise importance of market and cash flow liquidity

- Always consider market liquidity conditions before entering into a deal
- Assess costs of unwinding positions, especially in illiquid markets
- Implement policies and processes to manage liquidity and cash flow positions
- Prepare a liquidity contingency plan to be implemented in crisis situation

Consider impact of diversification and risk return trade-offs

- Returns should always be measured against market and other risks and risk weighted capital
- Ensure adequate diversification of trading and customer activities to reduce risk

Accept only the highest and most rigorous client relationship standards

- Promote highest standard of conduct with clients
- Ensure clients have the authority to undertake transactions
- Do not knowingly conduct business with clients involved in business activities known to be illegal or inconsistent with generally accepted standards of ethical or social behaviour in the community

Clients should understand transaction

- Ensure that clients have adequate information and understanding with regard to terms and conditions of all transactions
- Where requested, risk return information should be provided and explained clearly to clients
- Ensure that senior management of clients is aware of unusual or complicated transactions

Risk management based on sound legal foundations and documentation

- Ensure proper documentation of all transactions and counterparties

Sicherstellen eines zeitgerechten und genauen Risikomanagements

- regelmäßiges Mark-to-Market der Handelspositionen durch eine vom Handel unabhängige Stelle
- Häufigkeit der Bewertung in Abhängigkeit von Marktvolatilität, Volumen und institutionellem Risikoprofil
- wenn möglich, die Bewertung anhand unabhängiger Quellen prüfen
- eine verlässliche Methode zur Bewertung von Off-Market-Transaktionen sicherstellen
- Risikomessung mit Methoden, die auf allgemein akzeptierten statistischen Methoden und anerkannten Konfidenzintervallen beruhen
- Validierung der Marktmodelle vor Einführung

Marktrisikokontrolle durch Bestimmung maximaler Risikopositionen bei unterschiedlichen Szenarien

- Einschätzung negativer Entwicklungen auf Ertrags-, Liquiditäts- und Kapitalsituation
- regelmäßige Bewertung der Risikopositionen mit Stress-Szenarien
- kontinuierliche Updates der Volatilitätsmaßzahlen
- Förderung einer möglichst genauen Risikomessung

Ständiges Bewusstsein der Bedeutung von Markt- und Cashflow-Liquidität

- vor Transaktionen immer die Marktliquidität prüfen
- Einschätzung der Kosten zum Schließen einer Position, besonders in illiquiden Märkten
- Einführung von Verfahren zur Steuerung von Liquidität und Cashflow-Positionen
- Vorbereitung eines Liquiditätssteuerungsplanes in Krisensituationen

Einfluss von Diversifikationseffekten und Geschäften zur Risikokompensation

- Erträge sollen immer im Verhältnis zu den Risiken und dem risikogewichteten Kapital gemessen werden.
- Es sollte immer eine sinnvolle Diversifikation von Handels- und Kundenaktivitäten stattfinden, um eine Risikoverringerung zu erreichen.

Anlegen der höchsten und strengsten Standards bei Kundenbeziehungen

- Förderung der höchsten Verhaltensstandards gegenüber Kunden
- vergewissern, dass Kunden befugt sind, Transaktionen durchzuführen
- keine Geschäfte wissentlich mit Kunden abschließen, die in illegale oder dubiose („nicht mit den allgemein akzeptierten Standards ethischen oder sozialen Verhaltens in Einklang stehende") Geschäfte verwickelt sind

Kunden sollen die Transaktionen verstehen

- sicherstellen, dass der Kunde die adäquaten Informationen über die Bedingungen des Geschäftes hat und diese versteht
- wo erforderlich, dem Kunden Risiko-Ertrags-Informationen offenlegen und deutlich erklären
- sicherstellen, dass die Geschäftsleitung des Kunden sich ungewöhnlicher oder komplizierter Transaktionen bewusst ist

Risikomanagement auf soliden Rechtsgrundlagen und Dokumentationen aufbauen

- Gewährleistung einer geeigneten Dokumentation aller Transaktionen und Partner

- Prior to entering a transaction, ensure that customers and counterparties have the legal and regulatory authority to transact
- Ensure terms of contract are legally sound and enforceable
- Ensure timely confirmation of all transactions

Ensure adequate expertise supports trading and risk taking

- Resources to reflect demands of the position
- Right people to be placed in right positions
- Ensure proper position training and career planning
- All staff should understand policies, limits and compliance requirements

Use judgement and common sense

- Reliance on experience and expertise
- Strict adherence to the spirit as well as the letter of The Model Code

10.2. Guidelines for Dealing with Corporate/Commercial Clients

Authorisation

Both Principal and Client should exchange lists of the names of personnel authorised to deal clearly stipulating in which instruments/markets and amounts each individual is authorised to deal. However the existence of such a list should not necessarily negate a deal already done in good faith with an unauthorised party.

Segregation of duty

The segregation of front and back office duties and reporting lines should also be established in companies with their own dealing department.

Complex product information

It is the duty of the principal to be vigilant and fair to the customer at all times and to be mindful of the customer's interest. Banks should keep the following points in mind:

- The customer must understand the proposed transaction.
- Consequences and risks of a deal have to be clearly and understandably explained to the customer, in particular if the projected transaction includes a complex product or strategy.

Confidentiality

Banks and clients should not pass any information concerning the nature and conditions of a deal to a third party. If a product or strategy is individually designed for a customer, the technical details of the proposed transaction should not be divulged to any third party during the negotiation phase.

Entertainment and gifts

In addition to the provisions of the Model Code, principals should be aware that the excessive granting of entertainment and gifts by financial institutions can compromise a dealer's impartiality.

- vor Transaktionen die Handelsberechtigung des Partners bzw. Kunden prüfen
- sicherstellen, dass die Vertragsbedingungen rechtskonform und durchsetzbar sind
- Sicherstellen einer zeitgerechten Bestätigung der Transaktionen

Sicherstellen, dass Fachwissen den Handel und das Risikomanagement unterstützt

- Nur gut ausgebildete und qualifizierte Personen sollen auf Treasury-Positionen eingesetzt werden.
- richtiges Training und Karriereplanung gewährleisten
- Alle Beschäftigten sollen Limits, Erfüllungskriterien und die Geschäftspolitik verstehen.

Verwenden von Urteilskraft und Menschenverstand

- Vertrauen auf Erfahrung und Sachkenntnis
- Geist und Wortlaut des Model Codes sollen streng eingehalten werden.

10.2. Regeln für Geschäftsabschlüsse mit Firmen- bzw. Geschäftskunden

Berechtigung

Bank und Kunde sollen Listen austauschen, aus denen hervorgeht, welche Personen zum Handel in bestimmten Instrumenten bzw. Märkten berechtigt sind. Die Existenz einer entsprechenden Dokumentation bedeutet aber nicht, dass Geschäfte, die im guten Glauben mit einer nicht berechtigten Person abgeschlossen wurden, ungültig sind.

Trennung der Aufgabenbereiche

Die Trennung von Handel und Backoffice, getrennte Berichtslinien und wirksame Kontrollmechanismen sind auch von Unternehmen mit eigenem Handel einzuführen.

Information über komplexe Produkte

Es ist die Pflicht der Bank, jederzeit im Interesse des Kunden zu wirken und unter diesem Gesichtspunkt zu prüfen, ob ein Geschäft für den Kunden geeignet ist. Dabei soll die Bank folgende Punkte beachten:

- Der Kunde muss die vorgeschlagene Transaktion verstehen.
- Dem Kunden müssen die Auswirkungen und Risiken des Geschäftes klar und verständlich dargelegt werden, insbesondere wenn es sich um komplexe Produkte oder Strategien handelt.

Vertraulichkeit

Banken und Kunden sollen keine Informationen über ihre bilateralen Geschäfte und Geschäftsbedingungen an Dritte weitergeben. Wird für einen Kunden ein Produkt oder eine Strategie individuell zusammengestellt, sollen die technischen Details des Produkts während der Verhandlungen/Entwicklungen nicht an Dritte weitergegeben werden.

Unterhaltung und Geschäfte

Unternehmen sollen zusätzlich zu den Bestimmungen des Model Code beachten, dass die übermäßige Bereitstellung von Geschenken, Einladungen oder anderen Vergünstigungen die Unparteilichkeit des Händlers gefährden kann.

Historic exchange rates/FX rollovers

The prolongation of FX contracts should be executed by closing the open position at the existing spot rate and entering a new deal at current rates. This way, a proper image of realised gains and losses is ensured. Any deviation from this practice should be agreed and fully documented by the senior management of both counterparties.

Legal documentation

For particular or complex transactions not covered by standard documentation, the principal and client should ensure that they are in agreement on the terms of legal documentation and conditions of the transactions prior to dealing. An additional support or safeguard clause that insists that full written agreements and procedures should be in place before the second deal is transacted would be considered good practice.

Margin account/Collateralised trading

The establishment of a margin account should be fully documented and signed in advance of any trades. Close out procedures in the case of a customer's default should be clearly stipulated in the written agreement. There should be both a regular mark-to-market and reconciliation of all positions.

Know your customer

The provisions of the Model Code should be particularly carefully observed.

Internet/Online Trading

If internet trading facilities are established the recommendations and controls of the Model Code should be enforced.

FX-Rollovers/Historische Kurse

Die Verlängerung von Termingeschäften soll durch das Schließen der offenen Position zum aktuellen Kurs und den Abschluss eines neuen Geschäfts erfolgen, um eine korrekte Abbildung von Gewinn bzw. Verlust zu erhalten. Jede Abweichung von dieser Praxis muss in beiderseitigem Einverständnis erfolgen und durch die Geschäftsleitung beider Parteien dokumentiert werden.

Rechtliche Dokumentation

Kunde und Bank sollen im Fall von speziellen oder komplexen Geschäften, für die keine Standarddokumentation existiert, alle rechtlichen Bedingungen und Dokumentationen vor Geschäftsabschluss festlegen. Es ist gute Praxis, eine Bestimmung aufzunehmen, die den Abschluss eines zweiten Geschäftes nur dann gestattet, wenn alle Vereinbarungen und Abläufe vollständig in schriftlicher Form existieren.

Margin-Konten/Besicherte Geschäfte

Die Einrichtung von Margin-Konten muss vollständig dokumentiert und abgezeichnet sein, bevor ein Geschäft gemacht wird. Close-Out-Verfahren für den Fall des Konkurses eines Kunden, müssen in klarer Form schriftlich vereinbart werden. In regelmäßigen Abständen sollen die Positionen bewertet und zusammengeführt werden.

Kenne deinen Kunden

Die Bestimmungen des Model Codes sollen besonders aufmerksam befolgt werden.

Internet/Online-Trading

Werden internetbasierende Handelseinrichtungen angeboten, so ist den bereits oben ausgeführten Bestimmungen des Model Codes zu folgen.

11. Market Terminology and Definitions

In this chapter you learn ...
- which market terminology is used for FX and money market transactions.
- about the meaning of the different terms.
- about dealing periods and delivery/maturity dates.

Standard communication plays a vital role in avoiding misunderstandings and dissatisfaction with transactions. The currencies traded must be stated and specified without exception.

11.1. Market Terminology for FX and Money Market Transactions

Mine/I buy/I take

The trader buys at the quoted price the amount which has been quoted. In the foreign exchange spot market "mine"/"I buy" always refers to the base currency. In the FX forward market the trader saying "mine" buys the base currency forward.

"I take" is used in money market transactions. In this case the dealer borrows the quoted amount of money at the offered rate. The amounts traded are always quoted in millions.

Example
A trader receives a EUR/USD quote at 1.0100 – 05 and says "Five mine". He has bought EUR 5m at 1.0105

Yours/I sell/I give

The trader sells at the quoted price the amount which has been quoted. In the foreign exchange spot market "yours"/"I sell" always refers to the base currency. In the FX forward market the trader saying "yours" sells the base currency forward.

"I give" is used in money market transactions. In this case the dealer lends the quoted amount of money at the bid rate. The amounts traded are always quoted in millions.

Given

The deal has been proposed and agreed at the bid price quoted.

Taken

The deal has been proposed and agreed at the offer price quoted.

Join at/Support at

A commitment to putting an additional bid or offer at a current bid or offer price already quoted by the broker.

11. Marktterminologie und Definitionen

In diesem Kapitel lernen Sie ...

- welche üblichen Marktterminologien bei FX- und MM-Transaktionen verwendet werden.
- welche Bedeutung die einzelnen Termini haben.
- welche Valuta- und Laufzeitbestimmungen im Handel auftreten können.

Eine gemeinsame Sprache trägt wesentlich zur Vermeidung von Missverständnissen bei und hilft, Unzufriedenheit bei Geschäftsabschlüssen zu vermeiden. In jedem Fall ist (sind) die gehandelte(n) Währung(en) zu nennen und genau zu spezifizieren.

11.1. Terminologie bei FX- und MM-Transaktionen

Mine/I buy/I take

Der Händler kauft zum genannten Preis. Das Volumen muss genannt werden. Im FX-Kassamarkt bezieht sich „mine" oder „I buy" immer auf die quotierte Währung, bei FX-Swaps üblicherweise auf die Terminseite des Geschäftes. Sagt der Händler „I take", dann nimmt er im Geldmarkt zur Briefseite. Volumina des Geschäftes beziehen sich immer auf Millionen.

Beispiel

Ein Händler erhält EUR/USD zu 1,0100-05 quotiert und sagt „Five mine". Er hat dann EUR 5 Mio. zu 1,0105 gekauft.

Yours/I sell/I give

Der Händler verkauft zum genannten Preis. Das Volumen muss genannt werden. Im FX-Kassamarkt bezieht sich „yours" oder „I sell" immer auf die quotierte Währung, bei FX-Swaps üblicherweise auf die Terminseite des Geschäftes. Sagt der Händler „I give", dann gibt er im Geldmarkt zur Geldseite.

Given

Das Geschäft wurde zum Geldkurs vorgeschlagen und zum quotierten Geldkurs abgeschlossen.

Taken

Das Geschäft wurde zum Briefkurs vorgeschlagen und zum quotierten Briefkurs abgeschlossen.

Join at/Support at

Dieser Zusatz stellt eine Verpflichtung dar, zu einer gegebenen, aktuellen Quotierung mitzuquotieren.

> **Example**
>
> A broker quotes a deposit at 4.50-55. If a trader says "I join at the bid side 4.50 for 10" he also bids 10m at 4.50%.

Off

Cancellation of an existing quote (bid or offer).

Bid/Buy/Pay

Statement of a rate at which the dealer will buy the base currency in the spot market (or in the forward market in the case of an FX swap).

"Pay" is used in the money market and means that the dealer will borrow.

Offer/Sell

Statement of a rate at which the dealer will sell the base currency in the spot market (or in forward market in the case of an FX swap).

"Offer" is used in the money market and gives the interest rate at which the dealer will lend.

Under reference

A rate quoted in the market may no longer be valid and requires confirmation before it can be dealt.

Either way/Choice/Your choice

Same price for bid and offer.

Done

Deal agreed as proposed.

Firm/firm price

The rate quoted is valid and can be traded on.

For indication/Indication/For information/For level

The quote is indicative only and should be validated or confirmed before trades are proposed. It can indicate unwillingness to trade.

Checking

To check the availability of a credit line for the counterparty prior to conclusion of a deal. The term hints to the counterparty that there is a possibility of reducing the amount or declining the deal depending on the availability of the relevant credit line.

Your risk

The quoting dealer cautions the receiver of the quote that the price may have to be requoted at the receiver's risk.

My risk

The receiving dealer acknowledges the counterparty quotes at "your risk".

Beispiel

Ein Broker quotiert ein Depot zu 4,50-55. Sagt ein Händler, „I join at the bid side 4,50 for 10", bietet der Händler 10 Mio. zu 4,50% an.

Off

Widerruf einer Quotierung

Bid/Buy/Pay

ist der Preis, zu dem der Händler die quotierte Währung in der Kassa kauft. Das gilt auch für den FX-Swap. Pay bezieht sich auf den Geldmarkt und drückt den Zinssatz aus, zu dem der Händler nimmt.

Offer/Sell

ist der Preis, zu dem der Händler die quotierte Währung in der Kassa verkauft. Das gilt auch für den FX-Swap. Offer bezieht sich auf den Geldmarkt und drückt den Zinssatz aus, zu dem der Händler gibt.

Under reference

Wird eine Quotierung „under reference" gestellt, dann ist sie nicht länger gültig und muss nochmals bestätigt werden, wenn ein Geschäft abgeschlossen werden soll.

Choice/Your choice/Either way

Geld- und Briefkurs sind ident gestellt.

Done

Das Geschäft wird so, wie es angeboten wurde, abgeschlossen.

Firm/Firm price

Der quotierte Preis ist gültig und handelbar.

For indication/Indication/For information/For level

Die Quotierung dient als Indikation. Sie muss überprüft bzw. bestätigt werden, bevor gehandelt werden kann. Es drückt fehlenden Willen zum Handeln aus.

Checking

Die Verfügbarkeit der Kreditlinie muss überprüft werden, bevor die Zustimmung zum Geschäft gegeben werden kann. Dieser Zusatz kann der Gegenpartei andeuten, dass zu einem geringeren als zunächst vereinbarten Betrag abgeschlossen werden könnte.

Your risk

Der quotierende Händler weist die Gegenpartei darauf hin, dass sich die Quotierung noch auf Risiko des Partners ändern kann.

My risk

Die Geschäftspartei akzeptiert den Zusatz „Your risk".

All mine/all yours

Saying "all mine (yours)" commits a dealer to buying (selling) the counterparty's full amount.

Points/Pips

The smallest unit of an exchange rate.

Example
EUR/USD: 1/100th of a US Cent USD/JPY: 1/100th of a Yen GBP/USD: 1/100th of a US Cent USD/CHF: 1/100th of a Swiss Centime (Rappen)

Outright price

Any foreign exchange price for delivery on any date that is not part of an FX swap transaction. A spot transaction is in fact an outright price for delivery on the spot date. All other outright prices are calculated with a spot base, adjusted by the swap points (premium/discount).

Par

The spot and forward exchange rates for a specific period are the same.

Premium

The margin by which the forward exchange rate is dearer than the near date.

Discount

The margin by which the forward exchange rate is cheaper than the near date.

Basis point

1/100th of one percent (0.01%).

Yard

One billion (one thousand million = 1,000,000,000).

M

One million.

Plus/Minimum

Indicates that a minimum amount has to be traded.

Give-up

The loss of yield resulting from the sale of securities at one yield and purchase of securities at a lower yield.

Pick-up

Opposite of Give-up.

All mine/all yours

All mine (yours) bedeutet, dass man bereit ist, auf der Briefseite (Geldseite) der erhaltenen Quotierung den vollen Betrag zu kaufen (verkaufen), der von anderen Seite gewünscht wird.

Points/Pips

Die kleinste Einheit eines Wechselkurses.

Beispiel

EUR/USD: 1/100 eines US-Cent
USD/JPY: 1/100 eines Yen
GBP/USD: 1/100 eines US-Cent
USD/CHF: 1/100 eines Rappen

Outright-Preis

jeder Preis einer FX-Transaktion, der nicht Teil eines FX-Swaps ist. Theoretisch ist ein Kassapreis ein Outright-Preis für ein Geschäft mit Valuta am Spot Date. Alle anderen Outright-Preise werden auf Basis des Kassakurses und der Swappunkte (Auf-/Abschlag) ermittelt.

Par

Kassa- und Terminkurs für eine bestimmte Periode sind gleich.

Premium

Der Aufschlag, um den der Terminkurs höher ist als der Kassakurs.

Discount

Der Abschlag, um den der Terminkurs niedriger ist als der Kassakurs.

Basispunkt

Ein Hundertstel% (0,01%).

Yard

Eine Milliarde (eintausend Millionen = 1.000.000.000).

M

Eine Million.

Plus/Minimum

bedeutet, dass mindestens zu einem angegebenen Betrag abgeschlossen werden muss. Ten plus (minimum) heißt, dass mindestens 10 Mio. gehandelt werden müssen.

Give-up

Der Verlust durch den Verkauf eines Wertpapiers mit einer Rendite und dem Kauf eines Wertpapiers mit einer niedrigeren Rendite.

Pick-up

Gegenteil von Give-up

On-the-run

Most recently issued bills or bonds.

When Issued (WI)

Trades before debt security is issued. Settlement occurs when and if the security is issued, reflecting the period between the announcement of a security's auction and its issuance.

11.2. Terminology relating to Dealing Periods and Delivery/Maturity Dates

Spot

The purchase/sale of a currency for settlement two business days after transaction date (with certain exceptions, such as HKD, CAD).

Regular/fixed dates, Regular periods

1 week, 1 month, 2 months, 3 months, 6 months and 1 year usually from spot or occasionally from today in domestic money markets.

IMM dates

Third Wednesdays of March, June, September and December. These are the dates for which financial futures traded at the IMM (International Money Market) Division of the CME (Chicago Mercantile Exchange) are traded.

Odd/Broken/Cock dates

Dates other than regular dates.

Short dates

Maturity dates of less than one month.

Overnight, O/N

Deposit or swap transaction for settlement on transaction date to or against the next business day after transaction date.

Tomorrow/Next, T/N

Deposit or swap transaction for settlement on the next business day against the second business day after transaction date.

Spot/Next, S/N

Deposit or swap transaction for settlement on the second business day against the third business day after transaction date.

One week

Deposit or swap transaction for settlement spot (or today in domestic money markets) against one week after transaction date.

Tom/week, One week over tomorrow

Deposit or swap transaction for settlement tomorrow (or next business day) against one week from that date, i.e. the week starts on D + 1 and not on spot.

On-the-run

Die am kürzesten emittierten Anleihen und kurzfristigen Schuldtitel („bills").

When Issued (WI)

Geschäft, das vor Emission abgeschlossen wurde. Settlement erfolgt, nachdem das Wertpapier emittiert wurde, und berücksichtigt den Zeitraum zwischen Ankündigung und Emission.

11.2. Valuta- und Laufzeitbestimmungen

Spot

Bezeichnet generell die Lieferung zwei Banktage nach Geschäftsabschluss. Ausnahmen können der CAD und HKD darstellen.

Regular/fixed dates, Regular periods

Eine Woche, ein Monat, zwei Monate, drei Monate, sechs Monate und ein Jahr von Spot oder „heute" bei Geschäften am Inlandsmarkt.

IMM-Dates

Dritter Mittwoch im März, Juni, September und Dezember. Jene Tage, an denen Futureskontrakte an der IMM (International Money Market) Division des CME (Chicago Mercantile Exchange) gesettled werden.

Broken/Cock Dates/Odd

Alle nicht regulären Laufzeiten

Short Dates

Laufzeiten unter einem Monat

Overnight, O/N

Depot- oder Swaptransaktion, bei der das Settlement am Handelstag gegen den nächsten Handelstag durchgeführt wird.

Tom-next, T/N

Depot- oder Swaptransaktion, bei der das Settlement am nächsten Handelstag gegen den übernächsten Handelstag (= Spot) durchgeführt wird.

Spot-next, S/N

Depot- oder Swaptransaktion, bei der das Settlement-Spot gegen den nächsten Handelstag durchgeführt wird.

One Week

Depot- oder Swaptransaktion, bei der das Settlement-Spot (bei Inlandsgeschäften am Handelstag) gegen eine Woche durchgeführt wird.

Tom-week, One week over tomorrow

Depot- oder Swaptransaktion, bei der das Settlement am nächsten Handelstag gegen eine Woche ab morgen (bzw. nächster Handelstag) durchgeführt wird. D.h., die Woche beginnt nicht ab Spot zu laufen, sondern ab dem nächsten Handelstag.

Spot against end month, End of the month

Deposit or swap transaction for settlement spot against the last business day of the month.

End/End

Deposit or swap transaction for settlement on the last business day of a month against the last business day of a future month.

Turn of the month

Deposit or swap transaction for settlement on the last business day of a month against the first business day of the next month.

Turn of the year

Deposit or swap transaction wheresettlement takes place on the last business day of a year against the first business day of the next year.

Forward/forward, Fwd/Fwd

A foreign exchange or money market transaction where the settlement is for one forward date against another forward date.

Example

If you trade 3/6 Forward/forward FX-swap the transactions involved are settled in 3 and 6 months.

Mono

Transactions with a maturity of one month.

11.3. Practice Questions

1. What should a broker do if a dealer has interest on one side, and the other side is dealt away?
   a) enter into a deal at the dealer's price as soon as possible
   b) immediately put the price "subject to credit"
   c) put the price "under reference"
   d) put he price of the dealer "choice"
2. Your broker quotes you EUR/USD 1.1425-28. You respond by saying: "All yours". Which deal have you transacted?
   a) You are committed to buy the standard amount from the counterparty.
   b) You are committed to buy the counterparty's full amount.
   c) You are committed to sell all amounts to the counterparty at 1.1428.
   d) You are committed up to the amount permitted by your counterparty limit.
3. Your broker quotes you EUR/USD 0.9425-28. You respond by saying: "All mine". Which deal have you transacted?
   a) You are committed to buy the standard amount from the counterparty.
   b) You are committed to buy the counterparty's full amount.
   c) You are committed to sell all amounts to the counterparty at 0.9428.
   d) You are committed up to the amount permitted by your counterparty limit.

Spot against end month, End of the month

Depot- oder Swaptransaktion, bei der das Settlement-Spot gegen den letzten Handelstag im Monat durchgeführt wird.

End/End

Depot- oder Swaptransaktion, bei der das Settlement am letzten Handelstag eines Monats gegen den letzten Handelstag eines zukünftigen Monats durchgeführt wird.

Turn of the month

Depot- oder Swaptransaktion, bei der das Settlement am letzten Handelstag des Monats gegen den ersten Handelstag des Folgemonats durchgeführt wird.

Turn of the year

Depot- oder Swaptransaktion, bei der das Settlement am letzten Handelstag des Jahres gegen den ersten Handelstag des folgenden Jahres durchgeführt wird.

Forward/Forward

Eine FX- oder Geldmarkttransaktion, bei der das Settlement an zwei Valutatagen durchgeführt wird, die beide in der Zukunft liegen.

Beispiel

Bei einem 3/6-Forward/Forward-Swap werden die Geschäfte in drei Monaten und sechs Monaten gesettled.

Mono

Ein Geschäft mit einer Laufzeit von einem Monat.

11.3. Wiederholungsfragen

1. Was soll der Broker tun, wenn ein Händler eine Quotierung stellt und die Quotierung einer anderen Partei gehandelt wird?
    a) Er soll möglichst rasch zur Quotierung des Händlers abschließen.
    b) Er soll den Preis sofort „subject to credit" stellen.
    c) Er soll den Preis sofort „under reference" stellen.
    d) Er soll den Preis des Händlers „choice" stellen.
2. Ihr Broker quotiert Ihnen EUR/USD 1,1425-28. Sie sagen: All yours. Welche Transaktion haben Sie getätigt?
    a) den Standardbetrag an den Partner verkauft
    b) sich verpflichtet, den vollen Betrag an den Partner zu liefern
    c) sich verpflichtet, zu 1,1428 jeden Betrag zu verkaufen
    d) sich verpflichtet, jeden Betrag zu liefern, sofern es das Partnerlimit erlaubt
3. Ihr Broker quotiert Ihnen EUR/USD 0,9425-28. Sie sagen: All mine. Welche Transaktion haben Sie getätigt?
    a) den Standardbetrag vom Partner gekauft
    b) sich verpflichtet, den gewünschten vollen Betrag vom Partner zu kaufen
    c) sich verpflichtet, zu 0,9428 jeden Betrag zu verkaufen
    d) sich verpflichtet, jeden Betrag zu kaufen, sofern es das Partnerlimit erlaubt

4. Which terms are used if bid and offer rate are equal?
   a) choice
   b) your choice
   c) either way
   d) for level
5. What does the term "my risk" refer to?
   a) the risk that the broker may be stuffed
   b) the risk of the bank quoting the price
   c) the risk of the counterparty asking for a price
   d) the counterparty's inability to respond immediately, therefore taking the risk that the price may not remain the same
6. What is meant by the terms "premium" and "discount"?
7. What is meant by the addendum "checking" when concluding a deal?
8. How is the smallest unit of an exchange rate called?
9. When is the term "when Issued" used?
10. What is meant by "IMM dates"?
11. What is meant by "short dates"?

4. Welche Termini werden verwendet, wenn Geld- und Briefkurs ident gestellt sind?
   a) Choice
   b) Your choice
   c) Either way
   d) For level
5. Worauf bezieht sich der Ausdruck „My risk?"
   a) auf das Stuffing-Risiko des Brokers
   b) auf das Risiko der quotierenden Bank
   c) auf das Risiko des Partners, einen Preis zu fragen
   d) auf die Unmöglichkeit, sofort auf eine Quotierung antworten zu können und daher das Risiko eines sich ändernden Preises zu nehmen
6. Was bedeuten die Termini „Premium" bzw. „Discount"?
7. Was bedeutet der Zusatz „Checking" bei Abschluss eines Geschäftes?
8. Wie nennt man die kleinste Einheit eines Wechselkurses?
9. Wann wird der Terminus „When Issued" verwendet?
10. Was versteht man unter „IMM dates"?
11. Was versteht man unter „Short dates"?

PART VI: Risk Management

TEIL VI: Risikomanagement

In recent years risk management thinking has undergone dramatic changes, driven by the tremendous growth in derivatives trading, the development of modern approaches within finance theory, and also by an understanding that classic accounting approaches cannot adequately describe the risks involved in complex trading and hedging strategies. Today, the bank departments of strategic planning, system support, and controlling attempt to evaluate the impact of these new developments on the overall strategy of the banks, on the role of the management, and on the optimum allocation of the company's capital. With the help of risk measurement, risk assessment, and risk monitoring banks try to develop methods to adequately estimate market, credit, liquidity and operational risks. Furthermore, a clear limit system has been established that allows the bank's overall risks to move within given limits.

At present, legislation strongly favours statistical methods such as the value at risk (VaR) approach to quantify the risks of banks. These VaR approaches take several factors into account: possible fluctuations of individual risk positions and potential correlations between different positions. The role of the bank's management is to guarantee that the methods used match the risks that are taken on by the bank.

A very important source of bank revenues entails the assumption of risk; most risks should not be seen in a negative way. Banks must control risks so that trey are limited, but still allow banks to earn money on them. In order to achieve these two aims, risks must be measurable and thus manageable.

The majority of bank risks are controlled within trading and treasury. Since trading is one of the core areas of banking, it is strongly affected by the issue of limiting and measuring risks. Risks are always linked to uncertainty. Modern approaches of risk measurement try to quantify these uncertainties in order to compare different risk positions, and consequently the returns on risk.

Another important aspect of modern risk measurement methods is the idea that the total risk is lower than the sum of the single risks involved. This idea is based on the portfolio theory, whereby the total risk may be reduced by diversification. In the context of FX trades, this means that a single position (e.g., short USD position) bears a higher risk than a position that is composed of different individual positions (eg, the same amount composed of short positions in USD, GBP, JPY, and CHF). The probability that each position turns negative is lower than the probability that a single position will lead to a loss.

The same ideas apply also to credit risk, where the risk of a single credit is higher than a comparable risk that is based on a variety of borrowers (with comparable creditworthiness).

The tasks of the ALCO (Asset Liability Committee) and the frequency of their meetings normally depend on the structure of the bank. Normally the ALCO convenes monthly and the typical task is to control the bank's overall balance structure and market risk. Beyond this, the ALCO normally carries out the following tasks which are of great importance to

In den letzten Jahren hat sich das Wissen um das Risikomanagement rasant entwickelt. Das rasche Wachstum des Derivatehandels, die Entwicklung von modernen Ansätzen in der Finanztheorie und nicht zuletzt die Einsicht, dass die klassischen Methoden der Buchhaltung das Risiko von komplexen Handels- und Absicherungsstrategien nicht adäquat darstellen können, beschleunigten diesen Prozess. Derzeit stellen die Bankabteilungen Strategische Planung, Systemunterstützung, Mid-Office und Controlling Überlegungen an, welchen Einfluss die neuen Möglichkeiten auf die Gesamtbankstrategie, die Rolle der Geschäftsleitung und die optimale Zuordnung der Eigenkapitalressourcen in der Bank haben. In der Risikomessung, Risikobewertung und Risikokontrolle wird versucht, eine adäquate Quantifizierung der Markt-, Kredit-, Liquiditäts- und operationellen Risiken zu entwickeln. Ebenso wurden übersichtliche Limitsysteme in der Bank etabliert, die eine Bewegung des Gesamtbankrisikos innerhalb der vorgegebenen Grenzen erlauben.

Derzeit werden vom Gesetzgeber statistische Methoden wie der Value-at-Risk (VAR)-Ansatz wärmstens empfohlen, um die Risiken bei den Banken zu quantifizieren. Diese VAR-Ansätze berücksichtigen sowohl die Schwankungsmöglichkeiten der einzelnen Risikopositionen als auch Korrelationseffekte, die zwischen unterschiedlichen Positionen bestehen können. Die Rolle des Managements besteht darin sicherzustellen, dass die verwendeten Methoden den von der Bank eingegangenen Risiken entsprechen.

Eine wichtige Ertragsquelle der Banken ist das Risiko. Die meisten Risiken sind an sich nicht negativ zu sehen. Sie müssen von den Banken so gesteuert werden, dass sie einerseits begrenzt und andererseits so eingegangen werden, dass damit auch Geld verdient werden kann. Um beide Ziele erreichen zu können, müssen diese Risiken auch messbar und somit einschätzbar sein.

Der Großteil der wirtschaftlichen Bankrisiken wird im Handel/Treasury gesteuert. Da der Handel einer der Hauptnerven des Bankgeschäftes ist, betrifft ihn das Thema Risikomessverfahren besonders. Risiko wird immer mit Unsicherheit verbunden sein. Modernere Ansätze der Risikomessung versuchen, diese Unsicherheit zu quantifizieren. Durch einen einheitlichen Ansatz in der Risikomessung können unterschiedliche Risikopositionen und in weiterer Folge auch die Erträge, die durch dieses Risiko erwirtschaftet werden, miteinander verglichen werden.

Ein weiterer Kernpunkt moderner Verfahren der Risikomessung ist die Idee, dass das Gesamtrisiko normalerweise kleiner als die Summe der Einzelrisiken ist. Hier kommt das Gedankengut der modernen Portfoliotheorie zur Anwendung. Durch Diversifikation kann das Gesamtrisiko tendenziell verringert werden. Im Devisenhandel bedeutet dies, dass eine einzelne Position (z.B. USD-Short-Position) ein höheres Risiko aufzeigt, als eine Position, die sich aus unterschiedlichen Einzelpositionen zusammensetzt (z.B. USD-, GBP-, JPY-, CHF-Short-Position über die gleiche Gesamtsumme). Die Wahrscheinlichkeit, dass sich alle einzelnen Positionen negativ entwickeln, ist geringer als die Wahrscheinlichkeit, dass die Einzelposition zu Verlusten führt.

Die gleichen Überlegungen gelten für das Kreditrisiko. Hier ist das Risiko bei einem einzigen Kreditengagement ungleich höher als das vergleichbare Risiko einer Vielzahl unterschiedlicher Kreditnehmer mit vergleichbarer Bonität.

In der Bankbuchsteuerung werden sehr oft englische Begriffe verwendet. ALM heißt Asset Liability Management (Aktiv-/Passiv-Management – APM), das zugehörige Steuerungsgremium heißt öfters Asset Liability Committee (ALCO). Die Tagungsfrequenzen und Aufgaben des ALCO sind üblicherweise abhängig von der Struktur der Bank. Üblicherweise tagt das ALCO einmal pro Monat und die typische Hauptaufgabe ist die Steue-

the overall control of the bank: controlling the liquidity risk of the entire bank, equity management planning (solvency), establishing the transfer prices for interest and liquidity and monitoring the development of the bank's lending and deposit business

In chapter 1 we will first define and classify the various banking risks and then in chapter 2 present different measurement methods using the example of interest rate risk. We will then illustrate in chapter 3 how banks limit those risks internally. The chapter 4 and 5 will deal with the legal requirements banks have to adhere to regarding the measurement of banking risks and required minimum capital requirements.

Included in the following exams:
- **ACI Dealing Certificate (only chapter 1 and 3)**
- **ACI Diploma**
- **ACI Operations Certificate (only chapter 1 and 3)**

rung der gesamten Bilanzstruktur und des Marktrisikos der Bank. Darüber hinaus hat das ALCO üblicherweise folgende Aufgaben, die für die Gesamtbanksteuerung von großer Bedeutung sind: Steuerung des Liquiditätsrisikos der Gesamtbank, Planung der Eigenmittel (Solvabilität), Festlegung des Referenzsatzsystems und Monitoring der Aktiv- und Passivgeschäftsentwicklung der Bank.

In Kapitel 1 werden zunächst die unterschiedlichen Bankrisiken klassifiziert und definiert, um dann anschließend in Kapitel 2 – am Beispiel Zinsrisiko – die verschiedenen Messverfahren zu präsentieren. In weiterer Folge wird in Kapitel 3 aufgezeigt, wie die Banken intern diese Risiken begrenzen (Limits). Nachdem auch der Gesetzgeber Vorgaben macht, wie die Bankrisiken gemessen werden, und eine entsprechende Eigenmittelausstattung fordert, werden in den Kapiteln 4 und 5 die relevanten aktuellen gesetzlichen Bestimmungen präsentiert.

Prüfungsrelevant für:

- **ACI Dealing Certificate (nur Kapitel 1 und 3)**
- **ACI Diploma**
- **ACI Operations Certificate (nur Kapitel 1 und 3)**

1. Types of risk trading

In this chapter you learn ...
- what is meant by risk.
- which types of risks can arise in a bank.
- in which areas these risks mainly arise.
- what is meant by credit, settlement and replacement risk.
- which methods are used for measuring the replacement risk.
- which types of market risks can arise in a bank.
- what is meant by currency risk, interest rate risk, stock price risk and other price risks.
- what steps are necessary for calculating and valuating of open positions.
- about the possibilities to continue a position.
- about the possibilities to keep a closed position.
- which types of liquidity risk can arise in a bank.
- what is meant by operational risks.
- which operational risks can arise in a bank.

1.1. Overview

Risk is defined as the likelihood of a **loss or a lower than expected return**. Risk only applies to future and therefore uncertain events. Risks that have materialized are no longer classified as risks; rather they have been entered in the profit and loss account (as a loss).

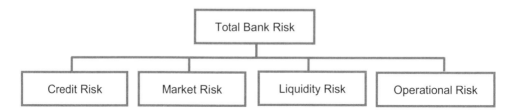

1.2. Credit risk

Credit risk is the **risk of loss due to a debtor's non-payment of a loan** or other line of credit or the **reduction of the expected return due to a so-called credit event**. A credit event may be the default of a debtor, a change in a debtor's creditworthiness (rating migration) or the movement of market credit spreads. Average expected losses in the credit business are covered by charging an expected loss premium to the debtor. Credit risk means therefore losses that exceed the expected loss.

Classic credit risk (counterparty risk)

The classic credit risk refers to the **loss of a transaction's total capital amount** (or parts of it) **due to the partner's inability to pay**. This classic credit risk exists for banks with **all as-**

1. Risikoarten im Handel

1.1. Übersicht

Risiko ist die **Gefahr einer möglichen Gewinnminderung.** Risiko bezieht sich ausschließlich auf die Zukunft und entspringt der Unsicherheit über die Zukunft. Alles, was an Risiken bereits schlagend geworden ist, ist nicht Risiko, sondern Verlust, der in der Buchhaltung bzw. im Ergebnis seinen Niederschlag findet.

1.2. Kreditrisiko

Das Kreditrisiko ist das **mit dem Verleihen von Geld verbundene Risiko des Gläubigers** bzw. das **Risiko einer Verringerung des Bankergebnisses aufgrund eines kreditbezogenen Ereignisses.** Unter kreditbezogenem Ereignis versteht man einen Kreditausfall, eine Veränderung der Bonität des Kreditnehmers (Wanderung) oder auch eine Veränderung der Credit-Spreads am Markt. Der durchschnittlich erwartete Verlust im Kreditgeschäft wird durch Zahlung einer Prämie (Standardrisikokosten) abgedeckt. Kreditrisiko bezieht sich somit auf negative Abweichungen vom erwarteten Verlust (unerwarteter Verlust).

Klassisches Kreditrisiko

Unter klassischem Kreditrisiko ist der **Verlust von Teilen oder des gesamten Kapitalbetrages eines Geschäftes bei Ausfall des Partners** zu verstehen. Dieses klassische Kreditri-

set deals, since all receivables are booked in the balance sheet with the capital amount. The same risk occurs with **warranties** that the bank has given.

With derivatives (off- balance sheet products), this classic credit risk is per se eliminated.

Example

Consider that the borrower defaults after the credit has been given but before it is paid back. This would mean that the bank loses the total amount of capital and the accrued interest. With an interest rate swap, the bank does not risk losing the underlying amount of capital in case of a default.

Settlement risk

Settlement risk represents a type of **credit risk that occurs with all exchange transactions**. The bank has already completed its part of the transaction while the partner's default prevents the completion of the transaction. Therefore, the extent of the settlement risk equals the **total value of the transaction**. The risk exists from the time the bank has done the transaction until the completion of the transaction by the counterparty.

If the payment arrangements differ due to different time zones, then settlement risk becomes a particular concern. If, for example, a EUR/USD spot transaction is settled, the payer of the EUR may complete his payment several hours before he can receive the USD in return.

The settlement risk should be particularly considered in the case of **FX transactions**. Here, on the one hand volumes are tending to increase, but on the other hand almost all transactions are settled over the counter. Settlement risk hit the headlines in 1974 with the bankruptcy of the Herstatt Bank, since then settlement risk has also been known as **"Herstatt risk"**.

Replacement risk

Replacement risk refers to a bank's **risk that due to counterparty´s default the position must be replaced at an extra cost in the market**. Replacement risk is therefore mainly an element of **OTC derivatives**. As for derivatives that are traded on the (stock) exchange there is assumed to be no credit risk (i.e. replacement risk), as the exchange provides for replacement risk by charging margins.

If the bank enters an interest rate swap and the counterparty defaults during the term, the bank has to arrange a new interest rate swap at current market rates for the rest of the term, in order to create the same interest position as before the default. Due to this new deal, additional costs can occur. Today, banks make use of **two common methods** to estimate replacement risk:

siko besteht bei allen **Aktivgeschäften in der Bilanz,** wo die Forderung der Bank über den Kapitalbetrag dokumentiert ist sowie bei **Garantiezusagen der Bank.**

Für derivative Produkte (Off-Balance-Produkte) ist dieses klassische Kreditrisiko per se ausgeschaltet.

Beispiel

In einem Kreditgeschäft, bei dem nach der Kreditvergabe und vor der Kreditrückzahlung der Partner ausfällt, verliert die Bank den gesamten Kapitalbetrag sowie die bis zu diesem Zeitpunkt angefallenen Zinsen. Bei einem abgeschlossenen Zinsswap besteht für die Bank kein Risiko, dass bei Ausfall des Partners der zugrundeliegende Kapitalbetrag verlorengeht.

Abwicklungsrisiko (Settlementrisiko)

Das Abwicklungsrisiko (Settlementrisiko) ist eine **Art von Kreditrisiko,** das **bei allen Tauschgeschäften** auftritt. Es besteht darin, dass die **Bank ihre Transaktion bereits angewiesen hat, der Partner in der Zwischenzeit jedoch ausfällt und seine Transaktion nicht durchgeführt hat.** Das Ausmaß des Settlementrisikos ist also der volle Tauschwert. Die Dauer, für die dieses Risiko anfällt, beginnt mit dem Zeitpunkt der eigenen Anweisung und endet zu dem Zeitpunkt, wo sichergestellt ist, dass der Partner seine Transaktion durchgeführt hat.

Besonders zu berücksichtigen ist das Settlementrisiko, wenn durch unterschiedliche Zeitzonen die Zahlungsmodalitäten bei einem Tauschgeschäft differieren. Wird beispielsweise ein EUR/USD-Kassageschäft abgeschlossen, wird der Zahler der EUR seine Zahlung einige Stunden vor dem möglichen Eingang der USD durchführen.

Das Settlementrisiko ist besonders bei **Devisengeschäften** (sowohl Kassa als auch Termin) zu berücksichtigen. Einerseits werden hier die Volumina größer, andererseits sind fast alle Geschäfte over the counter abgeschlossen. Das Abwicklungsrisiko wurde im Jahr 1974 mit dem Konkurs der Herstatt Bank eindrucksvoll aufgezeigt, sodass seit diesem Zeitpunkt der Begriff **„Herstatt-Risiko"** als Synonym für das Abwicklungsrisiko gebraucht wird.

Wiederbeschaffungsrisiko

Unter dem Wiederbeschaffungsrisiko ist das Risiko der Bank zu verstehen, dass **bei einem Ausfall eines Partners Zusatzkosten bei der Wiederbeschaffung der gleichen Position im Markt** anfallen. Wiederbeschaffungsrisiko entsteht damit **vor allem bei OTC-Derivativen.** Da bei börsengehandelten Produkten der Partner die Börse ist und die Börse sich ihrerseits über Margins gegen das Wiederbeschaffungsrisiko absichert, wird üblicherweise davon ausgegangen, dass die an der Börse gehandelten Kontrakte ohne Kreditrisiko (d.h. ohne Wiederbeschaffungsrisiko) sind.

Bei einem abgeschlossenen Zinsswap, wo der Partner während der Laufzeit ausfällt, muss die Bank, um wieder die gleiche Zinsposition wie vorher zu erhalten, einen neuen Zinsswap mit aktuellen Marktpreisen für die Restlaufzeit abschließen. Bei dieser Gegentransaktion können somit Kosten entstehen, die durch den Ausfall des Partners hervorgerufen wurden. Zur Bemessung dieses Wiederbeschaffungsrisikos werden in Banken derzeit **zwei übliche Verfahren** angewendet:

A simple and established method is the so-called **maturity method** whereby a specified percentage per year (of remaining maturity) is applied as a so-called credit equivalent. Usually different percentage rates are applied depending on whether the replacement risk stems from an interest rate instrument or a FX instrument (or both).

Example
A bank uses the following percentage rates to charge OTC derivatives against their (credit) limits: Interest rate instruments: 1% per year of maturity FX instruments: 3% per year of maturity Thus, 10% of the principal of an interest rate swap with 10 years of remaining maturity would be charged against the credit risk limit for the counterparty (for 100m IRS volume, 10m credit equivalent). As for a 2-year FX outright, 6% of the principal would be charged against the limit.

The second method, the **mark-to-market approach**, is more complex but also more accurate. In a first step, the current market values of all OTC derivatives are calculated. Only positive market values are used for the subsequent calculation of a risk figure, because the default of a counterparty would not result in a loss if the mark-to-market value was negative.

The positive mark-to-market value represents the loss that would be caused by the default of the respective counterparty today. Because MTM values are subject to volatility, the risk figure (= credit equivalent) is calculated by charging an add-on (calculated as a% of the principal) to the sum of positive OTC market values.

Example
IRS, 10 years, (fixed rate) receiver, rate: 4.00%, principal: 50m FX outright, EUR/USD at 1.1500, 2 years, principal: 50m Add-on: Interest rate transactions: 1%   FX transactions: 5%

Current MTM values:

	MTM	Positive MTM	Add-on	Credit Equivalent
IRS	+4,200,000	4,200,00	500,000	4,700,000
Outright	-2,342,000	0	2,500,000	2,500,000
			Sum	7,200,000

In total, EUR 7,200,000 would be charged against the credit limits of the counterparty. This methodology allows accounting for possible netting agreements.

Eine einfache und gängige Methode ist die sogenannte **Laufzeitmethode.** Hier wird ein bestimmter Prozentsatz pro Laufzeitjahr als Kreditäquivalent angesetzt. In der Praxis werden üblicherweise unterschiedliche Prozentsätze verwendet, je nachdem, ob das Wiederbeschaffungsrisiko nur Zinsrisiko, Wechselkursrisiko oder beides enthält.

Beispiel

Pro Jahr Laufzeit werden in der Bank folgende Prozentsätze für die Kreditlimitanrechnung von OTC-Derivativen vorgegeben:
Zinsinstrumente: 1% pro Jahr Laufzeit
FX-Instrumente: 3% pro Laufzeit

Dementsprechend würde ein Zinsswap mit zehn Jahren Laufzeit mit 10% vom Nominale in das Kreditrisikolimit des Partners eingerechnet werden (bei 100 Mio. IRS-Volumen, 10 Mio. Kreditäquivalent).
Ein zweijähriges Devisentermingeschäft würde mit dieser Regelung zu einer Limitanrechnung von 6% führen.

Eine komplexere, aber sauberere Anrechnung des Wiederbeschaffungsrisikos ist die sogenannte **MTM-Methode.** Hierbei werden in einem ersten Schritt für alle OTC-Geschäfte die aktuellen Marktwerte (Mark-to-Market) berechnet. Nur die positiven Marktwerte werden in den anschließenden Berechnungen verwendet, da nur hier ein entsprechender Verlust bei Ausfall des Partners entstehen würde.

Die positiven aktuellen Mark-to-Market-Werte sind gleichzusetzen mit dem Verlust, der heute entstehen würde, wenn der Partner ausfällt. Weil sich die Mark-to-Markets in der Zukunft noch ändern können, wird zusätzlich zu den positiven MTMs üblicherweise noch ein Sicherheitsaufschlag (in Prozent vom Nominale) berücksichtigt.

Beispiel

Festzinsempfänger IRS: zehn Jahre, Zinssatz 4%, Volumen 50 Mio., Partner X, Verkauf Devisentermingeschäft EUR/USD, zwei Jahre, Kurs 1,1500, Volumen 50 Mio., Partner X.

Add-on: Zinsgeschäfte: 1%
FX-Geschäfte: 5%

Aktuelle MTM-Werte:

	MTM	Anrechnung MTM	Add-on	Kreditäquivalent
IRS:	+ 4.200.000	4.200.000	500.000	4.700.000
Outright:	- 2.342.000	0	2.500.000	2.500.000
			Summe	7.200.000

In Summe würde also die Kreditlinie des Partners X mit EUR 7.200.000 belastet werden.

Mit dieser Methodik können auch etwaige Nettingvereinbarungen, die entweder einzelne Instrumente oder alle OTC-Derivative umfassen, jederzeit mitberücksichtigt werden.

1.3. Market risk

Market risk (also called price risk) is the risk that the bank suffers **losses on its open positions due to unfavourable market movements**. Especially in the trading section, market risks must be taken into account, since most open positions are found there.

Overview Market risks

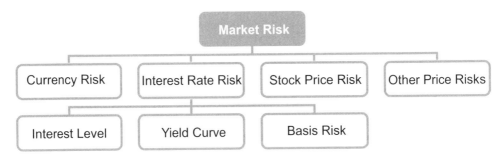

Market-based risks, which result from the change of the creditworthiness (e.g. special price risks respectively potential changes of creditworthiness spreads at securities or price risks at credit derivatives) or which are attributed to the market liquidity, should be considered in an appropriate way within the processes of risk management and risk controlling.

Currency risk

Currency risk is the **risk of loss due to changes in exchange rates**.

Interest rate risk

Interest rate risk is the **risk of loss due to interest rate movements**. It is possible to differentiate between the following "classes" of interest rate movements:

● change of the interest rate level (parallel shift of the yield curve)
● yield curve twist
● basis risk: The risk that the values of two similar, but not identical positions behave differently. For example different interest instruments (like deposits and FRAs) with the same term may still have an influence on the result in case of differing price movements of the 2 instruments involved.

Stock price risk

Stock price risk is the **risk of loss due to changes in stock prices.**

Other price risks

Other price risks are **risks of loss due to changes in gold and commodity prices or in prices of other positions** where market prices exist.

FX position keeping

Position keeping is a procedure where all transactions in a currency pair are recorded (e.g. GBP/USD) and the open balance is valued at the end of each time interval. This way, a bank has a comprehensive overview of its open positions and the risks it is currently running.

1.3. Marktrisiken

Unter Marktrisiko oder auch Preisrisiko ist das Risiko zu verstehen, dass die Bank **durch Marktbewegungen Verluste auf die eingegangenen offenen Positionen** erleidet. Dieses Risiko ist vorwiegend im Handel zu beachten, denn hier sind die offenen Positionen üblicherweise angesiedelt.

Übersicht Marktrisiken

Marktbezogene Risiken, die aus der Veränderung der Bonität einer Adresse resultieren (z.B. besondere Kursrisiken beziehungsweise potenzielle Änderungen von Bonitätsspreads bei Wertpapieren oder Preisrisiken bei Kreditderivaten) oder auf die Marktliquidität zurückzuführen sind, sind im Rahmen der Risikosteuerungs- und -controlling-Prozesse in angemessener Weise zu berücksichtigen.

Währungsrisiken

Währungsrisiken sind die **Risiken einer Verringerung des Bankergebnisses durch eine Veränderung von Wechselkursen.**

Zinsänderungsrisiken

Zinsänderungsrisiken stehen für das **Risiko einer Verringerung des Bankergebnisses durch Zinsänderungen.** Dabei wird unterschieden zwischen:

- Veränderung des Zinsniveaus (parallele Verschiebung der Zinskurve),
- Drehung der Zinskurve und
- Basisrisiko: Risiko der unterschiedlichen Kursentwicklung zweier ähnlicher, aber nicht identer Positionen. Beispielsweise können Zinsinstrumente gleicher Fristigkeiten unterschiedliche Wertentwicklungen aufweisen.

Aktienkursrisiken

Aktienkursrisiken stehen für das **Risiko einer Verringerung des Bankergebnisses durch Veränderungen von Aktienkursen.**

Sonstige Preisrisiken

Sonstige Preisrisiken stehen für das Risiko **einer Verringerung des Bankergebnisses durch Veränderung von Gold- und Rohstoffpreisen sowie der Preise für sonstige Positionen mit Marktpreisen.**

Positionsführung FX

Die Positionsführung ist ein Vorgang, bei dem alle Geschäfte in einem Währungspaar (z.B. GBP/USD) aufgezeichnet werden und der offene Saldo bewertet wird. So entsteht ein umfassender Überblick, welche offenen Positionen und Risiken gefahren werden.

Three steps are necessary in order to calculate and evaluate an open FX-position:

I. Calculation of the net position in the base currency

The net position in a currency is the amount by which a dealer is short or long of that currency after balancing out all deals. Long positions bear positive signs, short positions negative signs. If long and short positions cancel each other out the position is said to be closed.

II. Calculation of the net position in the quote currency

The volume of the base currency is multiplied by the price in order to get the volume of the quote currency. The volumes are then totalled.

III. Valuation at the average rate

The open net position is valued at the average rate. In order to calculate the average rate, the net position in the quote currency is divided by the net position in the base currency. The net position reflects the volume of the open position in the base currency. The average rate takes all transactions into account and can therefore be interpreted as the break-even rate. This means that if the position is closed at that rate there is neither a profit nor a loss. If the position is closed (or valued) at a better rate a dealing (or valuation) profit can be realised.

Example

You make the following USD/CHF transactions:
Sell USD 10 m at 1.4020
Sell USD 10 m at 1.4025
Buy USD 15 m at 1.4023
Buy USD 10 m at 1.4018

Your position:

Position base currency rate	Rate	Position quote currency	Total position	Average
-10,000,000	1.4020	+14,020,000	-10,000,000	1.40200
-10,000,000	1.4025	+14,025,000	-20,000,000	1.40225
+15,000,000	1.4023	-21,034,500	-5,000,000	1.40210
+10,000,000	1.4018	-14,018,000	+5,000,000	1.40150
+5,000,000		-7,007,500		1.40150

You have a long position of USD 5m at 1.4015.

By comparing your position with the current rate you can determine if the position is a profit or loss.

The following **principles** apply:

- In the case of **long positions** the **average rate is compared with the bid rate**. The question is if the base currency was bought cheaper than it can be sold now.
- In the case of **short positions** the **average rate is compared with the offered rate**. The question is if the amount sold can be repurchased cheaper.

In practice, the valuation of the position is done at the **mid rate**, though a valuation at the bid/offer rates is theoretically correct.

Die Ermittlung und Bewertung der offenen Position erfolgt in drei Schritten:

I. **Ermittlung der Nettoposition der quotierten Währung**

Um die Nettoposition in einer Währung zu ermitteln, werden die einzelnen Volumina der Geschäfte einfach saldiert. Long-Positionen tragen ein positives Vorzeichen, Short-Positionen ein negatives. Gleichen sich Long- und Short-Positionen aus, spricht man von einer geschlossenen Position.

II. **Ermittlung der Nettoposition in der Gegenwährung**

Um das Volumen der Gegenwährung zu ermitteln, wird das Volumen der quotierten Währung mit dem Preis (Kurs) multipliziert. Auch hier werden die Volumina saldiert.

III. **Bewertung zum Durchschnittskurs**

Die offene Nettoposition wird zum Durchschnittskurs bewertet. Die Nettoposition der Gegenwährung wird durch die Nettoposition der quotierten Währung dividiert. Die Nettoposition der quotierten Währung zeigt das Volumen der offenen Position. Der Durchschnittskurs berücksichtigt alle Transaktionen und kann als Break-Even-Kurs interpretiert werden. Kann die Position zu diesem Kurs geschlossen werden, so entsteht weder Gewinn noch Verlust. Wird die Position mit einem besseren Kurs geschlossen (oder bewertet), so ergibt sich ein Handelsgewinn (oder Bewertungsgewinn).

Beispiel

Sie führen folgende USD/CHF-Transaktionen durch:
Verkauf USD 10 Mio. zu 1,4020
Verkauf USD 10 Mio. zu 1,4025
Kauf USD 15 Mio. zu 1,4023
Kauf USD 10 Mio. zu 1,4018

Ihre Position sieht folgendermaßen aus:

Position quotierte Währung	Kurs	Position Gegenwährung	Gesamtposition	Durch-schnittskurs
-10.000.000	1,4020	+14.020.000	-10.000.000	1,40200
-10.000.000	1,4025	+14.025.000	-20.000.000	1,40225
+15.000.000	1,4023	-21.034.500	-5.000.000	1,40210
+10.000.000	1,4018	-14.018.000	+5.000.000	1,40150
+5.000.000		-7.007.500		1,40150

Das heißt, Sie sind long in USD 5 Mio. zu 1,4015.

Um zu ermitteln, ob Ihre Position ein Gewinn oder Verlust ist, muss sie mit dem aktuellen Kurs, zu dem Sie die Position schließen können, verglichen werden.

Folgende **Grundsätze** gelten:

- Bei **Long-Positionen** ist der **Durchschnittskurs mit dem Geldkurs zu vergleichen.** Die Frage ist, ob Sie die quotierte Währung günstiger gekauft haben, als Sie sie jetzt verkaufen können.
- Bei **Short-Positionen** ist der **Durchschnittskurs dem Briefkurs gegenüberzustellen.** Die Frage ist, ob Sie den gegebenen Betrag billiger kaufen können.

Obwohl die Bewertung der offenen Position mit dem jeweiligen Geld- und Briefkurs inhaltlich richtig ist, wird **in der Praxis die Nettoposition mit der Kassamitte bewertet.**

Example

Continued: Your net position is USD 5 m long at an USD/CHF average rate of 1.4015. The closing rate is 1.4017-19. Did you make a profit or loss?

You are USD 5m long, which you can sell at 1.4017. Since you have paid on average 1.4015 CHF per USD you cash in a profit of 0.0002 CHF per USD, i.e. CHF 1,000 (5,000,000 x 0.0002).

If you revalue the position at the mid rate (1.4018) your result is CHF 1,500 (5,000,000 x 0.0003).

Position keeping

If a closed position shall be valued again you can choose between two possibilities:

- You continue with the average rate of the net position
- The open net position is valued and the profit/loss booked. The starting point for next day's valuation is then the net position at the valuation rate.

Example

We continue with the USD/CHF example calculated above. You are USD 5 m long at 1.4015, valuation against 1.4017. Your next deal is the sale of USD 7 m at 1.4016. Value the position if the closing rate is 1.4016.

Option 1

Position base currency	Rate	Position quote currency	Total position	Average rate
+5,000,000	1.4015	-7,007,500	+5,000,000	1.40150
-7,000,000	1.4016	+9,811,200	-2,000,000	1.40185
-2,000,000		+2,803,700		1.40185

Average rate: 1.40185
Valuation rate: 1.4016
Result: Profit CHF 500 (2 m x (1.40185 – 1.4016))

Option 2

Position base currency	Rate	Position quote currency	Total position	Average rate
+5,000,000	1.4017	-7,008,500	+5,000,000	1.40170
-7,000,000	1.4016	+9,811,200	-2,000,000	1.40135
-2,000,000		+2,802,700		1.40135

Average rate: 1.40135 for 2 m
Valuation rate: 1.4016

Beispiel

Fortsetzung: Ihre Nettoposition ist USD 5 Mio. long bei einem USD/CHF-Durchschnitts-kurs von 1,4015. Die Schlussquotierung lautet 1,4017-19. Haben Sie einen Gewinn oder Verlust?

Sie sind USD 5 Mio. long und können diese zu 1,4017 verkaufen. Da Sie die USD zu durchschnittlich 1,4015 gekauft haben, erzielen Sie einen Gewinn von 0,0002 CHF pro USD. Das sind CHF 1.000 (5.000.000 x 0,0002).

Bei einer Bewertung zum Mittelkurs (1,4018) ist das Bewertungsergebnis CHF 1.500 (5.000.000 x 0,0003).

Weiterführen einer Position

Führt man eine bewertete Position weiter, bieten sich zwei Möglichkeiten:

- Man setzt auf der Nettoposition zum Durchschnittskurs auf.
- Die offene Nettoposition wird bewertet und der Gewinn/Verlust realisiert. Als Ausgangs-punkt für die nächsten Schritte dient jetzt die Nettoposition zum Bewertungskurs.

Beispiel

Fortsetzung: Sie sind USD 5 Mio. long zu 1,4015, Bewertung gegen 1,4017. Ihr nächstes Geschäft ist der Verkauf von USD 7 Mio. zu 1,4016. Die Bewertung erfolgt gegen 1,4016.

Variante 1

Position quotierte Währung	Kurs	Position Gegenwährung	Gesamtposition	Durchschnittskurs
+5.000.000	1,4015	-7.007.500	+5.000.000	1,40150
-7.000.000	1,4016	+9.811.200	-2.000.000	1,40185
-2.000.000		+2.803.700		1,40185

Schlusskurs: 1,40185 für 2 Mio.
Bewertungskurs: 1,4016
Ergebnis: Gewinn 500 CHF (2 Mio. x (1,40185 – 1,4016))

Variante 2

Gewinn von 1.000 festgeschrieben, Position 5 Mio. mit Bewertungskurs (1,4017) weiter-führen.

Position quotierte Währung	Kurs	Position Gegenwährung	Gesamtposition	Durchschnittskurs
+5.000.000	1,4017	-7.008.500	+5.000.000	1,40170
-7.000.000	1,4016	+9.811.200	-2.000.000	1,40135
-2.000.000		+2.802.700		1,40135

Schlusskurs: 1,40135 für 2 Mio.
Bewertungskurs: 1,4016

Result: Profit   1,000 (Valuation Day 1)
_____Loss_____500 (Valuation Day 2)___
Total: **Profit   CHF 500**

In option 1 all profits/losses of the past are incorporated in the average rate.

In the second possibility the result is locked in and the next average rate reflects the break-even for the new deals.

Position keeping if the base currency is the domestic currency

In continental Europe, the switch to the Euro poses the problem that the positions are kept and valued in the domestic currency. Thus, the position in the base currency is no longer automatically the open FX position. The open FX position is now the position in the base currency or profits/losses, which incur if the valuation is done at the valuation rate in the domestic currency.

Example

You buy EUR/USD 10 m at 1.1835 and buy EUR/USD 12 m at 1.1837. You sell EUR/USD 22 m at 1.1838. Furthermore, you buy EUR/USD 10m at 1.1840 and sell EUR/USD 5 m at 1.1842.

What is your position and result at the end of the day if you revalue your position against a EUR/USD closing rate of 1.1837?

Position base currency	Rate	Position quote currency	Total position	Average Rate
+10,000,000	1.1835	-11,835,000	+10,000,000	1.18350
+10,000,000	1.1837	-14,204,400	+22,000,000	1.18360
+10,000,000	1.1840	-11,840,000	+32,000,000	1.18370
-22,000,000	1.1838	+26,043,600	+10,000,000	1.18350
-5,000,000	1.1842	+5,921,000	+5,000,000	1.18296
+5,000,000		-5,914,800		1.18296

You are Euro 5m long at a EUR/USD rate of 1.18296. You earn a **profit** of 0.00074 Euro per USD (1.1837 – 1.18296). With 5 m Euro, that is **3,700 USD or 3,125.79 Euro**.

Keeping a closed position

Usually, positions are kept in the base currency. If the position in the base currency is closed you have **two possibilities to continue your position keeping**:

- You fix the result of the closed position and start with a new calculation of the average rate. In the final valuation the result of the closed position must be taken into account separately.

Ergebnis: Gewinn 1.000 (Bewertung Tag 1)

     Verlust 500 (Bewertung Tag 2)

Summe: **Gewinn 500 CHF**

In Variante 1 fließen alle Gewinne/Verluste der Vergangenheit in den Durchschnittskurs ein.

 In Variante 2 wird nach jeder Bewertung das Ergebnis festgeschrieben. Der nächste Durchschnittskurs zeigt den Break-Even für die neu getätigten Geschäfte.

Führen und Bewerten einer Position, wenn die quotierte Währung die Heimwährung ist

Im kontinentaleuropäischen Raum ergibt sich durch die Umstellung auf den Euro das Problem, dass bei der Positionsführung und der Bewertung die Heimwährung jetzt die quotierte Währung ist. Die ermittelte Position in der quotierten Währung ist dafür nicht mehr automatisch auch die offene FX-Position. Die offene FX-Position ist nunmehr die ermittelte Position in der quotierten Währung bzw. die Gewinne/Verluste, die in der Bewertung mit dem Bewertungskurs in der Heimwährung entstanden sind.

Beispiel

Sie kaufen EUR/USD 10 Mio. zu 1,1835 und kaufen EUR/USD 12 Mio. zu 1,1837. Sie verkaufen EUR/USD 22 Mio. zu 1,1838. Sie kaufen weiters EUR/USD 10 Mio. zu 1,1840 und verkaufen EUR/USD 5 Mio. zu 1,1842.
Was ist Ihre Position am Ende des Tages und das Ergebnis bei einer Bewertung gegen den Schlusskurs EUR/USD von 1,1837?

Position quotierte Währung	Kurs	Position Gegenwährung	Gesamtposition	Durchschnittskurs
+10.000.000	1,1835	-11.835.000	+10.000.000	1,18350
+12.000.000	1,1837	-14.204.400	+22.000.000	1,18360
+10.000.000	1,1840	-11.840.000	+32.000.000	1,18370
-22.000.000	1,1838	+26.043.600	+10.000.000	1,18350
-5.000.000	1,1842	+5.921.000	+5.000.000	1,18296
+5.000.000		-5.914.800		1,18296

Sie sind EUR 5 Mio. long zu einem EUR/USD-Kurs von 1,18296. Ihr Ergebnis ist ein **Gewinn** von USD 0,00074 pro EUR (1,1837 – 1,18296). Bei EUR 5 Mio. sind das **USD 3.700 oder EUR 3.125,79.**

Weiterführen einer geschlossenen Position

Häufig werden die Positionen in der quotierten Währung geführt. Ist jedoch die Position in der quotierten Währung geschlossen, so bestehen **folgende Möglichkeiten, die Position weiterzuführen:**

- Sie schreiben das Ergebnis auf die geschlossene Position fest und beginnen mit einer neuen Durchschnittskursermittlung. Bei der Schlussbewertung ist das Ergebnis der geschlossenen Position separat zu berücksichtigen.

- You skip the transaction that would close your position and re-insert it for valuation later. This way, you can calculate an average rate covering all transactions, against which you can make a valuation.

Example

In the morning you buy EUR/USD 10m at 1.1835 and EUR/USD 12m at 1.1837. You sell EUR/USD 22m at 1.1838. In the afternoon, you buy EUR/USD 10m at 1.1840 and sell EUR/USD 5m at 1.1842.
What is your position and result at the end of the day if you revalue your position at a EUR/USD closing rate of 1.1837?

Option 1

Step 1

Position base currency	Rate	Position quoted currency	Total position	Average Rate
+10,000,000	1.1835	- +11,835,000	+10,000,000	1.1835
+12,000,000	1.1837	-14,204,400	+22,000,000	1.18360909
-22,000,000	1.1838	+26,043,600	0	
0		+4,200		

Step 2

Position base currency	Rate	Position quoted currency	Total position	Average rate
+10,000,000	1.1840	+11,840,000	+10,000,000	1.1840
-5,000,000	1.1842	+5,921,000	+5,000,000	1.1838
+5,000,000		-5,919,000		1.1838

You have a loss of 500 USD (5,000,000 x (1.1837 – 1.1838) on the 5m Euro. If you add the profit of USD 4,200 from the first transaction, the total result is a **profit of USD 3,700 or 3125.79 Euro** (3,700/1.1837).

Option 2

Position base currency	Rate	Position quote currency	Total position	Average rate
+10.000.000	1,1835	-11.835.000	+10.000.000	1,18350
+12.000.000	1,1837	-14.204.400	+22.000.000	1,18360
+10.000.000	1,1840	-11.840.000	+32.000.000	1,18370
-22.000.000	1,1838	+26.043.600	+10.000.000	1,18350
-5.000.000	1,1842	+5.921.000	+5.000.000	1,18296
+5.000.000		-5.914.800		1,18296

Your **profit** is 5 m x 0.00074 = **USD 3,700**. Independently of the calculation you receive the same result.

- Man lässt die Transaktion, die zur Schließung der Position führt, weg, setzt sie jedoch zur Bewertung später wieder an. So ermittelt man über alle Positionen einen Durchschnittskurs, gegen den man bewerten kann.

Beispiel

Am Vormittag kaufen Sie EUR/USD 10 Mio. zu 1,1835 und kaufen EUR/USD 12 Mio. zu 1,1837. Sie verkaufen EUR/USD 22 Mio. zu 1,1838. Am Nachmittag kaufen Sie EUR/USD 10 Mio. zu 1,1840 und verkaufen EUR/USD 5 Mio. zu 1,1842.

Was ist Ihre Position am Ende des Tages und das Ergebnis bei einer Bewertung gegen den Schlusskurs EUR/USD von 1,1837?

Variante 1

1. Schritt

Position quotierte Währung	Kurs	Position Gegenwährung	Gesamtposition	Durchschnitts- kurs
+10.000.000	1,1835	-11.835.000	+10.000.000	1,1835
+12.000.000	1,1837	-14.204.400	+22.000.000	1,18360909
-22.000.000	1,1838	+26.043.600	0	
0		+4.200		

2. Schritt

Position quotierte Währung	Kurs	Position Gegenwährung	Gesamtposition	Durchschnitts- kurs
+10.000.000	1,1840	-11.840.000	+10.000.000	1,1840
-5.000.000	1,1842	+5.921.000	+5.000.000	1,1838
+5.000.000		-5.919.000		1,1838

Auf die EUR 5 Mio. haben Sie einen Verlust von USD 500 (5.000.000 x (1,1837 – 1,1838)). Dazu addieren Sie den Gewinn von USD 4.200 aus den oberen Transaktionen. In Summe beträgt Ihr **Gewinn** somit **USD 3.700 oder EUR 3.125,79** (3.700/1,1837).

Variante 2

Position quotierte Währung	Kurs	Position Gegenwährung	Gesamtposition	Durchschnittskurs
+10.000.000	1,1835	-11.835.000	+10.000.000	1,18350
+12.000.000	1,1837	-14.204.400	+22.000.000	1,18360
+10.000.000	1,1840	-11.840.000	+32.000.000	1,18370
-22.000.000	1,1838	+26.043.600	+10.000.000	1,18350
-5.000.000	1,1842	+5.921.000	+5.000.000	1,18296
+5.000.000		-5.914.800		1,18296

Ihr **Gewinn** beträgt **USD 3.700** (5 Mio. x 0,00074). Das Ergebnis bleibt also unabhängig von der Variante gleich.

1.4. Liquidity risk

As a basic principle, one distinguishes between **two basic types of liquidity risk**:

Refinancing or Funding Risk

Refinancing risk represents the **risk that liabilities cannot be met due to the lack of (regular) refinancing or funding sources**. This kind of risk might materialise in the form of unexpectedly high costs for (short-term) funding in the simplest case or in the form of illiquidity in the most extreme case. A shortage of funding need not be the result of a deteriorated credit quality of the bank but may also be caused by general market circumstances.

Refinancing risk exists whenever the **assets of a bank (e.g. loans) are committed for a longer maturity than liabilities** (e.g. savings), which means that the refinancing of the assets is not guaranteed for their whole maturity.

Asset Liquidity Risk

Asset liquidity risk stands for the risk that **certain assets of a bank cannot be sold or can only be sold at an extraordinarily high bid-ask spread**. This kind of liquidity risk may also be seen as a subcategory of market risk.

1.5. Operational Risks

The Basel II Committee distinguishes between operational risks that can be attributed to internal or external sources. The first class includes the risk of loss resulting from inadequate or failed

- people,
- internal processes and
- systems.

Operational risks represent all those **risks that are caused by malfunctioning systems** in banks. These may be computer shutdowns as well as inadequate organisational foundations within the banks. Even if banks are determined to establish the best systems and processes possible, the risk still exists that established procedures are bypassed with criminal intent by individuals.

Transaction risk

Transaction risk describes the risk that disadvantageous exchange rate movements may affect the income of an importer after he has delivered the goods.

Economic risk

The economic risk refers to a potential future loss of competitiveness due to a stronger currency.

1.4. Liquiditätsrisiko

Grundsätzlich können **zwei Arten von Liquiditätsrisiken** unterschieden werden.

Refinanzierungsrisiko (auch: bilanzielles Liquiditätsrisiko)

Refinanzierungsrisiko steht für die **Gefahr von fehlenden Refinanzierungsquellen der Bank, die notwendig sind, um ihren Verpflichtungen nachzukommen.** Der Bank können damit unerwartet hohe Kosten für die Beschaffung kurzfristiger finanzieller Mittel entstehen bzw. im Extremfall wird die Bank zahlungsunfähig (Illiquidität). Refinanzierungsrisiken können nicht nur durch eine Bonitätsverschlechterung der Bank schlagend werden, sondern auch durch allgemeine Marktilliquiditäten.

Refinanzierungsrisiko besteht immer dann, wenn die **Kapitalbindung auf der Aktivseite (z.B. im Kreditgeschäft) länger als die Kapitalbindung der Passivseite** ist. Für die Bank ist damit nicht sichergestellt, dass die Refinanzierung für die Gesamtlaufzeit zur Verfügung steht.

Instrumenten-Liquiditätsrisiko

Unter Instrumenten-Liquiditätsrisiko versteht man die **Gefahr fehlender Marktliquidität für Finanzinstrumente.** Von der Bank gehaltene Positionen können nicht oder nur unter Inkaufnahme einer außergewöhnlich hohen Kauf-/Verkaufsspanne geschlossen werden. Das Instrumenten-Liquiditätsrisiko kann auch als eine Unterkategorie vom Marktrisiko verstanden werden.

1.5. Operationale Risiken

Der Basler Ausschuss unterscheidet nach operationalen Risiken, die auf interne und externe Ereignisse zurückzuführen sind. Operationale Risiken, die auf **interne Ereignisse** zurückzuführen sind, sind die Gefahr von Verlusten als Folge der Unangemessenheit bzw. des Versagens von

● Mitarbeitern,
● internen Prozessen oder
● Systemen.

Unter operationalen Risiken sind üblicherweise alle **Risiken** zu verstehen, **die durch nicht funktionierende Systeme bei den Banken verursacht werden.** Dies können Computerausfälle oder auch ungenügende organisatorische Voraussetzungen der Banken sein. Auch wenn eine Bank sich bemüht, alle genannten Risiken zu vermeiden, existiert noch immer das Risiko, dass die etablierten Prozeduren von Einzelpersonen bewusst und in krimineller Art umgangen werden.

Transaktionsrisiko

Als Transaktionsrisiko bezeichnet man das Risiko eines Unternehmens, Waren geliefert zu haben und bis zum Zahlungseingang von einer negativen Wechselkursentwicklung betroffen zu sein.

Wirtschaftliches Risiko

Als wirtschaftliches Risiko bezeichnet man die Verschlechterung der zukünftigen Wettbewerbsfähigkeit aufgrund nachteiliger Wechselkursbewegungen.

The following risks fall within the class of **external operational risks**:

Political risks

Changes in the political landscape may have influences on the bank's business opportunities as well as on the business conditions which the bank's partners are facing.

Image risks

Due to the fact that banks are operating in a highly sensitive area (managing someone else's money), their business connections are very vulnerable to a possible loss of image. Rumours and/or scandals may lead to greater business losses, even though the economic effects themselves might be headed off easily by the bank.

Legal risks and risks of statutory regulations

Some risks cannot be influenced by banks, but could still play a role for the total risk of the bank. These risks could be legal uncertainties during the treaty's drafting as well as risks that are a result of possible changes in statutory regulations.

Summary

Risk is defined as the likelihood of a loss or a lower than expected return. Risk only applies to future and therefore uncertain events. Risks that have materialized are no longer classified as risks; rather they have been entered in the profit and loss account (as a loss). Credit risk is the risk of loss due to a debtor's non-payment of a loan or other line of credit or the reduction of the expected return due to a so-called credit event. The classic credit risk refers to the loss of a transaction's total capital amount (or parts of it) due to the partner's inability to pay.

Settlement risk represents a type of credit risk that occurs with all exchange transactions. The bank has already completed its part of the transaction while the partner's default prevents the completion of the transaction. Therefore, the extent of the settlement risk equals the total value of the transaction.

Replacement risk refers to a bank's risk that due to counterparty's default the position must be replaced in the market at extra cost. Today, banks make use of two common methods to estimate replacement risk: maturity method and mark-to-market approach.

Market risk (also called price risk) is the risk that the bank suffers losses on its open positions due to unfavourable market movements. The market risks are currency risk, interest rate risk, stock price risk and other price risks.

Currency risk is the risk of loss due to changes in exchange rates.

Interest rate risk is the risk of loss due to interest rate movements.

Stock price risk is the risk of loss due to changes in stock prices.

Unter **externen Ereignissen** werden verstanden:

Politische Risiken

Die Veränderung politischer Rahmenbedingungen kann sowohl die eigenen Geschäftsmöglichkeiten als auch die Rahmenbedingungen für die bestehenden Partner ändern.

Imagerisiken

Banken sind in einem hochsensiblen Geschäftsbereich tätig (Verwaltung von fremden Geldern). Ihre Geschäftsbeziehungen sind daher besonders anfällig für etwaige Imageverluste. So können Gerüchte und/oder Skandale – auch wenn der betriebswirtschaftliche Effekt von der Bank leicht kompensierbar ist – zu Geschäftseinbußen führen.

Rechtliche Risiken

Rechtliches Risiko beschreibt sowohl Rechtsunsicherheiten bei der vertraglichen Gestaltung als auch Risiken durch geänderte gesetzliche Bestimmungen. Risiken können auch außerhalb der direkten Einflusssphäre der Banken liegen. Dies können sowohl Rechtsunsicherheiten bei der vertraglichen Gestaltung als auch Risiken durch geänderte Bestimmungen sein.

Zusammenfassung

Risiko ist die Gefahr einer möglichen Gewinnminderung. Alles, was an Risiken bereits schlagend geworden ist, ist nicht Risiko, sondern Verlust, der in der Buchhaltung bzw. im Ergebnis seinen Niederschlag findet. Man unterscheidet zwischen Kredit-, Markt-, Liquiditäts- und operationalen Risiken.

Das Kreditrisiko ist das mit dem Verleihen von Geld verbundene Risiko des Gläubigers bzw. das Risiko einer Verringerung des Bankergebnisses aufgrund eines kreditbezogenen Ereignisses.

Unter klassischem Kreditrisiko ist der Verlust von Teilen oder des gesamten Kapitalbetrages eines Geschäftes bei Ausfall des Partners zu verstehen.

Das Abwicklungsrisiko (Settlementrisiko) ist eine Art von Kreditrisiko, das bei allen Tauschgeschäften auftritt. Es besteht darin, dass die Bank ihre Transaktion bereits angewiesen hat, der Partner in der Zwischenzeit jedoch ausfällt und seine Transaktion nicht durchgeführt hat. Das Ausmaß des Settlementrisikos ist also der volle Tauschwert.

Unter dem Wiederbeschaffungsrisiko ist das Risiko der Bank zu verstehen, dass bei einem Ausfall eines Partners Zusatzkosten bei der Wiederbeschaffung der gleichen Position im Markt anfallen. Zur Bemessung dieses Wiederbeschaffungsrisikos werden in Banken derzeit zwei übliche Verfahren angewendet, nämlich die Laufzeitmethode und die MTM-Methode.

Unter Marktrisiko oder auch Preisrisiko ist das Risiko zu verstehen, dass die Bank durch Marktbewegungen Verluste auf die eingegangenen offenen Positionen erleidet. Zu den Marktrisiken zählen Währungsrisiken, Zinsänderungsrisiken, Aktienkursrisiken und sonstige Preisrisiken.

Währungsrisiko ist das Risiko einer Verringerung des Bankergebnisses durch eine Veränderung von Wechselkursen.

Zinsänderungsrisiko steht für das Risiko einer Verringerung des Bankergebnisses durch Zinsänderungen.

Aktienkursrisiko steht für das Risiko einer Verringerung des Bankergebnisses durch Veränderungen von Aktienkursen.

Other price risks are risks of loss due to changes in gold and commodity prices or in prices of other positions where market prices exist.

Three steps are necessary in order to calculate and evaluate an open FX position: calculation of the net position in the base currency, calculation of the net position in the quote currency and valuation at the average rate. In practice, the valuation of the position is done at the mid rate, though a valuation at bid/offer rates is theoretically correct.

Should a closed position be valued again you may continue with the average rate of the net position or the open net position is valued and the profit/loss booked.

Usually, positions are kept in the base currency. If the position in the base currency is closed you can fix the result of the closed position and start with a new calculation of the average rate or you can skip the transaction that would close your position and re-insert it for valuation later.

As a basic principle, one distinguishes between two basic types of liquidity risk: Refinancing risk represents the risk that liabilities cannot be met due to the lack of (regular) refinancing or funding sources. Asset liquidity risk stands for the risk that certain assets of a bank cannot be sold or can only be sold at an extraordinarily high bid-ask spread.

Operational risks represent all those risks that are caused by malfunctioning systems in banks. The operational risks are transaction risk, economic risk, political risk, image risks and legal risks and risks of statutory regulations

1.6. Practice Questions

1. Which duties are assigned to the Asset Liability Committee (ALCO)?
   a) management and specification of the bank's market risk
   b) management of the bank's customer business
   c) supervision of the balance sheet accounting
   d) controlling and specification of the trader's limits
2. What is the difference between "risk" and "loss"?
3. Which risk arises from losses on open positions due to changes in exchange rate or interest rate?
   a) systemic risk
   b) market risk
   c) operational risk
   d) credit risk
4. What is meant by the classic credit risk?
5. What is meant by the settlement risk?
6. Which of the following positions entails NO basis risk?
   a) buy IRS/sell future strip
   b) borrowing 3 months/lending 6 months/purchase 3/6 FRA

Sonstige Preisrisiken stehen für das Risiko einer Verringerung des Bankergebnisses durch Veränderung von Gold- und Rohstoffpreisen sowie der Preise für sonstige Positionen mit Marktpreisen.

Die Ermittlung und Bewertung der offenen Position erfolgt in drei Schritten: Ermittlung der Nettoposition der quotierten Währung, Ermittlung der Nettoposition in der Gegenwährung und Bewertung zum Durchschnittskurs. Bei Long-Positionen ist der Durchschnittskurs mit dem Geldkurs zu vergleichen und bei Short-Positionen ist der Durchschnittskurs dem Briefkurs gegenüberzustellen. In der Praxis wird die Nettoposition oft mit der Kassamitte bewertet.

Wird eine bewertete Position weitergeführt, kann man einerseits auf der Nettoposition zum Durchschnittskurs aufsetzen oder die offene Nettoposition bewerten und den Gewinn/Verlust realisieren.

Häufig werden die Positionen in der quotierten Währung geführt. Um eine in der quotierten Währung geschlossene Position weiterzuführen, kann man einerseits das Ergebnis auf die geschlossene Position festschreiben und mit einer neuen Durchschnittskursermittlung beginnen oder andererseits die Transaktion, die zur Schließung der Position führt, weglassen und sie später zur Bewertung wieder ansetzen.

Grundsätzlich können zwei Arten von Liquiditätsrisiken unterschieden werden: Das Refinanzierungsrisiko steht für die Gefahr von fehlenden Refinanzierungsquellen der Bank, die notwendig sind, um ihren Verpflichtungen nachzukommen. Unter Instrumenten-Liquiditätsrisiko versteht man die Gefahr fehlender Marktliquidität für Finanzinstrumente. Von der Bank gehaltene Positionen können nicht oder nur unter Inkaufnahme einer außergewöhnlich hohen Kauf-/Verkaufsspanne geschlossen werden.

Unter operationalen Risiken sind üblicherweise alle Risiken zu verstehen, die durch nicht-funktionierende Systeme bei den Banken verursacht werden. Zu den operationalen Risiken zählen das Transaktionsrisiko, das wirtschaftliche Risiko, politische Risiken, Imagerisiken und rechtliche Risiken.

1.6. Wiederholungsfragen

1. Welche Aufgabe hat das Asset Liability Committee (ALCO)?
   a) Steuerung und Vorgabe des Marktrisikos der Bank
   b) Steuerung des Kundengeschäfts der Bank
   c) Aufsicht der Bilanzbuchhaltung
   d) Kontrolle und Vorgabe der Händlerlimits
2. Erklären Sie den Unterschied zwischen den Begriffen „Risiko" und „Verlust"!
3. Wie nennt man das Risiko, aufgrund von Wechselkurs- oder Zinsänderungen Verluste auf eine offene Position zu erleiden?
   a) Systemrisiko
   b) Marktrisiko
   c) operationales Risiko
   d) Kreditrisiko
4. Was versteht man unter dem klassischen Kreditrisiko?
5. Was versteht man unter dem Abwicklungsrisiko?
6. Bei welcher der folgenden Positionen besteht KEIN Basisrisiko?
   a) Kauf IRS/Verkauf Future-Strip
   b) 3 Monate genommen/6 Monate gegeben/3/6 FRA gekauft

　　c)　buy 3/6 FRA/sell 3/6 FRA
　　d)　buy FRA/buy future
7.　Name and decribe the two common methods for measuring replacement risks!
8.　Which of the following statements is true regarding market risks?
　　a)　It can be eliminated using a good VAR model.
　　b)　It is always equal to basis risk.
　　c)　It is the risk of negative price movements for open positions.
　　d)　It is the risk of the bank having to make a replacement deal if the counterparty fails to deliver on the original deal.
9.　What term would you use to describe the risk of an importing company that has to pay for goods in foreign currency?
　　a)　exchange rate risk
　　b)　transaction risk
　　c)　economic risk
　　d)　credit risk
10.　Having dealt a spot FX deal with a counterparty, on which day is your credit risk the greatest?
　　a)　tomorrow
　　b)　today
　　c)　The risk is equal on all days.
　　d)　on the spot date
11.　Which method can be used to continue a position that has already been valued?
　　a)　realize profit/loss and continue at valuation rate
　　b)　do not realize profit/loss and continue at the lowest rate
　　c)　do not realize profit/loss and continue at valuation rate
　　d)　realize profit/loss and continue at average rate
12.　What happens if the position in the base currency is closed?
　　a)　The average rate must be calculated using one less transaction.
　　b)　You can no longer keep the position.
　　c)　The offer rate is used instead of the mid rate to mark the position to market.
　　d)　The sequence of revaluating the transactions can be changed in order to enable the calculation of an average rate.
13.　At which rate is a long net position theoretically revalued?
　　a)　bid rate
　　b)　offer rate
　　c)　average rate
　　d)　All answers are false.
14.　What are the three steps to calculate and valuate open positions?
15.　You have a closed position in the base currency and have calculated a new average rate. What do you do in order to calculate the overall result?
　　a)　You add both results.
　　b)　You only take the result of the closed position into account.
　　c)　You only take the second result into account.
　　d)　You choose the rate that allows maximum tax evasion.
　　16.　Name and describe briefly the two types of liquidity risk!

    c) Kauf 3/6 FRA/Verkauf 3/6 FRA

    d) Kauf FRA/Kauf Future

7. Nennen und beschreiben Sie die beiden üblichen Verfahren zur Bemessung des Wiederbeschaffungsrisikos!

8. Welche der folgenden Aussagen trifft auf das Marktrisiko zu?

    a) Mit einem guten VAR-Modell kann es ausgeschaltet werden.

    b) Es ist immer gleich dem Basisrisiko.

    c) Es ist das Risiko nachteiliger Kursentwicklungen bei offenen Positionen.

    d) Es ist das Risiko, dass ein Geschäft nicht erfüllt wird, sodass die Bank gezwungen ist, ein Ersatzgeschäft zu tätigen.

9. Wie nennt man das Risiko, dem ein Importeur unterliegt, der für Waren in einer ausländischen Währung bezahlen muss?

    a) Umrechnungsrisiko

    b) Transaktionsrisiko

    c) wirtschaftliches Risiko

    d) Kreditrisiko

10. Sie haben ein FX-Kassageschäft abgeschlossen. An welchem Tag ist Ihr Kreditrisiko am höchsten?

    a) morgen

    b) heute

    c) an allen Tagen gleich

    d) am Spot-Tag

11. Welche Möglichkeiten haben Sie, bewertete Positionen weiterzuführen?

    a) Ergebnis festschreiben und mit Bewertungskurs weiterrechnen

    b) Ergebnis nicht festschreiben und mit Tiefstkurs weiterrechnen

    c) Ergebnis nicht festschreiben und mit Bewertungskurs weiterrechnen

    d) Ergebnis festschreiben und mit Durchschnittskurs weiterrechnen

12. Was können Sie tun, wenn bei der Berechnung des Durchschnittskurses die Position zwischenzeitlich geschlossen war?

    a) Man muss den Durchschnittskurs mit einer Transaktion weniger ermitteln.

    b) Die Position kann nicht mehr weitergeführt werden.

    c) Der Briefkurs wird statt der Kassamitte zur Bewertung herangezogen.

    d) Man kann die Reihenfolge der Bewertung so ändern, dass die Ermittlung eines Durchschnittskurses möglich ist.

13. Zu welchem Kurs wird eine Long-Nettoposition theoretisch bewertet?

    a) Geldkurs

    b) Briefkurs

    c) Durchschnittskurs

    d) Alle Antworten sind falsch.

14. Welche drei Schritte sind bei der Ermittlung und Bewertung der offenen Position erforderlich?

15. Sie haben eine geschlossene Position in der quotierten Währung und ermitteln einen neuen Durchschnittkurs. Was tun Sie, um das Gesamtergebnis zu ermitteln?

    a) beide Ergebnisse zusammenzählen

    b) nur das Ergebnis der geschlossenen Position berücksichtigen

    c) nur das zweite Ergebnis berücksichtigen

    d) den steuerlich besten Kurs wählen

16. Nennen und beschreiben Sie kurz die zwei Arten von Liquiditätsrisiko!

2. Risk Measurement Methods

In this chapter you learn ...

- about the methods for measuring market risk.
- how the risk is measured by the GAP Method, Duration Approach and Present Value of a Basis Point.
- what is meant by the concept of Key Rate Duration.
- which modern risk management methods are used.
- what are the basics of Probability Theory.
- what RiskMetrics stands for.
- what is meany by the GARCH Method.
- which methods are used for measuring credit risk.
- what is meant by Credit Value at Risk.
- what is meant by netting.
- which types of netting are used.
- what is meant by Central Clearing Counterparty.

2.1. Market risk

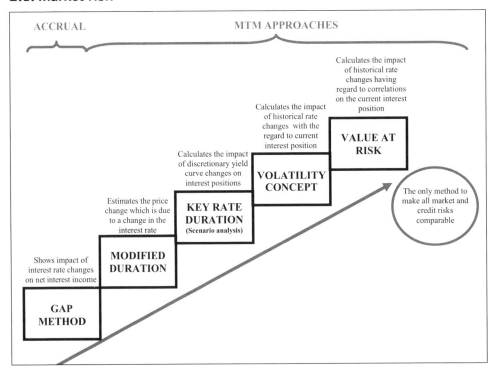

In the following section we would like to present different methods of risk measurement, using the example of interest rate risk measurement. The methods will be briefly explained

2. Methoden zur Risikomessung

In diesem Kapitel lernen Sie ...

- mit welchen Methoden das Marktrisiko gemessen werden kann.
- wie die Risikomessung mit der GAP-Methode, dem Durationsansatz und dem Present Value of a Basis Point erfolgt.
- was man unter dem Konzept der Key Rate Duration versteht.
- welche modernen Risikomanagementmethoden verwendet werden.
- die Grundlagen der Wahrscheinlichkeitstheorie kennen.
- wofür RiskMetrics steht.
- was man unter der GARCH-Methode versteht.
- mit welchen Methoden das Kreditrisiko gemessen werden kann.
- was man unter Credit Value at Risk versteht.
- was man unter Netting versteht.
- welche Arten von Netting verwendet werden.
- was man unter Central Clearing Counterparty versteht.

2.1. Marktrisiko

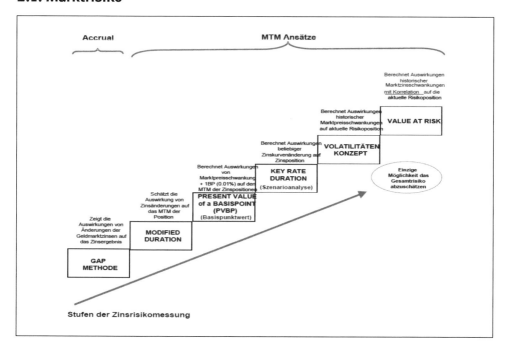

Am Beispiel Zinsrisikomessung möchten wir in der Folge die verschiedenen Verfahren der Risikomessung skizzieren. Die in der obigen Abbildung dargestellten Methoden werden jeweils kurz präsentiert, an einem einfachen Beispiel wird die Funktionsweise gezeigt und anschließend an einem durchgängigen Beispielportfolio angewendet. Zum Abschluss werden die Vor- und Nachteile der einzelnen Methoden aufgezeigt.

using a simple example and will then be applied to a standard example portfolio. Finally, the advantages and disadvantages of each method will be listed.

Our trading book

Position	Product	Volume	Rate	Term
1	Bond	-50,000,000	5.00%	3 years
2	Bond	-50,000,000	6.00%	7 years
3	Buy IRS[1]	+100,000,000	5.50%	5 years
4	Interbank	+100,000,000	3.50%	6 months

[1] 5-year fixed rate against 6-month EURIBOR

We assume the following yield curve for our example calculations:

Position	Yield
ON	2.25%
6 months	3.50%
1 year	4.00%
2 year	4.50%
3 year	5.00%
4 year	5.25%
5 year	5.50%
6 year	5.75%
7 year	6.00%

2.1.1. GAP Method

Basic Principle

The GAP Method assesses the **change in the annual profit and loss account that will be caused given a defined change in interest rates**. The basic underlying assumption is that the bank's interest rate positions are not sold before maturity. Therefore, possible market value changes of positions due to interest rate changes are neglected and only the impact on annual interest earnings and expenditures is taken into consideration.

The supposed interest rate change may be a parallel shift of the yield curve or more complex interest changes regarding the level of interest rates and the shape of the yield curve. Depending on the time horizon, the projected interest earnings will only be influenced by the changes of money market rates. The GAP analysis is therefore mainly used in **classic ALM of interest risk** and is only used for **positions of the banking book** (i.e. interest rate positions that are originated via the customer business and interest positions which the bank intends to hold unto maturity ("buy and hold")).

Example
Loan 12 months, 100 m, 3.00%   Deposit ON, 100m, 2.25%

Unser Handelsbuch

Position	Produkt	Volumen	Zinssatz	Laufzeit
1	Anleihe	-50.000.000	5,0%	3 Jahre
2	Anleihe	-50.000.000	6,0%	7 Jahre
3	Kauf IRS[1]	+100.000.000	5,5%	5 Jahre
4	Interbank	+100.000.000	3,5%	6 Monate

[1] 5 Jahre fix gegen 6-Monats-Euribor

Insgesamt nehmen wird dabei folgende Zinskurve an:

Laufzeit	Zins (Yield)
ON	2,25%
6 Monate	3,50%
1 Jahr	4,00%
2 Jahre	4,50%
3 Jahre	5,00%
4 Jahre	5,25%
5 Jahre	5,50%
6 Jahre	5,75%
7 Jahre	6,00%

2.1.1. GAP-Methode

Prinzip

Bei der GAP-Methode wird die **p.a.-Ergebnisveränderung anhand einer unterstellten Zinsänderung** berechnet. Dabei wird angenommen, dass die Positionen nicht vorzeitig aufgelöst werden und somit nur die jährliche Zinsertrags- bzw. Zinsaufwandsrechnung durch eine Veränderung der Marktzinsen beeinflusst wird.

Bei der unterstellten Zinsänderung kann entweder eine parallele Verschiebung der Zinskurve oder eine komplett geänderte Zinslandschaft vorausgesetzt werden, wobei je nach Zeithorizont jedoch nur die Veränderung der Geldmarktzinsen einen Einfluss auf das Ergebnis hat. Die GAP-Analyse wird derzeit hauptsächlich in der **klassischen ALM-Zinsrisikosteuerung** verwendet und bezieht sich üblicherweise nur auf die **Positionen des sogenannten Bankbuches** (also auf alle Zinspositionen, die sich aus Kundengeschäften ergeben, und alle Positionen, die die Bank beabsichtigt, bis zum Ende der Laufzeit zu behalten („buy and hold")).

Beispiel

Kredit zwölf Monate, 100 Mio., 3%
Einlage Taggeld, 100 Mio., 2,25%

GAP report:

	ON	12 months	Sum
Assets		100	**100**
Rate		3.00%	**3.00%**
Liabilities	100		**100**
Rate	2.25%		**2.25%**

Net interest income is projected to be 0.75%. In order to measure the risk of this projection, we suppose that short term rates change (here: increase).

Given a supposed interest rate increase of 1% we receive the following picture:

	ON	12 months	Sum
Assets		100	**100**
Rate		3.00%	**3.00%**
		+ 1%	
Liabilities	100		**100**
Rate	3.25%		**3.25%**

Net interest income has now been reduced to -0.25%. The risk of loss would therefore be EUR 0.25m (100 m x 0.25%)

Example GAP report for example portfolio

	6 months	3 years	5 years	7 years	Sum
Assets	100[2]	50[3]		50[4]	**200**
Rate	3.5%	5%		6%	**4.5%**
Liabilities	100[1]		100[2]		**200**
Rate	3.5%		5.5%		**4.5%**
				Net interest income:	0.00

[1] Interbank Refinancing
[2] Buy IRS
[3] Bond 3 years
[4] Bond 7 years

Given the current situation, net interest income is projected to equal 0%. The reason is that the weighted average interest of the bank's assets equals the weighted average interest of their liabilities.

Darstellung in GAPs:

	Taggeld	12 Monate	Summe
Aktiva		100	**100**
Zins		3,00%	**3,00%**
Passiva	100		**100**
Zins	2,25%		**2,25%**

Das Zinsergebnis dieser offenen Position beträgt somit 0,75%. Um das Risiko zu messen, wird unterstellt, dass sich die kurzfristigen Zinsen verändern (in unserem Fall ansteigen).

Bei einem unterstellten Zinsanstieg von 1% ergibt sich damit folgende Position:

	Taggeld	12 Monate	Summe
Aktiva		100	**100**
Zins		3,00%	**3,00%**
		+ 1%	
Passiva	100		**100**
Zins	3,25%		**3,25%**

Das Zinsergebnis geht somit auf -0,25% zurück und das Risiko würde entsprechend mit 0,25 Mio. (100 Mio. x 0,25%) dargestellt werden.

Beispiel GAP für Beispielportfolio

	6 Monate	3 Jahre	5 Jahre	7 Jahre	Summe
Aktiva	100[2]	50[3]		50[4]	**200**
Zins	3,5%	5%		6%	**4,5%**
Passiva	100[1]		100[2]		**200**
Zins	3,5%		5,5%		**4,5%**
				Zinsergebnis:	0,00

[1] Interbank Refinanzierung
[2] Kauf IRS
[3] Anleihe 3 Jahre
[4] Anleihe 7 Jahre

In der aktuellen Situation liegt der Beitrag des Zinsrisikos also bei 0, nachdem die Durchschnittsverzinsung der Aktivpositionen genau dem Durchschnittszins der Passivseite entspricht.

Because an increase or decrease in money market rates impacts the asset side and the liabilities side by the same amount, the projected net interest income will be the same for any scenario.

The GAP methodology therefore shows no interest rate risk for our example portfolio.

Advantages of the GAP Methodology

- **Simple handling**: If basis positions and their interest profiles are known, risk can be calculated in a relatively simple and straightforward way.
- The GAP methodology is the only kind of interest risk measurement that depicts **changes in the bank's net interest income**.

Drawbacks

- Assumptions have to be made on how expiring positions are renewed. The most basic **assumption** is to renew all expiring transactions on an ON basis.
- The GAP analysis **implies an unchanging risk structure**, so that effects of interest rate changes over the course of time cannot be illustrated (at least in a systematic way).
- **MTM effects are ignored.** The GAP analysis explains only the net interest margin or the part of the interest result that can be explained by interest rate risks which the bank has taken. As soon as interest rate products have to be mark-to-market (e.g. bonds in the trading book, derivatives …), the GAP analysis will only explain a certain part of the bank's interest result and thus its risk.
- The assumptions on how the yield curve will change are arbitrary. **Comparisons with other risks** (e.g. FX, stocks, trading book) **are not possible**.

Conclusion

It is **insufficient to quantify interest rate risk using the GAP analysis as the sole method**. The information of the GAP report on changes of the net interest margin, however, is an important decision criterion when managing the bank's banking book

2.1.2. Duration Approach

The duration approach is probably the best-known key figure for measuring interest rate risk. Originally, the duration was mainly used for fixed rate bonds. Now the duration is used for all interest rate positions. There are two types of duration: the **Macaulay Duration** (or: simple duration) and the so-called **Modified Duration**. The calculation of both durations is similar; their interpretation, however, differs significantly.

The Macaulay duration is de facto irrelevant for bank's internal risk measurement. However in order to explain the concept of duration in general, we will explain the basic principle and interpretation of the Macaulay duration and its application.

Da sich sowohl ein Anstieg als auch ein Rückgang der Geldmarktzinsen auf der Aktiv- und Passivseite der GAP-Positionen (sechs Monate) niederschlagen wird, ist unabhängig von der unterstellten Zinsänderung das Zinsergebnis immer 0. In der GAP-Methodik würde unser Beispielportfolio also kein Risiko verursachen.

Vorteile der Methode

- **Einfache Handhabung:** Sind die Grundpositionen und die Einstandspreise in den einzelnen Laufzeitbändern bekannt, so kann das Risiko relativ einfach berechnet werden.
- Die GAP-Methodik ist die einzige Form der Risikomessung, die mögliche **Veränderungen in der Zinsspanne der Bank darstellen** kann.

Probleme:

- Für die Verlängerung von auslaufenden Geschäften müssen **Annahmen** getroffen werden. Im einfachsten Fall werden alle Geschäfte, die auslaufen, mit Taggeld verlängert.
- Die GAP-Analyse unterstellt eine **gleichbleibende Risikostruktur,** sodass Reaktionen auf Zinsänderungen im Zeitablauf nicht bzw. nicht systematisch dargestellt werden können.
- **MTM-Effekte werden ignoriert:** Die GAP-Analyse erklärt nur die Zinsspanne bzw. den Teil der Zinsspanne, der sich durch eingegangene Zinsrisiken erklären lässt. Sobald in den Zinspositionen Produkte enthalten sind, die G&V-mäßig Mark-to-Market zu bewerten sind (z.B. Anleihen im Umlaufvermögen, derivative Produkte, ...), können mit der GAP-Analyse nur Teile des Bankergebnisses und damit des Risikos dargestellt werden.
- Die Unterstellung, wie sich die Zinsen im Zeitablauf verändern können, ist rein willkürlich, und etwaige **Vergleiche mit Risiken, die in anderen Abteilungen** (z.B. FX, Aktien, Handelsbuch, ...) **gefahren werden, sind nicht zulässig.**

Schlussfolgerung

Als ausschließliche Methodik zur Berechnung des Risikos ist die **GAP-Analyse unzureichend.** Die Zusatzinformation, wie sich die Zinsspanne der Bank bei etwaigen Zinsbewegungen verändern kann, ist jedoch ein relativ wichtiges Entscheidungskriterium, sobald es sich um die Positionen des Bankbuches handelt.

2.1.2. Durationsansatz

Der Durationsansatz ist die wohl bekannteste Kennzahl in der Risikomessung von Zinspositionen. Ursprünglich wurde das Konzept der Duration hauptsächlich für festverzinste Anleihen verwendet. Derzeit wird jedoch das Durationskonzept für alle Zinspositionen angewendet. Es gibt zwei Arten von Durations: **die einfache Duration (auch Macaulay Duration)** und die sogenannte **Modified Duration.** Die Berechnung beider Methoden ist zwar ähnlich, ihre Interpretation unterscheidet sich jedoch wesentlich.

Die einfache Duration ist de facto für die Risikomessung in Banken irrelevant. Um das Konzept zuordnen zu können, werden wir jedoch Prinzip, Anwendung und Interpretation kurz erläutern.

Simple Duration (Macaulay Duration)

Basic Principle

The Macaulay Duration of a bond is the length of time over which the losses/profits due to a one-time change in interest rates are offset by the higher/lower interest rate that the bond holder receives on reinvested coupon payments.

Formula: Macaulay Duration

$$D_{Macaulay} = \frac{\sum_{n=1}^{N} \frac{n \times CF_n}{(1+r)^n}}{\sum_{n=1}^{N} \frac{CF_n}{(1+r)^n}} \quad \text{or} \quad D_{Macaulay} = \frac{\sum_{n=1}^{N} \frac{n \times CF_n}{(1+r)^n}}{PV_0}$$

$D_{Macaulay}$ = Macaulay Duration
n = year index
N = total maturity in years
CF_n = Cash-Flow in year n
r = current yield for total maturity
PV_0 = current computed value of bond

Example

Simple example of application:
Bond 3 years; coupon 5%

1	2	3	4	5
Year	Cash-Flow	$(1+r)^t$	$\frac{(1 \cdot 2)}{3}$	$\frac{2}{3}$
1	5	1.05000	4.76190	4.76190
2	5	1.10250	9.07029	4.53515
3	105	1.15763	272.10884	90.70295
		Sum	**285.94104**	**100.00000**

Macaulay duration: $\dfrac{285{,}93986}{100} = 2{,}86$

Statement:
A yield of 5% is guaranteed over an investment horizon of 2.86 years.

Einfache Duration (Macaulay Duration)

Prinzip

Die einfache Duration (einer Anleihe) ist der Zeitpunkt, zu dem sich Kursverluste auf die Anleihe mit den höheren Zinserträgen bei der Weiterveranlagung der Kupons kompensieren (bzw. vice versa: Kompensation der Kursgewinne der Anleihe mit den niedrigeren Zinsen bei der Weiterveranlagung der Kuponserträge).

Formel: Macaulay Duration

$$D_{Macaulay} = \frac{\sum_{n=1}^{N} \dfrac{n \times CF_n}{(1+r)^n}}{\sum_{n=1}^{N} \dfrac{CF_n}{(1+r)^n}} \quad \text{bzw.} \quad D_{Macaulay} = \frac{\sum_{n=1}^{N} \dfrac{n \times CF_n}{(1+r)^n}}{PV_0}$$

$D_{Macaulay}$ = Macaulay Duration
n = fortlaufendes Jahr
N = Gesamtlaufzeit in Jahren
CF_n = Cashflow (auf Nominale 100) zum Zeitpunkt n
r = aktuelle Rendite in Dezimalen
PV_0 = aktueller rechnerischer Preis der Anleihe

Beispiel

Anwendung:
Anleihe, drei Jahre, Kupon 5%

1	2	3	4	5
Jahr	**Cashflow**	$(1+r)^t$	$\dfrac{(1 \cdot 2)}{3}$	$\dfrac{2}{3}$
1	5	1,05000	4,76190	4,76190
2	5	1,10250	9,07029	4,53515
3	105	1,15763	272,10884	90,70295
		Summe	**285,94104**	**100,00000**

Macaulay Duration: $\dfrac{285,93986}{100} = 2,86$

Aussage

Bei einem Investmenthorizont von 2,86 Jahren ist sichergestellt, dass die Rendite von 5% erzielt werden kann.

Example

fixed-rate bond at:	100
maturity:	3 years
coupon:	5%
duration:	2.86 years

Maturity	Cash-flow	Market yield 5% Price	Market yield 5% Interest	Price + interest	Market yield 6% Price	Market yield 6% Interest	Price + interest
1	5	100	5	105	98.17	5	103.17
2	5	100	5 + 0.25	110.25	99.06	5 + 0.30	109.36
2.86		100	4.3 + 0.44	114.99	99.86	4.3 + 0.53	114.99
3	105	100	5 + 0.51	115.51	100	5 + 0.56	115.56

coupon   interest on reinvested coupon
(50 x 5%)

The formula to calculate the Duration for bonds or interest rate positions where interest periods are shorter than one year looks the following:

$$D_{Macaulay} = \frac{\sum_{n=1}^{N \cdot ZP} \frac{\frac{n}{ZP} \times CF_n}{\left(1+\frac{r}{ZP}\right)^n}}{\sum_{n=1}^{N \cdot ZP} \frac{CF_n}{(1+\frac{r}{ZP})^n}} \qquad or \qquad D_{Macaulay} = \frac{\sum_{n=1}^{N \cdot ZP} \frac{\frac{n}{ZP} \times CF_n}{\left(1+\frac{r}{ZP}\right)^n}}{PV_0}$$

$D_{Macaulay}$ = Macaulay Duration
n = year index
IP = interest period (e.g. 2 for semi-annual payments)
N = total maturity in years
CF_n = Cash-Flow in year n
r = current yield for total maturity
PV_0 = current computed value of bond

Statement

Investors buying a 3-year fixed-rate bond should have an investment horizon of 2.86 years if they want to ensure a certain yield on their investment. If the bond is sold earlier, the investor is exposed to the risk of rising interest rates (which means falling bond prices), and the yield is thus not ensured.

Consequences

Therefore, the Macaulay duration should be read as an investment horizon and **cannot be used as a risk figure for professional trading**. What is more, the **assumptions** of a flat

Beispiel
Fixzins-Anleihe mit Kurs: 100
Laufzeit: 3 Jahre
Kupon: 5%
Duration: 2,86 Jahre

Laufzeit	Cashflow	Zinsen 5%		Preis + Zinsen	Zinsen 6%		Preis + Zinsen
		Preis	Zinsen		Preis	Zinsen	
1	5	100	5	105	98.17	5	103.17
2	5	100	5 + 0,25	110.25	99.06	5 + 0.30	109.36
2.86		100	4.3 + 0.44	114.99	99.86	4.3 + 0.53	114.99
3	105	100	5 + 0.51	115.51	100	5 + 0.56	115.56

Kupon   Zins auf Veranlagung
                 Kupon (50 x 5%)

Für Anleihen bzw. Zinspositionen mit unterjährigen Anleihen sieht die Formel für die Duration folgendermaßen aus:

$$D_{Macaulay} = \frac{\sum_{n=1}^{N*ZP} \frac{\frac{n}{ZP} \times CF_n}{\left(1+\frac{r}{ZP}\right)^n}}{\sum_{n=1}^{N*ZP} \frac{CF_n}{(1+\frac{r}{ZP})^n}}$$

bzw.

$$D_{Macaulay} = \frac{\sum_{n=1}^{N*ZP} \frac{\frac{n}{ZP} \times CF_n}{\left(1+\frac{r}{ZP}\right)^n}}{PV_0}$$

$D_{Macaulay}$ = Macaulay Duration
n = fortlaufende Periode
ZP = Zinszahlungsperiode (z.B. 2 für halbjährliche Zinszahlungen)
N = Gesamtlaufzeit in Jahren
CF_n = Cashflow (auf Nominale 100) für die Periode n (n-te Zinszahlung)
r = aktuelle Rendite in Dezimalen
PV_0 = aktueller rechnerischer Preis der Anleihe

Aussage

Kauft ein Investor eine dreijährige Anleihe, sollte er einen Investmenthorizont von 2,86 Jahren haben, wenn er sicher sein will, auf die beim Kauf der Anleihe dargestellte Rendite zu kommen. Wird die Anleihe vorher verkauft, so bleibt für den Anleger das Risiko steigender Zinsen (fallender Anleihekursen) bestehen, sodass die Rendite nicht gesichert ist.

Schlussfolgerung

Damit ist die Kennzahl einfache Duration ein Investmenthorizont und keine Risikokennzahl per se, sie **kann** daher **im professionellen Handel nicht verwendet werden.** Zusätz-

yield curve (i.e. coupons can be reinvested at the current bond yield) and only one change of the yield level **are quite unrealistic**. Therefore, the informative value of the Macaulay duration has to be questioned. In the worst case, interest rates fall at the beginning of the bond investment, so that the interest on the reinvested coupon is low, and rise at the end of the investment horizon, which causes the price of the bond to decline. Under this scenario, the bond investment would yield a lower return than 'promised' by the Macaulay duration.

Modified Duration

Basic Principle

The modified duration is an estimation of the price change of an interest instrument due to changes in the price of the respective market interest rates. Thus, the modified duration shows the sensitivity of interest instruments to supposed interest rate changes. In contrast to the GAP analysis, risk is not calculated as a change in the annual net interest income, but as the change of mark-to-market prices under specified (interest rate) scenarios.

$$MD = \frac{\sum_{n=1}^{N} \dfrac{n * CF_n}{(1+r)^n}}{\sum_{n=1}^{N} \dfrac{CF_n}{(1+r)^n}} * \frac{1}{1+r} \qquad \text{or} \qquad MD = \frac{\sum_{n=1}^{N} \dfrac{n * CF_n}{(1+r)^n}}{PV_0} * \frac{1}{1+r}$$

MD = Modified Duration
n = year index
N = total maturity in years
CF_n = cash-flow in year n
r = current yield (for total maturity)
PV_0 = current computed value of bond

Comparing the two duration formulas, one finds the following relationship:

$$MD = D_{Macaulay} * \frac{1}{1+r} \qquad \text{for annual interest payments}$$

$$MD = D_{Macaulay} * \frac{1}{1+\dfrac{r}{IP}} \qquad \text{for interest periods shorter than one year}$$

Looking at the formula for the Macaulay duration, one can see that the Macaulay duration could be also described as the maturity-weighted present value of the cash flows, or as the present value-weighted average capital tie-up.

lich sind die **enthaltenen Annahmen,** flache Zinskurve (d.h. Weiterveranlagung der Kuponerträge zum aktuellen langfristigen Zinssatz) und nur eine Zinsänderung im Zeitablauf, relativ unrealistisch, sodass die Aussagekraft der einfachen Duration **infrage zu stellen** ist. Im schlimmsten Fall fallen die Zinsen zu Beginn, sodass die Zinseinnahmen auf die Weiterveranlagung der Kupon relativ gering sind. Wenn die Zinsen dann gegen Ende noch ansteigen, fällt zusätzlich der Preis der Anleihe, sodass auf die berechneten Zeithorizont die versprochene Rendite nicht erwirtschaftet werden kann.

Modified Duration

Prinzip

Die Modified Duration ist eine Kennzahl zur Schätzung der Preisänderung einer Zinsposition bei einer Veränderung der entsprechenden Marktzinsen. Damit zeigt die Modified Duration den **Hebel von Zinsinstrumenten bei einer angenommenen Zinsänderung.** Zur Bemessung des Risikos wird nicht – wie bei der GAP-Analyse – die Veränderung des p.a.-Zinsergebnisses kalkuliert, sondern die Mark-to-Market-Veränderung bei geändertem Zinsszenario.

$$MD = \frac{\sum_{n=1}^{N} \frac{n \times CF_n}{(1+r)^n}}{\sum_{n=1}^{N} \frac{CF_n}{(1+r)^n}} \times \frac{1}{1+r} \quad \text{bzw.} \quad MD = \frac{\sum_{n=1}^{N} \frac{n * CF_n}{(1+r)^n}}{PV_0} * \frac{1}{1+r}$$

MD = Modified Duration
n = fortlaufendes Jahr
N = Gesamtlaufzeit in Jahren
CF_n = Cashflow (auf Nominale 100) zum Zeitpunkt n
r = aktuelle Rendite in Dezimalen
PV_0 = aktueller rechnerischer Preis der Anleihe

Vergleicht man die Formel, so stellt man fest, dass sie eine Modifikation der Macaulay Duration ist:

$$MD = D_{Macaulay} \times \frac{1}{1+r} \qquad \text{für jährliche Zinszahlungen bzw.}$$

$$MD = D_{Macaulay} \times \frac{1}{1+\frac{r}{ZP}} \qquad \text{für unterjährige Zinszahlungen}$$

Bei genauer Betrachtung der Berechnung kann man die Duration auch als laufzeitgewichteten Barwert der Cashflows oder, andersherum, als barwertgewichtete durchschnittliche Bindungsdauer bezeichnen.

Example

fixed rate coupon, price: 100
maturity: 3 years
coupon: 5%

1	2	3	4	5
Year	**Cash-flow**	**1/(1+r)^t**	**1*2*3**	**2*3**
1	5	0.95238	4.76190	4.76190
2	5	0.90703	9.07029	4.53515
3	105	0.86384	272.10960	90.70320
		Sum	**285.94179**	**100.00000**

$$MD = \frac{285{,}94179}{100{,}00} \times \frac{1}{(1+0{,}05)} = 2{,}72$$

The modified duration of the 3-year coupon equals **2.72**. Using this number, one is able to estimate the price change of the bond given a supposed change in market interest rates. Let's assume that the current price of the bond stands at 101.00. The modified duration of 2.72 means that a 1% change of the yield will change the price of the bond by 2.72%, i.e. 2.75 (= 101.00 x 2.72%).

By using the modified duration the price sensitivity for each single position is calculated. For the assumed interest changes the effects on the value of the portfolio are then calculated.

Example portfolio

Product	Volume	Interest rate	Maturity	MD
bond	-50,000,000	5.0%	3 years	2.72
Bond	-50,000,000	6.0%	7 years	5.58
buy IRS	+100,000,000	5.5%	5 years	3.78 (*)
Interbank	+100,000,000	3.5%	6 months	0.49

(*) Modified Duration of the IRS position calculated by synthetic positions (5.50% issue 5 years (fixed leg) and 3.5% asset 6 months (variable leg))

Product	Volume	MD	Profit/loss
bond 3 years	-50,000,000	2.72	-1,360,000
bond 7 years	-50,000,000	5.58	-2,790,000
IRS	+100,000,000	3.78	+3,780,000
Interbank	+100,000,000	0.49	+490,000
		TOTAL RISK	**+120,000**

(50,000,000 x 1% x 5,58)

Beispiel

Fixzins-Anleihe mit Kurs: 100
Laufzeit: 3 Jahre
Kupon: 5%

1	2	3	4	5
Jahr	**Cash-flow**	**1/(1+r) ^{t}**	**1*2*3**	**2*3**
1	5	0,95238	4,76190	4,76190
2	5	0,90703	9,07029	4,53515
3	105	0,86384	272,10960	90,70320
		Summe	**285,94179**	**100,00000**

$$MD = \frac{285{,}94179}{100{,}00} \times \frac{1}{(1+0{,}05)} = 2{,}72$$

Die Duration dieser dreijährigen Anleihe beträgt also **2,72**. Mithilfe der Duration kann nun die Preisänderung der Anleihe bei einer Änderung der Marktzinsen geschätzt werden. Angenommen, der aktuelle Preis der betrachteten Anleihe beträgt 101,00. Hat diese Anleihe nun eine Modified Duration von 2,72, so bedeutet das, dass sich bei einer Veränderung der Zinsen um 1 Prozentpunkt der Preis der Anleihe um 2,72% ändern wird, d.h. um 2,75 (= 101,00 x 2,72%).

Für die Modified Duration wird die Preissensitivität für jede einzelne Position berechnet. Mit einem unterstellten Zinsszenario werden dann die Effekte für den Gesamtwert des Portfolios simuliert.

Beispielportfolio

Produkt	Volumen	Zinssatz	Laufzeit	Modified Duration
Anleihe	-50.000.000	5,0%	3 Jahre	2,72
Anleihe	-50.000.000	6,0%	7 Jahre	5,58
Kauf IRS	+100.000.000	5,5%	5 Jahre	3,78 [*]
Interbank	+100.000.000	3,5%	6 Monate	0,49

[*] Berechnung der Modified Duration für den IRS über synthetische Positionen (5-Jahres-Emission zu 5,50% (Fixed Rate Payer-Position) und gegebenem Geld zu 3,50% (Short-Leg))

Produkt	Volumen	Modified Duration	Gewinn/Verlust
Anleihe 3 Jahre	- 50.000.000	2,72	- 1.360.000
Anleihe 7 Jahre	- 50.000.000	5,58	- 2.790.000
IRS	+ 100.000.000	3,78	+ 3.780.000
Interbank	+ 100.000.000	0,49	+ 490.000
		RISIKO GESAMT	**+ 120.000**

(50.000.000 x 1% x 5,58)

If interest rates increase by 1%, the MTM result will increase by 120,000. If interest rates decrease by 1%, the MTM result will be reduced by 120,000. Therefore, the risk assuming a 1% change in interest rates is established as 120,000.

Even though the modified duration was originally designed to measure the risk of fixed-rate bonds, the concept can nevertheless be applied to the total interest rate position of the bank. This applied to on-balance assets and liabilities positions as well as to derivative products.

The main advantages of this method are

- **simple handling** and calculation
- **high acceptance level** due to simple statements and interpretation
- **costs** due to any need to sell a position before maturity **are taken into account**
- **no assumptions necessary** regarding the **roll-over** of expiring positions

Drawbacks/points of criticism

- **flat yield curve** is assumed
- basic calculation does **not include the effect of yield curve changes**
- assumed interest rate changes are arbitrary and the resulting risk figures **cannot be compared to other risks**
- the calculated risk figure is a pure MTM risk containing **no information on net interest income**

Consequences

The duration approach is well-suited for the **estimation of the risk of individual positions** and thus for **determining the necessary volume of hedge transactions** (e.g. the hedge of a bond with futures). A simple duration approach, however, is not suited for the risk measurement of a complex trading book.

2.1.3. Present Value of a Basis Point

Basic Principle

As is the case with the duration approach, the Present Value of a Basis Point (PVBP) method does not estimate changes of the annual net interest income, but the **change in the present value of a position**. To do so, the exact times of the Cash-Flows of the position (nominal and coupon payments) are identified and mapped to an available number of zero rates. Then, value changes are calculated for each mapped amount of cash flow assuming a change of 1 basis point (BP) of the underlying zero rate.

The determined risk numbers of all positions are aggregated for each zero rate and used for the risk measurement. A final risk figure is attained by assuming interest rate changes (of the zero curve).

Steigen die Zinsen um 1%, so verbessert sich das MTM-Ergebnis um 120.000. Fallen die Zinsen um 1%, so verschlechtert sich das Ergebnis um 120.000. Dementsprechend wird das Risiko mit 120.000 bei einer 1%-Zinsänderung angesetzt.

Auch wenn die Duration ursprünglich für die Risikomessung von festverzinslichen Anleihen konzipiert wurde, kann sie jederzeit auf die gesamten Zinspositionen der Bank angewendet werden. Dies gilt sowohl für Aktiv- und Passivpositionen als auch für derivative Produkte.

Vorteile der Methode

- **einfache Handhabung** und Berechnung
- **hohe Akzeptanz** durch klare Aussagen und Interpretation
- Die **Kosten** bei einer eventuell vorzeitigen Schließung der Risikopositionen werden **abgeschätzt.**
- **keine Unterstellung bezüglich Weiterrollen** von auslaufenden Positionen

Kritikpunkte

- Für die Berechnung der Duration wird eine **flache Zinskurve** unterstellt.
- **Effekte von Zinskurvenänderungen** sind standardmäßig **nicht im Risiko enthalten.**
- Die Unterstellung, um wie viel sich die Zinsen ändern, ist rein willkürlich und lässt **keine Vergleiche mit sonstigen Risiken** zu.
- Das dargestellte Risiko ist ein reines MTM-Risiko, sodass **keine Aussagen über die Entwicklung der Zinsspanne** getroffen werden können.

Schlussfolgerung

Der Durationsansatz eignet sich gut für die **Abschätzung des Risikos von Einzelpositionen** und somit für die **Bestimmung des Volumens von Hedge-Transaktionen** (z.B. Absichern einer Anleiheposition mit Futures). Als Konzept für die Risikomessung eines komplexen Handelsbuches ist jedoch ein reiner Durationsansatz nicht geeignet.

2.1.3. Present Value of a Basis Point

Prinzip

Auch die Risikomessung mit dem Present Value of a Basis Point (PVBP) kalkuliert – analog dem Durationsansatz – nicht die p.a.-Veränderung des Zinsergebnisses, sondern die **Veränderung des Mark-to-Market-Wertes der Gesamtposition.** Dabei werden die Cashflows der Positionen (Kapital und Zinsen) zu den einzelnen Zeitpunkten festgelegt (Mapping) und die Wertveränderung bei einer Zinsveränderung von 1 BP wird (üblicherweise) mit der Zero-Kurve berechnet.

Die so ermittelten Risikowerte können nun auf einer aggregierten Basis (über alle Positionen und Laufzeiten) für die Risikomessung herangezogen werden. Die Risikomessung erfolgt dann wieder, indem das gesamte Zinsniveau verändert wird oder unterschiedliche Zinsszenarien unterstellt werden.

Example

position bond: 3 years
coupon: 5%
volume: 50 m

(1) Year	(2) Cash-flow	(3) Interest rate	(4) Discount factor	(5) Present value (2*3)
1	2,500,000	4.00%	0.96153846	2,403,846
2	2,500,000	4.50%	0.91553184	2,288,830
3	52,500,000	5.00%	0.86299665	45,307,324
			Sum	**50,000,000**

result for + 0.01% interest rate change

(1) Year	(2) Cash-flow	(3) Interest rate	(4) Discount factor	(5) Present value (2*3)
1	2,500,000	4.01%	0.96144601	2,403,615
2	2,500,000	4.51%	0.91535622	2,288,391
3	52,500,000	5.01%	0.86274851	45,294,297
			sum:	**49,986,302**
			differential:	**-13,698**

Interpretation: Given a shift in the zero curve of 1 bp (0.01%), there will be a MTM loss of 13,698 on the first bond position (50m, 3 years, 5% coupon).

Our Trading Book

Product	volume	rate	maturity	PVBP
Bond	-50,000,000	5.00%	3 years	-13,698
Bond	-50,000,000	6.00%	7 years	-28,419
buy IRS	+100,000,000	5.50%	5 years	+38,235
Interbank	+100,000,000	3.50%	6 months	+4,914

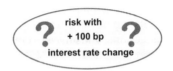

Beispiel

Position Anleihe: 3 Jahre
Kupon: 5%
Volumen: 50 Mio.

(1) Jahr	(2) Cash-flow	(3) Zinssatz	(4) Disk. Faktor	(5) Barwert (2*3)
1	2.500.000	4,00%	0,96153846	2.403.846
2	2.500.000	4,50%	0,91553184	2.288.830
3	52.500.000	5,00%	0,86299665	45.307.324
			Summe:	50.000.000

Ergebnis bei + 0,01% Zinsänderung

(1) Jahr	(2) Cash-flow	(3) Zinssatz	(4) Disk. Faktor	(5) Barwert (2*3)
1	2.500.000	4,01%	0,96144601	2.403.615
2	2.500.000	4,51%	0,91535622	2.288.391
3	52.500.000	5,01%	0,86274851	45.294.297
			Summe:	49.986.302
			Differenz	-13.698

Interpretation: Bei einem Zinsanstieg von 1 BP (0,01%) werden wir einen Kursverlust von 13.698 auf die Anleiheposition (50 Mio., 3 Jahre, 5% Kupon) haben.

Unser Handelsbuch

Produkt	Volumen	Zinssatz	Laufzeit	PVBP
Anleihe	- 50.000.000	5,00%	3 Jahre	-13.698
Anleihe	- 50.000.000	6,00%	7 Jahre	-28.419
Kauf IRS	+100.000.000	5,50%	5 Jahre	+38.235
Interbank	+100.000.000	3,50%	6 Monate	+4.914

product	volume	PVBP	profit/loss
bond 3 years	-50,000,000	-13,698	-1,369,800
bond 7 years	-50,000,000	-28,419	-2,841,900
IRS	+100,000,000	+38,236	+3,823,500
Interbank	+100,000,000	+4,914	+491,400
		TOTAL RISK	+103,200

(-28,419 x 100)

Interpretation

If interest rates increase by 100bp, the present value of the example portfolio will increase by 103,200. The risk (which is here the decrease of interest rates) is therefore established as 103,200.

Advantages (as with the Duration Method)

- **simple handling** and calculation
- **high acceptance level** due to simple statements and interpretation
- **costs** due to any need to sell a position before maturity **are taken into account**
- **no assumptions necessary** regarding the **roll-over** of expiring positions
- the **shape of the current zero curve** is taken into account

Drawbacks/points of criticism (as with the Duration Method)

- basic calculation does **not include the effect of yield curve changes**
- assumed interest rate changes are arbitrary and the resulting **risk figures cannot be compared to other risks**
- the calculated risk figure is a pure MTM risk containing **no information on net interest income**

Consequences

Basically, the PVBP approach is a refined duration approach that also takes the **present yield curve into account.** The basic drawbacks of the duration approach remain the same, however. Therefore, the PVBP approach may "only" be used as an alternative for the duration method that also allows the use of operative limits for maturity bands.

2.1.4. Key Rate Duration (Scenario Analysis)

Basic Principle

As for the Key Rate Duration, the Present Values of a Basis Point (or the respective Duration) are calculated and shown for the **cash-flows that are mapped to the different maturity bands** rather than on an aggregated basis for each individual position. Thus each position is divided up into its cash flows. The risk is then calculated by moving the interest rate curve and calculating the effect for the different maturity bands separately.

Produkt	Volumen	PVBP	Gewinn/Verlust
Anleihe 3 Jahre	- 50.000.000	-13.698	-1.369.800
Anleihe 7 Jahre	-50.000.000	-28.419	- 2.823.500
IRS	+100.000.000	+38.236	+3.823.551
Interbank	+100.000.000	+4.914	+491.400
		RISIKO GESAMT	**+103.200**

(-28.419 x 100)

Interpretation

Steigen die Zinsen um 100 BP, so verbessert sich das Ergebnis um 103.200. Das Risiko (bei Zinsrückgang) beträgt damit 103.200.

Vorteile (analog Durationsmethode)

- **einfache Handhabung** und Berechnung
- **hohe Akzeptanz** durch klare Aussagen und Interpretation
- Die **Kosten** bei einer etwaigen vorzeitigen Schließung der Risikoposition werden **abgeschätzt**.
- **keine Unterstellung bezüglich Weiterrollen** von auslaufenden Positionen
- Die **aktuelle Zinskurve** ist in der Ausgangsbewertung **berücksichtigt**.

Kritikpunkte (analog Durationsmethode):

- **Effekte von Zinskurvenänderungen** sind standardmäßig **nicht im Risiko enthalten.**
- Die Unterstellung, um wie viel sich die Zinsen ändern, ist rein willkürlich und lässt **keine Vergleiche mit sonstigen Risiken** zu.
- Das dargestellte Risiko ist reines MTM-Risiko, sodass **keine Aussagen über die Entwicklung der Zinsspanne** getroffen werden können.

Schlussfolgerung

Gegenüber der Duration sind die Aussagen der Risikomessung über den Present Value of a Basis Point ein bisschen verfeinert, indem die **aktuelle Zinskurve bei der Bewertung der Positionen mitberücksichtigt** wird. Generell bleiben jedoch die Probleme des Durationsansatzes bestehen, sodass der PVBP-Ansatz „nur" als Ersatz für die Durationsmethode bzw. als Möglichkeit, operative Limits in einzelnen definierten Laufzeitbändern festzulegen, herangezogen werden kann.

2.1.4. Key Rate Duration (Szenario-Analyse)

Prinzip

Bei der Key Rate Duration werden die Present Value of a Basis Point (oder die entsprechende Duration) nicht in Summe pro Einzelposition berechnet und dargestellt, sondern für die **Cashflows in den einzelnen Laufzeitbändern.** Jede Einzelposition wird somit in ihre Cashflows zerlegt. Das Risiko wird anschließend bestimmt, indem die Zinskurve verändert wird und der Effekt in den einzelnen Laufzeitbändern separat berechnet wird.

Example
bond: 3 years coupon: 5% volume: 50m In a first step, the PVBP of 13.698 (see previous calculation) is allocated to the different maturity bands.

Year	Cash-flow	Interest rate	Discount factor	Present value[1]	
1	2,500,000	4.00%	0.96153846	2,403,846	
2	2,500,000	4.50%	0.91553184	2,288,830	
3	52,500,000	5.00%	0.86299665	45,307,324	
Sum				**50,000,000[1]**	
result with + 0.01% interest rate change					
Year	Cash-flow	Interest rate	Discount factor	Present value[2]	Differential[2]-[1]
1	2,500,000	4.01%	0.96144601	2,403,615	-231
2	2,500,000	4.51%	0.91535622	2,288,391	-439
3	52,500,000	5.01%	0.86274851	45,294,297	-13,028
Sum				**49,986,302**	**-13,698**

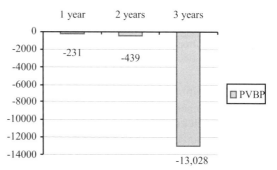

Subsequently, present value results are calculated for different supposed interest rate curves. In our simple example we assume a steepening interest rate curve for scenario 1 and an inverted interest rate curve for scenario 2.

Beispiel

Anleihe: 3 Jahre
Kupon: 5%
Volumen: 50 Mio.
In einem ersten Schritt wird der PVBP von 13.698 (siehe vorherige Berechnung) auf die
einzelnen Laufzeitbänder ermittelt.

Jahr	Cashflow	Zinssatz	Disk. Faktor	Barwert [1]	
1	2.500.000	4,00%	0,96153846	2.403.846	
2	2.500.000	4,50%	0,91553184	2.288.830	
3	52.500.000	5,00%	0,86299665	45.307.324	
Summe				**50.000.000[1]**	

Ergebnis bei + 0,01% Zinsänderung					
Jahr	Cashflow	Zinssatz	Disk. Faktor	Barwert [2]	Differenz [2]-[1]
1	2.500.000	4,01%	0,96144601	2.403.615	- 231
2	2.500.000	4,51%	0,91535622	2.288.391	- 439
3	52.500.000	5,01%	0,86274851	45.294.297	- 13.028
Summe				**49.986.302**	**- 13.698**

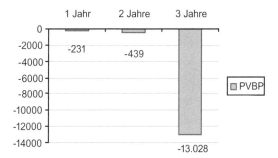

Anschließend wird das Ergebnis für unterschiedliche unterstellte Zinskurven berechnet. In
unserem einfachen Fall unterstellen wir in Szenario 1 eine steiler werdende Zinskurve und
in Szenario 2 eine inverse Zinskurve.

SCENARIO ANALYSIS	1 year	2 years	3 years	Key Rate Duration
current rates	4.00%	4.50%	5.00%	
PVBP	- 231	- 439	- 13,028	
scenario 1	4.00%	5.00%	6.00%	
Result	0	- 21,950	- 1,302,800	- 1,324,750
scenario 2	6.00%	5.00%	4.00%	
Result	- 46,200	- 21,950	+ 1,302,800	+ 1,234,650

-439 x 50

Scenario 1 would therefore cause a loss on the current positions, scenario 2 a profit. Consequently, a risk of 1,324,750 would be reported.

Our Trading Book

Product	Volume	Rate	Maturity
bond	-50,000,000	5.00%	3 years
bond	-50,000,000	6.00%	7 years
buy IRS	+100,000,000	5.50%	5 years
interbank	+100,000,000	3.50%	6 months

We get the following picture by calculating the PVBPs for the individual cash flows in the different maturity bands.

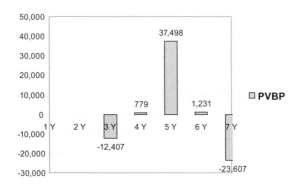

We assume again a steepening interest rate curve for scenario 1. Scenario 2 represents a parallel interest rate increase by 100 basis points.

SZENARIO-ANALYSE	1 Jahr	2 Jahre	3 Jahre	Key Rate Duration
Aktuelles Zinsniveau	4,00%	4,50%	5,00%	
PVBP	-231	-439	-13.028	
Szenario 1	4,00%	5,00%	6,00%	
Ergebnis	0	-21.950	-1.302.800	-1.324.750
Szenario 2	6,00%	5,00%	4,00%	
Ergebnis	-46.200	-21.950	+1.302.800	+1.234.650

-439 x 50

In Szenario 1 würden wir damit einen Verlust erleiden, in Szenario 2 einen Gewinn. Dementsprechend wird für die Risikoermittlung das Szenario 1 mit einem Risiko von 1.324.750 ausgewählt.

Unser Handelsbuch

Produkt	Volumen	Zinssatz	Laufzeit
Anleihe	-50.000.000	5,00%	3 Jahre
Anleihe	-50.000.000	6,00%	7 Jahre
Kauf IRS	+100.000.000	5,50%	5 Jahre
Interbank	+100.000.000	3,50%	6 Monate

Werden für die einzelnen Cashflows in den Laufzeitbändern die PVBPs ermittelt, so ergibt sich folgendes Bild:

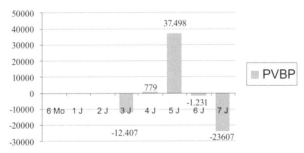

Szenario 1 wird wieder eine steilere Zinskurve unterstellt. Szenario 2 entspricht einem parallelen Zinsanstieg von 100 BP.

Scenario Analysis

	PVBP	current rates	scenario 1	profit/loss	scenario 2	profit/loss
6 months	0	3.50%	3.50%	0	4.50%	0
1 year	0	4.00%	4.00%	0	5.00%	0
2 years	0	4.50%	4.25%	0	5.50%	0
3 years	-12,407	5.00%	4.75%	+310,175	6.00%	-1,240,700
4 years	779	5.25%	5.25%	0	6.25%	+77,900
5 years	37,498	5.50%	5.75%	+937,450	6.50%	3,749,800
6 years	-1,231	5.75%	6.38%	-77,553	6.75%	-123,100
7 years	-23,607	6.00%	7.00%	-2,360,700	7.00%	-2,360,700
		Key Duration Rate		**-1,190,628**		**+103,200**

-12.407 x -25

Therefore, we would calculate a risk of 1,190,628 for our trading portfolio. Under scenario 2 (parallel shift), the result (= 103,200) equals exactly the risk that we received using the PVBP approach (assuming a 100bp shift).

Advantages

- **costs** due to any need to sell a position before maturity are **taken into account**
- **no assumptions necessary** regarding **the roll-over** of expiring positions
- **changes in the shape of the interest rate curve** can be **simulated**
- relatively **simple handling**: if the timetable of cash flows is known, risk can be calculated for a variety of possible scenarios in a straightforward way

Drawbacks/points of criticism

- **The possible interest curves can only be built up by scenarios.** As the number of possible yield curves is endless, we cannot ensure that the computed scenarios correspond to real life scenarios. Additionally changing the scenarios may lead to a changed risk figure even if the positions are not changed.
- The assumptions on how the interest rate curve changes are arbitrary and do **not allow comparisons to other risk figures**.
- The calculated risk figure is a pure MTM risk containing **no information on net interest income**.

Consequences

The key rate duration is the first of the approaches presented that allows the **quantifying of the interest curve risk**. Due to the arbitrary definition of scenarios, the use of the methodology as an objective and systematic risk measurement approach is very limited. The methodology is often used by banks for stress testing, where extreme yield curve movements are assumed and the reported risk figure is compared with the results of these scenarios.

Szenario-Analyse

	PVBP	Zinsen aktuell	Szena- rio 1	Gewinn/ Verlust	Szena- rio 2	Gewinn/ Verlust
6 Monate	0	3,50%	3,50%	0	4,50%	0
1 Jahr	0	4,00%	4,00%	0	5,00%	0
2 Jahre	0	4,50%	4,25%	0	5,50%	0
3 Jahre	-12.407	5,00%	4,75%	+310.175	6,00%	-1.240.700
4 Jahre	779	5,25%	5,25%	0	6,25%	+77.900
5 Jahre	37.498	5,50%	5,75%	+937.450	6,50%	3.749.800
6 Jahre	-1.231	5,75%	6,38%	-77.553	6,75%	-123.100
7 Jahre	-23.607	6,00%	7,00%	-2.360.700	7,00%	-2.360.700
		Key Duration Rate		**-1.190.628**		**+103.200**

-12.407 x -25

Für unser Handelsportfolio würden wir damit ein Risiko von 1.190.628 festlegen. Im Szenario 2 (parallel shift) entspricht das Ergebnis von 103.200 genau dem Risiko, das wir mit dem PVBP-Ansatz (bei 100 BP-Parallelverschiebung) ermittelt haben.

Vorteile

● Die **Kosten** bei einer etwaigen vorzeitigen Schließung der Risikopositionen werden **abgeschätzt.**

● **keine Unterstellung bezüglich Weiterrollen** von auslaufenden Positionen

● **Effekte von Zinskurvenänderungen** können **simuliert** werden.

● **relativ einfache Handhabung:** Sind die Cashflows zu den einzelnen Zeitpunkten bekannt, so kann das Risiko auch für eine Vielzahl von möglichen Szenarien einfach berechnet werden.

Kritikpunkte

● Die **möglichen Zinskurven können nur über Szenarien abgebildet** werden. Da die Anzahl der möglichen Zinskurven unendlich ist, kann nicht sichergestellt werden, dass die ausgewählten Szenarien der realen Entwicklung entsprechen. Auch führen neue Szenarien zu einem geänderten Risiko (auch bei gleichbleibenden Risikopositionen), sodass die Interpretation der Risikokennzahl erschwert wird.

● Die Unterstellung, um wie viel sich die Zinsen ändern, ist rein willkürlich und lässt **keine Vergleiche mit sonstigen Risiken** zu.

● Das dargestellte Risiko ist ein reines MTM-Risiko, sodass **keine Aussagen über die Entwicklung der Zinsspanne** getroffen werden können.

Schlussfolgerung

Die Key Rate Duration ist der erste Ansatz unter den präsentierten Methoden, der es erlaubt, **Zinskurvenrisiken** zu **quantifizieren.** Durch die relativ willkürliche Festlegung der Szenarien kann die Methodik jedoch nur sehr begrenzt als objektiver und systematischer Risikomessansatz verwendet werden. Die Methodik wird derzeit in Banken öfters bei der Berechnung von Stress-Tests verwendet, indem extreme Zinskurvendrehungen vorgegeben werden und die ausgewiesene Risikokennzahl mit den Ergebnissen dieser Extremszenarien überprüft wird.

2.1.5. Modern risk management methods (VaR-Approaches)

All of the above mentioned risk measurement methods focus only on individual types of risk. Therefore, the total risk can only be determined by adding these individual risks. Possible effects of diversification are not taken into account by these risk measurement methods. In risk measurement, the **value at risk approach (VaR)** is currently the most widely used method. Large banks use this approach mainly to **quantify the price risks** of their trading positions. Another incentive to use this approach is that it can also be used to determine the capital requirements (Capital Adequacy Directive).

The outstanding characteristic of all methods employed is to cover different types of risk – e.g. share risks, FX risks and interest rate risks – by a **standard measurement instruction** in order to consider diversification effects on the aggregation of risks.

Generally, the value at risk approach refers to the negative change in value (measured in absolute terms) of an individual position or of a portfolio, which is not exceeded during a certain time with a certain probability.

2.1.6. EXCURSUS: Probability theory

Modern risk management is based on statistical methods to a large degree. It is therefore important to have some knowledge of the relevant statistic basics.

The most important statistical key figures are the **mean** or **expected value** and the **variance**. The mean measures the average size of a number of values, while the variance measures to which degree these values vary around the mean.

A variable that randomly takes on different values is called random variable. The average value (result of a great number of observations) of such a random variable is called expected value or mean.

Example

In order to welcome their guests, a hotel in Las Vegas offers the following gamble:
Each guest is allowed to throw two dice. If the sum of pips exceeds seven, the guest receives the difference in USD. If the sum of pips falls short of seven, the guest has to pay the difference to the hotel. If the sum of pips equals seven, no payment is made.
We will now determine if this gamble is "fair" in the sense that the profit potential corresponds to the loss potential

---

2.1.5. Moderne Risikomanagementmethoden (VaR-Ansätze)

Alle bisher entwickelten Risikomessverfahren sind auf einzelne Risikoarten abgestimmt. Somit ist das Gesamtrisiko nur durch Addition der Einzelrisiken ermittelbar. Mögliche Diversifikationseffekte finden bei allen bisher ausgeführten Risikomessverfahren keine Berücksichtigung. Im Bereich der Risikomessung steht das **Value-at-Risk-Konzept (VaR)** derzeit im Mittelpunkt der Diskussion. Von größeren Banken wird es vor allem zur **Quantifizierung der Preisrisiken** aus ihren Handelsbeständen eingesetzt. Die Anwendungsmöglichkeiten zur Ermittlung der Eigenmittelerfordernisse (Kapitaladäquanzrichtlinie) verstärken das wachsende Interesse an dieser Methode.

Herausragendes Merkmal aller verwendeten Methoden ist die einheitliche Erfassung unterschiedlicher Risikoarten – wie beispielsweise Aktien-, Währungs- und Zinsrisiko – durch eine **einheitliche Messvorschrift.** Dabei können die Diversifikationseffekte bei der Aggregation der Risikoarten berücksichtigt werden.

Allgemein versteht man unter der Value-at-Risk-Methode die in absoluten Geldeinheiten gemessene negative Wertveränderung einer Einzelposition oder eines Portefeuilles, die mit einer bestimmten Wahrscheinlichkeit innerhalb eines festgelegten Zeitraumes nicht überschritten wird.

2.1.6. EXKURS: Wahrscheinlichkeitstheorie

Moderne Risikomessmethoden beruhen weitgehend auf statistischen Verfahren. Zum besseren Verständnis ist deshalb die Kenntnis der relevanten statistischen Grundlagen von besonderer Bedeutung.

Die wichtigsten statistischen Maßzahlen sind der **Mittelwert** bzw. der **Erwartungswert** und die **Varianz.** Während der Mittelwert die durchschnittliche Größe einer Anzahl von Werten darstellt, misst die Varianz, wie stark diese Werte um den Mittelwert streuen.

Vom Erwartungswert spricht man dann, wenn die Verteilungsfunktion der Werte, also die Eintrittswahrscheinlichkeit jedes einzelnen Wertes, bekannt ist. Den anhand der Wahrscheinlichkeiten berechneten durchschnittlichen Wert nennt man den Erwartungswert.

Beispiel

Um seine Gäste willkommen zu heißen, veranstaltet das Hotel Las Vegas folgendes Glücksspiel:
Der Spieler würfelt mit zwei Würfeln. Ist die Summe der Würfel größer als sieben, bekommt der Spieler die Differenz in EUR ausbezahlt. Ist die Summe kleiner als sieben, muss der Spieler die Differenz dem Hotel zahlen. Wird genau sieben gewürfelt, findet keine Zahlung statt.
Die Frage lautet nun: Ist das ein „faires" Spiel in dem Sinn, dass die Gewinnchancen und das Verlustrisiko gleich hoch sind?

Expected Value/Mean

In a first step, we will calculate the expected value of the sum of pips. We come to this number by multiplying all possible outcomes by their probabilities and summing them up.

$$EV = \sum_i p_i x_i$$

EV = expected value
p_i = probability of outcome i
x_i = value (sum of dips) of outcome i
i = index of outcomes

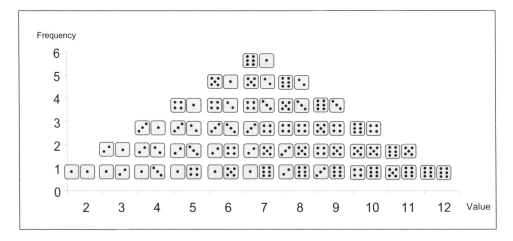

The probability of each outcome corresponds here to the relative frequency of each value. For one die, the probability for each value equals one sixth (1/6). As there are more combinations possible that yield a certain value when using two dice, the probabilities for the individual values differ.

The expected value equals the **sum of the probability weighted outcome values**. Here, the expected value equals seven. Because the profit/loss threshold is also seven, the gamble can be defined as "fair".

For a gambler, however, it is also important to know to what degree an outcome might deviate from the expected value, because the profit or loss that a gambler makes is not determined by the expected value of a game but by the actual outcome.

The two key figures from the field of statistics that are used to assess the variation of outcomes around the mean are called **variance (σ^2)** and **standard deviation (σ)**.

Variance

The dispersion of a random variable around the mean is measured as the deviation of outcomes from the expected value ($x_i - EV$). The variance is calculated as the **sum of probability-weighted squared deviations of the possible outcomes from the mean**. Squaring the deviations has the practical purpose that negative and positive deviations don't cancel each

Erwartungswert

Dazu muss als Erstes der Erwartungswert beim Würfeln berechnet werden. Den Erwartungswert erhält man, indem alle Werte des Würfelpaares mit ihren Eintrittswahrscheinlichkeiten multipliziert und anschließend summiert werden.

$$EW = \sum_i p_i x_i$$

EW = Erwartungswert
P_i = Wahrscheinlichkeit des Eintretens von (i)
X_i = Wert von (i)
i = Index der Werte

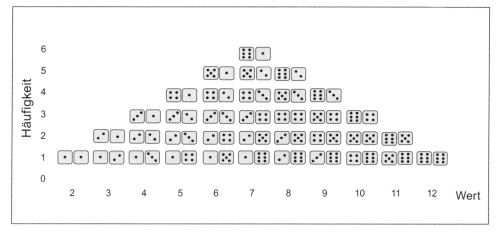

Die Eintrittswahrscheinlichkeit in diesem Zusammenhang entspricht der relativen Häufigkeit der jeweiligen Zahl. Bei einem Würfel hat jede Zahl eine Wahrscheinlichkeit von einem Sechstel (1/6). Für die verschiedenen Würfelpaare ergeben sich aufgrund der möglichen Kombinationen unterschiedliche Häufigkeiten und somit unterschiedliche Wahrscheinlichkeiten.

Der Erwartungswert ergibt sich als **Summe dieser wahrscheinlichkeitsgewichteten Werte.** Bei zwei Würfeln beträgt dieser Erwartungswert sieben. Da auch der Spieleinsatz bzw. die Zahlungsgrenze bei sieben liegt, kann man das Spiel durchaus als „fair" betrachten.

Zusätzlich zum Erwartungswert ist es für einen Spieler wichtig zu wissen, wie stark die Zahlen einzelner Würfe vom Erwartungswert abweichen. Denn der Gewinn bzw. Verlust eines Spielers ergibt sich schließlich aus der Zahl, die er tatsächlich würfelt, und nicht aus dem Erwartungswert. Zu diesem Zweck kann man zwei Streuungsmaßzahlen aus der Statistik, die **Varianz (σ^2)** und die **Standardabweichung (σ),** heranziehen.

Varianz

Die Streuung wird als Abweichung des eingetretenen Wertes vom Erwartungswert gemessen (x_i–EW). Um die Varianz zu erhalten, werden die **quadrierten Abweichungen mit ihren Wahrscheinlichkeiten multipliziert und zum Schluss summiert.** Die Quadrierung der Abweichungen hat ihren praktischen Grund darin, als sich andernfalls die positiven und negativen Abweichungen gegenseitig aufheben und so die tatsächliche Streuung nicht ge-

other out (in which case the true dispersion would not be measured) and that larger deviations receive a higher weighting than smaller ones.

$$Var = \sum_i p_i (x_i - EV)^2$$

Var = variance (σ^2)
EV = expected value
p_i = probability of outcome xi
x_i = value of outcome i
i = index of outcomes

Note: Whenever a distribution is unknown, the variance has to be estimated by making observations of outcomes (e.g. as is the case for volatile assets). Because the distribution is unknown, the formula for the estimation of the variance looks slightly different. Even though
the probability of one observation equals 1/n (where n is the number of observations), the observations are weighted using the term 1/(n-1).

$$Var = \sum_{i=1}^{n} \frac{(x_i - EV)^2}{n-1}$$

Var = variance (σ^2)
EV = expected value
n = number of observations
x_i = value of observation i
i = index of observations

Standard Deviation

The standard deviation equals the **square root of the variance**. In the financial world, the
term **volatility** is often used as a synonym for standard deviation. Compared with the variance, the standard deviation has the advantage that the dimension of the standard deviation
is the same as the dimension of the observed random variable (e.g. cm, kg or a monetary
unit) and that it can therefore be interpreted intuitively. The variance, on the other hand, represents a non-dimensional number.

$$Stdev = \sqrt{Var} = \sqrt{\sum_i p_i * (x_i - EV)^2}$$

Var = variance (σ^2)
Stdev = standard deviation
EV = expected value
p_i = probability of outcome xi
x_i = value of outcome i
i = index of outcomes

messen werden würde. Außerdem werden durch die Quadrierung größere Abweichungen stärker gewichtet als kleinere.

$$Var = \sum_i p_i \cdot (x_i - EW)^2$$

Var = Varianz (σ^2)
EW = Erwartungswert
p_i = Wahrscheinlichkeit des Eintretens von (i)
x_i = Wert von (i)
i = Index der Werte

Anmerkung: Wann immer man eine Verteilung nicht kennt und die Varianz über Beobachtungen geschätzt werden muss, wie etwa bei volatilen Assets, kommt bei der Berechnung der Varianz (und der daraus abgeleiteten Standardabweichung) ein korrigierender Faktor hinzu. Die Formel sieht dann folgendermaßen aus:

$$Var = \sum_{i=1}^{n} \frac{(x_i - EW)^2}{n-1}$$

Var = Varianz (σ^2)
EW = Erwartungswert
n = Anzahl der Beobachtungen
x_i = Wert von (i)
i = Index der Werte

Statt die einzelnen Beobachtungen mit ihrer Wahrscheinlichkeit, die dem Kehrwert der gemachten Beobachtungen (1/n) entspricht, zu multiplizieren, wird mit 1/(n-1) multipliziert.

Standardabweichung

Die Standardabweichung ist die **Quadratwurzel der Varianz**. In der Finanzwelt spricht man anstelle von Standardabweichung häufig von der **Volatilität.** Gegenüber der Varianz hat sie den Vorteil, dass sie dieselbe Dimension wie die Werte besitzt (wie z.B. cm, kg oder Geldeinheit) und damit intuitiv interpretiert werden kann. Die Varianz hingegen ist „dimensionslos".

$$Stdabw = \sqrt{Var} = \sqrt{\sum_i p_i \cdot (x_i - EW)^2}$$

Var = Varianz (σ^2)
Stdabw = Standardabweichung (σ)
EW = Erwartungswert
P_i = Wahrscheinlichkeit des Eintretens von (i)
X_i = Wert von (i)
i = Index der Werte

a	value	2	3	4	5	6	7	8	9	10	11	12	Summe
b	frequency	1	2	3	4	5	6	5	4	3	2	1	36
c	prob.	1/36	2/36	3/36	4/36	5/36	6/36	5/36	4/36	3/36	2/36	1/36	1
a * c	prob. weigh. values	2/36	6/36	12/36	20/36	30/36	42/36	40/36	36/36	30/36	22/36	12/36	252/36	=7
a- EW	deviation from EV	-5	-4	-3	-2	-1	0	1	2	3	4	5	0
$(a- EW)^2$	squard deviation	25	16	9	4	1	0	1	4	9	16	25	110
$c * (a- EW)^2$	prob. weigh. squared dev.	25/36	32/36	27/36	16/36	5/36	0/36	5/36	16/36	27/36	32/36	25/36	210/36	=5.83

variance   mean

(EV = 7, Variance = 5.83)

In the case of our gamble, the variance is calculated as 5.8. The standard deviation equals therefore 2.4.

$$Stdev = \sqrt{5.8} = 2.4$$

In order to get a better understanding of the standard deviation we will have a look at the probability distribution of the gamble.

The following illustration shows the probabilities for all possible outcomes of the gamble. Looking at the probability distribution of the gamble, one can calculate the probability that the outcome lies within a range of +/- 1 standard deviation around the mean.

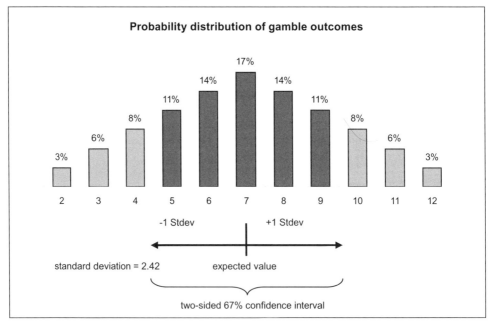

a	Wert	2	3	4	5	6	7	8	9	10	11	12	Summe	
b	Häufigkeit	1	2	3	4	5	6	5	4	3	2	1	36	
c	Wahrs.	1/36	2/36	3/36	4/36	5/36	6/36	5/36	4/36	3/36	2/36	1/36	1	
a * c	wahrs.gew. Werte	2/36	6/36	12/36	20/36	30/36	42/36	40/36	36/36	30/36	22/36	12/36	252/36	= 7
a - EW	Abweichung vom EW	-5	-4	-3	-2	-1	0	1	2	3	4	5	0	
$(a - EW)^2$	quadrierte Abw.	25	16	9	4	1	0	1	4	9	16	25	110	
$c * (a - EW)^2$	wahrs.gew. quadr. Abw.	25/36	32/36	27/36	16/36	5/36	0/36	5/36	16/36	27/36	32/36	25/36	210/36	= 5,83

(EW = 7, Varianz = 5,83)   Varianz   Erwartungswert

Bei unserem Würfelbeispiel ergibt sich eine Varianz von 5,8. Das entspricht einer Standardabweichung von 2,4.

$$\text{Stdabw} = \sqrt{5,8} = 2,4$$

Zur besseren Vorstellung der Standardabweichung kann man sich auch die Wahrscheinlichkeitsverteilung des Würfelbeispiels anschauen.

In der folgenden Grafik sind die möglichen Werte und ihre Wahrscheinlichkeiten angezeichnet. Daraus kann man ablesen, wie hoch die Wahrscheinlichkeit für den Bereich von +1 bis -1 Standardabweichungen ist.

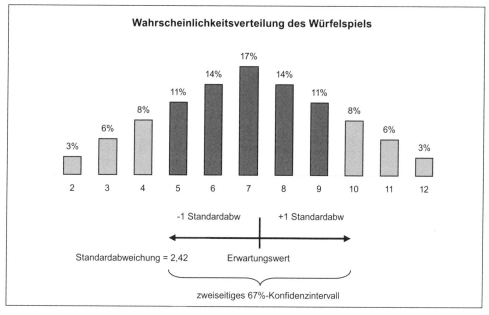

Wahrscheinlichkeitsverteilung des Würfelspiels

The range spans from 4.6 (= EV −1 Stdev) to 9.4 (= EV + 1 Stdev). Therefore, the outcomes 5 to 9 fall within this range. The summed up probability of these outcomes equals 67%. This means that one can expect the sum of pips to lie between 4.6 and 9.4 in 67 cases when throwing the dice one hundred times. Such a range is also called a confidence interval. A **confidence interval** states a range within which the outcome of a random variable will lie with a fixed probability. When looking at distributions, one generally distinguishes between **one-sided and two-sided confidence intervals**. The example at hand shows a two-sided confidence interval which states that the sum of pips will lie between 4.6 and 9.4 with a probability of 67% and with a probability of 33% either below or above that range.

From a risk point of view, however, only losses (in this case numbers below seven) are relevant, i.e. values that are smaller than the expected value. Therefore, it would be more interesting for the player to know what the possible loss is given a certain probability. Accordingly, mainly one-sided confidence intervals are used in risk measurement. A one-sided interval provides the information below which value a random variable will fall given a fixed probability (or which value it will exceed, respectively).

The next illustration shows that the probability that the sum of pips equals or exceeds 4 corresponds to 91%. The loss when throwing a four would equal (7–4=3) three USD. Therefore, we can make the statement that the maximum loss given a certainty of 91% equals three USD.

In other words, the probability for a loss greater than three USD equals 9%.

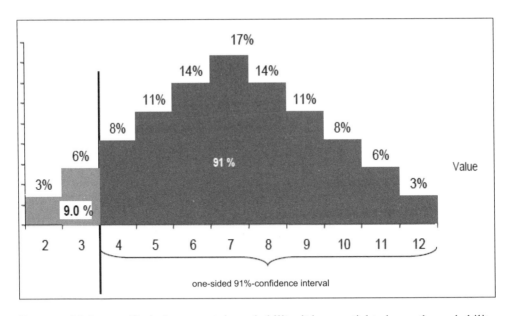

Because risk is quantified given a certain probability, it is essential to know the probability distribution of outcomes. The field of statistics offers a number of probability distributions with characteristic properties. One of the most important distributions is the **normal distribution** or **Gauss distribution**.

Dieser Bereich erstreckt sich von 4,6 (= EW –1 Standardabweichung) bis 9,4 (= EW +1 Standardabweichung). Da beim Würfeln nur ganze Zahlen möglich sind, zieht man die nächstgelegenen Werte von fünf bis neun heran, die alle zusammen eine Wahrscheinlichkeit von ca. 67% haben. Das bedeutet, dass die gewürfelte Zahl bei 67 von 100 Würfen im Bereich von 4,6 bis 9,4 liegt. Diesen Bereich nennt man auch Konfidenzintervall. Ein **Konfidenzintervall** gibt bei einer festgelegten Wahrscheinlichkeit an, innerhalb welcher Bandbreite ein Parameter mit eben dieser Wahrscheinlichkeit liegt. Bei Verteilungen unterscheidet man dabei zwischen **einseitigen und zweiseitigen Konfidenzintervallen.** Wir haben hier das Beispiel eines zweiseitigen 67%-Konfidenzintervalls gesehen, das zeigt, dass der Parameter Würfelzahl mit einer 67%-igen Wahrscheinlichkeit innerhalb der Bandbreite 4,6 bis 9,4 liegt bzw. mit einer 33% Wahrscheinlichkeit rechts oder links dieser Bandbreite liegt.

Aus einem Risikogesichtspunkt sind aber eigentlich nur die Verluste bzw. die Würfe, die geringer als der Erwartungswert sind, maßgebend. Deswegen wäre es für den Spieler hilfreich zu wissen, wie hoch der maximale Verlust in diesem Spiel mit einer gegebenen Wahrscheinlichkeit sein wird. In der Risikomessung werden deshalb hauptsächlich einseitige Konfidenzintervalle verwendet. Diese geben bei einer festgelegten Wahrscheinlichkeit an, über bzw. unter welcher Größe ein Parameter mit dieser Wahrscheinlichkeit liegt.

Aus der nächsten Grafik wird ersichtlich, dass man mit einer Wahrscheinlichkeit von 91% einen Vierer oder eine höhere Zahl würfelt. Der Verlust bei einem gewürfelten Vierer beträgt (7 – 4 = 3) EUR 3. Demzufolge kann man sagen, dass der maximale Verlust in dem Spiel mit 91%-iger Wahrscheinlichkeit EUR 3 beträgt. Oder anders ausgedrückt: Der Verlust von EUR 3 wird nur mit einer Wahrscheinlichkeit von 9% überschritten.

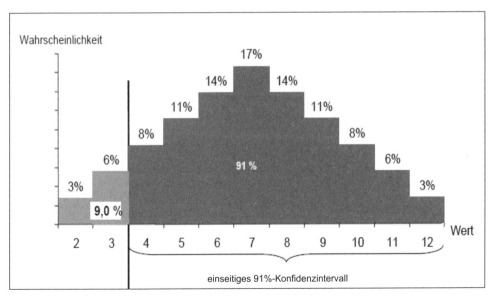

Für das Risiko aus statistischer Sicht ist es maßgebend, wie die Wahrscheinlichkeiten der Werte verteilt sind. Deswegen kommt der Wahrscheinlichkeitsverteilung eine besondere Bedeutung zu. In der Statistik findet man eine Anzahl spezieller Verteilungen mit charakteristischen Eigenschaften. Eine der wichtigsten Verteilungen ist die **Normalverteilung** oder auch **Gauß-Verteilung.**

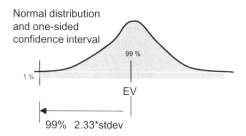

The normal distribution is **bell-shaped and symmetric** around the mean. This means that the probability of larger deviations is smaller than the probability of smaller deviations, and that the probability of a positive deviation of x equals the probability of negative deviation of x. Relating to market risk, this means that we assume no trend and that the risk of rising prices is the same as the risk of falling prices. The normal distribution also offers the advantage that the distribution can be completely described by its mean and its standard deviation. **Confidence intervals can therefore be calculated in a standardised way**, i.e. by subtracting or adding a certain multiple of the standard deviation to the mean.

A normal distribution is generated when a random variable (here: returns) depends on multiple, independent random variables (e.g. economic data, political decisions, management decisions, advances in technology, etc.). Such an assumption can be made for efficient markets.

The following table shows a number of commonly used confidence intervals and how they are calculated using the standard deviation:

	One-sided		Two-sided	
Confidence interval	Multiple of stdev σ	Interpretation	Multiple of stdev σ	Interpretation
90%	1.28	$P(z < EV - 1.28 * \sigma) = 10\%$	1.65	$P(z < EW - 1.65 * \sigma \text{ or } z > EW + 1.65 * \sigma) = 10\%$
95%	1.65	$P(z < EV - 1.65 * \sigma) = 5\%$	1.96	$P(z < EW - 1.96 * \sigma \text{ or } z > EW + 1.96 * \sigma) = 5\%$
99%	2.33	$P(z < EV - 2.33 * \sigma) = 1\%$	2.58	$P(z < EW - 2.58 * \sigma \text{ or } z > EW + 2.58 * \sigma) = 1\%$
99.9%	3.09	$P(z < EV - 3.09 * \sigma) = 0.1\%$	3.29	$P(z < EW - 3.29 * \sigma \text{ or } z > EW + 3.29 * \sigma) = 0.1\%$

where $P(z < EV - 2.33 * \sigma) = 1\%$ means that the probability that the value z is smaller than $EV - 2.33 * \sigma$ equals 1%.

Holding Period

In order to assess the risk of a trading position, it is essential to know (or to assume) how quickly it is possible to close that position. Here we will leave the example of the dice gamble behind us and will focus on trading examples.

In general, the risk of a position that can be closed from one day to the next is smaller than the risk of a position that can only be closed after 10 more trading days (e.g. because of a lack of market liquidity, the size of the position or the bank's possibilities to react). The

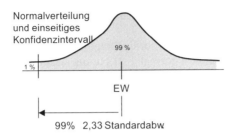

Die Normalverteilung hat die Form einer sogenannten **Glockenkurve** und ist symmetrisch um den Erwartungswert. Dies bedeutet, dass die Wahrscheinlichkeit von großen Bewegungen kleiner ist als von kleinen Bewegungen und dass die Wahrscheinlichkeit einer positiven Abweichung von x genauso groß wie die Wahrscheinlichkeit einer negativen Abweichung von x ist. Für das Marktrisiko bedeutet das, dass kein Trend unterstellt wird und das Risiko eines Anstiegs der Kurse genauso groß wie das Risiko von fallenden Kursen ist. Sie bietet unter anderem den Vorteil, dass man bei der **Berechnung der Werte für verschiedene Konfidenzniveaus standardisiert** vorgehen kann. Dazu wird die entsprechende Anzahl von Standardabweichungen vom Erwartungswert subtrahiert.

Eine Normalverteilung entsteht dann, wenn eine Zufallsvariable (hier: Returns) von vielen unabhängigen Zufallsvariablen (z.B. Wirtschaftsdaten, politischen Entscheidungen etc.) beeinflusst werden. Für effiziente Märkte trifft diese Annahme sehr gut zu.

Einige übliche Konfidenzniveaus bzw. ihre Berechnung mithilfe der Standardabweichung sind in der folgenden Tabelle zu finden:

Konfidenz-niveau	einseitig		zweiseitig	
	Anzahl der Stdabw σ	Interpretation	Anzahl der Stdabw σ	Interpretation
90%	1,28	$P(z < EW - 1,28 * σ) = 10\%$	1,65	$P(z < EW - 1,65 * σ$ oder $z > EW + 1,65 * σ) = 10\%$
95%	1,65	$P(z < EW - 1,65 * σ) = 5\%$	1,96	$P(z < EW - 1,96 * σ$ oder $z > EW + 1,96 * σ) = 5\%$
99%	2,33	$P(z < EW - 2,33 * σ) = 1\%$	2,58	$P(z < EW - 2,58 * σ$ oder $z > EW + 2,58 * σ) = 1\%$
99,9%	3,09	$P(z < EW - 3,09 * σ) = 0,1\%$	3,29	$P(z < EW - 3,29 * σ$ oder $z > EW + 3,29 * σ) = 0,1\%$

$P(z < EW - 2,33 * σ) = 1\%$ steht dafür, dass die Wahrscheinlichkeit, dass der Wert z kleiner ist als $EW - 2,33 * σ$, bei 1% liegt.

Haltedauer

Für die Bemessung des Risikos von Handelspositionen ist es wesentlich zu wissen (oder zu unterstellen), wie schnell der Handel aus einer bestehenden Position aussteigen kann. Um diesen Effekt zu argumentieren, müssen wir leider unser Würfelspiel verlassen und die weitere Argumentation für das Risiko von Handelspositionen erweitern.

Kann eine Position von einem Tag auf den anderen total geschlossen werden, so ist ihr Risiko geringer als das einer Position, die beispielsweise nur in einem Zeitintervall von zehn Tagen geschlossen werden kann (durch fehlende Marktliquidität, Größe der Position, Reak-

reason for that principle is that possible price changes become larger over a longer holding period.

Adapting the risk figure of a position for different holding periods is relatively straight forward when price changes follow a normal distribution. Assuming that the standard deviation (= volatility) is measured for daily price changes, we have to extrapolate that standard deviation in the following way:

Formula:
$$\sigma_n = \sigma_1 \times \sqrt{n}$$

σ_1 = (daily) standard deviation
n = holding period in (trading) days

Note: The holding period is counted in trading days. If a position can be sold in two weeks, the holding period counts 10 (trading) days. A year is generally counted as 252 (trading) days.

Example
EUR/USD position, 100 m standard deviation (volatility), 1 day: 0.50% What is the risk for a supposed holding period of 10 days?

● Calculation of the standard deviation for a holding period of 10 days:

$$\sigma_n = \sigma_1 \times \sqrt{n} = 0.50\% \times \sqrt{10} = 1.58\%$$

● Calculation of risk: 100,000,000 x 1.58% = 1,580,000

The general formula for adapting the volatility for holding periods that differ from the holding period which the volatility was measured for is as follows:

Formula:
$$\sigma_{t_1} = \sigma_{t_2} \times \sqrt{\frac{t_1}{t_2}}$$

σt = standard deviation for a holding period of t (trading) days

Example
EUR/USD position, 100 m standard deviation (volatility), 1 year: 5% What is the risk for a supposed holding period of 10 days?

● Calculation of the standard deviation for a holding period of 10 days

$$\sigma_{10} = \sigma_{252} \times \sqrt{\frac{10}{252}} = 5\% \times \sqrt{\frac{10}{252}} = 1.00\%$$

● Calculation of risk: 100,000,000 x 1% = 1,000,000

tionsmöglichkeiten der Bank). Der Grund für diesen Effekt: Bei längerer Haltedauer sind die möglichen Preisschwankungen im Markt auch entsprechend größer.

Bei der Unterstellung einer Normalverteilung ist die Hochrechnung auf eine längere Haltedauer relativ „straight-forward". Nachdem in der Risikomessung die Standardabweichung (Volatilität) üblicherweise für tägliche Preisschwankungen ermittelt wird, muss bei einer längeren Haltedauer die tägliche Preisschwankung hochgerechnet werden.

Formel:

$$\sigma_n = \sigma_1 \times \sqrt{n}$$

σ = Standardabweichung
n = Haltedauer in Tagen

Anmerkung: Nur Handelstage werden zur Haltedauer gezählt. Beträgt die Verkaufszeit für eine Position zwei Wochen, so bedeutet das eine Haltedauer von zehn (Handels-)Tagen. Für ein Jahr werden standardmäßig 252 Handelstage gerechnet.

Beispiel

EUR/USD-Position, 100 Mio.
Standardabweichung (Volatilität) 1 Tag: 0,50%
Wie hoch ist das Risiko bei einer unterstellten Haltedauer von zehn Tagen?

• Berechnung der Standardabweichung für eine Haltedauer von zehn Tagen:

$$\sigma_n = \sigma_1 \times \sqrt{n} = 0,50\% \times \sqrt{10} = 1,58\%$$

• Berechnung Risiko: 100.000.000 x 1,58% = 1.580.000

Die allgemeine Formel für das „Hoch- und Herunterrechnen" der Volatilität sieht folgendermaßen aus:

Formel:

$$\sigma_{t_1} = \sigma_{t_2} \times \sqrt{\frac{t_1}{t_2}}$$

σ_t = Standardabweichung für Haltedauer von t (Handels-)Tagen

---

Beispiel

EUR/USD-Position, 100 Mio.
Standardabweichung (Volatilität) 1 Jahr : 5%
Wie hoch ist das Risiko bei einer unterstellten Haltedauer von zehn Tagen?

• Berechnung der Standardabweichung für eine Haltedauer von zehn Tagen:

$$\sigma_{10} = \sigma_{252} \times \sqrt{\frac{10}{252}} = 5\% \times \sqrt{\frac{10}{252}} = 1,00\%$$

• Berechnung Risiko: 100.000.000 x 1% = 1.000.000

Correlation/Covariance

Correlation and Covariance are another two important and related parameters for the theory of probability. Both parameters quantify the relationship between two random variables, i.e. they describe how one random variable changes depending on the change of another random variable.

The **correlation** between random variables A and B corresponds to the **covariance** between A and B divided by the standard deviations of A and B. The correlation can be interpreted as a normed covariance and its values may **range from -1 to + 1** by definition. A correlation of +1 (-1) is called a perfect positive (negative) correlation, which means in other words a linear relation between two variables. A correlation of zero shows that there is no statistic interdependence between two normally-distributed random variables.

Therefore, correlation describes the **degree of the statistical interrelationship between two variables**. The following is a possible interpretation: Let ρ be the correlation between two variables. The ρ^2% of the variability of both variables can be attributed to the same (but not necessarily known) influencing factors. The number ρ^2 is called **coefficient of determination**.

Example: Let the correlation between the price movements of stocks A and B be 80%. The 80%^{2} = 64% of the variability of both stocks can be explained by the statistical interrelationship.

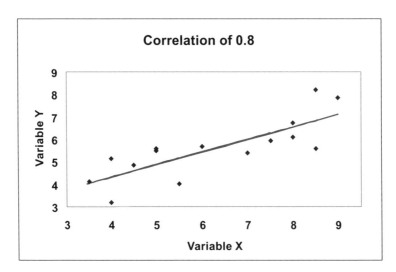

Note: The points in the graph show simultaneously observed values of two variables X and Y. The straight line shows how the interrelationship would look like with a correlation of 1 (linear relationship).

A negative correlation between different securities of an investor are quite desirable from an investor's point of view, as the investor can better diversify within the portfolio.

Korrelation/Kovarianz

Zwei weitere wichtige Maßzahlen aus der Wahrscheinlichkeitsrechnung sind die Korrelation und die Kovarianz. Beide geben den Zusammenhang zwischen zwei Variablen an, d.h., sie zeigen an, wie sich eine Variable ändert, wenn sich gleichzeitig eine andere Variable ändert.

Die **Korrelation** zwischen zwei Variablen A und B enstpricht der **Kovarianz** zwischen A und B dividiert durch die Standardabweichungen von A und B. Die Korrelation ist also eine Art normierte Kovarianz und liegt **zwischen +1 und -1**. Bei einer Korrelation von +1 bzw. -1 spricht man von einer perfekten (positiven bzw. negativen) Korrelation. Dies bedeutet, dass es einen eindeutigen linearen Zusammenhang zwischen den Variablen gibt. Eine Korrelation von 0 zeigt an, dass es keinen statistischen Zusammenhang zwischen den Variablen gibt.

Die Korrelation beschreibt also das **Ausmaß des statistischen Zusammenhangs von zwei Variablen**. Eine mögliche Interpretation ist die folgende: Sei die Korrelation zwischen zwei Variablen ρ, dann können ρ^2% der Variabilität der beiden Variablen durch dieselben (nicht notwendigerweise bekannten) Einflussfaktoren erklärt werden. Die Zahl ρ^2 wird dabei **Bestimmtheitsmaß** genannt.

Beispiel: Beträgt die Korrelation zwischen den Wertentwicklungen der Aktien A und B 80%, dann werden 80%² = 64% der Variabilität der beiden Aktien durch einen statistischen Zusammenhang erklärt.

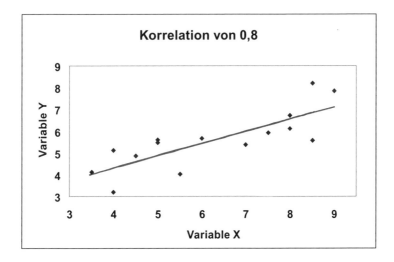

Anmerkung: Die Punkte stellen die zu gleichen Zeitpunkten beobachteten Werte von X und Y dar. Die Gerade illustriert eine Korrelation von 1, also einen perfekten linearen Zusammenhang.

Eine negative Korrelation zwischen den verschiedenen Finanztiteln ist aus Portfoliosicht für einen Anleger sehr wünschenswert, da dieser unter diesen Bedingungen am besten von der Diversifikation in mehrere Titel profitieren kann.

Example

You have a stock portfolio containing two titles with the following characteristics

Stock	Share W	Expected returns E (r)	Volatility (p.a.) σ	Correlation ρ
A	55%	10%	17.1%	0.15
B	45%	20%	20.8%	

We are interested in the expected return of the portfolio as well as in the risk of the portfolio (volatility).

The expected return of the portfolio is calculated as the sum of weighted stock returns.

$$E(r_p) = W_A \cdot E(r_A) + W_B \cdot E(r_B) = 0,55 \cdot 0,10 + 0,45 \cdot 0,20 = 14.5\%$$

When calculating the **risk of a portfolio**, the saying applies that the whole is more than the sum of its parts. It depends on the correlation to what degree the portfolio risk differs from the sum of the risks of the single positions. The portfolio risk, expressed with the standard deviation or volatility, is the **square root of the variance**.

$$\sigma^2_p = w^2_A \cdot \sigma^2_A + w^2_B \cdot \sigma^2_B + 2 \cdot (w_A \cdot \sigma_A \cdot CORR \cdot w_B \cdot \sigma_B)$$

$$\sigma^2_p = 0.55^2 \cdot 0.171^2 + 0.45^2 \cdot 0.208^2 + 2 \cdot (0.55 \cdot 0.171 \cdot 0.15 \cdot 0.45 \cdot 0.208) = 0.02025$$

$$\sigma_p = \sqrt{0,02025} = 14.2\%$$

The concept of volatility in market risk measurement

Calculating volatilities for market risk

When applying the concept of volatility (standard deviation) in market risk measurement, one usually has a history of daily prices (end-of-day or average) available. Based on these prices, a daily return is calculated by dividing the day's price by the price from the previous trading day and subtracting 1 (100%).

Example

EUR/USD	EOD price	return
day 1	1.2030	
day 2	1.2120	$0.0074813 = \left(\frac{1.2120}{1.2030}\right) - 1$

The calculated (discrete) return shows the percentage result of our position. If a history of such daily returns is available, the standard deviation can be calculated as shown in the previous chapter.

Beispiel

Ihr Aktienportfolio besteht aus zwei Titeln mit folgenden Merkmalen:

Aktie	Anteil W	Erwartete Rendite E (r)	Volatilität (p.a.) σ	Korrelation ρ
A	55%	10%	17,1%	0,15
B	45%	20%	20,8%	

Gefragt ist die erwartete Portfoliorendite sowie das Portfoliorisiko (Volatilität).
Die Portfoliorendite errechnet sich als Summe der gewichteten Einzelrenditen.

$$E(r_p) = W_A \cdot E(r_A) + W_B \cdot E(r_B) = 0,55 \cdot 0,10 + 0,45 \cdot 0,20 = 14,5\%$$

Beim **Portfoliorisiko** muss neben dem Einzelrisiko auch die Korrelation berücksichtigt werden. Das Portfoliorisiko, ausgedrückt mit der Standardabweichung bzw. Volatilität, ist gleich die **Quadratwurzel der Varianz.**

$$\sigma^2_p = w^2_A \cdot \sigma^2_A + w^2_B \cdot \sigma^2_B + 2 \cdot (w_A \cdot \sigma_A \cdot CORR \cdot w_B \cdot \sigma_B)$$

$$\sigma^2_p = 0,55^2 \cdot 0,171^2 + 0,45^2 \cdot 0,208^2 + 2 \cdot (0,55 \cdot 0,171 \cdot 0,15 \cdot 0,45 \cdot 0,208) = 0,02025$$

$$\sigma_p = \sqrt{0,02025} = 14,2\%$$

Das Konzept der Volatilität in der Marktrisikomessung

Berechnung von Volatilitäten für Marktrisiken

Verwenden wir jetzt das vorgestellte Konzept der Volatilität (Standardabweichung) im Marktrisikobereich, so hat man üblicherweise als Basisinformation die entsprechenden Kurse (Schlusskurse, Durchschnittskurse) der einzelnen Handelstage. Aus diesen Kursen wird dann der Return pro Handelstag errechnet, in dem der heutige Kurs durch den Vortageskurs dividiert wird und 1 (also 100%) abgezogen wird.

Beispiel

EUR/USD	Schlusskurs	Return
Tag 1	1,2030	
Tag 2	1,2120	$0,0074813 = \left(\dfrac{1,2120}{1,2030}\right) - 1$

Dieser errechnete (diskrete) Return zeigt uns also das tägliche Ergebnis für jeweils 1 Einheit. Auf diese so errechneten täglichen Returns wird dann das Konzept der Standardabweichung (wie im vorherigen Kapitel erläutert) angewendet.

Example

EUR/USD EOD prices for 7 trading days

	(1) Price	(2) Return	(3) Return - EV	(4) (3) 2
day 1	1.2030			
day 2	1.2120	0.007481	0.004142	0.000017
day 3	1.2010	-0.009076	- 0.012415	0.000154
day 4	1.2210	0.016653	0.013313	0.000177
day 5	1.2170	-0.003276	-0.006615	0.000044
day 6	1.2310	0.011504	0.008164	0.000067
day 7	1.2270	-0.003249	-0.006589	0.000043
Sum			Sum (5)	0.000502
Average/Expected Value (EV)		**0.003339**	**var = (5)/(6−1)**	**0.0001005**
		Standard deviation (volatility)		**1.002%**

The calculated volatility can be interpreted in the following way (under the assumption of normally distributed returns): with a probability of around 67% daily price changes will not exceed 1.002%. This translates into a price change of 0.0123 (= 1.002% x 1.2270) if there is an option position after day 7.

In order to quantify the risk, we have to look at a one-sided confidence interval, so that the 67% argued previously becomes around 83%. Having a 100m EUR/USD position, we would argue that the loss potential (= risk) would equal 1.23m USD (100m x 0.0123). Only in 17% of all cases would there be a loss on the 100m EUR/USD position that exceeds 1.23m USD.

Calculating log-normal returns

Often, instead of discrete returns, **continuous or log-normal returns** are used for the calculation of volatility.

There are two **arguments for using log-normal returns** for the calculation of volatility and risk:

- When using log-normal returns, a **continuous growth process** is assumed. When projecting risk based on continuous returns, **losses are never projected to exceed 100%**, which may happen with the discrete method when risk is linearly projected for longer holding periods.
- When using log-normal returns for FX price changes, the returns and thus the **measured volatility are independent from the quotation of the currency** (direct or indirect).

Beispiel

EUR/USD-Schlusskurse für sieben Tage

	(1) Kurse	(2) Return	(3) Return-EW	(4) (3)²
Tag 1	1,2030			
Tag 2	1,2120	0,007481	0,004142	0,000017
Tag 3	1,2010	-0,009076	- 0,012415	0,000154
Tag 4	1,2210	0,016653	0,013313	0,000177
Tag 5	1,2170	-0,003276	-0,006615	0,000044
Tag 6	1,2310	0,011504	0,008164	0,000067
Tag 7	1,2270	-0,003249	-0,006589	0,000043
Summe			**Summe (5)**	**0,000502**
Erwartungswert (EW)		**0,003339**	**Var = (5)/(6–1)**	**0,0001005**
			Standardabweichung (Volatilität)	**1,002%**

Die so ermittelte Volatilität kann unter der Annahme normalverteilter Returns nun folgendermaßen interpretiert werden:

Mit ca. 67% Wahrscheinlichkeit wird die tägliche Kursschwankung nicht größer als 1,002% sein. Haben wir also am siebenten Tag eine offene EUR/USD-Position, so ist die Schwankungsbreite (mit 67% Wahrscheinlichkeit) 0,0123 (1,002% x 1,2270).

Möchten wir jetzt das Risiko quantifizieren, so müssen wir auf ein einseitiges Konfidenzintervall wechseln, sodass aus den vorher argumentierten 67% jetzt ca. 83% werden. Bei 100 Mio. EUR/USD-Position würde also argumentiert werden, dass das Verlustpotenzial (= Risiko) 1,23 Mio. USD (100 Mio. x 0,0123) beträgt. Nur in 17% der Fälle werden wir also auf die 100 Mio. EUR/USD-Position innerhalb eines Tages einen Verlust machen, der größer als 1,23 Mio. USD ist.

Berechnen von lognormalen Returns

Bei der Berechnung der Volatilitäten werden im Marktbereich oft keine „normalen" Returns, sondern sogenannte **„lognormale" oder „stetige" Returns** verwendet.

Als **Vorteile** einer Berechnung der Volatilität auf Basis von lognormalen Returns können zwei Argumente aufgeführt werden:

- Bei der Berechnung von lognormalen Returns wird eine **stetige Verzinsung** angenommen. Beim Hochrechnen von stetiger Verzinsung können **Verluste nie 100% überschreiten,** was bei der linearen Hochrechnung diskreter Verzinsung theoretisch möglich ist, vor allem wenn man für längere Halteperioden rechnet.
- Bei der Verwendung von lognormalen Returns bei Währungskursentwicklungen kann die **gemessene Volatilität unabhängig der entsprechenden Kursnotierung** (EUR/USD oder USD/EUR) **verwendet** werden.

Example

EUR/USD	EOD price	return
day 1	1.2030	
day 2	1.2120	$0.007453 = \ln\left(\dfrac{1.2120}{1.2030}\right)$

Example

In our simplified example of 7 trading days, the calculation of the daily volatility when using log-normal returns looks as follows:

(1) Price	(2) Return	(3) LN (return)	(4) (3) – EV	(5) (4)²
1.2030				
1.2120	1.007481	0.007453	0.004161	0.000017
1.2010	0.990924	-0.009117	- 0.012410	0.000154
1.2210	1.016653	0.016516	0.013223	0.000175
1.2170	0.996724	0.003281	-0.006574	0.000043
1.2310	1.011504	0.011438	0.008146	0.000066
1.2270	0.996751	-0.003255	-0.006547	0.000043
Sum			**(5) Sum**	**0.000499**
Average/Expected Value (EV)		**0.003292**	**var = (5)/(6−1)**	**0.000100**
	Standard deviation (volatility)			**1.00%**

The interpretation of the volatility is the same as when using "normal" returns, except that an exponential function is used (instead of a linear one) to estimate risk figures.

Volatilities for interest rate positions

Whereas the calculation of a volatility or risk figure is quite straightforward for FX positions or stocks, the issue becomes a little more complicated for interest rate positions. This is because there is no direct interpretation for returns taken from historic interest rates. While the FX return equals the result of an open FX position, the return of historic interest rates only shows percentage changes of interest rates. The result (or indeed the risk) of an interest rate position, however, can only be determined taking the **influence on the price (duration, PVBP)** into account. Consequently, we have to distinguish between **interest rate volatilities** and **price volatilities**. Interest rate volatilities show how interest rates change while price volatilities show how prices of interest rate positions change (depending on the interest rate volatilities).

Beispiel

EUR/USD	Schlusskurs	Return
Tag 1	1,2030	
Tag 2	1,2120	$0,007453 = \ln\left(\dfrac{1,2120}{1,2030}\right)$

Beispiel

An unserem vereinfachten Beispiel einer Zeitreihe mit siebe Schlusskursen sieht die Berechnung der Volatilität mit lognormalen Returns folgendermaßen aus:

(1) Kurse	(2) Return	(3) LN (Return)	(4) (3) – EW	(5) (4)²
1,2030				
1,2120	1,007481	0,007453	0,004161	0,000017
1,2010	0,990924	-0,009117	- 0,012410	0,000154
1,2210	1,016653	0,016516	0,013223	0,000175
1,2170	0,996724	0,003281	-0,006574	0,000043
1,2310	1,011504	0,011438	0,008146	0,000066
1,2270	0,996751	-0,003255	-0,006547	0,000043
Summe			**(5) Summe:**	**0,000499**
Erwartungswert (EW)		**0,003292**	**Var = (5)/(6–1)**	**0,000100**
	Standardabweichung (Volatilität)			**1,00%**

Die Interpretation dieser Volatilitätskennzahl entspricht der Interpretation der Volatilität mit „normalen" Returns, wobei hier nicht linear, sondern exponential weitergerechnet wird.

Volatilitäten für Zinspositionen

Während die Berechnung und Anwendung der Volatilitätskennzahl für FX und Aktienrisiken relativ einfach ist, wird es im Zinsbereich schon schwieriger. Im Zinsbereich hat man zwar die Zeitreihen der Zinssätze für die verschiedenen Laufzeiten zur Verfügung, die Interpretation vom berechneten Return ist jedoch nicht so einfach. Während der Return im FX-Bereich auch das Ergebnis auf eine offene Position ist, ist im Zinsbereich der Return die prozentuelle Veränderung der Zinsen. Das Ergebnis (oder auch das Risiko) auf eine offene Position kann damit nur unter **Berücksichtigung des Preishebels (Duration, PVBP)** bestimmt werden. Dementsprechend unterscheidet man im Zinsbereich zwischen sogenannten **Zinsvolatilitäten** und **Preisvolatilitäten.** Bei der Preisvolatilität ist der Hebel des Instrumentes bzw. der Laufzeit berücksichtigt. Die Zinsvolatilität ist die reine Zinsänderung.

Example

3 year rates (fixing prices) for 7 days:

	(1) Rates	(2) Return	(3) Return – EV	(4) (3)²
day 1	4.78%			
day 2	4.81%	0.006276	-0.001347	0.000002
day 3	4.88%	0.014553	0.006929	0.000048
day 4	4.82%	-0.012295	-0.019919	0.000397
day 5	4.94%	0.024896	0.017273	0.000298
day 6	4.90%	-0.008097	-0.015721	0.000247
day 7	5.00%	0.020408	0.012785	0.000163
Sum		**0.045741**	**(5) Sum**	**0.001156**
Average/expected value (EV)			**var = (5)/(6–1)**	**0.000231**
	Standard deviation (volatility)		**1.52%**	

The calculated volatility can be interpreted in the following way (under the assumption of normally distributed returns):

Daily interest rate changes will not exceed 1.52% with a probability of around 67%. Given a current interest rate level of 5%, this translates into a level change of 0.076% (= 5% x 1.52%) or 7.6 basis points, respectively. The percentage volatility of 1.52% or the 7.6bp for the interest rate level represent the aforementioned interest rate volatility.

In our example portfolio, we have a 3-year bond (50m) with a PVBP of 13,698. Using the calculated interest rate volatility, we estimate a risk of 104,105 (13,698 x 7.6). We receive a similar result using the duration. We estimated a duration of 2.72 for the 3-year bond in the previous chapter. The duration shows the sensitivity of the price given a supposed interest rate change. An interest rate change of 7.6 bp leads to an estimated price change of 0.2067% (0.076% x 2.72). The risk for the total position of 50m equals then 103,360 (50,000,000 x 0.2067%), a similar number to the one received using PVBP for risk estimation. The risk of 103,360 or 0.2067% is called price volatility and takes maturity and interest rate sensitivity of the position into account.

Taking Holding Period and Confidence Interval into Account – Value-at-Risk (VaR)

There are two basic methods to measure financial risks: by **analytical solutions** or by **simulation**. The term analytical means that results can be directly attained by using (analytic) mathematic formulas. In practice the three following approaches to measure VaR are most commonly used:

- Variance-Covariance Method (analytic)
- Historical Simulation
- Monte Carlo Simulation

Beispiel
3-Jahres-Zinsen (Fixing Kurse) für sieben Tage:

	(1) Zinsen	(2) Return	(3) Return-EW	(4) $(3)^2$
Tag 1	4,78%			
Tag 2	4,81%	0,006276	-0,001347	0,000002
Tag 3	4,88%	0,014553	0,006929	0,000048
Tag 4	4,82%	-0,012295	-0,019919	0,000397
Tag 5	4,94%	0,024896	0,017273	0,000298
Tag 6	4,90%	-0,008097	-0,015721	0,000247
Tag 7	5,00%	0,020408	0,012785	0,000163
Summe			**(5) Summe:**	**0,001156**
Erwartungswert (EW)			**Var = (5)/(6 – 1)**	**0,000231**
	Standardabweichung (Volatilität)		**1,52%**	

Die so ermittelte Volatilität kann nun folgendermaßen interpretiert werden:

Mit ca. 67% Wahrscheinlichkeit wird die tägliche Schwankung nicht größer als 1,52% sein. Bei einem Zinsniveau von 5% bedeutet dies eine Schwankung von 0,076% (5% x 1,52%) oder von 7,6 BP. Die Volatilität von 1,52% bzw. die ermittelten 7,6 BP würden damit als Zinsvolatilität interpretiert werden.

Haben wir jetzt eine offene 3-Jahres-Anleihe-Position (50 Mio.) mit einem PVBP von 13.698, so ergibt sich ein Risiko von 104.105 (13.698 x 7,6). Auf ein ähnliches Ergebnis kommen wir über die Anwendung der Duration. Für die 3-Jahres-Anleihe haben wir im vorhergehenden Kapitel eine Modified Duration von 2,72 ermittelt. Diese Duration ermittelt – wie dargestellt – den Hebel der Kursänderung bezogen auf die Zinsänderung. Bei einer unterstellten Zinsänderung von 7,6 BP (= Zinsvolatilität) ist damit die Kursänderung 0,2067% (0,076% x 2,72). Bei 50 Mio. Anleiheposition würden wir damit das Risiko auf 103.360 (50.000.000 x 0,2067%) schätzen und sind somit auf einer ganz ähnlichen Dimension wie bei der Abschätzung mit dem PVBP. Die 103.360 bzw. 0,2067% werden als Preisvolatilität bezeichnet und berücksichtigen damit auch schon die Laufzeit und den entsprechenden Hebel der Zinsposition.

Berücksichtigung von Haltedauer und Konfidenzintervall – Value-at-Risk (VaR)

Die Messung finanzieller Risiken kann grundsätzlich auf zwei Wegen erfolgen, **analytisch** oder durch **Simulation**. Der Begriff analytisch bedeutet, dass ein Ergebnis explizit mit einer Formel berechnet werden kann. In der Praxis werden in den Banken hauptsächlich drei verschiedene VaR-Ansätze verwendet:

- Varianz-Kovarianz-Methode (analytisch)
- Historische Simulation
- Monte-Carlo-Simulation

Variance-Covariance method

The Variance-Covariance method uses the assumption of normally distributed random variables to calculate the VaR of individual position or portfolios with analytic formulas.

As has been already described, volatility can be easily adapted to different holding periods and confidence levels (assuming normal distribution). It has become standard to use a 99% confidence interval and a holding period of 10 (trading) days for market risk measurement (in the trading book).

Example

3 year bond
coupon: 5%
PVBP: 13,698
Interest rate volatility: 7.6bp

- Adjusting interest rate volatility for the 99% confidence interval:
  7.6 x 2.33(*) = 17.71
  (*) multiple of standard deviation for 99% confidence interval

- Adjusting 99% volatility for 10-day holding period
  $17.71 * \sqrt{10} = 56$

- Taking price sensitivity into account (here: PVBP, 3-year bond)
  56 x 13,698 = 767,088

The 3-year bond has therefore a VaR of 767,088, which means that with a probability of 99% there will be no loss exceeding 767,088 over a holding period of 10 days

Note: In this example, the random variable that is assumed to follow a normal distribution is not the price of the instrument but the interest rate, the so-called "risk driver". The price of the instrument can be directly related to (changes in) the interest rate. Possible changes of the interest rate are estimated by measuring its volatility and adjusting it for the holding period and confidence interval used.

The estimation of the risk of a portfolio using the variance/covariance method includes four (or five) main steps:

I.   **Calculating historic volatilities** either for the individual positions of the portfolio or for a set of risk drivers (e.g. stock indices, interest rates, FX prices, etc.). In the case that all price changes are attributed to risk drivers an additional step is needed to map all positions onto risk drivers. The advantage of using risk drivers and mapping are reduced computing time and data requirements. In particular, new data are usually unnecessary if a new position is added to the portfolio.

II. **Determining the holding period for a position.** The question that has to be answered is: How long does it take the bank to sell an existing position? The supposed holding period is determined based on type, size and market liquidity of the position.

III. **Determining the confidence interval:** Which probability represents a sufficient level of security?

Die Varianz-Kovarianz-Methode

Beim Varianz-Kovarianz-Modell wird der VaR einer Position oder eines Portfolios analytisch berechnet, und zwar unter Annahme von Normalverteilungen.

Wie im Kapitel „Statistische Grundlagen" beschrieben, kann so die ermittelte Volatilität jederzeit auf die gewünschte Haltedauer und das gewünschte Konfidenzintervall hochgerechnet werden. In der Risikomessung im Marktbereich haben sich als Standard ein Konfidenzintervall (einseitig) von 99% und eine Haltedauer von zehn Tagen als Standard etabliert.

Beispiel
3-Jahres-Anleihe
Kupon: 5%
PVBP: 13.698
Zinsvolatilität: 7,6 BP

- Umrechnung der Zinsvolatilität auf 99% Konfidenzintervall:
  7,6 x 2,33[*] = 17,71
  [*] Faktor für Umrechnung auf 99%

- Umrechnung der Zinsvolatilität (99%) auf zehn Tage Haltedauer:
  17,71 x Wurzel(10) = 56

- Berücksichtigung des Hebels (3-Jahres-Anleihe):
  56 x 13.698 = 767.088

Die 3-Jahres-Anleiheposition hat damit einen VaR von 767.088, was bedeutet, dass der Verlust mit 99% Wahrscheinlichkeit innerhalb eines Zeitraumes von zehn (Handels-)Tagen nicht größer als 767.088 sein wird.

Anmerkung: In diesem Beispiel wird nicht der Preis des Instrumentes direkt gemessen, sondern die Normalverteilungsannahme wird für einen Risikotreiber (hier: Zinssatz) gemacht, dessen Volatilität wird gemessen und aufskaliert und in Beziehung zum Preis des Instrumentes gebracht.

Die Berechnung des Risikos mit der Varianz-Kovarianz-Methode für ein komplettes Portfolio erfolgt in vier (oder fünf) Schritten:

I. **Berechnung der historischen Schwankungen** entweder für die einzelnen Portfolioinstrumente oder für eine Anzahl von Risikotreibern (z.B. Aktienindizes, Zinssätze, FX-Kurse etc.). Wird mit Risikotreibern gearbeitet, dann ist ein zusätzlicher Schritt notwendig, um einzelne Positionen auf Risikotreiber zu mappen (z.B. PVBP-Methode). Der Vorteil des Mappings auf Risikotreiber sind ein geringerer Rechenaufwand und reduzierte Datenanforderungen. Im Speziellen muss die Datenbasis üblicherweise nicht erweitert werden, wenn neue Positionen ins Portfolio aufgenommen werden.

II. **Festlegung der Haltedauer einer Position.** Die zu beantwortende Frage lautet: Wie schnell kann der Handel aus einer bestehenden Position aussteigen? Beeinflusst wird diese unterstellte Haltedauer von der Größe der Position und der Marktliquidität.

III. **Festlegung des Sicherheitsintervalls.** Wie viel Prozent aller historischen Fälle sollen bei der Risikomessung berücksichtigt werden?

IV. **Taking correlation effects between positions or risk drivers into account:** For example: If a bank has a 4-year receiver swap and a 5-year payer swap, the common risk of those two positions is lower than the sum of the individual positions' risks. The reason is that a scenario where the 4-year interest rate rises, and the 5-year interest rate falls is highly unlikely if not impossible. By taking correlation effects into account the risk of the given position would be significantly reduced and would no longer be comparable to the risk from two sold (or bought) interest swaps. When correlation effects are neglected, all individual positions' risks have to be aggregated, which will probably lead to a significant overestimation of total risk.

The great **advantages** of the Variance-Covariance method are its simplicity, minimal computing time, as well as the traceability of results by using (derivations of) the analytic formula.

A significant **disadvantage** of the model is the necessity of a number of assumptions that are not always met by reality. The most commonly challenged assumption is the assumption of normal distributions. Therefore, the risk of asymmetric instruments like options can only be measured to a limited degree.

A possibility to take advantage of the simplicity and traceability of the Variance-Covariance method is to use the model for initial solutions to get an overview of the risks. In practice, this could mean controlling risk daily using the Variance-Covariance method and applying more sophisticated and extensive risk measurement methods in defined time intervals.

EXCURSUS: Modern Portfolio Theory – Harry Markowitz

The basis of the Variance-Covariance model goes back to Harry Markowitz, who took as a basis for his portfolio theory, developed in 1952, that an **investment can be fully described by the two parameters variance (risk) and expected return**. The approach to optimising a portfolio on the basis of these two parameters is called the **"Mean Variance" Approach**. The core idea of Markowitz's theory is that investors are only interested in assets when purchasing them **improves the risk/return characteristic of the portfolio held**. One of the conclusions drawn from that assumption is that it makes no sense for investors to invest into unsystematic risk, but that an optimal portfolio is always composed of an investment into risk-free assets and an investment into a perfectly diversified market portfolio (of risky assets).

IV. Berücksichtigung von etwaigen Korrelationseffekten zwischen den Positionen bzw. Risikotreibern. Haben wir beispielsweise einen 4-Jahres-Swap (Kauf) und einen 5-Jahres-Swap (Verkauf) in den Büchern, so ist das Risiko der beiden Positionen nicht additiv zu sehen, sondern es gibt eine große (historische) Wahrscheinlichkeit, dass wenn der 4-Jahres-Satz ansteigt, der 5-Jahres-Satz nicht sinkt. Durch die Berücksichtigung der Korrelationseffekte würde das Risiko einer entsprechenden Position deutlich reduziert werden und wäre nicht mehr vergleichbar mit dem Risiko von zwei verkauften (oder gekauften) Zinsswaps. Bleiben diese Korrelationseffekte außer Acht, wäre im Extremfall jedes Risiko aufzuaddieren. Dies könnte je nach Handelsstrategie zu einer krassen Überschätzung des Gesamtrisikos führen.

Der große **Vorteil** der Varianz-Kovarianz-Methode besteht in ihrer einfachen Handhabung, dem geringeren Rechenaufwand sowie der „Rückverfolgbarkeit" der Ergebnisse mithilfe der für die VaR-Rechnung verwendeten Formel.

Ein erheblicher **Nachteil** des Modells ist die Notwendigkeit einer Reihe von Annahmen, die in der Realität nicht vollständig erfüllt werden. Am häufigsten wird dabei die Annahme normalverteilter Veränderungen der Risikofaktoren kritisiert. Im Speziellen können die Risiken asymmetrischer Produkte, wie z.B. Optionen, nur beschränkt erfasst werden.

Eine Möglichkeit, den Vorteil der einfachen Handhabung zu nutzen, ist es, das Varianz-Kovarianz-Modell als erste schnelle Lösung zu benutzen, um einen Überblick über Risiken zu bekommen. So kann die tägliche Risikoüberwachung mit dem Modell gemacht werden, kombiniert mit exakteren und aufwändigeren Risikomessungen in definierten Zeitabständen.

EXKURS: Moderne Portfoliotheorie – Harry Markowitz

Die Grundlagen des Varianz-Kovarianz-Modells gehen auf Harry Markowitz zurück, der seiner 1952 entwickelten Portfoliotheorie die Annahme zugrundelegt, dass ein **Investment durch die zwei Parameter Varianz und erwartete Rendite vollständig beschrieben** werden kann. Der Ansatz, ein Portfolio entsprechend diesen zwei Parametern zu optimieren, wird **„Mean-Variance"-Ansatz** genannt. Grundidee ist, dass für Investoren Titel immer nur dann interessant sind, wenn sie durch Hinzunahme des Titels die **Ertrags/Risiko-Charakteristik des gehaltenen Portfolios verbessern**. Im Weiteren kommt Markowitz zum Schluss, dass es für einen Investor keinen Sinn macht, unsystematisches Risiko zu halten, sondern ein optimales Portfolio sich aus risikolosen Titeln und einem perfekt diversifizierten Marktportfolio (riskanter Titel) zusammensetzt.

Example

VaR Calculation for our example portfolio using the Variance-Covariance method:

In order to calculate risk using the Variance-Covariance method, the following steps are necessary:
- Calculation of price volatilities (e.g. 99%, 10 days)
- Calculation of correlations
- Calculating portfolio risk using the formula

$$\sqrt{\text{Pricevola} * [C] * \text{Pricevola}^{T}}$$

Pricevola = Vector containing positions individual price risks
[C] = Correlation Matrix
T = transposed vector

Applying these steps to our example portfolio, we receive the following numbers:

Step 1: Calculation of price volatilities and mapping onto risk drivers (here: interest rates)

Product	Volume	Rate	Maturity
Anleihe	-50,000,000	5.0%	3 Jahre
Anleihe	-50,000,000	6.0%	7 Jahre
Kauf IRS	+100,000,000	5.5%	5 Jahre
Interbank	+ 100,000,000	3.50%	6 Monate

	1 PVBP	2 Interest volatility (99%, 10 days)	3 Price Vola/ Risk (1) x (2)
6 Monate	0	60 BP	0
1 Jahr	0	53 BP	0
2 Jahre	0	52 BP	0
3 Jahre	-12,407	50 BP	-620,350
4 Jahre	779	49 BP	+38,171
5 Jahre	37,498	48 BP	+1,799,904
6 Jahre	-1,231	47 BP	-57,857
7 Jahre	-23,607	45 BP	-1,062,315

Beispiel

VaR-Berechnung (Varianz-Kovarianz-Methode) für das Beispielportfolio:

Für die Bestimmung des Risikos mit der Varianz-Kovarianz-Methode sind folgende
Schritte notwendig:
- Bestimmung der Preisvolatilitäten (z.B. 99%, 10 Tage)
- Berücksichtigung der Korrelationen
- Berechnung des Risikos mit der Formel

$$\sqrt{\text{Preisvola} \cdot [\text{C}] \cdot \text{Preisvola}^{\,T}}$$

Preisvola = Vektor der einzelnen Preisrisiken
$[\text{C}]$ = Korrelationsmatrix
T = transponierter Vektor

Auf unser Handelsportfolio angewendet bedeutet das:

Schritt 1: Bestimmung der Preisvolatilitäten und Mapping auf Risikotreiber (hier: Zinssätze)

Produkt	Volumen	Zinssatz	Laufzeit
Anleihe	-50.000.000	5,0%	3 Jahre
Anleihe	-50.000.000	6,0%	7 Jahre
Kauf IRS	+100.000.000	5,5%	5 Jahre
Interbank	+ 100.000.000	3,50%	6 Monate
	1 **PVBP**	**2** **Zins-Volatilität** **(99%, 10 Tage)**	**3** **Preis-Volatilität/** **Risiko (1) x (2)**
6 Monate	0	60 BP	0
1 Jahr	0	53 BP	0
2 Jahre	0	52 BP	0
3 Jahre	-12.407	50 BP	-620.350
4 Jahre	779	49 BP	+38.171
5 Jahre	37.498	48 BP	+1.799.904
6 Jahre	-1.231	47 BP	-57.857
7 Jahre	-23.607	45 BP	-1.062.315

Step 2: Calculation of Correlations

A **correlation matrix** is necessary in order to calculate a portfolio VaR

Example

Pricevola	6 Mo	1 year	2 years	3 years	4 years	5 years	6 years	7 years
	0	0	0	-620,350	38,171	1,799,904	-57,857	-1,062,315

Correlation Matrix	6 Mo	1 years	2 years	3 years	4 years	5 years	6 years	7 years
6 Mo	1.00	0.76	0.73	0.70	0.65	0.63	0.62	0.62
1 years	0.76	1.00	0.85	0.80	0.78	0.76	0.72	0.70
2 years	0.73	0.85	1.00	0.89	0.86	0.81	0.78	0.77
3 years	0.70	0.80	0.89	1.00	0.94	0.90	0.88	0.87
4 years	0.65	0.78	0.86	0.94	1.00	0.95	0.93	0.90
5 years	0.63	0.76	0.81	0.90	0.95	1.00	0.94	0.93
6 years	0.62	0.72	0.78	0.88	0.93	0.94	1.00	0.96
7 years	0.62	0.70	0.77	0.87	0.90	0.93	0.96	1.00

Interpretation: $90\%^2 = 81\%$ of the variability of the 3-year rate and the 5-year rate can be explained by a statistic interrelationship.

Step 3: Calculating portfolio risk

The last step of calculating risk with the Variance-Covariance method is a bit more technical. We have to use matrix multiplication where the vector with the price volatilities is multiplied with the correlation matrix (which yields a vector). The result is then multiplied with the transposed vector for the price volatilities (which yields a number). The final result is received by extracting the root from that number.

6 Mo	1 year	2 years	3 years	4 years	5 years	6 years	7 years
0	0	0	-620,350	+38,171	+1,799,904	-57,857	-1,062,315

Pricevola	6 Mo	1 year	2 years	3 years	4 years	5 years	6 years	7 years
	0	0	0	-620,350	38,171	1,799,904	-57,857	-1,062,315

Correlation Matrix	6 Mo	1 years	2 years	3 years	4 years	5 years	6 years	7 years
6 Mo	1.00	0.76	0.73	0.70	0.65	0.63	0.62	0.62
1 years	0.76	1.00	0.85	0.80	0.78	0.76	0.72	0.70
2 years	0.73	0.85	1.00	0.89	0.86	0.81	0.78	0.77
3 years	0.70	0.80	0.89	1.00	0.94	0.90	0.88	0.87
4 years	0.65	0.78	0.86	0.94	1.00	0.95	0.93	0.90
5 years	0.63	0.76	0.81	0.90	0.95	1.00	0.94	0.93
6 years	0.62	0.72	0.78	0.88	0.93	0.94	1.00	0.96
7 years	0.62	0.70	0.77	0.87	0.90	0.93	0.96	1.00

Schritt 2: Bestimmung der Korrelationen

Zur VaR-Berechnung wird zusätzlich eine sogenannte **Korrelationsmatrix** benötigt:

Beispiel

Preisvola	6 Mo	1 Jahr	2 Jahre	3 Jahre	4 Jahre	5 Jahre	6 Jahre	7 Jahre
	0	0	0	-620.350	38.171	1.799.904	-57.857	-1.062.315

Korrelations Matrix	6 Mo	1 Jahr	2 Jahre	3 Jahre	4 Jahre	5 Jahre	6 Jahre	7 Jahre
6 Mo	1,00	0,76	0,73	0,70	0,65	0,63	0,62	0,62
1 Jahr	0,76	1,00	0,85	0,80	0,78	0,76	0,72	0,70
2 Jahre	0,73	0,85	1,00	0,89	0,86	0,81	0,78	0,77
3 Jahre	0,70	0,80	0,89	1,00	0,94	0,90	0,88	0,87
4 Jahre	0,65	0,78	0,86	0,94	1,00	0,95	0,93	0,90
5 Jahre	0,63	0,76	0,81	0,90	0,95	1,00	0,94	0,93
6 Jahre	0,62	0,72	0,78	0,88	0,93	0,94	1,00	0,96
7 Jahre	0,62	0,70	0,77	0,87	0,90	0,93	0,96	1,00

Interpretation: $90\%^2 = 81\%$ der Variabilität des 3-Jahres-Satzes und des 5-Jahres-Satzes werden durch einen statistischen Zusammenhang erklärt.

Schritt 3: Berechnung Risiko

Die Berechnung des Risikos mit der Varianz-Kovarianz-Methode ist etwas technisch. Es wird über eine Matrizenmultiplikation berechnet, indem der Vektor Preisvolatilität mit der Matrix Korrelationen multipliziert wird. Das Ergebnis wird dann noch einmal mit dem transponierten Vektor der Preisvolatilitäten multipliziert. Vom ermittelten Ergebnis wird dann die Wurzel genommen und als Risiko interpretiert.

6 Monate	1 Jahr	2 Jahre	3 Jahre	4 Jahre	5 Jahre	6 Jahre	7 Jahre
0	0	0	-620.350	+38.171	+1.799.904	-57.857	-1.062.315

Preisvola	6 Mo	1 Jahr	2 Jahre	3 Jahre	4 Jahre	5 Jahre	6 Jahre	7 Jahre
	0	0	0	-620.350	38.171	1.799.904	-57.857	-1.062.315

Korrelations Matrix	6 Mo	1 Jahr	2 Jahre	3 Jahre	4 Jahre	5 Jahre	6 Jahre	7 Jahre
6 Mo	1,00	0,76	0,73	0,70	0,65	0,63	0,62	0,62
1 Jahr	0,76	1,00	0,85	0,80	0,78	0,76	0,72	0,70
2 Jahre	0,73	0,85	1,00	0,89	0,86	0,81	0,78	0,77
3 Jahre	0,70	0,80	0,89	1,00	0,94	0,90	0,88	0,87
4 Jahre	0,65	0,78	0,86	0,94	1,00	0,95	0,93	0,90
5 Jahre	0,63	0,76	0,81	0,90	0,95	1,00	0,94	0,93
6 Jahre	0,62	0,72	0,78	0,88	0,93	0,94	1,00	0,96
7 Jahre	0,62	0,70	0,77	0,87	0,90	0,93	0,96	1,00

Pricevola (transposed)

6 Mo	0
1 year	0
2 years	0
3 years	620,350
4 years	+38,171
5 years	+1,799,904
6 years	-57,857
7 years	-1,062,315

$$RISK = \sqrt{\text{Pricevola} * [C] * \text{Pricevola}^{T}} = \sqrt{332,533,627,627} = \textbf{576,657}$$

We would therefore calculate a risk of 576,657 for our example portfolio (using the variance/covariance method and the supposed volatilities and correlations). As the volatilities were calculated for a confidence interval of 99% and a holding period of 10 days, the interpretation of the risk figure is the following:

A possible loss of the position will not exceed 576,657 over a period of 10 trading days with a probability of 99%. Or: The probability that a loss of the position will exceed the calculated risk figure over a period of 10 trading days equals 1%.

Historical simulation

If one cannot or does not want to make assumptions about risk factors, the historical simulation, a so-called model-independent method, may be used. When using historical simulation, no assumptions regarding the type, distribution, and volatility of risk factors and no assumptions about correlations have to be made. This methodology therefore **forgoes an analytic study of the risk factors**. In order make a historical simulation, you need the time series of the market prices of all underlying positions that are in the portfolio. The basic methodology consists of looking at how the value of the currently held portfolio has fluctuated during the chosen time slot.

For example, if you have all closing prices of the last 500 days, you determine the results of the portfolio for every day. The setting of a **confidence interval** decides how many of these days are to be eliminated from the risk calculation. If, in our example, the confidence interval is fixed at 99%, it means that the five days which constitute the worst results for our portfolio (500 x 0.01) are irrelevant. The sixth-worst day therefore serves as the basis for the portfolio risk measurement. Thereby, all historic correlation effects are automatically taken into consideration.

The challenge of the historical simulation lies in the **selection of the optimal time slot**. When choosing an extended period of time, the question has to be asked to what degree more dated observations are still relevant for current situation on the market. When choosing a shorter time slot it cannot be guaranteed that the observed values are representative for the underlying risk (e.g. if the time slot only covers a period of economic boom). Moreover, a small sample size increases estimation risk.

The **advantage** of this method lies in its independence from any models and their assumptions; these are all implicitly taken into account via historical correlations and prices.

Preisvolatilität (transponiert)

6 Mo	0
1 Jahr	0
2 Jahre	0
3 Jahre	620.350
4 Jahre	+38.171
5 Jahre	+1.799.904
6 Jahre	-57.857
7 Jahre	-1.062.315

$$\text{RISIKO} = \sqrt{\text{Preisvola} \cdot [C] \cdot \text{Preisvola}^T} = \sqrt{332.533.627.627} = \mathbf{576.657}$$

Anhand der Varianz-Kovarianz-Methode und mit den unterstellten Volatilitäten und Korrelationen würde sich somit ein Risiko von 576.657 für unser Beispielportfolio ergeben. Nachdem die Volatilitäten auf ein Konfidenzintervall von 99% und eine Haltedauer von zehn Tagen hochgerechnet wurden, ist die Interpretation folgende:

Der Verlust auf diese Position innerhalb von zehn Handelstagen wird mit 99-%iger Wahrscheinlichkeit nicht größer als 576.657 sein. Oder: Nur in 1% der Fälle wird der Verlust auf diese Position innerhalb von zehn Tagen größer sein als das berechnete Risiko.

Historische Simulation

Will bzw. kann man keine Annahmen über Risikofaktoren machen, so bietet sich als modellunabhängige Methode die sogenannte historische Simulation an. Es werden keine Annahmen über die Verteilung, die Volatilität, die Art der zugrundeliegenden Zufallsprozesse und Korrelationen getroffen, d.h., die Methode **verzichtet auf eine analytische Untersuchung der Risikofaktoren.** Für die historische Simulation ist es notwendig, über die Zeitreihen der Marktpreise aller im Portfolio enthaltenen Underlyings zu verfügen. Die Methodik besteht darin, zu betrachten, wie sich der Wert des aktuellen gehaltenen Portfolios während eines ausgewählten Zeitfensters verhalten hat. Hat man beispielsweise die Schlusskurse für die letzten 500 Tage zur Verfügung, so wird für das bestehende Portfolio das Ergebnis jedes Tages berechnet.

Die **Festlegung des Sicherheitsintervalls** bestimmt, wie viele der vergangenen Tage aus der Risikoberechnung zu streichen sind. Legen wir beispielsweise ein Sicherheitsintervall von 99% fest, so bedeutet das, dass die fünf schlechtesten Tage (500 x 0,01) für die Risikoermittlung irrelevant sind. Der sechstschlechteste Tag ist somit das Szenario, mit dem wir das Risiko aus unserem Portfolio bemessen würden. Damit sind automatisch alle historischen Korrelationseffekte berücksichtigt.

Die Herausforderung besteht in der **Wahl eines optimalen Zeitfensters.** Bei einem sehr langen Zeitfenster stellt sich die Frage, inwiefern weit zurückliegende Beobachtungen für die aktuelle Marktsituation noch relevant sind. Bei einer kurzen Historie tritt das Problem auf, dass die Anzahl der betrachteten Werte nicht repräsentativ ist (beispielsweise wenn das Zeitfenster nur eine Hochkonjunkturphase abdeckt). Außerdem vergrößert sich bei kleinen Stichproben der Schätzfehler.

Der **Vorteil** dieser Methode besteht in der Modellunabhängigkeit; Modellannahmen müssen nicht gemacht werden, sondern werden implizit über die historischen Korrelationen

Option risks (volatility, gamma), for example, are automatically taken into account when applying historical simulation. There is almost no statistical and mathematical knowledge required for implementing historical simulation.

There are also a number of significant **disadvantages** inherent in the historical simulation approach:

Data: Historical Simulation implicates high demands on data and computing time, especially if a portfolio is actively managed. Whenever a new position is added to the portfolio, it becomes necessary to expand the database and to rerun the complete historical simulation. The fact that each time the portfolio composition changes a completely new simulation has to be done may also lead to a situation where adding a position that should reduce total risk leads to a result with higher risk because a new simulation was used.

Backward Orientation: As the name implies, the approach relies fully on historical observation. The assumption that is used here states that what has not happened in the past will not happen in the future; Therefore, only value changes that have actually happened can be predicted.

New products/illiquid products: Historical simulation is not able to calculate a risk figure for newly or recently issued products or for illiquid products, because no suitable time series are available.

Monte Carlo simulation

The Monte Carlo simulation approach represents a simulation approach **based on random numbers**. The difference to the historical simulation is that the uncertainty about the future behaviour of risk factors is reproduced not with historical value changes but with random numbers.

As input for the Monte Carlo simulation the user has to make assumptions on volatilities, correlations and shape of the distribution in order to simulate the portfolio's future development via a random generator. Each of the simulations will be different, but the total of all simulations will fit the given statistical parameters. After finishing all simulations, the maximum loss is determined by choosing a desired confidence interval.

The most significant **advantage** of the Monte Carlo Simulation lies in its flexibility that allows the risk of complex instruments to be measured and random processes, for which there are no analytic formulas and solutions available, to be modelled. The main **disadvantages** are the complexity of calculations as well as the required computing time. Here it is necessary to find a compromise between speed (depending on the complexity of the assumptions and number of simulation runs) and accuracy.

The time and effort required to implement a Monte Carlo simulation are justified when **risk structures are complex**, e.g. when a portfolio includes a significant number of derivatives. For simpler risk structures, especially for those where there is a linear relationship between the changes of risk drivers and value changes, the Variance-Covariance method is sufficient.

Legislators generally stipulate as a minimum requirement that the **length of time series used for VaR models should be at least one year**. Bank-internal requirements should stipulate that the length of time series should be adequate to guarantee the validity of a VaR model.

und Preise berücksichtigt, d.h. zum Beispiel, dass verglichen mit einer Varianz-Kovarianz-Analyse etwaige Optionsrisiken (Volatilität, Gamma) bei der historischen Simulation ohne zusätzliche Modellannahmen berücksichtigt werden. Diese Aussage ist jedoch nur korrekt, wenn man von einer kurzen Haltedauer ausgeht; nicht berücksichtigt werden bei einer historischen Simulation nämlich Effekte, die sich aus einer Verkürzung der Restlaufzeit von Derivaten ergeben. Für die Implementierung einer historischen Simulation sind nahezu keine statistischen und mathematischen Kenntnisse erforderlich.

Die historische Simulation hat jedoch auch mehrere erhebliche **Nachteile:**

Daten: Insbesondere bei aktiv gemanagten Portfolios ist die Methode mit erheblichem Daten- und Rechenaufwand verbunden. Werden neue Positionen ins Portfolio aufgenommen, dann muss die Datenbasis erweitert werden und die gesamte Simulation neu gerechnet werden. Dies kann dazu führen, dass aufgrund einer neuen Position mit einem anderen Szenario gerechnet wird und diese Transaktion – obwohl vielleicht als risikomindernd gedacht – das Gesamtrisiko erhöht.

Vergangenheitsorientierung: Das Modell arbeitet ausschließlich mit historischen Beobachtungen, die Prämisse lautet: „Was es in der Vergangenheit nicht gab, kann es auch in Zukunft nicht geben"; es lassen sich also nur Dinge prognostizieren, die tatsächlich passiert sind.

Neue/illiquide Produkte: Die historische Simulation kann nicht auf neu emittierte bzw. illiquide Produkte, für die keine bzw. keine brauchbaren Zeitreihen zur Verfügung stehen, angewandt werden.

Monte-Carlo-Simulation

Bei der Monte-Carlo-Simulation handelt es sich um ein Simulationsverfahren **auf der Basis von Zufallszahlen.** Der Unterschied zur historischen Simulation ist, dass die Unsicherheit über das zukünftige Verhalten von Risikofaktoren nicht mit historischen Wertänderungen, sondern mit Zufallszahlen abgebildet wird.

Zur Berechnung des Risikos mit der Monte-Carlo-Simulation müssen Volatilitäten, Korrelationen sowie eine Verteilungsannahme vorgegeben werden. Mithilfe eines Zufallsgenerators wird dann die Weiterentwicklung des Wertes des Portfolios simuliert. Jede einzelne Simulation wird dabei unterschiedlich sein, aber die Summe der Simulationen wird den vorgegebenen statistischen Parametern entsprechen. Wenn alle Simulationen durchgeführt sind, wird der maximale Verlust über die Auswahl des gewünschten Konfidenzintervalls bestimmt.

Der größte **Vorteil** der Monte-Carlo-Simulation liegt in ihrer Flexibilität, die insbesondere bei der Risikomessung von komplexen Instrumenten und Prozessen immer dann gebraucht wird, wenn keine analytischen Formeln zur Darstellung zur Verfügung stehen.

Der **Nachteil** liegt jedoch in der extrem hohen Rechenintensität und den benötigten Computerkapazitäten. Hier muss man einen Kompromiss finden zwischen Geschwindigkeit (Komplexität der Darstellung und Anzahl der Simulationen) und Genauigkeit.

Der Aufwand einer Monte-Carlo-Simulation ist gerechtfertigt, wenn **komplexe Risikostrukturen,** insbesondere eine größere Anzahl von Derivaten, vorliegen. Für einfachere Risikostrukturen, insbesondere für solche, bei denen ein linearer Zusammenhang zwischen Veränderung der Risikofaktoren und Wertveränderung vorliegt, ist das Varianz-Kovarianz-Modell ausreichend.

None of the risk measurement methods quoted above work without limitations and assumptions. Therefore, it is important and necessary to understand the consequences if one or more of the underlying assumptions do not apply. The term **stress testing** refers to methods that simulate the effects of extreme market conditions and changes in assumptions. With stress testing, no particular procedure is laid down, but a number of requirements as to what stress testing scenarios should include are stipulated by supervisory authorities.

The term **back testing** refers to a reality test; where the predicted VaR values are, in retrospect, compared to the losses actually realised. Depending upon the comparison with the VaR value the results obtained yield information about the validity and quality of the applied risk model, and have to be provided to supervisory authorities.

Summary of the risk figures for our example portfolio

Key figure	Risk number	Assumption
GAP	0	change of money market rates, influence on annual net interest income
Duration	120,00	parallel interest rate shift (100% correlation between different terms
PVBP	103,222	
Scenario analysis	1,189,995	discretionary scenario risk figure may vary strongly
VaR	576,657	future same as history "black box"

2.1.7. Excursus: RiskMetrics and the spreading of the VaR concept

During the late 1980's, **JP Morgan** developed its own firm-wide Value at Risk system. This modelled **several hundred risk drivers** (e.g. interest rates, FX rates, etc.). A covariance matrix was updated quarterly from historical data. Each day, trading units would report by e-mail their positions' deltas with respect to each of the key factors. These were aggregated to express the combined portfolio's value as a linear polynomial of the key factors and a portfolio VaR was calculated using the assumption that the portfolio's value was normally distributed. The underlying idea here is the specifying of an **interdependency between the risk drivers and the value of the portfolio**. In this case the assumption of a **linear interdependency** (delta) and a **normal distribution** was used, as the risk was only estimated for an interval of one day.

With this VaR measure, JP Morgan replaced a **cumbersome system of notional market risk limits** with a simple system of VaR limits.

As this VaR system attracted plenty of interest from customers, JP Morgan developed a service called **RiskMetrics**. It comprised a detailed technical document as well as a covariance matrix for several hundred key factors.

Im Allgemeinen gibt der Gesetzgeber vor, dass der verwendete **Beobachtungszeitraum** für VaR-Modelle **mindestens ein Jahr** betragen muss. Dabei handelt es sich um eine Mindestanforderung. Für bankinterne Anforderungen sollte gelten, dass der Beobachtungszeitraum lang genug sein sollte, um inhaltlich die Validität eines VaR-Modells zu gewährleisten.

Keines der oben dargestellten Risikomessverfahren funktioniert ohne Begrenzung und Annahmen. Aus diesem Grund ist es wichtig und notwendig zu verstehen, was passieren kann, wenn eine oder mehrere Annahmen, die der Berechnung zugrundeliegen, nicht zutreffen. Unter dem Begriff **Stress-Testing** sind Verfahren zu verstehen, die die Effekte von extremen Marktkonstellationen und geänderten Annahmen simulieren. Beim Stress-Testing gibt es keine vorgeschriebenen Vorgangsweisen, jedoch eine Reihe von Vorgaben der Aufsichtsbehörden, was Stress-Szenarien beinhalten sollen.

Der Begriff **Back-Testing** bezeichnet einen Realitätstest, bei dem die prognostizierten VAR-Werte den tatsächlichen realisierten Verlusten im Nachhinein gegenübergestellt werden. Diese Ergebnisse müssen dem Gesetzgeber auch zur Verfügung gestellt werden, und abhängig von den Ergebnissen der Back-Tests im Vergleich mit dem berechneten VaR-Wert können Aussagen über die Güte des verwendeten Modells abgeleitet werden.

Zusammenfassung der Risikowerte für unser Handelsbuch:

Kennzahl	Risikowert	Annahme
GAP	0	Änderung der Geldmarktzinsen, Einfluss auf das jährliche Zinsergebnis
Duration	120.00	parallele Zinsbewegung
PVBP	103.222	(100% Korrelation zwischen den Laufzeiten)
Szenario-Analyse	1.189.995	willkürliches Szenario Risikokennzahl kann stark schwanken
VaR	576.657	Zukunft wie Vergangenheit, „Black Box"

2.1.7. EXKURS: RiskMetrics und die Verbreitung des VaR-Ansatzes

In den späten 80er-Jahren entwickelte **JP Morgan** sein eigenes konzernweites Value-at-Risk-System. Dabei wurden **mehrere hundert Risikotreiber** (z.B. Zinsen, FX-Kurse etc.) modelliert. Eine diesbezügliche Kovarianzmatrix wurde vierteljährlich upgedatet. Zum Zweck der Risikoabschätzung übermittelten die Handelsabteilungen täglich die Deltas ihrer Positionen hinsichtlich der verschiedenen Risikotreiber. Diese wurden aggregiert, und in einem darauf folgenden Schritt wurde das Risiko bzw. der Value-at-Risk des Gesamtportfolios unter Annahme einer Normalverteilung geschätzt. Die grundlegende Idee hier ist, einen **Zusammenhang zwischen den Risikotreibern und dem Wert des Portfolios** zu spezifizieren. In diesem Fall wurde die Annahme eines **linearen Zusammenhangs** (Delta) und einer **Normalverteilung** verwendet, da das Risiko nur für ein Tagesintervall geschätzt wurde.

Mithilfe dieser VaR-Maßzahl gelang es JP Morgan, ein **komplexes System nomineller Limite** mit einem einfachen VaR-Limit-System zu ersetzen.

Da dieses System auf großes Interesse bei Kunden von JP Morgan stieß, wurde ein Service unter dem Namen **RiskMetrics** entwickelt. Dieses beinhaltet sowohl die Veröffentlichung der technischen Unterlage für die Methodik als auch die Zurverfügungstellung einer Kovarianzmatrix für mehrere hundert Risikotreiber.

RiskMetrics was an important factor that to the widespread adoption of Value at Risk by both financial and non-financial firms during the mid 1990s. Even though RiskMetrics also describes historical and Monte Carlo simulation, it has been widely used as a **synonym for the covariance approach**.

2.1.8. GARCH Method

GARCH (**Generalized Autoregressive Conditional Heteroscedasticity**) represents an **advanced method of volatility measurement and prognosis**. The GARCH method is applied in risk management as well as in options trading.

Historical volatility is generally calculated by looking at a certain time window (e.g. the last year). This approach has the following disadvantages: The longer the time window used, the less will volatility figures react to the current market situation. When using time windows which are too short, volatility measurements become volatile and might change solely due to a number of observations falling out of the moving time window, without the current market situation actually changing.

The GARCH model corrects for these deficits. In doing so, it makes the following **assumptions**:

- **Market volatility** is **higher during certain periods** than in others
- There is a **natural long-term level of volatility**. The market tends to return to the natural volatility level after periods of higher or lower volatility

The GARCH model contains **parameters** which determine to what degree the average long-term volatility, the last measured volatility, and new observations are weighted. Observations are always weighted more heavily the more recent they are. Therefore, volatility figures based on a GARCH measurement will always react more strongly to current levels of volatility than the standard volatility measurement (given the same time window).

A drawback of the method is that the estimation of GARCH parameters is relatively complex and that there are no generally accepted market standards for the estimation of the parameters.

Note: Another model that weighs current volatility more heavily than historic volatility is the so-called **EWMA (Exponentially Weighted Moving Average)** model. Because EWMA does not provide an assumption about an average long-term volatility, it cannot be used for volatility prognosis.

The following illustration compares the volatility measure using GARCH, the standard volatility measure and realised volatilities for EUR/USD (all based on a 1-year window).

RiskMetrics spielte eine wichtige Rolle bei der verbreiteten Einführung des Value-at-Risk bei Finanz- und auch Nicht-Finanzdienstleistern im Laufe der 90er-Jahre. Obwohl RiskMetrics auch die Methodik für historische und Monte-Carlo-Simulation beschreibt, wird es bis heute als **Synonym für den Kovarianzansatz** verwendet.

2.1.8. GARCH-Methode

GARCH **(Generalized Autoregressive Conditional Heteroskedasticity)** stellt eine **fortgeschrittene Methode der Volatilitätsmessung und -prognose** dar. Anwendung findet die GARCH-Methode sowohl im Risikomanagement als auch bei Optionshändlern.

Klassisch wird die historische Volatilität auf Basis der Beobachtung eines bestimmten Zeitfensters berechnet. Diese Methode hat folgende Nachteile: Je länger die zur Berechnung der Volatilität verwendete Zeitreihe, desto weniger reagiert die Messung auf die aktuelle Marktsituation. Bei zu kurzen Zeitreihen kann sich die Volatilität durch Herausfallen von vergangenen Beobachtungen aus dem Beobachtungsfenster verändern, d.h., die gemessene Volatilität kann sich unabhängig von der aktuellen Marktsituation verändern.

Das GARCH-Modell korrigiert diese Defizite und geht dabei von **zwei grundlegenden Annahmen** aus:

- Die **Volatilität im Markt** ist **in bestimmten Perioden höher** als in anderen.
- Es gibt **langfristig ein natürliches Volatilitätslevel**, auf welches sich der Markt nach Phasen zu hoher bzw. zu niedriger Volatilität wieder hinbewegt.

Das GARCH-Modell beinhaltet **Parameter**, die festlegen, wie stark die durchschnittliche Volatilität, die zuletzt gemessene Volatilität und neue Beobachtungen gewichtet werden, wobei grundsätzlich Marktschwankungen umso stärker gewichtet werden, je aktueller sie sind. Daher reagiert eine GARCH-Messung stärker auf aktuelle Volatilitätsschwankungen als eine klassische Volatilitätsmessung.

Die Schätzung dieser GARCH-Parameter ist relativ aufwändig, es gibt auch keine allgemein anerkannten Marktstandards für diese Parameter.

Anmerkung: **EWMA (exponentially weighted moving average)** ist neben GARCH ein weiteres Modell, das aktuellere Marktschwankungen stärker gewichtet als vergangene. EWMA beinhaltet jedoch nicht die Annahme einer Langfristvolatilität und kann deshalb nicht für Volatilitätsprognosen verwendet werden.

Die folgende Abbildung vergleicht die mit GARCH gemessene Vola mit der Standard-Vola und den tatsächlich realisierten Volatilitäten des EUR/USD-Wechselkurses.

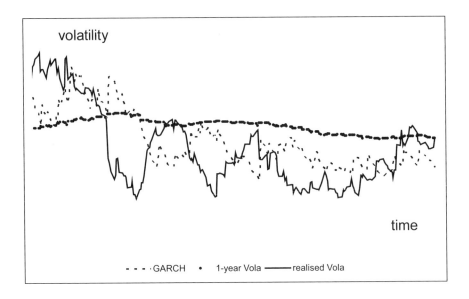

The assumed parameters in the GARCH are also used to make **forecasts regarding the future development of market volatility**. It predicts how quickly current market volatility will revert to the long-term average volatility. Based on these forecasts, it is possible to calculate future price movements for instruments of which the price is determined by volatility (e.g. options). The following illustration shows forecasts for the development of volatility given a lower current volatility (forecast 1) and a higher current volatility (forecast 2).

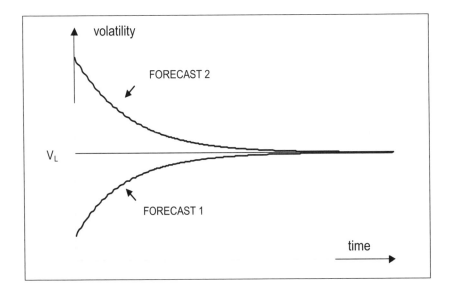

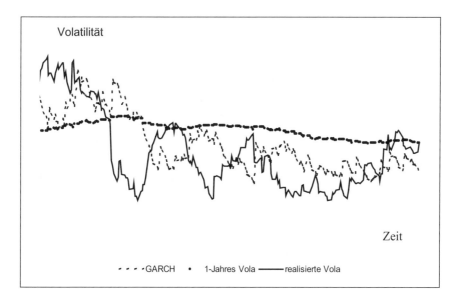

Die Parameter dienen auch dazu, **Vorhersagen bezüglich der zukünftigen Volatilitäts-entwicklung** zu treffen. Das GARCH-Modell sagt dabei voraus, mit welcher Geschwindig-keit sich die aktuelle Marktvolatilität an die langfristige Durchschnittsvolatilität wieder an-nähert. Daraus können Kursaussagen für Instrumente getroffen werden, deren Wert von der im Markt vorherrschenden Volatilität bestimmt wird (z.B. Optionen). Die nächste Abbil-dung zeigt Vorhersagen für die Entwicklung der Volatilität bei niedrigem Ausgangsniveau (Forecast 1) und hohem Ausgangsniveau (Forcecast 2).

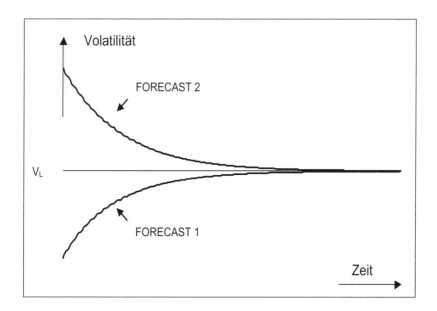

2.2. Credit Risk

2.2.1. Credit Value at Risk (CVaR)

Credit measurement has been an area of constant progress during the last years. The **application of the VaR approach in credit measurement** made it possible to measure credit risk so that results would be comparable with market risks, which marked a breakthrough in the area of risk management.

Alongside the thorough analysis of individual loans by means of balance sheet analysis, ratings, and ongoing credit surveillance, credit risk measurement and management at the portfolio level is arguably one of the most important components of credit risk management. In the same way as for individual loans, risk considerations are geared to the determination of the Probability of Default as well as the determination of Loss Given Default.

Thus, with regard to the whole loan portfolio, possible fluctuations in credit losses are quantified in addition to expected (credit) loss. Here, with the help of statistical methods, credit risk measurement aims to quantify unexpected loss as well as the credit loss distribution and thus the amount of economic capital necessary. Capital required to cover unexpected losses from an economic point of view is termed **economic capital**.

Credit Loss Distribution

Credit risk can be quantified based on a credit loss distribution. The credit loss distribution assigns a probability of occurrence to each possible amount of loss a loan portfolio might sustain. Determination of (the shape of) the credit loss distribution represents the pivotal element of all credit risk models. Irrespective of the underlying model assumptions, **two general distribution properties** can be observed:

- The credit loss distribution is **"skewed"**. This means that the distribution is **not symmetrical around the mean**, as is the case for the normal distribution. As a result, there is a high probability that no or only small losses will occur, while there is a low probability that very high losses will occur.
- The second property is the so-called **"fat tail"**, which means that the **possibility of extreme losses is still low**, but higher than in the case of a normal distribution.

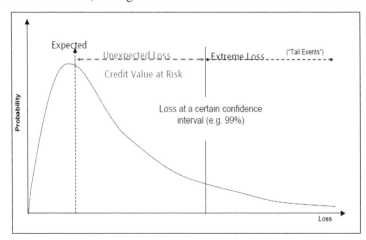

2.2. Kreditrisiko

2.2.1. Credit Value at Risk (CVaR)

Im Bereich Kreditrisikomessung wurden in den letzten Jahren sehr große Fortschritte erzielt. Während in der Vergangenheit kaum Ansätze bestanden, Kreditrisiken zu messen und miteinander vergleichbar zu machen, konnte der Durchbruch in der Risikomessung durch die **Übertragung des VaR-Ansatzes auf das Kreditrisiko** erzielt werden.

Neben der konsequenten Analyse von Einzelkrediten mittels Bilanzanalyse, Rating und laufender Kreditüberwachung ist die Messung und Steuerung des Kreditrisikos auf Portfolioebene einer der wohl wichtigsten Bestandteile im Kreditrisikomanagement. Bei der Einzelkreditentscheidung konzentriert sich die Risikobetrachtung auf die Bestimmung der Ausfallswahrscheinlichkeit und des zu erwartenden Verlustes im Falle des Ausfalls.

Betrachtet man in weiterer Folge das gesamte Kreditportfolio, wird neben dem erwarteten Verlust zusätzlich die mögliche Schwankung der Kreditverluste quantifiziert. In diesem Zusammenhang zielt die Kreditrisikomessung darauf ab, mittels statistischer Methoden den unerwarteten Verlust sowie die Kreditverlustverteilung und somit die Höhe der ökonomisch erforderlichen Eigenkapitaldeckung zu quantifizieren. Diese ökonomisch erforderlichen Eigenmittel, um unerwartete Verluste abdecken zu können, werden als **ökonomisches Kapital** bezeichnet.

Kreditverlustverteilung

Kreditrisiken lassen sich anhand der Kreditverlustverteilung quantifizieren. Diese Kreditverlustverteilung ordnet jedem denkbaren Verlust in einem Kreditportfolio die Wahrscheinlichkeit seines Auftretens zu. Die Bestimmung dieser Verteilung ist das zentrale Element sämtlicher Kreditrisikomodelle. Allerdings lassen sich unabhängig von den zugrundeliegenden Modellannahmen **zwei zentrale Verteilungseigenschaften** festhalten:

● Die Kreditverlustverteilung ist eine **„schiefe Verteilung"**. Das heißt, die Werte sind **nicht symmetrisch um den Erwartungswert verteilt,** wie es bei einer Normalverteilung der Fall ist. Daraus ergibt sich, dass mit hoher Wahrscheinlichkeit kein oder nur ein geringer Verlust, mit geringer Wahrscheinlichkeit jedoch ein sehr hoher Verlust eintritt.

● Die Kreditverlustverteilung besitzt einen **„Fat Tail"**, d.h., dass **extreme Verluste** zwar eine geringe, aber im Vergleich zu einer Normalverteilung doch **deutlich höhere Eintrittswahrscheinlichkeit** haben.

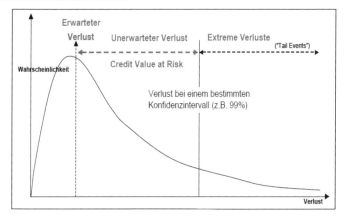

Credit Value at Risk (CVaR)

In recent years, the concept of Value at Risk has also established itself in the lending divisions of banks for the purpose of risk measurement.

Value at Risk measures risk potential, i.e. it quantifies to what degree actual losses might deviate from expected loss. Accordingly, Value at Risk (VaR) is defined as the **level of loss that will not be exceeded** over a specified period of time (e.g. one year) with a certain probability (e.g. 99%).

Example

A one-year VaR (99%) of 500,000 means that the bank will not suffer a loss higher than 500,000 within one year with a probability of 99%.

By calculating the ex-ante expected loss, a bank tries to compute an internal expected loss premium, while by calculating Value at Risk it aims to determine the **volume of economic capital** necessary. The VaR of a loan portfolio is termed **Credit Value at Risk (CVaR).**

Let's take a closer look at two parameters used in VaR calculation:

- the time horizon and
- the confidence interval

Time Horizon

The time horizon states the period for which risk is calculated. The time that is necessary to properly redeploy or liquidate a portfolio is the common benchmark when choosing the appropriate time horizon. As for the calculation of CVaR, the use of a **one-year time horizon** is common. It also corresponds to the frequency of the annual rating analysis of borrowers.

Confidence Interval

"Confidence interval" is a statistical term. It gives a **range within which credit loss will fall with a certain probability**. What the actual loss will be in the next year cannot be exactly predicted, but statistics allow the maximum loss possible to be estimated with a certain degree of confidence. The confidence interval chosen determines the **degree of certainty** of an estimate. It is common to use a confidence interval of 99% (or higher) to estimate CVaR.

2.2.2. EXCURSUS: Netting

In this paragraph we will discuss how to **reduce settlement and replacement risks**, which constitute a significant component of credit risk in trading. The basic principle is to conclude contracts with the respective counterparties which allow

- netting losses and profits that remain when deals have to be terminated prematurely due to the default of a counterparty **(replacement risk).**
- netting any receivables and liabilities that remain after a default between two or more counterparties **(settlement risk).**

Credit Value at Risk (CVaR)

Ein Konzept, das sich in den letzten Jahren auch im Kreditbereich zur Messung des Risikos durchgesetzt hat, ist Value at Risk.

Über den Value at Risk wird jenes Risikopotenzial gemessen, das angibt, inwieweit der tatsächliche Verlust von den erwarteten Verlusten abweichen kann. Dementsprechend wird der Value at Risk (VaR) definiert als der **maximale Verlust**, der mit einer bestimmten Wahrscheinlichkeit (z.B. 99%) über einen bestimmten Zeithorizont (z.B. ein Jahr) nicht überschritten wird.

Beispiel

Ein einjähriger 99%-VaR von EUR 500.000 bedeutet, dass der Verlust der Bank innerhalb des nächsten Jahres mit 99-%iger Sicherheit höchstens EUR 500.000 betragen wird.

Während über eine Ex-ante-Kalkulation des erwarteten Verlustes versucht wird, die Standardrisikokosten zu errechnen, wird über die Berechnung des Value at Risk die **Höhe des ökonomischen Kapitals** bestimmt. Der VaR eines Kreditportfolios wird als **Credit Value at Risk (CVaR)** bezeichnet.

Zwei Parameter in der Definition von VaR bedürfen einer genaueren Betrachtung:

- das Konfidenzintervall
- der Zeithorizont

Zeithorizont

Der Zeithorizont gibt an, für welchen Zeitraum das Risiko gemessen wird. Zur Wahl des Zeithorizontes orientiert man sich üblicherweise an der Zeit, die für die Umschichtung bzw. ordnungsgemäße Liquidierung des Portfolios notwendig ist. Im CVaR hat sich ein **Zeithorizont von einem Jahr** durchgesetzt und steht im Einklang mit der jährlichen Bonitätsüberprüfung der Kreditnehmer.

Konfidenzintervall

Das Konfidenzintervall ist ein Begriff aus der Statistik. Es gibt den **Wahrscheinlichkeitsbereich** an, in dem der geschätzte Wert des unerwarteten Kreditverlustes liegt. Wie hoch der tatsächliche Verlust in einem Jahr tatsächlich ist, kann niemand voraussagen. Die Statistik erlaubt uns jedoch mit einem (selbst) bestimmten Grad an Sicherheit zu schätzen, wie hoch dieser maximale Verlust sein wird. Das Konfidenzintervall bestimmt diesen **Grad an Sicherheit**. Auch im CVaR hat sich ein Konfidenzintervall von 99% etabliert.

2.2.2. EXKURS: Netting

Nachdem ein wesentlicher Bestandteil der Kreditrisiken des Handels aus Wiederbeschaffungs- und Settlementrisiken bestehen, möchten wir an dieser Stelle auf **Methoden zur Reduzierung dieser Risiken** eingehen. Das Grundprinzip ist immer, mit dem oder den entsprechenden Partnern Verträge abzuschließen, die es ermöglichen, dass

- im Konkursfall die etwaigen Kosten und Erträge bei vorzeitiger Beendigung von Kontrakten gegenverrechnet werden können (**Wiederbeschaffungsrisiko**).
- die Zahlungen, die sich zwischen zwei oder mehreren Partnern ergeben, saldiert werden (**Settlementrisiko**).

Basic Principle

In general, the term netting refers to **agreements between two or more counterparties that allow positive and negative values to be set off against each other given a certain event**. Thus, netting reduces a possibly large number of individual mutual commitments and positions to a smaller number. The main reasons for netting are the reduction of credit and settlement risk and a reduced amount of open commitments, reduced transaction costs and lower costs for nostro accounts (due to a reduced number of payments).

There are different types of netting agreements that differ with respect to

- the type and amount of the included payments
- the number of participants and the design of the netting system

The first feature distinguishes between netting by novation and close-out netting

Netting by novation

In this case existing **contractual obligations are satisfied or discharged by means of their replacement by new obligations**. Existing contracts are cancelled and replaced by **one new contract**. Since all payments are immediately included in the netting contract, the **administrative work is relatively high**. The advantage of netting by novation is that all claims covered by the netting agreement are legally enforceable if the counterparty goes bankrupt and no "cherry-picking" can take place.

Close-out netting

In practice, close-out netting is the preferred method. It is an **agreement to settle all contracted but not yet due liabilities and claims on an institution by one single payment, immediately upon the occurrence of a list of defined events**, such as the appointment of a liquidator to that institution. The settlement amount is determined by marking to market all open payments.

In case of OTC derivatives, close-out netting can be used for addressing counterparty risk if

- the deals were concluded with one counterparty
- the deals meet the netting criteria of the banking supervisory authorities.

The second feature distinguishes between **bilateral and multilateral netting.**

Bilateral Payment Netting

In the case of bilateral payment netting, **all transactions between two parties in one currency are netted and only the net balance is transferred**. This way, costs and risks are reduced. Payment netting is applied for transactions with the same value date. FX – Net and S.W.I.F.T Accord are examples of bilateral netting systems.

Multilateral Netting

In the case of multilateral netting, **all payments in one currency are netted** and the payments from all companies taking part in the multilateral netting system are taken into account. Multilateral netting systems are usually only set up for the most important curren-

Prinzip

Unter Netting versteht man die **vereinbarte Aufrechnung von gegenseitigen Positionen oder Verpflichtungen von Geschäftspartnern oder Teilnehmern eines Systems.** Das Netting verringert eine große Zahl von Einzelpositionen oder -verpflichtungen auf eine kleinere Zahl. Die wesentlichen Gründe für das Netting sind die Reduzierung des Kredit- und Settlementrisikos sowie die geringe Linienbelastung, geringere Transaktionskosten und günstigere Kosten für die Nostrokonten, weil weniger Zahlungen anfallen.

Beim Netting unterscheidet man

- Art und Umfang der inkludierten Zahlungsströme und
- Anzahl der Teilnehmer am und Ausgestaltung des Nettingsystems.

Zur ersten Gruppe zählen das Novations-Netting und Close-out Netting.

Novations-Netting

Darunter versteht man die **Erfüllung bestehender vertraglicher Verpflichtungen mit schuldbefreiender Wirkung mittels Ersatz durch neue Verpflichtungen.** Beim Novations-Netting werden die einzelnen Schuldverhältnisse in einem **Schuldumwandlungsvertrag** erfasst. Da die Ansprüche und Verpflichtungen immer schon zum Entstehungszeitpunkt saldiert werden, entsteht beim Novations-Netting ein **relativ hoher technischer Verwaltungsaufwand.** Der Vorteil des Novations-Nettings liegt darin, dass im Falle der Zahlungsunfähigkeit eines Unternehmens/Bank alle vom Nettingkontrakt abgedeckten Zahlungen durchsetzbar sind. Damit wird die Gefahr, dass im Konkursverfahren nur die profitablen Transaktionen durchgeführt werden, ausgeschaltet.

Close-out Netting

In der Praxis wird dem Close-out Netting (Liquidations-Netting) der Vorzug gegeben. Hier werden erst **bei Eintritt bestimmter Ereignisse (Kündigung oder Insolvenz) alle offenen Forderungen und Verbindlichkeiten aus Finanzgeschäften zum Marktwert zu einer Position saldiert.** Der Ausgleichsanspruch in Höhe des ermittelten Nettomarktwertes steht jener Partei zu, aus deren Sicht der Saldo positiv ist.

Mit dem Liquidations-Netting wird die Verrechnung von Adressausfallsrisiken bei OTC-Derivaten in allen Währungen ermöglicht, sofern

- die Geschäfte mit einem Partner abgeschlossen wurden und
- die Geschäfte nach den Vorschriften der Bankaufsicht für Aufrechnungsvereinbarungen anerkannt sind.

In der zweiten Gruppe unterscheidet man **bilaterales und multilaterales Netting.**

Bilaterales Payment Netting

Beim Payment Netting werden **alle Geschäfte zwischen zwei Parteien in einer Währung gegeneinander aufgerechnet und der Saldo transferiert.** Auf diese Weise sollen Kosten und Risiken reduziert werden. Das Payment Netting findet für Geschäfte mit der gleichen Valuta statt. FX-Net und S.W.I.F.T. Accord sind Beispiele für bilaterale Nettingsysteme.

Multilaterales Netting

Beim multilateralen Netting werden **Zahlungsströme in einer Währung saldiert**, wobei die Zahlungen an und von allen am multilateralen Nettingsystem beteiligten Unternehmen berücksichtigt werden. Multilaterale Nettingsysteme konzentrieren sich in der Regel auf die

cies in order to avoid clearing problems. The settlement risk for transactions that are executed outside of the netting system remains. Multilateral netting agreements are centred on a **clearing house** which handles all payments and is responsible for calculating the netting amounts.

The functionality of multilateral netting is illustrated by the following settlement matrix:

Sending bank	Receiving bank				Sum of liabilities
	A	B	C	D	
A	0	90	40	80	210
B	70	0	0	0	70
C	0	50	0	20	70
D	10	30	60	0	100
Sum of receivables (F)	80	170	100	100	450
Net position (V-F)	**-130**	**100**	**30**	**0**	**0**

The most important master agreements do also contain stipulations on netting. The **IFEMA** (International Foreign Exchange Master Agreement) allows for payment netting and netting by novation in the FX market, the **ICOM** (International Currency Options Market) for FX options. Close-out Netting is permitted given that it is also allowed under the applicable jurisdiction. IFEMA and ICOM were later merged into the **FEOMA** (Foreign Exchange and Options Master Agreement) which contains the same regulations as IFEMA and ICOM. The **ISDA Master Agreement** allows payment netting/netting by novation (point 2c of the ISDA Master Agreement) as well as close out netting (point 6e of the ISDA Master Agreement) for all products that are executed under an ISDA Master Agreement

The following table summarises the **advantages** of netting agreements and the considerations that should be made before entering into a netting agreement.

Advantages of netting by novation:

BILATERAL NETTING	MULTILATERAL NETTING
• settlement risk can be reduced up to 50% • different methods can be applied • no additional credit risk	• settlement risk can be reduced up to 90%. • open FX positions are transferred to a clearing house • time period of settlement risk is reduced to (less than) 24 hours

• Simplification of settlement because
   – of fewer payment orders
   – nostro account has to be settled less frequently
   – smaller amounts are transferred	

wichtigsten Währungen, um Probleme bei der Abwicklung zu vermeiden. Daher bleibt für alle außerhalb des Systems getätigten Transaktionen das Erfüllungsrisiko offen. Im Zentrum des multilateralen Nettings steht ein **Clearing House**, über das alle Zahlungsanweisungen laufen und in dessen Verantwortung es liegt, die Nettingbeträge korrekt zu berechnen.

Die Funktionsweise des multilateralen Nettings kann man anhand einer Settlement-Matrix illustrieren:

Sendende Bank	Empfangende Bank				Summe der Verbindlichkeiten
	A	**B**	**C**	**D**	
A	0	90	40	80	210
B	70	0	0	0	70
C	0	50	0	20	70
D	10	30	60	0	100
Summe der Forderungen (F)	80	170	100	100	450
Nettingposition (V-F)	**-130**	**100**	**30**	**0**	**0**

Die wichtigsten Rahmenverträge regeln auch das Netting. Das **IFEMA** (International Foreign Exchange Master Agreement) für den FX-Markt und **ICOM** (International Currency Options Market) für FX-Optionen sehen Novations-Netting und Payment Netting vor. Das Close-out Netting wird unter der Voraussetzung geregelt, dass Close-out Netting im Rahmen des anzuwendenden Rechts erlaubt ist. Das IFEMA und ICOM wurden zum **FEOMA** (Foreign Exchange and Options Master Agreement) verschmolzen, das dieselben Regelungen wie IFEMA und ICOM enthält. Das **ISDA Master Agreement** fasst alle Produkte, die unter den ISDA Rahmenverträgen abgeschlossen wurden, zusammen. ISDA sieht sowohl den Fall des Payment Nettings/Novations-Nettings (Punkt 2c des ISDA Master Agreements) als auch den Fall des Close-out Nettings/Liquidations-Nettings (Punkt 6e ISDA Master Agreement) vor.

In der folgenden Aufstellung sollen abschließend die **Vorteile von Nettingvereinbarungen** illustriert werden und den Überlegungen gegenübergestellt werden, die vor dem Eingehen einer Nettingvereinbarung angestellt werden sollen.

Vorteile Novations-Netting:

BILATERALES NETTING	MULTILATERALES NETTING
• Das Settlementrisiko kann betragsmäßig bis zu 50% reduziert werden. • Es können verschiedene Methoden verwendet werden. • kein zusätzliches Kreditrisiko	• Das Settlementrisiko kann betragsmäßig bis zu 90% reduziert werden. • Die offene Währungsposition wird zum Clearing House transferiert. • Das Settlementrisiko wird auf (weniger als) 24 Stunden verkürzt.

• Vereinfachung des Settlement, weil es
  – weniger Zahlungsanweisungen gibt,
  – der Abgleich der Nostrokonten weniger oft durchzuführen ist und
  – geringere Beträge transferiert werden.	

Netting is especially attractive for **banks with fewer locations and a limited number of counterparties** with whom a high number of mutual transactions are made. All these issues apply especially to market makers.

The most important netting services

Bilateral netting services

FX-Net and **S.W.I.F.T Accord** represent two of the best-known bilateral netting services.

FX-Net

FX-Net was founded in 1986 and belongs to FXNet Ltd., a consortium of 14 international banks. The system is operated by EBS Dealing Resources Inc. and features a fully automated netting process using S.W.I.F.T. MT codes. The system of FX-net is **two-tiered**:

I. **Recording of business transaction**
   Two counterparties confirm a transaction by using a number of electronic instructions and assigning them to the transaction. This first step is finished with the message **"MAC" (matched and confirmed) Status** (S.W.I.F.T. MT 300)

II. **Settlement**

III. The FX-Net system confirms the **net amounts** at the "cut-off" time agreed on by the counterparties and forwards payment orders and notes to the respective parties (S.W.I.F.T. MT 202 and 210). Additionally, a MT 950 statement, which is important for the settlement of the nostro account, is generated.

The **central points of FX-net** are:

- individually agreed upon cut-off times for payments to be delivered and received
- confirmations: real-time confirmation for the transaction, confirmation for the net amount on the value date

S.W.I.F.T. Accord

S.W.I.F.T. Accord is the name of a **netting function integrated in the S.W.I.F.T. system**. All payment messages of banks that are participants of Accord are saved separately and netted at the agreed booking time. The netting function also takes into account transactions with participants who are not participants of Accord, but who process their transactions via S.W.I.F.T. The extensive documentation about the status of confirmations and about the netting positions is delivered to Accord participants, but is also offered to non-participants.

The **central points of Accord** are:

- it comprises FX, money market and derivative transactions
- only S.W.I.F.T. MT codes are handled
- only one participant has to be an Accord member to make netting possible

Netting ist besonders für **Banken mit wenigen Standorten und einer begrenzten Anzahl von Gegenparteien**, mit denen viele gegenläufige Geschäfte abgeschlossen werden, interessant. Diese Punkte treffen besonders auf Market Maker zu.

Die wichtigsten Nettingdienste

Bilaterale Nettingdienste

Zu den bekanntesten bilateralen Nettingdiensten zählen **FX-Net** und **S.W.I.F.T. Accord.**

FX-Net

FX-Net wurde 1986 gegründet und ist im Besitz von FXNet Ltd., ein Konsortium von 14 weltweit aktiven Großbanken. Das System wird von EBS Dealing Resoruces, Inc. betrieben und basiert auf einem voll automatisierten Nettingprozess mithilfe von **S.W.I.F.T.-MT-Codes.** Das System von FX-Net funktioniert **zweistufig:**

I. **Geschäftserfassung**
   Über den Austausch mehrerer elektronischer Anweisungen bestätigen die Parteien das Geschäft, indem sie die Transaktion eingeben und dem Geschäft zuordnen. Der Schritt endet mit dem **„MAC"(matched and confirmed)-Status** (S.W.I.F.T. MT 300).

II. **Settlement**
   Zu dem von den Parteien vereinbarten „Cut-off"-Zeiten bestätigt das FX-Net-System die **Nettobeträge** und sendet die Zahlungsanweisungen bzw. -benachrichtigungen an die betroffenen Parteien (S.W.I.F.T. MT 202 und 210). Weiters wird eine MT 950 Statement Message generiert, die für den Abgleich der Nostrokonten bedeutend ist.

Die **Kernpunkte** von FX-Net sind:

● individuell vereinbarte „Cut-off"-Zeiten, selbst für zu leistende und empfangene Zahlungen
● Bestätigungen: Echtzeit für das Geschäft; am Valutatag für den Nettobetrag

S.W.I.F.T. Accord

S.W.I.F.T. Accord ist eine **in das S.W.I.F.T.-System integrierte Nettingfunktion.** Alle Zahlungsnachrichten von an Accord teilnehmenden Banken werden separat abgespeichert und zur vereinbarten Buchungsschlusszeit saldiert. Beim Netting werden auch Transaktionen mit Teilnehmern berücksichtigt, die nicht am Accord teilnehmen, aber über S.W.I.F.T. ihre Geschäfte abwickeln. Die umfangreichen Dokumentationen über den Status der Bestätigungen und der Nettingpositionen werden nur an die Teilnehmer von Accord gesendet, wobei S.W.I.F.T. bereit ist, diesen Dienst zu jedem gewünschten Zeitpunkt anzubieten.

Kernpunkte von Accord sind:

● Es umfasst FX-, Geldmarkt und Derivative.
● Nur speziell codierte S.W.I.F.T. MTs werden verarbeitet.
● Nur einer der Teilnehmer am Geschäft muss Accord-Mitglied sein, damit Netting stattfindet.

2.2.3. EXCURSUS: *Central Clearing Counterparty*

Definition

A clearinghouse acts as the Central Clearing Counterparty whenever it takes on the **role of the counterparty in a transaction for both sides**. Thus, the clearinghouse also takes on the credit risk of both counterparties.

CCPs have become common in Europe lately and concern not only the derivative market (OTC products) but also cash markets (deposits, repos, stocks, bonds). In Europe, the process of political integration, the development of an internal market for financial services and the objective of developing a pan-European infrastructure for payments and securities clearing and settlement have been the main driving factors for this development.

Because CCPs usually take on the credit risk of both counterparties, **requirements for membership are usually quite strict**, which results in counterparties only being accepted if they have excellent ratings and reputation. There is usually a group called "General Clearing Members" or "Direct Clearing Members" comprised of the only counterparties that are allowed to enter into direct transactions with the clearinghouse. Other participants are only allowed to do deals via a direct clearing member.

There are **sophisticated margin systems** in place to reduce the credit risk within CCP systems. As is customary at exchanges, the margin systems include initial and variation margins. Here, one can additionally distinguish between **net margins** (net balance of all margins) and **gross margins**. Currently, most systems work with net margins.

Most CCP systems automatically include netting agreements (both bilateral and multilateral) for managing payments.

The main **advantages** of CCP systems are:

- reduction of credit risk for all market participants
- reduction of global risk via margining and netting
- security and reliability by utilising margin systems of clearinghouses
- anonymity ("post trade anonymity")

The **biggest players in the European market** are:

- Euronext Cash Markets: stocks and bonds that are traded in Paris, Brussels and Amsterdam
- Eurex CCP: stocks traded on the Eurex
- LCH Equity Clear: stocks traded in London
- LCH RepoClear: bonds and repos
- LCH SwapClear: Plain Vanilla IRS in EUR, USD, GBP, JPY and CHF with a maturity up to 30 years.

Summary

When measuring market risk the following methods are used: GAP Method, Duration Approach, Present Value of a Basis Point, Key Rate Duration and Value at Risk calculations.

The GAP Method assesses the change in the annual profit and loss account that will be caused given a defined change in interest rates. The basic assumption is that the bank's interest rate positions are not sold before maturity. Therefore, possible market value chang-

2.2.3. EXKURS: Central Clearing Counterparty (CCP)

Definition

Ein Clearing House agiert als Central Clearing Counterparty, wenn es die **Rolle des Partners bei einem Geschäft für beide Seiten** übernimmt. Damit übernimmt das Clearing House das Kreditrisiko beider Partner.

CCP sind seit kurzem in Europa sehr üblich geworden und betreffen nicht nur den Derivativmarkt (OTC-Produkte), sondern auch die Geldmärkte (Depots, Repos, Aktien, Anleihen). In Europa sind die Hauptmotivatoren für die Entwicklung der Prozess der europäischen Integration die Entwicklung eines internen Marktes für Finanzdienstleistungen und die Zielsetzung der Entwicklung einer paneuropäischen Infrastruktur für Zahlungen und Wertpapierclearing und -abwicklung.

Da CCPs das gesamte Kreditrisiko der beiden Partner übernehmen, gibt es **üblicherweise sehr strenge Beitrittsbestimmungen,** die dazu führen, dass nur sehr finanzstarke Partner akzeptiert werden. Normalerweise gibt es die „General Clearing Members" oder auch „Direct Clearing Members", die als einzige direkt Geschäfte mit dem Clearing House abschließen können. Die anderen Teilnehmer können nur Geschäfte über die direkten Clearing Members abschließen.

Um das Kreditrisiko abzusichern, gibt es bei den CCP-Systemen **ausgefeilte Margin-Systeme.** Die Margin-Systeme bestehen – wie an der Börse üblich – aus Initial und Variation Margin, wobei hier noch einmal zwischen **Netto-Margins** (Saldierung aller Margins zu einer einzigen Margin) oder **Brutto-Margins** unterschieden werden kann. Derzeit basieren die meisten Systeme auf Netto-Margins.

Bezüglich der Zahlungen sind bei den meisten CCP-Systemen Nettingvereinbarungen automatisch inkludiert. Dies kann sowohl bilaterales Netting als auch multilaterales Netting sein.

Als **Vorteile** von CCP-Systemen gelten:

- Reduktion des Kreditrisikos für die Marktteilnehmer
- Reduktion des globalen Risikos durch Margining und Netting
- hohe Sicherheit durch das Ausnutzen der Margin-Systeme der Clearinghäuser
- Anonymität („post trade anonymity")

Die **großen Spieler am europäischen Markt** sind:

- Euronext Cash Markets: Aktien und Anleihen, die in Paris, Brüssel und Amsterdam gehandelt werden
- Eurex CCP: Aktien, die an der Eurex gehandelt werden
- LCH Equity Clear: Aktien, die in London gehandelt werden
- LCH RepoClear: Anleihen und Repos
- LCH SwapClear: Plain Vanilla Zinsswaps in EUR, USD, GBP, JPY und CHF bis zu einer Laufzeit von 30 Jahren

Zusammenfassung

Bei der Messung des Marktrisikos werden folgende Methoden verwendet: GAP-Methode, Durationsansatz, Present Value of a Basis Point, Key Rate Duration und VaR-Ansätze.
Bei der GAP-Methode wird die p.a.-Ergebnisveränderung bei einer unterstellten Zinsänderung berechnet. Dabei wird angenommen, dass die Positionen nicht vorzeitig aufgelöst

es of positions due to interest rate changes are neglected and only the impact on annual interest earnings and expenditures is taken into consideration. Advantages of the GAP Method are the simple handling and that it is the only kind of interest risk measurement that depicts changes in the bank's net interest income. Drawbacks are the necessity of assumptions, the implication of an unchanging risk structure, the fact that MTM effects are ignored and comparisons with other risks (e.g. FX, stocks, trading book) are not possible. The duration approach is probably the best-known key figure for measuring interest rate risk. Originally, the duration was mainly used for fixed rate bonds. Now the duration is used for all interest rate positions. There are two types of duration: the Macaulay Duration (or simple duration) and the so-called Modified Duration. The calculation of both durations is similar; their interpretation, however, differs significantly. The Macaulay Duration of a bond is the length of time over which the losses/profits due to a one-time change in interest rates are offset by the higher/lower interest rate that the bond holder receives on reinvested coupon payments. The modified duration is an estimation of the price change of an interest instrument due to changes in the price of the respective market interest rates. Thus, the modified duration shows the sensitivity of interest instruments to supposed interest rate changes. In contrast to the GAP analysis, risk is not calculated as a change in the annual net interest income, but as the change of mark-to-market prices under specified (interest rate) scenarios. The main advantages of this method are the simple handling, the high acceptance level, the fact that costs due to any need to sell a position before maturity are taken into account and no assumptions regarding the roll-over of expiring positions are necessary. Points of criticism are the assumption of a flat yield curve, the fact that the basic calculation does not include the effect of yield curve changes, the resulting risk figures cannot be compared to other risks and there is no information on net interest income.

As is the case with the duration approach, the Present Value of a Basis Point (PVBP) method does not estimate changes of the annual net interest income, but the change in the present value of a position. To do so, the exact times of the cashflows of the position (nominal and coupon payments) are identified and mapped to an available number of zero rates. The advantages and points of criticism are the same as in the case with the duration approach.

As for the Key Rate Duration, the Present Values of a Basis Point (or the respective Duration) are calculated and shown for the cash-flows that are mapped to the different maturity bands rather than on an aggregated basis for each individual position. Thus, each position is divided into its cash-flows. The risk is then calculated by moving the interest rate curve and calculating the effect for the different maturity bands separately. The advantages are that costs due to any need to sell a position before maturity are taken into account, no assumptions regarding the roll-over of expiring positions are necessary, changes in the shape of the interest rate curve can be simulated and the relatively simple handling. Points of criticism are that the possible interest curves can only be built up by scenarios, the assumptions on interest rate curve changes are arbitrary and do not allow comparisons to other risk figures and there is no information on net interest income.

In risk measurement, the value at risk approach (VaR) is currently the most widely used method. Generally, the value at risk approach refers to the negative change in value (measured in absolute terms) of an individual position or of a portfolio, which is not exceeded during a certain time with a certain probability.

werden und somit nur die jährliche Zinsertrags- bzw. Zinsaufwandsrechnung durch eine Veränderung der Marktzinsen beeinflusst wird. Vorteile dieser Methode sind die einfache Handhabung und dass man mögliche Veränderungen in der Zinsspanne der Bank darstellen kann. Als Probleme dieser Methode werden die Notwendigkeit von Annahmen für die Verlängerung von laufenden Geschäften, die Unterstellung einer gleichbleibenden Risikostruktur, die Ignoranz der MTM-Effekte und die Nichtvergleichbarkeit mit Risiken anderer Abteilungen genannt.

Der Durationsansatz ist die wohl bekannteste Kennzahl in der Risikomessung von Zinspositionen. Ursprünglich wurde das Konzept der Duration hauptsächlich für festverzinste Anleihen verwendet. Derzeit wird jedoch das Durationskonzept für alle Zinspositionen angewendet. Es gibt zwei Arten von Durations: die einfache Duration (auch Macaulay Duration) und die sogenannte Modified Duration. Die Berechnung beider Methoden ist zwar ähnlich, ihre Interpretation unterscheidet sich jedoch wesentlich. Die einfache Duration ist der Zeitpunkt, zu dem sich Kursverluste auf die Anleihe mit den höheren Zinserträgen bei der Weiterveranlagung der Kupons kompensieren. Die Modified Duration ist eine Kennzahl zur Schätzung der Preisänderung einer Zinsposition bei einer Veränderung der entsprechenden Marktzinsen. Damit zeigt die Modified Duration den Hebel von Zinsinstrumenten bei einer angenommenen Zinsänderung. Zur Bemessung des Risikos wird nicht die Veränderung des p.a.-Zinsergebnisses kalkuliert, sondern die Mark-to-Market-Veränderung bei geändertem Zinsszenario. Vorteile dieser Methode sind die einfache Handhabung und Berechnung, die hohe Akzeptanz, die Abschätzung der Kosten bei einer vorzeitigen Schließung der Risikopositionen und die Nichtunterstellung bezüglich Weiterrollen von auslaufenden Positionen. Als Kritikpunkte werden die Unterstellung einer flachen Zinskurve, die Nichtenthaltung von Effekten von Zinskurvenänderungen im Risiko, die Nichtvergleichbarkeit mit sonstigen Risiken und dass keine Aussagen über die Entwicklung der Zinsspanne getroffen werden können genannt.

Auch die Risikomessung mit dem Present Value of a Basis Point (PVBP) kalkuliert – analog dem Durationsansatz – nicht die p.a.-Veränderung des Zinsergebnisses, sondern die Veränderung des Mark-to-Market-Wertes der Gesamtposition. Dabei werden die Cashflows der Positionen (Kapital und Zinsen) zu den einzelnen Zeitpunkten festgelegt (Mapping) und die Wertveränderung bei einer Zinsveränderung von 1 BP wird (üblicherweise) mit der Zero-Kurve berechnet. Die Vorteile und Kritikpunkte gestalten sich analog dem Durationsansatz.

Bei der Key Rate Duration werden die Present Value of a Basis Point (oder die entsprechende Duration) nicht in Summe pro Einzelposition berechnet und dargestellt, sondern für die Cashflows in den einzelnen Laufzeitbändern. Jede Einzelposition wird somit in ihre Cashflows zerlegt. Das Risiko wird anschließend bestimmt, indem die Zinskurve verändert wird und der Effekt in den einzelnen Laufzeitbändern separat berechnet wird. Vorteile dieser Methode sind die Abschätzung der Kosten bei einer etwaigen vorzeitigen Schließung der Risikopositionen, die Nichtunterstellung bezüglich Weiterrollen von auslaufenden Positionen, die Simulation von Effekten von Zinskurvenänderungen und die relativ einfache Handhabung. Als Kritikpunkte werden die Abbildung der möglichen Zinskurven über Szenarien, die Nichtvergleichbarkeit mit sonstigen Risiken und dass keine Aussagen über die Entwicklung der Zinsspanne getroffen werden können genannt.

Im Bereich der Risikomessung steht das Value-at-Risk-Konzept (VaR) derzeit im Mittelpunkt der Diskussion. Von größeren Banken wird es vor allem zur Quantifizierung der

The most important statistical key figures are the mean or expected value and the variance. The mean measures the average size of a number of values, while the variance measures to which degree these values vary around the mean.

The dispersion of a random variable around the mean is measured as the deviation of outcomes from the expected value ($x_i - EV$). The variance is calculated as the sum of probability-weighted squared deviations of the possible outcomes from the mean.

The standard deviation equals the square root of the variance. In the financial world, the term volatility is often used as a synonym for standard deviation.

Because risk is quantified given a certain probability, it is essential to know the probability distribution of outcomes. The field of statistics offers a number of probability distributions with characteristic properties. One of the most important distributions is the normal distribution or Gauss distribution.

Correlation and covariance are two other important related parameters in the theory of probability. Both parameters quantify the relationship between two random variables, ie, they describe how one random variable changes depending on the change of another random variable. The correlation between random variables A and B corresponds to the covariance between A and B divided by the standard deviations of A and B. The correlation can be interpreted as a normed covariance and its values may range from -1 to +1 by definition.

There are two basic methods to measure financial risks: by analytical solutions or by simulation. In practice the three following approaches to measure VaR are most widely used: Variance-Covariance Method (analytic), Historical Simulation and Monte Carlo Simulation.

The Variance-Covariance method uses the assumption of normally distributed random variables to calculate the VaR of individual position or portfolios with analytic formulas.

If one cannot or does not want to make assumptions about risk factors, the historical simulation, a so-called model-independent method, may be used. When using historical simulation, no assumptions regarding the type, distribution, volatility of risk factors and correlations have to be made. This methodology therefore forgoes an analytic study of the risk factors. In order to make a historical simulation, you need the time series of the market prices of all underlying positions in the portfolio. The basic methodology consists of looking at how the value of the currently held portfolio has fluctuated during the chosen time slot.

The Monte Carlo simulation approach represents a simulation approach based on random numbers. The difference to the historical simulation is that the uncertainty about the future behaviour of risk factors is reproduced not with historical value changes but with random numbers.

As this VaR system attracted plenty of interest from customers, JP Morgan developed a service called RiskMetrics. The underlying idea here is the specification of an interdependency between the risk drivers and the value of the portfolio. During the late 1980's, JP Morgan developed its own firm-wide Value at Risk system. This modelled several hundred risk drivers (eg, interest rates, FX rates, etc).

GARCH (Generalized Autoregressive Conditional Heteroscedasticity) represents an advanced method of volatility measurement and prognosis. The GARCH method is applied in risk management as well as in options trading.

Preisrisiken ihrer Handelsbestände eingesetzt. Allgemein versteht man unter der Value-at-Risk-Methode die in absoluten Geldeinheiten gemessene negative Wertveränderung einer Einzelposition oder eines Portefeuilles, die mit einer bestimmten Wahrscheinlichkeit innerhalb eines festgelegten Zeitraumes nicht überschritten wird.

Die wichtigsten statistischen Maßzahlen sind der Mittelwert bzw. der Erwartungswert und die Varianz. Vom Erwartungswert spricht man dann, wenn die Verteilungsfunktion der Werte, also die Eintrittswahrscheinlichkeit jedes einzelnen Wertes, bekannt ist. Den anhand der Wahrscheinlichkeiten berechneten durchschnittlichen Wert nennt man den Erwartungswert.

Die Streuung wird als Abweichung des eingetretenen Wertes vom Erwartungswert gemessen (x_i–EW). Um die Varianz zu erhalten, werden die quadrierten Abweichungen mit ihren Wahrscheinlichkeiten multipliziert und zum Schluss summiert. Die Standardabweichung ist die Quadratwurzel der Varianz. In der Finanzwelt spricht man anstelle von Standardabweichung häufig von der Volatilität.

Für das Risiko aus statistischer Sicht ist es maßgebend, wie die Wahrscheinlichkeiten der Werte verteilt sind. Deswegen kommt der Wahrscheinlichkeitsverteilung eine besondere Bedeutung zu. In der Statistik findet man eine Anzahl spezieller Verteilungen mit charakteristischen Eigenschaften. Eine der wichtigsten Verteilungen ist die Normalverteilung oder auch Gauß-Verteilung.

Zwei weitere wichtige Maßzahlen aus der Wahrscheinlichkeitsrechnung sind die Korrelation und die Kovarianz. Beide geben den Zusammenhang zwischen zwei Variablen an, d.h., sie zeigen an, wie sich eine Variable ändert, wenn sich gleichzeitig eine andere Variable ändert. Die Korrelation zwischen zwei Variablen A und B enstpricht der Kovarianz zwischen A und B dividiert durch die Standardabweichungen von A und B. Die Korrelation ist also eine Art normierte Kovarianz und liegt zwischen +1 und -1.

Die Messung finanzieller Risiken kann grundsätzlich auf zwei Wegen erfolgen, analytisch (mit Formel) oder durch Simulation. In der Praxis werden in den Banken hauptsächlich drei verschiedene VaR-Ansätze verwendet: Varianz-Kovarianz-Methode (analytisch), historische Simulation und Monte-Carlo-Simulation.

Beim Varianz-Kovarianz-Modell wird der VaR einer Position oder eines Portfolios analytisch berechnet, und zwar unter Annahme von Normalverteilungen.

Will bzw. kann man keine Annahmen über Risikofaktoren machen, so bietet sich als modellunabhängige Methode die sogenannte historische Simulation an. Es werden keine Annahmen über die Verteilung, die Volatilität, die Art der zugrundeliegenden Zufallsprozesse und Korrelationen getroffen, d.h., die Methode verzichtet auf eine analytische Untersuchung der Risikofaktoren. Für die historische Simulation ist es notwendig, über die Zeitreihen der Marktpreise aller im Portfolio enthaltenen Underlyings zu verfügen. Die Methodik besteht darin zu betrachten, wie sich der Wert des aktuellen gehaltenen Portfolios während eines ausgewählten Zeitfensters verhalten hat:

Bei der Monte-Carlo-Simulation handelt es sich um ein Simulationsverfahren auf der Basis von Zufallszahlen. Der Unterschied zur historischen Simulation ist, dass die Unsicherheit über das zukünftige Verhalten von Risikofaktoren nicht mit historischen Wertänderungen, sondern mit Zufallszahlen abgebildet wird.

In den späten 80er-Jahren entwickelte JP Morgan sein eigenes konzernweites Value-at-Risk-System. Dabei wurden mehrere hundert Risikotreiber (z.B. Zinsen, FX-Kurse etc.) modelliert. Die grundlegende Idee hier ist, einen Zusammenhang zwischen den Risikotreibern und dem Wert des Portfolios zu spezifizieren. Da dieses System auf großes In-

Credit measurement has been an area of constant progress during the last years. The application of the VaR approach in credit measurement made it possible to measure credit risk so that results would be comparable with market risks, which marked a breakthrough in the area of risk management.

Value at Risk measures risk potential, ie, it quantifies to what degree actual losses might deviate from expected loss. Accordingly, Value at Risk (VaR) is defined as the level of loss that will not be exceeded over a specified period of time with a certain probability.

In general, the term netting refers to agreements between two or more counterparties that allow positive and negative values to be set off against each other given a certain event. There are different types of netting agreements that differ with respect to the type and amount of the included payments (netting by novations and close-out netting) and the number of participants and the design of the netting system (bilateral and multilateral netting).

FX-Net and S.W.I.F.T Accord represent two of the best-known bilateral netting services. A clearinghouse acts as the Central Clearing Counterparty whenever it takes on the role of the counterparty in a transaction for both sides. Thus, the clearinghouse also takes on the credit risk of both counterparties.

2.3. Practice Questions

1. To which purpose is normal distribution often assumed in trading?
   a) in order to calculate risk
   b) in order to confuse the traders
   c) in order to calculate the limits for traders
   d) in order to value positions marked-to-market
2. Explain briefly the basic principles of the GAP Method!
3. Name in two advantages and drawbacks each of the GAP Method!
4. Name three adavantages and points of criticism each of the concept of Modified Duration!
5. What is usually meant by the term VaR?
   a) risk measure for open trading positions
   b) expected value of an exchange rate
   c) normal distribution trading results
   d) mark-to-market of the daily position
6. What does the variance-covariance method in risk measurement take into account?
   a) future market movements
   b) historical losses of the trader
   c) non-linearity of the parameters
   d) correlation between positions
7. What are the three most commonly used approaches to calculate VaR in practice?
   a) Copula Approach
   b) Historical Simulation
   c) Monte Carlo Simulation

teresse bei Kunden von JP Morgan stieß, wurde ein Service unter dem Namen RiskMetrics entwickelt.

GARCH (Generalized Autoregressive Conditional Heteroskedasticity) stellt eine fortgeschrittene Methode der Volatilitätsmessung und -prognose dar. Anwendung findet die GARCH-Methode sowohl im Risikomanagement als auch bei Optionshändlern.

Im Bereich Kreditrisikomessung wurden in den letzten Jahren sehr große Fortschritte erzielt. Während es in der Vergangenheit kaum Ansätze gab, Kreditrisiken zu messen und miteinander vergleichbar zu machen, konnte der Durchbruch in der Risikomessung durch die Übertragung des VaR-Ansatzes auf das Kreditrisiko erzielt werden.

Über den Value at Risk wird jenes Risikopotenzial gemessen, das angibt, inwieweit der tatsächliche Verlust von den erwarteten Verlusten abweichen kann. Dementsprechend wird der Value at Risk (VaR) definiert als der maximale Verlust, der mit einer bestimmten Wahrscheinlichkeit über einen bestimmten Zeithorizont nicht überschritten wird.

Unter Netting versteht man die vereinbarte Aufrechnung von gegenseitigen Positionen oder Verpflichtungen von Geschäftspartnern oder Teilnehmern eines Systems. Beim Netting unterscheidet man bezüglich Art und Umfang der inkludierten Zahlungsströme (Novations-Netting und Close-out Netting) und Anzahl der Teilnehmer am und Ausgestaltung des Nettingsystems (bilaterales und multilaterales Netting).

Zu den bekanntesten bilateralen Nettingdiensten zählen FX-Net und S.W.I.F.T. Accord.

Ein Clearing House agiert als Central Clearing Counterparty, wenn es die Rolle des Partners bei einem Geschäft für beide Seiten übernimmt. Damit übernimmt das Clearing House das Kreditrisiko beider Partner.

2.3. Wiederholungsfragen

1. Wozu wird die Normalverteilung im Handel häufig angenommen?
   a) um das Risiko zu berechnen
   b) um die Händler zu verwirren
   c) um die Limite der Händler zu berechnen
   d) um die Positionen Mark-to-Market zu bewerten
2. Erklären Sie kurz das Prinzip der GAP-Methode!
3. Nennen Sie jeweils zwei Vorteile bzw. Probleme der GAP-Methode!
4. Nennen Sie jeweils drei Vorteile bzw. Kritikpunkte am Konzept der Modified Duration!
5. Was wird üblicherweise unter dem Begriff VaR verstanden?
   a) Risikomesszahl für die offenen Handelspositionen
   b) Erwartungswert eines Devisenkurses
   c) Normalverteilung der Ergebnisse des Handels
   d) Mark-to-Market der täglichen Position
6. Was berücksichtigt die Varianz-Kovarianz-Methode in der Risikomessung?
   a) zukünftige Marktschwankungen
   b) historische Verluste des Händlers
   c) Nicht-Linearität der Parameter
   d) Korrelationseffekte zwischen den Positionen
7. Welche sind die drei am häufigsten verwendeten Ansätze zur Berechnung eines VaR?
   a) Copula-Ansatz
   b) Historische Simulation
   c) Monte-Carlo-Simulation

    d) Variance-Covariance Approach

    e) Back-Testing

    f) Markowitz Model

8. Explain briefly the connection between correlation and covariance!

9. Which information do you need to be able to define confidence intervals for a normally distributed variable?

    a) only mean

    b) only standard deviation

    c) only variance

    d) mean, standard deviation and skewness

    e) mean, standard deviation and variance

10. How do historical simulations differ from other standard VaR measurement approaches?

    a) They have a higher accuracy.

    b) They take end of day prices into account.

    c) They take security intervals into account.

    d) No assumptions regarding the distribution of the values are made.

11. What does Monte Carlo Simulation in risk management stand for?

    a) stress testing

    b) taking into account the worst case scenario

    c) calculation of risk with the help of a random generator

    d) The trading results of the bank are as uncertain as a visit to the casino.

12. What does RiskMetrics stand for?

    a) market risk limit

    b) credit risk limit

    c) correlation matrix

    d) interpreation of a risk number

    e) value-at-risk model developed by JP Morgan

13. Which approach is the original value-at-risk calculation of JP Morgan based on?

    a) historical cimulation

    b) Monte Carlo Simulation

    c) GAP analysis

    d) variance-covariance approach

14. Name one advantage and disadvantage each of Monte Carlo Simulation!

15. Name two disadvantages of historical simulation!

16. What are the two main assumptions of the GARCH Model?

17. What is meant by economic capital?

18. What is meant by netting?

19. What are the two best-known bilateral netting services?

20. What does the term "mean variance" in the context of capital market theory stand for?

    a) tendency of market volatility to revert to a long-term mean

    b) for the variance of the mean depending on the observation period

    c) calculation of standard deviation as mean of the variance

    d) description of a risky investment with two parameters

d) Varianz-Kovarianz-Ansatz

e) Back-Testing

f) Markowitz-Modell

8. Erklären Sie kurz den Zusammenhang von Korrelation und Kovarianz!

9. Welche Informationen benötigen Sie, um Aussagen über Konfidenzintervalle einer normalverteilten Variable treffen zu können?

a) nur Erwartungswert

b) nur Standardabweichung

c) nur Varianz

d) Erwartungswert, Standardabweichung, Schiefe

e) Erwartungswert, Standardabweichung, Varianz

10. Wodurch unterscheiden sich historische Simulationen von den anderen klassischen VaR-Ansätzen?

a) durch eine höhere Treffsicherheit

b) durch die Berücksichtigung von Schlusskursen

c) durch die Berücksichtigung eines Sicherheitsintervalls

d) dadurch, dass keine Annahmen hinsichtlich der Verteilung der Werte vorgenommen werden

11. Was bedeutet Monte-Carlo-Simulation in der Risikomessung?

a) Stress-Testing

b) Berücksichtigung des Worst Case

c) Berechnung des Risikos mithilfe eines Zufallsgenerators

d) Die Handelsergebnisse der Bank sind so unsicher wie das Ergebnis im Spielcasino.

12. Wofür steht RiskMetrics?

a) Marktrisikolimit

b) Kreditrisikolimit

c) Korrelationsmatrix

d) Interpretation einer Risikokennzahl

e) Value-at-Risk-Modell von JP Morgan

13. Auf welchem Ansatz beruht die ursprüngliche Methodik von JP Morgan zur VaR-Ermittlung?

a) Historische Simulation

b) Monte-Carlo-Simulation

c) GAP-Analyse

d) Varianz-Kovarianz-Ansatz

14. Nennen Sie jeweils einen Vor- bzw. Nachteil der Monte-Carlo-Simulation!

15. Nennen Sie zwei Nachteile der historischen Simulation!

16. Von welchen zwei grundlegenden Annahmen geht das GARCH-Modell aus?

17. Was versteht man unter ökonomischem Kapital?

18. Was versteht man unter Netting?

19. Wie heißen die beiden bekanntesten bilateralen Nettingdienste?

20. Wofür steht der Begriff Mean-Variance in der Kapitalmarkttheorie?

a) dass die Marktvolatilität langfristig immer gegen eine bestimmte mittlere Varianz strebt

b) für die Schwankungen des Mittelwerts abhängig von der Beobachtungsperiode

c) steht für die Standardabweichung, die dem Mittel der Varianz entspricht

d) dass risikobehaftete Titel mit zwei Parametern beschrieben werden können

3. Limits

In this chapter you learn ...
- which types of limits exist.
- which credit risk limits are used.
- what is meant by a counterparty limit.
- what is meant by a country or industry limit.
- what should be considered at determining market risk limits.
- which trader limits are used.
- what is meant by an overnight limit.
- what is meant by an intraday limit.
- what is meant by a quotation limit.
- what is meant by a stop-loss limit.
- what is meant by a time mismatch limit.

Efficient risk monitoring needs **adequate risk measurement** as well as some **internal prerequisites**. The following points should be considered:

- back office support
- internal and external risk monitoring
- mark-to-market developments of the trading positions
- implementation of limit systems for trading

In this section, we want to discuss several **types of limits**. As far as the other prerequisites are concerned, we refer to the appendix that deals with internal surveillance requirements and the minimum requirements for trading operations.

Banks must not only measure, but also limit the risks that they are taking. How much risk is appropriate for a bank depends on the bank's **risk-bearing capacity**, which is closely linked to the bank's equity and equity structure, but also on the **strategies and the general risk attitude of the shareholders**. Generally, we distinguish between:

- limits that deal with credit risk
- limit that curtail market risk
- limits for liquidity risks of banks.

It should be noted that in practice there are a number of limits and systems. Therefore, we only want to discuss some of the limits and their possible forms.

3.1. Credit risk Limits

Counterparty limits

Typically, counterparty limits want to **limit the total position per counterparty**. They deal with classical default risk, replacement risks of derivatives and settlement risk. Within banks, counterparty limits have to be allocated within individual departments. In prac-

3. Limite

In diesem Kapitel lernen Sie ...

- welche möglichen Arten von Limiten es gibt.
- welche Kreditrisikolimite verwendet werden.
- was man unter Partnerlimit versteht.
- was man unter Länder- bzw. Branchenlimit versteht.
- was bei der Erstellung des Marktrisikos beachtet werden muss.
- welche Händlerlimite verwendet werden.
- was man unter Overnight-Limit versteht.
- was man unter Intraday-Limit bzw. Daylight-Limit versteht.
- was man unter Quotierungslimit versteht.
- was man unter Stop-Loss-Limit versteht.
- was man unter Laufzeit-Mismatch-Limit versteht.

Eine effiziente Risikokontrolle unterstellt sowohl eine **adäquate Risikomessung** als auch die notwendigen **internen Voraussetzungen**. Darunter sind unter anderem folgende Punkte zu subsumieren:

- Backoffice-Unterstützung
- Interne und externe Risikokontrolle
- Mark-to-Market-Bewertung der Handelspositionen
- Installation von Limitsystemen für den Handel

In diesem Kapitel möchten wir auf die möglichen **Arten von Limiten** eingehen. Hinsichtlich der anderen Voraussetzungen verweisen wir auf die in Teil V angeführten Prüfungsschwerpunkte der internen Revision sowie auf die Mindestanforderungen an das Betreiben von Handelsgeschäften.

Banken müssen die Risiken, die sie eingehen, nicht nur messen, sondern sie auch entsprechend begrenzen. Die Höhe des angemessenen Risikos hängt einerseits von der **Risikotragfähigkeit** der Bank ab, die mit dem Eigenkapital und der Struktur des Eigenkapitals eng verbunden ist. Andererseits spielt aber auch die **Strategie und die allgemeine Risikoeinstellung der Anteilseigner** eine wesentliche Rolle. Generell unterscheiden wir zwischen:

- Limiten, die das Kreditrisiko der Bank begrenzen sollen,
- Limiten, die das Marktrisiko begrenzen und
- Limiten, die das Liquiditätsrisiko begrenzen.

In der Praxis gibt es eine Vielzahl von Limiten und Zuordnungssystemen. Im vorliegenden Kapitel werden nur einige ausgewählte Beispiele näher dargestellt.

3.1. Kreditrisikolimite

Partnerlimite

Charakteristisch für Partnerlimite ist die **Begrenzung des Gesamtengagements pro Partner**. Ein weiteres Merkmal ist die Berücksichtigung des klassischen Risikos, des Wiederbeschaffungsrisikos bei derivativen Produkten und des Settlementrisikos. In Banken ist bei

tice, there are **rigid systems** that allot the total risk to individual products and departments, as well as **systems that set the total risk**, which is accessible to everyone on a first come first served basis. Both systems have **advantages and disadvantages**. With the rigid allotment, some departments do not strain their limits while others have to turn down profitable transactions due to their strained limits. As for the flexible system, it does not guarantee that the most profitable transactions eventually get carried out. If, in the extreme case, one negative credit transaction uses up the bank's total limit, none of the other departments will be able to carry out any transactions whatsoever. **Usually**, banks make use of **rigid systems**, which are however watered down internally, so that departments are able to pass on limits internally to others.

Country limits

Regardless of the individual customer, the **total credit risk that a bank is willing to take is limited by countries as well**. In addition to the counterparty risk, country limits can be added depending on the risk in a particular country. This way, it could become impossible to make a deal due to country limits, though the counterparty limit would still have allowed it.

Industry limits

Industry limits follow the same principle as country limits.

3.2. Market risk limits

Limit of the bank's total positions

When determining market risk limits, the aim should be to **take all the risks of the bank into account**. To make this limit operational, it must be **allocated to the individual organisational units**; depending on the organisational structure of the bank, one might, as a first step, divide the total risk limit into interest rate risks, currency risks, share risks and other risks.

Within the interest rate risk, risks in the money market and the capital market could be differentiated; and within the capital market one could further distinguish between single products or individual dealers.

den Partnerlimiten die interne Aufteilung auf einzelne Abteilungen festzulegen. In der Praxis gibt es sowohl **starre Systeme**, bei denen das Gesamtlimit auf einzelne Produkte und Abteilungen aufgeteilt wird, als **auch Systeme, bei denen alle auf ein Limit zugreifen und der Erste zum Zug kommt**. Beide Systeme haben **Vor- und Nachteile**. Bei einer starren Vergabe kann es passieren, dass einzelne Abteilungen ihre Limite nicht oder nicht voll ausnutzen, während in anderen Abteilungen gewinnbringende Geschäfte aufgrund des mangelnden Limits abgelehnt werden müssen. Bei der zweiten Variante ist für die Bank nicht sichergestellt, dass das für die Bank profitabelste Geschäft mit dem Kunden getätigt werden kann. Werden im Extremfall über ein für die Bank negatives Kreditgeschäft die gesamten Limite aufgebraucht, kommen alle anderen Abteilungen nicht mehr zum Zug. **Üblicherweise** findet man in den Banken das **System der starren Limitvergabe**. Dieses System wird jedoch dadurch flexibel, dass die einzelnen Abteilungen sich intern die Limite weitergeben können.

Länderlimite

Unabhängig vom Einzelkunden muss die Bank das **gesamte Kreditrisiko, das sie bereit ist, in einzelnen Ländern einzugehen, beschränken**. Je nach Einschätzung des Risikos in unterschiedlichen Ländern kann neben dem Partnerrisiko auch noch ein Länderlimit bestehen. So kann es vorkommen, dass ein Geschäft nicht gemacht werden kann, obwohl noch für den einzelnen Partner Platz im Limit bestehen würde, da das Gesamtengagement des Landes bereits erreicht ist.

Branchenlimite

Hier sind ähnliche Überlegungen wie beim Länderlimit anzusetzen.

3.2. Marktrisikolimite

Gesamtbankpositionslimit

Das Ziel bei der Erstellung des Marktrisikos muss die **Erfassung des Risikos für die gesamte Bank** sein. Um dieses Limit zu operationalisieren, muss es **auf die einzelnen organisatorischen Einheiten umgelegt** werden: So kann – je nach Organisationsform der Bank – das Gesamtrisikolimit in einem ersten Schritt auf Zins-, Währungs-, Aktien- und sonstige Risiken verteilt werden.

Im Zinsbereich könnte dann weiterhin die Unterteilung nach Geld- und Kapitalmarkt, im Geldmarkt dann möglicherweise eine Aufteilung zwischen einzelnen Produkten bzw. einzelnen Händlern vorgenommen werden.

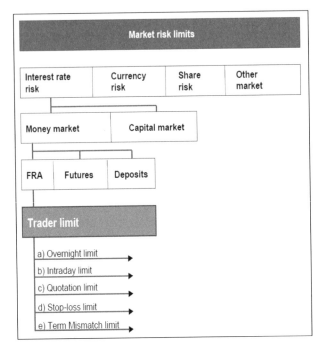

General requirements

- On the basis of the risk-taking capability, a system of limits for restricting the market price risks with consideration of risk concentrations should be established.
- It is not allowed to make a deal with market price risks without a market price risk limit.
- The methods for estimating the market price risks should be checked regularly. It should be checked, if the methods also lead to exploitable results in the case of serious market disruptions. For prolonged cases of missing, obsolete or distorted market prices alternative valuation methods should be determined for the main positions.
- The determined results of accounting and risk controlling should be made plausible regularly.
- In regular intervals, at least quarterly, a risk report about the market price risks incurred by the institution should be prepared and provided to the management. The report should contain the following information including the internal trades::
  a) an overview about the risk- and yield development of the positions with market price risks,
  b) significant limit exceedances,
  c) changes of the main assumptions or parameter, which are the basis for the methods of estimating the market price risks,
  d) conspicuousnesses at the reconciliation of the trading positions (e.g. concerning trading volumes, impacts on P&L, lapse ratios).
     For these purposes of the risk report you can either take into account on the development of the yield relating to commercial law (including executory profits and losses) or on the development of the economic yield.

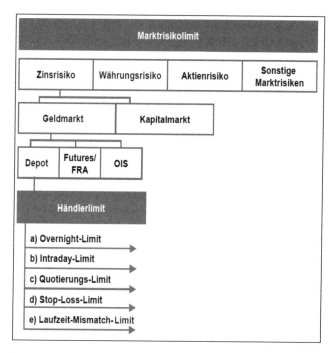

Allgemeine Anforderungen

- Auf der Grundlage der Risikotragfähigkeit ist ein System von Limits zur Begrenzung der Marktpreisrisiken unter Berücksichtigung von Risikokonzentrationen einzurichten.
- Ohne Marktpreisrisikolimit darf kein mit Marktpreisrisiken behaftetes Geschäft abgeschlossen werden.
- Die Verfahren zur Beurteilung der Marktpreisrisiken sind regelmäßig zu überprüfen. Es ist zu überprüfen, ob die Verfahren auch bei schwerwiegenden Marktstörungen zu verwertbaren Ergebnissen führen. Für länger anhaltende Fälle fehlender, veralteter oder verzerrter Marktpreise sind für wesentliche Positionen alternative Bewertungsmethoden festzulegen.
- Die im Rechnungswesen und Risikocontrolling ermittelten Ergebnisse sind regelmäßig zu plausibilisieren.
- In regelmäßigen Abständen, mindestens aber vierteljährlich, ist ein Risikobericht über die vom Institut eingegangenen Marktpreisrisiken zu erstellen und der Geschäftsleitung zur Verfügung zu stellen. Der Bericht hat unter Einbeziehung der internen Handelsgeschäfte folgende Informationen zu umfassen:
  a) einen Überblick über die Risiko- und Ergebnisentwicklung der mit Marktpreisrisiken behafteten Positionen,
  b) bedeutende Limitüberschreitungen,
  c) Änderungen der wesentlichen Annahmen oder Parameter, die den Verfahren zur Beurteilung der Marktpreisrisiken zu Grunde liegen,
  d) Auffälligkeiten bei der Abstimmung der Handelspositionen (z.B. hinsichtlich der Handelsvolumina, GuV-Auswirkungen, Stornoquoten).
  Für die Zwecke des Risikoberichts kann entweder auf die Entwicklung des unternehmensrechtlichen Ergebnisses (einschließlich schwebender Gewinne und Verluste) oder auch auf die Entwicklung des betriebswirtschaftlichen Ergebnisses abgestellt werden.

Trader limits

Overnight limit

The limit on the **open positions at the end of a day**. The overnight limit is equal to the position limit, i.e. the risk limit for the individual dealer. Depending on the market risk, the risk can be calculated per dealer by using a **scenario analysis** (e.g. 1% change in the interest rate, 5% change in exchange rate) or by using **complex methods** (e.g. the value at risk approach). In its simplest form, overnight limits may be plain volume limits (e.g. open position may not exceed 10m EUR/USD overnight).

Intraday limit

Even if a dealer is not allowed to have any open overnight positions, he still must be allowed to have open positions during the day. This intraday limit is fixed usually according to the dealer's qualification and position and **depends on the market liquidity of the instrument**. Besides, the limit will also **depend on the position of the bank in the market**, i.e. if it is market maker for the instrument or not.

Quotation limit

The quotation limit **limits the volume for which a dealer is allowed to quote**. Similar to the intraday limit, the quotation limit **depends on the dealer's qualification and position**, on the market liquidity for this instrument, and on the position of the bank in this market. For example, a EUR dealer might have a quotation limit of 100m, i.e. this dealer has the right to make FRA quotations up to DEM 100m per call.

Stop-loss limit

In addition to the overnight limit, there is the possibility of having a stop-loss limit. A stop-loss limit restricts the **maximum loss that the bank might be willing to accept on a particular position**. If this limit is exceeded, the dealer must close his position even if he has not exceeded his own position limit yet.

Term mismatch limit

In addition to the position's total limit, a **limit on open positions** can be fixed for individual terms. A FRA dealer's maximum open position can be limited, for example, in such a way that he can hold an open position of 1,000m for a term of six months, while for a term of one year the open position is limited to 500m. A similar limit may be implemented for an FX dealer, too.

Additional restrictions can be levied either by **instrument limits** that limit the liquidity risk in the individual markets, or by **term limits** that limit the maximum term of an instrument.

Market price risks of the trading book

It is recommended to treat the market price risks of the trading book in the following way:

- It should be secured that the deals with market price risks of the trading book are immediately taken into account on the relevant limits and furthermore that the responsible manager is prompt informed about his relevant limits and their current utilization. For exceeding limits appropriate measures should be taken. If necessary, an escalation procedure should be initiated.

Händlerlimite

Overnight-Limit

Unter Overnight-Limit versteht man die **Begrenzung der offenen Position am Ende des Tages.** Das Overnight-Limit entspricht dem Positionslimit, d.h. dem Risikolimit für den einzelnen Händler. Je nach Bemessung des Marktrisikos kann die Berechnung des Risikos pro Händler über eine **Szenarioanalyse (z.B.** 1% Zinsänderung, 5% Währungsänderung) oder aber über **komplizierte Verfahren (z.B. Value-at-Risk-Ansatz)** festgelegt werden. In seiner einfachsten Form kann das Overnight-Limit jedoch auch ein reines Volumslimit sein (z.B. offene Position darf über Nacht nicht größer als EUR/USD 10 Mio. sein).

Intraday-Limit/Daylight-Limit

Auch wenn beispielsweise ein Händler keine offene Overnight-Position fahren darf, so muss er doch die Möglichkeit haben, während des Tages zeitweise eine offene Position zu halten. Dieses Intraday-Limit wird üblicherweise **abhängig von der Qualifikation des Händlers und der Marktliquidität in dem gehandelten Instrument** festgelegt. Auch wird dieses Limit abhängig davon sein, **ob die Bank in diesem Instrument eine Market-Maker-Funktion innehat oder nicht.**

Quotierungslimit

Unter Quotierungslimit versteht man die **Begrenzung des Volumens, für das quotiert werden darf.** Ähnlich wie beim Intraday-Limit **hängt** das Quotierungslimit **von der Qualifikation und Funktion des Händlers, der Marktliquidität des Instrumentes und der Rolle der Bank in diesem Markt ab.** So kann beispielsweise das Quotierungslimit für einen EUR-FRA-Händler mit 100 Mio. begrenzt sein, d.h., dass dieser Händler das Recht hat, FRA-Quotierungen bis zu EUR 100 Mio. pro Anfrage abzugeben.

Stop-Loss-Limit

Zusätzlich zu dem Overnight-Limit kann es noch ein Stop-Loss-Limit geben. Ein Stop-Loss-Limit begrenzt den **maximalen Verlust, den die Bank bereit ist, auf eine Position zu akzeptieren.** Ist dieses Limit erreicht, muss der Händler seine Position schließen, auch wenn er noch Platz in seinem Positionslimit hat.

Laufzeit-Mismatch-Limit

Auch hier kann zusätzlich zum gesamten Positionslimit noch eine **Grenze für die offenen Risiken in den einzelnen Laufzeiten** festgelegt werden. So kann die maximale offene Position für einen FRA-Händler zusätzlich begrenzt werden, indem er beispielsweise eine offenen Position von 1.000 Mio. in einer Laufzeit bis sechs Monate fahren kann, während in der Laufzeit bis ein Jahr diese offene Position auf 500 Mio. begrenzt ist. Ein ähnliches Limit kann auch für einen Devisenterminhändler installiert werden.

Zusätzliche Begrenzungen können noch durch **Instrumentenlimite,** die das Risiko der Liquidität in den einzelnen Märkten begrenzen, und durch **Laufzeitlimite,** die für einzelne Instrumente die maximale Laufzeit eingrenzen, erreicht werden.

Marktpreisrisiken des Handelsbuches

Es wird empfohlen, die Marktpreisrisiken des Handelsbuches folgendermaßen zu behandeln:

* Es ist sicherzustellen, dass die mit Marktpreisrisiken behafteten Geschäfte des Handelsbuches unverzüglich auf die einschlägigen Limite angerechnet werden und der Positionsverantwortliche über die für ihn relevanten Limits und ihre aktuelle Ausnutzung zeitnah informiert ist. Bei Limitüberschreitungen sind geeignete Maßnahmen zu treffen. Gegebenenfalls ist ein Eskalationsverfahren einzuleiten.

- Positions with market price risks in the trading book should be valued daily.
- The yield for the trading book should be determined daily. The established risk positions should be consolidated to an aggregate risk position at least once a day at closing time. The aggregate risk positions, yield and limit capacity should be basically reported to the responsible manager for risk controlling prompt on the next day. The report should be matched with the trade areas. For non-trading book institutions with manageable risk positions in the trading book it is possible to renounce on the daily reporting in favour of a longer regular cycle.
- The determined risk values, calculated by a risk model, should be continuously compared with the real development.

Summary

Banks must not only measure, but also limit the risks they are taking. Generally, we distinguish between limits that deal with credit risk, limits that curtail market risk and limits for liquidity risks of banks. The credit risk limits are counterparty limit, country limit and industry limit.

Typically, counterparty limits aim to limit the total position per counterparty. In practice, there are rigid systems that allot the total risk to individual products and departments, as well as systems that set the total risk which is available to everyone on a first-come-first-served basis.

Regardless of the individual customer, the total credit risk that a bank is willing to take is limited by countries as well. When determining market risk limits, the aim should be to take all the risks of the bank into account. These market risk limits are used: overnight limit, intraday limit, quotation limit, stop-loss limit and time mismatch limit.

An overnight limit is the limit on open positions at the end of a trading day.

The intraday limit is usually fixed according to the dealer's qualification and position and depends on the market liquidity of the instrument.

The quotation limit restricts the volume at which a dealer is allowed to quote.

A stop-loss limit restricts the maximum loss that the bank might be willing to accept on a particular position.

In addition to the position's total limit, a limit on open positions can be fixed for individual terms with a term mismatch limit.

3.3. Practice Questions

1. What does a counterparty limit determine?
    a) maximum credit risk per counterparty
    b) number of transactions per counterparty
    c) maximum loss per counterparty
    d) maximum number of counterparties
2. Which other credit risk limits are used further to the counterparty limit?
3. What is meant by an overnight limit?
4. What does the intraday limit attempt to control?
    a) credit risk
    b) the size of the position at the end of the day
    c) market risk during a day
    d) the amount to be settled on a given day

- Die mit Marktpreisrisiken behafteten Positionen des Handelsbuches sind täglich zu bewerten.
- Es ist täglich ein Ergebnis für das Handelsbuch zu ermitteln. Die bestehenden Risikopositionen sind mindestens einmal täglich zum Geschäftsschluss zu Gesamtrisikopositionen zusammenzufassen. Die Gesamtrisikopositionen, Ergebnisse und Limitauslastungen sind grundsätzlich zeitnah am nächsten Geschäftstag dem für das Risikocontrolling zuständigen Geschäftsleiter zu berichten. Die Meldung ist mit den Handelsbereichen abzustimmen. Bei Nicht-Handelsbuchinstituten mit unter Risikogesichtspunkten überschaubaren Positionen im Handelsbuch kann auf die tägliche Berichterstattung zugunsten eines längeren Turnus verzichtet werden.
- Die modellmäßig ermittelten Risikowerte sind fortlaufend mit der tatsächlichen Entwicklung zu vergleichen.

Zusammenfassung

Banken müssen die Risiken, die sie eingehen, nicht nur messen, sondern sie auch entsprechend begrenzen. Generell unterscheiden wir zwischen Limiten, die das Kreditrisiko der Bank begrenzen sollen, Limiten, die das Marktrisiko begrenzen, und Limiten, die das Liquiditätsrisiko begrenzen. Zu den Kreditrisikolimiten zählen das Partnerlimit, das Länderlimit und das Branchenlimit.

Charakteristisch für Partnerlimite ist die Begrenzung des Gesamtengagements pro Partner. In der Praxis gibt es sowohl starre Systeme, bei denen das Gesamtlimit auf einzelne Produkte und Abteilungen aufgeteilt wird, als auch Systeme, bei denen alle auf ein Limit zugreifen und der Erste zum Zug kommt.

Ein Länderlimit bedeutet, dass die Bank, unabhängig vom Einzelkunden, das gesamte Kreditrisiko, das sie bereit ist, in einzelnen Ländern einzugehen, beschränken muss.

Das Ziel bei der Erstellung des Marktrisikos muss die Erfassung des Risikos für die gesamte Bank sein.

Im Geldmarkt werden folgende Händlerlimite verwendet: Overnight-Limit, Intraday-Limit/Daylight-Limit, Quotierungslimit, Stop-Loss-Limit und Laufzeit-Mismatch-Limit.

Unter Overnight-Limit versteht man die Begrenzung der offenen Position am Ende des Tages. Unter Quotierungslimit versteht man die Begrenzung des Volumens, für das quotiert werden darf. Wenn beispielsweise ein Händler keine offene Overnight-Position fahren darf, so muss er doch die Möglichkeit haben, während des Tages zeitweise eine offene Position zu halten. Hierfür wird ein Intraday-Limit verwendet, das üblicherweise abhängig von der Qualifikation des Händlers und der Marktliquidität in dem gehandelten Instrument festgelegt wird. Ein Stop-Loss-Limit begrenzt den maximalen Verlust, den die Bank bereit ist, auf eine Position zu akzeptieren. Mit einem Laufzeit-Mismatch-Limit kann zusätzlich zum gesamten Positionslimit noch eine Grenze für die offenen Risiken in den einzelnen Laufzeiten festgelegt werden.

3.3. Wiederholungsfragen

1. Was begrenzt ein Partnerlimit?
   a) maximales Kreditrisiko pro Partner
   b) Anzahl der Geschäfte pro Partner
   c) maximaler Verlust pro Partner
   d) maximale Anzahl möglicher Geschäftspartner

5. What does a volume limit restrict?
    a) minimum quotable spread
    b) maximum quotable spread
    c) the volume for which a quote can be made
    d) the quote when a certain price is reached
6. What is a stop-loss limit?
    a) the limit for the worst case result
    b) the maximum loss allowed for a year
    c) the volatility of the exchange rate at which the trader has to close his position
    d) the maximum loss at which a position must be closed
7. What is meant by a time mismatch limit?

2. Welche Kreditrisikolimite werden neben dem Partnerlimit noch verwendet?
3. Was versteht man unter einem Overnight-Limit?
4. Was versucht das Daylight-Limit zu kontrollieren?
   a) Kreditrisiko
   b) Größe einer Position zu Tagesende
   c) Marktrisiko während eines Tages
   d) Betrag, der an einem bestimmten Tag glattgestellt werden muss
5. Was begrenzt ein Quotierungslimit?
   a) minimal zu quotierenden Spread
   b) maximal zu quotierenden Spread
   c) Volumen, für das quotiert werden darf
   d) Quotierung, wenn ein vorgegebener Marktpreis erreicht wird
6. Was ist ein Stop-Loss-Limit?
   a) Ein Stop-Loss-Limit ist die Begrenzung des Worst-Case-Ergebnisses.
   b) Ein Stop-Loss-Limit ist der maximal budgetierte Verlust innerhalb eines Jahres.
   c) Ein Stop-Loss-Limit ist die Schwankung des Devisenkurses, bei der der Händler seine Position schließen muss.
   d) Ein Stop-Loss-Limit ist die Festlegung des maximalen Verlustes, bei dem die Position geschlossen werden muss.
7. Was versteht man unter dem Laufzeit-Mismatch-Limit?

4. Basel II

In this chapter you learn ...
- more about the motives and principles of Basel I.
- which methods are used for calculating capital requirements.
- which Basel I points are criticised.
- what are the basics and principles of Basel II.
- what are the three pillars of Basel II.
- about the differences between Basel I and Basel II.
- about the differences between standard approach and IRB approach.
- which risk asset classes are distinguished.
- about the input parameters for calculating risk-weighted assets.
- about the differences between the standard IRB approach and advanced IRB approach.
- which methods are used for calculating market and interest rate risk.
- which methods are used for calculating replacement risk.
- more about the calculation of replacement risk by means of maturity method and mark to market method.
- which modifications will arise in the calculation of replacement risk by Basel III.

4.1. The history of Basel II

Even though market risks still represent the biggest part of risks that are traded via a bank's treasury department, the role of **credit risks** has been constantly increasing. On the one hand, we have the credit risk stemming from OTC transactions, while on the other hand credit derivatives have been directly traded ever since the late nineties.

The following chapter deals with Basel II, the current international regulatory framework for the supervisory treatment of banking risks.

History, motives and principles

Because banks play a key role in the monetary system, governments are interested in a **stable banking system**. Therefore, banks should have **enough capital** at their disposal in order to be able to cover possible losses and to maintain their business operations at all times.

Before the introduction of the **1988 Basel Accord (= Basel I)**, countries had national regulatory frameworks which banks had to adhere to irrespective of their individual risk profiles. Off-balance sheet positions were generally ignored.

Following concerns about a constantly diminishing equity position due to increasing (international) competition among banks, the Basel Committee on Banking Supervision (founded in 1974) was assigned the duty to design an international regulatory framework for banks.

Basel I established **international minimum criteria for capital requirements** and made capital requirements dependent on a bank's specific receivables. At that time, credit risk was still considered to be the main risk in the banking business.

4. Basel II

In diesem Kapitel lernen Sie ...

- die Motive und Prinzipien von Basel I kennen.
- welche Methoden es zur Berechnung der Eigenmittel gibt.
- welche Punkte die Kritik an Basel I betrifft.
- die Grundlagen und Prinzipien von Basel II kennen.
- die drei Säulen von Basel II kennen.
- die Unterschiede zwischen Basel I und Basel II kennen.
- die Unterschiede zwischen Standardansatz und IRB-Ansatz kennen.
- welche Risikoaktivaklassen unterschieden werden.
- welche Inputparameter bei der Berechnung der risikogewichteten Aktiva verwendet werden.
- den Unterschied zwischen Basis-IRB-Ansatz und fortgeschrittenem IRB-Ansatz kennen.
- welche Methoden zur Berechnung des Markt- bzw. Zinsänderungsrisikos zur Verfügung stehen.
- welche Methoden zur Bemessung des Wiederbeschaffungsrisikos verwendet werden.
- die Bemessung des Wiederbeschaffungsrisikos mit Hilfe der Laufzeitmethode und der Marktbewertungsmethode kennen.
- welche Änderungen sich durch Basel III in der Bemessung des Wiederbeschaffungsrisikos ergeben werden.

4.1. Die Geschichte von Basel II

Obwohl Marktrisiken den größten Teil der über das Treasury gehandelten Risiken darstellen, spielen auch **Kreditrisiken** eine immer größere Rolle. Auf der einen Seite entstehen Kreditrisiken bei OTC-Transaktionen, auf der anderen Seite werden seit Ende der 90er-Jahre vermehrt Kreditderivate direkt gehandelt.

Der folgende Abschnitt beschäftigt sich mit Basel II, dem aktuell existierenden internationalen Regelwerk für die aufsichtliche Behandlung dieser Risiken.

Geschichte, Motive und Prinzipien

Da Banken eine Schlüsselrolle für das Geld- und Zahlungswesen spielen, sind Staaten an einem **stabilen Bankwesen** interessiert. Damit eine Bank stabil ist, muss sie jederzeit über **genügend Eigenkapital** verfügen, um mögliche Verluste abzudecken und den Geschäftsbetrieb weiterführen zu können.

Vor der Einführung der ersten **Basler Eigenkapitalvereinbarung von 1988 (= Basel I)** gab es länderindividuelle Eigenmittelvorschriften, die Banken unabhängig von ihrem Risikoprofil zu erfüllen hatten. Außerbilanzielle Positionen wurden dabei ignoriert.

Aus Besorgnis über eine durch den (internationalen) Wettbewerb immer dünner werdende Eigenmitteldecke wurde in den 80er-Jahren dem 1974 gegründeten **Basler Ausschuss für Bankenaufsicht (Basel Committee on Banking Supervision)** die Aufgabe übertragen, ein internationales Regelwerk für Bankaufsichten zu entwerfen.

Basel I etablierte internationale **Mindestkapitalrichtlinien**, die das Eigenkapital von Banken von ihren Kreditforderungen abhängig machten. Damals wurde Kreditrisiko noch als das beherrschende Risikoelement im Bankwesen betrachtet.

Demands were kept simple. Basel I determined that banks should hold **capital of at least 8% of their risk-weighted assets** (so-called **"Cooke Ratio"**). In order to determine the risk weights for specific assets banks have to assign their assets to one of **four asset classes** and multiply the nominal by a given percentage.

Risk weights and capital requirements under Basel I

Asset category	Risk weight	Capital requirement
(OECD) Sovereign	0%	0%
(OECD) Bank	20%	1.6%
Mortgage loan	50%	4%
Other	100%	8%

Methodology introduced to calculate capital requirements was the following:

1. step: risk weighted assets = nominal x risk weight
2. step: capital requirement = risk weighted assets x 8%

Basel I also introduced (rough) guidelines on capital requirements for **off-balance sheet positions** for the first time. Therefore, Basel I introduced so-called credit **conversion factors** in order to translate the nominal amount of derivatives, which have no direct relevance for credit risk, into meaningful credit risk equivalents. This means that an additional step is necessary when calculating capital requirements for off-balance sheet instruments:

Methodology to calculate capital requirements for off-balance sheet positions:

1. step: credit risk equivalent = nominal x credit conversion factor
2. step: risk weighted assets = credit risk equivalent x risk weight
3. step: capital requirement = risk weighted assets x 8%

In 1996, Basel I was amended for rules regarding market risk which had dramatically increased in relevance due to the banks' trading activities. As has been mentioned before, market risk had been neglected in the Basel 1988 Accord. The so-called **"market risk amendment"** became effective in 1998 and was implemented within the EU via the Capital Adequacy Directive.

The new regulations forced banks to **measure their exposure to market risks and to put capital aside for it**. Market risk was defined as the risk stemming from interest rate instruments and stocks in the trading book plus FX risks and commodity risks for the whole bank (trading book and banking book).

For the measurement of market risk, banks could use **standard risk measurement procedures** as suggested by the Basel Committee or **internal VaR models**. The application of internal models is thereby linked to a set of certain minimum criteria a bank has to fulfil.

How capital requirements have to be calculated for the trading book will be described in the section on Basel II.

Criticism of Basel I

Even though Basel I represented a significant improvement compared to previous regimes, it soon became clear that the ultimate goal of financial market stability could not be secured by Basel I.

Criticism of Basel I mainly concerned the following three points:

● **Misallocation of supervisory capital:** This misallocation was due to a lack of differentiation between risks (on the one hand the differentiation within an asset category, on the other hand the differentiation between the different asset categories) which lead to

Die Anforderungen wurden einfach gehalten. Basel I legte fest, dass Banken **Eigenmittel** in der Höhe von **mindestens 8%** ihrer risikogewichteten Aktiva zu halten hatten (sogenannte „**Cooke-Ratio**"). Um die Risikoaktiva zu bestimmen, mussten Banken ihre Kreditforderungen einer von **vier Forderungsklassen** zuordnen und den Forderungsbetrag mit einem vorgegebenen Prozentsatz multiplizieren.

Risikoaktiva und Eigenmittelunterlegung unter Basel I

Schuldnerkategorie	Risikogewicht	Eigenmittel
(OECD) Staat	0%	0%
(OECD) Bank	20%	1,6%
Hypothek besichert	50%	4%
sonstige Kredite	100%	8%

Methodik zur Berechnung der Eigenmittel:

1. Schritt: Risikoaktiva = Forderungsbetrag x Risikogewicht
2. Schritt: Eigenmittel = Risikoaktiva x 8%

Auch für **außerbilanzielle Positionen** wurden mit Basel I erstmals (grobe) Regelungen für die Eigenmittelunterlegung festgelegt. Dazu wurden sogenannte **Konversionsfaktoren** vorgegeben, mit denen die für das Kreditrisiko oft nicht aussagekräftigen Nominalen von außerbilanziellen Instrumente in Kreditäquivalent umgerechnet wurden. Bei außerbilanziellen Instrumenten benötigt man für die Berechnung der Eigenmittel also einen zusätzlichen Schritt:

Methodik zur Berechnung der Eigenmittel für außerbilanzielle Positionen:

1. Schritt: Kreditäquivalent = Nominale x Konversionsfaktor
2. Schritt: Risikoaktiva = Kreditäquivalent x Risikogewicht
3. Schritt: Eigenmittel = Risikoaktiva x 8%

Im Jahre 1996 wurde Basel I um Regelungen für das inzwischen durch die Handelsaktivitäten der Banken massiv angestiegene Marktrisiko ergänzt, welches im Entwurf von 1988 noch vernachlässigt worden war. Die Ergänzungen wurden im Jahre 1998 wirksam und wurden in der EU durch die sogenannte **Kapitaladäquanzrichtlinie** implementiert.

Die neuen Regelungen zwangen Banken dazu, das **Marktrisiko zu messen und mit Eigenkapital zu hinterlegen.** Die Änderungen der Eigenkapitalvereinbarung definieren dabei Marktrisiko als die Risiken aus Zinsinstrumenten und Aktien im Handelsbestand plus Fremdwährungsrisiken und Rohstofffrisken in der gesamten Bank.

Für die Messung des Risikos konnten Banken entweder **standardisierte Messverfahren des Basel-Kommittees** oder **interne VaR-Modelle** verwenden, wobei Banken für letztere Methodik bestimmten Anforderungen entsprechen mussten.

Welche Eigenmittelunterlegungen für Risiken im Handelsbuch berechnet werden müssen, wird genauer im Abschnitt über Basel II behandelt.

Kritik an Basel I

Auch wenn Basel I einen großen Fortschritt gegenüber früheren Regelungen darstellte, wurde bald klar, dass das Ziel der Finanzmarktstabilität nicht ausreichend sichergestellt werden konnte.

Die Kritik an Basel I betraf folgende drei Punkte:

- **Fehlallokation des aufsichtsrechtlichen Kapitals:** Diese Fehlallokation war begründet in der mangelnden Differenzierung von Risiken, einmal innerhalb der Forderungsklassen, aber auch zwischen den Forderungsklassen. Gute Bonitäten wurden dadurch

inflated capital charges for good credit qualities and insufficient capital charges for bad credit qualities. There was also no differentiation based on the maturity of credit claims and no supervisory incentives for banks to use credit mitigation techniques.

- **Incomplete coverage of banking risks:** A number of banking crises (e.g. Barings) showed that threatening losses were often triggered by operational risk.
- **No international standards** for supervisory review and disclosure in different countries.

In June 1999, the Basel Committee announced the development of a revised framework, which is known today as "Basel II".

4.2. Basics and Principles

The New Capital Accord – Basel II

Basel II stands for the Capital Adequacy Framework that was developed by the Basel Committee for Banking Supervision and was set in place on **January 1st 2007** within the European Union and worldwide for all international banks.

The goal of Basel II is to align capital adequacy assessment more closely with the fundamental risks in the banking industry. Furthermore, it provides incentives for banks to enhance their risk measurement and management capabilities.

Main methodological differences between Basel I and Basel II

BASEL I	BASEL II
focus on a single risk measure	– more emphasis on bank's own internal risk management methodologies – supervisory review – market discipline
one size fits all	– flexibility – banks select their own individual approach – Incentives for better risk management
broad brush structure	– more risk sensitivity

The main goal of Basel II remains the **soundness and stability of the financial system**. Minimum capital requirements alone are not sufficient to guarantee the achievement of this goal. Therefore, the new Capital Adequacy Framework consists of **three (equally important) pillars**:

- Pillar one: Minimum capital requirements
- Pillar two: Supervisory review process
- Pillar three: Market discipline

Pillar One: Minimum Capital Requirements

The minimum capital requirements outlined in pillar one certainly constitute the largest part of the Basel II regulations. The **calculation of capital requirements** (as the main point

benachteiligt, schwache Bonitäten begünstigt. Weiters wurde nicht nach den Laufzeiten von Forderungen differenziert und es gab keine aufsichtsrechtlichen Anreize für Banken, kreditrisikomindernde Techniken anzuwenden.

- **Keine komplette Erfassung von Risiken:** Die Erfahrung zeigte, dass Bankenkrisen oft durch operationelle Risiken (z.B. Barings) ausgelöst wurden.
- **Keine internationalen Standards** gab es für aufsichtsrechtliche Überprüfungen und Veröffentlichung in verschiedenen Ländern.

Im Juni 1999 kündigte das Basler Komitee schließlich an, eine neue Rahmenvereinbarung, heute bekannt unter dem Namen „Basel II", zu entwickeln.

4.2. Grundlagen und Prinzipien von Basel II

Die Neue Eigenkapitalvereinbarung – Basel II

Der Begriff Basel II bezeichnet die vom Basler Ausschuss für Bankenaufsicht vorgeschlagenen Eigenkapitalvorschriften, die seit dem **1. Januar 2007** in der EU und weltweit zumindest für international agierende Banken angewendet werden.

Basel II soll die Beurteilung der Angemessenheit des Eigenkapitals besser auf die wichtigsten Risikoelemente im Bankgeschäft abstimmen. Darüber hinaus sollen den Banken Anreize geboten werden, ihre Verfahren der Risikomessung und des Risikomanagements weiter zu verbessern.

Unterschiede Methodik Basel I – Basel II

BASEL I	BASEL II
Konzentration auf ein Risikomaß	– größere Bedeutung der bankinternen Methoden – Überprüfung durch die Aufsicht – Überprüfung der Marktdisziplin
Ein einziger Ansatz	– Flexibilität – Auswahl verschiedener Ansätze – Anreize für ein besseres Risikomanagement
Grobe Struktur	– risikogerechtere Ausrichtung

Die **Sicherheit und Solidität des Finanzwesens zu fördern** ist weiterhin das Hauptziel von Basel II. Die Mindestkapitalanforderungen alleine tragen jedoch zu diesem Ziel nicht ausreichend bei. Daher besteht die neue Eigenkapitalvereinbarung aus **drei tragenden Säulen**:

- Säule 1: Mindestkapitalanforderungen
- Säule 2: Aufsichtliches Überprüfungsverfahren
- Säule 3: Marktdisziplin

Säule 1: Mindestkapitalanforderungen

Die Mindestkapitalanforderungen, die unter Säule 1 untergebracht werden, stellen ohne Frage den umfassendsten Teil der Basel-II-Regelungen dar. Die **Berechnung der Eigenmittelunterlegung bzw. des regulatorischen Kapitals** ist dabei nach wie vor der zen-

of minimum capital requirements) was also the primary subject of discussion during the rounds of consultations.

One significant innovation with respect to minimum capital requirements is that **operational risk** will feature directly in the assessment of capital adequacy for the first time, so that it has to be quantified and translated into capital charges. Measurement approaches for operational risk are still in their fledgling stages as compared to those for credit and market risk. Nevertheless, Basel II was right to kick off this innovation in view of the fact that operational risk has the potential to significantly affect a bank's result.

The main principle of capital adequacy remained unchanged, i.e. at **8% in relation to total banking risks**:

$$\frac{\text{minimum capital requirement}}{\text{credit risk} + \text{market risk} + \text{operational risk}} = \text{capital adequacy (min. 8\%)}$$

The calculation method for credit risk also remained unchanged. The regulatory credit risk of a bank is equal to its risk-weighted assets (RWA). The most important innovation was the **assignment of different risk weights** to credit risks (ratings) that serve as an **input for the calculation of capital required**.

Example
Your bank's sum of risk-weighted assets for credit risk equals EUR 1.2 bn. Calculate the minimum capital requirement (market and operational risks are not considered in this example).   Capital requirement = 1.2 bn x 8% = EUR 96 m

In line with Basel II's aim of defining a more risk-oriented method for the calculation of capital requirements, the existing method, i.e. the standardised approach, was retained and developed further. Additionally, two **internal ratings-based (IRB) approaches** were also developed.

Based on the previous Capital Adequacy Framework (Basel I), the standardised approach uses ratings to determine risk weights, whereby only **external ratings**, i.e. ratings of internationally recognised rating agencies like Standard & Poor's or Moody's, are accepted.

On the other hand, the internal ratings-based approach (IRB approach) offers banks the opportunity to rely on their own internal ratings for calculating capital requirements. In taking this step, the Basel Committee also put forward a detailed set of minimum requirements designed to ensure the integrity of these internal assessments of credit risk, since these more complex internal approaches are still at a rather embryonic stage with regard to back-testing and evaluation.

Pillar Two: Supervisory Review

Supervisory review is regarded as an **important complement to minimum capital requirements and market discipline**. The second pillar aims to ensure that banks implement sound internal methods to measure risks and evaluate capital adequacy. Supervisors are expected to evaluate how well banks assess their capital needs in relation to their risks.

trale Punkt, über den die meisten Diskussionen während der Konsultationsphase ausgetragen wurden.

Die wesentliche Neuheit in Bezug auf die gesamten Mindestkapitalanforderungen ist, dass in Basel II **auch das operationelle Risiko quantifiziert und unterlegt** werden muss (obwohl hier die Messansätze im Vergleich zum Markt- und Kreditrisiko noch in den Kinderschuhen stecken).

Das Grundprinzip der Eigenmittelunterlegung blieb jedoch dasselbe. Die **Eigenkapitalquote** der Banken im Verhältnis zu ihren Risiken muss **mindestens 8%** betragen.

$$\frac{\text{Regulatives Eigenkapital}}{\text{Kreditrisiko} + \text{Marktrisiko} + \text{operationales Risiko}} = \text{Eigenkapital mind. 8\%}$$

Auch im Rahmen des Kreditrisikos blieb die prinzipielle Berechnungslogik erhalten: Das (regulatorische) Kreditrisiko der Bank entspricht der Summe der risikogewichteten Aktiva (RWA – engl.: risk-weighted assets). Die wesentliche Neuerung war die **Bestimmung der Risikogewichte**, die größere **Differenzierung nach Risikogehalt** bieten und gleichzeitig die Basis für die Berechnung des notwendigen Eigenkapitals darstellen.

Beispiel

Die Summe der risikogewichteten Aktiva für das Kreditrisiko (RWA) Ihrer Bank beträgt EUR 1,2 Mrd. Wie hoch ist die Eigenmittelunterlegung für das Kreditrisiko? (Markt- und operationelles Risiko werden hier nicht berücksichtigt.)

EM-Unterlegung = 1,2 Mrd. x 8% = 96 Mio. EUR

Mit dem Ziel einer risikogerechteren Berechnung der Eigenmittelunterlegung wurde einerseits die Basel-I-Methodik zum sogenannten Standardansatz weiterentwickelt und andererseits eine neue Methode – der **IRB-Ansatz** – entwickelt.

Aufbauend auf der alten Basel-I-Regelung werden im Standardansatz nach Ratingklassen standardisierte Risikogewichte angewendet, wobei nur **externe Ratings**, d.h. Ratings von aufsichtlich anerkannten Ratingagenturen wie Standard & Poor's oder Moody's zählen.

Der IRB-Ansatz (internal ratings based) hingegen gibt den Banken die Möglichkeit, ihre internen Ratings zur Eigenmittelberechnung heranzuziehen. Da interne Kreditrisikomodelle im Gegensatz zu Marktrisikomodellen im Sinne von Back-Testing und Evaluierung noch nicht ausgereift sind, wird den Banken nicht zur Gänze freie Hand gelassen und ein Regelwerk vorgegeben, wie die Berechnung des Kreditrisikos stattfinden soll.

Säule 2: Aufsichtliches Überprüfungsverfahren

Das aufsichtliche Überprüfungsverfahren wird als eine **wesentliche Ergänzung der Mindestkapitalanforderungen und Marktdisziplin** angesehen. Die zweite Säule stellt sicher, dass jede Bank solide interne Verfahren implementiert hat, mit denen die Angemessenheit ihres Eigenkapitals durch eine gründliche Bewertung ihrer Risiken beurteilt werden kann. Die Aufsichtsinstanzen sind dafür verantwortlich zu beurteilen, wie gut die Banken ihren Eigenkapitalbedarf im Verhältnis zu ihren Risiken abschätzen.

National supervisors are expected to review internal equity allocation. They are authorised to intervene by imposing additional capital charges when the risk of a bank is greater than its capital or when risks are not adequately controlled. Supervisors should also seek to intervene at an early stage to prevent capital from falling below the minimum levels required.

Supervisory review not only includes the **review of capital adequacy**, but also ensures that **quantitative and qualitative standards for the calculation of capital requirements** (for market, credit and operational risk) are met.

In general, the legal responsibilities of supervisors and their competencies to exert control over banks and intervene where necessary have been increased.

Pillar Three: Market Discipline

Guidelines under the third pillar require banks to **disclose up-to-date, relevant information on their financial situation and their risk exposure**. The motive was to increase the informative value of banks' balance sheets and enable market players to judge the adequacy of a bank's equity capitalisation. The increased transparency due to disclosure is aimed at strengthening the soundness and stability of the financial system.

There are qualitative and quantitative disclosure requirements depending on the measurement approaches applied. The information to be published relates to one of **four areas**:

- scope of application (within the banking group)
- capital structure
- capital adequacy
- risk exposure and assessment.

Systematic overview of the most significant changes in the three pillars for the measurement and control of risks in banking

Risiks / Pillars	Market Risk	Credit Risk	Operational Risk
Minimum Capital Requirements	no change	NEW: Standardised Approach IRB (Internal Ratings-Based) Foundation Approach IRB Advanced Approach	NEW: Basic Indicator Approach Standardised Approach Advanced Measurement Approaches (AMA)
Supervisory Review Process	NEW: interest rate risk in the banking book		
	NEW: supervisory review of compliance with minimum standards and capital requirements		
Market Discipline	NEW: disclosure requirements and recommendations for risk assessment processes and risk policies		

Die nationalen Aufsichtsbehörden überprüfen also die bankinterne Eigenmittelallokation und sind dazu ermächtigt, Banken mit unzureichender Eigenmittelausstattung eine über das gesetzliche Mindestmaß erforderliche Eigenkapitalquote vorzuschreiben. Dies inkludiert auch das frühzeitige Eingreifen der Aufsichtsbehörden, um zu verhindern, dass das Eigenkapital unter das Mindestmaß fällt.

Im Detail umfasst die aufsichtliche Überprüfung nicht nur das **Mindestmaß an Eigenmittelausstattung**, sondern auch die Sicherstellung, dass die **quantitativen sowie qualitativen Anforderungen zur Berechnung der Eigenmittelunterlegung** (für Markt-, Kredit- und operationelles Risiko) eingehalten werden.

Grundsätzlich wurde damit die Kompetenz der Aufsichtbehörden zur Durchsetzung von Kontroll- und Steuerungsmaßnahmen gegenüber den Banken erhöht.

Säule 3: Marktdisziplin

Die Richtlinien im Rahmen der Säule 3 erfordern von den Banken die **Offenlegung aktueller und aussagekräftiger Informationen zur finanziellen und risikopolitischen Situation**. Motivation ist die Aussagekraft von Bankbilanzen zu erhöhen und Marktteilnehmern eine Beurteilung der Angemessenheit der Eigenkapitalausstattung zu ermöglichen. Die gewonnene Transparenz soll zur Sicherheit und Solidität des Banken- und Finanzsystems beitragen.

Die Offenlegungsvorschriften, abhängig von den angewendeten Messansätzen, bestehen sowohl aus qualitativen als auch aus quantitativen Informationen und sind in folgende **vier Schlüsselgebiete** aufgeteilt:
- Anwendungsbereich der neuen Eigenkapitalvereinbarung (innerhalb der Bankengruppe)
- Eigenkapitalstruktur
- Eigenkapitalausstattung
- eingegangene Risiken und ihre Beurteilung

Wesentliche Neuerungen durch Basel II im Überblick

Risiken / Säulen	Marktrisiko	Kreditrisiko	Operationelles Risiko
Mindestkapitalanforderungen	unverändert	NEU: Standardansatz IRB-Basisansatz IRB fortgeschrittener Ansatz	NEU: Basisindikatorenansatz Standardansatz Fortgeschrittene Messansätze (AMA)
Aufsichtliches Überprüfungsverfahren	NEU: Zinsänderungsrisiko im Anlagenbuch		
	NEU: Überprüfung der Einhaltung der Mindestkapitalanforderungen und der Verfahren		
Marktdisziplin	NEU: Offenlegungsvorschriften und -empfehlungen für Risikomessverfahren und Risikopolitik		

While there has been a directive (the Capital Adequacy Directive) in place that addresses capital requirements for the trading book ever since 1996, Basel II does not stipulate standardised capital requirements for interest rate risk in the banking book. However, banks are obliged to control and disclose interest rate risk in the banking book and Basel II imposes a general limit on this type of risk.

As a consequence, banks are obliged to install an **effective asset/liability management system**. Control of risks in the banking book (= interest rate risk in the banking book) will be subject to supervision by the national regulatory bodies. In the event of large exposures, the authorities are also allowed to require banks to hold additional capital.

4.3. Capital Requirements for Credit Risk

The calculation of minimum capital requirements for credit risk in the banking book represents the most important part of pillar I.

The calculation is done in **two steps**. First, risk weights are calculated by multiplying the exposure by the respective **risk weight** (note that the exposure is pre-calculated in a separate step). The **capital requirement** is then the result of risk-weighted assets times 8%.

Example

$$RWA = RW \times E$$
$$CapReq = 8\% \times RWA$$

E = Exposure
RW = risk weight
RWA = risk-weighted assets
CapReq = capital Requirement

Calculate the minimum capital requirement for a corporate loan of EUR 800,000 and a risk weight of 50%.

$$RWA = 50\% \times EUR\ 800{,}000 = EUR\ 400{,}000$$
$$CapReq = 8\% \times EUR\ 400{,}000 = EUR\ 32{,}000$$

The difference to the 1988 Capital Adequacy Framework is the calculation of risk-weighted assets and, accordingly, the introduction of risk weights. More risk-sensitive regulations, the opportunity to choose from a range of approaches and the greater use of risk assessments made available by banks' own internal systems provide incentives for banks to improve their risk management systems. All this helps to ensure the stability of the financial system.

In line with Basel II's aim to define a more risk-oriented approach for the calculation of capital requirements, the previous Basel I methodology was modified and transformed into the standardised approach. Additionally, a new internal ratings-based approach (IRB approach), was also developed.

The Standardised Approach

The standardised approach is based on the capital adequacy regulation of 1988. In order to achieve better risk adjustment in a relatively simple way the standardised approach uses the external ratings of internationally recognised rating agencies to determine risk weights.

Während für das Handelsbuch einer Bank schon seit 1996 eine Richtlinie zur Eigenmittel-unterlegung besteht (Kapitaladäquanzrichtlinie), unterbleibt auch in Basel II eine einheit-liche Eigenmittelunterlegungspflicht für das Zinsrisiko im Bankbuch. Es bestehen jedoch strikte Kontroll- und Offenlegungspflichten der Bankbuchpositionen und das Zinsrisiko des Bankbuches wird begrenzt.

Zwangsläufig ist daher **gezieltes Aktiv-/Passiv-Management** in jeder Bank notwendig. Die Kontrolle des Bankbuchrisikos (= Zinsänderungsrisiko im Bankbuch) wird unter natio-naler Aufsicht stattfinden. Den Behörden ist im Falle großer Risikopositionen erlaubt, auch Eigenmittelerfordernisse zu verordnen.

4.3. Eigenmittelunterlegung für Kreditrisiko

Im Rahmen der Mindestkapitalanforderungen in Säule 1 stellt die Berechnung der Eigen-kapitalunterlegung des Kreditrisikos im Bankbuch (Anlagebuch) den wesentlichen Teil dar.

Die Berechnung der Eigenmittelunterlegung des Kreditrisikos erfolgt in **zwei Schritten**. Im ersten Schritt werden die **risikogewichteten Aktiva** berechnet, indem die Volumina mit den entsprechenden Risikogewichten multipliziert werden. Die **Mindestunterlegung** ergibt sich dann im zweiten Schritt mit der Berechnung von 8% der risikogewichteten Aktiva.

Beispiel

$$RWA = RW \times E$$
$$EM\text{-}Unt = 8\% \times RWA$$

E = Exposure (aushaftender Betrag)
RW = Risikogewicht (Risk Weight)
RWA = risikogewichtete Aktiva (Risk Weighted Assets)
EM-Unt = Eigenmittelunterlegung

Berechnen Sie die Mindesteigenmittelunterlegung für einen Kredit in der Höhe von EUR 800.000 an ein Unternehmen mit einem Risikogewicht von 50%.

$$RWA = 50\% \times 800.000\ EUR = 400.000\ EUR$$
$$EM\text{-}Unt = 8\% \times 400.000\ EUR = 32.000\ EUR$$

Der Unterschied zu der Eigenkapitalvereinbarung von 1988 besteht in der Berechnung der risikogewichteten Aktiva bzw. der Risikogewichte. Um die Stabilität des Finanzsystems zu gewährleisten, sollen durch risikogerechtere Ausrichtung, Auswahlmöglichkeit unter meh-reren Ansätzen und größere Bedeutung der bankinternen Methoden Anreize für ein besse-res Risikomanagement in den Banken geschaffen werden.

Mit dem Ziel einer risikogerechteren Berechnung der Eigenmittelunterlegung wurde ei-nerseits die alte Basel-I-Regelung zum sogenannten Standardansatz überarbeitet und eine neue Methode – der IRB-Ansatz – entwickelt.

Der Standardansatz

Der Standardansatz baut auf die Eigenkapitalvereinbarung von 1988 auf. Um eine risikoge-rechtere Behandlung zu ermöglichen, ohne die Berechnung übermäßig zu verkomplizieren, basieren die Risikogewichte beim Standardansatz auf externen Ratings.

The external ratings of **internationally recognised rating agencies** may be used. The best-known agencies are:

- Standard & Poor's
- Moody's
- Fitch IBCA

Standard risk weights not only depend on the respective rating but also on which **of 13 exposure classes** the respective exposure belongs to. These exposure/asset classes are:

- Claims on sovereigns
- Claims on non-central government public sector entities
- Claims on multilateral development banks
- Claims on banks
- Claims on securities firms
- Claims on corporates
- Claims included in the regulatory retail portfolio
- Claims secured by residential mortgage
- Claims secured by commercial real estate
- Past due loans
- Higher risk categories
- Other assets (including securitisation)
- Off-balance sheet items (including OTC derivatives)

The risk weights assigned to the three most important categories based on Standard & Poor's ratings are shown in Table 4 below. The task of supervisors is to assign the different rating notations of the various rating agencies to the standardised risk weights, according to the basic principle that capital requirements stemming from externally rated creditors mirror risks inherent in the exposure.

Als externe Ratings gelten die **Bonitätsbeurteilungen von aufsichtlich anerkannten internationalen Ratingagenturen**. Die bekanntesten Agenturen sind:

- Standard & Poor's
- Moody's
- Fitch IBCA

Die nach Ratings standardisierten Risikogewichte werden nach Art der Forderungen differenziert. **13 Kategorien von Forderungen (bzw. Aktiva)** sind zu unterscheiden:

- Forderungen an Staaten
- Forderungen an sonstige öffentliche Stellen
- Forderungen an multilaterale Entwicklungsbanken
- Forderungen an Banken
- Forderungen an Wertpapierhäuser
- Forderungen an Wirtschaftsunternehmen
- Kredite, die dem aufsichtlichen Retailportfolio zugeordnet werden
- durch Wohnimmobilien besicherte Forderungen
- durch gewerbliche Immobilien besicherte Forderungen
- Kredite im Verzug
- Forderungen mit höherem Risiko
- andere Vermögensgegenstände (inklusive Verbriefungen von Aktiva)
- außerbilanzielle Geschäfte (inklusive OTC-Derivate)

Die Risikogewichte der drei wichtigsten Kategorien sind in der folgenden Tabelle nach der Ratingsystematik von Standard & Poor's zu finden. Es ist die Aufgabe der Aufsichtsbehörden, die unterschiedlichen Notationen der Ratingagenturen den standardisierten Risikogewichten zuzuordnen. Wesentlich dabei ist, dass extern geratete Schuldner – unabhängig von der Ratingagentur – entsprechend ihrer Risiken unterlegt werden.

Risk weights under the standardised approach for sovereigns, banks and corporates

Rating	Sovereigns	Banks			Corporates
		option 1	option 2 normal	option 2 short-term	
AAA	0%	20%	20%	20%	20%
AA+					
AA-					
A+	20%	50%	50%	20%	50%
A					
A-					
BBB+	50%		50%	20%	100%
BBB					
BBB-		100%			
BB+	100%		100%	50%	100%
BB					
BB-					
B+					150%
B					
B-					
below B	150%	150%	150%	150%	150%
no rating	100%	100%	50%	20%	100%

Example

Calculate the minimum capital requirement for an AA-rated corporate loan of EUR 800,000.

$$CapReq = 8\% \times (20\% \times EUR\ 800{,}000) = EUR\ 12{,}800$$

Compared with the 1998 Capital Adequacy Framework, the **differentiation based on ratings** takes better account of the risk inherent in different assets. The standardised approach treats unrated assets (assets without an external rating) as one rating class and assigns them standardised risk weights. Internal ratings are not taken into account.

There are two options for **claims on banks**. National supervisors will apply one option to all banks in their jurisdiction. Under the first option, all banks incorporated in a given country will be assigned a risk weight one category less favourable than that assigned to claims on the sovereign of that country capped at 100%.

Risikogewichte im Standardansatz für Staaten, Banken und Unternehmen

Rating	Staat	Banken			Unternehmen
		Option 1	Option 2 normal	Option 2 kurzfristig	
AAA AA+ AA-	0%	20%	20%	20%	20%
A+ A A-	20%	50%	50%	20%	50%
BBB+ BBB BBB-	50%	100%	50%	20%	100%
BB+ BB BB-	100%	100%	100%	50%	100%
B+ B B-					150%
unter B	150%	150%	150%	150%	150%
kein externes Rating	100%	100%	50%	20%	100%

Beispiel

Berechnen Sie die Mindesteigenmittelunterlegung für einen Kredit in der Höhe von EUR 800.000 an ein Unternehmen mit einem Rating von AA.

$$\text{EM-Unt} = 8\% \times (20\% \times 800.000 \text{ EUR}) = 12.800 \text{ EUR}$$

Im Vergleich zu der Regelung von 1988 bringt die **Differenzierung nach Ratings** eine bessere Berücksichtigung des Risikogehalts der unterschiedlichen Aktiva. Der Standardansatz behandelt Aktiva ohne externes Rating wie eine Ratingstufe und gibt standardisierte Risikogewichte vor. Die bankinternen Bonitätsbeurteilungen der Kreditnehmer spielen diesbezüglich keine Rolle.

Für die **Forderungen an Banken** sind zwei Optionen vorgesehen. Die nationalen Aufsichtsbehörden entscheiden, welche dieser Optionen für alle Banken in ihrem Aufsichtsbereich gilt. Bei der ersten Option erhalten alle Banken ein um eine Stufe höheres Risikogewicht als der Sitzstaat, wobei das Risikogewicht auf 100% begrenzt ist.

Example

Your bank grants a loan of EUR 8 m to a domestic, unrated bank. National supervisors apply option 1 and your home country is rated AAA. Calculate the minimum capital requirement for this exposure under the standardised approach.

$$RWA = 20\% \times 8 \text{ m} = EUR \text{ } 1.6 \text{ m}$$
$$CapReq = 8\% \times EUR \text{ } 1.6 \text{ m} = EUR \text{ } 128{,}000$$

The second option bases the risk weighting on the external credit risk assessment of the bank itself, with claims on unrated banks being risk weighted at 50%. Under this option, a preferential risk weight may be applied to claims with an original maturity of three months or less.

As one can see, the treatment of exposures to unrated corporates remains the same as under Basel I; these loans are weighted at 100% with a capital requirement of 8%. Another innovation of the standardised approach, besides risk-sensitive risk weights, are improvements with respect to credit risk mitigants. Basel II allows a wider range of credit risk mitigants to be recognised for regulatory capital purposes, provided they meet a set of minimum requirements. Basically, three techniques can be distinguished for mitigating credit risk:

- on-balance sheet netting (use of net exposure of loans and deposits)
- guarantees and credit derivatives
- collateral

Basel II provides the rules for recognition of these techniques in the calculation of capital requirements. It stipulates how the effective risk weights for single exposures have to be calculated, starting from the standardised risk weights.

This revised version of the standardised approach is more risk sensitive than before due to the differentiation of ratings. However, it is not able to provide incentives for banks to improve their risk measurement and management practices. Additionally, only corporates that are externally rated are able to profit under the standardised approach. For these reasons, the IRB approach was developed.

The IRB Approach

The IRB approach for calculating minimum capital requirements was developed with the objective of further converging capital requirements and the individual risk profiles of banks.

In order to implement a precise risk adjustment, the risk weights are no longer standardised, but will be calculated using a **given mathematical function**.

As a result of using a mathematical function, risk weights may take on any value within a certain range. Both ratings and the specific characteristics of individual loans can thus be better accounted for than under the standardised approach.

As opposed to the standardised approach, the IRB approach relies on **banks' own internal estimates of risk components**, hence the name "internal ratings-based approach". Sub-

---

Beispiel

Ihre Bank hat an eine heimische, nicht geratete Bank einen Kredit in der Höhe von EUR 8 Mio. vergeben. Ihr Staat hat ein Rating von AAA und die Aufsichtbehörde hat sich für die Option 1 entschieden. Wie hoch ist die Eigenmittelunterlegung dieses Kredits im Standardansatz?

RWA = 20% x 8 Mio. = 1,6 Mio. EUR
EM-Unterlegung = 8% x 1,6 Mio. = 128.000 EUR

Bei der zweiten Option basiert das Risikogewicht auf dem externen Rating jeder einzelnen Bank, wobei Forderungen an Banken ohne Rating mit 50% zu gewichten sind. Bei dieser Option kann auf Forderungen mit einer Ursprungslaufzeit von maximal drei Monaten ein begünstigtes Risikogewicht angewendet werden. In Deutschland und Österreich haben sich die Aufsichtsbehörden für Option 1 entschieden.

Somit ist die Unterlegung bei Unternehmen ohne externes Rating dieselbe wie bei Basel I; diese Kredite sind mit 100% zu gewichten und mit vollen 8% zu unterlegen.

Zusätzlich zu den differenzierteren Risikogewichten bringt der Standardansatz auch wesentliche Neuerungen in Bezug auf Kreditrisikominderung. Unter Einhaltung von bestimmten Mindestbedingungen wird eine größere Bandbreite an kreditrisikomindernden Verfahren anerkannt. Grundsätzlich werden drei Arten von risikomindernden Verfahren unterschieden:

- Netting von Bilanzpositionen (Aufrechnen von Gegenpositionen)
- Garantien und Kreditderivate
- Sicherheiten

Zur Berücksichtigung dieser Verfahren bei der Berechnung der Eigenmittelunterlegung gibt Basel II ein Regelwerk vor. Es erklärt, wie, ausgehend von den standardisierten Risikogewichten, die effektiven Risikogewichte für einzelne Forderungen zu ermitteln sind.

Der Standardansatz in überarbeiteter Form ist dank der Differenzierung nach Ratings risikosensitiver als bisher. Er schafft jedoch nicht genügend Anreize, die Banken zu besseren Risikomessungen und Risikomanagement-Praktiken zu bewegen. Nur jene Unternehmen, die ein externes Rating besitzen, können vom Standardansatz profitieren. Daher wurde der IRB-Ansatz entwickelt.

Der IRB-Ansatz

Der IRB-Ansatz zur Berechnung des Mindesteigenkapitalerfordernisses für das Kreditrisiko wurde mit dem Ziel entwickelt, das individuelle Risikoprofil der Bank genauer widerzuspiegeln. Um eine größere Risikodifferenzierung zu ermöglichen, werden die Risikogewichte der einzelnen Forderungen nicht standardisiert, sondern über eine **vorgegebene mathematische Funktion** berechnet.

Aufgrund der Berechnung über eine mathematische Funktion können die Risikogewichte jeden möglichen Wert innerhalb einer gewissen Bandbreite annehmen. Sowohl die Ratings als auch die besonderen Merkmale einzelner Kredite können so besser als im Standardansatz berücksichtigt werden.

Im Unterschied zum Standardansatz basiert der IRB-Ansatz auf den **internen Ratings** der Banken, daher auch der Name „auf internen Ratings basierender Ansatz". Unter Einhal-

ject to a full set of regulations concerning methodology and disclosure, banks are allowed to use their own assessments of the credit quality of borrowers. The assessment of credit risk is thus more closely aligned to the individual risk profile.

The calculation of capital requirements follows the same principle as under the standardised approach. The capital charge for credit risk results from the risk-weighted assets being multiplied by 8%. However, under this approach the calculation of risk-weighted assets requires a few more steps.

Exposure Classes

In order to be able to calculate risk-weighted assets using the IRB approach, banks will have to slot their customers into one of several exposure classes, which represent varying credit risk characteristics:

- sovereigns
- banks
- corporates
  - small and medium-sized enterprises (SMEs)
  - specialised lending
    - project finance
    - object finance
    - commodities finance
    - income-producing real estate
    - high-volatility commercial real estate
- retail
  - residential mortgage
  - qualifying revolving loans
  - other retail
- equity exposure
- purchased receivables

In a second step the risk weights of each specific exposure must be calculated. The calculation depends on which exposure class and sub-exposure class an exposure is assigned to. However, the basic principle remains unchanged.

The first three exposure classes (sovereigns, banks and corporates) are treated in the same way apart from a few minor differences.

Risk-weighted assets are then calculated **using four different parameters** which serve as the input for the **risk-weight function** of the respective exposure class:

- Exposure at Default (EAD)
- Probability of Default (PD)
- Loss Given Default (LGD)
- Maturity (M)

Concerning these input parameters of the IRB approach, it is important to point out the difference between estimation and effective use of these variables. On the one hand, banks have to estimate the first three of these input parameters **at least once a year** for different asset classes.

This means the estimation of probability of default on each internal rating category, the estimation of loss given default according to internal collateral categories or LGD bands,

tung strenger Auflagen für Methodik und Offenlegung wird den Banken ermöglicht, ihre internen Bonitätseinschätzungen der Schuldner einzusetzen. Die Beurteilung des Kreditrisikos der Bank wird so dem individuellen Risikoprofil besser angepasst.

Die Berechnung der Mindesteigenmittelunterlegung im IRB-Ansatz erfolgt nach dem gleichen Prinzip im Standardansatz. Die risikogewichteten Aktiva multipliziert mit der Mindesteigenkapitalquote von 8% ergibt das Eigenkapitalerfordernis für das Kreditrisiko. Die Berechnung der risikogewichteten Aktiva erfordert jedoch einige Schritte mehr als im Standardansatz.

Risikoaktivaklassen (bzw. Forderungs- oder Assetklassen)

Für die Berechnung der risikogewichteten Aktiva im IRB-Ansatz müssen die Banken zuerst ihre Aktiva in die folgenden sechs Risikoaktivaklassen mit unterschiedlichen Kreditrisiko-Eigenschaften einordnen:

- Staaten
- Banken
- Unternehmen
  - KMU mit Risikoabschlag
  - Spezialfinanzierungen
    - Projektfinanzierungen
    - Objektfinanzierungen
    - Rohstoffhandelsfinanzierungen
    - Finanzierung von Mietimmobilien
    - hochvolatile gewerbliche Realkredite
- Privatkunden (Retail)
  - durch Wohnimmobilien besicherte Kredite
  - qualifizierte revolvierende Kredite
  - sonstiges Retail
- Beteiligungspositionen (Anteile an Unternehmen)
- angekaufte Forderungen

Im zweiten Schritt müssen die Risikogewichte für die einzelnen Kredite ermittelt werden. Die Formel zur Berechnung der Risikogewichte hängt im Detail von der jeweiligen Risikoaktivaklasse bzw. der Unterkategorie ab. Grundsätzlich erfolgt sie jedoch nach dem gleichen Schema. Die ersten drei Klassen Unternehmen, Banken und Staaten werden, abgesehen von geringfügigen Unterschieden, gleich behandelt.

Die risikogewichteten Aktiva werden durch das **Einsetzen von vier Inputparametern** in die für die jeweilige Risikoklasse anzuwendende **Risikogewichtsfunktion** ermittelt:

- Exposure at Default (EAD) = Forderungshöhe bei Ausfall
- Probability of Default (PD) = Ausfallswahrscheinlichkeit
- Loss Given Default (LGD) = Verlustintensität bzw. Verlusthöhe bei Ausfall
- Maturity (M) = Restlaufzeit

In Bezug auf die Inputparameter des IRB-Ansatzes muss der Unterschied zwischen der Schätzung und der effektiven Berechnung dieser Größen unterstrichen werden. Auf der einen Seite müssen die Banken – **mindestens einmal im Jahr** – die ersten drei dieser Inputparameter für bestimmte Klassen schätzen.

and the estimation of the amount outstanding at the point of default via credit conversion factors. These estimates then serve as the starting point for the capital requirement calculation.

On the other hand, banks have to compute **"effective" input parameters** for each individual calculation of capital requirements. Starting from the estimated parameter values, effective input parameters are calculated for each exposure allowing for credit risk mitigants. Risk weights are calculated by inputting these effective parameter values into the respective risk-weight function.

The estimation of input parameters places **high demands on data systems**. Not all banks were/are able to estimate all four parameters on the basis of internal data from the outset. For this reason, the Basel Committee has developed **two versions of the IRB approach**: the foundation IRB approach and the advanced IRB approach.

Foundation IRB Approach

Under the foundation IRB approach, banks will **only have to estimate the probability of default (PD) for each of their internal rating categories**. The remaining three input parameters and the methodology for recognising credit risk mitigation will be provided by the supervisory framework. Although a wider range of credit risk mitigation techniques will be eligible, some restrictions remain in the foundation IRB approach, e.g. restrictions on which guarantors and types of collateral will be recognised.

Advanced IRB Approach

Under the advanced IRB approach, **loss given default (LGD) and exposure at default (EAD) will also have to be estimated internally** in addition to the probability of default (PD). Likewise, banks will be allowed to use their **own methodology** when recognising credit risk mitigation techniques, provided they adhere to a set of stringent minimum requirements.

Similar to the standardised approach, both IRB approaches recognise **three types of credit risk mitigation technique**. Credit risk mitigation is taken account of via the respective input parameter:

- Netting via EAD
- Guarantees and credit derivatives via PD
- Collateral via LGD

Description of the Input Parameters

Exposure at Default (EAD) equals the amount outstanding at the point of default. For on-balance sheet products, the EAD equals the nominal amount of the loan. In the case of off-balance sheet products like credit lines or derivatives, the EAD or credit equivalent amount is calculated using a credit conversion factor. Netting is eligible as a credit risk mitigation technique for both on-balance sheet and off-balance sheet positions. Banks using the advanced IRB approach are free to provide their own estimates for the EAD of off-balance sheet positions.

Probability of Default (PD) is the likelihood that a borrower will default. More precisely, it defines the likelihood that a borrower will default within a specified period of time.

Darunter versteht man konkret die Schätzung der Ausfallswahrscheinlichkeit (PD) nach den internen Ratingklassen der Bank, der Verlustquoten im Ausfall (LGD) nach internen Sicherheitenklassen bzw. LGD-Bänder und auch die Schätzung der Aushaftung im Ausfall (EAD) mittels Kreditumrechnungsfaktoren. Diese Schätzungen dienen dann bei der Berechnung der Eigenmittelunterlegung als „Startwerte".

Auf der anderen Seite müssen die Banken bei jeder Berechnung der Eigenmittelunterlegung die **„effektiven" Inputparameter** berechnen. Ausgehend von den geschätzten Startwerten werden für jede einzelne Forderung unter Berücksichtigung von risikomindernden Verfahren die effektiven Inputparameter berechnet, die dann über die Risikogewichtsfunktion die jeweiligen Risikogewichte liefern.

Die Schätzung dieser Inputgrößen stellt vor allem **datentechnisch** einen **großen Aufwand** dar. Nicht alle Banken waren/sind in der Lage, von Beginn an alle diese vier Parameter auf Basis der internen Daten selbst zu schätzen. Aus diesem Grund hat der Basler Ausschuss **zwei Varianten des IRB-Ansatzes**, den Basis- und den fortgeschrittenen IRB-Ansatz, entwickelt.

Basis-IRB-Ansatz

Im Basis-IRB-Ansatz müssen die Banken **nur die PDs ihrer internen Ratingklassen schätzen**. Die restlichen drei Inputparameter bzw. das Regelwerk zur Berücksichtigung von Kreditrisikominderung werden vorgegeben. Der Umfang der anerkannten kreditrisikomindernden Verfahren ist breiter als im Standardansatz, trotzdem bleiben im Basis-IRB-Ansatz einige Beschränkungen aufrecht, wie z.B. welche Garantiegeber bzw. welche Arten von Sicherheiten anerkannt werden.

Fortgeschrittener IRB-Ansatz

Zusätzlich zur PD müssen im fortgeschrittenen IRB-Ansatz **auch die LGD und EAD von Banken intern geschätzt** werden. Ebenso dürfen sie bei der Berücksichtigung der Kreditrisikominderung unter Einhaltung strenger Mindestanforderungen ihre **eigene Methodik** anwenden.

In beiden Varianten des IRB-Ansatzes werden wie im Standardansatz **drei Arten von Kreditrisikominderung** anerkannt. Die Berücksichtigung dieser kreditrisikomindernden Verfahren erfolgt bei dem entsprechenden Inputparameter:

- Netting (Aufrechnen von Gegenpositionen) im EAD
- Garantien und Kreditderivate über die PD
- Sicherheiten im LGD

Beschreibung der Inputparameter

Exposure at Default (EAD) ist der aushaftende Kreditbetrag im Zeitpunkt des Ausfalls. Bei Bilanzpositionen entspricht EAD dem Buchwert des Kredits (Ausnutzung). Bei außerbilanziellen Geschäften wie Kreditlinien bzw. Derivaten wird der EAD über den Kreditumrechnungsfaktor bzw. den Kreditäquivalenzbetrag ermittelt. Das Aufrechnen von Gegenpositionen (Netting) als risikominderndes Verfahren wird sowohl bei Bilanzpositionen als auch bei außerbilanziellen Geschäften erlaubt. Den Banken, die den fortgeschrittenen IRB-Ansatz anwenden, ist erlaubt, die EADs von außerbilanziellen Positionen selbst zu schätzen.

Probability of Default (PD) ist die Ausfallswahrscheinlichkeit eines Kreditnehmers. Die PD besagt, mit welcher Wahrscheinlichkeit ein Kreditnehmer innerhalb eines be-

Here, Basel II specifies a period of one year, i.e. the **one-year PD** has to be used when calculating risk-weighted assets.

The **estimation of PDs** has to be made **for each individual risk category**, except in the case of a retail portfolio, where PDs are assigned to a pool of exposures on the assumption that all borrowers belong to the same rating category. Irrespective of which IRB approach is applied, banks have to estimate a PD for each of their internal rating categories.

As the probability of default only indicates the general credit quality of a borrower, transaction-specific exposure factors must not be taken into account when estimating the PD.

Guarantees and credit derivatives as credit risk mitigation techniques are taken account of via the PD. With respect to guarantees and credit derivatives, the foundation IRB approach applies the substitution approach, i.e. the (credit) exposure is split up into a protected portion and an unprotected one, and the probability of default of the counterparty is exchanged for that of the guarantor for the protected portion of the exposure. Banks using the advanced IRB approach are allowed to use their own methodology for recognising guarantees and credit derivatives as credit risk mitigants, provided they adhere to a stringent set of minimum requirements.

Loss Given Default (LGD) stands for the recovery rate in the event of default. More precisely, it states the loss as a percentage of total exposure. Under the foundation IRB approach, the Basel Committee sets forth supervisory LGD values depending on type of exposure as well as the methodology for calculating effective LGDs when allowing for credit risk mitigation. **Collateral** is the credit risk mitigation technique that is accounted for via LGD.

The foundation IRB approach recognises **four types of collateral**. Depending on the type of collateral, supervisory minimum LGDs are stipulated for exposures fully covered by collateral.

Type of Collateral	Required minimum collateralisation level	Required level of over-collateralisation for full LGD recognition	Minimum LGD
Eligible financial collateral	0%	100%	0%
Receivables	0%	125%	35%
CRE/RRE (mortgage)	30%	140%	35%
Other collateral	30%	140%	40%

This means that loans that are fully covered by financial collateral may have an LGD as low as 0%, while loans covered by other types of collateral cannot be assigned an LGD lower than 35% or 40% respectively. It is important to bear in mind that except for financial collateral, full collateralisation is obtained only when the value of the collateral amounts to at least 125% (in the case of receivables) or 140% (in the case of CRE/RRE and other collateral) of the value of the exposure (required level of over-collateralisation). Another restriction is that CRE/RRE and other collaterals are only recognised once they amount to at least 30% of the value of the exposure (minimum collateralisation level).

The supervisory LGD for unsecured exposures is 45%, and 75% for subordinated ones.

stimmten Zeitraums ausfällt. Als Zeitraum gibt Basel II ein Jahr vor, d.h., bei der Berechnung der Risikogewichte muss die **Wahrscheinlichkeit des Ausfalls innerhalb eines Jahres** herangezogen werden.

Die Schätzung der PDs hat **pro Ratingstufe** zu erfolgen. Dabei wird angenommen, dass alle Kreditnehmer einer Ratingstufe die gleiche Ausfallswahrscheinlichkeit haben. Unabhängig von der angewandten Variante des IRB-Ansatzes müssen die Banken schätzen, wie hoch die PDs der jeweiligen Ratingstufen ihres internen Ratingsystems sind.

Da die PDs ein Indiz für die allgemeine finanzielle Bonität der Kreditnehmer sind, werden bei der Schätzung der PDs pro Ratingstufe die transaktionsspezifischen Merkmale der Kredite nicht berücksichtigt.

Die Berücksichtigung von Garantien und Kreditderivaten als Kreditrisikominderung soll jedoch über die PDs erfolgen. Im Basis-IRB gilt in Bezug auf Garantien und Kreditderivate der Substitutionsansatz, d.h., der Kredit wird in einen garantierten und einen ungarantierten Teil aufgeteilt und die PD für den garantierten Teil wird mit der PD des Garantiegebers substituiert. Im fortgeschrittenen IRB-Ansatz hingegen dürfen die Banken unter Erfüllung strenger Mindestanforderungen ihre eigene Methodik zur Berücksichtigung von Garantien und Kreditderivaten anwenden.

Loss Given Default (LGD) ist die Verlustintensität bei Ausfall. Der LGD besagt, wie viel Prozent der Verlust betragen wird, wenn es zu einem Ausfall kommt. Für den Basis-IRB-Ansatz gibt der Ausschuss die LGD-Werte je nach Typ des Kredits sowie die Methodik zur Berechnung der effektiven LGDs unter Berücksichtigung der Kreditrisikominderung vor. Das im LGD zu berücksichtigende risikomindernde Verfahren ist die **Hereinnahme von Sicherheiten.**

Der Basis-IRB-Ansatz kennt **vier Arten von Sicherheiten**. Je nach Art der Sicherheit ist ein Minimum-LGD vorgesehen, den ein vollständig besicherter Kredit haben kann.

Art der Sicherheit	Mindestbe-sicherung	Vollständige Besicherung	Minimum LGD
finanzielle Sicherheit	0%	100%	0%
Forderungen	0%	125%	35%
Hypothek	30%	140%	35%
sonstige Sicherheiten	30%	140%	40%

Während der effektive LGD für Kredite mit vollständiger finanzieller Besicherung bis auf 0% hinuntergehen kann, ist der Minimum-LGD für andere Sicherheitenarten mit 35% bzw. 40% begrenzt. Dabei wird eine vollständige Besicherung außer bei finanziellen Sicherheiten erst dann erreicht, wenn der Sicherheitenwert 125% (Forderungen) bzw. 140% (Hypothek und sonstige Sicherheiten) des Kreditbetrages ausmacht. Noch dazu kommt, dass hypothekarische und sonstige Sicherheiten erst ab einer 30%igen Besicherung anerkannt werden.

Der vorgegebene LGD für unbesicherte Kredite beträgt 45%, im Falle von nachrangigen Krediten 75%.

Under the advanced IRB approach, banks have to estimate LGDs for their defined LGD categories internally. As opposed to the foundation IRB approach, there are no restrictions concerning the range of eligible types of collateral, nor on the method of calculating effective LGD. However, banks wishing to use internal LGD estimates for calculating risk weights are subject to stricter additional minimum requirements.

Maturity (M) stands for the residual maturity of an exposure. Under the foundation IRB approach the maturity is not explicitly taken into account, thus all exposures are assigned a standard maturity of **2.5 years**. Banks using the advanced IRB approach are required to measure the effective residual maturity for each facility, which is limited to a supervisory range of 1 to 5 years irrespective of the actual residual maturity.

Risk-Weight Function

Once the effective input parameters for the individual exposures have been determined, the risk weights may be calculated. The risk-weight function used for exposures to sovereigns, banks and corporates was calibrated in such a way that an unsecured loan (LGD = 45%) to a borrower with a PD of 1.06% and a residual maturity of 2.5 years would result in a risk weight of 100% and therefore a capital charge of 8%. This means that around 8% of equity still has to be set aside to cover the credit risk of this type of "benchmark loan".

$$RW = f (PD, LGD, M); \text{max. } 12.5 \times LGD$$
$$RWA = RW \times EAD$$
$$CapReq = 8\% \times RWA$$

RW   = Risk Weight
PD   = Probability of Default
LGD   = Loss Given Default
M   = Maturity
EAD   = Exposure at Default
RWA   = Risk-Weighted Assets
CapReq = Capital Requirement

The limitation to 12.5 times LGD is so that the **capital requirement will never exceed the exposure**.

The following figure 1 shows **the interrelationship between risk weights (or capital charges) and probability of default (PD)**. The risk-weight curve clearly shows that the IRB approach allows a better differentiation between risks inherent in individual exposures by comparison to the standardised approach.

Beim fortgeschrittenen IRB-Ansatz müssen die Banken intern die LGDs der selbst definierten LGD-Klassen schätzen. Im Gegensatz zum Basis-IRB-Ansatz gibt es weder Beschränkungen hinsichtlich der anerkannten Sicherheiten, noch wird vorgegeben, wie die effektiven LGDs zu berechnen sind. Banken, die bei der Berechnung der Risikogewichte ihre
internen LGD-Schätzungen verwenden wollen, haben jedoch strengere Mindestanforderungen zu erfüllen.

Maturity (M) ist die Restlaufzeit des Kredits. Die Restlaufzeit wird im Basis-IRB-
Ansatz nicht explizit berücksichtigt. Daher gilt für alle Kredite eine Restlaufzeit von **2,5
Jahren.** Im fortgeschrittenen IRB-Ansatz hingegen muss für jeden Kredit die effektive
Restlaufzeit berechnet werden, die unabhängig von der tatsächlichen Laufzeit auf zwischen
ein und fünf Jahre beschränkt ist.

Risikogewichtsfunktion

Nachdem die effektiven Inputparameter der einzelnen Kredite ermittelt worden sind, können die Risikogewichte berechnet werden. Die Funktion zur Berechnung der Risikogewichte für Unternehmen sowie Banken und Staaten ist so kalibriert, dass sich für einen Kredit
mit einer PD von 1%, einem LGD von 45% und einer M von 2,5 Jahren ein Risikogewicht
von ca. 100% und somit eine Eigenmittelunterlegung von 8% ergibt. Das bedeutet, dass das
Kreditrisiko dieses „Benchmark-Kredits" mit Eigenmitteln in der Höhe von 8% des Kreditbetrages zu unterlegen ist.

$$RW = \text{Funktion von (PD, LGD, M); höchstens } 12,5 \times LGD$$
$$RWA = RW \times EAD$$
$$EM\text{-}Unt = 8\% \times RWA$$

RW = Risikogewicht (Risk Weight)
PD = Ausfallswahrscheinlichkeit (Probability of Default)
LGD = Verlust im Ausfall (Loss Given Default)
M = Restlaufzeit (Maturity)
EAD = Aushaftung im Ausfall (Exposure at Default)
RWA = risikogewichtete Aktiva (Risk Weighted Assets)
EM-Unt = Eigenmittelunterlegung

Die Begrenzung des Risikogewichts mit dem maximal 12,5-Fachen des LGD hat den Zweck,
dass die **Eigenmittelunterlegung** eines Kredits **nie höher** wird **als der Kreditbetrag.**

Die folgende Grafik zeigt das **Risikogewicht für Unternehmen in Abhängigkeit von
der Ausfallswahrscheinlichkeit.** Diese Risikogewichtskurve macht deutlich, dass der IRB-
Ansatz im Vergleich zum Standardansatz eine weitgehend größere Differenzierung nach
Risikogehalt ermöglicht.

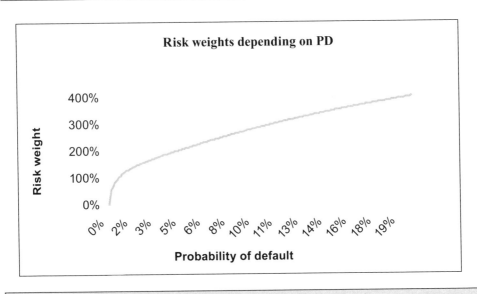

Example

Calculate the capital requirement for the following corporate loan:

EAD: EUR 2 m
PD: 0.5%
LGD: 40% $\Big\}$ RW resulting from RW function = 64%
M: 2.5 years

RWA = 64% x EUR 2 m = EUR 1,280,000
CapReq = 8% x EUR 1,280,000 = EUR 102,400

Comparing the IRB approach with the standardised approach

The advantage of the IRB approach is that it is based on (bank-) internal ratings and allows a **better differentiation of risks**. Actual capital requirements depend on the respective loan portfolio of a bank.

While banks can expect lower capital charges in the case of better-rated credit exposures, the opposite is likely for lower ratings. Under the standardised approach, a loan to an unrated company demands a risk weight of 100%. Under the IRB approach, a low internal rating for the same exposure will probably result in a risk weight higher than 100% and thus to a higher capital charge.

For this very reason, Basel II will increase the **importance of credit risk mitigation techniques**. Once it provides collateral, a company with a lower rating may receive a more advantageous risk weight under the IRB approach than it would under the standardised approach. And last but not least, providing collateral is a simpler and less time-consuming way for the borrower to receive more favourable conditions on a loan than via its rating.

Despite all the improvements with respect to capital requirements for credit risk, one essential issue (deliberately) remains untouched. The **correlation of risk between different borrowers** and thus any possible **benefits derived from diversification of a bank's loan**

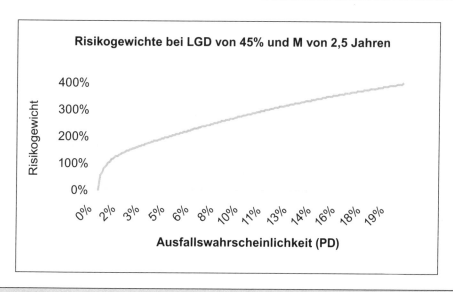

Risikogewichte bei LGD von 45% und M von 2,5 Jahren

Beispiel

Berechnen Sie die Eigenmittelunterlegung für den folgenden Unternehmenskredit:

EAD: 2 Mio. EUR
PD: 0,5%
LGD: 40%   } Risikogewicht aus der Funktion = 64%
M: 2,5 Jahre

RWA = 64% x 2 Mio. EUR = 1.280.000 EUR
EM-Unt = 8% x 1.280.000 EUR = 102.400 EUR

IRB-Ansatz im Vergleich zum Standardansatz

Der Vorteil des IRB-Ansatzes gegenüber dem Standardansatz ist, dass er auf den internen Ratings der Bank basiert und somit eine **größere Risikodifferenzierung** ermöglicht. Die tatsächliche Eigenmittelunterlegung hängt vom jeweiligen Kreditportfolio der Bank ab.

Während der IRB-Ansatz bei guten Bonitäten zu günstigerer Eigenmittelunterlegung führt, ist der Effekt bei schwächeren Bonitäten eher gegenläufig. Ein nicht extern geratetes Unternehmen hat im Standardansatz ein Risikogewicht von 100%. Ein schwaches internes Rating führt jedoch für dasselbe Unternehmen im IRB-Ansatz mitunter zu einem Risikogewicht von mehr als 100% und somit zu einer höheren Eigenmittelunterlegung.

Daher kommt im Rahmen von Basel II **der Sicherheit große Bedeutung** zu. Ein Unternehmen schwacher Bonität kann im IRB-Ansatz durch das Einbringen von entsprechenden Sicherheiten doch günstiger zu unterlegen sein als im Standardansatz. Und schließlich sind Sicherheiten jenes Gebiet, in dem der Kreditnehmer schneller und einfacher Einfluss auf seine Kreditkonditionen nehmen kann als auf sein Rating.

Trotz aller Entwicklungen in Bezug auf Unterlegung des Kreditrisikos bleibt ein wesentlicher Punkt (bewusst) unangetastet: Die **Risikokorrelationen zwischen unterschiedlichen Schuldnern** und jegliche **Diversifikationseffekte im Kreditportfolio der Bank wer-**

portfolio are not taken into account. In the long run, the goal is to calculate capital requirements on the basis of fully developed credit risk models. However, credit risk modelling is not yet considered to fulfil the necessary criteria. The most important deficiencies in the application of credit risk models as perceived by the Basel Committee relate to the quality of data and the ability of banks and supervisors to audit the results of such models.

Capital requirements for the trading book

A trading book consists of positions in financial instruments and commodities held either with trading intent or in order to hedge other elements of the trading book. To be eligible for trading book capital treatment, financial instruments must either be free of any restrictive covenants on their tradability, or be able to be hedged completely.

A trading book has to be frequently and accurately valued and should be actively managed.

Banks have to calculate capital requirements for three types of risk: for the **counterparty risk** of OTC derivatives, repo-style and other transactions, and for the **general market risk and specific (market) risk** of trading book positions.

Specific risk includes the risk that an individual debt or equity security moves by more or less than the general market and event risk, which also includes the risk of default. This means that the credit risk charge for trading book positions is already covered by the specific capital charges for trading book positions!

In measuring their trading book risks, banks have a choice between **two broad methodologies**. One alternative will be to measure the risks in a standardised manner, using a specified measurement framework. The alternative methodology allows banks to use risk measures derived from their own internal risk management models.

In the following, we will illustrate the calculation of capital requirements for the specific risk of interest rate instruments and FX instruments according to the standard methodology.

Specific risk charges for interest rate instruments in the trading book

Category	External Rating	Capital charge (specific risk)	Residual maturity
Sovereign	AAA to AA-	0.00%	all
	A+ to BBB-	0.25%	up to 6 months
		1.00%	6 to 24 months
		1.60%	above 24 months
	BB+ to B-	8.00%	
	below B-	12.00%	
	no rating	8.00%	
"Qualifying" assets (~investment-grade securities)		0.25%	up to 6 months
		1.00%	6 to 24 months
		1.60%	above 24 months
Other	same capital requirement as standardised approach for banking book		

For the calculation of the general risk charge for interest rate instruments, the market risk amendment provides two methodologies (the **maturity method** and the **duration method**), which will not be explained further here.

den nicht berücksichtigt. Obwohl es langfristig ein Ziel ist, vollständig ausgebaute Kreditrisikomodelle als die Grundlage für die Eigenkapitalberechnung einzusetzen, werden sie noch nicht als ausgereift betrachtet. Die wichtigsten Mängel, die der Ausschuss bei der Verwendung von Kreditrisikomodellen fand, bezogen sich auf die Datenqualität und die Fähigkeit von Banken und Aufsichtsbehörden, die Modellergebnisse zu überprüfen.

Eigenmittelunterlegung für das Handelsbuch

Dem Handelsbuch können Positionen zugeordnet werden, deren Handelbarkeit nicht eingeschränkt ist oder die (jederzeit) voll abgesichert werden können. Ein Handelsbuch muss häufig und exakt bewertet und aktiv verwaltet werden.

Banken müssen hier für drei Arten von Risiken Eigenmittelanforderungen berechnen; einerseits für die **Kontrahentenrisiken** aus außerbörslichen Derivaten, Wertpapierpensions- und ähnlichen Geschäften, andererseits für **allgemeine und spezifische Marktrisiken** (= besondere Kursrisiken) von Positionen.

Spezifisches Marktrisiko umfasst dabei das Risiko, dass sich einzelne Positionen stärker oder schwächer als der Gesamtmarkt bewegen. Hierzu gehört bei Handelsbuchpositionen auch das Kreditrisiko, das heißt, das Kreditrisiko von Handelsbuchpositionen ist bereits durch die Eigenmittelanforderung aus dem spezifischen Marktrisiko abgedeckt.

Die Banken haben hier die Wahl zwischen **zwei grundlegenden Verfahren.** Einerseits können die EM-Erfordernisse nach vorgegebenen Standardverfahren berechnet werden, als Alternative können die Banken interne Modelle für das Marktrisiko verwenden.

Im Folgenden wird die Berechnung der EM-Unterlegung für das spezifische Risiko von Zinsinstrumenten und für das Fremdwährungsrisiko nach dem Standardverfahren dargestellt.

EM-Unterlegung für das spezifische Risiko von Zinsinstrumenten im Handelsbuch

Kategorie	Externes Rating	Eigenmittelanforderung (spezifisches Risiko)	Restlaufzeit Instrument
Staat	AAA bis AA-	0%	alle
	A+ bis BBB-	0,25%	bis 6 Monate
		1,00%	6 bis 24 Monate
		1,60%	über 24 Monate
	BB+ bis B-	8%	
	Unterhalb B-	12%	
	ohne Rating	8%	
Qualifizierte Aktiva (~Investment-Grade Papiere)		0,25%	bis 6 Monate
		1,00%	6 bis 24 Monate
		1,60%	über 24 Monate
Andere	dieselbe Unterlegung wie beim Standardansatz für das Bankbuch		

Für die Berechnung des allgemeinen Zinsänderungsrisikos stehen eine sogenannte **Laufzeitmethode** und die **Durationsmethode** zur Verfügung, die hier jedoch nicht näher erläutert werden.

> **Example**
>
> Corporate bond in the trading book, coupon 4%, remaining maturity 18 months, Rating A-, EUR 10,000,000
> Capital requirement: EUR 100,000 (10,000,000 * 1.0%)
> Since the position is in the trading book and the rating corresponds to the rating of qualifying assets (investment grade), the capital requirement over the remaining term is predetermined (6-24 months → 1.00%).

Capital requirements for interest rate derivative

There are no capital charges for specific market risk for interest rate swaps, FX swaps, FRA, FX outrights and interest rate futures. As for contracts with an underlying obligation, the capital charge for the specific market risk is the same as for the underlying obligation.

Capital requirements for foreign exchange risk

Two processes are needed to calculate the capital requirement for foreign exchange risk. The first is to measure the exposure in single currency positions. The second is to measure the risks inherent in a bank's mix of long and short positions in different currencies. If banks do not use internal models for risk measurement, they can use a shorthand method provided by the Basel Market Risk Amendment.

Under the shorthand method, the nominal amount (or net present value) of the net position in each foreign currency and in gold is converted at spot rates into the reporting currency. The capital charge will be 8% of the overall net open position (i.e. whichever is the greater of the long and short positions).

> **Example**
>
> | | YEN | GBP | USD | RUB | AUD |
> |------------|------|-------|------|------|------|
> | Net Position | +50 | +100 | +20 | -30 | -40 |
> | Total | | 170 | | -70 | |
>
> The sum of the net-long positions (170) exceeds the sum of net-short positions (70). The capital charge for FX risk is therefore calculated as 170 * 8% = 13.60.

4.4. Legislator and Replacement Risk

The replacement risk of OTC derivatives is regulated under Basel II. In contrast to regular balance sheet instruments, a credit equivalent for the off-balance sheet products needs to be determined.

There are currently four different ways to measure this:

- maturity method
- mark-to-market method (MtM)

Beispiel

Unternehmensanleihe im HABU, Coupon 4%, Restlaufzeit 18 Monate, Rating A-, EUR 10.000.000
Eigenmittelunterlegung: EUR 100.000 (10.000.000 x 1,00%)
Da es sich um eine Position im Handelsbuch handelt und das Rating dem Rating von qualifizierten Aktiva (Investment Grade) entspricht, wird die Unterlegungspflicht über die Restlaufzeit bestimmt (6–24 Monate ➔ 1,00%).

EM-Unterlegung für Zinsderivate

Für Zinsswaps, Devisenswaps, FRA, Forward-Devisenkontrakte und Zinsfutures sowie Futures auf einen Zinsindex werden keine Eigenkapitalanforderungen für das spezifische Kursrisiko erhoben. Bei Kontrakten, denen eine Schuldverschreibung zugrunde liegt, muss das spezifische Kursrisiko mit Eigenkapital unterlegt werden, und zwar nach dem Risiko, das der Emittent darstellt (siehe Eigenmittelunterlegung für das Zinsänderungsrisiko).

EM-Unterlegung für Fremdwährungsrisiko

Hier müssen die Engagements in den einzelnen Währungen gemessen werden, um in einem folgenden Schritt die Risiken für die Gesamtheit der Long- und Shortpositionen zu berechnen. Verwenden die Banken keine internen Modelle zur Risikomessung, so sind nach einem vom Baseler Marktrisikopapier vorgegebenen Kurzverfahren.

Dabei werden alle in die Meldewährung umgerechneten Nettopositionen in den einzelnen Währungen long und short zusammengerechnet und die Position die größer ist (long oder short) mit 8% Eigenkapital unterlegt.

Beispiel

	YEN	GBP	USD	RUB	AUD
Nettoposition	+50	+100	+20	-30	-40
Gesamt	170			-70	

Die Summe der Netto-Long-Positionen (170) ist größer als die Summe der Netto-Short Positionen (70). Daher beträgt die Eigenmittelunterlegung für das Fremdwährungsrisiko 170 x 8% = 13,60.

4.4. Gesetzgeber und Wiederbeschaffungsrisiko

Unter Basel II wird auch das Wiederbeschaffungsrisiko bei derivativen OTC-Produkten geregelt. Dabei wird für derivative Produkte ein Kreditäquivalent ermittelt.

Aktuell gibt es vier unterschiedliche Bemessungsmöglichkeiten: Zusammenfassung

- Laufzeitmethode
- Marktbewertungsmethode (MtM)

- standardised method
- internal model

Maturity Method

Using the maturity method, a given percentage rate on the nominal amount, depending on the underlying and the term, is estimated as replacement risk.

Mark-to-market Method (MtM)

Using the mark-to-market method, only the current positive market values of the positions plus an add-on, depending on the underlying and the term, are estimated as replacement risk.

Standardised Method

Using the standardised method, current market values, the effect of netting agreements with the counterparty, the received and delivered collaterals per counterparty, the future market fluctuations and their effect on the MtM-values as well as the future market fluctuations and their effect on the value of collateral (with predetermined parameters) are considered.

Internal Model

Using so-called internal models (also called „expected positive exposure"), the bank can quantify the maximum exposure per counterparty for the entire term by considering the volatilities and correlations and the effects of netting and collateral agreements. As with the quantification of market risks with VaR-approaches, the parameters for the calibration of the model (confidence level, holding period, etc.) are predetermined by the legislator.

Since the evaluation with the standardised method as well as the so-called internal models (Expected Positive Exposure) are rather complex, only the first two methods are explained here.

The Maturity Method

Using the maturity method, credit risk for OTC derivatives is calculated in two steps.

Step 1

First, the nominal amounts of each instrument are multiplied by the following percentage rates:

Original term	Contracts on interest rates	FX rates contracts
Up to 1 year	0.5 %	2.0 %
More than 1 year and no longer than 2 years	1.0 %	5.0 %
For each additional year	1.0 %	3.0 %

- Standardmethode
- Interne Modelle

Laufzeitmethode

Bei der Laufzeitmethode wird abhängig vom Underlying und der Restlaufzeit der Position ein vorgegebener Prozentsatz auf den Nominalbetrag als Wiederbeschaffungsrisiko angesetzt.

Marktbewertungsmethode (MtM)

Bei der Marktbewertungsmethode werden nur die aktuellen positiven Marktwerte der Positionen plus ein Add-on, abhängig von der Restlaufzeit und dem Underlying, als Wiederbeschaffungsrisiko angesetzt.

Standardmethode

Bei der Standardmethode werden die aktuellen Marktwerte, der Effekt der Netting-Vereinbarungen mit dem Partner, die erhaltenen und eingelieferten Sicherheiten pro Partner, die zukünftigen Marktschwankungen und ihr Effekt auf die MtM-Werte sowie die zukünftigen Marktschwankungen und ihr Effekt auf die Sicherheiten, mit vorgegebenen Parametern, berücksichtigt.

Interne Modelle

Bei den sogenannten internen Modellen (auch „Expected Positive Exposure" genannt) kann die Bank mit einem internen Modell unter Berücksichtigung der Volatilitäten und Korrelationen und der Effekte von Netting und Collateral Agreements das maximale Exposure pro Kontrahent für die gesamte Laufzeit quantifizieren und als Risikoäquivalent ansetzen. Wie bei der Quantifizierung der Marktrisiken mit VaR-Ansätzen gibt es auch in diesem Falle vom Gesetzgeber vorgegebene Parameter (Konfidenzintervall, Haltedauer …), die bei der Kalibrierung des Modells mindestens zu erfüllen sind.

Da sowohl die Berechnungsmethodik mit der Standardmethode als auch die sogenannten internen Modelle (Expected Positive Exposure) relativ komplex sind, möchten wir hier nur auf die beiden ersten Ansätze eingehen.

Die Laufzeitmethode

Bei der Laufzeitmethode wird das Kreditrisiko für OTC-Derivate in zwei Schritten errechnet.

Schritt 1

Der Nominalwert jedes Instrumentes wird mit folgenden Prozentsätzen multipliziert:

Ursprungslaufzeit	Zinssatzverträge	Devisenkursverträge
höchstens 1 Jahr	0,5 %	2,0 %
mehr als 1 Jahr und nicht mehr als 2 Jahre	1,0 %	5,0 %
für jedes weitere Jahr	1,0 %	3,0 %

Note:

All derivatives that cannot be categorised as interest rate contracts fall into the category of FX contracts.

Step 2

The risk as determined in step 1 is multiplied by the counterparty weighting. This risk is capped at 50%.

Example

Capital requirement for an interest rate swap with 10 years maturity, volume EUR 100m; counterparty: OECD bank

Counterparty risk
weighting: 20% (OECD bank)
Capital adequacy: 8%
Credit risk equivalent: 9% (1% for the first two years plus 1% for each additional year) = 9,000,000 (100,000,000 * 9%)
Capital requirement: 144,000 (=9,000,000 * 20% * 8%)
                     (= credit risk equivalent * counterparty risk weighting * capital adequacy)

Example

Capital requirement for an FX outright transaction (EUR/USD), volume 10m, term 2 years, counterparty: corporate

Credit risk equivalent: 5% (2% for the first year and an additional 3% for the second year) = 500,000 (10,000,000 * 5%)
Counterparty risk
weighting: 50% (derivative, client)
Capital adequacy: 8%
Capital requirement: 20,000 (= 500,000 * 50% * 8%)
                     (= credit risk equivalent * counterparty risk weighting * capital adequacy)

Considering Netting Agreements in the Maturity Method

The authorities accept **offset agreements (close out netting)** if the maturity method is used, which means that one may reduce the percentage rates that are applied in step 1 according to the following table.

Anmerkung:

Alle sonstigen Derivative (außer reine Zinsderivate) fallen in die Kategorie von Devisen-kursverträgen.

Schritt 2

Im zweiten Schritt wird das Risiko, das sich aus dem ersten Schritt ergibt, mit der jeweiligen Adressgewichtung des Partners multipliziert. Zu berücksichtigen ist hier, dass die Adressgewichtung für das Wiederbeschaffungsrisiko mit 50 % begrenzt ist.

Beispiel

Unterlegungspflicht für einen Zinsswap mit 10 Jahren Restlaufzeit, Volumen 100 Mio. EUR, Partner OECD-Bank

Adressgewichtung	
Partner:	20 % (OECD-Bank)
Eigenmittel-unterlegungssatz:	8 %
Risikowert:	9 % (1 % für die ersten beiden Jahre, zuzüglich je 1 % pro weiteres Jahr Laufzeit) = 9.000.000 EUR (100.000.000 * 9 %)
Unterlegungspflicht (Eigenkapitalbedarf):	144.000 EUR (= 9.000.000 * 20 % * 8 %)
	(= Risikowert * Adressgewichtung * Eigenmittelunterlegungssatz)

Beispiel

Unterlegungspflicht für Devisentermingeschäft (EUR/USD), Volumen 10 Mio. EUR, Laufzeit zwei Jahre, Partner Unternehmen

Adressgewichtung	
Partner:	50 % (Derivativ, Kunden)
Eigenmittel-unterlegungssatz:	8 %
Risikowert:	5 % (2 % Jahr 1 zuzüglich 3 % für das zweite Jahr) = 500.000 EUR (10.000.000 * 5 %)
Unterlegungspflicht (Eigenkapitalbedarf):	20.000 (= 500.000 * 50 % * 8 %)
	(= Risikowert * Adressgewichtung * Eigenmittelunterlegungssatz)

Berücksichtigung von Netting-Vereinbarungen in der Laufzeitmethode

Bei von den Behörden anerkannten **Aufrechnungsvereinbarungen (Close Out Netting)** können bei der Verwendung der Laufzeitmethode die in Schritt 1 verwendeten Prozentsätze entsprechend der folgenden Tabelle reduziert werden.

Original term	Contracts on interest rates	FX rate contracts and contracts on gold
Up to 1 year	0.35 %	1.50 %
More than 1 year and no longer than 2 years	0.75 %	3.75 %
For each additional year	0.75 %	2.25 %

Example

Capital requirement for two interest rate swaps with a counterparty, which has conducted an accepted close out netting agreement with the bank:

Transaction 1:   fixed-rate payer swap 10 years, 100m EUR
Transaction 2:   fixed-rate receiver swap 5 years, 50m EUR

Credit risk equivalent (according to the table):
Transaction 1:   100m EUR * 6.75% (0.75% + 8 * 0.75%) = 6,750,000 EUR
Transaction 2:   50 * 3% (0.75% + 3 * 0.75%) = 1,500,000 EUR
Credit risk equivalent total: 6,750,000 + 1,500,000 = 8,250,000 EUR

Capital requirement:
8,250,000 * 50% * 8% = 330,000 EUR

Acknowledged **bilateral novation contracts (novation netting)** allow for a calculation based on the maturity method where the assumed nominal amount per partner takes into account the effects of the novation contract.

Mark-to-market Method (MtM)

The measurement of credit risk in the derivatives business is done in three steps:

Step 1

You determine the replacement value of contracts that have a positive MtM value.

Step 2

The notional amounts of all contracts are multiplied by the following percentage rates (to include all possible risks in the future)

Ursprungslaufzeit	Zinssatzverträge	Devisenkurs- und Goldverträge
höchstens 1 Jahr	0,35 %	1,50 %
mehr als 1 Jahr und nicht mehr als 2 Jahre	0,75 %	3,75 %
für jedes weitere Jahr	0,75 %	2,25 %

Beispiel

Unterlegungspflicht für zwei Zinsswaps, die mit einem Partner abgeschlossen wurden, mit dem die Bank eine anerkannte Close-Out-Netting-Vereinbarung abgeschlossen hat:

Geschäft 1:   Festzinszahler-Swap 10 Jahre, 100 Mio. EUR
Geschäft 2   Festzinsempfänger-Swap 5 Jahre, 50 Mio. EUR

Risikowerte (laut Tabelle):
Geschäft 1:   100 Mio. EUR * 6,75 % (0,75 % + 8 * 0,75 %) = 6.750.000 EUR
Geschäft 2:   50 * 3 % (0,75% + 3 * 0,75 %) = 1.500.000 EUR
Risikowert gesamt: 6.750.000 + 1.500.000 = 8.250.000 EUR

Eigenmittelunterlegung:
8.250.000 * 50 % * 8 % = 330.000 EUR

Bei anerkannten **bilateralen Schuldumwandlungsverträgen (Novation Netting)** kann bei der Berechnung mit der Laufzeitmethode der verwendete Nominalwert pro Partner unter Berücksichtigung des Schuldumwandlungsvertrages berechnet werden.

Marktbewertungsmethode (MtM)

Die Messung des Kreditrisikos aus Geschäften mit Derivaten erfolgt hier in drei Schritten:

Schritt 1

Der Wiederbeschaffungswert der Verträge wird ermittelt. Nur die positiven Wiederbeschaffungswerte werden weiter berücksichtigt.

Schritt 2

Die Nominalwerte aller Kontrakte werden mit folgenden Prozentsätzen multipliziert (um zukünftige potenzielle Risiken zu erfassen):

Term to maturity	Contracts on interest rates	FX contracts	Contracts on shares	Contracts on precious metals except gold	Contracts on commodities except gold
Up to 1 year	0%	1%	6%	7%	10%
More than 1 year and no longer than 5 years	0.5%	5%	8%	7%	12%
More than 5 years	1.5%	7.5%	10%	8%	15%

Exception:
This additional calculation does not apply to basis swaps.

Step 3
The risks determined in steps 1 and 2 are each multiplied by the counterparty weighting.

Example

Capital requirement for a fixed-rate payer swap with 10 years maturity, volume 100m EUR, interest rate 4.50%, market rate 4%, MtM +2,000,000, counterparty OECD Bank

Counterparty risk
weighting: 20% (OECD Bank)
Capital adequacy: 8%
Credit risk equivalent: 3,500,000 (= 2,000,000 + 1.5% * 100,000,000)
Capital requirement: 56,000 (=3,500,000 * 20% * 8%)
                         (= credit risk equivalent * counterparty risk weighting * capital adequacy)

Example

Capital requirement for an FX forward outright (sell EUR/USD), volume 10m EUR, price 1.1500, market price 1.2000,
MtM: - 395,833 EUR, term 2 years, counterparty corporate

Counterparty risk
weighting: 50%
Capital adequacy: 8%
Credit risk equivalent: 500,000 EUR (0 (as MTtM negative) + 500,000
                         (5% of 10,000,000)
Capital requirement: 20,000 EUR (= 500,000 * 50% * 8%)
                         (= Credit risk equivalent * Counterparty risk weighting * Capital adequacy)

Restlaufzeit	Zinssatz-verträge	Devisen-kursverträge und Gold	Beteiligungstitel	Edelmetalle außer Gold	Sonstige Warenverträge
höchstens 1 Jahr	0,0 %	1,0 %	6,0 %	7,0 %	10,0 %
mehr als 1 Jahr und nicht mehr als 5 Jahre	0,5 %	5,0 %	8,0 %	7,0 %	12,0 %
länger als 5 Jahre	1,5 %	7,5 %	10,0 %	8,0 %	15,0 %

Ausnahme:

Bei Basisswaps entfällt diese zusätzliche Berechnung.

Schritt 3

Die Risiken, die sich aus den Schritten 1 und 2 ergeben, werden mit der jeweiligen Adressgewichtung des Partners und dem Eigenkapitalunterlegungssatz multipliziert.

Beispiel

Unterlegungspflicht für einen Festzinszahler-Swap mit 10 Jahren Restlaufzeit, Volumen 100 Mio. EUR, Zinssatz 4,50 %, Marktsatz 4 %, MTM +2.000.000, Partner OECD-Bank
Adressgewichtung: 20 % (OECD-Bank)

Eigenmittel-
unterlegungssatz: 8 %
Risikowert: 3.500.000 (= 2.000.000 + 1,5 % * 100.000.000)
Unterlegungspflicht
(Eigenkapitalbedarf):   56.000 (= 3.500.000 * 20% * 8 %)
  (= Risikowert * Adressgewichtung * Eigenmittelunterlegungssatz)

Beispiel

Unterlegungspflicht für Devisentermingeschäft (Verkauf EUR/USD), Volumen 10 Mio. EUR, Kurs 1,1500, Marktkurs 1,2000,
MTM: -395.833 EUR, Laufzeit 2 Jahre, Partner Unternehmen

Adressgewichtung: 50 %
Eigenmittel-
unterlegungssatz: 8 %
Risikowert: 500.000 EUR (0 (da MTM minus) + 500.000 (5 % von 10.000.000)
Unterlegungspflicht
(Eigenkapitalbedarf):   20.000 EUR (= 500.000 * 50 % * 8 %)
  (= Risikowert * Adressgewichtung * Eigenmittelunterlegungssatz)

Unterlegungspflicht für Devisentermingeschäft (Verkauf EUR/USD), Volumen 10 Mio. EUR, Kurs 1,1500, Marktkurs 1,2000,
MTM: –395.833 EUR, Laufzeit 2 Jahre, Partner Unternehmen

Considering Netting Agreements in the Mark-to-market Method

The authorities accept **offset agreements** if step 1 of the mark-to-market method is based only on the net values of those contracts that are agreed upon. The possible future risk calculated in step 2 is reduced by the following formula:

40% Gross Risk + 60% * (Gross Risk * (Net MtM/Gross MtM))

where:

Gross risk = amount of add-ons of all transactions
Net MtM = amount of positive and negative MtM values, if the amount is positive, the value is set to 0
Gross MtM = amount of positive MtM values

Example
Capital requirement for two interest rate swaps with a counterparty, which has conducted an accepted close out netting agreement with the bank: Counterparty risk weighting 50%, capital adequacy 8%

Transaction 1:   fixed-rate payer swap 10 years, 100m EUR,
                      MtM + 2,000,000 EUR
Transaction 2:   fixed-rate receiver swap 5 years, 50m EUR,
                      MtM – 1,500,000 EUR

Step 1:   net MtM value: 500,000 (+ 2,000,000 – 1,500,000)
Step 2:   add-on transaction 1: 100m * 1.50% = 1,500,000
               add-on transaction 2: 50m * 0.75% = 375,000
               gross Risk: 1,500,000 + 375,000 = 1,875,000
               gross MtM: 2,000,000 + 0 = 2,000,000

Surcharge: 40% * 1,875,000 + 60% *(1,875,000*500,000/2,000,000)
               = 1,031,250 EUR
(40% * gross risk) + 60% * (gross risk * net MtM / gross MtM)

Credit risk equivalent:
500,000 + 1,031,250 = 1,531,250 EUR
(Net MtM-value + surcharge)

Capital requirement:
1,531,250 * 50% * 8% = 61,250 EUR
(Credit risk equivalent * Counterparty risk weighting * Capital adequacy)

Berücksichtigung von Netting-Vereinbarungen in der Marktbewertungsmethode

Bei von den Behörden anerkannten **Aufrechnungsvereinbarungen** wird bei der Verwendung der Marktbewertungsmethode im Schritt 1 nur mit dem Nettowert aller in der Vereinbarung einbezogenen Kontrakte gerechnet. Das im Schritt 2 berechnete zukünftige potenzielle Risiko wird mit folgender Formel reduziert:

$$\text{Zuschlag} = 40\% \text{ Bruttozuschlag} + 60\%\left(\text{Bruttozuschlag} * \frac{\text{Netto} - \text{MTM}}{\text{Brutto} - \text{MTM}}\right)$$

wobei:

Bruttozuschlag = Summe der Add-ons aller Geschäfte
Netto-MtM = Summe der positiven und negativen MtM-Werte, ist die Summe positiv, so wird der Wert mit 0 angesetzt
Brutto.MtM = Summe der positiven MtM-Werte

Beispiel

Unterlegungspflicht für zwei Zinsswaps mit einem Partner, mit dem die Bank eine anerkannte Close-Out-Netting-Vereinbarung abgeschlossen hat:
Adressgewichtung Partner 50 %, Eigenmittelunterlegung 8 %

Geschäft 1:	Festzinszahler-Swap 10 Jahre, 100 Mio. EUR, MtM + 2.000.000 EUR
Geschäft 2:	Festzinsempfänger-Swap 5 Jahre, 50 Mio. EUR, MtM – 1.500.000 EUR
Schritt 1:	Netto MtM-Wert: 500.000 (+ 2.000.000 – 1.500.000)
Schritt 2:	Add-on-Geschäft 1: 100 Mio. * 1,50 % = 1.500.000
	Add-on-Geschäft 2: 50 Mio. * 0,75 % = 375.000
	Bruttozuschlag: 1.500.000 + 375.000 = 1.875.000
	Brutto MtM: 2.000.000 + 0 = 2.000.000

Zuschlag: 40 %*1.875.000 + 60 %*(1.875.000 * 500.000/2.000.000)
                 = 1.031.250 EUR
(40 % * Bruttozuschlag) + 60 % * (Bruttozuschlag * NettoMtM/BruttoMtM)

Risikowert:
500.000 + 1.031.250 = 1.531.250 EUR
(Netto MtM-Wert + Zuschlag)

Eigenmittelunterlegungspflicht:
1.531.250 * 50 % * 8 % = 61.250 EUR
(Risikowert * Adressgewichtung * Eigenmittelunterlegung)

The relation (net MtM / gross MtM) used in the formula expresses the „efficiency" of the netting agreement. In the best case the net MtM is zero (if the negative MtM-values are higher than the positive MtM values). In this case only 40% of the calculated add-ons are included in the capital adequacy.

Acknowledged **bilateral novation contracts** allow for a calculation that is based on the mark-to-market method where net values per partner are used in steps 1 and 2 instead of gross values per contract.

4.4.1. Outlook: Expected Modifications Replacement Risk in Basel III / CRD IV

One of the most important lessons of the financial crisis in 2008 is the necessity of strengthening the Basel regulations regarding counterparty risks.

In June 2011 the Basel Committee on Banking Supervision has published its proposal for a new regulation of the banking sector under the title: "Basel III: A global regulatory framework for more resilient banks and banking systems". One of the essentially submitted amendments is the **change of capital adequacy for the counterparty risk of derivatives and financial transactions with securities**. These changes, known as CRD IV, will be effective for EU banks as of 1 January 2013.

According to the methods for equity requirement of OTC derivatives described in the previous chapter, the **additional adequacy of the so-called CVA (Credit Value Adjustment)** is of special importance. A big disadvantage of the current regulations for the quantification of the replacement risk is that losses resulting from the credit deterioration of the counterparty are not considered. Therefore, CRD IV has an equity requirement for OTC derivatives in addition to the calculated replacement risk which quantifies the **risk of a credit deterioration of the counterparty**. Currently, it is expected that the CVA will substantially increase the capital requirements of OTC derivatives (up to a factor of 10) and will put additional pressure on banks to enter into appropriate netting agreements with all counterparties (banks as well as corporates) and to conclude all transactions with collateral agreements.

Transactions with authorized **central counterparties (CCP)** are excluded from the regulation, which will lead to a **further shift of derivative transactions to the CCPs**. In our view, this will lead to a change of the OTC product range (interbank products as well as the appropriate customer products) in future years.

Die in der Unterlegungsformel verwendete Relation (Netto MtM/Brutto MtM) drückt hierbei die „Effizienz" der Netting-Vereinbarung aus. Im besten Fall ist der Netto MtM null (wenn die negativen MtM-Werte höher als die positiven MtM-Werte sind). In diesem Fall fließen nur 40 % der rechnerischen Add-ons in die Eigenmittelunterlegung ein.

Bei anerkannten **bilateralen Schuldumwandlungsverträgen** kann bei der Berechnung mit der Marktbewertungsmethode in den Schritten 1 und 2 statt mit Bruttowerten für die einzelnen Kontrakte mit Nettowerten pro Partner gerechnet werden.

4.4.1. Ausblick: Erwartete Änderungen Wiederbeschaffungsrisiko unter Basel III/CRD IV

Als eine der wichtigsten Lektionen der Finanzkrise von 2008 kann die Notwendigkeit einer Stärkung der Baseler Regelungen zu Kontrahentenrisiken gesehen werden.

Im Juni 2011 veröffentlichte das Basler Komitee für Bankenaufsicht unter dem Titel: „Basel III: A global regulatory framework for more resilient banks and banking systems" ihren Vorschlag zur Neuregulierung des Bankensektors. Einer der wesentlichen unterbreiteten Änderungsvorschläge ist die **Änderung der Kapitalanforderungen für das Kontrahentenrisiko aus Derivaten und Wertpapierfinanzierungsgeschäften**. Unter dem Namen CRD IV werden diese Änderungen voraussichtlich ab 1.1.2013 für die Banken im EU-Raum relevant werden.

Bezogen auf die im vorigen Kapitel dargestellten Methoden zur Eigenmittelunterlegung bei derivativen OTC-Produkten ist dabei vor allem die **zusätzliche Unterlegung des sogenannten CVA (Credit Value Adjustment)** zu sehen. Als großer Nachteil der aktuell geltenden Regelung wird bei der Quantifizierung des Wiederbeschaffungsrisikos das Fehlen der Berücksichtigung von Verlusten gesehen, die aus einer Bonitätsverschlechterung des Kontrahenten resultieren können. In der CRD IV wird dementsprechend ein Eigenmittelbedarf für OTC-Produkte eingeführt werden, der additiv zum berechneten Wiederbeschaffungsrisiko zusätzlich zu unterlegen ist und das **Risiko einer Bonitätsverschlechterung des Kontrahenten** darstellen soll. In der aktuellen Fassung der CRD IV wird erwartet, dass dieses CVA die Eigenmittelanforderungen für derivative OTC-Produkte wesentlich erhöhen (bis zu Faktor 10) und zusätzlichen Druck auf die Banken verursachen wird, mit allen Partnern in diesem Geschäftsbereich (sowohl Banken als auch Unternehmen) entsprechende Netting-Vereinbarungen zu treffen und alle Geschäfte mit Collateral Agreements abzuschließen.

Geschäfte mit anerkannten **zentralen Kontrahenten (Central Counterparty/CCP)** werden allerdings von dieser Regelung ausgenommen, sodass davon auszugehen ist, dass es mit den neuen Regelungen zu einer **weiteren Verlagerung des derivativen Geschäftes zu diesen CCPs** kommen wird. Dies wird unseres Erachtens dazu führen, dass sich in den kommenden Jahren die Produktlandschaft im OTC-Bereich (sowohl bei den Interbankprodukten als auch bei den entsprechenden Kundenprodukten) stark verändert.

Summary

Because banks play a key role in the monetary system, governments are interested in a stable banking system. Therefore, banks should have enough capital at their disposal in order to be able to cover possible losses and to maintain their business operations at all times.

Before the introduction of the 1988 Basel Accord (= Basel I) countries had national regulatory frameworks which banks had to adhere to irrespective of their individual risk profiles. Off-balance sheet positions were generally ignored. Following concerns about a constantly diminishing equity position due to increasing (international) competition among banks, the Basel Committee on Banking Supervision (founded in 1974) was assigned the duty to design an international regulatory framework for banks.

Basel I established international minimum criteria for capital requirements and made capital requirements dependent on a bank's specific receivables. At that time, credit risk was still considered to be the main risk in the banking business. Demands were kept simple. Basel I determined that banks should hold capital of at least 8% of their risk-weighted assets (so-called "Cook Ratio"). In 1996, Basel I was amended for rules regarding market risk which had dramatically increased due to the banks' trading activities. As has been mentioned before, market risk had been neglected in the Basel 1988 Accord. The so-called "market risk amendment" became effective in 1998 and was implemented within the EU via the Capital Adequacy Directive.

The new regulations forced banks to measure their exposure to market risks and to put capital aside for it. Market risk was defined as the risk stemming from interest rate instruments and stocks in the trading book plus FX risks and commodity risks for the whole bank (trading book and banking book). For the measurement of market risk, banks could use standard risk measurement procedures as suggested by the Basel Committee or internal VaR models. The application of internal models is thereby linked to a set of certain minimum criteria a bank has to fulfil.

Criticism of Basel I mainly concerned the following three points: misallocation of supervisory capital, incomplete coverage of banking risks and no international standards for supervisory review and disclosure in different countries.

In June 1999, the Basel Committee announced the development of a revised framework, which is known as "Basel II". Basel II stands for the Capital Adequacy Framework that was developed by the Basel Committee for Banking Supervision and was set in place on January 1st 2007 within the European Union and worldwide for all international banks. The goal of Basel II is to align capital adequacy assessment more closely with the fundamental risks in the banking industry. Furthermore, it provides incentives for banks to enhance their risk measurement and management capabilities. The new Capital Adequacy Framework consists of three (equally important) pillars: Pillar one: Minimum capital requirements; Pillar two: Supervisory review process and Pillar three: Market discipline.

One significant innovation with respect to minimum capital requirements is that operational risk will feature directly in the assessment of capital adequacy for the first time, so that it has to be quantified and translated into capital charges. In line with Basel II's aim of defining a more risk-oriented method for the calculation of capital requirements, the existing method, i.e. the standardised approach, was retained and developed further. Additionally, two internal ratings-based (IRB) approaches were also developed.

The calculation is done in two steps. First, risk weights are calculated by multiplying the exposure by the respective risk weight (note that the exposure is pre-calculated in a separate step). The capital requirement is then the result of risk-weighted assets times 8%.

Zusammenfassung

Da Banken eine Schlüsselrolle für das Geld- und Zahlungswesen spielen, sind Staaten an einem stabilen Bankwesen interessiert. Damit eine Bank stabil ist, muss sie jederzeit über genügend Eigenkapital verfügen, um mögliche Verluste abdecken und den Geschäftsbetrieb weiterführen zu können.

Vor der Einführung der ersten Basler Eigenkapitalvereinbarung von 1988 (= Basel I) gab es länderindividuelle Eigenmittelvorschriften, die Banken unabhängig von ihrem Risikoprofil zu erfüllen hatten. Aus Besorgnis über eine durch den (internationalen) Wettbewerb immer dünner werdende Eigenmitteldecke wurde in den 80er-Jahren dem 1974 gegründeten Baseler Ausschuss für Bankenaufsicht (Basel Committee on Banking Supervision) die Aufgabe übertragen, ein internationales Regelwerk für Bankaufsichten zu entwerfen. Basel I etablierte internationale Mindestkapitalrichtlinien, die das Eigenkapital von Banken von ihren Kreditforderungen abhängig machten. Damals wurde Kreditrisiko noch als das beherrschende Risikoelement im Bankwesen betrachtet. Die Anforderungen wurden einfach gehalten. Basel I legte fest, dass Banken Eigenmittel in der Höhe von mindestens 8% ihrer risikogewichteten Aktiva zu halten hatten (sogenannte „Cooke-Ratio").

Im Jahre 1996 wurde Basel I um Regelungen für das inzwischen durch die Handelsaktivitäten der Banken massiv angestiegene Marktrisiko ergänzt, das im Entwurf von 1988 noch vernachlässigt worden war. Die Ergänzungen wurden im Jahre 1998 wirksam und wurden in der EU durch die sogenannte Kapitaladäquanzrichtlinie implementiert.

Die neuen Regelungen zwangen Banken dazu, das Marktrisiko zu messen und mit Eigenkapital zu hinterlegen. Für die Messung des Risikos konnten Banken entweder standardisierte Messverfahren des Basel-Kommittees oder interne VaR-Modelle verwenden, wobei Banken für letztere Methodik bestimmten Anforderungen entsprechen mussten.

Es gab aber auch Kritikpunkte an Basel I: Fehlallokation des aufsichtsrechtlichen Kapitals, keine komplette Erfassung von Risiken und keine internationalen Standards für aufsichtsrechtliche Überprüfungen und Veröffentlichung in verschiedenen Ländern.

Im Juni 1999 kündigte das Basler-Komitee schließlich an, eine neue Rahmenvereinbarung, heute bekannt unter dem Namen „Basel II", zu entwickeln. Seit dem 1. Januar 2007 wird Basel II in der EU und weltweit zumindest für international agierende Banken angewendet. Basel II soll die Beurteilung der Angemessenheit des Eigenkapitals besser auf die wichtigsten Risikoelemente im Bankgeschäft abstimmen. Darüber hinaus sollen den Banken Anreize geboten werden, ihre Verfahren der Risikomessung und des Risikomanagements weiter zu verbessern. Die Neue Eigenkapitalvereinbarung besteht aus drei tragenden Säulen: Säule 1: Mindestkapitalanforderungen; Säule 2: Aufsichtliches Überprüfungsverfahren und Säule 3: Marktdisziplin.

Die wesentliche Neuheit in Bezug auf die gesamten Mindestkapitalanforderungen ist, dass in Basel II auch das operationelle Risiko quantifiziert und unterlegt werden muss. Mit dem Ziel einer risikogerechteren Berechnung der Eigenmittelunterlegung wurde einerseits die Basel-I-Methodik zum sogenannten Standardansatz weiterentwickelt und anderseits eine neue Methode – der IRB-Ansatz – entwickelt.

Die Berechnung der Eigenmittelunterlegung des Kreditrisikos erfolgt in zwei Schritten. Im ersten Schritt werden die risikogewichteten Aktiva berechnet, indem die Volumina mit den entsprechenden Risikogewichten multipliziert werden. Die Mindestunterlegung ergibt sich dann im zweiten Schritt mit der Berechnung von 8% der risikogewichteten Aktiva.

Der Standardansatz baut auf die Eigenkapitalvereinbarung von 1988 auf. Um eine risikogerechtere Behandlung zu ermöglichen, ohne die Berechnung übermäßig zu verkomplizieren, basieren die Risikogewichte beim Standardansatz auf externen Ratings.

The standardised approach is based on the capital adequacy regulation of 1988. In order to achieve better risk adjustment in a relatively simple way the standardised approach uses the external ratings of internationally recognised rating agencies to determine risk weights. The IRB approach for calculating minimum capital requirements was developed with the objective of further converging capital requirements and the individual risk profiles of banks. In order to implement a precise risk adjustment, the risk weights are no longer standardised, but will be calculated using a given mathematical function. As opposed to the standardised approach, the IRB approach relies on banks' own internal estimates of risk components, hence the name "internal ratings-based approach".

Risk-weighted assets are calculated using four different parameters which serve as the input for the risk-weight function of the respective exposure class: Exposure at Default (EAD); Probability of Default (PD); Loss Given Default (LGD) and Maturity (M). The estimation of input parameters places high demands on data systems. Not all banks were/are able to estimate all four parameters on the basis of internal data from the outset. For this reason, the Basel Committee has developed two versions of the IRB approach: the foundation IRB approach and the advanced IRB approach.

Under the foundation IRB approach, banks will only have to estimate the probability of default (PD) for each of their internal rating categories. The remaining three input parameters and the methodology for recognising credit risk mitigation will be provided by the supervisory framework.

Under the advanced IRB approach, loss given default (LGD) and exposure at default (EAD) will also have to be estimated internally in addition to the probability of default (PD). Likewise, banks will be allowed to use their own methodology when recognising credit risk mitigation techniques.

The advantage of the IRB approach is that it is based on (bank-) internal ratings and allows a better differentiation of risks. Actual capital requirements depend on the respective loan portfolio of a bank.

Banks have to calculate capital requirements for three types of risk: for the counterparty risk of OTC derivatives, repo-style and other transactions, and for the general market risk and specific (market) risk of trading book positions. In measuring their trading book risks, banks have a choice between two broad methodologies. One alternative will be to measure the risks in a standardised manner, using a specified measurement framework. The alternative methodology allows banks to use risk measures derived from their own internal risk management models.

For the calculation of the general risk charge for interest rate instruments, the market risk amendment provides two methodologies (the maturity method and the duration method). The maturity method, the mark to market method, the standard method and internal models can be used for calculating the replacement risk. As in the maturity method the replacement risk is formulated by a given percentage of the nominal value, the mark to market method uses the current positive market value plus an add-on for calculating the replacement risk.

4.5. Practice Questions

1. What are the four asset categories in order to determine the risk weights under Basel I?
2. Name three points of criticism of Basel I!
3. Name two differences between Basel I and Basel II!
4. What are the three pillars that form the Basel II Capital Accord?
   a) operational risk

Der IRB-Ansatz zur Berechnung des Mindesteigenkapitalerfordernisses für Kreditrisiko wurde mit dem Ziel entwickelt, das individuelle Risikoprofil der Bank genauer widerzuspiegeln. Im Unterschied zum Standardansatz basiert der IRB-Ansatz auf den internen Ratings der Banken, daher auch der Name „auf internen Ratings basierender Ansatz". Um größere Risikodifferenzierung zu ermöglichen, werden die Risikogewichte der einzelnen Forderungen nicht standardisiert, sondern über eine vorgegebene mathematische Funktion berechnet. Um die risikogewichteten Aktiva zu ermitteln, werden folgende vier Inputparameter in die für die jeweilige Risikoklasse anzuwendende Risikogewichtsfunktion eingesetzt: Exposure at Default (EAD) = Forderungshöhe bei Ausfall; Probability of Default (PD) = Ausfallswahrscheinlichkeit; Loss Given Default (LGD) = Verlustintensität bzw. Verlusthöhe bei Ausfall und Maturity (M) = Restlaufzeit. Die Schätzung dieser Inputgrößen stellt vor allem datentechnisch einen großen Aufwand dar. Nicht alle Banken waren/sind in der Lage, von Beginn an alle diese vier Parameter auf Basis der internen Daten selbst zu schätzen. Aus diesem Grund hat der Basler Ausschuss zwei Varianten des IRB-Ansatzes, den Basis- und den fortgeschrittenen IRB-Ansatz entwickelt.

Im Basis-IRB-Ansatz müssen die Banken nur die PDs ihrer internen Ratingklassen schätzen. Die restlichen drei Inputparameter bzw. das Regelwerk zur Berücksichtigung von Kreditrisikominderung werden vorgegeben.

Im fortgeschrittenen IRB-Ansatz müssen zusätzlich zur PD auch die LGD und EAD von Banken intern geschätzt werden. Ebenso dürfen sie bei der Berücksichtigung der Kreditrisikominderung unter Einhaltung strenger Mindestanforderungen ihre eigene Methodik anwenden.

Der Vorteil des IRB-Ansatzes gegenüber dem Standardansatz ist, dass er auf den internen Ratings der Bank basiert und somit eine größere Risikodifferenzierung ermöglicht. Die tatsächliche Eigenmittelunterlegung hängt vom jeweiligen Kreditportfolio der Bank ab.

Im Handelsbuch müssen Banken für drei Arten von Risiken Eigenmittelanforderungen berechnen; einerseits für die Kontrahentenrisiken aus außerbörslichen Derivaten, Wertpapierpensions- und ähnlichen Geschäften, andererseits für allgemeine und spezifische Marktrisiken (= besondere Kursrisiken) von Positionen. Die Banken haben hier die Wahl zwischen zwei grundlegenden Verfahren. Einerseits können die EM-Erfordernisse nach vorgegebenen Standardverfahren berechnet werden, als Alternative können die Banken interne Modelle für das Marktrisiko verwenden.

Für die Berechnung des allgemeinen Zinsänderungsrisikos stehen eine sogenannte Laufzeitmethode und eine Durationsmethode zur Verfügung.

Zur Bemessung des Wiederbeschaffungsrisikos können die Laufzeitmethode, die Marktbewertungsmethode (MtM), die Standardmethode oder interne Modelle verwendet werden. Während bei der Laufzeitmethode ein vorgegebener Prozentsatz auf den Nominalbetrag als Wiederbeschaffungsrisiko angesetzt wird, werden bei der Marktbewertungsmethode nur die aktuellen positiven Marktwerte der Positionen plus ein Add-on als Wiederbeschaffungsrisiko angesetzt.

4.5. Wiederholungsfragen

1. Welche vier Forderungsklassen wurden bei der Bestimmung der Risikoaktiva in Basel I verwendet?
2. Nennen Sie drei Kritikpunkte an Basel I!
3. Nennen Sie zwei Unterschiede zwischen Basel I und Basel II!
4. Aus welchen drei Säulen besteht die Basel-II-Eigenkapitalvereinbarung?
   a) operationelles Risiko

    b) market discipline

    c) market risk

    d) supervisory review process

    e) minimum capital requirements

5. What is the main principle of capital adequacy in Basel II?

    a) 99% credit value at risk

    b) avoidance of regulatory arbitrage

    c) provisions of 25% in the long-term receiveables of a bank

    d) capital ratio of 8% of risk-weighted assets

6. You are in charge of the regulatory capital. How do you calculate capital requirements for credit risk according to Basel II?

    a) 50% of a bank's tier 1 capital

    b) 100% of risk-weighted assets

    c) 8% of risk-weighted assets

    d) 50% of bank's total equity

    e) 20% of a bank's tier 1 capital

7. How are the capital requirements for credit risk calculated in Basel II?

8. Which three techniques can be distinguished for mitigating credit risk?

9. What is the basic feature of the standardised approach in Basel II compared to the IRB approaches?

    a) lower standard equity requirements

    b) standardised methods for market, credit and operational risk

    c) standardised risk weights according to type of exposure and rating

    d) risk weights geared to the notation of Standard & Poor's

10. What goal does the IRB approach pursue with respect to the calculation of capital requirements for credit risk?

    a) a simpler calculation model and improved methodology

    b) to create competitive advantages

    c) to make risks comparable

    d) the convergence of a bank's capital requirements and its individual risk profile

11. What are the advantages of the IRB approach over the standardised approach?

    a) a simpler calculation model and better methodology

    a) lower capital requirements

    b) better risk differentiation

    c) The calculation relies on internal ratings.

12. Which exposure classes does the standarised approach recognise?

    a) claims secured by residential mortgages

    b) equity exposures

    c) project finance

    d) claims on sovereigns

    e) corporate loans

    f) revolving credit

13. Which four input parameters are necessary to calculate risk-weighted assets (RWA) for corporate exposures in the IRB approach?

    a) Maturity (M)

    b) Exposure at Default (EAD)

    b) Marktdisziplin

    c) Marktrisiko

    d) aufsichtliches Überprüfungsverfahren

    e) Mindestkapitalanforderungen

5. Was ist das Grundprinzip der Eigenmittelunterlegung für Basel II?

    a) 99% Credit Value at Risk

    b) die Vermeidung von Regulatory Arbitrage

    c) Rückstellungen in Höhe von 25% der langfristigen Forderungen der Bank

    d) die Eigenkapitalquote bezogen auf die Risikoaktiva von mindestens 8%

6. Sie sind verantwortlich für die regulativen Eigenmittel. Wie berechnen Sie die Eigenmittelunterlegung für Kreditrisiko nach Basel II?

    a) 50% des Tier I Kapital der Bank

    b) 100% der risikogewichteten Aktiva

    c) 8% der risikogewichteten Aktiva

    d) 50% der gesamten Eigenmittel der Bank

    e) 20% des Tier I Kapital der Bank

7. Wie erfolgt die Berechnung der Eigenmittelunterlegung des Kreditrisikos in Basel II?

8. Welche drei Arten von risikomindernden Verfahren werden bei der Berechnung der Eigenmittelunterlegung unterschieden?

9. Was ist das Grundmerkmal des Standardansatzes in Basel II?

    a) standardmäßig geringere Eigenkapitalunterlegung

    b) standardisierte Methode für Markt-, Kredit- und operationelles Risiko

    c) nach Ratings und Forderungsarten standardisierte Risikogewichte

    d) nach der Notation von Standard & Poor's ausgerichtete Risikogewichte

10. Welches Ziel verfolgt der IRB-Ansatz für die Berechnung der Eigenmittelunterlegung für das Kreditrisiko?

    a) einfachere Berechnung bei besserer Methodik

    b) Wettbewerbsvorteile zu schaffen

    c) Risiken vergleichbar zu machen

    d) das individuelle Risikoprofil der Bank genauer widerzuspiegeln

11. Was sind die Vorteile des IRB-Ansatzes gegenüber dem Standardansatz?

    a) einfachere Berechnung bei besserer Methodik

    b) geringere Eigenmittelunterlegung

    c) größere Risikodifferenzierung

    d) Die internen Ratings werden berücksichtigt.

12. Welche Arten von Forderungen gehören zu den Forderungskategorien des Standardansatzes von Basel II?

    a) durch Wohnimmobilien besicherte Forderungen

    b) Beteiligungen

    c) Projektfinanzierungen

    d) Forderungen an Staaten

    e) Unternehmenskredite

    f) revolvierende Kredite

13. Welche vier Inputparameter sind zur Berechnung von risikogewichteten Aktiva (RWA) bei Unternehmenskrediten im IRB-Ansatz notwendig?

    a) Maturity (M)

    b) Exposure at Default (EAD)

    c) Loss Given Default (LGD)
    d) Confidence Level (CL)
    e) Recovery Rate (RR)
    f) Transition Probability (TP)
    g) Probability of Default (PD)

14. There are two versions of the IRB approach: the foundation IRB approach and the advanced IRB approach. How do these two versions differ from each other?
    a) with respect to the calculation of risk-weighted assets (RWA)
    b) with respect to minimum requirements
    c) with respect to minimum capital requirements
    d) with respect to the input parameters that have to be internally estimated
    e) with respect to the recognition of credit risk mitigation

15. Sort the following loans in ascending order according to their respective capital charge!
    loan 4: PD of 1.5% and LGD of 50%
    loan 3: PD of 0.7% and LGD of 40%
    loan 1: PD of 0.7% and LGD of 50%
    loan 2: PD of 0.09% and LGD of 32%
    a) loan 2 – loan 3 – loan 1 – loan 4
    b) loan 4 – loan 1 – loan 3 – loan 2
    c) loan 2 – loan 3 – loan 4 – loan 1
    d) loan 1 – loan 4 – loan 3 – loan 2

16. For which financial instruments does a replacement risk exist?
    a) for all customer deals
    b) for all derivative instruments
    c) for unsecured loans
    d) for OTC-derivatives

17. What is meant by Novations Netting?
    a) novation contract
    b) netting contract, which meets the novation conditions of ISDA
    c) contract about the netting out of current payments of an financial instrument
    d) contract about the netting out of receivables and liabilites in the case of insolvency

18. If the MtM method is used for calculating the replacement risk,
    a) the MtM values are ignored.
    b) only the positive MtM values are considered.
    c) only the balanced MtM values are considered.
    d) only the negative MtM values are considered.

   c) Loss Given Default (LGD)
   d) Confidence Level (CL)
   e) Recovery Rate (RR)
   f) Transition Probability (TP)
   g) Probability of Default (PD)

14. Es gibt zwei Varianten des IRB-Ansatzes, den Basis IRB-Ansatz und den fortgeschrit-
    tenen IRB-Ansatz. Wodurch unterscheiden sich die beiden Varianten?
   a) durch die Berechnung der risikogewichteten Aktiva (RWA)
   b) durch die Mindestanforderungen
   c) durch die Mindesteigenkapitalquote
   d) durch die intern zu schätzenden Inputparameter
   e) durch die Möglichkeit einer umfassenderen Berücksichtigung der Kreditrisikomin-
       derung

15. Reihen Sie die folgenden Kredite aufsteigend nach der erforderlichen Eigenmittelunter-
    legung!
    Kredit 4: PD von 1,5% und LGD von 50%
    Kredit 3: PD von 0,7% und LGD von 40%
    Kredit 1: PD von 0,7% und LGD von 50%
    Kredit 2: PD von 0,09% und LGD von 32%
   a) Kredit 2 – Kredit 3 – Kredit 1 – Kredit 4
   b) Kredit 4 – Kredit 1 – Kredit 3 – Kredit 2
   c) Kredit 2 – Kredit 3 – Kredit 4 – Kredit 1
   d) Kredit 1 – Kredit 4 – Kredit 3 – Kredit 2

16. Bei welchen Produkten besteht ein Wiederbeschaffungsrisiko?
   a) bei allen Kundengeschäften
   b) bei allen derivativen Produkten
   c) bei unbesicherten Krediten
   d) bei OTC-Derivaten

17. Was wird unter Novations Netting verstanden?
   a) Schuldumwandlungsvertrag
   b) Netting-Vertrag, der den Novationsbedingungen der ISDA entspricht
   c) Vertrag über die Saldierung von laufenden Zahlungen bei einem Produkt
   d) Vertrag über die Saldierung von Forderungen und Verbindlichkeiten im Konkursfall

18. Wird die MtM-Methode zur Quantifizierung des Wiederbeschaffungsrisiko verwendet,
    so werden
   a) die MtM-Werte ignoriert.
   b) nur die positiven MtM-Werte berücksichtigt.
   c) nur die saldierten MtM-Werte berücksichtigt.
   d) nur die negativen MtM-Werte berücksichtigt.

5. The Capital Adequacy Directive (CAD)

In this chapter you learn ...
- why it was necessary to publish the Capital Adequacy Directive.
- about the components of the trading book.
- which requirements have to be met in the trading book.
- about the main elements of the Capital Adequacy Directive.
- about the different equity tiers.
- what determines the credit risk.
- how replacement risk is measured using the maturity method and the mark-to-market method.
- about the advantages of netting agreements.
- which points should be considered when determining settlement risks and delivery risks on trading stock
- which large loan limits should be considered by the banks.
- how market risk (FX risk, interest rate risk, stock risk) is measured and limited.

Until the end of 1995, the statutory regulations were mainly in terms of the credit risk. In some countries, the interest rate risk and currency risk were limited by further regulations.

In 1993, the EU published the Capital Adequacy Directive (CAD), which was to be gradually **established in all EU countries from 1995 onwards**.

The Capital Adequacy Directive intends to create a uniform regulation for banks and financial institutions in all EU member states. Hereby, the determination of the equity requirement is **based on market risks as well as on credit risks**. Thus, CAD can be seen as an addition to the existing regulations for determining equity requirements in order to cover credit risks. Since the market risk is usually found in trading, the most important consequences of this new regulation are in the trading departments of the banks. Open positions that were taken by trading departments, as mentioned above, were already restricted in some countries but did not lead to higher equity requirements till today. Due to these new regulations, trading departments can expect higher equity requirements, which will lead to additional profit expectations within the trading departments.

A new feature of CAD is the **differentiation between a bank book** (strategic positions) **and a trading book**. In the trading book, an equity cover for the market risks (interest risk, share risk, and other market risks), credit risks, and settlement risks is required. Both the books have in common that they require a cover for currency risks. Within the bankbook, the credit risk must separately be covered by equity.

Components of the trading book

The trading book of a financial institution consists of:

- the bank's own trading of financial instruments
  - for re-selling

5. Die Kapitaladäquanzrichtlinie (KAR)

In diesem Kapitel lernen Sie ...

- warum der Erlass einer Kapitaladäquanzrichtlinie notwendig war.
- welche Bestandteile das Handelsbuch umfasst.
- welche Bedingungen bei der Festlegung des Handelsbuches zu berücksichtigen sind.
- welche wesentlichen Elemente die Kapitaladäquanzrichtlinie enthält.
- welche Arten von Eigenkapital unterschieden werden.
- wovon der Eigenkapitalbedarf für das Kreditrisiko beeinflusst wird.
- wie bei der Bemessung des Wiederbeschaffungsrisikos mittels Laufzeit- oder Marktbewertungsmethode vorgegangen wird.
- welche Vorteile die Anwendung von Nettingvereinbarungen haben.
- welche Punkte bei der Eigenkapitalunterlegung des Abwicklungs- und Lieferrisikos bei Geschäften des Handelsbestandes zu beachten sind.
- welche Großkreditgrenzen Banken zu beachten haben.
- wie bei der Messung und Begrenzung von Marktrisiken (Währungs-, Zins- und Aktienrisiko) vorgegangen wird.

Bis Ende des Jahres 1995 waren die gesetzlichen Bestimmungen hauptsächlich auf das Kreditrisiko abgestimmt. Durch international stark unterschiedliche Bestimmungen wurden Zins- und Währungsrisiken in manchen Ländern zusätzlich begrenzt (z.B. Grundsatz 1a in Deutschland, § 26 BWG in Österreich).

1993 publizierte die Europäische Union die Kapitaladäquanzrichtlinie (KAR; Capital Adequacy Direcitve, CAD), die **ab Ende 1995 in allen EU-Staaten sukzessive eingeführt** wurde.

Die Kapitaladäquanzrichtlinie bewirkte eine einheitliche Regelung für Banken und Finanzinstitute in allen Ländern. Bei der Eigenkapitalermittlung werden nun die **Marktrisiken** zusätzlich zu den Kreditrisiken **berücksichtigt**. Die KAR ist damit im Wesentlichen eine Ergänzung der bisher schon bestehenden Eigenkapitalbestimmungen für Kreditrisiken um das Marktrisiko. Da das Marktrisiko hauptsächlich im Handel angesiedelt ist, hatte diese neue Bestimmung auch ihre wichtigsten Konsequenzen in den Handelsabteilungen der Banken. Die offenen Positionen, die in den Handelsabteilungen eingegangen werden konnten, haben bis zur KAR nicht zu zusätzlichem Eigenkapitalbedarf geführt. Seit der KAR müssen die Handelsabteilungen mit höherem Eigenkapitalbedarf rechnen, der zu einem zusätzlichen Gewinnanspruch in den Handelsabteilungen führt.

Neu in der KAR war die **Unterscheidung zwischen** einem **Bankbuch** (strategische Positionen) und einem **Handelsbuch**. Im Handelsbuch gibt es eine Eigenkapitalunterlegungspflicht für das Marktrisiko (Zins-, Aktien- und sonstige Marktrisiken), für das Kreditrisiko und für das Abwicklungsrisiko. Gemeinsam für das Handels- und das Bankbuch gibt es eine Unterlegungspflicht für das Fremdwährungsrisiko. Im Bankbuch muss das Kreditrisiko separat mit Eigenkapital unterlegt werden.

Bestandteile des Handelsbuches

Der Handelsbestand eines Kreditinstitutes umfasst:

- Eigenhandel in Finanzinstrumenten
  - zum Wiederverkauf

- to take advantage of differences in selling and retail prices
- to take advantage of short-term fluctuations in prices and interest rates
- derivatives in combination with transactions in the trading book
- other positions connected with the trading of financial instruments
- stocks and operations to hedge or re-finance positions of the bond trading book
- sale and repurchase agreements (repos), reverse repos, bond-lending operations, and bond-borrowing operations of the trading book
- collateral for securities
- claims on pending transactions and advance payments for transactions in the bond's trading book

With the **trading book**, the following requirements have to be met:

- setting the bond trading book must follow internal criteria
- these internal criteria must be set in a way which is objectively comprehensible to third parties; the criteria should apply in general
- organisational precautions (trading room, "dealing table") are an indication for the trading book
- bonds that are part of the trading stock come under the trading book
- transfers are to be clearly documented and accounted for
- internal transactions to avoid risks in the bank book come under the trading book

National authorities have some freedom regarding the directive implementation; the regulations may therefore vary between the different EU countries. In this section, however, we present the most important and common elements of the CAD.

We focus on the following aspects:

- determination and use of the capital
- determination of the credit risk
  - credit risk for positions of the balance sheet
  - position risk
  - settlement risk
- methods to determine the market risk for
  - currency risk
  - interest rate risk
  - stock risk
- limits on large scale loans

5.1. Determining the equity cover and the use of equity

Under CAD, there has been a slight expansion in the definition of equity. CAD differentiates between three tiers of equity:

Tier 1

The **core equity** consists mainly of

- share capital
- free reserves minus possible losses or carried forward losses.

- – zur Nutzung der Unterschiede von Kauf- und Verkaufspreisen
- – zur Nutzung kurzfristiger Preis- und Zinsschwankungen
- derivative Instrumente in Verbindung mit Geschäften des Handelsbuches
- sonstige Positionen, die in Verbindung mit dem Handel in Finanzinstrumenten stehen
- Bestände und Geschäfte zur Absicherung oder Refinanzierung von Positionen des Wertpapierhandelsbuches
- Pensionsgeschäfte, umgekehrte Pensionsgeschäfte, Wertpapierleih- und Wertpapierverleihgeschäfte des Handelsbuches
- Übernahmegarantien für Wertpapiere
- Forderungen aus nicht abgewickelten Geschäften und Vorleistungen im Zusammenhang mit Geschäften

Bei der **Festlegung des Handelsbuches** sind zusätzlich folgende Bedingungen zu berücksichtigen:

- Die Festlegung des Wertpapierhandelbuches erfolgt nach internen Kriterien.
- Die internen Kriterien sind für außenstehende Dritte objektiv nachvollziehbar festzulegen; die Kriterien sind generell anzuwenden.
- Organisatorische Vorkehrungen (Trading-Raum, „Handelstisch") sind ein Hinweis auf das Handelsbuch.
- Wertpapiere im Handelsbestand zählen zum Handelsbuch.
- Umbuchungen sind nachvollziehbar zu dokumentieren und zu begründen.
- Interne Geschäftsabschlüsse zur Risikovermeidung im Bankbuch zählen zum Handelsbuch.

Die Bestimmungen in den einzelnen EU-Ländern weichen leicht voneinander ab, weil die nationalen Behörden bei der Umsetzung gewisse Freiräume hatten. Im folgenden Kapitel werden die wesentlichen und einheitlichen Elemente der KAR dargestellt.

Dabei werden folgende Punkte behandelt:

- Eigenkapitalermittlung- und verwendung
- Ermittlung des Kreditrisikos
  - – Kreditrisiko für Bilanzpositionen
  - – Wiederbeschaffungsrisiko
  - – Abwicklungsrisiko
- Methoden der Bestimmung des Marktrisikos für das
  - – Währungsrisiko
  - – Zinsrisiko
  - – Aktienrisiko
- Großkreditgrenzen

5.1. Eigenkapitalermittlung und -verwendung

In der KAR wird zwischen drei verschiedenen Arten von Eigenkapital unterschieden:

Tier 1

Das **Kernkapital**, bestehend aus:

- eingezahltem Stammkapital und
- freien Rücklagen abzüglich etwaiger Verluste und Verlustvorträge.

Tier 2

The **supplementary equity** is made up of

- shares without voting rights,
- subordinate debt with terms of more than five years and
- valuation reserves.

Tier 3

The **additional supplement capital** consists of

- subordinate debt with terms of more than two years and
- not yet realised net trading profits.

In addition to this, there are some more limits when **determining the equity cover for risks**:

- **At least 50%** of the equity requirement for **credit risk** has to be covered by core capital.
- **At least 28.5%** (the percentage may differ in some EU countries) of the equity requirement for **market risks** has to be covered by the remaining core capital (after having covered the credit risk).

5.2. Determination of the credit risk (Capital Adequacy Directive)

Almost all of the existing regulations on solvency (also known as Cooke Ratio or Basel I) were taken over by the CAD, but some aspects were refined, especially to take into account the requirements of the trading book. The equity requirement for credit risk – also called specific risk in combination with the positions of the trading book – depends on the **credit-worthiness of the partner** (counterparty weighting) as well as on the **risk of the particular instrument** (risk factor).

Equity requirement = Notional x counterparty weighting x risk factor x 8%

The counterparty weighting depends on the creditworthiness of the partner. The risk factor reflects the current value of the product credit risk.

5.2.1. Counterparty weighting

The counterparty weighting uses pre-defined, different weightings which express **credit risk in percent**. With possible guarantees or pledges, the lower weighting rate applies to those parts that are covered by the guarantee or pledge.

There are five different weighting rates applied:

Tier 2

Das **Ergänzungskapital**, bestehend aus:

- Aktien ohne Stimmrecht,
- den nachrangigen Titeln mit einer Ursprungslaufzeit von mehr als fünf Jahren und
- Bewertungsreserven.

Tier 3

Das **zusätzliche Ergänzungskapital**, bestehend aus:

- nachrangigen Emissionen mit mehr als zwei Jahren Ursprungslaufzeit und
- nicht realisierten Nettogewinnen aus dem Handelsbestand.

Zusätzlich gibt es bei der **Berechnung und Unterlegung der Risiken** Grenzen:

- Die sich aus dem **Kreditrisiko** ergebende Eigenkapitalanforderung muss zu **mindestens 50% aus dem Kernkapital abgedeckt** werden.
- Die sich aus den **Marktrisiken** ergebende Eigenkapitalanforderung muss zu **mindestens 28,5%** (Prozentsatz leicht unterschiedlich in den einzelnen EU-Ländern) **durch das restliche Kernkapital** (nach Abdeckung des Kreditrisikos) **abgedeckt** werden.

5.2. Ermittlung des Kreditrisikos

Die vor der KAR verwendeten Solvabilitätsrichtlinien (auch unter den Namen „Cooke Ratio" oder Basel I bekannt) wurden von der KAR fast vollständig übernommen und nur in einigen Punkten, die den speziellen Anforderungen des Handelsbuches Rechnung tragen, verfeinert. Der Eigenkapitalbedarf für das Kreditrisiko – im Zusammenhang mit den Positionen des Handelsbuches auch als spezifisches Risiko bezeichnet – wird durch die **Bonität des Kontrahenten (Adressgewichtung)** und durch das **Ausfallsrisiko, das durch das einzelne Produkt (Risikowert) entsteht**, beeinflusst.

Eigenkapital = Adressgewichtung x Risikowert x 8%

Die Adressgewichtung ist abhängig von der Bonität des Kontrahenten. Das Risiko gibt den Gegenwert des Kreditrisikos des Produktes wieder.

5.2.1. Adressgewichtung

Bei der Adressgewichtung gibt es vorgegebene, unterschiedliche Gewichtungsansätze, die in Prozent den **Kreditrisikograd** ausdrücken sollen. Bei etwaigen Garantien bzw. Verpfändungen wird das niedrigere Gewicht für den garantierten oder durch Verpfändung gesicherten Teil angesetzt.

Fünf unterschiedliche Gewichtungen sind vorgesehen:

- **Gewicht 0%:** Forderungen an (oder garantierte Forderungen von) Zentralregierungen und Zentralbanken sowie regionale und örtliche Verwaltungen der sogenannten Zone A (im Wesentlichen alle OECD-Staaten). In dieser Position enthalten sind auch Forderungen an staatlich anerkannte Börsen (betrifft das Wiederbeschaffungsrisiko bei börsengehandelten Produkten).

- **Weighting 0%:** Claims against (or guaranteed claims from) central governments and central banks as well as regional and local authorities of the so-called zone A (essentially all the OECD member countries). This weighting also applies to positions traded on officially recognised exchanges (relevant for replacement risk of products traded on exchanges)
- **Weighting 10%:** Claims against or sale-and-repurchase agreements from credit institutions of zone A if they are covered by corresponding securities (e.g. bonds in Germany "Pfandbriefe")
- **Weighting 20%:** Claims against debentures from credit institutions of zone A
- **Weighting 50%:** Claims that are covered totally by residential property mortgages, as well as those derivative instruments where the partner belongs to the 100% weighting category.
- **Weighting 100%:** all remaining assets of the bank

5.2.2. Risk factors

With the help of the risk factor, one can distinguish between

- risks of balance sheet instruments
- replacement risk for off-balance sheet instruments

Risks of instruments in the balance sheet

All positions in the balance sheet that are part of the banking book have a **risk factor of 100%**. There are some special regulations for those positions that are part of the trading book.

Share positions

The share positions of the trading book bear a specific risk (credit risk), that is 4% on the gross total position but only 2% on those shares

- whose issuers don't have a specific risk weighting of 100% for bonds
- that are highly liquid (e.g. DAX) and
- where the individual positions are no more than 5% of the stock portfolio.

Qualified assets

The CAD introduces to the securities trading book of a bank the term "qualified assets". For these, there is a **reduced equity requirement** of the credit risk (specific risk).

Qualified assets in the trading book are, for example:

- buying and selling positions on assets that bear a counterparty weighting of 20%.
- bonds with a counterparty weighting of 100%, if
  - they are accepted for trading at an recognised stock market
  - the respective bonds market is liquid
  - the partner's creditworthiness is considered satisfactory

Depending on the time to maturity and regardless of the original counterparty weighting, the following **total capital cover** is required:

- **Gewicht 10%:** Forderungen an und Schuldverschreibungen von Kreditinstituten, die ihren Hauptsitz in einem der OECD-Länder haben, wenn sie mit einer entsprechenden Sicherheit versehen sind (z.B. Pfandbriefe in Deutschland).
- **Gewicht 20%:** Forderungen an und Schuldverschreibungen von Kreditinstituten der Zone A.
- **Gewicht 50%:** Forderungen, die durch Hypotheken auf Wohneigentum in vollem Umfang gesichert sind, sowie derivative Produkte, bei denen der Kontrahent in die Kategorie von 100% fällt.
- **Gewicht 100%:** Alle anderen Aktiva der Bank.

5.2.2. Risikowert

Hier kann unterschieden werden zwischen

- Risiko bei Bilanzprodukten und
- Wiederbeschaffungsrisiko.

Risiko bei Bilanzprodukten

Alle Bilanzpositionen des Bankbuches sind mit **100% als Risikofaktor** anzusetzen. Bei der Bilanzposition des Handelsbuches gibt es einige Sonderregelungen.

Aktienpositionen

Bei Aktienpositionen des Handelsbestandes besteht ein spezifisches Risiko (Kreditrisiko), und zwar 4% Eigenmittel für die Bruttogesamtposition, jedoch nur 2% Eigenmittel für Aktien,

- für deren Emittenten das spezifische Positionsrisiko in Schuldverschreibungen nicht 100% beträgt,
- die hoch liquide sind (z.B. Dax-Werte) und
- deren Einzelposition 5% des Aktienportefeuilles nicht überschreitet.

Qualifizierte Aktiva

Im Wertpapierhandelsbuch der Bank führt die KAR zusätzlich den Begriff der qualifizierten Aktiva ein. Für sie gibt es eine **reduzierte Unterlegung des Kreditrisikos** (spezifisches Risiko).

Unter die Kategorie der qualifizierten Aktiva fallen unter anderem:

- Kauf- und Verkaufspositionen in Aktivposten, die mit 20% Adressgewichtung angesetzt werden;
- Schuldverschreibungen mit 100% Adressgewicht, falls
  - sie an einer anerkannten Börse zum Handel zugelassen sind,
  - der Markt in diesen Schuldverschreibungen liquide ist und
  - die Bonität des Kontrahenten als zufriedenstellend eingeschätzt wird.

Abhängig von der Restlaufzeit gibt es folgende **Gesamtunterlegungspflicht**, die unabhängig von der ursprünglichen Adressgewichtung anzusetzen ist:

Term to maturity	Cover
up to 6 months	0.25%
from 6 to 24 months	1.00%
more than 24 months	1.60%

Replacement risk

In general, replacement risk has to be **calculated for derivatives only**. In contrast to regular balance sheet instruments (where the total notional amount of capital is taken as credit risk) a **credit equivalent** for the off balance sheet products credit risk needs to be determined. This means that all claims in the balance sheet are weighted with 100%. For derivatives, there are two different possibilities of evaluation:

- the maturity method and
- the mark to market method.

I. The maturity method

With the maturity method, the credit risk for derivatives is calculated in two steps.

Step 1

First, all nominal amounts of each instrument are multiplied by the following% rates:

Original term	Contracts on interest rates	FX rates contracts
up to 1 year	0.5%	2.0%
more than 1 year and no longer than 2 years	1.0%	5.0%
for each additional year	1.0%	3.0%

Note: All other derivatives that cannot be categorised as interest rate contracts fall into the category of FX contracts.

Step 2

The risk that is determined by step 1 is multiplied by the counterparty weighting of the partner. The risk weighting for replacement risk is limited to 50%.

Example

Equity requirement for an interest 10-year, EUR 100m interest rate swap; counterparty: OECD bank

---

Credit risk equivalent: 9% (1% for the first two years plus 1% for each additional year) = 9,000,000 (100,000,000 x 9%)
Counterparty risk weighting: 20% (OECD bank)
Capital adequacy: 8%

Capital requirement: 144,000 (= 9,000,000 x 20% x 8%)
(= credit risk equivalent x counterparty risk weighting x capital adequacy)

Restlaufzeit	Unterlegung
bis zu 6 Monaten	0,25%
von 6 bis 24 Monaten	1,00%
über 24 Monate	1,60%

Wiederbeschaffungsrisiko

Generell wird das Wiederbeschaffungsrisiko nur für **derivative Instrumente** berücksichtigt. Dabei wird für derivative Produkte ein **Kreditäquivalent** ermittelt.

Es gibt zwei unterschiedliche Bemessungsmöglichkeiten:

- die Laufzeitmethode
- die Marktbewertungsmethode

I. Die Laufzeitmethode

Bei der Laufzeitmethode wird das Kreditrisiko für Derivate in zwei Schritten errechnet.

Schritt 1

Der Nominalwert jedes Instruments wird mit folgenden Prozentsätzen multipliziert:

Ursprungslaufzeit	Zinssatzverträge	Devisenkursverträge
höchstens 1 Jahr	0,5%	2,0%
mehr als 1 Jahr und nicht mehr als 2 Jahre	1,0%	5,0%
für jedes weitere Jahr	1,0%	3,0%

Anmerkung: Alle sonstigen Derivate (außer reine Zinsderivate) fallen in die Kategorie der Devisenkursverträge.

Schritt 2

Im zweiten Schritt wird das Risiko, das sich aus dem ersten Schritt ergibt, mit der jeweiligen Adressgewichtung des Partners multipliziert. Zu berücksichtigen ist hier, dass die Adressgewichtung für das Wiederbeschaffungsrisiko mit 50% begrenzt ist.

Beispiel

Unterlegungspflicht für einen Zinsswap mit zehn Jahren Restlaufzeit, Volumen EUR 100 Mio., Partner OECD-Bank.

Risikowert: 9% (1% für die ersten beiden Jahre, zuzüglich je 1% für jedes weitere Jahr Laufzeit) = 9.000.000 (100.000.000 x 9%)
Adressgewichtung: 20% (OECD-Bank)
Eigenmittelunterlegungssatz: 8%

Unterlegungspflicht (Eigenkapitalbedarf): 144.000 (= 9.000.000 x 20% x 8%)
(= Risikowert x Adressgewichtung x Eigenmittelunterlegungssatz)

Example

Equity requirement for a 2-year FX outright transaction (EUR/USD 10m), counterparty: corporate

---

Credit risk equivalent: 5% (2% for the first year and an additional 3% for the second year) = 500,000 (10,000,000 x 5%)
Counterparty risk weighting: 50% (derivative, client)
Capital adequacy: 8%

Capital requirement: 20,000 (= 500,000 x 50% x 8%)
(= credit risk equivalent x counterparty risk weighting x capital adequacy)

II. The mark-to-market method

The measurement of credit risk in the derivatives business is done in three steps:

Step 1

You determine the replacement value of contracts that have a positive MTM value.

Step 2

The notional amounts of all contracts are multiplied by the following% rates (to include all possible risks in the future)

Term to maturity	Contracts on interest rates	FX contracts	Contracts on shares	Contracts on precious metals except gold	Contracts on commodities except gold
up to 1 year	0%	1%	6%	7%	10%
more than 1 year and no longer than 5 years	0.5%	5%	8%	7%	12%
more than 5 years	1.5%	7.5%	10%	8%	15%

Exception: This additional calculation does not apply for basis swaps.

Step 3

The risks that are determined by steps 1 and 2 are each multiplied by the counterparty weighting of the partner.

Example

Capital requirement for a EUR 100m, fixed-rate (4.50%) receiver swap with 10 years of maturity; market rate: 4.00%, MTM 4,100,000; counterparty OECD bank.

Credit risk equivalent: 5,600,000 (= 4,100,000 + 1.5% x 100,000,000)

Beispiel

Unterlegungspflicht für Devisentermingeschäft (EUR/USD), Volumen EUR 10 Mio., Laufzeit zwei Jahre, Partner Unternehmen.

Risikowert: 5% (2% für das erste Jahr zuzüglich 3% für das zweite Jahr) = 500.000 (10.000.000 x 5%)
Adressgewichtung: 50% (Derivative, Kunden)
Eigenmittelunterlegungssatz: 8%

Unterlegungspflicht (Eigenkapitalbedarf): 20.000 (500.000 x 50% x 8%)
(= Risikowert x Adressgewichtung x Eigenmittelunterlegungssatz)

II. Marktbewertungsmethode

Die Messung des Kreditrisikos aus Geschäften mit Derivaten erfolgt in drei Schritten:

Schritt 1

Der Wiederbeschaffungswert der Verträge wird ermittelt. Nur die positiven Wiederbeschaffungswerte werden weiter berücksichtigt.

Schritt 2

Die Nominalwerte aller Kontrakte werden mit folgenden Prozentsätzen multipliziert (um zukünftige potenzielle Risiken zu erfassen):

Restlaufzeit	Zinssatz- verträge	Devisenkurs- verträge	Verträge über An- teilspapiere	Verträge über Edelme- talle außer Gold	Verträge über Roh- stoffe außer Gold
höchstens 1 Jahr	0%	1%	6%	7%	10%
mehr als 1 Jahr und nicht mehr als 5 Jahre	0,5%	5%	8%	7%	12%
länger als 5 Jahre	1,5%	7,5%	10%	8%	15%

Ausnahme: Bei Basisswaps entfällt diese zusätzliche Berechnung.

Schritt 3

Die Risiken, die sich aus den Schritten 1 und 2 ergeben, werden mit der jeweiligen Adressgewichtung des Partners multipliziert.

Beispiel

Unterlegungspflicht für einen Festzinsempfänger Zinsswap mit 10 Jahren Restlaufzeit, Volumen EUR 100 Mio., Zinssatz 4,5%, Marktsatz 4%, MTM 4.100.000, Partner OECD-Bank.

Risikowert: 5.600.000 (4.100.000 + 1,5% x 100.000.000)

Counterparty risk weighting: 20% (OECD bank)
Capital adequacy: 8%
Capital requirement: 89,600 (= 5,600,000 x 20% x 8%)
(= credit risk equivalent x counterparty risk weighting x capital adequacy)

Example

Capital requirement for a 2-year FX outright transaction (Selling EUR/USD 10m at 1.1500), market rate: 1.2000; MTM: EUR -395,833; counterparty: corporate

---

Credit risk equivalent: 500,000 (0 because MTM is negative) + 500,000 (5% of 10,000,000)
Counterparty risk weighting: 50%
Capital adequacy: 8%

Capital requirement: 20,000 (= 500,000 x 50% x 8%)
(= credit risk equivalent x counterparty risk weighting x capital adequacy)

5.2.3. EXCURSUS: Netting and novation

In the case of OTC derivatives, **counterparty risk** can be **reduced** via netting agreements. This means that counterparties agree to "net" their mutual claims and receivables under certain circumstances (e.g. the default of one counterparty). The CAD offers for derivatives the **possibility of a reduced equity** cover for the credit risk (replacement risk) in case of existing novations (bilateral contracts that allow the replacement of legal agreements by new obligations) or nettings (setting off matching sales and purchases against one another).
   Acknowledged **bilateral novation contracts** allow

- a calculation that is based on the market evaluation method where within steps 1 and 2 one makes use of **net values per partner** instead of gross values per contract
- a calculation that is based on the maturity method where the assumed **nominal amount per partner** takes into account the effects of the novation contract.

Authorities accept **offset agreements** if

- step 1 of the market evaluation method is based only on the net values of those contracts that are agreed upon. The possible future risk which is calculated in step 2 is reduced by the following formula:

40% Gross Risk + 60% x (Gross Risk x (Net Risk/Gross Risk))

- If the maturity method is used, one may reduce the% rates that are applied in step 1. The following table shows the reduced% rates.

Adressgewichtung: 20% (OECD Bank)
Eigenmittelunterlegungssatz: 8%
Unterlegungspflicht (Eigenkapitalbedarf): 89.600 (5.600.000 x 20% x 8%)
(= Risikowert x Adressgewichtung x Eigenmittelunterlegungssatz)

Beispiel
Unterlegungspflicht für Devisentermingeschäft (Verkauf EUR/USD), Volumen EUR 10 Mio., Kurs 1,1500, Marktkurs: 1,2000, MTM: EUR -395.833, Laufzeit zwei Jahre, Partner Unternehmen.

Risikowert: 500.000 (0 (da MTM minus) + 500.000 (5% von 10.000.000)
Adressgewichtung: 50%
Eigenmittelunterlegungssatz: 8%

Unterlegungspflicht (Eigenkapitalbedarf): 20.000 (500.000 x 50% x 8%)
(= Risikowert x Adressgewichtung x Eigenmittelunterlegungssatz)

5.2.3. EXKURS: Netting und Novation

Das **Adressausfallsrisiko** kann im Falle von OTC-Derivaten durch Nettingvereinbarungen **reduziert** werden. Dabei werden Forderungen und Verbindlichkeiten verrechnet oder saldiert. Die KAR räumte zusätzlich die **Möglichkeit einer reduzierten Eigenkapitalunterlegung** für das Kreditrisiko (Wiederbeschaffungsrisiko) bei derivativen Produkten im Falle von bestehenden bilateralen Schuldumwandlungsverträgen (Novation) oder Aufrechungsvereinbarungen (Netting) ein.

Bei anerkannten **bilateralen Schuldumwandlungsverträgen** kann:

- bei der Berechnung mit der Marktbewertungsmethode in den Schritten 1 und 2 statt mit Bruttowerten für die einzelnen Kontrakte mit **Nettowerten pro Partner** gerechnet werden.
- bei der Berechnung mit der Laufzeitmethode der verwendete **Nominalwert pro Partner** unter Berücksichtigung des Schuldumwandlungsvertrages berechnet werden.

Bei von den Behörden anerkannten **Aufrechnungsvereinbarungen** wird:

- bei der Verwendung der Marktbewertungsmethode im Schritt 1 nur mit dem Nettowert aller in der Vereinbarung einbezogenen Kontrakte gerechnet. Das im Schritt 2 berechnete zukünftige potenzielle Risiko wird mit folgender Formel reduziert:

$$\text{Zuschlag} = 40\% \text{ Bruttozuschlag} + 60\%\left(\text{Bruttozuschlag} * \frac{\text{Netto} - \text{MTM}}{\text{Brutto} - \text{MTM}}\right)$$

- Bei der Verwendung der Laufzeitmethode können die in Schritt 1 verwendeten Prozentsätze entsprechend der folgenden Tabelle reduziert werden:

Original term	Contracts on interest rates	FX rate contracts and con-tracts on gold
up to 1 year	0.35%	1.5%
more than 1 year and no longer than 2 years	0.75%	3.75%
for each additional year	0.75%	2.25%

5.2.4. Settlement risks and delivery risks on trading stock

To cover the settlement risks on trading stock, the CAD provides an additional equity cover-er. It differentiates according to the following criteria:

- **Transactions that were not settled by the counterparty on the agreed date**
  Equity requirement: fixed% rate (depending on the number of days between the agreed date and the current date) on the difference between current market rate and the agreed rate, or on the overall amount due.
- **Advance transaction**
  (e.g. payment of bonds before delivery)
  Equity requirement: cover similar to that for a credit (counterparty weighting x risk factor (100%) x 8%).
- **Repos, reverse repos, bond-lending and bond-borrowing operations**
  Equity requirement: in case of repos and bond-borrowing operations, the current market value is calculated including the securities clean price and accrued interest. The required equity for these positive market values is 8% of the market value multiplied by the counterparty risk of the partner.
- **Other risks**
  (e.g. claims in the form of fees and commissions)
  Equity requirement: further claims based on trading operations are weighted by the respective counterparty risk and are covered with 8%.

5.2.5. EXCURSUS: Large Loan Limits

For the sake of completeness, it has to be pointed out that additionally to stipulating general capital requirements; regulators also limit banks' exposures to single counterparties.
The following rules are to ensure banks' exposures to single counterparties:

- The **sum of all credit risks linked to a specific counterparty** or a group of affiliated counterparties may not exceed **25% of a bank's total capital.**
- The **sum of all credit risks against the parent company** (or the parent company's subsidiaries and the bank's own subsidiaries, respectively) may not exceed **20% of a bank's total capital**.

The sum of all large loans (credit risks against a customer exceeding 10% of the equity) may not exceed eight times of the equity of a bank.

Ursprungslaufzeit	Zinssatzverträge	Devisenkurs- und Goldverträge
höchstens 1 Jahr	0,35%	1,5%
mehr als 1 Jahr und nicht mehr als 2 Jahre	0,75%	3,75%
für jedes weitere Jahr	0,75%	2,25%

5.2.4. Abwicklungs- und Lieferrisiko aus Geschäften des Handelsbestandes

Für das Abwicklungs- und Lieferrisiko bei Geschäften des Handelsbestandes sieht die KAR eine zusätzliche Eigenkapitalunterlegung vor.

Folgende Punkte sind zu unterscheiden:

- **Geschäfte, die zum vereinbarten Zeitpunkt vom Partner nicht abgewickelt wurden**
  Eigenkapitalunterlegung: fixierter Prozentsatz, abhängig von der Anzahl der Tage zwischen dem vereinbarten Termin und dem aktuellen Datum (auf die Differenz zwischen Marktkurs und vereinbartem Kurs oder auf den gesamten ausstehenden Betrag)
- **Geleistete Vorleistungen**
  z.B. Zahlung von Wertpapieren vor der Lieferung
  Eigenkapitalunterlegung wie Kredit: Adressgewichtung x Risikofaktor (100%) x 8%
- **Repos und Reverse Repos (Wertpapierleih- und -verleihgeschäfte)**
  Eigenkapitalunterlegung: Im Falle von Repos und Wertpapierleihgeschäften ist der aktuelle Marktwert inklusive der Sicherheiten und der aufgelaufenen Zinsen zu berechnen. Für die so ermittelten positiven Marktwerte beträgt die Eigenmittelanforderung 8% des Marktwertes, multipliziert mit dem Adressrisiko der Gegenpartei.
- **Sonstige Risiken**
  z.B. Forderungen in Form von Gebühren und Provisionen
  Eigenkapitalunterlegung: Bei sonstigen Forderungen aus den Handelsgeschäften werden die Forderungen mit dem entsprechenden Adressrisiko gewichtet und mit 8% unterlegt.

5.2.5. EXKURS: Großkreditgrenzen

Der Vollständigkeit halber sei hier noch darauf hingewiesen, dass zusätzlich zu den dargestellten Eigenmittelunterlegungen der Gesetzgeber die Engagements der Banken bei einzelnen Adressen begrenzt.

Um das Risiko von Einzelengagements zu begrenzen, gibt der Gesetzgeber folgende Begrenzungen vor:

- Die **Gesamtheit der Kreditrisiken,** die **gegenüber einem Kunden** (bzw. einer Gruppe von verbundenen Kunden) bestehen, sind auf **25% der gesamten Eigenmittel** des Instituts begrenzt.
- Die **Gesamtheit der Kreditrisiken,** die **gegenüber dem Mutterunternehmen** (bzw. den eigenen Tochtergesellschaften und den Tochtergesellschaften des Mutterunternehmens) bestehen, sind auf **20% der gesamten Eigenmittel** des Instituts begrenzt.

Die Summe aller addierten Großrisiken (Kreditrisiko gegenüber einem Kunden, das größer als 10% der Eigenmittel ist) darf das Achtfache der Eigenmittel des Institutes nicht überschreiten.

5.3. Methods to determine the market risk

The CAD's fundamental innovations are mostly relevant for **measuring and limiting the market risks**. Here, FX risk, interest rate risk, and stock risk are differentiated. The CAD offers standard approaches for all three risk types. For each type, banks have the choice between applying the **standard approach** or measuring the risk via **internal models (VaR)** using specified parameters. Because most banks with an active trading book use internal models to quantify and report risk, the standard approaches will be only described briefly in the following paragraphs.

5.3.1. FX risk – Standard method

The calculation of the required equity cover for the FX risk follows three steps:

Step 1

Calculation of the open net position per currency.

Step 2

Calculation of the overall net position, where the net-long positions and net-short positions (exception: the currency of the balance sheet) are transferred into the balance sheet currency at the current spot rate. These positions are then added separately in order to arrive at the overall net amount of long positions and short positions. The larger of these amounts is taken as the overall net position of the institution's foreign currencies.

Step 3

Calculation of the required equity cover. This calculation includes an allowance of 2% of the overall capital available. This amount may be subtracted from the overall net position. The remaining position is weighted at 8%; the result is the required equity cover.

5.3.2. Interest rate risk – the standard approach

Under CAD's definition, the equity cover for interest rate risks is restricted to the positions in the trading book. Therefore, open interest rate risks of the bankbook do not require any equity cover. As far as the risk calculation is concerned, financial institutions are allowed to choose from different methods.

All these methods divide the interest rate risk into **three different categories**:

- basis risk: different instruments, coupons, and terms within a given maturity band
- yield curve risk: different changes of interest rates within the single terms
- interest level risk: the risk of a parallel shift of the yield curve

There are **two standard methods** (maturity band method and duration method) and the so-called sensitivity models that are allowed by the CAD to cover the interest rate risk. The two standard methods differ mainly in the complexity of the calculation. With the **maturity band method**, average risk factors are given for each term; with the duration method, the true risk factors of the positions are used for the calculation. Since the **duration method** is more precise, the CAD demands a lower equity cover.

5.3. Methoden zur Bestimmung des Marktrisikos

Wesentliche Neuerungen brachte die KAR hauptsächlich für die **Messung und die Begrenzung von Marktrisiken**. Dabei ist zwischen Währungsrisiko, Zinsrisiko und Aktienrisiko zu unterschieden.

Für alle drei Risikoarten werden in der KAR **Standardansätze** vorgegeben. Die Banken können sich jedoch bei allen Kategorien entscheiden, ob das Risiko mit den Standardansätzen oder mit sogenannten **internen Modellen (VaR)** unter der Berücksichtigung von vorgegebenen Parametern gemeldet und unterlegt wird. Da in der Praxis fast alle Banken, die über ein aktives Handelsbuch verfügen, das Risiko mit internen Modellen quantifizieren, werden die vorgegebenen Standardansätze hier nur kurz beschrieben.

5.3.1. Währungsrisiko – Standardansatz

Die Eigenmittelanforderung zur Deckung des Währungsrisikos erfolgt in drei Schritten:

Schritt 1

Berechnung der offenen Nettoposition pro Devise.

Schritt 2

Berechnung der Nettogesamtposition, indem die Netto-Long- und Short-Positionen (mit Ausnahme der Bilanzwährung) zum aktuellen Kassakurs in die Bilanzwährung umgerechnet werden. Diese Positionen werden anschließend getrennt summiert, um den Nettogesamtbetrag der Long- und Short-Positionen zu ermitteln. Der höhere der beiden Gesamtbeträge bildet die Nettogesamtposition in Devisen des Kreditinstitutes.

Schritt 3

Berechnung der Eigenmittelanforderung. Hier gibt es einen Freibetrag von 2% der gesamten verfügbaren Eigenmittel, der von der Nettogesamtposition abgezogen werden kann. Die restliche Position ist dann mit 8% zu gewichten und ergibt den Eigenmittelbedarf.

5.3.2. Zinsrisiko – Standardansatz

Die in der KAR definierten Eigenmittelanforderungen zur Abdeckung des Zinsrisikos beschränken sich auf die Positionen des Handelsbestandes. Damit sind offene Zinsrisiken aus dem Bankbuch von der Eigenkapitalunterlegung freigestellt. Auch bei der Berechnung des Zinsrisikos wird den Instituten freigestellt, unter unterschiedlichen Berechnungsmethoden auszuwählen.

Bei allen zur Verfügung gestellten Methoden wird das Zinsrisiko in **drei unterschiedliche Kategorien** eingeteilt:

- Zinsniveaurisiko: Risiko einer parallelen Verschiebung der gesamten Zinskurve
- Zinskurvenrisiko: unterschiedliche Zinsänderungen in den einzelnen Laufzeiten
- Basisrisiko: unterschiedliche Instrumente, Kupons und Laufzeiten innerhalb eines vorgegeben Laufzeitbandes

Bei der Unterlegung des Zinsrisikos sieht die KAR **zwei Standardverfahren** (Laufzeitband- und Durationsmethode) sowie die sogenannten Sensitivitätsmodelle vor. Die zwei Standardmethoden unterscheiden sich hauptsächlich hinsichtlich der Komplexität der Berechnungen.

5.3.3. Stock (price) risk

Stocks in this context are considered to be common shares, preference shares, convertible issues, participating preference shares, and all derivatives that are influenced by price changes in the above mentioned shares.

In this section, we discuss the cover for positions in the trading book. If certain shares are part of the bankbook, the cover is calculated like for an ordinary loan. In contrast, positions in the trading book need only a reduced cover for the credit risk (specific risk) but at the same time an additional cover for the market risk.

Step 1

First, you calculate the net positions for each instrument. The net positions are converted into the balance sheet currency according to the prevailing FX spot rates.

- Positions on indices are either split up into single positions according to the index composition or they are treated as an individual title.
- Derivatives are treated as positions in the underlying title.
- Options have to be taken into account with their delta.
- Sales and purchases (also spot and forward transactions) may be balanced if the papers are issued by the same issuing party, have the same conditions and are issued in the same currency.

Step 2

Secondly, the overall gross position and the overall net position are determined. The overall gross position is the sum of all net-long positions and net-short positions, ignoring the sign of the positions. The difference between the sum of net-long positions and the sum of net-short positions is the overall net position.

Step 3

Calculation of the required equity cover:

general position risk (market risk) = 8% of the overall net position

5.3.4. EXCURSUS: Suggestion of the Basle committee concerning equity cover of market risks

With its proposal in January 1996, the Basle committee of bank supervision explicitly allows internal risk models to be used in determining market risks. This proposal was the result of interventions of banks and financial market participants who strove for a more precise description of the risks involved in more complex trading strategies. With the proposed models, the CAD does take into account indirect correlation effects between positions but only if these positions are taken with the same market risk and in the same currency.

Internal models depend on the approval of the responsible authority. With internal models, banks may use historic volatilities and correlations to quantify their market risks. Thereby, correlations within the individual risk categories (e.g. 5-year interest rate position/ 10-year interest rate position) as well as adequately reliable correlations between the risk categories (e.g. USD interest position/ USD currency position; interest position/ share position) can be considered.

Bei der **Laufzeitmethode** werden durchschnittliche Risikofaktoren pro Laufzeit vorgegeben. Die **Durationsmethode** arbeitet mit dem echten Risikofaktor für die einzelnen Positionen. Durch die größere Genauigkeit der Durationsmethode wird der Eigenkapitalunterlegungssatz durch die KAR geringer angesetzt.

5.3.3. Aktienrisiko

Unter Aktien werden Positionen in Stammaktien, Vorzugsaktien, wandelbare Forderungstitel, durch Aktien unterlegte Partizipationsscheine sowie alle derivativen Instrumente, die von den Preisänderungen der angeführten Anteiltitel beeinflusst werden, verstanden.

In diesem Kapitel wird nur die Unterlegung von Positionen des Handelsbestandes dargestellt. Sind die Aktien Bestandteil des Bankbuches, so wird die Unterlegung entsprechend einem normalen Kredit durchgeführt. Demgegenüber kommt es bei Positionen des Handelsbestandes zu einer reduzierten Unterlegung für das Kreditrisiko (spezifisches Risiko), aber zusätzlich zu einer Unterlegung für das Marktrisiko.

Schritt 1

Die Nettoposition jedes Instruments ist zu berechnen. Die Nettopositionen sind mit den aktuellen Devisenkassakursen in die Bilanzwährung umzurechnen.

- Positionen auf Indizes sind entweder in die Einzelpositionen entsprechend der Zusammensetzung der Indizes zu zerlegen oder als eigener Titel zu verwalten.
- Derivative Instrumente sind als Positionen des zugrundeliegenden Titels zu behandeln.
- Optionen sind mit ihrem Delta zu berücksichtigen.
- Kauf- und Verkaufspositionen (auch Kassa- und Termingeschäfte) können saldiert werden, wenn der Titel auf den gleichen Emittenten lautet, die gleichen Merkmale hat und in der gleichen Währung emittiert wurde.

Schritt 2

Die Gesamtbrutto- und Gesamtnettoposition ist zu ermitteln. Man erhält sie durch die Addition sämtlicher Netto-Long-Positionen und Netto-Short-Positionen, ungeachtet des Vorzeichens. Die Differenz zwischen der Summe der Netto-Long-Positionen und der Netto-Short-Positionen ist die Nettogesamtposition.

Schritt 3

Berechnung der Eigenkapitalunterlegung:

Allgemeines Positionsrisiko (Marktrisiko) = 8% der Nettogesamtposition

5.3.4. EXKURS: Baseler Komitee zur Eigenkapitalunterlegung der Marktrisiken

Im Rahmen der Implementierung der KAR ist es den Banken erlaubt, die vom Baseler Komitee vorgeschlagenen internen Modelle zur Marktrisikomessung zu verwenden.

In seinem Vorschlag vom Januar 1996 sieht der Baseler Ausschuss für Bankenaufsicht die explizite Zulassung von internen Risikomodellen zur Ermittlung der Marktrisiken vor Dieser Vorschlag kam auf Intervention von Banken und Finanzmarktteilnehmern zustande, die sich bemühten, die Risiken aus komplexeren Handelsstrategien exakter darzustellen. Die KAR erlaubt in ihren vorgeschlagenen Standard-Modellen zwar indirekte Korrelationseffekte zwischen Positionen, jedoch ausschließlich dann, wenn die Positionen mit gleichem Marktrisiko und gleicher Währung eingegangen werden. So können beispielsweise keine Korrelationen zwischen Währungen und Zinsen (oder zwischen Zinsen und Aktienmärkten, ...) bei der Verwendung der Standardsätze berücksichtigt werden.

The use of internal models must follow the following quantitative parameters:

- assuming that the positions are held for 10 trading days
- a historic point of view of at least one year
- a one-sided confidence interval of 99 % (1 % probability that the loss is greater than the descried risk)

With regard to the qualitative criteria, the following requirements apply:

- independent department of risk management
- independent controls by the internal audit
- existing internal risk limits
- regular tests
- active participation of the management

The required equity cover for market risks is the larger of the two following values:

- average risk value of the last 60 days multiplied by a factor of 3
- risk value of the previous day

In addition to the above-mentioned factor of 3, the Basle Committee favours the introduction of a spread that depends on the individual reliability of the model in use.

When implementing the CAD, banks will be allowed to use the suggested internal models of risk measurement. Since Brussels currently recommends that the risk measured with internal models must meet at least the risk as measured by the CAD, banks can hardly reduce their equity cover by employing internal models The banks would thus have the single advantage that the internal risk measurement methods would then meet the statutory requirements.

Summary

Until the end of 1995, statutory regulations were mainly in terms of the credit risk. In some countries, the interest rate risk and currency risk were limited by further regulations. In 1993, the EU published the Capital Adequacy Directive (CAD), which was to be gradually established in all EU countries from 1995 onwards.

The Capital Adequacy Directive intends to create a uniform regulation for banks and financial institutions in all EU member states. Hereby, the determination of the equity requirement is based on market risks as well as on credit risks. A new feature of CAD is the differentiation between the banking book (strategic positions) and the trading book. In the trading book, an equity cover for the market risks (interest risk, share risk, and other market risks), credit risks, and settlement risks is required. Both books share the need for covering currency risks. Within the banking book, the credit risk must be separately covered by equity.

Durch die Verwendung von internen Modellen, die eine Zustimmung der zuständigen Behörde benötigen, können die Banken die auf historischen Daten basierenden Volatilitäten und Korrelationen anwenden. Dabei können sowohl Korrelationen innerhalb der einzelnen Risikokategorien (z.B. Fünf-Jahres-Zinsposition) wie auch die Korrelationen zwischen den Risikokategorien (z.B. USD-Zinspositionen/USD-Währungsposition, Zinsposition/Aktienposition), sofern sie hinreichend zuverlässig sind, berücksichtigt werden.

Bei der Verwendung interner Modelle sind folgende quantitative Parameter vorgegeben:

- Unterstellt Haltedauer von zehn Handelstagen
- Historischer Beobachtungszeitpunkt von mindestens einem Jahr
- 99,0 % einseitiges Konfidenzintervall (1,0 % Wahrscheinlichkeit, dass der Verlust größer als das dargestellte Risiko ist)

Bezüglich der qualitativen Kriterien sind folgende Anforderungen zu erfüllen:

- Unabhängige Risikokontrollabteilung
- Unabhängige Prüfung durch die interne Revision
- Existenz von internen Risikolimiten
- Regelmäßige Tests (sowohl Stress Tests als auch Back Tests)
- Aktive Teilnahme des Geschäftsleitung

Die Höhe des benötigten Eigenkapitals zur Abdeckung der Marktrisiken ist der höhere der beiden folgenden Werte:

- Durchschnittlicher Risikowert der letzten 60 Tage multipliziert mit dem Faktor von
- mindestens 3
- Risikowert des Vortages

Zusätzlich zum oben angeführten Faktor 3 hat sich der Baseler Ausschuss für die Einführung eines Zuschlags, abhängig von der individuellen Verlässlichkeit des verwendeten Modells, ausgesprochen.

Der Faktor von 3 kann von der Bankaufsicht bis zu einem Faktor von 4 erhöht werden, wobei die Festlegung dieses bankindividuellen Faktors von den Ergebnissen (Ausreißern) beim Back Testing abhängt.

Zusammenfassung

Bis Ende des Jahres 1995 waren die gesetzlichen Bestimmungen hauptsächlich auf das Kreditrisiko abgestimmt. 1993 publizierte die Europäische Union die Kapitaladäquanzrichtlinie (KAR; Capital Adequacy Direcitve, CAD), die ab Ende 1995 in allen EU-Staaten sukzessive eingeführt wurde.

Die Kapitaladäquanzrichtlinie bewirkte eine einheitliche Regelung für Banken und Finanzinstitute in allen Ländern. Bei der Eigenkapitalermittlung werden nun die Marktrisiken zusätzlich zu den Kreditrisiken berücksichtigt. Neu in der KAR war auch die Unterscheidung zwischen einem Bankbuch (strategische Positionen) und einem Handelsbuch. Im Handelsbuch gibt es eine Eigenkapitalunterlegungspflicht für das Marktrisiko (Zins-, Aktien- und sonstige Marktrisiken), für das Kreditrisiko und für das Abwicklungsrisiko. Gemeinsam für das Handels- und das Bankbuch gibt es eine Unterlegungspflicht für das Fremdwährungsrisiko. Im Bankbuch muss das Kreditrisiko separat mit Eigenkapital unterlegt werden.

Under CAD, there has been a slight expansion in the definition of equity. CAD differentiates between three tiers of equity: tier 1 (core equity): share capital and free reserves minus possible losses or carried forward losses; tier 2 (supplementary equity): shares without voting rights, subordinate debt with terms of more than five years and valuation reserves; tier 3 (additional supplement capital): subordinate debt with terms of more than two years and not yet realised net trading profits.

The equity requirement for credit risk – also called specific risk in combination with the positions of the trading book – depends on the creditworthiness of the partner (counterparty weighting) as well as on the risk of the particular instrument (risk factor).

The counterparty weighting depends on the creditworthiness of the partner. The risk factor reflects the current value of the product credit risk. The counterparty weighting uses pre-defined, different weightings which express credit risk in percent.

With the help of the risk factor, one can distinguish between risks of balance sheet instruments and replacement risk for off-balance sheet instruments. All positions in the balance sheet that are part of the banking book have a risk factor of 100%. There are some special regulations for those positions that are part of the trading book. The CAD introduces to the securities trading book the term "qualified assets". For these, there is a reduced equity requirement of the credit risk (specific risk). Qualified assets in the trading book are for example buying and selling positions on assets that bear a counterparty weighting of 20% and bonds with a counterparty weighting of 100%, if they are accepted for trading at a recognised stock market, the respective bonds market is liquid and the partner's creditworthiness is considered satisfactory.

In general, replacement risk has to be calculated for derivatives only. For off-balance sheet products a credit equivalent needs to be determined. For derivatives, there are two different possibilities of evaluation: the maturity method and the mark-to-market method. In the case of OTC derivatives, counterparty risk can be reduced via netting agreements. This means that counterparties agree to "net" their mutual claims and receivables under certain circumstances (eg, the default of one counterparty). For derivatives, the CAD offers the possibility of a reduced equity cover for the credit risk (replacement risk) in case of existing novations (bilateral contracts that allow the replacement of legal agreements by new obligations) or nettings (setting off matching sales and purchases against one another).

To cover the settlement risks on trading stock, the CAD provides additional equity cover.

The CAD's fundamental innovations are mostly relevant for measuring and limiting the market risks. Here, FX risk, interest rate risk, and stock risk are distinguished. The CAD offers standard approaches for all three risk types. For each type, banks have the choice between applying the standard approach or measuring the risk via internal models (VaR) using specified parameters.

All these methods divide the interest rate risk into three different categories: basis risk (different instruments, coupons, and terms within a given maturity band), yield curve risk (different changes of interest rates within the single terms) and interest level risk (the risk of a parallel shift of the yield curve).

In der KAR wird zwischen drei verschiedenen Arten von Eigenkapital unterschieden: Tier 1 (Kernkapital): eingezahltes Stammkapital und freie Rücklagen abzüglich etwaiger Verluste und Verlustvorträge; Tier 2 (Ergänzungskapital): Aktien ohne Stimmrecht, nachrangige Titel mit einer Ursprungslaufzeit von mehr als fünf Jahren und Bewertungsreserven; Tier 3 (zusätzliches Ergänzungskapital): nachrangige Emissionen mit mehr als zwei Jahren Ursprungslaufzeit und nicht realisierte Nettogewinne aus dem Handelsbestand.

Der Eigenkapitalbedarf für das Kreditrisiko – im Zusammenhang mit den Positionen des Handelsbuches auch als spezifisches Risiko bezeichnet – wird durch die Bonität des Kontrahenten (Adressgewichtung) und durch das Ausfallsrisiko, das durch das einzelne Produkt (Risikowert) entsteht, beeinflusst. Die Adressgewichtung ist abhängig von der Bonität des Kontrahenten. Das Risiko gibt den Gegenwert des Kreditrisikos des Produktes wieder. Bei der Adressgewichtung gibt es vorgegebene unterschiedliche Gewichtungsansätze, die in Prozent den Kreditrisikograd ausdrücken sollen.

Beim Risikowert kann unterschieden werden zwischen dem Risiko bei Bilanzprodukten und dem Wiederbeschaffungsrisiko. Alle Bilanzpositionen des Bankbuches sind mit 100% als Risikofaktor anzusetzen. Im Wertpapierhandelsbuch der Bank führt die KAR zusätzlich den Begriff der qualifizierten Aktiva (Kauf- und Verkaufspositionen in Aktivposten, die mit 20% Adressgewichtung angesetzt werden, und Schuldverschreibungen mit 100% Adressgewicht, falls sie an einer anerkannten Börse zum Handel zugelassen sind, der Markt in diesen Schuldverschreibungen liquide ist und die Bonität des Kontrahenten als zufriedenstellend eingeschätzt wird) ein. Für sie gibt es eine reduzierte Unterlegung des Kreditrisikos (spezifisches Risiko).

Generell wird das Wiederbeschaffungsrisiko nur für derivative Instrumente berücksichtigt. Dabei wird für derivative Produkte ein Kreditäquivalent ermittelt. Es gibt zwei unterschiedliche Bemessungsmöglichkeiten, nämlich die Laufzeitmethode und die Marktbewertungsmethode.

Das Adressausfallsrisiko kann im Falle von OTC-Derivaten durch Nettingvereinbarungen reduziert werden. Dabei werden Forderungen und Verbindlichkeiten verrechnet oder saldiert. Die KAR räumte zusätzlich die Möglichkeit einer reduzierten Eigenkapitalunterlegung für das Kreditrisiko (Wiederbeschaffungsrisiko) bei derivativen Produkten im Falle von bestehenden bilateralen Schuldumwandlungsverträgen (Novation) oder Aufrechungsvereinbarungen (Netting) ein.

Für das Abwicklungs- und Lieferrisiko bei Geschäften des Handelsbestandes sieht die KAR eine zusätzliche Eigenkapitalunterlegung vor.

Wesentliche Neuerungen brachte die KAR hauptsächlich für die Messung und die Begrenzung von Marktrisiken. Dabei ist zwischen Währungsrisiko, Zinsrisiko und Aktienrisiko zu unterscheiden. Für alle drei Risikoarten werden in der KAR Standardansätze vorgegeben. Die Banken können sich jedoch bei allen Kategorien entscheiden, ob das Risiko mit den Standardansätzen oder mit sogenannten internen Modellen (VaR) unter der Berücksichtigung von vorgegebenen Parametern gemeldet und unterlegt wird.

Bei allen zur Verfügung gestellten Methoden wird das Zinsrisiko in Zinsniveaurisiko (Risiko einer parallelen Verschiebung der gesamten Zinskurve), Zinskurvenrisiko (unterschiedliche Zinsänderungen in den einzelnen Laufzeiten) und Basisrisiko (unterschiedliche Instrumente, Kupons und Laufzeiten innerhalb eines vorgegeben Laufzeitbandes) eingeteilt.

There are two standard methods (maturity band method and duration method) and the so-called sensitivity models that are allowed by the CAD to cover the interest rate risk. The two standard methods differ mainly in the complexity of the calculation. With the maturity band method, average risk factors are given for each term; with the duration method, the true risk factors of the positions are used for the calculation. Since the duration method is more precise, the CAD demands a lower equity cover.

5.4. Practice Questions

1. What does the term capital adequacy refer to?
   a) total amount of shares in the free float of a bank
   b) ability of a bank to generate adequate capital
   c) ability of a bank to meet its dividend payments to shareholders
   d) a bank's capability to have sufficient capital to carry out normal business under internationally recognized rules
2. What determines the replacement risk according to the CAD?
   a) type of instrument
   b) equity of the bank
   c) liquidity of the market
   d) creditworthiness of the counterparty
3. What positions does the trading book of a financial institution include?
4. Which of these instruments has NO capital adequacy requirements under the BIS rules?
   a) OTC options
   b) exchange-traded products
   c) out-of-the-money swaptions
   d) any instrument which is marked-to-market
5. Which of the following products does not require capital backing if traded by banks?
   a) IRS
   b) FRAs
   c) futures
   d) forward/forward loans
6. What are the different equity tiers of the CAD?
7. What has an influence on the coverage of the credit risk?
8. What is meant by qualified assets?
9. What is the counterparty risk weighting for a loan to an AAA rated company under the CAD?
   a) 20%
   b) 100%
   c) 50%
   d) 10%
   e) 0%

Bei der Unterlegung des Zinsrisikos sieht die KAR zwei Standardverfahren (Laufzeit-band- und Durationsmethode) sowie die sogenannten Sensitivitätsmodele vor. Die zwei Standard-methoden unterscheiden sich hauptsächlich hinsichtlich der Komplexität der Berechnungen.

Bei der Laufzeitmethode werden durchschnittliche Risikofaktoren pro Laufzeit vorgegeben. Die Durationsmethode arbeitet mit dem echten Risikofaktor für die einzelnen Positionen. Durch die größere Genauigkeit der Durationsmethode wird der Eigenkapitalunterlegungssatz durch die KAR geringer angesetzt.

5.4. Wiederholungsfragen

1. Worauf bezieht sich der Begriff Kapitaladäquanz?
   a) auf die Summe der Aktien in Streubesitz einer Bank
   b) auf die Möglichkeit einer Bank, adäquates Kapital zu beschaffen
   c) auf die Möglichkeit einer Bank, den Dividendenzahlungen an die Aktionäre nachzukommen
   d) auf die Fähigkeit der Bank, genug Kapital zu haben, um unter international anerkannten Regeln ihre Geschäfte zu tätigen
2. Wovon hängt das in der Kapitaladäquanzrichtlinie fixierte Wiederbeschaffungsrisiko ab?
   a) Art des Instruments
   b) Eigenkapital der Bank
   c) Liquidität des Marktes
   d) Bonität des Partners
3. Welche Positionen umfasst der Handelsbestand eines Kreditinstituts?
4. Bei welchem Instrument ist nach den BIZ-Regeln der Kapitaladäquanzrichtlinie kein Kreditrisiko zu rechnen?
   a) OTC-Optionen
   b) börsengehandelte Kontrakte
   c) Swaptions aus dem Geld
   d) jedes Instrument, das Mark-to-Market ist.
5. Welches der angeführten Instrumente braucht keine Eigenkapitalunterlegung, wenn es von Banken gehandelt wird?
   a) IRS
   b) FRAs
   c) Futures
   d) Forward/Forward Anleihen
6. Welche Arten von Eigenkapital werden in der KAR unterschieden?
7. Wovon wird der Eigenkapitalbedarf für das Kreditrisiko beeinflusst?
8. Was versteht man unter qualifizierten Aktiva?
9. Wie groß ist die Adressgewichtung für einen Kredit an ein Unternehmen mit AAA-Rating in der KAR?
   a) 20%
   b) 100%
   c) 50%
   d) 10%
   e) 0%

10. Name and describe the two methods for the measurement of replacement risk!
11. Which limits did the legislator make in addition to the determination of credit risk?
12. Which of the following is true regarding netting agreements under the CAD?
    a) They have no effect on the CAD.
    b) The can lead to a reduced replacement risk.
    c) They can lead to reduced coverage against market risk.
    d) They can lead to reduced percentage for the coverage of counterparty risk.
13. What is true regarding novation agreements and utilisation of the market evaluation method?
    a) It uses gross amounts.
    b) It reduces the risk weightings.
    c) It uses net amounts.
    d) It allows for both gross and net amounts.
14. What is the equity requirement for coverage of open currency positions under the CAD?
    a) 0%
    b) 5%
    c) 100%
    d) 8%
15. According to the CAD, which of the following positions must be included when determining the market risk of stocks?
    a) positions in the banking book with a lower weighting
    b) positions in both the trading book and the banking book
    c) positions in the trading book only
    d) derivatives only
16. Which holding period is assumed when using internal models to determine the market risk?
    a) one year on average
    b) one trading day
    c) ten trading days
    d) The holding period is determined in accordance with the trading strategy of the bank.
17. Which statement is true regarding the determination of the equity cover for the market risk with the help of internal models?
    a) The risk value is normally adjusted for volatility.
    b) The risk value is normally multiplied by a factor of 3.
    c) The risk value is normally multiplied by a factor of 1.66.
    d) The risk value is normally adjusted using Gaussian normal distribution.
18. What are the three categories of interest rate risk?
19. What is the difference between maturity method and mark-to-market method!

10. Nennen und beschreiben Sie die beiden Methoden zur Bemessung des Wiederbeschaffungsrisikos!

11. Welche Begrenzungen gibt der Gesetzgeber zusätzlich zur Eigenmittelunterlegung bei der Kreditvergabe vor?

12. Was trifft auf Nettingvereinbarungen in der Kapitaladäquanzrichtlinie (KAR) zu?
    a) Sie haben keinen Einfluss auf die KAR.
    b) Sie können zu einem reduzierten Wiederbeschaffungsrisiko führen.
    c) Sie können zu reduzierten Eigenkapitalunterlegungen für das Marktrisiko führen.
    d) Sie können zu reduzierten Prozentsätzen für die Unterlegung des Adressrisikos führen.

13. Was ist beim Novations-Netting unter Verwendung der Marktbewertungsmethode zutreffend?
    a) Bruttowerte werden verwendet.
    b) Die Prozentsätze werden geändert.
    c) Nettowerte werden verwendet.
    d) Brutto- oder Nettowerte können verwendet werden.

14. Wie hoch ist die Eigenmittelunterlegung für offene Devisenpositionen in der KAR?
    a) 0%
    b) 5%
    c) 100%
    d) 8%

15. Was ist für die Ermittlung des Marktrisikos bei Aktien in der KAR zutreffend?
    a) Es gilt ein reduzierter Prozentsatz für die Positionen des Bankbuches.
    b) Es sind die Positionen des Handels- und des Bankbuches zu unterlegen.
    c) Es sind nur die Positionen des Handelsbuches zu unterlegen.
    d) Es werden nur die derivativen Instrumente berücksichtigt.

16. Welche Haltedauer wird bei der Verwendung von internen Modellen für die Ermittlung des Marktrisikos unterstellt?
    a) durchschnittlich ein Jahr
    b) ein Handelstag
    c) zehn Handelstage
    d) Die Haltedauer ist abhängig von der Handelsstrategie der Bank.

17. Zur Bemessung der Eigenkapitalunterlegung des Marktrisikos mit internen Modellen wird der ermittelte Risikowert im Normalfall …
    a) mit der verwendeten Volatilität korrigiert.
    b) mindestens mit dem Faktor 3 multipliziert.
    c) mit dem Faktor 1,66 multipliziert.
    d) mit der Gauß'schen Normalverteilung angepasst.

18. In welche drei Kategorien kann man das Zinsrisiko einteilen?

19. Erklären Sie den Unterschied zwischen Laufzeit- und Durationsmethode!

PART VII: Central Banks, Fundamental Analysis and Technical Analysis

TEIL VII: Notenbanken, fundamentale Analyse und technische Analyse

The main objective of the world's central banks is to ensure a relatively stable price level. Nevertheless, the ways in which central banks seek to achieve this goal are not always the same.

Statutory regulations of the countries provide the central banks with a number of instruments concerning interest or liquidity management to fulfil their objectives. Whereas the provision of central bank funds directly influences banks' liquidity, open market rates, discount and Lombard rates act more as signals and so influence the lending business of banks and the monetary and credit demands of the economy. Thereby, the central banks are in a position to influence interest rates and the liquidity situation in the money market in various ways according to their monetary objectives.

In contrast to some other countries, the monetary policy instruments of the European Central Bank are limited to interventions that leave the market forces and competition within the economy's financial sector largely untouched. Other central banks are able to directly limit the borrowing of non-banks (setting an asset ceiling) or they can lock in the interest rates of the financial market and the bonds market. Besides these rather strict methods the policy of most of the central banks is to indirectly steer the banks' credit policies and the demand for money by means of influencing the banks' liquidity and by the interest mechanism in the financial markets. This is made possible by using a wide range of instruments that are regulated by law.

These subjects are described in chapter 1 of this part. At the beginning the reader will get a historical overview about the foreign exchange and money markets. Afterwards, the main tasks and purposes of the Bank for International Settlements (BIS), the European Monetary Union (EMU) and the European System of Central Banks (ESCB) are described. Then the instruments and techniques that are available for interventions of central banks are explained. Chapter 2 deals with the basics of fundamental analysis. At the beginning of the chapter there is a short excursus on the balance of payments. Afterwards the reader will get an overview about the models of fundamental analysis. In addition to that you get detailed information about the different models: the monocausal models and the integrated models. At the end of this chapter there is a description of economic indicators which are used in fundamental analysis. The third chapter explains the basics of technical analysis. After an overview about the used methods of analysis these methods are described in detail.

Included in the following exams:
- **ACI Diploma**

Die aktuelle Hauptaufgabe der Notenbanken in aller Welt ist es, für ein möglichst stabiles Preisniveau zu sorgen. Die Art und Weise, wie die Notenbanken versuchen, ein stabiles Preisniveau zu erreichen, ist allerdings unterschiedlich.

Die gesetzlichen Regelungen der einzelnen Länder stellen den Notenbanken eine umfassende Auswahl an zins- und liquiditätspolitischen Instrumenten zur Erfüllung ihrer Aufgaben zur Verfügung. Während die Ausstattung mit Zentralbankgeld die Bankenliquidität direkt beeinflusst, haben Offenmarkt-, Diskont- und Lombardsatz Signalcharakter und beeinflussen auf diesem Weg das Kreditgeschäft der Banken bzw. die Geld- und Kreditnachfrage der Wirtschaft. So sind sie in der Lage, die Zinsen und Liquiditätsverhältnisse am Geldmarkt in vielfältiger Weise im Sinne ihrer geldpolitischen Zielsetzungen zu beeinflussen.

Im Gegensatz zu manchen anderen Ländern beschränken sich die Instrumente der EZB-Geldpolitik auf Eingriffsmöglichkeiten, die das freie Spiel der Marktkräfte und des Wettbewerbs im finanziellen Sektor der Wirtschaft weitgehend unangetastet lassen. Andere Zentralbanken verfügen beispielsweise über die Möglichkeit, die Kreditaufnahme der Nichtbanken unmittelbar zu beschränken (Kreditplafondierung) oder die an den Kredit- und Wertpapiermärkten geltenden Zinssätze administrativ festzulegen (Zinsbindung). Abgesehen von diesen streng restriktiven Maßnahmen zielt die Politik der meisten Notenbanken im Wesentlichen darauf, das Kreditangebotsverhalten der Banken und die Geld- und Kreditnachfrage der Wirtschaft mittelbar über Veränderungen der Bankenliquidität und den Zinsmechanismus an den Finanzmärkten zu steuern. Die dafür zur Verfügung stehenden Instrumente und Techniken, wie Währungsreservepolitik, Refinanzierungspolitik, Mindestreservepolitik, Offenmarktpolitik, Devisenmarkttransaktionen und bilaterale Geschäfte, sind gesetzlich geregelt.

Mit diesen Themen beschäftigt sich Kapitel 1 dieses Teiles. Zu Beginn bekommt der Leser einen kurzen historischen Überblick über die Geld- und Devisenmärkte. Anschließend werden ausführlich die Aufgaben und Ziele der Bank für Internationalen Zahlungsausgleich (BIZ), der Wirtschafts- und Währungsunion (WWU) und des Europäischen Systems der Zentralbanken (ESZB) behandelt. Anschließend werden die bereits oben angeführten verwendeten Instrumente und Techniken der Notenbanken näher erläutert. In Kapitel 2 werden die Grundlagen der fundamentalen Analyse dargestellt. Zu Beginn erfolgt ein kurzer Exkurs zur Zahlungsbilanz. Anschließend folgt eine Übersicht über die Modelle der fundamentalen Analyse. In weiterer Folge werden die Modelle, nämlich die monokausalen Erklärungsansätze und die integrierten Modelle, näher beschrieben. Den Abschluss dieses Kapitels bildet die Beschreibung von in der fundamentalen Analyse verwendeten volkswirtschaftlichen Kennzahlen. Das dritte Kapitel widmet sich der technischen Analyse. Nach einer Übersicht über die einzelnen Analyseverfahren werden diese anschließend ausführlich erläutert.

Prüfungsrelevant für:
- **ACI Diploma**

1. Central Banks

In this chapter you learn ...

- more about the history of foreign exchange and money markets.
- what is meant by the Bretton Woods System.
- about the aims of the Bretton Woods System.
- about the reasons for the collapse of the Bretton Woods System.
- what is meant by the Smithsonian Agreement.
- About the different types of exchange rate systems.
- why a European Monetary System was founded.
- why the Bank for International Settlements (BIS) was founded.
- which deals are allowed for the BIS and which deals are prohibited.
- about the tasks and purpose of the European Monetary Union.
- about the criteria for joining the European Monetary Union.
- which countries are members of the European Monetary Union.
- what is meant by the stability and growth pact.
- what is meant by the European System of Central Banks.
- which instruments and techniques are available for interventions of central banks.
- about the relevant characteristics of important international central banks.

1.1. EXCURSUS: History of Foreign Exchange and Money Markets

The practice of foreign exchange (FX) dealing goes back to the end of the 19th century. At that time the status of **gold as the reference currency** made it possible to carry out transactions via foreign accounts with ease. At the beginning of the 20th century, technical innovations led to great improvements in the area of completing and contracting money transactions. From telegraph and telephone to modern telecommunications, technical innovations have contributed to the modernisation and the acceleration of foreign exchange trading.

1.1.1. The Gold Standard (1880–1914)

The gold standard was a system of fixed exchange rates. The currencies' parities were fixed to gold; one differentiated between the **gold specie standard** and the **gold bullion standard**.

1.1.2. The Interwar Period (1918–1939)

The confusion and enormous costs resulting from World War I demanded **increased money creation** in almost all European countries. Different rates of inflation in these countries created a situation in which the international price structure diverged markedly.

To counteract the problems concerning foreign trade that resulted from their over-valued currencies, several countries carried out a massive devaluation of their currencies. The

1. Notenbanken

In diesem Kapitel lernen Sie ...

- wie sich die Geld- und Devisenmärkte historisch entwickelt haben.
- was man unter Bretton-Woods-System versteht.
- welche Ziele das Bretton-Woods-System hatte.
- warum es zum Zusammenbruch des Bretton-Woods-Systems kam.
- was man unter dem Smithsonian Agreement versteht.
- welche Arten von Wechselkurssystemen bestehen.
- aus welchen Gründen ein Europäisches Währungssystem gegründet wurde.
- welchen Zweck die Gründung der Bank für Internationalen Zahlungsausgleich (BIZ) hatte.
- welche Geschäfte die BIZ machen darf und welche ihr untersagt sind.
- welche Aufgaben und Ziele die Wirtschafts- und Währungsunion hat.
- welche Kriterien beim Beitritt zur Währungsunion zu erfüllen sind.
- welche Länder derzeit an der Währungsunion teilnehmen.
- was man unter dem Stabilitäts- und Wachstumspakt versteht.
- was man unter dem Europäischen System der Zentralbanken versteht.
- welche Instrumente bzw. Techniken den Notenbanken zur Intervention zur Verfügung stehen.
- welche marktrelevanten Merkmale die wichtigen internationalen Notenbanken aufweisen.

1.1. EXKURS: Die Geschichte der Geld- und Devisenmärkte

Die Technik des Devisenhandels geht bereits auf das Ende des 19. Jahrhunderts zurück, als es die **Referenzwährung Gold** ermöglichte, Zahlungen über ein Konto im Ausland problemlos abzuwickeln. Die technischen Errungenschaften zu Beginn des 20. Jahrhunderts brachten große Fortschritte bei der Abwicklung und Kontrahierung von Geldgeschäften mit sich. Vom Telegrafen über das Telefon bis zur heutigen modernen Telekommunikation leisteten viele technische Neuerungen ihren Beitrag zur Modernisierung und Beschleunigung des Devisenhandels.

1.1.1. Der Goldstandard (1880–1914)

Der Goldstandard bildete ein **System von festen Wechselkursen.** Die Paritäten dieser Währungen waren zum Gold fixiert, wobei zwischen der **Goldumlaufwährung** und der **Goldkernwährung** unterschieden wurde.

1.1.2. Die Zwischenkriegszeit (1918–1939)

Die Wirren und die enormen Kosten des Ersten Weltkriegs erforderten eine **erhöhte Geldschöpfung** in nahezu allen europäischen Ländern. Stark unterschiedliche Inflationsraten in den einzelnen Ländern hatten zur Folge, dass das internationale Preisgefüge auseinanderklaffte.

Um den außenwirtschaftlichen Problemen – bedingt durch die Überbewertung ihrer Währung – entgegenzuwirken, vollzog eine Reihe von Ländern massive Abwertungen der

fall in the exchange rate of one currency equalled the rise in the exchange rate of another. As a result, a race towards devaluation took place which carried with it all of the important world currencies. Triggered by the world economic crisis in 1931, European countries introduced **mechanisms to control foreign exchange**. To prevent a situation in which the savings of foreign currencies were insufficient to make the regular foreign currency payments, the monetary controllers felt obliged to permanently control import and export of foreign currencies.

1.1.3. The Exchange Standard – Bretton Woods System (1944–1970)

During the conference of **Bretton Woods in July 1944**, the US representatives brought up the basic idea of the gold standard again. Once this idea was commonly accepted, an internationally neutral monetary controller was agreed upon: the **International Monetary Fund (IMF)**, which was founded subsequently and is situated in Washington, D.C. The **main objectives** of this new order can be summarised as follows:

- establishment of an international monetary system with stable exchange rates
- relaxation of existing restrictions on foreign exchange
- introduction of the convertibility of all currencies

In 1961 the **Organisation for Economic Co-operation and Development (OECD)** was founded as a successor to the Organisation for European Economic Co-operation (OEEC), located in Paris. At present the OECD has 34 members.

The OECD's targets are the promotion of an optimal economic development among the member countries and the expansion of worldwide trade within a multilateral system. The OECD deals with the coordination of development aid; in particular it is a discussion forum for the western developed countries with a focus on the examination and informal reviewing of many international items.

1.1.4. The Collapse of the Fixed Exchange Rate System (1971–1973)

Due to a crisis in the international monetary system the Bretton Woods system finally collapsed at the beginning of the Seventies. **High deficits of the US balance of payments** caused confidence to be lost in the US dollar as the international key currency. Within a short time, enormous amounts of money were moved from the US to the European markets; there, the interest rates remained at a high level.

After heavy interventions by the German Bundesbank and the Swiss National bank, Switzerland and Austria revalued their currencies, while Germany and the Netherlands both let their currencies float for an indefinite period of time.

Within the **Smithsonian Agreement**, signed on the occasion of the monetary conference on the 17th/18th of December 1971, the United States obliged itself to raise the official gold price from USD 35 to USD 38 per troy ounce; this amounted to a nominal devaluation of 7.9%. At the same time, the European countries and Japan revalued their currencies by 8%, while Canada decided to stick to a floating exchange rate.

eigenen Währung. Die Wechselkurssenkung einer Währung entsprach aber wiederum der Höherbewertung einer anderen. Die Folge davon war ein regelrechter Abwertungswettlauf, in dessen Sog alle bedeutenden Weltwährungen gerissen wurden. Außerdem wurden ab dem Jahr 1931 in verschiedenen Staaten Europas **Devisenkontrollmechanismen** eingeführt, um zu verhindern, dass für die laufenden Auslandszahlungen keine ausreichenden Devisenreserven vorhanden sind.

1.1.3. Der Golddevisenstandard – Bretton-Woods-System (1944–1970)

Auf der **Konferenz von Bretton Woods im Juli 1944** brachten die amerikanischen Vertreter wieder die Grundidee des damaligen Goldstandardsystems ins Spiel. Nachdem diese Linie allgemein akzeptiert wurde, einigte man sich auch auf einen international neutralen Währungshüter, womit die Idee des damals noch zu gründenden **Internationalen Währungsfonds (IWF, International Monetary Fund IMF)** mit Sitz in Washington, D.C. ins Leben gerufen wurde. Die **Hauptziele** dieser neu geschaffenen Ordnung lassen sich wie folgt zusammenfassen:

- Errichtung eines internationalen Währungssystems mit stabilen Wechselkursen
- Abbau der noch vorhandenen Devisenrestriktionen
- Einführung der Konvertibilität aller Währungen

1961 wurde die **Organisation für wirtschaftliche Zusammenarbeit und Entwicklung (OECD)** als Nachfolgeorganisation der Organisation für Europäische Wirtschaftliche Zusammenarbeit (OEEC) mit Sitz in Paris geschaffen. Der OECD gehören derzeit 34 Mitglieder an.

Die Ziele der OECD sind die Förderung einer optimalen Wirtschaftsentwicklung in den Mitgliedstaaten und die Ausweitung des Welthandels in einem System des Multilateralismus. Die OECD befasst sich mit der Koordination der Entwicklungshilfe, vor allem aber ist sie als Diskussionsforum der westlichen Industrieländer mit der Untersuchung und informellen Vorabklärung vieler internationaler Fragen befasst.

1.1.4. Zusammenbruch des Systems fester Wechselkurse (1971–1973)

Durch eine Krise des internationalen Währungssystems brach das System von Bretton Woods schließlich zu Beginn der 70er-Jahre in sich zusammen. **Hohe Zahlungsbilanzdefizite der USA** führten dazu, dass das Vertrauen in den Dollar als internationale Leitwährung verlorenging. Enorme Kapitalbeträge flossen innerhalb kürzester Zeit aus den USA in die europäischen Märkte, deren Zinssätze weiterhin auf hohem Niveau waren.

Nach heftigen Interventionen der Deutschen Bundesbank und der Schweizerischen Nationalbank werteten die Schweiz und Österreich ihre Währungen auf, wogegen Deutschland und Holland ihre Währungen auf unbestimmte Zeit frei schwanken ("floaten") ließen.

Im Rahmen des **Smithsonian Agreements** verpflichteten sich daher die USA anlässlich der Währungskonferenz vom 17./18. Dezember 1971, den offiziellen Goldpreis von USD 35 auf USD 38 pro Unze zu erhöhen, was einer Dollarabwertung von 7,9% entsprach. Die europäischen Länder und Japan werteten ihre Währungen zusätzlich um fast 8% auf, während Kanada beschloss, den freien Wechselkurs beizubehalten.

1.1.5. The Monetary System since 1973

The collapse of the fixed rate system resulted in different developments; most of the industrial countries pursued a **controlled floating**. This meant that the exchange rate developments were not completely left to the free markets. Interventions by the central banks and the correct use of monetary instruments not only smoothed out daily fluctuations but also sought to prevent devaluations and revaluations.

The end of the Eighties was again characterised by relatively stable conditions partially as a result of the **Louvre agreement** in 1987. There, the seven most important economies (G7, USA, UK, Italy, Germany, Japan, Canada, France) agreed to stabilise their exchange rates by interventions, appeals, and interest rate policies. Only in 1990, the dollar came under pressure again due to fears of a recession and problems in the sector of the US savings banks.

Exchange Rate Systems

Two of the best known exchange rate systems are the Bretton Woods System and the former European Monetary System. There are two main types of exchange rates which also relate to different ways of compensating a deficit in the balance of payments: floating and fixed exchange rates.

Floating exchange rates are subject to demand and offer in the foreign exchange market, without any interfering of economic policy.

For **fixed** exchange rates economic policy defines a fixed exchange rate. Usually these are fixed but adjustable exchange rates, i.e. within a certain band the rates are allowed to float freely. Only the borders of the band are defended by the central banks (intervention band or upper and lower intervention points).

One hybrid system is **managed floating**. Basically the exchange rates are floating, but the central banks intervene (hidden or openly) to fulfil certain (silent or open) agreements.

A special form is the crawling peg, i.e. the adaption of an exchange rate at regular intervals (e.g. weekly) for a prearranged fixed amount (e.g. USD/HKD).

1.1.6. The European Monetary System (EMS)

On 13 March 1979, the **European Monetary System (EMS)** was introduced as the third attempt to establish a monetary union in Europe. The EMS is a **regional system of fixed but adaptable exchange rates**. Members of the EMS are all the countries of the European Union (EU). Those countries that do not belong to the EU but maintain tight economic and financial relations with the EU have the possibility to be associated to the system of exchange rates and interventions.

The main objective of the EMS was to create a **"zone of monetary stability in Europe"**, i.e. stability of exchange rates and prices, by means of monetary policy co-operation. The fixing of the exchange rates should help to strengthen the economic integration and to encourage trade within the EU.

1.1.5. Die Währungsordnung seit 1973

Nach dem Zusammenbruch des Fixkurssystems kam es zu unterschiedlichen Entwicklungen. Die meisten Industriestaaten betrieben ein **kontrolliertes Floating,** d.h., die Wechselkurse wurden nicht völlig dem freien Markt überlassen. Nach der Freigabe der Wechselkurse kam es zu einer massiven Abwärtsbewegung des Dollars. Dies war nur eine längst fällige Korrektur des durch das Fixkurssystem verzerrten Gefüges.

Das Ende der 80er-Jahre war dagegen von einer relativen Stabilität gekennzeichnet. Das war unter anderem das Resultat des **Louvre-Übereinkommens** aus dem Jahre 1987, in dem sich die sieben wichtigsten Wirtschaftsnationen (G7, das sind USA, Kanada, Japan, Großbritannien, Italien, Frankreich, Deutschland) einigten, ihre Wechselkursrelationen durch Interventionen, Appelle und zinspolitische Maßnahmen zu festigen.

Wechselkurssysteme

Die bekanntesten Wechselkurssysteme sind das Bretton-Woods-Abkommen sowie das frühere Europäische Währungssystem. Es werden zwei Grundformen unterschieden, mit denen auch unterschiedliche Zahlungsbilanzausgleichsmechanismen verbunden sind: flexible und fixe Wechselkurse.

Bei **flexiblen** („floating") Wechselkursen bildet sich der Wechselkurs allein aufgrund der Marktkräfte am Devisenmarkt, ohne Eingriff wirtschaftspolitischer Instanzen.

Bei **fixen** Wechselkursen wird von den wirtschaftspolitischen Instanzen ein fester Wechselkurs festgelegt. In der Regel handelt es sich dabei um feste, aber anpassungsfähige Wechselkurse, d.h., innerhalb bestimmter Bandbreiten können die Wechselkurse frei schwanken, die Zentralbanken verteidigen nur die Grenzen dieser Bandbreiten (Interventionsband bzw. obere und untere Interventionspunkte).

Eine Mischform ist das **kontrollierte Floating** („Managed Floating"). Die Wechselkurse bilden sich grundsätzlich frei, die Zentralbanken intervenieren aber (verdeckt oder offen), um bestimmte (stillschweigende oder offene) Absprachen zu realisieren.

Eine Sonderform ist die Gleitparität, d.h. die Anpassung des Wechselkurses in regelmäßigen Intervallen (z.B. wöchentlich) um einen im Voraus bestimmten Betrag (z.B. USD/HKD).

1.1.6. Das Europäische Währungssystem (EWS)

Das am 13. März 1979 in Kraft getretene **EWS (Europäisches Währungssystem),** der Nachfolger des EWV (Europäischer Währungsverbund), wurde als insgesamt dritter Anlauf zur monetären Integration ins Leben gerufen. Es war ein **regionales System fester, aber anpassungsfähiger Wechselkurse.** Mitglieder waren alle Staaten der Europäischen Union (EU), wobei aber grundsätzlich für all jene Länder, die nicht der EU angehörten, aber enge wirtschaftliche und finanzielle Beziehungen zu ihr unterhielten, die Möglichkeit bestand, sich durch Assoziierung am Wechselkurs- und Interventionsmechanismus zu beteiligen.

Ziel des EWS war es, durch eine engere währungspolitische Zusammenarbeit eine **„Zone der monetären Stabilität in Europa",** das bedeutet Wechselkurs- und Preisstabilität, zu schaffen. Die Fixierung der Wechselkurse sollte die wirtschaftliche Integration stärken und den Handel innerhalb der EU begünstigen.

Therefore an **"official" European Currency Unit (ECU)** that was mainly used as a clearing unit and as legal tender between the central banks was introduced in 1979. There were also several bonds denoted in ECU.

1.1.7. Table of Historic Development

System	Period	Characteristics	Reason for change
GOLD STANDARD	1880–1914	Gold specie standard and gold bullion standard; gold as legal tender and as reserve management	financing of World War I
INTERWAR PERIOD	1918–1939	inflation; devaluation; world economic crisis; foreign exchange management	outbreak of World War II
BRETTON WOODS	1944–1970	trial of a stable currency sys-tem; founding of the IMF; pegging of the USD to gold; system of fixed exchange rates; convertibility	deficits in the budget of the US, different growth rates in the most important industrial countries
SMITHSONIAN AGREEMENT	1971–1973	system of fixed exchange rates; interventions of the central banks	another devaluation of the USD and revaluation of the main currencies due to speculative transactions of capital
CONTROLLED FLOATING	since 1973	exchange rates float within a certain band; establishment of monetary unions	still in force; outside Europe
EUROPEAN MONETARY SYSTEM (EMS)	1979–1988	monetary basket (ECU); EMS-central banks; controlled floating	in Europe
EUROPEAN ECONOMIC AND MONETARY UNION; Treaty of Maastricht	since 1991	common economic and monetary policies; convergence criteria; European Central Bank, three stages within the schedule, from 1999 a single currency Since 1.1. 1999: EMS-II (between EUR and EU non-EUR currencies)	since 1.1.1999

1.2. Bank for International Settlements (BIS)

The Bank for International Settlements was founded to *"enhance the co-operation among central banks, to find new ways for international financial operations and to function as*

Zu diesem Zwecke wurde 1979 auch die Europäische **Währungseinheit (European Currency Unit = ECU)** als Rechen- und Bezugsmittel der Wechselkurse sowie als Zahlungsmittel und Reservewährung der Zentralbanken eingeführt.

1.1.7. Tabellarische Übersicht über die historische Entwicklung

System	Periode	Merkmale	Grund für Änderung
GOLDSTANDARD	1880–1914	Geldumlauf-, Goldkernwährung; Gold als Zahlungs- bzw. bloßes Reservemittel	Kriegsfinanzierung Erster Weltkrieg
ZWISCHEN-KRIEGSZEIT	1918–1939	Inflation; Abwertung; Weltwirtschaftskrise; Devisenbewirtschaftung	Ausbruch Zweiter Weltkrieg
BRETTON WOODS	1944–1970	Versuch eines stabilen Währungssystems; Gründung IWF; Gründung OECD; Bindung des USD an Goldpreis; Fixkurssystem; Konvertibilität	Zahlungsbilanzdefizite der USA, unterschiedliche Wachstumsraten der wichtigsten Industrieländer
SMITHSONIAN AGREEMENT	1971–1973	System fester Wechselkurse; Intervention der Zentralbanken	erneute Abwertung des USD und Aufwertung der Hauptwährungen aufgrund spekulativer Kapitalbewegungen
KONTROLLIERTES FLOATING	seit 1973	Wechselkurse schwanken frei innerhalb einer Bandbreite; Aufkommen von Währungsverbänden	noch wirksam, außer in Europa
EUROPÄISCHES WÄHRUNGS-SYSTEM (EWS)	1979–1998	Währungskorb (ECU); EWS-Zentralbanken; kontrolliertes Floating	in Europa
EUROPÄISCHE WIRTSCHAFTS- UND WÄHRUNGS-UNION; Vertrag von Maastricht	seit 1991	gemeinsame Wirtschafts- und Währungspolitik; Konvergenzkriterien; Europäische Zentralbank, Dreistufenplan, gemeinsame Währung ab 1999; seit 1.1.1999: EWS-II (EUR gegen EU-Währungen, die nicht am EUR teilnehmen)	seit 1.1.1999 in Kraft

1.2. Die Bank für Internationalen Zahlungsausgleich (BIZ)

Die Bank für Internationalen Zahlungsausgleich hat den Zweck, *„die Zusammenarbeit der Zentralbanken zu fördern, neue Möglichkeiten für internationale Finanzgeschäfte zu schaf-*

a trustee for international transactions between parties that had chosen the BIS as their agent." The BIS was **founded in Basle in 1930, on the basis of an agreement between Belgium, France, Germany, Great Britain, Italy, Japan, and the U.S.A.** (the Federal Reserve did not take up its rights as founder member until 1995). Its original objective was to manage the German reparation payments after the First World War as stated during the conference in The Hague in January 1930.

Nowadays, the BIS is a **public limited company** (stock corporation). Its nominal share capital is held by all European central banks (excluding the central banks of Albania and the countries of the former Soviet Union) and the central banks of Australia, Canada, Japan, South Africa, and the USA. The **BIS' bodies** are a supervisory council, which elects its chairperson and appoints the bank's president and chairperson, and a general assembly. Today, the council consists of 13 members; that is, the presidents of the most important European central banks, plus five experts from the spheres of finance, industry, and trade. The bank's chairperson is responsible to the bank's president for the bank's transactions.

Just before and during World War II, the bank's business almost came to a total standstill and its possible dissolution was discussed at the Bretton Woods conference, but shortly after this its importance began to grow again. In 1949, the bank became the agent for intra-European payment and co-operation agreements, and by mid 1950 for the European Payments Union. It served in just the same way as the European Monetary Co-operation Fund (EMCOF) and the multilateral system of settlement within the European currency agreement from 1958 until its end in 1972.

The bank also serves as agent for the OECD's agreement on guaranteed exchange rates between central banks and member countries. Since the establishment of the EMCOF in 1973, the BIS serves as its agent, too. It is also the bonds pledgee of the European Coal and Steel Community. According to a 1986 treaty with 18 European banks the BIS also serves as the clearing agent for private ECU.

1.2.1. The business policy of the BIS

The bank's businesspolicy must not counteract the monetary policies of the central banks. If BIS operations might cause unwanted reactions in any market, the central banks have the right to intervene before this transaction is actually done. The bank's statutes include a list of allowed transactions:

- gold and FX transactions on its own account or on account of the central banks.
- gold keeping on account of the central banks.
- discount and Lombard transactions with the central banks and
- buying and selling of negotiable securities (exception: stocks) on its own or on the central banks' account.

fen und als Treuhänder (Trustee) oder Agent bei den, ihr aufgrund von Verträgen mit den beteiligten Parteien übertragenen, internationalen Zahlungsgeschäften zu wirken". Sie wurde **1930 in Basel aufgrund eines Übereinkommens der Länder Deutschland, Belgien, Frankreich, Großbritannien, Italien, Japan und den USA** (wobei die amerikanische Notenbank ihre Rechte als Gründungsmitglied bis 1995 nicht wahrnahm) **gegründet.** Ursprünglich war sie von der Haager Konferenz im Januar 1930 dazu bestimmt, die deutschen Reparationszahlungen nach dem Ersten Weltkrieg zu regeln.

Die BIZ hat heute die Rechtsform einer **Aktiengesellschaft**, deren Nominalkapital von allen europäischen Zentralbanken (ausgenommen sind die Zentralbanken Albaniens und der Nachfolgestaaten der Sowjetunion) und den Zentralbanken Australiens, Japans, Kanadas, Südafrikas und der USA gehalten wird. Die **Organe der BIZ** setzen sich aus einem Verwaltungsrat, der seinen Vorsitzenden wählt und den Präsidenten der Bank sowie den Generaldirektor ernennt, und einer Generalversammlung zusammen. Der Verwaltungsrat ist ein Gremium von 13 Personen, das einerseits aus den Zentralbankpräsidenten der größten europäischen Notenbanken und andererseits aus fünf Vertretern aus Finanzwesen, Industrie und Handel besteht. Für die Durchführung der Geschäfte ist der Generaldirektor dem Präsidenten der Bank verantwortlich.

Nachdem die Geschäftstätigkeit der BIZ vor und während des Zweiten Weltkrieges fast zum Erliegen kam und auf der Bretton-Woods-Konferenz sogar ihre Auflösung ins Auge gefasst wurde, gewann sie kurz danach wieder an Bedeutung. So wurde sie 1949 Agent für die innereuropäischen Zahlungs- und Kompensationsabkommen und ab Mitte des Jahres 1950 für die Europäische Zahlungsunion (EZU). Sie erfüllte die gleiche Funktion für den Europäischen Fonds für währungspolitische Zusammenarbeit (EFWZ) und das multilaterale System des Zahlungsausgleichs im Rahmen des Europäischen Währungsabkommens (EWA) von 1958 bis zu dessen Beendigung Ende 1972.

Für das nach Beendigung des EWA abgeschlossene, jedoch mit Wirkung vom 1. Januar 1976 zunächst für drei Jahre suspendierte und dann Ende 1979 beendete Abkommen über eine Wechselkursgarantie zwischen Zentralbanken von Mitgliedstaaten der OECD wurde die BIZ gleichfalls als Agent bestellt. Seit dem Bestehen des EFWZ (1973) nimmt die BIZ auch die Aufgaben eines Agenten für ihn wahr. Für die von der Montanunion gewährten und von ihr aufgenommenen Anleihen ist die BIZ als Pfandhalter tätig. Aufgrund eines Vertrages mit 18 europäischen Banken Anfang 1986 war die BIZ auch Clearingstelle für private ECU.

1.2.1. Die Geschäftspolitik der BIZ

Die Geschäftspolitik der BIZ darf der Währungspolitik der einzelnen Zentralbanken nicht entgegenwirken. Sollte ein Finanzgeschäft der BIZ auf irgendwelchen Märkten eine unerwünschte Reaktion hervorrufen, so können die Notenbanken von ihrem Recht Gebrauch machen, vor der Durchführung dieser Transaktion Einspruch zu erheben. Die Statuten der Bank listen unter anderem folgende zulässige Geschäfte auf:

- Gold- und Devisengeschäfte auf eigene Rechnung und auf Rechnung von Zentralbanken,
- Verwahrung von Gold auf Rechnung der Zentralbanken,
- Diskont- und Lombardgeschäfte mit den Zentralbanken und
- Kauf und Verkauf von börsengängigen Wertpapieren (mit Ausnahme von Aktien) auf eigene und auf Rechnung von Zentralbanken.

Moreover, the BIS may keep accounts at the central banks and may take assets from them as well as serve as an agent or as a correspondent for the central banks. These transactions may – assuming that no central bank intervenes – also be done with other banks, trading and industrial companies as well as with the private sector. **Certain transactions are explicitly forbidden**, e.g. issuing banknotes, accepting of bills of exchange, and granting credits to governments.

1.3. The European Monetary Union (EMU)

1.3.1. Tasks and purposes of the EMU

On 9 and 10 December 1991, the heads of state of the EU member states approved an **outline of the treaty on the European Union in Maastricht**. This agreement served as the basis for the future development of the economic and monetary "zone" towards an **economic and monetary "union"**, which was realised on **January 1ˢᵗ 1999** through the introduction of the euro in (at that time) 11 member countries. The **euro** replaced the ECU at parity and established the so-called **Exchange Rate Mechanism II**. The latter is part of the euro convergence criteria and states that the exchange rate fluctuations of the member countries towards the euro must not exceed a deviation of ± 15% from the euro central rate. If a member risks exceeding this deviation limit the European Central Bank is contractually obliged to intervene.

The main purpose of the union is formulated in Article 2 of the treaty: the establishment of the EMU aims towards constant, non-inflationary, and ecological growth, a high level of the economies' convergence, a high level of employment, a high degree of social security, a rise of the standard of living and of life quality, and the promotion of economic and social cohesion and solidarity among the member states.

In order to achieve this, the member states are supposed to co-ordinate their economic and financial policies and to pursue a unified monetary and currency policy with **price stability as its main objective**. Furthermore, the member countries are obliged to maintain **discipline** when it comes to questions of **public spending**, and to strive for a **balanced foreign trade**. The member states must follow the general principles of an **open market economy** that is characterised by competition. The transfer of capital with regard to third countries is to be liberalised as well.

1.3.2. Convergence criteria

For countries to adopt the euro, they have to fulfil **four convergence criteria**, the so-called **Maastricht criteria**:

- **High degree of price stability:** The inflation rate may not exceed the average inflation rate of the three member countries with the lowest inflation rates by more than 1.5%.
- **Government finance:** The country's total outstanding government debt may not exceed 60% of its GDP and the country's budget deficit may not exceed 3% of its GDP.

Die BIZ darf ferner Konten bei Notenbanken unterhalten und ihrerseits Einlagen von Zentralbanken annehmen sowie als Agent und Korrespondent von Zentralbanken auftreten. Diese Geschäfte dürfen – wenn die Zentralbanken keinen Einspruch erheben – auch mit Banken, Handels- und Industrieunternehmen sowie Privatpersonen abgeschlossen werden. Eine **Reihe von Geschäften ist der BIZ ausdrücklich untersagt,** so z.B. die Notenausgabe, das Akzeptieren von Wechseln und die Gewährung von Krediten an Regierungen.

1.3. Die Wirtschafts- und Währungsunion (WWU)

1.3.1. Aufgaben und Ziele der WWU

Die EU-Staats- und Regierungschefs haben am 9./10. Dezember 1991 in **Maastricht** den Entwurf eines **„Vertrages über die Europäische Union"** gebilligt. Dieser Vertrag sah für den Wirtschafts- und Währungsbereich die Weiterentwicklung der Gemeinschaft zu einer **Wirtschafts- und Währungsunion (WWU)** vor und wurde durch den am **1. Januar 1999** durchgeführten Zusammenschluss der damals elf Teilnehmerstaaten Realität.

Zu diesem Zeitpunkt wurde der ECU durch den **Euro** ersetzt und der sogenannte **Wechselkursmechanismus II** eingeführt. Letzterer ist Teil der Konvergenzkriterien für die Einführung des Euro und legt fest, dass die Wechselkurse teilnehmender Länder nicht um mehr als +/-15% zueinander schwanken dürfen. Die EZB ist dabei vertraglich zur Intervention bei einem drohenden Überschreiten einer +/-15%-Abweichung verpflichtet.

Die vordringliche Aufgabe der Gemeinschaft ist in Artikel 2 des Vertrages formuliert, wonach die Errichtung der WWU zum Ziel hat, „... ein beständiges, nicht inflationäres und umweltverträgliches Wachstum, einen hohen Grad an Konvergenz der Wirtschaftsleistungen, ein hohes Beschäftigungsniveau, ein hohes Maß an sozialem Schutz, die Hebung des Lebensstandards und der Lebensqualität, den wirtschaftlichen und sozialen Zusammenhalt und die Solidarität zwischen den Mitgliedstaaten zu fördern."

Zur Erreichung dieser Ziele sollen die Mitgliedstaaten ihre Wirtschafts- und Finanzpolitik eng koordinieren und eine einheitliche Geld- und Wechselkurspolitik betreiben, die vorrangig auf das **Ziel der Preisstabilität** auszurichten ist. Des Weiteren wurde den Mitgliedstaaten auferlegt, bei den öffentlichen Finanzen **Haushaltsdisziplin** zu wahren und **außenwirtschaftliches Gleichgewicht** anzustreben. Die Mitgliedstaaten haben bei ihren Tätigkeiten die Grundsätze einer vom Wettbewerb geprägten **offenen Marktwirtschaft** zu beachten. Der Kapitalverkehr ist auch gegenüber Drittländern zu liberalisieren.

1.3.2. Konvergenzkriterien

Als Fundament für die Auswahl der Teilnehmer wurden **vier Konvergenzkriterien,** die sogenannten **Maastricht-Kriterien** entwickelt. Im Einzelnen gestalten sich die vier Kriterien wie folgt:

- **Hoher Grad an Preisstabilität:** Die Inflationsrate darf nicht mehr als 1,5 Prozentpunkte über den Inflationsraten der drei preisstabilsten Mitgliedstaaten liegen.
- **Öffentlicher Finanzhaushalt:** Die Gesamtverschuldung des Staates darf 60% des Bruttoinlandsproduktes nicht überschreiten und das laufende Defizit der öffentlichen Hand darf nicht mehr als 3% des Bruttoinlandsproduktes betragen.

- **Participation in the European Monetary System:** Applicant countries should have joined the exchange rate mechanism (ERM II) under the EMS for two consecutive years.
- **Long-term interest rates:** the nominal long-term interest rate must not be more than two percentage points higher than in the three lowest inflation member states.

The Gross Domestic Product (GDP) is the goods and services produced by the economy within a country's border. In contrast, the **Gross National Product (GNP)** includes all goods and services produced by the citizens of a country at home and abroad. The key difference between the two is that GDP is the total output of a region and GNP is the total output of all nationals of a region.

1.3.3. Members of the European Monetary Union

As of January 2012, the following **17 countries** participate in the European Monetary Union:

- Austria
- Belgium
- Finland
- Estonia (since 1st January 2011)
- France
- Germany
- Greece (since 1st January 2001)
- Ireland
- Italy
- Luxembourg
- Malta (since 1st January 2008)
- Netherlands
- Portugal
- Slovakia (since 1st January 2009)
- Slovenia (since 1st January 2007)
- Spain
- Cyprus (since 1st January 2008)

As of 1st January 2011 17 of the 27 Member States of the European Union participate in the European Monetary Union. The United Kingdom, Denmark and Sweden opted to stay out of the EMU. The European Commission irrevocably fixes the exchange rates of the "euro-in"-currencies to the euro:

Country	Rate
Austria	13.7603 ATS
Belgium	40.3399 BEF
Estonia	15.6466 EEK (since 1st January 2011)
Finland	5.94573 FIM
France	6.55957 FRF
Germany	1.95583 DEM
Greece	340.75 GRD (since 1st January 2001)
Ireland	0.787564 IEP

- **Teilnahme am Europäischen Währungssystem (EWS):** Für die Teilnahme an der EWU muss sich die betroffene Währung seit mindestens zwei Jahren innerhalb der Bandbreite des Wechselkursmechanismus des EWS bewegt haben.
- **Langfristiger Zinssatz:** Der Zinssatz langfristiger Staatsanleihen darf nicht höher liegen als zwei Prozentpunkte über dem Durchschnitt der drei preisstabilsten Mitgliedstaaten.

Das **Bruttoinlandsprodukt (BIP)** umfasst alle innerhalb der Landesgrenzen produzierten Güter und Dienstleistungen einer Volkswirtschaft. Das **Bruttonationalprodukt (BNP)** umfasst alle von Inländern (im Inland oder Ausland) produzierten Güter und Dienstleistungen. BNP und BIP unterscheiden sich um den Saldo der Erwerbs- und Vermögenseinkommen zwischen Inländern und der übrigen Welt. Das **Bruttosozialprodukt (BSP)** ist ein Synonym für BNP.

1.3.3. Mitglieder der Währungsunion

Folgende **17 Länder** nehmen derzeit an der Währungsunion teil (Stand Jänner 2012):

- Belgien
- Deutschland
- Estland (seit 1.1.2011)
- Finnland
- Frankreich
- Griechenland (seit 1.1.2001)
- Irland
- Italien
- Luxemburg
- Malta (seit 1.1.2008)
- Niederlande
- Österreich
- Portugal
- Slowakei (seit 1.1.2009)
- Slowenien (seit 1.1.2007)
- Spanien
- Zypern (seit 1.1.2008)

Seit 1.1.2011 nehmen 17 der 27 Mitgliedstaaten der Europäischen Union an der Europäischen Währungsunion teil. Großbritannien, Schweden und Dänemark bleiben vorläufig freiwillig der Währungsunion fern. Die Europäische Kommission fixiert die endgültigen Wechselkurse der „euro-in"-Währungen auf den Euro:

Land	Kurs
Belgien	40,3399 BEF
Deutschland	1,95583 DEM
Estland	15,6466 EKK (seit 1.1.2011)
Finnland	5,94573 FIM
Frankreich	6,55957 FRF
Griechenland	340,75 GRD seit 1.1.2001
Irland	0,787564 IEP

Italy	1936.27 ITL
Luxembourg	40.3399 LUF
Malta	0.429300 MTL (since 1st January 2008)
Netherlands	2.20371 NLG
Portugal	200.482 ESP
Slovakia	30.1260 SKK (since 1st January 2009)
Slovenia	239.640 SIT (since 1st January 2007)
Spain	166.386 PTE
Cyprus	0.585274 CYP (since 1st January 2008)

On 1 January 1999 the **European Central Bank (ECB)** started its operations in **Frankfurt/Main**.

1.3.4. Stability and growth pact

In order to curb fiscal laxity the EU designed the so-called **stability and growth pact**, which was introduced in 1997 at the Amsterdam summit. This pact determines high fines for countries that violate the budget and deficit criteria. Exceptions are made for countries in recession although these exceptions are very narrowly defined. The stability pact is often seen as a fiscal straightjacket and will certainly be an issue of discussion in the future.

Presumably, the question whether the criteria are fulfilled exactly might not be as important as the question whether the member states are willing to submit to the relatively strict regime of an independent central bank.

1.4. The European System of Central Banks (ESCB)

The European System of Central Banks (ESCB) consists of the **European Central Bank** and the **Central Banks of the member countries of the EMU**. The ECB is situated in Frankfurt/Main. The Central Banks of those EU countries whose currencies do not take part in the euro are also members of the ESCB but have no voting rights on the decisions about and implementation of the common monetary policy in the euro currency area.

The main goal of the ESCB is to **guarantee price stability** in the euro currency area. Additionally the ESCB supports the general economic policy of the European Union and acts in accordance with the fundamentals of an open market economy.

1.4.1. Tasks of the ESCB

The main tasks of the ESCB are:

- defining and implementing the monetary policy of the EU
- conducting FX operations
- holding and managing the official foreign reserves of the Member states
- promoting smooth operation of payment systems

Italien	1.936,27 ITL
Luxemburg	40,3399 LUF
Malta	0,429300 MTL (seit 1.1.2008)
Niederlande	2,20371 NLG
Österreich	13,7603 ATS
Portugal	200,482 ESP
Slowakei	30,1260 SKK (seit 1.1.2009)
Slowenien	239,640 SIT (seit 1.1.2007)
Spanien	166,386 PTE
Zypern	0,585274 CYP (seit 1.1.2008)

Mit 1.1.1999 nahm auch die **Europäische Zentralbank (EZB)** mit Sitz in **Frankfurt am Main** ihre Arbeit auf.

1.3.4. Stabilitäts- und Wachstumspakt

Um fiskalpolitischen Undiszipliniertheiten Einhalt zu gebieten, wurde beim EU-Gipfel in Amsterdam im Jahr 1997 der **Stabilitäts- und Wachstumspakt** verabschiedet. Er sieht teils strenge Strafen für jene Länder vor, die die Kriterien des Budgetdefizits und der Staatsverschuldung nicht erfüllen. Ausnahmen wurden für rezessionsgeplagte Länder vorgesehen. Diese nicht unumstrittene fiskalpolitische Zwangsjacke wird sicherlich noch für einige Diskussionen sorgen.

Für die Stabilität des Euros ist vermutlich weniger entscheidend, ob die Kriterien punktgenau erfüllt werden können, sondern ob die Teilnehmerländer tatsächlich bereit sind, sich dem relativ strengen Regime einer unabhängigen Zentralbank zu unterwerfen.

1.4. Das Europäische System der Zentralbanken (ESZB)

Das Europäische System der Zentralbanken (ESZB) besteht aus der **Europäischen Zentralbank (EZB),** die ihren Sitz in Frankfurt am Main hat, und den **nationalen Zentralbanken jener EU-Staaten, die an der Währungsunion teilnehmen**. Die Nationalbanken der restlichen Mitgliedstaaten sind Mitglieder des ESZB mit Sonderstatus: Sie beteiligen sich nicht an der Entscheidungsfindung betreffend der einheitlichen Geldpolitik für den Euro-Währungsraum und deren Umsetzung.

Vorrangiges Ziel des ESZB ist die **Gewährleistung der Preisstabiliät.** Weiters unterstützt das ESZB die allgemeine Wirtschaftspolitik in der Gemeinschaft und handelt im Einklang mit den Grundsätzen einer offenen Marktwirtschaft.

1.4.1. Aufgaben des ESZB

Zu den Aufgaben des ESZB zählen:

- Festlegung und Ausführung der Geldpolitik der Gemeinschaft
- Durchführung der Devisengeschäfte
- Haltung und Verwaltung der offiziellen Währungsreserven der Mitgliedstaaten
- Förderung des reibungslosen Funktionierens der Zahlungsverkehrssysteme

1.4.2. Decision-making bodies of the ESCB

There are three bodies within the ESCB: Executive Board, Governing Council where the votes on decisions are held and the General Council. The **Governing Council** is the **real decision-making body** and consists of the members of the Executive Board plus the presidents of the national central bank of those countries who take part in the European Monetary Union.

Tasks of the Governing council:

- Determining the monetary policy of the European Union
- Passing guidelines and directives that ensure the realisation of the tasks dedicated to the ESCB.
- Furthermore, the Governing council may change at its discretion in the monetary policy instruments employed, in the conditions of the monetary policy instruments, in the admission criteria to tenders, facilities, etc. and in the procedures associated with its monetary policy trades

1.5 Mechanisms of Interventions of Central Banks – Instruments and Techniques

1.5.1 Monetary Reserves Policy

The central banks' stock of foreign currency enlarges the scope of their currency policy and their international creditworthiness. Moreover, the stock of foreign currency **guarantees that payment transactions with foreign countries** (capital, services, and goods) **are completed properly**.

Foreign currency, gold, claims based on the respective country's share in the International Monetary Fund and its special drawing rights, as well as claims on the European Central Bank (ECB) are the major components of the **"international monetary reserves"**. A major part of the reserves is in US dollars, due to the dollar's leading position as an international currency for intervention and reserves.

It is the duty of the central banks to prevent unwanted consequences from the excessive flows of foreign exchange. In such cases, they make use of appropriate measures concerning foreign exchange, interest, or monetary policies.

Sudden excessive flows of foreign exchange can cause major problems for a country. Heavy influx of foreign exchange may raise the amount of cash in circulation, which may not suit the country's economic policies. Excessive draining away of foreign exchange may endanger the monetary reserves. An excessive demand for foreign exchange will push the central bank to a situation in which it has to pull out foreign exchange out of its reserves in order to steer against a fall of its own currency.

This automatically affects the domestic currency because any amount of bought and sold foreign exchange is settled in the domestic currency. If the central bank sells foreign exchange it receives domestic currency that is taken away from the amount of cash in circulation. If the central bank buys foreign currency the amount of cash in circulation is increased.

Sterilized Intervention

Sterilized intervention is a method used by monetary authorities to **equalize the effects of central bank intervention on the domestic monetary base by offsetting the purchase or**

1.4.2. Organe des ESZB

Das ESZB wird von den Beschlussorganen der EZB (EZB-Rat, Direktorium und erweiterter Rat) geleitet. Der **EZB-Rat** ist das **Entscheidungsorgan des ESZB.** Er besteht aus allen Mitgliedern des Direktoriums und den Präsidenten der nationalen Zentralbanken der an der Währungsunion teilnehmenden Mitgliedstaaten.

Aufgaben des EZB-Rates:

- Festlegung der Geldpolitik der Gemeinschaft
- Erlass von Leitlinien und Entscheidungen, die die Erfüllung der dem ESZB übertragenen Aufgaben gewährleisten
- Außerdem kann der EZB-Rat die Instrumente, Konditionen, Zulassungskriterien und Verfahren für die Durchführung von geldpolitischen Geschäften des ESZB jederzeit ändern.

1.5. Interventionsmechanismus der Notenbanken – Instrumente und Techniken

1.5.1. Währungsreservepolitik

Der Devisenbestand der Notenbanken vergrößert den Handlungsspielraum der Währungspolitik und die internationale Kreditwürdigkeit. Darüber hinaus soll der Devisenbestand den **reibungslosen Zahlungsverkehr mit dem Ausland** (Kapital-, Dienstleistungs- und Güterverkehr) **sicherstellen.**

Devisen, Gold, Forderungen aus der Beteiligung des jeweiligen Landes am Internationalen Währungsfonds und im Rahmen dieser Institution geschaffene Sonderziehungsrechte sowie Forderungen an die EZB bilden die wesentlichen Bestandteile der **„internationalen Währungsreserve".** Das Hauptgewicht der Devisenbestände nimmt der US-Dollar ein. Dies ergibt sich aus seiner dominierenden Stellung als internationale Interventions- und Reservewährung.

Aufgabe der Notenbanken ist es, unerwünschte Auswirkungen exzessiver Devisenzuflüsse und -abflüsse durch entsprechende währungs-, zins- oder devisenpolitische Maßnahmen zu verhindern.

Plötzlich vermehrte Devisenzuflüsse oder -abflüsse können ein Land vor ernste Probleme stellen. Überhöhte Devisenzuflüsse können den Geldumlauf in wirtschaftspolitisch unerwünschter Weise erhöhen. Abflüsse können sogar die Währungsreserven gefährden. Bei einer Übernachfrage nach Devisen muss (kann) die Notenbank Devisen aus ihren Währungsreserven anbieten, um ein Absinken des Heimwährungskurses zu vermeiden.

Automatisch ist damit die heimische Geldmenge berührt. Denn die gekauften oder verkauften Devisen werden in der Heimwährung abgerechnet. Verkauft die Notenbank Devisen, so fließen ihr Mittel in der Heimwährung zu, die so dem Geldumlauf entzogen werden. Kauft sie hingegen Devisen, so fließt Heimwährung in die Volkswirtschaft ein.

Sterilisierte Intervention

Eine sterilisierte Intervention ist die **Intervention einer Zentralbank am Devisenmarkt, bei der der Einfluss auf die inländische Liquidität (Zinsen) aufgehoben wird.** Eine Zentralbank verkauft z.B. die (steigende) Heimwährung – was die inländische Liquidität erhöht – und kauft die Fremdwährung. Gleichzeitig aber verkauft die Zentralbank Staatsanleihen,

sale of domestic assets within the domestic markets. E.g. a central bank sells the (increasing) domestic currency – raising domestic liquidity – and buys foreign currency. At the same time they sell government bonds, causing a decrease in domestic liquidity.

Unsterilized (or Non-Sterilized) Intervention

Unsterilized intervention is an intervention on the FX market whereby **central banks buy domestic currency, thereby withdrawing money from the market, but do not insulate their domestic money supplies against the influence of domestic liquidity** (interest) (e.g. by buying or selling government bonds). This procedure could imply that the central bank wants to induce a change in the market.

An indicator for the monetary reserves policy is the **effective exchange rate**. An effective exchange rate is the geometric weighted **average of different bilateral exchange rates** (calculated by the BIS).

Effective real exchange rates are effective nominal exchange rates excluding a weighted average of foreign prices and costs compared to the according domestic prices and costs.

They are **indicators for the competitiveness of a country** regarding prices and costs. The choice of currencies and weights depends on the specific economic background. Usually foreign trade weights are used for computing effective exchange rates.

However, the **prospects for the success of a policy of pure intervention are limited**. The currency disturbances under Bretton Woods as well as the EMS crises have shown that lasting tendencies of the market cannot be suppressed by the central banks' interventions in the foreign exchange market. At most, it is possible to let correcting interventions limit speculation that would otherwise occur due to major divergences between short-term development of the exchange rates and their long-term tendencies. Stable exchange rates are only possible if one successfully averts **permanent imbalances in the world economies** and by **coordinating the countries' economic development**, or if one counteracts against threatening adverse developments. During recent years these aims have been supported by the most intense efforts towards a better coordination of the economic and monetary policies among the seven leading western developed nations (G7) and the future EU countries.

1.5.2. Policy of Refinancing

On the one hand, the term refinancing is used when central banks give loans to banks by either buying bills (**Discount Policy**) or lending bonds (**Lombard Policy**). On the other hand, part of refinancing also is the regular availability of funds for revolving settled repurchase agreements (**Open Market Transactions**).

Discount Policy

Discount policy refers to the central bank's **right to purchase bills from other banks at a discount rate that is fixed by the central bank itself**. Bills that meet certain criteria are called eligible bills.

was Gelder aus dem Markt abzieht und somit die Liquiditätseffekte der Devisentransaktion ausgleicht.

Nicht-sterilisierte Intervention

Eine nicht-sterilisierte Intervention ist die **Intervention einer Zentralbank am Devisenmarkt, bei der der Einfluss auf die inländische Liquidität (Zinsen) nicht durch eine Offenmarkt-Transaktion aufgehoben wird.** Dies wäre der Fall, wenn z.B. eine Zentralbank die Heimwährung kauft und dadurch Gelder aus dem Markt abzieht, dies aber nicht durch den Kauf von Staatsanleihen wieder ausgleicht (was zu einem Zufluss an Geldern führen würde). Ein solches Vorgehen könnte bedeuten, dass die Zentralbank eine Veränderung der Geldmarktkonditionen wünscht.

Als Indikator für die Währungsreservenpolitik wird auf den **effektiven Wechselkurs** zurückgegriffen. Ein effektiver Wechselkurs beruht auf einem von der BIZ als geometrisches Mittel berechneten **Durchschnitt verschiedener bilateraler Wechselkurse.**

Effektive reale Wechselkurse sind effektive nominale Wechselkurse preisbereinigt mit einem gewogenen Durchschnitt von ausländischen Preisen oder Kosten, verglichen mit den entsprechenden inländischen Preisen und Kosten. Sie stellen **Indikatoren für die Wettbewerbsfähigkeit eines Landes** hinsichtlich der Preise und Kosten dar. Die Wahl der Währungen und Gewichte richtet sich nach der jeweiligen ökonomischen Fragestellung. Die gebräuchlichsten Berechnungsarten des effektiven Wechselkurses wenden Außenhandelsgewichte an.

Dennoch sind die **Erfolgsaussichten einer reinen Interventionspolitik begrenzt.** Sowohl die Währungsunruhen unter dem System von Bretton Woods wie auch die EWS-Krisen (Europäisches Währungssystem) der Jahre 1992 und 1993 haben gezeigt, dass sich nachhaltige Markttendenzen nicht durch Devisenmarktinterventionen der Notenbanken unterdrücken lassen. Allenfalls erscheint es möglich, bei starken Abweichungen der kürzerfristigen Wechselkursentwicklung vom Trend durch korrigierende Eingriffe spekulative Übersteigungen zu begrenzen. Stabile Wechselkursverhältnisse lassen sich dauerhaft nur erreichen, wenn es gelingt, **ausgeprägte und anhaltende Ungleichgewichte in der Weltwirtschaft zu vermeiden** und die **wirtschaftliche Entwicklung in den einzelnen Ländern stärker zu harmonisieren** bzw. sich abzeichnenden Fehlentwicklungen entgegenzuwirken. Diesen Zielen dienen auch die in den letzten Jahren gesetzten intensiven Bemühungen zur besseren Koordinierung der Wirtschafts- und Währungspolitik durch die sieben führenden westlichen Industrienationen (G7) und die EWWU-Staaten (Europäische Wirtschafts- und Währungsunion).

1.5.2. Refinanzierungspolitik

Mit dem Begriff Refinanzierung wird zum einen die Gewährung der Kredite durch die Notenbank an die Kreditinstitute im Wege des Ankaufs von Wechseln **(Diskontpolitik)** und der Beleihung von Wertpapieren **(Lombardpolitik)** bezeichnet. Zum anderen gehört zur Refinanzierung auch die laufende Mittelbereitstellung über die revolvierend abgeschlossenen Wertpapierpensionsgeschäfte mit Kreditinstituten **(Offenmarktgeschäfte).**

Diskontpolitik

Im Rahmen der Diskontpolitik haben Notenbanken das **Recht, von Geschäftsbanken Wechsel zu einem von ihnen festgelegten Diskontsatz zu kaufen.** Wechsel, die diesbe-

As a basic rule, three counterparties regarded as being solvent should guarantee for the redemption of the bill. The tendered bills acquired though the central bank must fall due within three months, and should be good commercial bills of exchange. The detailed prerequisites for exchange bills' suitability for acquisition are laid out in the credit policy regulations.

Usually, there are no limits (ceiling or floor) for the discount rate. Therefore, the central bank may autonomously fix the discount rate and is therefore able to act according to the current monetary policy. Being the lowest rate of refinancing, the discount rate includes a certain element of subsidy whose extent is determined by its divergence from other market interest rates. Due to this implied element of subsidy, discount policy is not used in the European System of Central Banks, while it stills plays a **prominent role in US central bank policy**.

Lombard Policy

One speaks of Lombard policy when central banks grant **interest-bearing loans** (**Lombard loans**) to other banks against **collateral** (certain securities, bonds and debts). Lombard loans are limited to short terms (usually of three months, e.g. in the Czech Republic).

However, a Lombard loan is only to be granted if it serves as a **short-term bridging of liquidity constraint** and if the loan's amount and term are appropriate and justifiable (= marginal lending facility). Therefore, Lombard loans should be used as current loans only.

Lombard loans may be granted against the transfer of bills, public bonds, government bonds, recovery claims, and bank bonds (however not against the debtor's own issue).

Consequences of a change of discount rate and Lombard rate

Fixing the **discount rate and the Lombard rate** lies at the heart of the central banks' interest rate policy. In a banking system where all banks are in permanent debt regarding the discount loan of the central bank, the discount rate represents the **floor for 1-month and 3-months interest rate**s. The overnight rate, however, may be below the discount rate for a short time since the banks can only pay back their discount loans gradually. In such cases the maturities are important.

Standing facilities

In the European Union, discount and Lombard policy were not included in the group of instruments available to the ECB. Instead, standing facilities were established which basically work **in the same way as the discount and Lombard policy**.

The idea of standing facilities is to **provide overnight liquidity** to banks as well as to offer banks with a liquidity surplus to place their money overnight for a (low) interest rate. They signal the trend of the ECB monetary policy and lay out the upper and lower boundaries of the money market rates for day funds. The **administration** of the facilities lies **locally with the national central banks**.

Marginal lending facility

The marginal lending facility enables commercial banks to bridge overnight liquidity shortages at a daily pre-fixed rate. The money received through the marginal lending facility

zügliche Mindesterfordernisse erfüllen, bezeichnet man als rediskontierbare Wechsel (in GB als „Eligible Bill").

Für die Wechsel sollen grundsätzlich drei als zahlungsfähig bekannte Verpflichtete haften. Die eingereichten Papiere müssen ferner bei Ankauf durch die Notenbank innerhalb von drei Monaten fällig werden und sollen gute Handelswechsel sein. Die detaillierten Voraussetzungen für die Ankaufsfähigkeit von Wechseln sind in den kreditpolitischen Regelungen festgelegt.

Für die Höhe des Diskontsatzes gibt es für gewöhnlich keine Ober- oder Untergrenze. Die jeweilige Notenbank ist somit bei seiner Festsetzung autonom. Sie kann sich nach den jeweiligen geldpolitischen Erfordernissen richten. Als traditionell niedrigster Refinanzierungssatz enthält der Diskontsatz eine Art Subventionselement, dessen Ausmaß vom Abstand zu den übrigen Marktzinssätzen bestimmt wird. Die Diskontpolitik ist **eines der wesentlichen Steuerungsinstrumente der Federal Reserve Bank.**

Lombardpolitik

Das im Rahmen der Lombardpolitik verwendete Instrument ist der **Lombardkredit.** Das sind **verzinsliche Darlehen**, die Notenbanken den Kreditinstituten gewähren, die dafür **bestimmte Sicherheiten (Wertpapiere oder Schuldbuchforderungen) zur Verfügung stellen** müssen.

Üblicherweise sind Lombardkredite **kurzfristige Kredite bis zu drei Monaten** (z.B. Tschechische Republik). Doch soll ein Lombardkredit grundsätzlich nur gewährt werden, wenn er der kurzfristigen Überbrückung eines vorübergehenden Liquiditätsbedarfs dient und die Lombardkreditaufnahme nach Umfang und Dauer angemessen und vertretbar erscheint. Daher sollen Lombardkredite kontokorrentmäßig in Anspruch genommen werden.

Lombardkredite können gegen Verpfändung von Wechseln, öffentlichen Anleihen, Schuldbuchforderungen, Ausgleichsforderungen und Bankschuldverschreibungen (jedoch nicht eigene Emissionen des Lombardschuldners) gewährt werden.

Auswirkungen der Veränderung von Diskont- und Lombardsatz

Die Festsetzung des **Diskont- und Lombardsatzes** stellt den Kern der Zinspolitik der Zentralbanken dar. Der Diskontsatz ist in einem Bankensystem, das permanent im Diskontkredit bei der Notenbank verschuldet ist, eine Art **untere Grenze der Zinssätze für Monats- und Dreimonatsgeld.** Hingegen kann der Tagesgeldsatz den Diskontsatz durchaus vorübergehend unterschreiten, da die Banken einmal in Anspruch genommene Diskontkredite nur schrittweise nach Maßgabe der Wechselfälligkeiten abbauen können.

Ständige Fazilitäten

Diskont- und Lombardsatz fanden keinen Eingang in das geldpolitische Instrumentarium des ESZB. Stattdessen wurden die ständigen Fazilitäten eingeführt, die eine **ähnliche Wirkung wie die Diskont- und Lombardpolitik** haben.

Zweck der ständigen Fazilitäten ist es, **Overnight-Liquidität bereitzustellen oder abzuschöpfen.** Sie signalisieren den Geldpolitikkurs des ESZB und stecken Ober- und Untergrenzen der Geldmarktsätze für Taggelder ab. Die ständigen Fazilitäten werden **dezentral von den nationalen Zentralbanken verwaltet.**

Spitzenrefinanzierungsfazilität

Die Geschäftspartner können sich zu einem vorgegebenen Zinssatz und gegen refinanzierungsfähige Sicherheiten Overnight-Liquidität beschaffen und so kurzfristige Liquidi-

must be backed by collateral, allowing unlimited credit. The marginal lending facility is generally the **interest rate ceiling for the overnight rate**.

Deposit facility

The deposit facility allows commercial banks to place a liquidity surplus at the central bank overnight at a pre-fixed rate. Generally, the deposit facility rate poses the **interest rate floor for the overnight rate**.

1.5.3. Minimum Reserve Policy

Organisation of the Minimum Reserve System

The minimum reserve policy obliges banks to maintain a **certain percentage of their own deposits at the central bank** (there are differences between national regulations, which are not dealt with here). These framework regulations once served as security for the **liquidity of customer deposits** at the banks.

The current system of minimum reserve is a **flexible and effective liquidity instrument** in the hands of the central bank.

The minimum reserve rate is to be held on the accounts of the national central banks and has to be fulfilled within a one-month settlement period under consideration of the average daily reserve assets (averaging provision). The reserve maintenance periods are determined in accordance with a calendar prepared by the ECB three months before the start of the year.

Each maintenance period begins on the settlement day of the first main refinancing operation following the meeting of the Governing Council, at which the monthly assessment of the monetary policy stance is pre-scheduled. The period ends the day before the next month's settlement day.

During this maintenance period banks must fulfil on average the reserve base. Therefore, banks can actively manage their liquidity over the time. Banks are not required to hold any "working balances" at the ECB, i.e. additional assets in order to ensure the settlement of regular payments. If banks do not cover their reserve base the ECB may fine them either by charging a margin over the marginal lending facility or by paying no interest on the deposit facility.

Transactions on the accounts with the central bank must be **recorded and managed every day**, because an overnight liquidity shortage incurs costs at the marginal lending facility while exceeding the minimum reserve requirement means forgoing the overnight rate.

Especially towards the end of the maintenance period, the money market situation depends on the degree to which the banks have maintained their minimum reserves until then. If there is a significant overall shortage, the overnight rate will rise, and with an expected surplus on the reserve balances the overnight rate will sharply fall. If a bank fails to meet its requirements, it has to pay a **special interest** rate on the difference between target and actual minimum reserve (in the ESCB this rate is marginal lending facility plus margin). A continuing non-compliance of the minimum reserve target is a violation against the central

tätsengpässe ausgleichen. Sofern ausreichend refinanzierungsfähige Sicherheiten vorhanden sind, gibt es keine Kreditobergrenze für diese Fazilität. Der Zinssatz für die Spitzenrefinanzierungsfazilität bildet im Allgemeinen die **Obergrenze des Taggeldsatzes.**

Einlagefazilität

Die Geschäftspartner können überschüssige Liquidität bei den nationalen Zentralbanken anlegen. Der Zinssatz für diese Einlagen wird im Voraus festgesetzt und bildet üblicherweise die **Untergrenze des Taggeldsatzes.**

1.5.3. Mindestreservepolitik

Die Ausgestaltung des Mindestreservesystems

Die Mindestreserveregelung verpflichtet Banken dazu, einen **gewissen Prozentsatz ihrer Einlagen als Guthaben bei der Zentralbank** zu halten (auf die Unterschiede zwischen den einzelnen Ländern geht das vorliegende Skriptum nicht ein).

Diese Rahmenvorschrift diente ursprünglich der **Liquiditätssicherung der Kundeneinlagen** bei den Banken. Das derzeit bestehende Mindestreservesystem soll dagegen den Notenbanken von vornherein als **flexibles und wirksames, liquiditätspolitisches Instrument** zur Verfügung stehen.

Die Mindestreserve-Erfüllungsperioden beginnen am Abwicklungstag des ersten Hauptrefinanzierungsgeschäfts, das auf die Sitzung des EZB-Rats folgt, in der die monatliche Erörterung der Geldpolitik stattfindet, und enden am Tag vor dem entsprechenden Abwicklungstag im Folgemonat. Die EZB veröffentlicht drei Monate vor Beginn des Jahres einen Mindestreserveperioden-Kalender.

Daher können die Banken ihre Zentralbankguthaben für Zahlungszwecke verwenden. Falls erforderlich, können sie kurzfristig abdisponieren, vorausgesetzt, dass sie an anderen Tagen des Erfüllungszeitraums entsprechend höhere Guthaben halten. Die Banken sind nicht gezwungen, zusätzlich zu den Mindestreserven besondere Guthaben bei der Zentralbank zur Abwicklung des laufenden Zahlungsverkehrs zu halten („working balances").

Die Bewegungen auf den Zentralbankkonten müssen täglich erfasst und disponiert werden. Tagesüberschreitende Unterdeckungen verursachen auf den Konten Kosten in Höhe der Spitzenrefinanzierungsfazilität.

Andererseits bedeutet eine Übererfüllung der Mindestreserve Rentabilitätsverzicht in Höhe des Tagesgeldzinses.

Die Mindestreserve ist auf Konten bei den nationalen Zentralbanken zu halten und muss unter Zugrundelegung der **tagesdurchschnittlichen Reserveguthaben** innerhalb einer einmonatigen Erfüllungsperiode erfüllt werden (Durchschnittserfüllung). Als **Sanktionen** für die Nichteinhaltung der Mindestreservepflicht sind **Sonderzinsen auf den Spitzenrefinanzierungssatz** oder **unverzinste Einlagen bei der EZB oder den nationalen Zentralbanken** vorgesehen.

Insbesondere gegen Ende der Erfüllungsperiode wird die Lage am Geldmarkt entscheidend davon bestimmt, inwieweit die Kreditinstitute ihre Mindestreserveverpflichtungen erfüllt haben. Bei großem Rückstand wird der Tagesgeldsatz anziehen, bei Übererfüllung möglicherweise aber stark nachgeben. Gelingt es einer Bank nicht, ihr Reserve-Soll bis zum Ende der Erfüllungsperiode zu erfüllen, so ist auf den Differenzbetrag, um den die Ist-Reserve das Reserve-Soll unterschreitet, ein Sonderzins zu leisten (im ESZB der Spitzenrefinanzierungssatz plus einer Marge). Eine fortgesetzte Nichterfüllung des Mindestreserve-

bank regulation and can lead to an exclusion from standing facilities or open market transactions.

The **minimum reserve rates** are **determined by the ESCB** and can be changed at any time. Changes are announced before the first minimum reserve period for which the change is valid.

Consequences of the Minimum Reserve

There are **two aspects of the minimum reserve that concern the liquidity policy**:

Firstly, an **additional demand of central bank money** (besides the already existing cash in circulation) is created, the amount is determined by the minimum reserve rates and the current total of reserve-bearing liabilities. The fluctuating demand of central bank money is the "lever" that enables the central bank to control the banks' money creation.

Secondly, **the minimum reserve instrument enables the central bank to correct the banks' long-term demand of central bank money by changing the reserve rates**. Since a change of the minimum reserve rates will make the central bank balances either rise or fall, the central bank may compensate transactions that will either create or destroy central bank money (e.g. foreign exchange interventions) by means of a minimum reserve policy. However, for technical reasons, changes in the minimum reserve rates come into effect only in the following month. If the money market situation requires fast action more flexible instruments like open market transactions are employed.

The average minimum reserve asset during the fulfilment period yields the **ESCB rate** (weighted with the number of calendar days) for the **main refinancing instrument** according to the following formula:

$$R_t = \frac{H_t * n_t * \sum\limits_{i=n}^{n} \dfrac{MRi}{n_t * 100}}{360}$$

Rt = Interest to be paid on the minimum reserve assets accumulated in the minimum reserve fulfilment period t
Ht = Minimum reserve assets in the minimum reserve fulfilment period t
nt = Number of calendar days of the minimum reserve fulfilment period t
I = calendar day i of the minimum reserve fulfilment period t
MRi = marginal interest rate of the current main refinancing operation at calendar day i

Any assets that exceed the minimum reserve requirement do not yield any interest.

For the calculation of the minimum reserve the liabilities against banks that are subject to the minimum reserve requirement are not taken into account.

The minimum reserve system should fulfil the following **money policy functions**:

- Stability of money market rates: The credit institutes are urged to absorb the effects of liquidity fluctuations with the aver-aging provision in the minimum reserve system. This leads to a stabilisation of the money market rates.
- Causing or increasing a structural liquidity shortage
- Managing the money supply, particularly through increasing interest elasticity of the money demand

Solls kann zum Ausschluss von den ständingen Fazilitäten und Offenmarktgeschäften führen.

Die **Mindestreservesätze** werden **von der Europäischen Zentralbank festgesetzt** und können jederzeit geändert werden. Änderungen werden vor der ersten Mindestreserveperiode, in der die Änderung gilt, bekanntgegeben.

Wirkungen der Mindestreserve

Das Instrument der Mindestreserve hat **zwei liquiditätspolitische Aspekte:**

Zum einen schafft es – neben dem Bargeldumlauf – einen **zusätzlichen Bedarf der Banken an Zentralbankgeld.** Seine Höhe hängt von den Mindestreservesätzen und vom jeweiligen Bestand an reservepflichtigen Verbindlichkeiten ab. Der entsprechend schwankende Zentralbankgeldbedarf ist der „Hebel", mit dem die Notenbank das Ausmaß der Geldschöpfung der Banken unter Kontrolle halten kann.

Zum anderen verschafft die Mindestreserve der Notenbank die Möglichkeit, **durch Veränderung der Reservesätze das Ausmaß des dauerhaften Zentralbankgeldbedarfs der Banken zu korrigieren.**

Durch eine Änderung der Mindestreservesätze werden Zentralbankguthaben der Banken unmittelbar gebunden oder freigesetzt. Mindestreservepolitik kann auch Vorgänge, mit denen eine Zentralbankgeldschaffung oder -vernichtung verbunden ist, ganz oder teilweise kompensieren, wie z.B. Devisininterventionen. Veränderungen der Mindestreservesätze sind allerdings aus technischen Gründen erst in der nächsten Reserveerfüllungsperiode wirksam. Für rasch wirksame Geldmarktsteuerungsmaßnahmen werden generell die flexibleren Offenmarktoperationen eingesetzt.

Die durchschnittlichen Mindestreserveguthaben während der Erfüllungsperiode werden zum **ESZB-Zinssatz** (gewogen mit der Anzahl der Kalendertage) für das **Hauptrefinanzierungsinstrument** gemäß folgender Formel verzinst:

$$R_t = \frac{H_t * n_t * \sum\limits_{i=n}^{n} \dfrac{MRi}{n_t * 100}}{360}$$

R_t = Zinsen, die für die Mindestreserveguthaben in der Mindestreserveerfüllungsperiode t anfallen
H_t = Mindestreserveguthaben in der Mindestreserveerfüllungsperiode t
n_t = Anzahl der Kalendertage der Mindestreserveerfüllungsperiode t
i = Kalendertag i der Mindestreserveerfüllungsperiode t
MRi = marginaler Zinssatz des aktuellsten Hauptrefinanzierungsgeschäftes am Kalendertag i

Guthaben, die die erforderliche Mindestreserve übersteigen, werden nicht verzinst.

Bei der Berechnung der Mindestreserve werden Verbindlichkeiten gegenüber mindestreservepflichtigen Kreditinstituten nicht berücksichtigt.

Das Mindestreservesystem soll folgende **geldpolitische Funktionen** erfüllen:

- Stabilisierung der Geldmarktsätze: Durch die Durchschnittserfüllung im Mindestreservesystem werden die Kreditinstitute dazu angehalten, die Auswirkungen von Liquiditätsschwankungen abzufedern. Dies führt zu einer Stabilisierung der Geldmarktsätze.
- Herbeiführung oder Vergrößerung einer strukturellen Liquiditätsknappheit
- Steuerung der Geldmenge, insbesondere durch Erhöhung der Zinselastizität

At present the FED, the BoJ and the ECB require minimum reserves. In contrary to the BoE where cash ratio deposits serve non-credit policy aims. For the SNB this instrument is not used currently (current regulations on "cash liquidity" pursue the same objectives).

1.5.4. Open Market Policy

The **buying and selling of bonds in the open market by the central bank** on its own account is called open market policy. The question regarding which securities may be bought depends on the legal regulations of the central bank concerned.

It must be added here, though, that even open market operations in long-term securities are **only permitted with the aim of influencing the money market**, i.e. the banks' liquidities. This excludes direct interventions by the central bank in the capital market that may be motivated by the wish to finance the public borrowing requirements or to support prices.

The instruction to buy and sell only in the open market is primarily a ban on central banks directly taking debts out of the hands of the issuer. Such a direct purchase would not be an open market transaction but in fact **granting of a credit to a government budget, which is prohibited**.

Short-term transactions are the key monetary instrument of the ECB. They are either under-taken as repo transactions or through the purchase/sale of mortgage loans ("Pfandbriefe").

Short-term transactions may be either :

* **Repo transactions** (assets are handed over as settlement of a sum owed, with the agreement that these assets will be returned at a specific time upon payment of the settlement sum or other agreed sum) or
* **Mortgage loan transactions** (property remains with the debtor if they discharge the debt).

It should be noted that in the US the repo terminology reverses if the FED becomes actively involved in the market. This means a System Reverse Repo of the FED is a sale and purchase of the bond, thus a measure to drain liquidity from the market and signalling rising interest rates.

Repurchase agreements are usually offered in form of a **tender** to banks. On the basis of the total amount of the banks' bids the effective amount to be passed on to the banks is determined. This is the result of the central bank's objectives regarding liquidity and the banks' demand for central bank money (e.g. to compensate fluctuations of the money in circulation or to balance the banks' minimum reserves). If there are more bids than needed, a scaling down takes place.

Repurchase agreements can be either **"volume-linked tenders"** or **"variable rate linked tenders"**. With a volume-linked tender the interest rate is already fixed. This means that banks have no way of influencing the volume quotation by their interest quotation. With

Derzeit werden sowohl von der FED, der BoJ und der EZB Mindestreserven gefordert. Im Gegensatz dazu dienen bei der BoE Cash-Ratio-Deposits nicht-kreditpolitischen Zwecken. Bei der SNB wird das Instrument derzeit nicht genutzt (aktuelle Bestimmungen über „Kassenliquidität" verfolgen jedoch die gleichen Ziele).

1.5.4. Offenmarktpolitik

Als Offenmarktgeschäfte bezeichnet man den **Kauf und Verkauf von Wertpapieren durch die Zentralbank auf eigene Rechnung am offenen Markt.** Welche Papiere angekauft werden können, ergibt sich aus den gesetzlichen Bestimmungen der jeweiligen Notenbanken.

Einschränkend ist hier jedoch zu bemerken, dass auch Offenmarktgeschäfte in langfristigen Papieren **nur zur Regelung des Geldmarktes, d.h. der Bankenliquidität, erlaubt** sind. Dies schließt beispielsweise direkte Notenbankinterventionen am Kapitalmarkt mit dem primären Ziel der Finanzierung des öffentlichen Kreditbedarfs oder der Kursstützung aus.

Die Vorschrift, nur „am offenen Markt" zu kaufen oder zu verkaufen, verbietet vor allem die Direktübernahme von Schuldtiteln durch die Notenbank aus der Hand der Emittenten. Bei einem solchen unmittelbaren Erwerb würde es sich nicht um ein Offenmarktgeschäft, sondern um die **Gewährung eines Kredits an einen öffentlichen Haushalt** handeln, die **untersagt** ist.

Befristete Transaktionen sind die wichtigsten Offenmarktgeschäfte. Das ESZB kauft oder verkauft refinanzierungsfähige Sicherheiten im Rahmen von Rückkaufvereinbarungen oder schließt Kreditgeschäfte gegen Verpfändung von refinanzierungsfähigen Sicherheiten ab.

Befristete Transaktionen können durchgeführt werden als

- **Pensionsgeschäfte** (Geschäfte, bei denen der Pensionsgeber dem Pensionsnehmer Vermögensgegenstände gegen Zahlung eines Betrages überträgt und in denen gleichzeitig vereinbart wird, dass die Vermögensgegenstände später gegen Entrichtung des empfangenen oder eines im voraus vereinbarten Betrages und zu einem bestimmten Zeitpunkt an den Pensionsgeber zurückbezahlt werden) oder
- **Pfandkredite** (das Eigentum am Vermögenswert bleibt beim Schuldner, wenn er seiner Verpflichtung nachkommt).

In den USA kehrt die Repo-Terminologie um, wenn die FED aktiv im Markt wird. Ein System Reverse Repo der FED ist – aus Sicht der FED – ein Verkauf und ein Kauf des Wertpapieres und daher eine Maßnahme, Liquidität aus dem Markt zu ziehen und einen Zinsanstieg zu signalisieren.

Wertpapierpensionsgeschäfte werden den Kreditinstituten üblicherweise in Form der **Ausschreibung** angeboten. Auf die Gesamtsumme der von den Banken abgegebenen Gebote wird der Betrag zugeteilt, der den liquiditätspolitischen Vorstellungen der Notenbank bzw. dem Bedarf der Banken an Zentralbankgeld (z.B. für die Auffüllung des Mindestreserve-Solls oder zum Ausgleich von Schwankungen des Bargeldumlaufs) entspricht. Gehen mehr Gebote ein, wird entsprechend repartiert (= Zuteilungsquote).

Wertpapierpensionsgeschäfte werden entweder als **Mengentender** oder als **Zinstender** angeboten.

Beim Mengentender ist der Zins fest vorgegeben. Das bedeutet, dass die Banken keine Möglichkeit haben, ihre Zuteilungsquote über ihre Zinsquotierung zu beeinflussen. Mit

a volume-linked tender at a fixed interest rate, the central bank can send signals in the market during times of volatile interest rates and, thereby, can stabilise the interest rates.

With a variable rate tender, the banks are enabled to quote a volume and an interest rate at which they are willing to settle repurchase agreements. Banks are allotted a share of the tender according to the competitiveness of their quote, i.e. the highest quote is satisfied first. The allotment finishes at the interest rate where the tender volume is completely placed. If, at the lowest interest rate, the quoted volume exceeds the remaining tender volume the bids are scaled down **("American tender")**. In contrast to American tenders, **Dutch tenders** allot to each bidder the requested volume at the marginal interest rate. The marginal interest rate is the lowest rate at which the tender volume can be placed in the market.

Another open market instrument to control market liquidity is the **issue of bonds**.

By means of open market operations the FED tries to keep the **Fed Funds Rate** within its designated limits. The Fed Funds Rate is the interest rate at which US banks lend to each other overnight.

1.5.5. FX Transactions

To avoid disturbances in the money market arising from FX market turbulence, during the period of fixed exchange rates central banks developed foreign exchange instruments which enabled them to influence international payment transactions.

These are **swap deals and outright operations** in the forward FX market. With a swap deal, one buys (sells) foreign currency from (to) the central bank at the spot rate and at the same time sells (buys) them as an outright. Therefore, one can speak of a **combination of spot and outright operation**, while the swap rate that is charged is equivalent to an interest rate. In contrast to a spot operation, an outright operation is to be carried out only at a later date (e.g. in 3 months). These operations are occasionally done to **counteract against speculative FX movements** or to **"silently" balance the exchange rate towards a foreign currency**, commonly the US dollar. With outright operations, one can influence the spot market indirectly, because a commercial bank will try to hedge against the FX risks out of the current outright operations by a reverse spot operation in order to avoid open FX positions.

Such transactions have a delayed influence on the banks' liquidity in the same way as a corresponding spot transaction in the FX market would have had. For example, if US dollars are sold with an outright transaction the central bank will withdraw the corresponding amount from the bank's account at the time the deal is carried out. This amount equals the amount the bank has to provide when the transaction effectively takes place.

FX swaps are quite flexible with respect to their construction. This includes the swaps' terms as well as the volumes that these transactions are based on. Furthermore, these transactions can be carried out very quickly.

For fine adjustment in the money market, central banks use this instrument as a "buffer" to counteract against unwanted fluctuations of the banks' accounts with the central bank as regards the required minimum reserve of the bank within its fulfilment period. Due to

dem Mengentender zum Festzins kann die Notenbank dem Markt in Phasen der Zinsunsicherheit ein Zinssignal geben und nachhaltig auf die Zinsentwicklung einwirken.

Beim Zinstender haben die Banken die Möglichkeit, neben dem Volumen auch den Zinssatz zu nennen, zu dem sie bereit sind, Pensionsgeschäfte abzuschließen. Bei der Zuteilung werden alle Offerten vom höchsten Zinssatz abwärts so lange voll bedient, bis die von der Notenbank bestimmte Betragshöhe erreicht ist. Gebote zum niedrigsten noch zum Zuge kommenden Satz werden gegebenenfalls repartiert, die Zuteilung erfolgt jeweils zu den individuellen Bietungssätzen der Banken (amerikanisches Verfahren).

Das ESZB kennt beim Zinstender auch das sogenannte **holländische Zuteilungsverfahren.** Es handelt sich dabei um ein Tenderverfahren, bei dem der Zuteilungssatz für alle zum Zuge kommenden Gebote dem marginalen Zinssatz (d.h. dem letzten Zinssatz, zu dem eine Zuteilung erfolgt) entspricht.

Ein weiteres Instrument der Offenmarktpolitik zur Steuerung des Liquiditätsbedarfes am Markt ist die **Emission von Schuldverschreibungen.**

Mithilfe von Offenmarktoperationen versucht die FED, die vorgesehene Bandbreite der **FED Funds Rate** zu halten. Die FED Funds Rate ist jener Zinssatz, zu dem im US Interbankmarkt Overnight-Geld genommen werden kann.

1.5.5. Devisenmarkttransaktionen

Um die von den Devisenmärkten ausgehenden möglichen Störungen der Geldpolitik zu beschränken, entwickelten die Notenbanken in Zeiten der festen Wechselkurse Deviseninstrumente, mit denen sie die internationalen Geldströme beeinflussen konnten.

Hierbei handelt es sich um **Swap- bzw. Outright-Geschäfte** am Devisenterminmarkt. Bei einem Swapgeschäft werden von der Zentralbank Devisen per Kasse gekauft (verkauft) und gleichzeitig per Termin verkauft (gekauft). Es handelt sich somit um eine **Koppelung von Kassa- und Termingeschäft,** bei der der in Rechnung gestellte Swapsatz ein Zinsäquivalent darstellt. Ein Outright-Termingeschäft unterscheidet sich von einem Kassageschäft durch den späteren Erfüllungstermin (z.B. in drei Monaten). Derartige Geschäfte werden verschiedentlich getätigt, um **spekulativen Devisenbewegungen entgegenzuwirken** oder um **Kursglättungsoperationen gegenüber einer Fremdwährung,** meist dem US-Dollar, möglichst „geräuschlos" durchzuführen. Durch Outright-Geschäfte werden nämlich mittelbar Wirkungen am Kassamarkt erzielt, weil die Geschäftsbank das Währungsrisiko aus dem mit ihr abgeschlossenen Termingeschäft durch ein entgegengesetztes Kassageschäft auszugleichen sucht, um eine offene Devisenposition zu vermeiden.

Die Bankenliquidität wird mit zeitlicher Verzögerung so beeinflusst, als ob ein entsprechendes Kassageschäft am Devisenmarkt abgeschlossen worden wäre. Werden beispielsweise US-Dollar im Rahmen eines Outright-Geschäftes verkauft und nicht per Kassa, so werden den Kreditinstituten am Erfüllungstermin im entsprechenden Gegenwert Zentralbankguthaben entzogen. Dieses müssen die Banken bei der effektiven Übernahme der Dollarbeträge bereitstellen.

Die Gestaltungsmöglichkeiten von Devisenswapgeschäften sind recht flexibel, sowohl im Hinblick auf die Laufzeit als auch auf das Volumen der Einzelabschlüsse. Außerdem sind diese Geschäfte rasch auszuführen.

Bei der Feinsteuerung des Geldmarktes haben die Notenbanken Devisenswapgeschäften eine Art Pufferrolle zugewiesen. Sie können unerwünschten Ausschlägen der Zentralbankguthaben der Kreditinstitute nach der einen wie der anderen Seite innerhalb einer laufen-

the settlement risk that must be in the range of the free marginal lending facility, only major banks are able to take part in these FX swap operations; the central bank has to address them individually to negotiate the price arrangements. As an alternative the ECB regularly uses **"quick tenders"** to influence the situation in the money market (quick tenders are only settled with chosen banks).

Overview: Open market operations

	Instrument	Term	Period	Method
Main refinancing operation[1]	Reverse transactions	1 week	weekly	standard tender
Longer-term refinancing operations[2]	Reverse transactions	3 months	monthly	standard tender
Fine-tuning operation[3]	• Reverse transactions • FX-swaps • Collection of fixed-term • deposits • Outrights	is not standardised	irregular	• Quick tender • bilateral procedure
Structural operations[4]	• Bond issues • Reverse transactions	• not standardised • standardised	• irregular • regular	• standard tender • bilateral procedure

[1]   regular open market transactions, short-term
[2]   regular open market transactions, longer-term
[3]   irregular open market transactions to counter unexpected liquidity movements
[4]   open market transactions in order to adjust the structural liquidity position of the financial sector towards the ESCB

1.5.6. Bilateral Procedures

The term "bilateral procedures" covers **all trades** of the ESCB **with one or more counterparties that are not undertaken in tender form**. The ECB deals either directly with the banks or through the stock exchange or brokers.

Bilateral procedures are used by national central banks for **fine-tuning monetary policy** or for **structural operations** through outright deals.

den Mindestreserve-Erfüllungsperiode entgegenwirken. Allerdings können an diesen Devisenswapoperationen (wegen des Settlementrisikos, das im Rahmen der freien Spitzenrefinanzierungsfazilität liegen muss) nur große Kreditinstitute teilnehmen, die von der Notenbank wegen der Preismodalitäten einzeln angesprochen werden müssen. Alternativ zum Devisenswap tätigt die EZB kurzfristige, nur über wenige Tage laufende Ausgleichsoperationen, die sogenannten **„Schnelltender"** (Schnelltender werden mit ausgewählten Kreditinstituten abgewickelt), um den Geldmarkt zu steuern.

Übersicht Offenmarktgeschäfte

	Instrumentenart	Laufzeit	Rhythmus	Verfahren
Hauptfinanzierungsinstrumente[1]	befristete Transaktion	eine Woche	wöchentlich	Standardtender
längerfristige Refinanzierungsgeschäfte[2]	befristete Transaktion	drei Monate	monatlich	Standardtender
Feinsteuerungsoperation[3]	• befristete Transaktionen • Devisenswaps • Hereinnahme von Termineinlagen • Outright-Geschäfte	nicht standardisiert	unregelmäßig	• Schnelltender • bilaterale Geschäfte
Strukturelle Operationen[4]	• Emission von Schuldverschreibungen • befristete Transaktionen • Outright-Geschäfte	• nicht standardisiert • standardisiert	• unregelmäßig • regelmäßig	• Standardtender • bilaterale Geschäfte

[1] regelmäßige, kurzfristige Offenmarktgeschäfte
[2] regelmäßige, längerfristige Offenmarktgeschäfte
[3] unregelmäßige Offenmarktgeschäfte zum Ausgleich unerwarteter Liquiditätsschwankungen
[4] Offenmarktgeschäfte zur Anpassung der strukturellen Liquiditätsposition des Finanzsektors gegenüber dem ESZB

1.5.6. Bilaterale Geschäfte

Bilaterale Geschäfte sind Verfahren, bei denen das ESZB ein **Geschäft mit einem oder mehreren Geschäftspartnern ohne Tenderverfahren** abschließt. Das ESZB spricht die Geschäftspartner direkt an, oder es werden Geschäfte über Börsen oder Marktvermittler durchgeführt.

Bilaterale Geschäfte setzen die nationalen Zentralbanken für Offenmarktoperationen zur **Feinsteuerung** oder für **strukturelle Operationen** mittels Outright-Geschäften ein.

Counterparties

Admission to be counterparty in open market transactions or to have access to the ECB's standing facilities is set up so as to guarantee a **large participant group**.

All institutions that must hold a minimum reserve with the ECB are entitled to be counterparty in open market transactions and to draw on the standing facilities.

For fine-tuning transactions, the ECB may only select a limited number of counterparties.

Collateral

All loans granted by the ECB have to be covered by collateral. There are two categories of collateral that meet central banks' requirements:

- **Tier 1 collateral**
  - ECB bonds
  - Other marketable debt instruments

- **Tier 2 collateral**
  - Marketable debt instruments
  - Non-marketable debt instruments
  - Shares traded on a stock exchange

The collateral must be either denominated in euro or one of the euro's national currencies.

Issuers of Tier 1 collateral:

- ESCB
- public sector
- private sector
- international and supranational institutions

Issuers of Tier 2 collateral:

- public sector and the
- private sector

1.6. Relevant Characteristics of Important International Central Banks Legend

Now the relevant characteristics of Federal Reserve System (FED), Bank of Japan (BoJ), European Central Bank (ECB), Bank of England (BoE), Schweizerische Nationalbank (SNB) are explained.

1.6.1. Organs with Authority over Monetary Policy

	Bodies
FED	Federal Open Market Committee (FOMC) = Central Bank's president + board of governors of the FED + president of the FED New York + 4 alternating FED presidents
BoJ	Policy Board = governor + 6 members
	Executive organ = governor + 2 deputy governors + 6 executive directors

Geschäftspartner

Die Zulassung von Geschäftspartnern zu Offenmarktgeschäften und ständigen Fazilitäten ist so gestaltet, dass ein **großer Teilnehmerkreis** gewährleistet ist.

Im ESZB werden jene Institute zu Offenmarktgeschäften und ständigen Fazilitäten zugelassen, die der Mindestreserve unterworfen sind.

Für die Teilnahme an Feinsteuerungsgeschäften kann das ESZB nur eine begrenzte Anzahl von Geschäftspartnern auswählen.

Sicherheiten

Das ESZB muss für alle Kredite ausreichend Sicherheiten verlangen. Zwei Gruppen von zentralbankfähigen Sicherheiten sind zu unterscheiden:

- **Tier-1-Sicherheiten**
  - EZB-Schuldverschreibungen
  - sonstige marktfähige Schuldtitel

- **Tier-2-Sicherheiten**
  - marktfähige Schuldtitel
  - nicht-marktfähige Schuldtitel
  - an einem geregelten Markt gehandelte Aktien

Die Sicherheiten müssen auf Euro oder nationale Denominierungen des Euro lauten.

Emittenten von Tier-1-Sicherheiten:

- ESZB
- öffentliche Hand
- privater Sektor
- internationale und supranationale Unternehmen

Emittenten von Tier-2-Sicherheiten:

- öffentliche Hand
- privater Sektor

1.6. Marktrelevante Merkmale wichtiger internationaler Notenbanken

Im Folgenden werden tabellarisch die marktrelevanten Merkmale der Federal Reserve Bank (FED), der Bank of Japan (BoJ), der Europäischen Zentralbank (EZB), der Bank of England (BoE) und der Schweizerischen Nationalbank (SNB) dargestellt.

1.6.1. Organe mit währungspolitischer Entscheidungsbefugnis

	Organe
FED	Federal Open Market Committee (FOMC) = Notenbankpräsident + Board of Governors of the FED + Präsident des FED New York + 4 wechselnde FED-Präsidenten
BoJ	Policy Board = Governor + 6 Mitglieder Executive Organ = Governor + 2 Deputy-Governors + 6 Executive Directors

ECB	Governing Council, Executive Board, General Council
BoE	Governor
	Executive directors
	Court of Directors = governor + deputy governors + 16 directors
SNB	Generalversammlung = shareholders
	Direktorium = president + vice-president + 1 member
	Bankbehörden = banking committee + revision committee + local committee

1.6.2. Main Purposes and Objectives

FED	guaranteeing the supply of lending and money to the economy in order to support economic growth while keeping price levels relatively stable
BoJ	securing the currency and controlling lending supply; the Bank of Japan should play its part in the constant growth of the Japanese economy
ECB	guaranteeing price stability, defining and implementing the EU's monetary policy; undertaking currency deals; maintaining and administrating the official currency deposits of EMU members; supporting smooth operation of payment systems
BoE	no legal purpose; national economic equilibrium, particularly money value stabilisation (the inflation target is determined by the government); functioning of the banking system
SNB	controlling the cash in circulation and a monetary and lending policy that serves the country's interest

1.6.3. Governmental Influence

FED	no influence
BoJ	far-reaching influence of the department of finance
ECB	no influence
BoE	no influence
SNB	mutual co-ordination of measures

1.6.4. Fiscal and Monetary Objectives

	Monetary aggregate targets	Other targets/indicators
FED	from July 1993: M2 concept is abolished (M2 and M3 are still used)	• "Estimate of multi-indicators", where the real interest rate is of growing importance
BoJ	observation of money supply is intensified since the end of the eighties (inflation of real value): M2 + CDs + deposits (Post Office savings bank, trustee funds) + bonds	• support of economic growth • stability of exchange rate • balanced foreign trade

EZB	EZB Rat, Direktorium, Erweitereter Rat
BoE	Governor
	Executive Directors
	Court of Directors = Governor + Deputy-Governors + 16 Directors
SNB	Generalversammlung = Aktionäre
	Direktorium = Präsident + Vizepräsident + 1 Mitglied
	Bankbehörden = Bankenausschuss + Revisionskommission + Lokalkommission

1.6.2. Hauptaufgaben und Ziele

FED	Gewährleistung der Geld- und Kreditversorgung der Wirtschaft mit dem Ziel, das Wirtschaftswachstum unter Wahrung einer angemessenen Preisstabilität zu fördern
BoJ	Währungssicherung und Kontrolle der Kreditversorgung; die Bank of Japan soll zur stetigen Entwicklung der japanischen Wirtschaft beitragen
EZB	Gewährleistung der Preisstabilität, Festlegung und Ausführung der Geldpolitik der EU, Durchführung der Devisengeschäfte, Haltung und Verwaltung offizieller Währungsreserven der Mitgliedstaaten, Förderung des reibungslosen Funktionierens der Zahlungsverkehrssysteme
BoE	kein gesetzlicher Auftrag; gesamtwirtschaftliches Gleichgewicht, insbesondere Geldwertstabilität (das Inflationsziel wird durch die Regierung vorgegeben); Funktionsfähigkeit des Bankensystems
SNB	Regelung des Geldumlaufs und eine dem Gesamtinteresse des Landes dienende Kredit- und Währungspolitik

1.6.3. Staatlicher Einfluss

FED	kein Einfluss
BoJ	weitreichender Einfluss des Finanzministeriums
EZB	kein Einfluss
BoE	kein Einfluss
SNB	gegenseitige Abstimmung der Maßnahmen

1.6.4. Geld- und währungspolitische Ziele

	Geldmengenziel	Sonstige Ziele/Indikatoren
FED	ab Juli 1993: M2-Konzept aufgegeben (aber nach wie vor Beobachtung von M2 und M3)	• „Multiindikatorenansatz", wobei Realzins an Bedeutung gewinnt
BoJ	Geldmengenbeobachtung seit Ende der 80er-Jahre (Sachwertinflation) intensiviert: M2 + CDs + Einlagen (Postsparkasse, Trustfonds) + Schuldverschreibungen	• Förderung des Wirtschaftswachstums • Wechselkursstabilität • außenwirtschaftliches Gleichgewicht

ECB	M3 = cash in circulation + demand deposits + time deposits with terms of less than 4 years + savings deposits of domestic non-banks	• direct inflation objective: 2%
BoE	Since 1992: no monetary aggregate targets (but the BoE's reports on growth of money supply are of great importance)	• direct inflation objective
SNB	central bank's money supply (cash in circulation, the bank's current account balance at the central bank) in mid-term 1% as annual average	

1.6.5. Instruments to Control the Money Market (without Minimum Reserve)

	General tuning	Fine tuning
FED	outright open market transactions (seasonal adjustments)	• repos • "discount window" • reverse repos (= matched sales purchases)
BoJ	rediscounting of bills	• interbank operations (secured and unsecured) • repos • outright open market transactions • • reverse repos
ECB	• bond issues • reverse transactions • outright deals • bilateral procedures • standard tender	• reverse transactions • quick tender • FX-swaps • standard tender • outright deals • bilateral procedures
BoE	interest oriented fine adjustment with initial basis refinacing on gilt-repo and secured loan facility	• outright open market transactions-(bill) purchases (terms up to 33 days) • repos • borrowing facilities (quasi Lombard on a bilateral basis) • outright open market transactions/ sales
SNB	FX swaps outright open market transactions cash liquidity	• lombard lendings • shifting of governmental time deposits • swaps on reversed transactions with government money market claims

EZB	M3 = Bargeldumlauf + Sichteinlagen + Termineinlagen bis 4 Jahre + Spareinlagen von inländischen Nichtbanken	• direktes Inflationsziel: 2%
BoE	ab 1992: kein Geldmengenziel (aber Geldmengenwachstum im Rahmen der regelmäßigen Inflationsberichte der BoE von großer Bedeutung)	• direktes Inflationsziel
SNB	Notenbankgeldmenge (Notenumlauf, Giroguthaben der Banken bei der Nationalbank) mittelfristig 1% im Jahresdurchschnitt	

1.6.5. Instrumente zur Steuerung des Geldmarktes

	Grobsteuerung	Feinsteuerung
FED	Outright-Offenmarktgeschäfte (seasonal adjustments)	• REPOS • „Discount-window" • Reverse REPOS (= Matched-Sales-Purchases)
BoJ	Wechselrediskont	• Interbankoperationen (besichert und unbesichert) • REPOS • Outright-Offenmarktgeschäfte • Reverse REPOS
EZB	• Emission von Schuldverschreibungen • befristete Transaktionen • Standardtender • Outright-Geschäfte • bilaterale Geschäfte	• befristete Transaktionen • Schnelltender • Devisenswaps • Outright-Geschäfte • Standardtender • bilaterale Geschäfte
BoE	Zinsorientierte Feinsteuerung mit ansatzweiser Basisrefinanzierung über Gilt-Repo und Secured loan facility	• Outright-Offenmarktoperationen-(Wechsel-)Käufe (Laufzeit bis 33 Tage) • REPOS • Borrowing Facilities (Quasilombard auf bilateraler Basis) • Outright-Offenmarktoperationen-Verkäufe
SNB	• Devisenswaps • Outright-Offenmarktgeschäfte • Kassenliquidität	• Lombardkredit • Verlagerung von Termineinlagen des Bundes • Swaps in Geldmarktbuchforderungen des Bundes (GMBF, Reversed Transactions with Government Money-Market Claims)

Summary

The practice of foreign exchange (FX) dealing dates back to the end of the 19th century. At that time the status of gold as the reference currency made it possible to carry out transactions via foreign accounts with ease. The gold standard was a system of fixed exchange rates. The confusion and enormous costs resulting from World War I demanded increased money creation in almost all European countries. Different rates of inflation in these countries created a situation in which the international price structure diverged markedly.

During the conference of Bretton Woods in July 1944, the US representatives brought up the basic idea of the gold standard again. Once this idea was commonly accepted, an internationally neutral monetary controller was agreed upon: the International Monetary Fund (IMF), which was founded subsequently and is situated in Washington, D.C.

Due to a crisis in the international monetary system the Bretton Woods system finally collapsed at the beginning of the Seventies. High deficits of the US balance of payments caused a loss of confidence in the US dollar as the international key currency. Within a short period of time, enormous amounts of money were moved from the US to the European markets; there, the interest rates remained at a high level.

The collapse of the fixed-rate system resulted in different developments; most of the industrial countries pursued a controlled floating. This meant that exchange rate developments were not completely left to the free markets.

On 13 March 1979, the European Monetary System (EMS) was introduced as the third attempt to establish a monetary union in Europe. The EMS is a regional system of fixed but adaptable exchange rates. The main objective of the EMS was to create a "zone of monetary stability in Europe", ie, stability of exchange rates and prices, by means of monetary policy co-operation. Therefore, an "official" European Currency Unit (ECU) was introduced in 1979 to bo mainly used as a clearing unit and as legal tender between the central banks.

The Bank for International Settlements was founded to "enhance the co-operation among central banks, to find new ways for international financial operations and to function as a trustee for international transactions between parties that had chosen the BIS as their agent." The BIS was founded in Basle in 1930, on the basis of an agreement between Belgium, France, Germany, Great Britain, Italy, Japan, and the USA. (the Federal Reserve did not take up its rights as founder member until 1995). The bank's business policy must not counteract the monetary policies of the central banks. If BIS operations threaten to cause unwanted reactions in any market, the central banks have the right to intervene before this transaction is actually done.

Zusammenfassung

Die Technik des Devisenhandels geht bereits auf das Ende des 19. Jahrhunderts zurück, als es die Referenzwährung Gold ermöglichte, Zahlungen über ein Konto im Ausland problemlos abzuwickeln. Der Goldstandard (1880–1914) bildete ein System von festen Wechselkursen.

Die Wirren und die enormen Kosten des Ersten Weltkriegs erforderten eine erhöhte Geldschöpfung in nahezu allen europäischen Ländern. Stark unterschiedliche Inflationsraten in den einzelnen Ländern hatten zur Folge, dass das internationale Preisgefüge auseinanderklaffte.

Auf der Konferenz von Bretton Woods im Juli 1944 brachten die amerikanischen Vertreter wieder die Grundidee des damaligen Goldstandardsystems ins Spiel. Nachdem diese Linie allgemein akzeptiert wurde, einigte man sich auch auf einen international neutralen Währungshüter, womit die Idee des damals noch zu gründenden Internationalen Währungsfonds (IWF, International Monetary Fund IMF) mit Sitz in Washington, D.C. ins Leben gerufen wurde.

Durch eine Krise des internationalen Währungssystems brach das System von Bretton Woods schließlich zu Beginn der 70er-Jahre in sich zusammen. Hohe Zahlungsbilanzdefizite der USA führten dazu, dass das Vertrauen in den Dollar als internationale Leitwährung verlorenging. Enorme Kapitalbeträge flossen innerhalb kürzester Zeit aus den USA in die europäischen Märkte, deren Zinssätze weiterhin auf hohem Niveau waren.

Nach dem Zusammenbruch des Fixkurssystems kam es zu unterschiedlichen Entwicklungen. Die meisten Industriestaaten betrieben ein kontrolliertes Floating, d.h., die Wechselkurse wurden nicht völlig dem freien Markt überlassen.

Das am 13. März 1979 in Kraft getretene EWS (Europäisches Währungssystem), der Nachfolger des EWV (Europäischer Währungsverbund), wurde als insgesamt dritter Anlauf zur monetären Integration ins Leben gerufen. Es war ein regionales System fester, aber anpassungsfähiger Wechselkurse. Ziel des EWS war es, durch eine engere währungspolitische Zusammenarbeit eine „Zone der monetären Stabilität in Europa", das bedeutet Wechselkurs- und Preisstabilität, zu schaffen. Zu diesem Zwecke wurde 1979 auch die Europäische Währungseinheit (European Currency Unit = ECU) als Rechen- und Bezugsmittel der Wechselkurse sowie als Zahlungsmittel und Reservewährung der Zentralbanken eingeführt.

Die Bank für Internationalen Zahlungsausgleich hat den Zweck, „die Zusammenarbeit der Zentralbanken zu fördern, neue Möglichkeiten für internationale Finanzgeschäfte zu schaffen und als Treuhänder (Trustee) oder Agent bei den, ihr aufgrund von Verträgen mit den beteiligten Parteien übertragenen, internationalen Zahlungsgeschäften zu wirken". Sie wurde 1930 in Basel aufgrund eines Übereinkommens der Länder Deutschland, Belgien, Frankreich, Großbritannien, Italien, Japan und den USA (wobei die amerikanische Notenbank ihre Rechte als Gründungsmitglied bis 1995 nicht wahrnahm) gegründet. Die Geschäftspolitik der BIZ darf der Währungspolitik der einzelnen Zentralbanken nicht entgegenwirken. Sollte ein Finanzgeschäft der BIZ auf irgendwelchen Märkten eine unerwünschte Reaktion hervorrufen, so können die Notenbanken von ihrem Recht Gebrauch machen, vor der Durchführung dieser Transaktion Einspruch zu erheben.

Die EU-Staats- und Regierungschefs haben am 9./10. Dezember 1991 in Maastricht den Entwurf eines „Vertrages über die Europäische Union" gebilligt. Dieser Vertrag sah für den Wirtschafts- und Währungsbereich die Weiterentwicklung der Gemeinschaft zu ei-

On 9 and 10 December 1991, the heads of state of the EU member states approved an outline of the treaty on the European Union in Maastricht. This agreement served as the basis for the future development of the economic and monetary "zone" towards an economic and monetary "union", which was realised on 1 January 1999 through the introduction of the euro in (at that time) 11 member countries. For countries to adopt the euro, they have to fulfil four convergence criteria, the so-called Maastricht criteria: high degree of price stability (max. 1.5% above the average inflation rate of the three member countries with the lowest inflation rates), sound government finance (government debt may not exceed 60% of its GDP), participation in the European Monetary System for minimum two years and low long-term interest rates (max. 2% above the nominal long-term interest rate in the three lowest inflation member states).

In order to curb fiscal laxity the EU designed the so-called stability and growth pact, which was introduced in 1997 at the Amsterdam summit. This pact determines high fines for countries that violate the budget and deficit criteria.

The European System of Central Banks (ESCB) consists of the European Central Bank and the central banks of the member countries of the EMU. The ECB is situated in Frankfurt/Main. The central banks of those EU countries whose currencies do not take part in the euro are also members of the ESCB but have no voting rights on the decisions about and implementation of the common monetary policy in the euro currency area. The main goal of the ESCB is to guarantee price stability in the euro currency area.

The central banks' stock of foreign currency enlarges the scope of their currency policy and their international creditworthiness. Moreover, the stock of foreign currency guarantees that payment transactions with foreign countries (capital, services, and goods) are completed properly. Foreign currency, gold, claims based on the respective country's share in the International Monetary Fund and its special drawing rights, as well as claims on the European Central Bank (ECB) are the major components of the "international monetary reserves". A major part of the reserves is in US dollars, due to the dollar's leading position as an international currency for intervention and reserves.

The term refinancing is used when central banks give loans to banks by either buying bills (Discount Policy) or lending bonds (Lombard Policy). Another part of refinancing is the regular availability of funds for revolving repurchase agreements (Open Market Transactions).

The minimum reserve policy obliges banks to maintain a certain percentage of their own deposits at the central bank (there are differences between national regulations, which are not dealt with here). These framework regulations once served as security for the liquidity of customer deposits at the banks. The current system of minimum reserve is a flexible and effective liquidity instrument in the hands of the central bank. The minimum reserve rate is to be held on the accounts of the national central banks and has to be fulfilled within a one-month settlement period under consideration of the average daily reserve assets (averaging provision). If a bank fails to meet its requirements, it has to pay a special interest rate on the difference between target and actual minimum reserve (in the

ner Wirtschafts- und Währungsunion (WWU) vor und wurde am 1. Januar 1999 durch den Zusammenschluss der damals elf Teilnehmerstaaten Realität.

Als Fundament für die Auswahl der Teilnehmer wurden vier Konvergenzkriterien, die sogenannten Maastricht-Kriterien entwickelt: hoher Grad an Preisstabilität (max. 1,5 Prozentpunkte über den Inflationsraten der drei preisstabilsten Mitgliedstaaten), öffentlicher Finanzhaushalt (max. Gesamtverschuldung 60% des BIP), mindestens zwei Jahre Teilnahme am Europäischen Währungssystem (EWS) und langfristiger Zinssatz (max. 2 Prozentpunkte über dem Durchschnitt der drei preisstabilsten Mitgliedstaaten).

Um fiskalpolitischen Undiszipliniertheiten Einhalt zu gebieten, wurde beim EU-Gipfel in Amsterdam im Jahr 1997 der Stabilitäts- und Wachstumspakt verabschiedet. Er sieht teils strenge Strafen für jene Länder vor, die die Kriterien des Budgetdefizits und der Staatsverschuldung nicht erfüllen.

Das Europäische System der Zentralbanken (ESZB) besteht aus der Europäischen Zentralbank (EZB), die ihren Sitz in Frankfurt am Main hat, und den nationalen Zentralbanken jener EU-Staaten, die an der Währungsunion teilnehmen. Die Nationalbanken der restlichen Mitgliedstaaten sind Mitglieder des ESZB mit Sonderstatus: Sie beteiligen sich nicht an der Entscheidungsfindung betreffend die einheitliche Geldpolitik für den Euro-Währungsraum und deren Umsetzung. Vorrangiges Ziel des ESZB ist die Gewährleistung der Preisstabiliät.

Der Devisenbestand der Notenbanken vergrößert den Handlungsspielraum der Währungspolitik und die internationale Kreditwürdigkeit. Darüber hinaus soll der Devisenbestand den reibungslosen Zahlungsverkehr mit dem Ausland (Kapital-, Dienstleistungs- und Güterverkehr) sicherstellen. Devisen, Gold, Forderungen aus der Beteiligung des jeweiligen Landes am Internationalen Währungsfonds und im Rahmen dieser Institution geschaffene Sonderziehungsrechte sowie Forderungen an die EZB bilden die wesentlichen Bestandteile der „nationalen Währungsreserve". Das Hauptgewicht der Devisenbestände nimmt der US-Dollar ein. Dies ergibt sich aus seiner dominierenden Stellung als internationale Interventions- und Reservewährung.

Mit dem Begriff Refinanzierung wird zum einen die Gewährung der Kredite durch die Notenbank an die Kreditinstitute im Wege des Ankaufs von Wechseln (Diskontpolitik) und der Beleihung von Wertpapieren (Lombardpolitik) bezeichnet. Zum anderen gehört zur Refinanzierung auch die laufende Mittelbereitstellung über die revolvierend abgeschlossenen Wertpapierpensionsgeschäfte mit Kreditinstituten (Offenmarktgeschäfte).

Die Mindestreserveregelung verpflichtet Banken dazu, einen gewissen Prozentsatz ihrer Einlagen als Guthaben bei der Zentralbank zu halten. Diese Rahmenvorschrift diente ursprünglich der Liquiditätssicherung der Kundeneinlagen bei den Banken. Das derzeit bestehende Mindestreservesystem soll dagegen den Notenbanken von vornherein als flexibles und wirksames, liquiditätspolitisches Instrument zur Verfügung stehen. Die Mindestreserve ist auf Konten bei den nationalen Zentralbanken zu halten und muss unter Zugrundelegung der tagesdurchschnittlichen Reserveguthaben innerhalb einer einmonatigen Erfüllungsperiode erfüllt werden (Durchschnittserfüllung). Als Sanktionen für die Nichteinhaltung der Mindestreservepflicht sind Sonderzinsen auf den Spitzenrefinanzierungssatz oder unverzinste Einlagen bei der EZB oder den nationalen Zentralbanken vorgesehen. Die Mindestreservesätze werden von der Europäischen Zentralbank festgesetzt und können jederzeit geändert werden. Änderungen werden vor der ersten Mindestreserveperiode, in der die Änderung gilt, bekanntgegeben.

ESCB this rate is the marginal lending facility plus margin). The minimum reserve rates are determined by the ESCB and can be changed at any time. Changes are announced before the first minimum reserve period for which the change is valid.

The buying and selling of bonds in the open market by the central bank on its own account is called open market policy. The question regarding which securities may be bought depends on the legal regulations of the central bank concerned.

To deal with disturbances in the money market caused by FX market turbulence, central banks developed foreign exchange instruments during the period of fixed exchange rates which enabled them to influence international payment transactions. These are swap deals and outright operations in the forward FX market. With a swap deal, one buys (sells) foreign currency from (to) the central bank at the spot rate and at the same time sells (buys) them as an outright. Therefore, one can speak of a combination of spot and outright operation, while the swap rate that is charged is equivalent to an interest rate.

The term "bilateral procedures" covers all trades of the ESCB with one or more counterparties that are not undertaken in tender form. The ECB deals either directly with the banks or through the stock exchange or brokers. Bilateral procedures are used by national central banks for fine-tuning monetary policy or for structural operations through outright deals.

1.7. Practice Questions

1. What were the main objectives of the Bretton Woods System?
2. Which city is the seat of the International Monteary Fund?
   a) London
   b) Paris
   c) New York
   d) Washington, D.C.
3. Why did the fixed exchange rate system collapse?
4. What is meant by the Smithsonian Agreement?
5. Name and describe the types of exchange rate systems!
6. What was the objective of the EMS?
7. Which states belong to the G7?
   a) G5 plus Italy and Spain
   b) G5 plus Canada and Mexico
   c) G5 plus Canada and Italy
   d) G5 plus Canada and Spain
8. Name and describe briefly the four convergence criteria!
9. Which of the following countries are members of the European Monetary Union?
   a) Norway
   b) Sweden
   c) Finland
   d) Malta
   e) Denmark
   f) Slovakia

Als Offenmarktgeschäfte bezeichnet man den Kauf und Verkauf von Wertpapieren durch die Zentralbank auf eigene Rechnung am offenen Markt. Welche Papiere angekauft werden können, ergibt sich aus den gesetzlichen Bestimmungen der jeweiligen Notenbanken.

Um die von den Devisenmärkten ausgehenden möglichen Störungen der Geldpolitik zu beschränken, entwickelten die Notenbanken in Zeiten der festen Wechselkurse Deviseninstrumente, mit denen sie die internationalen Geldströme beeinflussen konnten. Hierbei handelt es sich um Swap- bzw. Outright-Geschäfte am Devisenterminmarkt. Bei einem Swapgeschäft werden von der Zentralbank Devisen per Kasse gekauft (verkauft) und gleichzeitig per Termin verkauft (gekauft). Es handelt sich somit um eine Koppelung von Kassa- und Termingeschäft, bei der der in Rechnung gestellte Swapsatz ein Zinsäquivalent darstellt.

Bilaterale Geschäfte sind Verfahren, bei denen das ESZB ein Geschäft mit einem oder mehreren Geschäftspartnern ohne Tenderverfahren abschließt. Das ESZB spricht die Geschäftspartner direkt an, oder es werden Geschäfte über Börsen oder Marktvermittler durchgeführt. Bilaterale Geschäfte setzen die nationalen Zentralbanken für Offenmarktoperationen zur Feinsteuerung oder für strukturelle Operationen mittels Outright-Geschäften ein.

1.7. Wiederholungsfragen

1. Welche Hauptziele hatte das Bretton-Woods-System?
2. In welcher Stadt hat der Internationale Währungsfonds seinen Sitz?
   a) London
   b) Paris
   c) New York
   d) Washington, D.C.
3. Wodurch kam es zum Zusammenbruch des Systems fester Wechselkurse?
4. Was versteht man unter dem Smithsonian Agreement?
5. Nennen und beschreiben Sie die Arten von Wechselkurssystemen!
6. Welches Ziel hatte das EWS?
7. Aus welchen Staaten bestehen die G7?
   a) G5 plus Italien und Spanien
   b) G5 plus Kanada und Mexiko
   c) G5 plus Kanada und Italien
   d) G5 plus Kanada und Spanien
8. Nennen und beschreiben Sie kurz die vier Konvergenzkriterien!
9. Welche der folgenden Länder nehmen derzeit an der Währungsunion teil?
   a) Norwegen
   b) Schweden
   c) Finnland
   d) Malta
   e) Dänemark
   f) Slowakei

10. Which term can be connected with the Maastricht Agreement?
    a) introduction of EMS
    b) stability pact
    c) social protection
    d) All answers are false.
11. What is the effective exchange rate?
    a) fixed euro exchange rate
    b) nominal exchange rate adjusted by inflation
    c) weighted average exchange rate
    d) the PPP-adjusted exchange rate
12. What are the main tasks of the ESCB?
13. What are the main purposes of ECB?
    a) fixing of the gold price
    b) implementation of the EU's monetary policy
    c) support of a smooth working of payment systems
    d) guarantee of price stability
14. How is the minimum reserve requirement calculated?
    a) as a fixed nominal amount
    b) as a percentage of deposits
    c) as a percentage of equity
    d) as a percentage of cash-flow
15. Which liabilities are NOT taken into account by the minimum reserve requirement?
    a) demand deposits
    b) fixed deposits
    c) borrowed medium-term money
    d) short-term money borrowed from banks obliged to hold a minimum reserve
16. The ECD determines the minimum reserve ratio to be 2%. What does that mean?
    a) Banks have to hold 2% of their own bank deposits at the central bank.
    b) Banks have to hold 2% of their liabilities side at the central bank.
    c) Banks have to hold 2% of their own deposits at the central bank.
    d) Banks have to hold 2% of their customer loans at the central bank.
17. A sterilised intervention constitutes a central bank's course of action within its …
    a) policy of refinancing
    b) minimum reserve policy
    c) open market policy
    d) monetary reserves policy
18. What is the difference between a variable rate tender and a volume tender?
    a) The volume tender has a pre-determined interest rate.
    b) Volume tenders are allotted.
    c) In the case of a variable rate tender the bid does not include the requested volume.
    d) The variable rate tender is used by the central bank as an interest rate signal.
19. What does the initials BIS stand for?
    a) Bank for International Payment Systems
    b) Bank for International Settlements
    c) Basle International Settlement Bank
    d) Bank for Industry Settlements

10. Welcher Begriff kann mit dem Maastricher Vertrag in Verbindung gebracht werden?
    a) Einführung des EWS
    b) Stabilitätspakt
    c) sozialer Schutz
    d) Alle Antworten sind falsch.

11. Was versteht man unter dem effektiven Wechselkurs?
    a) fester Euro-Umrechnungskurs
    b) nominaler Wechselkurs minus Inflationsrate
    c) gewogener Durchschnitt verschiedener bilateraler Wechselkurse
    d) um die Kaufkraft angepasster Wechselkurs

12. Welche Aufgaben hat das ESZB?

13. Was gehört zu den Hauptaufgaben der EZB?
    a) Durchführung des Goldpreisfixings
    b) Ausführung der Geldpolitik der EU
    c) Förderung des reibungslosen Funktionierens der Zahlungsverkehrssysteme
    d) Haltung und Verwaltung offizieller Währungsreserven der Mitgliedstaaten

14. Wie wird die Mindestreserve berechnet?
    a) fixer Nominalbetrag
    b) Prozentsatz der Einlagen
    c) Prozentsatz des Eigenkapitals
    d) Prozentsatz des Cashflows

15. Welche Verbindlichenkeiten werden von der Mindestreservepflicht NICHT miteinbezogen?
    a) Sichteinlagen
    b) befristete Spareinlagen
    c) mittelfristig aufgenommene Gelder
    d) kurzfristig aufgenommene Gelder bei mindestreservepflichtigen Banken

16. Die EZB legt den Mindestreservesatz auf 2% fest. Was ist damit gemeint?
    a) Banken müssen 2% ihrer Bankeinlagen bei der Zentralbank als Guthaben halten.
    b) Banken müssen 2% ihrer Passivseite bei der Zentralbank als Guthaben halten.
    c) Banken müssen 2% ihrer Kundeneinlagen bei der Zentralbank als Guthaben halten.
    d) Banken müssen 2% ihrer Kundenkredite bei der Zentralbank als Guthaben halten.

17. Eine sterilisierte Intervention ist eine bestimmte Vorgehensweise einer Notenbank im Rahmen ihrer …
    a) Refinanzierungspolitik
    b) Mindestreservepolitik
    c) Offenmarktpolitik
    d) Währungsreservepolitik

18. Was ist der Unterschied zwischen Zins- und Mengentender?
    a) Der Mengentender hat den Zins fix vorgegeben.
    b) Mengentender werden repartiert.
    c) Beim Zinstender darf das Volumen nicht genannt werden.
    d) Der Zinstender wird als Zinssignal von der Notenbank verwendet.

19. Wofür steht die Abkürzung BIZ?
    a) Bank für Internationalen Zahlungsverkehr
    b) Bank für Internationalen Zahlungsausgleich
    c) Bank für Internationale Zusammenschlüsse
    d) Bank für Internationale Zusammenarbeit

20. Where are the BIS headquarters?
    a) The Hague
    b) Frankfurt
    c) Basel
    d) Washington, D.C.
    e) London
21. Which of the following organisations is the clearing bank of the central banks?
    a) BIS
    b) IMF
    c) BIL
    d) CEDEL
22. Which of these counts as Tier Two capital for a bank under the BIS rules?
    a) equity
    b) goodwill
    c) subordinated debt
    d) open reserves
23. Which instrument is NOT used in ESCB?
    a) minimum reserve
    b) rediscounting of eligible bills
    c) marginal lending facility
    d) open market transactions
24. What differentiates central banks from one another?
    a) degree of independence from the state
    b) ensuring a continous economic growth
    c) not all pursue the objective of price stability
    d) objectives regarding credit and exchange rate protection
25. Which of the following institutions CANNOT make independent decisions regarding its exchange rate policy?
    a) FED
    b) BIS
    c) SNB
    d) ECB

20. In welcher Stadt hat die BIZ seinen Sitz?
    a) Den Haag
    b) Frankfurt
    c) Basel
    d) Washington, D.C.
    e) London

21. Wer ist die Clearing-Bank der Notenbanken?
    a) BIZ
    b) IWF
    c) BIL
    d) CEDEL

22. Was zählt gemäß BIZ-Regeln zum Ergänzungskapital (Tier Two Capital) einer Bank?
    a) Eigenkapital
    b) Goodwill
    c) nachrangige Verbindlichkeiten
    d) offene Reserven

23. Welches Instrument ist im ESZB NICHT vorgesehen?
    a) Mindestreserve
    b) Rediskontierung von Wechseln
    c) Spitzenrefinanzierungsfazilität
    d) Offenmarktgeschäfte

24. Was unterscheidet Notenbanken voneinander?
    a) Unabhängigkeit vom Staat
    b) Gewährleistung eines kontinuierlichen Wirtschaftswachstums
    c) nicht alle verfolgen Preisstabilität
    d) Aufgaben bei der Kredit- und Währungssicherung

25. Welche der folgenden Institutionen hat KEINE währungspolitische Entscheidungsbe
    fugnis?
    a) FED
    b) BIZ
    c) SNB
    d) EZB

2. Fundamental Analysis

In this chapter you learn ...
- what is meant by fundamental analysis.
- which fundamental prediciting models are used.
- what is meant by the balance of payments.
- about the sub-balances of the balance of payments.
- what is meant by current account, trade balance, balance of goods (services), financial account and net change in official reserves.
- what is meant by the Purchasing Power Parity Theory.
- what is meant by the Interest Rate Theory.
- about the differences between flow models and stock models.
- about the main principles of integrated models.
- what is meant by the national income.
- which types of economic indicators can be distinguished.
- about the most important indicators.

Fundamental analysis explains **future movements in FX and interest rate markets with variations of the economies' macroeconomic indicators**.

The following **fundamental prediciting models** are distinguished:

- Monocausal Models: Purchasing Power Parity Theory, Interest Rate Parity Theory
- Integrated Models: Traditional Models: Keynesian Model, Monetary Approach, Asset Market Approach

First, fundamental analysis predicts the **changes in the indicators** so that it can determine the respective exchange rate. For this, information is gathered from publicly available data. Due to the time lag between collection and incorporation of the data about fundamental variables there is no immediate influence on exchange rates. Information about fundamentals often becomes really significant only when compared to older data.

In order to be able to use fundamental analysis to estimate or predict future exchange rate movements, an **interpretation of the currently available information is not sufficient**, for the reason that this (usually publicly available) information should already be part of the market's opinion and thus should have already manifested itself in current FX rates. When fundamental analysis is used for exchange rate prognosis it is necessary to make predictions about economic key indicators and estimate how the market's opinion deviates from one's own prediction.

2. Fundamentale Analyse

In diesem Kapitel lernen Sie ...

- was man unter Fundamentalanalyse versteht.
- welche fundamentalen Prognoseverfahren verwendet werden.
- was man unter Zahlungsbilanz versteht.
- aus welchen Teilbilanzen die Zahlungsbilanz besteht.
- was man unter Leistungs-, Handels-, Dienstleistungs-, Kapital- und Devisenbilanz versteht.
- was man unter Kaufkraftparitätentheorie versteht.
- was man unter Zinsparitätentheorie versteht.
- den Unterschied zwischen Stromgrößen- und Bestandsgrößenmodellen kennen.
- die Grundprinzipien der integrierten Modelle kennen.
- was man unter Nationaleinkommen versteht.
- welche Arten von Indikatoren unterschieden werden.
- die wichtigsten Indikatoren kennen.

Die **Untersuchung der ökonomischen Indikatoren, die Angebot und Nachfrage auf den Devisenmärkten bestimmen,** bezeichnet man als Fundamentalanalyse. Die Erkenntnisse über die Bestimmungsfaktoren und deren Zusammenwirken sollen Aufschluss über die zukünftige Entwicklung eines Währungskurses oder eines Zinssatzes geben.

Fundamentale Prognoseverfahren können in folgende Untergruppen geteilt werden:

- Monokausale Modelle: Kaufkraftparitätentheorie, Zinsparitätentheorie
- Integrierte Modelle: traditionelle Ansätze: keynesianischer Ansatz, monetärer Ansatz, Finanzmarktansatz

Die fundamentale Devisenkursprognose begründet **zukünftige Bewegungen auf den Zins- und Devisenmärkten** mit den Schwankungen makroökonomischer (= auf eine gesamte Volkswirtschaft bezogene) Bestimmungsfaktoren der betreffenden Volkswirtschaften.

Bei einer fundamentalen Prognose werden zunächst die **zukünftigen Veränderungen der Bestimmungsfaktoren** prognostiziert, um dann die Ausprägung des jeweiligen Devisenkurses bestimmen zu können. Die Informationen dazu stammen meist aus öffentlich zugänglichen Informationsquellen. Zwischen der Informationsaufnahme und ihrer Verarbeitung vergeht jedoch Zeit (Time Lag), sodass sich Informationen über fundamentale Variablen nicht unmittelbar auf den Devisenkurs auswirken. Ihre volle Bedeutung erlangen diese Informationen häufig erst, wenn sie mit älteren Daten verglichen werden.

Um die fundamentale Analyse zur Einschätzung zukünftiger Wechselkursbewegungen verwenden zu können, ist eine **Interpretation der vorliegenden Informationen üblicherweise nicht ausreichend,** da diese meist öffentlich zur Verfügung stehenden Informationen und die sich daraus gebildete Meinung des Marktes bereits in den Wechselkurs eingeflossen sind. Will man auf Basis der Fundamentalanalyse Wechselkursprognosen erstellen, so ist es notwendig, Prognosen für die volkswirtschaftlichen Bestimmungsfaktoren zu erstellen und abzuschätzen, ob die Meinung des Marktes davon abweicht.

The economic integration of an economy (and thus **demand and supply for domestic and foreign currency**) is measured in the balance of payments. The following chapter provides a description of the balance of payments and its sub-balances.

2.1. EXCURSUS: Balance of Payments and Sub-Balances

The balance of payments summarizes **all economic transactions between residents of a country and non-residents during a specific time period**, usually a year. The transactions are measured as income and outgoings of foreign exchange (measured in the domestic currency). Transactions are defined as the export and import of goods and services or financial capital in return for payment, or indeed free of charge (e.g. barter, financial transfers).

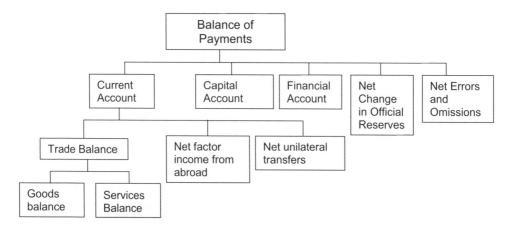

The Balance of Payments is composed of the following **sub-balances**:

- Balance on current account (with sub-accounts)
  - Trade Balance (Goods Balance + Services Balance)
  - Balance of factor income from abroad
  - Balance of unilateral transfers
- Balance on capital account
- Balance on financial account
- Balance on Official Reserves
- Balance on Net Errors and Omissions

The Balance of Payments follows the convention of double entry accounting, where all debit entries must be booked along with corresponding credit entries. It is therefore balanced in the sense that the sum of the entries is conceptually zero. Surpluses and deficits may only appear in the Balance of Payments' sub-balances.

The most common economic transactions of a country's residents with non-residents are non-gratuitous exports and imports of goods, services and financial capital. These transactions come with payments or liabilities to foreigners (debits) or payments or obligations received from foreigners (credits). The most important sub-accounts of the Balance of Payments are therefore the trade balance and the balance on financial account, especially when one wishes to evaluate the impact of fundamental economic transactions on ex-

Erfasst wird die ökonomische Verflechtung einer Volkswirtschaft und somit **Angebot und Nachfrage nach Heimwährung und Fremdwährungen in der Zahlungsbilanz.** Der folgende Exkurs gibt einen Überblick über die Zahlungsbilanz und ihre Teilbilanzen.

2.1. EXKURS: Zahlungsbilanz und Teilbilanzen

Die Zahlungsbilanz (balance of payments) einer Volkswirtschaft ist die **Zusammenstellung der außenwirtschaftlichen Transaktionen eines Landes während einer Periode** (üblicherweise ein Jahr). Diese werden als Einnahmen und Ausgaben von Fremdwährung (gemessen in der Heimwährung) erfasst. Transaktionen sind dabei der entgeltliche und unentgeltliche Übergang von Gütern (Waren und Dienstleistungen) und Forderungen zwischen Wirtschaftssubjekten. Die Transaktionen müssen also nicht unbedingt mit Zahlungsvorgängen verbunden sein (z.B. Realtausch, unentgeltliche Leistung von Gütern).

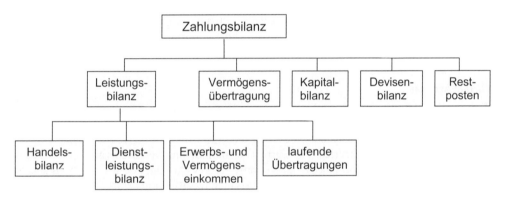

Die Zahlungsbilanz besteht aus folgenden **Teilbilanzen:**

- Leistungsbilanz (mit Teilbilanzen)
  - Handelsbilanz (HB)
  - Dienstleistungsbilanz (DB)
  - Erwerbs- und Vermögenseinkommen
  - laufenden Übertragungen
- Bilanz der Vermögensübertragung
- Kapitalbilanz
- (Gold- und) Devisenbilanz
- Restposten

Zu jeder Buchung in der Zahlungsbilanz muss eine Gegenbuchung erfolgen, die Bilanz als Ganzes ist also immer ausgeglichen. Überschüsse oder Defizite können nur bei Teilbilanzen auftreten.

Die Buchungen bestehen bei privaten Wirtschaftsakteuren hauptsächlich aus Leistungstransaktionen (die wertmäßige Erfassung eines Gutes) und/oder Finanztransaktionen (die Erfassung von Forderungen und Eigentumsrechten). Die wichtigsten Teilbilanzen der Zahlungsbilanz, insbesondere wenn es um die Auswirkungen von fundamentalwirtschaftlichen Vorgängen auf Wechselkurse geht, stellen demnach die Leistungsbilanz (Importe und Ex-

change rates. Based on that, one can make the following simplified illustration of the balance of payments:

Balance of Payments

		D	C
TB	GB	Export of goods	Import of goods
	SB	Export of services	Import of services
CB	FB	Import of capital	Export of capital
	OR	Reduction of official reserves	Increase of official reserves

The **debit (assets) side** of the Balance of Payments represents the **income of foreign exchange**, whereas the **credit (liabilities) side** is associated with **outgoing foreign exchange**.

In the following a more detailed description of the important sub-accounts of the balance of payments will be given. Sub-accounts with little or less relevance for exchange rate prognosis (capital account, factor income from abroad, errors and omissions) are ignored here.

Current Account

Transnational flows of goods and services as well as **transnational factor income** and **unilateral transfers** are entered in the current account. If the latter two are ignored, the current account becomes the trade balance, which represents the difference between a nation's exports and imports of goods and services. The Current Account Balance represents an important economic indicator of the performance of an economy. It shows to what extent a country is able to finance imports (and given transfers) with exports (and received transfers).

A **current account surplus** increases a country's net foreign assets by the corresponding amount. Net foreign assets are defined as the value of the assets that a country owns abroad, minus the value of the domestic assets owned by foreigners.

A **current Account deficit** increases the foreign indebtedness of an economy. A significant and permanent Current Account deficit is usually seen as a sign of a future devaluation of the domestic currency.

Trade Balance

The Trade Balance is the sum of the Balance of Goods and the Balance of Services and is thus the difference between the monetary value of all **exports** and **imports** of the economy. A positive trade balance is known as a trade surplus or as an **active trade balance**.

Balance of Goods (Services)

The Balance of Goods (Services) is a sub-account of the Current Account and stands for the **exports of goods (services) minus the import of goods (services)**.

A Balance of Goods (Services) **surplus** means that the value of exports of the period in question exceeded the **value of imports** (all measured in domestic currency). A **deficit** indicates that the value of exports fell short of the value of imports.

Factor income from abroad includes among others investment incomes including interests and dividends and earnings of residents working abroad. Net factor income from abroad therefore represents the difference between factor incomes of residents from abroad and the income accruing to foreign suppliers of factor services.

porte von Gütern) und die Kapitalbilanz (finanzielle Transaktionen) dar. Eine darauf abgestellte vereinfachte Darstellung der Zahlungsbilanz kann folgendermaßen aussehen:

		Zahlungsbilanz	
		S	H
Leistungsbilanz	Handelsbilanz	Warenexport	Warenimport
	DL-Bilanz	Dienstleistungsexport	Dienstleistungsimport
Kapitalbilanz i.w.S	Kapitalbilanz	Kapitalimporte	Kapitalexporte
	Devisenbilanz	Abnahme der Gold- und Devisenreserven	Zunahme der Gold- und Devisenreserven

Das **Soll** der Zahlungsbilanz stellt dabei **Deviseneinnahmen** dar und umgekehrt stellt das **Haben Devisenausgaben** dar.

Im Folgenden werden die einzelnen Teilbilanzen näher erläutert. Die vor allem für die Devisenkursprognose weniger relevanten Teilbilanzen (Übertragungsbilanzen, Erwerbs- und Vermögenseinkommen, Restposten) werden hier nicht behandelt.

Leistungsbilanz

In der Leistungsbilanz werden **internationale Güterströme** ebenso verbucht wie **Übertragungen zwischen In- und Ausland** und **grenzüberschreitende Erwerbs- und Vermögenseinkommen.** Der Saldo der Leistungsbilanz stellt eine wichtige ökonomische Größe zur Bewertung der Leistungsfähigkeit einer Volkswirtschaft dar. Sie zeigt, inwiefern ein Land Einfuhren (und geleistete Übertragungen) durch Ausfuhren (und empfangene Übertragungen) finanzieren kann.

Ein **Leistungsbilanzüberschuss** bedeutet eine Erhöhung der Auslandsposition, das ist die Netto-Vermögensposition einer Volkswirtschaft gegenüber dem Ausland.

Ein **Leistungsbilanzdefizit** bewirkt eine Zunahme der Auslandsverschuldung der Volkswirtschaft. Ein hohes andauerndes Leistungsbilanzdefizit wird üblicherweise als Indikator für eine bevorstehende Währungsabwertung angesehen.

Handelsbilanz

Die Handelsbilanz ist Teil der Leistungsbilanz und dient der Erfassung der **Wareneinfuhr und -ausfuhr.** Ein Handelsbilanzüberschuss (eine sogenannte **aktive Handelsbilanz**) liegt dann vor, wenn die Ausfuhren die Einfuhren übersteigen. Im umgekehrten Fall weist die Handelsbilanz ein Defizit auf (sogenannte **passive Handelsbilanz**).

Dienstleistungsbilanz

Die Dienstleistungsbilanz ist Teil der Leistungsbilanz und dient der **Erfassung aller Ex- und Importe von Dienstleistungen.**

Die Summe der Salden von Dienstleistungsbilanz und Handelsbilanz ergibt den **Außenbeitrag einer Volkswirtschaft.**

Weitere Teilbilanzen der Leistungsbilanz sind die Bilanz der Erwerbs- und Vermögenseinkommen (grenzüberschreitende Einkommen aus Faktorleistungen: unselbstständige Arbeit, Dividenden und Zinserträge) sowie die Bilanz der laufenden Übertragungen (Leistungen ohne direkte Gegenleistung, z.B. Zahlungen an internationale Organisationen).

The more important unilateral transfers are outright aid by the government, subscriptions to international agencies, grants by charitable foundations, and remittances by immigrants to their former home countries.

Financial Account

The financial account is the second of the two primary components of the balance of payments, the other being the current account. The financial account records **all transactions between domestic and foreign residents** that involve capital transfers receivable and payable and the acquisition and disposal of non-produced non-financial assets. There is usually a classification that distinguishes between short-term and long-term capital transfers (short-term usually being defined as having an original maturity of less than one year).

The situation on money and FX markets naturally has a strong impact on short-term capital transfer, as short-term investments can be quickly shifted between the domestic market and international markets.

The **main components** of the financial account are:

- Foreign direct investments (FDI): transnational participation in companies of at least 10%, reinvested profits, purchase and sale of real estate, ...
- Portfolio investments: investments in securities (stocks which do not fulfil the requirements of FDI and long-term bonds)
- Financial derivatives
- Credit transactions

From a domestic point of view, capital exports (imports) are defined as the increase (decrease) of claims and the decrease (increase) of liabilities against foreigners and are entered on the debits (credits) of the financial account.

Relationship between the sub-balances

General relationship between trade balance and the financial account: Purchases and sales of goods, financial assets or services are usually paid for with long- or short-term loans. Therefore a transaction entered in the trade balance and thus in the current account is usually offset by an entry in the financial account. The case is different if transactions are settled in cash via the FX market. Such a payment changes the official currency reserves (another sub-account of the balance of payments).

(Net Change in) Official Reserves

The **change of official national currency reserves** is booked in another sub-account of the balance of payments. Official reserves are foreign currency deposits and bonds held by central banks and monetary authorities. Gold, special drawing rights (SDRs) and the IMF reserve position are usually also included in the official reserves account.

The following example illustrates the booking of 2 typical economic cross-border transactions:

a) The export of machinery with a value of EUR 10m (on credit)
b) The import of raw materials with a value of EUR 5m (cash settlement)

Kapitalbilanz

Die Kapitalbilanz ist Teilbilanz der Zahlungsbilanz. Sie enthält die **Kapitalbewegungen von Inländern**, d.h. Änderungen in den Beständen der Forderungen und Verbindlichkeiten gegenüber dem Ausland. Dabei wird zwischen kurzfristigem und langfristigem Kapitalverkehr differenziert (die Grenze liegt üblicherweise bei einem Jahr der ursprünglichen Laufzeit). Der kurzfristige Kapitalverkehr wird dabei stark von der jeweiligen Situation an den Geld- und Devisenmärkten beeinflusst. Er erfasst die kurzfristigen Mittelverlagerungen zwischen dem inländischen Markt und dem internationalen Finanzmarkt.

Die **Hauptkategorien der Kapitalbilanz** sind:

- Direktinvestitionen: grenzüberschreitende Unternehmensbeteiligungen von über 10%, reinvestierte Gewinne sowie bereitgestellte Kreditmittel, Erwerb und Veräußerung von Immobilien etc.
- Wertpapieranlagen: langfristige Schuldverschreibungen und Dividendenpapiere, die nicht unter Direktinvestitionen fallen
- Finanzderivate
- Kreditverkehr

Als Kapitalexporte (-importe) werden Zunahmen (Abnahmen) von Forderungen gegen Ausländer sowie Abnahmen (Zunahme) von Verbindlichkeiten gegenüber Ausländern verstanden, sie scheinen als negative (positive) Position in der Kapitalbilanz auf.

Zusammenhang zwischen den einzelnen Teilbilanzen

Käufe und Verkäufe von Gütern, Vermögenswerten oder Dienstleistungen werden mit kurz- oder langfristigen Krediten bezahlt, somit findet grob gesprochen für eine Transaktion der Leistungsbilanz eine Gegenbuchung in der Kapitalbilanz statt. Eine Barzahlung am Devisenmarkt bewirkt eine Veränderung der Währungsreserven und wird in der Devisenbilanz ausgewiesen.

Gold- und Devisenbilanz (Reservebilanz)

Die Devisenbilanz ist Teil der Zahlungsbilanz und beschreibt die **Veränderung der offiziellen (nationalen) Währungsreserven der Zentralbank.** Zu den Währungsreserven zählen liquide Devisenbestände der Zentralbank, der Goldbestand, die Reserveposition im Internationalen Währungsfond sowie alle bestehenden Sonderziehungsrechte. Die Veränderung aller übrigen Forderungen und aller Verbindlichkeiten der Zentralbank werden in der Kapitalbilanz festgehalten.

Im folgenden Beispiel wird die Verbuchung von zwei typischen Transaktionen illustriert:

a) Export von Maschinen im Wert von EUR 10 Mio. (auf Kredit)
b) Import von Rohstoffen im Wert von EUR 5 Mio. (Barbezahlung)

Balance of Payments

		D	C	Balance
TB	GB	10 (a)	5(b)	+5
	SB			
CB	CB		10(a)	-10
	OR	5(b)		+5
	Balance	15	15	0

Explanation: The trade balance shows a surplus as the value of exports exceeds the value of imports. The capital account is negative, as 10m EUR of capital were exported (which means that net claims against foreigners have increased by EUR 10m). The balance of official reserves shows a surplus, which means that the foreign exchange reserves have decreased.

Now that we are familiar with the way that the balance of payments captures the cross-border transactions of an economy we will return to the subject of fundamental analysis.

Here, a distinction between

- monocausal (single variable) and
- integrated (multi variable) models is made.

2.2. Overview

Method	Model	Principle
Monocausal models		Explanation of exchange rate movements by one variable
	Purchasing Power Parity Theory	Exchange rates are determined by the real purchasing power
	Interest Rate Parity Theory	The exchange rate is the result of the relationship between interest rate differential and the swap rates
Integrated Models		Explanation of exchange rate movements by various variables
Traditional models	Keynesian model	Exchange rates are determined by supply and demand
	Monetary approach	Exchange rates are the results of portfolio decisions taken by investors
	Asset Market Approach	Further development of the monetary approach. Based on portfolio individual adjustments
New Models		Try to combine stock variables and flow variables in one model

| | | Zahlungsbilanz | | |
		S	H	Saldo
Leistungsbilanz	Handelsbilanz DL-Bilanz	10 (a)	5(b)	+5
Kapitalbilanz i.w.S	Kapitalbilanz		10(a)	-10
	Devisenbilanz	5(b)		+5
	Saldo	15	15	0

Erklärung: Die Leistungsbilanz ist positiv, da mehr exportiert als importiert wurde. Die Kapitalbilanz ist negativ, da Kapital exportiert wurde (das entspricht einer Zunahme von Forderungen gegenüber dem Ausland). Die Devisenbilanz ist positiv, das bedeutet, dass der Bestand an Devisen abgenommen hat.

Nachdem wir die Zahlungsbilanz und die darin enthaltene Erfassung der Außenbeziehungen einer Volkswirtschaft kennengelernt haben, wollen wir wieder zur fundamentalen Analyse zurückkehren.

Hier unterscheidet man

- den monokausalen (eine einzelne Erklärungsvariable) vom
- integrierten Ansatz (mehrere Variablen).

2.2. Übersicht

Methode	Modell	Prinzip
Monokausale Erklärungsansätze		Erklärung von Devisenkursveränderungen mit einer Variablen
	Kaufkraftparitäten-theorie	Devisenkurs wird durch reale Kaufkraft bestimmt
	Zinsparitätentheorie	Devisenkurs wird anhand des Zusammenhangs zwischen Zinsniveaudifferenz und Swapsätzen erklärt
Integrierte Modelle		Erklärung von Devisenkursveränderungen mit mehreren Variablen
Klassische Verfahren	Keynesianisches Modell	Devisenkurs wird durch Angebot und Nachfrage einer Währung bestimmt
	Monetärer Ansatz	Erklärung des Devisenkurses anhand der Portfolios einzelner Wirtschaftssubjekte am Geldmarkt
	Finanzmarktansatz (Asset Market Approach)	Weiterentwicklung des monetären Ansatzes, basiert auf Bestandsanpassungen (= Portfoliobestände der Individuen)
Neuere Ansätze		Versuch, Bestands- und Stromgrößen in einem Ansatz zu verknüpfen

2.3. Monocausal Models

2.3.1. Purchasing Power Parity Theory

The purchasing power parity theory states that the **exchange rate between two countries is determined by the real purchasing power of the countries' currencies**. If identical goods were traded on the world market at different prices, **arbitrage processes in goods** would cause the supply and demand of goods and consequently of currencies to change and thus the exchange rate to adjust. An arbitrage process is the cheap purchase of goods in a foreign country in order to sell them more expensively in the home country.

The **exchange rate assures that two currencies, adjusted by the exchange rate, buy the same amount of goods**. If, for example, the price level in one country rises relative to foreign countries' price levels, demand will shift from the now more expensive domestic goods and services to the now relatively cheaper foreign goods. Consequently, less domestic and more foreign currency is in demand. The theory of purchasing power parity therefore states that the currency of a country where prices increase will depreciate. In balance of payment terms this means that a (relative) increase in the domestic price level leads to a negative trade balance (or current account balance) and therefore to a depreciation of the domestic currency in the long run.

2.3.2. Interest Rate Parity Theory

The interest rate parity theory explains **exchange rate movements in the short term**. This theory is based on the assumption that **investors freely move their capital to where they expect the highest return**, whereby interest rate parity is the situation where the **same return can be expected in different (FX) markets**. Interest rate parity should be the standard situation in functioning markets. If the interest rate differential between two currencies changes, interest rate parity is no longer given. As investors shift their money now to where they expect a higher return, exchange rates adjust until a new parity is reached. Thus, short-term exchange rate movements can be explained by changes in interest rate differentials.

Let's take the example of domestic interest rates rising (relative to other interest rates). Investors will now move money into domestic investments as the higher interest rates attract them. The investments come with demand for the domestic currency and thus lead to its appreciation up to a level where new investments are not that attractive anymore.

In balance of payment terms, capital is imported and official reserves increase, which means a positive capital balance and a negative net change in official reserves.

Note: Because higher interest rates are usually linked to higher inflation, the purchasing power parity predicts long-term exchange rate movements in the opposite direction of the short-term movements predicted by the interest rate parity theory. Let's take the example of an increasing interest rate differential between domestic and foreign interest rates. The relatively higher domestic rates will attract short term investments and thus lead to an immediate appreciation of the domestic currency. In the long term, the domestic price level is expected to increase relative to foreign price levels, which will lead to a negative trade balance and with it, a depreciation of the domestic currency in the long term.

2.3. Monokausale Erklärungsansätze

2.3.1. Kaufkraftparitätentheorie

Die Kaufkraftparitätentheorie besagt, dass der **Devisenkurs zwischen zwei Ländern durch die reale Kaufkraft ihrer Währungen bestimmt** wird. Werden gleiche Güter auf dem Weltmarkt zu unterschiedlichen Preisen gehandelt, so führt dies zu **Güterarbitrageprozessen,** die eine Veränderung von Angebot und Nachfrage nach Gütern und daher auch nach Devisen verursachen. Sie lösen also eine Devisenkursänderung aus. Man spricht von Güterarbitrageprozessen, wenn Güter im Ausland preisgünstig eingekauft werden, um sie im Inland zu einem höheren Preis zu verkaufen.

Die Kaufkraftparitätentheorie besagt, dass **durch den Devisenkurs garantiert** ist, **dass man in beiden Ländern für einen bestimmten Geldbetrag die gleiche Gütermenge erwerben kann.** Steigt beispielsweise das Preisniveau im Inland (relativ zu einem anderen Land), so führt dies dazu, dass weniger der inländischen Güter und mehr der jetzt relativ günstigeren ausländischen Güter nachgefragt werden. Folglich wird weniger der heimischen Währung und mehr der ausländischen Währung nachgefragt. So wird beispielsweise die Währung des Landes, dessen Preisniveau sich erhöht, abgewertet. Auf die Zahlungsbilanz umgelegt bedeutet dies, dass durch eine Steigerung des heimischen Preisniveaus die Leistungsbilanz negativ wird und so langfristig zu einer Abwertung der Währung führt.

2.3.2. Zinsparitätentheorie

Die Zinsparitätentheorie ist ein **kurzfristiges Erklärungsmodell für Wechselkursbewegungen.** Die Theorie basiert auf der Annahme, dass **Anleger dort investieren, wo die höchste Rendite erwartet wird,** wobei in funktionierenden Märkten die Normalsituation jene einer Zinsparität ist. Eine Zinsparität im Sinne der Zinsparitätentheorie bezeichnet die **„Gleichheit der erwarteten Renditen auf Einlagen in zwei beliebigen Währungen".** Kurzfristige Wechselkursänderungen können daher durch Veränderungen der (relativen) Zinsniveaus erklärt werden.

Steigen beispielsweise die Zinssätze der heimischen Währung, so werden internationale Investoren aufgrund der jetzt fehlenden Zinsparität vermehrt ihr Geld in dieser Volkswirtschaft veranlagen. Die höhere Nachfrage nach der heimischen Währung hat damit ein Ansteigen dieser Währung zur Folge.

Auf die Zahlungsbilanz umgelegt bedeutet dieses Beispiel Kapitalimporte und eine Zunahme der Devisenreserven, also eine positive Kapitalbilanz und eine negative Devisenbilanz.

Anmerkung: Da höhere Zinsen üblicherweise auch mit höherer Inflation einhergehen, ist nach der Kaufkraftparitätentheorie langfristig eine der von der Zinsparitätentheorie kurzfristig vorhergesagten Wechselkursbewegung entgegengesetzte Bewegung zu erwarten. Beispielsweise bedeuten (relativ) steigende inländische Zinsen den Zufluss von kurzfristigen Geldern und damit eine Aufwertung der Währung. Langfristig würde das mit den hohen Zinsen einhergehende höhere Preisniveau zu einem Leistungsbilanzdefizit und damit zu einer Abwertung der Währung führen.

2.4. Integrated Models

2.4.1. Traditional Models

The traditional models are:

- the Keynesian Model
- the Monetary Approach and
- the Asset Market Approach

These models belong to either the group of flow models or of stock models. **Flow models** are based on changes of the indicators (e.g. income change, asset change), whereas **stock models** look at the absolute numbers of the indicators (e.g. level of the income or amount of assets).

2.4.2. Keynesian Model

The Keynesian model of **John Maynard Keynes** (British economist, politican and mathematican, 1883–1946) is a **flow model** and uses **mainly factors of the real economy** to determine the exchange rate. The exchange rate is a result of the supply and demand of currencies.

The supply and demand of currencies depends on the size and direction of the trade in goods and services (e.g. transfers of guest workers to their home country). Therefore the current account is the **dominant factor for the development of exchange rates**. When analysing exchange rates, the capital account is neglected because all capital flows are a result of activities in the real economy.

Therefore, the exchange rate always equals the relative prices of domestic and foreign goods. An exchange rate movement is caused either by a change in the domestic or foreign interest rate level that determines international capital flows, or a change in real income that influences the demand for exports and imports.

2.4.3. Monetary Approach

The monetary approach for determining the exchange rate is a **stock model**. It puts particular emphasis on the **stock of monetary assets**.

All balance of payments transactions are the result of **portfolio decisions** (investing money in different kinds of equity) **taken by domestic and foreign investors**. If there are disequilibria in the money market, investors adjust their portfolios accordingly. If there is an excess demand in the money market, portfolios are restructured and the foreign exchange demand increases (foreign exchange balance surplus). On the other hand, excess supply in the money market brings about a foreign exchange balance deficit.

2.4. Integrierte Modelle

2.4.1. Traditionelle Ansätze

Zu den traditionellen Ansätzen zur Erklärung der Währungskursbildung zählen:

- das keynesianische Wechselkursmodell
- der monetäre Ansatz und
- der Finanzmarktansatz.

Diese Modelle gehören entweder zur Gruppe der Stromgrößen- oder der Bestandsgrößenmodelle. **Stromgrößenmodelle** basieren auf Veränderungen der betrachteten Einflussgrößen (z.B. Einkommensänderungen, Änderungen der Vermögensbestände), während die **Bestandsgrößenmodelle** auf Beständen (z.B. Höhe des Einkommens oder des Vermögens) aufbauen.

2.4.2. Keynesianisches Modell

Das keynesianische Modell von **John Maynard Keynes** (britischer Ökonom, Politiker und Mathematiker, 1883–1946) gehört zur Gruppe der **Stromgrößenmodelle** und berücksichtigt vorwiegend **realwirtschaftliche Vorgänge als kursbestimmende Faktoren.** Der Kurs einer Währung wird durch Angebot und Nachfrage von Devisen bestimmt.

Devisenangebot und -nachfrage hängen wiederum vom Ausmaß und von der Richtung des Güter- und Dienstleistungshandels der beteiligten Länder sowie den Transferzahlungen (z.B. Geldüberweisungen von Arbeitsemigranten in ihr Heimatland) ab. Dominierender Faktor für die Devisenkursentwicklung ist daher der **Saldo der Leistungsbilanz einer Volkswirtschaft.**

Die Kapitalbilanz wird bei der Devisenkursanalyse vernachlässigt, da Kapitalströme aus realwirtschaftlichen Vorgängen resultieren.

Der Devisenkurs entspricht also stets den **relativen Preisen in- und ausländischer Güter.** Veränderungen des Devisenkurses resultieren entweder aus Änderungen des in- und ausländischen Zinsniveaus, die die internationalen Kapitalströme determinieren, oder aus Realeinkommensänderungen, die die Nachfrage nach Export- bzw. Importgütern beeinflussen.

2.4.3. Monetärer Ansatz

Der monetäre Ansatz zur Bestimmung des Devisenkurses ist ein **Bestandsgrößenansatz,** der insbesondere die **Bestände an Geldvermögen einer Volkswirtschaft** berücksichtigt.

Die in die Zahlungsbilanz eingehenden Leistungs- und Finanztransaktionen resultieren aus den **Portfolioentscheidungen** (Aufteilung des Geldvermögens auf Wertpapiere) **in- und ausländischer Wirtschaftssubjekte.** Herrscht ein Ungleichgewicht auf dem Geldmarkt, so passen die Wirtschaftssubjekte ihre Portfolios entsprechend an. Ein Nachfrageüberschuss auf dem Geldmarkt führt über eine Umstrukturierung der Portfolios zu einer Zunahme von Devisen (Devisenbilanzüberschuss). Ein Überangebot am Geldmarkt hat hingegen ein Devisenbilanzdefizit zur Folge.

2.4.4. Asset Market Approach

The Asset Market approach helps to determine **short-term foreign exchange rate movements**. It is a **further development of the monetary approach** and is based on **stock adjustments**. Four assumptions are made:

- complete substitution of domestic and foreign financial assets
- unlimited capital mobility
- immediate adjustments to relevant data changes in the money market
- delayed adjustments to new information in the goods markets

The last assumption allows **public income and real assets to be kept constant** in the short run. Thus, capital flows depend exclusively on the **portfolio decisions of investors**. The result of the portfolio restructuring depends mainly on the profit expectations and the characteristics of the assets (e.g. term structure of the investment opportunities, asset type). If monetary policy changes, investors adjust their financial assets. This leads to a change in the exchange rate.

2.4.5. New Models

New models **develop the traditional models further** by incorporating stock variables (asset structure) and flow variables (changes in the current account balance) as well as by including short-term, mid-term and long-term factors for determining exchange rates.

Exchange rate and interest rate movements are often a result of **readjustments by investors**. On the one hand, the new models are designed to include s**hort-term adjustments of financial markets** to changing structures. On the other hand, **changes in investor expectations** are also taken into account.

It is common for banks to produce fundamental analyses for different countries. For this, companies rely on various resources. For example,

- news agencies (e.g. Reuters or Telerate)
- centres for statistics
- central banks
- publicly available information (e.g. newspapers).

2.5. Measures of National Income and Output

National income

National income and output measures are used in economics to estimate the **total economic activity of a country**. National income is defined as the total net value of all goods and services produced over a specified period of time, representing the sum of wages, profits, rents, interest, and pension payments received.

The two most commonly used measures are the **gross domestic product (GDP)** and the **gross national product (GNP)**. The GDP is he value of all final goods and services produced in a country in one year and the GNP is the he value of all final goods and services produced in a country in one year by the nationals, plus income earned by its citizens abroad, minus income earned by foreigners in the country.

2.4.4. Finanzmarktansatz (Asset Market Approach)

Mithilfe des Finanzmarktansatzes (Asset Market Approach) lassen sich **kurzfristige Devisenkursbewegungen** bestimmen. Er gilt als **Weiterentwicklung des monetären Ansatzes** und basiert daher auf **Bestandsanpassungen.**

Dieser Ansatz unterstellt eine:

- vollständige Substitutionsmöglichkeit in- und ausländischer Finanzaktiva
- vollkommene Kapitalmobilität
- unmittelbare Anpassung auf dem Geldmarkt bei Änderung relevanter Daten
- verzögerte Anpassung auf dem Gütermarkt bei Datenänderungen

Die letzte Annahme führt dazu, dass **Volkseinkommen und Realvermögen kurzfristig** als **konstant** angesehen werden können. Kapitalbewegungen beruhen somit ausschließlich auf den **Portfolioentscheidungen der Anleger.** Dabei sind die Umstrukturierungsmaßnahmen der Anleger von den Ertragsaussichten und der Charakteristik der Vermögensgegenstände (z.B. Dauer der Kapitalbindung, Art der Vermögensgegenstände) der Wirtschaftssubjekte abhängig. Ergeben sich geldpolitische Veränderungen, führen diese unmittelbar zu einer Umstrukturierung der Finanzaktiva von Seiten der Anleger. Dies beeinflusst wiederum den Devisenkurs.

2.4.5. Neuere Ansätze

Neuere Ansätze zur Erklärung des Devisenkurses stellen **Weiterentwicklungen der traditionellen Modellansätze** dar. Neuere Ansätze verknüpfen die traditionellen Modelle so, dass einerseits Bestandsgrößen (Vermögensstruktur) und Stromgrößen (Leistungsbilanzveränderungen) berücksichtigt, andererseits kurz-, mittel- und langfristige Faktoren der Devisenkursbestimmung in einem Ansatz erfasst werden.

Anpassungsvorgänge der Anleger auf den Finanzmärkten sind die Ursache für Zins- und Devisenkursänderungen. Neuere Modellansätze sind darauf ausgerichtet, sowohl die **kurzfristige Anpassung der Finanzmärkte** an sich verändernde Strukturen zu erfassen, als auch **Änderungen der Erwartungen der Marktteilnehmer** zu berücksichtigen.

In der Praxis erstellen viele Banken Fundamentalanalysen für einzelne Länder. Die dafür erforderlichen Informationen beziehen die Unternehmen hauptsächlich

- von Nachrichtenagenturen (z.B. Reuters),
- von statistischen Ämtern,
- von den Zentralbanken,
- aus anderen öffentlich zugänglichen Informationsquellen (z.B. Zeitungen).

2.5. Volkswirtschaftliche Kennzahlen

Nationaleinkommen

Die Leistung einer Volkswirtschaft wird durch das sogenannte Nationaleinkommen (früher: Sozialprodukt) charakterisiert und stellt die **Summe aller Wertschöpfungen einer Volkswirtschaft** dar.

Bei Kennzahlen für das Nationaleinkommen kann man zwischen dem **Bruttonationaleinkommen** (BNE bzw. engl: GNP – Gross National Product) und dem **Bruttoinlandsprodukt** (BIP bzw. engl. GDP – Gross Domestic Product) unterscheiden.

The key difference between the two is that GDP is the total output of a region and GNP is the total output of all nationals of a region.

A number of other economic figures are derived from the GDP, one being the **net domestic product (NDP)**. The NDP is defined as the "GDP minus depreciation of capital".

2.5.1. Economic Indicators

The common method to evaluate the state of an economy more thoroughly and to make prognoses about its future development is to analyse individual economic parameters and project their future development.

The **most important macroeconomic parameters** are:

- Economic growth
- Inflation
- Interest level
- Exchange rates
- Productivity

As has been mentioned before, the prognosis made when carrying out fundamental analysis has to be compared to the market opinion in order to make a prognosis about future price (e.g. exchange rate) movements. The reason is that the market opinion on future economic development is already included in today's prices. A number of economic indicators are used as measurements for the abovementioned parameters. The importance of an indicator can be seen when the release of new indicator data leads to immediate and visible reactions in international market prices.

Economic indicators can be classified as follows:

- **Quantity indicators** give information about the quantitative development of a reference object (e.g. unemployment rate, new and unfilled orders).
- **Price indicators** give information about development or level of prices (e.g. inflation rate, stock prices).
- **Early indicators or leading indicators:** Indicators that change before the economy changes and thus give information about the future development of the economy (e.g. new and unfilled orders, stock prices).
- **Current and/or lagging indicators** show the present or past state of the economy (e.g. GDP, unemployment rate).

The following pages give a short description of the most important economic indicators:

Purchasing Managers Index (PMI)

The PMI is a composite index that is published **monthly** in the USA and is based on surveys among 400 purchasing managers. The purchasing managers can either respond with "better", "same", or "worse" to questions about the **future economic development**. The magic number for the PMI is 50. A reading of 50 or higher generally indicates that the industry is expanding.

It applies to the PMI, as for all other leading economic indicators, that a value that indicates strong economic future growth might be a warning signal for higher inflation in the case that economic growth is already strong.

Dabei wird beim Bruttoinlandsprodukt die Wertschöpfung innerhalb der Landesgrenzen erfasst, während das Bruttonationalprodukt Wertschöpfung über Produktionsfaktoren im Eigentum von Inländern beinhaltet.

Daneben gibt es auch noch den Begriff des **Nettonationaleinkommens**, das sich aus dem Bruttonationaleinkommen durch den Abzug der Abschreibungen ergibt.

2.5.1. Indikatoren

Um eine Volkswirtschaft im Detail und ihre zukünftige Entwicklung beurteilen zu können, betrachtet man einzelne gesamtwirtschaftliche Einflussfaktoren genauer und prognostiziert diese für die Zukunft.

Die **wichtigsten gesamtwirtschaftlichen Einflussfaktoren** sind:

- Wirtschaftswachstum
- Inflation
- Zinsniveau
- Wechselkurs
- Produktivität

Wie bereits erwähnt, geht es bei der fundamentalen Analyse zwecks Fremdwährungsprognose um eine Prognose der Entwicklung dieser Einflussfaktoren und eine Gegenüberstellung mit der Meinung des Marktes. Indikatoren dienen als Messgröße für gesamtwirtschaftliche Einflussfaktoren. Die große Bedeutung von Indikatoren kann man daran erkennen, dass deren Veröffentlichung sichtbare sofortige Auswirkungen auf die internationalen Märkte hat.

Folgende Klassifizierung von Indikatoren ist möglich:

- **Mengenindikatoren** geben Auskunft über die Mengenentwicklung eines Bezugsobjektes (z.B. Arbeitslosenquote, Auftragseingänge)
- **Preisindikatoren** informieren über Preisniveau oder -entwicklung (z.B. Inflationsrate, Aktienkurse)
- **Früh- bzw. vorlaufende Indikatoren** geben Hinweise auf die zukünftige Entwicklung der Wirtschaftslage (z.B. Auftragseingänge, Aktienkurse)
- **Präsens- und Spätindikatoren** zeigen die aktuelle und/oder vergangene wirtschaftliche Entwicklung (z.B. Bruttoinlandsprodukt, Arbeitslosenquote)

Im Folgenden werden die wichtigsten Indikatoren kurz beschrieben:

Einkaufsmanager Index (Purchase Managers Index – PMI)

In den USA wird **auf monatlicher Basis** durch Umfragen der „National Association of Purchase Managers" ermittelt, **welcher Prozentsatz der befragten Einkaufsmanager die künftige wirtschaftliche Entwicklung positiv einschätzt**.

Wie für alle volkswirtschaftlichen Kennzahlen gilt: Bei schlechter Wirtschaftslage ist ein hoher Indikatorwert sehr positiv, bei starkem Wirtschaftswachstum kann ein hoher Indikatorwert auf steigende Inflationsgefahr hinweisen und ist daher schlecht.

Auftragseingänge der Industrie (new and unfilled orders)

Die prozentuale Veränderung der Auftragseingänge (üblicherweise für langlebige Gebrauchsgüter) in der Industrie gegenüber dem Vorjahreszeitraum wird als Indikator aufgezeichnet und

New and unfilled orders

The percentage change of new and unfilled orders (usually for durable goods) for a month against orders one year ago is **published monthly**. An increase in orders indicates a strengthening in demand as serves as a **leading indicator for company profits as well as the development of the overall economy**.

Index of Leading Economic Indicators

The "Index of Leading Economic Indicators" is an American economic index intended to estimate future economic activity. The value of the index is composed of **ten key variables**, coming from both the supply side (production, investments, new orders) and the demand side (inflation, purchasing power, employment) as well as from monetary policies.

The indicator is geared towards estimating the **future development of the US economy**. The indicator also has a significant relevance for international markets due to the importance of the US market.

CRB Futures Index

The CRB Futures Index is an **index composed of 21 commodity futures**. The index serves as an **indicator of future inflation** (higher costs for raw materials lead to higher prices for final goods). The CRB Index is quoted **daily**.

Gold price

Gold historically **plays the role of a "safe harbour" investment in times of crisis**. On the other hand, rising gold prices may also be a **warning signal for rising inflation**.

Consumer Confidence Index (CCI)

The Consumers Confidence Index is a **monthly release** that is designed to assess the **overall confidence, financial health and spending power of the average US consumer**. The relation between positive and negative assessments is used as an indicator for future economic development.

Employment/Wages

Rising employment rates are generally seen as a positive sign because they **imply economic growth**. During an economic boom this can also be a **warning signal for rising inflation**. Indicators used are the unemployment rate, number of new employments, requests for unemployment support, salaries and wages overall and of different branches.

Import prices

Higher import prices for goods and services can lead to **higher inflation** as well as to **short-term deterioration in the trade balance**. Indicators are: Exchange rates, prices for imported goods.

monatlich veröffentlicht. Auftragseingänge in der Industrie sind ein **Frühindikator für die Unternehmensgewinne sowie für die Entwicklung der Gesamtwirtschaft.**

Index of Leading Economic Indicators

Der „Index of Leading Economic Indicators" wird vom US-Handelsministerium **auf monatlicher Basis** veröffentlicht. Der Indikator setzt sich aus **zehn Einzelindikatoren** zusammen, die von der Angebotsseite (Produktion, Investition, Auftragseingänge), der Nachfrageseite (Inflation, Beschäftigung, Kaufkraft) und von der Geldpolitik kommen.

Der Indikator zielt darauf ab, die **zukünftige Wirtschaftsentwicklung in den USA** abzuschätzen, hat aber aufgrund der Wichtigkeit des amerikanischen Marktes auch internationale Bedeutung.

IFO Geschäftsklima

In **monatlichen Zeitabständen** ermittelt das IFO-Institut in einer Umfrage **bei deutschen Unternehmen** deren **Einschätzung der Lage des eigenen Unternehmens sowie der Gesamtwirtschaft.** Das IFO Geschäftsklima ist ein wichtiger vorlaufender Indikator für die deutsche Wirtschaft.

Der Indikator wird aus dem Saldo aus optimistischer und pessimistischer Einschätzung gebildet. Bei einem Anstieg über 100 überwiegen die optimistischen, bei Werten unter 100 die pessimistischen Einschätzungen.

CRB Futures Index

Der CRB-Futures Index ist ein **Index für 21 Rohstoff-Futures.** Der Indikator dient der **Prognose der Inflation** (höhere Rohstoffkosten bedeuten höhere Produktionskosten). Der CRB Index wird **täglich** variabel notiert.

Goldpreis

Der Goldpreis hat traditionell eine **große Bedeutung in Krisenzeiten,** wo es häufig zu einem Anstieg des Goldpreises kommt. Andererseits hat das Gold aber auch zugleich eine **Warnfunktion für steigende Inflationsraten.**

Consumer's Confidence Index (CCI)/ICON-Konsumbarometer

Der „Consumer's Confidence Index" (CCI) wird in den USA **auf monatlicher Basis** veröffentlicht. Das deutsche Pendant ist das ICON-Konsumbarometer. Bei beiden wird das **Verbrauchervertrauen in die Wirtschaft** ermittelt.

Der Indikator wird aus dem Saldo der optimistischen und pessimistischen Einschätzungen gebildet. Bei einem Indikatorwert über null überwiegen die optimistischen, unter null die pessimistischen Einschätzungen.

Beschäftigung/Löhne

Ein **Ansteigen der Beschäftigung** ist grundsätzlich positiv, weil es ein **Zeichen für stärkeres Wirtschaftswachstum** ist. Bei Hochkonjunktur können (weiter) steigende Beschäftigung und Löhne aber auch ein **Warnsignal für Inflation** sein. Als Indikatoren sind geeignet: Arbeitslosenrate, Zahl der neu Beschäftigten, Anträge auf Arbeitslosenunterstützung, Löhne und Gehälter verschiedener Branchen oder der Gesamtwirtschaft.

Importpreise

Hohe Importpreise für Güter und Dienstleistungen werden in erster Linie durch eine **schwache Heimwährung** ausgelöst. Dies kann sowohl zu **höherer Inflation** als auch zu einer

Short-term interest rates

Central banks usually raise money market rates when there is a danger of rising inflation. Rates are lowered if the economy is slow and investments need to be stimulated. Possible indicators are: Prime rate, Lombard rate, repo rates or 3-month treasury securities.

Long-term interest rates

Rising long-term interest rates mean that the market expects a generally higher interest rate level in the future. Indicators are the yields of government bonds with a maturity ranging from 10 to 30 years.

Money Supply

The money supply is the **total amount of money available at a certain point in time that can be used for the exchange of goods and services**. The annual change of the money supply is **released monthly**.

The interest rate policy of the central bank is directly aimed at the management of money supply. The increase of money supply is synonymous with a decrease of interest rates. The central bank increases the money supply when the purpose is to stimulate the economy.

Producer Price Index (PPI)

The Producer Price Index (PPI) program measures the **average change compared to the previous year in the selling prices received by domestic producers for their output**. Increased prices for manufactured goods increase production costs for all companies, resulting in higher inflation. The indicator is used for the **prognosis of profits of certain branches** as well as for the **prognosis of future inflation rates and the monetary policy of the central bank**.

Summary

Fundamental analysis explains future movements in FX and interest rate markets with variations of the economies' macroeconomic indicators.

These fundamental prediciting models are distinguished: Monocausal Models (Purchasing Power Parity Theory, Interest Rate Parity Theory) and Integrated Models (Keynesian Model, Monetary Approach, Asset Market Approach).

Fundamental analysis predicts the changes in indicators so that it can determine the corresponding exchange rate.

The balance of payments summarizes all economic transactions between residents of a country and non-residents during a specific time period, usually a year.

The balance of payments is composed of these sub-balances: balance on current account (trade balance, goods balance + services balance, balance of factor income from abroad, balance of unilateral transfers), balance on capital account, balance on financial account, balance on official reserves, balance on net errors and omissions.

Transnational flows of goods and services as well as transnational factor income and unilateral transfers are entered in the current account.

The trade balance is the sum of the balance of goods and the balance of services and is thus the difference between the monetary value of all exports and imports of the economy.

The balance of goods (services) is a sub-account of the current account and stands for the exports of goods (services) minus the import of goods (services).

kurzfristigen Verschlechterung der Handelsbilanz führen. Als Indikatoren sind geeignet: Wechselkurse, Preise für importierte Waren.

Kurzfristige Zinsen

Sieht die Notenbank die Gefahr einer steigenden Inflation, so wird sie die kurzfristigen Zinsen anheben. Um Investitionen anzukurbeln, wird sie im Gegenzug die kurzfristigen Zinsen senken. Als Indikatoren sind geeignet: Leitsätze wie der Diskontsatz, Lombardsatz, Repo rates, 3-Monats-Zins staatlicher Obligationen.

Langfristige Zinsen

Steigen die langfristigen Zinsen stark an, so kann man daraus schließen, dass langfristig ein generell höheres Zinsniveau erwartet wird. Als Indikatoren sind die Renditen 10- bis 30-jähriger Staatsanleihen geeignet.

Geldmenge

Die Geldmenge ist die **Liquidität, die der Wirtschaft zum Austausch von Gütern und Dienstleistungen zur Verfügung steht.** Die jährliche Veränderung der Geldmenge wird **monatlich veröffentlicht.**

Die Zinspolitik der Notenbank ist unmittelbar mit der Steuerung der Geldmenge verbunden. Erhöht die Notenbank die Geldmenge, so ist dies gleichbedeutend mit einer Senkung der Zinsen. Die Notenbank wird dann die Geldmenge erhöhen, wenn sie der Wirtschaft stützend unter die Arme greifen will.

Erzeugerpreisindex (PPI = Producer Price Index)

Der Erzeugerpreisindex (PPI) erfasst die **Veränderung der industriellen Erzeugerpreise gegenüber dem Vorjahr.** Steigen die Preise der Güter und Dienstleistungen, die die Produzenten selbst einkaufen, hat dies einen Anstieg der Verbraucherpreise (Inflation) zur Konsequenz.

Der Indikator dient sowohl der **Prognose der Gewinne einzelner Branchen** als auch der **Prognose der zukünftigen Inflationsrate und Geldpolitik der Notenbank.**

Zusammenfassung

Die Untersuchung der ökonomischen Indikatoren, die Angebot und Nachfrage auf den Devisenmärkten bestimmen, bezeichnet man als Fundamentalanalyse.

Fundamentale Prognoseverfahren können unterteilt werden in monokausale Modelle (Kaufkraftparitätentheorie, Zinsparitätentheorie) und integrierte Modelle (keynesianisches Modell, monetärer Ansatz, Finanzmarktansatz, neuere Ansätze). Bei einer fundamentalen Prognose werden zunächst die zukünftigen Veränderungen der Bestimmungsfaktoren prognostiziert, um dann die Ausprägung des jeweiligen Devisenkurses bestimmen zu können.

Die Zahlungsbilanz (balance of payments) einer Volkswirtschaft ist die Zusammenstellung der außenwirtschaftlichen Transaktionen eines Landes während einer Periode (üblicherweise ein Jahr). Die Zahlungsbilanz besteht aus folgenden Teilbilanzen: Leistungsbilanz (Handelsbilanz, Dienstleistungsbilanz, Erwerbs- und Vermögenseinkommen, laufende Übertragungen), Bilanz der Vermögensübertragungen, Kapitalbilanz, (Gold- und) Devisenbilanz, Restposten.

The financial account is the second of the two primary components of the balance of payments, the other being the current account. The financial account records all transactions between domestic and foreign residents that involve capital transfers receivable and payable and the acquisition and disposal of non-produced non-financial assets.

The change of official national currency reserves is booked in another sub-account of the balance of payments.

The Purchasing Power Parity Theory states that the exchange rate between two countries is determined by the real purchasing power of the countries' currencies.

The exchange rate assures that two currencies, adjusted by the exchange rate, buy the same amount of goods.

The Interest Rate Parity Theory explains exchange rate movements in the short term. This theory is based on the assumption that investors freely move their capital to where they expect the highest return, whereby interest rate parity is the situation where the same return can be expected in different (FX) markets.

The integrated models belong to either the group of flow models or of stock models. Flow models are based on changes of the indicators (eg, income change, asset change), whereas stock models look at the absolute numbers of the indicators (eg, income level or amount of assets).

The Keynesian Model is a flow model and uses mainly factors of the real economy to determine the exchange rate. The exchange rate is a result of the supply and demand of currencies.

The Monetary Approach for determining the exchange rate is a stock model. It puts particular emphasis on the stock of monetary assets. All balance of payments transactions are the result of portfolio decisions (investing money in different kinds of equity) taken by domestic and foreign investors.

The Asset Market Approach helps to determine short-term foreign exchange rate movements. It is a further development of the monetary approach and is based on stock adjustments. Four assumptions are made: National income and output measures are used in economics to estimate the total economic activity of a country. The common method to evaluate the state of an economy more thoroughly and to make prognoses about its future development is to analyse individual economic parameters and project their future devel-

In der Leistungsbilanz werden internationale Güterströme ebenso verbucht wie Übertragungen zwischen In- und Ausland und grenzüberschreitende Erwerbs- und Vermögenseinkommen.

Die Handelsbilanz ist Teil der Leistungsbilanz und dient der Erfassung der Wareneinfuhr und -ausfuhr.

Die Dienstleistungsbilanz ist Teil der Leistungsbilanz und dient der Erfassung aller Ex- und Importe von Dienstleistungen.

Die Kapitalbilanz ist Teilbilanz der Zahlungsbilanz. Sie enthält die Kapitalbewegungen von Inländern, d.h. Änderungen in den Beständen der Forderungen und Verbindlichkeiten gegenüber dem Ausland. Die Hauptkategorien der Kapitalbilanz sind Direktinvestitionen, Wertpapieranlagen, Finanzderivate und Kreditverkehr.

Die Devisenbilanz ist Teil der Zahlungsbilanz und beschreibt die Veränderung der offiziellen (nationalen) Währungsreserven der Zentralbank.

Die Kaufkraftparitätentheorie besagt, dass durch den Devisenkurs garantiert ist, dass man in beiden Ländern für einen bestimmten Geldbetrag die gleiche Gütermenge erwerben kann. Außerdem besagt sie, dass der Devisenkurs zwischen zwei Ländern durch die reale Kaufkraft ihrer Währungen bestimmt wird.

Die Zinsparitätentheorie ist ein kurzfristiges Erklärungsmodell für Wechselkursbewegungen. Die Theorie basiert auf der Annahme, dass Anleger dort investieren, wo die höchste Rendite erwartet wird, wobei in funktionierenden Märkten die Normalsituation jene einer Zinsparität ist. Eine Zinsparität im Sinne der Zinsparitätentheorie bezeichnet die „Gleichheit der erwarteten Renditen auf Einlagen in zwei beliebigen Währungen".

Bei den integrierten Modellen wird zwischen Stromgrößen- und Bestandsgrößenmodellen unterschieden. Stromgrößenmodelle basieren auf Veränderungen der betrachteten Einflussgrößen (z.B. Einkommensänderungen, Änderungen der Vermögensbestände), während die Bestandsgrößenmodelle auf Beständen (z.B. Höhe des Einkommens oder des Vermögens) aufbauen.

Das keynesianische Modell von John Maynard Keynes gehört zur Gruppe der Stromgrößenmodelle und berücksichtigt vorwiegend realwirtschaftliche Vorgänge als kursbestimmende Faktoren. Der Kurs einer Währung wird durch Angebot und Nachfrage von Devisen bestimmt.

Der monetäre Ansatz zur Bestimmung des Devisenkurses ist ein Bestandsgrößenansatz, der insbesondere die Bestände an Geldvermögen einer Volkswirtschaft berücksichtigt. Die in die Zahlungsbilanz eingehenden Leistungs- und Finanztransaktionen resultieren aus den Portfolioentscheidungen in- und ausländischer Wirtschaftssubjekte.

Mithilfe des Finanzmarktansatzes (Asset Market Approach) lassen sich kurzfristige Devisenkursbewegungen bestimmen. Er gilt als Weiterentwicklung des monetären Ansatzes und basiert daher auf Bestandsanpassungen.

Die Leistung einer Volkswirtschaft wird durch das sogenannte Nationaleinkommen charakterisiert und stellt die Summe aller Wertschöpfungen einer Volkswirtschaft dar.

Um eine Volkswirtschaft im Detail und ihre zukünftige Entwicklung beurteilen zu können, betrachtet man einzelne gesamtwirtschaftliche Einflussfaktoren genauer und prognostiziert diese für die Zukunft. Die wichtigsten gesamtwirtschaftlichen Einflussfaktoren sind Wirtschaftswachstum, Inflation, Zinsniveau, Wechselkurs und Produktivität.

Folgende Arten von Indikatoren können unterschieden werden: Mengenindikatoren (z.B. Arbeitslosenquote, Auftragseingänge), Preisindikatoren (z.B. Inflationsrate, Aktienkur-

opment. The most important macroeconomic parameters are economic growth, inflation, interest level, exchange rates and productivity.

These are the most important economic indicators: Purchasing Managers Index (PMI), New and unfilled orders, Index of Leading Economic Indicators, CRB Futures Index, gold price, Consumer Confidence Index (CCI), employment/wages, import prices, short-term interest rates, long-term interest rates, money supply, Producer Price Index (PPI).

2.6. Practice Questions

1. What is recorded in the balance of payments?
   a) new indebtedness of a country
   b) all economic transactions between residents and non-residents
   c) purchasing power of an economy
   d) average payment period between economic units of a country

2. Which of the following are sub-balances of the current account?
   a) net change in offical reserves
   b) financial account
   c) net errors and omissions
   d) goods balance
   e) services balance
   f) net unilateral transfers

3. What does a passive trade balance mean?
   a) import of services exceeds export of services
   b) export of goods exceeds import of goods
   c) import of goods exceeds export of goods
   d) import of goods and services exceeds export of goods and services
   e) export of goods and services exceeds import of goods and services
   f) export of services exceeds import of services

4. What are the four main categories of the financial account?

5. Which economic balance is used as an economic indicator for the performance of a country's economy?
   a) balance of official reserves
   b) financial account
   c) balance of payments
   d) balance of current account

6. The export of goods in recorded in …
   a) the credit side of the financial account
   b) the credit side of the balance on official reserves
   c) the credit side of the trade balance
   d) the debit side of the balance on official reserves
   e) the debit side of the trade balance
   f) the debit side of the financial account

7. You spend your vacations in the Caribbean. Which one of your home country's balance is affected?
   a) balance on factor income from abroad
   b) services balance

se), früh- bzw. vorlaufende Indikatoren (z.B. Auftragseingänge, Aktienkurse) und Präsensindikatoren- und Spätindikatoren (z.B. Bruttoinlandsprodukt, Arbeitslosenquote). Beispiele für wichtige Indikatoren sind: Einkaufsmanager Index, Auftragseingänge der Industrie, Index of Leading Economic Indicators, IFO Geschäftsklima, CRB Futures Index, Goldpreis, Geldmenge, kurzfristige Zinsen, langfristige Zinsen, Importpreise, Consumer's Confidence Index (CCI), Erzeugerpreisindex.

2.6. Wiederholungsfragen

1. Was wird von einer Zahlungsbilanz erfasst?
   a) Neuverschuldung eines Staates
   b) Außenbeziehungen einer Volkswirtschaft
   c) Kaufkraft einer Volkswirtschaft
   d) durchschnittliche Zahlungsfristen zwischen Wirtschaftssubjekten einer Volkswirtschaft
2. Welche der folgenden Bilanzen sind Teilbilanzen der Leistungsbilanz?
   a) Devisenbilanz
   b) Kapitalbilanz
   c) Restposten
   d) Handelsbilanz
   e) Dienstleistungsbilanz
   f) Bilanz der laufenden Übertragungen
3. Was versteht man unter einer passiven Handelsbilanz?
   a) Dienstleistungsimporte übersteigen Dienstleistungsexporte.
   b) Güterausfuhren übersteigen Gütereinfuhren.
   c) Gütereinfuhren übersteigen Güterausfuhren.
   d) Wareneinfuhren übersteigen Warenausfuhren.
   e) Warenausfuhren übersteigen Wareneinfuhren.
   f) Dienstleistungsexporte übersteigen Dienstleistungsimporte.
4. Nennen Sie die vier Hauptkategorien der Kapitalbilanz!
5. Welche volkswirtschaftliche Bilanz wird meist als ökonomische Größe zur Bewertung der Leistungsfähigkeit einer Volkswirtschaft verwendet?
   a) Devisenbilanz
   b) Kapitalbilanz
   c) Zahlungsbilanz
   d) Leistungsbilanz
6. Wo wird der Warenexport einer Volkswirtschaft verbucht?
   a) im Haben der Kapitalbilanz
   b) im Haben der Devisenbilanz
   c) im Haben der Handelsbilanz
   d) im Soll der Devisenbilanz
   e) im Soll der Handelsbilanz
   f) im Soll der Kapitalbilanz
7. Sie verbringen Ihren Urlaub in der Karibik. Auf welche volkswirtschaftliche Bilanz Ihres Heimatstaates hat dies Auswirkungen?
   a) Bilanz der Vermögensübertragungen
   b) Dienstleistungsbilanz

    c) balance of payments

    d) balance of goods

8. Into which groups can fundamental predicting models be divided? Give two examples for each case!

9. What does the Purchasing Power Parity Theory indicate in a free market?

    a) the long-term trend of a currencys's exchange rate

    b) future relative inflation pressure

    c) future level of a country's saving ratio

    d) the speed of growth of a country's GDP

10. Which statements apply to the Interest Rate Parity Theory?

    a) explains short-term FX movements

    b) explains FX movements based on exports and imports of goods and services

    c) explains FX movements based on assumptions about investor behaviour

    d) explains long-term FX movements

11. What is the difference between flow models and stock models?

12. Which of the following models is a stock model?

    a) Monetary Approach

    b) Keynesian Model

    c) Asset Market Approach

    d) Barro Portfolio Model

13. What is the major factor used by the Keynesian Model in determing the exchange rate?

    a) the set of individual portfolio decisions

    b) the balance of trade

    c) the current account balance

    d) capital account balance

14. Explain briefly the Monetary Approach!

15. What does the national income measure?

    a) the sum of all wages received

    b) the sum of all tax revenues of an economy

    c) the sum of all tax expenses of an economy

    d) the sum of all goods and services produced

16. What are the different types of economic indicators?

17. Which of the following are early indicators (leading indicators)?

    a) new and unfilled orders

    b) stock prices

    c) national income

    d) Purchasing Manager Index

    e) industrial production

18. Which of the following are inflation indicators?

    a) balance of payments

    b) RPI

    c) PPI

    d) Average Earnings

  c) Zahlungsbilanz

  d) Handelsbilanz

8. In welche Untergruppen können fundamentale Prognoseverfahren unterteilt werden? Geben Sie jeweils zwei Beispiele!

9. Worüber gibt in einer freien Marktwirtschaft die Kaufkraftparitätentheorie Auskunft?

  a) über die langfristige Richtung der Wechselkurse

  b) über den künftigen Inflationsdruck

  c) über die Höhe der Sparquote eines Landes

  d) über die Wachstumsrate des BIP eines Landes

10. Welche Aussagen treffen auf die Zinsparitätentheorie zu?

  a) ist ein kurzfristiges Erklärungsmodell für Wechselkursbewegungen

  b) Wechselkursbewegungen werden durch Güterexporte und -importe erklärt.

  c) Wechselkursbewegungen werden durch Renditeerwartungen von Investoren erklärt.

  d) ist ein langfristiges Erklärungsmodell für Wechselkursbewegungen

11. Was unterscheidet Bestandsgrößenmodelle von Stromgrößenmodellen?

12. Welches der folgenden Modelle ist ein Stromgrößenmodell?

  a) Monetärer Ansatz

  b) Keynesianisches Modell

  c) Asset Market Approach

  d) Portfoliomodell von Barro

13. Was berücksichtigt das keynesianische Modell als wichtigsten Faktor für die Devisenkursentwicklung?

  a) individuelle Portfolioentscheidungen

  b) Saldo der Handelsbilanz

  c) Saldo der Leistungsbilanz

  d) Saldo der Kapitalverkehrsbilanz

  14. Erklären Sie kurz den monetären Ansatz!

15. Was wird durch das Nationaleinkommen gemessen?

  a) Summe aller empfangenen Löhne

  b) Summe aller Steuerleistungen einer Volkswirtschaft

  c) Summe aller Steuerausgaben einer Volkswirtschaft

  d) Summe aller Wertschöpfungen einer Volkswirtschaft

16. Welche Arten von Indikatoren kann man unterscheiden?

17. Welche der folgenden Indikatoren sind Frühindikatoren (vorlaufende Indikatoren)?

  a) Auftragseingänge der Industrie

  b) Aktienkurse

  c) Nationaleinkommen

  d) Einkaufsmanagerindex

  e) Industrieproduktion

18. Welche dieser Begriffe sind Inflationskennzahlen?

  a) Zahlungsbilanz

  b) RPI

  c) PPI

  d) Average Earnings

3. Technical Analysis

In this chapter you learn ...

- about the different methods of technical analysis.
- about their differences to fundamental analysis.
- which types of classical chart analysis are used.
- what is meant by line and bar charts.
- what is meant by trend lines and trend channels.
- what is meant by chart patterns.
- what is meant by a point & figure chart.
- what is meant by a candle chart.
- what is meant by the Elliott Wave Theory.
- what is meant by Gann Angles.
- which types of numerical models are used.
- what is meant by trend chasing systems.
- what is meant by anti-cyclical systems.
- what is meant by time series analysis.
- which innovative approaches are used.
- what is meant by pattern recognition.

Technical prediciting methods are based only on the **observation and analysis of historical price movements**. From the characteristic of past price cycles we can conclude on future developments.

The methods of technical analysis can be divided in two groups:

- classical chart analysis: line- and bar charts, candle charts,
  point & figure chart, Elliott Wave Theory, Gann Angles
- numerical methods: trend chasing systems as moving average, MACD,
  anti-cyclical systems as Momentum, RSI,
  time series analysis

Contrary to fundamental analysis, forecasting models of technical analysis are based on the **observation and registration of past exchange rates** in order to arrive at conclusions about future exchange rate developments from past movements. By tracking the exchange rate, trends and trend turning points should be recognized.

Technical analyses are often **self-fulfilling prophecies**. This is true if **many market participants interpret the signals the same way and therefore react also in the same way**, e.g. sell a currency. Although this criticism is justified, the broad range of technical forecasting models assures that not all people act at the same time in the same way because each model can give a slightly different signal. Furthermore, the users of technical models influence their analyses with individual opinions so that even with the same model two people can draw different conclusions. Finally, trading decisions in the currency markets do not depend solely on the result of one forecast.

3. Technische Analyse

In diesem Kapitel lernen Sie ...

- welche unterschiedlichen Verfahren der technischen Analyse unterschieden werden.
- welche Unterschiede es zur Fundamentalanalyse gibt.
- welche Arten von klassischen Chartanalysen verwendet werden.
- was man unter Linien- bzw. Balkenchart versteht.
- was man unter Trendlinien und Trendkanälen versteht.
- was man unter Formationen versteht.
- was man unter Point & Figure-Chart versteht.
- was man unter Candle Charts versteht.
- was man unter der Elliott-Wellen-Theorie versteht.
- was man unter Gann-Linien versteht.
- welche Arten von mathematischen Verfahren verwendet werden.
- was man unter Trendfolgesystemen versteht.
- was man unter antizyklischen Systemen versteht.
- was man unter Zeitreihenanalyse versteht.
- welche innovativen Verfahren verwendet werden.
- was man unter Mustererkennung versteht.

Technische Prognoseverfahren beruhen ausschließlich auf der **Beobachtung und Analyse historischer Kursbewegungen.** Aus der Charakteristik vergangener Kursverläufe werden Schlüsse für zukünftige Entwicklungen gezogen.

Die Verfahren der technischen Analyse lassen sich in zwei Gruppen einteilen:

- Klassische Chartanalyse: Linien- und Balkenchartanalyse, Candle Charts, Point & Figure-Chart, Elliott-Wellen-Theorie, Gann-Linien
- Mathematische Verfahren: Trendfolgesysteme wie gleitender Durchschnitt, MACD, antizyklische Systeme wie Momentum, RSI, statistische Zeitreihenanalyse

Im Gegensatz zur Fundamentalanalyse basieren die Prognoseansätze der technischen Devisenkursprognose auf der **Beobachtung und Registrierung des Devisenkurses** und ziehen aus dem bisherigen Kursverlauf Rückschlüsse auf zukünftige Kursausprägungen. Durch die Beobachtung des Devisenkursverlaufs sollen Trends und ihre Richtung sowie Umkehrpunkte erkannt werden.

Technische Analysen werden häufig als sich **selbst erfüllende Prognosen** (Self Fulfilling Prophecies) bezeichnet. Prognosen erfüllen sich selbst, wenn **viele Marktteilnehmer bestimmte Signale gleich deuten und auch gleich reagieren** (z.B. Devisen verkaufen). Dieser Kritikpunkt relativiert sich jedoch, da eine Fülle von Varianten technischer Prognoseansätze existiert und nicht alle Ansätze zum selben Zeitpunkt dieselben Handlungsempfehlungen (z.B. Kauf von Devisen) signalisieren. Auch die subjektiven Einflüsse der Anwender auf den Analysevorgang führen nicht immer unmittelbar zu einer einheitlichen Aussage der Prognoseverfahren. Außerdem werden die Entscheidungen zum Handeln auf dem Devisenmarkt nicht nur von Prognosen abhängig gemacht.

3.1. Overview

Overview technical analysis

Method	Model	Principle
Chart analysis	line chart	Individual prices are joined by a line
	bar chart	Highs and lows of an interval are joined by a vertical line; opening and closing prices are denoted by horizontal ticks
	candle chart	Price differences between opening and closing prices are marked by differently coloured candle bars
	point & figure chart	Crosses and circles are plotted in the chart as soon as prices changed by a pre-defined amount
	Elliott Wave Theory	Hypothesis that exchange rate movements follow a regularly repeating wave pattern
	Gann Angles	Allow short-term predictions based on reversal points with time
Numerical Models	trend chasing systems	Identification and chasing of exchange rate trends
	anti-cyclical systems	Systemizing of different price movements and patterns; recourse to price changes, not to absolute data
	time series analysis	statistical theory for analysis of a time series and division in trends, cycle and chance

Innovative Approaches

The latest developments in technical analysis (since about 1990) are characterized by the use of innovative methods to analyse time series. They often differ from statistical methods although they are no less complex. Their origin lies in science, particularly informatics and behaviourism.

Innovative methods can be divided in:

- neural networks
- fractal geometry
- pattern recognition

3.1. Übersicht

Übersicht technische Analyse

Verfahren	Modell	Prinzip
Klassische Verfahren	Linienchart	Devisenkurse werden als einzelne Punkte miteinander verbunden.
	Balkenchart	Höchst- und Tiefstkurs für ein Zeitintervall werden mittels vertikaler Linie verbunden; Eröffnungs- und Schlusskurs = horizontale Linien darauf
	Candle Chart	Preisunterschiede zwischen Eröffnungs- und Schlusskurs werden durch unterschiedliche Farben der Kerzenkörper eines Balkens signalisiert.
	Point & Figure-Chart	Kreuze bzw. Kreise werden in einen Chart eingetragen, sobald die Kursänderung ein bestimmtes Ausmaß übersteigt.
	Elliott-Wellen-Theorie	Hypothetische Annahme, dass der Devisenkursverlauf einer wellenförmigen Bewegung folgt und sich ständig wiederholt
	Gann-Linien	Erlaubt Kursprognosen, wenn der Zeitfaktor einen Wendepunkt signalisiert.
Mathematische Verfahren	Trendfolgesysteme	Identifizierung und Verfolgen der Trends des Devisenkurses
	Antizyklische Systeme	Systematisierung unterschiedlicher Kursverlaufsmuster; Bezug auf Kursveränderungen, nicht auf Kurse selbst
	Zeitreihenanalyse	Statistisch fundierte Theorie zur Untersuchung einer Zeitreihe und ihrer Zerlegung in Trends, zyklische Anteile und zufällige Komponenten

Innovative Prognoseverfahren

Innovative Prognoseverfahren sind in der Regel **mathematische Verfahren.** Sie basieren auf den Erkenntnissen der Informatik und der Lern- und Chaostheorie. Danach entwickelt sich der Devisenkurs in einem dynamischen, nichtlinearen System. Neuronale Netze und Prognosen auf Basis der Theorie der Fraktale sind die in der Praxis bereits verwendeten nichtlinearen Prognoseverfahren.

Innovative Prognoseverfahren werden folgendermaßen eingeteilt:

- künstliche neuronale Netze
- fraktale Geometrie
- Mustererkennung

Overview of Innovative Forecasting Methods

Method	Example	Principle
Innovative forecasting methods		Complex mathematical approaches to model non-linear dynamic relationships
	neural networks	"Learn" from the past experience, in order to react correctly in the current situation
	fractal geometry	Attempt to describe the inner structure of price developments, to get additional information about the distribution of price changes
	pattern recognition	Comparison of the current pattern with similar patterns from historical simulations, in order to model the future price

3.2. Chart Analysis

Chart analysis shows the movement of exchange rates graphically in order to forecast future trends from previous exchange rate developments.

The following charts are in general use

- line charts and bar charts
- candle Charts
- point & figure charts
- Elliott Wave Theory

The methods listed above help to determine, in advance, the right time for buying or selling a currency. Their forecasts are based solely on historical exchange rates, paying no attention to any other information. Additionally, we will briefly discuss the Candle Chart, which is popular in Japan.

3.2.1. Line Chart

The exchange rates for each time period are plotted in a diagram and the points are joined. Prices on the y-axis, time on the x-axis.

The line chart chooses for example the closing price of consecutive time periods, but can also work with daily, official fixings (e.g. ECB-Fixing at 13:15).

Übersicht innovative Prognoseverfahren

Verfahren	Beispiel	Prinzip
Innovative Prognoseverfahren		Komplexe mathematische Ansätze zur Modellierung dynamischer, nichtlinearer Zusammenhänge
	Neuronale Netze	„Lernen" aus Beispielen der Vergangenheit, um in aktueller Situation „angemessen" zu reagieren
	Fraktale Geometrie	Versuch, die innere Struktur von Kursbewegungen besser zu beschreiben, um zusätzliche Informationen über die Verteilung von Kursänderungen zu erhalten
	Mustererkennung	Vergleich des aktuellen Kursmusters mit ähnlichen Mustern historischer Situationen, um daraus auf ein zukünftiges Kursverhalten zu schließen

3.2. Klassische Chartanalyse

Klassische Verfahren stellen den Devisenkursverlauf in einem Chart grafisch dar, um anhand vergangener Kursverläufe eine Orientierung für zukünftige Kurstrends zu schaffen.

Hier wird unterschieden zwischen:

● Linien- und Balkencharts
● Candle Charts
● Point & Figure-Chartanalyse
● Elliott-Wellen-Theorie (Elliott Wave)

Alle Verfahren sollen eine Vorausbestimmung des richtigen Zeitpunktes für einen Devisenkauf bzw. -verkauf ermöglichen. Sie **stützen sich ausschließlich auf historische Devisenkurse** und verwenden diese – ohne Berücksichtigung weiterer Informationen – zur Prognose. Darüber hinaus soll noch das insbesondere in Japan verbreitete Candle Chart kurz angesprochen werden.

3.2.1. Linienchart

Die Devisenkurse bestimmter Zeitpunkte werden in ein Diagramm eingetragen (Zeitachse/Kursachse) und die einzelnen Punkte miteinander verbunden.

Bei den gewählten Kursen kann es sich z.B. um die Schlusskurse aufeinanderfolgender Zeitintervalle oder auch um den täglichen amtlichen Fixing-Kurs (z.B.: EZB-Fixing um 13:15 Uhr) handeln.

Example

Line chart

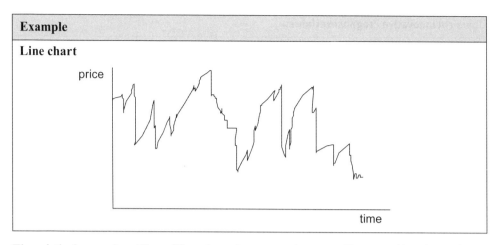

The relatively **easy handling** of line charts is a great advantage. However, line charts do not show price movements within a time period. This can be a problem because important information for exchange rate analysis can be lost. This problem was remedied with the development of **bar charts** that represent a more sophisticated form of line chart.

3.2.2. Bar Charts

The **highs and lows of a foreign currency** are plotted in a **diagram** and the points are joined with vertical lines (bars). A small horizontal line to the left of a bar denotes the opening level while a small horizontal line to the right represents the closing price of each interval.

Bar charts are **often depicted on a daily basis**, though professional traders often use shorter intervals.

Example

Bar chart

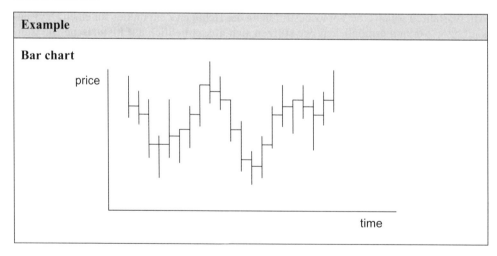

Beispiel

Linienchart

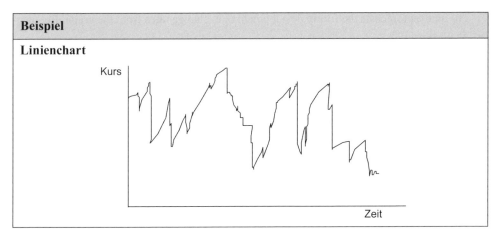

Liniencharts sind verhältnismäßig **einfach zu handhaben.** Devisenkursbewegungen inner-halb eines Zeitintervalls, die für die Kursanalyse von Bedeutung sein können, werden aber nicht in Liniencharts, sondern in **Balkencharts** erfasst. Die Balkenchartanalyse ist eine Er-weiterung der Linienchartanalyse.

3.2.2. Balkenchart

Die **Höchst- und Tiefstkurse** einer Währung für ein bestimmtes Zeitintervall werden in ein **Koordinatensystem** eingetragen. Beide Punkte werden mit einer vertikalen Linie (Bal-ken) verbunden. Ein kleiner horizontaler Strich auf der linken Seite des Balkens kennzeich-net den Eröffnungskurs, auf der rechten Seite des Balkens bezeichnet er den Schlusskurs des jeweiligen Zeitintervalls.

Balkencharts (Barcharts) werden **häufig auf Tagesbasis,** bei professionellen Devisen-marktteilnehmern sogar für noch kürzere Zeitintervalle erstellt.

Beispiel

Balkenchart

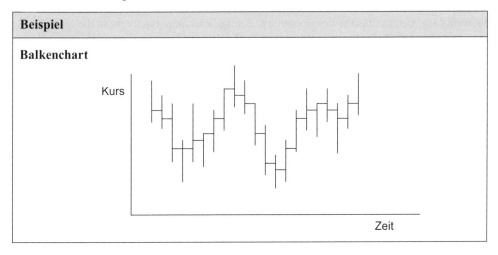

The analyst forecasts the future development of exchange rates from the graph. Requirements for this are:

- trends and trend channels
- resistance and support levels and
- chart patterns

3.2.3. Trend Lines and Trend Channels

Methods to determine a trend **assume that trends tend to continue until something seriously happens to change the trend**. By drawing lines that touch the **peaks and troughs of the chart**, trends can be made visible. This requires that the lines are tangent to all bars.

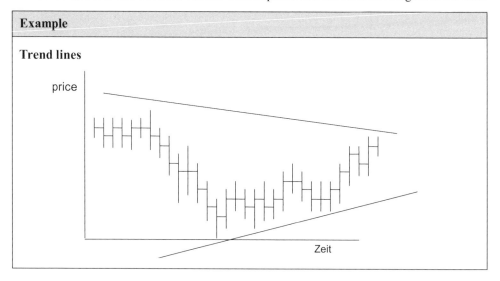

Example

Trend lines

price

Zeit

Despite daily movements the development of foreign exchange rates can, in the long run, be interpreted as a **system of overlapping trends of different lengths**. According to the length of the trend one distinguishes three types of trends:

- primary trends
- secondary trends
- tertiary trends.

If an identified trend continues, all future exchange rates are above or under the trend line. If the chart **intersects the trend line, the trend either reverses or is interrupted for a short time (consolidation phase)**. The chart analyst then has to judge the current market situation. He tries to identify certain chart patterns or employ other techniques to interpret the chart.

Aus der grafischen Darstellung prognostiziert der Analyst die zukünftige Entwicklung des Devisenkurses. Voraussetzung dafür ist die Ermittlung von:

- Trends und Trendkanälen
- Widerstands- und Unterstützungslinien
- Formationen

3.2.3. Trendlinien und Trendkanäle

Bei Verfahren zur Trendbestimmung geht man von der **Annahme** aus, **dass ein Trend eine einmal eingeschlagene Richtung wahrscheinlich beibehält.** Indem man Geraden an den Kursverlauf legt, werden Trends sichtbar. Dabei werden **zwei Extrempunkte derselben Art (Tiefst- bzw. Höchstkurse) miteinander verbunden.** Die beiden Punkte sind so auszuwählen, dass andere Balken höchstens tangiert werden.

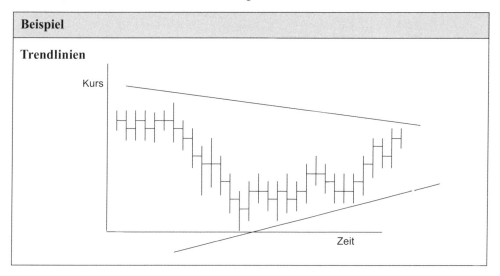

Beispiel

Trendlinien

Kurs

Zeit

Bei längerfristiger Beobachtung ist die Devisenkursentwicklung trotz der täglichen Schwankungen als ein **System von Überlagerungen unterschiedlich langer Trends** interpretierbar. Im Hinblick auf die Zeitdauer eines Trends unterscheidet man:

- Haupttrends (Primärtrends)
- Sekundärtrends
- Tertiärtrends

Hält ein festgestellter Trend an, so liegen alle zukünftigen Devisenkurse unter- bzw. oberhalb der Trendlinie. Schneidet der Chart dagegen die Trendlinie, so handelt es sich entweder um eine **Trendumkehr** oder eine **vorübergehende Trendunterbrechung (Konsolidierungsphase).** Der Chartanalytiker muss dann beurteilen, in welcher Situation sich der Markt augenblicklich befindet. Er versucht, bestimmte Formationen im Kursverlauf zu identifizieren oder greift auf weitere Verfahren zurück, die die Interpretation der Charts unterstützen.

In Point and Figure Charts trend lines can be drawn as fix 45° trend lines from every point in the chart. These draw a clear line between supply and demand and follow clear construction rules. **Fix 45° trend lines** cannot be used in time-related charts because a change in the scale, particularly on the time axis, would considerably distort the information received from trend lines.

If two parallel trend lines can be depicted in a chart and each of them is a tangent to either the peaks or the troughs, the formation is called a **trend channel**.

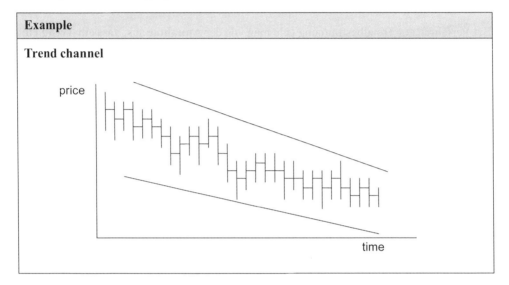

Example

Trend channel

3.2.4. Resistance and Support Levels

Support and resistance levels are levels that a foreign exchange rate cannot break through despite various movements in this direction. In the case of a **support level**, the exchange rate remains above the level for a considerable time, while a **resistance level** stops the upward trend of a currency.

If the exchange rate moves for a longer time within a trend channel the upper limit can be taken as the resistance level and the lower limit as the support level.

Resistance and support levels are widely used and are highly acclaimed references in the market because

- they deliver valuable information concerning the highs and lows of an exchange rate and
- because after a breakthrough a resistance level can become a support level and vice versa.

Trendlinien können auch als **starre 45°-Trendlinien** in Point & Figure-Charts von jedem beliebigen Chartpunkt gezogen werden. Sie grenzen Anbieter und Nachfrager klar ab und unterliegen eindeutigen Konstruktionsregeln. Starre 45°-Trendlinien sind für zeitabhängige Charts nicht geeignet, weil Änderungen im Darstellungsmaßstab, besonders auf der Zeitachse, die Auskunftsfähigkeit der Trendlinie stark reduzieren.

Können in einen Chart zwei parallel verlaufende Trendlinien eingezeichnet werden, eine oberhalb und die andere unterhalb der Balken, so liegt ein **Trendkanal** vor.

Beispiel

Trendkanal

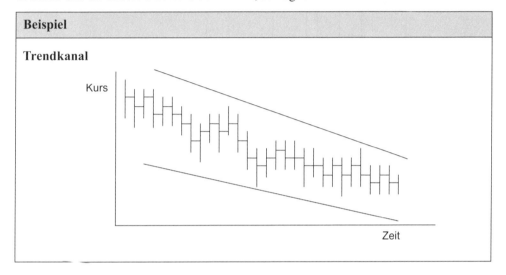

3.2.4. Widerstands- und Unterstützungslinien

Man spricht von einer **Unterstützungslinie,** wenn der Devisenkurs trotz mehrerer Abwärtsbewegungen ein gewisses Niveau nicht unterschreitet. Eine **Widerstandslinie** liegt vor, wenn der Kurs einen bestimmten Wert nicht überschreitet, obwohl er sich mehrmals aufwärts bewegt.

Bleibt beispielsweise ein Devisenkurs über einen längeren Zeitraum innerhalb eines Trendkanals, so lässt sich die obere Begrenzung des Kanals als Widerstandslinie und die untere als Unterstützungslinie auffassen.

Widerstands- und Unterstützungslinien sind für Devisenmarktteilnehmer häufig eine wertvolle Orientierungshilfe, weil

- sie Aufschluss über das Devisenkurspotenzial im Hinblick auf Höchst- und Tiefstkurse liefern können.
- sich Widerstandslinien nach einem Durchstoß als künftige Unterstützungslinien und umgekehrt Unterstützungslinien nach einem Durchdringen als Widerstandslinien erweisen können.

Example

Resistance level

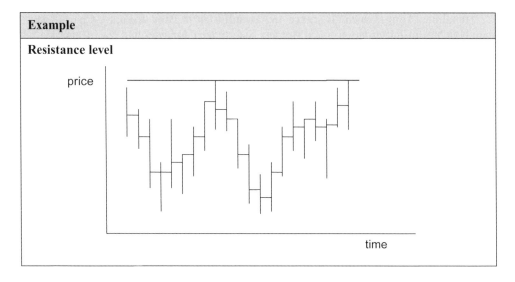

3.2.5. Chart Patterns

A chart pattern is a **typical, repeating price pattern** that can be shown in a chart. A developing chart pattern heralds a certain development of the exchange rate, though the interpretation demands a lot of experience from the analyst. A major distinction is made between

- trend sustaining patterns and
- trend reversal patterns.

Trend sustaining patterns confirm the continuation of the given trend. Trend sustaining patterns include **triangles (wedges)**. Triangles are formed by **two converging trend lines**.

Example

Triangles

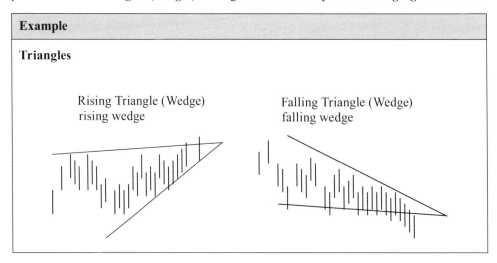

Rising Triangle (Wedge) rising wedge

Falling Triangle (Wedge) falling wedge

Beispiel

Widerstandslinie

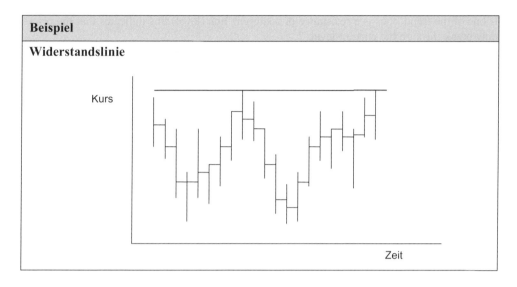

3.2.5. Formationen

Unter einer Formation versteht man ein **typisches, sich wiederholendes Kursbild**, das in einen Chart gelegt wird. Ein sich abzeichnendes Kursbild wird dann als Signal für eine bestimmte Fortentwicklung des Devisenkurses gewertet. Vorauszusetzen ist einige Fantasie des Analysten. Man unterscheidet zwischen

- Trendbestätigungsformation und
- Trendumkehrformation.

Trendbestätigungsformationen werden als Hinweis auf die Bestätigung und Fortsetzung des bisherigen Trends aufgefasst. Zu dieser Gruppe von Formationen zählen die **Dreiecksbilder** (engl.: wedge), sie entstehen durch **zwei aufeinander zulaufende Trendlinien.**

Beispiel

Dreiecksformationen

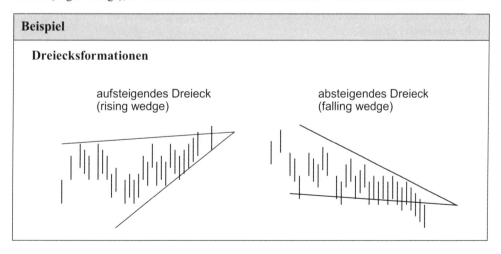

If one of the trend lines is a resistance or a support line (level) this indicates that the prices may break through the current level.

If an analyst spots a typical trend reversal pattern in his chart he expects a turn in the current trend. Major trend reversal patterns are shown in the illustrations below.

Example

Trend reversal patterns

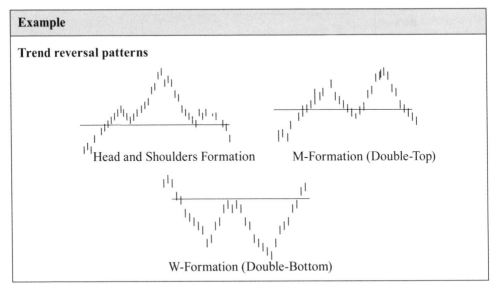

Head and Shoulders Formation   M-Formation (Double-Top)

W-Formation (Double-Bottom)

The best-known trend reversal pattern is the **head and shoulders formation**, which is similar to a head and two shoulders. It indicates a **downward trend**. It is formed by three upward movements and two downward movements.

By joining the base points of the formation (i.e. the shoulders) the neckline is formed. If the chart penetrates the neckline this is a signal to sell.

Besides head and shoulders formations there are also **reverse head and shoulder formations** (inverse head and shoulders, head and shoulders bottom formations) that are simply the reverse image of a head and shoulders. Consequently, it generates a buy signal as soon as the neckline is crossed.

3.2.6. Point & Figure Chart

Crosses and circles symbolize changes of the exchange rate. A **cross (x)** denotes a **rise in the exchange rate**, a **circle (o)** a **fall in the exchange rate**. Point and Figure Charts eliminate time and show instead price against price reversals. The price is plotted on the y-axis, price reversals on the x-axis.

New crosses or circles are plotted into the chart only if the change has reached a previously defined size ("box size", e.g. 10 pips). That way, negligible price changes are not considered. **Identical symbols are depicted in columns.** If the exchange rate changes by a multiple of the "box size", a new column with according symbols is started. Therefore the x- and o-columns change. The further to the right a column is situated, the more current are the price quotes.

Ist eine der Trendlinien Widerstands- oder Unterstützungslinie, so weist die Dreiecksformation auf die Tendenz des Kurses hin, das entsprechende Niveau zu durchbrechen.

Erkennt der Analyst im Kursverlaufsdiagramm eine typische Umkehrformation oder den Ansatz einer solchen Formation, dann rechnet er mit der Wende des bisherigen Kurstrends.

Beispiel

Trendumkehrformationen

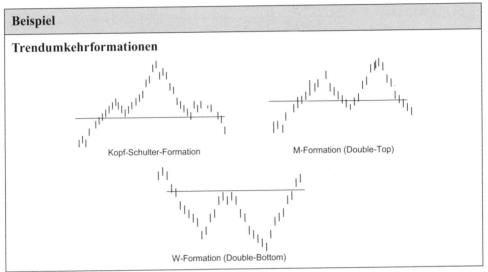

Kopf-Schulter-Formation   M-Formation (Double-Top)

W-Formation (Double-Bottom)

Die bekannteste Trendumkehrfunktion ist die **Kopf-Schulter-Formation.** Sie ähnelt einem Kopf mit zwei Schultern. Sie deutet einen **Abwärtstrend** an. Ihr Erscheinungsbild wird durch drei Aufwärtsbewegungen charakterisiert.

Verbindet man die Tiefstpunkte der Schultern durch eine Gerade, so entsteht die Nackenlinie, deren Durchbruch der Chartanalyst als Beginn einer Kursschwäche wertet.

Neben Kopf-Schulter-Formationen existieren auch **inverse Kopf-Schulter-Formationen,** die einem Spiegelbild herkömmlicher Kopf-Schulter-Formationen gleichen. Sie signalisieren einen **Aufwärtstrend.**

3.2.6. Point & Figure-Chart

Veränderungen des Devisenkurses werden durch Kreuz- und Kreissymbole dargestellt. Ein **Kreuz (x)** repräsentiert einen **Devisenkursanstieg,** ein **Kreis (o)** dagegen einen **Devisenkursrückgang.** Die Ausprägungen des Devisenkurses sind auf der Ordinate eines Point & Figure-Diagramms eingetragen. Points & Figure-Charts weisen keine lineare Zeitachse auf.

Neue Kreuze bzw. Kreise werden erst in ein Chart eingetragen, wenn die Änderung des Devisenkurses ein bestimmtes Ausmaß („Boxsize") erreicht hat (z.B. im Chart 10 Pips). Geringfügige Kursschwankungen bleiben so unberücksichtigt. **Gleichartige Symbole werden unter- und übereinander angeordnet, sodass sie die Form einer Säule annehmen.** Ändert der Devisenkurs seine Richtung um ein Vielfaches (Umkehrpunktzahl) der gewählten „Boxsize", so werden die entsprechenden Symbole in einer neuen Säule eingetragen. Auf diese Weise wechseln x- und o-Säulen. Säulen, die im Chart weiter rechts liegen, stellen demzufolge jüngere Kursnotierungen dar.

Example

Point & Figure Chart

GBP/USD quotes:

1.5930	X		
1.5920	X		
1.5910	X		
1.5900	X	O	
1.5890		O	X
1.5880		O	
1.5870		O	
1.5860		O	

Indications regarding the development of the exchange rate are derived from the **patterns of the consecutive columns**. For a simple buy or sell signal the analyst looks first at the current column. If a cross column exceeds the previous cross column by at least one cross it is a signal to buy (foreign exchange rate increase). If a circle column goes below the previous circle column, it is a signal to sell.

Like bar charts, Point and Figure Charts use trend lines, resistance and support levels.

In addition to simple buying and selling signals, triple tops and triple bottoms are major chart patterns. A **triple top** consists of **three upward trends** (three cross columns) and **two downward trends** (circle columns), whereas a **triple bottom** consists of **three downward trends** (three circle columns) and **two upward trends** (two cross columns). In each formation the columns alternate. At the triple top the last upward trend exceeds the levels of the two previous upward trends. This indicates a bull market and therefore the currency should be bought.

At the triple bottom the last downward trend breaks through the levels of the previous downward trends. This indicates a bear market and the currency is to be sold.

An additional bull signal in a triple top formation occurs if the bottom of the first circle column is lower than that of the second. Similarly, an additional bear signal occurs if in a triple bottom formation the first cross column exceeds the second cross column. Compare this situation to triangles with resistance or support lines as trend lines.

Beispiel

Point & Figure-Chart

Kurse für GBP/USD:

1,5930	X		
1,5920	X		
1,5910	X		
1,5900	X	O	
1,5890		O	X
1,5880		O	
1,5870		O	
1,5860		O	

Hinweise über die Entwicklung des Devisenkurses werden aus dem **Bild nebeneinander liegender Säulen** abgeleitet. Für ein einfaches Kauf- oder Verkaufssignal betrachtet der Analyst zunächst die aktuelle Spalte. Übertrifft eine aus Kreuzen aufgebaute Spalte die vorhergehende aus Kreuzen bestehende Säule um mindestens ein Kreuz, prognostiziert der Analyst einen Anstieg des Devisenkurses (Kaufsignal). Bei Kreissäulen ist es genau umgekehrt. Unterschreitet eine Kreissäule die vorhergehende Kreissäule um mindestens einen Kreis, so erhält der Chartanalyst einen Hinweis auf einen fallenden Devisenkurs (Verkaufssignal).

Der Umgang mit Point & Figure-Charts ist mit dem Umgang mit Balkencharts vergleichbar. Trend-, Widerstands- und Unterstützungslinien sowie Formationen lassen sich diagnostizieren.

Zu den bedeutenden Formationen zählen neben den einfachen Kauf- und Verkaufssignalen die Dreifachspitzen und Dreifachböden. Eine **Dreifachspitzenformation** setzt sich aus **drei Aufwärtstrends (Kreuzsäulen) und zwei Abwärtstrends (Kreissäulen)** zusammen. Hingegen besteht eine **Dreifachbodenformation** aus **drei Abwärtstrends und zwei Aufwärtstrends.** Die Kreissäulen (Kreuzsäulen) liegen jeweils zwischen den Kreuzsäulen (Kreissäulen). Bei der Dreifachspitze übersteigt der dritte Aufwärtstrend das Niveau der beiden ersten Aufwärtstrends. Dies deutet auf einen Anstieg des Devisenkurses hin (Hausse).

Der Dreifachboden besteht dagegen aus drei Abwärtstrends und zwei dazwischenliegenden Aufwärtstrends. Sobald der Boden der dritten Abwärtsbewegung den Boden der mittleren Abwärtsbewegung unterschreitet, liegt dem Analysten ein Signal für ein Sinken des Devisenkurses (Baisse) vor.

Liegt bei einer Dreifachspitze der Boden der ersten Kreissäule unterhalb desjenigen der zweiten Kreissäule, so wird dies als zusätzliches Haussesignal gewertet. Ein Dreifachboden liefert ein zusätzliches Baissesignal, wenn die erste Kreuzsäule die zweite überragt. Man vergleiche diese Situation mit der von Dreiecken, wenn eine der Trendlinien eine Widerstands- oder Unterstützungslinie ist.

Example

Triple Top Formation and Triple Bottom Formation

			K	X
X		X		X
X	O	X	O	X
X	O	X	O	X
	O		O	

Triple Top

	X		X	
O	X	O	X	O
O	X	O	X	O
O		O		O
			V	O

Triple Bottom

			K	X
				X
X		X		X
X	O	X	O	X
X	O	X	O	
X	O	X		
X	O			
X				

Triple Top with bull signal

O				
O	X			
O	X	O	X	
O	X	O	X	O
O	X	O	X	O
O		O		O
			V	O

Triple Bottom with bear signal

Point and Figure Charts differ from all other charts by using a **strict scheme**. This particularly helps in an unambiguous definition and recognition of chart patterns. This way, the drawing of arbitrary charts can be eliminated.

Moreover, they enable one to evaluate trading strategies based on Point and Figure Charts by simulating other strategies in the chart with historic data.

3.2.7. Candle Charts

A broad bar depicts the price change between opening and closing price. The colour of the bar shows if the price closed lower (black, dark) or higher (white, light).

A small and thin vertical line that is drawn above or below the bar creates the shape of a candle. It shows if the currency movements were within or outside a stated bandwidth.

Beispiel

Dreifachspitzen- und -bodenformationen

			K	X			X		X	
X		X		X		O	X	O	X	O
X	O	X	O	X		O	X	O	X	O
X	O	X	O	X		O		O		O
	O		O						V	O

Dreifachspitze   Dreifachboden

			K	X		O				
				X		O	X			
X		X		X		O	X	O	X	
X	O	X	O	X		O	X	O	X	O
X	O	X	O			O	X	O	X	O
X	O	X				O		O		O
X	O								V	O
X										

Dreifachspitze mit   Dreifachboden mit
Haussesignal   Baissesignal

Point & Figure-Charts unterscheiden sich von den bisher beschriebenen Charttypen durch eine **starke Schematisierung des Kursverlaufs.** Dies erleichtert insbesondere die eindeutige Definition und somit auch das Wiedererkennen von Chartformationen. Die Willkürlichkeit bei der Einzeichnung von Chartbildern kann so überwunden werden.

Auf diese Weise entsteht schließlich die Möglichkeit, Handelsstrategien zu überprüfen, die auf Point & Figure-Charts basieren, indem mithilfe historischer Kursverläufe ein entsprechender Handelsverlauf simuliert wird.

3.2.7. Candle Charts

Preisveränderungen zwischen dem Eröffnungskurs und dem Schlusskurs eines Zeitintervalls werden durch einen breiten Balken in einen Chart eingezeichnet. Die unterschiedlichen Farben des Balkens signalisieren, ob der Schlusskurs über (hell, weiß) oder unter (dunkel, schwarz) dem Eröffnungskurs liegt.

Die eigentliche „Kerzenform" erlangen die Candle Charts erst durch den Eintrag einer schmalen senkrechten Linie über oder unter dem Balken. Sie zeigt an, ob die Bewegungen der Währung innerhalb oder außerhalb des vorgegebenen Bereichs liegen.

Example

Candle Chart

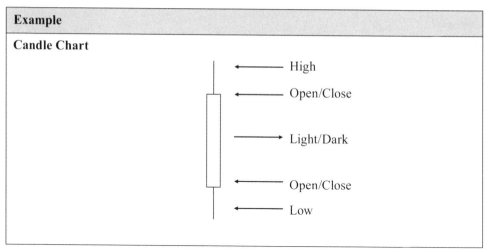

Generally, candle charts do not deliver **more information than bar charts** (the candle is determined by horizontal ticks that denote opening and closing price of the bar chart).

The main difference is the display of the price movements within the interval. The **coloured candle** makes it **easy to spot the direction of price movements**.

All analyses applicable to the bar chart can also be used in the candle chart. The coloured visualization enables the analyst to see additional chart patterns.

Often the sequence of colours and the characteristic shape of the candle lead to specific candle chart formations. If, for example, candles are based on daily data, the colour shows if the previous day was bullish (light candle) or bearish (dark candle).

Example

Engulfing Formation (bullish)

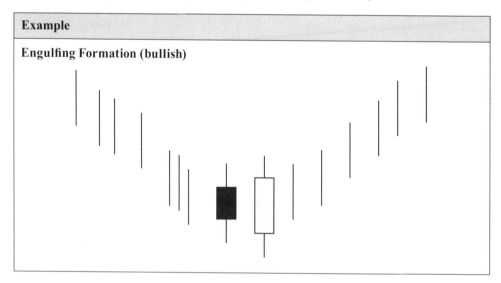

Beispiel

Candle Chart

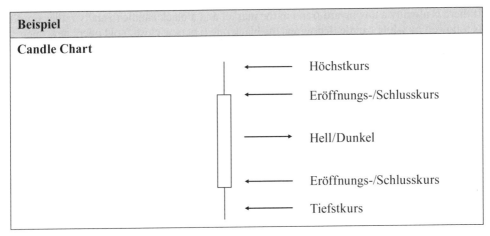

Höchstkurs

Eröffnungs-/Schlusskurs

Hell/Dunkel

Eröffnungs-/Schlusskurs

Tiefstkurs

Candle Charts vermitteln grundsätzlich nicht **mehr Informationen als Balkencharts** (der Kerzenkörper wird durch die waagerechten Striche für Eröffnungs- und Schlusskurse des Balkencharts festgelegt).

Der wesentliche Unterschied besteht in der Art der Darstellung der Kursbewegung innerhalb des Zeitintervalls. **Durch die farbliche Gestaltung** (hell/dunkel) des Kerzenkörpers sind diese **Bewegungen leichter erkennbar.**

Alle für die Balkencharts beschriebenen Analysetechniken können auch für Candle Charts benutzt werden. Durch die andere Art der Visualisierung sieht der Analyst jedoch zusätzliche Formationen.

So sind es oft die farbliche Aufeinanderfolge und das charakteristische Aussehen der Kerzen, die zur Unterscheidung der für Candle Charts typischen Formationen führen. Basieren die Kerzen z.B. auf Tagesdaten, dann zeigt ihre Farbe, ob innerhalb des jeweiligen Tages die Bullen (helle Kerzenkörper) oder die Bären (dunkle Kerzenkörper) zwischen Eröffnungs- und Schlusskurs die Oberhand gewinnen konnten.

Beispiel

Engulfing Formation (bullish)

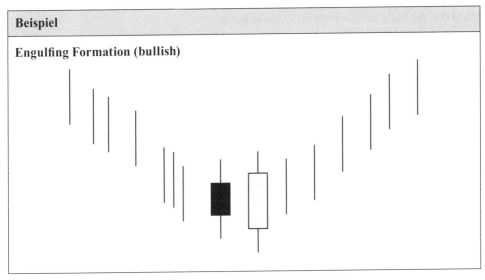

If there is already a downward trend in the market and a black candle (usually rather small) is followed by white candle that wraps the black one (i.e. new close > old open; new open < old close) one speaks of a **bullish engulfing formation**. It indicates the reversal from a current downward trend to an upward trend.

The reverse chart pattern in a market with a current upward trend is called a bearish engulfing formation (i.e. a white candle is followed by a black candle that wraps the white one). It indicates the reversal from a current upward trend to a downward trend.

A special situation occurs in the candle chart if bullish and bearish tendencies balance out and the opening price equals the closing price. The result is a candle that consists of a horizontal line only. This formation is called **Doji**.

Example

Doji Formation

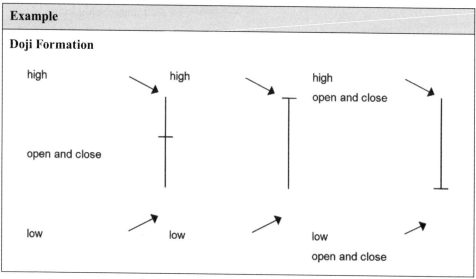

If there has been an upward trend before the Doji this is an indication of a ceasing of the trend (i.e. the bulls declined relatively to the bears).

Similarly, a consolidation phase can be expected if a Doji formation can be seen during a downward trend.

3.2.8. Elliott Wave Theory

The Elliott Wave Theory of **Ralph Nelson Elliot** (mathematican, USA, 1871–1948) assumes that **exchange rates move in waves**. These movements take place regularly and can be used for forecasting exchange rates. These assumptions are based on the **natural behaviour of the market participants**.

According to Elliott, prices move in **eight waves**, of which **five** are **impulse waves** and **three** are **corrective waves**. Impulse waves are usually denoted with numbers and correc-

Ist ein Markt im Abwärtstrend und folgt auf eine schwarze Kerze (mit in der Regel relativ kurzem Körper) eine weiße, deren Körper den vorangegangenen umfasst (neuer Schlusskurs > alter Eröffnungskurs; neuer Eröffnungskurs < alter Schlusskurs), so spricht man von einer **bullischen Engulfing Formation.** Sie deutet die Umkehr des aktuellen Abwärtstrends in einen Aufwärtstrend an.

In der gegensätzlichen Situation eines vorliegenden Aufwärtstrends ist die (bearische) Engulfing Formation gekennzeichnet, indem auf eine (kurze) weiße Kerze eine diese umfassende schwarze Kerze folgt, die den Trendwechsel einleiten soll.

Eine besondere Situation liegt im Candle Chart vor, wenn sich bullische und bearische Tendenzen die Waage halten und der Schlusskurs mit dem Eröffnungskurs übereinstimmt. Die zugehörige Formation wird als **Doji** bezeichnet. Sie besteht aus einer einzigen Kerze, deren Kerzenkörper auf eine waagerechte Linie zusammengeschrumpft ist.

Beispiel

Doji Formation

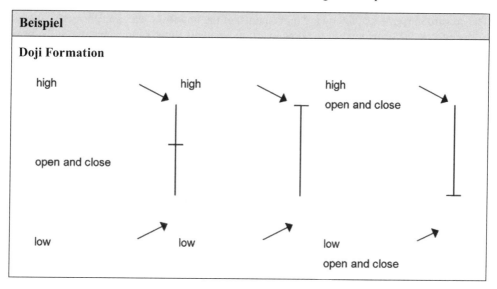

Lag zuvor ein Aufwärtstrend vor, so zeigt der Doji, dass die Kräfte der Bullen gegenüber den Bären nachgelassen haben, sich also ein Ende der Trendphase andeutet.

Ebenso muss man sich auf eine Konsolidierungsphase einstellen, wenn ein Doji im Verlauf eines Abwärtstrends auftritt.

3.2.8. Elliott-Wellen-Theorie

Die Elliott-Wellen-Theorie von **Ralph Nelson Elliot** (Mathematiker, USA, 1871–1948) basiert auf der Hypothese, dass der **Devisenkursverlauf einer wellenförmigen Bewegung folgt, die sich ständig wiederholt** und somit für Kursprognosen verwendet werden kann. Diese Annahme ist auf die **natürlichen Verhaltensweisen der Marktteilnehmer** zurückzuführen.

Die Kursbewegungen verlaufen nach Elliott in Form von **acht Wellen.** Die ersten fünf sind sogenannte **Impulswellen.** Die letzten drei bilden die sogenannten **Korrekturwellen.** Die Impulswellen werden üblicherweise mit Ziffern, die Korrekturwellen mit Buchstaben gekennzeichnet. Tabelle 1 enthält die Bewegungsrichtungen der einzelnen Wellen der Im-

tive waves with letters. The following table contains the directions of impulse waves and corrective waves in a bull market (rising exchange rates) and a bear market (falling exchange rates).

Direction of impulse waves and corrective waves:

	Bull cycle	Bear cycle
Impulse waves	First, third and fifth wave move up. Second and fourth down.	First, third and fifth wave move down. Second and fourth up.
Corrective waves	Waves a and c move down, wave b moves up.	Waves a and c move up, wave b moves down.

The wave pattern that is shown in the illustration below for a bull cycle looks similar for bull and bear cycle. The difference is the direction of the impulse waves and corrective waves. The upward movements (downward movements) of the impulse waves and corrective waves in the bull cycle correspond to the downward movements (upward movements) in the bear cycle.

Example

Wave pattern for a bull cycle

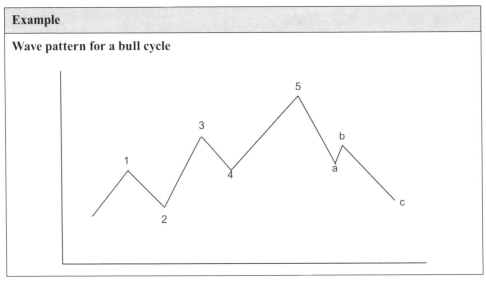

This basic pattern can be found in each wave movement and repeats constantly. Many small movements can be summed up as a big movement.

Elliott defined **nine categories of cycles**:

1. Grand supercycle (multi-century)
2. Supercycle (multi-decade)
3. Cycle (one year to several years)
4. Primary wave (a few months to a couple of years)
5. Intermediary wave (weeks to months)

puls- und Korrekturwelle für einen Hausse- (Devisenkursanstieg) und Baissezyklus (Kursrückgang).

Bewegungsrichtungen der Einzelwellen der Impuls- und Korrekturwelle:

	Haussezyklus	**Baissezyklus**
Impulswellen	Die erste, dritte und fünfte Welle vollziehen eine aufwärts gerichtete, die zweite und vierte dagegen eine abwärts gerichtete Bewegung.	Die erste, dritte und fünfte Welle vollziehen eine abwärts-, die zweite und vierte dagegen eine aufwärts gerichtete Bewegung.
Korrektur-wellen	Die Wellen a und c bewegen sich abwärts, die Welle b dagegen bewegt sich aufwärts.	Die Wellen a und c bewegen sich aufwärts, die Welle b dagegen bewegt sich abwärts.

Das Muster einer Wellenbewegung, das in der folgenden Abbildung für einen Haussezyklus dargestellt ist, verläuft für Hausse- und Baissezyklen ähnlich. Der Unterschied liegt in den entgegengesetzten Bewegungsrichtungen der Impuls- und Korrekturwellen. Die Aufwärtsbewegungen (Abwärtsbewegungen) der Impuls- und Korrekturwellen beim Haussezyklus entsprechen den Abwärtsbewegungen (Aufwärtsbewegungen) beim Baissezyklus.

Beispiel

Wellenbewegung für einen Haussezyklus

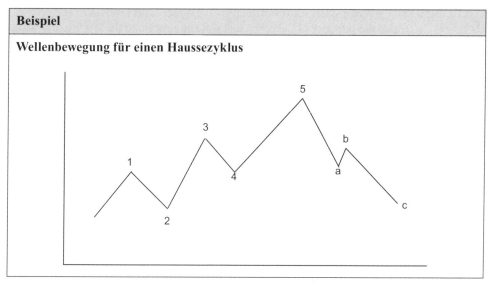

Das Grundmuster liegt jeder Wellenbewegung zugrunde und wiederholt sich ständig. Einzelne kleinere Wellenbewegungen können zu größeren Bewegungen zusammengefasst werden.

Elliot selbst formulierte folgende **neun Kategorien von Wellenbewegungen:**

1) Großer Superzyklus (über mehrere Jahrhunderte)
2) Superzyklus (mehrere Jahrzehnte)
3) Zyklus (ein bis mehrere Jahre)
4) Primärwelle (einige Monate bis einige Jahre)
5) Zwischenwelle (Wochen oder Monate)

6. Minor wave (weeks)
7. Minute wave (days)
8. Minuette wave (hours)
9. Subminuette wave (minutes)

The analyst must recognize from a bar or line chart the current state of the currency market in order to make a well-founded exchange rate forecast.

The so-called **Fibonacci numbers** play an important role in the Elliott Wave Theory. Fibonacci numbers are a mathematical sequence that follows the **natural law of the golden ratio**. It means that if one term is divided by its successor the ratio tends towards 0.618.

The Fibonacci Sequence is 1, 1, 2, 3, 5, 8, 13, 21, 34, 55, 89, 144... It is generated by the following formula:

$$Z(n) = Z(n-1) + Z(n-2) \text{ for } n > 2$$
$$Z(1) = Z(2) = 1$$

$$Z(n) = \text{n-th Fibonacci number}$$

A second peculiarity of the Fibonacci sequence is that the quotient of a term $Z(n)$ with the term $Z(n-1)$ converges to 0.382 (= 1 – 0.618). For $Z(1)$ and $Z(3)$ the ratio is 0.5. These three numbers (0.382, 0.618, 0.5) are used by technical analysis as **retracement levels**. Retracement levels help to determine the intensity of the corrective wave in relation to the last impulse wave. A retracement level of 0.382 means that the correction was 38.2% of the last upward trend.

3.2.9. Gann Angles

Gann Angles can be interpreted as **progressive support or resistance levels** and are **drawn ascending from price bottoms or descending from price tops in the form of a fan** (Gann fan).

The angles are drawn by **dividing the "price field", the difference between the two last opposite extreme points, by 8**. The most important angle is called the 1/1 angle (meaning: 1 unit of price for one unit of time) with a slope of 45°. Other angles are called the "1/8" angle (82.5°), "2/8" angle (75°) etc. until the "8/8" angle or the "8/1" angle (7.5°), "8/2" angle (15°) and so on. The most important ones should be the angles 3/8, 4/8 and 5/8, which remind one of Fibonacci numbers or the "Golden Ratio".

In a narrow sense, there are four types of Gann Angles:

- **Gann Angles from the division of the range between the highest and lowest price of a movement:** These are the most famous Gann Angles. The last movement is divided as shown above in the percentage of the appropriated resistance and support levels.
- **Gann Angles from the highest price:** This is the highest price divided as shown in the above scheme. The breakthrough by the 1/8- resp. the 7/8 angle is, particularly for commodities, a sure sign for a long bear market, the more secure the higher the price was before, so peak minus 1/8 of that price.

6) Miniwelle (Wochen)
7) Minutenwelle (Tage)
8) Minuettenwelle (Stunden)
9) Subminuettenwelle (Minuten)

Um eine Prognose des zukünftigen Kursverlaufes anstellen zu können, muss der Analyst anhand eines Linien- und Balkencharts erkennen, in welchem Stadium sich der Devisenmarkt befindet.

Im Rahmen der Elliott-Wellen-Theorie haben die sogenannten **Fibonacci-Zahlen** eine besondere Bedeutung. Sie bilden eine Zahlenfolge, die dem **Naturgesetz des Goldenen Schnitts** (entspricht ca. der Zahl 1,618; Kehrwert entspricht ca. 0,618) gehorcht. Das heißt, zwischen zwei aufeinanderfolgenden Zahlen der Fibonacci-Folge besteht ein konstanter Zusammenhang in der Form, als dass deren Quotient gegen 0,618 tendiert.

Die Fibonacci-Folge lautet 1,1,2,3,5,8,13,21,34,55,89,144, ... Sie gehorcht folgender Gesetzmäßigkeit:

$$Z(n) = Z(n-1) + Z(n-2) \text{ für } n > 2$$
$$Z(1) = Z(2) = 1$$

$$Z(n) = \text{n-te Fibonacci-Zahl}$$

Eine weitere Besonderheit der Fibonacci-Folge ist, dass der Quotient aus einer Zahl mit der übernächsten Zahl gegen 0,382 (= 1 – 0,618) tendiert. Bei $Z(1)$ und $Z(3)$ ist er 0,5. Diese drei Größen werden in der technischen Analyse als **Retracement Levels** verwendet.

Mithilfe der Retracement Levels wird versucht, die Stärke einer Korrekturwelle im Verhältnis zur letzten Impulswelle zu messen. Ein Retracement Level von 0,382 bedeutet, dass die Korrektur 38,2% des letzten Aufschwungs beträgt.

3.2.9. Gann-Linien (Gann Angles)

Gann-Linien sind als **fortschreitende Unterstützung bzw. fortschreitender Widerstand** zu interpretieren und verlaufen **fächerförmig von einem signifikantem Hoch- oder Tiefpunkt**. Ihre Lage wird errechnet, indem der „Preisraum", **also die betragsmäßige Differenz der zwei letzten entgegengesetzten Extrempunkte, durch die Zahl 8 dividiert** wird. Die wichtigste Linie ist dabei die 1/1-Linie (Bedeutung: eine Zeiteinheit je eine Preiseinheit) mit einem Winkel von 45% von einem Gipfel oder Boden. Nach Gann werden diese Linien als „1/8"-Linie (82,5°), „2/8"-Linie (75°) etc. bis zur „8/8"-Linie bzw. „8/1"-Linie (7,5°), „8/2" (15°) Linie usw. bezeichnet. Die höchste Aussagekraft sollen dabei die Linien 3/8, 4/8 und 5/8 besitzen, die an Fibonacci-Zahlen bzw. den „Goldenen Schnitt" erinnern. Insgesamt gibt es neun verschiedene Gann-Linien.

Im engeren Sinne gibt es vier Arten von Gann-Linien:

● **Gann-Linien aus der Teilung der Preisspanne zwischen dem höchsten und dem tiefsten Preis einer Bewegung:** Dies sind die bekanntesten Gann-Linien. Man teilt die letzte Bewegung gemäß obigem Schema prozentual in die entsprechenden Widerstands- und Unterstützungslinien.

● **Gann-Linien aus dem höchsten Preis:** Hier wird der höchste Preis nach dem obigen Schema aufgeteilt. Der Durchbruch durch die 1/8- bzw. die 7/8-Linie ist vor allem bei Rohstoffen ein sicheres Erkennungszeichen für eine längere Baisse, umso sicherer, je höher der Preis zuvor war, also Gipfel minus 1/8 dieses Preises.

- **Gann Angles from the division of the "price field" between the historical price minimum and price maximum of the market:** Gann considered these resistance- and support levels to be more important. So here you need to take the historical values to make accurate statements.
- **Gann Angles of historical movements, if they have taken more than a year:** You also work here with historical values, these values are particularly relevant in commodities.

As Gann lines in the broad sense, are also called two other groups of resistance- and supporprt levels, as they are also used by Gann:

- Gann lines based on historical small peaks and bottoms: The division into eights is usually performed only in a larger movement. This was also true for the above mentioned division into eights of the „price field", which always returns to the last major movement. For smaller movements in each case the levels of peaks and bottoms are used as support, as it is common practice.
- Various special lines emanating partly from the price, but by the time: Gann constructed with different rules a number of other resistance- and support levels.

Therefore Gann assumed that the ratio „price" to „time period" (day, week, month, year) is constant. Here is the rule that at a consilience of price and time, a change of the trend must be imminent. The construction of the Gann Angles is done by plotting certain time-cost ratios as a line in a chart.

Gann defined time as a major factor of future price movement and successful trading. Gann's price concept allows price forecasts, if the time factor signalizes a turning point. He divides the market into price zones based on major-, medium- and minor highs and -lows.

The Gann trader only watches the Gann angles as progressive supports and resistances. If the rate falls below a Gann angle, one would expect a drop onto the next lower Gann angle. If the rate rises above a Gann angle, one would expect a rise to the next higher Gann angle.

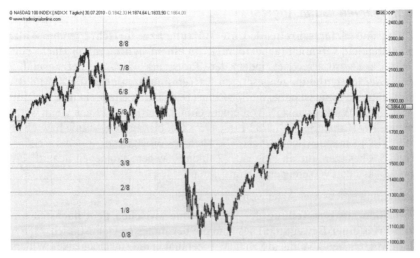

Gann Angles in Nasdaq

- **Gann-Linien aus der Teilung des „Preisraumes" zwischen dem historischen Tiefst- und Höchstpunkt des Marktes:** Gann hielt diese Widerstands- und Unterstützungslinien für wichtiger. Man benötigt hier also die historischen Werte um exakte Aussagen treffen zu können
- **Gann-Linien aus historischen Bewegungen, wenn diese mehr als ein Jahr gedauert haben:** Auch hier arbeitet man mit historischen Werten, besonders relevant sind diese Werte bei Rohstoffen.

Als Gann-Linien im weiteren Sinne kann man zwei weitere Gruppen von Widerstands- und Unterstützungslinien bezeichnen, da diese auch bei Gann Verwendung fanden:

- **Gann-Linien ausgehend von kleineren historischen Gipfeln und Böden:** Das Achteln wird normalerweise nur bei einer größeren Bewegung vorgenommen. Dies galt auch für das oben erwähnte Achteln des „Preisraumes", welches immer auf die letzte größere Bewegung zurückgeht. Bei kleineren Bewegungen werden jeweils die Niveaus der Gipfel und Böden als Unterstützung verwendet, so wie dies allgemein üblich ist.
- **Diverse Spezial-Linien, die teilweise nicht vom Preis, sondern von der Zeit ausgehen:** Gann konstruierte mit verschiedenen Regeln noch eine Reihe von anderen Widerstands- und Unterstützungslinien.

Gann unterstellte also, dass das Verhältnis „Preis" zu „Zeitraum" (Tag, Woche, Monat, Jahr) konstant ist. Dabei gilt, dass bei einem Zusammentreffen von Preis und Zeit eine Veränderung des Trends unmittelbar bevorstehen muss. Die Konstruktion der Gann-Linien erfolgt, indem bestimmte Zeit-Preis-Verhältnisse als Linie in ein Chart eingezeichnet werden.

Gann bestimmte Zeit als wesentlichen Faktor der zukünftigen Kursbewegung und erfolgreichen Handelns. Ganns Preis-Konzept erlaubt Kursprognosen, wenn der Zeitfaktor einen Wendepunkt signalisiert. Er unterteilt den Markt in Preiszonen, basierend auf Haupt-, Mittel- und Nebenhochs und -tiefs.

Der Gann-Trader achtet ausschließlich auf die Gann-Linien, als fortschreitende Unterstützungen und Widerstände. So ist nach dem Unterschreiten einer Gann-Linie mit einem Rückfall auf die nächste Gann-Linie zu rechnen und analog mit einem Überschreiten einer Gann-Linie ein Anstieg auf die nächstfolgende zu erwarten.

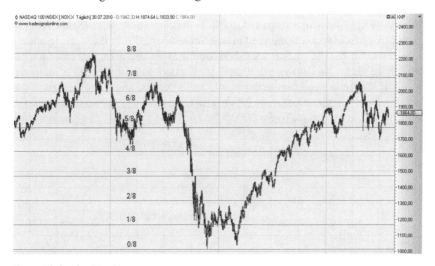

Gann-Linien im Nasdaq

As there is no reasonable explanation for the functioning of the Gann angles and no standard method for choosing time and price units, the approach has been seriously questioned and you will hardly ever find this kind of analysis in practice.

For drawing the Gann Angles you should proceed in the following way:

An upward trend angle is drawn upwards from the annual low. The opposite, the downward trend angle, is drawn downwards from the annual high.

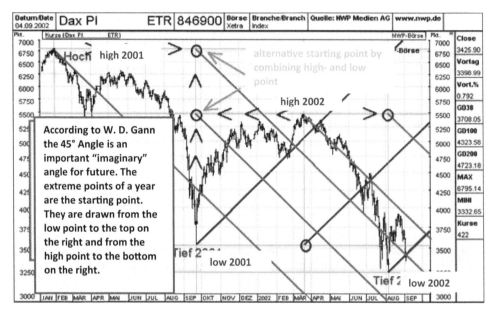

This chart shows on the example of DAX the above mentioned procedure. From the high in January 2001, a downward trend angle was drawn, which acted in the next two months as a resistance. In September of the same year, when there was a world-wide crash, this angle has been deceeded only for a few weeks despite massive stock price losses. Afterwards a new upward trend followed. The marked low in September 2001 is the starting point for the 45° Angle. It shows that the stock prices stabalised nearly exactly on this imaginary angle.

Furthermore Gann has shown additional application possibilities by combining high- and low points. Therefore you draw a horizontal and a vertical angle at the extreme points of each year. Where the angles cross, new 45° Angles are drawn. As shown in the turbulent price movements of the second half-year 2002 a Gann Angle has acted as big support in June.

Da es keine logische Erklärung für das Funktionieren der Gann-Linien und keine Standard-methode für die Auswahl der verwendeten Preis- und Zeiteinheiten gibt, ist diese Art der Devisenkursprognose in der Praxis eher selten und umstritten.

Beispiel
Bei der Einzeichnung der Gann-Linien wird folgendermaßen vorgegangen:
Eine Aufwärtstrendlinie wird vom Jahrestief nach oben eingezeichnet. Das Gegenstück, die Abwärtstrendlinie, wird vom Jahreshoch nach unten gezogen.

Dieses Chart zeigt am Beispiel des DAX die oben erläuterte Vorgangsweise. Vom Hoch im Januar 2001 wurde eine Abwärtslinie gezogen, die in den beiden nächsten Monaten als Wi-derstand fungierte. Im September des gleichen Jahres, als es weltweit zum Crash kam, wur-de eben diese Linie trotz massiver Kursverluste nur einige Wochen unterschritten. Danach folgte ein neuer Aufwärtstrend. Das im September 2001 markierte Tief dient als Startpunkt für die hochlaufende 45°-Linie. Und wie sich zeigt, fanden die Kurse im Februar 2002 fast genau auf dieser imaginären Linie Halt.

Gann hat zudem noch weitere Einsatzmöglichkeiten aufgezeigt, indem er Hoch- und Tiefpunkte kombinierte. Dabei zieht man eine waagerechte und eine senkrechte Linie an den Extremkursen der einzelnen Jahre. Wo sich diese Linien kreuzen, werden neue 45°-Li-nien eingezeichnet. Und wie sich zeigt hat in den turbulenten Kursbewegungen des zweiten Halbjahres 2002 wieder eine Gann-Linie im Juni als große Unterstützung gedient.

3.3. Numerical Models

Till now we have not distinguished between forecasting, interpretation and the actual trading strategy. But numerical models demand more accuracy. First, we discuss methods (trend chasing systems and anti-cyclical systems) that aim to pursue a particular trading strategy. In this case, particular price behaviour is assumed. Only in the section on time series analysis will we be dealing with forecasting.

The great advantage of numerical models is the necessity to **systemize and to formalize**. These requirements force you to describe the presumed and factual relations on financial markets in detail and to understand your own trading strategies.

If you have found a mathematical formula it is easier to check the ideas and strategies by applying them to past situations. Furthermore, simulations can be carried out and strategies can be optimised.

3.3.1. Trend Chasing Systems

Typical mathematical trend chasing systems are **Moving Averages**. Moving Averages are rather simple instruments that serve as the basis for more sophisticated methods. If you plot in a line chart on the price axis averages of the previous days instead of the daily quotes you get a new line that resembles the original chart but is a little smoother and has a time lag. The longer the average (i.e. the more data is used) the smoother the line and the bigger is the time lag.

Example

Moving Average

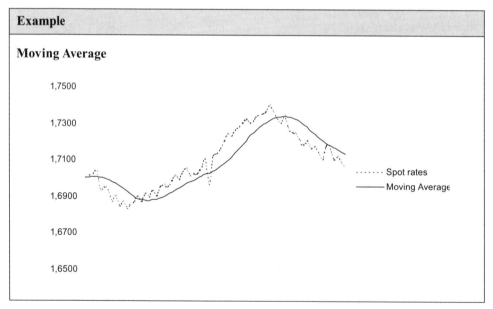

3.3. Mathematische Verfahren

Wurde bisher zwischen der Prognose, ihrer Interpretation und einer tatsächlichen Handelsstrategie nicht unterschieden, so zwingt der mathematische Ansatz hier dazu, genauer zu differenzieren. So werden zunächst Verfahren vorgestellt („Trendfolgesysteme" und „antizyklische Systeme"), deren Ziel es ist, eine bestimmte Handelsstrategie zu verfolgen. Dabei wird für die Zukunft eher ein bestimmtes Kursverhalten unterstellt, nicht aber prognostiziert. Auf eigentliche Prognosen geht ausschließlich der Abschnitt „Zeitreihenanalysen" ein.

Wesentlicher Vorteil aller mathematischen Verfahren ist die **Systematisierung und Formalisierung.** Um diese zu erreichen, ist es notwendig, die vermuteten oder tatsächlich bekannten Finanzmarktzusammenhänge genau zu beschreiben und die Strategien des eigenen Handels selbst zu verstehen.

Eine mathematische Formulierung ermöglicht die Überprüfung der Ideen oder Strategien für Situationen der Vergangenheit. Mit ihrer Hilfe können Strategien optimiert werden.

3.3.1. Trendfolgesysteme

Typische mathematische Trendfolgesysteme sind **gleitende Durchschnitte** (Moving Averages). Sie stellen zunächst einfache Komponenten dar, mit deren Hilfe auch komplexe Instrumente (z.B. MACDs) aufgebaut werden können. Man ordnet jedem Kurs eines Liniencharts den Durchschnitt (Mittelwert) der letzten Kurse (Länge des Durchschnitts) zu. Verbindet man diese Durchschnittswerte, so erhält man eine neue Linie, die der ursprünglichen Kurslinie ähnelt. Man stellt jedoch fest, dass die neue Linie geglättet erscheint und dem unterliegenden Kurs verzögert hinterherläuft. Glättung und Verzögerung werden stärker, wenn die Länge des Durchschnitts wächst.

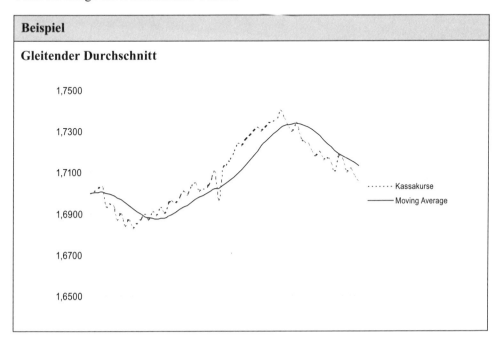

Beispiel

Gleitender Durchschnitt

The length of the average is appropriate if the price curve moves in an upward trend above the average and in a downward trend below the average. If the price crosses the moving average line from above, an upward trend has finished and a downward trend has begun. The reverse case is a signal for a starting bull market.

If trends shorten and the highs and lows change frequently, the time lag of moving averages can easily lead to a delayed signal. This is particularly true in sideways moving markets. Then, it can happen that trading strategies are executed if a new trend is already established. In an extreme case the investor buys always dearly and sells always cheaply.

To remedy this disadvantage, the concept of moving averages is adapted. Instead of looking at the position of price and moving average, one refers to the difference between price and moving average. The line generated by the difference between price and moving average fluctuates around the x-axis. This picture is called a **simple oscillator**.

Example

Oscillator

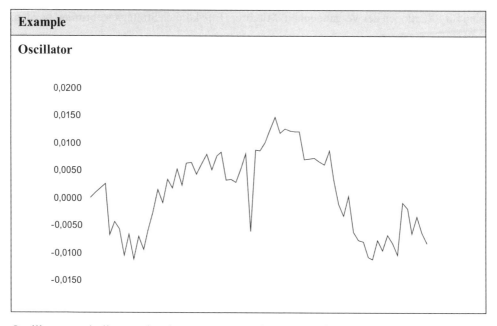

Oscillators are indicators that do **not react to price data**; rather they react to the changes in price data. Oscillators can have **positive or negative terms**. A positive difference indicates an upward trend, a negative difference a downward trend. The crossing of the x-axis denotes the trend reversal. A trading strategy based on this kind of oscillator resembles the corresponding **trading strategy based on moving averages**. Therefore, the time lag problem persists, i.e. trend reversals are shown too late. With the introduction of moving averages the significance of oscillators can be improved. This way a smoothed line follows the original curve. Now the crucial crossing is that of the moving average and not that of the x-axis.

Die Länge des Durchschnitts ist gut gewählt, wenn sich der Kurs in einem Aufwärts-trend oberhalb und in einem Abwärtstrend unterhalb der Durchschnittslinie bewegt. Schneidet der Kurs den Durchschnitt von oben nach unten, so ist der Aufwärtstrend been-det. Ein Abwärtstrend setzt ein. Durchstößt umgekehrt der Kurs die Linie der Mittelwerte von unten nach oben, so ist die Kursschwäche beendet und eine Hausse beginnt.

Verkürzen sich jedoch die Trendphasen, sodass Hoch- und Tiefpunkte des Kurses schnell aufeinanderfolgen, wie in seitwärtigen Märkten häufig der Fall, so kann der Verzögerungs-effekt der gleitenden Durchschnitte dazu führen, dass der Beginn zu spät erkannt wird. Die Handelsaktion wird vielleicht erst dann durchgeführt, wenn sich bereits der nächste (kurze) Trend etabliert hat. Im Extremfall kauft man dann stets teuer und verkauft billig.

Um diesen Nachteil zu beheben, betrachtet man zunächst folgende Abwandlung: Anstel-le der Lage von Kurs und Durchschnitt zueinander (Kurs liegt bei Aufwärtstrend über und bei Abwärtstrend unter dem zugeordneten Durchschnitt) betrachtet man ihre Differenz. So gelangt man zum **einfachen Oszillator.**

Beispiel

Einfacher Oszillator

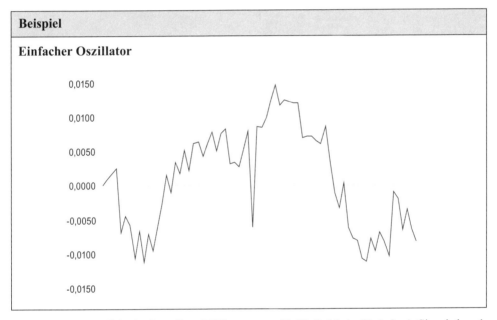

Im entstehenden Bild schwingt diese **Differenz um die Null-Linie (X-Achse).** Sie wird auch als einfacher Oszillator bezeichnet. Oszillatoren sind **Indikatoren, die nicht auf Kursda-ten selbst, sondern auf deren Veränderungen reagieren.** Der Oszillator kann positive und negative Werte annehmen. Ein **Aufwärtstrend** liegt vor, wenn dieser **Oszillator** (d.h. die Differenz) **positiv** ist, ein **Abwärtstrend,** wenn er **negativ** ist. Das **Überqueren der Null-Linie** beschreibt den **Trendwechsel.** Eine Handelsstrategie auf Basis eines solchen Oszil-lators entspricht exakt der auf Basis des zugehörigen gleitenden Durchschnitts. Der Makel der zeitlichen Verzögerung bleibt allerdings bestehen, d.h., der einfache Oszillator signali-siert die Trendumkehr zu spät. Die Idee einer Verbesserung besteht darin, nicht den Schnitt mit der Null-Linie als Kriterium für eine Trendwende zu benutzen. Stattdessen ordnet man dem einfachen Oszillator wieder einen gleitenden Durchschnitt zu, also eine Linie, die der ursprünglichen Kurve in geglätteter Form folgt. Das Ergebnis ist das **MACD.**

Example

MACD (Moving Average Convergence Divergence)

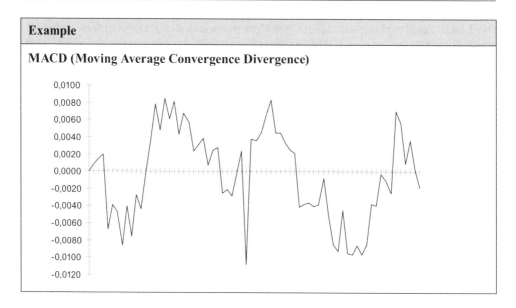

The basic idea behind MACD is that the oscillator cuts its own average rather than the x-axis.

Usually, the **difference between the 26-day and 12-day moving averages** is calculated, although these parameters can be altered. A **positive MACD** indicates the **12-day average is above the 26-day average** and points towards a **positive trend**.

Besides the variations based on moving averages, many other systems can be developed and are used in practice.

Among others, **oscillators are employed in combination with anti-cyclical systems** such as momentum and RSI of Welles Wilder.

3.3.2. Anti-cyclical Systems

Contrary to trend chasing systems, anti-cyclical systems refer to **exchange rate changes** rather than absolute exchange rates. Major anti-cyclical systems are:

- Momentum
- Relative Strength Index (RSI)

Momentum

The term momentum denotes the **absolute change between two exchange rate quotes within a fixed time interval** (e.g. price movements over the last 10 days).

The momentum is plotted in a chart where time is on the x-axis and price changes are on the y-axis. Linking the momentum points generates the **momentum curve**. If the individual opinion of the future price movements corresponds to the interpretation from the momen-

---

Beispiel

MACD (Moving Average Convergence Divergence)

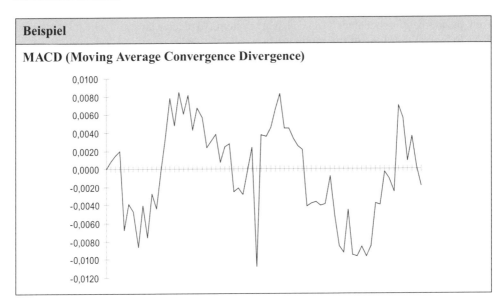

Die Grundidee des MACD besteht darin, dass der Oszillator seinen eigenen Durchschnitt in der Regel eher schneidet als die Null-Linie.

In der Regel wird beim MACD die **Differenz zwischen den gleitenden 26-Tages und 12-Tages Durchschnitten** betrachtet, wobei diese Parameter natürlich grundsätzlich auch anders gewählt werden können. Ein **positiver MACD** bedeutet, dass der **12-Tages Durchschnitt über dem 26-Tages Durchschnitt** liegt, und deutet auf einen **Aufwärtstrend** hin.

Neben den hier geschilderten Möglichkeiten der Abwandlung eines einfachen Systems, das auf einem gleitenden Durchschnitt basiert, sind noch viele andere denkbar und werden diese in der Praxis auch benutzt.

Unter anderem werden **Oszillatoren im Zusammenhang mit antizyklischen Systemen verwendet,** z.B. Momentum und RSI nach Welles Wilder.

3.3.2. Antizyklische Systeme

Im Gegensatz zu den Trendfolgesystemen beziehen sich antizyklische Systeme nicht auf den Devisenkurs selbst, sondern auf seine **Veränderungen.** Zu den bekanntesten antizyklischen Systemen gehören:

- das Momentum
- der Relative-Stärke-Index (RSI)

Momentum

Der Begriff Momentum bezeichnet die **absolute Veränderung zweier Devisenkurse mit einem festgelegten zeitlichen Abstand** (z.B. Kursänderung über die letzten zehn Tage).

Das Momentum wird in einen eigenen Chart eingezeichnet. Auf der Abszisse trägt der Analyst die Zeit, auf der Ordinate die Devisenkursänderung ein. Durch Verbindung der einzelnen Momentumpunkte entsteht die **Momentumkurve.** Folgt auch die Einschätzung des zukünftigen Kursverhaltens dieser Interpretation (d.h. Aufwärtstrend für positives Momentum, Abwärtstrend für negatives Momentum), so wird aus dem Momentum ein Trendfolge-

tum, the momentum becomes a trend chasing system. To receive an anti-cyclical system you have to look at the **slope of the momentum**.

Interpretations of the momentum

Momentum	Interpretation
> 0	Exchange rate rose
= 0	Exchange rate did not change
< 0	Exchange rate fell

Example

Momentum curve

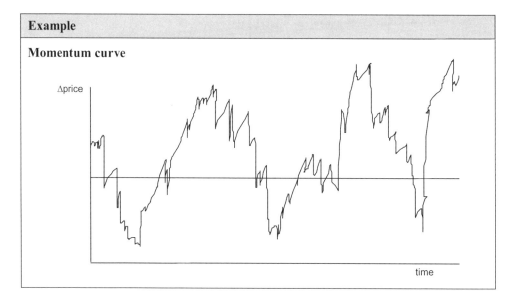

Momentum curves **indicate trend reversals very early**. If the momentum is positive (negative), the momentum curve falls (rises) even before the top (bottom) has been reached. The momentum should not be used as single trend indicator because it is prone to send wrong trading signals. Used **in conjunction with other forecasting methods** (e.g. moving averages) the momentum can be very useful as leading indicator.

Relative Strength Indicator of Welles Wilder

The Relative Strength Indicator is derived from an exchange rate comparison. Contrary to the momentum, the RSI **compares many different exchange rate quotes**. Moreover, the RSI **lies always between 0 and 1**.

The RSI is a ratio calculated by **dividing the average price increases by the average price decreases of the same period**. It is crucial to keep the time period between the compared prices constant (e.g. one day, one hour).

system. Um zu einem antizyklischen System zu gelangen, betrachtet man das **Steigungs-verhalten des Momentums** selbst.

Interpretationen des Momentums

Momentum	Interpretation
> 0	Der Devisenkurs ist gestiegen.
= 0	Der Devisenkurs hat sich nicht verändert.
< 0	Der Devisenkurs ist gefallen.

Beispiel

Momentumkurve

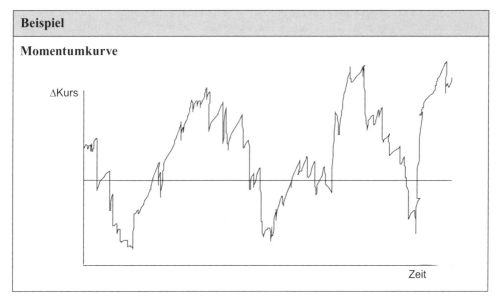

Die Momentumkurve **weist sehr früh auf Trendänderungen hin.** Bei einem positiven (negativen) Momentum fällt (steigt) die Momentumkurve schon bevor die Kurslinie ihren Hochpunkt (Tiefpunkt) erreicht hat. Als alleinige Trendindikatoren eignen sich Momentumkurven dennoch nicht, weil viele zum Teil unzutreffende Handelssignale ausgelöst werden. Momentumkurven können Prognosen jedoch gut unterstützen, wenn sie **in Verbindung mit einem anderen Verfahren** (z.B. gleitender Durchschnitt) eingesetzt werden.

Relative-Stärke-Index nach Welles Wilder

Der Relative-Stärke-Index (RSI) liefert eine Kennzahl, die aus einem Devisenkursvergleich resultiert. Im Unterschied zum Momentum werden jedoch nicht zwei Devisenkurse, sondern eine **Vielzahl von Kursänderungen miteinander verglichen.** Zudem nimmt ein RSI **ausschließlich Werte zwischen 0 und 1** an.

Die Werte des RSI werden durch die **Zerlegung eines Zeitraumes festgelegter Länge in Teilperioden** (z.B. Zeitraum = Monat, Teilperioden = Tage) gewonnen. Dann sind die in den Teilperioden ermittelten Kursgewinne und -verluste getrennt zu betrachten. So kann ein durchschnittlicher Kursgewinn und Kursverlust berechnet werden.

Die beiden Durchschnitte werden dann miteinander verglichen und mathematisch zum RSI-Wert umgeformt.

Interpretation of RSI values:

RSI	Interpretation
< 0.5	The average profit (profit per sub period) of the term was lower than the average loss.
= 0.5	The average profit (profit per sub period) of the term equalled the average loss.
> 0.5	The average profit (profit per sub period) of the term was higher than the average loss.

The RSI values are plotted periodically into the RSI Chart and the points are joined. The RSI is often quoted in **per cent**. Therefore, it takes on values between 0% and 100%.

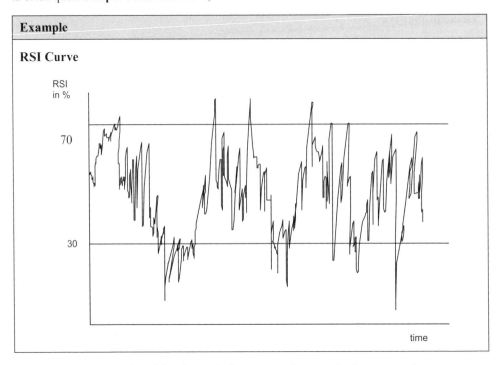

Example

RSI Curve

RSI values between 0.3 and 0.7 do not indicate a trend reversal whereas results

- lower than 0.3 or
- higher than 0.7

indicate consolidation and herald a trend reversal.

If the RSI is higher than 0.7 the currency market is said to be **"overbought"**. If the RSI is lower than 0.3 the market is said to be **"oversold"**.

Interpretation der RSI-Werte:

RSI	Interpretation
< 0,5	Der durchschnittliche Kursgewinn (Gewinn pro Teilperiode) des vergangenen Zeitraums war geringer als der durchschnittliche Kursverlust.
= 0,5	Der durchschnittliche Kursgewinn des vorhergehenden Zeitraums entsprach dem durchschnittlichen Kursverlust.
> 0,5	Der Kursgewinn des vergangenen Zeitraums war im Durchschnitt höher als der durchschnittliche Kursverlust.

Beim RSI-Chart werden die RSI-Werte periodisch eingetragen und die einzelnen Punkte miteinander verbunden. Der RSI ist häufig als **Prozentwert** angegeben. Das bedeutet, dass er zwischen 0% und 100% liegen wird.

Beispiel

RSI-Kurve

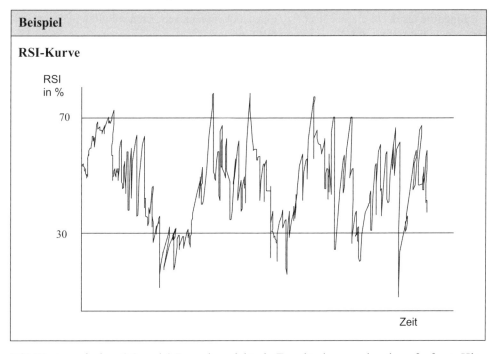

RSI-Werte zwischen 0,3 und 0,7 werden nicht als Trendänderungssignale aufgefasst. Hingegen indizieren Werte

- kleiner als 0,3 oder
- größer als 0,7

eine Konsolidierungsphase und lassen eine Trendumkehr erwarten.

Nimmt der RSI einen Wert größer als 0,7 an, dann spricht man von einem **„überkauften" Devisenmarkt (Overbought-Bereich).** Im Falle von RSI-Werten kleiner als 0,3 liegt dagegen ein **„überverkaufter" Markt (Oversold-Bereich)** vor.

3.3.3. Time Series Analysis

Time series analysis is a broad field in mathematics and statistics. A time series can simply be described as being the sequence of values pertaining to certain dates. A statistician then defines a **"stochastic process"**. A series of daily exchange rates is for him an outcome of the stochastic process.

The statistician aims to develop a mathematical model that can describe the stochastic process. If the description is also valid for the future one can also forecast the realizations. A time series analyst divides a time series into **three components**:

- trend
- cycle
- chance

His analyses focus on the exact identification and analysis of these components.

Since the results of the scientific work have not yet received much attention in daily business we do not want to dwell further on this topic.

3.3.4. Innovative Approaches

The latest developments in technical analysis (since about 1990) are characterized by the use of innovative methods to analyse time series. They often differ from statistical methods although they are no less complex. Their **origin lies in science, particularly informatics and behaviourism**.

Neural Networks

With the help of neural networks neurobiologists tried to simulate their models of human learning, thinking and forgetting using computers. Neural networks learn, generalize, can be trained and even learn by heart. These attributes serve rather to emphasize the image of neural networks than to describe their real characteristics. Neural networks neither think nor are they intelligent. Rather they are a research area within the field of **"artificial intelligence"**.

Neural networks are employed by several banks to forecast exchange rates (Commerzbank, Landesbank Hessen-Thüringen, WestLB). They are fed with historic price data and change their inner structure according to the deviation of the forecast from the actual price. Thus a model describing the **relationship between historic and future prices** is created. A continuation of these relations makes forecasts possible.

3.3.3. Zeitreihenanalyse

Die Zeitreihenanalyse ist ein weites Betätigungsfeld der mathematischen Statistik. Wenn eine Zeitreihe eine Abfolge von Werten darstellt, die jeweils gewissen Zeitpunkten zugeordnet sind, dann definiert der Statistiker zunächst den theoretischen Begriff des **„stochastischen Prozesses"**. Bei einem stochastischen Prozess ändert sich ein bestimmter Wert (z.B. Devisenkurs) zufällig. Eine Devisenkursreihe der täglichen Praxis ist für ihn dann nur eine Realisation dieses Prozesses.

Das Ziel des Statistikers ist es, ein mathematisches Modell zu entwickeln, das den stochastischen Prozess beschreibt. Behält diese Beschreibung dann auch in der Zukunft ihre Gültigkeit, so ist man auch in der Lage, für die Realisation Prognosen zu erstellen. Auf seinem Weg zur Prognose versucht der Zeitreihenanalytiker, die beobachtbare Zeitreihe in **drei Komponenten** zu zerlegen:

- Trend
- Zyklen
- Zufallsanteile („Störungen")

Seine Untersuchungen richten sich auf die Identifizierung und die genaue Analyse dieser Komponenten.

Weil die Ergebnisse dieser wissenschaftlichen Arbeiten kaum Bedeutung im Alltag des Devisenhandels erhalten haben, soll an dieser Stelle nicht weiter auf die Zeitreihenanalyse eingegangen werden.

3.3.4. Innovative Verfahren

Die jüngsten Entwicklungen im Bereich der technischen Analyse (etwa seit 1990) sind durch den Einsatz innovativer Methoden zur Zeitreihenanalyse gekennzeichnet. Sie heben sich von den statistischen Verfahren oftmals deutlich ab, sind jedoch in der Regel nicht weniger komplex. Ihren **Ursprung** finden sie häufig **in den Naturwissenschaften, im Bereich der Lerntheorie und in der Informatik.**

Neuronale Netze

Mithilfe erster künstlicher neuronaler Netze haben Neurobiologen versucht, die aus ihrem eigenen Wissenschaftsbereich und aus der Lerntheorie erwachsenen Modelle des menschlichen Lernens, Denkens und Vergessens mithilfe eines Computers zu simulieren. Diese Herkunft der neuronalen Netze verraten heute noch die Begriffe, die in ihrem Zusammenhang gerne benutzt werden: Neuronale Netze „lernen", „verallgemeinern", können „trainiert werden" und sogar „auswendig lernen". Dennoch dienen solche Attribute eher dazu, das Bild eines neuronalen Netzes plakativer erscheinen zu lassen, als die realen Eigenschaften eines neuronalen Netzes zu beschreiben: Neuronale Netze denken nicht, und sie sind auch nicht intelligent. Sie sind vielmehr ein Forschungsgegenstand einer wissenschaftlichen Disziplin mit dem Namen **„Künstliche Intelligenz"**.

Neuronale Netze zur Devisenkursprognose sind bereits bei verschiedenen Finanzinstituten im Einsatz. Sie werden mit historischen Kursinformationen gefüttert, ändern ihre innere Struktur nach einer zuvor festgelegten Methode, indem Prognose (Soll) und tatsächlicher Wert (Ist) abgeglichen werden. Auf diese Weise liefern sie wieder ein **Modell für den Zusammenhang zwischen historischen und zukünftigen Werten.** Ein Fortdauern dieses Zusammenhangs ermöglicht Prognosen.

To classify neural networks as a method of technical analysis is not exactly correct. If neural networks forecast prices, they use time series from other markets (e.g. stock market, interest market...) in addition to the historic price data. This way, neural networks can be seen as a hybrid of fundamental and technical analysis, accordingly they are also labelled **"synergetic analysis"**.

Fractal Geometry

The basic idea behind fractal geometry is that structures that appear in general (e.g. chart patterns in a monthly chart) also appear in detail (e.g. in a daily chart). If the relations between these structures (general and detailed) can be mathematically expressed, then additional information concerning these structures can be received.

The **average change of a time series** is a good example. This is certainly bigger if the time series is based on monthly data and not on daily data. The relationship between the average changes can be described by the relationship between the corresponding periods (month and day). This description discloses further information about the changes in the time series.

The **forecasting system of the Swiss company Olsen & Associates**, Zurich, pays attention to this kind of idea. In combination with other considerations the time axis is transformed. Various numerical methods are applied to analyse the resulting price series (with non-linear time axis) and to get forecasts and trading signals. To use the result also in the real-time (linear!) context, a **retransformation of the time axis** is necessary. Several banks employ the forecasting systems of Olsen & Associates.

3.3.5. Pattern Recognition

Statistics and applied informatics are the origins of pattern recognition methods. Like the classic chart analysis it also tries to **recognize patterns and formations in the price movements**.

Chart analysis defines formations (triangles, head and shoulder formations) and their meaning in order to compare the current chart pattern with defined patterns. Pattern recognition looks first at the **current situation** and **compares the observations with similar events in the past**. These systems learn from historic situations for the future. However the employment of pattern recognition in foreign exchange trading seems to be almost non-existent.

Summary

Technical prediction methods are based solely on the observation and analysis of historical price movements.The methods of technical analysis can be divided in two groups: classical chart analysis (line and bar charts, candle charts, point & figure chart, Elliott Wave Theory, Gann Angles) and numerical methods (trend chasing systems such as moving average, MACD, anti-cyclical systems such as Momentum, RSI, time series analysis).

Die Zuordnung der neuronalen Netze zu den technischen Analysen ist jedoch nicht ganz korrekt. Ein neuronales Netz kann nicht nur mit den historischen Werten des zu prognostizierenden Kurses gefüttert werden, sondern auch mit Kursreihen anderer Märkte (Aktien, Zinsen etc.). Auf diese Weise können neuronale Netze als Mischform der fundamentalen und technischen Analyse auftreten, für die bereits der Begriff **„synergetische Analyse"** vorgeschlagen wurde.

Fraktale Geometrie

Ein Grundpfeiler der fraktalen Geometrie ist die Erkenntnis, dass Strukturen, die im Großen erkannt worden sind (z.B. Charts mit Monatswerten), im Kleinen ebenfalls auftauchen (z.B. Charts mit Tageswerten). Lässt sich das Verhältnis dieser Strukturen (aus „groß" und „klein") mathematisch beschreiben, so erhält man zusätzliche Informationen über diese Strukturen.

Als Beispiel betrachtet man die **mittlere Änderungsrate einer Kursreihe.** Für Monatswerte ist sie größer als beim Zugrundelegen von Tageswerten. Das Verhältnis der mittleren Änderungsraten zueinander kann durch das Verhältnis der zugehörigen Perioden (Monat bzw. Tag) beschrieben werden. Die Art dieser Beschreibung gibt weiteren Aufschluss darüber, wie sich die Änderungsraten von Kursreihen verteilen.

In die **Prognosesysteme der Schweizer Firma Olsen & Associates,** Zürich, fließen derartige Überlegungen ein. Sie führen im Verbund mit anderen Ansätzen zu einer **Transformation der Zeitachse.** Auf die daraus resultierende Kursreihe (mit nichtlinearer Zeitachse) werden schließlich mathematische Verfahren (Abwandlung gleitender Durchschnitte) angewandt, um Prognosen und Handelssignale zu erhalten. Um diese auch in der realen Zeit (linear!) umsetzen zu können, ist eine Rücktransformation der Zeitachse notwendig.

Die Prognosesysteme von Olsen & Associates werden bei verschiedenen Banken genutzt.

3.3.5. Mustererkennung

Die Verfahren der Mustererkennung entstammen in der Regel der Statistik oder der angewandten Informatik. Sie versuchen ähnlich wie bei der klassischen Chartanalyse **Muster oder Formationen im Kursverlauf zu erkennen.**

Der Weg wird jedoch umgekehrt beschritten: Die klassische Chartanalyse postuliert Formationen (Dreiecke, Kopf-Schulter-Formationen) und ihre Bedeutung, sodass die aktuelle Chartsituation mit den vorgegebenen Mustern verglichen wird. Die Mustererkennung betrachtet hingegen zunächst **die aktuelle Situation,** fixiert diese und **vergleicht** sie dann **mit „ähnlichen" Situationen der Vergangenheit.** Aus solchen historischen Situationen „lernen" diese Systeme für die Zukunft. Der Einsatz der Mustererkennung in der Praxis des Devisenhandels scheint jedoch noch nicht fortgeschritten zu sein.

Zusammenfassung

Technische Prognoseverfahren beruhen ausschließlich auf der Beobachtung und Analyse historischer Kursbewegungen. Die Verfahren der technischen Analyse lassen sich in zwei Gruppen einteilen: klassische Chartanalyse (Linien- und Balkenchartanalyse, Candle Charts, Point & Figure-Chart, Elliott-Wellen-Theorie, Gann-Linien) und mathematische Verfahren (Trendfolgesysteme wie gleitender Durchschnitt, MACD, antizyklische Systeme wie Momentum, RSI, statistische Zeitreihenanalyse).

Contrary to fundamental analysis, forecasting models of technical analysis are based on the observation of past exchange rates in order to arrive at conclusions about future exchange rate developments from past movements.

The latest developments in technical analysis are characterized by the use of innovative methods (neural networks, fractal geometry, pattern recognition) to analyse time series. Their origin lies in science, particularly information technology and behaviourism.

In a line chart the exchange rates for each time period are plotted in a diagram and the points are joined, prices on the y-axis, time on the x-axis.

In a bar chart the highs and lows of a foreign currency are plotted in a diagram and the points are joined with vertical lines (bars). A small horizontal line to the left of a bar denotes the opening level while a small horizontal line to the right represents the closing price of each interval.

Methods to determine a trend assume that trends tend to continue until something seriously happens to change the trend. By drawing lines that touch the peaks and troughs of the chart, trends can be made visible. This requires that the lines are tangent to all bars. Despite daily movements the development of foreign exchange rates can, in the long run, be interpreted as a system of overlapping trends of different lengths. According to the length of the trend one distinguishes three types of trends: primary trends, secondary trends and tertiary trends. If two parallel trend lines can be depicted in a chart and each of them is a tangent to either the peaks or the troughs, the formation is called a trend channel.

In the case of a support level, the exchange rate remains above the level for a considerable time, while a resistance level stops the upward trend of a currency.

A chart pattern is a typical repeating price pattern that can be shown in a chart. A major distinction is made between trend sustaining patterns and trend reversal patterns. Trend sustaining patterns confirm the continuation of the given trend. Trend sustaining patterns include triangles (wedges). Triangles are formed by two converging trend lines.

The best-known trend reversal pattern is the head and shoulders formation, which is similar to a head and two shoulders. It indicates a downward trend. It is formed by three upward movements and two downward movements.

In a point & figure chart crosses and circles symbolize changes of the exchange rate. A cross (x) denotes a rise in the exchange rate, a circle (o) a fall in the exchange rate. Point and Figure Charts eliminate time and show instead price against price reversals. The price is plotted on the y-axis, price reversals on the x-axis.

In a candle chart a broad bar depicts the price change between opening and closing price. The colour of the bar shows if the price closed lower (black, dark) or higher (white, light).

Im Gegensatz zur Fundamentalanalyse basieren die Prognoseansätze der technischen Devisenkursprognose auf der Beobachtung und Registrierung des Devisenkurses und ziehen aus dem bisherigen Kursverlauf Rückschlüsse auf zukünftige Kursausprägungen. Innovative Prognoseverfahren (künstliche neuronale Netze, fraktale Geometrie, Mustererkennung) sind in der Regel mathematische Verfahren. Sie basieren auf den Erkenntnissen der Informatik und der Lern- und Chaostheorie.

Bei einem Linienchart werden die Devisenkurse bestimmter Zeitpunkte in ein Diagramm eingetragen (Zeitachse/Kursachse) und die einzelnen Punkte miteinander verbunden.

Die Balkenchartanalyse ist eine Erweiterung der Linienchartanalyse. Hier werden der Höchst- und Tiefstkurs einer Währung für ein bestimmtes Zeitintervall in ein Koordinatensystem eingetragen. Beide Punkte werden mit einer vertikalen Linie (Balken) verbunden. Ein kleiner horizontaler Strich auf der linken Seite des Balkens kennzeichnet den Eröffnungskurs, auf der rechten Seite des Balkens bezeichnet er den Schlusskurs des jeweiligen Zeitintervalls.

Bei Verfahren zur Trendbestimmung geht man von der Annahme aus, dass ein Trend eine einmal eingeschlagene Richtung wahrscheinlich beibehält. Indem man Geraden an den Kursverlauf legt, werden Trends sichtbar. Dabei werden zwei Extrempunkte derselben Art (Tiefst- bzw. Höchstkurse) miteinander verbunden. Im Hinblick auf die Zeitdauer eines Trends unterscheidet man Haupttrends (Primärtrends), Sekundärtrends und Tertiärtrends. Können in einen Chart zwei parallel verlaufende Trendlinien eingezeichnet werden, eine oberhalb und die andere unterhalb der Balken, so liegt ein Trendkanal vor. Man spricht von einer Unterstützungslinie, wenn der Devisenkurs trotz mehrerer Abwärtsbewegungen ein gewisses Niveau nicht unterschreitet. Eine Widerstandslinie liegt vor, wenn der Kurs einen bestimmten Wert nicht überschreitet, obwohl er sich mehrmals aufwärts bewegt.

Unter einer Formation versteht man ein typisches, sich wiederholendes Kursbild, das in einen Chart gelegt wird. Man unterscheidet zwischen Trendbestätigungsformation und Trendumkehrformation. Trendbestätigungsformationen werden als Hinweis auf Bestätigung und Fortsetzung des bisherigen Trends aufgefasst. Zu dieser Gruppe von Formationen zählen die Dreiecksbilder (engl.: wedge).

Die bekannteste Trendumkehrfunktion ist die Kopf-Schulter-Formation. Sie ähnelt einem Kopf mit zwei Schultern. Sie deutet einen Abwärtstrend an. Im Gegensatz dazu existieren auch inverse Kopf-Schulter-Formationen, die einem Spiegelbild herkömmlicher Kopf-Schulter-Formationen gleichen. Sie signalisieren einen Aufwärtstrend.

Bei einem Point & Figure-Chart werden Veränderungen des Devisenkurses durch Kreuz- und Kreissymbole dargestellt. Ein Kreuz (x) repräsentiert einen Devisenkursanstieg, ein Kreis (o) dagegen einen Devisenkursrückgang. Die Ausprägungen des Devisenkurses sind auf der Ordinate eines Point & Figure-Diagramms eingetragen. Gleichartige Symbole werden unter- und übereinander angeordnet, sodass sie die Form einer Säule annehmen.

In Candle Charts werden Preisveränderungen zwischen dem Eröffnungskurs und dem Schlusskurs eines Zeitintervalls durch einen breiten Balken in einen Chart eingezeichnet. Die unterschiedlichen Farben des Balkens signalisieren, ob der Schlusskurs über oder unter dem Eröffnungskurs liegt.

Die Elliott-Wellen-Theorie basiert auf der Hypothese, dass der Devisenkursverlauf einer wellenförmigen Bewegung folgt, die sich ständig wiederholt und somit für Kurspro-

The Elliott Wave Theory assumes that exchange rates move in waves. These movements take place regularly and can be used for forecasting exchange rates. These assumptions are based on the natural behaviour of the market participants.

According to Elliott, prices move in eight waves, of which five are impulse waves and three are corrective waves. Elliott defined nine categories of cycles: grand supercycle (multi-century), supercycle (multi-decade), cycle (one year to several years), primary wave (a few months to a couple of years), intermediary wave (weeks to months), minor wave (weeks), minute wave (days), minuette wave (hours), subminuette wave (minutes).

The so-called Fibonacci numbers play an important role in the Elliott Wave Theory. Fibonacci numbers are a mathematical sequence that follows the natural law of the golden ratio. It means that if one term is divided by its successor the ratio tends towards 0.618.

Gann Angles can be interpreted as progressive support or resistance levels and are drawn ascending from price bottoms or descending from price tops in the form of a fan (Gann fan). The angles are drawn by dividing the "price field" (the difference between the two last opposite extreme points) by 8.

The main advantage of numerical models is the necessity to systemize and to formalize. Typical mathematical trend chasing systems are Moving Averages. Moving Averages are rather simple instruments that serve as the basis for more sophisticated methods. The length of the average is appropriate if the price curve moves in an upward trend above the average and in a downward trend below the average.

Instead of looking at the position of price and moving average, one refers to the difference between price and moving average. The line generated by the difference between price and moving average fluctuates around the x-axis. This picture is called a simple oscillator. Oscillators are indicators that do not react to price data; rather they react to the changes in price data. Oscillators can have positive or negative terms.

A positive difference indicates an upward trend, a negative difference a downward trend. The basic idea behind MACD is that the oscillator cuts its own average rather than the x-axis.

Usually, the difference between the 26-day and 12-day moving averages is calculated, although these parameters can be altered. A positive MACD indicates the 12-day average is above the 26-day average and points towards a positive trend.

Contrary to trend chasing systems, anti-cyclical systems refer to exchange rate changes rather than absolute exchange rates. Major anti-cyclical systems are momentum and Relative Strength Index (RSI).

The term momentum denotes the absolute change between two exchange rate quotes within a fixed time interval (eg, price movements over the last 10 days). The momentum is plotted in a chart where time is on the x-axis and price changes are on the y-axis. Linking the momentum points generates the momentum curve.

The Relative Strength Indicator is derived from an exchange rate comparison. Contrary to the momentum, the RSI compares many different exchange rate quotes. Moreover, the RSI lies always between 0 and 1.

Time series analysis is a broad field in mathematics and statistics. A time series can simply be described as being the sequence of values pertaining to certain dates. A statistician then defines a stochastic process. A series of daily exchange rates is then an outcome of the stochastic process.

gnosen verwendet werden kann. Diese Annahme ist auf die natürlichen Verhaltensweisen der Marktteilnehmer zurückzuführen. Die Kursbewegungen verlaufen nach Elliott in Form von acht Wellen. Die ersten fünf sind sogenannte Impulswellen. Die letzten drei bilden die sogenannten Korrekturwellen. Elliot selbst formulierte folgende neun Kategorien von Wellenbewegungen: Großer Superzyklus (über mehrere Jahrhunderte), Superzyklus (mehrere Jahrzehnte), Zyklus (ein bis mehrere Jahre), Primärwelle (einige Monate bis einige Jahre), Zwischenwelle (Wochen oder Monate), Miniwelle (Wochen), Minutenwelle (Tage), Minuettenwelle (Stunden) und Subminuettenwelle (Minuten).

Im Rahmen der Elliott-Wellen-Theorie haben die sogenannten Fibonacci-Zahlen eine besondere Bedeutung. Sie bilden eine Zahlenfolge, die dem Naturgesetz des Goldenen Schnitts (entspricht ca. der Zahl 1,618; Kehrwert entspricht ca. 0,618) gehorcht.

Die Gann-Linien sind als fortschreitende Unterstützung bzw. fortschreitender Widerstand zu interpretieren und verlaufen fächerförmig von einem signifikantem Hoch- oder Tiefpunkt. Ihre Lage wird errechnet, indem der „Preisraum", also die betragsmäßige Differenz der zwei letzten entgegengesetzten Extrempunkte, durch die Zahl 8 dividiert wird. Der wesentliche Vorteil aller mathematischen Verfahren ist die Systematisierung und Formalisierung.

Typische mathematische Trendfolgesysteme sind gleitende Durchschnitte (Moving Averages). Sie stellen zunächst einfache Komponenten dar, mit deren Hilfe auch komplexe Instrumente (z.B. MACDs) aufgebaut werden können.

Die Länge des Durchschnitts ist gut gewählt, wenn sich der Kurs in einem Aufwärtstrend oberhalb und in einem Abwärtstrend unterhalb der Durchschnittslinie bewegt.

Wenn man anstelle der Lage von Kurs und Durchschnitt zueinander ihre Differenz betrachtet, gelangt man zum einfachen Oszillator. Oszillatoren sind Indikatoren, die nicht auf Kursdaten selbst, sondern auf deren Veränderungen reagieren. Der Oszillator kann positive und negative Werte annehmen. Ein Aufwärtstrend liegt vor, wenn dieser Oszillator (d.h. die Differenz) positiv ist, ein Abwärtstrend, wenn er negativ ist.

Die Grundidee des MACD besteht darin, dass der Oszillator seinen eigenen Durchschnitt in der Regel eher schneidet als die Null-Linie. In der Regel wird beim MACD die Differenz zwischen den gleitenden 26-Tages und 12-Tages Durchschnitten betrachtet, wobei diese Parameter natürlich grundsätzlich auch anders gewählt werden können. Ein positiver MACD bedeutet, dass der 12-Tages Durchschnitt über dem 26-Tages Durchschnitt liegt, und deutet auf einen Aufwärtstrend hin.

Im Gegensatz zu den Trendfolgesystemen beziehen sich antizyklische Systeme nicht auf den Devisenkurs selbst, sondern auf seine Veränderungen. Zu den bekanntesten antizyklischen Systemen gehören das Momentum und der Relative-Stärke-Index (RSI).

Der Begriff Momentum bezeichnet die absolute Veränderung zweier Devisenkurse mit einem festgelegten zeitlichen Abstand (z.B. Kursänderung über die letzten zehn Tage). Das Momentum wird in einen eigenen Chart eingezeichnet. Auf der Abszisse trägt der Analyst die Zeit, auf der Ordinate die Devisenkursänderung ein. Durch die Verbindung der einzelnen Momentumpunkte entsteht die Momentumkurve.

Der Relative-Stärke-Index (RSI) liefert eine Kennzahl, die aus einem Devisenkursvergleich resultiert. Im Unterschied zum Momentum werden jedoch nicht zwei Devisenkurse, sondern eine Vielzahl von Kursänderungen miteinander verglichen. Zudem nimmt ein RSI ausschließlich Werte zwischen 0 und 1 an.

Innovative approaches have their origin in science, particularly information technology and behaviourism. Neural networks are employed by several banks to forecast exchange rates (Commerzbank, Landesbank Hessen-Thüringen, WestLB). They are fed with historic price data and change their inner structure according to the deviation of the forecast from the actual price. Thus a model describing the relationship between historic and future prices is created. A continuation of these relations makes forecasts possible.

The basic idea behind fractal geometry is that structures that appear in general (eg, chart patterns in a monthly chart) also appear in detail (eg, in a daily chart). If the relations between these structures (general and detailed) can be mathematically expressed, then additional information concerning these structures can be gleaned.

Statistics and applied informatics are the origins of pattern recognition methods. Like the classic chart analysis it also tries to recognize patterns and formations in the price movements.

3.4. Practice Questions

1. Into which two categories can one divide the methods of technical analysis? Give three examples each!
2. What are the differences between fundamental analysis and technical analysis?
3. How is a trend channel created?
   a) by a trend reversal
   b) by parallel tangents along the highs and lows
   c) by two arbitrarily placed parallel trend lines
   d) by tangents with different slopes along the highs and lows
4. Which statement is true regarding bar charts?
   a) The bars are coloured differently according to their size.
   b) A horizontal tick is drawn on the left for the closing price.
   c) A horizontal tick is drawn on the left for the opening price.
   d) A horizontal tick is drawn on the right for the closing price.

Die Zeitreihenanalyse ist ein weites Betätigungsfeld der mathematischen Statistik. Wenn eine Zeitreihe eine Abfolge von Werten darstellt, die jeweils gewissen Zeitpunkten zugeordnet sind, dann definiert der Statistiker zunächst den theoretischen Begriff des „stochastischen Prozesses". Bei einem stochastischen Prozess ändert sich ein bestimmter Wert (z.B. Devisenkurs) zufällig.

Innovative Verfahren finden Ihren Ursprung häufig in den Naturwissenschaften, im Bereich der Lerntheorie und in der Informatik.

Neuronale Netze zur Devisenkursprognose sind bereits bei verschiedenen Finanzinstituten im Einsatz. Sie werden mit historischen Kursinformationen gefüttert, ändern ihre innere Struktur nach einer zuvor festgelegten Methode, indem Prognose (Soll) und tatsächlicher Wert (Ist) abgeglichen werden. Auf diese Weise liefern sie wieder ein Modell für den Zusammenhang zwischen historischen und zukünftigen Werten. Ein Fortdauern dieses Zusammenhangs ermöglicht Prognosen.

Ein Grundpfeiler der fraktalen Geometrie ist die Erkenntnis, dass Strukturen, die im Großen erkannt worden sind (z.B. Charts mit Monatswerten), im Kleinen ebenfalls auftauchen (z.B. Charts mit Tageswerten). Lässt sich das Verhältnis dieser Strukturen (aus „groß" und „klein") mathematisch beschreiben, so erhält man zusätzliche Informationen über diese Strukturen.

Die Verfahren der Mustererkennung entstammen in der Regel der Statistik oder der angewandten Informatik. Sie versuchen ähnlich wie bei der klassischen Chartanalyse, Muster oder Formationen im Kursverlauf zu erkennen.

3.4. Wiederholungsfragen

1. In welche zwei Gruppen lassen sich die Verfahren der technischen Analyse einteilen? Geben Sie jeweils drei Beispiele!
2. Welche Unterschiede gibt es zwischen fundamentaler Analyse und technischer Analyse?
3. Wie entsteht ein Trendkanal?
   a) durch eine Trendumkehr
   b) durch parallele Tangenten an Höchst- und Tiefstkursen
   c) durch zwei willkürlich gelegte, parallele Tangenten
   d) durch Tangenten mit unterschiedlichem Anstieg, die an Höchst- und Tiefstkurse gelegt werden.
4. Was trifft auf das Balkenchart zu?
   a) Der Balken wird je nach Größe unterschiedlich gefärbt.
   b) Für den Schlusskurs wird auf der linken Seite ein kleiner horizontaler Strich eingezeichnet.
   c) Für den Anfangskurs wird auf der linken Seite ein kleiner horizontaler Strich eingezeichnet.
   d) Für den Schlusskurs wird auf der rechten Seite ein kleiner horizontaler Strich eingezeichnet.

5. In the chosen interval you have observed the following price movements: open: 1.25; increase to: 1.35; fall to: 1.23; increase to: 1.50; fall to: 1.40; increase to: 1.45; close: 1.27. Which of these prices would you plot in a bar chart?
   a) 1.23
   b) 1.35
   c) 1.30
   d) 1.50
   e) 1.27
   f) 1.40
   g) 1.25
6. Which of the following is true regarding line charts?
   a) They are time-independent.
   b) They show patterns within the time interval.
   c) They only show one rate per interval.
   d) They show the lows of an interval.
7. What does a point & figure chart plot?
   a) daily price changes against time
   b) price against price reversals
   c) semi-logarithmic price against time
   d) closing price against time
8. USD/CHF falls to 1.4500 several times without breaking below it. What is the term used for this level?
   a) a resistance level for USD
   b) a double bottom
   c) a support level for CHF
   d) a support level for USD
9. What is a support level?
   a) a chart point above the current market
   b) a good level to sell dear
   c) a chart point where supply is anticipated
   d) a level below the current market price where buyers are anticipated
10. What does a double bottom usually indicate in chart analysis?
    a) a gradual flattening of a currently rising trend
    b) a trend reversal from a falling to a rising market
    c) a gradual flattening of a currently falling trend
    d) a trend reversal from a rising to a falling market
11. Which of the following statements about triangles (wedges) is NOT true?
    a) They are trend reversal patterns.
    b) They are trend confirmation patterns.
    c) They can be ascending or descending.
    d) They are created by tangents to high and low prices.
12. What is a Doji pattern?
    a) a square candle
    b) a candle which forms a horizontal line
    c) a candle in which the opening price and the low price are the same
    d) a candle in which the closing price and the peak price are the same

5. Sie haben im gewählten Zeitintervall folgende Kursentwicklungen beobachtet: Anfangs-kurs: 1,25; Kursanstieg auf 1,35; Kurs fällt auf 1,23; Kurs steigt auf 1,50; Kurs fällt auf 1,40; Kurs steigt auf 1,45; Kurs schließt bei 1,27. Welche Werte tragen Sie in das Balken-chart ein?
   a) 1,23
   b) 1,35
   c) 1,30
   d) 1,50
   e) 1,27
   f) 1,40
   g) 1,25

6. Was trifft auf Liniencharts zu?
   a) Sie sind zeitunabhängig.
   b) Sie zeigen Kursmuster innerhalb des Zeitintervalls.
   c) Sie weisen einem Zeitintervall nur einen Kurs zu.
   d) Sie zeigen Tiefstkurse eines Intervalles an.

7. Was bildet ein Point & Figure-Chart ab?
   a) tägliche Preisänderungen gegen die Zeit
   b) Preis gegen Preisrichtungsänderungen
   c) logarithmierte Preise gegen die Zeit
   d) den Schlusspreis gegen die Zeit

8. Wie nennt man das Niveau, wenn der USD/CHF-Kurs mehrere Male auf 1,4500 fällt, ohne diese Marke zu durchbrechen?
   a) eine Widerstandslinie für den USD
   b) ein Doppeltief
   c) eine Unterstützungslinie für den Schweizer Franken
   d) eine Unterstützungslinie für den USD

9. Was ist ein Unterstützungsniveau?
   a) ein Chartpunkt über dem aktuellen Marktniveau
   b) ein Niveau, um teuer zu verkaufen
   c) ein Chartpunkt, wo Angebot erwartet wird
   d) ein Niveau unter dem aktuellen Marktpreis, wo Käufer erwartet werden

10. Was bedeutet ein Doppelboden in der Chartanalyse?
    a) allmähliche Abflachung eines aktuellen Aufwärtstrends
    b) Wechsel von einem fallenden in einen steigenden Markt
    c) allmähliche Abflachung eines aktuellen Abwärtstrends
    d) Wechsel von einem steigenden in einen fallenden Markt

11. Welche Aussage können die bei Dreiecksformationen (Wedges) ausschließen?
    a) Sie sind Trendumkehrformationen.
    b) Sie sind Trendbestätigungsformationen.
    c) Sie können aufsteigend und absteigend sein.
    d) Sie entstehen durch Tangenten and Höchst- und Tiefstpunkten.

12. Was ist eine Doji-Formation?
    a) ein quadratischer Kerzenkörper
    b) ein Kerzenkörper, der aus einer waagrechten Linie besteht
    c) ein Kerzenkörper, bei dem Anfangskurs und Tiefstkurs zusammenfallen
    d) ein Kerzenkörper, bei dem Schlusskurs und Höchstkurs zusammenfallen

13. Which formation does not signal a trend reversal?
   a) Double Bottom
   b) Triangle
   c) Double Top
   d) Head and Shoulders

14. What does a head and shoulders combination show?
   a) three troughs and two peaks
   b) three peaks and two troughs
   c) four peaks and three troughs
   d) three peaks and four troughs

15. What is the principle behind the candlestick chart?
   a) The difference between the peak and low prices is coloured.
   b) The difference between the opening and closing prices is coloured.
   c) The difference between the closing and peak prices is coloured.
   d) All answers are false.

16. You see a downward trend in a candle chart. A black candle is followed by a white candle which embraces the black candle. What will you do?
   a) nothing
   b) wait
   c) go long in the market
   d) go short in the market

17. Which of the following statements is true according to the Elliot Wave Theory?
   a) It is impossible to forecast the length of waves.
   b) Prices are generally in a bear market.
   c) The most important aspect of price movements is the duration of each wave.
   d) The main patterns of price movements can be seen as five impulse waves followed by three corrective waves.

18. Which of the following are Fibonacci Retracement Levels?
   a) 50% and 75%
   b) 38.2% and 61.8%
   c) 25% and 50%
   d) 45.3% and 57.2%

19. What do oscillators indicate in technical analysis?
   a) trend
   b) volatility
   c) rising or falling wedge
   d) price momentum

20. What does a positive momentum indicate?
   a) a rising exchange rate
   b) a price peak
   c) a support level
   d) a change from upward trend to downward trend

21. Which of the following numbers is NOT important for RSI?
   a) 0.3
   b) 0.5
   c) 0.7
   d) 0.618

13. Welche Formationen stellen kein Signal für eine Trendumkehr dar?
    a) Double Bottom
    b) symmetrisches Dreieck
    c) Double Top
    d) Kopf-Schulter-Formation

14. Was zeigt eine Kopf-Schulter-Formation?
    a) drei Täler und zwei Spitzen
    b) drei Spitzen und zwei Täler
    c) vier Spitzen und drei Täler
    d) drei Spitzen und vier Täler

15. Auf welchem Prinzip beruhen Candle Charts?
    a) Die Differenz zwischen Höchst- und Tiefstkurs wird eingefärbt.
    b) Die Differenz zwischen Anfangs- und Schlusskurs wird eingefärbt.
    c) Die Differenz zwischen Schlusskurs und Höchstkurs wird durch einen gefärbten Balken dargestellt.
    d) Alle Antworten sind falsch.

16. Sie sehen auf Ihrem Candle Chart einen Abwärtstrend. Einer schwarzen Kerze folgt eine weiße Kerze, deren Körper die schwarze Kerze umfasst. Was werden Sie nun tun?
    a) nichts
    b) abwarten
    c) eine Long-Position aufbauen
    d) eine Short-Postion aufbauen

17. Was trifft laut Elliot-Wellen-Theorie zu?
    a) Es ist unmöglich, die Länge von Wellen vorherzusagen.
    b) Preise sind stets in einem fallenden Markt.
    c) Der wichtigste Aspekt von Preisbewegungen ist die Dauer jeder einzelnen Welle.
    d) Es können die Hauptmuster der Preisbewegung in fünf Impulswellen gesehen werden, die von drei Korrekturwellen gefolgt werden.

18. Welche Werte sind Fibonacci Retracement Levels?
    a) 50% und 75%
    b) 38,2% und 61,8%
    c) 25% und 50%
    d) 45,3% und 57,2%

19. Was zeigt der Oszillator in der technischen Analyse an?
    a) Trend
    b) Volatilität
    c) steigende und fallende Keile
    d) Preismomentum

20. Was bedeutet ein positives Momentum?
    a) einen steigenden Devisenkurs
    b) eine Kursspitze
    c) ein Unterstützungsniveau
    d) eine Trendumkehr von fallendem zu steigendem Trend

21. Welche Zahl ist beim RSI unwichtig?
    a) 0,3
    b) 0,5
    c) 0,7
    d) 0,618

22. What does a RSI value of 0.5 mean?
    a) You are overbought.
    b) You are oversold.
    c) The price has risen by 50%.
    d) The average price was equal to the average price decline.

23. Which term best describes a MACD?
    a) chart analysis
    b) fundamental analysis
    c) trend chasing system
    d) anti-cyclical system

22. Was bedeutet ein RSI-Wert von 0,5?
   a) Sie sind überkauft.
   b) Sie sind überverkauft.
   c) Der Kurs ist im Zeitintervall um 50% gestiegen.
   d) Der durchschnittliche Kursgewinn entsprach dem durchschnittlichen Kursverlust.
23. Zu welchen Analyseverfahren gehört der MACD?
   a) Chartanalyse
   b) Fundamentalanlayse
   c) Trendfolgesystem
   d) antizyklisches System

PART VIII: Annex

TEIL VIII: Anhang

1. Formulary

1.1. Financial Mathematics

1.1.1. Calculating Simple Interest

The formula for calculating simple interest (single payment of interest and a term of less than one year) is:

$$I = C \times r \times \frac{D}{B}$$

I = amount of interest
C = capital amount
r = interest rate in decimals (i.e. 5% = 0.05; 10.3% = 0.103; etc.)
D = number of days of interest period
B = day basis of calculation (fixed number of days per year)

Example

Bank A gives a 1-month deposit of Euro 5 m at 3%. Start date of this credit is October 1st and end date is November 1st. The actual number of days for this period is 31. Basis of term calculation is 360 days per year. The absolute interest of this credit is:

$$I = 5,000,000 \times 0.03 \times \frac{31}{360} = 12,916.67$$

On November 1st, the borrower will either
- pay interest of Euro 12,916.67 and roll over the credit, or
- settle the credit by paying back the principal plus interest: Euro 5,012,916.67

1.1.2. Average Interest

If different interest rates apply over several interest periods while giving or taking money, the average interest rate may be calculated like this:

$$r_{AV} = \left[\left(r_1 \times \frac{D_1}{B} \right) + \left(r_2 \times \frac{D_2}{B} \right) + \left(r_3 \times \frac{D_3}{B} \right) + \cdots + \left(r_n \times \frac{D_n}{B} \right) \right] \times \frac{B}{D_N}$$

r_{AV} = average interest rate
$r_1, r_2, \ldots r_n$ = interest rate of the respective terms of interest, in decimals
B = day basis of calculation
D_N = number of days of the total term
$D_1, D_2, \ldots D_n$ = number of days of the respective term

1. Formelsammlung

1.1. Finanzmathematik

1.1.1. Einfache Zinsberechnung

Die Formel für die einfache Zinsberechnung (einmalige Zinszahlung und Laufzeit unter einem Jahr) lautet:

$$Z = K \cdot r \cdot \frac{T}{B}$$

Z = Zinsbetrag
K = Nominalbetrag (Kapital)
r = Zinssatz (5% = 0,05; 10,3% = 0,103 etc.)
T = Anzahl der Tage für die Zinsberechnung (Laufzeit)
B = Berechnungsbasis (festgesetzte Anzahl der Tage pro Jahr)

Beispiel

Bank A gibt ein 1-Monats-Depot zu 3% (EUR 5 Mio.). Der Kredit startet am 1. Oktober und endet am 1. November. Die tatsächliche Laufzeit dieser Periode beträgt 31 Tage. Als Berechnungsbasis werden 360 Tage pro Jahr angenommen. Wie hoch sind die Zinsen in Absolutbeträgen auf diesen Kredit?

$$Z = 5.000.000 \times 0,03 \times \frac{31}{360} = 12.916,67$$

Am 1. November wird der Kreditnehmer entweder
• Zinsen von EUR 12.916,67 bezahlen und das Kapital verlängern („roll over") oder
• den Kredit mit Kapital inklusive Zinsen in Höhe von EUR 5.012.916,67 zurückzahlen.

1.1.2. Berechnung der Durchschnittszinsen

Wurden Gelder zu unterschiedlichen Zinsen über mehrere Zeitperioden aufgenommen oder veranlagt, kann der Durchschnittszinssatz folgendermaßen berechnet werden:

$$DZ = \left[\left(r_1 \times \frac{T_1}{B} \right) + \left(r_2 \times \frac{T_2}{B} \right) + \left(r_3 \times \frac{T_3}{B} \right) + \dots + \left(r_n \times \frac{T_n}{B} \right) \right] \times \frac{B}{T_N}$$

DZ = Durchschnittszins
$r_1, r_2, \dots r_n$ = Zinssätze in Dezimalen der einzelnen Perioden
B = Berechnungsbasis
$T_1, T_2, \dots T_n$ = Anzahl der Tage der einzelnen Perioden
T_N = Gesamtlaufzeit in Tagen

Bei dieser Durchschnittsberechnung werden keine Zinseszinsen berücksichtigt.

Example

You lent EUR at the following rates during the last year:
2 January – 2 April: (90 days) at 2.5%
2 April – 2 July: (91 days) at 2.75%
2 July – 2 October: (92 days) at 2.875%
2 October – 2 January: (92 days) at 3%

Calculate the average interest rate.

$$\left[\left(0.025\times\frac{90}{360}\right)+\left(0.0275\times\frac{91}{360}\right)+\left(0.02875\times\frac{92}{360}\right)+\left(0.03\times\frac{92}{360}\right)\right]\times\frac{360}{365}=2.78288\%$$

1.1.3. Calculating Compound Interest (Effective Interest)

If an amount is lent or borrowed over several terms and the interest payments are not paid out at the end of each term, the amount that is the basis for the interest calculation is raised by the amount of accrued interest. This is commonly known as capitalisation or compound interest.

The general formula for the calculation of compound interest is:

$$ER=\left\{\left[\left(1+r_1\times\frac{D_1}{B}\right)\times\left(1+r_2\times\frac{D_2}{B}\right)\times\left(1+r_3\times\frac{D_3}{B}\right)\times........\times\left(1+r_n\times\frac{D_n}{B}\right)\right]-1\right\}\times\frac{B}{D_N}$$

ER = effective interest rate
$D_1,....D_n$ = number of days of the respective term
B = day basis of calculation
D_N = number of days of the total term
$r_1.. ..r_n$ = interest rate of the respective terms of interest, in decimals

Example

Last year you invested CHF at the rates given below. The subsequent investment is made up of the original amount and the accrued interest:
2 January – 2 April: (90 days) at 2.5%
2 April – 2 July: (91 days) at 2.75%
2 July – 2 October: (92 days) at 2.875%
2 October – 2 January: (92 days) at 3%

What is the effective interest rate?

$$ER=\left\{\left[\left(1+0.025\times\frac{90}{360}\right)\times\left(1+0.0275\times\frac{91}{360}\right)\times\left(1+0.02875\times\frac{92}{360}\right)\times\left(1+0.03\times\frac{92}{360}\right)\right]-1\right\}\times\frac{360}{365}=2.8124\%$$

The effective interest rate is 2.8124%.

Beispiel

Sie haben CHF zu folgenden Zinssätzen für das letzte Jahr veranlagt:
2. Januar – 2. April: (90 Tage) zu 2,5%
2. April – 2. Juli: (91 Tage) zu 2,75%
2. Juli – 2. Oktober: (92 Tage) zu 2,875%
2. Oktober – 2. Januar: (92 Tage) zu 3%

Wie hoch ist der Durchschnittszinssatz?

$$\left[\left(0,025 \times \frac{90}{360}\right) + \left(0,0275 \times \frac{91}{360}\right) + \left(0,02875 \times \frac{92}{360}\right) + \left(0,03 \times \frac{92}{360}\right)\right] \times \frac{360}{365} = 2,78288\%$$

1.1.3. Berechnung der Zinseszinsen/Berechnung von Effektivzinsen

Wird ein Kapitalbetrag über mehrere Perioden veranlagt, ohne dass die Zinsen am Ende einer Periode gezahlt werden, so erhöht sich der in der nächsten Periode veranlagte Betrag um die Zinsen. Diese bilden dann ihrerseits einen Teil des Kapitals und damit der Verzinsungsbasis für die nächste Periode. Man spricht von Kapitalisierung bzw. Zinseszinsen.

Die allgemeine Formel für die Zinseszinsberechnung lautet:

$$EZ = \left\{ \left[\left(1 + r_1 \times \frac{T_1}{B}\right) \times \left(1 + r_2 \times \frac{T_2}{B}\right) \times \left(1 + r_3 \times \frac{T_3}{B}\right) \times \dots \times \left(1 + r_n \times \frac{T_n}{B}\right) \right] - 1 \right\} \times \frac{B}{T_N}$$

EZ = Effektivzins
$T_1, \dots T_n$ = Anzahl der Tage der einzelnen Perioden
B = Berechnungsbasis
T_N = Gesamtlaufzeit in Tagen
$r_1 \dots r_n$ = Zinssätze in Dezimalen der einzelnen Perioden

Beispiel

Sie haben CHF zu folgenden Sätzen für das letzte Jahr veranlagt. Die Anschlussveranlagung gilt jeweils für das Kapital und die bereits angefallenen Zinsen:

2. Januar – 2. April: (90 Tage) zu 2,5%
2. April – 2. Juli: (91 Tage) zu 2,75%
2. Juli – 2. Oktober: (92 Tage) zu 2,875%
2. Oktober – 2. Januar: (92 Tage) zu 3%

Wie hoch ist der Effektivzins?

$$EZ = \left\{ \left[\left(1 + 0,025 \times \frac{90}{360}\right) \times \left(1 + 0,0275 \times \frac{91}{360}\right) \times \left(1 + 0,02875 \times \frac{92}{360}\right) \times \left(1 + 0,03 \times \frac{92}{360}\right) \right] - 1 \right\} \times \frac{360}{365} = 2,8124\%$$

Der Effektivzins beträgt 2,8124%.

1.1.4. Calculating the Present Value (for terms ‹ 1 year)

The current value of a future cash flow is called present value. The present value is calculated by discounting the future value. Many markets, e.g. that for US T-bills, conventionally use discount rates.

$$PV=\frac{FV}{1+\left(r\times\dfrac{D}{B}\right)}$$

PV = present value (capital)
FV = future value
r = interest rate in decimals
D = number of days
B = day basis of calculation

Example

We know that the current yield of a US treasury bill is 5.50%. The future value is 1,000,000 in 2 months (61 days). Calculate the present value of the T bill.

$$PV=\frac{1,000,000}{1+\left(0.055\times\dfrac{61}{360}\right)}=990,766.61$$

The present value is 990,766.61

1.1.5. Calculating the Present Value (for terms › 1 year)

With a term of more than a year, the present value can be calculated in the following way:

$$PV=\frac{FV}{(1+r)^{N}}$$

Example

The present value of EUR 1 in five years at an interest rate of 6% is:

$$PV=\frac{1}{(1.06)^{5}}=0.74726$$

1.1.6. Calculating the Future Value (for terms ‹ 1 year)

Starting with the present value today (principal), the future value can be determined. The amount of money that is due at the end of the loan's or deposit's term is made up of the original amount of capital plus the interest. This amount is called the future value.

For example, if, today, you invest GBP 100 for 1 year at 4% p.a., you receive an amount of GBP 104 (Actual/365) at the end of the year.

1.1.4. Berechnung des Barwertes (unterjährig)

Als Barwert wird der heutige Wert eines zukünftigen Zahlungsstromes bezeichnet. Ausgehend vom Endwert wird also durch Abzinsen oder Diskontieren der heutige Wert ermittelt.

$$BW = \frac{EW}{1 + \left(r \times \dfrac{T}{B} \right)}$$

BW = Barwert (Kapital)
EW = Endwert
r = Zinssatz in Dezimalen
T = Anzahl der Tage
B = Berechnungsbasis

Beispiel

Wir wissen, dass die aktuelle Rendite eines EUR Commercial Papers 5,5% beträgt. Der Endwert in zwei Monaten (61 Tagen) beträgt 1.000.000. Was ist der aktuelle Wert dieses Commercial Papers?

$$BW = \frac{1.000.000}{1 + \left(0,055 \times \dfrac{61}{360} \right)} = 990.766,61$$

Der Barwert beträgt 990.766,61.

1.1.5 Berechnung des Barwertes (überjährig)

Bei mehrjähriger Laufzeit kann der Barwert folgendermaßen berechnet werden:

$$BW = \frac{EW}{(1+r)^N}$$

Beispiel

Der Barwert von EUR 1 in fünf Jahren beträgt bei einem Zinssatz von 6%:

$$BW = \frac{1}{(1,06)^5} = 0,74726$$

1.1.6 Berechnung des Endwertes (unterjährig)

Ausgehend vom heutigen Wert (auch Barwert oder Kapital) wird der zukünftige Wert ermittelt. Der Geldwert, der am Ende der Laufzeit eines Kredits oder eines aufgenommenen Depots fällig wird, beinhaltet Kapital plus angelaufene Zinsen. Dieser Wert wird auch Endwert des Kredits oder der Veranlagung genannt.

Wenn beispielsweise GBP 100 heute für ein Jahr zum Zinssatz von 4% p.a. investiert werden, erhält man nach Ende eines Jahres einen Betrag von GBP 104 (ACT/365).

The present value of this investment is GBP 100.
The future value of this investment is GBP 104.

Formula for the simple calculation of the future value:

$$FV=PV\times\left(1+\left(r\times\frac{D}{B}\right)\right) \quad \text{or} \quad FV=PV+\left(PV\times r\times\frac{D}{B}\right)$$

FV = future value of the investment
PV = present value
r = interest rate in decimals
D = number of days of the term of interest
B = day basis of calculation

In other words, the future value of an investment is the amount of capital (PV) plus accrued interest.

Example

You take a deposit of EUR 1 Mio at a rate of 6% p.a. for 92 days (Actual/360). At the end of its term, the value of the deposit will be:

$$FV=1,000,000\times\left(1+\left(0.06\times\frac{92}{360}\right)\right)=1,015,333.33$$

Note: When calculating future values that include compound interest, one has to first compute the effective interest rate from the nominal interest rate. Only after this has been done, you can use the above formula.

1.1.7. Calculating the Future Value (for terms > 1 year)

The formula for calculating the future value for terms > 1 year is:

$$FV = C \cdot \left(1+r\right)^N$$

FV = future value
C = capital amount
r = interest rate p.a. in decimals
N = total term in years

Note: It is also assumed that the re-investment is done at the same rate.

1.1.8. Interest Calculation with PV and FV (for terms < 1 year)

If we know the future value, the present value as well as the term of an investment and if there are no cash-flows during the term , we can calculate the current yield (current market interest rate).

$$r=\frac{\left(FV-PV\right)}{PV}\times\frac{B}{D}$$

FV = future value
PV = present value
B = day basis of calculation
D = number of days
r = current yield (current market interest rate)

Der Barwert dieser Veranlagung beträgt GBP 100.
Der Endwert dieser Veranlagung beträgt GBP 104.

Formel für die einfache Endwertberechnung:

$$EW = K \times \left(1 + \left(r \times \frac{T}{B}\right)\right) \qquad \text{oder} \qquad EW = K + \left(K \times r \times \frac{T}{B}\right)$$

EW = Endwert der Veranlagung
K = Kapitalbetrag
r = Zinssatz in Dezimalen
T = Anzahl der Tage der Zinsperiode
B = Berechnungsbasis

Also ist der Endwert einer Veranlagung der Kapitalbetrag (K) plus anteilige Zinsen.

Beispiel

Ein genommenes Depot über EUR 1 Mio. mit einem Zinssatz von 6% p.a. für 92 Tage (ACT/360) wächst am Laufzeitende zu einem Betrag von:

$$EW = 1.000.000 \times \left(1 + \left(0,06 \times \frac{92}{360}\right)\right) = 1.015.333,33$$

Anmerkung: Wenn Sie einen Endwert mit Zinseszinsen berechnen, müssen Sie zuerst den Effektivzinssatz aus dem Nominalzinssatz berechnen. Erst dann können Sie oben angeführte Formel verwenden.

1.1.7. Berechnung des Endwertes (überjährig)

Die Formel für die Berechnung des Endwertes für Laufzeiten länger als ein Jahr lautet:

$$EW = K \cdot (1 + r)^N$$

EW = Endwert
K   = Kapitalbetrag
r   = Zinssatz in Dezimalen p.a.
N   = Laufzeit in Jahren

Anmerkung: Diese Berechnung unterstellt, dass die Wiederveranlagung zum gleichen Zinssatz erfolgt.

1.1.8. Berechnung des Zinssatzes aus Barwert und Endwert (unterjährig)

Wenn wir Endwert, Barwert und Laufzeit eines Geschäftes kennen und es keine zwischenzeitlichen Cashflows gibt, kann aus den beiden Zahlungen auch die aktuelle Rendite (der aktuelle Zinssatz) herausgerechnet werden.

$$r = \frac{(EW - BW)}{BW} \times \frac{B}{T}$$

EW = Endwert
BW = Barwert
B = Berechnungsbasis
T = Anzahl der Tage
r = Zinssatz

Example

A EUR Commercial Paper with a time to maturity of 82 days has the stated cash flows. What is the yield?
present value: = 987,627
future value: = 1,000,000

$$r = \frac{(1,000,000 - 987,627)}{987,627} \times \frac{360}{82} = 5.5001\%$$

Note: You cannot use this formula if the investment has several cash-flows.

1.1.9. Interest Calculation with PV and FV (for terms > 1 year)

If present value, future value and the term of a deal are known, the interest rate can be calculated. Thereby, a re-investment of the coupon payments at the same interest rate is assumed.

$$r = \sqrt[N]{\frac{FV}{PV}} - 1 \quad \text{or} \quad \left(\frac{FV}{PV}\right)^{\left(\frac{1}{N}\right)} - 1$$

FV = future value
PV = present value
N = term

Example

At what interest rate do you have to invest EUR 50 mio in order to receive EUR 100 mio (incl. accrued interest) after 10 years?

$$r = \sqrt[10]{\frac{100}{50}} - 1 \qquad r = 7.17735\%$$

Note: The re-investment of the coupon payments at the same interest rate is assumed.

1.1.10. Conversion from Money Market Basis to Bond Basis and vice versa

$$r_{CM} = r_{MM} \times \frac{D_{MM}}{B_{MM}} \qquad\qquad r_{MM} = r_{CM} \times \frac{B_{MM}}{D_{MM}}$$

r_{CM} = interest rate in the capital market
r_{MM} = interest rate in the money market
D_{MM} = number of days per year, money market
B_{MM} = basis of term calculation, money market

Note: Formula fits only if the convention for CM is either ACT/ACT or 30/360.

Beispiel

Ein EUR Commercial Paper hat eine Restlaufzeit von 82 Tagen.
Barwert = 987.627
Endwert = 1.000.000

$$r=\frac{\left(1.000.000-987.627\right)}{987.627}\times\frac{360}{82}=5,5001\%$$

Anmerkung: Diese Berechnungsmethode gilt nicht bei Geschäften mit mehreren Cash-flows.

1.1.9. Berechnung des Zinssatzes aus Barwert und Endwert (überjährig)

Aus Barwert, Endwert und Laufzeit eines Geschäftes kann der Zinssatz ermittelt werden. Für zwischenzeitliche Zinszahlungen wird dabei eine Wiederveranlagung zum errechneten Zinssatz unterstellt.

$$r = \sqrt[N]{\frac{EW}{BW}} - 1 \quad \text{oder} \quad \left(\frac{EW}{BW}\right)^{\left(\frac{1}{N}\right)} - 1$$

EW = Endwert
BW = Barwert
N = Laufzeit

Beispiel

Zu welchem Zinssatz müssen EUR 50 Mio. heute angelegt werden, um nach zehn Jahren (inkl. Zinseszinsen) EUR 100 Mio. zurückzuerhalten?

$$r = \sqrt[10]{\frac{100}{50}} - 1 \quad r = 7,17735\%$$

Anmerkung: Diese Berechnungsmethode unterstellt die Wiederveranlagung der Zinszahlungen zum gleichen Zinssatz.

1.1.10. Umrechnung Geldmarktbasis/Kapitalmarktbasis

$$r_{KM} = r_{GM} \times \frac{T_{GM}}{B_{GM}} \qquad\qquad r_{GM} = r_{KM} \times \frac{B_{GM}}{T_{GM}}$$

r_{KM} = Zinssatz Kapitalmarkt
r_{GM} = Zinssatz Geldmarkt
T_{GM} = Anzahl der Tage pro Jahr Geldmarkt
B_{GM} = Berechnungsbasis Geldmarkt

Anmerkung: Die Formel gilt nur, wenn die Konvention für den Kapitalmarktzinssatz entweder ACT/ACT oder 30/360 ist.

1.1.11. Conversion of Non-Annual Payments into Effective Interest Rate

Interest payments not always are due annually but sometimes daily, weekly, monthly, quarterly, and semi-annual interest payments are also possible. With bonds, it is quite common that interest payments are made semi-annually. To be able to compare these non-annual interest payments to yearly payments (single payment of interest), one converts the nominal interest rate into the effective interest rate. With a single p.a. payment, the nominal rate equals to the effective rate of interest.

$$ER=\left(1+\frac{NR}{FIP}\right)^{FIP}-1$$

ER = effective rate of interest p.a. in decimals
NR = nominal rate of interest p.a. in decimals
FIP = frequency of interest payments p.a. (e.g. 2 for semi-annual, 4 for quarterly, etc.)

Example

You invest EUR at 6.00% for a period of 1 year and agree quarterly interest payments. What is the effective interest rate of this investment?

$$ER=\left(1+\frac{0.06}{4}\right)^{4}-1=6.13636\%$$

A quarterly interest rate of 6.00% corresponds to an annual rate of 6.14%.

1.1.12. Conversion of Annual into Non-Annual Interest Payments

We can also convert annual payments into non-annual payments:

$$r_{NA}=\left(\sqrt[FIP]{1+rA}-1\right)\times FIP$$

r_{NA} = non-annual rate of interest p.a., for the term of interest
FIP = frequency of interest payments p.a.
r_{A} = annual rate of interest p.a., in decimals

Example

You hold a bond with annual interest payments of 6.00%. Calculate the nominal interest rate, based on semi-annual interest payments.

$$r_{SA}=\left(\sqrt[2]{1+0.06}-1\right)\times 2=5.9126\%$$

The interest rate of 6.00% annual corresponds to a rate of 5.9126% semi annual.

1.1.11. Umrechnung von unterjährigen in ganzjährige Zinszahlungen

Zinszahlungen müssen nicht immer jährlich anfallen, sondern können auch täglich, wöchentlich, monatlich, quartalsweise oder halbjährlich ausbezahlt werden. Bei Anleihen fallen beispielsweise die Zinszahlungen mitunter halbjährlich an. Um diese unterjährigen Zinssätze mit Jahreszinssätzen (einmalige jährliche Zinszahlung) vergleichbar zu machen, wird aus dem Nominalzins der Effektivzinssatz errechnet. Bei einmaliger Zinszahlung p.a. ist der Nominalzins gleich dem Effektivzinssatz.

$$EZ = \left(1 + \frac{NZ}{ZP}\right)^{ZP} - 1$$

EZ = Effektivzins p.a. in Dezimalen
NZ = Nominalzins p.a. in Dezimalen
ZP = Zinsperioden p.a. (z.B. 2 für halbjährlich, 4 für quartalsweise etc.)

Beispiel

Sie legen EUR auf ein Jahr zu 6% an und vereinbaren quartalsweise Zinszahlungen. Welchen Effektivzinssatz ergibt diese Veranlagung?

$$EZ = \left(1 + \frac{0{,}06}{4}\right)^{4} - 1 = 6{,}13636\,\%$$

Ein Quartalszinssatz von 6% entspricht einem Jahreszinssatz von 6,14%.

1.1.12. Umrechnung von ganzjährigen in unterjährige Zinszahlungen

Um ganzjährige Zinszahlungen in unterjährige Zinszahlungen umzurechnen, verwendet man folgende Formel:

$$r_{UJ} = \left(\sqrt[ZP]{1 + rGJ} - 1\right) \times ZP$$

r_{UJ} = Zinssatz p.a., unterjährig, für Zinsperiode
ZP = Anzahl der Zinsperioden im Jahr
rGJ = Zinssatz p.a., ganzjährig, in Dezimalen

Beispiel

Der Zinssatz von 6% einer Anleihe mit ganzjähriger Zinszahlung soll in einen Nominalzinssatz mit halbjährigen Zinszahlungen umgewandelt werden.

$$r_{UJ} = \left(\sqrt[2]{1 + 0{,}06} - 1\right) \times 2 = 5{,}9126\,\%$$

Eine Anleihe mit 6% jährlich bringt den gleichen Ertrag wie eine Anleihe mit 5,9126% halbjährlich.

1.1.13. Zero Interest Rate Calculation (from yield to maturity rates)

Discount Factor

$$d_N = \frac{1 - r_N \cdot \sum_{j=1}^{N-1} d_j}{1 + r_N}$$

Zero Interest Rate

$$Z_N = \sqrt[i]{\frac{1}{d_N}} - 1$$

Z = Zero interest rate
r = interest rate in decimals
d = discount factor
N = maturity in year
j = current year

1.2. Money Market Calculations

1.2.1. Future Value of a CD

$$FV = PV \times \left(1 + \left(r \times \frac{D}{B}\right)\right)$$

FV = future value of CD
PV = present value of CD
r = interest rate in decimals (yield)
D = number of days of the term of interest
B = day basis for calculation

1.2.2. Secondary Market Price for Instruments on a Yield-base (CD)

$$PV = \frac{FV}{1 + \left(r \times \frac{D}{B}\right)}$$

PV = present value (secondary market price)
FV = future value (nominal value plus interest)
r = interest rate in decimals (yield)
D = number of days
B = day basis for calculation

1.1.13. Zero-Zinsberechnung (aus Yield-to-Maturity-Zinsen)

Diskontfaktor

$$d_N = \frac{1 - r_N \cdot \sum_{j=1}^{N-1} d_j}{1 + r_N}$$

Zero-Zins

$$Z_N = \sqrt[i]{\frac{1}{d_N}} - 1$$

z = Zerozins
r = Zinssatz in Dezimalen
d = Diskontfaktor
N = Laufzeit in Jahren
j = laufendes Jahr

1.2. Berechnungen für den Geldmarkt

1.2.1. Endwert eines Certificates of Deposit

$$EW = NW \cdot \left(1 + \left(r \cdot \frac{T}{B}\right)\right)$$

EW = Endwert CD
NW = Nominalwert CD
r = Zinssatz des CD
T = Anzahl der Tage der Zinsperiode
B = Berechnungsbasis

1.2.2. Sekundärmarkterlös für Instrumente auf Renditebasis

$$BW = \frac{EW}{\left(1 + \left(R \cdot \frac{T}{B}\right)\right)}$$

BW = Barwert (Sekundärmarktpreis)
EW = Endwert (Nominalwert plus Zinsen)
R = Rendite
T = Restlaufzeit
B = Berechnungsbasis

1.2.3. Secondary Market Price for Discount Instruments on a Yield-base

$$PV = \frac{FV}{1 + \left(r \times \dfrac{D}{B}\right)}$$

PV = present value (secondary market price)
FV = face value
r = interest rate in decimals (yield)
D = number of days
B = day basis for calculation

1.2.4. Secondary Market Price for Discount Instruments on a Discount-base

$$PV = FV - \left(\frac{FV \cdot r_d \cdot D}{B}\right)$$

PV = present value (capital)
FV = face value
r_d = discount rate, in decimals
D = number of days
B = day basis for calculation

1.2.5. Conversion Discount Rate/True Yield

$$r = \frac{r_d}{\left(1 - \left(r_d \cdot \dfrac{D}{B}\right)\right)}$$

r = interest rate, in decimals
r_d = discount rate, in decimals
D = number of days
B = day basis for calculation

1.3. Capital Market Calculations

1.3.1. Dirty Price Bond

$$DP\_Bond = \sum_{n=1}^{N} + \frac{CF_n}{(1+r)^n}$$

CF = Cash-flow
n = point of time in years
r = yield in decimals
N = total maturity
DB_Bond = Dirty Price Bond

1.2.3. Sekundärmarkterlös für Diskontinstrumente auf Renditebasis

$$BW = \frac{NW}{\left(1 + \left(R \times \frac{T}{B}\right)\right)}$$

BW = Barwert (Sekundärmarktpreis)
NW = Nominalwert
R = Rendite
T = Restlaufzeit
B = Berechnungsbasis

1.2.4. Sekundärmarkterlös für Diskontinstrumente auf Diskontbasis

$$BW = NW - \left(\frac{NW \cdot r_d \cdot T}{B}\right)$$

BW = Barwert (Sekundärmarktpreis)
NW = Nominalwert
r_d = Diskontsatz
T = Anzahl der Tage
B = Berechnungsbasis

1.2.5. Umrechnung Diskontsatz/Effektivzinssatz

$$r = \frac{r_d}{\left(1 - \left(r_d \cdot \frac{T}{B}\right)\right)}$$

r = Zinssatz p.a.
r_d = Diskontsatz
T = Anzahl der Tage
B = Berechnungsbasis

1.3. Berechnungen für den Kapitalmarkt

1.3.1. Dirty Price Bond

$$DP\_Bond = \sum_{n=1}^{N} + \frac{CF_n}{(1+r)^n}$$

CF = Cashflow
n = Zeitpunkt in Jahren
r = Rendite in Dezimalen
N = Gesamtlaufzeit
DB_Bond = Dirty Price Bond

1.3.2. Duration

$$D = \frac{\sum_{n=1}^{N} n \cdot \frac{CF_n}{(1+r)^n}}{\sum_{n=1}^{N} \cdot \frac{CF_n}{(1+r)^n}}$$

CF = Cash-flow
n = point of time in years
r = yield in decimals
N = total maturity
D = Duration

1.3.3. Modified Duration

$$MD = \frac{\sum_{n=1}^{N} n \cdot \frac{CF_n}{(1+r)^n}}{\sum_{n=1}^{N} \cdot \frac{CF_n}{(1+r)^n}} \cdot \frac{1}{1 + \frac{r}{NP}}$$

CF = Cash-flow
n = point of time in years
r = yield in decimals
N = total maturity
MD = Modified Duration
NP = number of interest payment periods in a year

1.4. Forward Rates – Forward Rate Agreement

1.4.1. Calculating Forward Rates (for terms < 1 year)

A forward-forward rate (or simply forward rate) is an interest rate for a future term of interest, e.g. an interest rate for a 6-month investment that will begin in 3 months. These forward rates can be derived from the interest rates prevailing in the market. By investing for 9 months and refinancing for 3 months the same effects can be achieved today.

The formula to calculate forward rates is as follows:

$$FR = \left\{ \left[\frac{1 + \left(r_l \times \frac{D_l}{B} \right)}{1 + \left(r_S \times \frac{D_S}{B} \right)} \right] - 1 \right\} \times \frac{B}{D_{l-S}}$$

FR = forward interest rate
r_l = interest rate in decimals, long-term
r_s = interest rate in decimals, short-term
D_l = number of days, long-term
D_s = number of days, short-term
B = day basis of calculation
D_{l-s} = difference between short term and long term (in days)

1.3.2. Duration

$$D = \frac{\sum_{n=1}^{N} n \cdot \dfrac{CF_n}{(1+r)^n}}{\sum_{n=1}^{N} \dfrac{CF_n}{(1+r)^n}}$$

CF = Cashflow
n = Zeitpunkt in Jahren
r = Rendite in Dezimalen
N = Gesamtlaufzeit
D = Duration

1.3.3. Modified Duration

$$MD = \frac{\sum_{n=1}^{N} n \cdot \dfrac{CF_n}{(1+r)^n}}{\sum_{n=1}^{N} \dfrac{CF_n}{(1+r)^n}} \cdot \frac{1}{1 + \dfrac{r}{AP}}$$

CF = Cashflow
n = Zeitpunkt in Jahren
r = Rendite in Dezimalen
N = Gesamtlaufzeit
MD = Modified Duration
AP = Anzahl Zinszahlungsperioden im Jahr

1.4. Forward-Sätze – Forward Rate Agreement

1.4.1. Berechnung von Forward-Sätzen (unterjährig)

Ein Forward-Forward-Satz (oder einfach Forward-Satz) ist ein Zinssatz für eine zukünftige Zinsperiode, z.B. ein Zinssatz für eine 6-Monats-Veranlagung, die in drei Monaten startet. Diese Forward-Sätze können von den aktuellen Zinssätzen abgeleitet werden. Durch eine 9-monatige Veranlagung und eine 3-monatige Refinanzierung ist dieser Effekt schon heute erzielbar. Somit ergeben sich Forward-Forward-Sätze direkt aus Niveau und Steilheit der Zinskurve.

Die Formel für die Berechnung der unterjährigen Forward-Sätze lautet:

$$FS = \left\{ \left[\frac{1 + \left(r_l \times \dfrac{T_l}{B} \right)}{1 + \left(r_k \times \dfrac{T_k}{B} \right)} \right] - 1 \right\} \times \frac{B}{T_{l-k}}$$

FS = Forward-Satz
r_l = Zinssatz in Dezimalen, lange Laufzeit
r_k = Zinssatz in Dezimalen, kurze Laufzeit
T_l = Anzahl der Tage, lange Laufzeit
T_k = Anzahl der Tage, kurze Laufzeit
B = Berechnungsbasis
T_{l-k} = Tage zwischen kurzer und langer Laufzeit

Example

Forward rate calculation for GBP, starting in 3 months for a term of 3 months.
Interest rates GBP: 3 months = 7½% (91 days)
6 months = 7¾% (183 days)

$$FR = \left\{ \left[\frac{1 + \left(0.0775 \times \dfrac{183}{365} \right)}{1 + \left(0.075 \times \dfrac{91}{265} \right)} \right] - 1 \right\} \times \frac{365}{92} = 7.85049\%$$

The forward rate for a 3 months deposit that starts in 3 months is 7.85049%.

1.4.2. Calculating Forward Rates (for terms > 1 year)

Given a short-term and a long-term interest rate it is possible to calculate a so-called forward rate (also called forward-forward rate).
    Formula:

$$FR = \left[\frac{(1+r_l)^N}{(1+r_s)^n} \right]^{\frac{1}{(N-n)}} - 1$$

FR = forward rate of interest
r_l = rate of interest in decimals, long-term
N = term in years, long term
r_s = rate of interest in decimals, short-term
n = term in years, short term

Note: The exact calculation is done on the basis of zero rates. For long terms, differences may become too big without using zeros.

1.4.3. FRA Settlement Payment

$$AD = \frac{(REF - FRA) \times (\pm VOL) \times \dfrac{D}{B}}{1 + \left(REF \times \dfrac{D}{B} \right)}$$

AD = amount due
REF = reference rate (e.g. LIBOR) in decimals
VOL = volume of the FRA (+ = buy; – = sell)
FRA = FRA rate in decimals
D = number of days of the FRA term
B = day basis for calculation

Beispiel

Berechnung des Forward-Satzes für GBP, startend in drei Monaten, für eine Laufzeit von drei Monaten.

Zinsen GBP: 3 Monate = 7½% (91 Tage)

6 Monate = 7¾% (183 Tage)

$$FS = \left\{ \frac{1 + \left(0,0775 \times \dfrac{183}{365} \right)}{1 + \left(0,075 \times \dfrac{91}{365} \right)} - 1 \right\} \times \frac{365}{92} = 7,85049\%$$

Der Forward-Satz für ein 3-Monats-Depot, das in drei Monaten startet, beträgt 7,85049%.

1.4.2. Berechnung von Forward-Sätzen (überjährig)

Aus einem kurzen und einem längeren Zinssatz kann ein sogenannter Forward-Zinssatz (auch Forward-Forward-Zinssatz) ermittelt werden.

Formel für die überjährige Ermittlung:

$$FS = \left[\frac{(1 + r_l)^N}{(1 + r_k)^n} \right]^{\frac{1}{(N-n)}} - 1$$

FS = Forward-Satz

r_l = Zinssatz in Dezimalen, lange Laufzeit

N = Laufzeit in Jahren, lange Periode

r_k = Zinssatz in Dezimalen, kurze Laufzeit

n = Laufzeit in Jahren, kurze Periode

Anmerkung: Die genaue Berechnung erfolgt mit Zero-Sätzen. Für längere Laufzeiten können die Abweichungen ohne Berücksichtigung von Zeros sehr groß werden.

1.4.3. Ausgleichszahlung Forward Rate Agreement

$$AZ = \frac{(REF - FRA)(\pm VOL) \dfrac{T_{FRA}}{B}}{\left(1 + \left(REF \cdot \dfrac{T_{FRA}}{B} \right) \right)}$$

AZ = Ausgleichszahlung

REF = Referenzsatz (z.B. LIBOR)

VOL = Volumen FRA

T_{FRA} = Anzahl der Tage im FRA

B = Berechnungsbasis

FRA = FRA-Zinssatz

1.5. Bond Market Calculations

1.5.1. Bond Price Calculation (on Coupon Date)

Note: Clean Price per 100 = Dirty Price per 100

$$\sum_{n=1}^{N} \frac{1}{(1+r)^n} \cdot CF_n$$

r = interest rate in decimals (yield)
n = ongoing period
N = total number of periods
CF_n = cash flow (at a nominal of 100) at time n

Dirty Price Calculation (Annual Coupon Payments)

$$P = \frac{CF_1}{(1+r)^{D/B}} + \sum_{n=2}^{N} \frac{CF_n}{(1+r)^{D/B} \cdot (1+r)^{n-1}}$$

D = days to the first cash flow
B = day basis for calculation (360/365/ACT)
r = interest rate in decimals (yield)
n = ongoing period
N = total number of periods
CF_n = cash flow (at a nominal of 100) at time n

1.6. FX Calculations

1.6.1. Calculating Swap Points from Interest Rates

$$\text{Premium/discount} = \text{SPOT} \times \left(\frac{1 + \left(r_V \times \dfrac{D}{B_V} \right)}{1 + \left(r_B \times \dfrac{D}{B_B} \right)} - 1 \right)$$

D = number of days
SPOT = spot rate
r_B = interest rate p.a. in decimals, base currency
r_V = interest rate p.a. in decimals, variable (quote) currency
B_B = day basis for calculation, base currency
B_V = day basis for calculation, variable (quote) currency

1.5. Berechnungen für den Anleihemarkt

1.5.1. Berechnung Anleihepreis (am Kupontag)

Anmerkung: Clean Preis per 100 = Dirty Preis per 100.

$$\sum_{n=1}^{N} \frac{1}{\left(1+r\right)^n} \cdot CF_n$$

r = aktuelle Rendite für die Periode
n = fortlaufende Periode
N = Gesamtanzahl Perioden
CF_n = Cashflow (auf Nominale 100) zum Zeitpunkt n

Dirty Price einer Anleihe (jährliche Kuponzahlungen):

$$P = \frac{CF_1}{(1+r)^{T/B}} + \sum_{n=2}^{N} \frac{CF_n}{(1+r)^{T/B} \cdot (1+r)^{n-1}}$$

P = Dirty Price
N = Anzahl der Zinsperioden
n = aktuelle Periode
CF = Cashflows (Kupon, Tilgung)
r = aktuelle Marktrendite
T = Tage bis zum ersten Cashflow
B = Berechnungsbasis Kapitalmarkt

1.6. Berechnungen für den FX-Markt

1.6.1. Berechnung der Swappunkte aus Zinssätzen

$$\text{Auf} - /\text{Abschlag} = \text{Spot} \cdot \left(\left(\frac{1 + \left(r_G \cdot \dfrac{T}{B_G} \right)}{1 + \left(r_Q \cdot \dfrac{T}{B_Q} \right)} \right) - 1 \right)$$

T = Anzahl der Tage
Spot = Kassakurs
r_Q = Zinssatz p.a., quotierte Währung
r_G = Zinssatz p.a., Gegenwährung
B_Q = Berechnungsbasis für die quotierte Währung
B_G = Berechnungsbasis für die Gegenwährung

1.6.2. Calculating Interest Rates from Swap Points (Outright)

Rate of the variable currency:
$$r_V = \left\{ \frac{\left[\left(1 + \left(r_B \times \dfrac{D}{B_B}\right)\right) \times O\right]}{S} - 1 \right\} \times \frac{B_V}{D}$$

Rate of the base currency:
$$r_B = \left\{ \frac{\left[\left(1 + \left(r_V \times \dfrac{D}{B_V}\right)\right) \times S\right]}{O} - 1 \right\} \times \frac{B_B}{D}$$

r_B = interest rate of base currency
r_v = interest rate of variable (quote) currency
O = outright
S = spot rate
D = days
B_B = day basis for calculation, base currency
B_v = day basis for calculation, variable (quote) currency

Note: e.g. for USD/JPY: USD is the base currency, JPY is the variable (or quote) currency.

1.6.3. Call Put Parity

$$Put = Call + \frac{(STR - Out)}{1 + \left(r_G \cdot \dfrac{D}{B_G}\right)}$$

Put = Put premium
Call = Call premium
STR = strike price
Out = outright
r = interest rate of variable (quote) currency
D = days
B_G = day basis for calculation, variable (quote) currency

1.7. Statistics

1.7.1. Estimated Standard Deviation

$$STDA = \sqrt{\sum_{t=1}^{N} \frac{\left(R_t - \tilde{R}\right)^2}{N-1}}$$

STDA = estimated standard variance
R_t = yield on day t
$\bar{R}$ = average yield
N = number of observations

1.6.2 Berechnung der Zinsen aus Swapsätzen (Terminkurse)

Zinssatz
Gegenwährung:

$$r_G = \left(\left[\frac{\left(1 + \left(r_Q \cdot \frac{T}{B_Q}\right)\right) \cdot TK}{SPOT} \right] - 1 \right) \frac{B_G}{T}$$

Zinssatz
quotierte Währung:

$$r_Q = \left(\left[\frac{\left(1 + \left(r_G \cdot \frac{T}{B_G}\right)\right) \cdot SPOT}{TK} \right] - 1 \right) \frac{B_Q}{T}$$

r_Q = Zinssatz quotierte Währung
r_G = Zinssatz Gegenwährung
T = Anzahl der Tage
B = Berechnungsbasis
TK = Terminkurs (Spot ± Auf-/Abschlag)
SPOT = Kassakurs

Anmerkung: Bei dem Währungspaar USD/JPY ist z.B. USD die quotierte Währung und JPY die Gegenwährung.

1.6.3 Call-Put-Parität

$$Put = Call + \frac{(STR - Out)}{1 + \left(r_G \cdot \frac{T}{B_G}\right)}$$

Put = Put Prämie
Call = Call Prämie
STR = Strike-Preis
Out = Outright
r = Zinssatz Gegenwährung
T = Tage
B_G = Berechnungsbasis Zinsen Gegenwährung

1.7 Statistik

1.7.1 Geschätzte Standardabweichung

$$STDA = \sqrt{\sum_{t=1}^{N} \frac{\left(R_t - \bar{R}\right)^2}{N-1}}$$

STDA = geschätzte Standardabweichung
R_t = Rendite am Tag t
$\bar{R}$ = durchschnittliche Rendite
N = Anzahl Beobachtungen

$$\sigma = \sigma_A \cdot \frac{\sqrt{x}}{\sqrt{252}}$$

σ_x = volatility for x days holding period
σ_A = volatility for 1 year

$$\sigma = \sigma_A \cdot \frac{\sqrt{x}}{\sqrt{252}}$$

σ_x = Volatilität für x Tage Haltedauer
σ_A = Volatilität für 1 Jahr

2. Guide programming HP-calculator

FX instruments

1

Outright

FWG=SPOT*((1+(%R2*(DAYS/BAS2)))/(1+(%R1*(DAYS/BAS1))))

2

Call/Put-Parity

PUT=CALL+(STRIKE−OUTR)/(1+(%R2*(DAYS/BAS2)))

Money market

3

Day calculation

DAYS=DDAYS(DAT1:DAT2:KAL)

[KAL1= act. calendar incl. leap year KAL2= 365-days calendar without leap year KAL3= 30/360 calendar]

4

discount/

effective rate

%R=%DISK/(1−(%DISK*(DAYS/BASIS)))

5

average rate

AR=((%R1*(D1/BASIS))+(%R2*(D2/BASIS))+(%R3*(D3/BASIS))+(%R4*(D4/BASIS))
+(%R5*(D5/BASIS)))*(BASIS/(D1+D2+D3+D4+D5))

6

effective rate

ER=((1+%R1*(D1/BASIS))*(1+%R2*(D2/BASIS))*(1+%R3*(D3/BASIS))*(1+%R4*(D4/
BASIS))* (1+%R5*(D5/BASIS)))-1)*(BASIS/(D1+D2+D3+D4+D5))

7

Interpolation

I=R%S+((R%L−R%S)/(DL−DS))*(DAYS−DS)

8

Forward/Forward

less one year

%FWD=(((1+(%RL*DL/BASIS))/(1+(%RS*DS/BASIS)))-1)*BASIS/(DL-DS)

2. Anleitung Programmierung HP-Rechner

FX-Instrumente

1

Outright

FWG=SPOT*((1+(%R2*(TAGE/BAS2)))/(1+(%R1*(TAGE/BAS1))))

2

Call/PutParität

PUT=CALL+(STRIKE–OUTR)/(1+(%R2*(TAGE/BAS2)))

Geldmarkt

3

Tageberechnung

TAGE=DDAYS(DAT1:DAT2:KAL)

[KAL1=akt. Kalender inkl. Schaltjahr KAL2=365-Tage Kalender ohne Schaltjahr KAL3=30/360 Kalender]

4

Diskont/

Effektivzins

%R=%DISK/(1–(%DISK*(TAGE/BASIS)))

5

Durchschnittszinssatz

DZ=((%R1*(T1/BASIS))+(%R2*(T2/BASIS))+(%R3*(T3/BASIS))+(%R4*(T4/BASIS))
+(%R5*(T5/BASIS)))*(BASIS/(T1+T2+T3+T4+T5))

6

Effektivzinssatz

EFFZ=((1+%R1*(T1/BASIS))*(1+%R2*(T2/BASIS))*(1+%R3*(T3/BASIS))*(1+%R4*(T4/
BASIS))* (1+%R5*(T5/BASIS))-1)*(BASIS/(T1+T2+T3+T4+T5))

7

Interpolation

ZINS=R%K+((R%L–R%K)/(TL–TK))*(TAGE–TK)

8

Forward/Forward

unter 1 Jahr

%FWD=(((1+(%RL*TL/BASIS))/(1+(%RK*TK/BASIS)))-1)*BASIS/(TL-TK)

9

FRA einfach

FRA=(((1+((%RL*TL)/BASIS))/(1+((%RK*TK)/BASIS)))–1)*(BASIS/(TL-TK))

9

FRA simple

FRA=(((1+((%RL*DL/BASIS))/(1+((%RS*DS)/BASIS)))–1)*(BASIS/(DL-DS))

10

FRA amount due

AD=((%REF-%FRA)*VOL*(DFRA/BASIS))/(1+(%REF*(DFRA/BASIS)))

Capital market

11

Bond

final maturity

PRICE=(%CPN*∑(YEAR:1:MAT:1:(1/(1+%R)^YEAR))+(1/(1+%R)^MAT))*100

12

Bond

semi-annually

PRICE=((%CPN/ZZ)*∑(year:1:(MAT*ZZ):1:(1/(1+(%R/ZZ))^year)))*100+(1/(1+(%R/ZZ))^(MAT*ZZ))*100

[ZZ: 1=annually; 2=semi-annually]

13

Money market/

Capital market-Rendite

%RKM=%RGM*(TGM/BGM)*(BKM/TKM)

14

Modified Duration,

annually/semi-annually

MD=((((%CPN/ZZ)*∑(Year:1:(MAT*ZZ):1:(1/(1+(%R/ZZ))^year*(year/ZZ)))+(1/(1+(%R/ZZ))^(MAT*ZZ)* MAT))*100)/(((%CPN/ZZ)*∑(Year:1:(MAT*ZZ):1:(1/(1+(%R/ZZ))^Jahr))+(1/(1+(%R/ZZ))^(MAT*ZZ)))*100)) * (1/(1+%R/ZZ))

[ZZ: 1=annually; 2=semi-annually]

15

2-year Zero of interest

Z2 = (1/((1-(R2*(1/(1+R1))))/(1+R2)))^(1/2)-1

16

3-year Zero of interest

Z3 =(1/((1-(R3*((1/(1+R1))+(1-(R2*(1/(1+R1))))/(1+R2))))/(1+R3)))^(1/3)-1

TIPS:

Calculation of days between two dates with the HP standard function TIME/CALC

Calculation of standard variance (volatility) with the HP standard function STAT/CALC/STAW

10
FRA-Ausgleichs-
zahlung
AUSZ=((%REF-%FRA)*VOL*(TFRA/BASIS))/(1+(%REF*(TFRA/BASIS)))

Kapitalmarkt

11
Bond
endfällig
KURS=(%CPN*∑(JAHR:1:LFZ:1:(1/(1+%R)^JAHR))+(1/(1+%R)^LFZ))*100

12
Bond
halbjährlich
Kurs=((%CPN/ZZ)*∑(Jahr:1:(LFZ*ZZ):1:(1/(1+(%R/ZZ))^Jahr)))*100+(1/(1+(%R/ZZ))^(LFZ*ZZ))*100
[ZZ: 1=jährlich; 2=halbjährlich]

13
Geldmarkt-/
Kapitalmarktrendite
%RKM=%RGM*(TGM/BGM)*(BKM/TKM)

14
Modified Duration,
jährlich/halbjährlich
MD=(((((%CPN/ZZ)*∑(Jahr:1:(LFZ*ZZ):1:(1/(1+(%R/ZZ))^Jahr*(Jahr/ZZ)))+(1/(1+(%R/ZZ))^(LFZ*ZZ)*   LFZ))*100)/(((%CPN/ZZ)*∑(Jahr:1:(LFZ*ZZ):1:(1/(1+(%R/ZZ))^Jahr))+(1/(1+(%R/ZZ))^(LFZ*ZZ)))*100)) * (1/(1+%R/ZZ))
[ZZ: 1=jährlich; 2=halbjährlich]

15
2-Jahres Zero aus Zins
Z2 = (1/(((1-(R2*(1/(1+R1))))/(1+R2)))^(1/2)-1

16
3-Jahres Zero aus Zins
Z3 =(1/(((1-(R3*((1/(1+R1))+(1-(R2*(1/(1+R1))))/(1+R2))))/(1+R3)))^(1/3)-1

TIPPS:

Berechnung Tage zwischen zwei Daten über die HP Standardfunktion ZEIT/RECH
Berechung der geschätzten Standardabweichung (Volatilität) über die HP Standardfunktion STAT/RECH/STAW

3. Solution to Practice Questions

PART I: THE MONEY MARKET

1. Methods of Interest Calculation, Yield Curve and Quotation

1. **ACT-method (Actual-method):** Counting the actual numbers of days that elapse.; **30-method:** Each month counts as 30 days (remaining days in a month are subtracted).; **30E-method:** Each month counts as 30 days (the 31st is treated as if it were the 30th; remaining days are subtracted).
2. **360-method:** Assuming that each year has 360 days.; **365-method:** Assuming that each year has 365 days.; **ACT-method:** in the money market (ISDA-method): The actual days per year are counted (leap year 366 days, "normal" year 365 days). If a deal runs over two years (one of them being a leap year), the interest calculation is divided into two parts.; in the capital market (ISMA-method): A year is counted with actual days of the term of interest (multiplied by the number of terms of interest).
3. d)
4. a)
5. c) and d)
6. d)
7. **Steep yield curve**: (normal or positive) short-term interest rates are lower than long-term interest rates; **flat yield curve**: interest rates for different terms are the same; **inverse yield curve**: short-term interest rates are higher than long-term interest rates.
8. c)
9. b)
10. c)
11. d)
12. 120-day interest rate = 0.0310 + [(0.035 – 0.0310)/(180 – 90)] x (120-90) = **3.23%**
13. One basis point is equal to $^{1}/_{100}$ of 1%, i.e. **0.01%.**
14. For money market transactions with a term of up to one year, the interest is paid **at the end of the term**.
15. For money market transactions where the term exceeds one year, interest is paid first after one year and then at maturity.

2. Money Market Cash Instruments

1. b)
2. EURIBOR (Euro Interbank Offered Rate)
3. b)
4. d)
5. LIBOR (London Interbank Offered Rate)
6. Most of the instruments are **coupon instruments,** ie, they are issued at an interest rate (coupon) and face value. Notional amount and interests are paid back at maturity. **Discount instruments** are issued with a discount from their notional value; at maturity the holder receives the notional amount. The difference between the issuing price and repayment is the buyer's interest result.
7. Coupon instruments are **Interbank Deposits, CDs and Repos**. Discount instruments are eg, **Commercial Papers, T-Bills and Eligible Bills**.

3. Lösung zu den Wiederholungsfragen

TEIL I: DER GELDMARKT

1. Zinsberechnung, Zinskurve und Quotierungen

1. **ACT-Methode (Actual-Methode):** Die tatsächlich verstrichenen Tage werden gezählt. **30-Methode:** Jeder Monat wird mit 30 Tagen gerechnet. Die Resttage innerhalb eines Monats werden subtrahiert. **30E-Methode:** Jeder Monat wird mit 30 Tagen gerechnet. Der 31. eines Monats wird mit dem 30. gleichgesetzt. Resttage werden subtrahiert.
2. **360-Methode:** Das Jahr wird mit 360 Tagen gerechnet. **365-Methode:** Das Jahr wird mit 365 Tagen gerechnet. **ACT-Methode:** <u>Geldmarkt (ISDA-Methode):</u> Gerechnet wird mit der Anzahl der tatsächlichen Jahrestage (Schaltjahr 366, normales Jahr 365). Fällt ein Geschäft in zwei Jahre, von denen ein Jahr ein Schaltjahr ist, wird die Zinsberechnung in zwei Teile geteilt, <u>Anleihemarkt (ISMA-Methode):</u> Das Jahr wird mit den echten Tagen der Zinsperiode (mal die Anzahl der Zinsperioden) gerechnet.
3. d)
4. a)
5. c) und d)
6. d)
7. **Ansteigende Zinskurve** (normale, steile, positive Zinskurve): Die Zinsen für kurze Laufzeiten sind niedriger als für lange Laufzeiten. **Flache Zinskurve**: Die Zinssätze für unterschiedliche Laufzeiten sind gleich hoch. **Inverse Zinskurve**: Die Zinssätze für kurze Laufzeiten sind höher als die Zinsen für lange Laufzeiten.
8. c)
9. b)
10. c)
11. d)
12. 120-Tage-Zinssatz = 0,0310 + [(0,035 – 0,0310)/(180 – 90)] x (120-90) = **3,23%**
13. Ein Basispunkt ist **1/100 von 1%, also 0,01%.**
14. Bei Geldmarktgeschäften mit einer Laufzeit von bis zu einem Jahr werden die Zinsen **im Nachhinein am Ende der jeweiligen Laufzeit** gezahlt.
15. Bei Geldmarktgeschäften mit einer Laufzeit von über einem Jahr werden die Zinsen **zunächst jährlich und dann bei Fälligkeit** bezahlt.

2. Cash-Instrumente im Geldmarkt

1. b)
2. EURIBOR (Euro Interbank Offered Rate)
3. b)
4. d)
5. LIBOR (London Interbank Offered Rate)
6. **Kuponinstrumente** werden zum Nennwert und mit einem Zinssatz (Kupon) emittiert. Am Ende der Laufzeit wird dann der Nennwert plus Zinsen zurückgezahlt. Im Gegensatz dazu werden **Abzinsungsinstrumente** (Diskontinstrumente) mit einem Abschlag vom Nennwert emittiert und zum vollen Nennwert zurückgezahlt. Aus der Differenz der beiden Beträge ergibt sich der Ertrag für den Käufer.
7. Zu den Kuponinstrumenten zählen **Interbank Depots, CDs und Repos.** Abzinsungsinstrumente sind z.B. **Commercial Papers, T-Bills und Wechsel.**

8. A **yield** (interest rate p.a., effective rate) is quoted on the basis of the invested capital (= present value), a **discount rate** is calculated on the basis of the future value. It is essential to differentiate between: coupon instrument ≠ discount instrument and yield ≠ discount rate.

9. **LIBOR (London Interbank Offered Rate)** is the most important reference rate, used when fixing certain maturities (FRAs, interest rate swaps, loans, etc.). It embodies the average interest rate of certain reference banks that are chosen for the daily fixing. LIBOR is called the interest rate at which top banks are willing to lend money to one another. **LIBID (London Interbank Bid Rate)**: In contrast to LIBOR, the LIBID represents the so-called deposit rate. LIBOR minus the usual spread yields the LIBID (eg, LIBOR USD 3-month = 3.50%, minus spread of 1/8% equals to LIBID of 3.375%). LIBID is the rate banks are willing to borrow money at.

10. The main advantage of CDs compared to clean deposits is that the bearer of a CD possesses a **negotiable liquid instrument in the secondary market**. Therefore, the bearer of a CD has the option to invest a deposit if there is sufficient demand. At the same time he retains a **flexible liquidity position** during the whole term of the CD. For this flexibility, the borrower usually has to accept **lower rates than the market interest rates**.

11. e)

12. d)

13. d)

14. b) 5,000,000 x [1+ (0.0615 x 181/360)]/[1+(0.0585 x 90/360)] = **USD 5,080,304.71**

15. An eligible bill is a certificate (several formal regulations have to be observed) by which the issuer obliges himself to pay a specific amount of money at a given place and time to the bearer. He has to fulfill this obligation either himself or through someone else.

16. a) and c)

17. b) 0.032/[1 − (0.032 x 91/360)] = **3.226%**

18. a) 20 m − (20 m x 0.037 x 35/360) = **USD 19,928,055.56**

19. d)

20. a)

21. a), c) and e)

22. a)

3. Short-term Interest Rate Derivatives

1. d)

2. b) and e)

3. d)

4. The FRA term is **the period from settlement date until maturity date**.

5. b)

6. c)

7. c)

8. a)

9. The **steeper** the yield curve the **higher** the FRA rates. The **flatter** the yield curve the **lower** the FRA rates.

8. Wird ein **Zinssatz (Rendite)** angegeben, so wird der Zinsbetrag auf der Basis des Anfangsbetrages berechnet. Wird ein **Diskontsatz** angegeben, so ist gemeint, dass der Abschlag (Zinsbetrag) auf Basis des Rückzahlungsbetrages berechnet wird und nicht auf Basis des Anfangsbetrages.

9. Der **LIBOR (London Interbank Offered Rate)** war vor Einführung des Euro der wichtigste Referenzzinssatz, der üblicherweise zum Fixieren bestimmter Fälligkeiten (FRAs, Interest-Rate Swaps, Kredite etc.) herangezogen wird. Er bildet den durchschnittlichen Zinssatz bestimmter Referenzbanken, die für das tägliche Fixing ausgewählt wurden. Der LIBOR wird auch häufig als jener Satz bezeichnet, zu dem erstklassige Banken bereit sind, untereinander Geld zu leihen. Der **LIBID (London Interbank Bid Rate)** stellt im Gegensatz zum LIBOR den sogenannten Einlagensatz dar. Der LIBOR abzüglich des üblichen Spreads ergibt somit den LIBID. Er wird auch als jener Satz bezeichnet, zu dem Banken bereit sind, Einlagen zu nehmen.

10. Der große Vorteil eines CDs gegenüber einem Depotgeschäft besteht darin, dass der Inhaber des CDs über ein **handelbares, liquides Instrument** verfügt, das er im Sekundärmarkt auch vor Fälligkeit bei Bedarf wieder verkaufen kann. Somit kann Cash kurzfristig mit einem für die Laufzeit des CDs fixierten Zinssatz angelegt werden und durch die jederzeitige Handelbarkeit die **Flexibilität in der Liquiditätsposition** trotzdem beibehalten werden. Als Preis für diese Flexibilität muss der Inhaber des CDs üblicherweise einen **niedrigeren Satz** als die im Geldmarkt quotierten Depotsätze akzeptieren.

11. e)
12. d)
13. d)
14. b) 5.000.000 x [1+ (0,0615 x 181/360)]/[1+(0,0585 x 90/360)] = **USD 5.080.304,71**
15. Ein gezogener Wechsel ist eine vom Aussteller unter Beachtung bestimmter Formvorschriften ausgestellte Urkunde, in der sich der Bezogene durch Akzept verpflichtet, eine bestimmte Geldsumme zu einer festgesetzten Zeit an einen bestimmten Ort an den als berechtigt Ausgewiesenen zu zahlen.
16. a) und c)
17. b) 0,032/[1 – (0,032 x 91/360)] = **3,226%**
18. a) 20 Mio. – (20 Mio, x 0,037 x 35/360) = **USD 19.928.055,56**
19. d)
20. a)
21. a), c) und e)
22. a)

3. Geldmarktderivate

1. d)
2. b) und e)
3. d)
4. Die Laufzeit eines FRAs ist die **Periode zwischen Settlement-Tag und Maturity-Tag.**
5. b)
6. c)
7. c)
8. a)
9. Je **steiler** die Zinskurve, desto **höher** die FRA-Sätze. Je **flacher** die Zinskurve, desto **niedriger** die FRA-Sätze.

10. a)
11. a)
12. a)
13. c)
14. a)
15. a)
16. b) and e)
17. d)
18. The **sum of all open contracts** is the open interest.
19. b)
20. c)
21. The value basis is the **difference between the implied forward rate** of the actual futures price in the market **and the "fair" forward rate**.
22. b)
23. d)
24. b)
25. In contrast to a strip hedge, where you trade a series of consecutive futures, for a stack hedge you only trade the **future with the closest delivery month**. Stack hedging is used when the futures which are needed for the hedge are not liquid enough (or are not traded at all). These futures are then replaced by futures with shorter periods and rolled over at maturity. Stack hedging is based on the underlying assumption that the price of the shorter future develops in the same way as the price of the longer future.
26. b)
27. a) and c)
28. a)
29. The simultaneous purchase and sale of futures contracts with **different times to maturity** and the **same underlying** is called an **intra-contract spread**.
30. An inter-contract spread is the simultaneous purchase and sale of futures contracts on **different underlyings**. Different times to maturity are not required.
31. c)
32. b)

4. Repurchase Agreements (Repos)

1. a)
2. a)
3. d)
4. d)
5. c)
6. b)
7. c)
8. The right of substitution allows the seller to recall collateral during a repo and substitute alternative collateral of equivalent value and quality.
9. b)
10. d)

10. a)
11. a)
12. a)
13. c)
14. a)
15. a)
16. b) und e)
17. d)
18. Als Open Interest wird die **Summe aller noch offenen Kontrakte** bezeichnet.
19. b)
20. c)
21. Die Wert-Basis ist die **Differenz zwischen dem implizierten Futures-Satz** (aus dem aktuellen Futures-Preis) **und dem rechnerischen Forward-Satz** (abgeleitet aus den aktuellen Cash-Sätzen).
22. b)
23. d)
24. b)
25. Beim Stack Hedging wird **nur der Future mit dem nächstgelegenen Delivery Month gehandelt**. Stack Hedging wird angewendet, wenn die für einen Hedge benötigten Futures entweder nicht gehandelt werden oder nicht ausreichend liquide sind. Es werden dann diese Futures durch solche mit einer kürzeren Laufzeit ersetzt und bei Fälligkeit weitergerollt. Beim Stack Hedging wird unterstellt, dass sich der Preis des kurzen Futures ähnlich wie jener des langen Futures entwickelt.
26. b)
27. a) und c)
28. a)
29. Wenn die Kontrakte **dasselbe Underlying** und **unterschiedliche Laufzeiten** haben, dann spricht man vom einem Intra-Kontraktspread.
30. Als Inter-Kontraktspread wird der gleichzeitige Kauf und Verkauf von Futures mit **unterschiedlichen Underlyings** bezeichnet. Anders als beim Intra-Kontraktspread sind **unterschiedliche Liefertage nicht erforderlich**.
31. c)
32. b)

4. Repurchase Agreements (Repos)

1. a)
2. a)
3. d)
4. d)
5. c)
6. b)
7. c)
8. Unter dem Recht zur Substitution versteht man das Recht des Verkäufers, das Collateral während der Laufzeit vom Käufer zurückzuverlangen und durch ein anderes Wertpapier von ähnlicher oder besserer Qualität zu ersetzen.
9. b)
10. d)

11. c)
12. d)
13. d)
14. **Bilateral repo (delivery repo):** the buyer takes custody of the collateral from the seller.; **Hold-in-custody (HIC) repo:** the seller retains custody of the collateral on behalf of the buyer.; **Tri-party repo:** collateral is transferred into the custody of the buyer across accounts held with an independent third-party custodian.
15. d)
16. b)
17. d)
18. see 4.6.1 Comparison of classic repos vs. sell/buy-backs
19. c)
20. a), b) and d)

5. Overnight Index Swaps (OIS)

1. The Overnight Index Swap **helps to vary interest rate positions** on a short-term basis and to **reduce the risk of varying overnight rates**.
2. d)
3. c)
4. d)
5. c)
6. a)
7. a) and d)
8. d)
9. c)

PART II: THE CAPITAL MARKET

1. Bonds

1. b)
2. b) and d)
3. government, banks and corporates
4. **Registered bonds:** The current owner of the bond and every change of ownership is recorded in a central register. Coupon payments and redemption are booked on the account of the current owner. **Bearer bonds:** The current bearer of the bond is entitled to receive the interest payments and redemption. The current owner is not registered. Interest payments are made to the bearer of the interest coupons and the repayment is to be made to the bearer or sender of the bond.
5. **Asset Backed Securities**: a bond which is securitised via certain assets (eg, loans, credit card outstandings, leasings etc.)
6. c)
7. d)
8. c)
9. a)
10. d)
11. a)

11. c)
12. d)
13. d)
14. **Bilaterales Repo (Delivery Repo):** Die Wertpapiere werden vom Verkäufer an den Käufer geliefert. **Hold-in-Custody (HIC) Repo:** Der Verkäufer behält die Wertpapiere und verwahrt sie treuhändisch für den Käufer. **Tri-party Repo:** Das Wertpapier wird dabei vom Konto des Verkäufers auf das Konto des Käufers übertragen, welche beide bei einem unabhängigen Clearing House – der dritten Partei – gehalten werden.
15. d)
16. b)
17. d)
18. siehe Punkte 4.6.1 Vergleich klassische Repos vs. Sell/Buy-Backs
19. c)
20. a), b) und d)

5. Overnight Index Swaps (OIS)

1. Der Overnight Index Swap bietet unter anderem die Möglichkeit, **Zinsbindungen kurzfristig zu variieren** und das **Risiko schwankender Taggeldsätze zu minimieren.**
2. d)
3. c)
4. d)
5. c)
6. a)
7. a) und d)
8. d)
9. c)

TEIL II: DER KAPITALMARKT

1. Anleihen

1. b)
2. b) und d)
3. Staat, Banken und Unternehmen
4. Eine **Namensschuldverschreibung** ist eine Anleihe, bei der der aktuelle Besitzer sowie jede Besitzänderung in einem Zentralregister aufgezeichnet werden. Zinszahlung und Rückzahlung erfolgen auf das Konto des aktuellen Besitzers. Eine **Inhaberschuldverschreibung** ist eine Anleihe, die den Überbringer berechtigt, Zins- und Rückzahlung zu erhalten. Der aktuelle Besitzer ist nicht dokumentiert, Zinszahlungen erfolgen an den Überbringer der Kuponabschnitte, die Rückzahlung erfolgt an den Überbringer oder Einsender der Schuldverschreibung.
5. **Asset Backed Securities:** eine Anleihe die durch bestimmte Aktiva (z.B. Kredite, Kreditkartenforderungen, Leasingfinanzierungen usw.) besichert ist
6. c)
7. d)
8. c)
9. a)
10. d)
11. a)

12. b)
13. **Flat yield curve:** All future cashflows are discounted with the same interest rate, the market yield for the bond's maturity.; **Re-investment of the interest returns at the same interest rate:** However, when calculating the present value with the formula $1/(1+r)^n$, you are assuming that interest payments can always be invested at the same rate during the term of the bond.
14. The zero curve is derived from one of these other curves, ie, the **zero rates can be calculated from the interest rates of coupon instruments**. This transaction is called boot-strapping.
15. d)
16. a)
17. b)
18. term of the bond, coupon and market yield
19. b)
20. a)
21. a)
22. b)
23. d)
24. b), c), d) and f)

2. Interest Rate Swap (IRS)

1. Public agent: The bank brokers a swap deal between two potential parties and supports them with its know-how during the negotiations of the contract. Legally, the bank is not involved in the contract and therefore does not take on any risk.
   Anonymous agent: The bank takes the role of an intermediary between two parties ("A" and "C"). With both parties, the bank concludes a contract separately. Parties "A" and "C" do not enter a legal agreement. In this case, the risks of creditworthiness are taken over by the bank.
2. a)
3. d)
4. For **spot swaps** the term usually starts two working days after the trade date (exception: GBP same day). For **forward Swaps**, it is fixed at another date than the usual two working days after trade date.
5. d)
6. d)
7. b)
8. b)
9. d)
10. d)
11. c)
12. **Initial transaction:** Exchange of the principal in different currencies 1 and 2 (initial exchange); **Interest payment:** Exchange of interest payments in different currencies during the swap term; **Final transaction:** Re-exchange of the principal in 1 and 2 (final exchange).
13. a)
14. c)
15. b) and c)

12. b)
13. **Flache Zinskurve:** Alle zukünftigen Cashflows werden mit dem gleichen Zinssatz, nämlich der Marktrendite für die Endfälligkeit der Anleihe, diskontiert. **Reinvestition der Zinserträge zum gleichen Zinssatz:** Bei Berechnung des Barwertes mit der Formel $1/(1+r)n$ wird unterstellt, dass **während der Laufzeit ausgezahlte Zinszahlungen immer zum gleichen Zinssatz wieder angelegt** werden können.
14. Die Zero-Kurve ist eine von den Zinskurven abgeleitete Zinskurve, d.h., die **Zero-Zinsen** können **aus den Zinssätzen von zinstragenden Instrumenten errechnet** werden. Dieser Vorgang wird Bootstrapping genannt.
15. d)
16. a)
17. b)
18. Laufzeit der Anleihe, Kuponhöhe und Marktrendite
19. b)
20. a)
21. a)
22. b)
23. d)
24. b), c), d) und f)

2. Zinsswapgeschäfte

1. Bei der **offenen Vermittlung** führt die Bank als Arrangeur zwei potenzielle Swappartner zusammen und unterstützt mit ihrem Know-how die Vertragsverhandlungen. Am Swapvertrag selbst ist sie jedoch rechtlich nicht beteiligt – sie übernimmt also kein Risiko. Bei der **anonymen Vermittlung** stellt sich die Bank als Mittler zwischen zwei Partner (A und C) und schließt mit jedem der beiden Kontrahenten einen separaten Vertrag ab. Die Partner A und C stehen in keiner direkten rechtlichen Verbindung zueinander. Die Bonitätsrisiken trägt in diesem Fall die Bank.
2. a)
3. d)
4. Bei **Spot Swaps** ist die Valuta üblicherweise zwei Bankarbeitstage nach dem Handelstag (Ausnahmen z.B. GBP gleichtägig). Bei **Forward Swaps** wird die Valuta zu einem anderen Datum als die üblichen zwei Bankarbeitstage festgelegt.
5. d)
6. d)
7. b)
8. b)
9. d)
10. d)
11. c)
12. **Anfangstransaktion:** Tausch der Kapitalbeträge in zwei unterschiedlichen Währungen 1 und 2 (Initial Exchange). **Zinstransaktion:** In der Zinstransaktion werden während der Laufzeit des Swaps Zinszahlungen in den zwei unterschiedlichen Währungen geleistet. **Schlusstransaktion:** Rücktausch der Kapitalbeträge in 1 und 2 (Final Exchange).
13. a)
14. c)
15. b) und c)

3. Interest Rate Options

1. An American option can be **exercised any time during the life of the option** and an European option can be **exercised only at expiry.**
2. The option's intrinsic value is **part of the option's premium**. For an in-the-money option, it represents the **amount by which the strike price is either below (call option) or above (put option) the price of the underlying**.
3. The option's time value is influenced by the **life of the option**, by the expectations on the **volatility** of the underlying, and by the **ratio between market price and strike price**.
4. c)
5. d) USD 50,000,000 x 0.035 = USD 1,750,000
6. b)
7. c)
8. d)
9. b)
10. d)
11. The **aim of a collar is to reduce the cost** (= premium) of the bought cap/floor by selling the floor/cap.
12. a)
13. The collar is usually **quoted in a "package"**. This means, that the **option premium is quoted in percentage for a collar** and not separately as two premiums for the used caps and floors.
14. The premium and thus the value of a bond option depends on the chosen strike price, the term, the volatility and the interest rate difference between money market and capital market.
15. The premium can either be quoted in **basis points** or can be computed with the **"futures style" method**. With the "futures style" method the premium is computed individually as a **percentage** depending on the risk of the whole options and futures portfolio.
16. d), f) and g)
17. A swaption offers **two possible forms of settlement**; **cash settlement** (settlement payment, with which the current present value of the swap is paid off) or **physical "delivery"** of a real interest rate swap.
18. a)
19. b)
20. b) and d)
21. b)

PART III: FOREIGN EXCHANGE & OPTIONS

1. FX Spot

1. The delivery of a spot transaction is normally **two bank days after the dealing date**.
2. **Monday, 21 December.** Since the "normal" **value date** (two days after the dealing date) falls on a public holiday, the next working day is taken as the value date for the transaction.
3. b)

3. Zinsoptionen

1. Während eine **amerikanische Option** an jedem Handelstag während ihrer Laufzeit ausgeübt werden kann, kann eine **europäische Option** nur am letzten Tag ihrer Laufzeit ausgeübt werden.
2. Der innere Wert einer Option ist ein **Teil der Optionsprämie.** Er ist der **Betrag, um den der Strike-Preis** einer In-the-money-Option beim Call unter bzw. beim Put **über dem Marktpreis des Underlying liegt.**
3. Er wird von der **Laufzeit**, der von den Marktteilnehmern erwarteten **Volatilität** des Basiswerts und vom **Verhältnis Marktpreis zu Strike-Preis** beeinflusst.
4. c)
5. d) USD 50.000.000 x 0,035 = USD 1.750.000
6. b)
7. c)
8. d)
9. b)
10. d)
11. Das Ziel eines Collars ist, die **Kosten** (= Prämie) für den gekauften Cap/Floor durch den Verkauf eines Floor/Cap zu **verringern.**
12. a)
13. Bei Collars erfolgt die Quotierung meist **„im Package".** Das bedeutet, es wird eine **Optionsprämie** in Prozent **für eine bestimmte Collar-Kombination** quotiert und nicht zwei Prämien für Cap und Floor, die dann saldiert werden, quotiert.
14. Die Prämie und damit der Wert einer Bond-Option hängt ab von dem gewählten Strike-Preis, der Laufzeit, der Volatilität und der Zinsdifferenz zwischen Geld- und Kapitalmarkt.
15. Die Prämie wird entweder in **Basispunkten** quotiert oder nach **dem „futures-style"-Verfahren** berechnet. Die Prämie wird bei einem „futures-style"-Verfahren als **Prozentsatz** in Abhängigkeit vom Risiko des Gesamtportfolios an Optionen und Futures individuell ermittelt.
16. d), f) und g)
17. Bei Swaptions gibt es **beide Möglichkeiten des Settlements.** Es kann sowohl ein **Cash-Settlement** (Ausgleichszahlung, bei der der aktuelle Barwert des Swaps ausbezahlt wird) als auch die **physische Lieferung,** bei deren Ausübung ein echter Zinsswap „geliefert" wird, vereinbart werden.
18. a)
19. b)
20. b) und d)
21. b)

TEIL III: FOREIGN EXCHANGE & OPTIONEN

1. Kassadevisenmarkt (FX Spot)

1. Die Lieferung findet bei einem Kassageschäft im Normalfall **zwei Bankarbeitstage nach Abschluss** statt.
2. **Montag, der 21.12.** Da der zweite Tag nach Geschäftsabschluss kein Banktag ist, ist der nächstfolgende Banktag der Valutatag.
3. b)

4. b)
5. d)
6. The broker's advantage is the **bigger market depth** compared to the one-to-one direct trading in the interbank market as with a broker you have many **more potential counterparties at the same time**.
7. A **voice broker** is a real human being who trades with banks via open telephone line (or Reuters conversation). He keeps his customers up-do-date on actual quotes. If a bank trades on a broker's price, a deal is done between this bank and the bank which quoted the price (if they both have enough limit for each other). The broker then confirms the deal with both of them and additionally sends a written confirmation to both counterparts as well.

   An **electronic broker** or electronic broking system works like a voice broker but the quotes and deals are done through a special system. The best known systems are Reuters 3000 and EBS. These systems also check whether both banks have enough limit to deal with each other. Then the system prints a confirmation for both counterparties.
8. c)
9. b)
10. d)
11. Big Figure = **2.59**
12. Pips = **70**
13. a)
14. b)
15. The spread is the **difference between the bid and offer rates**.
16. In a **direct quote** the home currency is the quote currency and the foreign currency is the base currency. In an **indirect quote** the home currency is the base currency and the foreign currency is the quote currency.
17. A **square or flat position** in one currency means that the dealer has **bought and sold the same** amount of currency and has no risk if the exchange rate changes.
18. a)
19. SEK/JPY rate = **18.4759**
20. c) and d)
21.

Country	ISO Code
New Zealand	NZD
Hungary	HUF
Sweden	SEK
Mexico	MXN
Macedonia	MKD
Australia	AUD
Argentina	ARS
South Africa	ZAR

4. b)
5. d)
6. Der Vorteil eines Brokers ist die **größere Markttiefe.** Während man beim direkten Interbankhandel immer nur eine begrenzte Anzahl von Banken gleichzeitig für einen Preis fragen kann, hat man über den Broker gleichzeitig Zugriff auf eine große Zahl von potenziellen Kontrahenten.
7. Ein **Voice Broker** ist ein Mensch aus Fleisch und Blut, der per Telefonstandleitung (auch via Reuters-Konversation) die Banken untereinander vermittelt. Er hält seine Kunden mit den aktuellen Quotierungen permanent auf dem Laufenden. Der Broker bestätigt dann beiden Banken mündlich den Geschäftsabschluss und sendet zusätzlich eine schriftliche Bestätigung an beide Kontrahenten. Ein **elektronischer Broker** bzw. ein elektronisches Broking-System funktioniert wie ein Voice Broker, nur erfolgen die Quotierungen und Abschlüsse in einem speziellen System. Die bekanntesten dieser Systeme sind Reuters 3000 und EBS. Zusätzlich prüfen diese Systeme vor Abschluss die Limite der Banken füreinander. Nach erfolgtem Abschluss erstellt das System eine schriftliche Bestätigung für beide Kontrahenten.
8. c)
9. b)
10. d)
11. Big Figure = **2,59**
12. Pips = **70**
13. a)
14. b)
15. Als Spread bezeichnet man die **Differenz zwischen dem Geldsatz und dem Briefsatz** (auch Geld-/Briefspanne).
16. Bei einer **direkten Quotierung** ist die Basiswährung (quotierte Währung) die Fremdwährung und die Heimwährung die Gegenwährung. Bei einer **indirekten Quotierung** ist die Heimwährung die Basiswährung (quotierte Währung) und die Fremdwährung die Gegenwährung. Die indirekte Quotierung entspricht dem reziproken Wert der direkten Quotierung.
17. Nimmt der Händler **weder eine Long- noch eine Short-Position** ein, so spricht man von einer Square- oder Flat-Position in einer Währung.
18. a)
19. SEK/JPY-Kurs = **18,4759**
20. c) und d)
21.

Land	ISO-Code
Neuseeland	**NZD**
Ungarn	**HUF**
Schweden	**SEK**
Mexiko	**MXN**
Mazedonien	**MKD**
Australien	**AUD**
Argentinien	**ARS**
Südafrika	**ZAR**

Egypt	**EGP**
Norway	**NOK**
Poland	**PLN**
Thailand	**THB**
Hong Kong	**HKD**

2. FX Outright and FX Swaps

1. b)
2. e)
3. d)
4. The Interest Rate Parity Theorem explains the **relation between interest rate and exchange rate**. The foreign exchange market is balanced if the deposits in all currencies have the same expected yield. This parity of expected yields for deposits in any two currencies, measured in the same currency, is called interest rate parity. According to this theorem the investor is indifferent concerning an investment in the home country and an investment in a foreign country.
5. The **"covered" Interest Rate Parity Theorem** is used in case of the currency risk of an asset being hedged in a foreign currency (eg, FX swap). In case of an unhedged currency risk, the so-called **"uncovered" Interest Rate Parity Theorem** (eg, carry trades) applies.
6. Outright forward FX transactions are usually quoted as **full forward exchange rate** to customers. In the interbank market outright forward FX transactions are quoted as **forward points** or full forward exchange rate.
7. a)
8. c)
9. d)
10. e)
11. spot basis: $[(1.5245 + 1.5255)/2] = 1.5250$
12. a)
13. c)
14. c)
15. c)
16. c)
17. b) and c)
18. b) and d) 10 m x 1.4250 = 14,250,000; 10 m x 1.4222 (1.4250 – 0.0028) = 14,222,000
19. d)
20. a)
21. b) and d)
22. The amount due is based on the **difference between the NDF rate and a reference FX spot rate** at the contract's maturity. It is usually paid in USD.
23. c) and d)
24. A SAFE (Synthetic Agreement for Forward Exchange) is a **synthetic agreement for an FX swap**. The purpose of SAFEs is the **fixing of future swap rates or outright prices**, without settlement risk (as is the case with all traditional FX swap).
25. If the settlement of the underlying contract is delayed (eg, through delivery problems, delayed finalisation), the forward deal has to be prolonged in order to **fix the hedge rate**

Ägypten	**EGP**
Norwegen	**NOK**
Polen	**PLN**
Thailand	**THB**
Hongkong	**HKD**

2. Devisentermingeschäfte und Devisenswaps

1. b)
2. e)
3. d)
4. Die Zinsparitätentheorie erklärt den **Zusammenhang zwischen Zinssatz und Wechselkurs.** Der Devisenmarkt befindet sich im Gleichgewicht, wenn die Anlagen in allen Währungen dieselbe erwartete Rendite bieten. Diese Gleichheit der erwarteten Renditen auf Anlagen in zwei beliebigen Währungen, gemessen in derselben Währung, bezeichnet man als Zinsparität.
5. Die sogenannte „gedeckte" **Zinsparitätentheorie** deckt den Fall ab, bei dem das Währungsrisiko einer Anlage in Fremdwährung abgesichert wurde (z.B. über FX-Swap). Von der **„ungedeckten" Zinsparitätentheorie** spricht man, wenn das Währungsrisiko nicht abgesichert wurde (z.B. bei sogenannten Carry Trades).
6. Devisentermingeschäfte werden gegenüber Kunden üblicherweise als **vollständiger Terminkurs** quotiert. Im Interbankenhandel werden Devisentermingeschäfte in Form von **Swappunkten** oder als vollständiger Terminkurs quotiert.
7. a)
8. c)
9. d)
10. e)
11. Kassabasis: [(1,5245 + 1,5255)/2] = 1,5250
12. a)
13. c)
14. c)
15. c)
16. c)
17. b) und c)
18. b) und d) 10 Mio. x 1,4250 = 14.250.000; 10 Mio. x 1,4222 (1,4250 – 0,0028) = 14.222.000
19. d)
20. a)
21. b) und d)
22. Die Ausgleichszahlung wird über die **Differenz zwischen NDF-Kurs und Referenzkurs,** bezogen auf das zugrundeliegende Kapital, berechnet. Die Ausgleichszahlung erfolgt üblicherweise in USD.
23. c) und d)
24. Ein SAFE (Synthetic Agreement for Forward Exchange) ist eine **synthetische Vereinbarung über einen FX-Swap.** Der Zweck von SAFEs ist die **Festsetzung von zukünftigen Swapsätzen bzw. Outrightkursen** unter Vermeidung der normalen Erfüllungsrisiken (Settlementrisiko), wie sie sonst bei traditionellen FX-Swaps bestehen.
25. Wenn die Erfüllung des durch den Devisenterminkontrakt abgesicherten Geschäftes verzögert wird, entsteht oft der Wunsch, das Devisentermingeschäft zu verlängern, um

until the final settlement of the underlying contract. Forward deals can be rolled over by FX swaps at maturity. Due to the difference between the original forward rate and the actual spot rate of the FX swap cash-flows are created on the date of the original maturity. To **avoid these cashflows** customers often ask for a **prolongation at historic rates** instead of trading an FX swap at actual rates.

3. FX Options

1. d)
2. b)
3. e)
4. a)
5. **1.5** → The put is out-of-the-money, ie, the intrinsic value is 0 and the premium is **only** the **time value**.
6. c)
7. a) and d)
8. a)
9. a)
10. A **Bermudan** style option **can only be exercised at certain dates during the option period**. It is a mix of a European and American style option.
11. d)
12. a)
13. c)
14. b)
15. c)
16. d)
17. a)
18. The option premium is also influenced by the moneyness of the option (ratio between strike and outright rate). Moneyness is a **description of an option's its strike price in relation to the price of its underlying asset**. Moneyness describes the intrinsic value of an option in its current state, that is it describes how closely an option is in-the-money, out-of-the-money or at-the-money.
19. b)
20. d)
21. d)
22. a)
23. d)
24. a)
25. a)
26. a)
27. d)
28. d)
29. In contrast to the Garman-Kohlhagen and the Black-Scholes models the Cox, Ross and Rubinstein model assumes a discrete random variable, ie, it does not assume a normal distribution like the other two models but a **binomial distribution.**
30. d)

den **Kurs bis zur endgültigen Erfüllung des abgesicherten Geschäftes zu fixieren.** Fällige Devisentermingeschäfte können mit FX-Swaps weitergerollt werden. Aufgrund von Kursunterschieden zwischen dem ursprünglichen Termingeschäft und der Kassabasis des FX-Swaps kommt es dabei jedoch zu **Cashflows zum Zeitpunkt der ursprünglichen Fälligkeit.** Zur **Vermeidung dieser Cashflows** besteht bei den Kunden oft der Wunsch, die Prolongation auf „alter Kursbasis" durchzuführen, anstatt einen FX-Swap auf aktueller Kursbasis abzuschließen.

3. Devisenoptionen

1. d)
2. b)
3. e)
4. a)
5. **1,5** → Der Put ist aus dem Geld, daher ist der innere Wert 0, und die Prämie besteht **nur** aus dem **Zeitwert.**
6. c)
7. a) und d)
8. a)
9. a)
10. Eine Bermudian Option kann **nur an bestimmten, im Voraus definierten Terminen während der Laufzeit der Option ausgeübt** werden. Sie ist also eine Mischform aus europäischer und amerikanischer Option.
11. d)
12. a)
13. c)
14. b)
15. c)
16. d)
17. a)
18. Die Moneyness ist eine Kennzahl, die quasi die **„Lage" (den aktuellen Börsenkurs) einer Option (oft auch eines Optionsscheines) in Bezug zum Geld (Basiskurs)** beschreibt. Genauer gesagt, wird durch die Kennzahl beschrieben, wie nah im Geld, am Geld oder aus dem Geld der Optionsschein notiert.
19. b)
20. d)
21. d)
22. a)
23. d)
24. a)
25. a)
26. a)
27. d)
28. d)
29. Im Gegensatz zum Garman/Kohlhagen- und Black & Scholes-Modell unterstellt das Cox-Ross-Rubinstein-Modell eine **diskrete Zufallsgröße,** d.h., es unterstellt keine Normalverteilung zur Beschreibung der Kursentwicklung wie die beiden anderen Modelle, sondern eine **Binomialverteilung.**
30. d)

4. Commodities

1. a)
2. d)
3. b), c) and e)
4. a)
5. a) and b)
6. c)
7. d)
8. d)
9. a)
10. c)
11. b)
12. a), b) and c)

PART IV: THE SETTLEMENT PROCESS

1. Introduction

1. The **increasing convergence** of different markets, a **tremendous rise of trading volume** (approx. USD 5 trillion per day in the G-10 countries) and the introduction of **new and complex FX and money market products** have required risk management to improve.
2. d)
3. Operational risk is the risk of incurring interest charges or other penalties for misdirecting or otherwise failing to make settlement payments on time owing to an error or technical failure.
4. Compensation payments for delayed or failed settlements, wrong portfolio decisions due to misleading position management, costs for investigating queries, costs for negotiating a resolution with counterparty
5. Systemic risk is the risk of one participant in a transfer system, or in financial markets generally, failing to meet its required obligations when due will cause other participants or financial institutions to be unable to meet their obligations when due.
6. b)
7. Segregation of back and front office duties; procedures in place for introducing new products; sophisticated model sign-off procedure; clear quantifiable operation performance measurement; recording all counterparty conversations; sophisticated, independent audit unit; contingency plans; disaster recovery plans; alternative communication channels for confirmations and settlement
8. These procedures should ensure that the bank is capable to price, value and settle the new types of transactions and to monitor the risks associated with the product launch.
9. **Direct model risks** occur when models are used to manage a bank's own positions and accounts. **Indirect model risks** occur when models are used in support of sales and advisory work and counterparty reporting.

4. Rohstoffe

1. a)
2. d)
3. b), c) und e)
4. a)
5. a) und b)
6. c)
7. d)
8. d)
9. a)
10. c)
11. b)
12. a), b) und c)

TEIL IV: DER SETTLEMENTPROZESS

1. Grundlagen

1. Mit der **zunehmenden Vernetzung** zwischen den unterschiedlichen Märkten, dem **gewaltigen Anstieg im Handelsvolumen** (ca. USD 5 Trillionen pro Tag in den G10-Staaten) und der **Einführung neuer, komplexer Produkte** auf den FX- und Geldmärkten sind auch die Herausforderungen an das Risikomanagement gestiegen.
2. d)
3. Operationales Risiko ist das Risiko, Zinsen oder andere Gebühren zahlen zu müssen, weil durch Irrtum oder technisches Versagen eine zur Erfüllung eines Geschäftes geleistete Zahlung fehlgeleitet wird oder auf eine andere Weise nicht rechtzeitig zustande kommt.
4. Kompensationszahlungen für ein verspätetes Settlement, eine falsche Portfolioentscheidung basierend auf einer falschen Position, Kosten für Untersuchungen der Vorfälle, Kosten für Verhandlungen mit der anderen Partei zur Schlichtung von Differenzen.
5. Unter Systemrisiko versteht man das Risiko, dass ein Marktteilnehmer seinen Verpflichtungen bei Fälligkeit nicht nachkommen kann (z.B. verspätete Zahlungsanweisung, Zahlungsunfähigkeit) und dadurch andere Marktteilnehmer bei Fälligkeit ebenfalls nicht erfüllen können.
6. b)
7. Trennung von Back- und Frontoffice-Aktivitäten, geeignetes Verfahren zur Einführung neuer Produkte, umfassende Einführungsverfahren für neue Modelle, Implementierung einer quantifizierte Leistungsmessung der Backoffice-Aktivitäten, Aufzeichnung von Gesprächen zwischen Händlern und Backoffices auf Band und ausreichend lange Aufbewahrung der Bänder, unabhängige Revisionseinheit, alternative Kommunikationswege zu Nostrobanken (z.B. Fax oder Telex), Organisation von Ausweichquartieren mit entsprechenden Backup-Systemen und Entwicklung von möglichen Katastrophenszenarien und Festlegung geeigneter Vorgehensweisen im Ernstfall.
8. Dadurch soll erreicht werden, dass die Bank das Pricing, die Bewertung und das Settlement der neuen Produkte durchführen kann und imstande ist, die mit dem neuen Produkt verbundenen Risiken zu überwachen und zu kontrollieren.
9. **Direkte Modellrisiken** betreffen Fehler bei der Positions- und Kontenführung, **indirekte Modellrisiken** beziehen sich auf Probleme beim Treasury Support, bei der Kundenberatung oder bei Berichten an den Partner.

10. The retention of data should be based on tax, regulatory and legal issues. Records may be kept on paper, electronic or magnetic media. Proper measures against theft and destruction have to be implemented. In case of computer-based data storage the compatibility of programs and media must be guaranteed.

11. Processing of transactions in the system; recording of the transactions in the books; making of payments; timely confirmation of all trades; timely settlement of transactions

12. Data entry and verification; data entry and confirmation; data entry and supervisory functions; generation of settlement instructions and release of payments; settlement and nostro reconciliation

13. b)

2. Deal Capture

1. If you deal through a broker, the **name of the counterparty is disclosed only after the deal has been executed**.

2. If credit lines turn out to be full or any other problems foil the deal with the counterparty, the broker will try to **find a suitable counterparty to sit** between the original counterparties. This practice is known as "switching".

3. There are two ways to capture a deal. The front office enters the deal into the **electronic dealing system** (eg, Reuters 2000, EBS) or **the trader writes a ticket.** This can be handwritten or computer-based. It is signed by the trader and passed to the back office where the trade data are captured.

4. Trade data; time of trade; settlement date; counterparty; financial instrument traded; amount; price/rate; netting indicators and settlement instructions (sometimes)

5. Online credit systems help to keep the credit limits with counterparties, especially if the bank trades with them on an aggregate basis, assess the creditworthiness of a counterparty and to adjust the limits if necessary and avoid deals with counterparties whose limits are almost filled.

6. Bulk trades should be **confirmed as soon as possible and no later than the end of the trade date.** All trade types, regardless of maturity (spot, forwards, tom/next) must be reported. If bulk trades are not properly allocated some **credit risk may remain**.

7. b)

8. d)

9. c)

10. Particular **care should be taken for amendments to FX swap transactions after settlement of the near leg**. Thus, also the offsetting currency and interest rate positions must be amended if the incorrectly captured deal is corrected, leading to an accurate P&L.

11. c)

12. Bilateral Key Exchange; Input and Output Sequence Numbers (ISNs und OSNs); Two-level system

13. Message type codes have a strict structure: **category** (market/product); **group** (general function of message); **type** (specific function of message)

14. c)

15. a)

10. Die Aufbewahrung hat nach steuerlichen und rechtlichen Gesichtspunkten zu erfolgen. Dokumente können auf Papier, elektronischen oder magnetischen Datenträgern abgelegt werden. Für jedes Speichermedium sind adäquate Schutzvorrichtungen gegen Zerstörung oder Diebstahl einzurichten. Im Falle computergestützter Aufbewahrung ist auf die Kompatibilität der Speichermedien und Programme zu achten.
11. Verarbeitung der Transaktionen im System, Aufzeichnung der Transaktionen in den Büchern, Durchführung der Zahlungen, pünktliche Bestätigungen aller Geschäfte, Erfüllung der Transaktionen zum vereinbarten Zeitpunkt.
12. Dateneingabe und -verifizierung, Dateneingabe und Bestätigung, Dateneingabe und Aufsichtsfunktionen, Erstellung von Settlementanweisungen und Freigabe der Zahlung, Settlement und Abstimmung der (Nostro-)Konten.
13. b)

2. Der Geschäftserfassungsprozess

1. Bei Geschäften über Broker ist zu beachten, dass der **Name des Geschäftspartners erst nach Abschluss des Geschäfts bekanntgegeben** wird.
2. Sollten Probleme mit Partnerlimits auftreten, so kann der Broker einen **geeigneten Partner zwischen die ursprünglichen Partner schalten.** Diese Vorgehensweise nennt man „Switching".
3. Entweder wird das Geschäft vom Frontoffice in ein **elektronisches Handelssystem** (z.B. Reuters 2000-2, EBS) eingegeben oder der Händler erfasst **schriftlich** (handschriftlich oder computergestützt) **auf einem Ticket** das Geschäft, bestätigt es durch seine Unterschrift und gibt das Ticket an das Backoffice weiter, das die Daten eingibt.
4. Handelstag, Uhrzeit, Settlement Date, Partner, Art und Umfang des Geschäftes, Preis, Netting-Indikatoren, Settlementanweisungen (fakultativ).
5. Mit einem Online-Kreditsystem soll ermöglicht werden, dass bei Geschäften mit einem Partner an verschiedenen Orten die Limits insgesamt eingehalten werden, im Frontoffice die Kreditlimite leichter eingehalten werden können und die Kreditwürdigkeit des Partners besser eingeschätzt werden kann und Limits angepasst werden können.
6. Fondsmanager sollen angehalten werden, **alle Informationen über „bulk trades" am Handelstag weiterzuleiten**, damit das **Kreditrisikomanagement aktualisiert** werden kann. Dabei sind alle Geschäfte, unabhängig von der Laufzeit (Spot, Tom/next, Forward), zu berücksichtigen.
7. b)
8. d)
9. c)
10. Im Fall von FX-Swaps, wo bereits das erste Geschäft geliefert wurde (und damit kein Fehler, z.B. falscher Spotkurs, behoben werden kann), muss bei Änderungen mit besonderer Vorsicht agiert werden, weil die **Devisen- bzw. Zinsposition zum Schließen des Geschäfts geändert werden muss.**
11. c)
12. Bilateral Key Exchange, Input und Output Sequence Numbers (ISNs und OSNs), Zweistufensystem.
13. Der dreistellige Code der Message Types setzt sich folgendermaßen zusammen: 1. Stelle: **Kategorie** (Markt/Produkt); 2. Stelle: **Gruppe** (Allgemeine Funktion der Mitteilung); 3. Stelle: **Typ** (Spezielle Funktion der Mitteilung)
14. c)
15. a)

16. d)
17. c)
18. d)
19. b), c) and d)
20. b)
21. d)

3. The Confirmation Process

1. a)
2. d)
3. Counterparties; nostro banks; broker (if applicable); trade date; value date; amount/currencies in the quoted as well as variable currency; buyer/seller; exchange rate/interest rate; settlement instructions
4. Telephone/oral; written; automated (S.W.I.F.T., TRAM, BART, ACS).
5. d)
6. d)
7. Brokers' agreements are not suitable for confirmation purposes because the deal was done between the counterparties and not with the broker. b) and d)
8. b) and d)
9. a)
10. d)
11. b)
12. d)
13. Auto confirmation and automated confirmation tracking (follow-up systems) help to reduce market risk and input errors, minimize settlement expenses and compensation payments, process larger volumes, check periodically if confirmations were re-affirmed, identify counterparties that did not confirm, reduce operational costs, escalate non-confirmation and increase the STP (straight-through processing) rate.

4. Netting

1. a)
2. In case of **novations netting** contractual obligations are satisfied or discharged by means of their replacement by new obligations. Since all payments are immediately included in the netting contract, the administrative work is relatively high. **Close-out netting** is an agreement to settle all contracted but not yet due liabilities and claims on an institution by one single payment, immediately upon the occurrence of a list of defined events, such as the appointment of a liquidator to that institution.
3. **Bilateral netting** is a legally binding agreement between two counterparties about the netting of amounts in the same currency for settlement of the same day under two or more trades. In a **multilateral netting** system, each bank in the system settles its overall net position in one currency with respect to all other members of the system.
4. **Bilateral netting:** settlement exposures can be reduced by up to 50%; a variety of methods are available; no additional credit risk; more efficient settlement due to a reduced number of payment instructions; fewer reconciliations and reduced amounts to be transfered
    Multilateral Netting: settlement exposure can be reduced by up to 90%; settlement exposure is transferred to clearing house; duration of settlement risk is reduced to 24 hours

16. d)

17. c)

18. d)

19. b), c) und d)

20. b)

21. d)

3. Der Bestätigungsprozess

1. a)

2. d)

3. Die im Geschäft involvierten Parteien, Nostrobanken, Broker (wenn vorhanden), Handelstag, Valuta, Betrag und Name der gehandelten Währungen, Rolle der Parteien im Geschäft (Käufer/Verkäufer), Wechselkurs und Settlementanweisungen.

4. Telefonisch/mündlich, schriftlich (Fax, Telex oder Post), automatisiert (S.W.I.F.T., TRAM, BART, ACS).

5. d)

6. d)

7. Die Verständigungen von Brokern sind als Bestätigung des Geschäftes nicht geeignet, weil nicht mit dem Broker, sondern einer anderen Bank das Geschäft gemacht wurde.

8. b) und d)

9. a)

10. d)

11. b)

12. d)

13. Mithilfe elektronischer Systeme zum Abgleich und zur Nachbearbeitung von Bestätigungen können Marktrisiken und Eingabefehler reduziert werden, Settlementkosten und Kompensationszahlungen minimiert werden, größere Volumina rascher verarbeitet werden, in regelmäßigen Abständen Geschäfte auf eine Gegenbestätigung geprüft und säumige Parteien identifiziert werden, operationale Kosten gesenkt werden sowie die STP(straight-through processing)-Rate erhöht werden.

4. Netting

1. a)

2. Beim **Novations-Netting** werden die einzelnen Schuldverhältnisse in einem Schuld-umwandlungsvertrag erfasst. Da die Ansprüche und Verpflichtungen immer schon **zum** Entstehungszeitpunkt **saldiert** werden, entsteht beim Novations-Netting ein relativ hoher technischer Verwaltungsaufwand. Beim **Close-out Netting** (Liquidations-Netting) werden **erst bei Eintritt bestimmter Ereignisse (Kündigung oder Insolvenz)** alle offenen Forderungen und Verbindlichkeiten aus Finanzgeschäften zum Marktwert zu einer Position **saldiert.**

3. Beim **bilateralen Netting** werden alle Geschäfte zwischen zwei Parteien in einer Währung gegeneinander aufgerechnet und der Saldo transferiert. Beim **multilateralen Netting** werden Zahlungsströme in einer Währung saldiert, wobei die Zahlungen von allen am multilateralen Nettingsystem beteiligten Unternehmen berücksichtigt werden.

4. **Bilaterales Netting:** Das Settlementrisiko kann betragsmäßig bis zu 50% reduziert werden; es können verschiedene Methoden verwendet werden; kein zusätzliches Kreditrisiko; Vereinfachung des Settlements, weil es weniger Zahlungsanweisungen gibt, der Abgleich der Nostrokonten weniger oft durchzuführen ist und geringere Beträge transferiert werden.
Multilaterales Netting: Das Settlementrisiko kann betragsmäßig bis zu 90% reduziert werden; die offene Währungsposition wird zum Clearing House transferiert; das Settle-

or less; more efficient settlement due to reduced a number of payment instructions, fewer reconciliations and reduced amounts to be transfered

5. c)
6. b), c) and d)
7. c)
8. Appropriate events of default (eg, insolvency, bankruptcy); conditions under which netting is applicable; method to calculate the netting amount; a clause stipulating that the netting amount includes all payments receivable and payable and that only a single net obligation is settled in case of default; optional clause to support payment netting
9. a)
10. a)
11. c)
12. a), c) and d)
13. c)
14. d)
15. a), b) and e)

5. Clearing and Settlement in Payment Systems

1. c)
2. All payments are exchanged through nostro accounts. **Nostro accounts** are denominated in the currency of the country where they are located. A **vostro account** is denominated in the domestic currency of the bank that runs the account on behalf of the foreign bank. Thus, each nostro account is also a vostro account. For example, if a German Bank A settles all USD trades through its USD account that it holds with the US-Bank B, this account is a nostro account for Bank A and a vostro account for Bank B. A bank may use more than one nostro account abroad for the payment or receipt of a currency although a sophisticated cash management will then be required to avoid overdrafts and/or excessive balances.
3. The clearing and settlement process comprises three stages: authorising and initiating the payment, transmitting and exchanging payment instructions and settlement between banks involved. Settlement can be undertaken on a bilateral basis or via a clearing house.
4. b)
5. **Owners** (central banks or private institutions); **settlement system** (net versus gross, sequential or simultaneous settlement systems); **operational area** (cross border/domestic/regional).
6. d)
7. a)
8. Settlement risk is the risk that a payment has been instructed irrevocably before the currency bought is received.
9. a), b) and d)
10. There are several ways to contain settlement risks: introduction of simultaneous settlement, payment/receipt relationship, introduction of a guaranteed refund system, introduction of a guaranteed receipt system, restricting membership of the payment system, establishment of bilateral and system-wide intra-day limits, loss/liquidity sharing agreements, recalculation of settlement amounts and real-time gross settlement (RTGS).
   Furthermore also legal risks, technical risks (breakdown of the payments system), fraud (wrong payment instructions or manipulated authenticated messages) or human error can occur.

mentrisiko wird auf 24 Stunden und weniger verkürzt; Vereinfachung des Settlements, weil es weniger Zahlungsanweisungen gibt, der Abgleich der Nostrokonten weniger oft durchzuführen ist und geringere Beträge transferiert werden.

5. c)
6. b), c) und d)
7. c)
8. Gründe für Zahlungsunfähigkeit, besonders Konkurs oder Ausgleich; Bedingungen, unter denen Netting angewendet werden kann; Verfahren, wie der Nettingbetrag zu errechnen ist; eine Klausel, die bestimmt, dass alle offenen Forderungen und Verpflichtungen im Falle der Zahlungsunfähigkeit einer Partei zur Berechnung des Ausgleichsbetrages herangezogen und zu einer Zahlung zusammengefasst werden; Option zur Verwendung von Payment Netting.
9. a)
10. a)
11. c)
12. a), c) und d)
13. c)
14. d)
15. a), b) und e)

5. Clearing und Settlement in Zahlungssystemen

1. c)
2. Das Settlement erfolgt über **Nostrokonten**, wobei die Nostrobanken am Tag vor dem Settlement-Tag Zahlungsinstruktionen erhalten, aus denen die zu leistenden und erhaltenden Zahlungen hervorgehen. Die Nostrokonten werden in den Heimwährungen jener Länder geführt, wo die Bank Geschäfte macht. Im Gegensatz dazu stehen **Vostrokonten**. Dabei handelt es sich um Konten in der Heimwährung einer Bank, die sie für andere Banken führt. Wenn beispielsweise Bank A aus Deutschland bei Bank B in den USA ein USD-Konto einrichtet, über das alle Zahlungsströme laufen, dann ist das Konto aus Sicht von Bank A ein Nostrokonto und aus der Sicht von Bank B ein Vostrokonto.
3. Der Clearing- und Settlementprozess erfolgt in drei Stufen: Bewilligung und Freigabe der Zahlung, Übertragung und Austausch der Zahlungsanweisungen und Zahlungsausgleich zwischen den Banken.
4. b)
5. **Eigentümer** (Zentralbanken oder private Institutionen), **Abwicklungssystem** (Nettobeträge vs. Bruttobeträge, gestaffelte vs. simultane Abwicklung), **Wirkungsbereich** (grenzüberschreitend oder regional).
6. d)
7. a)
8. Settlementrisiko bedeutet, dass die Zahlung unwiderruflich angewiesen wurde und der Gegenbetrag in der anderen Währung noch nicht erhalten wurde.
9. a), b) und d)
10. Um diese Risiken einzuschränken, gibt es folgende Möglichkeiten: Einführung einer simultanen Abwicklung, Verknüpfung von Zahlung und Gegenleistung, Einführung eines Systems mit Rückzahlungsgarantie, Einführung eines Systems mit Empfangsgarantie, Einschränkung des Teilnehmerkreises, Etablierung von bilateralen und systemweiten Intraday-Limits, Verlust- und Liquiditätsbeteiligung, Neukalkulation der Settlementbeträge (Rückabwicklung) und Abwicklung der Zahlung über ein Echtzeit-Bruttoabwicklungssystem („Real Time Gross Settlement" – RTGS).

11. It can occur legal risks, technical risks (breakdown of the payments system), fraud (deliberately wrong payment instructions or manipulated authenticated messages) or human error.

12. Net settlement, no unwinding, mandatory limit of EUR 5 million, changing the bilateral limits for the next business day until 6.00 p.m., when multilateral limit (EUR 1 billion) is exceeded the payment is queued, collateral pool of EUR 1 billion at the ECB

13. The settlement process is initiated by the **bilateral exchange of S.W.I.F.T. messages** between the banks involved. The balances are advised to the ECB and EBA-Clearing. The payment is sent via **TARGET** and takes place at the settlement accounts established by the banks at the ECB. EBA-Clearing informs the ECB who is a net creditor/debtor in the clearing and receives the payment confirmation from the ECB. Upon receipt of all confirmations, EBA-Clearing notifies all participants that the settlement operations are completed.

14. Operating hours: 7.00 a.m. to 4.00 p.m.; EAF-2 settles EUR payments only within Germany. Since there exists remote access, participants do not need to be physically present in the German market; participants provide a total liquidity of EUR 1.8 billion as collateral

15. In **phase 1 (delivery phase)** from 7.00 a.m. to 4.00 p.m. **payments are continually settled on a bilateral or multilateral basis**, depending on the instructions of the participants. **Phase 2 (settlement phase)** takes place between 4.00 and 4.30 p.m. and is designed as a two-stage **multilateral netting** process. In stage 1 liquidity from the Bundesbank accounts of participants can be used to cover any shortage though participants can limit access to them. If there are any debits left open after stage 1, the participants have 30 minutes to provide additional liquidity. If there remain any balances after stage 2 the payments are returned to the sender like they would be in a gross settlement system.

16. b)

17. d)

18. d)

19. a)

20. c)

21. c)

22. c)

23. d)

24. b)

25. a)

26. b), d) and e)

27. a)

6. Reconciliation of Nostro Accounts

1. d)

11. Es können auch rechtliche Risiken, technische Risiken (Ausfall des Zahlungssystems), Betrug (bewusst falsche Anweisungen oder Manipulationen authentischer Anweisungen) oder menschliches Versagen auftreten.

12. Netto-Settlement, keine Rückabwicklung, Rückabwicklungen müssen zwischen den beiden Parteien direkt vereinbart werden und in Form neuer Zahlungsanweisungen an das EBA-Clearing abgewickelt werden, die Teilnehmer müssen sich untereinander ein bilaterales Mindestlimit von EUR 5 Mio. einräumen, bilaterale Limits für den nächsten Tag können bis 18.00 Uhr geändert werden, die Summe aller eingeräumten Limits (credits) und erhaltener Limits (debits) ist auf je EUR 1 Mrd. beschränkt und EBA hat einen Pool an Sicherheiten im Wert von EUR 1 Mrd. bei der EZB hinterlegt.

13. Der Settlementprozess wird durch den **bilateralen Austausch von S.W.I.F.T.-Nachrichten** zwischen den Banken eingeleitet. Die Salden werden der EZB und EBA-Clearing avisiert. Der Zahlungsverkehr erfolgt über **TARGET** an die Zahlungsausgleichkonten bei der EZB. EBA-Clearing meldet der EZB, wer die Begünstigten beim Clearing sind und erhält von der EZB die Zahlungsbestätigungen. EBA-Clearing verständigt alle Mitglieder nach Durchführung über den Abschluss des Settlements.

14. Öffnungszeiten: 7.00 bis 16.00 Uhr; es sind nur Eurozahlungen in Deutschland möglich, jedoch ist ein Fernzugriff eingerichtet, d.h., es ist keine physische Präsenz in Deutschland erforderlich, um an EAF teilzunehmen. Die Gesamtsicherheit auf dem Liquiditätssammelkonto beträgt EUR 1,8 Mrd. und wird von den Teilnehmern bereitgestellt.

15. In der **Phase 1 (Einlieferungsphase)** werden von 7.00 bis 16.00 Uhr die **Zahlungen kontinuierlich bilateral oder multilateral abgerechnet,** wobei jeder Teilnehmer im Vorhinein bestimmt, mit welchem Partner multilateral bzw. bilateral gesettled wird. Die **Phase 2 (Ausgleichphase)** findet von 16.00 bis 16.30 Uhr statt. Dabei erfolgt in zwei Schritten **multilaterales Netting.** Im ersten multilateralen Netting wird zur Deckung von Sollsalden auch auf die Liquidität der Teilnehmer bei der Bundesbank zurückgegriffen, wobei die Teilnehmer den Zugriff begrenzen können. Sollten nach der ersten multilateralen Abrechnung noch offene Salden vorhanden sein, haben die betroffenen Teilnehmer 30 Minuten Zeit, um auf den Bundesbankkonten eine entsprechende Deckung bereitzustellen. Bleibt dann noch ein Saldo offen, werden Zahlungen als nicht ausgeführt an den sendenden Teilnehmer, wie in einem Bruttoabwicklungssystem, retourniert.

16. b)

17. d)

18. d)

19. a)

20. c)

21. c)

22. c)

23. d)

24. b)

25. a)

26. b), d) und e)

27. a)

6. Abgleich (Reconciliation) der Nostrokonten

1. d)

2. A bank should begin reconciliation **as soon as it receives notification from their nostro bank** that payment was received. If possible, reconciliation should be performed before the close of the currency's payments system enabling the bank to detect any problems in cash settlement and resolve them on settlement date.
3. b)
4. d)
5. First stage: On the day before value day the back office determines all **incoming and outgoing payments as well as the netting amounts**. This allows the bank to accurately fund its nostro accounts; Second stage: After settlement, **expected cashflows are compared to actual cash movements**. If any differences are detected the back office must contact the nostro bank or counterparty to resolve the difference. Typical causes for differences are wrong trade data capture, erroneous settlement instructions or that the nostro bank made an error. The counterparty that made the mistake has either to pay good value or compensation.
6. a), d) and e)
7. c)
8. b)
9. a)
10. This principle is important if other departments (eg, fixed income, emerging markets, derivatives) also use nostro accounts. Without consistent standards, it would be then very **difficult to establish a systematic and efficient settlement**.

7. Accounting and Financial Control

1. Accounting ensures FX transactions are properly recorded to the balance sheet and income statement. After a trade has been executed data are captured in subsidiary accounts that flow through to the **general ledger** at the end of each day. In order to ensure sub-ledgers reconcile to general ledger accounts a monthly check of all subsystem accounts is undertaken by an independent unit. All positions in the general ledger are **marked-to-market**. Once the position is closed out, realized gains or losses are calculated and reported. **Cashflow** movements on settlement date are **calculated** by the **back office** and posted to the general ledger.
2. Systematic reconciliation of the general ledger to the back office and of front office to the back office should be done on a daily basis.
3. b)
4. c)
5. Rates and prices should be fed **electronically from source systems.**

8. Money Laundering

1. d)
2. a)
3. d)
4. Vienna Convention
5. d)
6. Financial Action Task Force on Money Laundering
7. c)
8. b)

2. Der Abgleich beginnt, **sobald die Bank von ihrer Nostrobank über Zahlungseingänge/-ausgänge informiert wird.** Im Idealfall sollte der Abgleich erfolgen, bevor das Zahlungssystem schließt.

3. b)

4. d)

5. In der ersten Phase werden am Valuta vorliegenden Tag die zu **erwartenden Zahlungseingänge und -ausgänge bestimmt bzw. die Nettingbeträge für die Nostrokonten ermittelt.** Auf diese Weise kann die Bank ihre Nostrokonten mit der notwendigen Liquidität ausstatten. Nach dem Settlement werden die **tatsächlichen Geldflüsse mit den ursprünglichen Prognosen verglichen.** Werden Abweichungen festgestellt, so werden die Ursachen ermittelt und die Abweichungen behoben. Typische Fehlerquellen sind falsch erfasste Handelsdaten, fehlerhafte Settlement-Instruktionen oder Fehlverhalten der Nostrobanken. Jener Partner, auf dessen Seite der Fehler liegt, muss entweder eine Zahlung mit guter Valuta oder eine Kompensationszahlung leisten.

6. a), d) und e)

7. c)

8. b)

9. a)

10. Dieser Grundsatz ist wichtig, da neben dem FX-Bereich auch andere Abteilungen Emerging markets, Derivate, Bonds oder Nostrokonten verwenden. Ohne einheitliche Standards ist es **schwer, ein systematisches und effizientes Settlement zu schaffen.**

7. Buchhaltung

1. Die Buchhaltung verarbeitet die FX-Transaktionen in die **Bilanzkonten sowie in die G&V.** Nach Abschluss des Geschäftes werden die Daten in Unterkonten erfasst, die am Ende jeden Tages ins Hauptbuch zusammengeführt werden. Im Hauptbuch werden die **Positionen kontinuierlich Mark-to-Market bewertet,** bis die Position geschlossen wird. Dann wird der **Gewinn bzw. Verlust** festgeschrieben. Die am Settlement Date stattfindenden Cashflows werden vom Backoffice berechnet und direkt in das Hauptbuch übernommen.

2. **Der Abgleich zwischen Hauptbuch und Backoffice sowie Handel soll in systematischer Form erfolgen,** damit das Hauptbuch die aktuelle Lage der Bank korrekt widerspiegelt.

3. b)

4. c)

5. Die Preise und Zinssätze sollen **elektronisch von der Datenquelle** importiert werden, um Fehler zu vermeiden.

8. Geldwäsche

1. d)

2. a)

3. d)

4. Wiener Konvention

5. d)

6. Financial Action Task Force on Money Laundering

7. c)

8. b)

9. a) and d)
10. The FATF states explicitly that th recommendations should not only be followed by the **banking sector** only but also by all **other financial institutions** such as brokers or money exchange offices.
11. d), g) and h)
12. Development of internal policies; procedures and controls including the designation of compliance officers at management level and adequate screening procedures to ensure high standards when hiring employees; an ongoing employee training programme; an audit function to test the system.

9. Examples for Settlement Risk

1. Liquidity, credit and replacement risk
2. Existence of **bilateral credit limit systems** and the **right time to close down a bankrupt bank**
3. The member bank of the ECU Clearing wanted to revoke its payment. The bank learnt that the rules of EUR clearing did not permit this and **could not reverse the transaction**.
4. This example demonstrates that clearing participants must have a thorough **understanding of the rules of the clearing system** (eg, cut-off times) and that relatively **minor events can put the settlement at risk** (only 1% of the payments had to do with Barings).

PART V: THE MODEL CODE – INTERNATIONAL CODE OF CONDUCT
FOR FINANCIAL MARKETS

1. General Facts about the Model Code

1. c)
2. a), d) and e)
3. a)
4. a)
5. Over time the international dealing business has developed a standardised legal framework for different products with the aim of **creating a uniform arrangement and documentation of all deals** and to ensure the smooth settlement of deals.
6. Contents of the contract; payment; bank days; reference rate; interest calculation; termination; redemption; final payment; cover; other; appendix
7. The basic idea behind the minimum requirement is to assure that the trading department of a bank is technically and professionally able to run a **conclusive and controllable risk management system** that is based on the latest scientific findings in business administration.
8. d)
9. All business areas of a bank have to be covered; The method has to be described in detail and must be subject to continuous improvement; With the help of worst-case scenarios loss potentials should be assessed and presented to the management.
10. b)
11. c)

2. Business hours

1. d)

9. a) und d)
10. Die FATF sieht explizit vor, dass ihre Empfehlungen über den **Bankensektor** hinaus auch **alle anderen Finanzinstitute** (z.B. Broker oder Wechselstuben) betrifft.
11. d), g) und h)
12. Entwicklung interner Politiken, Verfahren und Kontrollen, einschließlich der Bestimmung von Personen auf Führungsebene, die für die Einhaltung der Verfahren sorgen, und geeigneter Verfahren, die bei der Personenauswahl höchste Ansprüche gewährleisten; Weiter- und Fortbildungsprogramm für Mitarbeiter; interne Revisionsstelle zur Überprüfung der Wirksamkeit des Systems.

9. Beispiele für Settlementrisiko

1. Liquiditäts-, Kredit- und Wiederbeschaffungsrisiko
2. **Kreditlimitsysteme im Zahlungssystem** und den **richtigen Zeitpunkt zur Schließung einer insolventen Bank** zu finden
3. Eine am ECU-Clearing beteiligte Bank wollte ihre Zahlung widerrufen. Da dies aber im Rahmen des Clearings nicht mehr möglich war, kam die Bank in eine **Nettoschuldnerposition**, die sie nur durch rasche kurzfristige Kreditaufnahmen decken konnte.
4. Dieser Vorfall zeigt einerseits, dass die Teilnehmer am Clearing die **genauen Vorschriften** (z.B. Buchungsschluss) **kennen** müssen und andererseits, wie **relativ kleine Ereignisse** (die Clearingzahlungen hatten zu weniger als 1% mit Barings zu tun) **das gesamte Settlement gefährden** können.

TEIL V: DER MODEL CODE – INTERNATIONALER VERHALTENSKODEX FÜR DIE FINANZMÄRKTE

1. Allgemeines zum Model Code

1. c)
2. a), d) und e)
3. a)
4. a)
5. Der Zweck der Rahmenverträge ist die **einheitliche Gestaltung und Dokumentation aller Geschäfte,** um eine reibungslose Abwicklung zu gewährleisten.
6. Vertragszweck, Zahlungen, Bankarbeitstage, Basissatz, Zinsberechnung, Beendigung, Schadenersatz, Abschlusszahlung, Deckung, Sonstiges, Anhang.
7. Die Mindestanforderungen stellen sicher, dass ein Institut für die Geschäftssparte Handel fachlich und technisch in der Lage ist, ein dem letzten Stand der Bankbetriebswirtschaftslehre entsprechendes **organisiertes, nachvollziehbares und kontrollierbares Risikomanagement** zu betreiben.
8. d)
9. Alle Geschäftsbereiche der Bank sind zu erfassen; die Methodik ist detailliert zu dokumentieren und fortlaufend weiter zu verbessern; zur Auslotung des Verlustpotenzials sind Worst-Case-Szenarien zu skizzieren und die Ergebnisse der Geschäftsleitung nahezubringen.
10. b)
11. c)

2. Handelszeiten

1. d)

2. d)
3. It would be prudent to have an **unofficial close for each trading day** against which end-of-day positions can be monitored or revalued, thus avoiding problems with determining intraday and overnight limits.
4. In the event of a country or state declaring a new national bank holiday the new value date will be the **first mutual business day** (for both currencies of the contract) **following the original value date** except where a bank holiday is declared on the last business day of a month, in which case the new value date will be the first mutual business day (for both currencies of the contract) prior to month end (ultimo).
5. The official opening of the currency markets is **5.00 AM Sydney time on Monday morning**, all year round. The recognised closing time for the currency markets is **Friday 5.00 PM New York time** all year round.
6. c)
7. **No**, the specified rate order does **not necessarily provide a fixed-price guarantee** to the counterparty. In accepting a stop-loss/profit order, an institution assumes an obligation to make every reasonable effort to execute the order quickly at the established price.
8. Position parking is the practice whereby two contract parties agree a deal, usually on the understanding that the contract will be reversed at a specified later date, at or near the original contract rate irrespective of the interim market rate change.
9. Management **should not allow** the parking of deals or positions with a counterparty because it can either lead to a **distorted risk position**.
10. a), b), d), e) and f)
11. a)

3. Personal Conduct Issues

1. d)
2. b)
3. a)
4. a)
5. Firms should adopt **appropriate procedures consistent with the G-10 governors statement and the FATF recommendations**, and also familiarise themselves with their legal responsibilities in this matter.
6. a)
7. d)

4. Back Office, Payments and Confirmations

1. b)
2. d)
3. b)
4. Date of transaction; system used (broker, phone, telex, dealing system); name and location of counterparty; rate, amount and currency; type and side of deal; value date; maturity date and all other relevant dates (eg, exercise date); standard terms/conditions applicable (eg, FRABBA, BBAIRS, ICOM, etc.); all other relevant information
5. d)
6. a)
7. c)

2. d)
3. Um Probleme mit der Behandlung von zu vermeiden, sollte ein **interner, inoffizieller Handelsschluss für jeden Tag** festgelegt werden, an dem die Positionen überprüft und bewertet werden.
4. Für den Fall neu eingeführter Bankfeiertage oder anderer öffentlicher Feiertage, die ein Settlement des Geschäftes nicht zulassen, gilt der **nächste gemeinsame Banktag (für beide gehandelten Währungen) nach der ursprünglichen Valuta als neue Valuta.** Fällt der neue Bankfeiertag auf einen Monatsultimo, so ist der letzte, für beide Währungen gültige Handelstag vor dem Ultimo zu wählen.
5. Die offizielle Beginnzeit für Währungsmärkte ist **Montagmorgen 5.00 Uhr, Sydney-Zeit.** Die offizielle Schlusszeit ist **Freitag, 17.00 Uhr, New-Yorker-Zeit.**
6. c)
7. **Nein**, der Auftraggeber darf eine Stop-Loss-Order **nicht als Fixpreis-Garantie ansehen.** Akzeptiert jedoch eine Institution eine Stop-Loss-Order, muss sie jede Anstrengung unternehmen, um sie beim vereinbarten Preis auszuführen.
8. Position Parking bedeutet, dass Positionen bei einer anderen Partei mit der Absicht, dieses Geschäft zu einem späteren Zeitpunkt zu historischen Kursen in die Bücher rückzuführen, geparkt werden.
9. Das Management sollte Position Parking **verbieten**, da dies zu einer **verfälschten Darstellung der Risikoposition führt.**
10. a), b), d), e) und f)
11. a)

3. Persönliches Verhalten

1. d)
2. b)
3. a)
4. a)
5. Jede Firma ist angehalten, **Prozeduren** zu entwickeln, die mit den **Empfehlungen der G10 bzw. G7** konform gehen und die **gesetzlichen Bestimmungen** zu beachten. Es soll im Ermessen der Geschäftsleitung liegen, ob mit Institutionen gehandelt wird, die für Dritte tätig werden.
6. a)
7. d)

4. Backoffice, Zahlungen und Bestätigungen

1. b)
2. d)
3. b)
4. Datum der Transaktion; verwendetes System (Makler, Telefon, Telex, Handelssystem); Name und Adresse des Geschäftspartners; Kurs, Betrag und Währung; Art und Seite (Kauf/Verkauf) des Geschäfts; Wertstellungsdatum, Ablaufdatum und alle anderen wichtigen Daten (z.B. Ausübungstag); angewandte Standardkonditionen (z.B. FRABBA, BBAIRS, ISDA, ICOM ...); alle sonstigen wichtigen Informationen.
5. d)
6. a)
7. c)

8. Market participants should aim to **reduce credit risk** by establishing bilateral currency netting agreements.

5. Disputes, Differences, Mediation, Compliance

1. a)
2. c)
3. c)
4. Disputes should be routinely referred to **senior management** for resolution, thereby transforming the dispute from an individual trader to broker issue to an inter-institutional issue. All compensation should take the **form of a bank cheque or wire transfer in the name of the institution or of adjustment to brokerage bills**. All such **transactions should be fully documented by each firm**. It is bad practice to refuse a broker's cheque or reduction in the brokerage bill for the amount concerned and to insist on a name at the original price.
5. The CfP is **not in favour of the settlement of differences by points**, but recognises that in those financial markets where the regulatory authority controls all participants in that market, this practice, properly regulated by the appropriate authority, is acceptable.

6. Authorisation, Documentation, Telephone Taping

1. General dealing policy including reporting procedures, persons authorised to deal, instruments to be dealt in, limits on open positions, confirmation and settlement procedures, relationships with brokers/banks, other relevant guidance as considered appropriate
2. c)
3. Documentation should be completed and exchanged as soon as possible after a deal is done. The use, wherever possible, of standard terms and conditions to facilitate this process is **recommended strongly**. When using such agreements, any proposed modifications or choices offered in the agreement must be clearly stated before dealing.
4. a)
5. Whether privately and/or company-owned devices can be used inside the dealing room and back office to transact, advise or confirm transactions; whether privately and/or company-owned devices are allowed inside the dealing room; terms, conditions and under which circumstances the use of such devices can be authorized by management; procedures to allow an end-to-end transaction audit trail, including where appropriate, call back or answerphone facilities and controls
6. a), d) and e)

7. Brokers and Brokerage

1. Brokers act as **intermediaries or arrangers of deals** and should aim to agree mutually acceptable terms between principals.
2. No, brokers are **forbidden to act in any discretionary fund management capacity**.
3. d)
4. Communication breakdown at the point of the consummation of trades; off-market discrepancies; software inadequacies or limitations ("bugs")
5. b)
6. In countries where brokers' charges are freely negotiable, such charges **should be agreed only by directors or senior management** on each side and recorded **in writing**. Any deviation from previously agreed brokerage arrangements should be expressly approved

8. Die Marktteilnehmer sollen darauf bedacht sein, **Settlement- und Kreditrisiken** durch bilaterale Nettingvereinbarungen zu **reduzieren**.

5. Konflikte, Differenzen, Vermittlung, Erfüllung

1. a)
2. c)
3. c)
4. Die Lösung soll **auf Ebene der Geschäftsführung** gesucht werden, um aus einem individuellen Streitfall einen institutionellen zu machen. Zahlungen sollen **in Form eines Bankschecks, einer Überweisung oder einer Reduzierung der Brokerrechnung** erfolgen. Alle mit dem Streitfall verbundenen **Transaktionen** sollen **vollständig dokumentiert** werden. Es ist unstatthaft, die Zahlung durch Bankscheck oder Reduzierung der Brokerrechnung abzulehnen und auf einen Namen zum vereinbarten Preis zu bestehen.
5. Das Committee for Professionalism **unterstützt nicht die Praxis des „Settlement of Differences by Points"**. Das CfP sieht jedoch diese Usance in jenen Märkten als akzeptable Praxis, wenn sowohl die Marktteilnehmer als auch der Prozess des „Settlement by Points" einer Aufsichtsbehörde unterliegen.

6. Autorisierung, Dokumentation, Telefonaufzeichnungen

1. Allgemeiner Handelsablauf inklusive Berichtsstruktur, zum Handel berechtigte Personen, gehandelte Instrumente, Limitstruktur, Bestätigungs- und Settlementprozess, Beziehung zu Brokern und Banken, andere relevante Punkte.
2. c)
3. Der Gebrauch von Standardbedingungen, die von verschiedenen Behörden herausgegeben werden, wird **dringend empfohlen**. Änderungen dieser Standardbedingungen müssen vor Geschäftsabschluss bekanntgegeben werden.
4. a)
5. Verwendung privater und/oder firmeneigener mobiler Endgeräte im Handelsraum und im Backoffice, um Geschäfte abzuschließen und zu bestätigen oder um Beratungs-gespräche zu führen; Zulassung von privaten und/oder firmeneigenen mobilen Endgeräten innerhalb des Handelsraums; Bestimmungen und Bedingungen für die Fälle, in denen diese Geräte von der Geschäftsleitung zugelassen werden; Verfahren, die einen Audit Trail für die gesamte Transaktion ermöglichen, gegebenenfalls einschließlich Rückruf- und Anrufbeantworterfunktionen.
6. a), d) und e)

7. Broker und Provisionen

1. Ein Broker wirkt als **Intermediär zwischen zwei Kontraktparteien** und soll die Über-ein-stimmung zwischen den Geschäftspartnern herbeiführen.
2. Nein, Broker dürfen **keine Eigenpositionen** handeln.
3. d)
4. Systemabsturz während eines Geschäftsabschlusses, Eingabe marktferner Preise, Softwaremängel oder -einschränkungen (Bugs).
5. b)
6. In Ländern, in denen Maklergebühren frei vereinbar sind, sollten solche Gebühren nur **vom Topmanagement oder von Direktoren festgelegt** werden. Dies sollte **schriftlich** geschehen. Jede Abweichung von diesen Gebühren muss im Einvernehmen mit dem Ge-

by both parties and clearly recorded in writing. **Failure to pay brokerage bills promptly is not considered good practice** as in some jurisdictions overdue payments are treated as a deduction from capital base for regulatory purposes, thus putting the broker at a disadvantage.
7. c)
8. c)
9. To ask the central bank to deal with another party
10. In the **deposit markets**, it is accepted that principals dealing through a broker have the right to turn down a name wishing to take deposits: this could therefore **require pre-disclosure of the name before closing the deal**.
11. d)
12. d)
13. Switching is acceptable practice if the **circumstances justify** it and if it is **approved by the parties whose names are substituted**.
14. Because the two offsetting transactions will **utilise credit lines** and because they are **often executed at an exchange rate that is off-market** due to the time it takes to arrange name substitution, such activities should be identified as switching transactions and they should be monitored and controlled.

8. Dealing Practice

1. c)
2. Deals at non-market rates should generally be avoided in order to avoid losses, fraud, tax evasion, and unauthorised extension of credit.
3. d)
4. a)
5. b)
6. In cases where a price being quoted by a broker is hit simultaneously by several banks for a total amount greater than what the price concerned is valid for, the broker should **apportion the amount the price is valid for proportionally among the banks concerned** in accordance with the amount hit by each.
7. d)
8. The price was dealt on; The deal was cancelled; His quote is superseded by a better bid/offer; The broker closes the transaction in that currency with another counterparty at a price other than that originally proposed.
9. When arranging a swap an unconditional firm rate will only be given where a principal deals **directly with a client** or when such a **principal has received a client's name or their rating from a broker**.
10. If transactions are conducted through fund managers/investment dealers, **traders should undertake all efforts to identify the principal counterparties as soon as possible** following a deal. Management at financial institutions engaged in trading with fund managers needs to be aware of the risks involved, particularly with respect to credit exposure and money laundering and should have in place a **written policy governing** such transactions.
11. Where Internet facilities are established by a bank for a client, the **conditions and controls should be comprehensively stated in the bank's rulebook**. There should be **appropriate security** in place governing access, authentication and identification of personnel who are authorised to use the facility.
12. b)

schäftspartner und schriftlich erfolgen. Es ist **unstatthaft, Brokergebühren nicht sofort zu bezahlen,** da in einigen Rechtsprechungen überfällige Zahlungen von der Eigenkapitalbasis in Abzug gebracht werden und somit den Broker benachteiligen.

7. c)
8. c)
9. die Zentralbank ersuchen, das Geschäft mit der anderen Partei zu machen
10. Im **Depotmarkt** ist es akzeptiert, dass Kunden, die durch einen Makler abschließen, gewisse Namen ablehnen können. Das führt dazu, dass der **Name vor Abschluss offenbart** werden muss.
11. d)
12. d)
13. Switching ist akzeptabel, wenn dies **nach den gegebenen Umständen gerechtfertigt** ist, und wenn der **Tausch von dazu befugten Personen genehmigt** wurde.
14. Da beim Switching sowohl **Kreditlinien beansprucht** werden als auch die dabei **verwendeten Kurse oft nicht mehr im Markt** sind, sollten diese Aktivitäten überprüft, kontrolliert und als Switching-Transaktionen ausgewiesen werden.

8. Handelspraxis

1. c)
2. Diese Geschäfte sind grundsätzlich zu vermeiden, da sie zur Verschleierung von Gewinnen bzw. Verlusten sowie zu Betrug, Steuerhinterziehung oder einer ungenehmigten Ausweitung von Kreditlinien verwendet werden können.
3. d)
4. a)
5. b)
6. Wird ein von Brokern quotierter Preis von mehreren Kunden gleichzeitig genommen und wird dadurch die Nachfrage größer als das Angebot, so soll der Broker den möglichen **Betrag proportional zu den gewünschten Beträgen aufteilen.**
7. d)
8. Es wird auf den Kursen gehandelt; der Händler widerruft; seine Quotierung wird durch eine bessere Quotierung ersetzt; der Broker hat eine andere Transaktion in derselben Währung mit einer anderen Partei zu einem anderen Preis abgeschlossen.
9. Eine fixe Preiszusage wird nur gegeben, wenn der **Name oder die Bonität des Geschäftspartners bekannt** ist bzw. eine **Bank direkt mit dem Kunden handelt.**
10. Handeln Banken mit Fondsmanagern, entsteht das Problem, dass der Händler bei Geschäftsabschluss nicht weiß, mit welcher Gegenpartei er das Geschäft abgeschlossen hat. **Händler sollten daher bestrebt sein, so rasch wie möglich die Namen zu ermitteln.** Das Management von Finanzinstitutionen, die mit Fonds handeln, soll sich der Risiken, insbesondere im Bereich Kreditrisiko und Geldwäsche, bewusst sein und **für Transaktionen mit Fonds Leitlinien in schriftlicher Form festlegen.**
11. Werden dem Kunden Leistungen angeboten, die auf dem Internet basieren, sind **Bedingungen und Kontrollen in einem bankinternen Regelbuch** zu dokumentieren. **Geeignete Sicherheitsmaßnahmen** sollen eingerichtet werden, die Zugang, Berechtigung und Identifikation des autorisierten Personals überprüfen.
12. b)

9. Dealing Practice for Specific Transactions

1. a)
2. d)
3. When a principal intends execute such a transfer it **must obtain the consent of the transferee before releasing its name**.
4. In the case of sale and repurchase agreements or stock lending or lending transactions, proper documentation including **written agreement of key terms and conditions** should be in place prior to the consummation of any trades.

10. Market Terminology and Definitions

1. c)
2. b)
3. b)
4. a), b) and c)
5. d)
6. **Premium** = The margin by which the forward exchange rate is dearer than the near date.
   Discount = The margin by which the forward exchange rate is cheaper than the near date.
7. To **check the availability of a credit line** for the counterparty prior to conclusion of a deal. The term hints to the counterparty that there is a possibility of reducing the amount or declining the deal depending on the availability of the relevant credit line.
8. The smallest unit of an exchange rate is called **points or pips**.
9. "When issued" is used for **trades before debt security is issued**. Settlement occurs when and if the security is issued, reflecting the period between the announcement of a security's auction and its issuance.
10. "IMM dates" are **the third Wednesdays of March, June, September and December**. These are the dates for which financial futures traded at the IMM (International Money Market) Division of the CME (Chicago Mercantile Exchange) are traded.
11. Short dates are **maturity dates of less than one month**.

PART VI: RISK MANAGEMENT

1. Types of risk trading

1. a)
2. **Risk** is defined as the likelihood of a loss or a lower than expected return. Risk only applies to future and therefore uncertain events. Risks that have materialized are no longer classified as risks; rather they have been entered in the profit and loss account (as a **loss**).
3. b)
4. The classic credit risk refers to the **loss of a transaction's total capital amount** (or parts of it) **due to the partner's inability to pay**.
5. Settlement risk represents a type of credit risk that occurs with all exchange transactions. The bank has already completed its part of the transaction while the partner's default prevents the completion of the transaction.

9. Handelspraxis für spezielle Transaktionen

1. a)
2. d)
3. Bevor die übertragende Partei das Assignment oder die Übertragung durchführt, soll sie die **Zustimmung des Übernehmers einholen, seinen Namen bekanntgeben zu dürfen.**
4. Bei Wertpapierpensionsgeschäften sollte eine **schriftliche Dokumentation** mit den wichtigsten Vertragsbedingungen vorhanden sein, bevor ein Geschäft abgeschlossen wird.

10. Marktterminologie und Definitionen

1. c)
2. b)
3. b)
4. a), b) und c)
5. d)
6. **Premium** = der Aufschlag, um den der Terminkurs höher ist als der Kassakurs.
   Discount = der Abschlag, um den der Terminkurs niedriger ist als der Kassakurs.
7. Die **Verfügbarkeit der Kreditlinie muss überprüft werden,** bevor die Zustimmung zum Geschäft gegeben werden kann. Dieser Zusatz kann der Gegenpartei andeuten, dass zu einem geringeren als zunächst vereinbarten Betrag abgeschlossen werden könnte.
8. Die kleinste Einheit eines Wechselkurses nennt man **Points bzw. Pips.**
9. „When issued" wird verwendet bei einem **Geschäft, das vor Emission abgeschlossen wurde.** Das Settlement erfolgt, nachdem das Wertpapier emittiert wurde und berücksichtigt den Zeitraum zwischen Ankündigung und Emission.
10. Als „IMM dates" bezeichnet man den **dritten Mittwoch im März, Juni, September und Dezember.** Dies sind jene Tage, an denen Futureskontrakte an der IMM (International Money Market) Division des CME (Chicago Mercantile Exchange) gesettled werden.
11. Unter „Short Dates" versteht man **Laufzeiten unter einem Monat.**

TEIL VI: RISIKOMANAGEMENT

1. Risikoarten im Handel

1. a)
2. **Risiko** ist die Gefahr einer möglichen Gewinnminderung. Risiko bezieht sich ausschließlich auf die Zukunft und entspringt der Unsicherheit über die Zukunft. Alles, was an Risiken bereits schlagend geworden ist, ist nicht Risiko, sondern **Verlust**, der in der Buchhaltung bzw. im Ergebnis seinen Niederschlag findet.
3. b)
4. Unter klassischem Kreditrisiko ist der **Verlust von Teilen oder des gesamten Kapitalbetrages eines Geschäftes bei Ausfall des Partners** zu verstehen.
5. Das Abwicklungsrisiko (Settlementrisiko) ist eine Art von Kreditrisiko, das bei allen Tauschgeschäften auftritt. Es besteht darin, dass die Bank ihre Transaktion bereits angewiesen hat, der Partner in der Zwischenzeit jedoch ausfällt und seine Transaktion nicht durchgeführt hat.

6. c)
7. Today, banks make use of two common methods to estimate replacement risk. A simple and established method is the so-called **maturity method** whereby a specified percentage per year (of remaining maturity) is applied as a so-called credit equivalent. Usually, different percentage rates are applied depending on whether the replacement risk stems from an interest rate instrument or an FX instrument (or both). The second method, the **mark-to-market approach**, is more complex but also more accurate. In a first step, the current market values of all OTC derivatives are calculated. Only positive market values are used for the subsequent calculation of a risk figure, because the default of a counterparty would not result in a loss if the mark-to-market value was negative.
8. c)
9. b)
10. d)
11. a)
12. d)
13. a)
14. Calculation of the net position in the base currency; calculation of the net position in the quote currency; valuation at the average rate
15. a)
16. As a basic principle, one distinguishes between two basic types of liquidity risk. **Refinancing risk** represents the risk that liabilities cannot be met due to the lack of (regular) refinancing or funding sources. This kind of risk might materialise in the form of unexpectedly high costs for (short-term) funding in the simplest case or in the form of illiquidity in the most extreme case. **Asset liquidity risk** stands for the risk that certain assets of a bank cannot be sold or can only be sold at an extraordinarily high bid-ask spread. This kind of liquidity risk may also be seen as a subcategory of market risk.

2. Risk Measurement Methods

1. a)
2. The GAP Method assesses the **change in the annual profit and loss account that will be caused given a defined change in interest rates**. The basic underlying assumption is that the bank's interest rate positions are not sold before maturity. Therefore, possible market value changes of positions due to interest rate changes are neglected and only the impact on annual interest earnings and expenditures is taken into consideration.
3. **Advantages: simple handling**, only kind of interest risk measurement that depicts **changes in the bank's net interest income**.
   Drawbacks: Assumptions have to be made on how expiring positions are renewed; The GAP analysis implies an **unchanging risk structure**; **MTM effects are ignored**; The assumptions on how the yield curve will change are arbitrary; **Comparisons with other risks** (eg, FX, stocks, trading book) **are not possible**.
4. **Advantages**: **simple handling** and calculation; **high acceptance level** due to simple statements and interpretation; **costs** due to any need to sell a position before maturity **are taken into account**; **no assumptions necessary** regarding the **roll-over** of expiring positions

6. c)
7. Zur Bemessung des Wiederbeschaffungsrisikos werden in Banken derzeit zwei übliche Verfahren angewendet. Eine einfache und gängige Methode ist die sogenannte **Laufzeitmethode**. Hier wird ein bestimmter Prozentsatz pro Laufzeitjahr als Kreditäquivalent angesetzt. Eine komplexere, aber sauberere Anrechnung des Wiederbeschaffungsrisikos ist die sogenannte **MTM-Methode**. Hierbei werden in einem ersten Schritt für alle OTC-Geschäfte die aktuellen Marktwerte (Mark to Market) berechnet. Nur die positiven Marktwerte werden in den anschließenden Berechnungen verwendet, da nur hier ein entsprechender Verlust bei Ausfall des Partners entstehen würde.
8. c)
9. b)
10. d)
11. a)
12. d)
13. a)
14. Ermittlung der Nettoposition der quotierten Währung, Ermittlung der Nettoposition in der Gegenwährung, Bewertung zum Durchschnittskurs
15. a)
16. Grundsätzlich können zwei Arten von Liquiditätsrisiken unterschieden werden. Das **Refinanzierungsrisiko** (bilanzielles Liquiditätsrisiko) steht für die Gefahr von fehlenden Refinanzierungsquellen der Bank, die notwendig sind, um ihren Verpflichtungen nachzukommen. Der Bank können damit unerwartet hohe Kosten für die Beschaffung kurzfristiger finanzieller Mittel entstehen bzw. im Extremfall wird die Bank zahlungsunfähig (Illiquidität). Unter **Instrumenten-Liquiditätsrisiko** versteht man die Gefahr fehlender Marktliquidität für Finanzinstrumente. Von der Bank gehaltene Positionen können nicht oder nur unter Inkaufnahme einer außergewöhnlich hohen Kauf-/Verkaufsspanne geschlossen werden.

2. Methoden zur Risikomessung

1. a)
2. Bei der GAP-Methode wird die **p.a.-Ergebnisveränderung bei einer unterstellten Zinsänderung** berechnet. Dabei wird angenommen, dass die Positionen nicht vorzeitig aufgelöst werden und somit nur die jährliche Zinsertrags- bzw. Zinsaufwandsrechnung durch eine Veränderung der Marktzinsen beeinflusst wird.
3. **Vorteile: einfache Handhabung**; einzige Form der Risikomessung, die mögliche **Veränderungen in der Zinsspanne der Bank darstellen** kann.
   Probleme: Für die Verlängerung von auslaufenden Geschäften müssen **Annahmen** getroffen werden; die GAP-Analyse unterstellt eine **gleichbleibende Risikostruktur,** so-dass Reaktionen auf Zinsänderungen im Zeitablauf nicht bzw. nicht systematisch dargestellt werden können; **MTM-Effekte werden ignoriert**; Unterstellung, wie sich die Zinsen im Zeitablauf verändern können, ist rein willkürlich und etwaige **Vergleiche mit Risiken, die in anderen Abteilungen gefahren werden, sind nicht zulässig.**
4. **Vorteile: einfache Handhabung** und Berechnung; **hohe Akzeptanz** durch klare Aussagen und Interpretation; **Kosten** bei einer eventuell vorzeitigen Schließung der Risikopositionen werden **abgeschätzt**; **keine Unterstellung bezüglich Weiterrollen** von auslaufenden Positionen.

Points of criticism: flat yield curve is assumed; basic calculation does not include the effect of yield curve changes; assumed interest rate changes are arbitrary and the resulting risk figures cannot be compared to other risks; the calculated risk figure is a pure MTM risk containing no information on net interest income.

5. a)
6. d)
7. b), c) and d)
8. The **correlation** between random variables A and B corresponds to the **covariance** between A and B divided by the standard deviations of A and B. The correlation can be interpreted as a normed covariance and its values may **range from -1 to + 1** by definition.
9. e)
10. d)
11. c)
12. e)
13. d)
14. **Advantage: flexibility** that allows the risk of complex instruments to be measured and random processes, for which there are no analytic formulas and solutions available, to be modelled.
   Disadvantage: complexity of calculations as well as the **required computing time**. It is necessary to find a compromise between speed (depending on the complexity of the assumptions and number of simulation runs) and accuracy.
15. **Data:** Historical Simulation creates high demands on data and computing time; **Backward Orientation:** The approach relies fully on historical observation; **New products/ illiquid products:** Historical simulation is not able to calculate a risk figure for newly or recently issued products or for illiquid products, because no suitable time series are available.
16. **Market volatility** is **higher during certain periods** than others; There is a **natural long-term level of volatility**. The market tends to return to the natural volatility level after periods of higher or lower volatility.
17. **Capital required to cover unexpected losses from an economic point of view** is termed economic capital.
18. In general, the term netting refers to **agreements between two or more counterparties that allow positive and negative values to be set off against each other given a certain event**.
19. **FX-Net** and **S.W.I.F.T Accord** represent two of the best-known bilateral netting services.
20. d)

3. Limits

1. a)
2. Country limits and industry limits
3. An overnight limit is the **limit on open positions at the end of a day**. The overnight limit is equal to the position limit, ie, the risk limit for the individual dealer.
4. c)
5. c)
6. d)

Kritikpunkte: Für die Berechnung der Duration wird eine flache Zinskurve unterstellt; Effekte von Zinskurvenänderungen sind standardmäßig nicht im Risiko enthalten; die Unterstellung, um wie viel sich die Zinsen ändern, ist rein willkürlich und lässt keine Vergleiche mit sonstigen Risiken zu; das dargestellte Risiko ist ein reines MTM-Risiko, sodass keine Aussagen über die Entwicklung der Zinsspanne getroffen werden können.

5. a)
6. d)
7. b), c) und d)
8. Die **Korrelation** zwischen zwei Variablen A und B entpricht der **Kovarianz** zwischen A und B dividiert durch die Standardabweichungen von A und B. Die Korrelation ist also eine Art normierte Kovarianz und liegt **zwischen +1 und -1**.
9. e)
10. d)
11. c)
12. e)
13. d)
14. **Vorteil: Flexibilität**, die insbesondere bei der Risikomessung von komplexen Instrumenten und Prozessen immer dann gebraucht wird, wenn keine analytischen Formeln zur Darstellung zur Verfügung stehen.
    Nachteil: extrem **hohe Rechenintensität und benötigte Computerkapazitäten.** Hier muss man einen Kompromiss finden zwischen Geschwindigkeit (Komplexität der Darstellung und Anzahl der Simulationen) und Genauigkeit.
15. **erheblicher Daten- und Rechenaufwand; Vergangenheitsorientierung:** Modell arbeitet ausschließlich mit historischen Beobachtungen; **neue/illiquide Produkte:** kann nicht angewandt werden auf neu emittierte bzw. illiquide Produkte, für die keine bzw. keine brauchbaren Zeitreihen zur Verfügung stehen.
16. Die **Volatilität im Markt** ist **in bestimmten Perioden höher** als in anderen; es gibt **langfristig ein natürliches Volatilitätslevel**, auf welches sich der Markt nach Phasen zu hoher bzw. zu niedriger Volatilität wieder hinbewegt.
17. Als ökonomisches Kapitel bezeichnet man die **ökonomisch erforderlichen Eigenmittel, um unerwartete Verluste abdecken zu können.**
18. Unter Netting versteht man die **vereinbarte Aufrechnung von gegenseitigen Positionen oder Verpflichtungen von Geschäftspartnern oder Teilnehmern eines Systems.**
19. Zu den bekanntesten bilateralen Nettingdiensten zählen **FX-Net** und **S.W.I.F.T. Accord.**
20. d)

3. Limite

1. a)
2. Länderlimite und Branchenlimite
3. Unter Overnight-Limit versteht man die **Begrenzung der offenen Position am Ende des Tages.** Das Overnight-Limit entspricht dem Positionslimit, d.h. dem Risikolimit für den einzelnen Händler.
4. c)
5. c)
6. d)

7. In addition to the position's total limit, a **limit on open positions** can be fixed for individual terms.

4. Basel II

1. (OECD) sovereign, (OECD) bank, mortgage loan, other loans
2. Misallocation of supervisory capital; incomplete coverage of banking risks, no international standards for supervisory review and disclosure in different countries
3. Focus on a single risk measure – more emphasis on bank's own internal risk management methodologies; supervisory review, market discipline; one size fits all – flexibility, banks select their own individual approach, incentives for better risk management; broad brush structure – more risk sensitivity
4. b), d) and e)
5. d)
6. c)
7. The calculation is done in two steps. First, risk weights are calculated by multiplying the exposure by the respective **risk weight** (note that the exposure is pre-calculated in a separate step). The capital requirement is the **result of risk-weighted assets times 8%.**
8. On-balance sheet netting (use of net exposure of loans and deposits), guarantees and credit derivatives, collateral
9. c)
10. d)
11. c) and d)
12. a), d) and e)
13. a), b), c) and g)
14. b), d) and e)
15. a)
16. d)
17. a)
18. b)

5. Capital Adequacy Directive (CAD)

1. d)
2. a)
3. The trading book of a financial institution consists of the bank's own trading of financial instruments, derivatives in combination with transactions in the trading book, other positions connected with the trading of financial instruments, stocks and operations to hedge or re-finance positions of the bond trading book, sale and repurchase agreements (repos), reverse repos, bond-lending operations and bond-borrowing operations of the trading book, collateral for securities and claims on pending transactions and advance payments for transactions in the bond's trading book
4. b)
5. c)
6. Tier 1 (core equity), tier 2 (supplement equity), tier 3 (additional supplement equity)
7. The equity requirement for credit risk – also called specific risk in combination with the positions of the trading book – depends on the **creditworthiness of the partner** (counterparty weighting) as well as on the **risk of the particular instrument** (risk factor).

7. Bei einem Laufzeit-Mismatch-Limit kann zusätzlich zum gesamten Positionslimit noch eine **Grenze für die offenen Risiken in den einzelnen Laufzeiten** festgelegt werden.

4. Basel II

1. (OECD-)Staat, (OECD-)Bank, Hypothek besichert, sonstige Kredite
2. Fehlallokation des aufsichtsrechtlichen Kapitals, keine komplette Erfassung von Risiken, keine internationalen Standards für aufsichtsrechtliche Überprüfungen und Veröffentlichung in verschiedenen Ländern
3. Konzentration auf ein Risikomaß – größere Bedeutung der bankinternen Methoden, Überprüfung durch die Aufsicht, Überprüfung der Marktdisziplin; ein einziger Ansatz – Flexibilität, Auswahl verschiedener Ansätze, Anreize für ein besseres Risikomanagment; grobe Struktur – risikogerechtere Ausrichtung
4. b), d) und e)
5. d)
6. c)
7. Die Berechnung der Eigenmittelunterlegung des Kreditrisikos erfolgt in zwei Schritten. Im ersten Schritt werden die **risikogewichteten Aktiva** berechnet, indem die Volumina mit den entsprechenden Risikogewichten multipliziert werden. Die Mindestunterlegung ergibt sich dann im zweiten Schritt mit der **Berechnung von 8% der risikogewichteten Aktiva.**
8. Netting von Bilanzpositionen (Aufrechnen von Gegenpositionen), Garantien und Kreditderivate, Sicherheiten
9. c)
10. d)
11. c) und d)
12. a), d) und e)
13. a), b), c) und g)
14. b), d) und e)
15. a)
16. d)
17. a)
18. b)

5. Die Kapitaladäquanzrichtlinie (KAR)

1. d)
2. a)
3. Der Handelsbestand eines Kreditinstitutes umfasst Eigenhandel in Finanzinstrumenten, derivative Instrumente in Verbindung mit Geschäften des Handelsbuches, sonstige Positionen, die in Verbindung mit dem Handel in Finanzinstrumenten stehen, Bestände und Geschäfte zur Absicherung oder Refinanzierung von Positionen des Wertpapierhandelsbuches, Pensionsgeschäfte, umgekehrte Pensionsgeschäfte, Wertpapierleih- und Wertpapierverleihgeschäfte des Handelsbuches, Übernahmegarantien für Wertpapiere und Forderungen aus nicht abgewickelten Geschäften und Vorleistungen im Zusammenhang mit Geschäften.
4. b)
5. c)
6. Tier 1 (Kernkapital), Tier 2 (Ergänzungskapital), Tier 3 (zusätzliche Ergänzungskapital)
7. Der Eigenkapitalbedarf für das Kreditrisiko wird durch die **Bonität des Kontrahenten** (Adressgewichtung) und durch das **Ausfallsrisiko**, das durch das einzelne Produkt (Risikowert) entsteht, beeinflusst.

8. Qualified assets in the trading book are **buying and selling positions** on assets that bear a counterparty weighting of 20% and **bonds** with a counterparty weighting of 100%, if they are accepted for trading at a recognised stock market, the respective bonds market is liquid and the partner's creditworthiness is considered satisfactory.

9. b)

10. There are two different ways of evaluation: the maturity method and the mark-to-market method. With the **maturity method**, the credit risk for derivatives is calculated in two steps. First, all nominal amounts of each instrument are multiplied by determined percentage rates. The risk that is determined by step 1 is multiplied by the counterparty weighting of the partner. The risk weighting for replacement risk is limited to 50%. With the **mark-to-market method** the measurement of credit risk in the derivatives business is done in three steps. In step 1 you determine the replacement value of contracts that have a positive MTM value. In the second step, the notional amounts of all contracts are multiplied by determined percentage rates (to include all possible risks in the future) and in the third step the risks that are determined by steps 1 and 2 are each multiplied by the counterparty weighting of the partner.

11. The sum of all credit risks linked to a specific counterparty or a group of affiliated counterparties may not exceed 25% of a bank's total capital. The sum of all credit risks against the parent company (or the parent company's subsidiaries and the bank's own subsidiaries, respectively) may not exceed 20% of a bank's total capital. The sum of all large loans (credit risks against a customer exceeding 10% of the equity) may not exceed eight times of the equity of a bank.

12. b)

13. c)

14. d)

15. c)

16. c)

17. b)

18. **Basis risk:** different instruments, coupons, and terms within a given maturity band; **yield curve risk:** different changes of interest rates within the single terms; **interest level risk:** the risk of a parallel shift of the yield curve

19. With the **maturity band method**, average risk factors are given for each term; With the duration method, the true risk factors of the positions are used for the calculation. Since the **duration method** is more precise, the CAD demands a lower equity cover.

PART VII: CENTRAL BANKS, FUNDAMENTAL ANALYSIS AND TECHNICAL ANALYSIS

1. Central Banks

1. Establishment of an international monetary system with stable exchange rates, relaxation of existing restrictions on foreign exchange, introduction of the convertibility of all currencies

8. Unter die Kategorie der qualifizierten Aktiva fallen unter anderem **Kauf- und Verkaufspositionen in Aktivposten,** die mit 20% Adressgewichtung angesetzt werden, und **Schuldverschreibungen** mit 100% Adressgewicht, falls sie an einer anerkannten Börse zum Handel zugelassen sind, der Markt in diesen Schuldverschreibungen liquide ist und die Bonität des Kontrahenten als zufriedenstellend eingeschätzt wird.

9. b)

10. Es gibt zwei unterschiedliche Bemessungsmöglichkeiten des Wiederbeschaffungsrisikos: die Laufzeitmethode und die Marktbewertungsmethode. Bei der **Laufzeitmethode** wird das Kreditrisiko für Derivate in zwei Schritten errechnet. Der Nominalwert jedes Instrumentes wird mit vorgegebenen Prozentsätzen multipliziert. Im zweiten Schritt wird das Risiko, das sich aus dem ersten Schritt ergibt, mit der jeweiligen Adressgewichtung des Partners multipliziert. Zu berücksichtigen ist hier, dass die Adressgewichtung für das Wiederbeschaffungsrisiko mit 50% begrenzt ist. Bei der **Marktbewertungsmethode** erfolgt die Messung des Kreditrisikos aus Geschäften mit Derivaten in drei Schritten. Im Schritt 1 wird der Wiederbeschaffungswert der Verträge wird ermittelt. Nur die positiven Wiederbeschaffungswerte werden weiter berücksichtigt. Im zweiten Schritt werden die Nominalwerte aller Kontrakte mit vorgegebenen Prozentsätzen multipliziert und im dritten Schritt werden die Risiken, die sich aus den Schritten 1 und 2 ergeben, mit der jeweiligen Adressgewichtung des Partners multipliziert.

11. Die Gesamtheit der Kreditrisiken, die gegenüber einem Kunden bestehen, sind auf 25% der gesamten Eigenmittel des Institutes begrenzt. Die Gesamtheit der Kreditrisiken, die gegenüber dem Mutterunternehmen bestehen, sind auf 20% der gesamten Eigenmittel des Instituts begrenzt. Die Summe aller addierten Großrisiken (Kreditrisiko gegenüber einem Kunden, das größer als 10% der Eigenmittel ist) darf das Achtfache der Eigenmittel des Institutes nicht überschreiten.

12. b)

13. c)

14. d)

15. c)

16. c)

17. b)

18. **Zinsniveaurisiko:** Risiko einer parallelen Verschiebung der gesamten Zinskurve; **Zinskurvenrisiko:** unterschiedliche Zinsänderungen in den einzelnen Laufzeiten; **Basisrisiko:** unterschiedliche Instrumente, Kupons und Laufzeiten innerhalb eines vorgegeben Laufzeitbandes.

19. Bei der **Laufzeitmethode** werden durchschnittliche Risikofaktoren pro Laufzeit vorgegeben. Die **Durationsmethode** arbeitet mit dem echten Risikofaktor für die einzelnen Positionen. Durch die größere Genauigkeit der Durationsmethode wird der Eigenkapitalunterlegungssatz durch die KAR geringer angesetzt.

TEIL VII: NOTENBANKEN, FUNDAMENTALE ANALYSE UND TECHNISCHE ANALYSE

1. Notenbanken

1. Errichtung eines internationalen Währungssystems mit stabilen Wechselkursen, Abbau der noch vorhandenen Devisenrestriktionen und Einführung der Konvertibilität aller Währungen

2. d)
3. Due to a **crisis in the international monetary system** the Bretton Woods system finally collapsed at the beginning of the 1970s. **High US balance of payments deficits** caused **confidence in the US dollar** as the international key currency **to be lost**. Within a short period of time, enormous amounts of money were moved from the US to the European markets; there, the interest rates remained at a high level.
4. Within the **Smithsonian Agreement**, signed on the occasion of the monetary conference on 17/18 December 1971, the United States obliged itself to **raise the official gold price from USD 35 to USD 38 per troy ounce**; this amounted to a nominal **devaluation of 7.9%**. At the same time, the European countries and Japan revalued their currencies by 8%, while Canada decided to stick to a floating exchange rate.
5. **Floating exchange rates** are subject to demand and supply in the foreign exchange market without any interfering economic policies. For **fixed exchange rates** economic policy defines a fixed exchange rate. One hybrid system is **managed floating**. Basically the exchange rates are floating, but the central banks intervene (hidden or openly) to fulfil certain (silent or open) agreements.
6. The main objective of the EMS was to create a "zone of monetary stability in Europe", ie, **stability of exchange rates and prices**, by means of monetary policy co-operation. The fixing of the exchange rates should help to strengthen the economic integration and to encourage trade within the EU.
7. c)
8. **High degree of price stability:** The inflation rate may not exceed the average inflation rate of the three member countries with the lowest inflation rates by more than 1.5%; **Government finance:** The country's total outstanding government debt may not exceed 60% of its GDP and the country's budget deficit may not exceed 3% of its GDP; **Participation in the European Monetary System:** Applicant countries should have remained within the exchange rate bandwidth for two consecutive years prior to joining the exchange rate mechanism (ERM II); **Long-term interest rates:** the nominal long-term interest rate must not be more than two percentage points higher than in the three member states with the lowest inflation.
9. c), d) and f)
10. c)
11. c)
12. Defining and implementing the monetary policy of the EU; conducting FX operations; holding and managing the official foreign reserves of the member states; promoting smooth operation of payment systems
13. b), c) and d)
14. b)
15. d)
16. c)
17. d)
18. a)
19. b)

2. d)
3. Durch eine **Krise des internationalen Währungssystems** brach das System von Bretton Woods schließlich zu Beginn der 70er-Jahre in sich zusammen. **Hohe Zahlungsbilanzdefizite der USA** führten dazu, dass das **Vertrauen in den Dollar** als internationale Leitwährung **verlorenging**. Enorme Kapitalbeträge flossen innerhalb kürzester Zeit aus den USA in die europäischen Märkte, deren Zinssätze weiterhin auf hohem Niveau waren.
4. Im Rahmen des Smithsonian Agreements verpflichteten sich die USA anlässlich der Währungskonferenz vom 17./18. Dezember 1971, den **offiziellen Goldpreis von USD 35 auf USD 38 pro Unze zu erhöhen**, was einer **Dollarabwertung von 7,9%** entsprach. Die europäischen Länder und Japan werteten ihre Währungen zusätzlich um fast 8% auf, während Kanada beschloss, den freien Wechselkurs beizubehalten.
5. Bei **flexiblen („floating") Wechselkursen** bildet sich der Wechselkurs allein aufgrund der Marktkräfte am Devisenmarkt, ohne Eingriff wirtschaftspolitischer Instanzen. **Bei fixen Wechselkursen** wird von den wirtschaftspolitischen Instanzen ein fester Wechselkurs festgelegt. Eine Mischform ist das **kontrollierte Floating („Managed Floating")**. Die Wechselkurse bilden sich grundsätzlich frei, die Zentralbanken intervenieren aber (verdeckt oder offen), um bestimmte (stillschweigende oder offene) Absprachen zu realisieren.
6. Ziel des EWS war es, durch eine engere währungspolitische Zusammenarbeit eine „Zone der monetären Stabilität in Europa", das bedeutet **Wechselkurs- und Preisstabilität**, zu schaffen. Die Fixierung der Wechselkurse sollte die wirtschaftliche Integration stärken und den Handel innerhalb der EU begünstigen.
7. c)
8. **Hoher Grad an Preisstabilität:** Die Inflationsrate darf nicht mehr als 1,5 Prozentpunkte über den Inflationsraten der drei preisstabilsten Mitgliedstaaten liegen. **Öffentlicher Finanzhaushalt:** Die Gesamtverschuldung des Staates darf 60% des Bruttoinlandsproduktes nicht überschreiten und das laufende Defizit der öffentlichen Hand darf nicht mehr als 3% des Bruttoinlandsproduktes betragen. **Teilnahme am Europäischen Währungssystem (EWS):** Für die Teilnahme an der EWU muss sich die betroffene Währung seit mindestens zwei Jahren innerhalb der Bandbreite des Wechselkursmechanismus des EWS bewegt haben. **Langfristiger Zinssatz:** Der Zinssatz langfristiger Staatsanleihen darf nicht höher liegen als 2 Prozentpunkte über dem Durchschnitt der drei preisstabilsten Mitgliedstaaten.
9. c), d) und f)
10. c)
11. c)
12. Festlegung und Ausführung der Geldpolitik der Gemeinschaft, Durchführung der Devisengeschäfte, Haltung und Verwaltung der offiziellen Währungsreserven der Mitgliedstaaten und Förderung des reibungslosen Funktionierens der Zahlungsverkehrssysteme
13. b), c) und d)
14. b)
15. d)
16. c)
17. d)
18. a)
19. b)

20. c)
21. a)
22. c)
23. b)
24. c)
25. b)

2. Fundamental Analysis

1. b)
2. d), e) and f)
3. d)
4. Foreign direct investments (FDI), portfolio investments, financial derivatives, credit transactions
5. d)
6. e)
7. b)
8. **Monocausal Models** (Purchasing Power Parity Theory, Interest Rate Parity Theory) and **Integrated Models** (Keynesian Model, Monetary Approach, Asset Market Approach)
9. a)
10. a) and c)
11. **Flow models** are based on changes of the indicators (eg, income change, asset change), whereas **stock models** look at the absolute numbers of the indicators (eg, level of the income or amount of assets).
12. b)
13. c)
14. The monetary approach for determining the exchange rate is a stock model. It places particular emphasis on the **stock of monetary assets**. All balance of payment transactions are the result of **portfolio decisions** (investing money in different kinds of equity) **taken by domestic and foreign investors**. If there are imbalances in the money market, investors adjust their portfolios accordingly.
15. d)
16. Quantity indicators, price indicators, early indicators or leading indicators, current and/or lagging indicators
17. a), b) and d)
18. b), c) and d)

3. Technical Analysis

1. **Classical chart analysis** (line and bar charts, candle charts, point & figure chart, Elliott Wave Theory, Gann Angles) and **numerical methods** (trend chasing systems as moving average, MACD, anti-cyclical systems as Momentum, RSI, time series analysis)
2. Contrary to fundamental analysis, technical analysis forecasting models are based on the **observation of past exchange rates** in order to arrive at conclusions about future exchange rate developments from past movements. By tracking the exchange rate, trends and trend turning points should be recognized.

20. c)

21. a)

22. c)

23. b)

24. c)

25. b)

2. Fundamentale Analyse

1. b)

2. d), e) und f)

3. d)

4. Direktinvestitionen, Wertpapieranlagen, Finanzderivate und Kreditverkehr

5. d)

6. e)

7. b)

8. **Monokausale Modelle** (Kaufkraftparitätentheorie, Zinsparitätentheorie) und **integrierte Modelle** (traditionelle Ansätze: keynesianischer Ansatz, monetärer Ansatz, Finanzmarktansatz)

9. a)

10. a) und c)

11. **Stromgrößenmodelle** basieren auf Veränderungen der betrachteten Einflussgrößen (z.B. Einkommensänderungen, Änderungen der Vermögensbestände), während die **Bestandsgrößenmodelle** auf Beständen (z.B. Höhe des Einkommens oder des Vermögens) aufbauen.

12. b)

13. c)

14. Der monetäre Ansatz zur Bestimmung des Devisenkurses ist ein Bestandsgrößenansatz, der insbesondere die **Bestände an Geldvermögen einer Volkswirtschaft** berücksichtigt. Die in die Zahlungsbilanz eingehenden Leistungs- und Finanztransaktionen resultieren aus den **Portfolioentscheidungen** (Aufteilung des Geldvermögens auf Wertpapiere) in- und ausländischer Wirtschaftssubjekte. Herrscht ein Ungleichgewicht auf dem Geldmarkt, so passen die Wirtschaftssubjekte ihre Portfolios entsprechend an.

15. d)

16. Mengenindikatoren, Preisindikatoren, Früh- bzw. vorlaufende Indikatoren, Präsens- und Spätindikatoren

17. a), b) und d)

18. b), c) und d)

3. Technische Analyse

1. **Klassische Chartanalyse** (Linien- und Balkenchartanalyse, Candle Charts, Point & Figure-Chart, Elliott-Wellen-Theorie, Gann-Linien) und **mathematische Verfahren** (Trendfolgesysteme wie gleitender Durchschnitt, MACD, antizyklische Systeme wie Momentum, RSI, statistische Zeitreihenanalyse)

2. Im Gegensatz zur Fundamentalanalyse basieren die Prognoseansätze der technischen Devisenkursprognose auf der **Beobachtung und Registrierung des Devisenkurses** und ziehen aus dem bisherigen Kursverlauf Rückschlüsse auf zukünftige Kursausprägungen. Durch Beobachtung des Devisenkursverlaufs sollen Trends und ihre Richtung sowie Umkehrpunkte erkannt werden.

3. b)
4. d)
5. a), d), e) and g)
6. c)
7. b)
8. d)
9. d)
10. b)
11. a)
12. b)
13. b)
14. b)
15. b)
16. c)
17. d)
18. b)
19. d)
20. a)
21. d)
22. d)
23. c)

3. b)
4. d)
5. a), d), e) und g)
6. c)
7. b)
8. d)
9. d)
10. b)
11. a)
12. b)
13. b)
14. b)
15. b)
16. c)
17. d)
18. b)
19. d)
20. a)
21. d)
22. d)
23. c)